GROWTH IN
AGREEMENT II

GROWTH IN AGREEMENT II

Reports and Agreed Statements of Ecumenical Conversations on a World Level, 1982-1998

Edited by
Jeffrey Gros, FSC
Harding Meyer
William G. Rusch

WCC Publications, Geneva

William B. Eerdmans Publishing Company
Grand Rapids, Michigan/Cambridge

Faith and Order Paper No. 187

© 2000 WCC Publications
World Council of Churches, 150 route de Ferney,
P.O. Box 2100, 1211 Geneva 2, Switzerland
Website: http://www.wcc-coe.org

Published jointly with William B. Eerdmans Publishing Co.
255 Jefferson Ave. S.E., Grand Rapids, Michigan 49503, USA/
P.O. Box 163, Cambridge CB3 9PU, UK
All rights reserved

This volume is based on the German language edition published as
Dokumente wachsender Übereinstimmung II: 1982-1990
© 1992 by Bonifatius GmbH Verlag, Paderborn,
and Verlag Otto Lembeck, Frankfurt a/Main

© Document 40 Paternoster Publishing, Carlisle, UK
Basil Meeking and J.R.W. Stott, eds
Reprinted by permission

WCC ISBN 2-8254-1329-1
Eerdmans ISBN 0-8028-4934-2

Cover design: Rob Lucas

Printed in Switzerland

Contents

General Introduction xv

PART A

I. ANGLICAN-LUTHERAN DIALOGUE

1. Report of the Working Group 2
   Cold Ash, England, 3 December 1983

2. Episcope 11
   Niagara Falls, USA, September 1987

3. The Diaconate as Ecumenical Opportunity 38
   Hanover, Germany, October 1995

II. ANGLICAN-METHODIST DIALOGUE

4. Sharing in the Apostolic Communion 55
   Kanuga, North Carolina, USA, January 1996

III. ANGLICAN-EASTERN ORTHODOX DIALOGUE

Historical Introduction 77

5. Agreed Statement, Anglican-Orthodox Dialogue 1976-1984 81
   Dublin, Ireland, 19 August 1984

6. Joint Communique: Robert A.K. Runcie, Archbishop of
   Canterbury, and Demetrios I, Ecumenical Patriarch, ... 105
   Lambeth Palace, London, England, 9 December 1987

vi   *Contents*

IV. ANGLICAN-ORIENTAL ORTHODOX DIALOGUE

Historical Introduction 108

7. Common Declaration: Shenouda III, Pope of Alexandria and Patriarch of the See of St Mark, and Robert A.K. Runcie, Archbishop of Canterbury 110
   Egypt, 1 October 1987

8. Joint Communique: George Carey, Archbishop of Canterbury, and Karekin I, Supreme Catholicos of All Armenians 112
   Lambeth Palace, London, England, 10 November 1997

V. ANGLICAN-REFORMED DIALOGUE

Historical Introduction 113

9. God's Reign and Our Unity 114
   Woking, England, January 1984

VI. BAPTIST-LUTHERAN DIALOGUE

10. A Message to Our Churches 155
    Geneva, Switzerland, 1990

VII. DISCIPLES OF CHRIST-REFORMED DIALOGUE

Historical Introduction 176

11. No Doctrinal Obstacles 178
    Birmingham, England, 4-11 March 1987

VIII. EASTERN ORTHODOX-ORIENTAL ORTHODOX DIALOGUE

Historical Introduction 187

12. Communique 190
    Chambésy, Geneva, Switzerland, 15 December 1985

13. Communique 191
    Anba Bishoy Monastery, Egypt, 24 June 1989

14. Second Agreed Statement and Recommendations
    to the Churches 194
    Chambésy, Geneva, Switzerland, 28 September 1990

IX. LUTHERAN-METHODIST DIALOGUE

15. The Church: Community of Grace 200
    Lutheran-Methodist Dialogue 1979-1984
    Bossey, near Geneva, Switzerland, June 1984

X. LUTHERAN-ORTHODOX DIALOGUE

Historical Introduction 219

16. Divine Revelation 222
    Allentown, USA, 30 May 1985

17. Scripture and Tradition 224
    Crete, Greece, 2 June 1987

18. The Canon and the Inspiration of the Holy Scripture 226
    Bad Segeberg, Germany, 8 September 1989

XI. LUTHERAN-REFORMED DIALOGUE

Historical Introduction 230

19. Towards Church Fellowship 233
    Geneva, Switzerland, Easter 1989

XII. OLD CATHOLIC-EASTERN ORTHODOX DIALOGUE

20. Ecclesiology 248
    Chambésy, Geneva, Switzerland, 7 October 1983

21. Soteriology 250
    Chambésy, Geneva, Switzerland, 7 October 1983

22. Sacramental Teaching 254
    Amersfoort, Netherlands, 3 October 1985
    and Kavala, Greece, 17 October 1987

23. Eschatology 264
    Kavala, Greece, 17 October 1987

24. Church Community 267
    Kavala, Greece, 17 October 1987

viii   *Contents*

XIII. REFORMED-METHODIST DIALOGUE

Historical Introduction 269

25. Together in God's Grace 270
    Cambridge, England, 27 June 1987

XIV. REFORMED-ORTHODOX DIALOGUE

Historical Introduction 275

26. Memorandum 277
    Leuenberg, Switzerland, 11 March 1988

27. Agreed Statement on the Holy Trinity 280
    Kappel, Germany, March 1992

28. Significant Features: A Common Reflection on the Agreed
    Statement 285
    Kappel, Germany, March 1992

29. Agreed Statement on Christology 288
    Limassol, Cyprus, January 1994

XV. REFORMED-ORIENTAL ORTHODOX DIALOGUE

Historical Introduction 291

30. Agreed Statement on Christology 292
    Driebergen, Netherlands, 13 September 1994

XVI. ADVENTISTS AND LUTHERANS IN CONVERSATION

31. Report of the Bilateral Conversation 1994-1998 295
    Cartigny, Switzerland, 15 May 1998

PART B

XVII. ANGLICAN-ROMAN CATHOLIC DIALOGUE

Historical Introduction 312

Contents   ix

32. Common Declaration: Pope John Paul II and Robert A.K. Runcie,
Archbishop of Canterbury 313
Canterbury, England, 29 May 1982

33. Salvation and the Church 315
Llandaff, Wales, 3 September 1986

34. Common Declaration: Pope John Paul II and Robert A.K. Runcie,
Archbishop of Canterbury,
Vatican, 2 October 1989 326

35. Church as Communion 328
Dublin, Ireland, 6 September 1990

36. Life in Christ: Morals, Communion and the Church 344
Venice, Italy, 5 September 1993

37. Common Declaration: George Carey, Archbishop of Canterbury,
and Pope John Paul II 371
Vatican, 5 December 1996

XVIII. BAPTIST-ROMAN CATHOLIC DIALOGUE

38. Summons to Witness to Christ in Today's World: A Report on
Conversations 1984-1988 373
Atlanta, USA, 23 July 1988

XIX. DISCIPLES OF CHRIST-ROMAN CATHOLIC DIALOGUE

39. The Church as Communion in Christ 386
St Louis, Missouri, USA, 7 December 1992

XX. EVANGELICAL-ROMAN CATHOLIC DIALOGUE

40. The Evangelical-Roman Catholic Dialogue on Mission 399
1977-1984

XXI. LUTHERAN-ROMAN CATHOLIC DIALOGUE

41. Martin Luther – Witness to Jesus Christ 438
Kloster Kirchberg, Germany, 6 May 1983

42. Facing Unity 443
Rome, Italy, 3 March 1984

43. Church and Justification 485
    Wurzburg, Germany, 11 September 1993

44. Joint Declaration on the Doctrine of Justification 566
    Augsburg, Germany, 31 October 1999

XXII. METHODIST-ROMAN CATHOLIC DIALOGUE

45. Towards a Statement on the Church – Fourth Series 1982-1986 583
    Nairobi, Kenya, 1986

46. The Apostolic Tradition – Fifth Series 1986-1991 597
    Paris, France, 15 April 1991

47. The Word of Life: A Statement on Revelation and Faith –
    Sixth Series 1991-1996 618
    Baar, Switzerland, 15 November 1995

XXIII. EASTERN ORTHODOX-ROMAN CATHOLIC DIALOGUE

Historical Introduction 647

48. The Mystery of the Church and of the Eucharist in the
    Light of the Mystery of the Holy Trinity 652
    Munich, Germany, 30 June-6 July 1982

49. Faith, Sacraments and the Unity of the Church 660
    Bari, Italy, June 1987

50. Common Declaration: Pope John Paul II and Patriarch
    Dimitrios I 669
    Vatican, 7 December 1987

51. The Sacrament of Order in the Sacramental Structure of the
    Church 671
    New Valamo, Finland, 26 June 1988

52. Uniatism: Method of Union of the Past, and the Present Search
    for Full Communion 680
    Balamand, Lebanon, 23 June 1993

53. Common Declaration: Pope John Paul II and Bartholomew,
    Ecumenical Patriarch 686
    Vatican, 29 June 1995

XXIV. ORIENTAL ORTHODOX-ROMAN CATHOLIC DIALOGUE

Historical Introduction 688

54. Common Declaration: Pope John Paul II and
    Mar Ignatius Zakka I Iwas 691
    Vatican, 23 June 1984

55. The Continuation of the Dialogue 694
    Cairo, Egypt, 12 February 1988

56. Report of the International Commission for Dialogue between
    the Coptic Orthodox Church and the Roman Catholic Church 695
    Monastery of St Bishoy, Egypt, 27 April 1990

57. Statement of the Joint Commission between the Roman Catholic
    Church and the Malankara Orthodox Syrian Church 696
    Kottayam, India, 3 June 1990

58. Report of the Second Meeting of the Joint International
    Commission between the Roman Catholic Church and the
    Malankara Orthodox Syrian Church 698
    Manganam, Kottayam, India, 9-12 December 1990

59. Pastoral Guidelines on Marriages between Members of the
    Catholic Church and the Malankara Syrian Orthodox Church 703
    Ernakulam, India, November 1993

60. Common Declaration: Pope John Paul II and Catholicos Karekin I 707
    Vatican, 13 December 1996

XXV. ASSYRIAN CHURCH OF THE EAST-ROMAN CATHOLIC DIALOGUE

Historical Introduction 709

61. Common Christological Declaration between the Catholic Church
    and the Assyrian Church of the East 711
    Rome, Italy, 11 November 1994

XXVI. PENTECOSTAL-ROMAN CATHOLIC DIALOGUE

62. Final Report 713
    Dialogue between the Secretariat for Promoting Christian Unity
    and Leaders of the Some Pentecostal Churches and Participants
    in the Charismatic Movement within Protestant and Anglican
    Churches
    1972-1976

63. Final Report 721
   Dialogue between the Secretariat for Promoting Christian Unity
   Some and Classical Pentecostals
   1977-1982

64. Perspectives on Koinonia 735
   Report from the Third Quinquennium of the Dialogue between the
   Pontifical Council for Promoting Christian Unity and Some
   Classical Pentecostal Churches and Leaders
   1985-1989

65. Evangelization, Proselytism and Common Witness 753
   1990-1997

XXVII. REFORMED-ROMAN CATHOLIC DIALOGUE

66. Towards a Common Understanding of the Church 780
   Second Phase, 1984-1990

PART C

XXVIII. WORLD COUNCIL OF CHURCHES AND ROMAN CATHOLIC CHURCH

Historical Introduction 820

67. Fifth Report of the Joint Working Group 821
   June 1982

68. Sixth Report of the Joint Working Group 842
   1990

69. The Church: Local and Universal 862
   A Study Document Commissioned and Received by the Joint
   Working Group
   1990

70. The Notion of "Hierarchy of Truths":
   An Ecumenical Interpretation 876
   1990

71. Ecumenical Formation: Ecumenical Reflections
   and Suggestions 884
   20 May 1993

Contents xiii

72. The Challenge of Proselytism and the Calling to Common Witness 891
   25 September 1995

73. The Ecumenical Dialogue on Moral Issues: Potential Sources of Common Witness or of Divisions 900
   25 September 1995

74. Seventh Report of the Joint Working Group 911
   1998

PART D

XXIX. WORLD COUNCIL OF CHURCHES

Historical Introduction 936

75. The Unity of the Church as Koinonia: Gift and Calling 937
   Canberra, Australia, February 1991

76. Message to the Churches 939
   Santiago de Compostela, Spain, August 1993

General Introduction

The goal of this volume is the same as that of *Growth in Agreement*, published in 1984 by Paulist Press and the World Council of Churches: to assemble and to make accessible to students, theologians and other ecumenically interested persons the results of international dialogues.[1] These materials have generally been published in a variety of places and are often not easy to locate or obtain.

The selection and division of the texts follow the principles of the earlier volume. Material, prepared and published by international dialogues from the years 1982 to 1 July 1998, is included. In order to facilitate the handling of the texts, they have been divided into four main sections:

- *Part A*, the results of conversations between churches and Christian world communions, which by and large belong to the World Council of Churches;
- *Part B*, the results of dialogues in which the Roman Catholic Church has taken part;
- *Part C*, the results of the activities of the Joint Working Group between the Roman Catholic Church and the World Council of Churches;
- *Part D*, documents from the World Council of Churches.

This work concentrates even more strongly than the earlier collection on the texts from the bilateral-interconfessional dialogues. These dialogues have been reviewed in the introduction to the first volume of *Growth in Agreement*, and the reader should consult what has been said there about the chief characteristics and role of dialogues in general and about the necessity of an inter-relation between bilaterals and multilaterals.[2] Also of continuing value is the earlier work of Nils Ehrenström and Günther Gassmann, and the several bibliographies edited by the Centro Pro Unione in Rome.[3]

One feature, which will be immediately noticed by any reader, is the amount of material produced in this period between 1982 and 1998. Yet since 1982 the number of dialogue partners has not varied significantly. This is not surprising and could hardly be otherwise, since all the larger Christian traditions and Christian world communions were already involved in dialogue prior to 1982. What is different is the evidence that many of these dialogues have entered into a second or even a third phase of their work. There is an expansion of themes, and where themes are revisited, there is a greater differentiation with discussion of individual aspects of the topic.

It is also clear that an increased inter-relatedness among the dialogues has occurred. In part this can be explained by the continuing function of *Baptism, Eucharist and Ministry* to orient the bilaterals.[4] The forum for bilateral conversations continues to survey in a helpful manner the inter-relatedness and coherence of the various dialogues.[5]

Even more so than in 1982 reception remains a major ecumenical challenge.[6] Indeed, more progress has been made in recent years than was true earlier. On the other hand, the difficulties of reception within and between the churches are more conspicuous.

It should be acknowledged in addition that dialogues and conversations between churches have taken place without using the classical model of dialogue with a final report available to the churches and larger public. Without such documentation, such activities cannot be recorded in this work. Yet such events have their importance and bear ecumenical fruit. They should not be overlooked.

The documents that follow have been reproduced in their entirety, in most instances with their preface, where these introductions give additional valuable information. In a few cases short "historical introductions" have been provided to show how a particular text or set of texts originated and developed.

Jeffrey Gros, FSC, Washington
Harding Meyer, Strasbourg
William G. Rusch, New York

March 1999

NOTES

[1] Harding Meyer and Lukas Vischer, eds, *Growth in Agreement: Reports and Agreed Statements of Ecumenical Conversations on a World Level*, New York, Ramsey and Paulist Press, and Geneva, WCC, 1984.
[2] *Ibid.*, pp.1-11. This volume is still available.
[3] Nils Ehrenström and Günther Gassmann, *Confessions in Dialogue*, Faith and Order Paper no. 74, 3rd ed. rev. and enlarged, Geneva, WCC, 1975; and J. Puglisi, *A Workbook of Bibliographies of Interchurch Dialogues*, Rome, Pro Unione, 1978, and "A Continuing Bibliography for Study of Interchurch Dialogues", in *Centro Pro Unione Bi-Annual Bulletin*, 1979, 1980 and onward.
[4] *Baptism, Eucharist and Ministry*, Faith and Order Paper no. 111, Geneva, WCC, 1982.
[5] Meyer and Vischer, *op. cit.*, pp.5-7. The forum continues to meet. Its most recent reports are found in Günther Gassmann, *Fourth Forum on Bilateral Conversations*; *Fifth Forum on Bilateral Conversations*; *Sixth Forum on Bilateral Conversations;* and Alan D. Falconer, *Seventh Forum on Bilateral Dialogues*, respectively Faith and Order Papers nos 125, 156, 168, 179, 1985, 1991, 1995, 1997, Geneva, WCC.
[6] Meyer and Vischer, *op. cit*, pp.7-9.

Part A

I. ANGLICAN-LUTHERAN DIALOGUE

1. Report of the Working Group

Cold Ash, England, 3 December 1983

I. Introduction

1. The last fifteen years [1968-83] have seen a remarkable convergence between the Anglican and Lutheran communions and their member churches. This applies both to theological understanding and practical contacts and exchange. The two Christian traditions have rediscovered a deep affinity in faith, worship, life and mission and a mutually enriching diversity of forms in expressing Christian faith and life.

2. In order to further this emergence of a new relationship between Anglicans and Lutherans, Anglican-Lutheran international conversations took place from 1970 to 1972. A small Anglican-Lutheran working group met in 1975. Official Episcopal-Lutheran conversations have been conducted in the USA since 1969. They led in September 1982 to the decision of three Lutheran churches and the Episcopal Church to enter into a relationship of "interim sharing of the eucharist". An Anglican-Lutheran European regional commission met from 1980 to 1982. Dialogues in other countries have begun. Many forms of closer fellowship and cooperation have emerged in all parts of the world.

3. This progress led the Anglican Consultative Council (ACC) in 1981 to recommend that the Lutheran World Federation (LWF) be invited to reconvene a joint Working Group. This initiative was welcomed by the executive committee of the LWF in 1982. Both sides appointed an Anglican-Lutheran joint working group and agreed that this group should receive information about the development of Anglican-Lutheran relations in different parts of the world, assess the results of Anglican-Lutheran dialogues, especially in Europe, Tanzania and the USA, make recommendations with the intention of proposing how the two communions might achieve full communion, suggest procedures that would assure closer cooperation between the two bodies.

4. The Anglican-Lutheran joint working group met from 28 November to 3 December 1983 at the Cold Ash Centre, Cold Ash, Berkshire, England. The meeting was marked by a spirit of joy and gratitude for a new era in Anglican-Lutheran relations. The participants now submit their report to the ACC and LWF and through them to the Anglican and Lutheran churches.

Cold Ash, Berkshire, England, 3 December 1983

II. The historical background of Anglican-Lutheran relations

5. In order to a assess adequately the significance of recent theological convergence and growing contacts, exchange and collaboration between Anglican and Lutheran

churches in many parts of the world, a glimpse at the history of our relations might be helpful.

6. In international, regional and national Anglican-Lutheran dialogues confidence is expressed that both churches are on the way towards full communion with each other. Such confidence is based on growing theological agreement and consensus. But it is also rooted in the rediscovery of common theological orientations, manifold contacts and sacramental sharing during the Reformation period and after. Today our churches, which had in many ways become strangers to each other during the intervening period, are discovering afresh their common convictions of faith, and a mutually enriching diversity in forms of worship, spiritual life, theological thinking and ethos, and in mission and service.

7. The following historical overview is taken from the report of the Anglican-Lutheran European regional commission (pp.4-6).

Our common heritage

8. In the early stages of the Reformation close ties existed between the Reformers in Britain and on the Continent. Under Henry VIII and Edward VI many English Reformers were strongly influenced by Luther's writings. Attempts were made, though politically motivated, to formulate an official consensus between English and German theologians and churchmen (*The Wittenberg Articles* 1536). This early Lutheran influence has left its mark on Archbishop Cranmer's first Book of Common Prayer, the Book of Homilies, English translations of the Bible, and, through a number of earlier doctrinal statements, on many of the thirty-nine articles of religion (*The Ten Articles* 1536, *The Bishops' Book* 1537, *The Thirteen Articles* 1538).

9. The theological common ground between Lutherans and Anglicans was soon superseded by the fast advance of Reformed, Calvinistic concepts. In England such views concerning the real presence in the eucharist and predestination found wide acceptance. Moreover, many of those who had been exiled on the Continent in the reign of Mary returned under Elizabeth I as zealous advocates for further reform of the English church, following the example of the church of Geneva.

The parting of the ways

10. From the second part of the 16th century the internal Puritan threat to abolish the episcopal system disturbed the unity of church and state in England and called forth a defence of the Church of England which emphasized its own identity by advocating its particular "middle way" between Rome and Geneva. In the same period some Lutheran churches on the Continent retained a similar structure to the English church, as in Sweden and Finland; others were forced to abandon the episcopal system. In either case the awareness of a family relationship between the Anglican and the Lutheran churches was still strong. Mutual recognition and intercommunion were freely practised.

11. But this period also witnessed the beginning of a separate development. The defence against puritanism was in the main directed against the Reformed and independent traditions, yet it also gave rise to critical attitudes towards all the Reformation churches on the Continent. The Anglican theological method had as its main criterion the interplay between scripture, Tradition and reason. The Lutheran criterion of sola scriptura did not exclude a high esteem for Tradition, but could not attribute to reason the same role as in English theological thinking.

12. Other developments and influences, many of them non-theological, led to further estrangement between the Anglican and Lutheran churches. Perhaps the most influential force in this development was the Oxford movement. Lutheranism was identified with Protestantism as it was encountered in England. Lutherans, on the other hand, tended to see in Anglicanism an expression of semi-Catholicism which they could not acknowledge. In practice this resulted in barriers to intercommunion and the failure to recognize each other as churches. The deepest difference was seen in the understanding and structure of the ministry with its wider implications for eucharistic theology and ecclesiology.

13. However, even during these centuries of separate development many relationships between Anglican and Lutheran churches continued. In both traditions there were individuals and groups who renewed contacts, enabled mutual theological exchange, and fostered a close relationship between Anglicans and Lutherans, especially in Scandinavia. The history of Anglican-Lutheran relations is a complex one and cannot be reduced to one simple pattern.

14. The inadequate and often distorted images of Anglicanism and Lutheranism created during these centuries are still present realities, and much needs to be done to correct them; but since the beginning of this century new developments have increased mutual knowledge and exchange, and have produced far-reaching changes in our relationship. This leads us to a new stage.

III. Anglican-Lutheran relationships today

15. Anglican-Lutheran relationships today are the result of several more general developments during the last few decades:
a) The ecumenical movement has provided many occasions for more frequent encounters between Anglicans and Lutherans. This has contributed to better mutual understanding between individuals and groups on both sides. A similar contribution has come from the conversations and the different arrangements for eucharistic sharing between the Church of England and the Scandinavian and Baltic Lutheran churches before and after the second world war.
b) Since the second world war, the translation of theological works, increased exchange through visits and study in the other church context, together with growing contact between both leaders and church members, has broadened mutual knowledge and understanding.
c) The ecumenical activity and the growing self-consciousness of Anglican and Lutheran churches in countries outside Europe has freed Anglican-Lutheran relations from their limited European perspective, and invests them with a special urgency, since Anglicans and Lutherans are living side by side in these countries and share common tasks of mission and service.

16. Together with this intensified exchange, there have been convergences resulting from general theological and ecumenical thinking, as well as the rediscovery of elements in our two traditions which indicate a close affinity. In addition to agreement on central Christian doctrines, these convergences include among others:
a) Becoming conscious that we share, as Anglicans and Lutherans, the same roots: emphasis on the witness of holy scripture as normative and on continuity with the apostolic faith and mission throughout the centuries and appreciation of the Reformation as a renewal movement within the church catholic and not as a beginning of a new church.

b) Realizing afresh that our two churches are marked by a high esteem for sacramental life and liturgical worship.
c) Affirming together the church as a community, constituted by Jesus Christ through his presence and action through the means of grace. This community, empowered by the Holy Spirit, is called to responsibility for the wider human community in which it lives.
d) Adopting similar views, assisted by the results of biblical and historical research, concerning the emergence of the Christian church and its institutions. This and basic agreements on the understanding of apostolicity and on the nature, place and function of the ordained ministry within the ministry of the whole people of God have removed many former differences.
e) Realizing that both Anglican and Lutheran churches comprehend convictions and forms of expression which are commonly associated with the "catholic" and with the Protestant traditions within Christianity. This enables them to exercise together a mediating role in efforts towards Christian unity.

17. Bilateral dialogues between our two churches have discovered, received, clarified and formulated these and other agreements and convergences. They are, therefore, playing an essential role in fostering the growing theological consensus between our two churches and in helping to broaden the awareness of the reality of such agreements and convergences. They challenge our churches to reconsider their relations and provide the necessary basis for decisions aiming at closer relationships with one another.

18. Increased contacts and exchange and theological dialogue and convergence have improved relationships between Anglican and Lutheran churches to a remarkable degree during recent years. But the forms of such relationships vary according to situations. A general, and far from complete, overview indicates the following types of relationships:
a) In many countries there exists eucharistic hospitality between our churches as part of a broader invitation to communicant members of trinitarian churches under the specific provisions/regulations of the respective churches. In these countries our churches also work together in specific projects and programmes.
b) A more specific relation between Anglican and Lutheran churches is found in situations where they have established bilateral contacts, cooperation, sharing in social work, assistance in pastoral work, mutual participation in worship and on special occasions, e.g. the consecration or installation of a bishop. These forms of relationships we find in all parts of the world, e.g. Europe, Canada, Latin America, Namibia, Tanzania, Madagascar, Papua New Guinea, Malaysia.
c) In some situations these contacts have led to the desire to enter into a theological dialogue with the purpose of deepening these contacts, of overcoming still existing differences and of moving to forms of official eucharistic sharing. This step has been taken or is planned, e.g. in Canada and Tanzania.
d) In other situations such a theological dialogue between Anglicans and Lutherans has already been conducted for several years and has resulted in reports and even in decisions by the churches involved. The two most significant examples of this dialogue are the Lutheran-Episcopal dialogue in the USA and the Anglican-Lutheran dialogue in Europe. Both dialogues built on the foundations laid by the *international Anglican-Lutheran conversations 1970-1972* and have enriched one another as well as profited from the multilateral dialogue in Faith and Order which resulted in *Baptism, Eucharist and Ministry*, 1982.

e) The *Lutheran-Episcopal dialogue in the USA* entered its third round in December 1983. After work between 1969 and 1972 the first dialogue commission presented a progress report in 1972. A new commission met between 1976 and 1980, and its report and recommendations were published in 1981. On the basis of these studies the conventions of the American Lutheran Church, the Association of Evangelical Lutheran Churches, the Episcopal Church in the USA and the Lutheran Church in America adopted in September 1982 an agreement. It expresses mutual recognition as churches in which the gospel is preached and taught, establishes a relationship of interim sharing of the eucharist and encourages forms of joint worship, mutual prayer, common study of holy scriptures, joint programmes of religious education, mission, social action, etc. This dialogue is of special significance because it is the first one which has led to action by the participating churches.

f) The *Anglican-Lutheran European commission* met between 1980 and 1982. Its report was published in 1983. The commission set its reflections on several doctrinal issues – justification, baptism, eucharist, spiritual life and liturgical worship, ordained ministry and episcopacy and the nature of the church – in the wider context of the challenges arising from the situation and mission of Anglican and Lutheran churches in present-day Europe. This dialogue, therefore, makes the affirmation that mission is the proper context of the search for unity. In its recommendations the commission stated its belief that "on the basis of the agreements we have reached, and in the light of the earlier agreement recorded by the international conversations together with the long-standing dialogue in the USA and the wider ecumenical consensus... there are no longer any serious obstacles on the way towards the establishment of full communion between our two churches". This conclusion goes somewhat beyond the actions resulting from the dialogue in the USA, but the recommendations of the European dialogue are basically pointing in the same direction. Another difference is that the report of the European dialogue has not yet been received or officially accepted by the churches concerned.

19. Though there are areas where closer Anglican-Lutheran relations are still non-existent or only in their initial stages, the overall development is remarkable and constitutes a new and highly significant stage in the history of the two communions. This development has also led to increasingly close relations between the Anglican Consultative Council and the Lutheran World Federation. The most advanced stage of relationships has been reached in the USA where the third round of Lutheran-Episcopal dialogue, begun in December 1983, may profit from the theological progress achieved in the European dialogue. It is to be hoped that these achievements serve as an impulse for Anglican-Lutheran relations in other parts of the world so that Anglicans and Lutherans also as two worldwide communions continue to move towards full communion in obedience to their common Lord and Saviour in serving together his mission in the world.

20. The relation between national and international dialogues is of great importance. National dialogue is naturally geared to a specific geographical location, but it provides the opportunity to apply the more general theological thinking of international dialogue to a specific situation. Conversely the national dialogue draws on the insights gained in other dialogues. This inter-relation is not just one of dependence of one upon another (national upon international) but a mutual activity both testing conclusions and ensuring consistency.

21. The active participation of both our churches in the multilateral Faith and Order conversations provides a common reference point and a wider framework for their dialogue. This is also important in view of the fact that Anglican-Lutheran discussions are conducted side by side with other interchurch dialogues of our churches and communions. Such parallel conversations may run the risk of pursuing different directions and of appearing to be saying different things to different partners. The broader multilateral conversations, together with the meetings of the forum on bilateral conversations and other efforts, help to maintain consistency and theological credibility. Increasing communication and exchange between the different dialogues also has the advantage of mutual enrichment. The Lutheran-Anglican dialogue has, for example, much profited from the statements on apostolicity, *episcope* and episcopacy in the Lutheran-Roman Catholic, Anglican-Roman Catholic and the Faith and Order conversations.

22. What has emerged from these different dialogues is that Anglicans and Lutherans have a distinctive role in ecumenical endeavours. Our traditions have a common root, and both our churches have been separated from communion with the Roman Catholic Church. Because of their history, therefore, both regard dialogue with the Roman Catholic Church as a principal responsibility. Between these churches an ecumenical breakthrough would heal a painful division with far-reaching consequences and would be of major importance for the unity of Christ's church. Such a consideration and commitment provides a strong link between us, but it also provides a link in the wider ecumenical scene, where both our churches, being catholic and reformed, are in dialogue also with the Orthodox, Reformed and other traditions.

23. In addition, our Anglican-Lutheran dialogue can now find a framework and a source of enrichment for its further development in the Faith and Order document *Baptism, Eucharist and Ministry* (*BEM*). This document has a different focus and status from the reports and recommendations coming from bilateral commissions, but it serves the same purpose of contributing to the movement towards visible unity. It will, therefore, be natural and helpful if our churches study and evaluate BEM together with the reports from their bilateral conversations. Since Anglicans and Lutherans appear to be adopting similar positions with regard to BEM, we hope that this will also be of assistance to their moving closer to one another on their path towards full communion.

IV. Goal of Anglican-Lutheran dialogue

24. We look forward to the day when full communion is established between Anglican and Lutheran churches.

25. By full communion we here understand a relationship between two distinct churches or communions. Each maintains its own autonomy and recognizes the catholicity and apostolicity of the other, and each believes the other to hold the essentials of the Christian faith:
a) subject to such safeguards as ecclesial discipline may properly require, members of one body may receive the sacraments of the other;
b) subject to local invitation, bishops of one church may take part in the consecration of the bishops of the other, thus acknowledging the duty of mutual care and concern;
c) subject to church regulation, a bishop, pastor/priest or deacon of one ecclesial body may exercise liturgical functions in a congregation of the other body if invited to do so and also, when requested, pastoral care of the other's members;

d) it is also a necessary addition and complement that there should be recognized organs of regular consultation and communication, including episcopal collegiality, to express and strengthen the fellowship and enable common witness, life and service.

26. To be in full communion means that churches become interdependent while remaining autonomous. One is not elevated to be the judge of the other nor can it remain insensitive to the other; neither is each body committed to every secondary feature of the tradition of the other. Thus the corporate strength of the churches is enhanced in love, and an isolated independence is restrained.

27. Full communion carries implications which go beyond sharing the same eucharist. The eucharist is a common meal, and to share in it together has implications for a sharing of life and of common concerns for the mission of the church. To be in full communion implies a community of life, an exchange and a commitment to one another in respect of major decisions on questions of faith, order and morals. It implies, where churches are in the same geographical area, common worship, study, witness, evangelism, and promotion of justice, peace and love. It may lead to a uniting of ecclesial bodies if they are, or come to be, immediately adjacent in the same geographical area. This should not imply the suppressing of ethnic, cultural or ecclesial characteristics or traditions which may in fact be maintained and developed by diverse institutions within one communion.

V. Moving towards full communion

28. Unity by stages is a concept that is gaining wide recognition, though not great clarity of definition. It implies that the end cannot be seen from the beginning, and that unity must be pursued in terms of movement and process. It does imply that we know the direction in which we wish to move, and that we take definite steps to break down the barriers which at present stand in the way of visible unity.

29. Lutherans and Anglicans concur that agreement in the faith is a proper prerequisite for unity: it is a stage on the way to its achievement. The agreed statements of dialogues carry the authority only of their members until they receive the approval of the appropriate juridical authorities of the churches. This approval should itself reflect a general consensus within the churches which must not only involve dialogue but also common prayer and practical collaboration.

30. An agreed statement is thus a crucial vehicle of consensus and provides grounds for decision-making about a changed relationship between churches: its "reception" by the churches is therefore a decisive stage on the way towards unity. The statements provide a basis for mutual recognition of churches and members and thus allow some degree of eucharistic communion.

31. Under certain conditions, individual or groups are admitted to holy communion in one another's churches before full communion has been achieved. One way to describe this initial stage is "limited eucharistic sharing". A specific example of this stage is the "interim sharing of the eucharist" that has been achieved in North America. In other Lutheran and Anglican churches those responsible should discuss and could adopt the same agreement or an adaptation. In so doing, they would accept the goal of full communion, committing themselves to resolve the remaining questions and work together. Some of these questions may only be resolved within the new relationship of limited eucharistic sharing.

32. The goal of full communion may be described as full mutual recognition of catholicity and apostolicity. That is to say, the churches become aware that they share a common identity in all essentials of the Christian faith, recognizing that they are in harmony and expressing their agreement in statements as well as in life. Full agreement in the faith should include proposals for implementation, that is, the implications of agreement on what is to be done.

33. At this time [1983] there are no Lutheran and Anglican churches in full communion with each other. To reach that goal, they must address and reach consensus on the following issues: authority in the church, the gospel and its implications, justification/salvation, the sacraments, the ministry and its ordering. In the process of reaching consensus of these issues, they may make their own the agreements which are already in place or develop future ones. They must also jointly address and act upon such concerns as witness and evangelism, worship and prayer, and service. The churches may well discover as they address and act on certain of these issues that this can best be done through their international institutions (the Lutheran World Federation and the Anglican Consultative Council).

34. It would be necessary before the goal of full communion to have developed some modus vivendi of worship and work. The tentative beginnings of common prayer, study, witness and evangelism as well as joint projects begun during the stage of interim eucharistic sharing should become the norm when the goal of full communion has been reached and hence must develop greatly before the step to full communion can be taken. The experience of the agreement in faith and recognition of ministries must be accompanied by genuine renewal for both Lutherans and Anglicans by which their constituencies can better see, understand and carry out the apostolic ministry in the service of the gospel.

Recommendations

On the basis of the international, regional and national dialogues between Anglicans and Lutherans and in the light of the communion centred around word and sacrament we have experienced in each other's traditions, we are mutually able to recognize the presence of the church of Jesus Christ in our respective communions. This recognition can be affirmed even if there is not as yet complete agreement on the ministerial expressions of apostolicity. But in spite of convergence rather than consensus on this sensitive issue, our mutual recognition of Christ prompts us to move with urgency towards the fullest possible ecclesial recognition and the goal of full communion.

To this end as first steps upon the way we recommend that:

I. (a) Anglican and Lutheran churches should officially encourage the practice of mutual eucharistic hospitality – if this is not already authorized – where pastoral need exists and when ecumenical occasions make this appropriate.

(b) The churches of our two communions should make provision for appropriate forms of "interim eucharistic sharing" along the lines of that authorized in the USA or recommended by the European regional commission as a further step towards full communion where there is a commitment to that goal.

We also recommend that:

II. (a) The ACC and the LWF should monitor the developing relationships between the two churches and encourage these relationships by communicating the information gathered to their member churches – in the first instance sending them this report.

(b) The ACC and the LWF should establish a permanent continuation committee to coordinate and assess developing Anglican-Lutheran relationships and dialogues.

(c) The ACC and the LWF should mutually invite consultants and observers to international bodies or consultations where they have not already done so.

(d) The ACC and the LWF should arrange a joint consultation (with advisers from their major dialogue partners) on the relation between apostolic succession, the ministry of the whole people of God, episcopacy and the historic episcopate, taking the BEM treatment of this issue as its framework together with the results of appropriate bilateral dialogues.

(e) The ACC and the LWF should encourage theological and pastoral exchanges and study at regional or church-to-church levels – such as the established Anglican-Scandinavian theological and pastoral conferences – in regions where this has not so far taken place, with a view to (i) examining and preparing ways to full communion, (ii) exploring jointly common pastoral and evangelistic challenges and opportunities.

(f) The ACC and the LWF should, in consultation with the World Council of Churches, cooperate more closely in political and social matters of mutual concern, especially in relation to urgent situations in countries (e.g. Namibia) where the two traditions exist in some strength.

I. ANGLICAN-LUTHERAN DIALOGUE

2. Episcope

Niagara Falls, September 1987

Preface

Two linked events took place at Niagara Falls in autumn 1987 in the course of the international dialogue between Anglicans and Lutherans. The first was a major consultation on *episcope* (24-29 September), and this was immediately followed (30 September-3 October) by a meeting of the Anglican-Lutheran International Continuation Committee to produce this report.

At the consultation some three dozen theologians, historians and church leaders met to tackle the issue of *episcope*, the chief remaining obstacle to full communion between Anglicans and Lutherans. The intention of this gathering may be summarized thus:

a) to shed some fresh light on the relationship between the topics of apostolic succession, the ministry of the whole people of God, episcopacy and the historic episcopate;
b) to set this material in the broad perspective of the church's mission, taking seriously the diversity of its cultural settings;
c) and to evaluate in the light of contemporary ecumenical dialogue the current practice of *episcope* amongst Anglicans and Lutherans, so as to offer pointers for the future reform and joint exercise of *episcope* in the service of our common mission.

A wealth of talent and wisdom was contributed to this task, and a real meeting of minds took place on several facets of the subject. There was strong representation from Asia and Africa, where the tempo of Anglican-Lutheran cooperation is visibly quickening. The active participation of Roman Catholic and Eastern Orthodox consultants proved to be very creative. Indeed, the emerging ecumenical consensus reassured Anglicans and Lutherans that their efforts to draw closer to one another in regard to the practical exercise of *episcope* was fully consistent with, and actually assisted by, their current bilateral dialogues with the Roman Catholic Church. Two other factors were specially helpful to the consultation: the daily sharing of worship according to the Anglican and Lutheran traditions, and the peaceful and hospitable atmosphere of Mount Carmel retreat house where we stayed.

Those who took part found this to be a fruitful and stimulating occasion, and it was agreed that the papers contributed should be made available in due course to a wider public by the Anglican Consultative Council (ACC) and the Lutheran World Federation (LWF).

The Anglican-Lutheran continuation committee met after the consultation to distil its findings and recommend attainable goals to the ACC and the LWF. It will be for these parent bodies as well as for individual member churches to decide whether this Niagara report represents any breakthrough in understanding, and how far and how soon its proposals should be implemented.

We wish to record our warm and grateful thanks to all who contributed to the consultation, and to the secretarial staff, Irmhild Reichen-Young and Vanessa Wilde.

      David Tustin   Sebastian Kolowa
      Bishop of Grimsby   Presiding Bishop
                                            Evangelical Lutheran Church in Tanzania
                                                                        Niagara Falls, October 1987

Introduction

1. Official Anglican-Lutheran conversations on the international level extend back over two decades. The first – the Anglican-Lutheran international conversations 1970-1972 (ALIC) – authorized by the Lambeth conference and the Lutheran World Federation (LWF) produced the Pullach report. Building upon it, the international relationship was intensified by a planning group meeting in 1975 and, more especially, by a joint working group in 1983, which recommended to the Anglican Consultative Council (ACC) and the LWF that they establish an international continuation committee. It should both enable further international conversation and help to make the results of the various national and regional Anglican-Lutheran dialogues contribute to progress elsewhere.

2. At its first meeting in Wimbledon, England, 1986, the Anglican-Lutheran International Continuation Committee (ALICC) laid plans for a joint consultation on *episcope*, regarded as the chief obstacle to full communion (see its report, appendix I). That international consultation took place in Niagara Falls, Ontario, Canada, in September 1987 and provided the basis for this report.

3. Numerous dialogues between Anglicans and Lutherans during the past twenty years have discovered how much we share in doctrine, worship, mission, and the understanding and functioning of ministry. The Anglican-Lutheran European Regional Commission (ALERC) concluded that "there are no longer any serious obstacles on the way towards the establishment of full communion between our two churches" (Helsinki report, 1982). A further expression of the wide extent of agreement is contained in section III (§§60-80) of this present report. But the documents resulting from these official encounters have repeatedly identified differences in the *practice* of *episcope* (that is, pastoral leadership, coordination and oversight), especially the presence or absence of bishops in the historic episcopate, as the chief (if not the only remaining) obstacle to full communion. By *historic episcopate* we mean an episcopate which traces its origins back through history to at least the end of the 2nd century. We use the phrase "apostolic succession" in the "substantive sense" identified by the Lutheran-Roman Catholic Joint Commission (LRCJC) document *The Ministry in the Church* (59,60) to signify "the apostolicity of the church in faith" (see further *Baptism, Eucharist and Ministry* (BEM) M34-35; §§19,20 below; *Helsinki Report*, 40 and 43; *Pullach Report*, 1973, 87-89; *LED II*, 1980, pp.61-62). Thus attention to this topic has been recognized as necessary if we are to:
a) continue movement towards full communion between our respective churches;
b) facilitate the ongoing development of common life and mission in various regions where our churches function in the same geographical areas; and

c) open up structural possibilities for the more complete future realization of full communion especially in the countries where our churches exist side by side.

4. The differences between us in the dimension of *episcope* include not only the presence or absence of bishops in the historic episcopate but also differences in the significance our churches attach to such bishops. These differences serve as the focal point for mutual fears and suspicions, prejudices and distorted perceptions. They also seem to threaten existing agreements with other churches as well as ecumenical expectations expressed in dialogues of both our churches with the Roman Catholic and Orthodox churches.

5. We have identified, through the work of our predecessors in dialogue and with the assistance of our colleagues in the most recent consultation, some perspectives on this topic which we believe can help our churches to overcome their differences, as well as ground and shape full communion, and assist its structural expression.

6. In the document which follows, initial and major attention is given to the mission of the church and its first realization in the communities of the New Testament period (section I). We give mission such prominence because at Wimbledon 1986 our survey of the situation of our churches throughout the world impressed upon us the fact that the agenda and the timetable for full communion between Anglicans and Lutherans is experienced differently in different parts of the world. However, the urgency of giving attention to the nature of the church's mission is universal. Indeed, the crisis of the church in mission is at least as great in those countries in Europe and North America where the need for full communion may be less urgently perceived. At Wimbledon, therefore, we determined that the theme for the consultation on *episcope* would be "*Episcope* in Relation to the Mission of the Church". What we are presenting in section I:
i) reflects a significant portion of our work at Niagara;
ii) offers a renewed perspective on the mission of the church as the *gift* of Christ; and
iii) provides the necessary context for both our understanding of *episcope* and our proposals for the realization of full communion between our churches.

We conclude that it is a mistake to hold that there is only one criterion which must be satisfied, that of an unbroken chain of ordinations from the apostles' time, if one church is to recognize another as truly apostolic.

7. Then we seek to identify the major requirements for carrying out the mission of the church in so far as they concern *episcope* or the ministry of pastoral leadership, cooperation and oversight (section II). These are doxology, continuity, disciplined life together, nurture, and faithfulness to the goal of human history given in Jesus Christ. We show how the office of bishop in the early church sought to hold local churches firm in the koinonia or communion of the faithful in all ages (diachronic catholicity) and in all places (synchronic catholicity). We consider subsequent developments in the episcopal office and evaluate Anglican and Lutheran forms of succession in the presiding ministry since the Reformation.

8. The document continues with a summary of "the truths we share", identifying the common tradition of faith, confession, sacramental life, and perspective on order which Anglicans and Lutherans have discovered in each other (section III).

9. All this is preparatory to the proposals we make to Anglicans and to Lutherans for the immediate establishment of full communion (section IV). We conclude this section with a series of proposals for reform which both traditions need to consider in order to renew the ministry of *episcope*.

10. Finally, we identify for our churches the legislative actions needed, the structures for shared mission and ministry, and the concrete liturgical recognition which would inaugurate our full communion (section V).

I. The nature of the church and its mission

11. "Praise be to the God and Father of our Lord Jesus Christ, who has bestowed on us in Christ every spiritual blessing in the heavenly realms" (Eph. 1:3).

The Christian church is first of all overwhelmingly conscious of the splendour of God's gifts – in Christ we have been chosen to be dedicated and full of love, to be accepted as heirs of God, to be forgiven, to be part of a plan that the whole universe be brought into a unity, and to receive the seal of the Holy Spirit as a pledge that we shall indeed enter into that inheritance. But to realize the magnificence of these gifts the church continually needs yet another gift, that of spiritual insight. Only so will we have any conception of the resources of power open to those who trust in Christ, resources the scale of which are only measured by the fact that everything has already been put in subjection to him, and that this same Christ is the supreme head of the church which is his body (Eph. 1:4-23).

12. The life of the church is based upon this already victorious engagement with the powers of sin and death. It is the free and unmerited grace of God which, through Christ's sacrificial death on the cross, once for all, brings us into union with him. This is how we come to be no longer aliens, but citizens together with God's own chosen people. To be the church is to be part of the story of the people of God entering into their inheritance within God's world.

13. But it is precisely that story which reminds us of the difficulties which are to be encountered. The people of Israel, God's chosen people, were repeatedly blind or disobedient, compromised with local rulers, persecuted prophets and suffered horrific disasters. Jesus' own life of teaching, healing and acceptance of the outcast and sinner brought him into deadly rivalry with the prevailing authorities. The disciples whom he sent out were instructed to expect to be rejected as well as received; and the New Testament communities which preserved the stories of Jesus did so in a form which illustrates the fact that jealousy, disputes and misunderstandings were part of their experience even after receiving the gift of the Holy Spirit.

14. There must therefore be a twofold consciousness in the mind of every Christian; on the one hand of the magnificence of God's gifts, on the other of the need to be prepared for difficulty, struggle and temptation. Honest reading of the history of the Christian church compels us to admit that that church, like the people of Israel, has repeatedly been blind or disobedient, has compromised with local rulers, persecuted its prophets and suffered horrific disasters. From that history we learn the necessity for continuous vigilance and the need for penitence.

15. It is the whole Christian church which has been sent on its mission and been given the necessary gifts. God's plan is the unification of all things in Christ; that, and nothing less, is the goal. Before that goal is realized the church has the task of embodying in all that it is, says and does the promise that the goal is realizable. The whole church is witness to that promise, and every member (limb or organ) of it is inescapably part of how that goal will be understood.

16. In this sense the church as a whole may be compared to a system of communication, no part of which is strictly irrelevant to the conveying of coherent meaning.

When human beings communicate with one another it is important, if one is to avoid confusion, that words, gestures, facial expressions and symbolic gifts should not contradict each other. Similarly when the church wishes to be heard in a given culture, it is important that the whole of its "language" be coherently inter-related so that its message makes sense.

17. Every member of the church is an integral part of its witness and its mission; and every member has received a gift of the Holy Spirit so that the whole may flourish. "All members are called to discover, with the help of the community, the gifts they have received and to use them for the building up of the church and for the service of the world to which the church is sent" (*BEM*, M5; see the whole section, M1-6, for an expression of the sense that every Christian is involved in the church's witness to God's plan for humankind).

18. The outbreak of misunderstandings, personal rivalries and disputes is a threat to the coherence of the Christian mission. It is already clear from the New Testament that the early Christian communities were having to resolve urgent and complex problems specifically relating to their mission and witness. The picture we gain from the study of the New Testament is of communities wrestling with the problems of internal discipline at the same time as carrying out their mission of witness to the love of God in Jesus Christ.

19. It is in this context that the development of an authoritative, but not authoritarian, ministry must be understood. It is plain that there were from the first those who held specific authority in the churches and who fulfilled their calling in and for the whole community (*BEM*, M9). Authority was not a matter of the acquisition of status, but the bestowal of responsibilities. These responsibilities were to be exercised in such a way as to serve the mission of the whole church in its numerous, diverse, but essentially inter-related acts and attributes. They included the maintenance of "witness to the apostolic faith, proclamation and fresh interpretation of the gospel, celebration of baptism and the eucharist, the transmission of ministerial responsibilities, communion in prayer, love, joy and suffering, service to the sick and the needy, unity among the local churches and sharing the gifts which the Lord has given to each" (*BEM*, M34).

20. Study of the life of the early Christian communities reflected in the pages of the New Testament should make it unthinkable for us to isolate ordination at the hands of someone in linear succession to the apostles as the sole criterion of faithfulness to the apostolic commission. So many investigations have now confirmed this conclusion that the burden of proof has passed to those who would argue otherwise. Ministries of pastoral leadership, coordination and oversight have continuously been part of the church's witness to the gospel. Indeed we may say that the mission of the church required the coherence of its witness in every aspect of its life, and that this coherence required supervision. But the New Testament does not entitle us to assert that such supervision was carried out by a uniform structure of government inherited directly from or transmitted by the apostles (on the development of structures see further §§41-59). Thus to speak of "apostolic succession" is to speak primarily of characteristics of the whole church; and to recognize a church as being "in the apostolic succession" is to use not one criterion of discernment, but many (cf. *BEM*, M35).

21. It is therefore essential for those Christian churches which do not enjoy full communion with one another to reappropriate the substantial basis for understanding the apostolic mission of the church with which the New Testament provides us. Mis-

sion indeed comes to special expression in the church's apostolicity. For apostolicity means that the church is sent by Jesus to *be* for the world, to participate in his mission and therefore in the mission of the One who sent Jesus, to participate in the mission of the Father and the Son through the dynamic of the Holy Spirit.

22. The church receives its apostolicity, its mission, as the gift of him who is "far above all rule and authority and power and dominion, and above every name that is named, not only in this age but also in that which is to come". For the Father "has put all things under his feet and has made him the head over all things for the church, which is his body, the fullness of him who fills all in all" (Eph. 1:21-23). Christ *can* confer his mission upon the church because by raising him from the dead the Father conferred the final *yes* upon Christ's way of self-offering love. All powers and dominions in *this* age believe, in the last analysis, that death has the last word. The appropriate expression of such belief is humanity's unrelenting drive for self-preservation. But if the Christ has the last word, then the appropriate expression is rather self-offering, confident in the knowledge that there is more to do with life than preserve it. Those who seek to save their lives will lose them anyway. But those who offer their lives for Christ's sake will find their true selves, will find life itself (Matt. 16:24-26 and par.).

23. The apostolicity of the church is the mission of self-offering (not self-preservation) for the life of the world. The church thus serves the reign of God, not the reign of sin and death. The church serves the mission of God's suffering and vulnerable love, not a mission of its own devising. The church serves the mission grounded in and shaped by Christ's way of being in the world.

24. The kingdom of God is thus the over-arching theme of history. The church's mission is to witness to that reign by its words and rites (proclamation and sacraments), by its structures and governance (Mark 10:35-45, esp. 43), by its *being* as well as its doing. The church has been given the insight into both the grounding and character of the kingdom of God (Christ as "Alpha" and "way") as well as the final eschatological victory of the kingdom of God (Christ as "Omega" and "fullness" or "consummation") Because of its *gift* of apostolic mission that church is called to apostolic mission. In the same way the gift of unity is the basis for the call to be unifying, the gift of holiness is the basis for the call to be consecrating, and the gift of catholicity is the basis for the call to be whole, orthodox and universal.

II. Requirements for the church's mission

25. The *gift* of Christ is that he sends his disciples as he has been sent (John 20:21), that they are to witness to God's forgiving judgment and verdict by setting at liberty all who are in the bondage of sin, that they are to witness to God's confounding and defeat of evil by unmasking the demonic powers and joining the struggle against them. In Christ the church is called to have and to serve the "keys" of the kingdom of God (Matt. 16:18). In Christ the church is called to be a sign, an instrument and a foretaste of the kingdom of God.

26. The church awakens to the astonishing discovery that its mission is a gift, that it has indeed been given the pearl of great price, the treasure hidden in a field (Matt. 13:44-46) and that this discovery is the reason for gathering others in order to participate in the joy (Luke 15:8-10). In order to *be* such a church it becomes conscious that certain things are required of it. These "requirements" follow as consequences upon the discovery that its mission is in fact a gift.

Doxology

27. The church praises God "for our creation, preservation, and all the blessings of this life; but above all for (God's) inestimable love in the redemption of the world by our Lord Jesus Christ; for the means of grace, and for the hope of glory" (Book of Common Prayer, General Thanksgiving). It has been given the word of Christ for teaching, admonition, wisdom as it sings and preaches, in prison and out of it (Acts 16:25), "with thankfulness... to God" (Col. 3:16). It is called "in word or deed (to) do everything in the name of the Lord Jesus, giving thanks to God the Father through him" (Col. 3:17). It has been baptized a royal priesthood as a people claimed by God for his own to proclaim the triumphs of one who has called us out of darkness into his marvellous light (1 Pet. 2:9). It has been given the meal by which it receives with thanksgiving the final, full and costly sacrifice of Christ on the cross. In this meal the church has been given its identity as the community which anticipates the heavenly banquet of consummated salvation (Isa. 25:6-8; Matt. 26:29; Mark 14:25; Luke 22:16,18; Matt. 14:19 and par.; Luke 13:29; 14:15-24; John 6:30-59; Rev. 19:9). In this meal the church has been given the promise that in Christ God will receive the offering of the whole people whom God calls and uses in the apostolic mission of the kingdom (Rom. 12:1-21). In the doxological prayer of the kingdom the Son gives the church the Father's name as the One who sent him in the power of the Spirit (Luke 11:1-13). The church praises the triune Name and prays in that name in order to be grasped and shaped by it for participation in the divine mission.

Continuity

28. The God who calls the church to its divine mission is faithful. God is faithful to God's own being and identity. The act of calling the universe into being is an act of vulnerable, risk-taking love (John 1:9-18; Col. 1:15-20; Heb. 13:8). God is faithful in covenant and promise, not abandoning Israel, but giving up the Son "for us all" (Rom. 8:31-39) so that the Gentiles might be grafted on to the "olive tree" of the people of God (Rom. 11:1-32). It is God's *faithfulness* which is "unsearchable" and "inscrutable" and which evokes our praise (Rom. 11:33-36). The church is given the gift of God's fidelity in order to be faithful. It has God's continuity in order to continue in Christ's word and to abide in koinonia or communion with Christ and with each other – and thus to experience and express both truth and freedom (John 8:31-33). The context in which the continuity of ministerial office is presented in the pastoral epistles is faithful teaching and confession (1 Tim. 4:6-16; 6:3-16; 2 Tim. 2:1-6; Titus 2:1).

29. Because the church's call to faithfulness and continuity is grounded in God's faithfulness and continuity, it is possible for the church to cherish both those symbols of continuity which the church has been given and also those experiences in its past in which God's faithfulness has persevered despite the church's brokenness, ambiguity, perversity and unfaithfulness. The church acknowledges with thanksgiving the canonical scriptures through which Torah and prophets, apostolic proclamation and gospel narrative have been identified, gathered and transmitted. The church exists because of the unbroken continuity of the gift of baptism and the Lord's supper. The church has been given the gift of orthodox confession in the form of dogmatic response to heresies which threatened the gospel. The church receives gratefully whatever historical continuity its bishops and presbyters have been given.

30. Such symbols of continuity are, however, only part of the life of the church, and need constantly to be interpreted afresh so that their meaning and impact may be always experienced as the liberating gospel of God's grace. Like any living being, the church only remains what it is through change and adjustment. The mere preservation of symbols of continuity may diminish their effectiveness. The history of the Christian church contains the record of God's faithfulness in spite of human faithlessness. God has persevered with the church even when the scriptures have been mutilated, ignored, traduced or idolized; even when baptism has been administered promiscuously or received frivolously; even when the Lord's supper has become routine or been neglected; even when the loss of the connection between gospel and dogma has led to inquisition and authoritarianism on the one hand, rejection and apostasy on the other hand. In the context of our study of *episcope* we have been led to trust God's faithfulness also when bishops in historic succession have been unfaithful in an effluvium of evil, or when churches forced to endure ruptures in the tradition grew comfortable with their supposed autonomy. The gospel of God's faithfulness is at the same time his call to the church to repent and be reconciled.

Disciplined life together as a community of disciples
31. The church's mission is given by God to a community. This has its basis in both the mission and the obedience of Jesus. The mission of Jesus was directed to Israel as a people, to Israel's renewal of and recalling of *its* mission (Luke 2:29-32; Matt. 10:5-15 and par.; 15:24). Through the renewal of Israel and the calling of the twelve the eschatological vision of the gathering of the Gentiles and the overcoming of alienation was to be realized (Eph. 2:11-3:13). The separate existence of synagogue (which does not acknowledge Jesus as Messiah) and church (which confesses Jesus as Messiah) is a painful reminder that our sinfulness continues to frustrate the mission of God, that we live in the tension between the inauguration and consummation of the kingdom of God, that the church itself is an ambiguous and incomplete sign of the kingdom of God. The temptation to autonomous individualism and anarchy on the one hand and to oppressive collectivism on the other hand means that the church requires discipline in its corporate life and at the same time that such discipline needs to be grounded in the obedience of Christ. The church is a community of disciples (Matt. 28:19-20). Its discipleship is described by the "Torah" of the kingdom of God (e.g. Matt. 5-7) and the apostolic description of life in the disciple community (e.g. Rom. 12-15; Gal. 5-6; Col. 2:20-4.6; Eph. 4-6). The discipline is both grounded in and shaped by Christ. Leadership is not to be like that of the Gentiles (Mark 10:43). It is "in the Lord" (1 Thess. 5:12-13; Eph. 5:21). It begins with the mind of Christ who took the form of a servant and was obedient to a slave's death (Phil. 2:1-11). Yet it is discipline replete with admonition (Mark and Matthew are written to communities to correct them and their leadership, as are Galatians, both Corinthian letters, 1 Thessalonians, and more) and making painful decisions necessary (e.g. 1 Cor. 5:1-2). The freedom of the gospel is the freedom of all in the community to be committed to the holiness of one another and the wholeness of the community (Gal. 6:1-5). Love is never indifferent.

Nurture
32. Here again the church discovers that the resource for its mission has already been given it. For Christ himself is the living bread, given for the life of the world

(John 6:51). He is the living water, of which, if anyone drinks, that person will never thirst again (John 4:14). Christ is, moreover, the door of the sheepfold, through which the sheep will pass to find somewhere safe to graze (John 10:9). These images of nurture become the task of the church by virtue of the commission to Peter to feed Christ's lambs (John 21:15). Nurture lies at the root of the exhortation for tenderness towards the "little ones", by which may be meant not just children but the young in the faith. Whether such persons may be fed milk or are ready for meat calls for the exercise of discernment (1 Cor. 3:2; Heb. 3:12).

33. The apparently reassuring imagery of shepherding conceals sharp judgments and urgent demands. The reason why sheep become the prey of wild beasts is because of bad shepherds who consume the milk, wear the wool, slaughter the fat beasts or drive them with ruthless severity (Ezek. 34:1-10). This indeed is the reason why the Lord himself is the shepherd of his people who, unlike the hireling, is ready to give his life for the sheep. Human shepherds of God's flock need to be reminded of his example and to guard against the temptations of power, if they are to receive the approval of the Chief Shepherd at his appearance (1 Pet. 5:1-4).

34. The life of the church can draw not merely upon Christ as a resource, but also must look towards Christ as the goal of its growth. Its maturity will be measured by nothing less than the full stature of Christ (Eph. 4:13). Nor is this conceived of as individual growth; it is, rather, the "building up of the body of Christ", in which there is a variety of gifts each designed "to equip God's people for work in God's service" (Eph. 4:12). There is, of course, a possibility, of which St Paul himself clearly has examples in mind, that such gifts might be deployed competitively: the eye and the hand in fact need each other and may have to be told so (1 Cor. 12:14-26). Even the simple acts of planting and watering the seed of the word need to be seen as cooperative ("they work as a team", 1 Cor. 3:8 NEB). The mission of the church requires a continuous effort to conceive all the Holy Spirit's gifts as part of a single enterprise and the overcoming of the tendency of human beings to jealousy and overbearing behaviour. The task of nurture is thus inseparable from that disposition of mind which is ready to reckon others better than oneself (Phil. 2:3).

Direction and goal

35. The journey on which the church is engaged has a goal and a direction which shape the whole character of the mission of the people of God from the beginning. In the ministry, death and resurrection of Jesus the church has been given a vision of the outcome of history. All things are to be brought into a unity in Christ (Eph. 1:10). It is, therefore, to Jesus Christ that we look while running with resolution the race for which we are entered (Heb. 12:1-2). In him we have the confidence to view the future as the triumph of the kingdom of God (Rev. 5; 7:13-17: cf. Isa. 25:6-8). We are the people who know the final outcome of the story, without yet knowing the details of the plot. Indeed, because the church has been let in on the outcome of the story of the world, the church's life and witness *change* the plot of history.

36. Because the outcome of history has been disclosed in Jesus, the church is called to anticipate the future of the Messianic age by sharing the Messianic banquet (see 27 above), the Lord's supper. But when the church does not include "those who have nothing", when it does not care about the world's poor, then it no longer partakes of the *Lord's* supper. The church not only profanes "the body and blood of the Lord", it also

denies its own identity as the people of the new age, the Messianic age (1 Cor. 11:17-34).

37. Because the outcome of history has been disclosed in Jesus, the church receives a *living hope* through the resurrection of Jesus Christ from the dead (1 Pet. 1:3-9). In Jesus' death and resurrection the power of death to determine the future has been broken. Death cannot have the last word for those who believe the resurrection. We now live towards the future differently, as a self-offering, not a self-protective, people. Our future is shaped by the one who has death behind him. He has become the "first-fruits" of those who sleep (1 Cor. 15:20-28). Hence the church is free to offer itself even to death, its ultimate witness (martyria) to its hope. The church is thus free to relate to enemies in a radically new way (1 Pet. 2:20-25; 3:9-12; Matt. 5:38-48; Luke 6:29-30; Rom. 12:17). The church witnesses to the Messianic age by its commitment to peace (Micah 3:3-4; Isa. 2:2-4).

38. Because the outcome of history has been disclosed in Jesus, the church is committed to justice for victims, and to liberation for the oppressed (Luke 1:51-53; 4:16-21; Matt. 11:5). The church seeks to express in its own life the overcoming of every alienation, whether racist, sexist or economic (Gal. 3:27-28).

39. Because the outcome of history has been disclosed in Jesus, the church is set free to view the past differently. The earliest disciples now could understand the cross of Jesus not as the rejection of his messianic mission but as the way of the Messiah. (Luke 24:26 is but one example; Isaiah 53 came to be understood as messianic only after the resurrection of Jesus.) Indeed, the cross of Christ is God's true glory (John 12:27-36; 17:1-15). Moreover, the disciples are called to the way of the cross, to suffer for the sake of the gospel (Mark 8:34-35 and par., Heb. 13:12-13). The disciples are also free to discern their *own* past differently, to confess sin rather than to deceive themselves by denying sin, to trust God's justification rather than their own self-contrived justifications.

40. Because of the vision which shapes its future the church recognizes that its mission is both necessary and limited; that the kingdom of God is served beyond the church; and that God may often have to work despite and against the church. Because the church betrays its mission it requires *episcope* to recall it, rebuke it and reform it.

Development of structure
41. All these requirements for the mission of the church in time are given in Christ, yet need to be realized in history. Each one – the praise of the community, its faithfulness and continuity, its disciplined life together, its activity of nurture and its sense of goal and direction – must be focused in symbolic acts and structures. As the church was launched outwards into the cultures of the ancient world and encountered new problems and dangers for which it had no ready-made solutions, these were the hallmarks of its common life.

42. As we have already remarked, there is no single pattern of leadership common to the early Christian communities (see §§19-20 above). Nevertheless, there was a serious and persisting need for wise and faithful leadership in the mission of the church. "Ministerial office played an essential part in the life of the church in the first century... Normative principles governing the purpose and function of the ministry are already present in the New Testament documents (e.g. Mark 10:43-45; Acts 20:28; 1 Tim. 4:12-16; 1 Pet. 5:1-4). The early churches may well have had considerable diversity in

the structure of pastoral ministry, though it is clear that some churches were headed by ministers who were called *episcopoi* and *presbyteroi*. While the first missionary churches were not a loose aggregation of autonomous communities, we have no evidence that 'bishops' and 'presbyters' were appointed everywhere in the primitive period. The terms 'bishop' and 'presbyter' could be applied to the same man or to men with identical or very similar functions" (Anglican-Roman Catholic International Commission [ARCIC], *The Final Report*, Ministry and Ordination 6).

43. The deaths of St Paul, St Peter and St James (the Lord's brother), who had exercised authoritative ministries in the churches, though in different places and in differing ways, left a vacuum in the church's life. The Book of Acts reflects the steps which were taken to supply this lack, by the appointment of presbyters (Acts 14:23). But the New Testament exhibits a striking absence of interest in titles or official designations when we compare the Christian writings with material concerning voluntary associations in the ancient world. The gospels of St Matthew and of St John show awareness of the danger inherent in developing structures and offices. 1 Peter warns against authoritarianism and money-making in the church leadership of northern Asia Minor. Though there is great interest in the pastoral epistles in the means for ensuring the succession of leadership by the laying-on of hands, there is no evidence to suggest that the bishop or presbyter had an exclusive role in relation to baptism and the eucharist.

44. There is a limited amount of testimony about the structures of Christian community in the 2nd century. All 4th-century and later testimony about this period must be handled with care because ancient writings about church history placed primary importance on proving there had been a consistent, unchanging Christian tradition. (In this, ancient Christian authors accepted the general cultural preference for what was old: the new was suspect on principle.) By the 4th century, the "monarchical episcopate" was so standard and unquestioned that it came to be regarded as having apostolic origins.

45. Ignatius of Antioch (c. 117) provides us with the earliest mention of the threefold ministry. But the episcopate he describes is what might be called a congregational episcopate as opposed to the later regional episcopate. Ignatius saw the bishops as standing in God's place, presiding over the community. The presbyters were seen either as "God's council" or the "council of apostles" – thus evoking the scene of the last judgment. The deacons represented either the commandment of God or Jesus Christ. In any case, "we are not certain how the Ignatian bishop was appointed or that he stood in a chain of historic succession to the apostles by means of ordination or even that the pattern described by Ignatius was universal in the church" (Lutherans and Catholics in Dialogue IV, *Eucharist and Ministry*, 39, reflections of the Roman Catholic participants).

46. Churches increasingly found that political or quasi political terminology expressed their sense of their own identity. This language was already to be found in the New Testament. Christians were a new people, or a new race, whose *politeuma* or commonwealth was in heaven (Phil. 3:20), strangers and sojourners in other people's cities in one sense, but looking forward to the city which God had prepared for them (Heb. 11:16) and thus in another sense at home in God's world. In their local communities, therefore, Christian people came to see themselves less and less as a specialized organization and more and more as a kind of tight-knit *polis* within a *polis* whose interests and activities embraced not some, but all, of the normal concerns of their mem-

bers. The church spread throughout the Roman world was one body, a single "people"; and it was of such a body that the bishop came to be recognized as leader and principal officer in each locality.

47. As time went on, the churches responded to the variety of gifts present in their midst by the creation of numerous other roles – readers, catechists, exorcists, acolytes, virgins and the like – all of whom were called *clerici*, in distinction to the ordinary citizenry, or *laici*. These developments indicate the openness of the churches to a variety of forms of ministry, not all of which needed to be perpetuated. But all alike, "clergy" and "laity", were first and foremost citizens of the commonwealth of heaven, all alike members of God's household (Eph. 2:19). When that household met together the bishop presided in a way which marked him out as the symbolic person in whom the identity of the community was focused and represented.

48. The significance of these developments is not that they can be extracted from the seamless web of church history and given normative status. Their importance lies rather in the basic intention to which they gave expression. The churches, in becoming discrete cultures within cultures, constituted a system of symbols. The office of bishop was valued because it expressed something important to the church's self-identity both within the community and in its external relations. It was a development relevant to a particular time and place, but with some surprising features – for example that bishops, unlike local magistrates, were elected for life. All our evidence confirms that, whatever the theological understanding of the office, it was open to gross abuse, as the New Testament documents already had made clear of earlier patterns of leadership.

49. But it had two clear advantages: first, that because the whole people was involved in the election (perhaps by shouting their votes – the potential for riotous disorder was always present), the authority of the bishop lay, in part, in the recognition accorded him by the community in its entirety; and secondly, ordinations entailed the participation of bishops from neighbouring congregations and thus elicited at least their consent. In the course of time, the role which neighbouring bishops played in the process of selection increased in importance, as stress was laid on the unity of the worldwide church. Thus the bishop embodied in his office the tension between locality and universality. In virtue of his election he represented the Christian people of his own town for the universal church; and in virtue of the assent of the larger church, symbolized by the mode of his ordination, he represented for his own flock the universal people of God, the whole body of local churches knit together in the communion of Christ.

50. The handling of this tension was no easy matter. Bishops installed by outside authority sometimes had great difficulty in governing their local churches; and bishops who were popular with their own flocks were sometimes judged unsatisfactory by synods of their peers. In the course of time more and more of the initiative for the election of bishops came to rest in the hands of regional authorities until the development reached the point that no bishop could be installed without the consent of the metropolitan.

51. By the 4th century also a significant realignment of responsibilities was occurring within the threefold ministry. The bishop, who had been in principle the leader of a single congregation, had become a regional overseer, while the presbyters, who had had no independent liturgical function, became the presidents of local eucharistic assemblies. By the middle ages this shift led to the presbyter's ministry being taken for

the normative form of ministry. The difference between bishop and presbyter was now a matter of jurisdiction. Jerome's opinion that bishops and presbyters were originally one and the same became widely accepted and played a role in both the Lutheran and Anglican Reformations.

52. Once again it must be said that this history is not invoked in order to give it normative status. There is too much variety for us to construct a single, synthetic picture of the episcopal office; and there is always a danger in anachronistically reading back the vastly changed scale of a modern bishop's activities into the ancient communities which were smaller. The point is rather that the symbolic position occupied by the bishop had two dimensions, the spatial and the temporal. The connections between the local and the universal, the present and the past, are both aspects of the one koinonia or communion. On the one hand, the bishop "is responsible for preserving and promoting the integrity of the koinonia in order to further the church's response to the lordship of Christ and its commitment to mission" (ARCIC, *The Final Report*, Authority I, 5); a koinonia which "is realized not only in the local Christian communities, but also in the communion of these communities with one another" (*ibid.*, 8). On the other hand the bishop as confessor of the faith links the church with its foundation in the prophetic and apostolic scriptures (Eph. 2:20).

53. What is essential to the life and mission of the church is that the connection between the universal and the local should be made, and that it should be effective. The question which has to be addressed to our own churches is not merely whether they intend such a link, but how it is allowed to be effective. The mere presence of a bishop as what is said to be "a focus of unity" will not *guarantee* the preservation of koinonia between local and universal; nor will the absence of such a bishop entail its destruction. The case is the same in relation to continuity. "Apostolic succession in the episcopal office does not consist primarily in an unbroken chain of those ordaining to those ordained, but in a succession in the presiding ministry of a church which stands in the continuity of apostolic faith and which is overseen by the bishop in order to keep it in the communion of the catholic and apostolic church" (LRCJC, *The Ministry in the Church*, 62).

54. Our brief reference to episodes in the history of the episcopal office highlights a telling fact. It is the oversight or presiding ministry which constitutes the heart of the episcopal office, and that oversight is never to be viewed apart from the continuity of apostolic faith. The fact of bishops does not by itself guarantee the continuity of apostolic faith. A material rupture in the succession of presiding ministers does not by itself guarantee a loss of continuity in apostolic faith. What evaluation is, then, to be given of a situation in which there is a material rupture in the succession of presiding ministers in the name of preserving the continuity of apostolic faith?

55. Clearly, no simple answer can be given. Where the rupture occurs, subsequent steps taken to secure the continuity of apostolic faith and to provide for a new succession in presiding ministry must weigh heavily in making that evaluation. In the English Reformation, it may be argued, the episcopal succession was secured in an uncanonical fashion in that no currently sitting diocesan bishops could be found who were willing to consecrate Matthew Parker. Whatever may be said about this and about the sufficiency of the 1550 ordinal for the transmission of the historic threefold ministry, the preface to the ordinal witnessed to the intention of the English Reformers to continue that ministry in a reformed manner. Thus the importance of the ordinal does

not lie in the historical accuracy of its claim that the offices of bishop, presbyter and deacon were present in the church from the beginning. Its importance lies rather in its expression of the intention to preserve continuity with traditional church structures.

56. For the Lutheran Reformation too the situation was complicated by the refusal of sitting bishops to ordain pastors for evangelical congregations. Faced with this emergency, "the Wittenberg Reformation sought a new understanding of ordained ministry by reaching back to the ordering of the ancient church. In so doing, the ministry of oversight in the (Wittenberg) *Stadtkirche* was described as an episcopal office and services of ordination were broadly structured to be a reappropriation of episcopal consecration in the ancient church" (*Kirchengemeinschaft in Wort und Sakrament*, Hanover, 1984, p.75). The Reformers "ordained through ordained pastors and thus laid claim to the episcopal structure of the office of pastors (ministers)" (H. Fries and K. Rahner, *Unity of the Churches*, Philadelphia, 1985, p.94).

57. It must be clearly noted that the Reformers believed themselves authorized to act in this manner in an emergency situation, appealing to Jerome's position on the original unity of the office of bishop and presbyter. The authority of a bishop's office is thus present in the pastors. The succession of a presiding ministry is thus preserved, though in an unaccustomed form. There was no objection to the office of bishop as such, as the Augsburg confession testifies:

> St Peter forbids the bishops to exercise lordship as if they had power to coerce the churches according to their will. It is not our intention to find ways of reducing the bishops' power, but we desire and pray that they may not coerce our consciences to sin. If they are unwilling to do this and ignore our petition, let them consider how they will answer for it in God's sight, inasmuch as by their obstinacy they offer occasion for division and schism, which they should in truth help to prevent (CA, XVIII, 76-78).

58. A similar problem faces both Anglicans and Lutherans, namely that the succession in the presiding ministry of their respective churches no longer incontestably links those churches to the koinonia of the wider church.

59. The comprehensive doctrinal agreement between Lutherans and Anglicans outlined in section III indicates a commonly held apostolic faith. In the light of this commonly held apostolic faith, neither tradition can, in good conscience, reject the apostolic nature of the other. In the light of the argument contained in the above sections, the ordained ministry is no longer an issue which need divide our two churches. In the light of the symbolic position of the bishop as reflecting both the universal and local koinonia, the continued isolation, one from another, of those who exercise this office of *episcope* in our two churches is no longer tolerable and must be overcome.

III. The truths we share

60. The Anglican-Lutheran European regional commission Helsinki report, of 1982, observed that "the history of Anglican-Lutheran relations is a complex one and cannot be reduced to one simple pattern" (§13). It is not necessary for us to trace all of the reasons for this observation. One fact, however, stands out. These two traditions have not officially engaged in any divisive theological or doctrinal controversies. They have not officially condemned each other as churches. Conversations in recent years in Europe, North America and Australia have resulted in identifying large areas of agreement in faith and life. Shared work and witness in Africa and Asia have revealed similar areas of agreement. In the USA, most Lutherans and the Episcopal Church have

entered into formal agreement of "interim eucharistic sharing" with each other. We wish here to specify the truths we share as disclosed by our official conversations.[1]

61. We accept the authority of the canonical scriptures of the Old and New Testaments. We read the scripture; liturgically in the course of the church's year (*Lutheran-Episcopal Dialogue II* [LED II], 1980, pp. 30-31; *Pullach Report*, 17-22).

62. We accept the Nicene-Constantinopolitan and Apostles' Creeds and confess the basic trinitarian and christological dogmas to which these creeds testify. That is, we believe that Jesus of Nazareth is true God and true Man, and that God is authentically identified as Father, Son and Holy Spirit (LED II, p.38; *Pullach Report*, 23-25).

63. Anglicans and Lutherans use very similar orders of service for the eucharist, for the prayer offices, for the administration of baptism, for the rites of marriage, burial, and confession and absolution. We acknowledge in the liturgy both a celebration of salvation through Christ and a significant factor in forming the *consensus fidelium*. We have many hymns, canticles and collects in common (*Helsinki Report*, 29-31).

64. We believe that baptism with water in the name of the triune God unites the one baptized with the death and resurrection of Jesus Christ, initiates into the one, holy, catholic and apostolic church, and confers the gracious gift of new life (*Helsinki Report*, 22-25).

65. We believe that the body and blood of Christ are truly present, distributed and received under the forms of bread and wine in the Lord's supper. We also believe that the grace of divine forgiveness offered in the sacrament is received with the thankful offering of ourselves for God's service (LED II, pp. 25-29; *Helsinki Report*, 26-28).

66. We believe and proclaim the gospel, that in Jesus Christ God loves and redeems the world. We "share a common understanding of God's justifying grace, i.e. that we are accounted righteous and are made righteous before God only by grace through faith because of the merits of our Lord and Saviour Jesus Christ, and not on account of our works or merit. Both our traditions affirm that justification leads and must lead to 'good works'; authentic faith issues in love" (*Helsinki Report*, 20; cf. LED II, pp.22-23).

67. Anglicans and Lutherans believe that the church is not the creation of individual believers, but that it is constituted and sustained by the triune God through God's saving action in word and sacraments. We believe that the church is sent into the world as sign, instrument and foretaste of the kingdom of God. But we also recognize that the church stands in constant need of reform and renewal (*Helsinki Report*, 44-51).

68. We believe that all members of the church are called to participate in its apostolic mission. They are therefore given various ministries by the Holy Spirit. Within the community of the church the ordained ministry exists to serve the ministry of the whole people of God. We hold the ordained ministry of word and sacrament to be a gift of God to his church and therefore an office of divine institution (*Helsinki Report*, 32-42).

69. We believe that a ministry of pastoral oversight (*episcope*), exercised in personal, collegial and communal ways, is necessary to witness to and safeguard the unity and apostolicity of the church (*Pullach Report*, 79).

---

[1] The most convenient collection of the relevant documents is to be found in *What Can We Share? A Lutheran-Episcopal Resource and Study*, William A. Norgren, ed., Cincinnati, Forward Movement Publications, 1985. Also *Growth in Agreement: Reports and Agreed Statements of Ecumenical Conversations on a World Level*, Harding Meyer and Lukas Vischer, eds, New York, Paulist, and Geneva, WCC, 1984.

70. We share a common hope in the final consummation of the kingdom of God and believe that we are compelled to work for the establishment of justice and peace. The obligations of the kingdom are to govern our life in the church and our concern for the world. "The Christian faith is that God has made peace through Jesus 'by the blood of his cross' (Col. 1:20) so establishing the one valid centre for the unity of the whole human family" (Anglican-Reformed International Commission 1984: *God's Reign and Our Unity*, 18 and 43; cf. *Pullach Report*, 59).

71. Because of all that we share, we concur with the conclusion of the Anglican-Lutheran European regional commission: "There are no longer any serious obstacles on the way towards the establishment of full communion between our two churches." We "acknowledge each other as true churches of Christ preaching the same gospel, possessing a common apostolic ministry, and celebrating authentic sacraments" (*Helsinki Report*, 62-63).

72. Furthermore, in addition to the common sharing of fundamental beliefs and practices which we have listed, we wish to make the affirmations which follow:

73. We recognize that in each other's churches there exists a sustained and serious commitment to the apostolic mission of the church.

74. We see ourselves already united by baptism in thankfulness to God for the gift of Jesus Christ, our Lord and Saviour, and for the sending of the Holy Spirit.

75. We acknowledge in each other's ministries of *episcope* the fruits of the presence of Jesus Christ and the activity of the Holy Spirit, in the offering of sacrifices of praise and thanksgiving, in the reflection of the faithful love of God towards the world, in care for the nurture and growth of all the faithful, and in commitment to the establishment of the kingdom of God in justice and peace for the whole earth.

76. We confess to God, to each other and to all Christian people how far, in our discharge of the ministry of *episcope*, our churches have fallen short of the unity and continuity of the apostolic commission. We ask of each other forgiveness for our disregard of each other's gifts, for our lack of humility, and for our past toleration of our division.

77. We earnestly desire to remove those barriers which prevent the life of our churches from reflecting that unity of heart and mind which is God's gift to the people of God.

78. We commit ourselves to the obligation to take counsel together in reaching a common mind on how the mission of the people of God can most fruitfully be served in every place, so that there may be a united witness to the gospel, in word and deed, and a common enjoyment of the means of grace.

79. We intend thereby also to promote the unity of all churches with whom we are seeking, or have already discovered, the faith of the catholic church.

80. We rejoice in rediscovering in each other our common inheritance of faith and of life, and in our unity in the one, holy, catholic and apostolic church.

> Praise be to the God and Father of our Lord Jesus Christ, who has bestowed on us in Christ every spiritual blessing in the heavenly realms.

IV. Application to Anglicans and Lutherans

81. At our consultation we addressed the question: "In the light of our common mission, what needs to be reformed in our respective expressions of *episcope*?" We also tried to visualize what patterns of leadership and oversight would be needed to meet the challenges of the next century. We were aware that all human institutions are sub-

ject to constant obsolescence and change. We cannot, therefore, commend uncritically either the reappropriation of historic episcopate or the perpetuation of existing forms of the exercise of *episcope*.

82. Neither of our churches is able to claim such a degree of faithfulness, that is, a continuity in either doctrine or order, as would enable it to sit in judgment on the other.

83. Nevertheless both our churches have been given by God sufficient faithfulness to the apostolic gospel that today we can recognize each other as sister churches.

84. The churches of the Lutheran tradition have received as the focus for God's faithfulness to them the creeds of the early church, the confessions of the 16th century, and the continuity of the ordained ministry through which the word of God has been preached and the sacraments and rites of the church have been administered.

85. The churches of the Anglican communion have received as the focus for God's faithfulness to them the creeds of the early church, the Book of Common Prayer from the 16th century (revised periodically and adapted regionally), and the continuity of the episcopal office through which clergy have been ordained for the preaching of the word of God and the administration of the sacraments and rites of the church.

86. Formal recognition of each other's ministries so that our churches acknowledge a relationship of full communion between them cannot simply mean that neither church changes. Nor can it mean that either church changes merely to meet the expectations and requirements of the other.

87. Rather churches of both communions are being called to acknowledge that the experience and practice of full communion will involve them both and simultaneously in changes and reforms.

88. Lutheran churches are being asked to make four changes in current practice, as follows:

89. All persons who exercise an ordained ministry of *episcope* should receive the title of bishop or suffragan bishop (see §57 [and Appendix IV] for historical and other information on the titles currently in use in some Lutheran churches.)

90. Because Lutherans understand the office of bishop as pastoral (CA, XXVIII, 5 *et passim*; cf. *Lutheran Understanding of the Episcopal Office*, 1983, which states that "episcopal ministry and episcopal office denote the task of pastoral leadership and spiritual supervision", pp.3ff.), constitutions should be revised so that bishops are elected to the same tenure of office as are congregational pastors, chaplains and other pastoral ministers in the church. That is, they should be elected and called until such time as death, retirement or resignation terminate their incumbency. This may mean that churches will also want to revise the procedures for identifying and nominating candidates for election to the ministry of bishop, so that God's gifts of leadership and governance (1 Cor. 12:28) are properly recognized and called to office. Where appropriate, bishops and churches should also establish and welcome structures for collegial and periodic review with the purpose of evaluating and improving the bishop's ministry.

91. In accordance with the canons of the council of Nicea the rites of installation for bishops should be revised so that there is a laying-on of hands by at least three bishops. The involvement of three bishops in the installation of a bishop is the liturgical form by which the church recognizes that the bishop serves the local or regional church through ties of collegiality which are links to the universal church. Such participation of three bishops should express liturgically the fact that genuine consultation among

bishops on the faith and life of the church is expected in structure and practice. If we are in full communion with each other, one or more of the bishops at a Lutheran installation should be from a church in the Anglican communion. Lutherans can invite such participation by Anglican bishops for two reasons. First, in recognizing and acknowledging "the full authenticity of the existing ministries of Lutheran churches" (see §94) Anglicans join Lutherans in affirming that bishops have authority only through the gospel (CA XXVIII, 5-8) and thus serve the identity and unity of the church given by the pure preaching of the gospel and the administration of the sacraments (CA VII, 2). Second, Lutherans have confessionally and historically recognized that the historic episcopate is a valuable symbol of unity and continuity in the church (cf. LRCJC, *The Ministry in the Church*, 65, 66 and 80, together with the documentation in the footnotes). Such participation of Anglican bishops must be a symbol for mandatory mutual consultation and real interaction in *episcope*.

92. It should become the unfailing practice that only bishops or suffragan bishops should preside at all ordinations of clergy in their respective regions (synods, dioceses, churches, districts). This is consistent with much current practice in Lutheran churches; and it is upheld in principle by the fact that Lutheran bishops or those who exercise *episcope* in Lutheran churches must now authorize all ordinations at which they do not themselves preside.

93. Anglican churches are being asked to make three changes in current practice, as follows:

94. Anglican churches should make the necessary canonical revisions so that they can acknowledge and recognize the full authenticity of the existing ministries of Lutheran churches. We believe that the basis for such action lies in the recognition that "the apostolic succession in the episcopal office does not consist primarily in an unbroken chain of those ordaining to those ordained, but in a succession in the presiding ministry of a church, which stands in the continuity of apostolic faith" (*The Ministry in the Church,* 62). Anglican churches are here being asked for a major canonical revision in ordering their relationships to those Lutheran churches which have bishops who are not in the historic episcopate and to those whose chief ministers exercising *episcope* are not called bishops. We believe that Anglicans are free to do this both by the grace and power of the Holy Spirit and because such action does not mean surrender of the gift of the historic episcopate. "Full communion", the consequence of such acknowledgment and recognition, does not mean the organizational merger of Anglican and Lutheran churches. Therefore Anglican churches would continue to consecrate their own bishops and ordain their own clergy according to the ordinals now in use.

95. Anglican churches and bishops should establish and welcome structures for collegial and periodic review with the purpose of evaluating and improving the bishop's ministry (see §90).

96. Anglican churches should regularly invite Lutheran bishops to participate in the laying-on of hands at the consecration and installation of Anglican bishops. Such participation must be a symbol for mandatory mutual consultation and real interaction in *episcope* (see §91).

97. We rejoice in the ways God's faithfulness has been manifested in our respective churches. We receive and cultivate the faithfulness of God evident in the historic episcopate. We recognize and praise God for his faithfulness in preserving the apostolic

mission and continuity of the church where the historic succession in the episcopate has been broken. We intend with these changes to enter into full communion, to create a single eucharistic community, to engage in fully shared mission, and thus to prepare for what structural implications may emerge. We trust that what we do will have significance for progress in other ecumenical relationships.

98. In all of this we wish to assure ourselves and our partners in ecumenical dialogue that these changes are not intended to imply and do not imply indifference to the gift and symbol of historic episcopate. We also assure our partners in bilateral and multilateral dialogue that we want to be mindful of our conversations with them and our commitments to them. No bilateral consensus or action can be blessed which ignores the church in its many traditions and manifestations. What we do is always done in the sight of all (*in conspectu omnium*) and – in so far as we are granted insight – on behalf of all.

99. In addition to the above changes proposed for each of our churches, we wish to pose questions which imply reform and renewal in the area of *episcope* to both of our churches.

100. Are those exercising pastoral leadership and oversight in our churches given the time and space to reflect on the priorities for mission in their regions, or have they become absorbed in and overloaded by administration? Is the administrative unit over which they preside frankly too big, so that their time and energy is all spent on the maintenance of a system rather than on the discernment of opportunity? Does the scale of their responsibilities make them inattentive to the experience of those whose daily witness involves their standing on the edge of church life? Has overfamiliarity with committee work, which indeed has its proper role, bred a lack of vision and of courage?

101. Are those in the episcopal office accessible enough to clergy and their families, not only in times of crisis but in an ongoing pastoral relationship? Do they take care not to foster an immature dependency, but rather encourage clergy to take responsibility for appraising their own ministry periodically, for reviewing their ministerial priorities, and for pursuing their own continuing education and spiritual refreshment? Do they also ensure that adequate resources are provided for offering personal help to clergy and their families in times of sickness, bereavement, domestic stress and financial difficulty?

102. Can those who exercise pastoral leadership and oversight escape the danger of being occupied too much with the affairs of the clergy, and also offer effective leadership in releasing and drawing together the talents of many individuals within the whole people of God? Can they set an example of leadership which is not autocratic but truly shared, facilitating collaborative styles of ministry and enabling the skills and insights of lay persons in every walk of life to be contributed to the church's common life?

103. Has the Anglican or Lutheran view of what it means to be in apostolic succession whether of pedigree or pure confession become such a matter of pride that the mission of the church has ceased to be a criterion by which the church is judged? Do those exercising *episcope*, whether Anglicans or Lutherans, consider they "possess" the apostolic entitlement, or do they see themselves challenged and outstripped by its demands and responsibilities?

104. Is it really the case that those exercising *episcope* consult with each other? Have they substituted the goal of denominational coherence for the wider vision of the unity of all Christians? Have they become so absorbed in consultative or legislative

problems and procedures within their own nation or province that they have ceased to care how their actions might influence other Christians in other parts of the world?

105. Has mutuality ceased between those exercising *episcope* in the church and their own local communities? Have leaders ceased to understand the changing needs of congregations? Have they become so remote from the poor and those on the margins of society that they can no longer represent the ministry of one who was the friend of, and host to, sinners? Or conversely, do local congregations keep those who exercise *episcope* at bay, as though their ministry were thought to be an intrusion upon, or competitive with, the self-sufficient organization of a parish?

106. Do those exercising *episcope* in the church expound and commend the Christian faith in a sustained way, not just preaching on special occasions or during isolated visits to congregations? Do they take real care to enlist the advice and help of those skilled in communications in the modern world, and to address those issues which are of urgent concern to people? Do they make the most of their corporate teaching role as a conference of bishops, and provide collegial support to one another in the exercise of their teaching responsibilities?

107. Do those who exercise *episcope* understand their liturgical role to be central to their responsibilities, and do they carry it out in a creative way? Do they lead the offering of prayer and praise with a sense of awe and reverence, inspiring clergy and congregations to offer well prepared and heartfelt worship to God? Do they maintain a proper balance between word and sacrament in their programme of public worship events? Do they encourage the renewal of liturgy, and hold together diverse styles of worship within the church's life? Do they take care to retain those skills which they now exercise less often than they did at an earlier phase of their ministries? Do they perform their liturgical tasks in a manner which symbolizes that all ministry is shared with others?

108. Do those exercising *episcope* show in their own personal lives Christ-like qualities? Do they give an example of holiness, love, humility and simplicity of life? Are they generous and hospitable? Is their style of life influenced too much by the patterns of leadership that are dominant in the culture where they live? Is it evident that they are dedicated to unselfish service, and are open to be touched by the sufferings of others? Do they give the time and space needed for prayer, study, rest, recreation and family life, and avoid being devoured by unreasonable public expectations of their office?

109. Are those chosen for leadership given the ceremonial trappings of prominence, but denied the ability to exercise their responsibilities? Is *effective* leadership vested in reality in persons who, by reason of their obscurity in a bureaucracy, are not accountable to the whole church? Are the realities of the exercise of power effectively disguised from view, and is it silently presumed that power can only be exercised competitively and never cooperatively? Are churches so frightened by the danger of authoritarianism that their systems of checks and balances destroy any capacity to respond in moments of special challenge and danger?

110. These are but some of the enquiries which follow from the argument we have advanced. They are based in the account we have given of the requirements for the mission of the church, on the understanding that the apostolic ministry must be a ministry engaged in, and facilitating the mission of the whole church. *Episcope* is a ministry of service, exercised with the cooperation of the whole community. Leaders

are to "manifest and exercise the authority of Christ in the way Christ himself revealed God's authority to the world, by committing their life to the community" (*BEM*, M16). When we ask whether leaders in communities other than our own do this with faithfulness, we are engaged in a process which inevitably involves self-examination. Our conclusion is that both our communions are called in the first place to penitence.

V. Practical steps

111. Here we consider by what practical steps Anglicans and Lutherans can realize full communion.

112. *Step 1:* Each regional or national church's governing body:
a) affirms the agreement in faith as expressed in certain specified documents (e.g. §§61-70 of this report);
b) recognizes the church of... as a true church of the gospel, etc. (see *BEM*, M53, [a] or [bl]).

113. *Step 2:* Create provisional structures to express the degree of unity so far achieved and to promote further growth. These could include the following examples, though the time scale could vary region by region:
a) eucharistic sharing and joint common celebration of the eucharist;
b) meetings of church leaders for regular prayer, reflection and consultation, thus beginning joint *episcope*;
c) mutual invitation of church leaders, clergy and laity, to synods, with a right to speak;
d) common agencies wherever possible;
e) explore the possibility of adjusting boundaries to assist local and regional cooperation;
f) covenants among church leaders to collaborate in *episcope*;
g) joint pastoral appointments for special projects;
h) joint theological education and training courses;
i) sharing of information and documents;
j) joint mission programmes;
k) agreed syllabuses for Christian education in schools, joint materials for catechesis and adult study;
l) cooperation over liturgical forms, cycles of intercession, lectionaries and homiletic materials;
m) welcoming isolated clergy or diaspora congregations into the life of a larger group (see ALERC, *Helsinki Report*, 5);
n) interchange of ministers to the extent permitted by canon law;
o) twinning (partnership) between congregations and communities;
p) joint programmes of diaconal ministry and reflection on issues of social responsibility;
q) joint retreats and devotional materials.

The ACC and LWF should be asked to give their full support to churches making such provisional arrangements.

114. *Step 3:* The actions taken in steps 1 and 2 form the basis and motivation for the implementation of the recommendations in §§88-96.

115. *Step 4:* Together representatives (including lay members, ordained ministers and church leaders) of both churches publicly celebrate the establishment of full communion. This liturgical occasion should include the following elements:
a) penitence for past shortcomings;
b) declaration of joint faith;
c) reaffirmation of baptismal vows;
d) mutual greeting by sharing the peace by the right hand of fellowship, so as to avoid any suggestion of reordination, mutual recommissioning of ministries, crypto-validation, or any other ambiguity;
e) a celebration of the eucharist;
f) a covenant to work together and become closely involved in one another's corporate life, with the long-term aim of fuller unity;
g) a personal covenant of the church leaders to collaborate in episcope (it is intended that new leaders should enter the same covenant on assuming office).

116. *Notes:* We understand these steps to be compatible with those proposed by LRCJC, *Facing Unity,* pp.58ff.

This process should be constantly open to further ecumenical initiatives with other churches, and is not intended to be exclusive (see above §97).

After step 4 joint consecration and installation of bishops and ordination of new ministers should be possible.

Appendix I: Report of the Anglican-Lutheran International Continuation Committee

Wimbledon, England, 13-17 October 1986

Background

1. The Anglican-Lutheran International Continuation Committee (ALICC) was appointed by the Anglican Consultative Council (ACC) and the Lutheran World Federation (LWF) on the recommendation (IIb) of the Anglican-Lutheran Joint Working Group, which met at Cold Ash, England, 28 November-3 December 1983. The meeting produced a report entitled "Anglican-Lutheran Relations: Report of the Anglican-Lutheran Joint Working Group" (the Cold Ash report), which provides essential background to the whole progress of Anglican-Lutheran relations in recent times. In it the group stated that "the last 15 years have seen remarkable convergence between the Anglican and Lutheran communions and their member churches" and recommended their respective bodies to "move with urgency towards the fullest possible ecclesial recognition and the goal of full communion" (p.16). The group had before it:
1. Anglican-Lutheran international conversations, 1970-72: *The Pullach Report;*
2. Lutheran-Episcopal Dialogue I, 1972, and Lutheran-Episcopal Dialogue II, 1981 (LED II);
3. Anglican-Lutheran dialogue, 1983: *The Helsinki Report* of the Anglican-Lutheran European regional commission.
4. The agreement adopted by the conventions of the American Lutheran Church, the Association of Evangelical Lutheran Churches, the Episcopal Church in the USA and the Lutheran Church in America, September 1982.

2. The task of the continuation committee is first to coordinate information about developments in Anglican-Lutheran relations in various parts of the world, and then, on the basis of an assessment of the total picture, to foster and to stimulate new initiatives. It reports to its parent bodies.

3. Recent developments

ALICC received the following reports:
- the final report of the Australian Anglican-Lutheran conversations, 1972-84;
- a report by the board for mission and unity of the Church of England on Anglican-Lutheran and other international dialogues (GS 685), June 1985;
- the report and recommendations of the Canadian Anglican-Lutheran dialogue, April 1986;
- a report from the eighth theological conversations between the Evangelische Kirche in Deutschland (EKD) and the Church of England, April 1986.

It also received William A. Norgren's study guide to Lutheran-Episcopal relations, *What Can We Share?* (1985); reports on the questionnaires regarding Anglican-Lutheran relations throughout the world, prepared by the ACC and the LWF; and the report of the archbishop of Canterbury's visit to and address at the Lutheran Church in America convention, Milwaukee, in August 1986; *Changing Anglican-Lutheran Relations,* William A. Norgren, 1985; *Towards Full Communion,* William G. Rusch, 1985; *Facing Unity: Models, Forms and Phases of Catholic-Lutheran Church Fellowship,* Roman Catholic-Lutheran Joint Commission, pub. by the Lutheran World Federation, 1985.

4. These documents by no means constitute a comprehensive coverage of all developments, and the committee acknowledges the difficulty in assembling all the relevant information, as the different member churches respond to international or national bilateral reports and other documents. It is also the case that from some smaller Lutheran and Anglican churches we have little or no information about ecumenical developments.

5. Oral reports were delivered by the members present at the ALICC of developments in a number of major theatres of Anglican-Lutheran interaction, including Tanzania, Malaysia, India (relations between Lutherans and the Church of South India), North America and Europe.

6. Assessment

It is clear from all the information before us that further highly significant steps are being taken on a regional basis to promote ever-increasing closeness of relationship, despite the lack of an international dialogue. We wish to draw attention to certain examples of this cooperation:

a) *Tanzania:* The Tanzanian Christian Council enables heads of all non-Roman Catholic churches to meet for two or three days every year to discuss things of mutual concern. Out of these annual contacts church leaders in Tanzania are very often great friends. On the basis of this friendship some Anglican bishops have received invitations to the consecration of Lutheran bishops and the same has been true of some Anglican consecrations.

b) *USA:* In its third series, the Lutheran-Episcopal dialogue in the USA (LED III) has nearly completed work on a document mandated by the churches: "The Gospel and

Its Implications". This is an attempt to make use of the eschatological perspective proving fruitful in current biblical and theological studies as the churches seek to be more faithful in engaging in mission in terms of ecumenism, evangelization and ethics. The dialogue has agreed to recommend to the respective churches some form of recognizing each other's central documents, that Lutherans recognize the Book of Common Prayer and Episcopalians recognize the Augsburg confession and Luther's Small Catechism. There are increasing instances of regular consultation between Episcopal and Lutheran bishops, of shared ministry by and in parishes, of regular study conferences of clergy from both churches and large gatherings for dialogue and worship. Virtually every part of the USA has had some formal joint celebrations of the eucharist by Lutheran and Episcopal bishops.

c) *Canada:* After a process beginning in October 1983, the Canadian Anglican-Lutheran dialogue has submitted a report to the churches containing brief agreed statements on justification, the eucharist, apostolicity and ordained ministry. The report proposes that the churches acknowledge each other "as churches where the gospel is truly preached and taught". The report requests the churches to initiate internally a period of study (1986-89) of the agreed statements and to declare a relationship of interim sharing of eucharist beginning in 1989 with an evaluation of this experience to be made in 1995. A number of other actions are also encouraged.

d) *Europe:* Study and preparatory work has been commissioned by the Church of England, the Evangelische Kirche in Deutschland and the Bund der Evangelischen Kirchen in der DDR for closer ecumenical relationships between these churches. A consultation of these churches is to be held in February 1987.

Pastoral and theological consultations and exchanges have been taking place every two years between the Church of England and the Scandinavian churches, drawing upon a long history of official Church of England relationships with the churches of Sweden and Finland.

e) *Australia:* Though the Australian Lutheran churches are not part of the LWF, we noted that a fruitful dialogue with Anglicans has been conducted since 1974, involving strands of Lutheranism not normally engaged in common ecumenical endeavour and covering a wide range of topics.

f) *India:* The Anglican dioceses became part of the Church of South India and the Church of North India. In 1947 the Lutheran churches in South India (about a million Christians) entered into union negotiations with the Church of South India, and they found a remarkable agreement in essential theological issues, but for reasons, largely non-theological, could not form one body. Nevertheless there are close relations between them in various aspects of life, especially in joint theological seminaries. Now the Lutheran churches in South India have become part of the United Evangelical Lutheran Churches in India.

7. It is apparent that the process of convergence described in *The Cold Ash Report* is continuing. The theological agreements reached in international and regional dialogues have facilitated shared life and, as so often happens, Christian living and theological reflection have mutually supported and enriched each other.

The present situation

8. In some contexts, it appears that shared life is a consequence of theological agreement and the process of reception. After the agreement reached in international

and regional dialogues it becomes possible for developments to occur in particular places, where responsible Christian judgment demands a new initiative. For instance, an Anglican bishop finds himself asking a Lutheran bishop to exercise oversight of churches in an emergency.

9. These developments are of different kinds, reminding us of the multi-faceted nature of the process of reconciliation. In some contexts, for good historical reasons, great emphasis has to be placed on theological discussion and the building of consensus; in other places what is crucial is making a reality of the sharing of oversight and mutual consultation; in other places, again, what is vital is breaking down cultural or communal barriers in the life of the whole church. It is our experience that the establishment of priorities in each situation has to be determined by the imperatives of the church's mission. Mission and ecumenism are inseparable, and have to be worked out region to region. Not all developments are capable of being applied universally. Some rest on understandings and judgments which are, as yet, incapable of verbal formulation, but which have resulted from responsible judgments in the face of particular needs or opportunities.

10. It is also true that there are places where the two churches live side by side and there are no signs of joint theological activity.

Future work

11. We have begun, and must continue, to identify the resources which we are discovering in one another. We have already received much from each other in our traditions of worship and liturgy, music and hymnody, historical and theological study, stewardship and spirituality. We continue to receive gifts through the lessons learned by sister churches in times of hardship and persecution, through the various ways our churches have sought to relate to social and political contexts with equally various degrees of faithfulness. It is a part of the task of this committee to discover and identify as many resources as God has given us, to evaluate their role in our common life and growing relationships, and to urge and facilitate the wider sharing of these resources between our communions. That these resources cannot always or easily be translated from one context to another must be remembered. The historical ambiguities present in our strengths and gifts dare not be ignored. But gifts remain gifts, even in brokenness and ambiguity, and they can be means used by God to further the great gifts of reconciliation and unity.

12. *Rethinking our goals:* Since the Cold Ash meeting, questions have surfaced about the way "full communion" is described and defined in the Cold Ash report and its relationship with the anticipated goal of other actual or potential forms or models of church unity. Because of these and other questions we recognize that one of our tasks must be the rethinking and reformulating of the meaning of "full communion". We are persuaded that such reformulation can take place only in the context of our growing common experience with one another.

13. *Consultation on episcope:* Another of our tasks must be to discuss the relationship between apostolic succession, the ministry of the whole people of God, episcopacy and the historic episcopate. We propose to do this in a consultation which would see ministry in relation to the mission of the church today. This consultation will be held in 1987 and our proposal for it is as follows:

Theme: Episcope in relation to the mission of the church today.
Questions to be addressed in the context of Anglican-Lutheran relations:

a) How was *episcope* exercised in the New Testament and the early church? How did it relate to mission?

This question demands that attention be paid to the sociological as well as theological factors underlying historical developments as the church moved towards more structured community life for the sake of mission, at varying rates of speed in different areas. It presupposes that there was no uniformity of development, all developments have equal or enduring validity.

b) What is the mission of the church in the 21st century? What is the church's prophetic role?

Both parts of this question demand answers set in a variety of cultural and geographical contexts. It cannot be fruitfully addressed in only abstract terms of global import.

c) How is *episcope* related to the ministry of the whole people of God?

Implicit in this question is the fact that the whole people of God exercises episcope in a variety of "styles" appropriate (or inappropriate!) to our different cultural contexts. It may be that some styles of leadership are more suitable in Christian communities than others. The consultation should keep the relation between leadership and service in mind.

d) In light of our common mission, what needs to be reformed in our respective expressions of episcope?

Discussion of this key question is central to the task of the consultation. Clearly it needs to take into account insights gleaned from the previous questions and answers. It asks, in effect, how can we do our job better?

e) What can we do together in episcope? How can we initiate and enable the joint exercise of episcope as a gradual process?

i) What light is thrown on this by our churches' responses to the Ministry section of the *BEM* document – especially paragraphs 23-25?

ii) What light is thrown on this by our respective bilateral dialogues with the Roman Catholic Church?

Again, this question presupposes a number of different answers for our different contexts. It follows that no single process can emerge, following a single timetable. Recognizing this, the question invites creative "dreaming".

f) How do we formulate attainable goals for our common mission?

The emphasis in this question is on attainable goals. What criteria are appropriate for judging whether a goal is attainable? That ours is a common mission is a presupposition, presumably needing no further elucidation.

14. *Further steps:* There are further concrete steps which we can take and/or propose to the churches on the way towards realization of the goal of full communion between our churches. We have identified the following tasks:

a) We should identify areas in which our churches need to be better informed about each other, where misleading or outdated perceptions inhibit trust and cooperation, understanding and commitment to unity. This is especially the case where geographical separation prevents continued living experience of one another, where common challenges and resources are not evident to one another, where stereotypes and caricatures prejudice our relationships and weaken our movement towards full communion.

b) We need to develop forms and forums for common attention to the scriptures, that is, letting ourselves be corporately challenged by what the scriptures have to say to us today. Increased joint work on lectionaries, homiletical studies, catechetical and adult study materials could be undertaken.

c) In so far as possible, members, clergy and leaders of our churches need encouragement to share in common worship, beginning with the eucharist hospitality which is now quite generally possible between Anglicans and Lutherans. We also need to cultivate mutual prayer and intercession for one another in concrete and specific ways. We need joint attention to the cultivation of discipleship grounded in our common and mutually recognized baptism.

d) One important and newly recognized way to understand the Lutheran reformation confession of "justification by faith" is that it is not so much a new or additional doctrine, but rather it is an instruction to pastors about how they are to preach and teach the Christ of the ancient classic doctrines so that Christ is encountered as promise, not threat, and so that Christ is therefore received by faith, not by some inappropriate response (e.g. "works"). This creates an opportunity for renewed and common theological and catechetical attention to the Apostles' and Nicene Creeds, that is, to the classical christological and trinitarian dogmas, so that they are experienced as gospel confession rather than as ecclesiastical ideology. This is a common study task in which our traditions both need and can assist each other.

e) Even though our churches do not agree fully on the meaning or expression of episcopacy, we can give attention to the development and cultivation of forms for consultation of leaders with each other. Simultaneously, the leadership needs to encourage the interaction of clergy, congregations, seminarians and theologians for purposes of shared experience in worship, study and mission.

f) We need to look at the authentic apostolic continuity which both our churches evidence, although not always in identical forms, and which links us both to the church of all ages. Simultaneously we need to increase our awareness of the diversity of contexts throughout the world in which our churches live and function, often side by side.

g) We intend to ask how the practice of interim sharing of the eucharist, begun in the USA, could be effected in other contexts.

h) We intend to describe and propose theological and pastoral exchanges in regions where these are not already taking place as a way of implementing the concrete steps identified above because shared life is reciprocally related to theological agreement.

15. *Our witness:* All these tasks are to be understood in terms of the church's witness and evangelism, which includes worship and prayer, diaconic service, and attention to issues of peace with justice.

16. *Lay leadership:* We regard as fundamental to the relationship of our churches that the laity exercise responsibility for leadership in ecumenical mission and that our envisioning of concrete steps into the future make provision for such exercise of lay responsibility

I. ANGLICAN-LUTHERAN DIALOGUE

3. The Diaconate as Ecumenical Opportunity

Hanover, Germany, 1995

Foreword

Lutherans and Anglicans, like Christians of many other traditions, have been engaged during recent decades in much debate about the nature of ministry – both the ministry of the whole people of God and that of specific ordained ministers. This debate was intensified by the publication in 1982 of the Lima document *Baptism, Eucharist and Ministry (BEM)*, which intentionally raised many fundamental issues of ecclesiology, ministry and ordination.

A new approach was pioneered by the Anglican-Lutheran International Commission (ALIC) in *The Niagara Report* (1987), which tackled the question of *episcope*, or pastoral oversight, from the perspective of the church's mission. This produced a breakthrough in Anglican-Lutheran understanding which has already borne fruit in the proposed concordat of agreement (1991) in the USA and the Porvoo common statement (1992) between the British and Irish Anglican churches and the Nordic and Baltic Lutheran churches.

ALIC believed that the next logical step would be to undertake a fresh joint study of the *diaconate*, especially since the threefold ordering of the ordained ministry had long been a central issue in Anglican-Lutheran dialogue. The atmosphere of openness and growing trust between us has given us the confidence to work together on this question, where perplexities and real differences are evident, yet without their being church-dividing. Our desire has been to learn from each whatever could be useful for the common mission we share, and to avoid unnecessary duplication of effort.

From the outset of this project we were aware that our theological reflection needed to be rooted in the experience and concerns of those who actually exercise various diaconal ministries. We record our gratitude to the consultants, to whose evidence and convictions we paid serious attention.

We were equally aware that some churches do not have an ordained ministry distinct from that of the presbyter/pastor. The subject matter of this report is, nevertheless, directly relevant where, in response to specific needs, forms of ministry have sprung up which could be better recognized and utilized if seen in the context of diaconal ministry. Not only those people engaged in such work, but those whom they serve and with whom they cooperate, can be helped to value this diaconal ministry more highly.

Our aim is to offer a theological rationale which follows a clear line of argument: from Christ and the Spirit, through the ministry of the whole people of God (including ordained ministry) to an understanding of the diaconate. The latter part of this study focuses on the role of the ordained deacon in particular, as distinct from the broader understanding of diaconia.

We desire to know far more than we have yet discovered about the impressive range of diaconal ministries, and are sorry that our limited resources did not permit us to make a wider factual survey. We have been glad to discover that a number of working parties and research projects on this theme are already under way in various churches throughout the world. This reinforces our conviction that a particular ecumenical opportunity lies in developing the diaconate, and we indicate in appendix I the main factual points on which we would welcome information from church leaders and the chairpersons of diaconal associations and communities.

We recommend this Hanover report to our parent bodies, the Anglican Consultative Council and the Lutheran World Federation, and through them to their member churches throughout the world. We hope that it will serve as a catalyst for both joint study and joint action. We also dare to believe that it may have significance beyond these two world communions, and ask our ecumenical partners to study it in the context of the search for closer visible unity and of common service to God's world.

By common consent the members of ALIC dedicate this report to the memory of the late Deacon Tom Dorris of the Evangelical Lutheran Church in America. For many years Tom exercised a skilled ministry in the Communications unit of the World Council of Churches in Geneva, reporting and interpreting church affairs to the media. He was a keen advocate of a restored diaconate, and carefully collated the responses of all churches to the paragraphs in the Lima document on this subject. Not long after moving to new work with the Life and Peace Institute in Sweden he was tragically killed in a car accident in 1994. We hope that this report will further the concerns to which he dedicated his life.

We wish to express our particular thanks to those who played a key role in drafting and editing this report: Prof. Michael Root (Strasbourg, France), the Very Rev. William Petersen (Rochester, NY, USA) and the Rev. Dr Walter Bouman (Columbus, Ohio, USA). We also pay a special tribute to our co-secretaries, the Rev. Dr Eugene Brand and the Rev. Dr Donald Anderson; for each of them the publication of this book coincides with their retirement from a long and distinguished period of ecumenical service at the international level.

Rt Rev. David Tustin
Bishop of Grimsby, England

Rev. Prof. Ambrose Moyo
University of Harare, Zimbabwe

I. Introduction

1. The diaconate, an institution of great importance in the early church, is again coming to life in the church as a ministry and office closely related to central aspects of the church's identity: service, outreach, humility, concern for human needs. This reinvigoration of the diaconate has various roots: liturgical revival, a livelier sense of the church's mission in the world, and a renewed perception of rightful diversity in the church's ministries. These sources have together shaped the many forms of diaconate and diaconal ministry current today or under consideration in our churches.

2. No ecumenical consensus has yet emerged on the nature and forms of the diaconate and diaconal ministry. Not only have different churches made different deci-

sions about the diaconate, but debates continue within the churches about such fundamental questions as whether the diaconate is appropriately an ordained or lay ministry and whether those who intend to be ordained priest or pastor should first be ordained to the diaconate (the so-called "transitional diaconate"). The diaconate and diaconal ministries are still in flux in many churches. New forms of diaconate have been recently introduced in some churches, with varying degrees of acceptance, and are under study in other churches. While the nature of the diaconate is not an issue which lies at the centre of the faith, the restoration and reinvigoration of the diaconate affects the structure of the whole church's ministry. It not only reshapes mission, but directly touches the vocational lives of persons engaged in ministry. The debate over the diaconate thus has highly practical implications.

3. Transition and flux in the diaconate have been heightened by recent exegetical work on the meaning of the word "diakonia" in the New Testament and early church. Earlier work had argued that waiting at table and service of a humble sort was the term's paradigmatic sense. Diakonia as a term for Christian ministry was thus taken to refer especially to a character of humble service that should be typical of all ministry in the name of Christ.

4. More recent exegetical work, especially by John Collins in his *Diakonia: Reinterpreting the Ancient Sources* (Oxford, 1990) has called this earlier consensus into doubt. In the world in which the early church lived, diakonia seems to have referred to the service of a "go-between" or agent who carries out activities for another. In the letters of Paul, it also appears that diakonia is used to describe Paul and some of his associates as the "go-between" who carries the gospel from God or Christ to those who are to hear the message of salvation. Diakonia seems more concerned with apostleship than with our present understanding of the diaconate. Though scholars continue to debate, their findings cannot be ignored and have played an important part in this study.

5. Institutional and conceptual change in relation to the diaconate and diaconal ministry should be grasped as an opportunity to explore new forms of mission. This study has been especially concerned to consider the diaconate and diaconal ministry as an ecumenical opportunity, an opportunity for common mission among the churches. Ecumenical progress must not remain a matter of theological discussions or formal agreements, but needs to reach into and be nourished by common life and mission. In moving from its earlier study of *episcope* (*The Niagara Report: Report of the Anglican-Lutheran Consultation on Episcope 1987*) to its present study of the diaconate, the Anglican-Lutheran International Commission (ALIC) has not moved from issues of primary ecumenical importance to secondary issues, but rather has moved deeper into the heart of the one church's mission. In addition, while this study was carried out by a bilateral commission, observers from other ecclesial traditions were involved in the commission's preliminary work and ALIC hopes that the study's results will be relevant well beyond the two traditions.

6. Within both the Anglican and Lutheran communions, the nature of the diaconate and the possibilities of its renewal have been much discussed in recent years. A study at the international level was requested by the 1988 Lambeth conference and by a Lutheran World Federation (LWF) consultation on ministry held in 1992 in Cartigny, Switzerland. In response to these requests, the following study was proposed by ALIC at its meeting in Johannesburg in February 1993 and approved by the standing committee of the Anglican Consultative Council and primates meeting in March 1994 and

by the council of the LWF in June 1994. Background papers were commissioned for a preparatory consultation in April 1995 in West Wickham, Kent, England. This consultation produced the outline of a statement on the diaconate. On the basis of the papers and outline from the earlier consultation and with the participation of four expert consultants, ALIC developed the following text at their meeting at Kloster Wennigsen, near Hanover, Germany, in October 1995. The West Wickham papers are available from the Anglican communion office in London.

7. As the Niagara report did with *episcope*, this study seeks to place the diaconate in the context of a more comprehensive vision of the mission of God in the world. It thus begins with a consideration of Christ and the Holy Spirit as the agents who always drive the church's ministry. The church is then discussed as the sign and instrument of the work of Christ and the Spirit. The church's mission and ministry then form the context for the discussion of the diaconate and diaconal ministry in the remainder of the text.

II. Theological foundations for the diaconate and diaconal ministry

A. Christ, kingdom and Spirit

8. Faithful diaconal ministry has been done and is being carried out under a great variety of circumstances and forms by the church and its members. In this document the Anglican-Lutheran International Commission uses a theological model which it believes is especially suitable for locating diaconal ministry within the mission and ministry of the church as a whole. The church has both its historical and its theological basis in the resurrection of Jesus Christ. The resurrection of Jesus is the eschatological event (1 Cor. 10:11) which discloses the crucified one as "both Lord and Messiah" (Acts 2:36); which identifies him as the one who determines the ultimate destiny of the universe (1 Cor. 15:24-28); and which discloses that he is "the head over all things for the church" (Eph. 1:22). He is eschatological Lord because "death no longer has dominion over him" (Rom. 6:9). All powers of the "old age" are dominated by death and are characterized by an unrelenting drive for self-preservation, at whatever cost to others. But if Jesus Christ has the last word, then he confers the freedom for self-offering on behalf of the world in the conviction that there is more to do with life than to preserve it (Matt. 16:24-26 and parallels; cf. *The Niagara Report*, 22-23).

9. The resurrection of Jesus Christ is the lens through which the church perceives Jesus' own mission and ministry, and retells the story. The historical mission of Jesus was to announce the good news of the reign of God in proclamation and parables, to embody the reign of God in signs and actions, and to be the historical fulfilment of the promised final victory of the reign of God through his death and resurrection (Mark 1:14-15; Luke 17:21-22; Matt. 11:2-6; Luke 11:20). In a slave's death (Phil. 2:6-8) on the cross he endured the consequence of his own diaconal ministry. For Jesus was crucified because his messianic mission was to be God's saving embrace of all Israel and of all the world. On the cross Jesus was obedient to the sending and mission of the Father (Mark 14:32-37) in the power of the Holy Spirit (Mark 1:9-11). Jesus was sent by the Father to reconcile the whole creation to God (2 Cor. 5:17-19).

10. In Christ the victory of the reign of God over the powers of death and sin has begun. The leadership ministry of Christ is therefore not like leadership in the world of death and sin (Mark 10:41-45). It has a character and quality determined by Christ's

way of being in and for the world, in the service of his Father. Christ is determinative for the ministry and ministries of the church. He is the basis for the *leitourgia*, the worship, of the church, for he offers and gives himself in free obedience (Heb. 9:14; Gal. 2:20; 1 Cor. 11:23-26; John 12:20-33, etc.). He is the basis for the *martyria*, the witness, of the church, for he is the foundational witness to the everlasting love of the triune God (John 3:16; Rom. 5:8). As the incarnate Word sent by the Father, Jesus is the basis for the church's *diakonia*, the freedom to announce and act out God's eschatological salvation (Rom. 15:8). Christ is diakonos, servant, as the agent and image of the One who sent him, acting and forgiving with his Father's own power, mediating the Father's will to the world. Being diakonos does not mean that the roles of leader and servant are reversed or abolished, but rather that those who lead and rule do so as servants, that is, as agents of Christ's salvation (Luke 22:27).

11. The outpouring of the Holy Spirit is the sign promised by Christ that the eschatological reign of God has come. At every point the presence and power of the Holy Spirit testifies that the final act of history has occurred in Jesus. The Holy Spirit came upon Mary in the conception of Jesus (Matt. 2:18-20; Luke 1:35). The Holy Spirit descended upon Jesus at his baptismal commissioning (Mark 1:10 and par.). The Holy Spirit was promised as Christ's eschatological gift to his disciples (Acts 1:8; John 14:15-17, etc.).

12. Thus the outcome of the mission and ministry of Christ is nothing less than a new creation. The entire universe is encompassed by the love and care, the redeeming commitment and creative salvation of the Holy Trinity.

B. The church

13. *The church is both designated and called to be the effective sign and instrument of the reign of God.* The eschatological reign of God, inaugurated by and inseparable from Jesus Christ, is the goal and promise of God in history. The reign of God is being served wherever institutions, communities, movements and individuals contribute to peace with justice, to compassion for the suffering, to preservation and care of the creation, and to admonition and conversion of sinners.

14. The church is called and admonished to reflect in its being and worship, its life and ministry, what God has done and is doing (Eph. 4:1-6; Rom. 12; Col. 3:1-4:1; *The Niagara Report*, 24). The pattern of apostolic writing in Ephesians, for example, is that the church is exhorted and admonished on the basis of what God has done. In Christ the reign of God has already come. That means, among other things, that God has already broken down the wall of hostility between Jew and Gentile, male and female, slave and free (Gal. 3:28; Eph. 2:11-22).

15. The church is called to witness to the reign of God. In this witness, the church confesses that Jesus is the Christ, even beyond the church where he is not recognized as such. One aspect of the church's witness to the reign of God is a critical recognition of where the reign of God is being served. The church is called to cooperate in humility with institutions, communities, movements and individuals contributing to the vision of the reign of God. The church is called to identify, warn against and oppose the powers of death and sin, without counting the cost.

16. *The church is created by the Holy Spirit.* On the basis of the promise of Christ (John 14:15-17, etc.) the community of disciples experienced the Holy Spirit (Acts 2:1-4; John 20:22-23). Acts 2:17 uses an eschatological formula, "in the last days", to intro-

duce the vision of the prophet Joel. The Holy Spirit is now the dynamic of the entire community, young and old, women and men, and not just the dynamic of charismatic individuals. The Holy Spirit is the *arrabon*, the "down payment" on God's final future (Eph. 1:14; 2 Cor. 1:22 and 5:5). As "down payment" the Holy Spirit empowers and calls the church to live in anticipation of the consummation of the reign of God. The evidence of the Holy Spirit's presence is behaviour determined by being "in Christ" (Gal. 5:22-26). Jesus' disciples are promised the Holy Spirit as the answer to their prayer (Luke 11:13). The church is therefore called to receive the prayer which Jesus taught it to pray (Luke 11:1-4) as the way Jesus shares with the church his own mission and ministry. The church prays for the Holy Spirit when it asks that God's name be holy, that God's reign come, that it eat the messianic bread of the future, and that it anticipate God's final forgiveness by forgiving all who sin against it.

17. The church is called to trust God's promise that the Holy Spirit will be given. The church is called to be open to the Holy Spirit, to receive the gift and the gifts of the Spirit, to recognize and seize the opportunities to serve the reign of God, and to accept with thanksgiving the ministries which serve the reign of God.

18. *The church becomes visible in its gathering as a eucharistic assembly.* When the church gathers for "the Lord's supper" (1 Cor. 11:19), it becomes especially visible "as a church" (1 Cor. 11:18). In Corinth it was evident that some of the members were not caring for other members in that meal which anticipates the consummation of the reign of God when God will be "all in all" (1 Cor. 15:28). Just so, the church was not diaconal, was not proclaiming the Lord's self-offering for the world "until he comes" (1 Cor. 11:26). It is precisely in the eucharistic celebration that the eschatological consummation of the reign of God is anticipated (*BEM*, Eucharist 21).

19. The eucharistic celebration involves five actions: (1) The gathering of the baptized in one place as the koinonia of Christ with his people and as the koinonia of the people in Christ (Acts 2:42, 46; 1 Cor. 10:16-17); (2) attention to the word of God; (3) the offering, in which the baptized offer themselves through prayer and gifts for service to the reign of God; (4) the meal of the presence of the eschatological Christ which anticipates the messianic banquet; (5) the sending of the baptized into their daily mission and ministry.

20. The eucharistic assembly as koinonia participates in and manifests the leitourgia, martyria and diakonia of the Christ who is present to it and through it. It is in the eucharistic assembly that the church receives its identity (body of Christ) and its mission (to be offered for one another and for the world; 1 Cor. 10:16-17; 11:17-26). In gathering, word, prayer, meal and sending the church is called and embraced by Christ for his mission and ministry in the world.

C. Diaconal ministry

21. *The liturgy provides the context for understanding the church's diaconal ministry.* The celebration of the eucharist (see above, 18) has, in significant ways, shaped the governing structures of the church. In the Lutheran tradition, bishops (Augsburg confession XXVIII) and ordained ministers in general (Augsburg confession V) are defined by their connection with word and sacrament. In the Anglican tradition, bishops, priests and deacons are ordained into ministries that have to do with word and sacrament. Both of these traditions reflect the vision and practice which comes to expression in ancient Christian documents (e.g., the *Apology of Justin Martyr*, the *Didache*, the *Apostolic Constitution* of Hippolytus).

22. The celebration of the eucharist is a paradigm for the inter-relationship of various ministries in the church. It is, among other things, a kind of "dress rehearsal" for life.

23. The liturgy is the work of the whole people of God. Ministry is, first, ministry of the church as a whole. The whole community is a priestly people (1 Pet. 2:9). Hebrews, in one passage, brings together the ministry of Christ and the inter-related ministries of leitourgia, martyria and diakonia on the part of the people: "Therefore Jesus also suffered outside the city gate in order to sanctify the people by his own blood. Let us then go to him outside the camp and bear the abuse he endured. For here we have no lasting city, but we are looking for the city that is to come. Through him, then, let us continually offer a sacrifice of praise to God, that is, the fruit of lips that confess his name. Do not neglect to do good and to share what you have, for such sacrifices are pleasing to God" (Heb. 13:12-16).

24. *The ministry of the whole people of God requires the ministries of individuals.* Through baptism persons are initiated into the ministry of the whole church. Incumbent upon all the baptized is the exercise of leitourgia, martyria and diakonia. However, baptism itself does not confer office in the church. "What is the common property of all, no individual may arrogate to himself, unless he is called" (*Luther's Works*, WA 6:566; American edition 36:116). Office must be given by the church. Within the liturgy there are a variety of specific tasks to be performed; these tasks have traditionally been correlated with distinct roles in the liturgical celebration, e.g., that of presider and deacon, which have a symbolic function.

25. There are some offices in the church which enact and bring into focus central aspects of the mission of the entire church and also form the identity of the person involved. This description applies particularly to ordained ministries. Such ministries involve an appointment or call from the church and a rite which includes prayer and the laying-on of hands. In the church's rite, God is active, giving the gifts needed for ministry. Through leitourgia, martyria and diakonia persons designated as God's gifts to the church become symbols of Christ and his church (*BEM*, Ministry 12,15).

26. *A close relationship exists between liturgical celebration and diaconal ministry.* The baptized have been given their calling and ministry by virtue of their baptism. That calling is renewed and reshaped by the liturgical celebration of the eucharist. The diaconal ministry of the laity receives encouragement and, where appropriate, leadership from the deacons of the church.

27. The ministry of deacons was traditionally, and in some places is at present, expressed within the liturgical celebration of the gathered eucharistic assembly by assigning elements of the rite to the deacon: reading the gospel, leading the intercessions of the people, receiving the gifts of the people and "setting the table" for the meal, serving the eucharistic meal, sending the people from the eucharistic assembly into the world, administering the ceremonial. In the early church the social service carried on by deacons seems to have been rooted in the liturgical celebration (see the *Apology* of Justin Martyr).

28. The social services so central to the diaconal communities and ministries founded in the 19th century continue to be a vital aspect at the church's witness and ministry. These services were rooted in a rich worship and community life. The integration of worship and service remains a concern for the various diaconal ministries of the church.

III. Diversity and commonality of present forms of diaconal ministry

A. Diversity and unity

29. In some traditions and congregations, recent liturgical renewal has included a revival of the specific liturgical role of the deacon (cf. 27). In other traditions, various members of the laity have assumed one or more of these ritual elements. Representatives of the laity served to encourage all the laity in their daily ministries. The revival of the deacon's specific liturgical role need not exclude liturgical expressions of lay ministry. It should give appropriate leadership to the diaconal dimension and character of the daily ministry of all the baptized.

30. The diaconate and other diaconal ministries have taken highly diverse forms in the Lutheran and Anglican Communions. Not only have the differences existed between the two traditions, but diaconal ministries within each tradition have been so multiform that they are difficult to categorize. Some generalizations can, however, be made about diaconal ministry in each tradition.

31. The Anglican tradition has preserved an ordained diaconate, whether transitional or permanent, and "deacon" in an Anglican context usually refers to someone in this office. But Anglican churches also have deaconesses and other especially designated persons who carry out diaconal ministry (e.g., licensed lay workers, communities of religious).

32. At the time of the Reformation, Lutheran churches did not preserve an ordained diaconate within a threefold ordering of ministry. "Deacon" in most Lutheran traditions refers to a person consecrated or commissioned to a ministry focused on parish work or social service, but not ordained, i.e., their ministry has not generally been seen as a form of the single ordained ministry, usually understood by Lutherans to be the office of word and sacrament. Some deacons or diaconal ministers have liturgical roles. Deaconesses are known in many countries, many churches have a variety of diaconal ministries, and the ordained diaconate has been revived in some Lutheran churches.

33. The diversity of diaconal ministries in the Anglican and Lutheran churches is not a difference that breaks or blocks communion between our churches. The possibility of diversity in the diaconate and diaconal ministries has been affirmed in Anglican-Lutheran dialogues since their beginnings in 1909 (Anglican Communion-Church of Sweden).

34. To be ecumenically fruitful, diversity must be open to cooperation and mutual enrichment. Our traditions have influenced each other in diaconal ministry in the past. The Anglican tradition has held up the model of an ordained diaconate for all churches shaped by the Reformation of the 16th century. The deaconess movement that arose in 19th-century German Lutheranism found an echo in the founding of similar communities in some Anglican churches.

35. Diversity is always to be seen against the background of the one church of Jesus Christ, to which both Anglicans and Lutherans belong. On the one hand, diversity should thus be recognizably rooted in a shared set of beliefs and commitments about the mission and ministry of the church (see above, section II). Unity must not exclude diversity, but diversity should be transparent to unity.

36. On the other hand, cooperation and enrichment are significantly furthered when our various diaconal ministries are informed about and can recognize each other. Some Lutheran-Anglican agreements have provided for a mutual canonical recognition of

ordained deacons (e.g., the Northern European Porvoo common statement). Mutual acquaintance and recognition in diaconal ministries, however, should reach further than just canonical measures. Possibilities of common learning and work need to be explored. Deacons and diaconal ministers from our traditions already meet in national and international organizations devoted to diaconal ministry. A deeper knowledge of one another would further mutual support and encouragement, which might be especially important in places where only a few deacons from each tradition are present. If communion is truly a growing together into a common life, then a lively sense of a common diaconal mission, carried out in many ways, is an important aspect of communion.

B. Various forms of diaconal ministry

37. Many of the diaconal ministries within our churches arose in response to specific needs in our societies. The dominant factors in the diversity of diaconal ministries have been the various needs which they have sought to meet and the historical contexts in which they arose and which shaped their character. Diaconal ministries are thus often expressions of particular historical and cultural realities.

38. While a clearer sense of the nature of the diaconate and diaconal ministry is needed, the flexibility and spontaneity that have characterized the development of many diaconal ministries over the last two hundred years should not be lost. While respecting cultural and historical diversity, our churches must also be ready to reflect critically on these forms. Some may have outlived their usefulness. Some may need to be reformed. The churches need to be open to the development of new forms of diaconal ministry, as needs and the moment require.

39. Certain forms of diversity need here to be especially noted in order to avoid misunderstanding, to further mutual recognition and to avoid distortions.

40. The most obvious diversity within and between our churches is between the diaconate as an ordained ministry and forms of diaconal ministry commissioned, set apart or consecrated in other ways. The issues related to ordination are discussed below in section IV.

41. An important variable in diaconal ministry is the form of commitment called for by different ministries. A significant number of such ministries call for extended or life-long commitment. Some call for commitment to life in community, in various forms and for various lengths of time. The form of commitment tends to reflect the inter-relation of ministry and personal identity. When diaconal ministry involves personal identity and is not just a task (cf. §25), long-term or open-ended commitment is particularly appropriate.

42. Different forms of diaconal ministry relate in different ways to the leadership and decision-making structures of the churches. Some were initially mandated by the central structures of church authority and are immediately responsible to those structures. Others arose as grassroots initiatives responsible to the church in more indirect ways.

43. A relative freedom from the central decision-making structures of the churches has permitted some diaconal ministries to be spaces where excluded groups (e.g., women) have been able to shape and exercise their own ministries. These ministries have addressed concerns sometimes ignored by the church leadership.

44. The danger should be recognized that such ministries can become places where the ministries of women and other marginalized groups can be isolated and limited.

Diaconal ministries with a specific focus should not be shaped in ways that reinforce oppressive stereotypes. Just as the entire life of the church, including its leadership structures, is being opened to all within it, so diaconal ministries which may previously have been identified with certain groups should be opened to all. For example, forms of diaconal ministry that have traditionally been seen as appropriate only for women can be seen as possible for men also.

45. Some forms of diaconal ministry have been defined by specific tasks, e.g., work with youth or the sick. Others have been defined by a community, fellowship or association which has then taken up a variety of tasks, e.g., some orders of deaconesses. There is no need to choose between these two forms of diaconal self-definition. The church at various times needs both forms of ministry, which to a degree relate to different forms or ways of life to which individuals feel themselves called.

46. Different forms of diaconal ministry call for different sorts of preparation and engagement. Some depend extensively on previous experience in church and world, and do not require a special preparation of the sort now associated with seminaries and university theological faculties. Others employ a more "professional" model of education and certification. Again, no universal judgment should be made that any particular model is the only one appropriate. Rather, careful consideration needs to be given to what forms of preparation and examination a particular task and role calls for.

C. Common principles

47. Within the diversity of present forms of diaconal ministries, some common principles can be recognized, applicable to both lay and ordained diaconal ministries. These common principals form a background against which we can recognize the various diaconal ministries in our midst. By identifying theological concerns related to various forms of diaconal ministry, they can also provide guidance in thinking about and shaping such ministries. Taken together, these principles do not provide an exhaustive description or definition of the diaconate or the diaconal ministry. The variety that has typified and should typify diaconal ministries rules out such an exhaustive definition. That the relation of some ministries to what is here and elsewhere described as diaconal ministry is sometimes unclear is in itself not a problem.

48. A general description of diaconal ministers can be given: *Diaconal ministers are called to be agents of the church in interpreting and meeting needs, hopes and concerns within church and society.*

49. As agents of the church, deacons and diaconal ministers do not pursue a simply self-initiated and self-accountable ministry. While traditionally deacons were understood to be agents of the bishop, diaconal ministers today are often agents of congregations or other church bodies. In all cases, however, diaconal ministry is carried out in the name of the church.

50. Such a relation of agency implies a relation of accountability. Accountability is a many-sided relation. Diaconal ministers must account to the church for their ministries. The church, however, is also accountable for providing adequate support and preparation for diaconal ministries carried out in its name. Accountability should not become a relation of subservience which would hinder the spontaneity and flexibility which diaconal ministry often needs, and which would rule out the possibility of diaconal ministry expressing a prophetic critique of the church. Diaconal ministers can also at times model special forms of Christian life. Such critique and modelling must

be for the sake of the wider church, however, if diaconal ministry is to be understood as ministry that represents the church.

51. Diaconal ministry typically not only seeks to mediate the service of the church to specific needs, but also to interpret those needs to the church. The "go-between" role of diaconal ministry thus operates in both directions: from church to the needs, hopes and concerns of persons in and beyond the church; and from those needs, hopes and concerns to the church.

52. Precisely as ministry that represents and is an agency of the church, diaconal ministries are not only ministries of service (diakonia), but also of witness (martyria) and worship (leitourgia). If diaconal ministry is carried out in the name of the church, then it is only rightly carried out in the name of Christ and to the praise and glory of God. The revival of a specific liturgical role for deacons in some churches points to the witness and worship which occur throughout their ministry.

53. The inter-relation of service, witness and praise may vary widely in different forms of diaconal ministry. Though the present understanding of the meaning of diakonia in the New Testament is undergoing change, service typically forms the central emphasis of diaconal ministry. This service is liturgically focused and brought to the recognition of the church in the various roles of the deacon in the eucharist.

54. The church's service, however, must not cease to be a witness to the Christ who is among us as one who serves. Diaconal ministry is a form of discipleship and should be recognizable as such. The witnessing aspect of diaconal ministry was, and in some of our churches still is, symbolized by the deacon reading the gospel within the church's liturgy. This role symbolizes the witness of diaconal ministry, which nevertheless finds its centre in the witnessing character of its service.

55. Like all aspects of the Christian life, diaconal ministry is to the praise and glory of God. This aspect of diaconal ministry should be particularly evident in the joy and hope which should shine through diaconal ministry, even in situations which would seem to induce despair. Again, this doxological aspect of diaconal ministry is symbolized by specific roles deacons and diaconal ministers can and have played in the liturgy of the church, e.g., proclaiming the resurrection in the Easter vigil through the *Exultet*. The leitourgia of diaconal ministry also includes lament and intercession. The deacon thus traditionally, and today again in some churches, gathers and leads the congregation's intercessory prayers. Again, however, these liturgical roles symbolize the true centre of the leitourgia of the diaconal ministers, which is to be found in their daily ministry.

56. As a specific and focal form of a task to which all Christians are called, the service of one's neighbour, diaconal ministry should foster and bring to wider recognition the ministry of others, rather than making their ministries redundant or superfluous. The diaconal minister should lead and inspire the wider church in its service. Here the interpretive role of diaconal ministry plays a special role. Diaconal ministries will have their own specific tasks which are their own responsibility. As a ministry of the whole church, however, this ministry should have a multiplying effect, leading others to their own specific tasks of service.

57. As a ministry of the church, diaconal ministry is not the ministry of isolated individuals, but should reflect the personal, collegial and communal aspects of the church's ministries (cf. *BEM*, Ministry 26). One possible form of such collegiality is the mutual support and communal life of the various communities, associations and

mother houses that have proved important to the vitality of many diaconal ministries. These forms of life have provided important opportunities for mutual support in often invisible and thankless work, have called forth special gifts, and have provided examples of committed community for other ministries and the church.

IV. An ordained diaconate

A. The question of an ordained diaconate

58. Previous sections have laid the foundation for a more focused consideration at this point of a renewed or re-established diaconate within the ordained ministry. Unless otherwise specified, in this section the terms "deacon" and "diaconate" refer to an ordained ministry.

59. It is important to reiterate here that questions surrounding the renewal or the re-establishment of the diaconate as an ordained ministry in the contemporary church do not constitute a church-dividing problem for Lutherans and Anglicans. The way in which Lutherans and Anglicans today hear the questions surrounding the diaconate is coloured by their differing histories. These questions are, nevertheless, addressed in the context of remarkable ecumenical agreements already existing between the two traditions as they move towards the explicit goal of full communion. Such agreements, on the one hand, fully document mutual concern for the historical ordering of ministry as a sign of apostolicity and, on the other hand, find in such a common grounding the basis for a certain freedom to address critically the issues around the effective ordering of ministries in the contemporary church as it seeks to serve and proclaim the gospel.

60. Contemporary discussion about a renewed or re-established diaconate is, of course, by no means limited to our two traditions. Wider catholic tradition, contemporary scholarship and ecumenical conversation place before Lutherans and Anglicans questions concerning a renewed diaconate. Three sources in particular inform present reflections: (1) the insights of *BEM* on the diaconate (Ministry 31); (2) the historical-philological corrective to earlier understandings of the *diakon-* words provided by John Collins' *Diakonia* (see above, 3f.); and (3) the long tradition that finds the paradigm for the entire ministry of the deacon in the deacon's liturgical role in and about the paschal proclamation (*Exultet*) at the great vigil of the resurrection.

61. From these sources there emerges a renewed definition of diaconate for our time that understands deacons to be not merely an inferior order of ministers exercising lowly service, but agents ordained to assist the community's presider (bishop/presbyter), both in the proclamation and celebration of word and sacrament, as well as in the coordinating of the community's diakonia in Christ. As in the paschal liturgy, the deacon not only proclaims "the light of Christ", inviting the people to join in praise and thanksgiving, but also leads the community into ministry with "the light of Christ". While remaining faithful, then, to ancient theological understandings and structures of ministry, such a definition, in fact, provides challenges as well as opportunities for both the Lutheran and Anglican traditions as they have historically addressed and carried out the diaconate and diaconal ministries.

62. In both traditions the distinctive role of the diaconate within the ordained ministry has been absorbed into the presbyterate on the basis of developments that obtained in the Western church from the middle ages to the eve of the 16th-century reformations. The Anglican tradition, for instance, preserved the form of the diaconate,

while the Lutheran tradition for the most part did not. Furthermore, where Anglicans retained some semblance of a liturgical role for the diaconate in word and sacrament, pastorally they treated the order essentially as an apprenticeship for presbyterate. Among Lutherans the diaconate as an order within the one ministry of word and sacrament did not survive. Rather, a revival of lay diaconal ministries, carrying out socio-caritative-educational work without a liturgical base in the church, has characterized most Lutheran practice since the 19th century.

B. The meaning of ordination in relation to the diaconate

63. In the contemporary situation the meaning of ordination in relation to the diaconate is an issue of central importance.

64. For many (but not all) Lutheran churches, the ordination of deacons would be a new development requiring a convincing rationale. Specifically, such a proposal would require a broader understanding of the traditional Lutheran doctrine of ordained ministry. For many (but not all) Anglican churches, whether they are for or against the renewal of the diaconate, retention of it in "form only" has grown increasingly problematic in the contemporary situation. Thus it becomes necessary to reconsider the language used in relation to ordination itself. In the case of a renewed or re-established diaconate, ordination (1) is into both an activity and an identity; (2) calls for some kind of open-ended or life-long commitment; (3) includes recognition as being within the one ordained ministry of word and sacrament; and (4) entails a symbolic as well as a practical relationship to the whole community that provides for the public exercise of this ministry as well as for its accountability. Such a way of talking about the diaconate has the advantage of going through and beyond the old dichotomies of "functional" versus "ontological" by giving the diaconate a specifically ecclesiastical location and expression (see above, 25).

65. In this regard, appropriate reference can be made to those significant statements in *BEM* (M29-31) that deal with the unity as well as particular characteristics of ordained ministry, whether of the bishop, presbyter or deacon. Here within the one ordained ministry may be found a threefold expression on the basis of the principle "distinction without separation". Yet with respect to a renewed or re-established diaconate, it is precisely here that challenging issues arise for Lutherans and Anglicans. In addition, both traditions also face questions about the relation of this order to (1) the presbyterate, (2) those already exercising non-ordained diaconal ministries, and (3) all the baptized (laos). In each, there exist both problems and opportunities.

66. Thus, for instance, Lutheran churches without an ordained diaconate are challenged to consider whether such a diaconate as has been described above (including a liturgical grounding in the ministry of word and sacrament) would be of value in their service of the gospel and, if so, whether a diaconal ministry more reflective of the practice of the wider church and Christian tradition could appear as a legitimate development for Lutherans.

67. Anglican churches are challenged to restore to the diaconate (as defined above) its character as a lifelong and distinct form of ordained ministry, including with its liturgical function a pastoral focus on *caritas* and *justitia* in church and society. Such a restoration would imply both a reconsideration of the transitional diaconate and the possibility of direct ordination to the priesthood of persons discerned to have presbyteral vocations without their "passing through" the diaconate. The possibility of such direct ordination is not excluded on historical or theological grounds.

68. In both traditions, the presbyters may perceive a renewed diaconate as a threat to their own identity and role. This will be especially so where the presbyteral office is seen as the embodiment of all ordained ministry. If, however, presbyters can welcome deacons as partners-in-ministry, both liturgically and within the church's mission, then they may themselves be freed to exercise a more focused ministry, bearing responsibility for the life of the community in word and sacrament. In this way, too, the diaconate can stand as a witness against the perennial threat of clericalism, an ecclesiastical distortion rooted in exclusivist attitudes and practices. Deacons are called by the very nature of their order to stand as a witness to presbyters and bishops that the authority of all ordained ministry is for service alone.

69. The re-establishment of a diaconate within the ordained ministry need not appear as a denigration of the work of diaconal orders, agencies, or persons who exercise ministries to, for and with the oppressed, the marginalized or the poor. It would be surprising, rather, if deacons did not urgently strive to link these diaconal groups with the life of the congregations they serve in order more effectively to carry out together the church's mission. It might also occur through such contact that diaconal orders, agencies or persons would, over time, come to a new appreciation of the connection between the worship that is at the heart of Christian communities and their own life of service. In turn, they might seek creative ways to connect this service with the liturgical life of congregations.

70. In our own day, one of the chief arguments against a renewed diaconate is often a concern that various ministries in worship now exercised by lay persons as the result of movements of liturgical renewal might be reabsorbed into a clerical order. It is asked whether a re-established diaconate will more generally usurp lay ministries. These concerns have arisen to the extent that laity have ceased in our age to be the passive recipients or consumers of ministry at the hands of the ordained and become active participants in the church's mission. If, however, deacons are understood as the very persons who (1) "represent to the church (laos) its calling as servant", and (2) "exemplify the interdependence of worship and service" (*BEM*, Ministry 31), then we can address the concern that what deacons do is the same as what Christians in general could or should do. In fact, deacons have no special powers or activities exclusively reserved to them. What is, however, distinctive is their call to be publicly accountable servants of the church who have a charge to model, encourage and coordinate diakonia. This is the particular call or vocation of the deacon that is not shared by all Christians.

71. There are also professional implications in regard to a renewed or re-established diaconate in the contemporary church. Questions and concerns here, in fact, are often voiced prior to any sustained theological or ecclesiological reflection on the diaconate. At this point it must simply be indicated that a great diversity of approach is possible in dealing with a renewed diaconate according to ecclesiastical circumstances and missionary need. Thus a renewed diaconate could be exercised as full-time or part-time, stipendiary or non-stipendiary. When paid, remuneration could be from either church or non-church sources. Whatever the case, these questions are secondary to theological, liturgical and ecclesiastical considerations.

72. Finally, both traditions would be challenged to ensure that appropriate forms of education and formation for this ministry are developed within their various agencies of theological education. In such planning and development it will be important to consider what aspects of diaconal formation and education will best be done in conjunc-

tion and community with those preparing for presbyteral or lay ministries and which parts solely with candidates for the diaconate. Given the nature of ordained diaconal ministry, the bulk of the preparation probably will need to occur in the former manner. In any case it will be important that formation in diakonia, as well as in the ability to form others in diakonia, occurs.

C. The renewal of the diaconate as an opportunity for unity and joint mission

73. The renewal of the church's diaconate at this time presents a unique opportunity for deepened unity and joint endeavour in the life and mission of the Anglican and Lutheran, as well as other churches.

74. The process of ecumenical dialogue and theological reflection is one which itself helps to build and deepen koinonia among Christians of different communions. Discussions about the place and practice of diakonia in baptized and ordered Christian life can positively influence the future of the church and how the church is seen and manifested in the world. Not only do such discussions help to further the work on ministry begun in *BEM*, they also contribute to an overarching ecclesiological vision which can strengthen the bonds among Christians of the Lutheran, Anglican and other traditions.

75. The diaconate offers a theme for ecumenical exploration which can result in a more effective coordination of efforts to renew mission and liturgy both within and among these differing traditions. It is an exploration which pushes churches to rethink existing assumptions, and to reach greater clarity in their theological and functional understanding of the offices of presbyter and bishop. Such clarity can only help to enhance liturgical practices and the way in which they shape the intentional daily ministry of all baptized Christians.

76. The contribution of the diaconal movement initiated in the 19th century by the churches in Germany and spread throughout the Lutheran communion has set an inspiring example of diaconal works already being performed by many Christians, both individually and corporately, both unofficially and in the name of the church. Raising the possibility of an ordained diaconate, visibly incorporated into ordered ministry and eucharistic liturgy, challenges the church in every location both to take greater ownership of diakonia as a sign of apostolicity and to encourage the whole people of God to understand their daily life as an arena for Christian service. Likewise, the emergence of a distinctive, lifelong ordained diaconate in the Anglican church invites all Christians better to integrate worship and service in their daily lives. A revitalized diaconate can be a means for equipping the laity to become serving leaders in their various callings and for mobilizing them to become effective agents for the transformation of worldly structures and institutions.

77. The church's diakonia is characterized by practical expressions of God's redeeming love in concrete acts of justice, reconciliation and healing. A renewed diaconate can effectively strengthen these acts with the church's authority and blessing by linking them with the eucharistic meal. Such a renewal opens the door for shared endeavours which can be undertaken locally and by the wider church. Indeed, such associations of diaconal communities as the Kaiserswerthe Diakonieverband, Diakonia, the World Federation of Diaconal Associations and Diaconal Communities and its regional bodies, represent ecumenical and collaborative possibilities which should be further explored.

78. Regardless of differing practices and assumptions, deacons and diaconal ministers of all traditions are closely bound together by their common awareness of exercising servanthood within and beyond the church, wherever hope and suffering present opportunities for justice and healing. There is a powerful potential for further initiatives along these lines:
- Anglican and Lutheran parishes and congregations sharing the ministry of deacons and diaconal ministers of either tradition, borrowing or seconding deacons and diaconal ministers in areas where one or the other tradition is sparsely represented;
- joint presentations at synodical or convention gatherings on the "needs, hopes and concerns of the world" as perceived and experienced by deacons and diaconal ministers;
- invitations to deacons or diaconal ministers of one tradition to participate in the liturgies of the other, particularly on major occasions;
- opening up diaconal associations of a "third order" type to women and men of both traditions exercising diaconal ministry;
- initiating joint pilot or demonstration projects using pooled resources from Anglican and Lutheran jurisdictions to encourage experimentation and learning with regard to:
  - new patterns of stipendiary and non-stipendiary ministry;
  - ways of discerning diaconal as distinct from presbyteral vocations and encouraging churches, where ready, to ordain accordingly;
  - theological and ministerial training and formation;
  - encouraging and supporting churches which may not at this time have a diaconate to initiate a diaconate as appropriate to their ministry needs.

V. Conclusion

79. This study has been conducted under the theme of the diaconate and diaconal ministries as an ecumenical opportunity for the contemporary life and mission of the churches. If diaconal ministry is to be pursued in the name of the wider church, it must be ecumenically open. In a situation of division, most diaconal ministries will be rooted in and accountable to a particular church body. Nevertheless, the mandate of diaconal ministry is laid upon the entire church of Jesus Christ. The call to witness to the unity we have been given and to contribute to the unity we seek is also addressed to deacons and diaconal ministers. Precisely because diaconal ministry is not burdened with the problems of validity and canonical recognition which hinder our visible unity in the exercise of presbyteral and episcopal ministry, we are called all the more to take up the possibilities before us for common diaconal ministry. The question and opportunity thus become clear: Could forms of joint, common or united diaconal ministry precede and clear the way for a joint, common or united presbyterate or episcopacy? Joint oversight of diaconal ministries could provide a focus for movement into a joint exercise of *episcope*. Our churches and our diaconal ministers need to be imaginative in shaping diaconal ministries ecumenically.

Appendix I: Factual Survey

We extend an open invitation to church leaders and the chairpersons of diaconal associations and communities throughout the world to assist this project by reporting briefly on the following points:

- What publicly accredited forms of diaconal ministry exist in your church?
- What kind of diaconal work is done by other persons in the name of your church?
- Since when has this been so? (key dates in development)
- What numbers of women and men are engaged in these ministries?
- Are they full-time or part-time; paid from church/other sources or unpaid?
- Are these ministries inter-related with other church structures?
- What are the educational requirements and training provisions for these ministries?
- How are they commissioned, e.g. ordination, licensing, commissioning, consecration, etc.?

Any contributions to this enquiry will help to throw further light on the extent and variety of diaconal ministry of our churches' life.

4. Sharing in the Apostolic Communion

Kanuga, North Carolina, USA, January 1996

Preface
The international dialogue between Anglicans and Methodists had its beginning in the Lambeth conference of 1988. The invitation by the Anglican bishops to begin formal conversations was enthusiastically accepted by the World Methodist Council.

The dialogue began with Anglican and Methodist leaders from around the world coming together with diversity in theology and practice, even within the two communions. As we continued our common journey, prayer, worship and work became increasingly intermingled. We began as separate sides. We concluded as one community.

Our methodology included three specific elements:

1. We produced an interim report which was widely distributed within both communions, including guided questions for responses. This report received 21 responses from every level of our two communions. We especially acknowledge that three of our responses came from joint bodies of Anglicans and Methodists in Great Britain, Ireland and Southern Africa. We are grateful to those who responded and we have incorporated many of their suggestions into this final report.

2. We used numerous recent ecumenical texts, most notably *Baptism, Eucharist and Ministry* (Lima, 1982) and even more recent fruits of bilateral dialogues involving Anglicans and Lutherans such as the Porvoo common statement and the Methodist-Roman Catholic dialogue which have produced further convergences that we have built upon.

3. We found that, in light of the responses to questions raised by the interim report, more time and attention had to be spent on matters that divided our two communions than on those upon which we are already happily agreed. Therefore, more has been said about the ministry than about doctrine.

We commend this document to our two sponsoring bodies, to the World Methodist Council meeting in Rio de Janeiro in August 1996 and to the Anglican Consultative Council for presentation to the Lambeth conference in July 1998. We also urge that Anglicans and Methodists in every place study the text together as in itself a step towards unity.

It is our hope that the proposals and the enabling steps at the conclusion of the document will be carefully considered and affirmed and, under God's guidance, enacted by the appropriate bodies in each communion.

Our divided family is being drawn towards fuller communion by our common heritage and our desire to be faithfully together in worship, mission and witness. Ultimately, it is the Holy Spirit who calls us into a bold and new journey towards visible unity.

Very Rev. Justus Marcus   Bishop Willian Oden
Co-chairmen, Anglican-Methodist International Commission

Sharing in the Apostolic Communion

Introduction

1. Appointed representatives of the worldwide Anglican communion and the World Methodist Council met in Jerusalem (March 1992), in Dublin, Ireland (April 1993) and Kanuga, North Carolina (January 1996) to consider the common tradition shared by Methodists and Anglicans, and to consider ways the two churches might, in our time, forge new relationships that will signal greater unity and more effective Christian witness to the world.

2. There have been dialogues between Anglicans and Methodists at the national level in different parts of the world. Yet although the World Methodist Council was organized in 1881, and the Lambeth Conference of the Anglican Communion has met since 1867, this is the first time an international Anglican-Methodist commission has been established to focus on the Methodist-Anglican separation of more than two hundred years. The Lambeth Conference, meeting at Canterbury in 1988, noted with regret that there was no international dialogue between us. The bishops recommended that steps be taken to begin such a dialogue, and the executive committee of the World Methodist Council readily agreed.

3. This document is the product of that dialogue. It reflects large areas of agreement between the two communions, suggesting a growing together of Anglicans and Methodists in recent years. This document is offered for consideration both to the World Methodist Council and its member churches, and to the 1998 Lambeth Conference and the provinces of the Anglican Communion. The purpose is to test if there is sufficient agreement, in this description of Methodist-Anglican relationships, for our churches to engage themselves together more fully in faith, mission and sacramental life.

4. The concern that Christian believers be seen as one in Christ is urgent at this particular time. We are faced by growing secularism and the loss of social cohesion in the older Christian world. At the same time other religious faiths are everywhere challenging Christianity with alternative visions of the human condition and destiny. Thus the present Anglican-Methodist dialogue is more than Christians talking to themselves about internal ecclesiastical arrangements. The integrity of Christian witness is at stake.

5. Denominations and ecclesial traditions have developed as ways to understand, express and live the gospel. They provide a heritage to be honoured and even celebrated. But all such bodies are incomplete and limited by our sinfulness and finitude, and ultimately by the ideal of Christian unity. Christians believe there is "one Lord, one faith, one baptism, one God and Father of all, who is above all and through all and in all" (Eph. 4:5-6). Confessing this oneness together, to the highest achievable degree, is crucial for our evangelization, and may mitigate our disunity which now detracts from

the presentation of the gospel of reconciliation. We seek to be obedient to the will of Christ both in our confession of God's saving word and in our witness to the one Lord of the church and Saviour of the world.

6. The present report has benefited from the responses of the churches to an interim draft. The text bears the following structure. The first main section describes the present situation (I). The following three sections address the goal of fuller communion in faith, mission and sacramental life: faith and doctrine (II), mission and ministry (III), sacraments and the life of the Spirit (IV). A concluding fifth section offers proposals to enable our two communions to grow in worship, mutual care and mission together (V).

I. The present situation

7. With the historical memory of our separation and the perception of growing convergence, the Anglican and Methodist communions have been encouraged to seek fuller communion in faith, mission and sacramental life as a stage towards the visible unity of all Christians. We see that the work of the Spirit has not always been acknowledged in the ordered life of the church. The evangelical revival, the rise of Methodism and the Tractarian movement are eminent examples of the inbreaking of the Spirit. Recognizing our common baptism, we now hear the Holy Spirit calling us to fuller communion. We yearn to respond to this divine call which prompts us to reclaim one another. We recognize that we are called to fuller communion not only by practical considerations, but also by the very nature of our gospel faith, which calls us into communion with the triune God and with one another (koinonia). The scriptures portray the unity of the church as a joyful communion with the Father and with his Son Jesus Christ in the Holy Spirit, as well as communion among its members (1 John 1:1-10; cf. 2 Cor. 13:14). Jesus prays that the disciples may be one as the Father is in him and he is in the Father, so that the world may believe (John 17:21). Our quest is to share more fully life in the triune God. The fuller communion to which we believe we are now being called includes:
– agreement in core doctrines;
– the foundation of our common baptism and the mutual recognition of membership;
– a eucharistic communion going beyond mutual hospitality;
– mutual recognition and interchangeability of ministries and rites;
– the fellowship of help, encouragement and prayer for one another;
– collaboration in evangelism, mission and service;
– national, regional and local structures of common decision-making.

8. Our history provides a strong foundation of shared faith on which to build. The history of God's people as recorded in holy scriptures and in the experience of the church during the patristic, medieval and Reformation periods has formed us. While the exigencies and decisions of the 18th century separated Anglicans and Methodists, other factors, geographical, cultural and religious, kept us in a constant interaction. "Anglican", for example, at one time referred to the Church of England and its chaplaincies overseas. Now, however, it refers to more than 35 national and multinational churches throughout the world, in communion with the see of Canterbury and each other. Anglicans consider the Lambeth Conference, the Anglican Consultative Council and the primates meeting together with the archbishop of Canterbury to be the "instruments" of Anglican unity. Similarly, Methodism spread from England to Ireland,

North America and the West Indies, and thence by missionary endeavours to many other parts of the world. Today 68 Methodist bodies are found witnessing in almost a hundred countries. They join together in the World Methodist Council for consultation, fellowship and mutual encouragement and cooperation. Methodists and Anglicans have contact with each other in most places, and while these contacts have often been positive, sometimes they have not. Both Methodist and Anglican churches have joined united and uniting churches, some of which are members both of the World Methodist Council and the Anglican "instruments". While each communion has institutions and practices of its own, we have also shared together in the experience of the wider Christian community in recent times.

9. In Methodism, two historic black churches (the African Methodist Episcopal Church and the African Methodist Episcopal Zion Church) emerged as protests against acts of injustice, and another (the Christian Methodist Episcopal Church) at its own request. As denominations, they have continued to share in the full life and work of the worldwide church. A characteristic contribution has been their vibrant preaching and worship, and their intentional focus on social ministries.

10. On the common grounds of faith and baptism, Methodists and Anglicans already meet and recognize Christ in each other through personal relationships, common work in ecumenical councils, community ministries, joint worship and local ecumenical projects. The united churches of North and South India and Pakistan include Anglicans and Methodists in wider unions. In a real sense, therefore, a degree of communion already exists between Anglicans and Methodists. It is this reality which we seek to expand and deepen between our two communions.

11. Achieving fuller communion calls us to build on the God-given reality of variety and difference. Difference is not something we merely tolerate, it is our gift to each other for pleasure, for learning, for enrichment in the faith. There are differences in doctrine and ethos between Anglicans and Methodists that might be mutually enriching but which hamper our present relationships. These need to be understood. Because we moved apart from a common milieu, both Anglicans and Methodists sought to justify positions, and in the process tended to caricature the other. Each took on characteristics and attitudes that need to be re-examined. In order to be reconciled with each other, our first task will be to reach a common understanding of our past with integrity, and affirm each other's contributions to the fullness of Christ's church. In order to interact fully as people of God, we need to understand our differences and build on our positive diversity towards a common mission and life together in Christ.

12. We are beckoned by the Spirit to exercise a disciplined imagination as we seek to be faithful in the contexts we are given, to identify achievable goals and be swift to grasp opportunities to reach them. In all of this, the very nature of our world community demands that our thinking and acting be both local and global.

13. During the period of growing together as communions, prayer, study and common endeavour are essential. We offer the following as examples from a rich range of possible actions:

a) In worship
i) Joint worship on such significant occasions for our traditions as the Easter vigil, All Saints' day, patronal festivals, Aldersgate Sunday, Richard Allen day (AME), James Varrick day (AMEZ), covenant service, and other local observances.

ii) Mutual eucharistic hospitality, when members in good standing of each communion are welcomed to receive at the Lord's table in the communion of the other.
iii) Mutual invitations to attend and participate where possible in ordinations and consecrations.

b) In study and discussion
i) Promotion of opportunity for ecumenical studies in formal and informal gatherings. Joint courses might be offered in theological schools, continuing education and lay training programmes. Such courses might include mission, evangelism, worship and social ethics. Study in shared living situations is to be encouraged.
ii) Joint study or discussion groups on a parish or regional basis may gather to tell our stories and to share our experience of fire in the Spirit. Groups might have a specific timetable or goal as, for example, meeting during Lent, or focusing on a Christian approach to such issues as peace, justice and the environment.

c) In cooperation
i) The formation of a contact group or joint committee between churches in the two communions. This contact group might suggest specific ways in which members of the other communion could participate in decision-making groups at various levels.
ii) Cooperation between the Anglican parish and the Methodist church in an area in one common project, either continuing or annual (e.g. day-school, evangelistic campaign, homeless shelter).
iii) The creation of new Anglican-Methodist long-term cooperative partnerships in mission, evangelism and pastoral care at the local level and the encouragement of existing projects and covenants such as Local Ecumenical Projects in England, or local covenants in the USA.

II. Faith and doctrine
14. Doctrinal issues touch all areas of our churches' lives and inevitably affect all steps in the growing relationship between our two communions. The following concerns engage attention: the central or core doctrines on which agreement is evident; the official doctrinal texts or standards in each communion's churches; the location of decision-making on doctrinal matters in each communion's churches; the doctrinal emphases that may be considered characteristic of and particular to either family of churches; our respective ecclesiologies, including our understandings of unity and the relation of the church to the kingdom of God; the ways in which our changing contexts and priorities necessitate and make possible a re-examination of doctrines that have been controversial between us.

Agreement in the core of doctrine
15. The following can be affirmed as central or core doctrines that we share in common: we believe in God the eternal and undivided Trinity, Father, Son and Holy Spirit; in the work of God as Creator of all that is; in the saving work of our Lord Jesus Christ, true God and truly human; in the sanctifying and liberating work of the Holy Spirit. We recognize the fallenness of humankind and the need for redemption. We believe in the sufficiency of Christ's redemptive work; justification by grace through faith; the church as the body of Christ; the sacraments of baptism and the Lord's supper as instituted by Christ; the final judgment; and the hope of eternal life in God's kingdom.

16. As an instance of the existing agreement between us in core doctrines, we gladly note the resolution of the Church of England general synod, meeting at York in 1978, which declared that the Church of England required no further doctrinal assurances from the Methodist Church of Great Britain beyond those it had already received through the Methodist approval of the Anglican-Methodist plan of unity in 1969 and 1972. We also rejoice that the Church of Ireland and the Methodist Church in Ireland report that "as far as Ireland is concerned, no further doctrinal assurances are needed from either communion". Further, the Episcopal Church, the United Methodist Church and the three historic black Methodist churches in the USA have all given their approval to the doctrinal consensus of the Consultation on Church Union (1984).

17. Provided agreement remains firm on central or core doctrines, it is important that we do not demand of each other a greater uniformity of interpretation than we experience in our own separate communions.

Official doctrinal texts and standards

18. The churches of our two communions hold in common a number of official doctrinal texts and standards. We all affirm the scriptures as the supreme rule of faith and life and their sufficiency as containing all things necessary to salvation. We all affirm the beliefs contained in the Apostles' and Nicene-Constantinopolitan Creeds which we employ in our services of worship. We all affirm the fundamental principles of the English Reformation, to which the formularies of the 16th century, homilies, prayer book and articles bear historic testimony. Both Anglicans and Methodists have used the rites of the Book of Common Prayer as received and adapted by the various churches in the two communions. Our contemporary revisions of the liturgy all draw on commonly shared research in the context of the modern liturgical movement.

19. In addition to these texts held in common, Methodists are also guided in various ways by John Wesley's standard sermons, his explanatory notes upon the New Testament, and by the hymns of the Wesley brothers – all elements believed to be consonant with scripture, with early Tradition and with the English Reformation. Similarly, Anglicans look to their prayer books, both to the Book of Common Prayer and to the prayer books currently authorized for use by the various provinces, for guidance in matters of faith and practice.

20. In addition, the historic black Methodist churches have drawn on the authenticity of the experiences of their respective founders. The founders withdrew themselves from the mother church either for reasons of racial discrimination or for the freedom of worshipping "under their own vine and fig tree".

21. When churches of our two communions have become part of united churches in various lands, their doctrinal texts and standards have been respected as an important part of the common tradition in the united churches.

The location of doctrinal decision-making

22. There are certain common features among the churches in the two communions concerning the making of decisions on doctrinal matters. In Methodism the final authority in the interpretation of doctrine resides at the highest level of Conference in each particular denomination, with certain items being protected by restrictive clauses. For instance, the General Conference of the African Methodist Episcopal (AME)

Church restricts its own right to "repeal or change the articles of religion, establish any new rules of doctrine, or alter any rule of government to the effect of doing away with episcopacy or general superintendency" (AME *Discipline*). Anglicans also see doctrinal authority as residing in synodical procedures at the diocesan and provincial levels, with each diocese or province taking care to act in consultation with others. A special place is occupied by the bishops in the Anglican Communion acting collegially in doctrinal decisions.

Characteristic doctrinal emphases
23. Certain doctrinal emphases have historically been perceived as characteristic of, and sometimes peculiar to, the two families of churches. It is important to ensure that these are correctly understood by the other family and to avoid the danger of caricature. Many Anglicans for example insist strongly upon the efficacy of grace in the sacraments, but this should not be seen as calling into question the fact that Methodists also hold the sacraments as "outward and visible signs of inward and spiritual grace". Methodists, for their part, have preached a doctrine of Christian perfection, but this should not cast doubt on the fact that Anglicans also have pursued holiness of life.

The church, its unity, and the kingdom of God
24. Concerning ecclesiology, neither communion claims to be the whole church, though each claims to be part of the church catholic. All agree that certain elements and activities are essential to the being and life of the church: the perseverance of the baptized community in the teaching of the apostles; proclamation of the gospel to the world; faithful worship of God, including the breaking of bread and common prayer; order and discipline in our corporate existence; openness to the operation and gifts of the Holy Spirit. Both Anglicans and Methodists recognize that there are divisions in Christianity that run counter to the gospel, compromising and damaging its proclamation and credibility. We each recognize that the restoration of unity, under the guidance of the Holy Spirit, is an urgent imperative laid upon us to bring us into greater conformity with Christ's will for his church and strengthen our witness to the world.

25. We can agree in seeing the living church, Christ's body, as by God's grace the sign, instrument and foretaste of God's kingdom: "The church is sent into the world as sign, instrument and first-fruits of a reality which comes from beyond history – the kingdom, as reign of God. The unity of the church is not simply an end in itself because the church does not exist for itself but for the glory of God and as a sign, instrument and first-fruits of his purpose to reconcile all things in heaven and earth through Christ. Nor is the unity of the church merely a means to an end, for the church already enjoys a foretaste of that end, and is only a sign and instrument in so far as it is a foretaste. Life in Christ is the end for which all things were made, not a means to an end beyond it" *(God's Reign and Our Unity,* the report of the Anglican-Reformed International Commission 1984, §29). While we recognize with humble thanksgiving that the church is the body of Christ and therefore of divine origin as God's church, we also agree that both Anglican and Methodist churches, as human institutions, are incomplete, frail and provisional, and will still be so even if united. We remain under the calling to become with all God's people ever more fully the one holy, catholic and apostolic church until God's final kingdom should come.

Changing contexts and priorities

26. In the 20th century our changing contexts have affected our understanding of matters which divided us in the past and demand that we set about resolving the differences that have divided us. We note, first, the modern *ecumenical* movement, which was prompted by the need for united witness, especially on the mission field. In some places, churches of our two communions have already entered into unions, e.g., in South India and in North India; and in many other places there has been increasing cooperation in missionary endeavours. In the spirit of ecumenism, we look more for the things that unite us than for those that divide us.

27. Second, scholars of both communions have contributed to our understanding *of the Bible and of Christian origins* in ways which have shed fresh light on ecumenical questions.

28. Third, the modern *liturgical* movement has brought our churches together in renewed understandings of worship on the basis of scripture and the early church and has enabled the revision of our liturgies along very similar lines. It has also fostered within our two communions a common appreciation for different cultural styles and heritages in worship. Our two communions participated in the "Lima process" from its very beginnings and most of our churches have made generally favourable responses to the WCC Faith and Order text of 1982 on *Baptism, Eucharist and Ministry* (*BEM*).

29. Fourth, churches in both our communions have come to see the urgency of *evangelism* in a world of secularism and of the growth of populations who have never heard the gospel. The differing responses to the evangelistic needs and opportunities of the 18th century eventually contributed to our going separate ways; it would be appropriate if, in our time, a joint recovery of our evangelistic responsibilities helped towards the restoration of unity between us.

30. Fifth, churches in both communions have become increasingly aware of the everyday *needs of the world* and have already begun to find unity in joint service to people in distress; they have committed themselves in the causes of justice and peace.

III. Mission and ministry

A. MISSION

31. God's concern is for the whole world and he first chose the ancient people of Israel as the light to lead all peoples to the true light of his knowledge. Because of human failure to come to the light, in mercy God sent his Son. "For God so loved the world that he gave his only Son, so that everyone who believes in him may not perish but may have eternal life" (John 3:16).

32. "As the Father sent me," said the crucified and risen Jesus, "so I send you", and he breathed on his disciples the Holy Spirit (John 20:21-23). Thus were the apostles, as their title suggests, "sent out" as witnesses to the Easter faith. Since at that moment they also represented the entire church (*BEM*, M10), the whole body of believers was thereby commissioned and empowered for mission in Christ's name and in his way.

33. Anglicans and Methodists have sought in history to be faithful to this missionary calling. Both share as their heritage the ancient evangelization of Britain by Celtic and Roman missionaries. The reformation brought a renewed grasp of the gospel. In the 18th century, the differing expressions of the evangelical revival among Anglicans

included the call of the Methodist societies to "spread scriptural holiness over the land".

34. From both churches arose extensive missionary enterprises in every part of the world. The fruit is that in both communions, there are churches, especially in Asia and Africa, which are growing rapidly, and call us to new patterns and styles of worship, nurture and community, and challenge us how to bring to contemporary situations "things both old and new". Our various approaches to mission have been partial, bound by time and culture, and yet blessed.

35. Anglicans and Methodists were also part of later revivals and awakenings in North America and elsewhere. Most recently, both communions have been touched by contemporary movements of renewal in the Holy Spirit. Both face the failure of traditional structures and styles of life and worship to contain these and other movements, and both have experienced division and disunity as a result. We recognize our need to explore the way in which the apostles understood their calling both as apostles and evangelists, and how contemporary churches are "sent" in continuity with the church and the apostolic witness of all ages. As disciples of Christ, commissioned to participate in the faithful mission of the church, we seek together to deepen our understanding of our calling to be Christ's witnesses.

36. Both Anglicans and Methodists have acknowledged that the gospel calls us to confess Christ both in word and deed. John Wesley and William Wilberforce, for example, stood together in the movement to abolish slavery. In the same tradition, Anglo-Catholic and evangelical missions made distinctive contributions among both rural and urban poor in many parts of the world. One recent statement, developed at the Lambeth conference of Anglican bishops in 1988, urges us to include in mission: proclaiming the gospel and enabling response; teaching, baptizing and nurturing new believers; response to human need by loving service; challenging and transforming unjust structures of society.

37. All of this leads us to recognize our need to articulate from our common experience a trinitarian theology of mission so that we may witness together to the one God who calls us all into the mission of the Son for the sake of the whole world in the power of the Holy Spirit. We acknowledge that mission is both empowered by God's gift of unity within the church and implements and makes visible the church's unity for the world to see and believe. The unity of the church, in the imperfect present and as promised by God, empowers the church to be a prophetic sign of the kingdom in every place.

38. Throughout the world, our churches relate to the state in a variety of ways, from establishment of the church to persecution. Some of these past and present relationships affect our life together, and invite prayerful and honest mutual exploration. In our life as churches, we affirm that we are equal partners in Christ's mission, united in prayer and service.

B. MINISTRY

The calling of the whole people of God

39. Anglicans and Methodists begin their consideration of ministry at a common point: the calling of the whole people of God to be engaged in the ministry and mission of Jesus Christ to the world. In this calling, God the Spirit draws all people through Christ into a holy community which gives glory to God the Father. The call to

mission is a call to common worship of the triune God, to holiness of life, and to the conversion of the world, both the structures of society and individual human beings. The church, while always in need of reformation, is the first-fruits of the unity which God desires for the whole creation. Thus the call to mission is also a call to penitence and Christian unity.

40. Both Methodists and Anglicans recognize baptism as the sacrament of our union with Christ in his death and resurrection by which we are admitted to the church and are called to participation in Christ's mission in the world. "As the Father sent me, so I send you" (John 20:21). The church is one, holy and catholic, and it is apostolic. The risen and ascended Christ continues his work now in constant intercession for the world and in drawing all people to reconciliation with God and with each other. All who believe are caught up into this priestly work of Christ, and called to maintain this apostolic task, as the people of God. Thus "apostolic tradition in the church means continuity in the permanent characteristics of the church of the apostles: witness to the apostolic faith, proclamation and fresh interpretation of the gospel, celebration of baptism and the eucharist, the transmission of ministerial responsibilities, communion in prayer, love, joy and suffering, service to the sick and needy, unity among the local churches and sharing the gifts which the Lord has given to each" (*BEM*, M34).

The calling of the ordained ministry

41. Anglicans and Methodists recognize that it is God who provides all that the church needs for its work and worship. Every Christian has been given grace according to God's providence and the measure of Christ's gift. Therefore it is said, "when he ascended on high he made captivity itself a captive; he gave gifts to his people" (Eph. 4:7-8). God has not left the world without witnesses, and to this end calls men and women into particular ministries to equip the saints (Eph. 4:12) for their apostolic task. Whereas in baptism all of the people of God are turned outwards towards the world where Christ leads us, in ordination some of the baptized are called and set apart to serve the gospel and the people gathered by Christ's gospel: by the faithful preaching of the word and administration of the sacraments, by regularly recalling the people of God to their apostolic task in and for the world, leading and encouraging them in it and pointing them to the God who guides and sustains them. John Wesley affirmed that "the end of all ecclesiastical order" is "to bring souls from the power of Satan to God, and to build them up in his fear and love" (letter of 25 June 1746 to "John Smith"). The ordained ministry is never an end in itself; nor is it within and for the church alone. It is a providential servant leadership within and for the people of God in the world.

42. "The church ordains certain of its members for the ministry in the name of Christ by the invocation of the Spirit and the laying-on of hands (1 Tim. 4:14; 2 Tim. 1:6)" (*BEM*, M39). Our churches ordain in the context of the worship assembly; this signifies that ordination is the act of the whole community, and it publicly claims the promises of Christ, "the risen Lord, who is the true ordainer and bestows the gift. In ordaining, the church, under the inspiration of the Holy Spirit, provides for the faithful proclamation of the gospel and humble service in the name of Christ" (*BEM*, M39). In the Anglican communion, bishops are always the ministers of ordination. In Methodism, ordination always takes place by authority of the Conference, which entrusts

presidency of the rite of ordination to bishops, presidents or other ordained ministers. The laying-on of hands by those duly appointed is, at the same time, a sign of the Spirit's gift and "an acknowledgment by the church of the gifts of the Spirit in the one ordained, and a commitment by both the church and the ordinand to (their new mutual) relationship" (M44c).

Historical origins of the ordained ministry

43. Biblical scholars have in recent times called attention to the great variety of ways in which the early church ordered its life for its apostolic work. Some of these reflect the patterns inherited from the Jewish community in Jerusalem or new communities developing in the Roman world. "During the 2nd and 3rd centuries," as *BEM* M19 phrases it, "a threefold pattern of bishop, presbyter and deacon became established as the pattern of ordained ministry throughout the church". This ministry is to be seen as a single ministry, its basic oneness expressed in the service of word and sacrament. In the differentiated threefold form it has existed, though with many changes and further developments, until today (see *BEM,* M19-21 and *The Niagara Report,* report of the Anglican-Lutheran consultation on *episcope* 1987, §§41-55).

44. Other patterns of ministry exist which emerged in Christian history and which God has blessed. The Lima document says: "At some points of crisis in the history of the church, the continuing functions of ministry were in some places and communities distributed according to structures other than the predominant threefold pattern. Sometimes appeal was made to the New Testament in justification of these other patterns. In other cases the restructuring of ministry was held to lie within the competence of the church as it adapted to changed circumstances" (*BEM,* M19). Both Richard Hooker and John Wesley allowed for the existence of such variations within Christian ecclesial bodies.

45. A new type of ministry arose in Methodism in this way. Laypeople with the requisite gifts were used "in connexion with Mr Wesley" as preachers and as pastors for the care and nurture of local societies. Some were itinerant, and some local, preachers. This development was not by reaction against Anglican forms, nor was appeal made to other "biblical patterns" such as presbyterian or congregational: it developed to serve the needs of the growing church.

46. In those patterns that have emerged in the Methodist tradition as well as in the Anglican Communion, the intention has been to provide *episcope* for the particular Christian community. *Episcope* is a gift of the Holy Spirit and involves the maintenance and furtherance of the apostolicity, catholicity, unity and discipline of the church; it is given to nurture the church's koinonia: "We declare to you what we have seen and heard so that you also may have fellowship with us; and truly our fellowship is with the Father and with his Son Jesus Christ" (1 John 1:3: the word "fellowship" translates "koinonia").

47. The threefold ordering of the ministry as bishop, presbyter (elder, priest) and deacon is familiar to all Anglicans and to those Methodists whose tradition flows from Wesley's provisions for the Methodists in North America. In Britain and in churches elsewhere that have continued the British polity, the Conference exercises *episcope* over the people called Methodists, with pastoral care being exercised beyond the local church through persons who bear varying titles (including superintendent minister, district chair, and even bishop). *Episcope* in these latter churches is primarily understood in corporate terms.

48. It is important to understand that, whatever the exigencies of history, departure from a threefold or personal-episcopal form of ministry did not imply any less a commitment to the provision of faithful *episcope* for the congregations of Christ's people. Whether a church claims an episcopal succession from apostolic times, or whether a church has formed a new pattern for itself out of its experience and particular need, its intention, we believe, has been to safeguard the faithful witness to the gospel, of which Jesus Christ is the foundation and to which prophets and apostles bore the same witness in their day. We recognize in each other's churches, within the Anglican and Methodist families, that intention being faithfully carried out in the faith and life and work of each church. At the same time we acknowledge that, in both families, we have fallen short of the apostolic charge laid upon the people of God.

Episcope as carried out in the threefold ministry

49. Those churches in our two communions which have carried out *episcope* by means of the threefold order of bishops, presbyters (priests or elders) and deacons value this personal ministry in respect of *episcope* as one sign of the apostolicity of the church and of its succession from the calling and commissioning of the earliest disciples by Jesus Christ during his earthly ministry and after his resurrection.

50. The church is a sign, instrument and foretaste of God's kingdom, and a means whereby Christ continues his saving work in the world. Because of their particular calling within Christ's body, the church, ordained ministers are first and foremost and always servants of the people of God, as Jesus was in his earthly ministry. Servanthood is an essential part of all ordained ministry, whether that of bishop, presbyter or deacon.

51. There is, therefore, within ordained ministry an office of deacon in the church, which sets forth the essential sign of Christ's work and purpose for the world (Mark 10:35-45). In both our communions there is creative work in progress in discovering afresh how this servanthood is to be understood and practised. It has liturgical, pastoral and proclamatory aspects; it is to be exercised both within the body of believers and more broadly in the world. It is a distinctive and often life-long ministry. It is traditionally closely associated with the work of the bishop.

52. The bishop is seen as the focus of the exercise of *episcope* as described above in paragraphs 46 and 49. Bishops do not exercise their ministry in isolation, either from the other ordained ministers or from the laity. They work in collaboration and consultation; as servants of the servants of God they never lose their participation in the diakonia of Christ. Their marks have been usefully set out for us in the *Anglican-Methodist Ordinal* drawn up for the English plan of union in 1968: "A bishop is called to be a chief minister and chief pastor and, with other bishops, to be also a guardian of the faith, the unity and the discipline which are common to the whole church, and an overseer of her mission throughout the world. It is his duty to watch over and protect the congregations committed to his charge and therein to teach and to govern after the example of the apostles of the Lord. He is to lead and guide the presbyters and deacons under his care and to be faithful in ordaining and sending new ministers. A bishop must, therefore, know his people and be known by them; he must proclaim and interpret Christ's gospel to them; and lead them in the offering of spiritual sacrifice and prayer. He must take care for the due ministering of God's word and sacraments; he must also be diligent in confirming the baptized and whenever it shall be required of

him, in administering discipline according to God's holy word" (*Anglican-Methodist Ordinal*, pp.30-31). The COCU Consensus describes bishops functioning as "liturgical leaders, teachers of the apostolic faith, pastoral overseers, leaders in mission, representative ministers in the act of ordination, administrative leaders, servants of unity, participants in governance" (*The COCU Consensus: In Quest of a Church of Christ Uniting* [1984], Ministry, §§45-51). The bishop has been the principal minister of the sacraments, sharing many of his duties collegially with presbyters.

53. Just as the bishops have a special collaborative link with the deacons, so they share some of their responsibilities with the presbyters. In the early church, presidency at the eucharist was often a mark of the episcopate, but with the growth of the church, and the increasing need of the bishop to exercise responsibility for larger groupings of Christians, so presbyters would take up the role of presiding at the eucharist of the church in one place, nurturing its life and, in collaboration with the bishop, building, guiding and guarding its order, life and faith. In time the church developed a broader conception of the meaning and function of presbyteral order, and priests became the most common ministers of sacramental grace for all the people of God. In all this the presbyters, too, should never lose their primary character as servants. Just as they support, serve and lead the whole people of God, together with the bishop and the deacons, so they in their turn are supported and held to their work by the whole people of God.

54. Anglicans continue to speak of presbyters as priests. As they use the language of ministerial priesthood, they recognize that they must distinguish this secondary and derivative language of priesthood both from the high priesthood of Christ and the royal priesthood of the people of God. The *Anglican-Methodist Ordinal* of 1968 put it this way: "The royal priesthood which the whole church has received from Christ her Lord, and in which each member of his body shares, is exercised by the faithful in different ways. The distinctive ministry is a special form of this participation. It is in this way that the priesthood of bishop and presbyter should be understood. The ministry is thus a divinely appointed organ which acts in relation to the whole body in the name of Christ and which represents the priestly service of the whole body in its common worship. Ministers are, as the Methodist statement on ordination says, both Christ's ambassadors and the representatives of the whole people of God" (*Anglican-Methodist Ordinal*, p.12).

The ministry of women

55. God's calling of women to serve the ministry in all its forms is accepted throughout Methodism.

56. In the Anglican Communion, women have been ordained in ever-increasing numbers in a growing number of provinces as bishops, presbyters and deacons in recent years, though not universally, and not without substantial differences of opinion and some variety of practice. The Anglican communion is dealing with the effects of these decisions made in some of its provinces on its own unity as a communion.

Formal lay ministries

57. The apostolate of laypeople is primarily in the world. But just as ordained ministers live and witness in the world beyond the institutional church, so many laypeople offer their gifts within the work of the visible church with a commitment growing from

their baptismal responsibilities. This is to be welcomed as signs of the Spirit's abundant work. In the experience of our churches, and especially in Methodism, laypeople have had the role of pioneers and preachers in the founding of churches.

58. All laypeople have their proper roles in the life, governance and work of the church today. Some laypeople are called to share in various major responsibilities in the institution alongside ordained ministries. Lay readers, catechists, local preachers and pastors, class leaders, musicians, administrators of various sorts and other such leaders give their time and talents generously in local congregations and other levels of church work. Both our communions affirm their work and acknowledge its value in the total ministry of the church.

59. Both our communions are concerned in our time to articulate an adequate theology of ministry, lay and ordained, and create the necessary conditions to foster a prepared and committed laity and clergy, both being necessary for the life and mission of a faithful church.

Episcope in Anglicanism and Methodism since the 18th century

60. While John Wesley lived, the Methodist people remained a society within the Church of England, attending worship and receiving the sacraments at Anglican hands. At the same time that Wesley insisted on this loyalty to Anglican ways, he found his hand forced by the needs of his societies in America and elsewhere to provide for the faithful preaching of the word and administration of the sacraments. Being a presbyter of the Church of England, believing himself a "scriptural *episcopos*", and acting in an emergency situation, Wesley appointed two men, Thomas Coke and Francis Asbury, as "superintendents" for the American church to provide there the same kind of oversight that he was able to provide in England; at the same time he ordained two other men as deacon and then elder for ministry in North America. In the American church, the superintendent came to be known as bishop.

61. In England, Wesley made provision however for a continuance of the societies after his death through the *episcope* of a body of itinerant preachers known as the "legal hundred", which in turn became the conference as we know it today. For over forty years, from 1795 to 1836, the main Wesleyan body on the whole avoided actions which would prejudice a living relationship with the Church of England. In 1836, the Wesleyans accepted the necessity to act separately as a church, and decided to ordain the itinerant preachers by prayer and the imposition of hands. This was in part a response to a more exclusive understanding of church and ministry which arose from the Oxford Movement in the mid-19th century. Anglicans and Methodists began to define themselves as churches over against each other's claims, which made mutual acceptance very difficult. In recent decades, we have learned to see each other as churches in a different perspective. In the Methodist family, whether episcopal or not, the churches have enjoyed complete acceptance of each other as churches, including full communion and mutual interchangeability of ministries.

The present convergence of our communions leading to the mutual recognition of their apostolicity

62. We have already spoken of the new situation which has been developing in the past decades bringing our two communions closer together in a number of very important ways (see above, §§27-31).

63. This growing convergence means, amongst other things, that old contrasts between episcopal churches, themselves with different understandings of episcopacy, and churches with non-episcopal polities, might be viewed in a broader perspective, namely, the perspective of common loyalty to the apostolic faith, and obedience to and trust in the faithfulness of God who does not leave the world without witnesses. As Anglicans and Methodists we in the commission, like many in our communions, have come to view the histories of our respective communions, including our separation from one another, in this light, and therefore regard the time as right to move towards fuller communion in faith, mission and sacramental life with each other.

64. At the same time, we welcome the statement in *BEM* that the historic episcopate is "a sign, though not a guarantee, of the continuity and unity of the church" (M38). And, having in mind the resolution of the Church of England general synod of 1978 (cf. §16 above), we recall with equal gratitude the decision of the British Methodist Conference in 1981 to be ready to receive the historic episcopate into its life and ministry, recalling what those who proposed this step said in relation to it: "There are times when someone has to take the initiative. This is especially true in the healing of broken relationships. We believe that this is such a moment in the growing together of Christians and the Christian churches. The Methodist Church is perhaps uniquely fitted to take a step that would be a sign of our faith in the future of the church and a help to others. We use the word sign in two senses: as an indication of what we think the church of the future will be like and as an act or symbolic gesture which will help towards a future that never seems to come nearer."

65. While the expression of penitence by both Methodists and Anglicans for our separation and continuing division is a necessary and rightful step in the restoration of the unity which Christ desires for his church, and for which we long, the Anglican members of our commission in particular wish to confess our penitence for the fact that, along with other examples of the maintenance of division in the Anglican Communion, the Church of England was unable to respond positively to the covenant proposals which were before the churches in Britain at the time of that resolution of the British Methodist Conference.

66. We cannot emphasize strongly enough the fundamental statement made earlier, and expressed clearly in the Lima document and in the statements of various bilateral conversations made by both our communions, that the apostolic commissioning by the risen Christ was to the people of God as a whole. It is the church as the whole people of God which is apostolic.

67. We also reaffirm that Christ calls the church to his mission in the world, renewing it in every generation. The Anglicans in our commission recognize the development of Methodism in the 18th and 19th centuries as being carried out in faithful response to that charge of the risen Christ, and recognize the central importance of the apostolic practice of mission and evangelism in the life and work of the Methodist people, from those days until now. Equally, the Methodists in our commission recognize the authenticity and reality of the Anglican Communion's commitment to mission and evangelism as demonstrated, for example, by the historic missionary societies, the work of Anglo-Catholic and evangelical parishes in urban areas, and most recently the decade of evangelism.

68. In this document we have also set out the substantial agreement that exists between us on matters of faith, doctrine, and life in Christ, and on the basis of this we

believe we are in a position to move towards full recognition of the apostolicity of each other's churches.

Moving towards the recognition of each other's ministry including the re-establishment of the historic episcopate

69. We believe the recognition of each other's apostolicity as churches should include the recognition of the apostolicity of each other's ministry and allow us to work towards the establishment of that ministry in its traditional threefold form, including, in ways which still need to be worked out, the historic episcopate.

70. We see the historic episcopate as one sign of the continuity, unity and catholicity of the church. We look forward to entering into fuller communion with one another in faith, mission and sacramental life and to the historic episcopate becoming again, for all of us, one element in the way by which the ordained ministry is transmitted with due order. John Wesley himself was concerned with this matter. We recognize that this process will be perceived differently by those Methodist churches which have had a personal episcopal ministry within Conference for two hundred years, and those whose episcopal oversight has been carried out through Conference itself. We recognize that we have many gifts to share with each other within the apostolicity of the church including the historic episcopate and corporate or conciliar *episcope*. But we are quite clear, in the light of all our work, and the whole of this report, that this must be done in such a way as not to call into question the ordination or apostolicity of any of those who have been ordained as Methodist or Anglican ministers according to the due order of their churches.

71. The whole commission realizes that the historic succession of bishops from the earliest times raises important questions which need to be addressed by our two communions as they move towards fuller communion in faith, mission and sacramental life. Responses to our interim report also made clear the importance of clarifying the meaning and significance of the historic episcopate. The following paragraphs (in particular 72 to 78) therefore address the subject, dwelling particularly on Anglican and Anglican-Lutheran agreed statements in addition to *Baptism, Eucharist and Ministry*.

72. We return to the important paragraph M38 of *BEM* quoted earlier (§64). There it is observed that "today churches, including those engaged in union negotiations, are expressing willingness to accept episcopal succession as a sign of the apostolicity of the life of the whole church", and "as a sign, though not a guarantee, of the continuity and unity of the church". The Methodist Church of Great Britain, in union negotiations with the Church of England, responded positively to Archbishop Fisher's invitation in 1946 "to take episcopacy into their system" by twice voting in 1969 and 1972 to adopt a form of church government that included the episcopate as understood by the Church of England. Unions with Anglicans (and Presbyterians and Congregationalists) in South India, and in North India (with these churches and with Baptists), have also demonstrated this willingness.

73. The phrase "historic episcopate" has been used regularly within Anglicanism at least since the second half of the 19th century, but is not used by the Roman Catholic Church or the Orthodox churches. Nor does the Lima text use it, generally preferring to speak of the "apostolic tradition" when referring to the church's apostolicity as a whole, and of "episcopal succession" when referring specifically to the continuity in handing on personal *episcope* from one generation to another in the life of the church.

In early ecumenical dialogue, Anglicanism began to use the term "historic episcopate" when commending the importance of episcopal ministry to other parts of the church.

74. In this context the term appears as the fourth element in the so-called Chicago Quadrilateral, adopted by the bishops of the Episcopal Church of the USA in 1886, and offered by them as a basis for the creation of a united church within the USA. The quadrilateral, slightly modified, was then adopted by the Lambeth Conference of Anglican bishops in 1888, as the basis on which Anglicans would enter into negotiations with other churches for the eventual visible unity of the church worldwide. All four elements were deemed essential principles of unity within an apostolic church; the historic episcopate was not to be taken on its own.

75. The resolution of 1888 states:

> That, in the opinion of this Conference, the following articles supply a basis on which approach may be by God's blessing made towards home reunion:
>
> a) the holy scriptures of Old and New Testaments, as "containing all things necessary to salvation", and as being the rule and ultimate standard of faith;
> b) the Apostles' Creed as the baptismal symbol; and the Nicene Creed, as the sufficient statement of the Christian faith;
> c) the two sacraments ordained by Christ himself – baptism and the supper of the Lord – ministered with unfailing use of Christ's words of institution, and of the elements ordained by him;
> d) the historic episcopate, locally adapted in the methods of its administration to the varying needs of the nations and peoples called of God into the unity of his church.

76. Within Anglicanism, the historic episcopate denotes the continuity of oversight in the church through the ages from the earliest days, expressed in a personal episcopal ministry, the intention of which is to safeguard, transmit and restate in every generation the apostolic faith delivered once for all to saints. It is not the only way by which the apostolic faith is safeguarded and transmitted, nor is it exercised apart from the church as a whole. It is exercised within the church, recalling the people of God (§41 above) to their apostolic vocation. It is exercised in an interplay with the whole people of God, in which their reception of that ministry is a crucial element. Anglicans see the Lima text's description of the exercise of *episcope* collegially, personally and communally (*BEM,* M26) as essential to their understanding of the ministry of the historic episcopate. It is a personal episcopal ministry, but always exercised collegially (i.e., together with other bishops, and with the clergy within each diocese), and also communally (i.e. together with the laity and clergy in synod, convention or council).

77. Anglicans have come to use the language of "sign" when referring to the historic episcopate, in harmony with the Lima text, which speaks of "episcopal succession as a sign of the apostolicity of the life of the whole church" (*BEM,* M38). We have already quoted the phrase in which episcopal succession is said to be a "sign" though not a guarantee of the continuity and unity of the church (*BEM,* 38). The Lima text also speaks of ordination as (a) invocation to God that the one to be ordained "be given the power of the Holy Spirit in the new relation which is established between this minister and the local Christian community and, by intention, the church universal" (*BEM,* M42), and (b) as a "sign" of God's granting of this prayer (*BEM,* M43). Anglicans speak both of the episcopal succession, or in their terms the historic episcopate, as a sign of the apostolicity and continuity and unity of the church, and also more narrowly, of the act of ordination as itself a "sign". The Porvoo agreement of the British and Irish

Anglican churches with the Nordic and Baltic Lutheran churches refers to the act of the laying-on of hands with prayer in ordination as follows:

> The precise significance or intention of the laying-on of hands as a sign is determined by the prayer or declaration which accompanies it. In the case of the episcopate, to ordain by prayer and the laying-on of hands is to do what the apostles did, and the church through the ages.
>
> In the consecration of a bishop the sign is effective in four ways: first it bears witness to the church's trust in God's faithfulness to his people and in the promised presence of Christ with his church, through the power of the Holy Spirit to the end of time; secondly, it expresses the church's intention to be faithful to God's initiative and gift, by living in the continuity of the apostolic faith and tradition; thirdly, the participation of a group of bishops in the laying-on of hands signifies their and their churches' acceptance of the new bishop and so of the catholicity of the churches; fourthly, it transmits ministerial office and its authority in accordance with God's will and institution. Thus in the act of consecration a bishop receives the sign of divine approval and a permanent commission to lead his particular church in the common faith and apostolic life of all the churches.
>
> The continuity signified in the consecration of a bishop to episcopal ministry cannot be divorced from the community of life and witness of the diocese to which he is called. In the particular circumstances of our churches, the continuity represented by the occupation of the historic sees is more personal. The care to maintain a diocesan and parochial pattern of pastoral life and ministry reflects an intention of the churches to continue to exercise the apostolic ministry of word and sacrament of the universal church.

The Porvoo document continues by describing the historic episcopal succession as a "sign":

> The whole church is a sign of the kingdom of God; the act of ordination is a sign of God's faithfulness to his church, especially in relation to the oversight of its mission. To ordain a bishop in historic succession (that is, in intended continuity from the apostles themselves) is also a sign. In so doing the church communicates its care for continuity in the whole of its life and mission, and reinforces its determination to manifest the permanent characteristics of the church of the apostles. To make the meaning of the sign fully intelligible it is necessary to include in the service of ordination a public declaration of the faith of the church and an exposition of the ministry to which the new bishop is called. In this way the sign of historic episcopal succession is placed clearly in its full context of the continuity of the proclamation of the gospel of Christ and the mission of his church.
>
> "The use of the sign of the historic episcopal succession does not by itself guarantee the fidelity of a church to every aspect of the apostolic faith, life and mission. There have been schisms in the history of churches using the sign of historic succession. Nor does the sign guarantee the personal faithfulness of the bishop. Nonetheless, the retention of the sign remains a permanent challenge to fidelity and to unity, a summons to witness to, and a commission to realize more fully, the permanent characteristics of the church of the apostles" (*Together in Mission and Ministry: The Porvoo Common Statement with Essays on Church and Ministry in Northern Europe*, London, Church House Publishing, 1993, §§47-51).

78. In the present context of this Methodist-Anglican dialogue, it has to be admitted that the Methodists have not always seen episcopal consecration as the Porvoo common statement describes it, or experienced the historic episcopate as a sign of the unity, continuity or apostolicity of the church. To the extent that they have in their history experienced it otherwise, the effectiveness of the sign has been de facto called in question. A sign, even when it is given by God, can become in the fallenness of human life, even life within the church, an occasion of disunity rather than unity. By the same token, in the mercy and calling of God, it can become again a gift of grace. Anglicans who treasure the historic episcopate within the polity they believe God has given them,

seek to offer it to Methodists in the hope that it become again for all of us a gracious sign of the unity and continuity Christ wills for his church.

79. The Lambeth conference of 1920 sent out an appeal to all Christian people for the "reunion of Christendom", in which it reaffirmed the Chicago-Lambeth Quadrilateral of 1888, but substituted a different wording for the fourth element of the Quadrilateral as follows:

> A ministry acknowledged by every part of the church as possessing not only the inward call of the Spirit, but also the commission of Christ and the authority of the whole body.

It then asked, "May we not reasonably claim that the episcopate was the one means of providing such a ministry? It is not that we call in question for a moment the spiritual reality of the ministries of those communions which do not possess the episcopate. On the contrary, we thankfully acknowledge that these ministries have been manifestly blessed and owned by the Holy Spirit as effective means of grace." Having thus acknowledged the positive status of the ministries of churches that do not possess the historic episcopate, the Lambeth resolution urged that the historic episcopate "is now and will prove to be in the future the best instrument for maintaining the unity and continuity of the church". At the same time it emphasized that "the office of a bishop should be everywhere exercised in a representative and constitutional manner".

80. The commission believes that the historic episcopate will be one sign of the unity and continuity of the church, as it moves into greater unity in the future. The commission reiterates the view of the Lambeth Quadrilateral that fundamental to that unity and continuity is the authority both our churches ascribe to the Bible and to the creeds, and to the continuing celebration of the sacraments of baptism and the holy communion. These are indeed effective signs of the church, through the grace of God, constituting its unity and continuity. Ministerial order is a further sign, and within that, the historic episcopate is also such a sign. In the due transmission of ministerial order we recognize that, following the mutual recognition of our two churches, a bishop of the historical episcopate as we have described it will always take part in the ordination of ministers of the word and sacrament by the laying-on of hands. At the same time we reaffirm the principle accepted in the British Anglican-Methodist scheme of 1963-72 that liberty of interpretation of the meaning of such participation is to be fully respected (cf. §17 above).

81. The commission sees the exercise of *episcope* focused in the personal ministry of the bishop – never forgetting that it is to be exercised "in a collegial and communal way" – as having particular importance in relation to the disciplinary and pastoral care of the church and especially of the clergy, and also in the representative role which the bishop carries in relation to the world outside the church. The bishop is there to speak and act and suffer for the apostolic faith, as the church's representative recognizable and known inside and outside the church. The bishop of course does not do this exclusively; many others, lay and ordained, bear witness to the apostolic faith by their life and action and words, but the bishop is charged by the church to take the lead. The public exercise of this ministry of oversight is inaugurated in each time and place by the public act of consecration through the laying on of hands accompanied by the prayer of the whole people of God.

82. We commend this portraiture of the "historic episcopate" as Anglicans understand it and wish to share it as a sign and pledge of wider Christian unity. Much of what

Anglicans value in the episcopal succession, Methodists have sought to ensure in their own succession of ministries: first, collegially and communally in the decisions of conference governing the life of local churches; and then personally in the prayer and laying-on of hands as the normal sign of maintaining a faithful ministry in the church in every generation (cf. *BEM,* M38). Moreover, in American Methodism and in those places which have adopted its order, and more recently in South Africa and Nigeria, ordained ministries with the title and tasks of "bishop" have been intended as personal signs of apostolicity and of the continuity of faith and ministry.

83. A review of recent ecumenical conversations, undertaken by the house of bishops in the Church of England, reveals broad ecumenical agreement that:

> The witness of the gospel has been entrusted to the churches as a whole. Therefore, the whole church as the *ecclesia apostolica* stands in the apostolic succession. Succession in the sense of succession of ordained ministries must be seen within the succession of the whole church in the apostolic faith *(Apostolicity and Succession,* House of Bishops Occasional Paper, General Synod of the Church of England, Misc. 432, 1994, §11, p.4).

84. Methodist churches have shared in this growing convergence. In every way, they understand the primary calling of the church to be to witness to the apostolic faith in all ages. In every generation Methodist churches have appointed ministers to proclaim that faith in word and sacrament, and understand those ministers to be in true succession from the Wesleyan preachers and ministers, and before them from the historic church reaching back to Pentecost. For the sake of the unity of the church, it is open to Methodists to reclaim the historic episcopate as a rich sign of the continuity and faithfulness of the church which within their own life they have solemnly sought to maintain. Embracing this sign may also be a step towards the possibility of wider union with other episcopal churches, chiefly Orthodox and Roman Catholic. This union may appear at this point to lie far in the future; nevertheless, both Methodist and Anglican international dialogues and local experience have produced remarkably fruitful results.

85. None of our churches, viewed from the human perspective, can claim to have been fully obedient to the call of Christ; no ministry has perfectly pointed the church to the faithfulness of Christ; yet both our churches recognize the presence of the crucified and risen One in our midst, and the guiding and healing hand of the Holy Spirit. In repentance and faith therefore, this commission encourages Methodist and Anglican churches everywhere, at the appropriate level of decision-making, to recognize formally the apostolicity of each other's churches and our common intention to maintain the apostolic faith. Following this mutual recognition the churches together may institute a united ministry which includes the historic succession as we have described it.

IV. Sacraments and the life of the Spirit

86. Methodists and Anglicans share a common belief that the Christian life is faith working through love (Gal. 5:6). That life is expressed and nurtured in many ways: through preaching, teaching, education programmes, action and service in the world, prayer and adoration personal or corporate, and particularly in the celebration of the Lord's sacraments of baptism and holy communion. It is here that the local community of believers is linked with the universal church, round the world and through the ages, and enabled to look forward to the coming of the kingdom.

87. In our local Anglican and Methodist communities those who are baptized are baptized into the universal church of Christ; they are made Christians and members of the body of Christ. We have referred to baptism earlier in this report, identifying its context and meaning in God's mission to the world (§§40,41), and have listed baptism and the Lord's supper as instituted by Christ as elements within the core of doctrine upon which we are agreed (§15).

88. The Lima text on *Baptism, Eucharist and Ministry* declares that the eucharist, or Lord's supper, is essentially the sacrament of the gift which God makes to us in Christ through the power of the Holy Spirit. It expounds the meaning of the holy communion as "thanksgiving to the Father, memorial of Christ, invocation of the Spirit, communion of the faithful, and meal of the kingdom". According to *BEM*, "the church confesses Christ's real, living and active presence in the eucharist. While Christ's real presence in the eucharist does not depend on the faith of the individual, all agree that to discern the body and blood of Christ, faith is required... Christian faith is deepened by the celebration of the Lord's supper" (*BEM*, E13). The commission endorses this statement.

89. The eucharist is the sacrament commanded by Christ for the continual remembrance of his life, death and resurrection, until his coming again. It is the church's sacrifice of praise and thanksgiving by which the sacrifice of Christ is made present in its effects, and in which he invites us to unite ourselves to his one offering of himself. The outward and visible sign of the eucharist is bread and wine given and received at Christ's command, while the inward and spiritual grace is the body and blood of Christ given to his people and received by faith. By it we receive from God forgiveness of sins, the strengthening of our union with Christ and one another, and the foretaste of the heavenly banquet which is our nourishment in eternal life. It is required that we examine ourselves, repent of our sins, and be in love and charity with our neighbour when we come to the Lord's table.[1]

90. In every celebration of the eucharist, we believe the local community to be joined to the universal church. It is primarily because the risen Christ is the true president at each celebration of the eucharist that this is the case. Both our churches take care to see that the persons who preside in each community are duly authorized and commissioned so to do by those exercising *episcope* in each church. In the Anglican communion this is always a presbyter or bishop; in the Methodist churches this is also the norm, though those exercising *episcope* can authorize others so to do in particular situations.

91. As we look together at the developing of our life as members of the body of Christ, certain key issues emerge in connection with the life of the Spirit and its sacramental expressions. Anglican and Methodist churches alike practise the baptism of infants, children and adults. However, we find ourselves facing common problems: the need to ensure the growth in faith of children in our midst; to find ways of affirming and deepening the faith declared in baptism – in personal commitment, in confirma-

---

[1] The matters of the disposal of elements remaining after the communion service on the one hand, and of the extra-liturgical uses of the sacrament on the other, have been sensitive issues between Anglicans and Methodists. We note that *BEM* recommends that in regard to the practice of reserving the elements, "each church should respect the practices and piety of the others", while declaring that "the best way of showing respect for the elements served in the eucharist celebration is by their consumption without excluding their use for communion of the sick" (E32).

tion, and in regular times of recommitment such as the Easter vigil or the covenant service; to develop means for the nurture of personal holiness and service to others.

92. In some countries fewer are brought to baptism as infants in both communions than used to be the case. In the present missionary situation that exists in all countries, both Anglicans and Methodists are challenged to order church life and liturgy so that youth and adults may come to faith, and may find ways of marking their continuing spiritual journey once they have been baptized.

93. Anglicans historically have found a unity in worship through a Book of Common Prayer. Methodists also have drawn on this heritage, but have modified it in their own situations, especially in the use of extempore prayer and hymnody. There have been differences of emphasis, but our common search for a living spirituality has challenged us to rediscover the deep sources of our own heritage, to use them creatively, and to receive with gratitude the riches and wisdom of the wider church.

94. For both Methodists and Anglicans, worship is at the heart of our Christian vocation. As churches, we are wrestling with the character and quality of the liturgy of word and sacrament at the heart of the church's life and the norm for Sunday worship: "The eucharist, which always includes both word and sacrament, is a proclamation and a celebration of the work of God... Its celebration continues as the central act of the church's worship" (*BEM,* E3 and 1). In practice, for most Methodists and many Anglicans, the preaching of the word is the primary focus of Sunday worship. For many other Anglicans and a growing number of Methodists, the eucharist, with biblically centred preaching, is the ordinary Sunday worship.

V. Proposals to enable our two communions to grow in worship, mutual care and mission together

95. The commission requests the two responsible bodies to adopt the following two resolutions:

I. As the basis for growth into fuller communion between Anglicans and Methodists in faith, mission and sacramental life, we the Lambeth Conference/the World Methodist Council; together with the World Methodist Council/the Lambeth Conference; affirm and recognize that:
– Both Anglicans and Methodists belong to the one, holy, catholic and apostolic church of Jesus Christ and participate in the apostolic mission of the whole people of God.
– In the churches of our two communions the word of God is authentically preached and the sacraments instituted by Christ are duly administered.
– Our churches share in the common confession and heritage of the apostolic faith.

II. In virtue of this recognition of each other's apostolicity as churches we, the Lambeth Conference/the World Methodist Council, agree to establish a joint working group:
i) to prepare a way of celebrating this mutual recognition;
ii) to prepare, in full accordance with the principles agreed in the report of the Anglican-Methodist International Commission, guidelines for procedures whereby the competent authorities at appropriate geographical levels would be enabled to implement:
– the mutual recognition of members;
– eucharistic communion going beyond mutual hospitality;
– mutual recognition and interchangeability of ministries and rites;
– structures of common decision-making.

Historical Introduction

The earlier theological dialogue between the Orthodox and Anglican churches was summarized in the agreed statement of Moscow (1976) which was composed from statements drawn up by the Joint Theological Commission and the joint sub-commissions on the following subjects:
1) the knowledge of God;
2) the inspiration and authority of holy scripture;
3) scripture and Tradition;
4) the authority of the councils;
5) the filioque clause;
6) the church as eucharistic community;
7) the invocation of the Holy Spirit in the eucharist.

The three joint sub-commissions, which usually met three times a year, continued to share in the work of the Joint Theological Commission by each providing suggestions for common theological statements, chiefly in three areas: (1) the mystery of the church; (2) faith in the Trinity; and (3) worship and Tradition. These texts, in the preparation of which both parties in each sub-commission had a hand, were afterwards discussed at a meeting of the full joint commission; the commission then produced the definitive text of the communique on all the subjects proposed by the three sub-commissions. The communique, along with the texts of the three sub-commissions and other relevant material, formed the basis for the writing of the agreed statement.

The work of the three sub-commissions and the Joint Theological Commission prepared the way for the text of the Dublin agreed statement (1984), into which the jointly produced texts were inserted at points dictated by their subject matter:

I. The mystery of the church: (1) approaches to the mystery; (2) the marks of the church; (3) communion and intercommunion; (4) wider leadership within the church; (5) witness, evangelism and service

II. Faith in the Trinity, prayer and holiness: (1) participation in the grace of the Holy Trinity; (2) prayer; (3) holiness; (4) the filioque.

III. Worship and Tradition: (1) paradosis – Tradition; (2) worship and the maintenance of the faith; (3) the communion of saints and the departed; (4) icons.

From the texts of the Dublin agreed statement, which was signed by the chairmen of the inter-Orthodox and Anglican commissions, it is clear that a consensus was reached on important dogmatic subjects, while on other points existing disagreements continued unchanged, for example, in the understanding of the marks of the church that are set down in the creed, the ordination of women, the meaning of eucharistic communion, and others.

After the signing of the Dublin agreed statement the theological dialogue continued, inspired by the same hopes and following the same method, but the problem inherent in the ordination of women and the final decision of the Anglicans in favour of such ordinations led to a corresponding reduction in the work of the sub-commissions and the Joint Theological Commission. The third preconciliar pan-Orthodox conference (1986) rated "the work thus far done by the Joint Theological Commission as satisfactory"; it also pointed to "tendencies" among the Anglicans "to undervalue this dialogue", stressed the negative effects that might be produced by further ordinations of women and by the incorrect ecclesiological suppositions at work in some churches of the Anglican Communion, and recommended that an effort be made to achieve a theological consensus "in dogmatic questions that divide the two churches".

The decision of the Lambeth Conference of the Anglican Communion in favour of the ordination of women (1988) augmented the already existing obstacles to progress in the dialogue, which continued indeed but now in a different spirit and with different prospects. Characteristic in this regard were the positions taken by the Lambeth Conference in regard to the continuation of the theological dialogue; these were published in *Ecumenical Bulletin* (Nov.-Dec. 1988), a periodical that enjoys the approval of the Anglican Episcopal Church in the United States. According to these positions, the Anglican church "emphatically approves, because of its importance, the Dublin agreed statement of 1984, which followed upon the Moscow agreed statement of 1976. With special joy it notes the extent of the theological agreement attested in the Dublin statement, the honesty with which this statement gives detailed expression to divergent viewpoints, and the special emphasis it places on prayer and worship as the setting for the continuing theological dialogue... It joyfully welcomes the renewal of joint theological discussion between Anglicans and Orthodox and encourages the work of its own commission...; in particular it notes the intention of the commission to focus on the subject of ecclesiology."

The position taken by the Lambeth Conference on the filioque is of special significance for the Orthodox church and the dialogue with the Anglicans. The Conference attempts, among other things, to go more deeply into the filioque clause. It determines that above and beyond its real meaning the clause has become a sign of conflict. (1) In particular, it recalls the resolution of the Lambeth Conference of 1978 (art. 35,5), as well as the relevant reactions of the provinces of the Anglican Communion, all of which complied with the call to remove this clause from liturgical texts. (2) It also points out that the position taken by the Faith and Order commission of the World Council of Churches in regard to "an ecumenical examination of the apostolic faith as set down in the Nicene-Constantinopolitan Creed (381)" has reference to the original text of this creed. (3) The Conference also believes that all the "Western churches" can act uniformly in this matter and accept the original form of the creed, without thereby betraying their theological heritage. (4) The Conference recommends that the provinces of the Anglican Communion henceforth publish revised liturgical texts of the Nicene-Constantinopolitan Creed that do not contain the filioque clause.

The pan-Orthodox conference, which was academic in character, was convened in Rhodes in 1988. It studied the Orthodox tradition on the question of the place of women in the church and their relationship to the priestly office. The theological papers that were read there showed how many-faceted the teaching of the fathers on this subject is. The papers were published along with the conclusions in the communique; they made clear the negative position of the Orthodox church on the question of the ordination of women. From this point of view it is possible that theological dialogue might lead to a new appreciation of the importance of this question as well as of the theological themes already discussed in the Moscow and Dublin statements.

The third preconciliar pan-Orthodox Conference (1986) has already given its assessment: that Anglican trends in the matter of the ordination of women "can have negative repercussions on the course of the dialogue", in the sense that any and every unilateral tendency which seeks to limit interest in the purposes of the dialogue has negative repercussions on the dialogue. The difficulty has meanwhile intensified as a result of the continuing ferment and tensions within the Anglican communion that have resulted from various statements. A report signed by 141 Anglican bishops from Australia, Brazil, Canada, Great Britain, the Middle East, New Zealand, Scotland, Spain, numerous African countries, and the United States, describes the ordination of women as "a natural development of the institution of ecclesiastical office" and as a question having to do with "the living meaning of the church's mission". The statement was an indirect disapproval of the positions taken by another 52 bishops, who opposed the ordination of women to priestly and episcopal office.

This ferment within the Anglican Communion is due chiefly to the recommendations of the Joint Theological Commission of Anglicans and Lutherans, which was chaired by Anglican Bishop David Tustin (Great Britain) and Lutheran Bishop Sebastian Kolowa (Tanzania). In the joint communique which this commission issued in June 1988 it was recommended that there be "an immediate restoration of full communion" between the two ecclesial communities. This recommendation was then to be presented to the council of the Anglican Communion and to the Lutheran World Federation. The principal cause of the existing separation was considered to be "the difference in the practical implementation of the episcopal office". Anglicans emphasize its beginning in "apostolic succession", while Lutherans have a much broader conception of "bishop" and "episcopal office" – especially in relation to pastors, who exercise a full episcopal supervision over the faithful entrusted to their care. It was considered necessary for the envisioned "full communion" that the Lutherans adopt the primitive method of ordination, in which episcopal consecration is given through the laying-on of hands by three bishops.

This approach to the matter did not lead to a breaking off of the work of the Joint Theological Commission [of Anglicans and Orthodox], though it did have a negative influence on the spirit in which the work was carried on. The commission met at the monastery of New Valaamo in Finland (1989) and decided on the framework within which work on the theme "Theology of the Church" was to be carried on. The meeting held at the Anglican monastery of John the Evangelist (Toronto, 10-17 September 1990) dealt with the theology of the dogma of the Trinity; the chairmen were Metropolitan John of Pergamon and Anglican Bishop Mark Dyer. The theological discussions, in which both sides took the creeds as their basis, had to do with the following subjects:

1) icons;
2) symbolization and graphic representation of the mystery of the Holy Trinity; the Trinity as community;
3) the filioque and the inner life of the Trinity.

During the discussions the subject also came up of the effects which certain trends within the Anglican communion might have on the further course of the dialogue. In addition, the commission approved the recent decision of the Lambeth Conference to undertake a new assessment of the filioque question.

Damaskinos Papandreou

5. Agreed Statement
Anglican-Orthodox Dialogue 1976-84

Dublin, Ireland, 19 August 1984

Preface

It was Archbishop Basil of Brussels, one of the most revered Orthodox members of the Anglican-Orthodox Joint Doctrinal Commission, who remarked that the aim of our dialogue is that we may eventually be visibly united in one church. We offer this report in the conviction that although this goal may presently seem to be far from being achieved, it is nevertheless one towards which God the Holy Spirit is insistently beckoning us. Those who have served on the commission at every stage since its inception in 1966, and since our own co-chairmanship began in 1980, have been aware that this is the case, although we may sometimes have been tempted to think otherwise. Not only is there a long-standing friendship between the Anglican Communion and the Orthodox churches but we have not been allowed to forget that the continuation of such friendship is both costly and demanding.

As those who read this document will see, we have been studying for eight years some of the basic aspects of our holy faith. As bishops, clergy and lay theologians representing our churches in many parts of the world, we have not hesitated to voice our differences as well as our agreements. There are still more to be faced. Yet, as we debate together, and above all as we celebrate the holy liturgy and other services daily during the week-long meetings according to the rites of our churches, we are convinced that we are being slowly but surely moulded by the Spirit into the patterns of love and understanding which, when God knows we are ready for it, will eventually lead to visible unity.

Such experiences do not achieve their true end unless they are shared with the bishops, clergy and faithful people of our respective churches. We hope that this new agreed statement completed in Dublin will provide a fresh opportunity for many Anglicans and Orthodox to study our faith together. For while we press on in the work of our commission we are equally anxious to do all we can to encourage visits among the bishops of our churches; and also the participation of synodical, diocesan and parish gatherings, wherever our churches live side by side, in the exciting tasks of rediscovering one another in Christ; of sharing in the richness of each other's traditions; and, as we recognize the poverty caused by our long separations, together serving others in the Name of the One who prayed to his Father:

> I do not pray for these only, but also for those who believe in me through their word, that they may all be one; even as thou, Father, art in me, and I in thee, that they also may be in us, so that the world may believe that thou hast sent me (John 17:20-21).

Bishop Henry Hill
Co-chairmen

Methodios of Thyateira and Great Britain
Dublin, 19 August 1984

Introduction: Anglican-Orthodox dialogue 1976-84

1. Background

As a result of the talks in 1962 between the archbishop of Canterbury, Dr Michael Ramsey, and the ecumenical patriarch, Athenagoras I of Constantinople, the primates of the Anglican Communion were approached and agreed unanimously to the setting up of an Anglican theological commission to confer with theologians of the Orthodox churches. In 1964 the third pan-Orthodox conference at Rhodes unanimously decided officially to resume dialogue with the Anglican Communion, and this was ratified by all the Orthodox churches. After a preparatory phase (1966-72) in which the Anglican and Orthodox commissions met separately, the first series of joint conversations took place (1973-76) and resulted in the production of the Moscow agreed statement on the knowledge of God, the inspiration and authority of holy scripture, scripture and Tradition, the authority of the councils, the filioque clause, the church as the eucharistic community, and the invocation of the Holy Spirit in the eucharist.[1]

2. From Moscow to Lambeth (1976-78)

The Ecumenical Patriarch Athenagoras I described Archbishop Michael Ramsey's 1962 visit to Constantinople as "the beginning of a new spiritual spring that may lead to greater rapprochement and the closer collaboration of all churches".[2] During his visit to the Ecumenical Patriarch Demetrios I in 1982 Archbishop Robert Runcie of Canterbury referred to that earlier remark and then spoke of the first series of Anglican-Orthodox conversations as a "spiritual summer" with the Moscow agreed statement as its "first-fruits". He next went on to speak of a "wintry season" of difficulties experienced in Anglican-Orthodox relations.[3] For when the Anglican-Orthodox Joint Doctrinal Commission met at Cambridge in 1977 to study the subjects agreed at the conclusion of the Moscow conference (1: the church and the churches; 2: the communion of saints and the departed; 3: ministry and priesthood),[4] a "thunderstorm" broke out presaging the onset of "winter". For the Orthodox members "realized with regret" that the ordination of women was "no longer simply a question for discussion but an actual event in the life of some of the Anglican churches" and asked themselves "how it will be possible to continue the dialogue, and what meaning the dialogue will have in these circumstances".[5] It was therefore agreed that the 1978 meeting would take place "before the Lambeth Conference, in order, by expounding the Orthodox position, to enable their Anglican brethren to come to what, in their view, would be a proper appreciation of the matter. For the Orthodox the future of the dialogue would depend on the resolutions of the Lambeth Conference."[6] In February 1978 the bishop of St Albans told the general synod of the Church of England that "the future as well as the character of these valuable doctrinal discussions now hangs in the balance".

The main part of the 1978 conference at Moni Pendeli, Athens, was devoted to setting out the Orthodox and Anglican positions on the ordination of women to the priesthood. In its report the Orthodox members said: "We see the ordination of women, not as part of the creative continuity of tradition, but as a violation of the apostolic faith and order of the church... This will have a decisively negative effect on the issue of the recognition of Anglican orders... By ordaining women Anglicans would sever themselves from continuity in apostolic faith and spiritual life." They added: "It is obvious that, if the dialogue continues, its character would be drastically changed." The joint conclusions to the report stated: "We value our dialogue together and we are encouraged that our churches and their leaders, as well as the members of our commission, hope that it may continue under conditions acceptable to both sides."[7]

Following the 1978 Lambeth Conference's resolution 21 on the ordination of women,[8] the Orthodox co-chairman of AOJDD, Archbishop Athenagoras, expressed his view that "the theological dialogue will continue, although now simply as an academic and informative exercise, and no longer as an ecclesial endeavour aiming at the union of the two churches". He later recommended that Orthodox professors rather than bishops should take part in the dialogue as an indication of its changed status and purpose. Some Orthodox agreed with this. However, as the bishop of St Albans discovered during his visits to the Orthodox churches in the spring of 1979, other Orthodox felt there was no need to change the standing of the talks and wished the dialogue to be resumed in order, as the Lambeth Conference 1978 resolution 35:2 put it, "to explore the fundamental questions of doctrinal agreement and disagreement in our churches".[9] This view prevailed, and in July 1979 the steering committee of AOJDD met and agreed that the full commission should continue its work in July 1980. "The ultimate aim remains the unity of the churches," it affirmed. But "the method may need to change in order to emphasize the pastoral and practical dimensions of the subjects of theological discussions". it concluded: "Our conversations are concerned with the search for a unity in faith. They are not negotiations for immediate full communion. When this is understood the discovery of differences on various matters, though distressing, will be seen as a necessary step on the long road towards that unity which God wills for his church."

3. From Llandaff to Dublin (1980-84)

During his visit to the ecumenical patriarch of Constantinople in 1982, the archbishop of Canterbury, Dr Robert Runcie, "spoke with gratitude of His All Holiness' encouragement to continue the dialogue particularly when facing difficulties, which had led to the second spring which these official conversations were now experiencing".[10] The commission resumed its work at St Michael's College, Llandaff, in July 1980, and welcomed as its new co-chairmen Bishop Henry Hill of Ontario, Canada (following the appointment of the bishop of St Albans as archbishop of Canterbury), and Archbishop Methodios of Thyateira and Great Britain (following the death of his predecessor Archbishop Athenagoras). The commission approved a report on "The Communion of Saints and the Departed", and continued work on "The Church and the Churches" and on the filioque clause in the creed. This was continued and extended at subsequent meetings at the Orthodox patriarchal centre at Chambésy in Geneva 1981, and at Canterbury in 1982 where the first sub-commission focused on "The Mystery of the Church", the second sub-commission on "Participation in the Grace of the Holy Trinity and Christian Holiness", and the third sub-commission on "Tradition, Christian Worship, and the Maintenance of the Christian Faith". At the commission's meeting at Odessa in the Soviet Union in 1983, particular attention was given to new material on primacy (seniority); witness, evangelism and service; and prayer, icons and family devotion; and discussion of the topics already on the agenda was continued. The 1984 meeting at Bellinter near Dublin has had the task of finalizing an agreed report and statement on "The Mystery of the Church", "Faith in the Trinity, Prayer and Holiness", and "Worship and Tradition".

4. Conclusion

After the difficulties of the fairly recent past, the Anglican-Orthodox Joint Doctrinal Commission has re-established itself and has now developed a productive and satisfactory way of working. There is a freshness and liveliness brought into the commission by the presence of so many new members both Anglican and Orthodox, as well as much valued continuity and a wealth of experience provided by its older and longer-serving members. There is a prayerfulness which permeates its whole work, and which has brought the commission to a new stage of fellowship in Christ. Also, some of the pressures of the past have gone. We are not required to solve outstanding problems (such as the ordination of women) as a condition of continuing the dialogue. Nor are we trying to produce too quickly materials that might be used as the basis for early decisions to enter a new stage of relationships between our churches. Instead, the commission is more free to explore together and understand better the faith we hold and the ways in which we express it. It is also noteworthy that far more consideration has been given to prayer and spirituality than is usual in interchurch encounters of this type. If we accept that Anglican-Orthodox dialogue is still in the *first* stage of exploring each other's faith and seeking cooperation in mission and service,"[11] then it can perhaps be seen that much good work is being done by this particular bilateral conversation to help bridge the ancient divide between Eastern and Western churches.

During the archbishop of Canterbury's visit to Constantinople in 1982, Archbishop Methodios of Thyateira and Great Britain, the Orthodox co-chairman of the Joint Doctrinal Commission, said: "There is positive progress towards the first stage of common prayer and cooperation."

Members of the commission are convinced, as an Anglican Consultative Council report has said, that their work contributes greatly to "the mission and peace of the churches after the ancient division of East and West", and to the church's ministry of reconciliation and peace "in the midst of world political tensions and their resulting pressures".[12]

International Anglican-Orthodox dialogue both draws from and seeks to promote local Anglican-Orthodox dialogue, remembering that the latter's task is not to duplicate but to make known international agreements and to develop relationships between the people of the two churches.

Anglican-Orthodox discussions take place in the context of Anglican-Roman Catholic, Orthodox-Roman Catholic and other bilateral and multilateral conversations. Each draws from and contributes to the other. We are convinced that our discussions have a further part to play in East-West relations, in interchurch relations and in theological explorations from which we all benefit.

The Agreed Statement

Method and approach

1. In our discussions since the adoption of the Moscow agreed statement, and especially during the last four years, our joint commission has endeavoured to keep constantly in mind the essential link that exists between theology and sanctification through prayer, between doctrine and the daily life of the Christian community. Keenly aware how dangerous it is to discuss the Christian faith in an abstract manner, we have

sought always to understand how theological principles are expressed in the living experience of the people of God.

I. The mystery of the church

Approaches to the mystery

2. We live in a deeply divided world. We are aware that Christian disunity, as well as being contrary to the will of God and a sin against the very nature of the church, has often contributed towards the divisions of the world. We know that the church is entrusted with a message of reconciliation. This drives us to seek unity amongst ourselves, in order to contribute to the healing of the divisions of humankind, as well as to stand together as Christians who face difficulties and pressures, and who witness to Christ's truth in a hostile or indifferent world. We know the temptation for Christian communities to avoid this challenge. But Christ has poured out his Spirit on his people, to transform them "into his likeness from one degree of glory to another" (2 Cor. 3:18), and to incorporate them in his mission of love and reconciliation to the world (2 Cor. 5:18; John 20:21).

3. The mystery of the church cannot be defined or fully described. But the steadfast joy of people who discover new life and salvation in Christ through the church reminds us that the church itself is a lived experience. The church is sent into the world as a sign, instrument and first-fruits of the kingdom of God. The New Testament speaks about it primarily in images, such as the following:

4. (a) The church is "the body of Christ" (1 Cor. 12:27). The head is Christ (Eph. 1:22; Col. 1:18), and his members are those who in faith respond to the gospel (Rom. 10:17), are baptized in the name of the Father, the Son and the Holy Spirit (Matt. 28:19), and are united with Christ and with each other through participation in the eucharist (1 Cor. 10:16-17). Through this union they are being conformed to his true humanity, filled with his divinity, and made "partakers of the divine nature" (2 Pet. 1:4) (θέωσις). In its totality the church incorporates both living and departed in the communion of the saints.

5. (b) The church is the messianic gathering, the gathering in Christ of all nations into the people of God (Matt. 8:11; Gal. 3:8), and, as the new Israel, completes the special sign of God's grace given in the election of the ancient people of Israel as God's chosen and beloved (Gal. 3:8; Rev. 21:2-3).

6. (c) The church is the holy temple of God, indwelt by his Spirit (1 Cor. 3:16; Eph. 2:22). It is a spiritual house, a royal priesthood appointed to declare to the world the wonderful deeds of him who called them out of darkness into light (1 Pet. 2:5-9).

7. (d) The New Testament also speaks of the church as Christ's bride, whom he presents to himself "without spot or wrinkle or any such thing" (Eph. 5:27; cf. 2 Cor. 11:2). In this connection scripture looks forward to the consummation of history as "the marriage of the Lamb", when the bride will be prepared to meet her bridegroom in glory (Rev. 19:6-8).

The marks of the church

8. In the creed we proclaim the church to be one, holy, catholic and apostolic.

(a) The church is one, because there is "one Lord, one faith, one baptism, one God and Father of us all" (Eph. 4:5), and it participates in the life of the Holy Trinity, one

God in three persons. The unity of the church is expressed in common faith and in the fellowship of the Holy Spirit; it takes concrete and visible form as the church, gathered round the bishop in the common celebration of the holy eucharist, proclaims Christ's death till he comes (1 Cor. 11:26). The unity of Christians with Christ in baptism is a unity of love and mutual respect which transcends all human division, of race, social status and sex (Gal. 3:28). This unity in Christ is God's gift to the world by which men and women may learn to live in unity with one another, accepting one another as Christ has accepted them.

9. Nevertheless, we find ourselves in an abnormal situation. We are a disrupted Christian people seeking to restore our unity. Our divisions do not destroy but they damage the basic unity we have in Christ, and our disunity impedes our mission to the world as well as our relationships with each other. Anglicans are accustomed to seeing our divisions as within the church: they do not believe that they alone are the one true church, but they believe that they belong to it. Orthodox, however, believe that the Orthodox church is the one true church of Christ, which as his body is not and cannot be divided. But at the same time they see Anglicans as brothers and sisters in Christ who are seeking with them the union of all Christians in the one church.

10. (b) The church is holy (1 Cor. 3:17) because its members are in Christ, the head, who is holy and who lives in them (Eph. 3:17). The church's holiness can be obscured but cannot be destroyed by the sins of its members. Christ's holiness is shown, not in drawing apart from outcasts and sinners but in calling them (Mark 2:15-17), and most fully in his becoming sin for us in order to deliver us from sin (2 Cor. 5:21). For through his life, death and resurrection he overcomes, redeems and sanctifies the world, and by his justifying grace transforms forgiven sinners into "a holy people" (1 Pet. 2:9). The church's holiness springs from the action of God's Holy Spirit whom Christ sends to purify his people, to draw them into the reality of his risen life, and to conform them to his compassion and love for the world.

11. The pursuit of holiness challenges the world and may bring Christians into conflict with it, as they carry on Christ's spiritual warfare with the powers of evil. In this they are following the saints of the church who have shared in Christ's resurrection and sufferings (Col. 1:24), "in honour and dishonour, in ill repute and good repute" (2 Cor. 6:8).

12. (c) The church is catholic because by word and life it maintains and bears witness to the fullness of the faith, and because people of all nations and conditions are called to participate in it. Catholicity stands in contrast to schism and heresy. If Christians cease to love each other or to respect church order they are in danger of schism. If they depart from the essentials of the apostolic faith they become guilty of heresy. The catholicity of the church is shown in the multiplicity of particular local churches, each of which, being in eucharistic communion with all the other local churches, manifests in its own place and time the one catholic church. These local churches, in faithful response to their own particular missionary situation, have developed a wide diversity in their life. As long as their witness to the one faith remains unimpaired, such diversity is to be seen, not as a deficiency or cause for division, but as a mark of the fullness of the one Spirit who distributes to each according to his will (1 Cor. 12:11).

13. At each local eucharist, celebrated within the catholic church, Christ is present in his wholeness, and so each local celebration actualizes and gives visible expression to the church's catholicity.[13] Communion in the eucharist is also the outward manifes-

tation of the common faith and the Christian love which binds together all the local churches in the one catholic church. Their communion is likewise expressed in the constant contact and communication between the bishops and members of different local churches through meetings in council, exchange of letters, mutual visits, and prayer for each other.

14. (d) The church is apostolic because it is built on the foundation of the apostles (Eph. 2:20; Rev. 21:14) who are the primary and authoritative witnesses to the crucified and risen Lord. Their authority lies in the fact that they were sent by Jesus Christ, who was himself sent by the Father (Matt. 28:19-20; John 20:21). Christ gave them the Holy Spirit, who maintains the apostolic word as a living force within the church, evoking faith and discipleship. The church's apostolicity is manifested chiefly in three ways:

15. (i) The church maintains the apostolic tradition by its preaching and teaching and by a constantly renewed understanding and living of scripture. By critical discernment it rejects inauthentic ways of thought and life.[14]

16. (ii) The church in each generation participates in the apostolic mission to the world. The church is "not of the world" (John 17:14), but it is in, with and for human society. Its mission is to save and transform society by the power of the Holy Spirit. This mission includes preaching, teaching, worship, diakonia, testimony against injustice, also the hidden life of prayer, and martyrdom.

17. (iii) The apostolicity of the church is manifested in a particular way through the succession of bishops. This succession is a sign of the unbroken continuity of apostolic tradition and life. Through prayer and the laying-on of hands, the bishop receives the Holy Spirit, who bestows on him a *charisma* giving him the grace and responsibility to uphold and testify to the authority of the apostolic word (2 Tim. 1:6). The local bishop can only perform his ministry: (1) in unity with his brother bishops, especially when meeting synodically; (2) in unity with his flock, both clergy and laity. In exercising the ministry of oversight he should pay heed to the prophetic and other gifts which Christ gives his people (Rom. 12:6-8; Eph. 4:11-12).

Communion and intercommunion

18. (a) The several provinces of the Anglican communion have their own synodical regulations governing eucharistic hospitality and relationships of reciprocal intercommunion and full communion with other churches. There are some instances where the pastoral concern for individuals is uppermost. There are others where there have been specific joint declarations of intent to work together locally or nationally to seek unity (such as that between members of local ecumenical projects in England or between Anglicans, Methodists, Presbyterians and Congregationalists in South Africa). There are still others where unity of faith, ministry and sacraments is accompanied by growth in conciliarity and common mission. From all of these it is clear that there has been a considerable development in ecumenical and interchurch relations in recent years, which has resulted in Anglicans sharing in the eucharist with members of other churches on special ecumenical occasions, in times of special need, or on a more regular basis.

19. Anglicans have come to recognize different stages in which churches stand in a progressively closer relationship to each other, with a corresponding and consequent degree of eucharistic sharing which is viewed as both "a proper manifestation of such

unity in Christ as they already share" and as "creative of even greater unity".[15] However, "for a church officially to authorize intercommunion (whether "reciprocal" or "limited") as a *means* to unity, or for an individual to practise it, where there is already some agreement in faith and commitment to unity, is not to deny that a more complete expression, such as full communion or organic union, is also a goal to be sought".[16]

20. (b) For the Orthodox, "communion" involves a mystical and sanctifying unity created by the body and blood of Christ, which makes them "one body and one blood *(σύσσωμοι καὶ σύναιμοι)* with Christ",[17] and therefore they can have no differences of faith. There can be "communion" only between local churches which have a unity of faith, ministry and sacraments. For this reason the concept of "intercommunion" has no place in Orthodox ecclesiology.

Wider leadership within the church

21. (a) Throughout the history of the church, from the New Testament onwards, there can be seen varying patterns of wider leadership. Anglicans often refer to these as levels of "primacy", whereas Orthodox generally prefer to speak about an order of "seniority" *(πρεσβεία)*. Despite differences in the outward forms in which this wider leadership is expressed, there is fundamental agreement between the way in which Anglicans understand "primacy" and the way in which Orthodox understand "seniority".

22. (b) In the New Testament there are certain persons within the church who are vested with special authority, such as Peter, Paul, James and John, but none of these acts in isolation. The entire New Testament points to the independence or autonomy of local churches, which live together in unity, yet with no single church possessing permanent pre-eminence. Following the adoption of Christianity as the official religion of the Roman empire, an order of seniority became established, involving five great sees in the following sequence: Rome, Constantinople, Alexandria, Antioch, Jerusalem (see the canons of the ecumenical councils, especially canon 2 of Constantinople [381] and canon 28 of Chalcedon [451]). Both the apostolic foundation of sees and the civil status of cities as centres of communication influenced the development of this order of seniority.

23. (c) This wider leadership, whether described as "seniority" or "primacy", is to be understood in terms not of coercion but of pastoral service. Jesus warned his apostles, both by word and by example, to exercise their authority not by lording it over the flock but by being servants of all (Mark 10:42-45; John 13:12-17); and the same warning was repeated to those who succeeded the apostles in the oversight of the church (1 Pet. 5:1-4). Since in practice this teaching has often been forgotten, it is good that the Anglican-Roman Catholic International Commission has called attention to it, noting that "truly to lead is to serve and not to dominate others", and that the bishop has his authority in order to serve his flock as its shepherd.[18] This is to be kept in mind whenever the word "honour" is applied to a bishop, as in the phrase "seniority of honour" *(πρεσβεία τῆς τιμῆς)*.

24. (d) Wider leadership exists at various levels:

> (i) There is first the seniority of the bishop who presides over a group of diocesan bishops. Such seniority is held in modern Orthodox practice by the patriarch within each patriarchate, or by the presiding archbishop or metropolitan within each autocephalous or autonomous church; in Anglican practice, by the archbishop or presiding bishop within each province of the Anglican Communion.

(ii) Secondly, there exist various different forms of seniority on the universal level, such as that of the pope within the Roman Catholic Church (and throughout the whole Christian church prior to the schism); that of the ecumenical patriarch within the Orthodox church; and that of the archbishop of Canterbury within the worldwide Anglican Communion.

25. (e) It is the purpose of wider leadership to strengthen unity and to give brotherly help to the bishops of the local churches in the exercise of their common ministry which exists to safeguard scriptural truth whenever it is threatened, to promote right teaching and living, and to further the church's mission to the world. This the bishop who has seniority does chiefly in two ways:

(i) He encourages Christian fellowship and collaboration by initiating procedures which will lead to the summoning of a council or synod, and presiding over it.

(ii) In certain situations, when appeals are made to him from the decisions of a diocesan bishop or a group of bishops, he initiates procedures whereby these decisions may be reviewed.

But the bishop who has seniority does not have the right to intervene arbitrarily in the affairs of a diocese other than his own.[19]

26. (f) In exercising his ministry the bishop who has seniority should respect the proper authority and freedom of each diocese or local church. He should always act in collegiality with his brother bishops; equally he should take account of the gifts of understanding and discernment entrusted to the whole people of God, clergy and laity together.

27. (g) The ecumenical councils ascribe a position of special seniority, within the wider leadership of the universal church, not only to the see of Rome but also to that of Constantinople; and this fact needs to be taken into account in any Christian reunion.[20] The ecumenical patriarch does not, however, claim universal jurisdiction over the other churches, such as is ascribed to the pope by the First and also the Second Vatican Council; and Orthodox see any such claim as contrary to the meaning of seniority, as this was understood in the early centuries of the church.

28. The Anglican churches of the British Isles, since their separation from the see of Rome, have developed into an international communion; and within this communion a position of seniority has come to be ascribed to the ancient see of Canterbury. But this seniority is understood as a ministry of service and support to the other Anglican churches, not as a form of domination over them; and, like the ecumenical patriarch, the archbishop of Canterbury makes no claim to a primacy of universal jurisdiction. Thus, even though the seniority ascribed to the archbishop of Canterbury is not identical with that given to the ecumenical patriarch, the Anglican Communion has developed on the Orthodox rather than the Roman Catholic pattern, as a fellowship of self-governing national or regional churches.

29. (h) According to Roman Catholic teaching the primacy of the pope is closely linked to his infallibility. Both Orthodox and Anglicans consider that infallibility is not the property of any particular person within the church.[21] it is significant that the Anglican-Roman Catholic International Commission has stated clearly: "This is a term applicable unconditionally only to God, and... to use it of a human being, even in highly restricted circumstances, can produce many misunderstandings".[22]

30. Anglicans and Orthodox are both firmly convinced that the Holy Spirit will guide the church into all truth and "the powers of death shall not prevail against it" (Matt. 16:18). We believe that all bishops are empowered by the Holy Spirit to bear

witness to the truth; but if the doctrine of infallibility means that it is possible to guarantee by external criteria that certain statements of a particular bishop are safeguarded from error, we cannot accept this. Equally no such guarantee can be given concerning the statements of an episcopal assembly, since the ecumenicity of a council is manifested through its acceptance by the body of the church.

Witness, evangelism and service

31. God bears witness to himself by his revelation in creation (Rom. 1:19-20; Acts 14:17), through the patriarchs and prophets and finally through his Son Jesus Christ (Heb. 1:1-2), who is "the faithful and true witness" (Rev. 3:14). Christ is also the true Servant, who turned upside down our ideas of leadership by becoming "the servant of all"[23] and by serving mankind in his obedient and sacrificial ministry, suffering and death. God's revelation of himself in Christ necessarily involved conflict with evil, which brought him to the cross. So God's highest service to mankind – the bringing of salvation in Christ – is at the same time his profoundest witness to himself in and through Christ's sacrifice on the cross. Christ is witness ($\mu\acute{\alpha}\rho\tau\upsilon\varsigma$) as well as teacher, healer and saviour. The primary movement of witness and service is therefore from God to the world, and it includes his affirmation of the sanctity of life, his testimony against all that is evil, and also his call to all mankind to "repent, and believe in the gospel" (Mark 1:15).

32. This movement is continued in the church, the body of Christ, when in the power of the Holy Spirit it responds to God's call and offers itself in witness and service to the world. The church's witness and evangelism call men to hear the good news and to receive the saving grace of Christ. The apostolic church exists by mission as fire exists by burning. Mission is not merely one of many items of business for the church or for a department of the church. The members of the church are to be judged not least by what they do to reach unbelievers. The evangelizing of one person by another is the responsibility of laypeople and clergy alike. The church's mission also includes its service of mankind, which brings the healing, forgiveness, love and compassion of Christ to people in need, people in conflict and people in the grip of sin and evil.

33. Witness, evangelism, service, worship and sacrifice belong together, for these are different sides of the same reality. So testimony in the name of Jesus rightly given is also a service to one's neighbour; ministry rightly performed in the name of Christ constitutes a witness to Jesus. Worship ($\lambda\varepsilon\iota\tau\omicron\upsilon\rho\gamma\acute{\iota}\alpha$) involves service of the people (its ancient meaning), when we worship Christ by ministering to him in the sick, the prisoner and the needy (Matt. 25:37-40). Where the church is not at liberty to organize developed social and philanthropic programmes of its own or to take part in those organized jointly with others, its witness is carried out through worship, prayer and personal ministry. The church can bear witness not only in word and deed but also in silence. Lives dedicated to service proclaim the gospel. Sacrificial self-giving, suffering and death may result from testimony to the truth of the gospel – or from testimony against injustice, which is also testimony to the truth of God's concern for the poor and the oppressed.

34. Evangelism involves the church in social action which can be an authentic witness to the gospel and should not be separated from it or contrasted with it. The church should not engage in a social programme that becomes an end in itself, for "man shall not live by bread alone, but by every word that proceeds from the mouth of God"

(Matt. 4:4). The spirit in which Christians act is different from that of humanism or secularism. It is informed by a sense of God's grace, of sin and the need for repentance and by an eschatological perspective. Nevertheless Christians are right to be involved in the life of the world and in the wider struggle for justice, freedom and peace, and for the removal of everything which threatens the sacred gift of life to all mankind.

35. The church's witness and service minister to people's deepest spiritual, physical and social needs. But in carrying out this mission the church's stance should be one of continual vigilance, as it lives "in the world", but is "not of the world" (John 17:11-16) and as it seeks to be faithful to Christ the true witness and servant.

II. Faith in the Trinity, prayer and holiness

Participation in the grace of the Holy Trinity

36. Trinitarian doctrine presupposes participation in the grace of the Holy Trinity. The doctrine One God in Trinity is not an abstract philosophical formula. It originates in the personal and corporate experience of the grace of the triune God which has been and is communicated to us in Jesus Christ. This experience is not to be understood in a merely subjective way. It is rooted in the historic fact of the incarnation and God's revelation of himself in Christ. Doctrine is the attempt to express this revelation in such a way as both to safeguard it from misunderstanding and to enable others to share in it. The formulation of doctrine, which is based on the scriptures and on a tradition of careful theological reflection, should in no way be seen as an independent intellectual exercise. Ultimately, as St Gregory the Theologian (of Nazianzus) says, "It is impossible to express God and yet more impossible to conceive him."[24] Thus doctrinal formulae should in no way detract from the mystery of God which is handed down in the church from the apostles by the Fathers. It is not the doctrine of the Trinity but the One God in Trinity, the Father, Son and the Holy Spirit, that constitutes the object of Christian worship and faith. Although we may sometimes speak separately of God the Father, sometimes of God the Son and sometimes of God the Holy Spirit, it is always understood that there is no division of one person from another, but all and each reveal in unity the grace and glory of the one Godhead.

37. Christians participate in the grace of the Holy Trinity as members of the Christian community. It is the church which is filled by the Holy Spirit and it is precisely for this reason that every human person has the possibility of becoming a partaker of the divine nature (2 Pet. 1:4). The Holy Spirit praying in us heals and renews us at the centre of our being, that is to say in our hearts. The healing character of the grace of the Holy Trinity in the life of the individual believer and of the church has important implications for the whole life of contemporary society.

Prayer

38. Christian prayer to God is always offered to the Holy Trinity. It is usually addressed to the Father through the Son in the Holy Spirit, although it is also addressed to the Son and sometimes to the Holy Spirit. Although prayer is at one level a human activity, at a deeper level it is the activity in us of God the Holy Spirit, who dwells in our hearts by faith. As St Paul says in Romans 8:26-27: "Likewise the Spirit helps us in our weakness; for we do not know how to pray as we ought, but the Spirit himself

intercedes for us with sighs too deep for words." So prayer becomes "... a possibility by the boundless excellence of the grace of God".[25]

39. Common to East and West alike is the experience of the Holy Spirit praying in us of which St Paul speaks in Galatians 4:6-7: "God has sent the Spirit of his Son into our hearts, crying 'Abba! Father!' So through God you are no longer a slave but a son, and if a son then an heir." This prayer is described in the Christian tradition in a variety of ways. In Greek patristic writings it is often spoken of as "prayer of the mind" (νοερὰ προσευχή) where "mind" is not understood as "intellect" (in the modern sense) but rather as what St Paul calls "the heart". Very similar descriptions of the same experience of prayer are to be found in early Latin authors like St John Cassian, St Gregory of Tours and St Patrick.[26]

40. In the Eastern church one of the traditional forms of this prayer is the "Jesus prayer". But prayer of the heart can take other forms, which equally lead to the same experience of the glory of Christ seen and declared by the patriarchs, prophets, apostles, fathers and all the saints.

41. Prayer of the Holy Spirit in the heart of the individual Christian is inseparable from the common liturgical prayer of the Christian community. It is particularly related to the grace given in baptism, chrismation (confirmation) and eucharist and, generally, to the whole sacramental life of the church and to common prayer and the reading of scripture. Both common liturgical prayer and personal prayer are informed and shaped by the church's faith in God, the Father, the Son and the Holy Spirit.

42. Prayer, both corporate and individual, is an integral part of the life of all Christians. The contemplative and active aspects of Christian life should always be held together, although in the life of each Christian one way or other may predominate at different times, and in the life of some Christians one or the other may predominate throughout their life. For all Christians progress in prayer and obedience involves readiness to take up the cross, and commitment to a disciplined life, whose purpose is their own personal growth in holiness and their more effective witness and service in the church and in society at large.

Holiness

43. The fruit of the Spirit praying in us is holiness, and at the heart of holiness is love for God and neighbour. God's love works in us to produce holiness, restoring in us the image of God and making us and all things whole. In this life, Christians experience a tension between the call to holiness and the power of sin, the struggle between "flesh" and Spirit (Gal. 5:17) which requires continual repentance and the assurance of God's forgiveness. God's call to holiness is also a call to work for justice, so that the church's prayer for the coming of God's reign on earth as in heaven requires of Christians that they cooperate with God in the world. God's love for the world, embodied in Jesus Christ, works through the Holy Spirit to transfigure all things into the new creation, and we are to make manifest that love in the life of the world.

The filioque

44. Further discussions on the filioque led to the reaffirmation by both Anglicans and Orthodox of the agreement reached in Moscow in 1976 that this phrase should not be included in the Nicene-Constantinopolitan Creed.[27] Certain Anglican churches have already acted upon this recommendation, whilst others are still considering it.

45. From the theological point of view the Orthodox stated that the doctrine of the filioque is unacceptable, although as expressed by Augustine it is capable of an Orthodox interpretation. According to the Orthodox understanding the Son cannot be considered a cause or co-cause of the existence of the Holy Spirit. In spite of this we find in certain fathers, for example St Maximus the Confessor (7th century),[28] as explained by Anastasius the Librarian (9th century),[29] the opinion that the filioque, as used in early Latin theology, can be understood in an Orthodox way. According to this interpretation a distinction should be made between two senses of procession, one by which the Father causes the existence of the Spirit (ἐκπόρευσις) and the other by which the spirit shines forth from the Father *and* the Son (ἐκφανσις). This second sense of procession must be clearly differentiated from the later Western use of the filioque which observed no such distinction but rather confused "cause of existence" with "communication of essence" (ἐκπόρευσις) with (ἐκφανσις). Some Orthodox theologians, while affirming that the doctrine of the filioque is unacceptable for the Orthodox church, at the same time, having in mind the position of Prof. Bolotov (1854-1900) and his followers, regard the filioque as a "theologoumenon" in the West.[30]

46. On the Anglican side it was pointed out that the filioque was not to be regarded as a dogma which would have to be accepted by all Christians. It was emphasized, however, that the following points are important for a correct understanding of its intention:

(a) although the Western tradition has spoken from time to time of the Son as a "cause" (causa) of the Spirit, this language has not met with favour and has fallen into disuse;
(b) the Western tradition has continued to maintain that the Father is the sole "fount of deity" (*fons deitatis*/πηγὴ Θεότητος) at the same time as it has associated the Son with the Father as the "principle" (*principium*) of the Spirit;
(c) the Western tradition, in speaking of the Father and the Son as "one principle", has not meant to imply that the Spirit proceeds from some undifferentiated divine essence (οὐσία), as opposed to the persons (ὑποστάσεις) of the Father and the Son.

The Anglicans on the commission put on record that they do not wish to defend the use of the term "cause" in this context.[31]

III. Worship and Tradition

Paradosis – Tradition

47. Looked at from outside, the two churches appear to be very different in their attitude to Tradition, the Anglicans allowing a great variety of attitude and teaching, the Orthodox being strongly attached to the definitions and the structures of the Tradition, especially to those established in the ecumenical councils and by the church fathers.

48. Nevertheless within the freedom existing in the Anglican Communion there is a commitment and responsibility to the Tradition, and a conviction that there are elements in the Tradition, for instance the historic creeds and the Chalcedonian definition, of permanent validity. On the Orthodox side, there exists freedom and understanding of Tradition as the constant action of the Holy Spirit in the church, an unceasing presence of the revelation of the word of God through the Holy Spirit, ever present, here and now. Tradition is always open, ready to embrace the present and accept the future.

49. The Anglicans share this understanding of Tradition. Tradition, with scripture as the normative factor within it (see Moscow agreed statement, section III), is that

which maintains our Christian identity, which develops and nurtures our Christian obedience, and makes our Christian witness effective in the power of the Holy Spirit.

50. The Tradition of the church flows from the Father's gift of his Son "for the life of the world", through the sojourning of the Holy Spirit in the world to be a constant witness to the truth (John 15:26). The church draws its life and being from this same movement of the Father's love; that is to say, the church too lives "for the life of the world". Its Tradition is the living force and inexhaustible source of its mission to the world.

51. The presence of the Holy Spirit in the church enables the whole body of the faithful, the *pleroma* of the church, to be enriched and strengthened in facing the problems of our time, both within the church and outside it. There are a variety of gifts of the Spirit which work together for the building up of the Christian people for their work of witness and service in the world for the common good. Both Anglicans and Orthodox see in their fidelity to Tradition a mutual bond, and a strong incentive to closer cooperation in witness and service to the world.

52. One aspect of the dynamic nature of Tradition is to be seen in the way in which the church assimilates and sanctifies certain elements of the cultures of the various societies in which the church lives. The fathers of the church, under the guidance of the Holy Spirit, exercised a careful discrimination in their use of material from the society around them. The church at the present time needs to exercise a similar discrimination, remaining true to the mind (φρόνημα) of the fathers and facing the new questions with which our century confronts us.

Worship and the maintenance of the faith

53. Faith and worship are inseparable. Dogmas are not abstract ideas existing in and for themselves, but revealed and saving truths and realities intended to bring mankind into communion with God. Through the liturgical life of the church creation comes to share in this saving reality. Thus in worship the church becomes what she really is: body, fellowship, communion in Christ. She maintains the true faith and is maintained in the truth faith by the action and work of the Holy Spirit.

54. The great affirmations of Christian doctrine have their liturgical formulation and expression; all the saving truths of the faith are doxologically and liturgically appropriated. The catholic faith is this, that we worship God, Father, Son and Holy Spirit, Trinity consubstantial and undivided.

55. Liturgy is the action by which the community celebrates the events which created it, sustain it, and give it its future. In both churches corporate and personal worship are inseparable. It is only as members of the worshipping church that we can make a true confession of the faith. For example, in the Orthodox liturgy the creed is introduced with the words: "Let us love one another so that with one mind we may confess." Moreover, because of the nature of man and more especially the incarnation of the Word, the tradition of Christian worship is outward as well as inward, involving bodily gestures and material signs and objects as well as spiritual attitudes.

56. The liturgical life of the church is the very heart of Tradition. The church in the celebration of its liturgy recalls the mighty acts of God in the past, experiences them as present and living realities, and anticipates the coming of the Lord in glory. In the presence of the risen Christ we receive the promise of the coming kingdom. Liturgical time is no cold and lifeless representation of past events, nor simply an historical

record. In it Christ himself is living in his church. Liturgical time is time transfigured through liturgical act, for it is time animated by "the fervour of faith full of the Holy Spirit" (liturgy of St John Chrysostom). Thus by worship we live in the new time of the kingdom. That implies two things: first, the entrance of the Lord of glory into our history as the Saviour of the world, and second, our entrance into the eternal kingdom of the Holy Trinity by grace.

57. Liturgy and all Christian worship are rooted in salvation history. Salvation history with all its mighty events in both the old and new covenants is confessed, celebrated and appropriated by means of the liturgical year. The centre of that year, as of salvation history itself, is the saving person and work of Jesus Christ present in the power of the Holy Spirit.

58. In the eucharist we become partakers of the Lord's supper. The eucharist is anamnesis and participation in the death and resurrection of Christ, liturgically affirmed and realized in the annual celebration of the paschal mystery. This is renewed every week in the feast of the Lord's day and in every celebration of the holy eucharist. The fact of the resurrection of Christ is the basis of Christian faith and worship, since as St Paul says: "If Christ has not been raised... your faith is in vain" (1 Cor. 15:14).

59. The significance of the resurrection is liturgically experienced and expressed in the preparatory season of Lent and in the season which follows, from Easter through the Ascension to Pentecost. In the coming of the Paraclete, the whole mystery of Christ is realized: the Holy Spirit takes the things of Christ and shows them to us, making them real in every age; the Paraclete is thus the constant source of life in the Tradition of the church.

60. The church baptizes her members into the death and resurrection of her Lord, bringing them from the state of sin and death into membership of his body and participation in his eternal life. The centrality of the Easter solemnity has made Easter the supreme occasion for the administration of the rites of Christian initiation.

61. As in the divine economy of salvation, the atonement achieved by the death and resurrection of Christ presupposes the incarnation and the incarnate life of Christ, so in the Christian year, the feast of Easter presupposes the feasts of the Nativity and the Epiphany and the other feasts related to the life of our Saviour. Thus we have the yearly cycle of the feasts of our Lord. In the West the season of Advent prepares Christians to celebrate Christ's coming as Saviour, and reminds them of his future coming in judgment and glory.

62. Finally the liturgical year includes the feasts of the Blessed Virgin Mary, Mother of God, and of the saints, witnessing thus to the dogmatic truth that Christ the head of the church remains always united with the members of his body and that there is no separation between the militant and triumphant church. "The Lord is wonderful in his saints", and in the communion of the saints we see again the power of the resurrection in the life and Tradition of the church destroying death and transfiguring time.

63. Anglicans and Orthodox hold that the liturgy and all worship are essentially for the expression, maintenance and communication of the true faith. Liturgical texts are thus fundamental doctrinal standards for both. Both recognize the possibility of the church making liturgical revisions according to the necessity of the times, and with a view to the salvation of the people of God. They differ only in their estimation of the need for such revisions in the present situation, this difference reflecting their diverse historical experiences and situations.

64. In both Anglican and Orthodox traditions, prayers and devotions in the family are understood as an extension of the corporate worship of the church. From New Testament times onwards the Christian family has been considered to be a household church. The rite of marriage, a sign or image of the spiritual union between Christ and his church, initiates a relationship within which children may be nurtured and where the faith is taught, lived and communicated to others.

65. The traditions of both churches are rich in a variety of family devotions and customs which include the use of parts of the divine office, reverence of icons, use of crosses and pictures, grace at meals, Bible reading, as well as blessings of events and turning points of family life. Both Anglican and Orthodox members are convinced of the importance of the family and the household church as a vehicle of the Tradition of the church and wish to explore this further.

The communion of saints and the departed

66. All prayer is ultimately addressed to the triune God. We pray to God the Father through our Lord Jesus Christ in the Holy Spirit. The church is united in a single movement of worship with the church in heaven, with the Blessed Virgin Mary, "with angels and archangels, and all the company of heaven". The Orthodox also pray to the Blessed Virgin Mary and Theotokos and the saints as friends and living images of Christ.

67. Those who believe and are baptized form one body in Christ, and are members one of another, united by the Holy Spirit. Within the body each member suffers and rejoices with the others, and in each member the Holy Spirit intercedes for the whole. These relationships are changed but not broken by death. "He is not God of the dead, but of the living" (Matt. 22:32), for all live in and to him. This is the meaning of the communion of saints.

68. God is "the God of Abraham, the God of Isaac, and the God of Jacob" (Exod. 3:6), "the Lord of hosts" (Isa. 6:3), "the God and Father of our Lord Jesus Christ" (Rom. 15:6). Our God is not an abstract idea, but the God of persons, revealing himself in and to particular men and women. Union with God therefore involves us in a personal relationship with all who belong to him through the grace of the Holy Spirit who both unites and diversifies: and this personal relationship, which is not broken by death, is precisely the communion of saints.

69. Our experience of the communion of saints finds its fullest expression in the eucharist, in which the whole body of Christ realizes its unity in the Holy Spirit. We see this in ancient eucharistic prayers of East and West, which commemorate the saints and intercede for the departed as well as for the living.

70. "Christ is risen from the dead trampling down death by death..." By virtue of Christ's cross and resurrection, death is no longer an impassable barrier. It is this sense of our continuing union in the risen Christ that forms for all Orthodox the basis of prayer for the dead and the invocation of the saints. Mainly as a result of the abuses of the medieval West, and the consequent Reformation in the 16th century, Anglicans rejected much of the practice and teaching of the church of that time. The cult of the saints and prayer for the departed were criticized on the grounds of the all-sufficiency of Christ's redeeming work. Today there is a variety of practice among Anglicans on these matters. All remain careful in the language which they use in prayer for the departed, being anxious not to return to the errors of the Western middle ages. But all affirm our union with the departed in the risen Christ.

71. God's love is present everywhere and is offered to everybody, but not everyone accepts it. According to some fathers, even those in hell are not deprived of the love of God but by their own free choice they experience as torment what the saints experience as joy. The light of God's glory is also the fire of judgment. God's wrath is no other than his love; how we experience that love, in this life and after death, depends on our attitude. The Orthodox church in the prayers of Pentecost, believing that Christ has the keys of death and hell (Rev. 1:18), and hoping that the love of God will find a response in the souls even of some who are in hell, prays for their salvation, although their ultimate destiny remains a mystery (Matt. 25:31-46 as understood by the fathers).[32]

72. "... from one degree of glory to another" (2 Cor. 3:18): for the righteous, in the view of the Orthodox and also of many Anglicans, further progress and growth in the love of God will continue for ever. After death, this progress is to be thought of in terms of healing rather than satisfaction or retribution. Other Anglicans think of perfection in Christ as an immediate gift in the life to come. As Anglicans and Orthodox we are agreed in rejecting any doctrine of purgatory which suggests that the departed through their sufferings are making "satisfaction" or "expiation" for their sins. The traditional practice of the church in praying for the faithful departed is to be understood as an expression of the unity between the church militant and the church triumphant, and of the love which one bears to the other.

73. Prayers for the departed are therefore to be seen, not in juridical terms, but as an expression of mutual love and solidarity in Christ: "we pray for them because we still hold them in our love" (Catechism of the Episcopal Church, USA).

74. The prayers of the saints on our behalf are likewise to be understood as an expression of mutual love and shared life in the Holy Spirit. Such a term as "treasury of merits" is foreign to both our traditions. "There is one God, and there is one mediator between God and men, the man Christ Jesus" (1 Tim. 2:5): the intercession of the saints for us is always in and through this unique mediation of Christ. The saints reign with Christ (cf. Luke 22:29-30): Christ is the King, and the saints share in his kingly rule.

75. The Blessed Virgin Mary played a unique role in the economy of salvation by virtue of the fact that she was chosen to be Mother of Christ our God. Her intercession is not autonomous, but presupposes Christ's intercession and is based upon the saving work of the incarnate Word.

76. The Orthodox practice of commemorating the saints of the Old Testament powerfully affirms the way in which the whole history of salvation is made present in the liturgy of the church.

77. All Anglican liturgies refer to the communion of saints by thanking God for that communion and for the lives and examples of particular saints, and some refer to the saints' prayers for us, but very few contain invocations addressed directly to saints.

78. Much of the language in which we speak of the saints and the departed is derived from the life of prayer and piety. Many of the church's affirmations concerning the communion of saints are in hymnography and iconography. At the same time there is an appropriate doctrinal reserve which reflects the mystery of our relationship with the departed. It is in God alone that we have communion with them.

Icons

79. In the incarnation human nature, body as well as soul, was assumed into the life of the Word of God; and in the renewed creation, which this incarnation has effected,

the whole material world is sanctified, and the destructive opposition of matter and spirit overcome.

80. In the Orthodox tradition the depiction and use of icons has a christological foundation. The icon is understood as an important means whereby we confess and appropriate the mystery of the incarnation.

81. Anglicans have in the past felt serious difficulties about this question. For example a committee of the Lambeth Conference in 1888 said: "It would be difficult for us to enter more intimate relations with that (sc. Orthodox) church as long as it retains the use of icons." These difficulties are part of a larger history of the West. The decrees of the seventh ecumenical council were not properly understood in the West owing to the unfortunate translation of the Greek word προσκύνησις (veneration) by the Latin word *adoratio* (worship). The subsequent uncontrolled development of visual imagery later in the middle ages in the West led to strong reactions, above all at the time of the Reformation. The Reformers understood the prohibition of idolatry in the ten commandments as applying to the practices of their own day. They sought to purify and simplify the worship of the church, in order that glory might be given to God alone. In particular they rejected the worship of images.

82. Anglicans however did not reject all use of bodily gestures and images in the worship of the church. The Book of Common Prayer retains, for example, the use of the sign of the cross in baptism, and the giving of a ring in marriage. In the controversies in the century following the Reformation, Anglicans constantly appealed to the words of St Paul, "All things should be done decently and in order" (1 Cor. 14:40). In his exposition of the church catechism, *The Practice of Divine Love*, Bishop Thomas Ken (1637-1711) prays, "give me grace to pay a religious, suitable veneration to all sacred persons or places or things which are thine by solemn dedication and separated for the uses of divine love, and the communications of thy grace, or which may promote the decency and order of the worship, or the edification of faithful people". In fact a distinctive Anglican tradition of religious art developed. During the last hundred years increasing contact with the Orthodox churches and a fuller knowledge of their tradition have brought new light to this question.

83. In the light of the present discussion the Anglicans do not find any cause for disagreement in the doctrine as stated by St John of Damascus: "In times past, God, without body and form, could in no way be represented. But now since God has appeared in flesh and lived among men, I can depict that which is visible of God. I do not venerate matter, but I venerate the creator of matter, who became matter for me, who condescended to live in matter, and who through matter accomplished my salvation; and I do not cease to respect the matter through which my salvation is accomplished."[33]

84. By the incarnation of the Word who is the image of the Father (2 Cor. 4:4; Col. 1:15; Heb. 1:3) the image of God in every man is restored and the material world itself sanctified and again made capable of mediating the divine beauty. Icons are used as a means of expressing, as far as it can be expressed, the glory of God seen in the face of Jesus Christ (2 Cor. 4:6), and in the faces of his friends. Icons are words in painting, referring to the history of salvation and its manifestation in specific persons. Icons have always been understood as a visible gospel, as a testimony to the great things given to us by God the Word incarnate. In the council of 860 it was stated that "all that is uttered in words written in syllables is also proclaimed in the language of colours". From this

perspective icons and scripture are linked through an inner relationship; both coexist in the church and proclaim the same truths. "Just as in the Bible we listen to the word of Christ and are sanctified... in the same way through the painted icons we behold the representation of his human form... and are likewise sanctified" (St John of Damascus).[34]

85. An icon is a means of entering into contact with the person or event it represents. It is not an end in itself. In the words of St Basil: "The honour shown to the icon passes to the prototype."[35] It guides us to a vision of the divine kingdom where past, present and future are one. It makes vivid our faith in the communion of the saints. In the definition of the seventh ecumenical council we read: "The more frequently they (sc. icons) are seen, the more those who behold them are aroused to remember and desire the prototypes and to give them greeting and the veneration of honour; not indeed true worship which, according to our faith, is due to God alone."[36]

86. Just as scripture is understood within the community of faith, so too the icon is understood within the same community of faith and worship. It is an essentially liturgical form of art. In response to the faith and prayer of the believers, God, through the icon, bestows his sanctifying and healing grace. Thus the icon serves to promote the communication of the gospel and hence its making and use must always be controlled by theological criteria. It is not a random decoration, but an integral part of the church's life and worship. In this respect its place in the church's worship can be compared with the place of music and chant and with the faithful preaching of the word of God.

87. In our time, when visual imagery plays a more and more important part in people's lives, the tradition of icons has acquired a startling relevance. It presents the church with a new possibility of proclaiming the gospel in a society in which language is often devalued.

Epilogue

88. At this point in our work, after twelve years of discussion, we feel it right to attempt a summary of the progress that, as Anglicans and Orthodox, we have been able to achieve with God's help. We note in particular the following points over which we agree or disagree, or which we see as requiring further exploration.

I. The knowledge of God

89. Here we have discovered a difference in terminology, but no difference in fundamental belief. The normal Orthodox ways of speaking about the essence and energies of God, and about "divinization" (Θέωσις), are not employed by most Anglicans, but Anglicans do not reject the underlying doctrine which this language expresses.[37]

II. Scripture and Tradition

90. (a) We agree in our basic understanding of the inspiration and authority of scripture, and we agree more particularly that the church gives attention to the results of scholarly research concerning the Bible. But we have not attempted to state in detail how critical methods of historical research are to be applied to the Bible, for we see this as a task outside the scope of a commission such as our own. We have noted a minor difference over the distinction which both churches make between the canonical books of the Old Testament and the deutero-canonical books: the Orthodox church has not pronounced officially on the nature of the distinction, as is done in the articles of the Church of England.[38]

91. (b) We agree likewise in our view of the fundamental relationship between scripture and Tradition: they are not two sources, but correlative. We agree that the church cannot define dogmas which are not grounded both in scripture and in Tradition. We agree that the "mind" (φρόνημα) of the fathers is of lasting importance for our understanding of the Christian faith.

92. We agree that tradition is to be seen in dynamic terms, as the constant action of the Holy Spirit in the church; and therefore both our delegations accept that there exist freedom and variety within the one Tradition of the church. But we have not yet attempted to state in detail what are the limits of that freedom and variety in regard to every specific point of doctrine.[39]

III. The Holy Trinity

93. (a) We agree in affirming that prayer and sanctification are founded upon the grace of the Holy Trinity.[40]

94. (b) We agree that the original form of the Nicene-Constantinopolitan Creed referred to the origin of the Holy Spirit from the Father. For this reason, because the filioque was introduced into the creed without the authority of an ecumenical council and without due regard to catholic consent, the Anglicans agree with the Orthodox that the filioque should not be included in the creed.[41]

95. (c) We have discussed how far the doctrine implied by the filioque (as distinguished from the inclusion of the filioque in the creed) is acceptable to our two churches. Here we have failed to reach full agreement. The Anglican delegates regard the filioque as a valid theological statement, though not as a dogma. The Orthodox delegates regard the doctrine of the filioque as unacceptable, but they note that according to some Eastern fathers, the use of the filioque in early Latin theology can be understood in an Orthodox way.[42]

IV. The church

96. (a) We agree in our fundamental understanding of the church as one, holy, catholic and apostolic.[43]

97. (b) Despite differences in the outward forms of wider leadership within our two communions, there is fundamental agreement between the way in which Anglicans understand "primacy" and the way in which Orthodox understand "seniority". We agree more particularly that all levels of wider leadership within the church are to be envisaged in terms not of coercion but of pastoral service.[44]

98. (c) We agree in our basic understanding of witness, evangelism and service within the church. More especially we affirm that missionary witness to unbelievers, and sacrificial service to those in need, are the shared responsibility of all church members, clergy and laypeople alike.[45]

99. (d) But while we agree that the church is one, holy, catholic and apostolic, we are not agreed on the account to be given of the sinfulness and division which is to be observed in the life of Christian communities. For Anglicans, because the church under Christ is the community where God's grace is at work, healing and transforming sinful men and women; and because grace in the church is mediated through those who are themselves undergoing such transformation, the struggle between grace and sin is to be seen as characteristic of, rather than accidental to, the church on earth. Orthodox, while agreeing that the human members of the church on earth are sinful, do not

believe that sinfulness should be ascribed to the church as the body of Christ indwelt by the Holy Spirit.

100. (e) As regards the first of the four marks of the church, its oneness, we disagree in our view of the relationship between the church's basic unity and the present state of division between Christians. The Anglican members see our divisions as existing within the church while the Orthodox members believe that the Orthodox church is the one true church of Christ, which as his body is not and cannot be divided.[46]

101. (f) With this is linked a further disagreement, concerning communion and intercommunion. The Anglican tradition accepts as legitimate, in certain situations, the use of intercommunion as a means towards the attainment of full organic unity. The Orthodox reject the notion of intercommunion, and believe that there can be communion only between local churches that have a unity of faith, ministry and sacraments.[47]

102. (g) As regards the fourth of the four marks of the church, its apostolicity, we agree that this is manifested in a particular way through the succession of bishops and that this succession is a sign of the unbroken continuity of apostolic tradition and life.[48] But we have not so far discussed what is the attitude of our two churches towards such communities as have not preserved the succession of bishops in an outward and visible form. Nor have we discussed the Orthodox view of the validity of Anglican ordinations.

103. (h) We have failed to reach agreement concerning the possibility, or otherwise, of the ordination of women to the priesthood. The Orthodox affirm that such ordination is impossible, since it is contrary to scripture and Tradition. With this some Anglicans agree, while others believe that it is possible, and even desirable at the present moment, to ordain women as priests.[49] There are, however, many related issues that we have not so far examined in any detail, particularly the following: how we are to understand the distinction within humanity between man and woman; what is meant by sacramental priesthood, and how this is related to the unique high priesthood of Christ and to the royal priesthood of all the baptized; what, apart from the sacramental priesthood, are the other forms of ministry within the church.

V. Councils

104. (a) We agree that the ecumenical councils provide an authoritative interpretation of scripture in order to safeguard the salvation of the people of God.

105. (b) We differ, however, in our understanding of the relative importance of the councils. While the Anglican members lay greater emphasis upon the first four councils, and less upon on the fifth, sixth and seventh, applying to conciliar decisions the concept of an "order" or "hierarchy of truths", the Orthodox members find this concept to be in conflict with the unity of the faith as a whole.

106. (c) We are agreed in considering that infallibility is not the property of any particular person in the church. But we consider that the implications of the terms "infallible" and "indefectible" need to be further explored.

107. (d) We are agreed that the ecumenicity of councils is manifested through their acceptance by the church. But we feel that further discussion is needed of the processes whereby the teaching of councils is recognized and accepted.[50]

VI. Faith and worship, church and eucharist

108. (a) We are agreed about the integral link between faith and worship, between the Tradition of the church and its liturgical life. We are agreed in our general under-

standing of baptism, although we have not discussed this in detail. We are agreed in describing the eucharist as an anamnesis and participation in the death and resurrection of Christ.[51]

109. (b) We are agreed in regarding the church as a eucharistic community: the eucharist actualizes the church. In each local eucharistic celebration the visible unity and catholicity of the church is fully manifested. The question of the relationship between the celebrant and his bishop and that among bishops themselves requires further study.[52]

110. (c) We are agreed in attaching cardinal importance to the action of the Holy Spirit in the eucharist, as also throughout the entire life of the church. In the Orthodox eucharistic liturgy this is an invocation (ἐπίκλησις) of the Holy Spirit; in some Anglican liturgies there is no such explicit epiclesis, but all Anglicans are agreed that the operation of the Holy Spirit is essential to the eucharist.[53]

111. (d) We are agreed that through the consecratory prayer, addressed to the Father, the bread and wine become the body and blood of the glorified Christ by the action of the Holy Spirit in such a way that the faithful people of God receiving Christ may feed upon him in the sacraments.[54] But we have not yet discussed in detail what is the nature of the ineffable change effected through the consecratory prayer, nor have we considered how far the eucharist may be regarded as a sacrifice.[55]

112. (e) We have reached basic agreement on the communion of saints and the departed. All of us believe that the communion of the Holy Spirit joins in unity the members of the body, whether living or departed, and this unity is expressed in prayer and thanksgiving. There remains, however, a certain difference here between Orthodoxy and Anglicanism, since in most Anglican churches, requests to the saints to pray for us are not made, and also prayers for the faithful departed, though common, are by no means universal; and some Anglicans believe that only thanksgiving for the departed is appropriate. Moreover, not all Anglicans agree with the Orthodox patristic understanding of endless progress after death.[56]

113. (f) In regard to icons we have found that notwithstanding past Anglican objections and despite differences in liturgical practice, there is no serious disagreement here between Anglicanism and Orthodoxy. It is true that Anglicans do not believe that the veneration of icons, as practised in the East, can be required of all Christians. But Anglicans agree that the theology of the icon is founded upon, and intended to safeguard, the doctrine of the incarnation. They also accept that it is legitimate to regard the icon, not merely as a decoration, but as a means of entering into relationship with the person or event it represents; and to hold that in response to the faith and prayer of the believers, God through the icon bestows his sanctifying grace. We have not yet adequately discussed the difference between two- and three-dimensional images.[57]

114. None of the points of disagreement mentioned above is to be regarded as insoluble, but each is to be regarded as a challenge to this commission, or to some similar body to be appointed in the future by our two churches, to advance more deeply in its understanding of the truth. Anglicans and Orthodox alike, we are called to "reach out towards that which lies ahead, pressing forward to win the prize which is God's call to the life above, in Christ Jesus" (Phil. 3:13-14).

NOTES

1. Published with introductory and supporting material in *Anglican-Orthodox Dialogue: The Moscow Agreed Statement*, K. Ware and C. Davey, eds, London, SPCK, 1977; also published in *Growth in Agreement*, vol. I, H. Meyer and L. Vischer, eds, Geneva, WCC, pp.41-46.
2. Colin Davey, "Anglican-Orthodox Relations during the Patriarchate of His All-Holiness Athenagoras I (1948-72)", in *Athenagoras, the Epirote Ecumenical Patriarch*, Ioannina, 1976, p.417.
3. Communiqué, 1 August 1982, §4, *Episkepsis*, no. 278, 1 Sept. 1982, p.2.
4. *Anglican-Orthodox Dialogue*, p.78.
5. Communiqué from Cambridge conference.
6. *Ibid.*
7. Report of the Athens meeting, §§III 4,5,6; V.
8. *The Report of the Lambeth Conference* 1978, pp.45-47.
9. *Ibid.*, p.51.
10. Communiqué, §4, *Episkepsis*, no. 278, 1 Sept. 1982, p.2.
11. See Anglican Consultative Council 1982 consultation, "Unity by Stages", section III (a).
12. *Steps towards Unity*, report of the ACC preparatory group on ecumenical affairs, Woking, UK, Feb. 1984, p.14.
13. See the Moscow agreed statement, section VI, "The church as the eucharistic community".
14. See the Moscow agreed statement, section III, "Scripture and Tradition".
15. *Intercommunion: A Scottish Episcopalian Approach*, 1969, p.10.
16. ACC study paper on "Full Communion", 1981, p.7.
17. *PG* 33, 1100 A7, or *PG* 96, 1409 D8,9.
18. "Authority in the Church II", 5 and 17, in *The Final Report of ARCIC*, pp.83,89.
19. The statement in "Authority in the Church II", 20, *ibid.*, p.90, requires further elucidation.
20. In this connection we would wish to qualify what is said in the ARCIC report "Authority in the Church I", 23, *ibid.*, p.64.
21. See the Moscow Agreed Statement, IV, §§17-18.
22. "Authority in the Church II", 32, *op. cit.*, p.97.
23. Polycarp, *Letter to the Philippians*, 5:2; cf. Mark 10:45.
24. *Theological Orations*, II, 4.
25. Origen, *PG* 11, 416A.
26. St John Cassian, *Collations*, X, 10. St Gregory of Tours, *History of the Franks*, V, 10. St Patrick, who writes in his *Confession*, ch. 25: "And another time I saw him praying in me and I was as it were within my body and I heard above me, that is above my inner man, and there he was praying earnestly with groans, and while this was going on I was in amazement and I was wondering and I was considering who it could be who was praying in me but at the end of the prayer he spoke to the effect that it was the Spirit, and at that I woke." Trans. in R.P.C. Hanson, *The Life and Writings of the Historical Saint Patrick,* New York, 1983, p.94.
27. Moscow agreed statement, section V, 19-21.
28. St Maximus the Confessor, *Letter to Marinos*, *PG* 91, 133D-136B, *PG* 90, 672 CD.
29. Migne, *PL* 129, 560D-561A.
30. See Archpriest Liveriy Voronov, "The Filioque in the Ecumenical Perspective", in the *Journal of the Moscow Patriarchate*, 5, 1982, pp.66-68; AOJDD 313: L. Voronov, on the theses of Bolotov; and AOJDD 283: a translation, taken from Prof. V.V. Bolotov's book *On the Question of the Filioque* (published in 1914), of his "theses on the filioque" together with a passage (pp.30-36) defining terms, which include Bolotov's own definition of a theologoumenon as follows: "But I may be asked what I mean by Θεολογούμενον. In essence it is also a theological opinion, but only the opinion of those who for every catholic are more than just theologians: they are the theological opinions of the holy fathers of the one undivided church; they are the opinions of those men, among whom are those who are fittingly called 'ecumenical doctors'. Θεολογούμενα I rate highly, but I do not in any case exaggerate their significance, and I think that I 'quite sharply' distinguish them from dogmas. The content of a dogma is truth: the content of a Θεολογούμενον is only what is probable. The realm of a dogma is *necessaria*, the realm of a Θεολογούμενον is *dubia: In necessariis unitas, in dubiis libertas!*"
31. For an outline of traditional Anglican views see AOJDD 213, "The Filioque in Ecumenical Perspective: A Preliminary Anglican Response", by Prof. Eugene Fairweather.
32. E.g. *PG* 57-8, 717ff.
33. On Holy Icons I, *PG* 94, 1245B.
34. On Holy Icons III, *PG* 94,1333D.
35. On Holy Spirit 18, *PG* 32, 149 C8f.

[36] Mansi, *Concilia*, XIII, 482.
[37] Moscow agreed statement, §§1-3.
[38] MAS, §§4-8.
[39] MAS, §§9-12; Dublin agreed statement, §§47-52.
[40] DAS, §§36-43.
[41] MAS, §§19-21.
[42] DAS, §§44-46.
[43] DAS, §§2-17.
[44] DAS, §§21-30.
[45] DAS, §§31-35.
[46] DAS, §§8-9.
[47] DAS, §§18-20.
[48] DAS, §§14-17.
[49] DAS, appendix 2.
[50] MAS, §§13-18; DAS, §§29-30.
[51] DAS, §§53-65.
[52] MAS, §§22-27.
[53] MAS, §§29-32.
[54] MAS, §§25-26.
[55] MAS §22 refers to the Bucharest statement of 1935 on the eucharist, which is printed with an introduction on pp.92-93 of *Anglican-Orthodox Dialogue: Moscow Agreed Statement*, London, SPCK, 1977. However we have not discussed it in detail, nor, acting as a joint commission, have we as yet expressed our agreement or otherwise with the six points that it contains.
[56] DAS, §§66-78.
[57] DAS, §§79-87; MAS, §15.

6. Joint Communique
Robert A.K. Runcie, Archbishop of Canterbury, and Demetrios I, Ecumenical Patriarch

Lambeth Palace, London, England, 9 December 1987

At the invitation of the Archbishop of Canterbury, the Ecumenical Patriarch Demetrios I, Archbishop of Constantinople and New Rome, paid a visit to England, 7-10 December 1987. The Patriarch was accompanied by their Eminences Chrysostomos, Metropolitan of Myra; Gabriel, Metropolitan of Colonia; Evangelos, Metropolitan of Perga; Bartholomew, Metropolitan of Philadelphia; Methodios, Archbishop of Thyateira and Great Britain; the Very Rev. the Great Archdeacon Demetrios; the Very Rev. Meliton, Under-Secretary of the Holy Synod; the Very Rev. Chrysostomos, third deacon; Prof. Basil Istavridis; and Dr Theodosios Karamouratoglos.

On Monday, 7 December, the Ecumenical Patriarch and the Archbishop of Canterbury joined together in private prayer in the chapel of Leeds Castle, Kent, en route for Canterbury. At Canterbury the Patriarch and the Archbishop, together with their companions, were greeted by the dean and chapter of the Metropolitical Cathedral Church of Christ. The cathedral choir sang the "Ton Despotin" in honour of the Ecumenical Patriarch (to specially commissioned music by John Tavener) as the Patriarch and the Archbishop processed through the cathedral church to the high altar, from where they exchanged formal greetings. The Anglican eucharistic liturgy followed, according to the contemporary rite of the Church of England, presided over by the Archbishop of Canterbury. The creed was recited in its ecumenical form as authorized by the councils of Nicea and Constantinople. The celebration was of the conception of the blessed Virgin Mary. At the conclusion of the eucharist, the Patriarch blessed the large congregation in Greek after the Archbishop had done so in English. A festal banquet was given by the Archbishop of Canterbury in honour of the Ecumenical Patriarch at St Augustine's College, Canterbury.

On Tuesday, 8 December, the Ecumenical Patriarch and the Archbishop, accompanied by their Eminences Chrysostomos, Metropolitan of Myra, Gabriel, Metropolitan of Colonia, Evangelos, Metropolitan of Perga, and Bartholomew, Metropolitan of Philadelphia, paid a courtesy call on His Excellency Mr Rahmi Gumrukcuoglu, the Turkish ambassador, and on His Excellency Mr Stephanos G. Stathatos, the Greek ambassador.

The Ecumenical Patriarch was received in private audience at Buckingham Palace by Her Majesty Queen Elizabeth II.

In the afternoon the Patriarch and his party were introduced to personalities of the Church of England and of other churches at a luncheon at Church House, Westminster.

Later in the day the Ecumenical Patriarch was received by the dean and chapter of the Collegiate Church of St Peter at Westminster. The Patriarch prayed at the Tomb of the Unknown Warrior and then attended evensong with the Archbishop and those who accompanied them. After evensong the Patriarch and the Archbishop prayed together in silence at the shrine of St Edward the Confessor. They presided at a lecture given at Church House, Westminster, by Canon Rowan Williams, professor of divinity of the Lady Margaret Chair in the University of Oxford. A reception for the Patriarch followed at Thyateira House, given by His Eminence Archbishop Methodios of Thyateira and Great Britain.

On Wednesday, 9 December, the Ecumenical Patriarch and the Archbishop of Canterbury, together with those who accompanied them, in particular the co-chairmen and other members of the Anglican-Orthodox Joint Doctrinal Commission, spent the morning together in conversation about Anglican-Orthodox relations, the official dialogue between the two churches, and other matters of mutual concern. At the request of the Ecumenical Patriarch, His Eminence Metropolitan Chrysostomos of Myra, in his capacity as chairman of the commission on inter-Christian affairs of the Ecumenical Patriarchate, gave a report on the visits of the Ecumenical Patriarch to the churches of Alexandria and Jerusalem, Russia and Georgia, Serbia and Romania, and Greece and Poland, as well as to His Holiness Pope John Paul II at the Vatican. He said that in spite of the many obstacles to be overcome, notably for the Orthodox the inadmissibility of the ordination of women to the priesthood and to the episcopate, the Orthodox churches were unanimous in wishing to maintain and develop the dialogue which is at present being carried on and has been approved and affirmed by the third Pan-Orthodox preparatory commission. This commission – as is known – had expressed its satisfaction with the work accomplished to date by the Anglican-Orthodox Joint Doctrinal Commission. On the Anglican side it was reported that at its recent meeting the Anglican Consultative Council, presided over by the Archbishop of Canterbury, officially recommitted the churches of the Anglican Communion to the Anglican-Orthodox dialogue.

In the light of these facts, the Ecumenical Patriarch and the Archbishop of Canterbury reaffirmed their fullest commitment to the official dialogue between the churches and expressed their desire for the reinforcement of the dialogue, which neither of the churches wished in any way to downgrade: the dialogue is aimed at nothing less than that visible and sacramental unity which Christ wills for his one, holy, catholic and apostolic church. Metropolitan Chrysostomos said that the Orthodox churches intended to hold a pan-Orthodox symposium in 1988 to discuss the theological presuppositions for the inability of the Orthodox churches to accept the ordination of women, and to prepare a fuller statement of the Orthodox position on this matter. The Anglicans were asked to provide the Orthodox with full information on all reports and papers relating to both sides of this question at present under discussion in the Anglican Communion. The Archbishop of Canterbury stressed the importance of sharing full and accurate information on both sides, so that the question might be discussed and resolved within the context of the present dialogue.

In spite of obstacles past and present, the Ecumenical Patriarch and the Archbishop of Canterbury wished to encourage all Anglicans and Orthodox to take the search for unity between Eastern and Western Christians ever more seriously. They reminded the faithful of the two communions that within this pilgrimage, Anglican-Orthodox relations have a historic and time-honoured place. Anglicans recognize in Orthodoxy great theological treasures and richness of spirituality; Orthodox value the pastoral experience of Anglicans in secularized societies. To enable a mutual exchange of these gifts, the Ecumenical Patriarch and the Archbishop of Canterbury wished to foster more pastoral visits and exchanges between the two churches as well as maintaining the official theological dialogue. They agreed that such contacts should not be limited to leaders of the church, but should also include priests and laypeople, young and old, women and men.

The concluding part of the visit consisted of a doxology in honour of the Patriarch of St Sophia's Cathedral and a Nikaean dinner at Lambeth Palace at which farewell speeches were made and gifts exchanged. The gift of the Archbishop of Canterbury to the Ecumenical Patriarch took the form of a glass trophy engraved in Greek and English with the opening verse of Psalm 133:2: "Behold how good a thing it is, brothers, to dwell together in unity." The Ecumenical Patriarch presented to the Archbishop of Canterbury a copy of a 6th-century cross of the Emperor Justin with the inscription: "To the Archbishop of Canterbury, Dr Robert Runcie, from Demetrios of Constantinople, the Kiss of Peace – 1987."

IV. ANGLICAN-ORIENTAL ORTHODOX DIALOGUE

Historical Introduction

The idea of an official theological dialogue between the Oriental Orthodox churches and the Anglican Communion emerged spontaneously in the atmosphere created by the recent trend to promote bilateral relations between the churches. The earlier, unofficial contacts took more concrete form in a meeting, sponsored by the Anglican Consultative Council, of representatives of the Oriental Orthodox churches and the Anglican Communion at St Albans, England, 7-11 October 1985. The following representatives of the Oriental Orthodox churches took part: Bishop Bishoy of Damietta and Father Tadros Malaty (Coptic Orthodox Church), Archbishop Bozabalian of Nerses (Armenian Orthodox Church of Etchmiadzin), Datev Sarkissian (Armenian Orthodox Church of Cilicia), Rabban Abdulahad Shado (Syrian Orthodox Church), Metropolitan Paulus Mar Gregorios (Syrian Orthodox Church of India), and Archbishop Shoa Gregorios (Ethiopian Orthodox Church). Bishop Henry Hill of Canada was chairman of the group, made up of eminent theologians, that represented the Anglican Communion.

The purpose of the meeting was to determine the concrete procedure to be followed in the collaboration of the two families of churches, especially with regard to jointly issued documents and pastoral problems. The following possibilities were discussed:
a) a theological collaboration through exchange of scholarships for the study of theology, and through joint initiatives;
b) collaboration at the pastoral level in areas in which the faithful of both churches are living, so that common problems arising in practice may be more easily solved;
c) a theological dialogue to investigate differences that have been handed down in divergent ways in the two churches.

The discussions were, generally speaking, conducted in a positive spirit. Also suggested was the establishment of a joint theological commission for the opening of an official theological dialogue, but conditions were not yet sufficiently ripe for this idea in the Oriental Orthodox churches. It is evident that this meeting eased the way for a rapprochement between the two church families in the area of theological collaboration, in the approach to practical problems, and at the level of mutual contacts.

At the same time, a number of the Oriental Orthodox churches had reservations in view of the debate within the Anglican Communion regarding the official introduction of ordination for women and the admission of women to all degrees of orders. But these reservations did not lessen the positive attitude towards contacts and pastoral collaboration in regions in which the faithful of both churches are living. The establishment of a "forum" of Anglicans and Oriental Orthodox for the purpose of coordinating practical pastoral collaboration led ultimately to the suggestion that a corresponding theological "forum" also be established. The purpose of this would be to undertake a systematic study of differences in belief and practice in the area of baptism and the other sacraments, since it is these differences that hinder the development of closer relations between the two churches and the implementation of the idea of ecclesial communion.

An important step in the rapprochement of the two churches was the common declaration issued by Shenouda III, Patriarch of the Coptic Orthodox Church, and Dr Robert Runcie, Archbishop of Canterbury (1 October 1987). In this common declaration emphasis was placed on the Nicene-Constantinopolitan Creed as the basis of the common faith, without the addition of the filioque and taken as parallel to the other two confessions of faith of the early centuries: "This is the faith of the church. This is our faith: belief in one God, Father, Son and Holy Spirit which Anglicans and Coptic Orthodox confess in the early three ecumenical creeds." In dogmatic Christology the point was emphasized that "in spite of past misunderstandings Anglicans and Coptic Orthodox also confess together their faith that our Lord and God, the Saviour and Sovereign of all, Jesus Christ, is perfect in his divinity and perfect in his humanity. In him his divinity is united with his humanity in a real perfect union without mingling or commixture, without confusion or change, without division or separation, his divinity did not separate from his humanity for an instant... In him are preserved all the properties of the divinity and all the properties of the humanity, together in a real, perfect, indivisible and inseparable union."

This common declaration is a sufficiently broad basis on which the leaders of the two churches can encourage their faithful to look for a proximate rapprochement between the two churches and for their collaboration at the pastoral level. The discussion of the question of ordination of women at the twelfth conference of the Anglican Communion (Lambeth 1988) was of special importance for these relations. When the time came for interventions by representatives of the other churches, Bishop Bishoy of Damietta read the "Message" which Coptic Patriarch Shenouda III addressed to the conference and in which he rejected the ordination of women with an appeal to sacred scripture and to the Tradition of the church. The decision taken by the Lambeth Conference in this matter had a negative influence not only on these bilateral relations but also on the relations of the Anglican Communion with the other ecclesial families in the Oriental Orthodox churches.

Damaskinos Papandreou

7. Common Declaration
Shenouda III, Pope of Alexandria and Patriarch of the See of St Mark, and Robert A.K. Runcie, Archbishop of Canterbury

Egypt, 1 October 1987

Shenouda III, Pope of Alexandria and Patriarch of the See of St Mark, and Robert, Archbishop of Canterbury and President of the Anglican Consultative Council, give thanks to God in the Holy Spirit for our meeting in Egypt both in Cairo and at the Monastery of St Bishoi in the Wadi El Natroun for common prayer and conversation to further closer relations between the churches of the Anglican Communion and the Coptic Orthodox Church in accordance with the prayer of our Lord for the unity of all his disciples (John 17:21).

Our desire for mutual understanding and closer cooperation has for its foundation the basic conviction that in spite of many centuries of isolation from each other and the separate development of our two traditions, we nevertheless still share an essentially common faith.

The heart of this faith is to be found in the Christian profession of faith in one God the Father Almighty, Maker of heaven and earth, and of all things visible and invisible: and in one Lord Jesus Christ, the only begotten Son of God, begotten of his Father before all worlds, God of God, Light of Light, very God of very God, begotten not made, being of one substance with the Father, by whom all things were made: who for us men, and for our salvation, came down from heaven, and was incarnate by the Holy Ghost of the Virgin Mary, and was made man, and was crucified also for us under Pontius Pilate; he suffered and was buried, and the third day he rose again according to the scriptures, and ascended into heaven, and sitteth on the right hand of the Father, and he shall come again with glory to judge both the quick and the dead: whose kingdom shall have no end.

And we believe in the Holy Spirit, the Lord, the Giver of life, who proceedeth from the Father, who with the Father and the Son together is worshipped and glorified, who spoke through the prophets; and in one holy, catholic and apostolic church: acknowledging one baptism for the remission of sins, and looking for the resurrection of the dead, and the life of the world to come, Amen.

This is the faith of the church. This is our faith: belief in one God, Father, Son and Holy Spirit which Anglicans and Coptic Orthodox confess in the early three ecumenical creeds.

In spite of past misunderstandings Anglicans and Coptic Orthodox also confess together their faith that our Lord and God, the Saviour and Sovereign of all, Jesus Christ, is perfect in his divinity and perfect in his humanity. In him his divinity is united with his humanity in a real perfect union without mingling or commixture, without confusion or change, without division or separation, his divinity did not separate from his humanity for an instant, he who is God eternal and invisible became visible in the flesh, and took upon himself the form of a servant. In him are preserved all the properties of the divinity and all the properties of the humanity, together in a real, perfect, indivisible and inseparable union.

Though Anglicans and Coptic Orthodox recognize with humility the theological differences which have sadly separated Christians since 451, they also now recognize that some divisions had cultural and political origins rather than real differences in faith. Nevertheless, as a result of their separate histories, Anglicans and Coptic Orthodox need to examine their differences to overcome difficulties and misunderstandings; for example regarding the sacrament of holy baptism. The recently established Anglican-Oriental Orthodox pastoral forum has proposed a future theological forum which should provide a place for this discussion so that existing difficulties over the doctrine and practice of holy baptism may be overcome, together with any other perceived differences of faith or sacramental life which would prevent closer relations and ultimate communion between our two churches.

Pope Shenouda III and Archbishop Robert also express deep thankfulness for the good relations which are now well established between the local Anglican diocese in Egypt, and its bishop, the Right Rev. Ghais Malik, and the Coptic Orthodox Church. These same good relations characterize Anglican-Coptic cooperation in other regions, principally Western Europe, North America and Australia. We call on the two churches to continue to give each other brotherly mutual support and help. We recognize the great significance of the Coptic Church in the wider context of Christianity in the Middle East. Christians throughout the world have the duty to support their Christian brothers and sisters in the original homelands of the Christian church.

Above all we call upon the faithful of the Anglican Communion and the Coptic Orthodox Church to pray for each other as fellow members of the household of faith. This will be the true basis for the increased theological understanding, consultation and social collaboration which should characterize the relations between the two churches. In conclusion we commend the sacred cause of the unity of Christians to the prayers of all the saints, and especially to St Mark the Evangelist, St Clement of Alexandria, St Athanasius, St Cyril, St Anthony of Egypt, St Bishoi, and above all to the Blessed Virgin Mary, Theotokos, in whose company and fellowship we are supported in the communion of saints.

May God, the Giver of all good gifts, answer our prayers for unity through Jesus Christ our Lord in the power of the Holy Spirit.

8. Joint Communique

George Carey, Archbishop of Canterbury,
and Karekin I, Supreme Catholicos of All Armenians

Lambeth Palace, London, England, 10 November 1997

During this historic visit we have had the opportunity to pray and talk together, we have been mindful not only of the long-standing relationship between the Armenian Apostolic Church and the Anglican Communion, but also of the new situation that now exists in the independent Republic of Armenia – a cause of great joy.

Our thoughts and discussions have turned towards our hopes for the deepening relations between our two churches around the world and our common commitment to the mission of Christ's church in conformity to his command to baptize and make disciples of all nations (Matt. 28:19).

We give thanks for our theological discussions, especially those of the Anglican-Oriental Orthodox international forum. We hope that, building on the work of this forum and that of other ecumenical dialogues, we will soon be able to reach a consensus indicating substantive convergence on the formerly divisive christological issue.

We give thanks for the close relationships between provinces of the Anglican Communion and the Armenian Apostolic Church throughout the world and encourage the deepening of these relationships in life and witness at the local level.

We recognize that all churches are faced with common challenges in an increasingly secular culture, and we commit ourselves to bilateral discussions and work together where possible on these issues. Further, we commit ourselves to developing partnerships and sharing resources and insights particularly in Christian education, sector ministries and chaplaincies and other similar areas.

We rejoice that we have had the opportunity to meet and pray together. Especially we were privileged to join together on Remembrance Sunday in common prayer for the victims, not only the dead of all wars but in particular for those victims of the Armenian genocide. In faithfulness to the saints and martyrs who have gone before us and mindful of the dawning of the third Christian millennium and the 1700th anniversary of the foundation of Christianity in Armenia in 2001, we recommit ourselves and our churches to the search for unity in Christ, our resurrection and our life.

V. ANGLICAN-REFORMED DIALOGUE

Historical Introduction

The initiative for this dialogue came from the World Alliance of Reformed Churches in 1974. The executive committee of the World Alliance hoped that an official dialogue with the Anglican Communion would be of help to those Reformed and Anglican churches that belong to a union of churches or are taking part in negotiations for union. The fact that numerous efforts to achieve union had failed had raised the question of the deeper reasons for the failures. The proposal had a positive reception. The executive committee of the Anglican Consultative Council gave its consent to the project in 1977. Both partners were in agreement that the focus should be on the following tasks:
a) an assessment of those dialogues concerned with union in which Anglican and Reformed churches had participated or were now participating;
b) an analysis of the specific points of dispute between the two families;
c) an exchange of views on questions of methodology and strategy, for example, on the advantages and drawbacks of bilateral and multilateral dialogues;
d) an examination of shifts in ecclesiology, especially the dwindling interest in the question of the oneness of the church;
e) consideration of future relations between the two families.

A first consultation was devoted to securing a detailed agreement on the mandate of the commission (1978). In the following year the members of the commission for dialogue were appointed. The commission then met four times between 1981 and 1984 for sessions lasting several days.

The Lambeth Conference of 1988 examined the report. It was especially appreciative of the fact that in the report the unity and mission of the church were seen and described in the perspective of the kingdom of God. It expressed its satisfaction that ways had been found of jointly accepting the traditional threefold office. It recommended study of the report and its acceptance by the synods of the Anglican Communion. In addition, it suggested the establishment of a small continuation committee that would monitor further developments. The general assembly of the World Alliance of Reformed Churches, meeting in Seoul, Korea, in 1989, accepted this proposal.

Lukas Vischer

V. ANGLICAN-REFORMED DIALOGUE

9. God's Reign and Our Unity

Woking, England, January 1984

Preface

This report is the result of work spread over four years (1981-84) by the Anglican-Reformed Commission which was set up after preliminary consultation in 1978. We were appointed by the Anglican Consultative Council and the World Alliance of Reformed Churches.

Those appointed to this commission have greatly valued the growing and deepening fellowship which has developed during our meetings and we owe much in particular to the worship in daily prayer and eucharist in which we have shared together and which remained the context in which we sought to do our work.

From the outset we sought to go behind the historical and traditional problems which have divided us since Reformation times and to put our quest for unity in new perspectives. We sought to do this by enquiring into the relationship between the church and the kingdom of God, the priority of grace, the trinitarian and christological basis of ministry, the mission of the church.

We were fortunate in having in our membership representatives from Africa and Latin America and in being reminded by them that the divisions and differences that stemmed from the Reformation are not felt to be as important in many regions of the world as the divisions between rich and poor, black and white, men and women.

We were aware that our membership was not representative of continental Europe or Asia, and was entirely male. Nevertheless we hope our findings will prove to be sensitive to the wide varieties of situations in which our member churches find themselves. A single report cannot, of course, do justice to every local situation but we hope groups will find in the report things to challenge them, and that they will also be aware of factors that are inadequately handled by us.

In submitting this report, we recommend that, in receiving and studying it, members of the Anglican and Reformed traditions will discuss this not only between themselves but where possible with other traditions too.

In our earlier meetings we were greatly helped by the Rev. Dr John Huxtable who was the first co-chairman for the Reformed side and we regret that health reasons compelled him to resign from the commission.

We should wish to thank also the Rev. Richmond Smith, theological secretary for the World Alliance of Reformed Churches until 1983, who acted as co-secretary and who was succeeded by the Rev. Dr Alan Sell for our final meeting.

We are indebted to our Anglican secretaries, the Rev. David Chaplin who served us in the preliminary stage and the Rev. George Braund who was with us throughout the four years of our commission's life.

A special word of appreciation is due to Deirdre Hoban, Vanessa Wilde of London and Colette Jacot of Geneva who served our meetings so efficiently in the secretarial office.

    John Tinsley   Roy F. Wilson
    Bishop of Bristol   United Church of Canada
    Anglican Consultative Council   World Alliance of Reformed Churches
    Co-chairmen   *Woking, England, January 1984*

I. Our task

ORIGINS OF THE PRESENT REPORT

1. The World Alliance of Reformed Churches (WARC) represents 157 churches with about 70 million members. The Anglican Consultative Council (ACC) represents 27 provinces with about 65 million members. There are some parts of the world where only one of these two families of churches is represented. In Uganda and Tanzania, for example, there are large Anglican churches but no Reformed. In many countries of Europe, and in Indonesia, there are strong Reformed churches but few, if any, Anglicans. But there are large parts of the world where the two live side by side. Their distinctive and divergent styles of life and witness were developed during the struggles of the Reformation in Europe, and reflect the circumstances of that time and place. Now, four centuries later, they have become world communions. Both are committed to the ecumenical movement and have taken a leading part in it. Both have long been involved in discussions with each other and with other churches, in negotiations for union and – in the Indian sub-continent – in the formation of united churches.

2. These facts, and especially the fact that certain Anglican and Reformed churches have been actually united and now form together large and growing churches covering the whole of the Indian sub-continent, place our two communions in a relationship with each other which implies an obligation to press towards fuller unity. Both communions had their origin as distinct entities in the events of the Reformation, but both confess themselves part of the one catholic church, even though there are important differences between them in the ways they understand their continuity with the pre-Reformation Western church. We are agreed that the unity we seek must be that of all Christian people, and it follows that "the test of all local schemes of union is that they should express locally the principle of the great catholic unity of the body of Christ" (Church of South India, Basis of Union, §1). But since that ultimate aim cannot be achieved in one leap, it is proper to ask that churches should at all times be ready to look for opportunities for small advances towards it. We believe that our two communions, within the wider fellowship of the universal church, are well placed to take such steps in the many parts of the world where our member churches live side by side. We offer this report in the hope that it will serve to encourage and guide such steps.

3. During the last sixty years Anglican and Reformed churchmen have taken a full part in multilateral discussions of the matters of faith and order which divide them, and

have shared in the production of the recently published joint statement on *Baptism, Eucharist and Ministry* (1982). Both have also been involved in bilateral conversations. The WARC has had such conversations with Lutherans, Baptists and Roman Catholics, and is exploring the possibility of dialogue with the Orthodox, Mennonites, Methodists and Churches of Christ (Disciples). Anglicans have had extensive dialogue with Lutherans, Old Catholics, Orthodox and Roman Catholics – the last of these having produced its *Final Report* in 1982.

4. In spite of all this activity, and in spite of the achievement of full organic union in North and South India, Pakistan and Bangladesh, recent years have seen a series of failures and disappointments in the quest for unity between our two communions. Plans for organic union between Anglican and Reformed churches which at one time seemed very promising have collapsed in Nigeria, Ghana, Sri Lanka, the Sudan, Canada, Australia and New Zealand. The United States Consultation on Church Union (COCU) has been at work for more than twenty years and has been obliged to move from the search for full organic union to exploring the idea of a covenant as a first stage, but progress towards this intermediate goal is uncertain. Proposals for covenanting in England and New Zealand have failed, and those in South Africa have suffered a serious setback. Committed as our two communions are to the quest for visible unity, we are bound to feel disappointed by this record of failure.

5. Accordingly the WARC and the ACC decided to call the first international consultation between the two bodies. A preliminary meeting was held in 1978, and subsequently four residential meetings of five to seven days each were held from 1981 to 1984. All of these meetings took place at St Columba's House, Woking, England. Throughout the meetings the members were able to share together in eucharistic worship and in morning and evening prayer according to the several traditions of our two communions. This shared worship has been of fundamental importance for the work of the commission. It is only as we meet in adoration of our one Lord that our minds are drawn into unison. It is necessary to make this point clear at the outset since, in our view, the fruitfulness of the report will depend in large measure on the extent to which its examination and reception in the member churches takes place within the same ambience of worship.

WHAT KEEPS ANGLICANS AND REFORMED APART?

6. Anglican and Reformed churches have found it possible to come together in united churches and to develop a common life in which both traditions could continue to play a part. Although representative theologians of both communions have been able to agree on the terms for proposed unions covering the matters of faith and order which have divided us, nevertheless, as we have seen, in most of the world these verbal agreements have not been enough to create unity. Is it possible to identify the factors which are still, apparently, stronger than the theological agreements which have been reached in some places? No doubt these factors are as varied as human nature itself, but some which are common to many situations can be listed even though they may apply in very different degrees in the many different places where our churches live and work. There are, of course, many controversies which occur within both our communions as well as between them. Some of these arise from the diversities of insight which will always characterize the life of the church. Others need to be resolved within both our communions. We wish in this report, however, to look at things which divide our two

communions from one another. Some of these are specific to our two communions; others are things which apply generally to the life of churches.

Specific obstacles

7. (a) Our two communions define themselves in different ways, and this makes mutual understanding difficult. Many churches within the Reformed tradition have defined themselves in terms of subscription to a written confession, while those of the Congregational faith and order (many of whom are represented in the WARC), though never reluctant to devise declarations of the faith commonly held among them, have not made confessional subscription into a test of church membership. Anglicans have rather found their identity in a common liturgy and a common adherence to the three-fold ministry. The thirty-nine articles of the Church of England do not figure as largely in the self-understanding of Anglicans as the Book of Common Prayer does. In modern times Reformed churches have devoted much time and effort to the preparation of confessional documents restating the faith in contemporary terms, or else (as at Barmen in 1934 and at Ottawa in 1982) declaring heretical certain doctrines or practices. Anglican churches, meanwhile, have laboured to revise their forms of worship in the light of changing situations. Much might be written about the relative importance of these two exercises, and there is much need on each side to reflect on the value of the other. The fact remains, however, that this difference is expressive of a deep divergence of the ways in which the two churches understand themselves, and a correspondingly serious difficulty in understanding the other. The difference separates what belongs together. The danger here is of a kind of "nominalism" – the confusing of form and substance. We have tended, in scholastic fashion, to identify too absolutely our formulations of the truth with the truth as it is in Jesus, and our forms of worship as the definitive ways of participating in him. We have thus judged one another by our outward forms. When the late Pope John XXIII had the courage to say that the substance of ancient doctrine is one thing but our formulations are another, he opened the door for reformation and the reformulation of doctrine, and so for the renewal sought in Vatican II. It was a plea for a "realist" understanding which broke with Tridentine "nominalism" and dogmatism. So, as Anglicans and Reformed, we must look together beyond our rigid formulations of doctrine and forms of worship to the reality of what we are in Christ, so that we may find formulations of doctrine and forms of worship which truly bear witness to the gospel of grace. The church is *semper reformanda* in the light of Christ and the gospel. We must learn to accept one another for what we are in God's grace, and not simply judge one another by our outward forms, important as these are.

8. (b) Both our communions affirm the centrality of word and sacrament in the life of the church, but the accent falls differently. At their best Anglicans honour the faithful preaching of the word and Reformed have a deep reverence for the sacraments. But it cannot be denied that we habitually fall short of our best, and because we fail in different ways we are very conscious of the failures of the other. Reformed churchmen can point to the meagre quality of some Anglican preaching, and Anglicans can point to the shallowness of some eucharistic practice in Reformed churches.

9. (c) The role of the bishop in Anglican piety and churchmanship has no exact parallel in Reformed experience. We are not speaking here of the strictly ecclesiological and theological factors involved in the difference between Anglican and Reformed pat-

terns of oversight. Even when these are reconciled, there remains as a point of real difference the importance given to the bishop as the one who, in a more than functional sense, stands as a personal symbol of the catholicity and apostolicity of the church. Reformed churchmanship has not developed anything exactly comparable to this, and perhaps it is at this point that one of the deepest emotional barriers to union lies.

10. (d) The tradition of the Anglican churches was initially shaped in the 16th century by the Elizabethan settlement, and in the 17th century by the antagonism created by the civil war and the restoration. The worldwide development of the Anglican Communion in the 18th and 19th centuries was intimately connected with the expansion of British imperial power. The fact that the Church of England has thus such intimate relations with the state, and that until recently the Anglican churches in many parts of the world were seen as closely related to the colonial power, has strongly affected relations with other churches. The Reformed churches have had in the past, and still have in Scotland and in some parts of Europe, a comparable (though not identical) bond of union with the state. In the British Isles these close bonds between church and state are still important obstacles to full mutual acceptance, and their consequences in other parts of the world are not irrelevant.

11. (e) More subtle, but not less important, are the bonds which tie our two communions to the national feeling and the folk religion of the people to whom we minister. The feeling, in England, for example, that the Anglican form of worship and church order is "the religion of the English people", and in Scotland that the Presbyterian forms similarly embody the proper religion of the Scots, is often deep and enduring. English and Scots people who have migrated to other parts of the world have carried these sentiments with them, and they have lost none of their strength on the journey. In North America the different denominational forms tend to be seen as optional varieties of one common religion which is proper to the nation as a whole. In some parts of the third world, through the accidents of missionary history, membership in an Anglican or a Reformed church is intimately related to membership in a particular tribal or ethnic group, and – in such places – the church can be defined as the church of that people more appropriately than as the church of a confession.

General obstacles

12. (a) There are obstacles to unity which operate in all encounters between churches and are not confined to the Anglican-Reformed dialogue; they need, however, to be recognized. One of the most important of these is the fear that union means loss of identity. This fear goes very deep. No one becomes a Christian, and no one grows up into mature Christian discipleship except through forms of teaching, worship, practice and piety which have been developed in a particular tradition. Apart from an encounter with Christians nurtured in another tradition, there is no occasion for making a distinction between the substance and the form – between the presence of Christ himself and the forms in which he has made himself present to the disciple. In this sense there is a "natural fundamentalism" in regard to the forms of churchmanship which is quite proper. When the encounter takes place with a Christian nurtured in another tradition, there arises the painful necessity of going beyond and behind the received form to a new apprehension of the substance – of the presence of Christ himself. This is a kind of fresh conversion. It cannot be easy. It should not surprise us that it is resisted with passionate intensity, because resistance seems to be required by

fidelity to Christ as he has made himself known to us in the past. As with all true conversion, this can only be the work of the Holy Spirit, for which we have to pray.

13. (b) A further difficulty which besets all moves towards organic union is the widespread and well-grounded fear of large organizations. In spite of many disclaimers, it is widely feared that organic unity will lead to the uniformity which frequently seems to be the inevitable – even if unintended – consequence of large-scale organization. While we cannot admit a dichotomy between "visible unity" and "spiritual unity", we must both insist that a deep spiritual unity in Christ is the necessary precondition of unity of structure, and also devote more effort to the adumbration of structures designed to ensure that "visible unity" does not mean bureaucratically controlled uniformity.

14. (c) Among the most pervasive and powerful of all the factors which combine to paralyze the movement towards unity is a false understanding of the nature of the church and of God's calling to the church. For too many Christians the church is seen only in static terms, the religious aspect of society, a home of refuge from the storms of life, a bark to carry the passengers safely into harbour – or rather a flotilla of boats among which each person is free to choose the most attractive. So long as the church is seen in this way there will be no urgency about the quest for unity. Our report is written in the conviction that the church is to be understood in a much more dynamic way, as a pilgrim people called to a journey whose goal is nothing less than God's blessed kingdom embracing all nations and all creation, a sign, instrument and foretaste of God's purpose "to sum up all things with Christ as head" (Eph. 1:10). It is only in this missionary and eschatological[1] perspective that the question of unity is rightly seen.

CHRISTIAN UNITY AND HUMAN UNITY

15. From this perspective it is possible to look in a new way at the disappointments and obstacles to which we have referred in the previous section. In the course of our report we shall suggest ways in which some of these difficulties may be met, but at the outset we must confess that many of these arise because of a wrong understanding of the nature and calling of the church. When the church is understood as an end in itself and not as a sign and foretaste of the kingdom, then the quest for ecclesiastical unity is seen as irrelevant to the great issues of God's rule of justice and peace. For, as has to be sadly confessed, the church itself has often been guilty of complicity in and perpetration of all kinds of injustices to those who – for whatever reason – are pushed to the margins of society. It has sometimes condoned and even called down God's blessing on violence. Too often its theological statements have pretended to a universal truth above all party conflict, but in fact they have reflected the interests of those who wielded power. They have been ideologically tainted.

16. In this situation, it is often said, discussions about the respective merits of bishops and presbyteries are an irrelevance. The unification of these corrupted churches would make matters not better but worse. The real divisions are not the traditional ones of faith and order, but the divisions on issues of justice and peace. The first need, therefore, is that the churches themselves should be liberated from captivity to the interests of the powerful in order to become instruments of liberation for others.

---

[1] Eschatology is that part of Christian doctrine which concerns the last things – the coming again of Christ, judgment, the kingdom of God and eternal life.

17. These often passionate affirmations must serve to call us back from a false view of the church to one which is dynamic and missionary. This will mean that our quest for Christian unity is seen steadily in the context of God's purpose to reconcile all people and all things in Christ. According to the fourth gospel Jesus said: "I, when I am lifted up will draw all men to myself" (John 12:32). The church is called to be the first-fruits and sign of that promise which is for all mankind. Its disunity is a sin against that promise. Church unity would be a false unity if it were not for the sake of the fulfilling of that promise in all its universal scope. The Faith and Order movement was born in the context of a missionary concern. The pioneers of the movement drew their inspiration and their guidance from the prayer of Jesus that his disciples might be one "so that the world may believe" (John 17:21). They sought unity not as an end in itself but for the sake of mission. Yet it must be acknowledged that this perspective has sometimes been lost. It needs to be reaffirmed that if we seek for unity among Christians it can only be in order that the church may become a more credible sign, instrument and foretaste of God's purpose to "unite all things with Christ as head" (Col.1:19f.; cf. Eph. 1:10).

18. If it is wrong to separate the question of church unity from the question of the unity of humankind, it is also wrong and delusive to propose "justice" and "peace" as goals to be sought apart from a shared life in Christ. If "justice" is conceived as an abstract principle, the pursuit of it is a recipe for endless war, because all human beings overestimate what is due to themselves and underestimate what is due to others. Belligerents invariably claim to be fighting for justice. The Christian faith is that God's justice has been made manifest and available in the actual event of Christ's atonement, and that it is here at the cross that it can be received as a gift by faith and become the basis for actual justice among human beings. So also "peace" pursued as an abstract concept can only delude us. The most devastating wars are fought among the promoters of rival programmes for peace. The Christian faith is that God has made peace through Jesus "by the blood of his cross" (Col. 1:20), so establishing the one valid centre for the unity of the whole human family. But these statements are mere words unless they are embodied (even if only provisionally) in a visible community in which the righteousness of God and the peace of God are actually known and experienced in reality – even though it is only a foretaste of the full reality. The church is not authorized or empowered to represent a justice and a peace other than the justice and peace offered to the world in the atoning work of Christ. But it contradicts its own nature and calling when its members are unable to live together in a reconciled fellowship. Concern for the unity of all humankind is the only proper context for the quest of church unity, it is not a reason for abandoning that quest.

A WIDER PERSPECTIVE

19. It may help the reader of this report to understand its main thrust if we record how we came to put together our dual concern for the unity of the church and for the unity of humanity. The initial approach of our European and North American members was to look again at the theological and sociological factors which have kept our churches apart (see, for example, §§6-14 above). Such topics as "establishment" in England and "subscription to confessions" in the Reformed churches of Great Britain, have too often been examined politically and ecclesiastically rather than theologically and pastorally. This has impeded ecumenical advance, the phrase "national church" being so differently understood in diverse denominational settings.

20. The commission was made very conscious of the need to distinguish the purely cultural and political factors in the traditions of separated Anglican and Reformed churches. The disentangling of some of these factors gave a new reality to the commission's task, helping us to focus more clearly on the biblical and theological basis for the exchange of views, and so to follow a properly theological line in the faith and order discussion.

21. These theological and sociological factors had their sources in Europe and North America; but it was disturbing to recognize just how many of the ecclesiastical, political, social and national tensions and misunderstandings, which affect relationships among our member churches in the United Kingdom churches, had been exported to territories of the British Commonwealth and elsewhere, affecting indigenous churches, both Anglican and Reformed, in such areas. These inherited prejudices and divisions still cause perplexity and leave traces of strain and antagonism in many third-world churches.

22. The initial approach of those coming from Anglican and Reformed churches in the third world, to serve on this small international group, was to stress the seeming irrelevance of many traditional discussions on Christian unity and church reunion in the face of the desperate social problems facing their countries. From South Africa we were warned of new and perhaps graver threats to the unity of the churches based on racial discrimination, and from Latin America we were made aware of the divisions between Christians, some supporting oppressive systems and others opting for the struggle to end them. The North Americans warned of sexual discrimination in the church. The plea of our members from the third world was to make "orthopraxis" the significant issue between divided churches, notably the position taken by individual churches on the issue of apartheid in Southern Africa. Agreement on Christian principles and practice was presented as the first priority in bringing churches together. A response to this third-world sense of urgency over "orthopraxis" in a threatened world introduced a salutary note of realism into the discussions, and led the participants to take a fresh look at priorities in the ecumenical movement.

23. All this meant a new emphasis on the unity of the human race as the goal of the Christian gospel, with the kingdom of God restored as a focus for ecclesiology. The commission proceeded with its task with a world-related feeling of urgency, seeing its theological task to be not so much academic as essentially evangelical. The faith and order task was then taken up in terms of the final goal of the kingdom. This numerically small Anglican-Reformed International Commission worked in this freshly discovered worldwide context and within the ultimate dimension of the kingdom of God – that is to say, the reign of God in which creation and human community are renewed by the Spirit through their transformation in Christ.

24. This concern for the unity of humanity in the purpose of God provided the antidote to the self-centredness referred to in paragraph 14 above. We realized that the most effective way of overcoming the apathy which is threatening the ecumenical movement is to put much more closely together concern for the unity of the church and for the unity of humanity in the purpose of God. The rest of our report attempts to do this.

II. The church: God's apostolic people

Debtors to grace

25. In spite of all the factors which continue to keep our two traditions apart, we join with the whole Christian family in confessing one, holy, catholic and apostolic

church. The goal of church unity is the reconciliation of humanity and the whole universe to God, and the source and impetus for that unity are to be found in God himself; for the gospels testify to the unity between Jesus Christ and the Father (John 10:30; Matt. 11:27), and between the Father and the Spirit (John 15:26), and Jesus prays that his disciples may be drawn into that unity (John 17:21). The pattern of unity in diversity is thus in the Godhead. The God whose being is holy love, uniting the Father, Son and Spirit, draws us by the work of the Spirit into participation in the Son's love and obedience to the Father. This same holy love draws us to one another. This is grace, and to reject one another is to reject God's grace. The reason why we can never rest content in our separation is the unlimited grace of God the Father, who has accepted us in the beloved Son and bound us together in his own life by the power of the Holy Spirit – a life in which we are called to reflect both the unity and diversity of the Godhead. If then we refuse to accept one another in Christ we flout the grace by which he has accepted us and by which we live.

26. God by this sheer grace has called a people to be bound to him in total fidelity. The Old Testament portrays the Lord as the lover who for ever seeks the faithfulness of his own bride. The New Testament bears witness to the decisive events in which the Father sent forth his own beloved Son to take upon himself and redeem our sin-stained humanity, and anointed him by the Spirit to do the mighty works which manifest his kingly presence. The climax of these mighty works was the victorious passion in which the ruler of this world was cast down from his seat of power. With that victory accomplished, Jesus sent forth his disciples, empowered by the Spirit, to continue that which he had been sent by the Father to do (John 20:19-23). This purpose of the Father is nothing less than "to reconcile all things to himself, whether on earth or in heaven" in Christ who is both the head of the whole cosmos and also the head of that body which is sent into the world as the first-fruits of his reconciling work (Col. 1:15-23). As those who have been "reconciled in his body of flesh by his death" (v.22) they are to 'hold fast to the head', from whom the whole body, nourished and knit together through its joints and ligaments, grows with a growth that is from God" (Col. 2:19). They thus belong already to the new creation in which all the natural barriers that hold human beings apart are transcended (Col. 3:11).

27. All of our life in Christ – as Paul never tires of insisting – is based on "the immeasurable riches of (God's) kindness towards us in Christ Jesus" (Eph. 2:7). This kindness is despised and flouted when we fail to live together in that unity which his unconditional kindness both enables and requires. We are summoned to accept one another as freely as God in Christ has accepted us (Rom. 15:7). If we have been "reconciled to God in one body through the cross" (Eph. 2:16), then to break into fractions is to commit the enormity of dismembering the body of our Saviour (1 Cor. 1:13). The life which we share in Christ is both deeply personal and inescapably corporate. The love of God poured into our hearts by the Spirit binds us at the same time to our brothers and sisters. This love is continually renewed through an interior commitment in love and obedience to the Saviour. This is something profoundly personal. But it expresses itself in a commitment of love and obedience to the other ("be servants one of another") which issues in the life of a visible human community. Hence it is that in that prayer in which Jesus consecrated himself as an offering to the Father, and in the same act consecrated his disciples to be offered in him, he also prayed that they might be kept in the same unity which binds him to the Father. Their corporate life is to be

nothing less than a real participation in the life of the triune God – a life lived always in Christ and offered to the Father through the power of the Spirit. When it is so, there will be a credible witness to the world of God's action in Christ (John 17:21).

28. The prayer of Jesus from which these words are taken acknowledges, as does the whole gospel, the darkness in which the light shines. The gospel of God's grace can be rejected and seen not as good news but as threat. People may choose darkness rather than light, and the church, which is sent not to judge but to bring the word of salvation, can become the occasion for conflict and rejection. Christ, who is the rock on whom we build, is the stone of stumbling for those who reject his invitation to enter the new age and become children who live only by grace. We are warned at many points in scripture that judgment begins with the house of God and not all who say "Lord, Lord" will be acknowledged by the Lord at the end as his. We are not permitted to prescribe limits to unity or to pretend that there are none. This does not lessen but heightens the urgency of the quest for unity. We are sent to call all people to the faith and obedience of Christ and we must trust him to gather his own at the end.

First-fruits of a new creation

29. It is essential to approach the question of unity among Christians in this missionary and eschatological context. The church is sent into the world as sign, instrument and first-fruits of a reality which comes from beyond history – the kingdom, or reign of God. The unity of the church is not simply an end in itself because the church does not exist for itself but for the glory of God and as a sign, instrument and first-fruits of his purpose to reconcile all things in heaven and earth through Christ. Nor is the unity of the church merely a means to an end, for the church already enjoys a foretaste of that end, and is only a sign and instrument in so far as it is a foretaste. Life in Christ is the end for which all things were made, not a means to an end beyond it.

30. The church is thus a provisional embodiment of God's final purpose for all human beings and for all creation. It is an embodiment because it is a body of actual men and women chosen by God to share through the Spirit in the life of Christ and so in his ministry in the world. It is provisional in a double sense: only part of the human family has been brought into its life, and those who have been so brought are only partly conformed to God's purpose. If they were fully conformed they would be fully reconciled to one another. The quest for unity is one aspect of the church's acting out of her unceasing prayer: "Your kingdom come." By holding steadily in view both the corporeality of the church, its embodiment of Christ's life in the life of an actual community, and its provisionality in relation to the kingdom, we are able to expose the fallacies underlying the three following arguments which are often directed against the quest for visible unity.

31. (a) Some affirm that concern for unity deflects attention from the more urgent business of evangelism, and they (correctly) point out that groups less interested in unity are often among the most successful in achieving numerical growth. To this it must be replied that if the church were an end in itself then it would follow that multiplication of numbers would be the criterion by which priorities should be judged, but if the church is a sign and first-fruits of the reconciliation of all things in Christ, the fruit of evangelism should be communities reconciled to one another in Christ. If men and women are not being drawn into the one body, we must ask whether in fact their growth in Christ is not being stunted. "Rather, speaking the truth in love, we are to

grow up in every way into him who is the head, into Christ, from whom the whole body, joined and knit together by every joint with which it is supplied, when each part is working properly, makes bodily growth and upbuilds itself in love" (Eph. 4:15-16). The mere multiplication of cells, unrelated to the purpose of the body, is a sign not of life and health, but of cancer and death.

32. (b) Others declare that issues of justice and peace are more important from the viewpoint of the kingdom than the ecclesiastical issues of faith and order. To this it must be replied that if the church were merely a means to an end, then it would have to be judged by its effectiveness in promoting a more just and free social order. But even the best social order is not the final goal of human existence. Christians have sometimes forgotten that the church, while it is only a provisional embodiment of the new creation, is nevertheless a real embodiment enjoying by God's grace a real foretaste here and now of the righteousness and peace and joy of journey's end. When this is forgotten, Christianity is turned into a mere ideological crusade, and its actions for justice and peace are robbed of their essential and distinctive character – namely the presence here and now of the peace and righteousness of God given freely to sinful men and women. The church is a sign and the first-fruits of the ultimate order which transcends history. In so far as it is a true sign and the true first-fruits, it will also have an instrumental value in promoting justice and freedom in the transient social order of history, but in so far as it contradicts in its own life the order which it is called to signify and (provisionally) embody, it fails in the one task which is entrusted to it.

33. (c) Still others say that unity must not be pursued at the expense of truth. This is right. But if the church is a sign and the first-fruits of God's purpose to reconcile all things in Christ, then all formulations of truth must be judged by their relation to the central reality of God's redeeming and reconciling work in Christ. Doctrines which deny or devalue this must – in the name of faithfulness – be resisted. Nevertheless it is not required that all doctrinal matters must be agreed before unity is possible. That would be to deny the provisionality of the church in relation to the kingdom. In fact it frequently happens that, when matters of doctrine and practice are held to justify continued separation, the supreme truth, which is Christ himself, is publicly denied in the name of lesser truths which are held in separation. We are more likely to reach unanimity as a result of accepting one another in Christ and then working out our differences in one fellowship than by giving them in effect a status higher than that of the one supreme truth given to us in Christ. The experience of churches which have taken the risk of union even when there had been wide disagreement abundantly confirms this.

34. Too often the concerns for evangelism, social justice and church unity are set against each other, different groups demanding that primary or exclusive attention be given to one or another of these concerns. The Father, however, sent his Son to preach the gospel, to proclaim justice for the oppressed and to draw together all his disciples into the unity of the Godhead. He has enlisted us to participate in his work through the power of the Spirit. He gives gifts so that all his disciples may perform their distinctive work as different members of his one body. Evangelism, social justice and church unity are not conflicting concerns, but are complementary aspects of the one mission of God in which we participate as accountable stewards. To restrict our concern to any one of them would be to abridge the gospel.

Sent to all the nations

35. As a provisional embodiment of God's purpose of reconciliation, the church must understand itself as a people in pilgrimage, accepting with gratitude the resting places given on the way, but always ready to move when it is clear that faithfulness to the one calling of the one Lord requires it, an Abrahamic community, ready to live in tents, looking always to the city whose builder and maker is God (Heb. 11:10). The decisions required with regard to the reunion of our separated communions have to be made in the context of pilgrimage towards a goal which no one has yet reached. This pilgrimage is a missionary pilgrimage. The church is apostolic both in tracing its origin through the first apostles and in continuing that apostolate today. The church's journey is both to the ends of the earth and to the end of the age. The disciples were called by Jesus to be with him and to be sent in the power of the Spirit. In the same way the church abides in Christ through the Spirit only as it goes with him on the mission entrusted to him by the Father.

36. This missionary perspective is being rediscovered in contemporary teaching about the church. (Consider the opening words of the Second Vatican Council's Constitution on the Church: "Christ is the light of the nations".) This rediscovery was necessary because the ecclesiastical forms which developed at the time of the Reformation (our own included) were shaped by the "Christendom" perspective of that time. Although the great reformers were seeking to return to scripture and the fathers to find models on which reformation could be based, their thinking was inevitably shaped by the society in which they lived, a society understood as Christian in which all (except Jews) were baptized, in which church and society were effectively coterminous, and which had no regular contact with the world of the non-Christian religions – apart from the military encounter with Islam as the enemy on the frontiers of Christendom. Consequently our theologies and ecclesiologies have been developed in dialogue (often polemical) between different versions of churchmanship rather than in missionary encounter with the unevangelized world. The rediscovery of a missionary perspective has been made possible by the experience of the worldwide church during the recent centuries of missionary expansion. This has helped us to enter again into the perspective of the New Testament, where the church is a small evangelizing community in a pagan society, ministry is primarily leadership in mission, baptism is commitment to that mission, and eucharist is the continual renewal of that commitment.

37. This missionary context provides new perspectives for the controversies about ministry, word and sacrament which have traditionally divided our two communions. We hope that our present report illustrates the validity of these new perspectives as we come to deal with these matters. It is important to hold this missionary perspective in close relation to what has been said about the provisionality of the church in relation to the kingdom. It has been said that there are two aspects of this provisionality; only *part* of the human family has been enlisted for Christ, and those who have been enlisted show only a very *partial* obedience. These two aspects are mutually related. As the church goes out to bear witness to Christ among the nations, its own partial understanding of God's purpose is corrected and enlarged.

38. This is because mission is not simply the action of the church enlarging its own borders. Mission is the sovereign action of the Holy Spirit who, through the faithful words and deeds of the church, bears witness to Jesus (John 15:26) and does his own work of convicting the world (John 16:8-11) and of leading the church into a fuller

understanding of the Father's will (John 16:12-15). As in the Old Testament, so also in the New, the work of gathering all the nations to become God's people and to worship him from whom their life comes, is the work of God himself. It is the presence of the Spirit, foretaste of the eschatological kingdom, which constitutes the effective witness to Jesus. The human occasions for the Spirit's work include both words and deeds, all springing from and expressing the life of the one body which lives for the praise and adoration of God. Where there is a shared life centred in the worship and service of God the Father, rooted in Christ as he is made known to us in scripture, interpreted in the teaching of faithful witnesses all down the ages, and sustaining the free exercise of the Spirit's varied gifts of speech and action among all the members, there the sovereign Lord, the Spirit, both gathers the peoples and leads the church into fuller understanding. It is within this missionary perspective that we can begin to overcome the partial understandings which have kept our two communions apart.

III. Life in the church

Orthodoxy and orthopraxis

39. The church owes its being to that which has been done once for all in the incarnation, ministry, passion, resurrection and ascension of the Lord Jesus Christ whom we acknowledge and confess as the Son, the second person of the triune God. The church lives only in dependence upon him, the head, and this dependence consists in faith, love and obedience. It has therefore been at all times the necessary concern of the church that faith, love and obedience should be directed exclusively to their true object. The church has sought, and must always seek, both in its worship and in its teaching, to find words which are faithful to the church's Lord. Orthodoxy means both true teaching and true worship. As we have noted above (§7), Reformed churches have tended to emphasize the former and Anglicans the latter, but we agree that both are essential and that in this respect each of our communions can learn from the other.

40. Orthodoxy is not maintained simply by repeating the same words. In its missionary advance the church is always required to find in the languages of those who are brought to faith from many cultures, words which direct their minds in teaching and worship to the one true God. Likewise, as the church continues to hand on the faith in each new age, it is required to find new words which, in the language of these new generations, will rightly express that faith. Both our communions, receiving the scriptures as the authoritative standard of faith, acknowledge the need for this continuing effort of reformulation both in teaching and in worship.

41. Although our predecessors took different paths at the time of the Reformation, they had a common concern to restore "the face of the ancient Catholic church" (Calvin), through a return to scripture and the fathers. Today both our communions acknowledge our dependence on the credal and liturgical formulations of the earliest centuries. Both recognize our need to remain open to the witness of Christians of other traditions and – since we contain within our membership people of many different cultures – to learn from Christians of all continents and of all races, so that our contemporary teaching and worship may truly express the fullness of God's purpose to reconcile all humankind in Christ. All of this is implicit in our commitment to the ecumenical movement.

42. Within this movement new contacts with the Orthodox churches have placed some of the interconfessional conflicts of the Western churches in fresh perspective. They have stimulated thought on the doctrine of the Trinity and its centrality by reopening discussion of the filioque clause[2] in the Western version of the Nicene Creed. Though this doctrine of the Trinity, fundamental to our faith, has never been denied in either the Anglican or Reformed tradition, yet we confess that it has not occupied the central place which belongs to it and which it has held among the Orthodox. The image of God in the minds of many people in our churches is a unitary one – the solitary creator, the prime mover of the philosophers. Consequently the doctrine of the Trinity has been regarded as an incomprehensible mystification of something simple.

43. Nevertheless it lies at the very foundation of our life in Christ, as well as of the faith which sustains it, that God – the one and only God – is Father, Son and Spirit in the perfect unity of love; that the divine being is therefore not solitary but always and from eternity a being in love; and that in our life in Christ we are made participants in this being-in-love – as Christ prayed for believers that they might be made one in the unity which he has with the Father (John 17:21). Just as we believe that man has been created by God to have his being-in-love, so in the church we participate in the life of the triune God in fulfilment of the purpose of creation. This must govern decisively our life in the church and our concern for the world.

44. Orthodoxy, which is both right believing and right worshipping – that is to say, belief and worship directed to the truth, the reality of the triune God – cannot be severed from right practice. Faith and love belong together with obedience. "If you keep my commandments", said Jesus, "you abide in my love." The church is under obligation to guard the true faith expressed, and constantly needing fresh expression, in teaching and worship. It must be able, when need arises, to warn against forms of teaching and worship which lead those who use them away from the true God, and if necessary to draw a line of demarcation at the point where falsehood threatens truth. But if faith, love and obedience belong inseparably together, it follows that the church may have to take like action in respect of conduct which contradicts the truth by which the church lives. The World Alliance of Reformed Churches has recently acted – after years of unproductive discussion – to suspend from its membership churches which adhere to the ideology and practice of apartheid. The breach has occurred in this case not because of differences about the doctrines which have traditionally divided the churches, but because of adherence to a practice held to be incompatible with obedience to Christ. It is a matter of orthopraxis rather than of orthodoxy. There are many Christians who think that racial separation is not the only issue of praxis on which the church may have to use the word "heresy" and exercise the discipline of suspension from communion. The continued acquiescence of churches in the monstrous injustices of the present international economic order may well be another such matter.

45. No discussion of Christian unity in the contemporary world can escape this question. True believing (orthodoxy) should bear fruit in right action (orthopraxis). Yet, because Christians are sinners, they fail to embody in their conduct what they profess in their creed. The church is a fellowship in which Christ consents to eat and drink with

---

[2] In the original form of the Nicene Creed, still used in the Eastern Orthodox churches, it is said that the Spirit proceeds from the Father. The Western churches subsequently added the words "and from the Son" (Latin filioque). This addition, made without the agreement of a universal council, has been a cause of disagreement been the Eastern and Western churches ever since.

sinners. But the church is also called to be a school of holiness in which the members "teach and admonish one another in all wisdom" (Col. 3:16) in order that its members may be "presented holy and blameless and irreproachable" before its Lord (Col. 1:22). Conduct contradictory of our faith which refuses correction and which, as in both the examples we are considering, entrenches itself in a false theology or ideology, cannot indefinitely be held within the Christian fellowship.

46. We have to confess that our search for ecclesiastical unity will be disobedience to the church's Lord if it does not go hand in hand with the mutual correction and admonition of which the apostle speaks, and if it is not ready to face the painful possibility of excommunication where this correction is refused, or where the wrong practice is entrenched and defended within a doctrinal formulation which fails to acknowledge Christ as the sole Lord of both church and world. Such a painful possibility must be recognized. So far as our two communions are concerned, the division – if it occurred – would not be between but within each of them.

Baptism

47. Baptism has not been an issue in dispute between our two traditions, yet our common practice of baptism has not led us into that unity which is stated by St Paul to be the necessary implication of one baptism. According to him, all who are baptized into Christ constitute in him one body in which there cannot be divisions (Gal. 3:27f.; 1 Cor. 12:13; Eph. 4:4f.). We have to ask whether our failure to draw the proper conclusions from our common baptism is evidence of failure in both our communions to understand fully its meaning.

48. (a) According to all the four gospels, the beginning of the public ministry of Jesus was his baptism by John in the River Jordan. The practice of Christian baptism in water, which we share with the universal church, looks back to this decisive event, and it is here that we must begin to understand its meaning. John's message concerned the imminence of the day of the Lord. It was a call to repentance in view of threatened judgment. The baptism in water which John administered was a prophetic sign accompanying and enforcing the message. Jesus, the sinless one, went down into the waters of Jordan in solidarity with our sinful race, submitting vicariously to the judgment of God upon guilty sinners. The coming judge was the man judged for sinners, the Lamb of God who takes away the sin of the world. In that action Jesus was acknowledged by the Father as the beloved Son and anointed by the Spirit for his mission. This is the event which marks "the beginning of the gospel" (Mark 1:1; cf. Acts 1:22; 10:37). The triune God has taken up into his own being the sinful history of the world. "For our sake he made him to be sin who knew no sin, so that in him we might become the righteousness of God" (2 Cor. 5:21).

49. The baptism of Jesus looked towards its fulfilment in his total life and ministry. From his baptism Jesus is driven by the Spirit first into the desert to meet and master in single combat the power that opposes God's purpose, and then, having "bound the strong man" (Mark 3:27), into the towns and villages of Galilee to release those who had been his captives. The baptism had to be implemented in this active engagement with the prince of this world, consummated on the cross where the "ruler of this world" is cast out (John 12:31), and vindicated in the resurrection.

50. Jesus' baptism as the servant (cf. Isa. 42:1ff.) is thus a baptism into death, and he speaks during his ministry of his coming death as his baptism (Luke 12:50, Mark

10:38). In the Marcan phrase just referred to, Jesus warns his disciples that they will be required to share this baptism into death, and in St Paul's writings we are likewise reminded that our baptism is into his death (Rom. 6:3), so that as we die with him we may also rise with him (Rom. 6:5). The "one baptism", which following St Paul we confess in our creed, is the entire event begun in Jordan, completed on Calvary, and proclaimed in the resurrection.

51. (b) Until that event was complete the new dispensation of the Spirit could not begin. Pentecost presupposes Calvary and Easter (John 7:39). It is when the baptism of Jesus is complete that he can and does return to bestow upon his disciples the gift of the Spirit so that they in turn can become part of the mission from the Father and agents of his liberating power for those held in the grip of sin (John 20:22-23). And those who accept the call to follow Jesus are in turn incorporated by baptism in water in the triune Name to become, by the indwelling of the Spirit, part of his liberating mission, made members together in the one body of Christ and acknowledged as children of the one Father (Acts 2:38; Rom. 8:14-17; 1 Cor. 12:13; Gal. 3:27). In our water-baptism we are brought sacramentally into union with the once-for-all baptism of Jesus on behalf of all mankind, ourselves and our children, and we claim the Father's promised gift of the Spirit.

52. (c) Baptism means, therefore, the participation of believers through the Spirit in what Christ has done for us and continues to do for us as he shares with us his communion with the Father and his mission to the world. It is thus incorporation into Christ, into a life of dying and rising with Christ (Rom. 6:1-11; 2 Cor. 4:7-15), sharing with him his ministry as the servant in the fellowship of his sufferings and the power of his resurrection, immersed in his liberating death where our sins are buried, where the "old Adam" is crucified with Christ and the power of sin is broken. In baptism Christ identifies us with himself in his victory over the powers of evil, his ministry of reconciliation, and we believe that we shall be one with him in the final resurrection. The one baptism is therefore our common incorporation into Christ, into this common life of shared worship and mission in him. It is the visible and effective sign and seal of that gracious work of the Spirit by which the church is constituted.

53. (d) Baptism, by which Christ incorporates us into his life, death and resurrection, is thus, in the strictest sense, constitutive of the church. It is not simply one of the church's practices. It is an event in which God, by engaging us to himself, opens to us the life of faith and builds the church. As Jesus was baptized, anointed by the Spirit from the Father, and declared to be the Son, so we are incorporated into the church in the triune Name, and are commanded: "Go therefore and make disciples of all nations, baptizing them in the name of the Father and of the Son and of the Holy Spirit, teaching them to observe all that I have commanded you" (Matt. 28:19f.). Baptism is therefore never an uninterpreted action. As the voice from heaven proclaimed its meaning, so in preaching we proclaim in the power of the Spirit that "this Jesus is the Christ", and in every baptism proclaim his name. Word and action are inseparable.

54. (e) The gospel invites from us the response of faith and repentance. When Christ vicariously submitted for us to the baptism of repentance, and accepted the consequences of human sin for us on the cross, it was not to exonerate us from the need for personal faith and repentance but to bring us to faith and repentance in the assurance that our sins are forgiven. Hence we must not separate baptism from faith and repentance. With all Christians we acknowledge the necessity of faith for the reception

of the salvation set forth and embodied in baptism. Our practice of infant baptism does not deny this, but rests upon the priority of what Christ has done once for all on behalf of the whole human family, and upon the conviction that "the act of God in baptism finds its response of faith not only from the one baptized but also from the community of faith which includes the child's family. It is in this community, the church, that a child develops as a person to the point where, later in time, he or she personally appropriates the response of faith" (WARC-BWA report, 1973-77, section VI).

55. It has to be confessed that in both our communions many baptized as infants have not in fact been led to make this personal appropriation. This has caused some who have come in later life to a living faith to ask for a second baptism on the ground that their baptism as infants was invalid. We are agreed, on the one hand, that this situation is a summons to re-examine our baptismal discipline and the care given to the Christian nurture of those baptized as infants. On the other hand we must insist that the call for a second baptism rests on a failure to understand that baptism is primarily the work of God in Christ. The apostolic writers speak of baptism with the utmost realism (Rom. 6:3ff.; 1 Cor. 6:11; Col. 3:12; Titus 3:5). Something irreversible was done when we were baptized: God, through the Spirit, drew us into the death and new life of his Son. But, like the baptism of Jesus, our baptism is not an end but a beginning. We are committed to follow Jesus in his engagement with the prince of this world. Our baptism is to be completed, as his was, by going the way of the cross. This is true whether we are baptized as adults or as infants. It is therefore possible to betray our baptism – to become apostate. It is not possible either to undo it or to repeat it.

56. As the baptism of Jesus was a beginning, prophetically embracing both its fulfilment in his ministry and its consummation in his death and resurrection, so the baptism of a Christian is likewise the beginning of a process. It looks forward to a life of developing discipleship in the continual offering up of life itself until at death we say by grace: "Father, into your hands I commit my spirit." There is considerable debate within both our communions about the conditions under which baptism should be administered, and the ways in which its fulfilment in mature discipleship should be marked. We are agreed that baptism is the essential rite of initiation into the life in Christ; that baptism is in water and the Spirit; and that it is the beginning of a life in Christ which has to grow and reach full maturity. Beyond this there are matters which are the subject of discussion. While both communions have traditionally baptized the infant children of Christian parents, there is discussion within our churches of the propriety of this. Some churches permit both infant baptism and the postponement of baptism until the child of Christian parents can make a personal confession of faith. All our churches, moreover, seek to bring those baptized in infancy to confirmation or an analogous rite in which prayer is made for strengthening by the Holy Spirit (with or without the imposition of hands), and the person concerned is admitted to the full responsibilities of membership.

57. Further there are differences between and within our traditions about the meaning and conditions of membership. These have been shaped not only by our differing theological confessions but even more by our differing relations to society. Even in those parts of the world which were formerly identified as "Christendom", it is no longer possible seriously to think of baptism as the customary rite immediately following birth, and of confirmation as the customary rite marking entry into adult status – even though these ideas persist in some places. All our churches are, and increasingly

know themselves to be, in a missionary situation. Membership in the church, therefore, is seen as distinct from membership in the civil society. In this respect our two communions share a common experience. There are indeed places where baptism may result in a person being cast out of his society, and even in his death. But separation is for the sake of a true solidarity, for Christ was cast out in order to draw all humankind into its true unity. We are being reminded again that baptism is into his death. There is a difference between our two communions in the way they define membership. Reformed churches have tended to define it primarily as membership in a local congregation, while Anglicans, by the practice of episcopal confirmation, have emphasized membership in the wider church. These emphases, however, are complementary rather than contradictory and require further exploration by our churches.

58. The scene is further complicated by the rise of the "charismatic" movement within both our communions, which has led to an emphasis on recognizable tokens of the Spirit's presence as the proper mark of full membership. In some places this leads to a denial of the validity of the baptism received in infancy and the demand for baptism anew. On the one hand we must welcome and cherish all the signs in our time of a new quickening by the Spirit in the lives of members. On the other hand we must steadily maintain the eschatological perspective which we have tried to outline in this report. Our perspective is controlled by the hope of God's perfect kingdom. Our life in Christ is a growing up, a journeying towards that blessed consummation. Whether we speak of the baptism of infants or of believers, or of a "second blessing" by the Spirit, none of these is the end of the journey. All of these are markers pointing the way towards a goal which lies beyond our sight, but is known and cherished in faith.

59. These differences are for the most part not between but within our communions. A report such as ours cannot pretend to resolve them. In part they arise from a fresh sense of the missionary calling of the church, and are therefore to be welcomed. We believe that, in the perspective of a dynamic understanding of the church as the provisional incorporation of humankind into Christ, while not all our differences are resolved, we can together acknowledge our one baptism as a gift of God's sheer grace to those who can never be more than beginners in their grasp of it, as God's calling to grow up into the fullness of Christ and as the sign of God's purpose of redemption for all humankind through the passion and victory of Christ.

60. (f) At the heart of the New Testament teaching about baptism lies the biblical concept of "the one for the many" and "the many in the one" – that the one Christ gave his life for the many and that the many have their life in the one Christ. In the Old Testament God elected the one nation of Israel to be a royal priesthood on behalf of all nations, that in Abraham all nations might be blessed. This election of Israel to the royal priesthood found its fulfilment in the incarnation, in Christ's anointing by the Spirit to be the high priest of humanity, that God's purpose for all nations might be brought to fulfilment in and through him. God's purpose in the gospel is to restore our true humanity in Christ, that what was lost in Adam might be restored in Christ as the head of the race, the head of a new humanity. When Christ, therefore, calls the church to be a royal priesthood and baptizes the one church by the one Spirit at Pentecost, it is that the church may be the one people of God for all nations, sent out to preach the gospel and baptize the nations, that God may call the whole of humanity to become his people. It is in these terms that we understand baptism – the baptism of Christ for us and our common baptism into Christ. When Christ was baptized for us in the waters of

Jordan and in blood on the cross, we were baptized into his baptism. When he died we died in him. When he was buried we were buried in him. When he rose we rose in him. And now our life is hid with Christ in God. "For the love of Christ controls us, because we are convinced that one has died for all; therefore all have died. And he died for all, that those who live might live no longer for themselves but for him who for their sake died and was raised" (2 Cor. 5:14f.). This Christ, the one for many, baptizes the church by the Spirit, that as one body we may participate with him in his ministry of reconciliation, to restore to all nations their true humanity as the children of one father (2 Cor. 5:18-21).

61. (g) This understanding of our common baptism has very great practical consequences. If we are as realistic about baptism as the apostolic writers are, then we are already by our baptism one body, and the continued separation of our two communions is a public denial of what we are already in Christ. Moreover, there are consequences beyond these ecclesiastical ones. In the one man Jesus we see our common humanity taken up, redeemed and given back to us so that we can share it together – Jew and Gentile, man and woman, slave and free, rich and poor, white and black. Fidelity to our baptism commits us to affirm in word and practice the full, equal and God-given humanity of every person, to embody that affirmation in our public and political life, and to oppose and resist all that denies this shared humanity. Our baptism commits us to follow Jesus on the way of the cross, in warfare against the world, the flesh and the devil, until everything will be subject to the Father and own Jesus as lord.

The eucharist

62. As in our understanding of baptism, so with reference to the eucharist, it is in the missionary and eschatological context that we are enabled to see beyond the things which create divisions between and within our two communions. While there is, and has always been, a very great measure of agreement between us on the doctrine of the eucharist, it would be idle to deny that divergent practices and, even more, divergent styles of spirituality in regard to the eucharist have often made mutual understanding difficult. With regard to these differences, we acknowledge that we have much to receive from each other. We seek here to state what we hold in common.

63. (a) Baptism and eucharist rest alike upon the finished work of Christ in his incarnation, death, resurrection and ascension. Our baptism is a participation in the baptism of Jesus begun in Jordan and consummated on Calvary. By the same token when we are obedient to the words and deeds of Jesus on the eve of his passion, our celebration of the eucharist is a participation in the benefits of his death and resurrection. Both have, therefore, their basis in the one work of Jesus, accomplished once for all, proclaimed and made effective for us by the continuing work of the Spirit. Our baptism engages us to follow Jesus on the way of the cross; when we share in the eucharist Christ renews that same engagement with us and enables us to renew our engagement to him. He feeds his pilgrim people. Like the Passover, the eucharist is to be received as provision for an urgent journey (Exod. 12:11). Christ fulfils the eucharist in his people when the communicants go into the world to their daily tasks as his servants and as witnesses to the kingdom of God. This makes no light claim upon our discipleship. As the Lima report puts it: "The eucharist shows us that our behaviour is inconsistent in the face of the reconciling presence of God in human history: we are placed under continual judgment by the persistence of unjust relationships of all kinds in our society, the

manifold divisions on account of human pride, material interest and power politics..." (BEM, p.14, §20).

64. (b) At every celebration of the eucharist we rehearse the deeds and words of Jesus on the night of his passion. At that moment too there was urgency. It was a moment of separation when Jesus had to go alone to his death, leaving the disciples behind. But his leaving them was in order that, having won the victory, he might return to lead them on the way, the "new and living way" which he himself is (Heb. 10:19ff.; John 14:1-6). He must go alone, but it is in order that they may follow afterwards (John 13:36). So it is "for their sake" that he consecrates himself to the Father, in order that "they may also be consecrated in the truth" (John 17:19). And in this moment of urgency, of separation, and of perplexity, Jesus gives to the disciples the bread and wine of their shared meal with the words, "This is my body", "This is my blood", and adds the solemn command: "Do this in remembrance of me." This is the visible enactment of what is expressed in the words of the consecration prayer as given by St John (John 17:18). The disciples, who do not now understand the words or the intention of Jesus, are made participants in the action of Jesus to which he must now go alone, and they are commanded to do this thing through which he will become present with them and unite them with him in his consecration to the Father. And it was as the disciples obeyed this command that they came to know that he was alive with them in his risen life (Luke 24:35). In this sense we must say that the eucharist is constitutive of the church because in it Christ unites the disciples with himself.

65. (c) The eucharist is a memorial (anamnesis) of the unique sacrifice of Christ. This is more than a mere mental action of recollection. It is the "living and effective sign of Christ's sacrifice, accomplished once for all on the cross, and still operative on behalf of all humankind" (*BEM*, p.11, §5). When we "do this" in obedience to his command, we know that his words are true: "This is my body. This is my blood." We know that in the action of the eucharist Christ is truly present to share his risen life with us and to unite us with himself in his self-offering to the Father, the one full, perfect and sufficient sacrifice which he alone can offer and has offered once for all. And as he, the risen Lord, ever lives at the Father's side to make intercession for us, so we, united with him, offer up in this action of the eucharist our intercessions for the church and the world.

66. We have frequently been divided in our understanding of this point because of a pervasive dualism which separates what scripture holds together – visible and invisible, outward and inward, objective and subjective. We are of course all agreed that in the eucharist God is truly "with us": that he joins us to himself in Christ in and through created realities. There is a real presence of Christ which "does not depend upon the faith of the individual", even though "to discern the body and blood of Christ faith is required" (*BEM*, p.12, §13). The trouble begins, however, when we commence to argue whether this presence is associated with the outward, visible elements of bread and wine, or whether it is an inward, invisible presence received in the heart through faith. The fact is that both statements are true; neither should be so asserted as to exclude the other. "Eucharistic doctrine must hold together these two movements since in the eucharist, the sacrament of the new covenant, Christ gives himself to his people so that they may receive him through faith" (ARCIC Elucidations, §7).

67. There has also been a destructive polarization in our common history between emphasis on the preached word and emphasis on the sacrament. This is to put asunder

what is given to us in scripture and in the gospel as one. The gospel is news of the Word made flesh. The preached word is an anamnesis of Christ just as is the eucharistic meal. Hence "the celebration of the eucharist properly includes the proclamation of the word" (*BEM*, p.12, §12). Both word and sacrament have their actualization in the presence of the risen Lord. Our two traditions have tended to emphasize the one side or the other of this single reality – the word acted or the word proclaimed. We need each other's help to restore at this point the unity which should never have been lost (see §§8 and 39 above).

68. (d) Our being united to Christ in his offering of himself to the Father is a work of the Holy Spirit. The prayer of invocation (epiclesis) is therefore a proper part of the eucharistic action. "The church prays to the Father for the gift of the Holy Spirit in order that the eucharistic event may be a reality: the real presence of the crucified and risen Christ giving his life for all humanity" (BEM, p.13, §13). The eucharist is a making present of the once-for-all sacrifice of Christ. Joined to Christ in that sacrifice, the church makes an acceptable offering of itself in thanksgiving to the Father. We therefore invoke the gift of the Spirit from the Father to sanctify both us and the elements of bread and wine, so that in our eating and drinking we may be united with the one sacrifice of Jesus. "Sanctified by his Spirit, the church, through, with and in God's Son Jesus Christ, offers itself to the Father. It thereby becomes a living sacrifice of thanksgiving through which God is publicly praised" (WARC/RC, section 81).

69. (e) The presence of the Spirit is the foretaste, pledge and first-fruits of God's coming kingdom. At every eucharist the church looks forward to the consummation of that reign. "In this union of the church on earth with the risen and ascended Christ, which he continues to sustain through its eucharistic communion with him, the church is enabled by grace to participate in his reconciling mission to the world. Christ and his church share in this in different ways: Christ vicariously as Mediator and Redeemer, the church as the community of the redeemed to whom he has entrusted the ministry of reconciliation (2 Cor. 5:18), and stewardship of the mysteries (cf. 1 Cor. 4:1). "As often as you eat this bread and drink this cup, you proclaim the Lord's death till he comes" (1 Cor. 11:26). Thus precisely because the mission of the church is grounded in, and sustained through, the eucharistic communion with Christ, [the church] is sent out by Christ into all the nations and all ages in the service of the gospel, in reliance upon his promise that he will be present to it always to the end of the world" (*ibid.*, section 86).

70. (f) The eucharist which unites us with Christ and feeds us with his own life in his body and blood, unites us at the same time with one another and with the whole company of Christ's people in every age and place. It is therefore a condition for participation in the eucharist that we have forgiven one another and are in love and charity with our neighbours. Participation in the eucharist commits us to the ceaseless search for reconciliation among all for whom Christ died, and is incompatible with the exclusion of any person on grounds of race, sex, social distinction or culture as well as with the refusal to share material resources given by God for the benefit of all. In relation to all that divides Christians at the Lord's table we have to ponder the grave words of St Paul about those who eat and drink judgment to themselves (1 Cor. 11:17-32).

71. (g) Along with baptism, the eucharist is fundamental to and constitutive of the life of the church. It is the sacrament given to the church by her Lord for the continual renewal of her life in him. It is therefore the proper form of worship for the weekly

assembling of the church on the Lord's day, the day of resurrection, the birthday of the new creation. In neither of our traditions were the first reformers successful in persuading the great mass of Christians that it was their privilege to share in the eucharist every Sunday. Recent decades have seen in both our communions a recovery of the integral relationship between Sunday worship and the eucharist, but recovery is far from universal. We believe that it should be accepted as the norm in both our traditions.

72. (h) Churches as a whole have long been divided on the question whether participation in the eucharist should be open to all the baptized including infants and children, or whether it should be limited to those able to understand a course of teaching about its meaning. In common with the rest of Western Christendom, our two traditions have followed the second alternative, but in both there is a growing questioning of it. Some in both our traditions have been impressed by the example of Eastern churches which receive baptized infants to communion with their parents. It is indeed difficult to defend the practice of admitting children to baptism while denying them the eucharist. However, all of us would wish to affirm the need for a rite in which those baptized as infants, whether they have been accepted as communicants or not, are enabled, after due preparation, to make their own confession of faith and commitment to Christ, and are renewed by the grace of God through a further invocation of the Spirit, so that they can commit themselves freely and deliberately to share in God's mission to the world. The remaining questions about the relation of confirmation to baptism are not, in our judgment, such as to prevent mutual recognition of one another's members by the churches of our two communions. There are, however, questions concerning the ministry which still prevent such mutual recognition, and we turn now to consider these.

IV. Ministry in the church

Ministry of the church and in the church

73. The church is sent by God to witness in the world to his unlimited grace. Only in this double perspective of mission and of the new life in Christ experienced as the free gift of grace can ministry in the church and the ministry of the church be adequately understood. The church as a whole, and all ministry within and on behalf of the church, have one source in the action of the Father in sending the Son into the world anointed by the Spirit to announce and embody God's blessed reign over all humankind and all creation. For the fulfilment of this mission Jesus called others to follow him and – in particular – appointed twelve "to be with him and that he might send them out to preach and to have authority to cast out demons" (Mark 3:14f.). After his final victory over the powers of evil, Jesus returned to assure these disciples that he was still with them, giving them the gift of his peace, sending them into the world to continue his mission, giving to them his Spirit, and entrusting to them the ministry of release from sin and reconciliation with the Father (John 20:19-23). As he thus commissioned them, he showed them the scars of his passion, a reminder to them of the way his mission went and theirs must go – the way of the cross. The kingship of God and his victory over the powers of evil will be made manifest to the world only under the sign of the cross.

74. The company gathered behind closed doors on that first Easter evening was the church in embryo. It is to the whole church that the commission is given and it is to the

whole church that the gift of the Spirit is made. The church as a whole is constituted by this act of sending and anointing. It exists, therefore, not for itself but for the glory of God in the fulfilment of that mission for which Jesus was sent from the Father. The primary ministry is that of the risen Christ himself, and we are enabled to participate in it by the power of the Spirit. His ministry is entrusted to sinful men and women and it is only as debtors to grace that we can fulfil it. The mission of the church is an overflow of the grace of God. It is only as those whose sins have been freely forgiven that we can be the bearers to others of God's gift of forgiveness. This ministry is exercised by and through the entire membership of the church in the course of their daily work in the world. Every member of the church, therefore, abiding in Christ, shares in this ministry.

75. The same company gathered in that shuttered room was also the ministry in embryo. Those who were there commissioned and anointed were sent to call others to be with Jesus and, in their turn, to be sent. The disciples are to "make disciples of all nations" (Matt. 28:19). As they have heard and obeyed the call of Jesus, "Follow me", so they in turn are to call others, and these others are, in their turn, both to "be with Jesus" and to "be sent" in the service of God's kingdom.

76. Thus from the very beginning there is a pattern of ministerial leadership in the life of the church. It is to the whole church that the commission is given, but the church was never an unstructured aggregate of individual believers out of which a ministerial structure had to develop. On the contrary there was from the beginning a pattern of calling and following. The first disciples are both the first followers and the first apostles sent to call others to follow. And this calling is always to a double relationship with Jesus: to be with him and to be sent. As he sends them he promises to be with them – to the ends of the earth and the end of the world (Matt. 28:19f.). Leadership in the church means leading others into the company of Jesus so that – in him and by the working of the Spirit – their lives may be offered to the Father, and also leading others into the world to challenge the dominion of evil in the name of Christ and in the power of the Spirit. This double calling finds its unity in the cross which was at the same time Jesus' total offering of himself to the Father on behalf of all humankind, and the decisive victory of God's kingdom over the dominion of evil. Ministerial leadership in the church may therefore be defined as following Jesus in the way of the cross so that others in turn may be enabled to follow in the same way.

77. If ministry is understood in this way, the church is protected from two opposite tendencies: on the one hand, the tendency to regard the ordained ministry as something separate from the church, having its being independently of the whole body; on the other hand, the tendency to regard the ordained ministry as something created by the church in the course of historical development. The scriptures show us that "the church has never been without persons holding specific authority and responsibility" (*BEM*, p. 21, §9). Certainly, however, the varied forms of ordained ministry have evolved in the course of history. On this three things may be said: (i) The particular ministerial structures which are now embodied in our different communions cannot claim the direct authority of scripture. The New Testament cannot be held to prescribe a threefold ministry of bishops, priests and deacons, a presbyterian or congregational form of government, or the primacy of the see of Rome. All attempts to read off one divinely authorized form of ministry from the New Testament are futile. (ii) The church is a living body which should combine continuity of tradition with adaptation to new situa-

tions under the guidance of the Holy Spirit. (iii) Not all the developments of the past nineteen centuries are to be regarded as divinely sanctioned simply because they have occurred. The ministerial forms which we inherit have been developed in the course of the church's missionary advance through the centuries and among the nations. They are neither to be treated as immutable because they exist, nor to be rejected because they are not explicitly authorized by scripture. Our duty is first to receive and cherish them with gratitude, and then to learn, as those before us have done, to adapt and reform them under the guidance of the Spirit in faithfulness to the apostolic witness, and in accordance with the missionary needs of our day.

78. In both our traditions a wide variety of words is used to describe the work of the ordained ministry. Anglicans widely use the word "priest", but this has never been used in the Reformed tradition. Both our communions make use of the pastoral image of the ministry, but it is often used in a way which contradicts its missionary thrust. "Shepherd" in the Old Testament is the familiar title for the kings and other rulers who led their people, ruled them, guarded them and went before them into battle. The Good Shepherd in Jesus' language is the one who is willing for the sake of the sheep to meet the attacking wolves and give his life in the combat (John 10:7-15). And when Jesus entrusts to Peter the pastoral care of his flock he immediately tells Peter that it will entail learning to follow him on the way that leads to the cross (John 21:15-19).

79. The word priest is used in the New Testament of Christ himself, and of his whole body, the church. The New Testament does not use the word "priest" to designate any Christian minister. The word came into use early in the church's history to designate the bishop, and was then extended to his presbyters. Anglicans, in common with most Christians, have continued this usage. The Reformed, in common with other churches of the Reformation, abandoned the usage on account of its connection with a particular doctrine of eucharistic sacrifice, and also because it was not authorized by scripture. We are, however, agreed that since it is acknowledged that the whole church is called to be in Christ a priestly people (1 Pet. 2:5,9), and since ministers are called to lead, enable and equip the church for this priestly office, the priestly nature of the ministry cannot be denied. We can accept all the following words of the WCC statement: "Ordained ministers are related, as are all Christians, both to the priesthood of Christ and to the priesthood of the church. But they may appropriately be called priests because they fill a particular priestly service by strengthening and building up the royal and prophetic priesthood of the faithful through word and sacraments, through their prayers of intercession, and through their pastoral guidance of the community" (*BEM*, p.23, §17). We recognize however that the word "priest", used of an ordained minister, has acquired overtones which render it unacceptable to many Christians. We would not in such circumstances expect the word to be universally used. We would, however, wish to insist that while the word may appropriately be used, other words, such as pastor, presbyter, minister, are no less appropriate.

Ordination, authority, continuity

80. Those who may thus be called "priests" exercise their priestly ministry neither apart from the priesthood of the whole body, nor by derivation from the priesthood of the whole body, but by virtue of their participation, in company with the whole body, in the priestly ministry of the risen Christ, and as leaders, examples and enablers for the priestly ministry of the whole body in virtue of the special calling and equipment

given to them in ordination. The one so ordained is called to be a focus of unity for the whole body. Ordination is the act which constitutes and acknowledges this special ministry of representation and leadership within the life of the church both locally and universally. In the act of ordination, the church in Christ prays to the Father to grant his Spirit to the one ordained for the office and work to which that person is called, accompanying the act with a sacramental sign which specifies by the imposition of hands the one for whom the prayer is made, and – in faith that the prayer is heard – commits to the person ordained the authority to act representatively for the universal church in the ways proper to that particular office.

81. The Spirit gives gifts to all members of the church, equipping them for many kinds of ministry. All are called to be good stewards of God's varied gifts (1 Pet. 4:10). But not all are ordained. The New Testament does not give us direct guidance as to who should be ordained. From very early times ordination has been connected with the eucharist. In the eucharist Christ himself is present in his fullness, and the company which shares in it is therefore the catholic church in that place. It is not the branch of an organization of which the centre is elsewhere, for where Christ is, there is the catholic church – God's gathering together of the people into their true Head. But even in the New Testament itself we find that a problem arises where groups of Christians propose to celebrate the supper in separation from their fellow members. This seems to be the situation envisaged in Paul's remonstrance to the Corinthians (1 Cor. 11:17-22). How is the distinction to be made between the eucharist in which Christ is present in the midst of his universal church, and the celebration of a divisive group which is in the apostle's word "not the Lord's supper" (v.20)? This was a practical question which had to be answered. At an early stage Ignatius of Antioch formulated the answer in the general provision that a "valid" eucharist is one presided over by the one acknowledged by the congregation and by neighbouring congregations as its leader, or by one authorized by him.

82. It is clear, on the one hand, that this is a matter of the harmonious ordering of the life of the church. The one who presides does so, not in virtue of a different relationship to the life of the risen Christ from the rest of the body, but because – as a matter of order – he has been so authorized. But, on the other hand, it is clear that this ordering is of central importance for the very life of the church. It arises from a genuine concern that what is celebrated should truly be the Lord's supper. For order is love in regulative operation, and love is the fundamental reality of the church's being.

83. It is in this context that we must consider what is sometimes called "lay presidency" at the eucharist, which has been at various times a matter of dispute between Anglican and Reformed Christians. The practice of "lay celebration" has sometimes been advocated because it was held to be a necessary witness to the "priesthood of all believers". This advocacy clearly rests on a misunderstanding, since it implies that it is the president who is alone the priest. The practice thus contradicts the doctrine which it is intended to support. On the other hand there have been and there still are situations where, because of a shortage of ordained ministers, or because of very rapid missionary advance, there are congregations which must either have the eucharist without an ordained minister, or else have no eucharist at all except on rare occasions. In some cases it may be said that this indicates a lack of proper foresight on the part of the church's leadership, but this observation does not meet the immediate pastoral need. Reformed churches have therefore frequently taken the view that a layperson should

be given authority by the church to preside at the eucharist in such circumstances. This is justified on the ground that the orderly modification of normal practice may meet particular pastoral needs, and fulfil the intention which the general practice is intended to serve. The general rule should remain that the president at the eucharist should be the person who has, by ordination, received the authority so to preside, and the church ought to order its affairs in such a way that this proper rule may be kept. The presidency of the ordained person does not depend upon his possessing a priesthood which others lack; it depends upon the good ordering which is essential to the life of the church as it exercises corporately the priesthood given to it by the one who is alone the good High Priest.

84. We associate ourselves with the following exposition of the threefold nature of ordination as given in the WCC statement:

a) Ordination is an invocation to God that the new minister be given the power of the Holy Spirit in the new relation which is established between this minister and the local community and, by intention, the church universal. The otherness of God's initiative, of which the ordained ministry is a sign, is here acknowledged in the act of ordination itself. "The Spirit blows where it will" (John 3:3). The invocation of the Spirit implies the absolute dependence upon God for the outcome of the church's prayer. This means the Spirit may set new forces in motion and open new possibilities "far more abundantly than all that we ask or think" (Eph. 3:20).

b) Ordination is a sign of the granting of this prayer by the Lord who gives the gift of the ordained ministry. Although the outcome of the church's epiclesis depends on the freedom of God, the church ordains in confidence that God, being faithful to his promise in Christ, enters sacramentally into contingent, historical forms of human relationship and uses them for his purpose. Ordination is a sign performed in faith that the spiritual relationship signified is present in, with and through the words spoken, the gestures made and the forms employed.

c) Ordination is an acknowledgment by the church of the gifts of the Spirit in the one ordained, and a commitment by both the church and the ordinand to the new relationship. By receiving the new minister in the act of ordination, the congregation acknowledges the minister's gifts and commits itself to be open towards these gifts. Likewise those ordained offer their gifts to the church and commit themselves to the burden and opportunity of new authority and responsibility. At the same time, they enter into a collegial relationship with other ministers (*BEM*, pp.30-31, §§42-44)

85. In the ministry of the word and sacrament the whole church is again and again enabled to receive forgiveness and to renew its participation in Christ's ministry in the world. The minister as leader has a representative character, to act as "the one on behalf of the many", so that the whole church is represented in his person as he carries in his heart the concerns of all his people. He does not act in his own name, but in the name of Christ, and in the name of the whole body of Christ, so that he is at once the mouthpiece of our Lord and the mouthpiece of his flock. This is acknowledged in ordination, both in the case of those who ordain and of those who are ordained. Those who ordain act in the name of Christ and of the whole catholic church, and the one who is ordained is set apart to act as a minister, not of one denomination, but of the one body of Christ.

86. Ordination involves as part of its essential nature the entrusting of authority to the ordained person to act focally and representatively for the whole church. The ordained ministry has therefore always been seen as both a sign of unity in the church and a means of maintaining it. For the same reason the ordained ministry is inevitably the point at which issues arising from the disunity of the church are most sharply

focused. Ministry, which is properly a sign of unity and continuity, has become the most obvious symbol of division.

87. We confess one holy catholic and apostolic church. In the ordination rites of both our traditions, we make our invocation to the Father in the name of Christ and therefore intend that the ordination is to the ministry of his universal church carrying an authorization universally valid. In fact, because we are divided, the prayers are not the prayers of the whole church and the authorization is not acknowledged by the whole church. In particular our two communions are divided at this point because of different views about the role of the continuity of ordination in signifying and safeguarding unity.

88. The church lives in historic continuity from Christ's coming until his coming again. This continuity is grounded in the gift to the church of the Spirit through whom we participate in Christ's continuing ministry. In maintaining this continuity the church depends upon the written scriptures, the sacraments of baptism and the eucharist, the ecumenical creeds and the continuing transmission of teaching and practice from generation to generation, wherever Christian parents and teachers hand on to their children and pupils that which they have received. In this process of transmission there is always the possibility of distortion. As a corrective of this, the early church prized the continuity of public teaching in the great centres of Christian life focused in the personal teaching ministry of the bishops. This succession of public episcopal ministry could be appealed to as a ground of assurance that what was being taught was the authentic message of Jesus and the apostles. The acceptance of the canon of the apostolic writings in the New Testament provided a written record to which this appeal could be made.

89. Related to this appeal, but distinct from it, is the appeal to the continuity of succession in ordination. In so far as ordination involves committing of authority to certain persons to act representatively for the whole church, it is obvious that it can only be properly performed by those who have received authority thereto. Churches normally decline to acknowledge ordinations carried out by persons who have not been authorized by the church to act in this way. Historic continuity of office-holders is, in fact, the normal way by which the continuity of any corporate body is secured and signified. Anglicans preserve this continuity or succession through episcopal ordination; in the Reformed tradition it is preserved through ministerial ordination.

90. But ordination is not simply the committing of authority by the church. It is first of all an invocation to the Father asking for the gift of the Spirit to the ordinand. The answering of that prayer lies within the sovereign freedom of the Father to whom the prayer is addressed. In our divided state the prayers which we offer are not the unanimous prayer of the catholic church. Nevertheless, it is not open to us to say that the answer of the Father is defective. Our two communions, in common with others, have been led through our participation in the ecumenical movement to acknowledge that ordinations which were defective, both in that they were the prayers of divided churches and in that the authority of those ordaining was not the authority of the universal church, have been acknowledged and blessed by God who, being faithful to his promises, has entered sacramentally into these acts and used them for his gracious purpose. We have been led to acknowledge this in humble gratitude, and thus to acknowledge the reality of one another's churchly life. But this gives us no ground for concluding that the historic continuity of ordinations is an irrelevance. On the contrary it

is an element in the proper visible form of the church's unity in space and time, to the end of the age and the ends of the earth. We therefore affirm that the ways by which our separated churches are brought into unity must be such as to ensure (a) that the reality of God's gift of ministry to the churches in their separation is unambiguously acknowledged; and (b) that the continuity of succession in ordination with the undivided church is – so far as lies in our power – visibly restored and maintained.

Patterns of ministry

91. The patterns of the ordained ministry in the Anglican and Reformed traditions are on the surface very different. Beneath the differences, however, there can be discerned a common pattern which involves, in each local church, a chief pastor who works with a body of colleagues and a staff of helpers or assistants to forward the work of Christ in church and world. This pattern first appeared in the early church's division of the ordained ministry into the work of bishop, presbyter and deacon. While the tendency in both our traditions has been to truncate this pattern by effectively reducing the orders to two (bishop-priest, minister-elder), the classic pattern reflects an ordering which developed and was found appropriate in the life of the church – those, namely, of pastor, a collegial association for the pastor, and pastoral assistants to carry out ministry in the world. This threefold pattern cannot claim to be the only one authorized in scripture. The various authors of the New Testament point rather to a variety of patterns which existed in the earliest period of the church. But the threefold pattern eventually prevailed and was generally adopted by the church. The large majority of churches have maintained it in one form or another to the present day.

92. In both our traditions this pattern has suffered deformation in the course of history. We believe, however, that it should be accepted in some form for the sake of the unity and continuity of the church, both locally and universally, and for the sake of its missionary calling. But if it is to serve these ends, the ministry must conform to that of Christ. Christ has given the gift of ministries to the church "to equip the saints for the work of ministry, for building up the body of Christ, until we all attain to the unity of the faith and of the knowledge of the Son of God, to mature manhood, to the measure of the stature of the fullness of Christ" (Eph. 4:12f.). To the extent that ministry conforms to Christ, it reflects the character of God as revealed in the incarnation. As God in Christ deals with us in a personal way, so all ministry must have a *personal* character, providing in a specific person a focus for the unity and witness of the community. As God calls us into a reconciled fellowship, so all ministry must have a *collegial* character – exercised not by one person alone but in shared responsibility with colleagues. As the church is the body of Christ quickened by the Spirit, so the ministry must have a communal character, so that every member is enabled to exercise the gifts which the Spirit gives and so that the whole community is, as far as possible, associated in the process of teaching and decision-making. And as the work of Christ was that of the servant Lord who gave his life a ransom for many, so these three characteristics must combine in a ministry of service to the world for which Christ died.

93. How can the ministry of bishops, presbyters and deacons fulfil these three requirements? In the beginning these three ministries were the ministries of the local church. The bishop was the shepherd and leader of the local community; he presided over the celebration of the eucharist. He was surrounded by a college of presbyters who with him had the responsibility of teaching, preaching and leadership. He was assisted

by deacons who gave special attention to the diaconal witness of the community. Evidence for this pattern can be found in the letters of Ignatius. As the church grew, congregations multiplied in each place. This led to a shift of responsibilities. The bishop became the leader of several congregations while the presbyters became the shepherds of these congregations. In this way, and no doubt for good reasons, the bishop's office gradually became a regional one. It is evident that by this shift of responsibilities the balance between the personal and collegial dimensions of the exercise of the ordained ministry was destroyed. The question therefore arises for both our communions: How can this balance be restored at all levels of the church's life? As the churches of our two families try to answer this question, the movement towards unity will become easier.

94. In their attempt to return to the origins of the church, the Reformers of the 16th century reintroduced the threefold ministry in the local church. In each congregation of the Reformed tradition there was to be a pastor for the proclamation of the word of God and the administration of the sacraments. He was to be surrounded by a group of elders and deacons. Most churches in the Reformed tradition adhere to this pattern today, though the diaconate as a separate ministry has not been maintained in all places. In the Congregational tradition, however, lay leadership in the local church is normally entrusted to deacons, not elders. At the regional level the government is exercised by presbyters or representative groups elected by synods. The participation of the community finds expression at the local level through church assemblies and at the regional level through representative synods or councils in both the Presbyterian and Congregational traditions. Thus the personal, collegial and communal elements in the governance of the church are adequately expressed at the local level. But the Reformed churches have to ask themselves whether they attach enough importance to the personal dimension of the ordained ministry at the district or presbyterial level – that is to say, to the exercise of oversight in a particular way through one person together with and within a college.

95. In considering guidelines for the union of Anglican and Reformed churches, we call attention to the considerable variations of existing practice within both our communions. For example, in the Anglican communion the personal nature of episcopacy is substantially affected by the geographical size of the diocese and the number of people in the pastoral care of the bishop, and the office of deacon has taken new shape in Papua New Guinea and the United States; in some Reformed churches, elders are ordained for life and in some elected for a fixed term, while the name "deacon" in Switzerland and Holland signifies a much fuller and more active form of service than is found in the Reformed diaconate in other parts of the world.

96. Keeping in mind what is said above (§92) about the personal, collegial and communal dimensions of ministry, we must consider what changes would be involved in Reformed practice if a moderator of presbytery or synod were to become a bishop-in-presbytery, and in Anglican practice if elders were to be introduced in congregations as a welcome embodiment of aspects of service which Anglicans recognize to have been present among the many activities of deacons in the history of the church. As Anglican and Reformed churches unite in different parts of the world, there will be considerable variety in styles of ministry, corresponding to the variety that already exists within each communion. We expect Anglican-Reformed united churches to go on learning from each other's experience, particularly in the initial decades, within the forms of mutually recognized ministry on the way to a universally recognized ministry.

More detailed suggestions, no doubt limited in application because of the limitations of the membership of this commission, are offered in chapter V (§§110ff.).

97. Both our communions need to give urgent thought to the renewal of other forms of ministry. It is also perhaps necessary that both should consider afresh, in the light of contemporary circumstances, the relevance of the various ministries which are described in the New Testament under the names of prophets and evangelists. The role of the theologians in the life of the church could well be considered afresh in the light of the teaching of the Geneva reformers on the "doctors" (i.e. theological teachers) and of the teaching role of bishops.

Women and the ordained ministry

98. Our two traditions have not reached a common mind on the ordination of women to the threefold ministry. Practice varies in different cultural situations, but the Reformed churches in membership of WARC do not generally have theological objections to the ordination of women. In the course of the last fifty years most Reformed churches have begun to ordain women ministers, and they have taken this step out of conviction, and not because of a shortage of ministers. Where there is a theological objection to the ordination of women, it is usually based on biblical teaching emphasizing the headship of the male (see §103 below). However, even where there is no theological objection to women's ordination, it is not always accepted sociologically and emotionally. There is a substantial minority of Reformed Christians who do not accept women ministers. Even where there are women ministers there has been little serious consideration of the distinctive contribution that women might make in the ordained ministry.

99. Of the twenty-seven Anglican provinces three (including two large ones) have ordained women priests, as have a few dioceses in other provinces. Of those provinces which do not ordain women eight have formally stated that they have no fundamental objections to the ordination of women to the priesthood, others have stated that they do have fundamental objections, and others have made no decision. At present there are no Anglican women bishops. Some provinces, who do not ordain women to the priesthood, have ordained women deacons, and others are considering doing so. This difference of theology and practice has not broken communion within the Anglican Communion. In the USA a few Anglicans have left the Episcopal Church because it has ordained women; and it has caused tension and heart-searching more widely.

100. As a joint commission of the two communions we can neither ignore this question, nor pretend to settle it. It is an issue which affects the unity of the church both *within* our separate communions and *between* them. Differences of doctrine and practice on this issue have not yet substantially broken communion *within* either confessional family. However, it is the judgment of some that it was a major factor which told against the acceptance of the English covenant proposals for unity between member churches of our two communions. It is clearly impossible for churches which exist in the same geographical area but which take different stands on this issue to enter into complete union. It is therefore an issue the solution of which cannot be postponed much longer. We see no contradiction between the concept of the ordained ministries expressed in this document and the ordination of women. This matter is of equal concern to both traditions, and one on which we must work together.

101. The debate about the ordination of women to the ministry focuses upon three areas:

(a) Those opposed to the ordination of women argue that the force of nineteen centuries of tradition should not lightly be set aside; and that a decision on such an issue should not have been taken by one denomination on its own, but only by a universal council of all the churches. All those concerned for Christian unity will take this argument seriously, so long as it is not simply a device to block all discussion and change. How long is it right to expect those in favour of the ordination of women to wait, bearing in mind that there has not been a universally recognized general council for a thousand years? If they are truly concerned for Christian unity, both those churches who do ordain women and those who do not will desire urgently to meet and discover one another's motives and reasons for the stand they take on this issue.

102. (b) Some of those opposed to the ordination of women to the priesthood base their argument upon the maleness of Jesus, our one High Priest. They deny that a woman can preside at the Lord's supper, since the president at the eucharist in some respects re-presents Christ at the last supper. Those who support the ordination of women claim that the exclusion of women from this role is inconsistent with the fact that men and women share equally in the life in Christ and therefore in his priesthood.

103. (c) All those opposed to the ordination of women point to passages in the Bible which teach that women are to be subordinate to men both in the world and in the church. This subordination is traced to one of the two stories in Genesis of the creation and fall. It is reinforced by some of the practical teaching found in the Pauline corpus of letters, according to which women should not speak or teach in the church. Those in favour of the ordination of women claim that woman's subordination to man was overcome in Christ (Gal. 3:28), and they point out that very few churches now carry out to the letter all the practical teaching found in the Pauline letters. In most of our churches, for instance, women have very important teaching roles, and are often admitted to the diaconate. The debate on this issue is closely tied to a particular interpretation of the authority of scripture.

104. Whatever the outcome, we believe that this debate should be carried on in the context of the mission of the Christian church to the whole of humanity. What kind of ministry in the church will witness most faithfully and effectively to the fullness of Christ's ministry? What kind of ministry will enable the church to convey to contemporary society the good news that in Christ God has reconciled the whole of humanity to himself? The debate is not simply about the ministry. It concerns the nature of the church and of Christ's salvation of humanity, and is indeed central to our understanding of the nature and being of God.

V. Our goal

The form of unity

105. We are at one in believing that God intends the unity of his church, but along with our partners in the ecumenical movement we still struggle to understand and express the form which unity should take. It is clear that the church – like the human family as a whole – is and will always be characterized by great diversity. People differ according to national and political allegiance, ethnic and cultural character, and the thought forms embodied in their various languages. These differences will always be present among Christians, both within denominations and between them. Because the church is called to be a sign and the first-fruits of God's purpose to reconcile all things

in Christ, its provisional character will only be truly expressed if these diversities are also present in its life, and are yet at the same time held within a unity which bears witness to God's final purpose. Its life must, if it is to be true to its nature, neither destroy this diversity by the imposition of a false and premature unity which pretends to embody what will only be truly known at the end, nor absolutize the diverse elements by allowing them to destroy the unity which is Christ's gift. To put the matter another way: the sovereign grace of God in Christ which holds us together must not be regarded as a wholly hidden reality which does not have to be expressed in visible unity; nor, on the other hand, must we allow our premature vision of the final unity to deny the possibility that other visions may contain elements of truth.

106. What visible form of unity will correspond to this character of the church as the provisional embodiment of an eschatological unity? During the greater part of the church's history, when human society was less mobile than it is now, the divisions of the church were mainly geographical. The separated communions occupied, as a general rule, distinct areas. In the last three hundred years, however, and especially since the creation of new nations in America by the emigration of peoples from many different areas of Europe, the church in each area has been characterized by a plurality of confessional allegiances. And because a mobile society necessitates large-scale organization, denominational structures have been developed to support and unify the local congregation scattered throughout a religiously plural society and to coordinate their activities. The "denomination" as we know it is essentially a product of the North American experience during the past two hundred years, and has now become the dominant form of the church in most parts of the world. No one can deny that denominational organizations have enabled the churches to act effectively in many ways, and it is difficult to imagine the church today without them. Yet, as theologians have pointed out, their ecclesial status is very questionable. In the New Testament the word *ecclesia* is used to denote the local fellowship, the church in a region (Acts 9:31) or the universal church. It is a questionable use of biblical language to use the word "church" for the entities which we now call "denominations". Nevertheless there are some who affirm that the form of visible unity to be sought is the reconciliation of these denominations in such a way as to enable them to continue to exist in their present form while recognizing and accepting one another as optional alternative manifestations of the one holy catholic church.

107. At its third assembly in New Delhi (1961), the WCC made the following statement about the form of visible unity:

> We believe that the unity which is both God's will and his gift to his church is made visible as all in each place who are baptized into Jesus Christ and confess him as Lord and Saviour are brought by the Holy Spirit into one fully committed fellowship, holding the one apostolic faith, preaching the one gospel, breaking the one bread, joining in common prayer, and having a corporate life reaching out in witness and service to all and who at the same time are united with the whole Christian fellowship in all places and all ages in such wise that ministry and members are accepted by all, and that all can act and speak together as occasion requires for the tasks to which God calls his people. (New Delhi report, p.116)

108. At the fourth assembly in Uppsala (1968), this was further developed with special emphasis on its second part – namely the call to the "churches in all places to realize that they belong together and are called to act together". The assembly went on:

> The ecumenical movement helps to enlarge this experience of universality, and its regional councils and its World Council may be regarded as a transitional opportunity for eventually

actualizing a truly universal, ecumenical, conciliar form of common life and witness. The members of the World Council of Churches, committed to each other, should work for the time when a genuinely ecumenical council may once more speak for all Christians and lead the way into the future. (Uppsala report, p.17)

109. In later discussions this concept of "conciliar fellowship" was further developed, not as an alternative to the model set forth at New Delhi but as the drawing out of one of its implications. The fifth assembly at Nairobi (1975) further clarified this concept in the following words:

> The one church is to be envisioned as a conciliar fellowship of local churches which are themselves truly united. In this conciliar fellowship, each local church possesses, in communion with the others, the fullness of catholicity, witnesses to the same apostolic faith, and therefore recognizes the others as belonging to the same church of Christ and guided by the same Spirit. (Nairobi report, p.60)

In the Vancouver assembly (1983) the WCC recommitted itself to three things: (1) visible unity, (2) mission and evangelism, and (3) justice and peace. It recommitted itself to visible unity in the following words:

> The Lord prays for the unity of his people as a sign by which the world may be brought to faith, renewal and unity. We take slow, stumbling steps on the way to the visible unity of the church, but we are sure the direction is essential to our faithfulness. Since the Nairobi assembly there have been movements in many places, new united churches, acts of common witness, local ecumenical projects. There is a new theological convergence which could enable decisive steps towards one eucharistic fellowship. We especially thank God for the hope given to us by the *BEM* document and seek widespread response to it. (Vancouver report, p.2)

110. We believe that our two communions should endorse these ecumenical findings. This would imply that we are not simply seeking a modus vivendi between two globally organized denominations which would continue their separate though reconciled existence. Since we see the denomination not as by itself "the church", but as a family or fellowship of churches, we are agreed that Christian unity must in the last resort be discovered and actualized at the local level. Hence we seek the emergence of reconciled local communities, each of which is recognizable as "church" in the proper sense: i.e. communities which exhibit in each place the fullness of ministerial order, eucharistic fellowship, pastoral care and missionary commitment and which, through mutual communion and cooperation, bear witness on the regional, national and even international levels. Such churches would express both the unity to which God calls his whole creation in Christ and the diversity which properly characterizes the human family as God intends it to be. While we can only speak as members of our two communions, our intention in speaking of "locally recognizable forms of the universal church" is obviously directed to all who are called by Christ's name. Our hope is that our member churches might play a part in drawing together others also into something which might express locally the wholeness of the catholic church.

111. But what, exactly, is meant by the use of the word "local" in this connection? This question raises complex issues. Anglican polity implies a diocesan structure based on the bishop, a Reformed, a presbyterial or congregational one. In both traditions, however, popular understanding regards the local congregation meeting weekly for worship as the basic unit, and this should not be written off as a complete misunderstanding, since the fullness of the catholic church is there in the eucharistic celebration

of the Sunday assembly of the people of God. But if the church is to be truly the sign and foretaste of God's kingdom for the place where it is, we have to take into account not only our church traditions but the realities of the secular world in which the "local" church must make its witness. Except in very simple static societies, modern communities consist of various overlapping groups whose members are related through language, work, culture and common interest. In order to be effective in missionary outreach the church may have to encourage the formation of distinct forms of ministry and eucharistic fellowship for different groups in the same area. Yet these must be enabled to realize their unity through sharing the life of a diocese, presbytery or association. But even a large diocese, if it is small enough to have the real experience of unity, may be too small to embrace the life of a modern city. There is thus no simple definition of the phrase "local church" which is applicable to all situations, but we commend the following statement by a recent WCC consultation on the subject:

> The term refers to an area where Christians can easily meet and form one committed fellowship in witness and service. Every local church will normally gather in one eucharistic service. The conditions of the area may be such that there is need of several separate services. Even then it must be made evident that these communities understand themselves as one eucharistic fellowship.
>
> The area to be served may vary in size. It may be a village or a small town; it may be a city or part of a city. It should not be so large that the Christian community loses coherence, nor yet so small that its homogeneity favours separatism in the human community. The area should be so chosen that the power of the gospel to cross human barriers will be made manifest. (*In Each Place: Towards a Fellowship of Local Churches Truly United*, WCC, 1977, pp.8-9)

Our differing structures, congregational and diocesan, have arisen in the course of seeking to be faithful to our calling to manifest the new life in Christ in and for each local community. As we seek together the proper forms of a locally united church we cannot give exclusive importance either to the single congregation or to a larger diocese or presbytery. We must recognize the secular realities of each place, and seek forms of local unity and ministerial order which will manifest for each place the fullness of Christ's redeeming presence and power.

Practical suggestions
112. If our two communions are to become one, Reformed churches will have to face the question of bishops, Anglican churches will have to reconsider the diaconate and take into account the Reformed experience of the eldership, and both communions will have to take more seriously the role of the whole membership in the governance of the church. The following suggestions will not fit all the circumstances but are set out in order to stimulate study of workable structures which may be appropriate in each area.
a) It is recognized in both communions that the Reformed pattern, in which each local congregation has a minister assisted by a body of elders, is in conformity with a pattern which seems to have been common in the earliest times. The Reformed minister occupies a place analogous to that of the primitive bishops. In this sense the Reformed may rightly say: "We have bishops already."
b) It is recognized that the concept of the "local church" is different in the two traditions: for Anglicans it is the diocese centred in the bishop; for Reformed it is the congregation meeting weekly for the sharing of word and sacrament under the

presidency of the minister. However we define the "local church", we all believe that in every such gathering the full ministry of word and sacrament ought to be available as an integral part of the life of the congregation.

c) Even though the Reformed might rightly say that they have bishops already, it is accepted in most Reformed churches that some form of oversight is needed at a supra-congregational level. Normally this oversight is exercised by a corporate body – presbytery or synod. We think that Reformed churches should accept the fact that, at every level, oversight needs to be exercised in a way that is both personal and corporate. Personal oversight apart from the wisdom of a corporate body is apt to become arbitrary and erratic; oversight by a corporate body without a personal pastor is apt to become bureaucratic and legalistic. In fact many Reformed churches have developed forms of oversight at the regional level which combine both elements effectively.

d) It is agreed by all that personal oversight is to be exercised by participation in the one Good Shepherd; if not it is corrupted and corrupting.

113. What changes would be involved in Reformed practice if the moderator of presbytery or synod were to become a bishop-in-presbytery? We think that the following would be involved:

a) He would have to hold office for a substantial period, sufficient to enable him to develop a real pastoral relationship with ministers and people and to be known widely in the community as the representative of the church in the particular area.

b) The bishop would have to be relieved of other duties in order to fulfil this role.

c) The bishop's role would be more than that of presiding at meetings. The following extract from the ordination prayer for a bishop from the Church of England's Alternative Service Book may indicate the most important elements in the work of a bishop:

> Almighty Father, fill this your servant with the grace and power which you gave to your apostles, that he may lead those committed to his charge in proclaiming the gospel of salvation. Through him increase your church, renew its ministry and unite its members in a holy fellowship of truth and love. Enable him as a true shepherd to feed and govern your flock; make him wise as a teacher, and steadfast as a guardian of its faith and sacraments. Guide and direct him in presiding at the worship of your people. Give him humility, that he may use his authority to heal, not to hurt; to build up, not to destroy.

In other words, the one so ordained would be called to ministerial leadership in the whole life of the church in his area.

d) The bishop would need to have opportunities to share with his colleagues in other presbyteries in order to seek help and wisdom in dealing with pastoral problems. It is a matter for discussion whether this should take the form of a "college of bishops" exercising a distinct role in the constitutional government of the church, as in Anglican practice; or whether it should take the form of provision for regular consultation on pastoral problems without such a separate governing role as in the CSI.

114. Such a suggestion may not commend itself initially to some Reformed ministers. We would, however, commend it on the following grounds: that in every walk of life there ought to be a visible element of personal accountability; that every minister, including the bishop, needs personal pastoral support and help in his ministry; and that in his exercise of personal oversight the moderator/bishop would really be acting pastorally.

115. We also anticipate that the suggestions may meet with resistance from presbyteries on the ground that something of their present authority would be diminished. We believe, on the contrary, that an effective and sustained personal leadership, if rightly exercised, is the best way to ensure the authority and effectiveness of a corporate body such as a synod or presbytery.

116. In many languages there are several words which are used or may be appropriately used for the office of chief pastor. Each word has its distinctive overtones of meaning. It is not necessary that the same word should always be used, provided that the substance of the office is recognizably the same. There have been and are great variations in the ways in which the episcopal office is exercised, and while Reformed churches ought not necessarily to copy any existing Anglican model, there ought to be discussion among the churches with a view to developing styles of oversight which are congruous with the biblical witness and the practice of the universal church, and which are appropriate to contemporary circumstances.

117. If the two traditions are to come together in united churches, Anglicans will have to consider both the meaning and practice of the diaconate and also the significance of the eldership as it has been developed in the Reformed tradition. Anglicans are aware of the fact that the diaconate as at present exercised in many of their churches is not a genuine diaconate in any classical or biblical sense, but is rather a period of probation and preparation for the priesthood. Many Anglicans have been much concerned for a long time to seek the restoration of a genuine diaconate, and there are parts of the communion where this is taking place. In the eldership God has raised up collegial ministry which has clear mandate in the New Testament and which has proved effective in the contemporary world in many different situations. We think that Anglicans should adopt the eldership as it has developed in the Reformed tradition in order to give shape to emerging movements of lay leadership in the Anglican churches. This would mean the development of a number of elders in every congregation, normally non-stipendiary and not intending to serve later as priests, sharing with the priest in the pastoral care of the congregation in a manner which might follow in large measure the pattern offered by the present Reformed eldership. It is recognized, of course, that the words "deacon" and "elder" in the early church stand for quite distinct offices. But it is also recognized (e.g. in *BEM*, p.24, §22) that "the Spirit has many times led the church to adapt its ministry to contextual needs", and that the present function of the deacon in the Anglican church is pastoral rather than "diaconal" in the classical sense. There is therefore no reason why the experience of the Reformed eldership should not be made use of to enrich a renewed Anglican diaconate.

118. If such an office of elder/deacon is to be accepted for all congregations in future united churches, it would be essential to ensure that the entire membership of the congregation is enabled to take its proper share in the governance of the church. This would require provision for regular meetings of the whole congregation to consider matters affecting the life and witness of the church, and regular opportunities for the entire membership to choose representatives to act on its behalf in the governance of the congregation and of the wider church. The question whether such representatives should or should not necessarily be elders/deacons is one which would have to be discussed. We cite here the model of the congregation in the Uniting Church of Australia:

> The congregation is the embodiment in one place of the one holy catholic and apostolic church, worshipping, witnessing and serving as a fellowship of the Spirit in Christ. Its mem-

bers meet regularly to hear God's word, to celebrate the sacraments, to build one another up in love, to share in the wider responsibilities of the church, and to serve the world. The congregation will recognize the need for a diversity of agencies for the better ordering of her life in such matters as education, administration and finance. (Basis of Union)

119. Nothing said in this report should be taken to imply that ordained ministry is all we need. In concentrating attention on the steps required towards unity, we take it for granted that the life of the churches will be sustained as in any period of Christian history, by a great variety of lay ministries, full-time, part-time and voluntary – ministries raised up to meet needs, giving effective service and not to be regretted when their time passes.

Expectations of the present report

120. In offering this report to our parent bodies, we recognize that our member churches are in many vastly different cultural and political situations. We hope that the report will, so far as possible, be studied by Anglican and Reformed congregations together in each place. We hope that the guidelines we have suggested will be useful to Anglican and Reformed churches in different parts of the world who are seeking unity. We are encouraged by the degree of convergence already visible as each of our two communions seeks to reform itself. For example, the Reformed welcome the Anglican trend towards ministering baptism in the Sunday assembly of the people of God, and Anglicans welcome the trend towards more frequent celebration of the eucharist in Reformed churches.

121. The movement for unity has suffered in recent years because bilateral international discussions between confessional families have dealt mainly with theological questions, while the many multilateral discussions between churches in each place (e.g. in local councils of churches) have dealt mainly with practical issues, and the two have not been brought together. We hope that the theological work done in this report will be studied in relation to the practical problems in each place, and that, if possible, it will be studied by groups representing more than our two communions. In such local discussions the work of these bilateral theological discussions and the WCC document on *Baptism, Eucharist and Ministry* should be made use of. In order to facilitate discussion and promote the consideration of possible action, we have appended a number of questions to the report. We would welcome responses to these questions not only from our member churches but also from any national or local councils of churches which see fit to study our work.

122. We are aware of the fact that the things which keep Anglicans and Reformed in any particular place apart are often not the things dealt with in "faith and order" documents. The divisive factors are often of other kinds – cultural, social and political. We have to ask whether the widespread failure of our member churches to act on the convictions which they hold in common is not the result of lethargy, of timidity, or unwillingness to face change and, above all, of an acquiescence in social injustice and a lack of missionary zeal. In the present report we have repeatedly stressed the fact that it is in a missionary context that the true nature of the church, sacraments and ministry are understood. We cannot receive our proper unity without this missionary context. It is because we have been grasped by the vision of the kingdom of God that we are motivated to overcome divisions. As the churches in each place study this report together, they should ask one another whether this missionary perspective is in fact controlling their study.

123. We hope that those who study this report will have in mind seven things which we have tried to keep in view:
a) Participation in Christ and in the life of the triune God. In our different communions we are all participating, in the Spirit, in what Christ has done and is doing, and in his communion with the Father and his mission to the world and his will for peace and justice.
b) The primacy of grace. We are in Christ simply by the sheer unconditioned grace of our Lord who has taken us, unworthy as we are, into his company. We do not seek unity because we can approve of one another. We seek it because, when we refuse to do so, we treat with contempt the immeasurable kindness of our Lord who has accepted us as we are in order that he may make us what he would have us to be.
c) The world is torn apart and threatened with destruction by our selfish passion, greed and fear. The church cannot be the sign of God's reconciling grace for all humankind while itself remaining unreconciled, stubbornly clinging to the past.
d) The missionary calling. The church is the first-fruits of God's gracious purpose to embrace his whole human family in the arms of his love. While we think only of ourselves and of what is helpful to us, we miss what he has in store for us. It is when we turn towards the world as witnesses, heralds and servants of his kingdom, that we shall learn the secret of unity.
e) The other discussions – bilateral and multilateral in which our two communions have taken part.
f) The experience of united churches. Our two traditions are represented (with others) in the united churches of the Indian sub-continent, the formation of which was inspired by the vision of a church locally united and reflecting in its local unity the unity of the universal church. These churches have now a long and precious experience of living and growing together in unity. Those who laboured and prayed for the union of these churches believed that their example would encourage others to follow, but this hope has been disappointed. The united churches, instead of being the vanguard of a movement for unity, have become isolated. In contradiction of their own purpose, they are in danger of being seen as just a new denomination. We think it imperative that, as far as possible, they should be drawn into the further discussions with us, both so that their experience may be available to us, and also that their threatened isolation may be avoided. We would hope that other world confessional families which are involved in the Indian unions (Methodists, Baptists, Disciples, Lutherans) would wish to take similar actions in so far as they are involved in bilateral conversations.
g) The experience for many of our member churches who have received mutual encouragement and correction through their membership in the World Council of Churches.

124. Throughout our conversations we have been led to see all our work in the perspective of the church's missionary calling, acknowledging that the church is but a provisional embodiment of what is promised at the end. The church is – to use again the familiar image – a pilgrim people. The church must therefore be willing to move when the Lord calls it to do so. This is our final, and perhaps most important word. Many of the gravest warnings in scripture are addressed to those who are unwilling to move forward in response to the call and promise of God (e.g. Heb. 3:12-19). The call to unity challenges our sloth and unbelief with a summons to look up and listen to the voice of

the living God who has called us to be one as he is one, and who is able to complete what he has begun in us. We may well take to ourselves the call addressed to an unbelieving company on the brink of the Red Sea: "Tell the people of Israel to go forward" (Exod. 14:15).

VI. Recommendations

1. We invite Anglican and Reformed churches to pray for each other regularly. To this end we ask the Anglican Consultative Council and the World Alliance of Reformed Churches to find ways of encouraging the widest possible use of the ecumenical prayer cycle, and we ask the Anglican Consultative Council to relate the Anglican prayer cycle more closely to the ecumenical prayer cycle.
2. Having regard to the differing degrees of relationship between the churches of our two communions in various parts of the world, we urge them to embark on the next stage towards unity, in the light of the findings of this report.
3. We recommend that our member churches examine carefully the issues raised under the heading "What keeps us apart" (§§6-14).
4. We recommend that the churches of both traditions undertake a fresh examination of the implications of our common practice of baptism – wherever possible together, but certainly sharing their findings.
5. We recommend that where churches of our two communions are committed to going forward to seek visible unity, a measure of *reciprocal* communion should be made possible; for communion is not only a sign of unity achieved, but also a means by which God brings it about.
6. We recommend that the churches of our two communions examine their structures to see if the personal, collegial and communal aspects of oversight are adequately represented at every level; and that if they are not, they give serious attention to such revisions as are applicable in their regions.
7. We recommend that our member churches in each place explore the possibility of moving towards the formation of united churches as envisaged in section V in this report.
8. In the light of what we have said in paragraphs 22, 44, 45, 61 and 70 of this report we recommend that, wherever possible, Anglican and Reformed churches seek together ways in which all forms of discrimination which devalue persons may be eliminated. As a step in this direction we urge our churches around the world:
    a) to work together to overcome those barriers which exist between privileged and underprivileged, black and white, male and female;
    b) to share their human, spiritual and material resources with those in need.
9. We recommend that our churches discuss the following questions at all levels – in joint groups where possible.

General questions
1. God has accepted us and made us one in Christ. Therefore we are bound to accept one another and live together in one body. How must we change in order to enable us to be one body in each place (§§19ff.)?
2. Are the concerns for evangelism, social justice and doctrinal purity compatible with the active struggle for unity? How in your experience are they held together (§§29ff.)?

3. Does your church engage in mission? Why is mission important? Are the motives for mission the same as, or different from, the motives for unity (§§35ff.)?
4. Are the obstacles listed in section I a sufficient ground for our remaining separate (§§6ff.)?
5. What form and extent of doctrinal agreement is necessary for the reunion of separate Christian churches? What relation does your answer have to the measure of agreement within your own church?
6. How far is folk religion a barrier to unity?
7. For good and for ill, in what ways is your church bound to and moulded by your culture, or by an alien culture?
8. How is your church conditioned by a sense of national identity?
9. In what ways is your church related to the state?
10. What are the implications of your answers to questions 7, 8 and 9 for your understanding of:
    i) the nature of the church;
    ii) the lordship of Christ in his church;
    iii) the prophetic role of the church vis-a-vis the state;
    iv) the mission of the church?
11. What importance has historic continuity in the church for the life of the ordinary Christian? How is this continuity maintained (section IV)?
12. What difference does the consciousness of belonging to a universal church make to the ordering of your church life and mission (section V)?

Questions relating to worship and the sacraments
1. What is the significance of people feeling uncomfortable in each other's worship for relations between the churches? Should sharing in each other's worship enrich us, or give us reasons for remaining apart?
2. To what extent do stereotyped images of other people's practices and institutions constitute a barrier to reunion, and what can be done to correct these?
3. Since baptism, as the rite of Christian initiation, is sufficient to constitute a person a full member of Christ and his church, what is the theological and pastoral purpose of confirmation or any analogous rite, and how are both related to participation in the eucharist (§§55ff.,72)?
4. The report states that Christ constitutes his church in the eucharist. What are the implications of this for the regularity and frequency of communion (§§62ff.)?
5. For participation in the eucharist it is required that we be in love and charity with our neighbours. We are in fact involved in structures of violence and oppression. What steps are you taking to deal with this contradiction?
6. Is the statement about "lay celebration" of the Lord's supper (§83) acceptable? If not, why not?
7. What does your church do with the consecrated elements left over after communion? What does this imply concerning your understanding of Christ's presence?

Questions on ministry and church membership
1. Since both our communions recognize each other's baptism, what prevents us from establishing full communion, accepting each other's members and mutually exchanging ministers as vital steps on the road to full unity?

2. To what extent does the kind of ministry exercised by your ordained ministers encourage or inhibit the ministry of the whole body?
3. Of the names you normally use for the ordained minister which do you think most appropriate to the task of the ministry of word and sacrament and of Christian leadership? What is the value in the names you do not normally use (§79)?
4. In any plan of union in your area how could the continuity of ordination with the undivided church be restored, whilst the reality of God's gift of ministry to all participating churches is acknowledged?
5. Is the description of ordination given in paragraphs 80-90 acceptable to both our communions?
6. To what extent is the ministry of your church at every level effectively personal, collegial and communal?
7. What changes would be needed in your area for Reformed churches to adopt a "bishop-in-presbytery" and for Anglican churches to accept the office of elder, as suggested in paragraphs 112-16?
8. What patterns of ministry would be appropriate for a united church in your area, given the missionary task of the church, the existing patterns in both communions, and the need for ministries to be acceptable to both world communions?
9. How should the ordained and non-ordained ministries at all levels be ordered so that ministers are always mutually accountable and responsible?
10. Does the practice of your church bear witness to the equal partnership of women and men in God's covenant? How could your church incorporate women more fully into every facet of its ministry and governance (§§98-104)?
11. There are some who believe that it is God's will to ordain women to the ministry, and others who do not. There will not be full unity between our two communions until we reach a common mind on this issue. What steps are our churches in your area taking together to seek God's will on this matter? Are women represented in all your discussions of this issue?
12. In the discussion of the ordination of women, what weight ought to be given to the effects of our decisions on other churches?

10. A Message to Our Churches

Geneva, Switzerland, 1990

Introduction

Baptists and Lutherans worldwide have, as a result of the work of the Baptist-Lutheran Joint Commission, caught up with their common history. That history stretches back to the relationships between Lutherans and Anabaptists at the time of the 16th-century Reformation. While present-day Baptist churches are not directly descended from the Anabaptists, this document indicates a sense of kinship. One historical reason for our international conversations has been the Lutheran condemnations of Anabaptists in 16th-century confessional documents.

The conversations of the present joint commission, 1986-89, have their immediate roots in correspondence between the Baptist World Alliance (BWA) and the Lutheran World Federation (LWF) which began in 1975. On the basis of contacts between officials of the two international bodies, and noting that regional/national dialogues had been taking place, it was decided that plans for more widely based conversations should be laid. The plans were twice postponed, but finally began to be implemented in 1984.

The first meeting of the joint commission was held in Rummelsberg, Federal Republic of Germany, in 1986. Subsequent meetings were in Wildbad, Federal Republic of Germany (1987), Dresden, German Democratic Republic (1988), and Smidstrup Strand, Denmark (1989). In each meeting place we reserved time to meet, to exchange views and to discuss matters of common interest with local Baptist and Lutheran church leaders.

As stated by the parent bodies, the aim of the four-year round of conversations has been "to clarify differences, convergences and agreements in thought and practice between our churches... findings should outline our present view of former condemnations, suggest ways of overcoming present difficulties and recommend ways to improve mutual knowledge, respect and cooperation between our churches".

As the present document indicates, members of the joint commission adopted a plan for their meetings which corresponded to a suggestion from the BWA that discussion topics include "faith, grace, baptism, ecclesiology and ministry". The multilateral Lima paper of Faith and Order, *Baptism, Eucharist and Ministry*, has been a significant point of reference during our work. We have also found common Bible study of pericopes pertinent to our discussions to deepen and enrich our mutual understanding of God's word, and also to help us break through barriers of terminology and customary habits of expression.

What we have written is the fruit of our discussions and of much preparatory work between sessions. It must now stand on its own as our report to the BWA and the LWF who appointed us. We have not been able to solve the problem of baptism, the problem which has come to symbolize theological differences between us. That solution awaits future leading of God's Spirit. But we have been able to say much together about matters at the heart of our common Christian faith.

It is a limitation of ecumenical documents that by them we cannot communicate successfully what these four years have meant to us as participants. We have been privileged to grow together in bonds of Christian understanding and affection, to recognize in one another members of the faithful people of Christ. We have prayed together, meditated together on the holy scriptures, sung God's praises with one voice. We have shared our visions of the church's mission and our calling as Christian sisters and brothers. We have sought to "bear one another's burdens, and so fulfil the law of Christ" (Gal. 6:2).

Our prayer is that our report may be the catalyst to bring together Baptists and Lutherans in various parts of the world who through their own common study might have similar experiences of unity in the one Spirit.

    Thorwald Lorenzen   Marc Lienhard
    Baptist chair   *Lutheran chair*

I. Authority for preaching and teaching in the Baptist and Lutheran traditions

1. THE NATURE OF AUTHORITY

1. Authority for preaching and teaching in both our communions resides ultimately in God who has revealed himself in Jesus Christ, and who is present with us in the saving and liberating power of the Spirit. This authority is grounded in the good news of God's love and grace; therefore it is authoritative, but not authoritarian. For both communions Christ himself is the embodiment of authority for preaching and teaching.

2. SCRIPTURE AND TRADITION

Scripture alone (sola scriptura)

2. Authority is necessarily linked to the Bible, because the biblical testimonies witness to God's saving and liberating activity in the history of humanity.

3. The scriptures belong to the Tradition of the Christian church. Within that Tradition the scriptures function to protect the gospel of Jesus as the Christ against influences foreign to the gospel and the Bible.

4. In the development of the biblical canon (the determination of which writings are included in the holy scriptures) the church sees the work of God's Spirit. By recognizing the canon, the church confesses that the scriptures, i.e. the biblical part of Tradition, are the measure of the rest of Tradition. The scriptures alone can ascertain that the Tradition remains true to the gospel. They alone can assure that the Tradition continues to tell the story of Jesus as Redeemer and Liberator. This is the meaning of the Reformation emphasis on sola scriptura which both Lutherans and Baptists affirm. This formula is open for misunderstanding, however, and therefore calls for interpretation.

Christ alone (solus Christus)

5. As Baptists and Lutherans we look with gratitude and reverence to the great cloud of witnesses that has gone before us. By preserving the integrity of the gospel through the turbulences of history, and by passing the gospel on to us, they have become to us fathers and mothers in the faith. We owe much to Tradition and therefore do not want to depreciate it.

6. We recognize, however, that not all traditions are in harmony with the ground and content of our faith, Jesus Christ. Our common Reformation heritage points to the fact that in addition to legitimate developments of the reality to which the Bible witnesses, teachings and practices have also evolved which we cannot understand as consonant with the biblical witness. Our churches therefore recognize and accept the gift "to distinguish between spirits" (1 Cor. 12:10) and "test the spirits to see whether they are of God" (1 John 4:1).

7. The Spirit of God and the scriptures point therefore to Jesus Christ as the content of our faith. In Jesus Christ the scriptures and Tradition have their centre and their norm.

8. Sola scriptura is not directed against Tradition as such, but against a tradition that departs from the biblical witness to Jesus Christ, or attempts to identify the living reality of the gospel with dogmatic formulations. Sola scriptura points us to Jesus Christ, as he is proclaimed in the scriptures, as the ground, content and norm of faith.

9. Jesus Christ is God's gift of salvation for humanity and all of creation. In and through Christ we are reconciled with God, our sins are forgiven, and we are liberated to become instruments of reconciliation (2 Cor. 5:18-20).

10. While Baptists and Lutherans agree on the authority of scripture for revealing the love of God in Jesus Christ, they may differ in the way they use scripture as norm for Christian life and practice. Baptists tend to seek explicit warrants in scripture for their faith, practice and doctrines, while Lutheran practice and tradition allow for greater freedom in matters which are not explicitly commanded in scripture. Both Baptists and Lutherans strive to live and work in harmony with the gospel as it is revealed in the scriptures.

The interpretation of scripture

11. As Lutheran and Baptist Christians we confidently point all persons to the scriptures with the conviction that there they can find the way of salvation, and be strengthened for their Christian life.

12. Some parts of the Bible are difficult to understand because they were written long ago in historical and cultural settings which are different from ours. Different readings in the received manuscripts of the biblical writings raise questions about the original texts. Biblical research and interpretation are therefore helpful in discovering the depth and riches of the biblical message. The authentic message of the Bible, however, is clear to everyone who wants to hear.

13. Since the Bible witnesses to historical events, and since we confess that in Jesus Christ God has become a human person, and that in the Holy Spirit God has become part of our human historical life, we must read and interpret the biblical writings not only in light of their historical context, but also in light of our own experience and historical circumstances, in order to allow the divine message to become a living reality ever again.

14. When we relate the divine message to the human context, we must be aware that we are always prone to use the Bible to validate our preconceived doctrines and practices. In confessing with the church through the ages that the message of the Bible stands over against us in grace and in judgment, we seek to protect the divine message from human distortions.

15. We believe that the scriptures have only been rightly understood when they lead us to Christ and instruct us for the obedience of faith in everyday Christian life.

The function of theology

16. Faith may go astray: we are aware of the constant temptation to compromise the lordship of Jesus Christ by protecting what has become important to us in our life and in our church. Our theological task is to discern what doctrines and practices are legitimate expressions of the Christ-centred biblical message and which are distortions. At the same time we must constantly resist the temptation to identify the living reality of the gospel with human formulations and structures.

17. Beyond this critical task, theologians have the constructive task of shaping fresh theological expressions which seek to refocus the gospel that we have received to meet the challenges of the present and the demands of the future, thus serving the tasks of preaching and teaching. Together we recognize the specific challenge of our time to provide an authoritative theological basis for our churches' involvement in the struggle for peace, justice and the integrity of creation.

18. Theology aims at enabling the church effectively to fulfill its function to proclaim and manifest the gospel in word and deed.

The role of creeds and confessions

19. Both our churches have written creeds and confessions,[1] but these have no independent authority alongside the Bible. They help churches and church members properly to interpret and understand the scriptures. They are "signposts" to point us towards the centre of the biblical message, where we find the basis and content of our faith, Jesus Christ. They are "guard rails" to keep us on the main road of Christian convictions. They are "road maps" that help us to reach the goals of our faith. They also function to help the churches preserve continuity within the discontinuity of time. Although creeds and confessions have their own historical *Sitz im Leben*, they serve to express the churches' identities, to explain the faith to others, and to fend off illegitimate traditions and practices.

20. A difference between Baptists and Lutherans can be found in the relative importance which they ascribe to such confessions. The Lutheran confessions were statements that articulated the reforms which their writers and endorsers wanted to bring about in the medieval church. Consequently these confessions were intensely formative of Lutheranism, and remain an inextricable part of Lutheran identity and theology. Lutheran pastors promise at their ordination to preach and teach in conformity with some or all of the Lutheran confessions.

---

[1] The major Lutheran confessions are accessible in Theodore G. Tappert, ed., *Book of Concord*, Philadelphia, Muhlenberg, 1959. For Baptist confessions see W.L. Lumpkin, *Baptist Confessions of Faith*, Valley Forge, PA, Judson, rev. ed. 1969; G. Keith Parker, *Baptists in Europe: History and Confessions of Faith*, Nashville, Broadman, 1982.

21. Although Baptists have regional confessions written at different times and for different purposes, they have no confessional documents that apply worldwide. The authority of these confessions is limited. Baptists generally refer directly to the authority of the scriptures.

3. FAITH AND PRACTICE

22. The Holy Spirit, working through the gospel of Jesus Christ, creates the community of faith, the church. Both Baptists and Lutherans affirm that all Christians live in direct relationship with God through Christ in the Spirit. They are called to be part of the community of the redeemed, and as true priests and prophets to lead lives that are characterized by discipleship and witness to the world. In their fellowship with one another believers are called to seek the will of God and then to order their church life in a way which best witnesses to Jesus Christ as Saviour and Lord.

23. Both Lutherans and Baptists affirm a "special" ministry, also called by God and marked by ordination, within the "general" ministry of witness and discipleship which is incumbent upon all members. With reference to the ordained ministry Lutherans have stressed its role within the church, while Baptists have tended to emphasize the evangelistic and missionary thrust of the ministry.

24. In principle, the Lutheran confessions (CA 7) do not prescribe any particular church structure, whether congregational, presbyterial or episcopal, but they insist that whatever structures are utilized they must allow the gospel to have free course and not hinder it. Thus the office of the ordained ministry is held to be given by God for the sake of the gospel, that is, to ensure both the free course and the purity of the gospel as word and sacrament. Therefore the ordained minister's authority for public preaching and teaching of the word and the administration of the sacraments is lodged not in the church structure but in the gospel; the structure mediates that authority, which is to say that the structure is always subservient to the gospel.

25. Baptist practice is diverse. Although theological training is often seen as a condition for ordination, and preaching and the administration of baptism and the Lord's supper are normally carried out by ordained ministers, there is a great openness to and respect for laypersons who preach and serve in the churches alongside the ordained ministers. For Baptists, authority to designate men and women to lead in worship, preach and administer baptism and the Lord's supper is vested in the local congregation. The authority of the ordained ministry is grounded in God who calls men and women to the gospel ministry; this call is confirmed by the church.

4. CONCLUSION

26. From our discussions it has become clear that Baptists and Lutherans agree that all authority resides ultimately in God's revelation in Jesus Christ. We regard the scriptures as the distinctive witness to Jesus Christ by which all other expressions of the Tradition are judged. We affirm historical and contemporary efforts of Christians to formulate the faith for their time in creeds, confessions and theological statements.

Recommendations

27. On the basis of our substantial agreement in matters of authority for preaching and teaching, we recommend:

- that our churches be encouraged to participate in interdenominational pastors' meetings, pulpit exchanges, and joint worship and evangelistic services;
- that our churches encourage their theological faculties, theological students and Christian educators to rediscover our common historical roots in the 16th century, to investigate the histories of relationships between Baptists and Lutherans wherever they have occurred, and thus to become aware that there is much more that unites than divides us;
- that our respective communions be encouraged to continue further study and conversations about our similarities and differences in doctrines and practice and thereby develop bridges of understanding for the future.

II. Faith-baptism-discipleship

1. THE STATE OF THE QUESTION

28. In discussing faith-baptism-discipleship our Baptist-Lutheran conversation touched upon its most crucial and controversial subject, the problem of the baptism of infants. Though unresolved questions remain, the many aspects of the issue which Baptists and Lutherans share in common should be accorded proper emphasis. These joint affirmations cover not only faith and discipleship; we found them in baptism too, so long as the particular issue of infant baptism was bracketed out.

29. We emphasize together the intimate relationship among faith, baptism and discipleship. Baptism must be understood within such a broad life context, not in isolation as a separate entity. It was, therefore, of utmost importance for us to discuss faith and baptism in relation to Christian discipleship. This underlines our conviction that faith in Jesus Christ and baptism are essentially linked to our mission and service in the world and to our hope in the coming Lord. Whatever is said about faith, baptism and discipleship must be in accord with the biblical testimony, according to which they all have their place in God's saving activity. By grace God calls men and women to become disciples of Jesus Christ; God forgives their sin, renews their lives, endows them with the Holy Spirit, makes them members of the body of Christ. The initiative always comes from God. The human response is a reaction made possible by the Holy Spirit.

30. On the one hand, both Baptists and Lutherans are inheritors of long and living traditions which influence our convictions, arguments, practices and perspectives. On the other hand, both face together new and ever-changing situations which call for a renewed theological perspective on faith-baptism-discipleship. Among Lutherans one sees both a growing reluctance to practise an indiscriminate baptism of infants and an increasing number of adult baptisms. Among Baptists one notes a continuing debate both about the extent of God's activity in baptism, and about the transferal of membership from other churches. But the traditional point of disagreement between Lutherans and Baptists still remains. Though Lutherans increasingly are baptizing adults, they maintain the basic practice of baptizing infants. Baptists, on the other hand, practise believer's baptism only.

31. Lutherans and Baptists have basically the same understanding of faith and discipleship. Our discussions showed that inherited reservations and fears on either side do not affect the substance of the issues, but rather signal dangers of one-sided emphases arising as the traditions have developed.

32. We both regard faith as the appropriate answer to God's gracious invitation. It is both a life-renewing event and a lifelong process. It is total and confident commitment to God, practised in discipleship. There are some differences of emphasis. While Lutherans have emphasized that the response of faith is not our doing nor is faith our possession, Baptists have emphasized the present reality and personal experience of faith. From Lutherans, Baptists may learn to regard faith as God's gift; from Baptists, Lutherans may learn that this gift calls for human response and enables a transformed life. We both regard discipleship – following Jesus wherever he calls us, even if it is to bear his cross – as a lifelong process, encompassing our entire existence: in fellowship with the people of God, in doing God's will, in prayer and worship and in service and mission to the world.

33. The chief issue between Lutherans and Baptists is how faith relates to baptism. For Baptists, personal and conscious faith prior to baptism is indispensable. For Lutherans, on the other hand, baptism may antedate a personal, self-conscious response of faith provided that the person is surrounded and upheld by the faith of the church and the family. Our conversations concentrated on this difference, but could not bridge the gap. The various reasons are given in the second part of this chapter.

34. Although there is much in the theology of baptism which Lutherans and Baptists hold in common, Baptists in general cannot regard the baptism of infants and the baptism of adults as two different forms of one baptism. They are regarded as the results of two different theological positions. In general, Baptists are unable to acknowledge infant baptism as baptism. That believing adults should be baptized is disputed by neither side. Baptist inability to acknowledge the baptism of infants as Christian baptism causes Lutherans to question whether Baptists understand baptism as a means of grace.

2. THE UNDERSTANDING OF BAPTISM

Biblical

35. Baptists and Lutherans both build their theological understanding of baptism on the New Testament. No single passage of the New Testament includes all the aspects of a systematic doctrine of baptism. However, it is clear that baptism is grounded on Jesus Christ (Matt. 28:18-20). It is related to the gift of the Holy Spirit, received by faith and lived in Christian discipleship (Acts 2:38). By baptism "we were buried... with him... into death, so that as Christ was raised from the dead by the glory of the Father, we too might walk in newness of life" (Rom. 6:4). Other themes giving content to Christian baptism include new life (Eph. 2:5f.), new birth (John 3:5; Titus 3:5; 1 Pet. 1:3f., 2:1f.), conversion and forgiveness of sins (Acts 2:38), incorporation into the body of Christ (Acts 2:41; 1 Cor. 12:13), salvation (Eph. 2:5; 1 Pet. 3:20f.), justification (1 Cor. 6:11; Titus 3:7), sanctification (1 Cor. 6:11), washing away of sins (Acts 22:16; 1 Cor. 6:11; Heb. 10:22; 1 Pet. 3:21), becoming heirs of the kingdom of God and of eternal life (John 3:5; Titus 3:5-7; 1 Pet. 1:3f.), putting on Christ (Gal. 3:27; Col. 3:9f.), a new humanity without any barriers of division (1 Cor. 12:13; Gal. 3:27f.; Col. 3:9-11), new obedience to Christ (Rom. 6:6ff.; Col. 3:5ff.; 1 Pet. 2:1ff.), Christian unity (Eph. 4:4-6). This survey of New Testament aspects and references demonstrates the intimate connection of baptism with faith and discipleship. We find the emphasis on the initial experience of conversion as well as on the ongoing process of living in Christ and on the activity of the Holy Spirit.

36. Though the relationship between God's act and the human response cannot be sorted out in a neatly schematic manner, it is clear that everywhere the New Testament begins with God's initiative in sending the Son, in giving divine grace, in forgiving sin, in renewing lives. A biblical theology of baptism must never separate baptism from God's initiative nor from the variegated relationships of the context of faith and discipleship. Baptism has its place within that framework; it cannot be regarded as a mere expression of human obedience, nor as a ceremony which is effective in and of itself. Rather baptism is a divine ordinance by which God accepts us into the kingdom and sets us within God's people. It gives public expression to God's covenant and commissions us to service in the world.

37. Lutherans and Baptists agree that there is no reference to the baptism of infants in the New Testament, though some Lutherans see in the accounts of the baptism of the Philippian jailer and "all his family" (Acts 16:33) and of "the household of Stephanas" (1 Cor. 1:16) implicit references. It is indisputable, however, that the theological affirmations about baptism in the New Testament assume the baptism of believing adults. Therefore, Baptists baptize believers only. Lutherans, on the other hand, argue that a theological understanding of baptism which is thoroughly biblical is not contradicted by the baptism of infants.

38. Both Lutherans and Baptists accept that the missionary situation in which the biblical statements about the relationship of faith and baptism are made requires that a confession of faith in response to the proclamation of the gospel precede baptism. Though faith matures and grows following baptism (it is not gift in the static sense), faith must be in evidence when someone requests baptism. Baptists regard this New Testament situation as normative, thus finding it impossible to baptize infants. Lutherans, however, have maintained that once the question of children being born into Christian families had to be faced by the growing church, that church rightly modified its view that a personal confession of faith had to precede baptism. Lutherans have, therefore, been open both to the fundamental New Testament sequence (proclamation, conversion/faith, baptism) and to the baptism of infants. Moreover, Lutherans have not wanted to equate the gift of faith with the personal confession of it, and have, therefore, not thought of the biblical sequence as a series of separate steps.

Theological

39. Lutherans stress that baptism is a form of God's word – a visible word, the expression of the priority of divine grace. It is God who through baptism incorporates the person baptized into the kingdom and thus into the community of the church. In baptism, therefore, God gives the gift of salvation, a gracious gift which only faith can receive. Baptism and faith belong together for without faith God's baptismal gift is of no use. But lack of faith cannot nullify God's action; as God's gracious action baptism remains valid even without faith. That is why baptism must not be repeated. Nonbelievers who have been baptized are to be called to recognize what God has accomplished in them, and to respond in faith. The priority of God's gracious action is unmistakable in the baptism of infants: infant baptism becomes a special testimony that baptism is a gift, something to be received. Lutherans think it not without significance that Jesus called children prototypes of God's kingdom (Matt. 19:14).

40. Baptists do not recognize a biblical foundation for such an interpretation of baptism as a visible word of prevenient grace. They do not attribute to baptism the place

the gospel occupies, the gospel which is proclaimed and testified to. Baptists must regard the Lutheran understanding as altering the character and place of baptism in the biblical order of salvation. Baptism is not the first step. For Baptists, the Lutheran view isolates and over-estimates baptism, giving it an independent theological weight and function. They fear this could lead to attributing to baptism the place reserved for Christ and his cross.

Anthropological

41. Anthropology also plays a role in the differing Lutheran and Baptist positions, particularly the issue of freedom of choice. It is, of course, difficult to make a clean distinction between the theological and anthropological aspects of that issue, but freedom of choice is not a theological issue alone. Baptists emphasize a person's innate freedom to choose baptism. That decision must not be made for a person either by parents or by the church, especially not before a person is able to make his or her own decisions. Of course, Baptists are aware that no one is absolutely free of environmental and social pressures, but they maintain that it belongs to the individual rights of a human being to decide whether or not to become a member of a church. Baptists know too that people do not have an inherent capacity to decide to become members of the kingdom of God, that such decisions are the result of the work of the Holy Spirit. But Baptists nevertheless maintain that God created us as human beings who can and should respond personally. Though there is a danger of overstating the subjective and active aspects of the responding person, Baptists regard it to be important not to surrender these aspects altogether.

42. While Lutherans can make many of the same affirmations about human nature, they would nevertheless contend that infant baptism does not rob one of personal decision. God who offers salvation in baptism calls for the response of faith. That response can be refused. So the personal character of faith is maintained even when it is the primary role of faith to receive the baptismal grace already bestowed. Lutherans cannot accept that infant baptism violates human rights; in this instance Lutherans locate the issue of human rights in the dialectical relationship between the gift of grace and the response of faith. The relationship must be dialectical because while grace and faith are distinct they are necessarily inter-related.

43. Positions taken by Baptists and Lutherans can be discussed further in terms of the place of baptism in one's life. We both agree that baptism and faith are components of the lifelong process of discipleship.

44. Lutherans develop this further by speaking of living out of one's baptism for the rest of one's life. They see baptism as initiation into a lifelong process; what was once given must be actualized again and again: "... a Christian life is nothing else than a daily baptism, once begun and ever continued" (Luther, Large Catechism, IV, 65). This process will reach its completion only at the end of time in the new creation. Baptism is a paradigm of the Christian life, assuring us that, by God's grace, "in the midst of death we are surrounded by life".

45. While Baptists also speak of baptism as initiation into a lifelong process, they stress conversion-faith-baptism as a spiritual event (rebirth) which must not be confused with a natural event (birth). Therefore, they fear that infant baptism becomes, though unintentionally, a cultural-religious *rite de passage* connected with natural birth.

46. Lutherans too differentiate natural and spiritual events. When parents and godparents disregard the insoluble connection between baptism and faith, Lutherans know that infant baptism can be misunderstood as a *rite de passage*. For that reason there is a growing hesitancy among Lutherans to baptize infants indiscriminately, and a growing insistence on the importance of the environment of faith in family and church. But Lutherans must ask Baptists whether a practice of baptism at other points in life (e.g. between childhood and adolescence) cannot also be misunderstood as a *rite de passage*.

Ecclesiological and sociological

47. Finally, differences between Lutherans and Baptists regarding baptism may be expressed in ecclesiological and sociological terms, especially in regard to the role of the family. This becomes evident in the following three problems. First: Lutherans proceed from the birth of a child into a Christian family. This situation replaced the New Testament missionary situation. That change, in turn, calls for a change in the order of steps in becoming a Christian. Baptists, on the other hand, do not exclude Christian families from the general missionary situation. Second, Baptists reserve the concept "family of God" for the church only, distinguishing it from the natural family. Of course, Lutherans are also aware of the difference between spiritual and natural kinship, and that the division may run right through a family. They nonetheless regard the Christian family as part of the family of God. Thus, Lutherans hold that Christian parents and the church, supporting the parents, provide a faith context for baptizing their children. Third, theologically, what is the position of children in a Christian family and environment? Lutherans ask whether Baptists underestimate or even disregard the position of children. Baptists answer that they are concerned for the education of their children in a Christian spirit, but that instead of infant baptism they practise prayers of intercession and blessing. Most Baptists would regard the baptism of infants as an act of blessing, nothing more.

3. CONCLUSION

48. The rather lengthy sections of part two of this chapter on faith-baptism-discipleship are an attempt to clarify and shed light on the major disagreement between Baptists and Lutherans regarding baptismal theology and practice. Section two would be misinterpreted, however, were it to leave the impression that our conversations were deadlocked in theological controversy. On the contrary, the overwhelming impression of both partners has been that we share so much in common that we gladly recommend greater efforts towards a common Christian witness to the world. Our wish is that the warm spirit of fellowship and love which we ourselves have come to experience could characterize Baptist-Lutheran relationships everywhere. On the basis of our mutual understanding of faith and discipleship, we see a firm basis for increasing cooperation. Our meetings showed that we have much to learn from each other. Our differences constitute a mutual challenge to search for greater clarity in our praxis, convictions and traditions. Our conversations took place in an atmosphere of mutual trust and concern strong enough to guard us from mere self-justification. We see this as a sign of hope. Even where we have been unable to share each other's convictions, we have gained respect for each other's consciences.

Recommendations

49. We have struggled at length with the issues of faith-baptism-discipleship, and have come to respect deeply the integrity of one another's tradition. We have also come to regret the pain our baptismal practices cause one another. We therefore recommend:

- That Baptists and Lutherans in neighbouring parishes/congregations meet to study their baptismal theology and practices in order to come to greater understanding and appreciation of their respective traditions. This would enhance their Christian fellowship, heighten their awareness of the riches of the body of Christ and strengthen them in their common mission in the world.
- That both Baptists and Lutherans reject a recent practice by some independent evangelists of encouraging successive baptisms of the same person upon successive conversion experiences.
- That Lutherans develop and practise a firm baptismal discipline in a secular society in which the community of faith presupposed by infant baptism cannot simply be assumed.
- That Baptists recognize the validity of the baptism of Lutherans who have been baptized as confessing believers, and later apply for membership in a Baptist church.
- That the most controversial question in this context (i.e. the evaluation of infant baptism by Baptists), which could not be solved in our dialogue, be treated in a spirit of mutual respect, whenever such a case of conflict occurs in church practice. Both Lutherans and Baptists should be aware of each other's grief: on the Lutheran side, when a Lutheran convert is "re-baptized" by Baptists because for Lutherans that places the integrity of the one baptism in jeopardy; on the Baptist side, when Lutherans call the Baptist practice "rebaptism", and when Baptists see their missionary witness deflected by unbelievers who plead infant baptism – a special problem in folk and state churches. Both Lutherans and Baptists should place their common Christian witness to the world first and not let their differences on baptism become a stumbling block.
- That Baptists further study and evaluate different practices currently used by various Baptist churches: some Baptists do not accept Lutherans who were not baptized as confessing believers as church members, because these Baptists do not acknowledge infant baptism; others accept them as full church members upon their confession of faith, without acknowledging their infant baptism, however; others respect a person's affirmation of his/her own infant baptism without agreeing to the doctrine of infant baptism; others accept them as members, acknowledging also their infant baptism as "valid, though unclear" baptism; still others try to find an intermediate solution by granting associate, guest or fraternal membership, providing an opportunity for common worship and service, but so marking the difference in baptismal doctrine. Lutherans would be grateful if a solution could be found whereby the membership practice does not question the integrity of their baptism.
- That Lutherans continue their efforts to overcome the problem of indiscriminate baptism which is particularly acute in folk church situations, and to clarify what that practice implies for church membership.
- That our inability to find a solution to the issue of infant baptism challenge us to study further and at greater depth the theological basis for infant baptism and the implications of the present socio-cultural context of that practice. We recommend that such a study be done jointly.

III. The church

1. THE UNDERSTANDING OF THE CHURCH

Our common biblical heritage

50. In their ecclesiology both Baptists and Lutherans rely on the emphasis of the Reformation that the Bible is the source and the judge of what the church is and ought to be. Both have attempted to unfold the riches of the New Testament teaching on the church as much as possible.

51. The early church is the continuation of the group of disciples around Jesus, called anew after his resurrection and enabled through the gift of the Holy Spirit. Most of its self-designations, however, point to continuity with the Old Testament "people of God", the people of God's covenant and promise (1 Pet. 2:10; Rom. 9:25f.), thus being the true children of Abraham and the true Israel (Rom. 2:28f.; Gal. 6:16). This means that the ecclesiology of the early church is theocentric and formulated in awareness of the church's place in salvation history. The church is made up of "those who... call on the name of our Lord Jesus Christ" (1 Cor. 1:2; Acts 9:21); it is the "royal priesthood" and "holy nation" (1 Pet. 2:9; Rev. 1:6); it is the "salt of the earth" and "light of the world" (Matt. 5:13f.).

52. The special relation of the church to Jesus Christ is expressed in several ways. Jesus chose his disciples that they should be with him and that he might send them, endowed with authority from him (Mark 3:14f.; John 15:16). He "loved the church and gave himself up for her, that he might sanctify her, having cleansed her..." (Eph. 5:25f.). He is the Lord of the church, calling it to obedience. He is the "shepherd of the sheep" (John 10:2ff.). The church is dependent on him, just as branches depend on the vine (John 15:1ff.). It is his table around which the church assembles (1 Cor. 11:17ff.). The church lives "in Christ", "in the Lord" (Phil 1:1; 4:4). In particular the term "body of Christ" underlines both the unity of all the different members in Christ and the lordship of Christ, the head of the body (Rom. 12; 1 Cor. 12; Eph. 1:22f.; Col. 1:18). Discipleship also includes following Jesus' footsteps and his example in bearing the cross, in suffering for his name's sake, and in serving (Mark 8:34f.; 10:43-45; 1 Cor. 4:9ff.).

53. The church is a creation of the Holy Spirit, poured upon God's people at Pentecost. The Holy Spirit conveys the new life and the power manifested in Christ's resurrection from the dead (Acts 2:32f.). Church members thus become "living stones", built up as a "spiritual house" and temple, whose character is holiness (1 Pet. 2:5ff.; Col. 1:22).

54. The New Testament church exhibits several characteristics. It is universal, encompassing all nations, without any barriers of division between "Jew nor Greek,... slave nor free,... male nor female" (Gal. 3:28). The church is "one in Christ" (Gal. 3:28; Eph. 4:3ff.). Its very unity is a sign to the unbelieving world so that it may believe (John 17:21). Likewise the love within and of the church is a sign of invitation to all people (John 13:34f.). The church is missionary, called by Christ to participate in his service to the world. It is a society in contrast to the practices of worldly rulers, "not exercising dominion", but rendering humble service to one another (Matt. 20:25-28). The church is a fellowship of love, compassion and forgiveness, living from Christ's own mercy (Matt. 18). It is engaged in the ministry in glory, but has the "treasure in earthen vessels" (2 Cor. 3:8f.; 4:7), often in the form of a paradox: "as sorrowful, yet always rejoicing; as poor, yet making many rich" (2 Cor. 6:10).

55. The New Testament church is a pilgrim people, moving towards the day of the Lord Jesus Christ, when "he who began a good work... will bring it to completion" (Phil 1:6). The eschatological perspective enables the church to persist in the "work of faith and labour of love and steadfastness of hope" (1 Thess. 1:3). The church is the pilgrim people of God, having the promise of the great "sabbath of God" (Heb. 4), expecting "always [to] be with the Lord" (1 Thess. 4:17). Therefore, the church must not become proud (1 Cor. 4:7); rather, with Paul it is summoned to "know him [Christ] and the power of his resurrection, and may share his sufferings", and "straining forward to what lies ahead" (Phil. 3:10-14).

56. Although both Lutherans and Baptists accept the authority of the biblical message and seek in their traditions to remain faithful to it, different emphases have emerged in their understanding and experience of being the church.

Lutheran understanding

57. *The marks of the church:* Following the Lutheran Reformers, Lutherans accept the ecumenical understanding of the church expressed in the Nicene Creed. The four attributes of oneness, holiness, catholicity and apostolicity are taken for granted. What is distinctive within the Lutheran tradition is the identification of the marks of the church primarily with the word and sacraments. Without these means there would be no believers and consequently no church. "The church is the assembly of saints in which the gospel is taught purely and the sacraments are administered rightly. For the true unity of the church it is enough to agree concerning the teaching of the gospel and the administration of the sacraments. It is not necessary that human traditions or rites and ceremonies, instituted by men, should be alike everywhere. It is as Paul says, 'One faith, one baptism, one God and Father of all...'" (CA 7). That is why Lutherans look upon these visible, effective means as essential to the nature of the church. When Luther expanded his catalogue of the marks of the church, he included also manifestations of faith: prayer, praise, thanksgiving and the suffering implied in discipleship.

58. The Lutheran Reformers insisted on making the manifestations of the gospel (i.e. word and sacraments) rather than the manifestations of faith the essential marks of the church, because of their essential insight that salvation is a free gift of God and cannot be achieved through human activity, and because the means of grace are visible and concrete. Characteristically, then, Lutherans give priority to what is given by God and only secondarily mention the fruits of faith that are manifest in the assembly of believers. They have also insisted that in this world the church is never exclusively a church of believers. In its midst are also nominal Christians (hypocrites). Only at the time of the last judgment will they be separated from each other.

59. *Diversity of practice:* A church cannot be identified as Lutheran only on the basis of style, practice or custom. Lutheran unity does not depend on conformity in such matters. Out of the common heritage of medieval catholicism, Lutheran practice has been shaped by 16th-century reforms and later by the influences of pietism and the Enlightenment. As Lutheran churches spread from Europe to other continents, they transplanted some of the flavour of the home church while adopting new practices to meet the challenges and opportunities of their new context. Nonetheless, a fundamental emphasis on word and sacraments shapes Lutheran church life wherever Lutherans are found.

60. *Worship:* The prominence of word and sacraments is evident first in worship. Lutherans regard people assembled for worship as the heart of what the church is. The

sacraments are regarded as equal in importance and efficacy with the proclaimed word in communicating the gospel. Bread and wine and water connected with the word become the vehicles of Christ's forgiving and liberating presence in the believer. In many Lutheran churches continuity with the ancient and medieval European church is evident in the use of visual arts, liturgical vestments and music, and a high degree of ritual in worship. While Lutherans are increasingly open to variety in worship forms in response to the mission imperative to reach out to people from other cultural heritages, they are also influenced by recent liturgical renewal movements towards greater appreciation of classical liturgical forms.

61. Still the preaching of the word is the most regular feature of Lutheran worship. Lutherans understand preaching as encounter with the living voice of God through the gospel *(viva vox evangelii)*. Lutheran preaching is characteristically exegetical in nature, expounding a biblical text, often taken from a schedule of texts assigned for the Sundays of the church year (lectionary). Laypersons may sometimes preach in Lutheran churches, but as a rule those who preach or administer the sacraments do so under regular call as ordained ministers or under the supervision of an ordained minister.

62. *Catechesis:* The centrality of the word is evident also in the emphasis on catechesis in Lutheran churches. From the time of Luther, study of the catechism in the home was encouraged as well as instruction by one's pastor. Still today Lutheran churches require a period of serious study of scripture and the catechism of persons preparing for confirmation. As a remembrance of baptism confirmation marks a major transition in the life of a believer, though it has often acquired cultural overtones as well. Christian education for adults is a common element in the life of Lutheran parishes and institutions.

63. *Polity:* In Lutheran churches authority is exercised through the ministry of word and sacraments. A Lutheran congregation does not regard itself as autonomous since it derives its life and being from these means of grace, which are entrusted to regularly called and ordained pastors. The authority of the pastor for leadership in the parish, however, is shared with the congregational council. Both congregations and pastors share doctrinal and administrative authority with synods or other supra-congregational structures. By such interdependent arrangements of checks and balances, churches of the Lutheran tradition seek to avoid the extremes of congregationalism on the one hand, and of clerical hierarchy on the other. Almost all Lutheran churches enjoy communion with one another and participate in ecumenical organizations at the local, national and international levels.

64. Lutheran churches do exist as folk churches but they also exist where strict separation of church and state obtains, and where Lutherans are one of many denominations.

65. The great contribution and strength of the Lutheran confessional heritage is the emphasis on gift. Yet in focusing too narrowly on proclaimed word and sacraments, Lutherans run the risk of forgetting that these precious gifts are not ends in themselves, but means to the end of creating and sustaining faith. The word must not only be preached, but believed, professed and lived. A constant Lutheran temptation is to stress justification by grace through faith as the essence of the gospel without following through to sanctification, thus cheapening the very saving grace we extol. This in turn has the consequences, on the one hand, of intellectualizing theology by removing it

from the practice of discipleship and, on the other hand, of encouraging an attitude of quietism with respect to justice, peace and the care of the creation. Furthermore, the stress on the pure proclamation of the gospel and the proper administration of the sacraments tends to nurture a certain clericalism which is antithetical to the exercise of the gifts of every Christian. Thus, there is often among Lutherans a weakness in the expression of fellowship and in the missionary vision.

Baptist understanding

66. *The marks of the church:* Baptists generally affirm the traditional characteristics of the church, that it is one, holy, universal and missionary/apostolic. Their theological approach to ecclesiology is, however, more easily discernible in their intention to follow the Bible as closely as possible; it is their intention to be "church according to the New Testament". In particular the first chapters of Acts, the Pauline image of the "body of Christ", the description in Ephesians 4 and regulations for church life as found in Matthew 18 and in the pastoral epistles have shaped Baptist ecclesiology. In interpreting such passages the Baptist emphasis has been on the living character of the church, as distinct from a mere outward form of Christianity. From their beginnings Baptists have been engaged in the quest for the "true church".

67. Due to the heritage of congregationalism, Baptists stress that the church is made up of people; Baptists intend to be the "people of God". Neither must church organization deteriorate into institutionalism nor church life to routine. Personal elements are regarded as primary, in particular personal faith and commitment. Baptists like the term "free church", indicating free decision as well as freedom from non-church influences.

68. Historically it should be noted that Baptists have attempted to be heirs of the "radical reformation"; they like to quote Luther's preface to the "Deutsche Messe" (1526) where he speaks of those "who want to be Christians in earnest". Furthermore, Baptist ecclesiology partly developed in reaction to that of the established churches; hence its anti-hierarchical and anti-sacramental aspects; hence also the emphasis on the local church with close personal relationships over against folk-church anonymity. The Baptist movement took shape during the ascendance of democracy; several aspects of that are reflected in Baptist church life, for example the strong championing of religious liberty.

69. Baptist ecclesiology has taken over much from the Reformed tradition: from Zwinglianism some of its emphasis on the role of the Holy Spirit, from Calvinism its emphasis on sanctification and practical Christian activity. Therefore, the communion table is not so much the centre of Baptist worship as the pulpit is; biblical instruction is regarded as important. The emphasis on personal activity was combined with that of pietism, revival movements, and missionary and diaconic work.

70. Baptist ecclesiology might be described by the words of Galatians 4:19: that "Christ be formed in you". This implies concrete Christian discipleship, the character of a living organism, and the visible form of the church in terms both of the experience of the assembling congregation and of being a sign to the world. The church exists to make Jesus Christ manifest; it is not to put forward itself, of course, but his grace and gifts.

71. *Church practice:* Baptist church practice is rooted in the basic conviction that the church is the body of Christ and God's instrument for the salvation of the world.

72. Through personal faith which is publicly confessed in believers' baptism persons become members of the body of Christ and as such also members of the local

church (local church in Baptist usage corresponds to local congregation in Lutheran usage). The experience of Jesus Christ as Saviour and Lord and the public confession of this faith in baptism is fundamental to the Baptist understanding of being the church.

73. Life in the local church is marked by a spirit of intentional community. This becomes evident in regular worship services, Bible study, prayer meetings, personal and family relationships, and the care for the sick and needy. Emphasis is also placed upon personal commitment and a credible Christian life-style. Church members are encouraged to meet regularly for worship, the preaching of the word, instruction and the Lord's supper. In all of these there is a strong emphasis on the Bible as the basis of Baptist life and worship.

74. Although Baptists emphasize the priesthood of all believers and the equality of all members, there are organizational structures to serve the life and ministry of the church. Central is the ministry of the whole congregation. The church meeting (congregational assembly) serves to structure this ministry. The church elects deacons and sometimes elders for the spiritual and administrative leadership of the church. The pastors, also elected and appointed by the church, serve to enable the church to fulfill its ministry. All members are expected and encouraged to discern their personal gifts and talents, and with them to participate actively in the ministry of the church.

75. Important is the conviction that the church does not exist for itself; therefore Baptists regard evangelism, mission and social ministries as essential tasks of the church. To follow Jesus Christ also means to take up the cross. Like other Christians Baptists have experienced the reality of this biblical truth and have thereby been reminded to accept it as one of the characteristics of the church.

76. For Baptists, all authority is vested in the local church, though local churches may delegate authority to such other organizational structures as unions of churches in order to achieve a more efficient way to exercise their ministry.

77. Although the church becomes manifest in the local community, most Baptists are aware of the wider Baptist constituency and of the universal Christian church. They cooperate therefore in regional, national and international structures to coordinate their work and make their ministry efficient. Their participation in various ecumenical projects and organizations is also an expression of understanding themselves as part of the universal body of Christ.

78. Baptists have placed great emphasis on the separation of church and state and on religious liberty because they are convinced that the gospel must be received and lived in freedom from political, social, national, legal and religious coercion or bondage.

79. Looking back on our doctrinal statements about the church, Baptists share with Lutherans the awareness that the church, whose identity is in Jesus Christ and in him alone, is always also a frail, sinful and human community. In light of Christ we become aware of our shortcomings, and we need to bring to our common attention the following: the emphasis on our church affairs makes us sometimes reluctant to engage in the struggle for justice and peace in the world. Sometimes we too easily identify our faith in Christ with our socio-economic and cultural concerns and interests. Often we are so caught up with our own church life that we show insufficient interest in our ecumenical responsibilities. Baptists should be aware that their emphasis on piety easily leads to moralism. Baptists should realize that they are inconsistent when they emphasize the priesthood of all believers and the equality of all members and yet are reluctant to encourage the full ministry and ordination of women.

2. THE MISSION OF THE CHURCH

80. We are grateful to God that the gospel of Jesus Christ has freed us from our estrangement and self-interest, and has made us open to worship God, to love our fellow human beings and to accept responsibility for the environment in which we live. In sharing his life with us in Christ and in the Spirit, God has called us as individuals and as churches to become "fellow workers" (1 Cor. 3:9). Through the ages we hear the invitation and challenge of our Lord: "Let your light so shine before men, that they may see your good works and give glory to your Father who is in heaven" (Matt. 5:16).

81. As Lutherans and Baptists we joyfully acknowledge the call to be the people of God and, as such, to participate in God's mission to call people to faith in Jesus Christ, to be agents of his power to heal human life wherever it is broken or breaking, and to shoulder responsibility as stewards of his creation. God who loves the world (John 3:16) and has reconciled it with himself through Christ, calls us to the ministry of reconciliation (2 Cor. 5:18-20). This ministry of reconciliation becomes concrete in the many different ways in which our churches minister to the needs around them. In all different forms of ministry we want to give expression to God's passion for our world, and as such we aim to be witnesses to the "reign of God".

82. In our evangelistic ministries of proclamation we tell the story of Jesus as the story of God's unconditional love. We believe that the gospel is God's power unto salvation, that through faith in Jesus Christ people find forgiveness for their sin, hope in times of despair, meaning when meaninglessness seems to engulf them. We are grateful to God for the many signs in the lives of people that demonstrate the power of the gospel today.

83. With our missionary ministries we join with Christian brothers and sisters everywhere in the common task of witnessing to the gospel in word and deed. As people who know that the God whom we have experienced as Redeemer, is also the Creator and Sustainer of the world, and as recipients of his healing and reconciling love, we cannot but share with others the love that we have experienced ourselves. In doing so, we want to respect people's cultural heritages. We realize that coercion and proselytism contradict the gospel. At the same time we affirm that missionary passion belongs to the nature of the gospel. In confessing the church as "apostolic", we acknowledge that we belong to the company of those who are "sent" to witness to the good news declared in Jesus Christ. Like the apostle Paul we feel a divine necessity (1 Cor. 9:16) and obligation (Rom. 1:14) to be witnesses to the gospel "in Jerusalem and in all Judea and Samaria and to the end of the earth" (Acts 1:8).

84. Part of our participation in God's mission is our concern for and support of the present ecumenical process towards justice, peace and integrity of creation. We are sadly aware of the many ways in which the dignity of the human person, human society and the environment are threatened by the selfishness, materialism, militarism and the self-interest of nations. The arms race and the ecological crisis threaten the survival of the human race. Racism, apartheid, sexism, human ideologies, torture and unemployment deny the dignity and equality of human beings. Poverty, hunger and sickness force millions to exist in inhuman conditions. Refugees, asylum-seekers and the unemployed have become the outcasts of modern human society. Child prostitution, child labour and the dissolution of the family sap the energy and creativity of the next generation. Complacency, negligence, individual and collective selfishness have resulted in grievous damage to nature, thus undermining the very basis of life on our planet. In

this situation, as part of our response to God, we as individuals and as churches are to be agents of peace and reconciliation, we are to heal those who are broken in body and spirit, we are to invest our time, money and energy to bring justice to the oppressed, to bring food and medical care to those who are hungry and sick. Accordingly, we are committed to the implementation of human rights. Equally we are committed to the care of nature because nature partakes with us in creation and redemption (Rom. 8:19-22). Therefore, we call upon our churches to see the struggle for the implementation of human rights, the pursuit of peace and the care of the earth as intrinsic to our faith in Jesus Christ.

85. We have understood our conversations as a response to our Lord's desire that in the process towards unity we may better reflect the very being of God, and thus become a more credible witness to a world that has a great need to hear words and see deeds of reconciliation, healing and forgiveness (John 17:20f.; Eph. 4:4-6).

3. THE LORD'S SUPPER

86. Together Baptists and Lutherans confess that the Lord's supper was instituted by Jesus Christ as the meal of the new covenant between God and his people and as a meal of communion (koinonia) among believers.

87. In conformity with its institution by Jesus Christ, the celebration of the Lord's supper brings the congregation together to eat and drink the bread and the cup, to listen to the word of promise and to pray. By this prayer we give thanks to God for his work accomplished in creation, redemption and sanctification. We remember the suffering, death and resurrection of Christ and ask for the coming of the Holy Spirit. We celebrate Christ's presence and look towards the time when communion with him shall be fulfilled in his kingdom. We are equipped and sent into this world as witnesses and instruments of the coming kingdom of Christ.

88. Together we confess the presence of Jesus Christ in the midst of the worshipping congregation celebrating the Lord's supper. There are, however, differences in the understanding of the mode of his presence. In Lutheran perspective the Lord imparts himself in his body and blood with bread and wine through the word of promise and the work of the Holy Spirit. In this way he wills to give himself to us. This receiving of Christ does not depend on the faith of the individual person, although only believers can receive Christ for their salvation. Baptists relate the presence of Christ to the celebration of the Lord's supper as a whole: breaking the bread and drinking the cup, the worshipping community remembers the crucified and risen Lord sharing his life with us in the power of the Holy Spirit.

89. What does the Lord give to his people? He gives himself. In communion with him we receive forgiveness of sins, freedom for a sanctified life and service in the world, a renewed fellowship among sisters and brothers, and hope in the life to come. This is our common belief, although in the past Lutherans put more emphasis on the forgiveness of sins and the certitude of salvation, whereas Baptists have emphasized (according to 1 Cor. 11) reconciliation among the church members and the spiritual strengthening for a life in sanctification and witness.

90. At the celebration of the Lord's supper Christ is the host. All who confess him as Lord and Saviour are invited. For Lutherans and Baptists participation in the Lord's supper confirms and confesses ever anew that through faith and baptism we have been incorporated into the body of Christ and are his people.

RECOMMENDATIONS

91. On the basis of mutual understandings achieved with respect to the church and its mission, we recommend:
- that we mutually recognize each other as communions within the church of Christ;
- that we encourage our churches to participate in the ongoing struggle for the implementation of human rights, for the establishing of justice and peace and for the preservation of creation;
- that we encourage the efforts of our churches to win the world to an authentic commitment to Christ; as all genuine Christian witness is participation in the mission of the one Christ, we urge increased coordination in the missionary activities of our churches.

92. On the basis of our discussion of the Lord's supper we recommend that the already existing practice of mutual hospitality at the communion table be endorsed and encouraged.

IV. Lutheran condemnations of the Anabaptists in the 16th century and the relationship of Lutherans and Baptists today

1. THE LUTHERAN CONFESSIONS

93. Lutheran confessional writings of the 16th century contain condemnations of Anabaptists and their teaching.

94. *Augsburg confession, 1530 (CA):* Anabaptists and their teachings are specifically mentioned and rejected in five of the articles. Article 5: "Condemned are the Anabaptists and others who teach that the Holy Spirit comes to us through our own preparations, thoughts and works without the external word of the gospel" (German text). Article 9: "... the Anabaptists who teach that infant baptism is not right are rejected" (German text). The Latin text adds: "and [who] declare that children are saved without baptism". Article 12: "Our churches condemn the Anabaptists who deny that those who have once been justified can lose the Holy Spirit..." (Latin text). Article 16: "Condemned here are the Anabaptists who teach that none of the things indicated above (i.e. occupy civil offices, serve as princes and judges, render decisions and pass sentence according to imperial and other existing laws, punish evildoers with the sword, take required oaths...) is Christian" (German text). Article 17: "Rejected... are the Anabaptists who teach that the devil and condemned men will not suffer eternal pain and torment" (German text).

95. *Formula of Concord, 1580, Epitome, chapter 12:* The section "Errors of the Anabaptists" criticizes the Anabaptist anthropology in its presumed denial of the doctrine of original sin as well as Anabaptist refusal to baptize infants. Also criticized is the view that "a congregation is not truly Christian if sinners are still found in it". The section repeats the condemnations of CA 16.

96. The Lutheran Reformers rarely distinguished between the various streams of the "left wing" of the Reformation, but tended to lump even conflicting groups together under the Anabaptist label (e.g. violent Enthusiasts and pacifist biblical Anabaptists).

2. THE IMPACT OF THE CONDEMNATIONS

97. The condemnations of the CA and FC were aimed at teachings and teachers who stood in opposition to the Lutheran understanding of the gospel. In fact, however, they had an impact far beyond the arena of theological debate, and played a role in fur-

thering a mentality which had serious social and legal consequences for Anabaptists including confiscation of property, torture, expulsion and execution. The persecution of Anabaptists in the 16th century reflects a lack of commitment to religious liberty, a principle affirmed today by both Lutherans and Baptists.

98. While the relationship between the modern Baptist movement which began in the 17th century and the Anabaptists of the 16th century is disputed, many Baptists today increasingly make a connection and see the roots of their identity and self-understanding in the 16th-century Anabaptists. Whichever position is taken, it is demonstrably true that Baptists have themselves also suffered discrimination and legal problems as a result of the Lutheran condemnations.

3. THE LUTHERAN CONFESSIONS AND LUTHERANS TODAY

99. Contemporary Lutherans consider themselves to stand in continuity with the confessional writings of the 16th century. Being confessional, however, does not require theologians simply to reiterate every affirmation of the confessions. The spirit of the confessions themselves compels the person of faith to reject or modify any human formulation of faith which is found to be in conflict with the gospel as it applies to the world today. For example, the doctrine of the "just war" referred to in article 16 of the Augsburg confession must be reinterpreted in our time in response to the changing nature of war itself. Similarly, article 9 of the Augsburg confession, which has been used to support the notion that all infants must be baptized or that infant baptism is the only legitimate form of baptism, must be reinterpreted to meet the situation of a secularized society. In this context, many faithful Lutherans hold that it is not appropriate to baptize infants from families where there is no Christian commitment.

100. In the relationship of Lutherans and Baptists today only the teaching about baptism in the Augsburg confession, paragraph 9, remains controversial. The other condemnations do not apply to Baptists today, and even in the 16th century they were often based on an undifferentiated view of the various streams of the "left wing" of the Reformation. Today we recognize that it is not helpful to address differences with condemnations. The remaining differences in the understanding of baptism should be further discussed with reference to our common commitment to the authority of the scriptures and to the lordship of Christ, and in the awareness of travelling together towards our coming Lord in common witness and service.

101. Lutherans today recognize and deplore the role their doctrinal condemnations played in the persecution of Anabaptists. They regard what happened then as a warning to abstain from discrimination against those of different beliefs and ways of thinking.

4. THE LUTHERAN CONFESSIONS AND BAPTISTS TODAY

102. In predominantly Lutheran countries, Baptists sometimes still experience discrimination by Lutheran institutions (e.g. schools) and publications.

103. Lutherans recognize and deplore that the condemnations against the Anabaptists have contributed to discrimination against today's Baptists, and they beg forgiveness. The situation requires continuing vigilance to prevent such violations of fundamental Christian fellowship.

104. Baptists recognize and deplore an attitude of superiority which overlooks the spiritual treasure God has produced within the Lutheran churches. There have been unfair and distorted depictions of other churches. And for this they beg forgiveness.

5. Divergences and convergences between Baptists and Lutherans today

105. Previous chapters have shown that differences remain between Baptists and Lutherans today. But the convergences between Baptists and Lutherans are greater than these differences. They reveal us both to be pilgrim people in and for the world, moving towards God's future with a common commitment to the one Lord Jesus Christ. We are, therefore, committed to address our differences from within a fellowship of churches.

106. Together we accept the appropriateness of a "No" between sisters and brothers to doctrinal expressions we cannot accept, but we seek to affirm that the body of Christ has many members, and that neither Baptists nor Lutherans can presume to exclude the other from that body. We therefore commit ourselves to labour together as children of God, brothers and sisters in Jesus Christ.

Recommendations

107. On the basis of our acknowledgment of the pain caused by the Lutheran condemnations of the Anabaptists in the 16th century, we recommend:
- that Lutherans and Baptists take up what was said in paragraphs 103-104, and use it in an appropriate form in their communities in worship services celebrated jointly whenever possible;
- that further editions of the Lutheran confessions contain a statement indicating that the condemnations no longer apply in our interdenominational relations (cf. §§97,99,100,103); the consequences of this should be made clear especially in ministerial training, in the context of ordination and in other instances of the official use of the confessions;
- that acknowledged differences in doctrine and practice be treated with a friendly "No" and be made the occasion of deeper mutual study; the language we use should reflect our mutual Christian commitment avoiding any condemnation of persons, even where doctrinal positions cause objection.

VII. DISCIPLES OF CHRIST-REFORMED DIALOGUE

Historical Introduction

There is a close kinship between the Reformed churches and the Churches of Christ (Disciples). The Churches of Christ (Disciples) emerged from a revivalist movement of the 19th century. Their roots are in the Reformed tradition. Their founders were ordained Presbyterian pastors, and the movement received its impress from disagreement with a form of Presbyterianism that was characterized by a narrow orthodoxy in both its teaching and its constitution. Although the movement developed many traits of its own in the course of time, it can be understood as being in more than one respect a secessionist movement within the Reformed tradition.

From the outset the Churches of Christ (Disciples) laid a strong emphasis on the call to unity. They understood themselves to be instruments of unity within divided evangelical Christianity. Many Disciples have taken an active part in the ecumenical movement. The churches entered into international dialogue for the purpose of determining the extent to which the reasons which led to division are still valid and, even more, of determining what steps can be taken to bring the two groups of churches closer together. Much has changed since the time when the Churches of Christ came into existence. The Presbyterianism from which the Churches of Christ (Disciples) separated themselves at the beginning of the 19th century is a thing of the past. In many countries Reformed churches and the Churches of Christ work closely together and have even become members of united churches. The international dialogue was therefore faced from the outset with the question of how the two traditions could be brought together in a comprehensive reconciliation.

The dialogue began in 1984. Representatives of the World Alliance of Reformed Churches and the Disciples' Ecumenical Consultative Council met in Geneva in order to reach an agreement on the present state of relations between the two groups. Both sides prepared careful analyses of the situation. In the course of the conversations the conviction grew that the time for a rapprochement had come. A small booklet, *Reformed and Disciples of Christ in Dialogue*, was prepared and sent to all the member churches of both organizations for their views (Studies from the World Alliance of Reformed Churches, no. 6, 1985). In March 1987 a second and larger consultation was held in Birmingham, England. A detailed examination was made of the differences between the two traditions, and the conclusion reached was that the division between the two traditions need no longer exist today. The report expresses this conviction with great frankness (no. 37). The consultation confronted both churches with the question of how they would deal with this unanimous finding. The papers and reports of the consultation were published in *Mid-Stream: An Ecumenical Journal*, 27/2, April 1988.

The executive committees of both the Disciples' Ecumenical Consultative Council and the World Alliance of Reformed Churches decided to present the report to their member churches. The executive committee of the World Alliance of Reformed Churches invited the Disciples' Ecumenical Consultative Council to send a strong delegation to its general assembly in Seoul (August 1989). Numerous churches of the World Alliance of Reformed Churches announced their express approval of the Birmingham report, and the general assembly of Seoul consequently saw itself as in a position to approve the recommendations of the report and to instruct the executive committee to continue the dialogue. On the one hand, still unresolved questions were to be clarified; on the other, communion between the churches at the national and local levels was to be promoted. The general assembly asked the Disciples' Ecumenical Consultative Council to participate in the work of the executive committee of the World Alliance of Reformed Churches by appointing a permanent delegate to that committee. The invitation was accepted. With it is associated the hope that a closer collaboration between the two partners may gradually develop.

Lukas Vischer

11. No Doctrinal Obstacles

Birmingham, England, 4-11 March 1987

1. Introduction

1. The church of Jesus Christ is one, but the different Christian communions are separated from one another. The Reformed churches and the Disciples of Christ have entered into a dialogue in the hope of healing their own divisions and so more nearly manifest the unity in which both so firmly believe. This is a report of that dialogue.

2. The Reformed Christians were represented by a delegation from the World Alliance of Reformed Churches, a family of some 160 Presbyterian, Reformed, Congregational and United churches from throughout the world. Their origins, in some cases, even precede the Protestant Reformation of the 16th century, and all recognize some form of historical relationship to the Swiss Reformation. Their global expansion has taken place largely as a result of the missionary efforts of the 19th century.

3. The Disciples delegation represented the Disciples Ecumenical Consultative Council. The Disciples of Christ are a family of churches with origins in the 19th century in the United States, Great Britain and Australasia. They quickly spread to various parts of the world, also largely through missionary efforts. From the beginning they emphasized Christian unity as one of their fundamental concerns. Today there are about 3 million Disciples in some 35 different countries.

4. The dialogue began to take serious form with a meeting in Geneva, Switzerland, in the summer of 1984, when representatives of the Reformed and Disciples met to explore the possibility of a consultation between these two families of Christians. The results of that meeting were presented in *Reformed and Disciples of Christ in Dialogue*, published by the World Alliance of Reformed Churches in 1985. Included in this booklet is a survey of the history of relations between the Disciples and Reformed, and lists of places where the two have cooperated and currently work together. Also there is a response by a Reformed theologian to this history of relationships.

5. Both sides discussed with their appropriate governing bodies the possibility of a dialogue, and received approval to proceed. Plans were then made for a formal gathering in Birmingham, England, 4-11 March 1987. During this meeting the two delegations, involving over twenty participants, engaged in wide-ranging, searching conversations, listened to and discussed papers, learned about cooperative activities and actual unions of churches. Each day included worship, and there was an opportunity to worship in churches in the region around Birmingham.

6. The dialogue is seen by the Disciples as an opportunity to make clear the international character of their own commitment to unity, particularly as they learn about the

uniting and united ventures of Reformed and Disciples in many parts of the world. Also, by engaging the Reformed churches in conversation the Disciples might be able to reappropriate their own historic emphasis on the grace of God experienced and made known especially in baptism and the Lord's supper. For the Reformed, dialogue with the Disciples represents an opportunity to explore some issues of concern in their heritage. The Disciples separated from the Reformed precisely over some of the issues that have continued to be divisive in the Reformed churches, including the authority of creeds, the nature of the church and ministry. By talking with the Disciples, the Reformed will be able to reconsider these issues. Also, conversations with the Disciples reinforces an increasing awareness among the Reformed of the significance of the unity of the church and the centrality of the sacraments in the life of the church. For both groups, the dialogue has provided an occasion to examine critically a wide range of issues over against and in tandem with another community of God's people. It is an encouragement to participate in what is fittingly called "a reconciliation of memories" over past divisions.

7. One of the results of this dialogue has been the discovery that there is great diversity within each church family, so much so that serious questions must be raised about the validity of any purported church-dividing issues. At each place where there seems to have been a grave impasse, it is found that there are some groups within both the Disciples and Reformed that stand on either side of the issue. Even on such a question as baptism, where the practices and theology appear to be so different, we learn that the sides are already living together in united churches where such issues have been overcome. The dialogue has led to better understanding and provides the basis for further cooperative efforts in mission and witness. This report thus reflects differences and diversity along with delight at the level of unity thus far achieved, and great hope for the future relations of the Reformed and Disciples as they seek to be faithful people in God's world.

II. Our common faith

8. On both sides Disciples and Reformed share certain fundamental commitments which deserve to be reaffirmed as guidelines for the future. These commitments have to do with the calling and mission of the church itself. Among other things the church is called to be:

9. A. A community living by God's word in holy scripture

The church lives by faithful hearing of the word of God, as the testimony of the Bible is witnessed to afresh in its bearing upon today and tomorrow. This also involves listening receptively and critically to the witness of past generations to that testimony; but it requires more than merely traditional reliance on past interpretations. The range and power of God's word is not confined to the understanding unfolded in any one age or time – whether the early church, the middle ages, the Reformation or the 19th century. We are certainly called to hear and respect the witness of our ancestors in the faith, and to learn from it. But to do this in order to engage in faithful hearing of God's word *today*. The reason is not simply that times change; it is that the gospel is always calling us forward towards the kingdom of Jesus Christ. Therefore, the church should always be:

10. B. A community in reformation

Our communions owe a particular debt to the movement of Reformation which began in Western Europe in the 16th century. Much of our institutions, order and practice derive from that beginning which retains special significance for us, whether we trace our historical origins to it more or less directly as some Reformed churches do, or only indirectly as the Disciples and newer Reformed churches do. These churches share a complex, diverse common heritage. But they also share the awareness that the church is continually called to reappraisal and renewed reformation. Complex social, political, cultural and intellectual developments since the 16th century have affected us all. Particularly important have been the Enlightenment, the evangelical awakening, and the global expansion of Christianity. The enslavement and oppression of racial groups during the period of colonization has also had far-reaching consequences. All these challenge us to look self-critically on the ways in which our churches have developed and identified themselves throughout the centuries, and in particular on the long history of Christian separation, subdivision and denomination-building. Disciples and Reformed alike are increasingly aware today that the church is called to be:

11. C. A community visibly united in the faith and service of Jesus Christ

This certainly involves the quest for unity among all Christians and churches, for ways of discovering and expressing that unity even now, albeit this is often only possible in fragmentary and provisional forms. But it is also a challenge to those churches which, like ours, are especially closely related to each other to engage seriously in the search for visible unity between themselves. Current ecumenical encounters, local, regional and international, have already increased our appreciation of each other's tradition and testimony and invite us both to critical appraisal of our own heritage and to a renewed search for a greater unity.

12. D. Lord's supper

Disciples and Reformed are in basic agreement about the meaning of the Lord's supper. We celebrate it in obedience to the command of Christ as a "sacrament" or "ordinance" instituted by him. By partaking of it we remember him and his sacrificial death, but the significance of the Lord's supper, for us, is by no means restricted to its commemorative aspect. The dominant theological position in both traditions has always stressed that the Lord's supper as a sacrament is a means of grace, a sign and seal which makes Christ's presence known to us through the invocation of the Holy Spirit (epiclesis). Whilst the Lord's supper is a memorial (anamnesis) in that it brings to redemptive memory the earthly life and death of Christ, it goes far beyond memorial, bringing the participant into communion with the One who not only died but rose again from the dead and with whom we can have a living relationship. The experience of communion with Christ, who is present in the Lord's supper, therefore evokes praise and thanksgiving (eucharistia). It also reaffirms for us that the church is a "covenant community" as we respond in a covenant meal to God's initiative. Such a response entails a commitment on the part of the eucharistic community to be a prophetic sign of God's presence with, and loving care for, humankind. Moreover, the supper, for both traditions, is a sign of the unity of believers and a means of proclaiming the significance of the death and resurrection of Christ "until he comes". This eschatological dimension not only points to future aspects of the Lord's supper as the "meal of the kingdom" but emphasizes that, through Christ, we already participate in the present reality of the kingdom of God.

13. The issue of "closed communion" which in the 19th century was instrumental in causing the Disciples to disassociate themselves from current Presbyterian practices, is no longer an issue dividing Disciples and Reformed. For the most part, Reformed churches welcome to the table members of other Christian communities, as do the Disciples. Both traditions recognize that the table is the Lord's, not ours, and that all Christians may approach that table on Christ's own invitation.

14. Both traditions affirm the importance of the Lord's supper for the life and witness of the community of faith. Reformed ministers are ordained as ministers of "word and sacrament" and Disciples ministers are ordained to these same functions. Both traditions, therefore, affirm the centrality of the Lord's supper for their understanding of the nature of church.

15. Another way of affirming the centrality of the Lord's supper for Disciples is weekly communion. Frequency of the Lord's supper has never been a divisive issue between Disciples and Reformed, although Disciples would encourage all Reformed churches to celebrate the supper more frequently than quarterly or monthly. Weekly celebration is already the practice in a number of Reformed churches. Such weekly communion, of course, has always been part of the Reformed ethos, if not of Reformed practice, as Calvin strongly (though unsuccessfully) argued for weekly communion in Geneva. The Reformed tradition, for its part, would encourage the Disciples to take even more seriously the link between the preaching of the word and the Lord's supper.

III. Issues we face together

16. A. The nature of the church

Disciples and Reformed both affirm that God's free act of grace brings the church into being. God has remained faithful to the covenant established for God's people, even when they have rebelled against it. In the fullness of time God sent his Son, Jesus Christ, to unite all in heaven and on earth in one body, giving access in one Spirit to the Father (Eph. 1:3-10, 2:11-22).

17. Thus there is only one church of God. The church is holy because God has redeemed and consecrated it through the death and resurrection of Jesus Christ. The church is catholic because Christ calls it to express the fullness of his own life and ministry, drawing all peoples into one fellowship in all places and times. The church is apostolic because Christ commissions it to proclaim to all peoples the gospel first entrusted to the apostles.

18. The church is called to a continual offering of itself and the world to God in a life of worship, prayer and praise; it receives and expresses the renewing life of the Holy Spirit in word and sacrament; it declares the reconciling and saving power of Christ in preaching and service; it bears witness to Christ's sovereignty over all the nations.

19. Hence the church, called into being by God's word, becomes visible as the local community of faith gathers around the Lord's table, receives those newly baptized into his name, studies the word of God, hears the gospel proclaimed, helps the poor and needy, and is sustained by the ministry of those called and set apart for that service. Christ has promised to be in the midst where two or three are gathered in his name, and where two or three are so gathered they are necessarily united with all others so gathered through space and time (cf. Disciples-Roman Catholic International Dialogue:

Agreed Account of Nashville Meeting, 1984, *Mid-Stream: An Ecumenical Journal*, vol. XXV, no. 4, 1986, p.417).

20. Disciples and Reformed have generally found no difficulty in relating their understanding of the church either to the local congregation or to the church universal. But it has sometimes been difficult to express the reality of the church in a way which does full justice to its nature beyond the local congregation. Moreover, particular emphases or concerns can distort the understanding of the whole. For example, the notion of a covenant people causes problems if that people is identified with a particular nation, race or state. Again, the voluntary principle, classically expressed by John Locke, that a church is a voluntary society of those who join together of their own accord to worship God, can obscure God's initiative in calling the church, and blind local congregations to their involvement with other congregations in mutual support and service. Finally, the identification of a church with a particular culture, way of life, race or social grouping, obscures God's intention that all shall be one in Christ. We recognize and confess that such partial understandings have existed in both our traditions, and that we can only realize and embody the unity God intends as we progress beyond them. Thus, although the church already is the body of Christ, in its existing forms it is a provisional embodiment of the kingdom. (cf. Anglican-Reformed international dialogue, *God's Reign and Our Unity*, §§30,35).

21. Historically the church has made affirmations of its faith in the Apostles and Nicene Creeds as a way of manifesting its unity. From the 16th century onwards the Reformed churches believed it important to express their witness to the gospel and its implications for their day in particular confessions of faith. The way such confessions of faith were sometimes used as exclusive tests of fellowship led Disciples in the 19th century to reject them and to prefer only the simplest confession of faith in Jesus Christ as the Son of God, found in the gospels and elsewhere in the New Testament.

22. Changes in biblical and theological hermeneutics have led increasing numbers in both traditions to recognize the difficulty of claiming that one particular credal formulation is an adequate statement of the truth for all peoples and times. Changes in Western culture and an increasing awareness of the challenge of other faiths and cultures have enabled us to recognize that the church needs to confess its faith today in a way which relates it both to scripture and to the contemporary world. Disciples have been reconsidering their attitude to creeds and confessions of faith. Several Reformed churches have found it necessary to confess their faith in the midst of political crisis. Several united churches have found the occasion of union to be a valuable opportunity to confess their faith. Such confessions always need to have as their purpose the building up of the body of Christ, and their authority lies in their faithfulness to the gospel rather than in the human wisdom involved in their compilation. God's grace remains primary.

23. B. Baptism

From the responses of Disciples and Reformed to the World Council of Churches' text, *Baptism, Eucharist and Ministry*, as well as from various teaching documents or common statements of churches in various national settings, it becomes clear that agreement exists on central theological convictions concerning baptism, namely that:
a) Baptism is the unique initiatory act which makes explicit for the recipient God's gracious act of redemption in Christ. It signifies dying with Christ to sin and being

raised with Christ to new life; it marks a union with Christ, and in it is promised the sanctifying power of the Holy Spirit.
b) Baptism also requires the response of faith to God's gracious action. It is administered by and within the church as the community of faith. At every baptism, the faith is confessed.
c) The difference between infant and believers' baptism becomes less sharp when it is recognized that both forms of baptism embody God's own initiative in Christ and express a personal response of faith made within a believing community. Personal confession of faith normally takes place in the presence of the congregation, either at the time of baptism in the case of the believer, or at a later time by those who are baptized as infants.
d) Baptism is the entrance to a life of discipleship within the shared ministry of the whole people of God. It bears witness to the church as a confessing community in which members are led by the Holy Spirit towards lifelong growth in faith.

24. In most places, Disciples and Reformed recognize each other as baptized members of the body of Christ and admit one another freely to their respective eucharistic celebrations.

25. They agree that teaching concerning baptism is never to be developed in a way which undercuts the centrality of justification by grace through faith.

26. Thus also neither tradition can be content with a baptismal theology which excludes children from the Christian community. Reformed affirm that children belong to the covenant people of God and signify their belonging through infant baptism. Disciples affirm that they have a place within the kingdom, which is confirmed in the face of human sin and rebellion, by baptism as a believer for the remission of sins. For a united church to have a double practice is to assert the legitimacy of both these theological views. There is need for fuller discussion in this setting of traditional teaching on original sin.

27. It is consistent with the agreed theology of baptism to perceive baptism as a once-for-all event in the life of the Christian, leading into a continued reception of grace focused by the repeated sacrament of the Lord's supper. To uphold this theology of grace, Disciples and Reformed should refuse to practise rebaptism. Recognizing that such refusal creates pastoral problems of great difficulty to some individuals and churches, they should support one another in theological and pastoral consistency.

28. C. Ministry
Our dialogue has confirmed and strengthened the sense, already developed through ecumenical discussion, cooperation and participation in uniting churches, that Disciples and Reformed are in fundamental agreement on the theology of ministry. We share the conviction that the ministry of the church has as its basis the ministry and "self-emptying" of Jesus Christ which the proclamation, witness and conduct of the life of the community is to reflect. Into this ministry, Christians are incorporated in baptism. The calling of ministry is thus given to the whole people of God, and constitutes a "priesthood of all believers" in which each Christian ministers to the other and pursues his or her vocation in the world. We believe and experience the empowering of the Holy Spirit in enabling the fulfilment of the various vocations of Christians which together comprise the ministry of the whole church.

29. Within this mutual ministry of the people of God, our traditions have reaffirmed the necessity of a ministry of word and sacrament, through which the community is challenged to be faithful, is nurtured, and proclaims the grace and presence of God. Both traditions have always affirmed that such a ministry is to be exercised collegially. They have also seen the need, through various patterns, for an expression of the church's diakonia. They have also been concerned with provisions for helping the community and communities to be built up so that they might participate more effectively in the ministry of Jesus Christ.

30. Historical experience, theological principles and the needs of ministry have led us to establish and make subject to reform, the patterns of our ministry. Despite claims in the past, Disciples and Reformed have come to acknowledge that there is no single pattern of ministry set down in the New Testament and that no exclusive claims on behalf of any of the historic patterns developed by our churches, or others, are warranted by biblical scholarship, ecumenical consensus, or the challenge of ministry. There are no differences between us to keep us apart, as is illustrated by the instances in which we are already in union.

31. Since the forms of ministry which exist at present are different at various points, despite remarkable similarities, certain issues deserve continued mutual reflection and clarification. Our efforts to deal with these issues must be set within the larger context of theological reflection on the nature of ministry carried out in ecumenical discussion today. Among the matters to be clarified are the following.

32. *The theological meaning of ordination:* Disciples and Reformed share the conviction that the ordering of the ministry of the church justifies certain ministries "set apart" within the ministry of all by the act of ordination, which must be understood in the context of the one ministry of the people of God. Our churches, like all others, are challenged to rediscover the theological meaning of ordination so that it will not be confused either with induction to a pastoral charge or with matters of practice, however significant, such as terms of employment, salary, part-time and full-time service, and standards of accreditation.

33. *Presbyteral ministry:* In our traditions ministry within the local congregation has been shared among a group of people who have overall responsibility for ensuring that the word is preached, the sacraments are administered, and discipline, governance and oversight are exercised. To care for this cluster of services our churches have developed certain "offices", e.g., the minister or pastor, the Reformed "elder" and the Disciples "elder" – which in various ways require clarification through further ecumenical dialogue.

34. *Diaconal ministry:* The Reformed in the 16th century and the Disciples in the 19th century retained, in a revised form, the office of deacon as an integral part of the ministry of the whole people of God. Both of our traditions have valued a diaconate as a means of linking the worshipping community with care for the poor and needy of the world and as a means of ordering the life of the local congregation in a way which links the ordained to the whole people of God. Since within and between our two traditions there are and have been different understandings and practices of the role and function of the diaconate, revitalization of this ministry warrants our further mutual attention.

35. *Oversight ministry:* Disciples and Reformed acknowledge, implicitly and explicitly, the need for oversight (*episcope*) within the church. Within the local congregation this has been focused in the pastors, and shared with elders. Beyond the local

congregation oversight has been exercised in a variety of ways with different combinations of individual and collegial ministry. In the light of ecumenical dialogue (e.g., *Baptism, Eucharist and Ministry*), and practical experience of cooperation with other church traditions (e.g., local ecumenical projects in England), both Disciples and Reformed are called upon to consider anew the provisions for *episcope* present within their bodies.

36. Both the Disciples and many of the Reformed ordain women, in keeping with their understanding of oneness in Christ, the inclusiveness of the ministry to the gospel, and the gifts of ministry given to Christians regardless of their sex, race, and other natural and social distinctions. Although we have not considered the *ordination of women* to be an obstacle to mutual recognition between our churches and those which cannot yet in conscience affirm the ordination of women, we cannot consider the issue to be in any way secondary or expendable in the effort for unity in the church, and we therefore press in ecumenical dialogue to keep this concern before all churches of Jesus Christ. We also press to keep before our own churches the concern that all prejudices be eliminated and full equality of opportunity be obtained in our responses to God's call to women in ministry.

IV. Recommendations

37. On the basis of these discussions we believe there are no theological or ecclesiological issues which need to divide us as churches. Consequently we request the Disciples Ecumenical Consultative Council and the World Alliance of Reformed Churches call upon their member churches to say whether or not they can accept the following declaration:

> The Disciples of Christ and the Reformed churches recognize and accept each other as visible expressions of the one church of Christ.

Acceptance of this declaration presses us beyond our divided histories towards a common ecumenical future. We believe that this declaration has several specific implications. It implies sufficient consensus between our two traditions on the meaning of the gospel, on baptism, the Lord's supper and ministry to enable our churches to recognize and accept each other's members and ministries, to share reciprocally the Lord's supper, and to engage in common mission, evangelism and service in the world. The acceptance of each other as churches also implies our commitment to remove other obstacles which keep us from sharing full fellowship and mission in the name of Christ.

38. This unity will clearly need to be expressed in each local and national context where Disciples and Reformed exist. Its form will vary in different situations. Faithfulness to God's call to visible unity may encourage some of our churches to achieve *some form of visible unity* in their national or regional situation. Our member churches may also be drawn into *closer cooperation* (e.g., local covenants, shared buildings, shared ministries, united congregations, joint mission beyond the congregations, and joint theological education) and into *costly solidarity* with the poor, oppressed and marginalized. Our churches may further be drawn into dialogue on specific theological and missional issues, e.g., the presidency of the Lord's supper, the crisis of the environment, peace and justice, the witness of the disabled, the use of inclusive language in theology and liturgy.

39. We trust our common declaration will lead the Disciples Ecumenical Consultative Council and the World Alliance of Reformed Churches to work more deliberately to express their unity in Christ. In anticipation of a growing relationship of unity, we propose several new links, namely that the Disciples Ecumenical Consultative Council and the World Alliance of Reformed Churches:

i) establish regular communication between each other, especially about the major activities, programme strategies and ecclesiological developments in each tradition, and involving reports to their plenary meetings;
ii) send special delegations to each meeting of the DECC's assembly (every 5-7 years) and the WARC's general council (every 5-7 years): these delegations should include persons from diverse constituencies, such as women and men, those from the third world, as well as Europe and North America, and those of different races and ethnic groups;
iii) encourage awareness and learning experience from those united churches in which Disciples and Reformed have lived together in faith and witness (viz., United Kingdom, North India, Zaire, Jamaica, Japan, Southern Africa);
iv) pursue common theological work, focusing upon common concerns which emerge from our participation in the wider ecumenical movement;
v) give attention to the widespread distribution of this report of the Birmingham international consultation, calling upon the churches to study its issues and proposals and to offer their counsel about the future between these two families of churches.

Historical Introduction

The way to dialogue between the Orthodox church and the Oriental-Orthodox church was opened up by many official and unofficial initiatives on both sides, as well as by important theological meetings in the context of the ecumenical movement. The pan-Orthodox conferences of 1961, 1962, 1963 and 1968 encouraged the idea of an official theological dialogue, as did the first preconciliar pan-Orthodox conference of 1976. But the official announcement of such a dialogue was postponed for numerous non-ecclesiastical reasons. After a series of consultations, the joint theological commission was convened for dialogue; it met for its first plenary session at Chambésy, Geneva, in 1985.

This first session proceeded to examine and evaluate earlier ecclesial and theological meetings, for it regarded these as providing useful material for the commission's work. It discussed and agreed upon basic principles of methodology for the conduct of the dialogue, and decided on a first set of subjects, as follows:

The way to a common Christology
1) problems of terminology;
2) conciliar formulations;
3) historical factors;
4) interpretation of christological dogmas today.

In the theological discussions of this first session it was established, on the basis of the results achieved in previous theological meetings, that the two ecclesial families (1) both represent and express the ancient patristic and general church tradition, and (2) despite their different approaches and their divergent interpretation of the inherited christological concepts, are in agreement on the content of their christological teaching. There was thus a positive desire for rapid progress in the work of the joint theological commission, a desire expressed by both sides in statements of the heads of the Oriental Orthodox churches and in the official position taken by the Orthodox church at the third preconciliar pan-Orthodox conference. The latter greeted "with special satisfaction" the opening of the official theological dialogue, and stressed that the prospects for this dialogue "give justified hope that the two churches will together find a solution to questions which have to do with statements of the fourth ecumenical council and are indissolubly connected with the christological decisions of the other ecumenical councils" and that "the (Oriental Orthodox) churches will come to accept the fourth, fifth, sixth and seventh ecumenical councils, so that the reciprocal excommunications may be lifted".

The second meeting of the joint theological commission took place at the monastery of Anba Bishoy in Egypt (June 1989) and continued its work on the basis of a document drafted by a joint theological sub-committee (Corinth 1987) concerning christological terminology. During the first session Shenouda, Patriarch of the Coptic Church, called upon the members of the joint theological commission to find a way of restoring communion between the two ecclesial families. After lengthy and intense discussions of the draft document a small committee composed a final text which, after some changes, was unanimously accepted by all members.

The joint theological commission appointed a joint sub-committee to study and draw up concrete proposals for dealing with the common pastoral problems that had been brought to light. It also determined the subjects and appointed the speakers for the next meeting, which was to take place in September 1990 at Chambésy, Geneva, and discuss the following:
1) report of the joint sub-committee on pastoral problems;
2) conciliar formulations and anathemas;
3) historical factors;
4) interpretation of christological dogmas today;
5) future steps.

I call attention here to the conclusion of the joint text accepted by both sides, in which emphasis is placed on the awareness of the members that "our mutual agreement is not limited to Christology, but encompasses the whole faith of the one undivided church of the early centuries". This statement gained a highly positive acceptance from both Orthodox and Oriental Orthodox churches.

The joint sub-committee for pastoral problems met at the monastery of Amba Bishoy in Egypt (31 January-4 February 1990) and conducted its work in accordance with the guidelines set down at the plenary session of the joint theological commission. The fruits of its discussions were assembled in a joint statement which the sub-committee forwarded to the plenary session of the joint theological commission. The intention was to promote fraternal relations and collaboration between the two churches. For the future this meant concretely: bridging the gap created by past misunderstandings; proclaiming complete agreement on christological dogma; and giving reciprocal recognition to baptisms and pastoral undertakings. Theological collaboration was to proceed in a systematic way; ecumenical relations with the rest of the Christian world were to be coordinated; and there was to be more extensive collaboration, so that the common inheritance from the fathers and the common spirituality might find useful expression.

The third session of the joint theological commission was held at the Orthodox Centre of the Ecumenical Patriarchate in Chambésy, Geneva (23-28 September 1990). The subject of its discussions was the suggestions made by the sub-committees for pastoral themes and for theological discussion. These sub-committees had likewise met at the Orthodox Centre, but before the work of the plenary assembly began (20-23 September 1990). After detailed theological discussions a joint communique was composed, in which the communion in faith that had been revealed was confirmed:
a) Those errors are condemned which have habitually been attributed by each side to the other and have for a long time burdened the consciousnesses of the churches with polemical theological confrontations and conflicts.

b) All the solidly established criteria that reflect conciliar decisions and/or the patristic tradition and that confirm the agreement of the two dialoguing churches on Orthodox christological doctrine are specified and listed.
c) Complete agreement on the essential elements of the faith (elements that are also necessarily presupposed in the restoration of eucharistic communion) is likewise emphasized.
d) Emphasis is also placed on everything that is necessary from the ecclesial point of view as well as everything that must be regarded as theologically possible, so that the anathemas imposed by both sides (whether by councils or by persons of the two churches) may be lifted.
e) There is unanimous agreement that the manner in which each church lifts the anathemas issued by both sides should make clearer the way to a reciprocal enrichment of Orthodox spirituality and the strengthening of Orthodox witness in the contemporary world.

The joint statements unanimously accepted by the members of the joint theological commission rightly emphasize the point that the theological labours of this commission have been completed, since there are no further serious and essential theological problems requiring investigation. The norm of a common response to the common patristic tradition also determines the importance of any partially divergent practices; these cannot be regarded as valid grounds for the further postponement of ecclesial communion.

Damaskinos Papandreou

12. Communique

Chambésy, Geneva, Switzerland, 15 December 1985

After two decades of unofficial theological consultations and meetings (1964-85), moved forward by the reconciling grace of the Holy Spirit, we, the representatives of the two families of the Orthodox tradition, were delegated by our churches in their faithfulness to the Holy Trinity, and out of their concern for the unity of the body of Jesus Christ, to take up our theological dialogue on an official level.

We thank God, the Holy Trinity, the Father, the Son and the Holy Spirit, for granting us the fraternal spirit of love and understanding which dominated our meeting throughout.

The first part of our discussions centred on the appellation of the two families in our dialogue. Some discussion was also devoted to the four unofficial consultations of Aarhus (1964), Bristol (1967), Geneva (1970) and Addis Ababa (1971). It was thought that the studies and "agreed statements" of these unofficial consultations as well as the studies of our theologians could provide useful material for our official dialogue.

A concrete form of methodology to be followed in our dialogue was adopted by the joint commission. A joint sub-committee of six theologians was set up, three from each side, with the mandate to prepare common texts for our future work.

For the next meetings, whose aim would be to rediscover our common grounds in Christology and ecclesiology, the following main theme and subsequent sub-themes were agreed upon:

Towards a Common Christology
1) problems of terminology;
2) conciliar formulations;
3) historical factors;
4) interpretation of Christological dogmas today.

Special thanks were expressed to the Ecumenical Patriarchate for convening this official dialogue, as well as for the services and facilities which were offered for our first meeting here in Chambésy, Geneva, at the Orthodox Centre.

We hope that the faithful of our churches will pray with us for the continuation and success of our work.

Prof. Dr Chrysostomos Konstantinidis
Metropolitan of Myra
Ecumenical Patriarchate

Bishop Bishoy
Coptic Orthodox Church

Co-presidents of the commission

13. Communique

Anba Bishoy Monastery, Egypt, 24 June 1989

The second meeting of the joint commission of the theological dialogue between the Orthodox church and the Oriental Orthodox churches took place at the Anba Bishoy Monastery in Wadi-El-Natroun, Egypt, from 20 to 24 June 1989.

The official representatives of the two families of churches of the Orthodox churches met in an atmosphere of warm cordiality and Christian brotherhood for four days at the guest house of the patriarchal residence at the monastery, and experienced the gracious hospitality and kindness of the Coptic Orthodox pope and patriarch of Alexandria and his church.

His Holiness Pope and Patriarch Shenouda addressed the opening session of the meeting and appealed to the participants to find a way to restore communion between the two families of churches. The participants also travelled to Cairo to listen to the weekly address of Pope Shenouda to thousands of the faithful in the great cathedral of Cairo. Pope Shenouda also received the participants at his residence later.

The twenty-three participants came from thirteen countries and represented thirteen churches. The main item for consideration was the report of the joint sub-committee of six theologians on the problems of terminology and interpretation of christological dogmas today. The meetings were co-chaired by His Eminence Metropolitan Damaskinos of Switzerland and His Grace Bishop Bishoy of Damiette. In his response to Pope Shenouda, Metropolitan Damaskinos appealed to the participants to overcome difficulties caused by differences of formulation. Words should serve and express the essence, which is our common search for restoration of full communion. "This division is an anomaly, a bleeding wound in the body of Christ, a wound which, according to his will that we humbly serve, must be healed."

A small drafting group composed of Metropolitan Paulos Mar Gregorios of New Delhi, Prof. Vlassios Phidas, Prof. Fr John Romanides, Prof. Dimitroff and Mr Joseph Moris Faltas produced a brief statement of faith based on the report of the joint sub-committee, in which the common christological convictions of the two sides were expressed. This statement, after certain modifications, was adopted by the joint commission for transmission to our churches for their approval and as an expression for our common faith, on the way to restoration of full communion between the two families of churches. The statement follows:

Agreed statement

We have inherited from our fathers in Christ the one apostolic faith and Tradition, though as churches we have been separated from each other for centuries. As two families of Orthodox churches long out of communion with each other, we now pray and trust in God to restore that communion on the basis of the common apostolic faith of the undivided church of the first centuries which we confess in our common creed. What follows is a simple reverent statement of what we do believe, on our way to restore communion between our two families of Orthodox churches.

Throughout our discussions we have found our common ground in the formula of our common father, St Cyril of Alexandria: *mia physis (hypostasis) tou Theou Logou sesarkomené*, and in his dictum that "it is sufficient for the confession of our true and irreproachable faith to say and to confess that the Holy Virgin is Theotokos (Hom. 15, cf. Ep. 39)".

***

Great indeed is the wonderful mystery of the Father, Son and Holy Spirit, one True God, one *ousia* in three *hypostases* or three *prosopa*. Blessed be the Name of the Lord our God for ever and ever.

Great indeed is also the ineffable mystery of the incarnation of our Lord Jesus Christ, for us and for our salvation.

The Logos, eternally consubstantial with the Father and the Holy Spirit in his divinity, has in these last days become incarnate of the Holy Spirit and Blessed Virgin Mary Theotokos, and thus became man, consubstantial with us in his humanity but without sin. He is true God and true man at the same time, perfect in his divinity, perfect in his humanity. Because the one she bore in her womb was at the same time fully God as well as fully human we call the Blessed Virgin Theotokos.

When we speak of the one composite *(synthetos)* hypostasis of our Lord Jesus Christ, we do not say that in him a divine hypostasis and a human hypostasis came together. It is that the one eternal hypostasis of the Second Person of the Trinity has assumed our created human nature in that act uniting it with his own uncreated divine nature, to form an inseparably and unconfusedly united real divine-human being, the natures being distinguished from each other in contemplation *(theoria)* only.

The hypostasis of the Logos before the incarnation, even with his divine nature, is of course not composite. The same hypostasis, as distinct from nature, of the incarnate Logos, is not composite either. The unique theandric person *(prosopon)* of Jesus Christ is one eternal hypostasis who has assumed human nature by the incarnation. So we call that hypostasis composite, on account of the natures which are united to form one composite unity. It is not the case that our fathers used *physis* and *hypostasis* always interchangeably and confused the one with the other. The term hypostasis can be used to denote both the person as distinct from nature, and also the person with the nature, for a hypostasis never in fact exists without a nature.

It is the same hypostasis of the Second Person of the Trinity, eternally begotten from the Father who in these last days became a human being and was born of the Blessed Virgin. This is the mystery of the hypostatic union we confess in humble adoration – the real union of the divine with the human, with all the properties and functions of the uncreated divine nature, including natural will and natural energy, inseparably and unconfusedly united with the created human nature with all its properties and functions, including natural will and natural energy. It is the Logos incarnate who is the subject of all the willing and acting of Jesus Christ.

We agree in condemning the Nestorian and the Eutychian heresies. We neither separate nor divide the human nature in Christ from his divine nature, nor do we think that the former was absorbed in the latter and thus ceased to exist.

The four adverbs used to qualify the mystery of the hypostatic union belong to our common tradition – without commingling (or confusion) *(asyngchytós)*, without change *(atreptós)*, without separation *(achoristós)* and without division *(adiairetós)*. Those among us who speak of two natures in Christ do not thereby deny their inseparable, indivisible union; those among us who speak of one united divine-human nature in Christ do not thereby deny the continuing dynamic presence in Christ of the divine and the human, without change, without confusion.

Our mutual agreement is not limited to Christology, but encompasses the whole faith of the one undivided church of the early centuries. We are agreed also in our understanding of the Person and work of God the Holy Spirit, who proceeds from the Father alone, and is always adored with the Father and the Son.

The joint commission also appointed a joint sub-committee for pastoral problems between churches of the two families, composed of the following ten persons:

Metropolitan Damaskinos, co-president, ex officio
Bishop Bishoy, co-president, ex officio
Prof. Vlassios Phidas, co-secretary, ex officio
Bishop Mesrob Krikorian, co-secretary, ex officio
Metropolitan Georges Khodr of Mount Lebanon
Metropolian Petros of Axum
Prof. Gosevic (Serbia)
Prof. Dr K.M. George (India)
A nominee of Patriarch Ignatius Zakka Iwas of Syria
Metropolitan Gregorios of Shoa

This joint sub-committee will have its first meeting from 5 to 9 December in Anba Bishoy Monastery and will prepare a report for the next meeting of the joint commission.

It was also decided that the next meeting of the joint commission would be held in September 1990 at Chambésy, Geneva, to consider:
1) the report of the joint sub-committee on pastoral problems;
2) conciliar formulations and anathemas (Rev. Prof. John S. Romanides, H.E. Dr Paulos Mar Gregorios);
3) historical factors (Prof. Vlassios Phidas, Rev. Father Tadros Y. Malaty);
4) interpretation of christological dogmas today (Metropolitan Georges Khodr of Mount Lebanon, Bishop Mesrob Krikorian and Mr Joseph Moris);
5) future steps.

It was also decided that the name of the joint commission would be Joint Commission of the Orthodox Church and the Oriental Orthodox Churches.

VIII. EASTERN ORTHODOX-ORIENTAL ORTHODOX DIALOGUE

14. Second Agreed Statement and Recommendations to the Churches

Chambésy, Geneva, Switzerland, 28 September 1990

Introduction

The third meeting of the joint commission of the theological dialogue between the Orthodox church and the Oriental Orthodox churches took place at the Orthodox Centre of the Ecumenical Patriarchate, Chambésy, Geneva, from 23 to 28 September 1990.

The official representatives of the two families of the Orthodox churches and their advisors met in an atmosphere of prayerful waiting on the Holy Spirit and warm, cordial, Christian brotherly affection. We experienced the gracious and generous hospitality of His Holiness Patriarch Dimitrios I, through His Eminence Metropolitan Damaskinos of Switzerland in the Orthodox Centre of the Ecumenical Patriarchate. We were also received at two grand receptions, one at the residence of Metropolitan Damaskinos and the other at the residence of His Excellency, Mr Kerkinos, the ambassador of Greece to the United Nations, and Mrs Kerkinos.

The 34 participants came from Austria, Bulgaria, Cyprus, Czechoslovakia, Egypt, Ethiopia, Finland, Greece, India, Lebanon, Poland, Switzerland, Syria, UK, USA, USSR (Russian church, Georgian church and Armenian church), and Yugoslavia. The six days of meetings were co-chaired by His Eminence Metropolitan Damaskinos of Switzerland and His Grace Metropolitan Bishoy of Damiette. His Eminence Metropolitan Damaskinos in his inaugural address exhorted the participants to "work in a spirit of humility, brotherly love and mutual recognition" so that "the Lord of the faith and Head of his church" will guide us by the Holy Spirit on the speedier way towards unity and communion.

The meeting received two reports, one from its theological sub-committee, which met at the Orthodox Centre, Chambésy (20-22 September 1990), and the other from its committee on pastoral relations, which met at the Anba Bishoy Monastery, Egypt (31 January to 4 February 1990). The following papers which had been presented to the theological sub-committee were distributed to the participants:
1) dogmatic formulations and anathemas by local and ecumenical synods within their social context: Rev. Prof. John S. Romanides, Church of Greece;
2) anathemas and conciliar decisions — two issues to be settled for restoration of communion among Oriental Orthodox and Eastern Orthodox churches: Dr Paulos Mar Gregorios, Metropolitan of Delhi, Orthodox Syrian Church of the East;
3) historical factors and the council of Chalcedon: Fr T. Malaty, Coptic Orthodox Church;

4) historical factors and the terminology of the synod of Chalcedon (451): Prof. Dr Vlassios Phidas, Greek Orthodox Patriarchate of Alexandria;
5) interpretation of christological dogmas today: Metropolitan Georges Khodr, Greek Orthodox Patriarchate of Antioch;
6) interpretation of christological dogmas today: Bishop Mesrob Krikorian, Armenian Apostolic Church of Etchmiadzin.

The six papers and the two sub-committee reports, along with the "summary of conclusions" of the fourth unofficial conversations at Addis Ababa (1971) which was appended to the report of the theological sub-committee, formed the basis of our intensive and friendly discussion on the issues and actions to be taken. A drafting committee composed of Metropolitan Georges Khodr, Metropolitan Paulos Mar Gregorios, Archbishop Keshishian, Archbishop Garima, Rev. Prof. John Romanides, Metropolitan Matta Mar Eustathius (Syria), Prof. Ivan Dimitrov (Bulgaria) with Prof. V. Phidas and Bishop Krikorian as co-secretaries, produced the draft for the second agreed statement and recommendations to churches. Another drafting committee composed of Prof. Papavassiliou (Cyprus), Bishop Christoforos (Czechoslovakia), Metropolitan Paulos Mar Gregorios and Liqaselttanat Habtemariam (Ethiopia), with Fr Dr George Dragas as secretary, produced the draft for the recommendations on pastoral issues.

The following is the text of the unanimously approved second agreed statement and recommendations:

Second Agreed Statement and Recommendations to the Churches
The first agreed statement on Christology adopted by the joint commission of the theological dialogue between the Orthodox and Oriental Orthodox churches, at our historic meeting at the Anba Bishoy Monastery, Egypt, from 20 to 24 June 1989, forms the basis of this second agreed statement on the following affirmations of our common faith and understanding, and recommendations on steps to be taken for the communion of our two families of churches in Jesus Christ our Lord, who prayed "that they all may be one".

1. Both families agree in condemning the Eutychian heresy. Both families confess that the Logos, the Second Person of the Holy Trinity, only begotten of the Father before the ages and consubstantial with him, was incarnate and was born from the Virgin Mary Theotokos; fully consubstantial with us, perfect man with soul, body and mind ($νοῦς$); he was crucified, died, was buried, and rose from the dead on the third day, ascended to the heavenly Father, where He sits on the right hand of the Father as Lord of all creation. At Pentecost, by the coming of the Holy Spirit, he manifested the church as his body. We look forward to his coming again in the fullness of his glory, according to the scriptures.

2. Both families condemn the Nestorian heresy and the crypto-Nestorianism of Theodoret of Cyrus. They agree that it is not sufficient merely to say that Christ is consubstantial both with the Father and with us, by nature God and by nature man; it is necessary to affirm also that the Logos, who is by nature God, became by nature man, by his incarnation in the fullness of time.

3. Both families agree that the hypostasis of the Logos became composite ($σύνθετος$) by uniting to his divine uncreated nature with its natural will and energy, which he has in common with the Father and the Holy Spirit, created human

nature, which he assumed at the incarnation and made his own, with its natural will and energy.

4. Both families agree that the natures with their proper energies and wills are united hypostatically and naturally without confusion, without change, without division and without separation, and that they are distinguished in thought alone (τῇ θεωρίᾳ μόνῃ).

5. Both families agree that he who wills and acts is always the one hypostasis of the Logos incarnate.

6. Both families agree in rejecting interpretations of councils which do not fully agree with the horos of the third ecumenical council and the letter (433) of Cyril of Alexandria to John of Antioch.

7. The Orthodox agree that the Oriental Orthodox will continue to maintain their traditional Cyrillian terminology of "one nature of the incarnate Logos ("μία φύσις τοῦ θεοῦ Λόγου σεσαρκωμένη"), since they acknowledge the double consubstantiality of the Logos which Eutyches denied. The Orthodox also use this terminology. The Oriental Orthodox agree that the Orthodox are justified in their use of the two-natures formula, since they acknowledge that the distinction is "in thought alone" ("τῇ θεωρίᾳ μόνῃ"). Cyril interpreted correctly this use in his letter to John of Antioch and his letters to Acacius of Melitene (PG 77,184-201), to Eulogius (PG 77,224-228) and to Succensus (PG 77,228-245).

8. Both families accept the first three ecumenical councils, which form our common heritage. In relation to the four later councils of the Orthodox church, the Orthodox state that for them the above points 1-7 are the teachings also of the four later councils of the Orthodox church, while the Oriental Orthodox consider this statement of the Orthodox as their interpretation. With this understanding, the Oriental Orthodox respond to it positively.

In relation to the teaching of the seventh ecumenical council of the Orthodox church, the Oriental Orthodox agree that the theology and practice of the veneration of icons taught by that council are in basic agreement with the teaching and practice of the Oriental Orthodox from ancient times, long before the convening of the council, and that we have no disagreements in this regard.

9. In the light of our agreed statement on Christology as well as of the above common affirmations, we have now clearly understood that both families have always loyally maintained the same authentic Orthodox christological faith, and the unbroken continuity of the apostolic tradition, though they may have used christological terms in different ways. It is this common faith and continuous loyalty to the apostolic Tradition that should be the basis of our unity and communion.

10. Both families agree that all the anathemas and condemnations of the past which now divide us should be lifted by the churches in order that the last obstacle to the full unity and communion of our two families can be removed by the grace and power of God. Both families agree that the lifting of anathemas and condemnations will be consummated on the basis that the councils and fathers previously anathematized or condemned are not heretical.

We therefore recommend to our churches the following practical steps:
A. The Orthodox should lift all anathemas and condemnations against all Oriental Orthodox councils and fathers whom they have anathematized or condemned in the past.

B. The Oriental Orthodox should at the same time lift all anathemas and condemnations against all Orthodox councils and fathers, whom they have anathematized or condemned in the past.

C. The manner in which the anathemas are to be lifted should be decided by the churches individually.

Trusting in the power of the Holy Spirit, the spirit of truth, unity and love, we submit this agreed statement and recommendations to our venerable churches for their consideration and action, praying that the same Spirit will lead us to that unity for which our Lord prayed and prays.

Signatures of the second agreed statement and recommendations to the churches, Chambésy, 28 September 1990

Metropolitan Damaskinos   Metropolitan Bishoy
Co-president, Ecumenical Patriarchate Co-president, Coptic Orthodox Church

Recommendations on Pastoral Issues

The joint commission of the theological dialogue between the Orthodox church and the Oriental Orthodox churches, at its meeting at the Orthodox Centre of the Ecumenical Patriarchate, in Chambésy, Geneva, from 23 to 28 September 1990, received a report from its joint pastoral sub-committee which had met at the Anba Bishoy Monastery in Egypt from 31 January to 4 February 1990. The report was the starting point for an extended discussion of four types of pastoral issues:

I. Relations among our two families of churches, and our preparation for unity.
II. Relations of our churches with other Christian churches and our common participation in the ecumenical movement.
III. Our common service to the world of suffering, need, injustice and conflicts.
IV. Our cooperation in the propagation of our common faith and tradition.

I. Relations among our two families of churches

1. We feel as a joint theological commission that a period of intense preparation of our people to participate in the implementation of our recommendations and in the restoration of communion of our churches is needed. To this end we propose the following practical procedure.

2. It is important to plan an exchange of visits by our heads of churches and prelates, priests and laypeople of each one of our two families of churches to the other.

3. It is important to give further encouragement to exchange of theological professors and students among theological institutions of the two families for periods varying from one week to several years.

4. In localities where churches of the two families co-exist, the congregations should organize participation of one group of people-men, women, youth and children, including priests, where possible from one congregation of one family to a congregation of the other to attend in the latter's eucharistic worship on Sundays and feast days.

5. Publications:
a) We need to publish, in the various languages of our churches, the key documents of this joint commission with explanatory notes, in small pamphlets to be sold at a reasonable price in all our congregations.

b) It will be useful also to have brief pamphlets explaining in simple terms the meaning of the christological terminology and interpreting the variety of terminology taken by various persons and groups in the course of history in the light of our agreed statement on Christology.
c) We need a book which gives some brief account, both historical and descriptive, of all the churches of our two families. This should also be produced in the various languages of our peoples, with pictures and photographs as much as possible
d) We need to promote brief books of church history by specialist authors giving a more positive understanding of the divergencies of the 5th, 6th and 7th centuries.

6. Churches of both families should agree that they will not rebaptize members of each other, for recognition of the baptism of the churches of our two families, if they have not already done so.

7. Churches should initiate bilateral negotiations for facilitating each other in using each other's church premises in special cases where any of them is deprived of such means.

8. Where conflicts arise between churches of our two families, e.g. (a) marriages consecrated in one church being annulled by a bishop of another church; (b) marriages between members of our two families being celebrated in one church over against the other; (c) or children from such marriages being forced to join the one church against the other, the churches involved should come to bilateral agreements on the procedure to be adopted until such problems are finally solved by our union.

9. The churches of both families should be encouraged to look into the theological curriculum and books used in their institutions and make necessary additions and changes in them with the view to promoting better understanding of the other family of churches. They may also profitably devise programmes for instructing the pastors and people in our congregations on the issues related to the union of the two families.

II. Relations of our churches with other Christian churches in the world

10. Our common participation in the ecumenical movement and our involvement in the World Council of Churches needs better coordination to make it more effective and fruitful for the promotion of the faith which was once delivered to the saints in the context of the ecumenical movement. We could have a preliminary discussion of this question at the seventh assembly of the WCC at Canberra, Australia, in February 1991 as well as in regional and national councils of churches and work out an appropriate scheme for more effective coordination of our efforts.

11. There are crucial issues in which our two families agree fundamentally and have disagreements with the Roman Catholic and Protestant churches. We could organize small joint consultations on issues like:
a) the position and role of the woman in the life of the church and our common Orthodox response to the contemporary problem of other Christian communities concerning the ordination of women to the priesthood;
b) pastoral care for mixed marriages between Orthodox and heterodox Christians;
c) marriages between Orthodox Christians and members of other religions;
d) the Orthodox position on dissolution or annulment of marriage, divorce and separation of married couples;
e) abortion.

12. A joint consultation should be held on the burning problem of proselytism, vis-a-vis religious freedom to draw up the framework of an agreement with other churches, for the procedure to be followed when an Orthodox or Oriental Orthodox person or family wants to join another (Catholic or Protestant) church or vice versa.

13. A special joint consultation should be held on the theology and practice of uniatism in the Roman Catholic Church, as a prelude to a discussion with the Roman Catholic Church on this subject.

14. We need to have another joint consultation to coordinate the results of the several bilateral conversations now going on or held in the past by churches of our two families with other Catholic and Protestant churches.

III. Our common service to the world of suffering, need, injustice and conflicts

15. We need to think together how best we could coordinate our existing schemes for promoting our humanitarian and philanthropic projects in the socio-ethnic context of our peoples and of the world at large. This would entail our common approach to such problems as:
a) hunger and poverty,
b) sickness and suffering,
c) political, religious and social discrimination,
d) refugees and victims of war,
e) youth, drugs and unemployment,
f) the mentally and physically handicapped,
g) the old and the aged.

IV. Our cooperation in the propagation of the Christian faith

16. We need to encourage and promote mutual cooperation as far as possible in the work of our inner mission to our people, i.e., in instructing them in the faith, and how to cope with modern dangers arising from contemporary secularism, including cults, ideologies, materialism, aids, homosexuality, the permissive society, consumerism, etc.

17. We also need to find a proper way for collaborating with each other and with other Christians in the Christian mission to the world without undermining the authority and integrity of the local Orthodox churches.

15. The Church: Community of Grace
Lutheran-Methodist Dialogue 1979-84

Bossey, near Geneva, Switzerland, June 1984

Preface

It is with deep gratitude and joy that we are able to present the results of the dialogue between the Lutheran World Federation and the World Methodist Council to the decision-making bodies and member churches of our two communions.

During five well-prepared meetings between 1979 and 1984, our joint commission has been able to discuss a wide range of questions which are central to our faith and Christian life as individuals and churches. Our report witnesses to important agreements and convergences and indicates the ways in which we express our common faith differently. On that basis the joint commission recommends steps towards closer fellowship between our churches, including pulpit exchanges and mutual hospitality at the table of the Lord.

It is our hope and wish that the results of this dialogue will be used in our churches as a source and impulse for closer relations in life, witness and service and as a basis for further dialogue where the need to achieve an even fuller agreement is felt.

May the Holy Spirit whose power and guidance we celebrate again at this Pentecost time lead us towards that visible unity of all Christians for which our Lord prayed.

Dr Carl H. Mau   Dr Joe Hale
General secretary   General secretary
Lutheran World Federation   World Methodist Council

Introduction

A. History of the dialogue

1. The bilateral dialogue between the Lutheran World Federation (LWF) and the World Methodist Council (WMC) on the theme "The Church: Community of Grace" traces its origin to the conference of secretaries of Christian world communions in Rome, 1977. On the evening of 17 May a small group of Methodists and Lutherans met to discuss the arrangements for an exploratory conversation between their two confessional families.[1] The officers of the LWF and WMC decided to send seven participants

---

[1] The Methodists were Bishop William R. Cannon, member of the Presidium of the World Methodist Council; Dr Joe Hale, general secretary of the WMC; and Mr Frank Northam, secretary, Geneva office, WMC. Representing the Lutherans were Dr Carl H. Mau, Jr, general secretary of the Lutheran World Federation; Dr Daniel Martensen, secretary for interconfessional research, LWF; and Dr Harding Meyer, research professor, Institute for Ecumenical Research, Strasbourg.

from each side to an exploratory consultation 5-9 December 1977 at Epworth-by-the-Sea, St Simons Island, Georgia, USA.

2. The Epworth-by-the-Sea consultation was organized around four topics: basic commonalities, issues needing clarification, common tasks confronting Lutherans and Methodists, and methodological and practical implications of a Lutheran-Methodist dialogue at the world level. The participants concluded that such a dialogue could contribute to the progress of ecumenism to a degree that would justify the required scholarly effort and financial expenditure. Thus they prepared a statement of purpose and a five-part programme of discussion for submission to their respective executive committees.

3. The purpose of the dialogue would be:
a) to contribute to mutual understanding and respect between Methodists and Lutherans for both their similarities and their differences;
b) to help demonstrate that Lutheranism and Methodism are parts of one community in Christ and seek to stand together in their witness and service in the world;
c) to strengthen possibilities for practising fellowship in word and sacrament between Lutheranism and Methodism;
d) to provide theological support for church cooperation and unity according to local needs and possibilities.

4. Further, under the theme "The Church: Community of Grace", five topics would be explored:
a) biblical authority and the authenticity of the church;
b) the gospel of grace;
c) the Holy Spirit in the church, the communion of saints, the body of Christ;
d) the sacraments of the gospel;
e) the mission of the church in today's world.

5. The Lutheran-Methodist joint commission would be comprised of six to eight members from each side (not including staff), with special attention to world geographical inclusiveness.

6. Both the LWF and the WMC gave approval to this proposal. They appointed a joint commission of 16 members, representing Methodist and Lutheran churches in Africa, Asia, Europe, North America and Latin America, and a significant sequence of consultations followed.

The *first* session of the joint commission was held at Dresden, 20-26 January 1979. The main topics of this meeting were the authority of scripture, the role of human reason, and the nature of Christian experience.

The *second* session was held at Bristol, England, 12-16 May 1980. Issues discussed there were Christian experience, justification and sanctification.

The *third* session was held in Oslo, Norway, 3-9 October 1981. Topics discussed were the Holy Spirit and ecclesiology.

The *fourth* session was held at Lake Junaluska, North Carolina, 20-26 March 1983. The means of grace, baptism and eucharist, church order, and the discussion of a first draft of this common statement were the main themes.

The *fifth* session was held at Bossey near Geneva, Switzerland, 3-8 March 1984, at which time evangelization, social ethics and adoption of a final report were the agenda items.

7. For the Lutheran World Federation, this dialogue with the World Methodist Council was part of a series of official dialogues with other Christian world commu-

nions, including the Roman Catholic Church, the Anglican Communion, the Orthodox churches and (from 1985) the Baptist World Alliance. In 1967 the World Methodist Council began an official bilateral dialogue with the Roman Catholic Church. The dialogue with the Lutheran World Federation was the second international dialogue of the WMC. The present dialogue must be seen not only in the context of worldwide ecumenicity but also as related to a considerable number of Lutheran-Methodist bilateral dialogues on the national level and to other expressions of increasing contacts and improving relationships between churches of our two confessional traditions.

B. Background and experience of the dialogue

8. The background of and reason for the dialogue is the recognition that while Lutheran and Methodist churches differ from one another in expressions of faith, life, ethos and order, these differences are often the result of the specific origins and subsequent developments of both churches.

– Lutheranism started as a reform movement within the late medieval church and assumed its specific identity in the conviction that it had rediscovered and restated fundamental Christian truths in obedience to the word of God and in continuity with the early fathers of the church. Its identity was also shaped by its distinction from and conflict with the Roman Catholic Church on the one hand, and the Anabaptist and in part also the Reformed tradition on the other hand.

– Methodism emerged in a completely different context and in a later era. The context of its origin was the Anglican tradition. Methodism was a reform movement which desired to spread scriptural Christianity to all, especially to the neglected multitudes both inside and outside the church; it assumed its specific identity in response to the developing unbelief of the Enlightenment mentality and within the rapidly changing human and social conditions of the new era of industrialization and urbanization.

9. The differences between the Methodist and Lutheran churches, therefore, cannot simply be identified by reference to a series of specific points of doctrinal conflict and controversy. Rather, both churches represent traditions which are committed to faithful service and proclamation of the gospel of Jesus Christ in and for this world.

10. Lutheran and Methodist churches have lived side by side in many countries, and often for a long time. Their relationship has on the whole been marked neither by open doctrinal controversy nor by forms of mutual recognition or fellowship. The purpose of our dialogue has accordingly been to clarify the agreements and convergences in faith between us and to examine whether the differences between us are divisive or mutually challenging and enriching.

11. As members of the body of Christ, we share our faith in worship and service, in thought and love, in prayer and neighbour-care. Through these diverse ways we participate in the fullness of Christian life with one another, and especially in our sense of common mission. In this context we have explored our respective understandings and interpretations of Christian faith. We have welcomed the opportunity for such theological focus and have pursued it vigorously, but we also recognize that this discussion is only a part of the larger context of Christian faith and life.

12. In order to realize our purpose, papers were presented by each side on the main topics of our agenda. Our intense discussions have helped to clarify our respective positions, to discover a wide range of agreement, and to achieve a clearer view of the

character and significance of our identity as Christians and as churches. We also have made an attempt to combine with our dialogue possibilities of encounter with local churches in the areas of our meetings in order that our theological debates could be informed and enriched by the experience of the actual life of our churches and that we could communicate something of our work and expectations to the people in the congregations.

13. In the process of our dialogue we have grown in mutual respect, understanding and fellowship. Behind different theological expressions and forms of Christian life, we have discovered basic common convictions; we have experienced agreements and disagreements, some of which run along our confessional lines, while others cut across our confessional alignments. Such experiences and insights have reached a deep level and can be communicated only insufficiently to others who have not gone through a similar process. We hope, therefore, that our common statement will be studied, wherever possible, in the context of dialogues and encounters between Lutherans and Methodists on local and national levels so that similar experiences and new insight may become possible.

14. In this common statement we intend to set down the results of our dialogue. The topical sections represent developed refinements and modifications of the original outline. In each case we seek to communicate our points of agreement, to delineate our distinctive emphases, and to acknowledge what we have found to be unresolved issues between Lutheranism and Methodism as two ways of being communities of grace. Our statement concludes with recommendations followed by a select bibliography.

I. The authority of the scriptures

15. Lutherans and Methodists confess Jesus Christ to be the word of God incarnate, and we acknowledge the scriptures of the Old and New Testament as faithful witnesses to this central revelation. The historic collection of the books of the Bible has been commended by the ancient Christian churches and confirmed by the Holy Spirit as the most authentic, faithful and trustworthy bearer of the word of God. We must each judge our own traditions and hold one another accountable to the criterion of this scriptural testimony.

16. The scriptures provide the primary authoritative standards for faith and life, witness and work. Written for diverse historical needs and occasions, the scriptures continue to proclaim the word of God as addressed to people in their special times and situations. The long history of the formation, composition, transmission and proclamation of these texts further demonstrates that God uses human words, authors and witnesses, and has called and sanctified their many efforts to proclaim his word of justice and mercy.

17. The faithful interpretation of the scriptures must acknowledge their historical diversity and attend carefully to the specific formulations, testimonies and messages of individual passages, books and literatures. Moreover, the scriptures must be read with reference to Jesus Christ as Lord and Saviour, its authentic centre and content. But the Word of God, revealed in Christ Jesus once for all, is also eternal. Hence the Word of God speaks to each age, and those who bear their witness in new times and occasions must be held accountable for the appropriate use and interpretation of the scriptures.

18. Methodists and Lutherans rejoice in the rich tradition of the one, holy, catholic church and trace their deep convictions about the authority of the scriptures to the

founders of their distinctive traditions and beyond them to the faith of the earliest Christian communities. Both Luther and Wesley grounded their efforts to reform and renew the church in disciplined scriptural study. In his *Explanatory Notes upon the New Testament* and in his *Sermons*, Wesley faithfully acknowledges the norm of scriptural authority. Luther repeatedly appealed for an examination of the scriptures that was directed and authorized by that which presents Christ.

19. As auxiliary keys to interpreting the scriptures we have explored tradition, reason and experience. Both church families acknowledge the three creeds of the ancient church (Apostles', Nicene, Athanasian). Because we believe that these ancient creeds authentically interpret the New Testament witness to Jesus Christ, we maintain that theological positions must be developed in continuity with them. Lutherans also give a special place to the Augsburg confession and Luther's Small Catechism (and some Lutheran churches to the entire *Book of Concord*) as a faithful explication of the teaching of the scriptures and the ancient church, and they hope to engage in dialogue with other Christians, using these confessions as a basis for the conversation. Methodists give a special place to John Wesley's *Sermons* and *Explanatory Notes upon the NT* as standards of doctrine and use them as a basis for ecumenical conversation (and some Methodist churches to the *Twenty-Five Articles on Religion*, the Evangelical United Brethren *Articles on Religion*, and the *General Rules*). The hymns of Charles Wesley also have importance for doctrinal discussion. The confession of apostolic faith today is being raised currently both in our churches and in the larger ecumenical movement with its research project "Towards the Common Expression of the Apostolic Faith Today". Such confession requires careful study in view of the changed historical and cultural circumstances in which both churches find themselves. All such theological work, we agree, must be primarily and constantly governed by the scriptures in critical relation to each context.

20. Lutherans and Methodists agree that human reason is a divine gift which helps to clarify and communicate the word of God for the teaching of the church and its mission to the world. Wesley, who was the author of "Appeals to Men of Reason and Religion", shared the appeal to reason of his age. But, as against the Deists, he gave priority to revelation and stressed the need of reason to be illuminated by the Holy Spirit. Luther reacted against the rationalism of medieval scholasticism. He did not attribute to reason any role in human salvation. But he valued reason as a human capacity for the ordering of personal and social life. Therefore, both traditions treat reason with respect and caution. They are also aware of its capacity for being misused and perverted. As critically self-aware, human reason is indispensable for life in this world and, in this way, is in the service of God's purposes.

21. Methodists and Lutherans recognize that experience will always be a significant factor in the understanding of the scriptures – and this in a twofold sense. It is a vital medium through which the Holy Spirit confirms the gospel in the lives of believers. And, at the same time, the gospel witnessed by the scriptures critically interprets experience. Methodists generally have emphasized more than Lutherans the role of experience in confirming Christian interpretation, but both Methodists and Lutherans agree that all experience claiming to be distinctively Christian must be judged by criteria drawn from the scriptures. The social and cultural contexts within which our churches live deeply affect our Christian experience, our interpretation of the scriptures, and our theological reflection. These diverse social and cultural settings of our

churches are also subject to critique and interpretation according to the authoritative standards of our faith. New questions arise in each age which require new answers. The question of whether certain interpretations or theological innovations are faithful to the gospel must always be carefully pursued. Nevertheless, evangelical fidelity leads us to expect and welcome new understandings of God's word of justice and mercy as the Holy Spirit leads us to proclaim it in the midst of various occasions and social contexts throughout the world.

22. For both Lutherans and Methodists the personal experiences and the theological thinking of Luther and Wesley have influenced the spirituality that is vital in and characteristic of the respective church families. In addition to these lasting influences, social, cultural, political and ecclesiastical contexts have contributed to differing practices of faith. Christian life has been expressed in a variety of styles of piety in our two traditions.

II. Salvation by grace through faith

23. We agree that, in accordance with the scriptures, justification is the work of God in Christ and comes through faith alone. Within the context of justification, faith comprises both assent and trust. Persons as sinners are justified by God's gracious love in Christ, and not on the basis of human efforts or worthiness. Christ's righteousness is imputed and imparted to them by an act of God as they are enabled by the Holy Spirit to trust in God. Justification is dependent upon Christ's atoning death. In Christ, God reconciled the world and conquered the evil forces that dominate human life and the created order.

24. Wesleyans stress the prevenient grace of God which prepares humans for acknowledgment of justifying grace. They also affirm justification as the foundation for full redemption in Christ. Thus Methodists tend to understand justification by faith in Jesus Christ as initiating and, as such, determining the whole Christian life through God's action and personal appropriation. Lutherans believe that in justification, at once and constantly, God gives forgiveness, righteousness and eternal life. Christians therefore are in every moment dependent on God's justifying grace and never move beyond or above the position of justified sinners. For both traditions, Christians throughout their whole life are in need of God's forgiving grace.

25. Reflection upon justification leads to consideration of sanctification. Sanctification is also a work of God's grace. Both traditions agree that sanctification is, on the one hand, seen as God's completed and anticipated act when God justifies and reconciles human beings. On the other hand, sanctification is God's work which is continuously going on in the Christian's life led by the Holy Spirit. In this way human beings are both drawn closer to God in faith and nearer to the neighbour in love. Lutherans stress that in Christ people are justified and sanctified while at the same time they remain sinners before God (*simul justus et peccator*). Methodists speak of this drastic change as a new birth in consequence of which the regenerated Christian lives in ever deepening and more fruitful love of God and neighbour. Methodists dare set no limit to what the grace of God can do for people in this present life. And it was a part of the original tradition received through John Wesley to believe that perfect love should be earnestly sought by believers and might be received in this life.

26. Furthermore, we agree on the basis of scripture that a Christian lives by God's grace received through faith. For Christian life, authentic faith inevitably yields obedi-

ence. Christian faith is faith that is active in love and is ever anew called to do good works because of God's command and for the sake of the neighbour. New being in Christ is the result of justification through the Holy Spirit. Methodists emphasize the positive condition of that new creation. Consequently they hold that, transformed by Christ, the believer is set free to be conformed to the will of God. Lutherans also emphasize the positive conditions of new creation and understand the Christian life as daily conversion (recognition of our continuing sin and continuous call upon the forgiving grace of God) and as faithful following of Christ in daily obedience. The law stands as claim and judge; the awareness of the law leads to the renewed trust in Christ's righteousness as the only ground of salvation, life and confidence.

27. There is common agreement that God's creating and sustaining grace is continuously present in the world and in human life. Lutherans maintain that in creation God gives human beings material goods necessary for our living, and as the Lord of nature and all people, God fights against forces that would destroy the creation. In this saving action, however, God gives to people the fruits of Christ's saving work, such as forgiveness of sins and eternal life. Methodists also stress God as creator and moral governor of the world. The presence of God in the world is centred in Christ's redeeming work. From this centre God graciously blesses all life. The original significance of this prevenient grace for human beings is the development of a sense of right and wrong, the recognition of fallen life as under the wrath of God, and the drawing of people to the saving grace given to us through word and sacrament and received by faith.

III. The church

28. The church is the community of Jesus Christ called into being by the Holy Spirit. Those who respond in faith to the gospel of Christ, proclaimed in word and sacrament, are brought into a new relationship with God and with each other. All that divides people from each other has been overcome by Christ who binds men and women together into a new community of love, across the barriers of nation and race, colour and class, age and sex and wealth. As we are made one in the body of Christ we share in the one Spirit, by whom our unity in Christ is sustained and our life in Christ continually renewed.

29. At the heart of the Christian life is the worship of God in which we proclaim what God has done in creation and redemption and offer in response our thanksgiving. The Spirit who enables us to offer ourselves in joyful thanksgiving to God also frees us to give ourselves in service and witness to each other and to the world. The centre of our witness, as of our worship, is what God has done in Jesus Christ. The power of our witness comes from the Spirit who uses our words and our deeds to manifest Christ to the world.

30. Our churches, as historical institutions, have been both appropriately and inappropriately responsive to their social contexts. Hence, while the existence of the church is in the world and for the world, it must be constantly self-critical and critical of the whole life of society, exercising its divinely constituted vocation in obedience to the word of God. Thus in its origin, its worship and its service the church is the community of grace.

31. In speaking of the church as the communion of saints, both Lutheran and Methodist churches affirm the Holy Spirit's initiative in constituting and sanctifying

the community of believers in the one, holy, catholic, apostolic church. Definitions of the church in our two traditions indicate basic agreement:

a) Article 13 in the *Articles of Religion*, as edited by John Wesley, reads: "The visible church of Christ is a congregation of faithful men in which the pure word of God is preached and the sacraments duly administered according to Christ's ordinance, in all those things that of necessity are requisite to the same."
b) The confession of faith of the Evangelical United Brethren Church, article 5: "We believe the Christian church is the community of all true believers under the lordship of Christ... in which the word of God is preached... and the sacraments are duly administered according to Christ's own appointment. Under the discipline of the Holy Spirit the church exists for the maintenance of worship, the edification of believers and the redemption of the world."
c) The Augsburg confession, article 7: "It is also taught among us that one holy Christian church will be and remain forever. This is the assembly of all believers among whom the gospel is preached in its purity and the holy sacraments are administered according to the gospel. For it is sufficient for the true unity of the Christian church that the gospel be preached in conformity with a pure understanding of it and that the sacraments be administered in accordance with the divine word."

32. Special emphases has been placed on the corporate nature of Christian life. To be "in Christ" is to be bound together in the family of God, and it is to be bound in service to the human family. Both traditions have been aware of the personal impact of excessive individualism, and both, while desiring to affirm the significance of the personal dimensions of the life of faith, also emphasize the corporate and communal dimensions of Christian existence.

33. Methodists and Lutherans include the elements of word, sacraments, faith and community in their articulation of what the church is. Lutherans and Methodists hold that the church also shall exercise church discipline even though they may understand and exercise such discipline in different ways. They also recognize that in situations of oppression or discrimination by secular powers the exercise of discipline can become a form of costly confession to Jesus Christ.

34. Historically, both confessional families started as movements within existing churches. Neither of the movements intended to become a separate church. While the Methodists grew into churches which were independent of the state, the Lutherans largely were organized as majority churches and state churches in wide regions (Scandinavian *Statskirker*, German *Landeskirchen*; ethnic/religious predominance in American upper Midwest). Methodist and Lutheran members of the commission affirm that Methodist or Lutheran churches, which are minorities in a situation where the other church is in a majority or privileged position, are to be recognized as fully legitimate churches and should enjoy equal rights and possibilities. We encourage a relationship to secular rule in which the church is independent and all denominations enjoy parity before the state. We rejoice that progress towards better understanding is being made in many of the places where Methodists and Lutherans have experienced problems in their formal relationships. The exchanges we have had in this dialogue itself have contributed positively to the growth of such understanding.

35. The foundation of the church is Jesus Christ, mediated through the means of grace. Baptism marks entry into this community. There is mutual recognition that persons are called to live out their baptism in a daily life of faith and their active partici-

pation in the life and mission of the Christian community. In both traditions there is an understanding of the need for persons to affirm and to appropriate the meaning of their faith. The Wesleyan tradition places great weight upon growth towards Christian maturity through the constant use of the means of grace. Both church families recognize that there are different legitimate patterns of living the Christian life. This variety should be recognized not only to continue our faithfulness and make us open to other witnesses but also to prevent our tendencies to impose our way upon others.

36. Lutherans and Methodists believe that it is God's will for the word to be proclaimed and that the word of God accomplishes that for which God sends it – the creation of a faithful people, the salvation of the world, and life according to God's law. Both sides agree that neither baptism nor holy communion are, in themselves, a guarantee of salvation. Under God the church has responsibility for pastoral care and instruction to assist the baptized to live as Christians in the fellowship of the church. There are times when the church must officially decide that a person has removed himself or herself from that fellowship. Even so discipline is always pastoral and the church must seek ways to bring about repentance and reconciliation.

37. Our two traditions have emphasized the ministry of all the people of God both in their everyday vocations and in particular responsibilities within the Christian community. Accordingly our insistence on the importance of the ordained ministry goes together with our recognition of the manifold lay ministries. Ministries of laity share in the wholeness of the ministry of Christ who bears the form of a servant in the church and in the world. In this broader perspective of ministry we acknowledge God's gift of the ordained ministry, which in both our churches is exercised by women and men. The ordained minister presides in the proclamation of the word, the celebration of the sacraments and the exercise of pastoral care. Since the New Testament presents diverse forms of ministry, we hold that no particular form of ordained ministry or church order is prescribed by the New Testament as necessary for the church. In obedience to their God-given mission, our churches have developed particular patterns of ministry. The unity of the church is given by Christ. This unity also requires the mutual recognition of the ministries of our churches.

38. For Lutherans ordained ministry is an office and a service decreed by God for the administration of the means of grace for the salvation of the people. Such administration is public and takes place after ordination. Lutherans emphasize the call of God through the church to the office of ministry. A person remains in this office as long as he or she exercises the functions of this office with the approval of the church. Methodists place great stress on the call of God through the Holy Spirit to people who offer themselves for the ordained ministry. The conviction of this call must be tested by the church. Methodists distinguish between a call to preach (service of the word) and a call to ordained ministry (service of word, sacrament and order).

39. Methodists and Lutherans regard oversight (*episcope*) as fundamental in the life of the church. This ministry is exercised in a variety of ways. In most Lutheran and Methodist churches oversight is exercised by bishops. We value this episcopal ministry, which is, however, not regarded as being an essential mark of the church. Where such a rank and title is employed, both Lutherans and Methodists view the bishop as a minister set aside for superintending pastoral function. We recognize ordination under either Lutheran or Methodist discipline as having continuity with the apostolic tradition, and we recognize our ministries to be ministries in the church of Christ.

IV. Means of grace

40. The Holy Spirit creates the body of Christ and communicates God's grace through means that are ordained and made effective by God. Lutherans and Methodists agree that the word of God and the sacraments of baptism and eucharist are the fundamental means of grace by which the gospel of God's redeeming love in Christ is conveyed to people to be received in faith, and by which Christ through the Holy Spirit constitutes, preserves and sends the church into the world.

41. By means of grace we understand certain external words, tangible signs, or acts instituted by Christ and conveying God's grace to human beings and to strengthen them for a life in faith and service. Lutherans and Methodists highly esteem the use of these means because of God's ordination and promise to act through them. On the other hand, they believe that there is no effect or merit in the means as human actions, but God's promise is to work, to strengthen, and to nurture faith in those who receive them according to his order. Their benefit can only be received by faith as confidence in God's effective presence.

42. In bestowing his unmerited love upon people God's sovereign freedom is not limited to certain means. Yet we as his children and Christ's disciples are not free to choose whether or not to use the means ordained by our Lord. Because he has commanded them we neglect them at our peril.

43. Lutherans and Methodists agree that preaching, baptism and the Lord's supper are the central means of grace because of their divine appointment and clear relation to the objective character of the gospel. The two traditions differ, however, in their opinions about the extent and the content of the range of means. Lutherans prefer to look upon preaching, baptism and eucharist as means of grace in a proper sense because of their clear historic institution according to the scriptures. Methodists also use the expression "means of grace" for a wider range of institutions and practices such as prayer, Bible study, class meetings, fasting, vigils, love feasts. God is free to use any means, whether biblically instituted or not, in order to grant his grace to human beings. For the Christians' use of the means of grace it is important to act according to God's commands as well as to rely not on any human action, conviction or worthiness, but solely on God's promise.

A. Baptism

44. There is agreement among Methodists and Lutherans that baptism is a sacrament instituted by Jesus Christ. Baptism is not primarily a human act, but God's gift of salvation for men and women who are sinners. Baptism is not only a mark of Christian profession, it is an effective sign of God's grace.

45. Through baptism we are given a new relationship with God, the Father, the Son and the Holy Spirit. In baptism we are united with Jesus Christ in his death and resurrection and are incorporated into the body of Christ which is the church. Therefore baptism is an unrepeatable act. In this sacrament the Holy Spirit is given to renew the life of the baptized. Forgiveness of sins and justification are given. Baptism is the sacrament of entrance, not only into a particular denomination, but into the holy, catholic church and, consequently, is a sacrament of fundamental unity in Christ and in the one Spirit.

46. Baptism is inseparably linked with faith. The Holy Spirit enables human beings to rely faithfully upon God's promise of grace expressed in the sacrament. Baptism is

the sacrament of the beginning of Christian life and has lasting significance for our continual repentance and daily reception of forgiveness and for our growth in faith and obedience. The benefits of baptism are forgiveness of sins, life and salvation. These benefits may be lost through unbelief and persistent disobedience. Therefore both Lutherans and Methodists will call for repentance and the conversion of the non-believing baptized person as a return to the promised gift of grace in baptism.

47. We recognize as valid all acts of baptism in the name of the Trinity using water and administered according to Christ's command and promise. We affirm one another's baptism as prescribed in the present baptismal liturgies of our churches. We also recognize baptism as valid when, in unusual circumstances, it is administered by laypeople.

48. Because baptism is God's act of salvation it is intended for all persons without regard to age, mental capacity or other such factors. Consequently, all the baptized are incorporated into covenant with God, into the church of Christ as the divine promise has reference also to them.

49. Baptism is usually administered by an ordained minister in a congregational service of public worship. Further, baptism is connected with the nurturing task of a Christian congregation. In this way baptized persons can be supported in Christian faith and life. We recognize our common need for strengthening this nurture by our churches in today's secularized society.

50. On the other hand there are divergences and disagreements among us on the following points.

We share the understanding that humanity's relationship to God, to one another, and to oneself has been broken and that sin now belongs to all humankind. Methodists, however, assert that God's reconciling work in Christ has an anticipatory effect enabling positive response of human beings (prevenient grace). God's gracious action which bestows salvation upon humankind is not bound to particular human words or actions. Consequently, emergency baptism is infrequent among Methodists. Lutherans put a specific emphasis on the necessity of baptism for salvation because baptism is understood as the fundamental application of God's atonement in Christ to the individual. This does not however involve a conviction that unbaptized infants are outside the love of God.

51. We agree in looking upon baptism as entrance into the church. However, there is a difference among us about the way in which we more precisely define the relationship between baptism and church membership. For Lutherans, baptism establishes church membership. Most Methodists distinguish between preparatory and full membership. The former is given through baptism, the latter through explicit admission on profession of faith. In a historic perspective this is rooted in Methodism as a revival movement which often incorporated new members after conversion. Theologically regarded this divergence among us is due to different understandings of faith in relation to the baptismal act. The concern of both Lutherans and Methodists is to hold closely together God's action and human faith. But while Methodists stress the necessity of a personal faith for receiving salvation, Lutherans look upon faith as confidence in God's promise given in the baptismal act.

B. The eucharist

52. Eucharistic theology and practice in their particular Methodist and Lutheran forms developed with different presuppositions and in different historical contexts.

Lutherans reformed eucharistic doctrine and practice on the basis of the biblical witness and in accordance with their emphasis on the priority of the gospel of God's free grace in Jesus Christ. This implied a critique of what they regarded as errors and false developments in late medieval eucharistic doctrine and practice as well as of certain developments and convictions in the Reformed tradition. The understanding of the eucharist in Methodism has its roots in the Anglican tradition, which at the Reformation introduced new liturgies which were influenced by the teaching and liturgies of the Reformers. This background in the Anglican tradition received a new expression in the deep eucharistic spirituality of the Wesleys in their hymns and sermons. For Methodists in the evangelical revival the eucharist was itself a means of conversion, and this evangelical dimension of the sacrament deserves consideration of those concerned with evangelism in the present day.

53. Both our traditions regard the Lord's supper as one of the fundamental means of grace. They stress Christ's institution of his supper, his command to continue to celebrate it according to his institution until he comes again, and the promise that he has bound himself to this meal. The action of the eucharist becomes such a means of grace through the power of Christ's creative and promising word, which is the Lutheran emphasis, and through the action of the Holy Spirit in it, which is the Methodist emphasis. But for both word and Holy Spirit belong together in the sacramental action.

54. We affirm together that the eucharist is not only an outward but an effective sign of the saving presence of the risen Lord Jesus Christ. His presence is real here and now. Jesus Christ, with all that he has achieved for us in his life, death and resurrection, gives himself to us in this meal. He offers his life-giving body and blood with bread and wine to all who partake in the meal and receive him in faith. While both traditions believe in Christ's presence in the whole sacramental action, Lutherans tend to emphasize also the real yet mysterious union between Christ's body and blood and the elements of bread and wine more strongly than Methodists generally do. One consequence of the Lutheran view is that for them even unbelievers do in fact receive the body and blood of Jesus Christ, but to their condemnation/judgment. Methodists, while recognizing the need to receive the sacrament worthily, speak of believers but not of unbelievers as receiving the body and blood of Christ. We are, however, convinced that such differences are less significant than the agreements between us.

55. In the Lord's supper we receive forgiveness of sins, the assurance of our acceptance by God for Christ's sake. In this encounter with the living Christ, we are strengthened in our faith and hope and love; and our communion with the Lord of the church and with the members of his body is renewed and deepened. We believe that the Holy Spirit enables us to partake in the eucharist with the confidence that we truly receive Jesus Christ present for us with his good gifts for life in this world and for hope in the world to come. Strengthened by this meal, we are sent forth into the world again to be messengers and servants of God's love through commitment to peace, justice and reconciliation in the midst of the conflicts, struggles and hopes of our world and time.

56. In both of our confessional traditions recent developments in eucharistic doctrine and practice are rather similar. There is an increase in the frequency of the celebration of the Lord's supper. We recognize that the service with word and sacrament is the central act of worship of the Christian community. There is a new awareness of the corporate character of this act of worship, expressing and making real the communion (koinonia) with Jesus Christ and with one another. We recognize in the eucharist an

anticipation of God's kingdom and therefore a challenge to the injustices of the world in which we live looking forward to a world in which people are truly reconciled to each other and share in justice and generosity all the gifts of God. We also realize afresh the character of the eucharist as an act of praise and thanksgiving for all that we have received from God in creation and in the history of his gracious dealings with his people until the day when God will create a new heaven and a new earth.

V. The mission of the church

A. *Evangelization*

57. The church has received the joyful commission to preach the gospel to all humankind (Matt. 28:18-20). Thus engaged in the service of the world, the Christian church gives this commission its highest priority. Methodism began as part of the evangelical revival in 18th-century England. Its special apostolate has always been to be an evangelistic and missionary movement within the church catholic, calling persons everywhere in their various situations to faith and to holiness of heart and life. In Lutheranism the all-encompassing emphasis on the proclamation of the gospel in word, sacrament and deed constitutes an eminent missionary and evangelistic impulse within that tradition. Methodism may profit from Lutheran concern for the clarity of the gospel; Lutherans may be inspired by Methodism to implement their evangelistic impetus.

58. The evangelization of the world is a divine project which involves human beings. Jesus Christ, God's great missionary to a lost world, was the supreme revelation of God's heart and expression of divine love. Evangelism is indeed the heartbeat of God! God sends Christian disciples as missionaries to the world.

59. Proclamation is announcement – the announcement of God's offer and invitation – all centring in Jesus Christ. God's proclamation is not just words. It is the offer of liberation and deliverance. The announcement of God's call of love and offer of forgiveness looks for a response of repentance, faith and obedience in love.

60. The movement of the Spirit of God is evident in our world today as people are drawn to faith in God. In many places the membership of the church is growing. In other places where churches face the experience of decreasing numbers, there is at the same time a rediscovery of the gospel as a missionary message which leads to further proclamation of God's love to people. In many places, church membership involves hardship or persecution. But even there we find often a renewed vitality of faith leading to a missionary witness.

61. The surrounding spiritual climate of an age has sometimes assisted but more often has made difficult the progress of Christian mission. In our world such hostile elements include secularism of society, especially in the Western world; the spread of scepticism and unbelief and the suspicion of traditional structures and expressions of religion; the existence of great political systems avowedly based on materialistic atheism (liberal capitalism and Marxism), the indifference to spiritual values resulting from the distractions of an affluent and technological society. In other parts of the world deep social and political depravation along with the failure of the churches to champion freedom and justice have resulted in a crisis of confidence between the missionary church and those who listen to its message with a suspicion arising from a defective Christian witness. In recent years new cults and ancient religions have conducted

an impressive and challenging missionary enterprise. The distribution in Europe of great numbers of people of other faiths has posed questions in what have previously been nominally Christian lands. Taken together, these considerations involve problems that are likely to increase.

62. We strongly feel our commitment for common witness to the gospel when we read the prayer of our Lord in John 17. We are glad to discover that there is fundamental agreement in the understanding of evangelization; although there is a variety of forms and expressions in both our traditions.

63. "All this is from God, who through Christ reconciled us to himself and gave us the ministry of reconciliation... So we are ambassadors for Christ... We beseech you on behalf of Christ, be reconciled to God" (2 Cor. 5:18ff.). There is no doubt about what the task is of all Christians in the world. We are sent to bring every day to all human beings this message of their reconciliation to God.

64. We proclaim this message of reconciliation and invite people to accept their salvation by faith. There is no other way than to trust in God's action on the cross and in the resurrection of Jesus Christ. Evangelization is the call to persons to believe in Christ. Incorporated into his body through faith we are given a vision of the world for which he died and are linked with him in love for all people. "Because God's love has been poured into our hearts through the Holy Spirit" (Rom. 5:5).

65. When the message of Christ is accepted by faith, there is a conversion of the person with the whole life now coming under the reign of the Lord. This experience is also described in the Bible as the new birth, beginning a new life as a disciple of Christ. Life in the Spirit is the consequence.

66. The purpose of evangelization is to help people enter into fellowship with God in this life and to receive eternal salvation in the life to come. The urgency of evangelization arises both from our obedience to our Lord's commission and from our awareness of God's righteous judgment upon sinful humanity. In Christ God has justified the ungodly, giving repentance unto forgiveness of sins to all who believe and are baptized. This justification means we are accepted in God's judgment, we are redeemed for the service of God in this world and delivered from wrath in the age to come. This future aspect of life beyond death is a part of the biblical message and also speaks to life today.

67. Becoming a faithful disciple of Jesus Christ has implications for the way one lives in society. Christians are called to be responsible, active and critical members of the society in which they live, whether their contributions are appreciated or not. The biblical understanding of salvation must be reclaimed today in its bold announcement of God's ultimate dominion over all idols and systems of domination and dependency. Just as Isaiah and the psalmist announced God's salvation as critique of the absolutization of power by the Assyrian and neo-Babylonian empires, so also the prophetic Christian witness of today is a critique of all systems and structures which oppress people, exploit the poor, deny human rights and justify violence. Thus the proclamation of salvation will constantly bring the Christian witness into conflict with such powers.

68. The question is also before us of how we speak of the salvation of the world, when today we are facing a possible nuclear holocaust. The Lutheran understanding of the two realms might be taken into account here because it stresses God's good purpose for his world. In this world there always will be struggle between good and evil. The complete and final realization of the will of God belongs to the last day, beyond the limits of our world. Nevertheless, Christians are called upon to be penetrating fac-

tors in the world – as salt, light and leaven – to realize the will of God in society as far as possible within the context of history. God's love and victory revealed in Jesus Christ give us courage, hope and joy in our social activities and tasks, one of which is unity in our mission.

B. Ways of evangelization today
69. The New Testament gives us the pattern for evangelization in a specific culture and context. The Son of God "pitched his tent among us" to make it possible for us to be redeemed. The Word made flesh in Jesus Christ is the supreme example of "contextualization". For us, the proclamation of this gospel may involve the adaptation of liturgy, dress, language, music and other forms of expression. It is essential that persons are approached as persons, so that we are willing to listen to their concerns and questions and to respect their cultural identity. The *content* of the gospel is a "given"; the *form* of teaching, preaching, service is then fitted to the situation.

70. Ways of evangelization – though not applicable everywhere in the same way – may include the following:
– The worshipping community of God is primary in evangelization. Believers, refreshed in their witness to Christ by participation in vital worship, move into the world reflecting the love of God to unbelievers through their behaviour and their explicit witness. "By this all men will know that you are my disciples, if you have love for one another" (John 13:35).
– The apostles called those who believed to be baptized. Baptism as one of the means by which God gives his grace and signifies his great love is an important element of evangelization. Evangelization also involves calling baptized persons who have ceased to claim the benefits of all that is offered in baptism to enter anew into the church, its sacraments and the Christian life in the Spirit.
– Personal witness in which Christians share their experience of the good news of Jesus Christ with others is indispensable to the Christian life. The New Testament provides several examples in which language and thought patterns were adopted to address various audiences (e.g. Jews, Greeks, Samaritans and Gentiles).
– Service which expresses Christian concern for the whole person has been an instrument of evangelization throughout the history of the church.
– The invitation to all people to commit themselves to God and thereby find their true human being, dignity and a direction for life results in the multiplying of the witness and service of responsible men and women. This is of special significance for young people in many parts of the world.
– Through Christian ashrams (in India, for example) the gospel is presented to non-Christians through indigenous methods. Christian and non-Christian children learn about the Lord Jesus Christ by having devotional life in the ashram hostels and consequently whole families are influenced.
– Efforts to support a renewed spirituality and a deep identification with the people are fundamental to the witness of the gospel in every society. This implies cooperation with all Christians to reinforce the Christian conscience in society.
– Evangelistic campaigns have long been effective means of preaching the good news of Jesus Christ to large gatherings of people.
– Preaching the gospel that Jesus is the Saviour and the Master of the world also denotes that Jesus Christ and those who follow him come in conflict with all the

forces which work against God's plan for the world. The church recognizes that in the resurrection, Jesus is victorious over these forces, including death.

71. Often, as evangelization is undertaken, new leadership for the church is discovered. Natural leaders whose gifts have been hidden or unused are put to work in the service of Christ.

72. Evangelization is an essential part of the church's mission. Evangelism must not be defined in terms of methods. The "evangel" itself is definitive of what is said and how it is communicated in word and deed. As Lutherans and Methodists seek to discharge the commission to evangelize with zeal, they must continually test all means by a clearly discriminated grasp of the gospel. Thus theological reflection must be held accountable to the great commission, and evangelistic methods must be held accountable to theological reflection. We can evangelize by word of mouth, by printed word, by means of visuals, by dramatization, by story-telling, by good works of love, by having exemplary Christian homes, and at times by silent witness and suffering.

C. Christian ethics in the modern world

73. As Christians in the tradition of the Reformation, Lutherans and Methodists bear witness to the gospel of God's liberation of humanity and the whole creation in Christ Jesus for the sake of whom God justifies the ungodly. This action of God breaks the enslaving bonds of sin and grants new possibilities for life and is therefore fundamental to any subsequent description of the Christian ethic. Thus, human moral behaviour is never understood as an effort to earn God's grace, nor is obedience to divine commands regarded as a means to salvation. Christian ethics is grounded in the joy of salvation in Jesus Christ.

74. The joy and freedom of the Christian life are consistently prized in Methodism and Lutheranism. Recognizing humanity's bondage to sin, both Wesley and Luther were eloquent in describing the freedom of Christian living which relies upon the calling, sustaining and sanctifying work of the Holy Spirit. Christians, individually and corporately, are called to witness and service in personal and public arenas of life. Therefore, Lutherans and Methodists stand together in the affirmation of trusting obedience to God as fundamental to the Christian ethic. This ethic is distinguished from others by responding faithfully to the word of God and by recognizing freedom as a gift from God which is exercised with the guidance of the Spirit.

75. Methodists affirm that the wisdom of God is displayed in the natural world and that God created its laws. God's nature revealed in Jesus Christ is the source of universal moral law. God has given conscience to sinful humanity through prevenient grace as a universal work of Christ. Thus, even so-called "natural man" possesses an ethical capability on both the personal and the social level.

Lutherans also affirm that all people have a concept of right and wrong according to God's law, and even though they are sinners they are capable of doing God's will in many ways, although such moral consciousness is present only in limited degrees. Both approaches make it possible for Christians to communicate and cooperate with others in ethical affairs.

76. Both Luther and Wesley believed that Christian obedience involves more than the acceptance of conventional patterns of moral behaviour. Both fought an unending battle against lowered ethical standards. Luther's concern for ethical instruction in the congregations required him to produce catechisms both as a corrective to the devalua-

tion of secular vocation and as a description of the exercise of Christian freedom. In Wesley's era when vast forces of social change and moral indifference were crushing the people, Methodists recognized their vocation to the service of love to their neighbours and to a living witness to the will of God in society. Their high moral standards and personal virtues sometimes led to conflict and even persecution by unbelievers and nominal Christians.

77. Christian service, exercise of love, obedience and discipleship are rooted in God's commandments and reconciling love as attested in scriptures and disclosed in Christ Jesus who "came not to be served but to serve, and to give his life as a ransom for many" (Mark 10:45). Christians and Christian communities are called to discern what is "good and acceptable and perfect" (Rom. 12:2) as guided by biblical norms and the considerate love of the neighbour. Christian ethical standards are not simply a set of rules or laws. Nor can Christians in any part of the world or in any society or culture insist that all others conform to all their moral traditions or practices. Nevertheless, there are basic orientations and goals of Christian commitment which are of universal relevance and which make common worldwide Christian witness and service possible.

78. Lutherans and Methodists understand the vocation of the church in society in the light of God's history of salvation in Christ. Justification by faith necessitates engagement with fellow human beings. Having been freed by God, Christians find their noblest vocation in the service of the neighbour.

79. Many ethical values and practices will be shared with other persons of good will and serious moral purpose so that Christians readily acknowledge their debt to other systems of high ethical standards (see Paul's use of moral catalogues in Galatians 5). In fact, Christians will in particular circumstances find themselves in solidarity with diverse groups who advocate justice, peace and reconciliation. They may share the stigma of exclusion with those whose moral actions have placed them at odds with prevailing authorities and powers. On the other hand, as believing communities come to have the mind that was in Christ, they also confront and challenge other concepts of human life. In learning from Jesus Christ the Lord of the church who became obedient unto death, Christians also come to understand that the goals of life are no longer privilege, self-interest or power, but service in Christian love and self-giving. These goals are in striking contrast to standards so highly prized in the world, such as dominance and material success.

80. Lutherans and Methodists agree that justification by faith inevitably requires personal and corporate works of mercy. Life in Christ includes ministry to human need. Thus the church sets up and encourages secular agencies to establish institutions and programmes to provide direct assistance to people. The church also speaks to and tries to influence public policy about war and peace, racism, human rights, the rights of women and of children, the distribution of wealth, ecology and other matters of public policy which affect the quality of life and being for all parts of God's creation. We acknowledge that we have often allowed our churches to live in comfortable cultural captivity rather than to risk unpopularity and internal tension. We affirm that discipleship includes stewardship of our personal and communal resources in the continuing struggle for peace and justice.

81. Christian service and obedience in its social orientation seeks to preserve and strengthen the wellbeing of societies and to heal their weaknesses and defects. In this

way Christians serve in cooperation with God in God's sustaining and preserving work in the world. In doing this we together emphasize that God's justice has been revealed in the vindication of the suffering and death of Jesus Christ. Thus in Christ, God has conquered the human and cosmic forces of evil. Thereby Christians are enabled to struggle with the powers of death and destruction in freedom from fear and in hopeful confidence of the final realization of Christ's victory.

VI. Suggestions for the future

82. At the close of our second meeting (Bristol 1980) we said: "The important point is that conversations are underway between two traditions of the one, holy, catholic church. These are traditions which by history and present existence should be talking together... both similarities and differences have been located, and a promising future lies ahead." Although our work as a joint commission will not continue beyond 1984, we are convinced that there is a promising future for Lutheran-Methodist dialogue, diaconal involvement, eucharistic fellowship and visible unity.

83. To widen that dialogue we send to our respective constituencies this common statement. We hope that its use among seminary faculties, seminarians, interested laypersons and pastors will result in a greater consciousness of the other tradition and a greater appreciation of one another's theology, spirituality and historic apostolate. The bibliography [not included here] is designed to indicate where our reading about one another should begin.

84. We testify that ecumenical discussion also helps us to grow in the knowledge and understanding of our own traditions. In working to pull down the walls that have separated Christians, we are forced to define the core of our own ecclesial identity. Thus a double blessing comes from ecumenical dialogue: greater love both for our own church and for other churches.

85. We have been pleased to take notice of Lutheran and Methodist dialogues on the regional level. We have been assisted in our task by the statement on baptism that came from the USA discussions. We hope that such contacts will continue within our two world communions and that regional dialogues will make use of our work.

86. Since our dialogue began the World Council of Churches' Faith and Order paper *Baptism, Eucharist and Ministry* has been published. Although this document was not introduced formally into our discussions, we note similarities between some of our conclusions and those of this major theological convergence statement. We add our voice to the call for the churches to respond to *Baptism, Eucharist and Ministry*. Therefore, we have included it and selected related titles in the bibliography.

87. We also urge Methodist and Lutheran parishes to engage in dialogue. Pastors might organize joint meetings for conversion by using this document or by reading and discussing selected writings of Luther and Wesley from the bibliography. Pastors might also meet regularly for exegesis of the lectionary as they prepare sermons. We recommend that our churches provide for pulpit and altar fellowship exchanges and mutual hospitality at the table of the Lord. We encourage the use of Lutheran pastors to interpret Lutheranism to Methodist lay groups and the use of Methodist ministers to do the same for their tradition to Lutheran congregations. We urge the formation of lay groups of Lutherans and Methodists to read together the Bible, the writings of Luther, of Wesley, and confessional and doctrinal documents as well as to pray and worship together. We request the education boards of our respective constituent bodies to prepare local

church study units on themes similar to those discussed in this dialogue. We urge Methodist and Lutheran churches to give leadership in local ecumenical diaconal consortia and to assume together the leadership in forming such consortia where they do not now exist.

88. There are some issues which we believe merit further exploration and discussion. Especially the topics of providence and two kingdoms, aspects of anthropology, and forms of unity require such further study. We hope that these will be pursued in appropriate settings.

VII. Recommendations

89. From the beginning one purpose of the dialogue has been to assist Methodist and Lutheran churches to move towards greater fellowship in faith, witness and service. Such fellowship finds visible expression in full sacramental communion.

90. We gratefully acknowledge that our dialogue has led us a significant way towards this because we were able to discover a great amount of agreement and convergence between us. We regard this theological discussion to have achieved sufficient agreement to make the following recommendations:

91. 1. We recommend that our churches take steps to declare and establish full fellowship of word and sacrament; we recommend that as a first and important step our churches officially provide for pulpit exchanges and mutual hospitality at the table of the Lord. We rejoice that full fellowship of word and sacrament is currently practised in some of our churches.

92. 2. We recommend that in every place our churches work together to manifest their unity in common efforts of witness and service in the world.

93. 3. We recommend that our churches receive and use the results of this theological dialogue in seeking the visible unity of all Christians.

94. Finally, we hope that our churches may find common mission and life together by the sharing of our lives with the world for which Christ died. We covet for our people that in mind, heart and service they may grow together in experiencing the reality of THE CHURCH: COMMUNITY OF GRACE. We trust the Holy Spirit to lead Lutherans and Methodists in forms of witness, service and fellowship that will demonstrate our obedience and love for the same Lord Christ.

X. LUTHERAN-ORTHODOX DIALOGUE

Historical Introduction

As is well known, the dialogue between the Orthodox church and the Lutherans had its roots in the Reformation period. The way was prepared for the contemporary dialogue by the rapprochement that occurred due to ecumenical undertakings in the period between the two world wars and to the work of the World Council of Churches. The fourth pan-Orthodox conference (Chambésy, Geneva, 1968) passed a positive judgment on the preceding academic discussions and unofficial contacts and decided to encourage the process by establishing an inter-Orthodox commission that would prepare for an official dialogue; this dialogue finally began in 1981.

The first plenary session of the joint theological commission was held in Espoo, Finland, in 1981, after preparatory contacts had been completed. The discussions focused on the theme of "participation in the mystery of the church" and were based on the papers read there, while at the same time the search for the theological presuppositions required for the advancement of these joint labours and for the restoration of ecclesial communion was chosen as the perspective within which the work of the commission would continue. With this in view, the idea of "participation in the mystery of the church" was chosen as the theme for the next meeting, and a joint sub-commission was established to set forth the basic positions. The sub-commission met in the monastery of Penteli near Athens in 1982 and drafted texts on the following subjects:
1) the Holy Trinity and the church;
2) the church in the history of salvation;
3) the marks of the church;
4) the way in which the salvation of humanity which Christ wrought is communicated in and through the church.

The second plenary session of the joint theological commission took place in Limassol, Cyprus, in 1983. The members discussed the papers delivered there as well as a proposed text, the drafting of which was entrusted to four representatives from both sides, who took as their basis the four documents previously drafted by the sub-commission. In the course of the discussions serious disagreements and differences of theological opinion arose regarding the proposed draft of a joint text; in the end, the draft was not accepted. "Divine revelation" was chosen as the subject of the next plenary session.

The third plenary session took place in Allentown, Pennsylvania, USA, in 1985. A small committee composed a draft of a joint statement on "divine revelation" again on the basis of the papers delivered by members of the joint theological commission and of the discussion that followed upon these papers. The draft was submitted to the full commission and discussed at length. After some changes and clarifications it was unanimously accepted by the members of the commission. The unanimous acceptance of the first joint statement was especially important because it broadened the scope of the dialogue by showing that the common theological fundamentals of the two traditions needed to be studied in a systematic way. "Scripture and Tradition" was chosen as the subject of the next meeting. The third preconciliar pan-Orthodox conference (1986) approved the course being taken in the dialogue, but also expressed the hope that "in the bilateral discussions and the composition of joint statements the academic and the ecclesiastical aspects would be given equal emphasis".

The fourth plenary session took place in Crete, Greece, in 1987 and based its work on the short draft which a small joint sub-commission had composed at Bossey, Switzerland, in 1986. There was an important discussion of this text; the communiqué of the joint theological commission says of the document: "The joint commission does not intend the statement on 'Scripture and Tradition' to be taken as expressing a complete agreement on the subject. Its role in the ongoing dialogue is rather to show the present stage of agreement and thus to lay the foundation for subsequent stages. Moreover, the statement being issued also points to areas in which further discussion between Lutherans and Orthodox is needed." The commission also pointed out that there are important areas in which agreement reigns because, as the statement itself says, "the holy Tradition is the authentic expression of divine revelation in the living experience of the church". The statement continues: "This 'euagelion' of salvation is the content of the holy Tradition, preserved, confessed and transmitted in scripture, in the lives of the saints in all ages, and in the conciliar tradition of the church."

The fifth plenary session took place in Bad Segeberg, Germany, in 1989. The subject discussed was "the canon and inspiration of holy scripture", and the basis for the discussion was provided by a joint statement drafted by a joint sub-commission that met in Venice, Italy, in 1988. The emphasis in the papers read and in the discussions was on the make-up of the canon and the meaning of inspiration. The final text as reformulated after clarifications and additions was accepted as a joint statement. The statement studies the theme of "inspiration of the holy scripture" in relation to the theological tradition and to the faith professed on both sides. Inspiration is explained as an instruction which the individual authors of the Bible receive "from the experience of the revelation of God's glory through the Holy Spirit" and is understood to be an ongoing activity of the Holy Spirit whereby the church is led to a correct interpretation of the scriptures.

The sixth plenary session of the joint theological commission was planned for 1991 to discuss "authority in the church and the authority of the church". In order that the joint sub-commission might prepare more thoroughly for the discussion of this topic, it was sub-divided into three.

The joint sub-commission met in Paris (Châtenay Malabry), 26-30 June 1990, and studied the first of the three topics, namely, "the authority of ecumenical councils", in light of four introductory papers prepared by both sides. As a result of the discussion a number of basic theses on councils were accepted; for example, that councils "are special gifts of God to his church and an integral part of the church's life". They are not to be taken, however, "as institutions detached from the church and working against it, as though they were independent supreme courts". The authority of the church is rooted rather in the authority of our Lord Jesus Christ, "which is bestowed on the church as a whole" and "finds expression in the canon of sacred scripture, the life of the faithful, and the synodal life of the church". Furthermore, "the office given through ordination exercises a special responsibility in the synodal life of the church". It was also decided, however, that no general statement should be issued on this subject; the four introductory papers were to be examined once again in light of the objections mentioned above and to be discussed at the sixth plenary session.

Damaskinos Papandreou

16. Divine Revelation

Allentown, USA, 30 May 1985

I. (1) God, whom no one has ever seen (John 1:18), reveals himself in history to human beings through his word and power (energies). This revelation of God which begins with the creation of the world (Acts 14:15-17) is fulfilled through his saving work (oikonomia) in Christ, in the outpouring of the Holy Spirit and in the promise of a new creation.

(2) The triune God in whom we believe and whom we confess has revealed his divine wisdom and gracious will in his saving work which manifests him to us as Creator, Redeemer, Perfector, and the One who will be the judge of all humanity. God's promise in the Old Testament, when he spoke to the fathers by the prophets in many and various ways (Heb. 1:1) and its fulfilment in Jesus Christ is not only the history of the revelation of God but also the history of the salvation of humankind. Revelation is the word of God and the word about God; it is simultaneously the word for the destiny and the salvation of all people.

(3) God himself saves human beings from their lostness and alienation from him and brings them into the authentic life of the new creation (2 Cor. 5:17). The centre of his saving work is the sending of his Son who "for us and for our salvation came down from heaven; by the power of the Holy Spirit he became incarnate from the Virgin Mary, and was made man. For our sake he was crucified", raised to new life "in accordance with the scriptures; he ascended into heaven and is seated at the right hand of the Father". Through the exalted Lord the Father pours out the Holy Spirit upon his people and thereby leads his revelation to completion. The same Holy Spirit who has spoken through the prophets is effective in the apostolic kerygma by glorifying the Son and granting saving knowledge to all believers (John 14:13-16) until the fulfilment of all promises is attained in the kingdom of God on the last day.

II. (4) God's revelation in Jesus Christ is realized and actualized in the church and through the church as the body of Christ. The paschal and pentecostal mysteries instituted the church of the New Testament in which the revelation is lived, proclaimed and transmitted. The Holy Spirit sustains the church's life and growth until the last day through the proclamation of the gospel in the fullness of the apostolic tradition and its transmission from place to place and from generation to generation, not only by words but also by the whole life of the church.

(5) The holy scriptures are an inspired and authentic expression of God's revelation and of the experience of the church at its beginnings. In the church's ongoing experience of its life in Christ, in the faith, love and obedience of God's people and their wor-

ship, the holy scriptures become a living book of revelation which the church's kerygma, dogma and life may not contradict. Because through the guidance of the Holy Spirit the dogma of the church is in agreement with the holy scriptures, therefore the dogma itself becomes an unchangeable witness to the truth of revelation. Thus under the guidance of the Holy Spirit, divine revelation is living in the church through holy scripture and holy Tradition.

(6) "The sacred and divinely inspired scriptures are sufficient for the exposition of the truth, but there also exist many treatises of our blessed teachers composed for this purpose, and if one reads them he will gain somehow the right interpretation of the scriptures" (St Athanasius, c. gent. 1,3, *PG* 25,4).

(The original of paragraph 6 is the Greek text; the translation is provisional.)

17. Scripture and Tradition

Crete, Greece, 2 June 1987

1. The divine revelation in the Old and in the New Testament of the saving intervention of God (oikonomia), consummated in the person of Jesus Christ, is communicated to the world through the operation of the Holy Spirit. This saving intervention of God through the Son in the Holy Spirit is the essence of the "euangelion" of salvation.

2. The word of God made known to the prophets is revealed to us through the incarnation, the life and teaching, the passion, resurrection and ascension of Jesus Christ and the sending of his Spirit at Pentecost. By all this Jesus Christ accomplished and secured the unity of the testaments and the continuity of the once and for all offering of his body and blood for our salvation and his abiding presence with us to the end of the ages. Therefore, the "euangelion" of salvation, to which holy scripture bears witness, is not simply speech from or about God but the hypostatic Word of God incarnate. This "euangelion" of Jesus Christ, which by the operation of the Holy Spirit is communicated to us by the church to the end of the ages, is the holy Tradition.

3. The holy Tradition is the authentic expression of divine revelation in the living experience of the church, the body of the Word incarnate. The church in its sacraments and spiritual life transmits this "euangelion" of our salvation through the operation of the Holy Spirit. Therefore, apostolic faith is not only a matter of proclamation but an incarnate faith (Heb. 11:1; cf. *enhypostatos pistis*, Maximus Confessor, *Quaestiones* 25, *PG* 90,336D) in the church.

4. This "euangelion" of salvation is the content of the holy Tradition, preserved, confessed and transmitted in scripture, in the lives of the saints in all ages, and in the conciliar tradition of the church.

5. The Orthodox and the Lutheran churches have the same Bible, comprising the Old and New Testament, but the following ten books of the Old Testament have varying degrees of authority in our churches: Judith, 1 Ezra, 1 Maccabees, 2 Maccabees, 3 Maccabees, Tobit, Eccleslasticus, Wisdom of Solomon, Baruch and the Letter of Jeremiah. In the future we will have to discuss the problem of the canon in more detail.

6. The same triune God is revealed in the Old and in fullness in the New Testament. The Old Testament contains God's unconditional promise of salvation, and the New Testament contains its fulfilment in Christ through the Holy Spirit. Both Testaments reveal God's judgment of the sin inside and outside God's people and God's saving grace in Christ. Holy scripture, being the work of the Holy Spirit in holy Tradition, has as criterion for its true understanding Jesus Christ himself in the life and teaching of the one, holy, catholic and apostolic church.

7. The revelation of God, even as contained in scripture, transcends all verbal expressions. It is hidden from all creatures, especially from sinful human beings (*palaios anthropos*). Its true meaning is revealed only through the Holy Spirit in the living experience of salvation, which is accomplished in the church through the Christian life. This catholic experience of salvation in the church is at the same time the only authentic expression of the true understanding of the word of God.

8. The holy Tradition as ongoing action of the Holy Spirit in the church expresses itself in the church's whole life. The decisions of the ecumenical councils and local synods of the church, the teaching of the holy fathers and liturgical texts and rites are especially important and authoritative expressions of this manifold action of the Holy Spirit. However, not every synod claiming to be orthodox, not every teaching of an ecclesiastical writer, not all rites are expressions of the holy Tradition, if they are not accepted by the whole church. They may be only human traditions, lacking the presence of the Holy Spirit. That is why the problem of the criteria for determination of the presence of the holy Tradition in the traditions of churches is of great importance and needs further study.

9. Therefore, those church decisions which have been received by the catholic church as true expressions of the intent of the holy scripture can be considered authentic criteria of the church's faith and its confession (cf. Vincent of Lérins, *Commonitorium*, 2,3; *PL* 50,640). The church's doctrinal definitions which confess the holy Trinity and God's saving act in Jesus Christ by the Holy Spirit are guidelines for defending truth against falsehood. Proclaiming, confessing and living in Christ, the church communicates the mystery of God's revelation. The church's doctrinal statements are rooted in its whole spiritual life and at the same time are shaped by it. As St Basil affirmed about holy scripture and holy Tradition:

> ...regarding the true faith, both of these have the same value (St Basil the Great, *On the Holy Spirit*, XXVII, 66; *PG* 32,188A).

In another place St Basil argued for the formula "the glory is common to the Father and to the Son" (*he doxa koine Patri kai Hyio*) first on the basis of some of the fathers; then he continued:

> But it is not sufficient for us that it is a tradition of the fathers. For even they followed the intent (*boulema*) of the scriptures because they have used as principles the testimonies of the scriptures as mentioned shortly before (St Basil the Great, *On the Holy Spirit*, VII,16; *PG* 32,96).

10. The function of holy scriptures is to serve the authenticity of the church's living experience in safeguarding the holy Tradition from all attempts to falsify the true faith (cf. Heb. 4:12, etc.), not to undermine the authority of the church, the body of Christ.

11. Regarding the relation of scripture and Tradition, for centuries there seemed to have been a deep difference between Orthodox and Lutheran teaching. Orthodox hear with satisfaction the affirmation of the Lutheran theologians that the formula "sola scriptura" was always intended to point to God's revelation, God's saving act through Christ in the power of the Holy Spirit, and therefore to the holy Tradition of the church, as expressed in this paper, against human traditions that darken the authentic teaching in the church.

12. Pointing to scripture is pointing to the "euangelion" of salvation, to Christ and therefore to the holy Tradition which is the life of the church, to act as criterion of its authenticity and so to stress the church's unity and catholicity for the joyful common praise of the triune God.

18. The Canon and the Inspiration of the Holy Scripture

Bad Segeberg, Germany, 8 September 1989

1. The holy scripture is a great treasure of the church and serves as norm for its faith and life. The Old Testament bears witness to the self-revelation of the triune God in the prophets to the fathers (Heb. 1:1). It witnesses to God's acts of deliverance and judgment, to God's demands for faithful obedience and to God's promise of the coming Saviour of the world. The New Testament bears witness that God the Father sent his Son into the world to become a human being, born of the Virgin Mary (Luke 1:30-31; Gal. 4:4) and that God raised him from the dead in the power of the Holy Spirit (Rom. 1:3). Thus the triune God opened the door to life eternal for all believers from all nations. The one church of Jews and Gentiles, gathered in the Holy Spirit as the body of Christ, received the Hebrew scriptures which St Paul called "the old covenant" or "the Old Testament" (2 Cor. 3:14) or "holy scriptures" (Rom. 1:2; cf. "the scripture", John 2:22; Acts 8:32; "the scriptures", Mark 12:24; 1 Cor. 15:3f.) and later established the canon of the books of the New Testament. The Old and the New Testaments together comprise the holy scripture, the church's Bible.

A. The canon of holy scripture

2. The Bible of our Lord Jesus Christ and his apostles was the holy scripture of Israel (cf. Luke 4:16-21). It included the law and the prophets and comprised other writings such as the Psalms which had pre-eminence among them. Thus from the beginning the church had a fixed common nucleus of the canon of the Old Testament. Concerning the inclusion of some writings of Jewish origin, different usages existed side by side in the church. The council of 691-692 (Quinisextum) sanctioned various usages of local churches which included the short canon, a medium canon and an all-inclusive canon.

3. According to the common faith of the church, God's revelation in the holy scriptures of the Old Testament points to the incarnation of his Son, Jesus Christ, who was crucified and who rose from the dead for our salvation. The church teaches that the Son of God was the revealer to the prophets even before his incarnation (1 Cor. 10:4; John 8:58). The saving work of the triune God (oikonomia) is completed in the outpouring of the Holy Spirit at Pentecost and in the gathering of the church (Acts 2:1,17) which awaits the consummation. The traditions regarding the incarnate Lord himself and the message of the apostles were joined to the holy scriptures of Israel as their fulfilment and completion (Heb. 10:11; 2 Cor. 3:3-18). These new writings, a deposit of the apostolic oral tradition, became the New Testament.

4. The beginning of the New Testament canon dates back to the time of the apostles. By the end of the 2nd century its basic parts were established: the four gospels and the Acts, the Pauline epistles and the major catholic epistles. The church defined the canon because it heard in these writings the divine revelation in the authentic voice of the apostles as chosen witnesses of Jesus Christ. Later, the church in synods established the exact limits of the New Testament.

5. The recognition of the holy scriptures of the Old and New Testaments, the Christian Bible, is one of the most important decisions of the church on its way from Pentecost to the last judgment. We believe and teach together that the church was led by the Holy Spirit in this decision.

6. The early church recognized in these writings the prophetic promise and the original apostolic proclamation by which the church lives, and it acknowledges the normative authority of these scriptures. The consensus of the church under the guidance of the Holy Spirit decided finally the canonicity of the books of holy scripture. This consensus remains valid for us independent of judgments reached by contemporary historical research concerning the authorship of individual biblical writings. With regard to the content of the New Testament canon there are no differences between our churches.

7. The Old Testament comprises the following 39 canonical books: Genesis, Exodus, Leviticus, Numbers, Deuteronomy, Joshua, Judges, Ruth, 1 Kings (1 Samuel), 2 Kings (2 Samuel), 3 Kings (1 Kings), 4 Kings (2 Kings), 1 Chronicles, 2 Chronicles, 2 Ezra (Ezra), Nehemiah, Esther, Job, Psalms, Proverbs of Solomon, Ecclesiastes, The Song of Solomon, Isaiah, Jeremiah, Lamentations of Jeremiah, Ezekiel, Daniel, Obadiah, Joel, Jonah, Amos, Hosea, Micah, Nahum, Zephaniah, Habakkuk, Haggai, Zechariah, Malachi; and the ten *anagignoskomena* (also called "deuterocanonical") which correspond to the Lutheran "apocrypha". In the Orthodox tradition they are: Judith, 1 Ezra, 1 Maccabees, 2 Maccabees, 3 Maccabees, Tobit, Ecclesiasticus (Jesus Sirach), Wisdom of Solomon, Baruch and Letter of Jeremiah.[1]

8. The New Testament comprises 27 writings: Matthew, Mark, Luke, John, Acts, Romans, 1 Corinthians, 2 Corinthians, Galatians, Ephesians, Philippians, Colossians, 1 Thessalonians, 2 Thessalonians, 1 Timothy, 2 Timothy, Titus, Philemon, Hebrews, James, 1 Peter, 2 Peter, 1 John, 2 John, 3 John, Jude, Revelation.

9. We have one common holy scripture. We read it in our worship services; we use it catechetically. In the liturgy the reading of the gospel is always the conclusion and the high-point in a series of biblical texts. Jesus Christ is the centre of the holy scripture, the key to its understanding, the fulfilment of all of God's promises.

10. From the beginning the Old Testament existed in the church in Hebrew and in Greek. The New Testament was written in Greek. The church translated the holy scripture again and again into the languages of many peoples. The many languages in which

---

[1] The confessions of the Evangelical Lutheran Church do not contain a list of biblical books because the canon of the holy scripture was received by the Reformation as a given entity. Accordingly, there is also no delimitation of the canon of the Old Testament which is binding for all Lutheran churches. In Martin Luther's translation which became normative for German-speaking lands, the following books and texts which "are profitable and good to read" are reckoned as the Apocrypha (this name does not here mean writings rejected by the church): Judith, Wisdom of Solomon, Tobit, Jesus Sirach, Baruch, 1 Maccabees, 2 Maccabees, Additions to Esther, Susanna, Bel and the Dragon, Prayer of Azariah, Song of the Three Young Men, Prayer of Manasseh.

the one holy scripture appeared express the life of the one church in many languages and cultures. This also discloses that the canon of the holy scripture is a special fruit of the church's life and a special gift for the church.

B. The inspiration of scripture

11. "All scripture is inspired by God and profitable for teaching, for reproof, for correction, and for training in righteousness that the man of God may be complete, equipped for every good work" (2 Tim. 3:16f.). "No prophecy of scripture is a matter of one's own interpretation, because no prophecy ever came by the impulse of man, but men moved by the Holy Spirit spoke from God" (2 Pet. 1:20f.). To speak of inspiration (*theopneustia*) of the holy scripture is to speak of the work of the Holy Spirit. When Christians declare scripture to be inspired, they are making a statement about the way God has chosen to work among his people. Holy scripture is one of the means by which the Holy Spirit bears witness to the truth, inspires and sustains the faith of believers.

12. The question regarding the inspiration of the books of the holy scripture points back to the working of the Spirit in their production, that is to say, the inspiration of the authors, and points forward to the working of this same Spirit in the church who teaches how the scriptures are to be understood and leads the faithful to their goal.

13. According to the apostolic witness and the teaching of the fathers, this goal is participation in God's glory. "And those whom he justified he also glorified" (Rom. 8:30; cf. 1 John 3:2). It is the theme of all divine revelation that the triune God himself saves the creation from its lostness and alienation and leads it to true life. The holy scripture is the divinely inspired and canonical witness to revelation which nevertheless transcends all possibilities of concepts and expressions. As witness to revelation the holy scripture is God's word. Inspiration is the operation of the Holy Spirit in the authors of the holy scripture so that they may bear witness to the revelation (John 5:39) without erring about God and God's ways and means for the salvation of humankind. Therefore the authors of holy scripture describe God's ways with his creation and his people and thereby witness to God's glory which is hidden from the eyes of unbelievers. Inspiration comes from the experience of the revelation of God's glory through the Holy Spirit. To the Old Testament prophets, to the apostles and prophets of the new covenant (Eph. 2:20; 3:5), God revealed his glory. It is important to note that glorification is inseparable from the cross and from suffering not only with respect to our Lord Jesus Christ (John 12:23f.,32) but also with respect to his followers (Gal. 2:19-20). Glorification is the transformation and renewal of the whole person (Rom. 12:2). It empowered the authors of holy scripture to proclaim and to write the word of God.

14. Prophets, apostles and saints who have experienced God's glory and witnessed to it in holy scripture declare the truth of God and the ways of communion with him. It is about them that St Paul wrote: "The spiritual man... is himself to be judged by no one. 'For who has known the mind of the Lord so as to instruct him?' But we have the mind of Christ" (1 Cor. 2:15-16). Orthodox and Lutheran theologians agree that there is no similarity or analogy of being (*analogia entis*) between God and creation, even though the created depends on God. This is why St Gregory the Theologian wrote: "It is impossible to express God and even more impossible to conceive him" (*Oratio Theologica* 2,4).

15. Those who have experienced the glory of God, which experience in itself cannot be expressed in words or conceived in thoughts, are yet inspired to use expressions

and concepts of ordinary language in order to guide others to the same experience. St Paul wrote: "Because you are sons, God has sent the Spirit of his Son into our hearts, crying 'Abba! Father!'" (Gal. 4:6). This coming of the Spirit into the heart is the normal form of inspiration in the faithful (Rom. 8:14-17,26-27). The Holy Spirit effects this through preaching and teaching and the life of those who are already inspired (Rom. 10:13-15; 1 Cor. 4:16; 11:1).

16. The Old Testament period prepared the way for the acceptance of the incarnation of the Son of God by the prophetic tradition represented by St John the Baptist and by Mary, the mother of God, and by other believers who found their place in the early Christian community. Christ revealed himself as having by nature the same glory with his Father by his teaching, his miracles and especially by revelation of his glory in his baptism and transfiguration, crucifixion, resurrection, ascension and by Pentecost. It is by Pentecost that the church became the body of Christ, thus being led into all truth.

17. The interpenetration of revelation and inspiration consummated in Pentecost continues in the life of the church. Within the life of the church Christians who become "a temple of the Holy Spirit" (1 Cor. 6:19) and therefore are members of the body of Christ are led into all the truth in the experience of glorification, as the Lord prayed to the Father: "Father, I desire that they also, whom thou hast given me, may be with me where I am, to behold my glory which thou hast given me in thy love for me before the foundation of the world" (John 17:24).

18. Expressions and concepts of biblical authors about God are inspired because they are unerring *guides* to communion with God. But the authors did not receive inspiration about created truths except that God created the world out of nothing (ex nihilo). Also the human words of Christ are guides to pentecostal glorification and not this glorification itself since God as revealed in glorification cannot be conceived or expressed. For this reason holy scripture is not to be used as a substitute for scientific research. Some books of the Bible are written by those authors who themselves have reached glorification, while other books were written about them or about historical events.

19. Authentic interpreters of the holy scripture are persons who have had the same experience of revelation and inspiration within the body of Christ as the biblical writers had. Therefore it is necessary for authentic understanding that anybody who reads or hears the Bible be inspired by the Holy Spirit. The Orthodox believe that such authentic interpretation is the service of the fathers of the church especially expressed in the decisions of the ecumenical councils. Lutherans agree in principle. Lutheran confessional writings affirm that no one can believe in Jesus Christ by one's own reason or abilities but that it is the Holy Spirit who calls, gathers and illuminates believers through the gospel even as he calls, gathers and enlightens the whole church on earth keeping it in union with Jesus Christ in the one true faith (Luther's *Small Catechism*).

XI. LUTHERAN-REFORMED DIALOGUE

Historical Introduction

The report presented here is the result of theological conversations which the Lutheran World Federation and the World Alliance of Reformed Churches held from 1985 to 1989. It may come as a surprise that an official Lutheran-Reformed dialogue at the world level came about only so late in time. The reason is certainly not to be looked for in any special distance between the two families. For in fact the opposite is true: they are so close to each other that the need of a special dialogue was not obvious.

The dialogue had a lengthy and complex prehistory. A breakthrough in relations between the Lutheran and Reformed churches was achieved at the European level in 1973. After prolonged theological conversations a doctrinal agreement, known as the Leuenberg agreement, was worked out and presented to the Lutheran, Reformed and United churches of Europe for ratification. The great majority signified their acceptance within a relatively short time and declared their agreement on pulpit and table fellowship as well as their reciprocal recognition of ordinations. Ever since this agreement was reached, representatives of the churches involved have met regularly for doctrinal conversations that have for their purpose to consolidate and deepen the communion achieved (Sigtuna 1976, Friebergen 1981, Strasbourg 1987).

The theological conversations that would eventually produce the Leuenberg agreement began back in the 1950s. They took place under the aegis of the Faith and Order commission of the World Council of Churches and were supported by both the World Federation and the World Alliance. In North America, too, conversations were initiated at the beginning of the 1960s. A first series concluded with the publication of *Marburg Revisited* (ed. Paul C. Empie and James McCord, Minneapolis, 1966). A second series took place in the 1970s and a new effort in the years 1981-83 produced a report presented to both churches.

Quite early on, both world organizations were faced with the question of what importance these conversations in Europe and North America were to have for the two sides. In 1967 a small group was commissioned to go into this question. A year later the group became a true joint committee. Its purpose was:
1) to continue the theological dialogue;
2) to achieve clarity on the practical implications of the theological consensus that might be obtained;
3) to reach agreement on the role of the two world organizations in the life of newer churches; and

4) to define more fully the idea of "closer working relations".

This last charge makes clear what the two executive committees had in mind: they wanted to find out whether and to what extent the agreement achieved would make a rapprochement of the two world organizations possible or even mandatory. The joint committee focused especially on the question of how the two families could effectively contribute to the further development of the ecumenical movement; in this connection it devoted a great deal of attention to the goals that might be set for a "truly ecumenical council". In order to give this committee greater authority, two members of the each executive committee were appointed to it.

Meanwhile a further initiative had been added. In 1969 the Lutheran World Federation and the World Alliance of Reformed Churches had decided to hold joint conversations with the Roman Catholic Church on the subject of interconfessional marriages. These conversations were completed in 1976 (see *Growth in Agreement I*, pp.277-306).

In 1973 the joint committee was in a position to submit a report to the executive committees of the two world organizations. In its response the Lutheran World Federation put itself on record as saying that "in the future the two world organizations... should plan their meetings jointly and should collaborate with the other two partners in theological studies and ecumenical dialogues". At the same time the World Federation recommended the appointment of a new joint committee which would have a threefold purpose:
1) to examine the theological and ecclesiastical implications of the Leuenberg agreement,
2) to undertake a series of case studies on Lutheran-Reformed relations, and
3) to continue studying the idea of a "universal council".

In 1974 the World Alliance of Reformed Churches accepted these recommendations.

But the work of the new joint committee soon ran into problems. It quickly became clear that however important the development of Lutheran-Reformed relations might be in Europe, the Leuenberg agreement could not without further ado be applied to other areas of the world. At the same time dialogues, and especially that of the Lutheran World Federation with the Roman Catholic Church, were becoming ever more important, so that interest in a privileged relationship between the two families issuing from the Reformation began to wane. In 1976 the committee offered a new suggestion: a "consultative team" should be created that would promote Lutheran-Reformed relations in individual countries. The idea was to start undertakings that would be geared to the situation in specific regions. The suggestion fell through because the two world organizations in fact had other priorities and lacked the financial means required for such an expensive programme. The joint committee was dissolved in 1979.

The executive committee of the World Alliance of Reformed Churches now decided to form a small working group. This group was to survey the state of relations and develop recommendations for the future. Two years later (1981) it presented its report. In this it came to the plain conclusion that new conversations were needed. The general assembly of the World Alliance of Reformed Churches, held in Ottawa in 1982, agreed with this view. It was recommended that the theological section of the World Alliance be commissioned to undertake conversations with the Lutheran World Federation and thus give new life to the interrupted dialogue. The seventh plenary assembly of the Lutheran World Federation (Budapest 1984) had this to say: "The anticipated new dialogue with the World Alliance of Reformed Churches is meant to help in the process of extending to the two worldwide Christian communities the ecclesial reality that has emerged in regional arrangements which accord with the Leuenberg agreement" (LWF Report, no. 19-20, 1985, p.227).

The report presented here appeared in spring 1989, in time for the general assembly of the World Alliance of Reformed Churches, which was held in August of that year, to take cognizance of it. The assembly recommended that the report be delivered to the member churches for their comments. The hope was expressed that official conversations between the Lutheran World Federation and the World Alliance of Reformed Churches might be undertaken in the near future (*Proceedings of the 22nd General Council*, Seoul 1989, p.229).

Lukas Vischer

XI. LUTHERAN-REFORMED DIALOGUE

19. Towards Church Fellowship

Geneva, Switzerland, Easter 1989

Foreword

After a decade of conversation between representatives of the World Alliance of Reformed Churches and the Lutheran World Federation, enabling action to pursue a theological dialogue on the international level was taken in 1982. In 1983 and 1984 the WARC and the LWF agreed to a series of recommendations stipulating the make-up and mandate for a Lutheran-Reformed joint commission. The international dialogue was intended to build on regional agreements already reached – notably the Leuenberg agreement in Europe – and to respond to needs of member churches, especially in Asia, Africa and Latin America.

The joint commission was subsequently appointed and held its first meeting in Geneva, 1985. The three additional annual meetings called for by the approved design were held in Chicago (1986), Driebergen (1987) and Budapest (1988). The meetings featured not only theological discussion but also efforts to assess concrete Lutheran-Reformed relationships in various parts of the world. Therefore our report combines theological affirmation, reporting and recommendations. We have attempted to place these in the context of our contemporary understanding of the gospel and of the church's mission in the world.

We commend this report to the member churches of our sponsoring world bodies in the hope that it will affirm relationships already achieved, further relationships still in various stages of development, and stimulate efforts towards relationships where none presently exist. We prize our common Reformation heritage and are confident that it has an important and dynamic contribution to make not only to Lutheran-Reformed relationships, but also within the larger oikoumene in which both Lutheran and Reformed churches are committed participants.

James B. Torrance
Reformed chair

Gyula Nagy
Lutheran chair

Introduction

1. The passion for renewal of the church in the light of the gospel which brought into being the Lutheran and Reformed churches four and a half centuries ago remains alive today among us, the heirs of the Reformation. Both of our traditions are deeply engaged in the ecumenical movement, seeking to renew our faithfulness of Christian witness and service and to make the unity of Christ's church visible.

2. Therefore it is with dismay that we must acknowledge the estrangement that we have so often experienced since the earliest years of our churches' existence, despite our common historical and theological roots in the 16th-century Reformation and despite the profound agreement we see also today in our teaching of the gospel and worshipping life.

3. Our estrangement can be seen in:

4. – the mutual condemnations by Lutheran and Reformed churches in the 16th century;

5. – the continuing failure of our churches in many parts of the world to declare pulpit and altar/table fellowship: as a result the Lord's supper, an anticipation of our unity in God's final reign, becomes a sign of our brokenness; Christ's intention that we should share the sacramental meal as brothers and sisters is contravened;

6. – the unwillingness of some of our churches to accept fully each other's ordained ministries, as evidenced by the practice of reordaining those ministers who seek entry into the other's ministry;

7. – the widespread failure to pursue the opportunities that exist for joint action of witness, service and mission, for expression of our common faith.

8. We recognize that such separated existence is simply no longer acceptable. We are called so to live as churches that our life is in accord with the coming reign of God of which Jesus Christ is the harbinger and first-fruits. Such a vision calls us to live in unity as brothers and sisters in Christ. Today we understand more clearly and more urgently the path towards unity which the message of Christ proclaims and which the reign of God requires. The grounds for our present clarity and sense of urgency can be noted.

9. – From our Reformation heritage, we have a common concern to bear witness to the unconditional character of the free gift of grace; God accepts us by grace alone. If we are to be faithful to this witness, we must accept one another as freely and unconditionally as God in Christ accepts us. God does not accept us because we offer Lutheran or Reformed worship. There is only one offering acceptable to God, that which has been provided for us by God in Christ. We have nothing to offer except in him. Continued estrangement in the life of word and sacrament, witness and service among those who see that their teaching of the gospel is substantially in unity is a denial of the very meaning of grace. In gratitude for Christ's free offer to us of reconciliation in his body, we believe that we must exhibit a reconciled style of life in our existence as churches.

10. – In the present world the call to mission urgently requires our fuller fellowship. To live otherwise than as reconciled sisters and brothers weakens our witness and our capacity to act effectively in mission. Already significant steps have been taken in several countries by our churches to unite more closely in view of the mission opportunities presented. Around the globe we sense this urgency whether the mission context is secularized indifference and opposition to religion, the vital presence of other religions, or great and desperate social need and suffering. We shall be found inadequate to our mission if we fail to respond together to today's pressing opportunities for witness.

11. – The persistent and impressive outcome of dialogues between our churches in the past twenty years has been the conclusion that no insuperable barrier to fuller fellowship exists. The 16th-century condemnations have been declared no longer applicable by many Lutheran and Reformed churches today. Remaining theological differences have been recognized as important, but not church-dividing. Full pulpit and

altar/table fellowship or organic union already shapes the churchly life of several millions of our Lutheran and Reformed church members today.

12. We interpret these developments and deepened insights as urgings of God, and they can be obeyed only by resolute and energetic efforts to make our unity more visible and more deeply experienced. Conventional or lukewarm efforts at rapprochement will not suffice. We must move actively through the doors which God is opening for us today, seizing the opportunities that God places before us.

13. We rejoice in the progress of some of our churches towards fuller fellowship and common mission. We feel ourselves privileged, on the one hand, to join and affirm their witness; and we seek, on the other hand, to embolden those of our churches that find the way towards unity more difficult.

14. We recognize that Lutheran-Reformed unity will be pursued under the larger obedience to seek unity with all of our Christian sisters and brothers. Our churches are in dialogue and intercommunion with other partner churches, and we believe that our calling to unity as co-heirs of the Reformation is consonant with the larger ecumenical movement of which we are a part. In fact, we believe that only as we take each step of obedience immediately visible to us will we be able to find our way through the complexities which lie ahead on the path to the full unity of the church.

15. In this report our goal is to make clear the distinctive nature of Lutheran-Reformed unity, to explore the diversities we experience which sometimes enrich and sometimes hinder our life together, and to make recommendations for full church fellowship among all our churches. We intend these recommendations to be compatible with the position each of us has taken with other partners in dialogue.

16. Our common concern in seeking unity in our two communions is to image that unity in diversity which is in God, that our churches might be a sign and witness to the world of that unity and communion which God wills for all.

I. Our common faith

17. We Lutheran and Reformed churches throughout the world profess that we are one in Jesus Christ, with a common heritage in the Reformation of the 16th century. Within the one, holy, catholic and apostolic church, by the light of the gospel and the creeds of the undivided church, with the saints of all ages, we believe in one God, Father, Son and Holy Spirit.

18. The world and the human family owe their existence to the grace of this triune God who created us in the divine image. We acknowledge that, despite our misuse of the creation and our disregard of human communion, the future of the world and our destiny as human beings are defined by the grace which surpasses all understanding and merit. God's purposes have been revealed and lived out as gracious promise in Jesus Christ our Lord. We believe that the Holy Spirit will empower the fulfilment of this promise in the coming kingdom of God of which the risen Christ is the first-fruits.

19. Jesus Christ is the church's one foundation. He lived a life of healing and teaching, was crucified and rose again for us, reveals himself in the holy scriptures and is confessed in the creeds of the church. Together we share the evangelical concern of the Reformation to proclaim the life, death and resurrection of Jesus Christ for us as the gospel, the centre of the scriptures.

20. Our salvation is complete in Christ who has fulfilled the promises and the law for us, reconciled us to God and one another and made us one in his one body. Christ

now calls us by the Holy Spirit, in union with himself, to participate in his communion with the Father, his intercessions for the world, his mission from the Father to the world, and his continuing ministry of service to the needs of all humanity.

21. We are justified by the grace of God and not by our own works, and are therefore called to communion with God and one another, not on the basis of our own achievement but on the strength of the divine gift. God accepts us into his fellowship, not because we are acceptable in terms of his norms of acceptance – God's law – but because in Christ, by grace, God has broken down the barriers which separate us from God. So we are called to accept one another in costly discipleship as freely and unconditionally as God in Christ has accepted us.

22. We live by faith alone, receiving God's forgiveness in daily repentance and the gift of new life in Christ, in the hope of the fulfilment of God's purposes for all creation in his kingdom.

23. Jesus Christ alone is the word of God. Christ gives himself to us to be known and loved in the prophetic and apostolic witness of Old and New Testaments. Christ comes to us through the Holy Spirit, in all ages, in the proclamation of the gospel and the administration of the sacraments, baptism and Lord's supper.

24. In worship, in the richness and variety of our different traditions, we participate by the Spirit in the worship and intercessions of Christ who is the only priest in the church, by whose offering alone we are accepted, and through whom as members of one body we have access to the Father by the one Spirit. The proclamation of the gospel, together with baptism, eucharist and ministry are Christ's gifts to his one church. By these gifts through the Spirit Christ makes us participants of his one baptism, nourishes us at his table as members of his one body, and shares with us his ministry of reconciliation. These gifts are essential to our identity as the Christian church, for its continuity and constant renewal.

25. There is no area in life, indeed in all creation, which does not belong to Jesus Christ who sends us into all the world to be a sign of God's kingdom and to preach and live the gospel of reconciliation in a common concern for justice, freedom, peace and care for the creation.

26. Finally as Lutheran and Reformed churches we affirm that full agreement in the right teaching/preaching of the gospel and the right administration of the sacraments is necessary and sufficient for the true unity of the church.

II. On the way to church fellowship

27. Though some forms of Lutheran-Reformed church fellowship have existed since the 19th century, it is in recent decades that the basic agreement in our common faith has been discovered which motivates a new concern for the unity of the church and has furthered full communion among our two branches of the Reformation heritage. In some parts of the world Lutheran and Reformed churches exist side by side. In other parts one or the other confessional tradition is in the majority with the other as distinct minority. In still other parts only one partner is to be found. The history which has produced these varying situations and the attitudes they engender is not an insignificant factor on the way to church fellowship.

28. The present state of Lutheran-Reformed relations cannot, therefore, be described in a uniform manner. We must content ourselves with selected situational reports.

Concord at Leuenberg and church fellowship

29. After long negotiations representatives of the Lutheran, Reformed and union churches in Europe have formulated their common mind in the Leuenberg agreement (1973) and proposed that on this basis these churches should declare themselves to be in full communion with one another. The agreement has a very simple structure. It begins with the change in conditions since the Reformation, and then describes the common understanding of the gospel: God justifies in Jesus Christ all who believe, and graciously gives himself through the Holy Spirit in the proclamation of the word and the celebration of the sacraments. Next the document examines the doctrinal condemnations pronounced in the course of history and shows that they no longer apply to the partners in dialogue today. The themes addressed here are: the Lord's supper, Christology and predestination. In a final section the churches declare:
– that they are one in their understanding of the gospel;
– that the condemnations expressed in the old confessional documents no longer apply to the contemporary doctrinal positions of the assenting churches;
– that they offer each other pulpit and table fellowship; this includes the mutual recognition of ordained ministries and the freedom to provide for intercelebration of holy communion.

30. Now this fellowship has to be realized and strengthened in the life of the churches and congregations. The common understanding of the gospel on which church fellowship is based must be further deepened, tested in the light of the witness of holy scripture and its relevance continually shown on the contemporary scene. For this reason the Leuenberg churches are engaged in continuing theological dialogue and in a search for common witness and service in the world. Because they are done *within* a communion, these common efforts are arguably the most significant result of the agreement.

31. The Leuenberg agreement poses many questions about fellowship between the Lutheran and Reformed churches throughout the world. In the first place, of course, it must be seen as a positive advance: the Leuenberg discussions must be counted among the few bilateral dialogues which have produced a declaration of church fellowship. The European churches thereby took a step which no Lutheran or Reformed church in any other part of the world can simply ignore.

32. The Leuenberg agreement, however, also poses difficult questions to the subscribing churches. In some places the declaration of church fellowship has had hardly any consequences in the life of local congregations, even after fifteen years. Theological agreement in itself is not enough; it must be translated into concrete situations, with its liturgical, spiritual, practical or organizational consequences. At the moment the Lutheran and Reformed churches in Europe find themselves on this difficult path from the mere declaration to the realization of church fellowship. Seventy-six European churches and four Latin American churches have signed the agreement. Some of these include it in their constitutions. In the Netherlands, on the basis of the Leuenberg agreement, the minority Lutheran church has joined the two majority Reformed churches in a process towards church union.

Union churches

33. In some places Reformed and Lutheran churches have come together in union churches. The oldest examples are churches in the German Democratic Republic and the Federal Republic of Germany. They reflect historical developments in Germany at

the beginning of the 19th century and can only be properly understood against that political background. The formation of these churches, it should be noted, was a major factor in the emigration of Lutherans to North America and elsewhere and triggered in Germany a movement towards greater Lutheran self-consciousness.

34. Typical of the constitutions of these German union churches is their reference to both Lutheran and Reformed confessions. Ordination to the ministry takes place on the basis of either confession according to the wish of the ordinand. In recent times this union model has scarcely found acceptance anywhere. A more homogeneous European model is the Church of Czech Brethren when both traditions are embraced. Still another model is found in Austria where Reformed and Lutheran congregations have an organizational union but retain their separate confessional character.

35. Another type of church union took place in Ethiopia in 1973. During the period of mission preceding the Italian occupation, virtually total parity existed between "evangelical" groups which remained uninfluenced by particular confessional issues. This sense of unity increased during the occupation when missionaries left the country. After the occupation, efforts to achieve church unity were thwarted by the confessional sensitivities of the returned missionaries. The result was the formation of two churches: Bethel (Presbyterian) and Mekane Yesus (Lutheran). In 1973 Bethel became two synods among the autonomous Lutheran synods of the Ethiopian Evangelical Church Mekane Yesus. Though Lutheran and Reformed congregations retain their distinctive flavours, they are one church.

Churches in dialogue

36. A third group of Lutheran and Reformed churches is striving, through their common understanding of the gospel, towards future church fellowship. The two examples offered here indicate how geography and history are influential factors. They may stand for other similar situations.

37. *Indonesia:* The Protestant churches in Indonesia in general express not a confessional but an ethnic or regional character in their respective names. This is the result of the former colonial government policy to allow only one missionary society to work among people of one ethnic community. Because of this the self-understanding of the Indonesian churches in general has been as much ethnic or regional as confessional. It has also been determined, however, by the religious pluralism of the nation where, in addition to Christianity (officially sub-divided as Catholic and Protestant religions), Islam (the majority religion), Buddhism and Hinduism are recognized religions.

38. In 1950 a council of churches was established to express and to further a movement towards one church. But a more decisive step occurred in 1984 with the establishment of the Communion of Churches based on a consensus documented in "Five Documents on Unity". The documents are:
1) guidelines on the common mission of the churches;
2) common apprehension of our universal Christian faith in Indonesia;
3) mutual recognition and acceptance of all member churches;
4) basic (church) order of the Communion of Churches;
5) self-reliance in theology, forces and funds.

39. The guidelines on common mission begin with the basic statement that each church is a manifestation of the one, holy, catholic and apostolic church, and as such is called upon in every place and throughout all ages:

- to proclaim the good news to the whole creation (Mark 16:15);
- to manifest the unity of the body of Christ with a variety of gifts, but in the same Spirit (1 Cor. 12:4);
- to render service in love to everybody and to implement justice for all (Mark 10:45; Luke 4:18; 10:25-37; John 15:16).

40. Based on that statement, the guidelines contain chapters on unity, on witness and proclamation, on participation and service in development, on relations and cooperation with the government, on relations with other communities, on ecumenical relations and on the implementation of the guidelines. In the section on mutual recognition and acceptance pulpit and table/altar fellowship is also officially acknowledged.

41. The starting point for the Communion of Churches was the need for a common mission in Indonesia. In part it parallels government efforts to form a cohesive nation from the variety of resident ethnic groups. The churches together face the challenge of being obedient to the missionary command in a religiously pluralistic society while still affirming the building of a cohesive society in the nation. The Communion of Churches is therefore engaged in an open-ended and ongoing process.

42. For Reformed and Lutheran churches in particular these developments have led to full communion, including the mutual recognition of ordained ministries. Through common programmes of education both for laypeople and clergy, attempts are made to resolve such remaining differences as marriage discipline and other ethical-political issues.

43. *United States of America:* The first Lutheran-Reformed dialogue in the United States resulted in the document *Marburg Revisited* (1966).[1] Based on substantial theological research, this dialogue saw "no insuperable obstacles to pulpit and altar fellowship" and recommended to the North American bodies "that they encourage their constituent churches to enter into discussions looking forward to intercommunion and the fuller recognition of one another's ministries" (p.52). No official decision to do so was taken by any of the participating churches which were members of the Caribbean and North American area council of the World Alliance of Reformed Churches and of the USA national committee of the Lutheran World Federation (p.54: actions were taken, but not to enter discussions...). It should be noted, however, that "Marburg conversations" took place against the background of de facto church fellowship on several levels, and that these conditions still prevail.

44. A second round of conversations (1972-74) was less productive. The participants studied the newly published Leuenberg agreement (see above) and concluded that its approach, being so focused on classical 16th-century issues, was inappropriate to the very different American scene. They "observed that while the American Lutheran Church and the Lutheran Church in America and the Reformed churches adhere to the *doctrine* of the Lord's supper expressed in their respective confessions of faith, in *practice* they are saying that the confessional differences concerning the *mode* of Christ's presence ought not to be regarded as obstacles to pulpit and altar fellowship" (pp.57f.). Expressing some frustration at their "inability to make theological headway" the participants recommended an approach to each other "at every level of life, through a fresh hearing of the gospel... as well as in terms of their confessional and

---

[1] The documents referred to below are collected in *An Invitation to Action*, Philadelphia, 1984. Quotations are cited from that book.

ecclesiastical traditions". Any resultant declarations of altar fellowship were to be handled on "a church body to church body basis" (p.58).

45. In the recent third round of dialogue (1981-83), participants focused on the central issues of justification, the Lord's supper and ministry. The latter had not been discussed previously in American dialogues. The group built on the previous theological work which in its judgment had prepared a sound foundation of agreement between the Reformed and Lutherans – an agreement so compelling that it mandated urgent action. There was agreement that the old condemnations no longer applied to the current partners, but the group felt strongly that a declaration of fellowship would be, as such, insufficient. What was needed was new life in common worship, study and mission.

46. Recommendations sent to the churches in *An Invitation to Action* (1984) urged them to take action providing for:
- mutual recognition as churches;
- mutual recognition of their ordained ministries which are responsible for preaching and the sacraments;
- mutual recognition of their churches' celebrations of the Lord's supper "as a means of grace in which Christ grants communion with himself, assures us of the forgiveness of sins, and pledges life eternal";
- establishment of a process of reception of the report which would engage Lutherans and Reformed people in common study, worship (both joint celebrations of holy communion and the preaching and presiding of ministers of one tradition in congregations of the other are mentioned) and mission at every judicatory level, and which would refer unresolved theological issues to a subsequent dialogue in he context of the new relationship (pp.4-6).

47. Participants from the Lutheran Church-Missouri synod submitted a minority report, declining to recommend full communion. In 1984 the Cumberland Presbyterian Church approved *An Invitation to Action* for study in the church but has not participated in further dialogue. In 1986 representatives of the Lutheran Church in America, the American Lutheran Church, the Association of Evangelical Lutheran Churches, the Reformed Church of America, and the Presbyterian Church (USA), all of whose national assemblies were to meet the same summer, negotiated a common statement based on the *An Invitation to Action* text, slightly modified with reference to the Lord's supper: "... a means of grace in which Christ, truly present in the sacrament, is given and received, forgiveness of sin is declared and experienced, and a foretaste of life eternal is granted". Through a related amendment, provision was made for "occasional joint services of the Lord's supper" and for sharing of pastors "where appropriate and desirable, and in accordance with the disciplines of our several churches". All those churches except the Lutheran Church in America approved this common text. The Lutheran Church in America modified the recommendations still further, omitting recognition of the Lord's supper but encouraging communion with members of the Reformed Church in America and the Presbyterian Church (USA) under present church disciplines, retaining provision for occasional joint services of the Lord's supper "where appropriate and desirable, and in accord with the disciplines of our several churches", looking forward to establishment of "full communion" with those Reformed churches, and calling for further discussion of the Lord's supper, Christology and predestination.

48. The formation of the Evangelical Lutheran Church in America (1988) from the AELC, ALC and LCA created a new structure for Lutheran-Reformed relations in the

United States. Currently discussions are being held between its representatives and those of the United Church of Christ, the Reformed Church in America and the Presbyterian Church (USA) to determine the extent and character of work required before fellowship between the two traditions can be declared.[2]

Other patterns of relationship

49. Many levels of Lutheran-Reformed relations exist which stop short of involving the churches themselves in dialogue. Yet these can be important stepping stones to unity. Examples are joint theological faculties or common social-service institutions. Through such cooperative efforts, churches which live side by side without much concern for or knowledge of each other may find ways of overcoming mistrust or difficult past histories so as to recognize ever more fully their baptismal bond of unity in Christ.

50. Some Reformed and Lutheran churches are geographically separate from each other and have few immediate possibilities to practise fellowship. That should not, however, mean that this document is irrelevant to them. For such separated churches the world Lutheran and Reformed bodies have a special function. They serve as instruments of contact worldwide, thus connecting all their member churches with issues of church fellowship, even churches far distant from those of the ecumenical partner.

III. Unity in diversity

51. Following the historical confessions, as Lutheran and Reformed churches we affirm that agreement in the right preaching of the gospel and the administration of the sacraments in accordance with God's word is necessary and sufficient for the true unity of the church (cf. §26 above).

52. This understanding of the unity of the church makes clear that, rather than unity and diversity being opposites, diversity is part of the richness of our unity in Christ. One needs however to make a distinction where diversity is concerned. A difference which compromises full agreement in the right preaching of the gospel and the right administration of the sacraments makes church fellowship impossible and thus becomes a church-dividing difference, and an instance of illegitimate diversity.

53. The divisive nature of such differences must be surmounted if unity is to be achieved. When full agreement in word and sacrament is reached and no longer affected by the remaining differences, these differences lose their church-dividing character and become legitimate parts of the life of our churches. These differences are borne by the deeper agreement in word and sacrament and express our unity in diversity.

54. In the 16th century there was a sad collapse of fellowship between the churches. The differences had become church-dividing. Accordingly, the confessions of that period enshrine mutual condemnations. These condemnations dealt with the understanding of the Lord's supper, which was closely linked to christological issues and the doctrine of double predestination. In the past forty years representatives of our two churches have examined these difficult issues in great depth in many national and international dialogues. Above all there were studies carried out in the Netherlands, France and West Germany, which made possible the dialogue in Europe, and also the Leuen-

---

[2] In 1991 these four churches voted to declare full communion the basis of the dialogical results.

berg agreement, as well as the studies made in Indonesia and the USA (see §§27-50 above). The result was a far-reaching consensus on all these church-dividing issues.

Word and sacrament

55. The fundamental agreement of the Lutheran and Reformed traditions concerning word and sacrament has been demonstrated in historical and theological studies produced in the United States and Europe, e.g. *Marburg Revisited* (1966), *Arnoldshainer Thesen* (1960), *Auf dem Weg* (1967) and *Auf dem Weg II* (1971). These studies have not only examined areas of traditional condemnations, but have restated the fundamental consensus in the gospel of justification by faith expressed in a common understanding of word, baptism and eucharist.

56. – This gospel is the good news that for us and for our salvation God's Son became human in Jesus the Christ, was crucified and raised from the dead. By his life, death and resurrection he took upon himself God's judgment on human sin and proved God's love for sinners, reconciling the entire world to God.

57. – For Christ's sake we sinners have been reconciled to God, not because we earned God's acceptance but by an act of God's sheer mercy. The Holy Spirit calls and enables us to repent of our sin and accept God's gracious offer. Those trusting in this gospel, believing in Christ as Saviour and Lord, are justified in God's sight.

58. – Both the Lutheran and Reformed traditions confess this gospel in the language of justification by grace through faith alone (p.9, cf. pp.67f.).

59. – Baptism is administered in the name of the Father and of the Son and of the Holy Spirit with water. In baptism, Jesus Christ irrevocably receives man, fallen prey to sin and death, into his fellowship of salvation so that he may become a new creature. In the power of his Holy Spirit, he calls him into his community and to a new life of faith, to daily repentance, and to discipleship (p.68).

60. – In the Lord's supper the risen Christ imparts himself in his body and blood, given up for all, through his word of promise with bread and wine. He thereby grants us forgiveness of sins, and sets us free for a new life of faith. He enables us to experience anew that we are members of his body. He strengthens us for service to all men.

61. – When we celebrate the Lord's supper we proclaim the death of Christ through which God has reconciled the world with himself. We proclaim the presence of the risen Lord in our midst. Rejoicing that the Lord has come to us, we await his future coming in glory (p.68) (Leuenberg agreement).

62. These strong declarations of our common understanding of word and sacrament, based on prior studies, are sufficient testimony to justify our conviction that the agreement between the two traditions is not merely grounded in concurrence on certain points concerning word and sacrament, but represents an agreement in the gospel of Jesus Christ itself. While differences remain, on the basis of this consensus in the gospel nothing now stands in the way of church fellowship. In the light of this full agreement the condemnations previously expressed are no longer applicable to our partner churches.

Church and ministry

63. Our agreement in word and sacrament implies a necessary consequence: accord in our view of the fundamental character of the church. The church is the community of believers created by Jesus Christ through the gospel rightly preached and the sacraments rightly administered.

64. While concurring in this basic understanding of the church, we recognize that we have exhibited a number of varying ecclesiological practices as evidenced in the various understandings of polity, worship and mission. One may observe them in churches of the Lutheran and Reformed traditions.

65. Such differences, however, are appropriate expressions of our diversity and do not compromise our fundamental agreement in the gospel.

66. Is that true, however, concerning ministry? One of the points of discussion and concern arising between our two confessional traditions has been in this area. Recently, discussions of ministry as understood by Lutherans and Reformed have been undertaken. A number of foundational points of agreement have been identified:
- all ministry in the church derives from and expresses the ministry of Jesus Christ by the Holy Spirit;
- the ministry is given to the whole church, and its central mission is to preach the gospel to all the world;
- by baptism all believers are called to be priests and participate in the ministry of Jesus Christ;
- within the priesthood of all believers God has given a particular ministry of word and sacrament conferred on men and women by ordination which is expressed in the public preaching of the gospel, the administration of the sacraments and pastoral service; the priesthood of all believers cannot exist apart from the ministry of word and sacrament, but neither can there be a ministry of word and sacrament apart from the priesthood of all believers;
- ministry cannot exist without form, order, structure, office and oversight;
- all ministry participates in the ministry of the apostolic faith;
- ministry is a gift of God but not one form or structure is definitively established by the biblical testimony.

67. These points of fundamental agreement are expressed in a variety of ways in the churches of our traditions. Difference in emphasis has led to practices which may appear to be contradictory. For example, Lutherans have traditionally understood oversight (*episcope*) in terms of a distinct office while the Reformed churches have invested this responsibility in an ecclesiastical body usually called presbytery or classis. Recent studies have demonstrated that such differences pertain both to form and structure and to legitimate differences in theological interpretation, but do not challenge our common understanding of the gospel.

68. This last observation should show us that despite the necessary distinction, no false separation should be made between the church-constituting elements (word and sacrament) and the questions of structure and organization. It is imperative for the realization of church fellowship that in all areas we make sure that the existing church structures and traditions in no way jeopardize the consensus on word and sacrament nor obscure our unity in Christ. This can happen when these structures directly oppose the consensus or when human organization of the church is either over- or underestimated. Therefore constant vigilance is necessary in all local situations. It is important to continue theological study of these ecclesiological issues so that the legitimate diversity we have does not once more become divisive. In its present form the whole church has the duty so to structure its ministry, both corporate and personal, that the transmission of the gospel of reconciliation and love may become known throughout the entire world.

Witness and service in this world

69. Our common understanding of the gospel liberates and binds the churches to common service and common witness in the world. Our traditions emphasize the new obedience of faith active in love and the inseparability of justification and sanctification. The struggle for justice, human rights, peace and the care of creation demands of the church acceptance of a common responsibility.

70. In the 16th century this teaching was expressed by Lutherans in terms of two kingdoms and by Reformed in terms of Christ's sovereignty. Both of these forms of expression, however, were misunderstood when interpreted apart from the historical context in which they were formulated.

71. In today's church which is called to witness to Christ in a large variety of situations, 16th-century formulations may not be directly applicable. What they were meant to affirm, however, is still utterly relevant. As Christians we are called to proclaim and live the love of God to humanity in its need, to remove the causes of human suffering, to defend justice and peace in the community and in the whole of creation. Failure to take up this duty, tolerance of injustice and all forms of suppression, become counter-witnesses which contradict our faith. This is a particular challenge for our churches today.

72. On ethical issues, too, there is legitimate diversity between churches, communities and individual Christians. The consensus in word and sacrament which binds us together can find expression in various ways both politically and socially. But here too diversity can become illegitimate; there are certain ethical beliefs which cease to express the agreement reached on the understanding of the gospel. This obstructs the path leading to the common table of the Lord and thereby breaks church fellowship, as illustrated by the actions of the Lutheran World Federation and the World Alliance of Reformed Churches suspending the rights of membership of those churches defending and practising apartheid. It is therefore important that, both within our churches and communities, as well as between our churches, we engage in a common search for common witness and service where the important issues of our day are concerned (peace, justice, race, gender, bio-ethics, etc.). Our church fellowship is a community which knows and accepts variety. But that does not imply undifferentiated acceptance of any or all attitudes or opinions.

Language, ethnicity and sectarianism

73. The distinctiveness of each tradition cannot be measured through doctrine alone. It is important to note that factors such as politics, social order, economics and ethos which have to a degree shaped the life and thought of the church, have themselves been shaped by theological assumptions, and that even today they may be nurtured by hidden religious roots. The tenacity with which we cling to our Lutheran and Reformed distinctiveness may well be more a matter of self-interest, nationalism or cultural chauvinism than faithfulness to the gospel.

74. Language itself, while a gift from God, is an imperfect vehicle for the communication of our understanding of the gospel and its implications. The meanings of words shift over the centuries, and the same terms used in one culture may have different connotations in another. Almost every word we use in church and theology has at least one translation behind it, and theologians today are increasingly aware of the complexity of the metaphorical language used in our discourse concerning God. Lan-

guage pertaining to faith, including that of the Bible itself, has been used to justify injustice and self-interest. We believe that the imperfection and misuse of language are in part responsible for our historic divisions and regret that we have not in the past duly recognized this. At the same time, as a gift of God language is an instrument of the Holy Spirit. Lutheran and Reformed Christians recognize in the words of their respective confessions the biblical truth which draws us together in the gospel. We affirm that Jesus Christ alone is the Word and that the confessions of the Lutheran and Reformed traditions point to him and him alone.

75. Ethnic and racial factors have also played a role in dividing our traditions. While race and ethnicity may draw people together and contribute to their sense of identity, they have also created suspicion in our churches and become instrumental in perpetuating divisions. Our common confession of the gospel challenges any separation based on race, gender, ethnicity or class. We affirm that the church's one foundation is Christ (cf. §19 above); that we are justified not by who or what we are in the world, but by God's grace in Christ (§21 above); and that our whole life belongs to him alone (cf. §25 above). Thus our common confession calls in question all doctrines of racial superiority or ethnic domination. At the same time, we recognize that racial and ethnic identity are gifts of the Lord and rejoice in God's creation with its wonderful variety of races, peoples and nations. Moreover ethnicity may become a means through which the gospel is given witness, and through which culture serves Christ.

76. Unlike ethnicity which sometimes unites, sectarianism always divides. We become sectarian when we allow formulations made to express the gospel to stand as a barrier dividing us from those who formulate differently. Our common affirmation testifies that the wall separating us from the Father has been broken by Jesus, and therefore the walls dividing us from one another must also be destroyed (cf. §21 above). We therefore urge Lutheran and Reformed Christians throughout the world not only to pray that the Spirit guide them to recognize Christ and the gospel in one another's confessions, but also to search their hearts to determine if confessions and doctrines intended for reconciliation have degenerated into systems fortifying positions of power and privilege. While we affirm the rich diversity of our churches, we deplore the sectarian use of scripture and confession to justify division. In Christ we are reconciled and called to be agents of reconciliation.

77. Our one Lord, by the gift of his one Spirit, can use our diversities to exercise Christ's ministry of reconciliation, build up Christ's one body, and use the church as a witness to all nations to bring to fulfilment God's purposes for all creation in the kingdom of God.

78. We believe that unity, diversity and harmony are all God's gifts to the church. Therefore diversity must not obscure unity, nor concern for unity deny diversity. Together we serve one Lord, through whom we alone have access by the one Spirit to the Father.

IV. Recommendations

79. In light of the discovery that nothing stands in the way of church fellowship, we urge Lutheran and Reformed churches throughout the world who are members of the Lutheran World Federation and the World Alliance of Reformed Churches to declare full communion with one another. By this we mean:

80. – Acknowledging that the condemnations pronounced upon one another in former times are no longer to be regarded as applicable in today's situation.

81. – Establishing full pulpit and altar/table fellowship, with the necessary mutual recognition of ministers ordained for word and sacrament.

82. – Committing themselves to growth in unity through new steps in church life and mission together.

83. We have come to this recommendation on the basis of our belief that both Lutheran and Reformed churches agree on those matters which are necessary and sufficient for the true unity of the church: the right preaching of the gospel and the administration of the sacraments in accordance with the word of God (cf. §26 and §§51-78 above). Those differences in preaching and sacrament which remain among us should no longer be regarded as church-dividing (cf. §52 above).

84. We rejoice that some Lutheran and Reformed churches have already declared church fellowship with churches of the other tradition. Among these are the Lutheran and Reformed churches which have signed the Leuenberg agreement (1973), the Lutheran and Reformed churches of Indonesia, and the Ethiopian Evangelical Church Mekane Yesus. Representatives of these churches participating in our dialogue witnessed to the meaning of this new relationship for their churches. We encourage other churches to confirm for themselves the reality of their unity in Christ through such a declaration of full communion.

85. *We call upon* all Lutheran and Reformed churches to make their unity more real and visible to their members and to the world. Whether a church is taking its first steps of rapprochement or has already declared church fellowship with the other tradition, continuing growth in unity will be a faithful response to Christ's will for unity.

86. As intentional continuing steps in realizing our unity, we encourage the churches:

87. – To take the initiative in reaching out to the other in any area where churches of both traditions are to be found.

88. – To engage in ongoing theological work and reflection together on the central doctrines of our faith, on the life of worship and our liturgical traditions, and on church structures, learning from one another, and familiarizing ourselves with the range of Lutheran-Reformed dialogue around the world.

89. – To develop a common witness and service to the world, involving both evangelism and practical response to the challenges of contemporary society.

90. – To incorporate learning about the fellowship between our churches into our total educational programme: theological education for the ministry, continuing education for pastors, lay education for children and adults. This should include re-examining old stereotypes of one another. It will become natural for such education to be increasingly done together.

91. – To work out whatever new common organizational structures may be necessary for the sake of witness to the new relationship.

92. – To carry out the actions mentioned above in ways that are consonant with our commitments to other churches in the larger ecumenical movement.

93. *We propose* that at every level of church life, member churches of the two traditions explore together what is needed in that particular situation for further growth in unity. Situations around the world are so diverse that new forms and styles of life together must be tailored to each context.

94. – In the local churches, emphasis must be placed on devising useful ways to encounter personally members of churches of the other tradition. The suggestions in paragraphs 85-92 all lend themselves to local churches. But on special occasions common celebrations of worship may be developed. In some places, for example, an annual Sunday of ecumenical sharing might become a significant tradition, with exchanges of pastors and worshippers among the congregations.

95. – At the regional or national level, the suggestions of paragraphs 85-92 would take different forms but remain equally important. Emphasis here might be placed on developing structures for regular exchange among the churches and developing common witness.

96. – At the international level, we call upon the Lutheran World Federation and the World Alliance of Reformed Churches to collaborate whenever possible in their work, studying what appropriate conclusions should be drawn for their life from the new relationship existing between Lutheran and Reformed member churches. We urge particularly that efforts be made in every ecumenical dialogue of either tradition to explore fully the implications for that dialogue of what has been said to other dialogue partners by both Lutheran and Reformed churches. In this way the churches can intentionally evaluate the consistency and compatibility of various relationships of ecumenical dialogue.

97. We request all Lutheran and Reformed churches to place this report on their agenda for study and to transmit their responses to the recommendations to the Lutheran World Federation or the World Alliance of Reformed Churches.

20. Ecclesiology

Chambésy, Geneva, Switzerland, 7 October 1983

THE HEAD OF THE CHURCH

The head of the church is Christ, the first-born of all creation through whom and for whom all things were created and through whom God decided to reconcile all things to himself by making peace by the blood of his cross (cf. Col. 1:15-20). Out of the fullness of the life of the head, Christ, the members of the body have new life in Christ through the Holy Spirit (cf. Rom. 6:11; 2 Cor. 5:17; Col. 2:9f.). "And God has put all things under his feet and has made him the head over all things for the church which is his body, the fullness of him who fills all in all" (Eph. 1:22f.). Christ is in fact the "one Lord" (Eph. 4:5), the only head of the body, the church, from whom "the entire body, nourished and knit together through its joints and ligaments, grows with a growth that is from God" (Col. 2:19; cf. Eph. 4:15). Therefore Christ cannot be thought of without the church, the head not without the body and vice versa, because Christ and the church are joined with one another and abide in absolute, inseparable and eternal union. The faithful, justified by the blood of Jesus Christ, are saved by him, have peace with God and boast of the hope of the glory of God. This hope cannot be destroyed because the love of God has been poured into their hearts by the Holy Spirit who has been given to them (cf. Rom. 5:1-5). So the church as the body of Christ is joined with its head by the Holy Spirit and together with him is the whole Christ (cf. Eph. 1:22f.). In him the members have new life and grow through the Holy Spirit towards perfection in divine grace in the firm hope that they shall be like him for they shall see him as he is (1 John 3:2).

The focus of the new life is the holy eucharist in which the inner form of the bond between the body and the head shows itself. The bishop who celebrates the eucharist presides in the place of Christ, and by bringing to God in this manner the sacrifice which has been wrought by Christ once and for all, he represents Christ as the head of the church assembled around him in whose name he celebrates.

The bishops, as the successors of the apostles who carry on the apostolic ministry, are faithful guarantors of the catholicity and apostolicity of the church. According to divine law, the bishops among themselves are of the same rank because they all have received the same episcopal grace by the lawful sacramental laying-on of hands and stand in the apostolic succession. They take part in the same way without quantitative or qualitative difference in one and the same episcopal authority. They are bishops among bishops, servants of Christ and the church. They, too, are members of the body, i.e. the church, holding a special position in it.

Even though the bishops are equal to one another in episcopal authority, the life of the church during the first three centuries evidenced a differentiation in the positions of honour granted to the various episcopal sees. The bishops of certain local churches, who had gained greater authority for various reasons, held a special position of honour and exercised a greater influence in ecclesiastical matters. The position of honour of the bishops of these sees was unfolded in ecumenical synods since the 4th century to a presidency of honour (presbeia timēs) in the church (third canon of the second ecumenical synod – Mansi 3,560). The bishop of Rome enjoyed such an honorary position because the see of Rome took the first place in the order of episcopal sees: Rome was the capital of the empire and its church preserved the apostolic tradition – still without any innovations; it brought the gospel of salvation to peoples and nations who had not yet heard of Christ and it was rich in church life and works of love. So the bishop of Rome possesses the presidency of honour in the church. But with regard to episcopal authority, he does not differ whatsoever from his brother bishops. The same is valid for the other bishops who hold honorary rank in the church.

According to the teaching of the Orthodox and the Old Catholic Church, all the decrees of later dates therefore, which ascribe a monocratic and absolute authority over the whole church to the bishop of Rome and which regard him as infallible when he defines doctrine in the exercise of his office "as shepherd and teacher of all Christians" (*ex cathedra*), are regarded as unacceptable. With their unwavering striving for unity, both churches hope that the existing difficulties and divisions will be overcome by the head and Lord of the church, so that according to his word those who believe in him may all be one and thus the world may come to faith (cf. John 17:20f.).

In the view of the joint Orthodox-Old Catholic theological commission, the above text on "The Head of the Church" represents the teaching of the Orthodox and Old Catholic churches.

Chambésy, Geneva, 7 October 1983

21. Soteriology

Chambésy, Geneva, Switzerland, 7 October 1983

CHRIST'S WORK OF SALVATION

"God so loved the world that he gave his only Son that whoever believes in him should not perish but have eternal life" (John 3:16). God in his love and mercy wanted to save man who had lost the communion with God through sin and so was condemned to destruction and death. This decision of God was carried out by God's Son and Logos who, in the fullness of time, "for us men and for our salvation" was sent into the world and was made man, "humbled himself and became obedient unto death, even death on a cross" (Phil. 2:8).

The Son of God completed the work of salvation by his incarnation and his entire earthly life, his baptism, his word and his deeds, his suffering, his death on the cross, his descending to the realm of the dead, his resurrection and ascension and the sending of the Holy Spirit.

By his incarnation, the Lord began to fulfill the great mystery of salvation. In the person of God the Logos, the hypostatic union of the human and divine natures came about forming the foundation and starting point for the salvation of the whole human race, which is understood as one organic and unified whole (cf. Gregory of Nyssa, *Hom. opif.* 16 – *PG* 44.185). God the Logos assumed a special human nature in his incarnation but because of the unity of the human race he united all humanity within himself, the "one united and undivided nature" (Gregory of Nyssa, *Tres dii* – *PG* 45.120) which he redeemed and restored to its original beauty. The Lord has recapitulated and united to himself "the original form of man" so that we gain in him what we have lost in Adam: the freedom from sin and death and eternal life in fellowship with God (cf. Irenaeus of Lyons, *Haer.* 3.18.1, 7 – *PG* 7.932,938; cf. also Cyril of Alexandria, Jo. 9 – *PG* 74.273; Leo I of Rome, *Sermo* 12.1 – *PL* 54.168f). In the last Adam the image of God which had been darkened and distorted by sin in the first Adam has been restored, renewed and made richer.

Furthermore the message, which Jesus Christ, as the greatest prophet and teacher of mankind, has proclaimed in word and deed, has a saving power for man in order to liberate the spirit of man from the darkening effect and the error that came from sin. What he taught he confirmed through signs and predications about what was to come. Through his entire earthly life he proved himself to be the best and unsurpassable example of holiness and obedience to the will of God. The message of the Lord, which is indestructible (cf. Matt. 24:35; Mark 13:31; Luke 21:33) and not in need of perfection, is offered by a gracious God to all men without distinction. It is the call of God directed to all to turn back "out of darkness into his marvellous light" (1 Pet. 2:9), to the truth and salvation in Christ which has absolute and universal character and is meant for all at all times.

The divine Saviour achieved the salvation of the human race by humbling himself and by his total obedience which he demonstrated during his entire life, particularly by his suffering and his death on the cross by which he has freed the human race of sin and "became the source of eternal salvation to all who obey him" (Heb. 5:9). The sacrifice made on the cross by Jesus Christ as the eternal High Priest and mediator of the new covenant (cf. Heb. 9:11-15) in our place and for our sins was an atonement. He became "the expiation for our sins, and not for ours only but also for the sins of the whole world" (1 John 2:2). By his sacrifice he redeemed and saved us because he offered his life out of love as a ransom. By his death on the cross the Lord took upon himself the sins of men (cf. Isa. 53:4f.; 2 Cor. 5:21; 1 Pet. 2:24) and washed them from us by his blood "that we might die to sin and live to righteousness" (1 Pet. 2:24). The power of the sacrifice offered on the cross at Calvary once and for all embraces humanity of all ages, giving to them the saving grace flowing from it.

The Lord completed his work of salvation in glory. This is evident in his descending to the realm of the dead, in his resurrection and ascension to heaven, in his sitting at the right hand of the Father, in his capacity as future judge of the living and the dead, as well as in the church founded by him. In it he continues the redemption of the world through the work of the Holy Spirit sent at Pentecost to remain in it forever, by giving of himself to those for whom he continuously intercedes before God (cf. Heb. 9:24). The resurrection of the Lord is the confirmation and certain guarantee that man is freed from sin, corruption and death, and it is at the centre of the Christian faith (cf. Rom. 8:11; 1 Cor. 15:20-23). It is the pledge and the beginning of the resurrection and immortality of all, for the Lord is "the first-fruits of those who have fallen asleep" in which "all shall be made alive" (1 Cor. 15:20-22; cf. Col. 1:18).

The last manifestation of the glory of the Lord is his coming again at the end of time, for he will judge the living and the dead, renew heaven and earth and reign with the elect in the kingdom of the Father to all eternity.

In the view of the joint Orthodox-Old Catholic theological commission, the above text on "Christ's Work of Salvation" represents the teaching of the Orthodox and Old Catholic churches.

Chambésy, Geneva, 7 October 1983

THE WORK OF THE HOLY SPIRIT IN THE CHURCH AND THE APPROPRIATION OF SALVATION

Out of love for sinful man (cf. John 3:16), God our Lord sent his Son into the world, who reconciled all things in heaven and on earth (cf. Col. 1:20) and renewed creation by his resurrection (cf. 2 Cor. 5:15-18). Jesus Christ commanded his disciples to proclaim the gospel to all nations (cf. Matt. 28:19f.) so that his salvation may give light to all who sit in darkness and in the shadow of death (cf. Luke 1:79).

The appropriation of salvation by individual human beings takes place in the church through the work of the Holy Spirit who grants his grace. The Holy Spirit, who proceeds from the Father and rests in the Son and is given and has appeared through the Son to the faithful (cf. John of Damascus, f.o. 8 – PG 94.821,833) always remains in the church, fills it and builds it up, renews and sanctifies it and makes it into an "ark of salvation" for the whole world. He is the Paraclete who is sent by the Lord to lead the church into all truth (cf. John 16:13). All that the Saviour brings about in the church for the well-being of men is, according to the holy fathers, "fulfilled by the grace of the Spirit" (Basil the Great, *Spir.* 16/39 – *PG* 32.140). The Holy Spirit is as it were the soul of the church, the life-giving, sanctifying and unifying power of its body. The Holy Spirit and the church are inseparable: "for where the church is, there the Spirit of God is also, and where the Spirit of God is, there the church is and all grace" (Irenaeus of Lyons, *Haer.* 3.24.1 – *PG* 7.966). The Holy Spirit is fundamental for the new existence of man in the church whose rebirth occurs by water and the Spirit (cf. John 3:5f.).

We humans receive the gift of the Holy Spirit in the church through Christ, and thus become children of God and fellow heirs with Christ (cf. Rom. 8:15-17); we are brought back into communion with God, for which he has created us. The spirit of sonship lives in our hearts and cries: "Abba, Father" (cf. Rom. 8:15; Gal. 4:6). He "helps us in our weakness; for we do not know how to pray as we ought, but the Spirit himself intercedes for us with sighs too deep for words" (Rom. 8:26). The Spirit lives in the body of the faithful as in a temple (cf. 1 Cor. 6:19). He unites them in the celebration of holy eucharist to the one body in the fellowship of the church. He allows Christians to take part in his holiness; they become "partakers of the divine nature" (2 Pet. 1:4), i.e. "deified through the partaking of the divine shining of the light and not changed into the divine being" (John of Damascus, f.o. 26 – *PG* 94.924). He imparts to each individual his gift of grace for the building up of the body of Christ: the gift of speaking wisdom, the gift of speaking knowledge, the gift of healing, the gift of discerning spirits, and especially the gift of ordained ministry as an organ for building up this body (cf. 1 Cor. 12:4-11,28f.).

God saves man without violating his free will. "He wants all to be saved but he forces nobody. God is willing... to save man not against his will and determination, but with his will and freely made decision" (John Chrysostom, *Hom.* 3.6 in Ac. 9.1 – PG 51.144). The appropriation of salvation in Christ by man occurs by the cooperation of the Holy Spirit and man. The Holy Spirit effects the vocation, the illumination, the conversion, the justification, the rebirth in baptism and the sanctification in the church; man, for his part, accepts the grace offered and participates freely by faith and his good works, in other words, by "faith working through love" (Gal. 5:6). This cooperation is not to be understood as if God alone achieves one part of the work and man alone another; rather all things are achieved by God, without whose help man can do nothing for his salvation. But man also participates in all things, he is moved to act himself and not to remain inactive (cf. Augustine, *Corrept.* 2/4 – *PL* 44.918: *aguntur ut agant, non ut ipsi nihil agant*). "From the God of the universe, who works all in all, we must believe that he does it in the manner that he awakens, protects and strengthens the free will which he himself once granted and not in such a way that he nullifies it" (John Cassian, *Coll.* 13.18 – *PL* 49.946; cf. Augustine, *Spir. et litt* 34/60 – *PL* 44.240). This cooperation of God and man embraces the entire new life in Christ. One cannot say that man behaves passively in any act of faith – and were it even the first one – and that God alone works in him.

Correspondingly, the church rejects any teaching according to which God alone grants his saving grace to some but not to others, thus by his decree predestinating some to salvation, others to damnation. God is not the originator of evil but the source of life and salvation. That is why he desires "all men to be saved and to come to the knowledge of the truth" (1 Tim. 2:4).

The rebirth and sanctification of men is the special work of the Holy Spirit. The outpouring of the Holy Spirit expected at the end of time has already occurred in the church since the day of Pentecost (cf. Acts 2:16-18). The glory of the end of time is no longer merely a hope but already a present reality. The presence of the Holy Spirit in the church offers certain guarantee for this. If we have in our hearts the part, which is the pledge of the Spirit, we will not doubt the whole, which is the perfection of the gift in the blessedness of eternal life (cf. Rom. 8:23; 2 Cor. 1:22f.; 5:5; Eph. 1:13f.; 4:30; Tit. 3:6f.; cf. also John Chrysostom, *Res. mort.* 8 – *PG* 50.431).

In the view of the joint Orthodox-Old Catholic Theological commission, the above text on "The Work of the Holy Spirit in the Church and the Appropriation of Salvation" represents the teaching of the Orthodox and Old Catholic churches.

Chambésy, Geneva, 7 October 1983

22. Sacramental Teaching

Amersfoort, Netherlands, 3 October 1985
Kavala, Greece, 17 October 1987

THE SACRAMENTS OR MYSTERIES OF THE CHURCH

1. In the New Testament the word "mysterion" refers to the inconceivable act of God's work of salvation in Christ. The church, in which Christ remains for ever, is a continuation of the mystery of Christ, of the wonderful union of the divine and human nature. The invisible, uncreated salutary grace of the triune God is manifested in the church in connection with physical means, historical institutions and concrete acts, that is with natural and real signs. This grace is bestowed by the Holy Spirit who is sent to the church and gives all in it.

2. The Holy Spirit, leading the church into all truth (cf. John 16:13), guarantees it the divine grace necessary for the salvation of men. This grace is manifold and is bestowed abundantly.

3. During his earthly ministry, which had its noblest expression in the cross and resurrection, Christ created the salvific means of sharing with us grace: the holy sacraments or mysteries. Christ imparted these sacraments to the church. As regards the fundamental and essential aspects of their liturgical realization in prayer and visible signs connected with it they received their shape through the apostles. In this way then the institution and arrangement of the sacraments are derived from the New Testament: in part expressly and directly from the words and actions of Jesus, in part from indirect references and actions of Jesus as well as the conviction of his disciples and apostles that whatever they were instituting and directing to be done in the life of the church was in union with the will and direction of the Lord. And so they do not offer of themselves anything new or arbitrary regarding the fundamentals and essentials of salvation.

4. The sacraments with which the church was endowed are: baptism, confirmation, eucharist, penance, unction, ordination and marriage. Even though this list of sacraments can neither be found in a systematic way in the New Testament nor in the tradition of the fathers, it reflects the uninterrupted conviction and practice of the church.

5. The sacraments as specific sanctifying actions lead to the new creation and unfolding of life in Christ through the incorporation of the recipients into the church as the body of Christ, this being effected by the Holy Spirit. Through the sacraments of the church each individual achieves his development to life in Christ in all the manifestations of his or her personal and corporate existence. This whole new existence and development of the believers to life in Christ gained by the sacraments is a reliable way to the heavenly kingdom and leads to eternal life.

6. The sacraments are not mere symbols of grace but their reliable instruments and transmitters. The physical elements of the sacraments are consecrated through prayers and sacred actions of the church and are connected with the communication of grace in different ways in the individual sacraments.

7. The use of physical elements in the sacraments is necessary because of the psychosomatic condition of human beings: "If you were incorporeal he would have given you naked incorporeal gifts; but as the soul is connected with the body he gives you the spiritual in the physical" (John Chrysostom, *Hom.* 82.4/83.4 in Mt. – PG 58.743).

8. The physical means are not effective by themselves but in virtue of the presence of the Holy Spirit: "If there is grace in the water it does not come from the nature of water but from the presence of the Spirit" (Basil the Great, *Spir.* 15/35 – PG 32.132).

9. It is the general view of the church that the sacraments in themselves are effective for salvation. Grace comes from the giver and actual liturgist of the sacraments, Jesus Christ, who remains in the church forever and continues his work through it, and it is bestowed by the Holy Spirit who is effective in the celebration of the sacraments. In order that the sacraments accomplish their salutary purpose, people must express their inner readiness to receive them.

10. The liturgists of the church are necessary for the celebration of the sacraments. These are the bishops and priests who assume this task through the sacrament of ordination. The efficacy of the sacraments is not invalidated by the imperfection or unworthiness of the liturgists.

11. It is the triune God who performs the holy sacraments as well as the whole work of salvation: "The Father and the Son and the Holy Spirit administer all things, the priest lends his tongue and makes his hand available" (John Chrysostom, *Hom.* 87.4/86.4 in Jo. – PG 59.472; cf. also the same, *Hom.* 2.4 in 2 Tim. – PG 62.612; Augustine, *Tract.* 6.7 in Jo. – PL 35.1428).

In the view of the joint Orthodox-Old Catholic theological commission, the above text on "The Sacraments or Mysteries of the Church" represents the teaching of the Orthodox and Old Catholic churches.

Amersfoort, 3 October 1985

BAPTISM

1.1. Baptism is that God-given sacrament of the church through which the one baptized in the name of the holy and life-giving Trinity becomes a member of the church of Christ, is freed from the dominion of sin and is born again to a new creature in Christ by partaking of the mystery of the divine work of salvation in Christ.

1.2. The necessity of the sacrament of baptism, already prefigured in the Old Testament, was proclaimed by Jesus Christ by his baptism in the Jordan as well as by his commission to the apostles to make all nations disciples by "baptizing them in the name of the Father and of the Son and of the Holy Spirit" (Matt. 28:18-20). Without being born again of water and the Spirit man cannot enter the kingdom of God (John 3:5).

1.3. According to the Tradition of the ancient undivided church, the believer who is submerged in consecrated water and emerges three times in the name of the Father and the Son and the Holy Spirit is buried with Christ and rises with him (cf. Col. 2:12; Rom. 6:3-5).

1.4. The physical elements with which the sacrament of baptism is carried out and through which God's almighty grace works in the baptized cannot be regarded as mere symbols or changeable external material elements of the ecclesiastical practice of baptism passed on by the apostles. They are connected with the event in which the baptized is washed clean of original sin and personal sins and is renewed in Christ. In this sense, the perseverance of the church concerning the observance of the apostolic practice (submerging three times in consecrated water) should be understood. The practice of the undivided church is baptism by immersion three times. Baptism by pouring water three times is also known in the church as emergency baptism.

2.1. The baptized is reborn by the operation of divine grace and is joined with Christ in one body and enjoys the status of a child of God. By this connection to one body he is united with the faithful of all ages and nations and lives this fellowship in the church; he becomes a citizen of the kingdom of God and realizes his salvation in spiritual battles in the hope of partaking in the life of the world to come. Although these effects of baptism are a gift of the triune God and are founded in the mystery of the divine work of salvation in Christ, in order to become fruitful they assume the personal acceptance of the divine gift in faith, conversion and works of love on the part of the baptized.

2.2. Adult baptism and infant baptism effectuate the same gift of divine grace. The only difference concerns the time at which the divine grace given through baptism can become available for the baptized and yield spiritual fruits. The fact that such spiritual fruit for adults as well as for small children is only possible in the unbroken unity with the Christian fellowship in the one, holy, catholic and apostolic church makes the necessity obvious that the baptized, whether adults or small children, must be led by the church's community; in the case of small children, the godparents confess the faith of the church in the name of the baptized.

2.3. Participating in the mystery of the life, death and resurrection of Christ through baptism has as a natural and immediate consequence the possibility and necessity of the baptized partaking in the gift of the Holy Spirit poured out at Pentecost and acceding to the sacrament of eucharist.

2.4. Baptism is administered by the bishop or a presbyter (priest) and only in emergency cases by deacons or laity.

In the view of the joint Orthodox-Old Catholic theological commission, the above text on "Baptism" represents the teaching of the Orthodox and old Catholic churches.
Amersfoort, 3 October 1985

CONFIRMATION

1. In baptism man is born again in the power of the Holy Spirit to life in Christ. Thereby he receives a new spiritual existence. His spiritual progress and the growth of what he has acquired through baptism likewise require the presence and the work of the Holy Spirit. Confirmation bestows the gifts of the Holy Spirit on the baptized, allows them to take part personally in the event of Pentecost and at the same time guarantees this gift, according to the words of the Orthodox liturgy: "Seal of the gift of the Holy Spirit. Amen."

2. According to the unanimous faith of the ancient and undivided church, in the celebration of confirmation the practice of the apostles is carried on, who laid hands on

the baptized in order that the Holy Spirit come upon them (cf. Acts 8:14-17; 19:1-7). In order that the new life of man in Christ may grow, confirmation immediately followed baptism, as is witnessed to by the Eastern and Western fathers of the church: "Those who are baptized in the church are brought before the leaders of the church and receive the Holy Spirit by our prayer and the laying-on of hands and are thus perfected through the seal of God" (Cyprian of Carthage, ep. 73.9 – *PL* 3.1115/1160). "Spiritual sealing follows... for after baptism by water perfection occurs when at the bishop's prayer the Holy Spirit is poured out" (Ambrose of Milan, *Sacram.* 3.2.8 – *PL* 16.434/453). "After having bathed himself in the river Jordan and brought the waters into contact with his deity, he emerged from them and the Holy Spirit in substance came upon him, like resting on like. In the same manner to you also, after you had emerged from the pool of the sacred waters, was given the unction, the image of that wherewith Christ was anointed" (Cyril of Jerusalem, *Catech.* 21.1 – *PG* 33.1088f.). "The illuminated ones must be anointed with the heavenly unction after baptism and partake of the kingdom of Christ" (Synod of Laodicea, canon 48 – Mansi 2.571).

3. Only the bishops as those who followed in the apostolic ministry were to lay hands on the baptized in order that the gift of the Holy Spirit be transmitted to them. When the number of believers grew beyond the ability of bishops to fulfill this task, the practice of chrismation of the baptized by presbyters developed early in the East and for a while partially in the West. The blessing of the oil of chrism though remained under the sole responsibility of the bishop (cf. Synod of Carthage a.419, canon 6 – Mansi 4.424). As a rule confirmation was reserved for the bishop throughout most of the West; the arrangement enjoined by synods that the baptized have to be confirmed as soon as possible after their baptism points out that baptism and confirmation belong together by necessity. The view and practice of the ancient undivided church requires the three sacraments of initiation – baptism, confirmation and eucharist – to be celebrated in conjunction with each other, for even though each is complete in itself and theologically distinguishable from the others they still belong inseparably together and form a homogeneous whole.

In the view of the joint Orthodox-Old Catholic theological commission, the above text on "Confirmation" represents the teaching of the Orthodox and Old Catholic churches.

Amersfoort, 3 October 1985

HOLY EUCHARIST

1. The sacrament of holy eucharist is the focal point of the entire life of the church. In this sacrament Christ is present in reality and essence. He offers himself in a bloodless way and shares himself with the faithful in an ever new and real representation of his bloody sacrifice on the cross offered once and for all. So the eucharist is at the same time sacrament and real sacrifice. In this sacrament the faithful receive the body and blood of Christ and by it are united with him and through him with one another and take part in the power of his work of salvation that has its climax in his sacrifice on the cross and in his resurrection.

2. The Lord himself instituted the eucharist. Before the Passover during the meal, the Lord took bread, gave thanks, broke it and gave it to the disciples saying: "This is

my body." And he took the cup, gave thanks and gave it to them saying: "Drink ye all of it; for this is my blood, the blood of the new covenant, which is shed for many for the forgiveness of sins. Do this in remembrance of me" (cf. Matt. 26:26-29; Mark 14:22-25; Luke 22:14-23; 1 Cor. 11:23-25).

3. In bread and wine, which are consecrated and changed in the eucharist, the Lord himself is really and truly present in a supernatural way and imparts himself to the faithful. Bread and wine are, after the consecration, the body and blood of Christ and not mere symbols of his body and blood. "The bread and the wine are not images of the body and blood of the Lord – certainly not! – but the deified body of the Lord himself; the Lord himself said: 'This is' not the image of my body but 'my body' and not the image of my blood, but 'my blood'" (John of Damascus, f.o. 86 – *PG* 94.1148f). According to the proclamation of the seventh ecumenical synod "neither the Lord nor the apostles and fathers have called the bloodless sacrifice offered by the priest an image, but the body and the blood themselves... before the consecration they were called images, after the consecration they are called, in an actual sense, body and blood of Christ; this is what they are and believed to be" (Mansi 13.265).

4. The eucharist represents the whole work of the divine economy in Christ that has its climax in his sacrifice on the cross and in his resurrection. The eucharistic sacrifice stands in direct relationship to the sacrifice on the cross. The sacrifice of Calvary is certainly not repeatable. It happened once and for all (Heb. 7:27). But the eucharist is much more than a symbolic image or an image that reminds us of that sacrifice. It is the same sacrifice celebrated sacramentally. It is celebrated as a commemoration of the Lord ("Do this in remembrance of me") and is not a mere, but a true and real commemoration and representation of Christ's sacrifice. Before us are the body and blood of the Lord themselves. "That (sacrifice) we now also offer, namely the one once offered, the inexhaustible one. This happens to commemorate that which once happened; for he says 'Do this in remembrance of me'. Not an ever different sacrifice as the (Jewish) high priest of those times, but we always offer the same one; or rather we effect a memorial of the sacrifice" (John Chrysostom, *Hom.* 17.3 in Heb. – *PG* 63.131). "And as we commemorate his suffering in all our celebrations of the sacrifice – for the suffering of the Lord is the sacrifice that we offer – we may not do anything else than what he has done" (Cyprian of Carthage, *Ep.* 63.17 – *PL* 4.387/398f.).

5. The priest officiating at each eucharist is the Lord himself. "You are the one who offers and is offered, who accepts and is imparted, Christ, our God" (Prayer of the Cherubic Hymn). "He is the priest; it is he himself who offers, and he himself is the offered gift" (Augustine, *Civ.* 10.20 – *PL* 41.298; cf. Ambrose of Milan, *Enarr.* 25 in Ps. 38 – *PL* 14.1051f/1102; the same, *Patr.* 9/38 – *PL* 14.686/720). The whole eucharistic community, clergy and people, has an organic part in the performance of the eucharistic celebration. The liturgists of the sacrament are bishop and priest. The practice of the church and the canons forbid deacons "to offer" (cf. first ecumenical synod, canon 18 – Mansi 2.676).

6. According to apostolic tradition and practice, leavened bread is used in the eucharist. The use of unleavened bread in the West is a later practice. In addition wine is used – "the fruit of the vine" (Mark 14:25) – that from ancient times is mixed with water (cf. Irenaeus of Lyons, *Haer.* 5.2.3 – *PG* 7.1125; Cyprian of Carthage, *Ep.* 63 – *PL* 4.372-389/383-401).

7. The consecration of bread and wine in the eucharist takes place through the entire eucharistic prayer. The words of the Lord "Take, eat... drink ye all of it" in the eucharistic prayer, which has a consecratory character as a whole, do not themselves effect the transformation of the bread and wine into the body and blood of Christ. The transformation is effected by the Holy Spirit whose descending is being prayed for in the epiclesis.

8. After appropriate preparation all believers take part in the eucharist; for who does not take part at the table of the Lord does not take part in the life in Christ: "unless you eat the flesh of the Son of man and drink his blood, you have no life in you" (John 6:53). According to the practice of the church prevailing since ancient times not even infants and much less children are kept away from the eucharist. Only the unbaptized, heretics, those separated from the church and those restrained by church discipline for any reason are excluded from the partaking of the sacrament (cf. John of Damascus, f.o. 86 – *PG* 94.1153). The faithful communicate under both kinds as was the case at the last supper.

9. In the eucharist the faithful are united with their Lord and with one another by the communion in his body and blood and together form one body. "Because there is one bread, we who are many are one body, for we all partake of the one bread" (1 Cor. 10:17). "Because we partake in the one bread, we all become one body of Christ and one blood and members amongst each other and are thus united with Christ in one body" (John of Damascus, f.o. 86 – *PG* 94.1153). In union with Christ, the believer is filled with grace and with all spiritual gifts and blessings that union with Christ involves. He makes progress in spiritual life, grows in perfection and thus has the hope of resurrection to eternal life and the full participation in the glorious and blessed kingdom of Christ.

In the view of the joint Orthodox-Old Catholic theological commission, the above text on "Holy Eucharist" represents the teaching of the Orthodox and Old Catholic churches.

Amersfoort, 3 October 1985

PENANCE

1. In the sacrament of penance the sins committed by those believers who sincerely repent and confess them to a priest are forgiven. "The manifold mercy of God reaches out to a fallen mankind not only in the grace of baptism, but the healing remedy of penance also restores the hope of eternal life" (Leo I of Rome, *Ep.* 108 – *PL* 54.1011).

2. The Lord promised the authority to forgive sins to the apostles (Matt. 16:19; 18:18) and invested them with this authority after the resurrection: "If you forgive the sins of any, they are forgiven; if you retain the sins of any, they are retained" (John 20:23). This authority was passed on by the apostles to their successors. On the basis of this authority, the sacrament of penance developed as a God-given, permanent institution in the life of the church, as is attested to by the writings of the fathers and the liturgical and canonical tradition of the church.

3. Administrators (liturgists) of the sacrament of penance are the bishop and those priests authorized by him.

4. Sincere hearty repentance and confession to a priest are indispensable for the forgiveness of sins. The original form of public penance was later replaced by a form of private confession before a priest.

5. God offers forgiveness of sins to the penitent through the priest: "What is done below by priests, God makes into a reality above; and so the Lord confirms the judgment of his servants" (John Chrysostom, *Sac.* 3.5 – *PG* 48.643) "Whatever has been loosed by these keys (of the church) on earth, has every promise of also being loosed in heaven" (Augustine, *Sermo* 351.5/12 – *PL* 39.1549).

6. The priest who dispenses the sacrament of penance may, in his pastoral judgment, impose an act of penance not only on those on whom forgiveness of sins has not yet been pronounced, but also on those who have already been forgiven. The imposition of an act of penance, as attested to in scripture and Tradition (cf. 2 Cor. 2:6-8; Apostolic Constitutions 2.16,18,41 – *PG* 1.625ff., 629ff., 696ff.), aims at the spiritual improvement of the sinner and is designed to help guard against a repetition of the same sin. Penance, therefore, does not have the character of punishment but rather of a means of grace (Basil the Great, Can. 65 – *PG* 32.797).

7. The sacrament of penance was instituted for all baptized who, after baptism, committed venial or mortal sins and then demonstrated remorse for their failings. There are no sins or failings which, after repentance has been expressed, cannot be forgiven through the sacrament of penance. "For the Lord who forgave all sins did not exclude any transgression" (Ambrose of Milan, *Paen.* 1.2/5 – *PL* 16.467).

In the view of the joint Orthodox-Old Catholic theological commission, the above text on "Penance" represents the teaching of the Orthodox and Old Catholic churches.

Kavala, 17 October 1987

UNCTION

1. During his redeeming ministry on earth our Saviour healed those who suffered from diseases of body and soul. He commissioned his disciples to do the same (cf. Mark 6:7,13; 9:35). Following the example of the Lord and of the apostles, the church performs the sacrament of unction [anointing the sick], in which the faithful are prayed for and anointed with oil for the healing of body and soul: "We pray to you, Lord of all might and power, send forth the healing power of the only-begotten from heaven on this oil, so that it may be to those who are anointed with it the means for driving out every form of sickness and weakness... every form of fever and suffering, for healing grace and the forgiveness of sins, as the medicine of life and salvation for the healing and wholeness of soul, body and spirit, and for complete and total strengthening" (Serapion of Thumis, *Euch.* 29[17].1; cf. Innocence I of Rome, *Ep.* 25.8/11 – *PL* 20.560).

2. The apostle James affirms: "Is any among you sick? Let him call for the presbyters of the church, and let them pray over him, anointing him with oil in the name of the Lord; and the prayer of faith will save the sick man, and the Lord will raise him up. And if he has committed sins, he will be forgiven" (James 5:14-16).

3. Anointing the sick with oil consecrated for this purpose, and prayer, are required for the performance of this sacrament. The administrators of this sacrament are the leaders of the church, i.e. the bishop and the priests. If possible there should be, as James suggests, more than one administrator participating, although one will suffice if no more are available.

4. The fruits of this sacrament are the healing of diseases and the forgiveness of sins. Due to this twofold healing effect, the Orthodox church also makes this sacrament

available to its people in good health preparing themselves for holy communion; however, this does not serve as a substitute for the sacrament of penance.

5. The sacrament of unction is to be received by all baptized, not only those suffering from terminal conditions.

In the view of the joint Orthodox-Old Catholic theological commission, the above text on "Unction" represents the teaching of the Orthodox and Old Catholic churches.
Kavala, 17 October 1987

ORDINATION

1. The ordained ministry (ordo) is a fundamental institution in the life of the church and has its origin and continuing basis in the commissioning of the apostles by the resurrected Lord who bestowed on them the Holy Spirit for the fulfilment of their mission. This ministry must be understood in connection with apostolic succession (cf. Commission Text III/7), through which the saving work of Christ in the church continues. The New Testament witnesses that through prayer and the laying-on of hands the apostles transmitted to other men the authority conferred on them and that through this prayer and laying-on of hands the latter were granted by God the gifts of grace necessary for the spiritual office (1 Tim. 4:14; 2 Tim. 1:6-14; 2:2; Acts 14:23; 20:28-32).

2. That special apostolic characteristic, namely the apostolic ministry itself as a service to the entire church which the apostles embody as universal shepherds of the church, is not part of the authority of the office of bishop received from the apostles in the consecration as bishop. No single bishop has received this apostolic office for himself on the basis of [apostolic] succession, but rather, all bishops share in the apostolicity in and through the church.

3. In spite of a certain degree of unclarity in the vocabulary used, the ordained ministry as a special spiritual function appears quite early in the form of bishop, priest (presbyter) and deacon. The bishop as teacher, liturgist and shepherd of the local church under his guidance, guards and preserves its unity and the truth of its teaching. Since he possesses the fullness of ordained ministry, he also performs all sacramental acts and other liturgical functions, and exercises the work of shepherd in all its fullness. The priests (presbyters) support the bishop by performing the sacraments (with some specific exceptions) and other liturgical functions and participate in the proclamation of the gospel and the spiritual instruction of the faithful. The deacons assist the bishop and the priests (presbyters) in the performance of sacraments, participate in social ministries and assist in the work of the church in general.

4. Except for the as-yet-not-fully-understood arrangement of deaconesses, the undivided church did not permit the ordination of women.

5. The candidate who has been determined to be worthy for ordained ministry is ordained by the bishop, with prayer and the laying-on of hands, in a eucharistic gathering of the church, whereby the bishop prays, together with the clergy and the faithful gathered, that the grace of the Holy Spirit who heals what is sick and supplies what is lacking may descend on the ordinand. The practice attested to in the "Apostolic Tradition" of Hippolytus (c. 7f) and known only in the West that the priests (presbyters) present lay their hands on the head of the ordinand together with the bishop is a sign of their union with the bishop and their approbation of the admission of the ordinand

to their collegium. This is not intended to raise any doubt about the full and exclusive authority of the bishop in matters of ordination. The prayer of the entire congregation and the approbation expressed in this prayer also demonstrates the cooperation and participation of all the people.

6. The divine grace received in ordination grants the authority for a particular service in the proclamation of the gospel, in the liturgical sacramental life of the church and in the gathering and upbuilding of the faithful. This service has a differing form and purpose depending on whether it is performed by a bishop, a priest (presbyter) or a deacon. The gift of ordained ministry granted in the grace of ordination has a threefold purpose because it continues the threefold ministry of the Lord in the church: the kingly, the sacerdotal and the prophetic.

7. The efficacy of the sacraments administered by those in ordained ministry is not dependent on their personal holiness or unworthiness, "for it is God who sanctifies us in his mysteries" (John Chrysostom, *Hom.* 8.1 in 1 Cor. – *PG* 61.69).

In the view of the joint Orthodox-Old Catholic theological commission, the above text on "Ordination" represents the teaching of the Orthodox and Old Catholic churches.

Kavala, 17 October 1987

MARRIAGE

1. Marriage is an institution given by God. It was founded by God at creation as a fellowship of love and for the mutual support of husband and wife (Gen. 2:18), then reaffirmed by the Lord (Matt. 19:4-6) and blessed by his presence at the wedding at Cana (John 2:1-11).

God created man as male and female (Gen. 1:27) and placed their common life under his special protection and blessing. Already under the old covenant the marital union represents a characteristic image of the union between God and his people. Under the new covenant marriage, in which union man and woman are bound together in mutual love and in faith, represents as an image the great mystery of the love and unity which exists between Christ and the church he founded (cf. Eph. 5:32).

2. In his blessing of the first human couple God has associated the propagation of children with marriage: "Be fruitful and multiply and fill the earth" (Gen. 1:28). In bringing children into the world and raising them in the "discipline and instruction of the Lord" (Eph. 6:4), man has become a partner of God in continuing God's work of creation. Through children, man experiences the gift of fatherhood and motherhood and, together, spouses and children form a family which is a kind of small church, the house church.

Marriage is the mystery of love par excellence (cf. John Chrysostom, *Laud. Max.* 3 – *PG* 51.230). It fulfills its purpose as a fellowship of love of spouses, not only by bearing children and sharing life (cf. Eph. 5:25, 1 Sam. 1:8). This love and unity between spouses as the principal purpose of marriage is achieved when they remain in the grace of the Holy Spirit.

3. The church, which has blessed marriage since ancient times, "so that it responds to the Lord and not to lust" (Ignatius of Antioch, *Polyc.* 5.2 – *PG* 5.724), is not simply giving its blessing to the natural union of man and woman, but rather is uniting the new couple in the eucharistic fellowship and thereby placing the marriage in the context of

the mystery of the church. The consent of the bridal couple is indispensable for marriage which is concluded as a sacrament by the blessing of a lawfully ordained minister.

4. The sanctity of marriage and the spiritual character of the union and fellowship of persons in a marriage blessed according to the pattern of the union between Christ and his church is the basis for the church's conviction that marriage is a life-long union and indissoluble. The Lord proclaimed the sanctity and indissolubility of marriage (Matt. 19:6), but admitted the possibility of its dissolution for reasons of adultery (Matt. 5:32; 19:9). The apostle Paul says that a second marriage after the death of a spouse is permissible, although he expresses his preference that widowed persons not marry again (1 Cor. 7:39).

In the strict sense, therefore, a marriage cannot be dissolved for reasons other than adultery or the death of one of the spouses; but the church, out of forbearance and love for people, acknowledges other, analogous reasons. In its pastoral care the church is guided by divine commandment and the divine disposition to forgive as it deals with marriages which have failed due to human shortcomings.

5. In its pastoral care the church emphasizes the fact that husband and wife are equally (cf. 1 Cor. 7:3f.; Eph. 5:21-33; 1 Pet. 3:1-7) responsible for the grace which is theirs in marriage as well as in their vocation to glorify God also in their bodies (1 Cor. 6:12-20; cf. also Heb. 13:4).

6. Marriage and ordination are not mutually exclusive. The ancient church allowed the ordinand a free choice between marriage and celibacy and forbade only widowed persons from marrying after ordination. With regard to marriage after ordination, the tradition of the ancient church held the "promise of celibacy" at ordination as an impediment to marriage. Marriage and celibacy are not placed in opposition to each other nor do they abrogate each other. They represent parallel paths of Christian perfection.

In the view of the joint Orthodox-Old Catholic theological commission, the above text on "Marriage" represents the teaching of the Orthodox and Old Catholic churches.
Kavala, 17 October 1987

23. Eschatology

Kavala, Greece, 17 October 1987

THE DOCTRINE OF THE LAST THINGS

1. The church and the end time

Christian life points towards the kingdom of God and the return of the Lord in glory. The faith of the apostles that "here we have no lasting city, but we seek the city which is to come" (Heb. 13:14), and that "the form of this world is passing away" (1 Cor. 7:31), determines the content of Christian hope and produces a sense for the transitory and provisional nature of this world. The church has always emphatically clung to the eschatological hope and thereby has stamped the character of the life of the faithful.

Eschatological hope is no empty experience, since the end time has already commenced in the midst of the life of the church, which represents the continued unfolding reality of the kingdom of God in historical time. The resurrection of Christ already ushers in his return in glory, and the outpouring of the Holy Spirit inaugurates the last times which Joel prophesied (Joel 3:1-5; Acts 2). The Christian lives in the period of time between Pentecost and the second coming of the Lord as on the "eighth day of creation". We in the church receive through the sacraments and the other divine means of grace the pledge of the Spirit, in the hopeful anticipation of the joyous experience of the whole which is yet to come.

Therefore the Christian does not press forward as though rejecting the experience of this world, but rather bears witness to God's love through activity in this world; beyond that, however, he desires to enjoy something even greater: "We ourselves, who have the first-fruits of the Spirit, groan inwardly as we wait for adoption as sons, the redemption of our bodies" (Rom. 8:23). "We do not reject the present, but we strive for the greater" (John Chrysostom, *Hom.* 14.6 in Rom. – *PG* 60.531). For Christians, death has laid aside its terrible mask. For them it is the passage from the transitory to the eternal, the corruptible to the incorruptible. The day on which martyrs and saints died is the day on which the church celebrates their birthday in the other life.

2. Life after death

Death, which is a consequence of Adam's sin, concludes the period of trial and spiritual progress for man. This is why the New Testament and the fathers of the church warn the faithful not to disregard God's grace as long as they live. After death there will no longer be an opportunity for salvation, only judgment and scrutiny of past deeds will follow (cf. 2 Cor. 6:2; Gal. 6:10; Basil the Great, *Moral.* 1.2,5 – *PG* 31.700f,704).

Men will be judged by God immediately after death on the basis of their deeds performed during their lifetime (cf. 2 Cor. 5:10; 11:15; Rom. 2:5-11). The righteous and the saints will be brought near to God; sinners, however, will be led far from God to Hades, as depicted in the parable of the rich man and Lazarus (Luke 16:19-31). "While waiting for the final judgment the souls of the faithful wait in a finer place, the sinners and evil ones in a worse place" (Justin Martyr, *Dial.* 5.3 – *PG* 6.488). The honour which the church accords the saints rests on the belief that they are already in God's presence and, in a certain sense, are already enjoying the divine glory, the full enjoyment of which at the general resurrection at the last day they still await. Prayers to the Mother of God and the saints to intercede for us with God in whose presence they live and are continuously heard by him rest on the same assumptions. The supplication of the saints contributes to God's mercy being bestowed on the living. This forms a strong and perpetual bond between the church militant and the church triumphant.

Even though believing and teaching that, after death, it is not possible for those in the ranks of the sinners to cross over to join the righteous, the church, following an ancient tradition, celebrates eucharist in the faith, and with the hope, that God will remember those fallen asleep in mercy; it also conducts memorial services and commends acts of charity to the faithful. This gives expression to the loving fellowship between the living and those who have already passed on, together with the hope of one's own resurrection. "We believe that the prayer will be a very great advantage to those on whose behalf it has been brought" (Cyril of Jerusalem, *Catech.* 23.9 – *PG* 33.1116f).

3. The resurrection of the dead and the renewal of the world

The entire divine plan of salvation will find its historical fulfilment in the coming of the Lord in glory. The resurrection of the dead and the renewal of the world will accompany the Lord's appearance. These are fundamental truths of the faith as they are contained in the creeds of the ancient church. The Nicene-Constantinopolitan Creed declares of Christ that "he will come again with glory, to judge the living and the dead", and concludes with an expectation of resurrection. "We look for the resurrection of the dead and the life of the world to come."

The moment of the second coming of the Lord is unknown (Mark 13:32); therefore the church admonishes the faithful always to be prepared and to watch, for the day of the Lord is coming as a thief in the night, at an hour when no one is expecting him (Mark 13:33-37; Matt. 24:42-44; 1 Thess. 5:2; 2 Pet. 3:10). The church has rejected all attempts to determine the exact moment of the Lord's return.

The final judgment will be preceded by the resurrection of the dead and the renewal of the world. The return of the Lord coincides with the transformation of all mankind and the world from a condition of corruption to one of incorruption (cf. 1 Cor. 15:51f.; 1 Thess. 4:17). The bodies of those who have already fallen asleep will be raised and indestructibly reunited with their souls in that intimate relationship which it had enjoyed earlier; the bodies of the living will be transformed and creation will be renewed (cf. Rom. 8:19-22; 2 Pet. 3:13). The church believes that the resurrected bodies will be like that of their glorified Lord (cf. also John Chrysostom, *Delic.* 6 – *PG* 51.352).

All will experience the resurrection of the body, so that they may appear before the Lord with body and soul reunited and after the final judgment enjoy either blessedness or eternal damnation. The eternal happiness of the righteous as well as the eternal punishment of the wicked is a constant teaching of holy scripture and the fathers of the church.

Our daily prayer for the coming of his kingdom will be fulfilled at the return of Christ, as is attested in the Book of Revelation: "I saw a new heaven and a new earth; for the first heaven and the first earth had passed away... and death shall be no more... and he who sat upon the throne said: Behold, I make all things new" (Rev. 21:1-5).

In the view of the joint Orthodox-Old Catholic theological commission, the above text on "The Doctrine of the Last Things" represents the teaching of the Orthodox and Old Catholic churches.

Kavala, 17 October 1987

24. Church Community

Kavala, Greece, 17 October 1987

ECCLESIAL COMMUNION: PRESUPPOSITIONS AND CONSEQUENCES

1. The church is the one body of Christ, animated by the one Holy Spirit. In this body, by the work of the Spirit, the faithful are bound together in the unity of faith, worship and church order.

2. Every local church has its centre in the holy eucharist. It is Christ who invites to his meal. Therefore it is celebrated by his church under the direction of the bishop or a priest commissioned by him; and indeed it is the church as the one body of Christ which performs this celebration, and all who receive this eucharist become one body, the body of Christ. "The bread which you see on the altar, sanctified by the word of God, is the body of Christ. The cup, or more precisely what the cup contains, sanctified by the word of God, is the blood of Christ... If you have received properly you are what you have received. For the apostle says: we, the many, are one bread, one body" (Augustine, *Sermo* 227 – *PL* 38.1099). "The bread which we break, is it not communion in the body of Christ? Why didn't he [Paul] say: take part in? Because he wanted to say more than that and indicate how profound the connection is. For communicating is not only taking part and receiving a portion but also being united to. As that body is united to Christ so are we united to him through this bread... For after he said: communion in the body, he attempts to express the close connection and therefore adds: because there is one bread, we who are many are one body. What do I mean by communion (koinonia)? he says. We ourselves are that body. For what is that bread? The body of Christ! But what do those who partake become? The body of Christ! Not many bodies, but one body... For you are not nourished from one body, and he by another, but all are fed by the same body" (John Chrysostom, *Hom.* 24.2 on 1 Cor. – *PG* 61.200f).

3. Because it is Christ who invites, the church invites participation in the table fellowship. This connects participants to the church's task of proclaiming the gospel, building up the body of Christ and preserving its unity in true faith and in love.

4. As being admitted into the church does not occur without confession of the true faith, so the eucharist is not celebrated as the centre of the church without the true faith. The Christ of the sacraments is none other than the Christ of faith whom the church has confessed at all times and in all places with unanimity.

5. Fellowship includes the entire life of the church. Therefore it is said about the members: "They devoted themselves to the apostles' teaching and fellowship, to the breaking of bread and the prayers" (Acts 2:42). St Ignatius wrote: "... gather together,

all of you, each and every one of you without exception, experiencing a common grace, in one faith, and in Jesus Christ, of David's lineage according to the flesh, Son of man and Son of God, to obey the bishop and the presbyterium with undivided allegiance, breaking one bread, which is the medicine of immortality, antidote to death, a gift which supports life in Jesus Christ for evermore" (Ignatius of Antioch, Eph. 20:2 – *PG* 5.661).

6. The supper of the Lord can no longer be celebrated together where fellowship is broken. The re-establishment of eucharistic fellowship during continuing separation in faith is in itself a contradiction since, in spite of common reception of the eucharist, the churches will continue to live in separation from one another. Such behaviour will accept the existence of separated churches as normal and then may lead to the sense that the sorrow and remorse necessary to overcome separation are, in fact, superfluous. Indeed eucharistic fellowship is an expression of fellowship in the faith of the one church.

7. Whenever fellowship is broken the church has the responsibility to heal the wound. The re-establishing of fellowship is not possible outside of the one body of Christ because the unity of faith and the fellowship of the Holy Spirit is given only in this body. In order to re-establish fellowship it is necessary not only to check carefully whether we are close enough to each other but also whether the differences are so significant that separation must continue to exist.

8. The consequence and expression of reciprocally recognized fellowship in the faith is the full liturgical-canonical communion of churches, the realization of organic unity in the one body of Christ. The liturgical and canonical consequences, which result from ecclesial fellowship, will be elucidated and regulated by the church on the basis of the Tradition of the undivided church. This fellowship does not signify uniformity in liturgical order and ecclesial practice, but rather embodies an expression of the fact that the historically legitimated development of the one faith of the ancient and undivided church is preserved in each of the participating churches. This fellowship also does not require the subjection of one church with its tradition to the other church, for this would contradict the reality of the fellowship. The churches united in full communion will fulfill their responsibilities in the world not isolated from each other, but on principle together.

In the view of the joint Orthodox-Old Catholic theological commission, the above text on "Ecclesial Communion: Presuppositions and Consequences" represents the teaching of the Orthodox and Old Catholic churches.

Kavala, 17 October 1987

XIII. REFORMED-METHODIST DIALOGUE

Historical Introduction

Although the Reformed and Methodist traditions are close in many respects, it is only recently that an official dialogue has been undertaken between the World Methodist Council and the World Alliance of Reformed Churches. In many countries conversations have been carried on between Methodists and Reformed; in a number of countries Methodist and Reformed churches have joined united churches. The question therefore arises of the extent to which the two are to remain separated in the future.

The initiative for an international dialogue came from the World Alliance of Reformed Churches. It soon became clear that detailed conversations extending over many years would not be required for establishing mutual agreement on doctrine and order. A first meeting took place in St Albans, England, 20-23 July 1985. Its purpose was to formulate both shared convictions and differences and to survey the state of reciprocal relations. In the report an attempt was made to state the common faith. At the same time, the group suggested that it draw up a more comprehensive report on the basis of a lengthier consultation (see *Reformed World*, 38, 8, Dec. 1985, pp.444ff.). The suggestion won the agreement of both the plenary assembly of the World Methodist Council and the executive committee of the World Alliance of Reformed Churches. This second meeting took place at Cambridge, 20-23 July 1987. It resulted in the report that follows.

The group came to the conclusion that the classical doctrinal differences between the two families should not be regarded as impediments to unity. It urgently asked both churches to come to grips with this observation. A series of concrete questions were formulated which were to guide the churches in their reflection on the subject. The general assembly of the World Alliance of Reformed Churches (Seoul, 15-26 August 1989) took an explicit position on the report. It expressed its happiness with the results of the group's work and suggested the appointment of a small joint group; this new group would enquire into the conclusions to be drawn from the agreement thus far reached.

Lukas Vischer

XIII. REFORMED-METHODIST DIALOGUE

25. Together in God's Grace

Cambridge, England, 27 July 1987

Introduction

The second international consultation of the World Alliance of Reformed Churches and the World Methodist Council met in Cambridge from 23 to 26 July 1987. We took up the central questions committed to us by the first consultation in 1985 as the principal issues requiring further discussion. Within the context of broad general agreement on the nature of the gospel and the church, the following main questions were those which were addressed by means of papers and discussion: the Christian Tradition and our particular traditions within it; fundamental questions about salvation and, particularly, its origins in the grace of God and its realization in the Christian life; the nature of the church as a covenant community; and the ways in which our churches have lived and understood their diverse relationships with the state.

Affirmation

These conversations have reassured us of our common rootage in the gospel and of the compatibility of our expressions of it. In many places in the world, churches in our two traditions have already entered into close relationships, including both federal and organic unions. These unions were entered after due doctrinal discussions; we wish to affirm that there is sufficient agreement in doctrine and practice between our two positions to justify such answers to the Lord's call to unity for the sake of mission and our common praise of God. Being convinced of the urgency of manifesting the unity God has given, we wish also to affirm that in all places churches in our two traditions are already in a position mutually to recognize membership and ministry, to join in common tasks of evangelism and service, and to share fellowship in word and sacrament. Historic differences of theological perspective and practice still maintain their influence, but are not of sufficient weight to divide us. More positively, they should be regarded as mutually corrective and enriching. Under present conditions, both traditions are increasingly benefiting from our common appropriation of new insights into the gospel granted through theological teaching in this century, through common worship and witness, and through our participation in the wider ecumenical movement.

Explication

1. The Tradition and the traditions

All Christian traditions convey distinctive ways of proclaiming and living the gospel. Both of our traditions regard the scriptures as the primary authority in matters of faith and practice and confess the shared faith of the universal church expressed in ecumenical creeds and by witnesses to it through the centuries.

Within the broad Tradition, however, our two traditions originate in different historical circumstances and tend to refer themselves to different kinds of secondary authority. For the Reformed, the major orientation is to "the deeper plunge into the gospel" which was the Reformation, and to the great confessions of the 16th and 17th centuries. These have often operated, under scripture, as subordinate standards for the teaching and government of the church. Methodists look to the figures of the Wesleys and to their work on behalf of evangelistic and sacramental renewal within a church already heir to the Reformation.

Wesley's standard sermons, his explanatory notes on the New Testament, and his abridgment of the Anglican articles have provided the formal doctrinal basis for the various Methodist churches. In worship, a large part has been played by the Wesleyan hymns which, along with the adaptation of the *Book of Common Prayer*, have directed and nourished the faith of the people. Both traditions testify to the priority of God's grace, the sufficiency of faith, the call to holy living, and the imperative to mission. The ways in which these realities have been expressed have differed, so that distinctions of ethos, liturgical expression and church order have resulted, both between and within our traditions.

2. Grace

Grace has been a principal emphasis in both our traditions. From first to last our salvation depends on the comprehensiveness of God's grace as prevenient, as justifying, as sanctifying, as sustaining, as glorifying. Nevertheless, in seeking to preserve this primary truth, our traditions have tended to give different accounts of the appropriation of saving grace, emphasizing on the one hand God's sovereignty in election, and on the other, the freedom of human response. This gave rise to the dispute between "Calvinism" and "Arminianism" which has often been seen as a dividing line between the Reformed and Methodist traditions, although in fact not all in the Reformed tradition subscribe to double predestination, nor all Methodists to the Arminian alternative.

In "Calvinism" it is the elect who come to faith and therefore receive saving grace, while in "Arminianism" it is those who in freedom "will to be saved". Despite the apparent contradiction between Calvin and Wesley (who followed Arminius at this point), the debate presupposes agreement on several fundamental matters. Wesley himself affirmed his agreement with Calvin: "(1) in ascribing all good to the free grace of God; (2) in denying all natural free will, and all power antecedent to grace; (3) in excluding all merit from man, even for what he has or does by the grace of God".

It was only when, from the basis of this fundamental agreement, the question "who are the saved?" was approached, that the conflicting stances identified as Calvinist and Wesleyan were adopted. In each case the stance taken leaves questions that demand answers consistent with the three accepted tenets just mentioned. Methodists who follow Wesley must face two objections in particular from Calvinists. First, Calvinists object that the necessary freedom to choose salvation was lost in the fall, and that to claim otherwise is Pelagian. Wesley in response agreed that all are dead in sin by nature, but maintained that none is now in a mere state of nature. Prevenient grace, which he saw as the universal inheritance of Christ's atoning work, restores this lost freedom of choice, while not guaranteeing salvation. Calvinists then object that this dishonours God by denying his sovereignty, since it claims that human freedom to deny is greater than God's will to save. Wesley's reply was that in creating people with free will, God chose to limit his power at this point. Therefore the human capacity to say no to saving grace is, according to Wesley, just as compatible with God's sovereignty as is the human capacity to sin.

In their turn, the Reformed who follow Calvin must face two questions in particular from Wesleyans. First, Wesleyans ask how the predestinarian approach avoids understanding God's freedom as anything more than arbitrariness, and human freedom as anything other than illusion, if the eternal destiny of every creature is already determined. The Calvinist answer is that since God as Creator is the author of justice and his ways are not our ways, it is a fundamental categorical mistake for us to judge him at the bar of our human and limited reason. The second Wesleyan question is how can the missionary and evangelical imperative be maintained if, no matter what, the saved will be saved and the lost lost? Calvinists affirm in reply that obedience to the sovereign God commits the church to proclamation of the gospel so that people may hear and believe, and thus God's will to save be fulfilled. Consequently, impetus for and result of missionary and evangelistic outreach are evident no less in the Reformed than in the Methodist tradition, although the motivation may be understood and expressed somewhat differently.

These questions that we put to each other lie in the realm of theological problems, and answers can be given which in each case are consistent with the basic agreed affirmations and find scriptural support. But for both Methodists and Calvinists there is a question which cannot be answered, not because it is difficult, but because to propose an answer would be to destroy the very terms of the problem. Those who claim that prevenient grace gives to all the freedom to come to faith cannot answer the question "why do these choose salvation, and not those?", without denying the very human freedom they wish to affirm. Those who contend that only the elect may come to faith, and thus be saved by grace, cannot answer the question "why does God choose these and not those?" without limiting God's sovereign freedom which above all they wish to maintain. That these questions, which are unanswerable in principle, exist at all, points to the fundamental mystery underlying both the theological problem and the answers. Both traditions have gone wrong when they have claimed to know too much about this mystery of God's electing grace and of human response.

Therefore, that Wesley and Calvin advocated conflicting ways of holding together what they affirm in common should not constitute a barrier between our traditions. Even if Wesley and Calvin are followed without modification (which gives their approaches greater authority than they themselves allowed any human interpretation), what they both affirmed is not only the fundamental mystery of God's saving grace witnessed to in scripture. It is also the underlying theology of grace that was stated in three points at the beginning of this section and that provides the context without which that mystery is to be recognized, received and celebrated.

3. The church as covenant community

Both traditions have found the concept of covenant to be a central way of understanding the church. Nevertheless, there has been diversity of understanding even within the traditions, and our conversations have sought clarification and common ground. The Reformed tradition began as an attempt to reform and restore the Western church on the basis of the newly perceived word of God and in new obedience to that word. The Reformed family understands the church as a covenant community called together by

God's grace. Election and covenant find their expression in the existence of the church. The church is grounded in the eternal purpose of God to send Jesus Christ into the world as the head and saviour of all things. The Methodist movement began as a mission to the unevangelized, and saw itself at first as a society within the established church. In different places and at different times, it came to understand itself as a distinct church. John Wesley thought of Christian community as a means by which members build each other up in faith and life. Within Methodism, covenanted life has been realized through societies, conferences and Christian fellowship, and is reaffirmed in annual covenant services.

Both traditions confess that we have allowed individualism to undercut our sense and practice of corporate churchly life. Often our religion, under the influence of contemporary culture, has retreated into a merely private realm. The recovery of the centrality of covenant is therefore urgent. Through a conversion of the heart, one appropriates the covenant relationship with God and with other people. Thus, the sacraments are to be understood as signs and seals of faithful participation in the covenant community, and not individualistically. Accordingly, baptism is the sacrament of adoption into the family of God, incorporation into the body of Christ, and reception into the koinonia of the Spirit. Likewise, our communion with the Lord and with one another in him is expressed and sustained at his table. We acknowledge that our life together in our present church structures is in constant need of re-evaluation and reformation as we look forward to the consummation of the covenant when Christ will be all in all. Our acting as if we could exclude others from the covenant, and our failure to exercise our stewardship of the world and its resources, are both a denial of the covenant which God has established with humankind and all creation.

4. Church and state

Our concern to honour God's covenant in the practical implementation of the faith necessarily involves some form of relationship with civil authorities. Within both our traditions there is a wide variety of relationships, ranging from forms of establishment to contexts in which there is considerable tension with the powers that be. We confess that among ourselves there are places where those who are in a position of privilege give less than due respect to Christian minorities. We also acknowledge that the Christian church has repeatedly used its privileged position for social and political aggrandizement. While the church has the permanent responsibility to challenge and to let itself be challenged by society, the form of challenge and response vary from time to time and from place to place. Both of our traditions share a conviction of the power of Christ as prophet, priest and king to transform all life in the world.

5. Perfect salvation

Both Reformed and Methodist traditions affirm the real change which God by the Spirit works in the minds and hearts and lives of believers. By the sanctifying grace of God, penitent believers are being restored to God's image and renewed in God's likeness. To imitate God, says Wesley, is the best worship we can offer. What God is in heaven, says Calvin, he bids us to be in this world: the loving kindness of God is to be reflected in the love Christians bear towards their neighbours. Our traditions agree that, on the human side, salvation consists in the perfect love of God and neighbour, which is to have the mind of Christ and fulfill his law. We are to love God with singleness of heart, and to seek God's glory with a single eye. We are to love without reserve the sisters and brothers for whom Christ died.

The work which God has begun in us, says Calvin, he will surely complete. What God has promised, says Wesley, he is ready and willing to realize now. In the two traditions we are taught to strive and pray for entire sanctification. The Reformed stress on election and perseverance gives believers the confidence that God will keep them to the end. The Methodist preaching of perfection affirms that we may set no limit to the present power of God to make sinners into saints.

Methodists and Reformed agree that "man's chief end is to glorify God and to enjoy him forever". The heavenly fellowship of praise and bliss is, by God's grace, to be anticipated now, as we "with one heart and one voice glorify the God and Father of our Lord Jesus Christ" and together share his benefits. We are saved into community; and, as Jesus prayed that his disciples might be "perfected into one", so the closer sharing of life between Christians in the Reformed and Methodist traditions will be evidence of growing participation in the communion of the triune God.

Conclusions and recommendations

We report, as a result of our conversations, a new-found confidence that our two traditions witness to a common gospel and embody authentic forms of obedience and faithful discipleship. Our complementary ways of Christian thought and life are built upon a foundation in God's grace, in covenant existence, and in the goal of perfect salvation. We have found in each other faithful witness to the Christian gospel, and we have been renewed in our sense of oneness in Christ. In particular, we have found that the classical doctrinal issues which we were asked to review ought not to be seen as obstacles to unity between Methodists and Reformed. Certain implications flow from this conviction for the development of our relations to one another as Christian world communions. We therefore recommend:

1. That our world bodies invite their member churches to consider the implications of our findings and to communicate their responses. Possible questions for consideration are:

a) Can Reformed and Methodist churches cooperate more closely in local worship, study and witness?
b) Can Methodist and Reformed churches cooperate more closely regionally and nationally – for example, in joint doctrinal commissions, evangelistic outreach and social service?
c) Are there countries in which Reformed/Methodist union negotiations might be initiated?
d) Ought our two international bodies to grow closer together by tackling common tasks and by sharing human and other resources?

2. That where one or other of our churches is a majority church, the utmost care should be taken to ensure that the smaller partner or partners not be given reason to feel unwanted or undervalued.

3. That in each nation our member churches should together examine the question, "How can the covenant people of God relate to the state and bear faithful witness to their society in a rapidly changing and divided world?"

The people of our two traditions, to whom this report is addressed, exist in varying relationships to each other. It is our earnest prayer that whether they find themselves within a church union, are contemplating such a step, do not have the other partner as a neighbour, or are not yet part of a wider union, they will find both encouragement and challenge in this report.

XIV. REFORMED-ORTHODOX DIALOGUE

Historical Introduction

The dialogue between the Orthodox and the Reformed churches was the ripe fruit produced by preceding local dialogues or contacts, whether in the framework of the ecumenical movement or outside it. It was the result in particular of contacts between the ecumenical patriarchate and the World Alliance of Reformed Churches; a detailed report on these contacts was read at the first meeting of the joint theological commission (1986). The benevolent view taken of this dialogue by the Orthodox church found expression at the third preconciliar pan-Orthodox conference (1986) in the wish that the dialogue "might be officially begun and might develop in a positive and creative spirit". The conference also expressed the hope that "this dialogue might take into account the experience gained in other dialogues, profiting by the positive results achieved there and avoiding the negative aspects".

A preparatory meeting took place at the Orthodox Centre of the Ecumenical Patriarchate in Chambésy, Geneva, in March 1986. Several theological papers were read, and questions about method and the list of subjects were discussed at length. It was decided to suggest the opening of an official dialogue and the formation of a joint commission which would develop the programme for the dialogue. This commission made concrete suggestions and in particular outlined the first subject for the official dialogue:

"The Doctrine of the Trinity on the Basis of the Nicene-Constantinopolitan Creed"
1. The Trinity as source of the church's faith, worship, and life
   a) the incarnation of Christ: revelation of the triune God as love;
   b) the divine-human life of Christ, communicated to humankind by the Holy Spirit.
2. The church as body of Christ: experience of, and witness to, the new life in Christ through the centuries
   a) the sacraments in the life of the church;
   b) royal priesthood and priestly office.
3. The church's mission in the world: reconciliation, service, work for justice and peace

At the same time it was decided that in order more fully to prepare the members of the commission for their work, papers on two subjects should be readied: (1) "who are we?", and (2) "evaluation of the papers read at earlier local dialogues". This suggestion was consonant with the common persuasion that the official theological dialogue should, "on the one hand, be regarded as the goal towards which the results of local and other meetings had been leading and, on the other, should be such as to promote and deepen relations between the two traditions at the local and regional levels".

On the basis of these preparations both the Orthodox churches and the World Alliance of Reformed Churches agreed to begin an official dialogue and appointed their delegations.

The first plenary session of the official joint theological commission took place in Leuenberg, Switzerland, in March 1988. The discussion focussed on three papers dealing with the following subjects: (1) ecclesiological profiles of the Orthodox and Reformed traditions; (2) information on earlier conversations at the local and regional levels; (3) examination of the doctrine of the Trinity in the Nicene-Constantinopolitan Creed on the basis of some patristic texts and the dogmatic teaching of the Orthodox and Reformed traditions.

The discussions of ecclesiology and theology cleared up many points in both traditions, although they also brought to light a number of matters on which different views were taken, for example the relation between sanctification and divinization, the meaning of Tradition, the ecclesial nature of theology, the structures of the church, and so on. Discussion of these topics was postponed and is to be taken up during the discussion of ecclesiology. In dealing with the third subject mentioned above, the basis of the discussion was the Nicene-Constantinopolitan Creed in its original and authentic form, that is, without the addition of the filioque, although it was agreed that the theology of the filioque would have to be investigated at some point in the dialogue. The four theological papers on this third subject, together with the ensuing discussion of the doctrine of the Trinity during the 4th century, could not deal exhaustively with the problems involved. A significant agreement was evidenced on essential points, but a number of questions were also raised concerning, for example, the relation of the teaching of the fathers to the faith and tradition of the church; causality and monarchy in the Trinity; the biblical basis for the doctrine of the Trinity; the working of the Holy Spirit outside the church; the relation between scripture and dogma or confession of faith; the Trinity and feminism; and so on. It was decided to continue the discussion of trinitarian dogma.

The second meeting of the official commission took place 1-8 October 1990, in Minsk, Byelorussia. In the interim, a small sub-committee had drafted a statement expressing the common understanding of the doctrine of the Trinity. Further, more advanced papers on certain aspects of the problem were delivered. The following matters in particular were discussed:
1) the biblical basis for the doctrine of the Trinity;
2) the Trinity and the worship of the church.

After thorough discussion the commission was able to reach agreement on the report printed below. A small sub-committee was charged with the stylistic improvement of the text (March 1991).

The dialogue has continued to meet: in 1992 in Kappel, Switzerland, which produced the "Significant Features" text included here, following up the earlier work on the Trinity, making more explicit its salient points; in 1994 in Limassol, which produced the "Agreed Statement on Christology"; and in 1996 in Aberdeen, Scotland. A small executive group regularly evaluated the meetings and proposed next steps. The dialogue hopes to go on to deal with questions of the church and ministry (Lukas Vischer, ed., *Agreed Statements: From the Orthodox Reformed Dialogue*, Geneva, World Alliance of Reformed Churches, 1998).

Jeffrey Gros
Damaskinos Papandreou

XIV. REFORMED-ORTHODOX DIALOGUE

26. Memorandum

Leuenberg, Switzerland, 11 March 1988

Some forty theologians representing the Orthodox church and the World Alliance of Reformed Churches met for the first round of their official theological dialogue in Leuenberg, Switzerland, 7-11 March 1988.

The theological commission reaffirmed their faith in the Holy Trinity as expressed in the Nicene-Constantinopolitan Creed, which they used as the starting-point to their discussions.

There were three main areas on which papers by Orthodox and Reformed members were read and discussions were held in plenary sessions: (a) ecclesiological profiles of the Orthodox and the Reformed traditions (papers were read by Prof. V. Pheidas and Prof. B. Rigdon); (b) information on earlier discussions between Orthodox and Reformed theologians and churches on a local or regional level (papers by H.E. Metropolitan Damaskinos of Switzerland [invited] and Prof. J. Pasztor); and (c) an examination of the doctrine of the Trinity in the Nicene-Constantinopolitan Creed on the basis of certain patristic texts and the dogmatic teaching of the Orthodox and Reformed traditions (papers by Prof. T.F. Torrance, Prof. G.D. Dragas, Prof. T. Koev and Prof. L. Vischer).

As regards the first topic it became apparent that historical/ecclesiological considerations were unavoidable. For instance the Orthodox theologians are accustomed to appeal to the tradition of the "undivided church" which preceded the great schism between the Eastern and the Western churches in the 11th century because of their attachment to the common faith of Christendom and their rejection of the Western scholastic theology. On the other hand, the Reformed have shaped their theology and tradition in conflict with mediaeval scholasticism and in their attempt to recover the original tradition of Christianity by looking afresh at the scriptures and the early church. There was preliminary discussion on the Orthodox understanding of the "undivided church" and on the Reformed principle of "reform" but it became clear that both notions required further and thorough examination.

In the course of this discussion several ecclesiological implications were drawn and questions were asked from both sides, but it was agreed that all these, together with the whole topic of ecclesiology, should be discussed at a later stage, once the topic of the "Holy Trinity as the source of faith, worship and life of the church" (cf. the decision of the 1986 meeting mandated by the churches as the basis of the dialogue) was adequately discussed and clear conclusions were drawn.

As far as previous Orthodox-Reformed local dialogues were concerned, two papers were read and several points emerged for discussion touching on such subjects as the relation of nature to grace, or the relation of sanctification to deification, the notion of Tradition, the ecclesial contexts and structures of theology, etc. Though both papers were received with gratitude as providing valuable material for the official dialogue, which has just begun, they too were filed for treatment or use at a later stage.

As regards the third topic the members used the Nicene Creed as their starting-point though its status in the two traditions was understood to be different. The Reformed members explained in a preliminary way that the ecumenical creed was accepted and used by the Reformed churches, but was not regarded as a primary standard. As regards the filioque clause, the Reformed members stated the prevailing position among the Reformed churches, according to which the above clause should be removed since it did not belong to the original version, but that the theological issues relating to the filioque controversy should be discussed with the view to reaching a common mind.

In connection with this third topic four papers were read and discussed, two from each side, which dealt with the 4th-century treatises on the Holy Spirit of St Athanasius, St Basil and St Gregory the Theologian (Nazianzen), and with the Nicene triadology in Orthodox dogmatic theology and in the theology of Calvin. A broad agreement was reached about the essential elements of the doctrine of the Trinity, especially on the point that there is in God unity in Trinity and Trinity in unity. Several questions were asked from the two sides which were related to such topics as:
- the character of patristic teaching and its relation to the Tradition and faith of the church;
- "causality" and "monarchy" in the Trinity;
- the distinction between *ousia* and *hypostasis* and between *ousia* and *energeia*;
- whether the name "Father" could refer to the Trinity as a whole, or to the divine *ousia*;
- the biblical basis of the Nicene doctrine of the Trinity, especially that which relates to the Old Testament;
- the hermeneutics of the fathers as contrasted to that of contemporary Western scholars;
- the relation of scripture to dogma or the creed;
- "kerygma" and "dogma" in St Basil's teaching;
- the character of the dogmatic utterances of the fathers or the creed;
- whether the Spirit works outside the church;
- the relation between the trinitarian dogma and experience or Trinity and spirituality;
- the Trinity and other religions;
- Trinity and feminism;
- Trinity and cosmology;
- Trinity and the kingdom of God (eschatology), etc.

All these questions made it clear that the discussion on the doctrine of the Trinity on the basis of the Nicene-Constantinopolitan Creed had been inaugurated and should continue in future meetings.

After some discussion, following a request on the part of the Orthodox, it was agreed that proselytism against each other should cease so that all members from both sides may feel free to attend the dialogue and so that mutual trust might increase and the dialogue might yield positive results. In this connection it was also agreed that our rapprochement and common affirmation should not be used or become a pretext for proselytizing.

With regard to future meetings it was agreed that a small sub-committee, consisting of the two co-chairmen plus Prof. T.F. Torrance, Prof. J. Van Hoeven, Prof. G. Dragas and Prof. D. Ciobotea, should meet to expound more systematically the discussion on the Trinity and arrange the questions raised above into topics to be treated in future meetings. It was also agreed that this sub-committee should arrange the programme for the next meeting and duly inform the members of the full commission.

27. Agreed Statement on the Holy Trinity

Kappel, Germany, March 1992

We confess together the evangelical and ancient faith of the catholic church in "the uncreated, consubstantial and coeternal Trinity", promulgated by the councils of Nicea (AD 325) and Constantinople (AD 381). "This is the faith of our baptism that teaches us to believe in the name of the Father, of the Son and of the Holy Spirit. According to this faith there is one Godhead, Power and Being of the Father, of the Son, and of the Holy Spirit, equal in honour, majesty and eternal sovereignty in three most perfect subsistences (ἐν τρισὶ τελειοτάσεσιν ὑποστάσεσιν), that is, in three perfect Persons" (ἤγουν τρισὶ τελείοις προσώποις) (*Ep. Syn. Constantinopolitanae*, AD 382).

The self-revelation of God as Father, Son and Holy Spirit

According to the holy gospel God has revealed himself in the Father, the Son and the Holy Spirit, as "through the Son we have access to the Father in one Spirit" (Eph. 2:18). Of decisive importance in the church's formulation of belief in the Holy Trinity was the dominical institution of baptism "in the name of the Father and of the Son and of the Holy Spirit" (Matt. 28:19). As Basil expressed it: "We are bound to be baptized in the terms we have received and to profess faith in the terms in which we have been baptized" (*Ep.* 125.3). Other triadic formulations in the New Testament reinforced this belief, such as the benediction: "The grace of the Lord Jesus Christ and the love of God and the communion of the Holy Spirit be with you all" (2 Cor. 12:14). The ancient catholic church laid great stress on the words of our Lord: "All things have been delivered to me by my Father; and no one knows the Son except the Father; and no one knows the Father except the Son, and any one to whom the Son chooses to reveal him" (Matt. 11:27; Luke 10:22). With this they conjoined the words of St Paul about "what God... has revealed to us through the Spirit; for the Spirit searches everything, even the depths of God" (1 Cor. 2:10) (thus John of Damascus, *De fide orthodoxa* 1.1). This is the foundation of the apostolic doctrine of the Trinity in unity and the unity in Trinity: one Being, three Persons.

To believe in the unity of God apart from the Trinity is to limit the truth of divine revelation. It is through the divine Trinity that we believe in the divine unity, and through the divine unity that we believe in the divine Trinity. "There is one eternal Godhead in Trinity, and there is one glory of the Holy Trinity... If the doctrine of God (ἡ Θεολογία) is now perfect in Trinity, this is the true and only divine worship (Θεοσέβεια), and this is the beauty and the truth, it must have always been so" (Athanasius, *Con. ar.* 1.18).

Three Divine Persons

In the New Testament witness to God's revelation "the Father", "the Son", and "the Holy Spirit" are unique and proper names denoting three distinct Persons or real hypostases which are neither exchangeable nor interchangeable while nevertheless of one and the same divine Being. There is one Person of the Father who is always the Father, distinct from the Son and the Spirit; and there is another Person of the Son who is always the Son, distinct from the Father and the Spirit; and another Person of the Holy Spirit who is always the Spirit distinct from the Father and the Son. In this Trinity "one is not more or less God, nor is one before and after another", "for there is no greater or less in respect of the Being or the consubstantial Persons" (Gregory the Theologian, *Or.* 31.14; 40.43). All three Persons are co-eternal and co-equal. They are all perfectly one in the identity of their nature and perfectly consubstantial in their Being. Each Person is himself Lord and God, and yet there are not three lords or gods, but only one Lord God, and there is only one and the same eternal Being of the Father, the Son and the Holy Spirit. The Father, the Son and the Holy Spirit are perfectly and completely consubstantial in their mutual indwelling of one another and in their containing (περιχώρησις) of one another. "The Trinity praised, worshipped and adored, is one and indivisible and without degrees (ἀσχημάτιστος), and he is united without confusion, just as the Monad also is distinguished in thought without division. For the threefold doxology, 'holy, holy, holy is the Lord' offered by those venerable living beings, denotes the three perfect Persons, just as in the word 'Lord' they indicate his one Being" (Athanasius, *In ill. om.* 6). The Holy Trinity is thus perfectly homogeneous and unitary, both in the threeness and oneness of God's activity, and in the threeness and oneness of his own eternal unchangeable Being. What God the Father is towards us in Christ and in the Spirit he is inherently and eternally in himself, and what he is inherently and eternally in himself he is towards us in the incarnation of his Son and in the mission of the Spirit. "As it always was, so it is even now; and as it now is, so it always was and is the Trinity, and in him (ἐν αὐτῇ) Father, Son and Holy Spirit" (Athanasius, *Ad ser.* 3.7). "In the Godhead alone the Father is properly Father, and since he is the only Father, he is and was, and always is. And the Son is properly the Son, and the only Son. And of them it holds good that the Father is always called Father, and the Son is always called Son. And the Holy Spirit is always the Holy Spirit, whom we have believed to be of God, and to be given from the Father through the Son. Thus the Holy Trinity remains invariable, known in one Godhead" (Athanasius, *Ad ser.* 4.6).

While the three Divine Persons differ from one another precisely as Father, Son and Holy Spirit, they are nevertheless conjoined in all their distinctiveness, for the entire and undivided Godhead resides in each Person, and each Person dwells in or inheres in the Other; so that the whole of one Person is imaged in the whole of the Other. In the terms used by Athanasius, "There is only one form (εἶδος) of Godhead" (Athanasius, *De syn.* 52; *Con. ar.* 3.16). Thus the Son reveals the Father as his complete image, and the Spirit does the same to the Son. The Father is revealed through the Son in the Holy Spirit, and it is in the Spirit and through the Son that we come to the Father. Each and all reveal the whole Godhead, and thus none can be regarded as being partial in any way as compared with the other two: each Person is "whole God" and the "whole God" is in each Person. Since "God is Spirit" (John 4:24) the "whole God" and "each Person" and all relations within the Holy Trinity are to be understood in a completely spiritual way.

Eternal relations in God

The three Divine Persons are also conjoined through their special relations. Thus the Son is eternally begotten of the Father and the Spirit eternally proceeds from the Father and abides in the Son, in ineffable ways that are beyond all time (ἀχρόνως), beyond all origin (ἀνάρχως), and beyond all cause (ἀναιτίως). The generation of the Son and the procession of the Spirit are unknowable mysteries which cannot be explained by recourse to human or creaturely images, although some images (e.g. Light from Light) may provide a way for us to grasp some aspects of the reality to which they are used to refer (cf. Athanasius, *Con. ar.* 2.36; Cyril of Jerusalem, *Cat.* 11.11). They indicate distinctions in relations not partitions or divisions. "Differentiated as the Persons are, the entire and undivided Godhead is one in Each." "Each of these Persons is entirely united to those with whom he is conjoined, as he is with himself, because of the identity of Being and Power that is between them" (Gregory the Theologian, *Or.* 31.14,16). The three Persons of the Holy Trinity are thus to be heard and known, worshipped and glorified "as one Person (πρόσωπον)" (Didymus, *De trin.* 2.36; Cyril of Alexandria, *In Jn.* 15.1).

The three Divine Persons are also inseparably conjoined in all the manifestations of God's activity, in creation, providence, revelation and salvation, as they are consummated in the incarnate economy of the Son. In fact all divine activity begins with he Father, extends through the Son and reaches its fulfilment in the Spirit. Thus, as St Basil taught, creation is initiated by the Father, effected by the Son and perfected by the Spirit (*De spir. sanct.* 16.38).

The order of Divine Persons in the Trinity

In the trinitarian formulae of the New Testament, as Gregory the Theologian, among others, pointed out, there is a variation in the order in which "the Father", "the Son", and the "Holy Spirit" are mentioned, which indicates that the order does not detract from full equality between the three Divine Persons (Gregory the Theologian, *Or.* 36.15). Nevertheless, as we learn from the institution of holy baptism, there is a significant coordination which places the Father first, the Son second, and the Spirit third (cf. Athanasius, *Ad ser.* 3.5 ; Basil, *Ep.* 125.3). The priority of the Father does not imply that there is something more in him compared to the Son, for all that the Father is the Son is apart from "Fatherhood", and likewise all that the Son is the Spirit is apart from "Sonship". Thus the order inherent in the trinitarian relations is grounded on the fact that the Son is begotten of the Father and the Spirit proceeds from the Father. This applies also to the unique revelation of the Father through the incarnation of his only begotten Son and the sending of the Holy Spirit by the Father in the name of the Son.

This priority of the Father or monarchy of the Father within the Trinity does not detract from the fact that the Father is not properly (κυρίως) Father apart from the Son and the Spirit, that the Son is not properly Son apart from the Father and the Spirit, and that the Spirit is not properly Spirit apart from the Father and the Son. Hence the *monarchia* of the Father is perfectly what it is in the Father's relation to the Son and the Spirit within the one indivisible Being of God. "The perfection of the Holy Trinity is an indivisible and single Godhead" (Athanasius, *Ad ser.* 1.33).

Trinity in unity and unity in Trinity, the one monarchy

Since there is only one Trinity in unity, and one unity in Trinity, there is only one indivisible Godhead, and only one *arche* (ἀρχή) or *monarchia* (μοναρχία). As such, however, Gregory the Theologian reminds us, "It is a monarchy that is not limited to one Person" (*Or.* 29.2). "The Godhead is one in Three, and the Three are One, in whom all the Godhead is, or, to be more precise, who are the Godhead" (*Or.* 39.11). "Each person is God when considered in himself; as the Father, so the Son, and as the Son, so the Holy Spirit; the Three One God when contemplated together; each God because consubstantial; one God because of the monarchy. I cannot think of the One without being enlightened by the splendour of the Three; nor can I distinguish them without being carried back to the One" (Gregory the Theologian, *Or.* 40.41). "In proclaiming the divine *monarchia* we do not err, but confess the Trinity, and Trinity in Unity, One Godhead of the Father, Son and Holy Spirit (τὴν Τριάδα, Μονάδα ἐν Τριάδι, καὶ Τριάδα ἐν Μονάδι, μίαν Θεότητα Πατρὸς καὶ Υἱοῦ, καὶ Ἁγίου Πνεύματος) (Epiphanius, *Haer.* 62.3). The μία Ἀρχή or Μοναρχία is inseparable from the Trinity, the Μονάς from the Τριάς. As such the monarchy of the Father within the Trinity is not exclusive of the monarchy of the whole undivided Trinity in relation to the whole of creation. Hence all worship and glorification by the creature is offered "to God the Father through the Son and in the Spirit" or "to the Father with the Son and together with the Holy Spirit", that is, to the one indivisible God who is Three in One and One in Three, the Holy Trinity who is blessed for ever.

Perichoresis: the mutual indwelling of Father, Son and Holy Spirit
The Holy Trinity remains invariable, known in one Godhead and one monarchy, but in which each of the three Divine Persons indwells and is indwelt by the Others. "They reciprocally contain One Another, so that One permanently envelopes, and is permanently enveloped by, the Other whom he yet envelopes" (Hilary, *De trin.* 3.1). It is in the light of this eternal περιχώρησις of the three Divine Persons in God, or the co-indwelling and co-inhering of the Father, the Son and the Holy Spirit in One Another, that we are to understand the mission of the Holy Spirit from the Father and the gift of the Holy Spirit by the Son. The Holy Spirit proceeds from the Father, but because of the unity of the Godhead in which each Person is perfectly and wholly God, he proceeds from the Father through the Son for the Spirit belongs to and is inseparable from the Being of the Father and of the Son. He receives from the Son and through him is given to us. Thus, "We believe in the Holy Spirit, the Lord and Giver of Life, who proceeds from the Father, who with the Father and the Son is worshipped and glorified, who spoke by the prophets" (the Nicene-Constantinopolitan Creed). It is precisely with the doctrine of the consubstantiality and deity of the Holy Spirit that the proper understanding of the Holy Trinity is brought to its completion in the theology and worship of the church. And it is with the doctrine of the Trinity that the adoration and knowledge of God reach their perfection. This is the faith of the one, holy, catholic and apostolic church, that we worship one God in Trinity and Trinity in unity.

One Being, three Persons
The faith and confession of the "One Being (οὐσία), three Persons" (Synod of Alex, 362/1) does not rest on any preconception or definition of the Divine Being, but on the very Being of God as he has named himself "I am who I am/I shall be who I shall be" (Ex. 3:14), the ever-living and self-revealing God who truly and really is, besides whom there is no other God. This revelation of God as "he who is who he is" is mediated to us in the gospel through the one act of God the Father, through the Son

and in the Spirit. Thus in the doctrine of the Holy Trinity the "One Being" of God does not refer to some abstract essence, but to the "I am" (Ἐγώ εἰμι) of God, the eternal living Being which God is of himself (Athanasius, *Con. ar.* 3.6; 4.1; *De syn.* 34-36; *De decr.* 22). Similarly the faith and confession of the unity in Trinity and Trinity in unity does not presuppose some prior definition of the relation of the three Divine Persons to the one Divine Being or vice versa; it rests on the one revelation of God the Father which is given us through Jesus Christ and his Spirit.

Thus in confessing the divine unity in Trinity we do not presuppose precise knowledge of "what" God is in his One Being or "how" he is Three in One and One in Three, but we believe in him as One God, the Father, the Son and the Holy Spirit, and profess knowledge of him in accordance with this one revelation handed on to the church through the apostles. That is the one faith in which we are baptized and on which the whole church rests.

The apostolic and catholic faith

In the words of St Athanasius: "It is the very tradition, teaching and faith of the Catholic church from the beginning, which the Lord gave, the apostles preached and the fathers kept upon which the church is founded... that there is a Trinity, holy and complete, confessed to be God in Father, Son and Holy Spirit, having nothing foreign or external, nor composed of one who creates and one who is originated, but all creative, consistent, indivisible in nature, one in activity. The Father does all things through the Word in the Holy Spirit. Thus, the unity of the Holy Trinity is preserved and thus one God is preached in the church, who is over all and through all and in all (Eph. 4:16) – 'over all' as Father, as beginning and fountain; 'through all' through the Word; but 'in all' in the Holy Spirit. It is a Trinity not only in name and form of speech, but in truth and actuality. For as the Father is he who he is, so also his Word is one who is God over all, and the Holy Spirit is not without existence but truly exists and subsists" (*Ad ser.* 1.28).

28. Significant Features
A Common Reflection on the Agreed Statement

Kappel, Germany, March 1992

The theological orientation of the agreed statement [on the Holy Trinity] is governed by the fact that it is only through God that God may be known. The self-revelation of God as the Father, the Son and the Holy Spirit provides the framework within which alone it is to be interpreted. It is fidelity to the supreme truth that through Christ and in one Spirit we have access to the Father which opens a way through divergent traditions in the East and West for ecumenical agreement.

Trinitarian language
Throughout the statement attention is given to the fact that human language when applied to God is inevitably and rightly stretched beyond its ordinary or conventional sense if it is to serve the purpose intended. Accordingly terms like $οὐσία$, $ὑπόστασις$ and $Φύσις$ borrowed by the church from Greek are consistently handled in the new shape given to them as they are harnessed in the service of God's trinitarian self-revelation. Thus no use is made of Aristotle's distinction between primary and secondary substance which has troubled Western theology, while Latin translations like "substance" or "essence" of more concrete Greek notions of being are usually avoided. Similarly the terms $οὐσία$ and $Φύσις$ are not used in an abstract generic sense. The doctrine of the Holy Trinity expounded here is: one God, three Persons, not three Persons, one nature.

Care has been taken in this statement to recall our Lord's teaching that "God *is* Spirit". This means that terms like $οὐσία$, $ὑπόστασις$ or $Φύσις$ when applied to God must be understood in a wholly spiritual, personal yet genderless way. It also means that any images taken from creaturely being have to be understood in a diaphanous or "see-through" way, in which they are used like lenses through which vision of truth may take place, but which are not themselves projected into deity. They are used like all biblical and theological terms to point spiritually beyond the images themselves to truth independent of them. Hence when the incarnate Son is said to be the image of the Father, and the Holy Spirit is spoken of as the image of Christ, stress is laid upon a wholly spiritual way of understanding the consubstantial relation of the incarnate Son to the Father and of all hypostatic relations in God, which cuts away the arguments advanced by the Arians in reading back the images of creaturely sonship and fatherhood into God.

Of particular significance is the deepening of the Nicene conception of $οὐσία$ through its coordination with the divine "I am who I am/I shall be who I shall be", on the one hand, and with the co-inherence of the three Persons in the unity of the Godhead, on the other hand. The effect of this is to give the term οὐσία a personal meaning under the impact of divine revelation, and to develop the understanding of οὐσία as being in its internal relations along with ὑπόστασις as being in its objective relations. Thus ὑπόστασις is used to denote the three divine Persons in the distinctive otherness of their relations with one another within the oneness of the οὐσία of the Godhead. The words for "face" (πρόσωπον) and "name" are also allied to ὑπόστασις which has the effect of giving it the meaning of self-identifying personal being. It was through this unique coordination of the concepts of οὐσία and ὑπόστασις together with the co-inherent relations of the divine hypostases who are the consubstantial Trinity, that birth was given to the concept of "person" and of "personal" unknown before in the ancient tradition of either the Hebrews or the Greeks. The relations between persons are integral to what persons are – which holds in an uncreated way in the Trinity and in a creaturely way in human being. It is in this sense, not in a subjective or psychological sense, that the statement on the Holy Trinity uses the terms "person" and "personal".

The monarchy

Of far-reaching importance is the stress laid upon the monarchy of the Godhead in which all three divine Persons share, for the whole indivisible Being of God belongs to each of them as it belongs to all of them together. This is reinforced by the unique conception of co-inherent or perichoretic relations between the different Persons in which they completely contain and interpenetrate one another while remaining what they distinctively are in their otherness as Father, Son and Holy Spirit. God is intrinsically triune, Trinity in unity and unity in Trinity. There are no degrees of deity in the Holy Trinity, as is implied in a distinction between the underived deity of the Father and the derived deity of the Son and the Spirit. Any notion of subordination in God is completely ruled out. The perfect simplicity and the indivisibility of God in his triune Being mean that the ἀρχη or μοναρκία cannot be limited to one Person, as Gregory the Theologian pointed out. While there are inviolable distinctions within the Holy Trinity, this does not detract from the truth that the whole Being of God belongs to each divine Person as it belongs to all of them and belongs to all of them as it belongs to each of them, and thus does not detract from the truth that the monarchy is One and indivisible, the Trinity in unity and the unity in Trinity.

The doctrine of the monarchy that is not limited to one Person, and the doctrine of the περιχωρησι of the three divine Persons, or their reciprocal containing of one another, when taken together, may help towards a fuller understanding of the mission of the Holy Spirit from the Father and gift of the Holy Spirit by the Son. As the agreed statement says: "The Holy Spirit proceeds from the Father, but because of the unity of the Godhead in which each Person is perfectly and wholly God, he proceeds from the Father through the Son for the Spirit belongs to and is inseparable from the Being of the Father and of the Son." A further study in depth of this procession might help us to find ways of cutting behind the division between the East and the West over the so-called "filioque", for it does not allow of any idea of the procession of the Spirit from two ultimate principles or ἀρχαί.

Ecumenical significance

The statement on the Holy Trinity is thus of considerable ecumenical significance in offering an approach to the doctrine of the Trinity which is neither from the three

Persons to the one Being of God, nor from the one Being of God to the three Persons. The account of the Trinity given by the statement stresses at one and the same time the Trinity and the unity of God, through guidance taken mostly from Athanasius and Gregory the Theologian. As such, it cuts across mistaken polarized views of the doctrine of the Holy Trinity according to which Latin theology moves from the oneness of God to the three Persons of the Father, the Son and the Holy Spirit, while Greek theology moves from the three Persons of the Father, the Son and the Holy Spirit to the oneness of God. What is provided by the agreed statement of the Orthodox theologians in the East and the Reformed theologians in the West is pre-eminently a statement on the tri-unity of God as Trinity in unity and unity in Trinity.

29. Agreed Statement on Christology

Limassol, Cyprus, January 1994

1. In accordance with the Nicene Creed we affirm the basic interconnection between the doctrine of the Trinity and the doctrine of Christ. Our common belief in one God, the Holy Trinity of the Father, the Son and the Holy Spirit is bound up with our belief in Jesus Christ who reveals the mystery of the Holy Trinity. It affirms that the God of the Old Testament scriptures who led his people Israel from oppression to new shores of freedom is the Father of Jesus of Nazareth who sends forth his life-giving Spirit. He is one and the same God who encounters us in the resurrected Christ and in the Holy Spirit acting in his church.

As regards the connection between the doctrine of the Trinity and the doctrine of the incarnation, Orthodox and Reformed seem to follow two different kinds of approach which, however, are not incompatible. The Orthodox approach takes its beginning in the mystery of the incarnation which includes the whole saving economy as it is proclaimed in the Bible, confessed in the patristic tradition and experienced in the divine liturgy. The starting point of the Reformed approach to Christology and the mystery of the Trinity is the scriptural witness to the life, death and resurrection of Jesus of Nazareth. Both agree that their teaching about Trinity and incarnation reflects the encounter with the reality of God as revealed in Christ.

2. Following the witness of the gospel as it is declared in the second article of the Nicene Creed, Orthodox and Reformed confess that Jesus Christ is the eternal and only-begotten Son and Logos of God, the second Person of the Holy Trinity, who became fully human, without ceasing to be God, by being conceived by the Holy Spirit and born of the Virgin Mary. Both confess the apostolic faith that the incarnation took place in the fullness of time, when God "sent his own Son to be born of a woman under the law to redeem those under the law and grant to us adoption as children" (Gal. 4:4-5). Thus understood, the incarnate Son is the manifestation of the Holy Trinity in the sphere of earthly human history. The incarnate Son as a concrete historical person demonstrates that human nature is not fundamentally foreign to God. It reveals rather what was hidden in the primordial nature of the Logos. Through the incarnation the life of God is manifested under the conditions of human existence. God assumes the human condition and nature in all their aspects and dimensions. All this takes place for us human beings and for our salvation, so that we may become participants in the "treasures of wisdom and knowledge" (Col. 2:3) hidden in Christ.

3. The incarnation of the Son of God belongs to the very same existence and life of God. As the divine will to create the world and humanity is connected with God's

being, so also the will to save them was "a mystery hidden before the ages in God who created all things" (Eph. 3:9). Creation and incarnation, then, belong together to God's original plan. Thus, Christ's redemptive work "was predestined before the foundation of the world, but was manifested in the end of time" (1 Pet. 1:20). Being the Head of all creation by whom all things were formed, the Son who was by nature eternally of the same uncreated nature with the Father and the Spirit, received to himself the created human nature and became fully human in body and soul so that through it he might unite himself with the entire creation.

4. In the language of the fathers and the councils of the early church, Jesus Christ as the incarnate Son of God unites human and divine natures in his own single person (*hypostasis*). The properties of each nature belong to the whole person in whom both natures are united without being confused or separated. So Jesus Christ acts both as divine and as human, exercising both kinds of properties as appropriate in communion with each other. In this sense there is a "communication of attributes" within the hypostatic union as the divine nature acts through the human and the human under the guidance of the divine. Strictly speaking, however, it is to the *person* of Jesus Christ as the incarnate Word that the properties of both natures are correctly ascribed. The distinct properties of the one nature are not transferred to the other *nature*: the divine nature does not acquire human characteristics nor the human nature divine attributes. What can be said is that through the *perichoresis* or interpenetration of the two natures in the unity of Christ's person the human nature is restored, sustained and glorified as the *new and perfect humanity* of the last Adam, recapitulating the history of the first Adam. In the Orthodox tradition this is called *theosis* (commonly rendered as "deification"), but this does not imply that Christ's humanity ceases to be creaturely or becomes divine in essence. Reformed theology shares this understanding but avoids the language of *theosis*. It treats the theme more in terms of the *sanctification* of human nature in Christ. In both traditions this renewal of our common humanity in the person of the incarnate Word is affirmed and venerated as the decisive saving action of divine grace and the pledge of the renewal and restoration of all who are united to Christ as members of the body of which he is the Head.

Speaking of the union of natures in the person of Jesus Christ is normative for both the Orthodox and Reformed traditions. However, the term "nature" should not be understood statically, or abstractly, nor as if the human and divine natures were two individual instances of a generic concept of "nature". What this language directs us towards is the reality of God assuming the reality of humanity in Jesus Christ, a movement of God to humanity and humanity to God in the unity of his person and history.

The divergent conclusions drawn by the Orthodox and Reformed traditions on the subject of iconography is a subject related to the above statement which might well form a point of entry for discussion at a future dialogue.

5. According to the Nicene Creed it was "for us and for our salvation" that the eternal Son of God became flesh, lived, died and rose again. The ontological ground of our salvation is the hypostatic or personal union of the Word and flesh, or divine and human natures, in Jesus Christ. Conversely, the hypostatic union is worked out in the economy of salvation. The New Testament presents this economy in terms of the three offices (*triplex munus*) of prophet, priest and king. This threefold office continues its activity in the church. Each of these offices provides a particular model – witness, sacrifice, service – for the restoration of the divine image in humanity through participa-

tion in Christ. At the same time each office points us to the deity of Christ who is eternal Word, Son and wisdom of God. All three offices thus show the unity of true historical humanity and true eternal deity in the person of Jesus Christ, and also how the divine calling should be exercised in all aspects of our lives from birth to death.

6. The Holy Trinity is presupposed by the incarnation, but the incarnation enables us to approach the Trinity at a deeper level. The incarnation shows us, as nothing else, the nature and path, the range and depth of God's love. It shows us that God, though complete in himself in the loving fellowship of Father, Son and Holy Spirit, loved us so much that he sent his only-begotten Son to enter and redeem his creation. The creation is not part of the eternal nature of God. We understand it to be a deliberate act of God that he might share that love which he is with that which he is not. Creation is then rooted in the mutual love of the persons of the triune God. Thus understood the incarnation is the key which opens to us the intention, plan, meaning and goal of the creation. In the incarnation of the Son the purpose of creation is fully revealed. The Spirit acting in Christ penetrates the *cosmos*. The Spirit groans with all creatures and leads them to the promised goal of their perfection. This is why the relationship between the world and God receives its true form in the incarnate son; from the incarnation it obtains its direction and identity. "In him all things have their being" (Col. 1:17).

In Christ we understand that God cannot bear to be absent from his creation and through his Spirit constantly strives to bring it to share his freedom and joy. As the community of the redeemed, set free by the incarnation of the eternal Son, we are caught up in that love, trust and freedom. We see the teeming creation with new eyes as God's bountiful world. We are summoned to share his purpose, to be liberated, healed and restored, to celebrate and rejoice, to worship and share creation's praise for its maker.

7. The understanding common to Orthodox and Reformed of the revelation of the three persons of the Trinity makes them crucially aware of the connection between Christology and pneumatology and of the specific role of the Holy Spirit in the incarnation of the Word of God and in the history of salvation. Both Orthodox and Reformed recognize the Spirit's creative activity in the birth of Christ from the Virgin Mary as the first-fruits of the new creation. It is the Holy Spirit who glorifies Christ and through his sending at Pentecost bears witness to Christ in the world. It is the Holy Spirit who brings about the communion of all believers both with the head of the body of Christ and between themselves. It is the Holy Spirit who summons all Christians to the confession of the same Christ and communicates to us the very life of Christ through word and sacrament. It is the Holy Spirit who unites word and sacrament in the living experience of the church and leads the church to the realization of the kingdom of God in the eschaton. It is the Holy Spirit who enables us to discern the authentic relationship between the paschal and the pentecostal mysteries in the history of salvation, because "one can say Jesus is Lord, except in the Holy Spirit" (1 Cor. 12:3).

XV. REFORMED-ORIENTAL ORTHODOX DIALOGUE

Historical Introduction

The Oriental Orthodox churches – Coptic, Syrian, Armenian, Ethiopian and (Indian) Malankara – and the Reformed churches have been in dialogue over the years in the context of the World Council of Churches, and in many parts of the world they live side by side. In 1991, through the initiative of the World Alliance of Reformed Churches, the five Oriental Orthodox churches showed their openness to enter into a bilateral dialogue.

Planning began in August 1992 and the first meeting was co-chaired by Dr Milan Opocensky, general secretary of the World Alliance, and Pope Shenouda III, pope and patriarch of Alexandria. Dialogue sessions were held in Wadi-El-Natroun, Egypt, in 1993, Driebergen, Holland, in 1994, Kottayam, India, in 1997, Richmond, Virginia, USA, in 1998, and Damascus, Syria, in 1999.

The highlight of the dialogue to date is the 1994 "Agreed Statement on Christology" and the 1998 "Draft Common Statement" summarizing the elements of discussion to that date. Numerous papers were presented explaining the two traditions to one another and outlining the theological background for the agreements reached and the issues to be treated in the future (H.S. Wilson, ed., *Oriental Orthodox-Reformed Dialogue: The First Four Sessions*, Geneva, WARC, 1998).

Jeffrey Gros

30. Agreed Statement on Christology

Driebergen, Netherlands, 13 September 1994

Introduction
In our search for a common understanding of differences in Christology that have existed between us, we have thought it appropriate to focus upon the formula of union, AD 433. This formula represents an agreement reached by Antioch and Alexandria following the third ecumenical council in 431 and, as such, provides a common point of departure for both parties. We find the interpretations in this agreement to be in accord with the christological doctrines in both of our traditions.

Agreed statement
"We confess our Lord Jesus Christ, the only-begotten Son of God, perfect in divinity and perfect in humanity, consisting of a rational soul and a body, begotten of the Father before the ages according to his divinity, the Same, in the fullness of time, for us and for our salvation, born of the Virgin Mary, according to his humanity; the Same consubstantial with the Father according to his divinity, and consubstantial with us according to his humanity. For a union has been made of two natures. For this cause we confess one Christ, one Son, one Lord.

"In accordance with this sense of the unconfused union, we confess the holy Virgin to be Theotokos, because God the Word became incarnate and was made human, and from the very conception united to himself the temple taken from her. As to the expressions concerning the Lord in the gospels and epistles, we are aware that theologians understand some as common, as relating to one Person, and others they distinguish, as relating to two natures, explaining those that befit the divine nature according to the divinity of Christ, and those of a humble sort according to his humanity" [based on the formula of union, AD 433]

The four adverbs used to qualify the mystery of the hypostatic union belong to our common christological tradition: "without commingling" (or confusion) (*asyngchtos*), "without change" (*atreptos*), "without separation" (*achoristos*), and "without division" (*adiairetos*). Those among us who speak of two natures in Christ are justified in doing so since they do not thereby deny their inseparable indivisible union; similarly, those among us who speak of one united divine-human nature in Christ are justified in doing so since they do not thereby deny the continuing dynamic presence in Christ of the divine and the human, without change, without confusion.

Both sides agree in rejecting the teaching which separates or divides the human nature, both soul and body in Christ, from his divine nature or reduced the union of the natures to the level of conjoining. Both sides also agree in rejecting the teaching which confuses the human nature in Christ with the divine nature so that the former is absorbed in the latter and thus ceases to exist.

The perfect union of divinity and of humanity in the incarnate Word is essential for the salvation of the human race. "For God so loved the world, that he gave his only begotten Son, that whosoever believeth in him should not perish, but have everlasting life" (John 3:16 KJV).

Conclusion

In offering this statement, we recognize the mystery of God's act in Christ and seek to express that we have shared the same authentic christological faith in the one incarnate Lord.

We submit this statement to the authorities of the Oriental Orthodox churches and to the executive committee of the World Alliance of Reformed Churches for their consideration and action.

His Grace Metropolitan Bishoy
General Secretary of the Holy Synod
of the Coptic Orthodox Church
Co-chairman

Rev. Dr Milan Opocensky
General Secretary of the World
Alliance of Reformed Churches
Co-chairman

Areas of emerging convergence on holy scripture and Tradition

Both sides acknowledge the deep relationship between the early traditions (the total life) of the church, as guided by the Holy Spirit, and the emergence of written holy scripture. The incarnate word of God is both the source and the judge of the tradition and the holy scripture of the church which bear witness to him.

The Oriental Orthodox distinguish the Tradition of the entire church regarding matters of faith from local traditions of the various churches. They understand both Tradition and holy scripture as constituting one reality emerging from the continuing life of the church. Tradition must be essentially in agreement with the intention of holy scripture, and the authority of the fathers of the church is recognized from their acceptance by the church as a whole. The Reformed side respects this understanding.

The Reformed churches affirm the critical distance of holy scripture in relation to tradition. The church must always examine and reform their traditions in the light of holy scripture. The Oriental Orthodox side respects this emphasis.

Both sides agreed on the normative function of holy scripture for the life of the church. The Word incarnate makes use of human means, including human language and culture. So holy scripture and its correct interpretation, guided by Tradition, witnesses to the word of God in our different contexts.

Areas that need further clarification:
1) our concepts of history and revelation;
2) methods of interpreting holy scripture and evaluating tradition;
3) how do our historical contexts affect our understandings of holy scripture?
4) the question of canonical books in our respective traditions.

Suggested topics for future meetings:
1) understandings of holy scripture and its inspiration in our respective traditions;
2) the function of theological reflection and the work of theologians in our traditions;

3) understandings of revelation and history;
4) the work of the Holy Spirit in the early church: the question of the normative status of the early church for our respective traditions;
5) holy scripture and tradition and how they are correlated: (a) what do we mean by "Tradition?" (b) results from previous ecumenical meetings, e.g. at Montreal; see the book edited by Ellen Flesseman-van Leer;
6) the role of the present historical context in the interpretation of holy scripture – the hermeneutical problem;
7) introduction to liturgical practices of the Oriental Orthodox church on the premises of our next meeting;
8) our views on the sacraments and the ministry of the church (for a later meeting).

31. Report of the Bilateral Conversation 1994-1998
Cartigny, Switzerland, 15 May 1998

Preamble

While the *Seventh-day Adventist Church* (SDA) with its 10 million members is a comparatively strong Christian denomination, it is extraordinary in its worldwide missionary thrust. Rooted in more than 200 countries, the SDA Church is today the most widespread Protestant denomination. The 19th-century origins of the church were marked by the strong expectation of the second coming of Christ. The Adventist teachings concerning the sabbath and the second coming have, in spite of their strong biblical foundations, traditionally created a distance between the SDA and other Christian denominations. Today the SDA, while maintaining its distinctive emphases, welcomes opportunities for fellowship, meeting human needs, and exchange of viewpoints with other Christians.

Born as the first-fruits of the 16th-century German Reformation, the *Lutheran churches* are today present in all continents. The Lutheran World Federation (LWF), a worldwide communion of Lutheran churches, comprises with its 124 member churches and nearly 58 million members more than 95 percent of today's Lutheranism. In Northern Europe Lutheran churches are still regarded as national or "folk" churches. Lutheran concentration is likewise strong in Germany and in some parts of North America. Strong Lutheran churches are also found in many parts of Africa and, to a lesser extent, in Asia and South America. For the most part Lutherans have been active in the ecumenical movement.

During the last decades, the officers of the LWF and the SDA have met regularly in meetings of the secretaries of the Christian world communions. As a result of these contacts and also because Adventists recognize their Reformation heritage, the idea arose of a joint theological consultation in order to achieve a better mutual understanding. This proposal was approved in 1993 by leaders of the general conference of SDA and the LWF council.

The initial consultation was held 1-5 November 1994 in Darmstadt, Germany. It defined the following as its goals:
- achieve better mutual understanding;
- break down false stereotypes;
- discover the bases of belief;
- discover points of real and imaginary friction.

The discussions in Darmstadt were open, frank and friendly. It quickly became clear that the strong appreciation among the SDA theologians for the work of Martin

Luther formed a natural starting point for the interchange. The experience of worshipping together also led to a sense of deep spiritual fellowship. By the end of the consultation participants felt that an excellent beginning had been made on all of the goals set for the gathering. Both Lutheran and SDA representatives were in agreement that further discussion, building on this beginning, would be a very positive step for both churches.

To that end the members of the consultation recommended to both the SDA and the LWF that three further consultations be held between 1996 and 1998. The proposal for the themes of these three meetings was as follows:
- first session: justification by faith; the law; law and gospel
- second session: ecclesiology and the understanding of church authority
- third session: eschatology

This proposal was approved by both world communions. The objectives of the conversations were to remain the same as in Darmstadt. The report from the Darmstadt meeting explained the reasons for selecting the three topics:

1. The doctrine of justification by grace through faith alone is central to both Lutherans and Adventists. A discussion of this central tenet seems a good place to begin theological reflection. In the same way, the understanding of law and gospel is one of the defining doctrines of Lutheranism. Adventists, on the other hand, have often been called legalistic because of the central place they give to law and obedience as the logical result of their stress on justification. A careful discussion of these issues, including sabbath/Sunday observance, would be a good foundational starting-point for further theological exploration.

2. The SDA Church has frequently been designated as a "sect". Where it fits in the spectrum of Christian churches needs to be explored. A thorough look at the Adventists' self-understanding as a church with a view to determining the extent to which they see themselves as part of the worldwide Christian church or as a special movement apart from it is important. To this end a discussion of both SDA and Lutheran understanding of the church and authority is essential. Included should be the understanding of the role of the confessions for Lutherans, and the writings of Ellen G. White for Adventists.

3. In view of the extensive biblical witness to eschatology and the current interest in the topic, we need to explore whether the Lutheran eschatology is too indefinite and whether the Adventist eschatology is too definite. The SDA fundamental belief concerning the "remnant" and the theological terms such as "Babylon" and "mark of the beast" shall be included in this study. Furthermore, the SDA views of the heavenly sanctuary and the preadvent judgment need to be discussed in the wider context of the once-for-all atonement at the cross and Christ's high priestly activity.

The issues of the *first thematic session* were discussed in a consultation held in Mississauga near Toronto, Canada, 17-21 June 1996. On the basis of several background papers and extensive discussions a common statement (ch. I below) was drafted and approved. Delegations had been appointed by the respective world communions. The Lutheran delegation was chaired by Faith Rohrbough (USA and Canada), and the Adventist delegation by Bert B. Beach (USA).

The same style of work was continued in the *next meeting* held in Jongny, Switzerland, 1-6 June 1997, in which the second thematic part was drafted, discussed and approved (ch. II below). Furthermore, a small drafting group was appointed which met at Silver Spring, USA, 29-30 October 1997, in order to prepare for the last consultation and the resulting publication.

The *final consultation* was held in Cartigny, Switzerland, 10-16 May 1998. It completed work on the common statement (ch. III below), and made *recommendations* (after ch. III below) for the future life of our churches. The Cartigny meeting was also visited by the president of the SDA, Dr Robert S. Folkenberg, and the general secretary of the LWF, Dr Ishmael Noko. The consultation closed with an Adventist worship service at Collonges, France, on 16 May.

We came together in 1994 as strangers, we parted in 1998 as friends. We came with questions, we parted with appreciation. While significant doctrinal differences remain, we found much in common: a love for the word of God, a shared heritage from the Reformation, a deep appreciation for the work and teachings of Martin Luther, a concern for religious freedom and, above all, the gospel of justification by grace through faith alone. By spending many hours together in listening and seeking to understand, in agreeing and disagreeing, in eating and especially praying, we experienced the bonding of the Spirit under our one Lord Jesus Christ. Each of us who was given the opportunity to be part of these common conversations feels enriched intellectually and spiritually by this adventure of faith, and we give thanks to our God from whom all blessings flow.

I

Justification by faith

Both Lutherans and Adventists teach that justification is the work of God in Christ and comes through faith alone. We are justified by the grace of God and not by our own works. The Lutheran Augsburg confession (CA, art. IV) holds that "we cannot obtain forgiveness of sin and righteousness before God by our own merits, works, or satisfactions, but that we receive forgiveness of sin and become righteous before God by grace, for Christ's sake, through faith..." According to the 10th Fundamental Belief (FB) of the Seventh-day Adventists, we "exercise faith in Jesus as Lord and Christ, as Substitute and Example. This faith which receives salvation comes through the divine power of the word and is the gift of God's grace. Through Christ we are justified, adopted as God's sons and daughters, and delivered from the lordship of sin."

During our conversations it has become obvious that both Lutherans and Adventists unconditionally affirm the inter-related principles of the Reformation: sola scriptura, solus Christus, sola fide, sola gratia. Both churches regard themselves as heirs of the Protestant Reformation and as children of Luther. This shared understanding of justification by faith gives us today the possibility to say that both churches teach salvation in an essentially congruent manner. This understanding is founded on the biblical truth: "For we hold that a person is justified by faith apart from works prescribed by the law" (Rom. 3:28 NRSV). Both Lutherans (CA IV) and Adventists (FB 10) refer to Romans 3:21-26 as foundational for their teaching.

Different confessional emphases concerning salvation do exist, but in the light of this shared understanding they need not be incompatible. Lutherans have traditionally understood the correct teaching on justification by faith as the criterion of all other central issues of belief. Adventists do not speak of a criterion but put the notions of righteousness and justification in the wider context of the experience of salvation. But nevertheless salvation in Christ and justification by faith alone are at the heart of Adventism also.

Further, Adventists teach: "Salvation is all of grace and not of works, but its fruitage is obedience to the commandments" (FB 18). Lutherans also teach the "new obedience", i.e., that "faith should produce good fruits and good works and that we must do all such good works as God has commanded" (CA VI). However, as the Augsburg confession immediately continues, "we should do them for God's sake and not place our trust in them as if thereby to merit favour before God". Both sides agree in that they do not speak of good works as requirements or merits but as fruits. Adventists call these works "an evidence of our love for the Lord" (FB 18); Lutherans customarily refer to the "new obedience". A special Adventist emphasis on the commandments can here be found, whereas the Lutherans have a special stress on the freedom of the Christian. But since both churches speak of obedience and fruits instead of requirements and merits, we agree that neither side teaches a justification by works of the law.

Both churches understand justification as God's gracious declaration of the forgiveness of sins for the sake of Jesus Christ, crucified and risen, and at the same time as the free gift of new life in him. Justification in the full sense of the word consists in the fundamental imputation of God's righteousness for the sake of Jesus Christ and in the indwelling of Christ in the heart of the repentant believer. This "gift of new life" or "indwelling of Christ" can be called sanctification; although it can thus be conceptually distinguished from the fundamental declaration of the forgiveness of sins, these two aspects of justification are inseparable in the believer's experience.

Both Lutherans and Adventists characterize the new life or the sanctifying aspect of justification as the indwelling of Christ or as new life in the Spirit. Lutherans tend to understand this new life essentially as receiving the Holy Spirit in the word and sacraments of the church, thus following Luther's exposition of the Apostles' Creed in his Large Catechism: "The Holy Spirit effects our sanctification through the following: the communion of saints or Christian church, the forgiveness of sins, the resurrection of the body, and the life everlasting." Adventists describe sanctification in a slightly more immediate manner: "Through the Spirit we are born again and sanctified; the Spirit renews our minds, writes God's law of love in our hearts, and we become partakers of the divine nature and have the assurance of salvation now and in the judgment" (FB 10).

In spite of these emphases both churches agree that this new life "in Christ" or "in the Spirit" is not something which comes through one's own strength or effort. The new life is a transforming gift of God; and precisely for this reason it is a life in Christ or in the Spirit, not a life centred around ourselves. As a safeguard against perfectionism, Adventists teach that the new life does not exclude the possibility of sinning, while Lutheran tradition stresses that even as justified the believing person remains a sinner.

In the light of this mutual understanding we can say that both Lutherans and Adventists can hear a truly biblical witness in each other's proclamation. Lutherans can say this on the basis of their traditional criterion for accepting other Christians by determining whether they preach the gospel "with a pure understanding of it" (CA VII). Affirming this convergence in the central Christian message of justification by faith alone can be regarded as an important milestone in breaking down false stereotypes between our churches and in building up relations which allow us conscientious cooperation in some areas of Christian witness and service.

We are aware that justification of the sinner is a living reality that should shape our whole Christian experience here and now. This Christian life is a life in the Spirit and by the Spirit (Gal. 5:16-25). At the same time it is a life of faith, a life in which Christ's kingdom is hidden under the cross: "... it is no longer I who live, but it is Christ who lives in me. And the life I now live in the flesh I live by faith in the Son of God, who loved me and gave himself for me" (Gal. 2:20).

The law
Our conversations concerning the law reveal four areas of note. In these Lutherans and SDAs have significant agreement, as well as differing nuances and emphases, and some divergences.

1. Both Lutherans and SDAs categorically affirm that justification rests wholly on the grace of God, so that keeping of the law cannot bring merit or contribute to salvation. Obeying the law must be understood as the result of, and response to, God's free gift of salvation. On this point Lutherans and SDAs are in complete agreement.

2. Lutherans and SDAs recognize the importance of the ten commandments, but the connotations of law differ in each communion.

Adventist concern for the law is demonstrated as follows: "The great principles of God's law are embodied in the ten commandments and exemplified in the life of Christ. They express God's love, will and purposes concerning human conduct and relationships and are binding upon all people in every age. These precepts are the basis of God's covenant with his people and the standard in God's judgment. Through the agency of the Holy Spirit they point out sin and awaken a sense of need for a Saviour. Salvation is all of grace and not of works, but its fruitage is obedience to the commandments. This obedience develops Christian character and results in a sense of well-being. It is an evidence of our love for the Lord and our concern for our fellow men. The obedience of faith demonstrates the power of Christ to transform lives, and therefore strengthens Christian witness" (FB 18).

Lutherans' appreciation for the ten commandments is shown by Luther's exposition of them in both of his catechisms. In Lutheran families, congregations and schools they have always been an essential ingredient of religious instruction. In this larger context of instruction Lutherans see the commandments as providing valuable principles for Christian life.

The connotations of law, however, differ significantly between Lutherans and Seventh-day Adventists. For Lutherans "law" has a wider reference than the decalogue and can be a negative term contrasting with grace. Lutherans tend to be careful in regard to the so-called didactic use of the law, i.e., law as a guide for the Christian life. While affirming the validity of the content of the ten commandments and the necessity of the "new obedience" for Christians, Lutherans at the same time also want to affirm Christian freedom. Lutherans consistently see the law in the context of law and gospel, with the over-riding concern to protect justification as sola gratia and sola fide. In this emphasis Lutherans reflect the apostle Paul's concerns in Romans and Galatians, and also the roots of their communion in the Reformation.

Adventists, however, see the law in a more positive context. They tend to view the law in terms of God's revealed will focused in the giving of the ten commandments in the Old Testament and the ongoing role of law in the New Testament. By this emphasis Adventists reflect their concern to show the perpetuity of the ten commandments and obedience to them as the fruit of sanctification.

3. Lutherans and Adventists agree that the life of the justified person will be demonstrated by deeds of faith. The Holy Spirit brings forth "fruit" to God's glory (Gal. 5:22-23) in a spontaneous manner that cannot be reduced to a written code.

Adventist concern for deeds of faith is shown in FB 18 (quoted above). Lutheran concern for deeds of faith is reflected e.g. in CA XX: "Our teachers have been falsely accused of forbidding good works. Their writings on the ten commandments, and other writings as well, show that they have given good and profitable accounts and instructions concerning true Christian estates and works... It is also taught among us that good works should and must be done, not that we are to rely on them to earn grace but that we may do God's will and glorify him. It is always faith alone that apprehends grace and forgiveness of sin. When through faith the Holy Spirit is given, the heart is moved to do good works."

SDAs see the ten commandments as playing a greater role in deeds of faith. Adventists understand the new life in Christ, sanctification, to be a spiritual, lived expression of the principles of the law (Rom. 8:1-3), in which love to God and love to fellow humans is the ruling motivation. For Adventists, the law provides a framework for the life of love.

Both communions teach the doctrine of the final judgment (Lutherans: CA XVII; SDAs: FB 10,23), although SDAs place more emphasis on this belief. While both Lutherans and SDAs agree that the Christian's works come under review in the judgment (cf. Acts 17:31; Rom. 14:10; 2 Cor. 5:10), both parties hold that it is the Christian's standing in Christ (justification) that alone gives hope.

4. Both communions take seriously the third/fourth commandment. However, the practical conclusions drawn from this commandment diverge.

Lutherans keep, following the traditional practice of the Christian church, the holy day on the day of resurrection, the first day of the week. In Lutheran proclamation and piety Sunday has always been understood as a day of rest and worship. In fact Sunday has for Lutherans appropriated much of the function of sabbath (see Luther's Large and Small Catechisms).

Adventists see the sabbath as an essential part of the divine design in creation. The third/fourth commandment of the Decalogue returns human beings to this truth, leading them to treat sabbath observance as a vital element in the expression of loving obedience to God as Creator and Redeemer. For Adventists sabbath-keeping is neither a meritorious work nor something that makes them alone God's people; rather it is a grateful acceptance of a divine gift. Adventists do not claim that only sabbath-keepers can be saved. They acknowledge that Lutherans in their observation of Sunday will appeal to biblical arguments as well as to ancient Christian tradition; however, they hold firm to their conviction that the scriptures, both Old and New Testaments, call us to observe the seventh day as the sabbath. Nevertheless Adventists recognize that great servants of God have sincerely kept Sunday in honour of their Lord's resurrection throughout the Christian era.

For Lutherans, their practice is based on the apostle Paul's teaching of the role of law in the life of Gentile Christians. In Christ, Christians are not under the law in the same manner as the Jews, and the law is seen from the perspective of Christian freedom. Paul opposes all attempts to impose the Jewish law on the Gentile Christians. These Pauline guidelines have shaped the understanding of the third/fourth commandment from the early church to the Reformation. Today, Christ's resurrection on the one hand shapes the Lutheran view of Sunday. On the other hand, Paul's acceptance of the Jewish Christians who keep the law also calls Lutherans to respect the Adventist view.

II

Scripture and authority in the church

Both Lutherans and Adventists look to scripture as the foundation of church authority. The Reformation principle of sola scriptura lies at the heart of both communions, with scripture as the basis for their respective proclamation.

Lutherans have an organic concept of authority, as authority is exercised through the ministry of word and sacrament. In this organic understanding, the gospel is the essence of authority; scripture its documented basis; the sacraments its external signs; synods, other ecclesial bodies and the ordained ministers its public bearers; and the Spirit its acting agent. For Adventists, the authority Christ delegates to his church is diffused through the whole body. All teachings, practices and decisions are accountable to the word of God. The article on the holy scriptures appears as the first in the Fundamental Beliefs of the church and reads in part: "The holy scriptures are the infallible revelation of his [God's] will. They are the standard of his character, the test of experience, the authoritative revealer of doctrines, and the trustworthy record of God's acts in history."

In both confessions, Christ alone is the head of the church. All aspects of ministry are derived from him, including the priesthood of all believers and the delegated authority of ordained ministers. The authority structures of the church differ from Lutherans to Adventists: Lutheran church structures are more diverse, corresponding to the history and cultural contexts of the churches; the Adventist church, although present in many countries, has an essentially unified structure.

While both Lutherans and Adventists affirm scripture as the foundation of all authority, their respective approaches to scripture differ in significant aspects. For Lutherans, the gospel understood as unmerited justification is the organic centre of scripture; it is the hermeneutical key to the study and interpretation of scripture. Adventists look to the totality of scripture, seeking to find Christ as the centre and the New Testament as the summit of scripture. Further, in their study Adventists tend to seek explicit biblical proofs, whereas Lutherans leave more room for what is not explicitly stated (e.g. Sunday observance). Thus, Adventists, while alert to the historical background of the biblical writings, apply scripture more directly to life today. Lutherans tend to relate specific passages to the total message of scripture and also give particular attention to the changed conditions of today's world.

Both Lutherans and Adventists hold to the Bible as the decisive norm – *norma normans* – but both assign authority to other documents as the derived norm – *norma normata*. The churches of the Lutheran Reformation adhere to five credal or confessional documents – the ancient creeds (Apostolicum, Nicaenum, Athanasium), the Augsburg confession, and Luther's Small Catechism. The Apostolic and Nicene Creeds have a natural place in the liturgy of the Lutheran churches, Luther's Small Catechism is used in general Christian education, and the Augsburg confession has its primary role in theological training and orientation.

Adventists affirm the biblical content of the ancient creeds. Furthermore, their Fundamental Beliefs explicitly confess belief in the Trinity (FB 2-5).

Although Adventists do not look to confessional documents, they place high value on the writings of Ellen G. White, in whom they believe the biblical gift of prophecy was manifested. Her work consisted principally in counselling the church and providing spiritual nurture. Adventists regard her writings as "a continuing and authoritative source of truth, which provide for the church comfort, guidance, instruction and correction" (FB 17). Ellen G. White's authority is a derived authority: she firmly endorsed the sola scriptura principle, and Adventists test her writings by the scripture.

Thus, Lutherans and Adventists differ widely in their approach to scripture, authority structures of the church and authoritative documents outside of scripture. However, both communions have the same essential source of authority at the core – the holy scriptures.

Ecclesiology

Both Adventists and Lutherans understand the church as community of believers. The church exists in historical continuity from biblical times to our days.

Adventists hold that: "The church is the community of believers who confess Jesus Christ as Lord and Saviour. In continuity with the people of God in Old Testament times, we are called out from the world" (FB 11).

Lutheran confessions state that: "One holy Christian church will be and remain forever. This is the assembly of all believers among whom the gospel is preached in its purity and the holy sacraments are administered according to the gospel" (CA VII).

Even though Lutherans nowadays seldom speak of the church in the Old Testament, this way of speaking also belongs to the tradition of Lutheran confessions (e.g. Apol. VII, 14-19; XXVII, 98). The roots of the Christian church are found in Old Testament times and the Christian church manifests God's new covenant with God's people. The principle of continuity within this community of believers is thus for both churches of great importance.

As CA 7 points out, Lutherans identify the Christian church through the so-called marks of the church which are the gospel and the two sacraments: baptism and the Lord's supper. Adventists also regard parallel marks as important for the life of the church: "We join together for worship, for fellowship, for instruction in the word, for the celebration of the Lord's supper, for service to all mankind, and for the worldwide proclamation of the gospel" (FB 11).

Both communions affirm that the proclamation of the gospel, worship life, personal prayer, participation at the Lord's supper and service for the world are central elements of each Christian's life in the church. These features also make the church a living Christian communion, a community of believers.

Together we affirm the biblical descriptions of the church as people of God, as body of Christ and as temple of Holy Spirit. The Christian church is neither a static entity nor a merely external organization: it is an assembly of believers, a spiritual community, God's holy people who expect the coming of their Lord Christ. In the church Christians confess Jesus Christ as Saviour and Lord, look forward to his coming kingdom and proclaim the gospel message to all the world. Recognition of this mission is essential for the self-understanding of the church.

We thus share a basic understanding of the church in biblical terms. We agree that the word of God, the gospel message of Jesus Christ should always be at the centre of our understanding of the essence and tasks of the church.

An important aspect of how Adventists and Lutherans evaluate each other as churches concerns our views regarding baptism and the Lord's supper. For Lutherans, it is sufficient for the true unity of the church to agree concerning the teaching of the gospel and the administration of the sacraments (CA VII). These two sacraments are thus for Lutherans of decisive significance in the identification of the church. For Adventists, the ordinances of baptism and the Lord's supper are important but do not have the same relative significance in ecclesiology as they do for the Lutherans.

This does not mean, however, that the Adventists would downplay the role of baptism and the Lord's supper as such. In their Fundamental Beliefs the articles on these two ordinances (FB 14-15) immediately follow the articles (FB 1113) on the church. As a part of Protestant Christianity, Adventists reflect many aspects of Reformation theology concerning baptism and the Lord's supper.

We can together affirm that baptism and the Lord's supper are at the heart of the New Testament expression of Christian faith. They are closely connected with salvation and newness of life in Christ.

In both churches we baptize in the name of Father, Son and Holy Spirit. We agree that God's initiative is essential for every Christian understanding of baptism. God offers the gift of salvation.

Whereas Lutherans follow the practice of the majority of the churches in baptizing infants, Adventists have consistently adhered to believers' baptism by immersion. Our theological disagreements in regard to baptism are basically similar to the larger interconfessional debates concerning the differences between these two Christian baptismal traditions (see *Baptists and Lutherans in Conversation*, LWF, Geneva, 1990). Today we realize that both infant baptism and believers' baptism have long roots and are received traditions within major Christian churches. Lutherans admit that there is no clear reference to the baptism of infants in the New Testament. While Adventists do not accept infant baptism, they acknowledge it as an early and widespread practice among Christians.

We agree that baptism can never be separated from faith. Although we adhere to different practices, we both affirm that baptism must be accompanied by faith. Lutherans may claim that baptism is "valid, even though faith be lacking" (Luther, Large Catechism IV,53); nevertheless, baptism must lead into faith in order to be effective; Adventists teach that faith must precede baptism.

Lutheran confessional writings condemn diverse "Anabaptist" practices. For reasons stated in other dialogues involving Lutherans (See *Baptists and Lutherans in Conversation*), most of these condemnations do not apply to today's Christian churches which practise believers' baptism. CA IX formally applies to these churches; even there, however, Lutherans recognize today that in a secular world believers' baptism reminds traditional Christian churches of their obligation to connect personal faith with baptism.

Concerning the Lord's supper, both Adventists and Lutherans speak of the presence of Christ at the communion table. Whereas Lutherans stress the real and corporeal presence, Adventists speak in terms of spiritual presence and spiritual experience, thus approaching to some extent the Calvinist terminology. We both agree that the Lord's supper contains a strong spiritual dimension which Lutherans refer to as visible word and mystery.

Adventists teach that "preparation for the supper includes self examination, repentance and confession" (FB 15). Lutherans fully agree in regard to the necessity and usefulness of these preparations. For Adventists, the Lord's supper is preceded by the service of foot washing which expresses this preparation. In the Lutheran church the Lord's supper is in a parallel manner most often preceded by a confession of sins and absolution.

Adventist self-understanding has a broad base. It includes four main elements: Adventists' relation to the Reformation, the concept of a cosmic conflict between good and evil, mission, and their view of the "remnant". Adventists have a high appreciation for the Reformation. They see themselves as heirs of Luther and other Reformers, especially in their adherence to the great principles of *sola scriptura, sola gratia, sola fide, solo Christo*. Teachings which others may view as distinctive of Adventists are seen by them as the continuation of the Reformations' recovery of biblical truth.

Adventists also see themselves as part of an ongoing struggle between good and evil. They derive this apocalyptic worldview from scripture. In this view Christ as victor at Calvary and Lord of the church assures the ultimate triumph of good and the end of evil. Christ uses various agencies on behalf of the good and Adventists understand themselves as one of these agencies but not the only one.

A third critical element in Adventists' self-understanding is the importance that they give to mission, including evangelism. They are impelled by the vision of Revelation 14 in which the everlasting gospel is to be given "to every nation, kindred, tongue and people" prior to the second coming of Christ. For this reason Adventists tend to think in global terms and give mission priority.

Adventists' self-understanding also expresses itself in the concept of the remnant. This term with deep biblical roots designates a group who survived a crisis (historical remnant), as well as those who are faithful to the Lord (faithful remnant). Adventists focus on the use of this term in the Apocalypse. They see themselves as instruments of God in gathering the faithful remnant. Adventists recognize that God's faithful remnant whose identity is known only to God includes Christians in many churches throughout the world. They understand that in the final crisis before the return of Jesus, God's faithful remnant will be clearly identified as those who are committed to Christ as Saviour and Lord, and who keep the commandments of God and the faith of Jesus.

Although the concept of remnant is not current in Lutheranism, the Lutheran tradition has often seen the Christian church in strongly eschatological terms. In Lutheran Pietism it was and to some extent still is believed that only a small flock of true believers will be faithful to Christ in the last times.

Lutherans appreciate the Adventist attempts to differentiate in their use of the remnant concept. A possible point of comparison is offered in CA VIII in which a distinction is made between the theological understanding of the Christian church as assembly of believers and saints and the situation "in this life" in which "many false Christians... remain among the godly".

Both for Adventists and Lutherans the historical church is thus not identical with the true church as "assembly of believers and saints" or "faithful remnant". Moreover, faithful Christians can be found in other churches. Affirming this state of affairs can open possibilities for interchurch relations. For Lutherans, this affirmation also means that the Adventist view is not to be counted among such false ecclesial self-understandings which identify an external church body with the assembly of all true believers (cf. CA VIII). At the same time our churches attempt to make manifest the gospel and the people of God. Although the borders of the true church are in the final analysis invisible, the Christian church in its mission to the world should not remain invisible. The church ought to be visible and present as the light of the world (Matt. 5:14), since it proclaims Christ who is the true light, which enlightens everyone (John 1:9).

III

Eschatology

Both Lutherans and Adventists affirm that Jesus Christ is the centre of eschatology. He is the Lord of time and space, and his atoning death on the cross has won the decisive battle over the forces of evil and ensured the ultimate restoration of all things. "For God was pleased to have all his fullness dwell in him, and through him to reconcile to himself all things, whether things on earth or things in heaven, by making peace through his blood, shed on the cross" (Col. 1:19,20).

For the believer in Jesus, eschatology has both a present and a future dimension. The person who is justified by grace alone through faith alone has already passed from death to life (Col. 3:3) and already sits with Christ in the heavenly places (Eph. 2:6). One who is so justified is a new creation (2 Cor. 5:17), a citizen of the divine commonwealth (Eph. 2:19), and a child of God (1 John 3:1,2), no longer living in terror or uncertainty before God.

Nevertheless, the Christian lives between the times, already in "the last days" (Heb. 1:2) that began with the first coming of Jesus, and yet still awaiting the consummation of all things when Christ shall be all in all. Thus Adventists and Lutherans affirm not only the present reality of justification but also the hope of the second coming of Jesus in glory. This "blessed hope" (Titus 2:13) is reflected in the very name "Adventist", and is shared by Lutherans who live in expectation of "the dear last day" (Luther, WA Br 9, 175).

In many respects the two communions have similar understandings of salvation history. Lutherans and Adventists affirm that history is not cyclical but linear, not random but moving towards its *telos* (goal) in a cosmic restoration. "We know that the whole creation has been groaning as in the pains of childbirth right up to the present time" (Rom. 8:22).

As regards eschatology on the individual level, both Lutherans and Adventists affirm that the witness of scripture points to the resurrection of the body rather than the immortality of the soul.

Both Lutherans and Adventists likewise attest that scripture teaches the judgment in association with the second coming of Christ (2 Tim. 4:1), even as the ancient creed declares: "[Christ] comes to judge the living and the dead." The "rewards" or "inheritance" that God's people receive at that time is given to them wholly by the merits of Christ and is in no manner the result of their own good works. The reception of faith in Christ, the fundamental basis of eternal life, is itself a divine gift and mystery. Lutherans affirm that the individual person cannot make a choice on a free basis for or against Christ, but is already here totally dependent on God, the Holy Spirit (cf. Luther, *Small Catechism*, II,6.).

In awaiting the consummation of all things, Lutherans and Adventists seek to avoid the extremes of a complacent attitude on the one hand, and overheated expectation of the second coming on the other. Both communions have had to deal with over-zealous members who resorted to setting dates and propounding various calculations that were not helpful in building up the body of Christ. Rather than such behaviour, Lutherans and Adventists advocate a life of active Christian service to the world. While both emphasize daily readiness, Adventists stress the nearness of the return of the Lord. Both communions seek to take seriously the scriptural admonitions to be faithful, to take a critical stand towards the prevailing culture, and they call both clergy and laity to proclaim and teach the coming of the kingdom as a source of hope and joy.

As Lutherans and Adventists seek to understand scriptural prophecy, they agree on several principles of interpretation. First, that scripture must be permitted to interpret itself; second, that we should exercise due humility in claiming to know the future, and third, that prophecy is only clearly understood after it has been fulfilled. "I have told you now before it happens, so that when it does happen, you will believe" (John 14:29).

Adventists and Lutherans share certain convictions concerning biblical apocalyptic literature. They regard such literature as important for study, proclamation, and instruction for Christian living; they recognize that such literature, as indeed all biblical literature, is rooted in a historical setting and that it not only addresses the context out of which it emerged but also carries an important message for generations still to come. Concerning the Apocalypse, they agree that Christ is the centre of this book and that it portrays the conflict between good and evil in the format of a cosmic drama.

In spite of the considerable convergence between Lutherans and Adventists in their respective understandings of eschatology, significant areas of divergence have become apparent in our discussions. These differences emerge sharply in the respective understandings and exposition of biblical apocalyptic literature.

While both communions believe that history is moving towards a climax and that scripture prepares Christians for events yet to come, Adventists give stronger emphasis to these matters. Five articles of their 27 Fundamental Beliefs focus on eschatology (FB 23 – the ministry of Christ in the heavenly sanctuary; FB 24 – the second coming of Christ; FB 25 – death and resurrection; FB 26 – the millennium and the end of sin; and FB 27 – the new earth), whereas the confessional statements of Lutheranism say little beyond that which is affirmed in the ancient creeds. For Adventists the question of the historical accuracy of scripture is crucial and, while they agree that prophecy can only be fully understood as such after it has been fulfilled, they do not accept the notion of prophecy written *ex eventu* (after the event).

Lutherans have traditionally been rather cautious in their interpretation of apocalyptic literature. Rather than reading the book of Revelation as a prediction of specific historical events which were to happen after the book was written, they tend to see in it references to events which were of critical significance to the early church.

Adventists, however, view biblical apocalyptic literature as having a significant predictive element. The books of Daniel and Revelation have played, and continue to play, a major role in their self-understanding. Beyond the spiritual and ethical values of these books, Adventists look to them as given by divine intent so that God's people may gain a grasp of the broad outlines of history moving relentlessly towards the Eschaton. This knowledge is not for the purpose of satisfying idle curiosity, but to confirm faith in Christ as Lord of history.

Thus, Adventists understand the book of Daniel to have been written, as it claims, in the 6th century B.C. They read its stories as instructive history, not as court tales. And, in keeping with a long line of interpreters of the book from the early church to the 19th century, they do not understand the "little horn" in chapters 7 and 8 to indicate events in the 2nd century B.C.

Adventists hold that the symbols, numbers and beasts of Daniel and the Apocalypse give – in the broad sense, not in detail – the course of human history. This they do by letting scripture interpret itself and considering the historical setting of each document. At times, some Adventists have erred in claiming to understand details rather than the broad sweep, and have made misguided statements about the future, which only God can know. Adventists seek to avoid such excesses; nevertheless, they are convinced that their historicist approach to interpretation remains valid.

Adventists' interest in apocalyptic has led to a distinctive eschatological teaching – the pre-Advent judgment (FB 23 – the ministry of Christ in the heavenly sanctuary). The thrust of this teaching is to view the judgment as beginning at a particular time in history (1844), arrived at on the basis of studies in Daniel, Hebrews and other scriptures.

While Lutherans affirm the Christology which portrays Jesus as High Priest (Heb. 7-9), they find no biblical basis for a doctrine which intimates that this High Priest began a new phase of his ministry at a specific time in recent history. However, they acknowledge that Adventists appeal to biblical and theological evidence.

Adventists maintain that this teaching does not threaten the gospel, since the judgment in the heavenly sanctuary identifies those whose assurance rests on justification by grace alone. Christ does not cease to be intercessor when he enters upon the work of judgment. And the heavenly sanctuary itself is to be understood in terms of function more than form.

For Adventists this teaching is important for their self-understanding. It conveys hope because of the prospect of the near return of Jesus; it assures that heaven and earth are linked, and that their Saviour is also their intercessor; and it comforts because God is about to bring to a close the long conflict between good and evil.

Two other Adventist teachings concern the symbols of Babylon and the mark of the beast. Adventists believe that Babylon as used in Revelation represents an apostasy manifested during the Christian era that will culminate in an eschatological apostasy in the Christian world. Then a political and religious alliance will form resulting in the great persecution (Rev. 13:15-17).

Adventists have historically identified the mark of the beast with the future, worldwide, oppressive government enforcement of Sunday observance at the end of time. They do not believe that Sunday observance today constitutes the mark of the beast or that those who observe Sunday have the mark of the beast (see section *"the law"*, part 4).

Because of time constraints, the consultation did not address some other topics related to eschatology, such as the millennium.

Despite differences in emphasis and understanding of eschatology, Lutherans and Adventists affirm their common faith in Jesus as Saviour, Justifier, and Lord of history. They await the full realization of Christ's prayer for oneness among his people (John 17:23) when "the kingdom of the world has become the kingdom of our Lord and of his Christ, and he will reign for ever and ever" (Rev. 11:15).

RECOMMENDATIONS

In our conversations we have achieved significant convergences in our understanding of the Christian faith. We do not want to conceal the existing doctrinal differences, but we nevertheless think that the following recommendations can be made to our churches:

1. We recommend that Adventists and Lutherans mutually recognize the basic Christian commitment of each other's faith communions. This general recognition is specified as follows:
   a) We recommend that Lutherans in their national and regional church contexts do not treat the Seventh-day Adventist church as a sect but as a free church and a Christian world communion. This recommendation is based both on the Adventist understanding of water baptism in the name of the triune God, an understanding which for Lutherans means that baptism is valid, and further on the joint conviction that "faithful Christians can be found in other churches" (see chapter II, section "Ecclesiology"), a view which is compatible with CA VIII.
   b) We also recommend that Adventists in their relationship with other Christian churches seek to have this conviction consistently affirmed. This recommendation can be seen as an expression of the *SDA General Conference's Working Policy* 1996/1997 § O 75 which unequivocally speaks of "other Christian churches" and recognizes "those agencies that lift up Christ before men as a part of the divine plan for evangelization of the world". Furthermore, according to the Adventist understanding of the Lord's supper, Lutherans as "believing Christians" (FB 15) are welcome to participate in the Adventist communion service.

2. In our discussions we have reached a comprehensive consensus on scripture as the sole foundation of church authority and on Christ as the head of the church. The credal and confessional documents are for Lutherans derived norms of faith *(norma normata)*. In an analogous manner the writings of Ellen G. White represent for Adventists an authority which is derived from scripture and which is to be tested by the scripture.

On the basis of this consensus we urge Adventists and Lutherans in their public teaching and theological education to present the other faith communion's view of church authority truthfully and unpolemically and in a manner which corresponds to their self-understanding.

We reaffirm the importance of giving scripture priority in preaching and daily life. We consider personal Bible study to be a fundamental part of Christian life and encourage members of our churches to engage in joint study of the Bible.

3. While each faith communion will continue to maintain its identity and convictions, we recommend that Lutherans and Adventists encourage and nurture consultative linkage for the good of the total Christian community, understanding, and the betterment of humanity. Several areas of cooperation for a joint witness suggest themselves, such as in:
   a) alleviating the suffering of humanity
   b) religious liberty endeavours
   c) ministerial associations / pastoral gatherings
   d) joint prayer events
   e) Bible Society work

4. As a sequel to the already concluded conversations, we recommend that Lutherans and Adventists meet in occasional bilateral consultations to explore topics of mutual interest. We further recommend that a first such consultation should deal with the theological foundations and the spiritual dimension of our observance of the day of rest and worship, with particular reference to modern society. Such a consultation should include a cross section of theologians, pastors, church leaders, and laypeople from the two churches with the possibility of other invitees.

5. We recommend that both the Lutheran World Federation and the General Conference of Seventh-day Adventists develop plans for the dissemination and study of this report among their churches in order that members of both communions may acquire a better understanding of each other's views and spiritual concerns.

PART B

Historical Introduction

In many Anglican responses to the results of the first round of Anglican-Catholic dialogues the request was made that the subject of justification be included. The request came not only from the more "evangelical" circles within Anglicanism but was also surely inspired by memories which had been revived not least by dialogue and other kinds of relations with the Reformed churches. Anglicans remembered once more that early Anglicanism had accepted the Reformers' teaching on justification and that this teaching is an element both in past controversies with which the churches must come to grips and in the faith which is still to be jointly confessed today. Between 1970 and 1981 the Anglican-Roman Catholic International Commission (ARCIC I) produced four reports: eucharistic doctrine; ministry and ordination; and authority in the church I and II (see *Growth in Agreement I*, pp.62-129). In 1982 it was decided to form a new international commission (ARCIC II). In four meetings (Venice, Italy, 1983; Durham, England, 1984; Graymoor, USA, 1985; and Llandaff, Wales, 1986) this commission produced an agreed statement on "Salvation and the Church", which was published in January 1987. The commission went on to devote four more meetings to the study of questions of ecclesiology (Palazzola, Italy, 1987; Edinburgh, Scotland, 1988; Venice, Italy, 1989; and Dublin, Ireland, 1990). The result of these consultations was published in January 1991 in the report on "Church as Communion".

When the responses to the final report emerged from Lambeth (1988) and the holy see (1991), ARCIC II felt the need to provide some clarifications in 1993, which elicited a positive response from the Catholic Church (1994) (Christopher Hill and Edward Yarnold, SJ, *Anglicans and Roman Catholics: The Search for Unity. The ARCIC Documents and Their Reception*, London, SPCK/CTS, 1994).

During that same period the full commission was working on the theme of ethics and produced *Life in Christ* in 1993. The next stage of the work of this dialogue continued on the issue of authority in the churches.

Jeffrey Gros

32. Common Declaration
Pope John Paul II and Robert A.K. Runcie, Archbishop of Canterbury

Canterbury, England, 29 May 1982

1. In the Cathedral Church of Christ at Canterbury the pope and the archbishop of Canterbury have met on the eve of Pentecost to offer thanks to God for the progress that has been made in the work of reconciliation between our communions. Together with leaders of other Christian churches and communities we have listened to the word of God; together we have recalled our one baptism and renewed the promises then made; together we have acknowledged the witness given by those whose faith has led them to surrender the precious gift of life itself in the service of others, both in the past and in modern times.

2. The bond of our common baptism into Christ led our predecessors to inaugurate a serious dialogue between our churches, a dialogue founded on the gospels and the ancient common traditions, a dialogue which has as its goal the unity for which Christ prayed to his Father "so that the world may know that thou has sent me and has loved them even as thou hast loved me" (John 17:23). In 1966, our predecessors Pope Paul VI and Archbishop Michael Ramsey made a common declaration announcing their intention to inaugurate a serious dialogue between the Roman Catholic Church and the Anglican communion which would "include not only theological matters such as scripture, Tradition and liturgy, but also matters of practical difficulty felt on either side" (Common Declaration, §6). After this dialogue had already produced three statements on eucharist, ministry and ordination, and authority in the church, Pope Paul VI and Archbishop Donald Coggan, in their common declaration in 1977, took the occasion to encourage the completion of the dialogue on these three important questions so that the commission's conclusions might be evaluated by the respective authorities through procedures appropriate to each communion. The Anglican-Roman Catholic International Commission has now completed the task assigned to it with the publication of its final report, and as our two communions proceed with the necessary evaluation, we join in thanking the members of the commission for their dedication, scholarship and integrity in a long and demanding task undertaken for love of Christ and for the unity of his church.

3. The completion of this commission's work bids us look to the next stage of our common pilgrimage in faith and hope towards the unity for which we long. We are agreed that it is now time to set up a new international commission. Its task will be to continue the work already begun: to examine, especially in the light of our respective judgments on the final report, the outstanding doctrinal differences which still separate us, with a view towards their eventual resolution; to study all that hinders the mutual

recognition of the ministries of our communions; and to recommend what practical steps will be necessary when, on the basis of our unity in faith, we are able to proceed to the restoration of full communion. We are well aware that this new commission's task will not be easy, but we are encouraged by our reliance on the grace of God and by all that we have seen of the power of that grace in the ecumenical movement of our time.

4. While this necessary work of theological clarification continues, it must be accompanied by the zealous work and fervent prayer of Roman Catholics and Anglicans throughout the world as they seek to grow in mutual understanding, fraternal love and common witness to the gospel. Once more, then, we call on the bishops, clergy and faithful people of both our communions in every country, diocese and parish in which our faithful live side by side. We urge them all to pray for this work and to adopt every possible means of furthering it through their collaboration in deepening their allegiance to Christ and in witnessing to him before the world. Only by such collaboration and prayer can the memory of the past enmities be healed and our past antagonisms overcome.

5. Our aim is not limited to the union of our two communions alone, to the exclusion of other Christians, but rather extends to the fulfilment of God's will for the visible unity of all his people. Both in our present dialogue, and in those engaged in by other Christians among themselves and with us, we recognize in the agreements we are able to reach, as well as in the difficulties which we encounter, a renewed challenge to abandon ourselves completely to the truth of the gospel. Hence we are happy to make this declaration today in the welcome presence of so many fellow Christians whose churches and communities are already partners with us in prayer and work for the unity of all.

6. With them we wish to serve the cause of peace, of human freedom and human dignity, so that God may indeed be glorified in all his creatures. With them we greet in the name of God all men of good will, both those who believe in him and those who are still searching for him.

7. This holy place reminds us of the vision of Pope Gregory in sending St Augustine as an apostle to England, full of zeal for the preaching of the gospel and the shepsherding of the flock. On this eve of Pentecost we turn again in prayer to Jesus, the Good Shepherd, who promised to ask the Father to give us another Advocate to be with us for ever, the Spirit of truth (cf. John 14:16), to lead us to the full unity to which he calls us. Confident in the power of this same Holy Spirit, we commit ourselves anew to the task of working for unity with firm faith, renewed hope and ever deeper love.

33. Salvation and the Church

Llandaff, Wales, 3 September 1986

The status of the document
The document published here is the work of the Second Anglican-Roman Catholic International Commission (ARCIC II). It is simply a joint statement of the commission. The authorities who appointed the commission have allowed the statement to be published so that it may be discussed and improved by the suggestions received. It is not an authoritative declaration by the Roman Catholic Church or by the Anglican communion, who will evaluate the document in order to take a position on it in due time.

The commission will be glad to receive observations and criticisms made in a constructive and fraternal spirit. Its work is done to serve the progress of the two communions towards unity. It will give responsible attention to every serious comment which is likely to help in improving or completing the result so far achieved. This wider collaboration will make its work to a greater degree work in common, and by God's grace will "lead us to the full unity to which he calls us" (common declaration of Pope John Paul II and the Archbishop of Canterbury, Pentecost 1982).

Preface
The 29th of May 1982, the eve of the feast of Pentecost, was a day of great significance for the Anglican and Roman Catholic churches on their path towards unity. In the footsteps of St Augustine of Canterbury whom his predecessor Pope Gregory the Great had sent from Rome to convert the English, Pope John Paul II visited Canterbury. There, in the church founded by Augustine, he and the present Archbishop of Canterbury, Dr Robert Runcie, along with representatives of the English churches and of the whole Anglican Communion, proclaimed and celebrated the one baptismal faith which we all share. The pope and the archbishop also gave thanks to God for the work of the first Anglican-Roman Catholic International Commission (ARCIC I) whose "Final Report" had just been published, and agreed to the establishment of a new commission (ARCIC II) to continue its work.

The primary task of ARCIC II is to examine and try to resolve those doctrinal differences which still divide us. Accordingly, at the request of the Anglican Consultative Council (Newcastle, September 1981), we have addressed ourselves to the doctrine of justification, which at the time of the Reformation was a particular cause of contention. This request sprang out of a widespread view that the subject of justification and salvation is so central to the Christian faith that, unless there is assurance of agreement on this issue, there can be no full doctrinal agreement between our two churches.

We have spent more than three years on this task. The doctrine of justification raises issues of great complexity and profound mystery. Furthermore it can be properly treated only within the wider context of the doctrine of salvation as a whole. This in turn has involved discussion of the role of the church in Christ's saving work. Hence the title of our agreed statement: "Salvation and the Church". We do not claim to have composed a complete treatment of the doctrine of the church. Our discussion is limited to its role in salvation.

In our work, particularly on the doctrine of justification as such, we have been greatly helped by the statement "Justification by Faith" agreed in 1983 by the Lutheran-Roman Catholic consultation in the USA (Minneapolis, Augsburg, 1985). This illustrates the interdependence of all ecumenical dialogues – an interdependence which is an expression of the growing communion which already exists between the churches. For the search for unity is indivisible.

A question not discussed by the commission, though of great contemporary importance, is that of the salvation of those who have no explicit faith in Christ. This has not been a matter of historical dispute between us. Our ancestors, though divided in Christian faith, shared a world in which the questions posed by people of other faiths, or none, could scarcely arise in their modern form. Today this is a matter for theological study in both our communions.

Although our first concern has been to state our common faith on the issues in the doctrine of salvation which have proved problematic in the past, we believe that the world, now as much as ever, stands in need of the gospel of God's free grace. Part of the challenge to Christians is this: How can we bear true witness to the good news of a God who accepts us, unless we can accept one another?

The purpose of our dialogue is the restoration of full ecclesial communion between us. Our work has recalled for us still wider perspectives – not only the unity of all Christian people but the fulfilment of all things in Christ.

We trust that God who has begun this good work in us will bring it to completion in Christ Jesus our Lord.

Bishop Cormac Murphy-O'Connor   Bishop Mark Santer
Co-chairman   *Co-chairman*

Llandaff, 3 September 1986, Feast of St Gregory the Great

Salvation and the Church

Introduction

1. The will of God, Father, Son and Holy Spirit, is to reconcile to himself all that he has created and sustains, to set free the creation from its bondage to decay, and to draw all humanity into communion with himself. Though we, his creatures, run away from him through sin, God continues to call us and opens up for us the way to find him anew. To bring us to union with himself, the Father sent into the world Jesus Christ, his only Son, in whom all things were created. He is the image of the invisible God; he took flesh so that we in turn might share the divine nature and so reflect the glory of God. Through Christ's life, death and resurrection, the mystery of God's love is

revealed, we are saved from the powers of evil, sin and death, and we receive a share in the life of God. All this is pure unmerited gift. The Spirit of God is poured into the hearts of believers – the Spirit of adoption, who makes us sons and daughters of God. The Spirit unites us with Christ and, in Christ, with all those who by faith are one with him. Through baptism we are united with Christ in his death and resurrection, we are by the power of the Spirit made members of one body, and together we participate in the life of God. This fellowship in one body, sustained through word and sacrament, is in the New Testament called "koinonia" (communion). "Koinonia with one another is entailed by our koinonia with God in Christ. This is the mystery of the church" (ARCIC I, *The Final Report*, introduction 5). The community of believers, united with Christ, gives praise and thanksgiving to God, celebrating the grace of Christ as they await his return in glory, when he will be all in all and will deliver to the Father a holy people. In the present age the church is called to be a sign to the world of God's will for the healing and recreation of the whole human race in Jesus Christ. As the church proclaims the good news which it has received, the heart of its message must be salvation through the grace of God in Christ.

2. The doctrine of salvation has in the past been a cause of some contention between Anglicans and Roman Catholics. Disagreements, focusing on the doctrine of justification, were already apparent in the church of the later middle ages. In the 16th century these became a central matter of dispute between Roman Catholics and continental Reformers. Though the matter played a less crucial role in the English Reformation, the Church of England substantially adopted the principles expressed in the moderate Lutheran formulations of the Augsburg and Württemberg confessions. The decree on justification of the Council of Trent was not directed against the Anglican formularies, which had not yet been compiled. Anglican theologians reacted to the decree in a variety of ways, some sympathetic, others critical at least on particular points.[1] Nevertheless, in the course of time Anglicans have widely come to understand that decree as a repudiation of their position. Since the 16th century, various debates on the doctrine of justification and on related issues (such as predestination, original sin, good works, sanctification) have been pursued within each of our communions.

3. In the area of the doctrine of salvation, including justification, there was much agreement. Above all it was agreed that the act of God in bringing salvation to the human race and summoning individuals into a community to serve him is due solely to the mercy and grace of God, mediated and manifested through Jesus Christ in his ministry, atoning death and rising again. It was also no matter of dispute that God's grace evokes an authentic human response of faith which takes effect not only in the life of the individual but also in the corporate life of the church. The difficulties arose in explaining how divine grace related to human response, and these difficulties were compounded by a framework of discussion that concentrated too narrowly upon the individual.

4. *One* difficulty concerned the understanding of the *faith* through which we are justified, in so far as this included the individual's confidence in his or her own final salvation. Everyone agreed that confidence in God was a mark of Christian hope, but some feared that too extreme an emphasis on assurance, when linked with an absolute doctrine of divine predestination, encouraged a neglect of the need for justification to issue in holiness of life. Catholics thought that this Protestant understanding of assurance confused faith with a subjective state and would actually have the effect of under-

mining hope in God. Protestants suspected that Catholics, lacking confidence in the sufficiency of Christ's work and relying overmuch on human efforts, had lapsed either into a kind of scrupulosity or into a mere legalism and so lost Christian hope and assurance.

5. A *second* difficulty concerned the understanding of *justification* and the associated concepts, righteousness and justice. Fearing that justification might seem to depend upon entitlement arising from good works, Reformation theologians laid great emphasis on the imputation to human beings of the righteousness of Christ. By this they meant that God declared the unrighteous to be accepted by him on account of the obedience of Christ and the merits of his passion. Catholics took them to be implying that imputed righteousness was a legal fiction, that is, a merely nominal righteousness that remained only external to the believer. They objected that this left the essential sinfulness of the individual unchanged, and excluded the imparted, or habitual and actual, righteousness created in the inner being of the regenerate person by the indwelling Spirit. Anglican theologians of the 16th and 17th centuries saw imputed and imparted righteousness as distinct to the mind, but indissoluble in worship and life. They also believed that, while we are made truly righteous because we are forgiven, we know ourselves to be in continuing need of forgiveness.

6. A *third* difficulty concerned the bearing of *good works* on salvation. Reformation theologians understood the Catholic emphasis on the value of good works and religious practices and ceremonies to imply that justification in some degree depended upon them in such a way as to compromise the sovereignty and unconditional freedom of God's grace. Catholics, on the other hand, saw the Reformation's understanding of justification as implying that human actions were of no worth in the sight of God. This, in their judgment, led to the negation of human freedom and responsibility, and to the denial that works, even when supernaturally inspired, deserved any reward. The Anglican theologians of the Reformation age, taking "by faith alone" to mean "only for the merit of Christ", also held good works to be not irrelevant to salvation, but imperfect and therefore inadequate. They saw good works as a necessary demonstration of faith, and faith itself as inseparable from hope and love.

7. Although the 16th-century disagreements centred mainly on the relationship of faith, righteousness and good works to the salvation of the individual, *the role of the church* in the process of salvation constituted a *fourth* difficulty. As well as believing that Catholics did not acknowledge the true authority of scripture over the church, Protestants also felt that Catholic teaching and practice had interpreted the mediatorial role of the church in such a way as to derogate from the place of Christ as "sole mediator between God and man" (1 Tim. 2:5). Catholics believed that Protestants were abandoning or at least devaluing the church's ministry and sacraments, which were divinely appointed means of grace; also that they were rejecting its divinely given authority as guardian and interpreter of the revealed Word of God.

8. The break in communion between Anglicans and Roman Catholics encouraged each side to produce caricatures of the other's beliefs. There were also extremists on both sides whose words and actions seemed to confirm the anxieties of their opponents.

The renewal of biblical scholarship, the development of historical and theological studies, new insights gained in mission, and the growth of mutual understanding within the ecumenical movement enable us to see our divisions in a new perspective. We have explored our common faith in the light of these shared experiences and are able in what follows to affirm that the four areas of difficulty outlined above need not be matters of dispute between us.

Salvation and faith

9. When we confess that Jesus Christ is Lord, we praise and glorify God the Father, whose purpose for creation and salvation is realized in the Son, whom he sent to redeem us and to prepare a people for himself by the indwelling of the Holy Spirit. This wholly unmerited love of God for his creatures is expressed in the language of grace, which embraces not only the once for all death and resurrection of Christ, but also God's continuing work on our behalf. The Holy Spirit makes the fruits of Christ's sacrifice actual within the church through word and sacrament: our sins are forgiven, we are enabled to respond to God's love, and we are conformed to the image of Christ. The human response to God's initiative is itself a gift of grace, and is at the same time a truly human, personal response. It is through grace that God's new creation is realized. Salvation is the gift of grace; it is by faith that it is appropriated.

10. The gracious action of God in Christ is revealed to us in the gospel. The gospel, by proclaiming Christ's definitive atoning work, the gift and pledge of the Holy Spirit to every believer, and the certainty of God's promise of eternal life, calls Christians to faith in the mercy of God and brings them assurance of salvation. It is God's gracious will that we, as his children, called through the gospel and sharing in the means of grace, should be confident that the gift of eternal life is assured to each of us. Our response to this gift must come from our whole being. Faith, therefore, not only includes an assent to the truth of the gospel but also involves commitment of our will to God in repentance and obedience to his call; otherwise faith is dead (James 2:17). Living faith is inseparable from love, issues in good works, and grows deeper in the course of a life of holiness. Christian assurance does not in any way remove from Christians the responsibility of working out their salvation with fear and trembling (Phil. 2:12-13).

11. Christian assurance is not presumptuous. It is always founded upon God's unfailing faithfulness and not upon the measure of our response. God gives to the faithful all that is needed for their salvation. This is to believers a matter of absolute certitude. The word of Christ and his sacraments give us this assurance. Throughout the Christian tradition there runs the certainty of the infinite mercy of God, who gave his Son for us. However grave our sins may be, we are sure that God is always ready to forgive those who truly repent. For the baptized and justified may still sin. The New Testament contains warnings against presumption (e.g. Col. 1:22 ff.; Heb. 10:36ff.). Christians may never presume on their perseverance but should live their lives with a sure confidence in God's grace. Because of what God has revealed of his ultimate purpose in Christ Jesus, living faith is inseparable from hope.

Salvation and justification

12. In baptism, the "sacrament of faith" (cf. Augustine *Ep.* 98.9), together with the whole church, we confess Christ, enter into communion with him in his death and resurrection, and through the gift of the Holy Spirit are delivered from our sinfulness and raised to new life. The scriptures speak of this salvation in many ways. They tell of God's eternal will fulfilled in Christ's sacrifice on the cross, his decisive act in overcoming the power of evil and reconciling sinners who believe. They also speak of the

abiding presence and action of the Holy Spirit in the church, of his present gifts of grace, and of our continuing life and growth in this grace as we are transformed into the likeness of Christ. They also speak of our entry with all the saints into our eternal inheritance, of our vision of God face to face, and of our participation in the joy of the final resurrection.

13. In order to describe salvation in all its fullness, the New Testament employs a wide variety of language. Some terms are of more fundamental importance than others: but there is no controlling term or concept; they complement one another. The concept of salvation has the all-embracing meaning of the deliverance of human beings from evil and their establishment in that fullness of life which is God's will for them (e.g. Luke 1:77; John 3:16-17; cf. John 10:10). The idea of reconciliation and forgiveness stresses the restoration of broken relationships (e.g. 2 Cor. 5:18ff.; Eph. 2:13-18). The language of expiation or propitiation (*hilasterion*, etc.), drawn from the context of sacrifice, denotes the putting away of sin and the re-establishment of right relationship with God (e.g. Rom. 3:25; Heb. 2:17; 1 John 2:2, 4:10). To speak of redemption or liberation is to talk of rescue from bondage so as to become God's own possession, and of freedom bought for a price (e.g. Mark 10:45; Eph. 1:7; 1 Pet. 1:18ff.). The notion of adoption refers to our new identity as children of God (e.g. Rom. 8:15-17,23; Gal. 4:4ff.). Terms like regeneration, rebirth and new creation speak of God's work of recreation and the beginning of new life (e.g. John 3:3; 2 Cor. 5:17; 1 Pet. 1:23). The theme of sanctification underlines the fact that God has made us his own and calls us to holiness of life (e.g. John 17:15ff.; Eph. 4:25 ff.; 1 Pet. 1:15ff.). The concept of justification relates to the removal of condemnation and to a new standing in the eyes of God (e.g. Rom. 3:22ff., 4:5, 5:1ff., Acts 13:39). Salvation in all these aspects comes to each believer as he or she is incorporated into the believing community.

14. Roman Catholic interpreters of Trent and Anglican theologians alike have insisted that justification and sanctification are neither wholly distinct from nor unrelated to one another. The discussion, however, has been confused by differing understandings of the word justification and its associated words. The theologians of the Reformation tended to follow the predominant usage of the New Testament, in which the verb *dikaioun* usually means "to pronounce righteous". The Catholic theologians, and notably the Council of Trent, tended to follow the usage of patristic and medieval Latin writers, for whom *iustificare* (the traditional translation of *dikaioun*) signified "to make righteous". Thus the Catholic understanding of the process of justification, following Latin usage, tended to include elements of salvation which the Reformers would describe as belonging to sanctification rather than justification. As a consequence, Protestants took Catholics to be emphasizing sanctification in such a way that the absolute gratuitousness of salvation was threatened. On the other side, Catholics feared that Protestants were so stressing the justifying action of God that sanctification and human responsibility were gravely depreciated.

15. Justification and sanctification are two aspects of the same divine act (1 Cor. 6:11). This does not mean that justification is a reward for faith or works: rather, when God promises the removal of our condemnation and gives us a new standing before him, this justification is indissolubly linked with his sanctifying recreation of us in grace. This transformation is being worked out in the course of our pilgrimage, despite the imperfections and ambiguities of our lives. God's grace effects what he declares:

his creative word imparts what it imputes. By pronouncing us righteous, God also makes us righteous. He imparts a righteousness which is his and becomes ours.[2]

16. God's declaration that we are accepted because of Christ together with his gift of continual renewal by the indwelling Spirit is the pledge and first instalment of the final consummation and the ground of the believer's hope. In the life of the church, the finality of God's declaration and the continuing movement towards our ultimate goal are reflected in the relation between baptism and the eucharist. Baptism is the unrepeatable sacrament of justification and incorporation into Christ (1 Cor. 6:11, 12:12-13; Gal. 3:27). The eucharist is the repeated sacrament by which the life of Christ's body is constituted and renewed, when the death of Christ is proclaimed until he comes again (1 Cor. 11:26).

17. Sanctification is that work of God which actualizes in believers the righteousness and holiness without which no one may see the Lord. It involves the restoring and perfecting in humanity of the likeness of God marred by sin. We grow into conformity with Christ, the perfect image of God, until he appears and we shall be like him. The law of Christ has become the pattern of our life. We are enabled to produce works which are the fruit of the Holy Spirit. Thus the righteousness of God our Saviour is not only declared in a judgment made by God in favour of sinners, but is also bestowed as a gift to make them righteous. Even though our acceptance of this gift will be imperfect in this life, scripture speaks of the righteousness of believers as already effected by God through Christ: "he raised us up with him and seated us with him in the heavenly realms in Christ Jesus"(Eph. 2:6).

18. The term justification speaks of a divine declaration of acquittal, of the love of God manifested to an alienated and lost humanity prior to any entitlement on our part. Through the life, death and resurrection of Christ, God declares that we are forgiven, accepted and reconciled to him. Instead of our own strivings to make ourselves acceptable to God, Christ's perfect righteousness is reckoned to our account. God's declaration is sometimes expressed in the New Testament in the language of law, as a verdict of acquittal of the sinner. The divine court, where the verdict is given, is the court of the judge who is also Father and Saviour of those whom he judges. While in a human law court an acquittal is an external, even impersonal act, God's declaration of forgiveness and reconciliation does not leave repentant believers unchanged but establishes with them an intimate and personal relationship. The remission of sins is accompanied by a present renewal, the rebirth to newness of life. Thus the juridical aspect of justification, while expressing an important facet of the truth, is not the exclusive notion in the light of which all other biblical ideas and images of salvation must be interpreted. For God sanctifies as well as acquits us. He is not only the judge who passes a verdict in our favour, but also the Father who gave his only Son to do for us what we could not do for ourselves. By virtue of Christ's life and self-oblation on the cross we are able with him to say through the Holy Spirit, "Abba, Father" (Rom. 8:15; Gal. 4:6).

Salvation and good works

19. As justification and sanctification are aspects of the same divine act, so also living faith and love are inseparable in the believer. Faith is no merely private and interior disposition, but by its very nature is acted out: good works necessarily spring from a living faith (James 2:17ff.). They are truly good because, as the fruit of the Spirit, they are done in God, in dependence on God's grace.

The person and work of Christ are central to any understanding of the relation between salvation and good works. God has brought into being in the person of his Son a renewed humanity, the humanity of Jesus Christ himself, the "last Adam" or "second man" (cf. 1 Cor. 15:45,47). He is the firstborn of all creation, the prototype and source of our new humanity. Salvation involves participating in that humanity, so as to live the human life now as God has refashioned it in Christ (cf. Col. 3:10). This understanding of our humanity as made new in Christ by God's transforming power throws light on the New Testament affirmation that, while we are not saved *because of* works, we are created in Christ *for* good works (Eph. 2:8ff.). "Not because of works": nothing even of our best achievement or good will can give us any claim to God's gift of renewed humanity. God's recreating deed originates in himself and nowhere else. "For good works": good works are the fruit of the freedom God has given us in his Son. In restoring us to his likeness, God confers freedom on fallen humanity. This is not the natural freedom to choose between alternatives, but the freedom to do his will: "The law of the Spirit of life in Christ Jesus has set me free from the law of sin and death... in order that the just requirement of the law might be fulfilled in us" (Rom. 8:2,4). We are freed and enabled to keep the commandments of God by the power of the Holy Spirit, to live faithfully as God's people and to grow in love within the discipline of the community, bringing forth the fruit of the Spirit.[3]

Inasmuch as we are recreated in his "own image and likeness", God involves us in what he freely does to realize our salvation (Phil. 2:12ff.). In the words of Augustine: "The God who made you without you, without you does not make you just" (*Sermons* 169.13). Thus from the divine work follows the human work: it is we who live and act in a fully human way, yet never on our own or in a self-sufficient independence. This fully human life is possible if we live in the freedom and activity of Christ who, in the words of St Paul, "lives in me" (Gal. 2:20).

20. To speak thus of freedom in Christ is to stress that it is in Jesus Christ that the shape of human life lived in total liberty before God is decisively disclosed. Our liberation commits us to an order of social existence in which the individual finds fulfilment in relationship with others. Thus freedom in Christ does not imply an isolated life, but rather one lived in a community governed by mutual obligations. Life in Christ sets us free from the demonic forces manifested not only in individual but also in social egotism.

21. The growth of believers to maturity, and indeed the common life of the church, are impaired by repeated lapses into sin. Even good works, done in God and under the grace of the Spirit, can be flawed by human weakness and self-centredness, and therefore it is by daily repentance and faith that we reappropriate our freedom from sin. This insight has sometimes been expressed by the paradox that we are at once just and sinners.[4]

22. The believer's pilgrimage of faith is lived out with the mutual support of all the people of God. In Christ all the faithful, both living and departed, are bound together in a communion of prayer. The church is entrusted by the Lord with authority to pronounce forgiveness in his name to those who have fallen into sin and repent. The church may also help them to a deeper realization of the mercy of God by asking for practical amends for what has been done amiss. Such penitential disciplines, and other devotional practices, are not in any way intended to put God under obligation. Rather, they provide a form in which one may more fully embrace the free mercy of God.

23. The works of the righteous performed in Christian freedom and in the love of God which the Holy Spirit gives us are the object of God's commendation and receive his reward (Matt. 6:4; 2 Tim. 4:8; Heb. 10:35, 11:6). In accordance with God's promise, those who have responded to the grace of God and consequently borne fruit for the kingdom will be granted a place in that kingdom when it comes at Christ's appearing. They will be one with the society of the redeemed in rejoicing in the vision of God. This reward is a gift depending wholly on divine grace. It is in this perspective that the language of "merit"[5] must be understood, so that we can say with Augustine: "When God crowns our merits it is his own gifts that he crowns" (*Ep.* 194.5.19). Christians rest their confidence for salvation on the power, mercy and loving-kindness of God and pray that the good work which God has begun he will in grace complete. They do not trust in their own merits but in Christ's. God is true to his promise to "render to everyone according to his works" (Rom. 2:6); yet when we have done all that is commanded we must still say: "We are unprofitable servants, we have only done our duty" (Luke 17:10).

24. The language of merit and good works, therefore, when properly understood, in no way implies that human beings, once justified, are able to put God in their debt. Still less does it imply that justification itself is anything but a totally unmerited gift. Even the very first movements which lead to justification, such as repentance, the desire for forgiveness and even faith itself, are the work of God as he touches our hearts by the illumination of the Holy Spirit.

The church and salvation

25. The doctrine of salvation is intimately associated with the doctrine of the church, which "is the community of those reconciled with God and with each other because it is the community of those who believe in Jesus Christ and are justified through God's grace" (ARCIC I, *Final Report,* introduction 8). The church proclaims the good news of our justification and salvation by God in Christ Jesus. Those who respond in faith to the gospel come to the way of salvation through incorporation by baptism into the church. They are called to witness to the gospel as members of the church.

26. The church is itself a *sign* of the gospel, for its vocation is to embody and reveal the redemptive power contained within the gospel. What Christ achieved through his cross and resurrection is communicated by the Holy Spirit in the life of the church. In its life the church signifies God's gracious purpose for his creation and his power to realize this purpose for sinful humanity. It is thus a sign and foretaste of God's kingdom. In fulfilling this vocation the church is called to follow the way of Jesus Christ, who being the image of the Father took the form of a servant and was made perfect by suffering. When for Christ's sake the church encounters opposition and persecution, it is then a sign of God's choice of the way of the cross to save the world.

27. This once-for-all atoning work of Christ, realized and experienced in the life of the church and celebrated in the eucharist, constitutes the free gift of God which is proclaimed in the gospel. In the service of this mystery the church is entrusted with a responsibility of *stewardship*. The church is called to fulfil this stewardship by proclaiming the gospel and by its sacramental and pastoral life. The church is required to carry out this task in such a way that the gospel may be heard as good news in differing ages and cultures, while at the same time seeking neither to alter its content nor

minimize its demands. For the church is servant and not master of what it has received. Indeed, its power to affect the hearer comes not from our unaided efforts but entirely from the Holy Spirit, who is the source of the church's life and who enables it to be truly the steward of God's design.

28. The church is also an *instrument* for the realization of God's eternal design, the salvation of humanity. While we recognize that the Holy Spirit acts outside the community of Christians, nevertheless it is within the church, where the Holy Spirit gives and nurtures the new life of the kingdom, that the gospel becomes a manifest reality. As this instrument, the church is called to be a living expression of the gospel, evangelized and evangelizing, reconciled and reconciling, gathered together and gathering others. In its ministry to the world the church seeks to share with all people the grace by which its own life is created and sustained.

29. The church is therefore called to be, and by the power of the Spirit actually is, a *sign*, *steward* and *instrument* of God's design. For this reason it can be described as *sacrament* of God's saving work. However, the credibility of the church's witness is undermined by the sins of its members, the shortcomings of its human institutions, and not least by the scandal of division. The church is in constant need of repentance and renewal so that it can be more clearly seen for what it is: the one, holy body of Christ. Nevertheless the gospel contains the promise that despite all failures the church will be used by God in the achievement of his purpose: to draw humanity into communion with himself and with one another, so as to share his life, the life of the Holy Trinity.

30. The church which in this world is always in need of renewal and purification, is already here and now a foretaste of God's kingdom in a world still awaiting its consummation – a world full of suffering and injustice, division and strife. Thus Paul speaks of a fellowship which is called to transcend the seemingly insuperable divisions of the world; where all, because of their equal standing before the Lord, must be equally accepted by one another; a fellowship where, since all are justified by the grace of God, all may learn to do justice to one another; where racial, ethnic, social, sexual and other distinctions no longer cause discrimination and alienation (Gal. 3:28). Those who are justified by grace, and who are sustained in the life of Christ through word and sacrament, are liberated from self-centredness and thus empowered to act freely and live at peace with God and with one another. The church, as the community of the justified, is called to embody the good news that forgiveness is a gift to be received from God and shared with others (Matt. 6:14-15). Thus the message of the church is not a private pietism irrelevant to contemporary society, nor can it be reduced to a political or social programme. Only a reconciled and reconciling community, faithful to its Lord, in which human divisions are being overcome, can speak with full integrity to an alienated, divided world, and so be a credible witness to God's saving action in Christ and a foretaste of God's kingdom. Yet, until the kingdom is realized in its fullness, the church is marked by human limitation and imperfection. It is the beginning and not yet the end, the first-fruits and not yet the final harvest.

31. The source of the church's hope for the world is God, who has never abandoned the created order and has never ceased to work within it. It is called, empowered and sent by God to proclaim this hope and to communicate to the world the conviction on which this hope is founded. Thus the church participates in Christ's mission to the world through the proclamation of the gospel of salvation by its words and deeds. It is called to affirm the sacredness and dignity of the person, the value of natural and polit-

ical communities and the divine purpose for the human race as a whole; to witness against the structures of sin in society, addressing humanity with the gospel of repentance and forgiveness and making intercession for the world. It is called to be an agent of justice and compassion, challenging and assisting society's attempts to achieve just judgment, never forgetting that in the light of God's justice all human solutions are provisional. While the church pursues its mission and pilgrimage in the world, it looks forward to "the end, when Christ delivers the kingdom to God the Father after destroying every rule and every authority and power" (1 Cor. 15:24).

Conclusion

32. The balance and coherence of the constitutive elements of the Christian doctrine of salvation had become partially obscured in the course of history and controversy. In our work we have tried to rediscover that balance and coherence and to express it together. We are agreed that this is not an area where any remaining differences of theological interpretation or ecclesiological emphasis, either within or between our communions, can justify our continuing separation. We believe that our two communions are agreed on the essential aspects of the doctrine of salvation and on the church's role within it. We have also realized the central meaning and profound significance which the message of justification and sanctification, within the whole doctrine of salvation, continues to have for us today. We offer our agreement to our two communions as a contribution to reconciliation between us, so that together we may witness to God's salvation in the midst of the anxieties, struggles and hopes of our world.

NOTES

[1] The council of Trent's decree on justification was issued after seven months' work on 13 January 1547 and should be read as a whole. It is printed in Denzinger-Schönmetzer, *Enchiridion Symbolorum Definitionum et Declarationum* (=DS) (Herder, Freiburg, 1965), DS 1520-1583. English translation in H. Schroeder, ed., *The Canons and Decrees of the Council of Trent*, USA, Tan Books and Publ., 1978; extracts in J. Neuner and J. Dupuis, eds, *The Christian Faith in the Doctrinal Documents of the Catholic Church*, Collins, 1983, nos 1924-83. The principal documents and authors for Anglican consideration of the subject in the period before 1661 are the Thirty-nine Articles (1571); Cranmer's Homily "Of Salvation" (1547), to which article 11 refers; Richard Hooker's *Learned Discourse of Justification* (1586); Richard Field, *Of the Church* III, appendix, ch. 11 (1606); John Davenant, *Disputatio de Iustitia Habituali et Actuali* (1631, transl. Allport, 1844 as *Treatise on Justification*); William Forbes, *Considerationes Modestae et Pacificae* I (posthumously published 1658, transl. 1850 as *Calm Considerations*).

[2] For Richard Hooker, "we participate in Christ partly by imputation, as when those things which he did and suffered for us are imputed unto us for righteousness; partly by habitual and real infusion, as when grace is inwardly bestowed while we are on earth, and afterwards more fully both our souls and bodies made like unto his in glory" (*Laws of Ecclesiastical Polity* V.lvi.11).

[3] Cf. article 10 of the Thirty-nine Articles: "We have no power to do good works pleasant and acceptable to God, without the grace of God by Christ preventing us, that we may have a good will, and working with us (*cooperante*), when we have that good will." This echoes Augustine's language about "prevenient" and "cooperating" grace (*De gratia et libero arbitrio* 17.33).

[4] *Simul iustus et peccator* is a Lutheran not a characteristically Anglican expression. It does not appear in Trent's decree on justification. The Second Vatican Council (*Lumen Gentium* 8) speaks of the church as "holy and at the same time always in need of purification" (*santa simul et semper purificanda*). The paradox is ultimately of Augustinian inspiration (cf. *En. in Ps.* 140.14 f and *Ep* 185.40).

[5] Misunderstanding has been caused by the fact that the Latin *mereor* has a range of meanings, from "deserve" to "be granted" and "obtain". This range is reflected in patristic and mediaeval Christian Latin usage. By "merit" the council of Trent (DS 1545) did not mean the exact equality between achievement and reward, except in the case of Christ, but the value of goodness, as being, in the divine liberality, pleasing to God who is not so unjust as to overlook this work and love of the justified (Heb. 6:10).

34. Common Declaration
Pope John Paul II and Robert A.K. Runcie, Archbishop of Canterbury

Vatican, 2 October 1989

After worshipping together in the Basilica of Saint Peter and in the Church of Saint Gregory, from where Saint Augustine of Canterbury was sent by Saint Gregory the Great to England, Pope John Paul II, Bishop of Rome, and His Grace Robert Runcie, Archbishop of Canterbury, now meet again to pray together in order to give fresh impetus to the reconciling mission of God's people in a divided and broken world, and to review the obstacles which still impede closer communion between the Catholic Church and the Anglican Communion.

Our joint pilgrimage to the Church of Saint Gregory, with its historic association with Saint Augustine's mission to baptize England, reminds us that the purpose of the church is nothing other than the evangelization of all peoples, nations and cultures. We give thanks together for the readiness and openness to receive the gospel that is especially evident in the developing world, where young Christian communities joyfully embrace the faith of Jesus Christ and vigorously express a costly witness to the gospel of the kingdom in sacrificial living. The word of God is received, "not as the word of man, but as what it really is, the word of God" (1 Thess. 2:13). As we enter the last decade of the second millennium of the birth of Jesus Christ, we pray together for a new evangelization throughout the world, not least in the continent of Saint Gregory and Saint Augustine where the progressive secularization of society erodes the language of faith and where materialism demeans the spiritual nature of humankind.

It is in such a perspective that the urgent quest for Christian unity must be viewed, for the Lord Jesus Christ prayed for the unity of his disciples "so that the world may believe" (John 17:21). Moreover, Christian disunity has itself contributed to the tragedy of human division throughout the world. We pray for peace and justice, especially where religious differences are exploited for the increase of strife between communities of faith. Against the background of human disunity the arduous journey to Christian unity must be pursued with determination and vigour, whatever obstacles are perceived to block the path. We here solemnly re-commit ourselves and those we represent to the restoration of visible unity and full ecclesial communion in the confidence that to seek anything less would be to betray our Lord's intention for the unity of his people.

This is by no means to be unrealistic about the difficulties facing our dialogue at the present time. When we established the Second Anglican-Roman Catholic International Commission in Canterbury in 1982, we were well aware that the commission's task would be far from easy. The convergences achieved within the report of the First

Anglican-Roman Catholic International Commission have happily now been accepted by the Lambeth conference of the bishops of the Anglican Communion. This report is currently also being studied by the Catholic church with a view to responding to it. On the other hand, the question and practice of the admission of women to the ministerial priesthood in some provinces of the Anglican Communion prevents reconciliation between us even where there is otherwise progress towards agreement in faith on the meaning of the eucharist and the ordained ministry. These differences in faith reflect important ecclesiological differences and we urge the members of the Anglican-Roman Catholic International Commission and all others engaged in prayer and work for visible unity not to minimize these differences. At the same time we also urge them not to abandon either their hope or work for unity. At the beginning of the dialogue established here in Rome in 1966 by our beloved predecessors Pope Paul VI and Archbishop Michael Ramsey, no one saw clearly how long-inherited divisions would be overcome and how unity in faith might be achieved. No pilgrim knows in advance all the steps along the path. Saint Augustine of Canterbury set out from Rome with his band of monks for what was then a distant corner of the world. Yet Pope Gregory was soon to write of the baptism of the English and of "such great miracles... that they seemed to imitate the powers of the apostles" (Letter of Gregory the Great to Eulogius of Alexandria). While we ourselves do not see a solution to this obstacle, we are confident that through our engagement with this matter our conversations will in fact help to deepen and enlarge our understanding. We have this confidence because Christ promised that the Holy Spirit, who is the Spirit of Truth, will remain with us forever (cf. John 14:16-17).

We also urge our clergy and faithful not to neglect or undervalue that certain yet imperfect communion we already share. This communion already shared is grounded in faith in God our Father, in our Lord Jesus Christ, and in the Holy Spirit; our common baptism into Christ; our sharing of the holy scriptures, of the Apostles' and Nicene Creeds; the Chalcedonian definition and the teaching of the fathers; our common Christian inheritance for many centuries. This communion should be cherished and guarded as we seek to grow into the fuller communion Christ wills. Even in the years of our separation we have been able to recognize gifts of the Spirit in each other. The ecumenical journey is not only about the removal of obstacles but also about the sharing of gifts.

As we meet together today we have also in our hearts those other churches and ecclesial communities with whom we are in dialogue. As we have said once before in Canterbury, our aim extends to the fulfilment of God's will for the visible unity of all his people.

Nor is God's will for unity limited exclusively to Christians alone. Christian unity is demanded so that the church can be a more effective sign of God's kingdom of love and justice for all humanity. In fact, the church is the sign and sacrament of the communion in Christ which God wills for the whole of his creation.

Such a vision elicits hope and patient determination, not despair or cynicism. And because such hope is a gift of the Holy Spirit we shall not be disappointed; for "the power at work within us is able to do far more abundantly than all we ask or think. To him be glory in the church and in Christ Jesus to all generations, for ever and ever. Amen" (Eph. 3:20-21).

35. Church as Communion

Dublin, Ireland, 6 September 1990

Preface
During the past four years the members of the Anglican-Roman Catholic International Commission have considered the mystery of communion which is given and made visible in the church. This has not been an easy task, because of the inherent complexity and depth of the mystery. For the same reason, our study cannot be complete or perfect. We have paid particular attention to the sacramentality of the church; that is, to the church as a divine gift, grounded in Christ himself and embodied in human history, through which the grace of Christ is mediated for the salvation of humankind. In doing this, we believe that we have laid a necessary foundation for further work on vital topics which were broached by our predecessors in the first Anglican-Roman Catholic International Commission. In particular we look forward to deeper study of the nature of the authority of Christ, the living Word of God, over his church, and of the means through which he exercises that authority and his people respond to it.

In considering the church as communion we have drawn upon thinking in both our churches and in the dialogues with other Christian bodies in which both are engaged. We offer the outcome of our labours not only to our own respective churches, but to all who are concerned with the common search for that full ecclesial unity which we believe to be God's will for all his people. We do this in the hope of study and response.

The members of the commission have not only been engaged in theological dialogue. Their work and study have been rooted in shared prayer and common life. This in itself has given them a profound experience of communion in Christ; not indeed that full sacramental communion which is our goal, but nevertheless a true foretaste of that fullness of communion for which we pray and strive.

We are painfully aware of the difficulties which still lie in our way. Nevertheless, we are heartened and encouraged by the words of Pope John Paul II and Archbishop Robert Runcie in their common declaration of 2 October 1989:

> Against the background of human disunity the arduous journey to Christian unity must be pursued with determination and vigour, whatever obstacles are perceived to block the path. We here solemnly recommit ourselves and those we represent to the restoration of visible unity and full ecclesial communion in the confidence that to seek anything less would be to betray our Lord's intention for the unity of his people.

The pope and the archbishop also declared: "The ecumenical journey is not only about the removal of obstacles but also about the sharing of gifts." That indeed has been the experience of the members of the commission. In giving we receive. That is of the essence of communion in Christ.

        Bishop Cormac Murphy-O'Connor   Bishop Mark Santer
        Co-chairman   *Co-chairman*

The status of the document

The document published here is the work of the Second Anglican-Roman Catholic International Commission (ARCIC II). It is a joint statement of the commission. The authorities who appointed the commission have allowed the statement to be published so that it may be widely discussed. It is not an authoritative declaration by the Roman Catholic Church or by the Anglican Communion, who will evaluate the document in order to take a position on it in due time.

Church as Communion

Introduction

1. Together with other Christians, Anglicans and Roman Catholics are committed to the search for that unity in truth and love for which Christ prayed. Within this context, the purpose of the Anglican-Roman Catholic International Commission is to examine and try to resolve those doctrinal differences which stand in the way of ecclesial communion between Anglicans and Roman Catholics. The "Final Report" of ARCIC I and the publication of ARCIC II's statement on "Salvation and the Church" have contributed to progress in mutual understanding and growing awareness of the need for ecclesial communion. We believe it is time now to reflect more explicitly upon the nature of communion and its constitutive elements. This will enable us to meet the requests that have been made for further clarification of the ecclesiological basis of our work.

2. This statement on communion differs from previous ARCIC reports in that it does not focus specifically on doctrinal questions that have been historically divisive. Nor does it seek to treat all the issues pertaining to the doctrine of the church. Its purpose is to give substance to the affirmation that Anglicans and Roman Catholics are already in a real though as yet imperfect communion and to enable us to recognize the degree of communion that exists both within and between us.[1] Moreover, we believe that within the perspective of communion the outstanding difficulties that remain between us will be more clearly understood and are more likely to be resolved; thus we shall be helped to grow into a more profound communion.

3. There are advantages in adopting the theme of communion in an exploration of the nature of the church. Communion implies that the church is a dynamic reality moving towards its fulfilment. Communion embraces both the visible gathering of God's people and its divine life-giving source. We are thus directed to the life of God, Father, Son and Holy Spirit, the life God wills to share with all people. There is held before us the vision of God's reign over the whole of creation, and of the church as the first-fruits of humankind which is drawn into that divine life through acceptance of the redemption given in Jesus Christ. Moreover, this focus on communion enables us to affirm that

which is already realized in the church, the eucharistic community. It enables us also to acknowledge as a gift of God the good that is present in community life in the world: communion involves rejoicing with those who rejoice and being in solidarity with those who suffer and those who search for meaning in life. To explore the meaning of communion is not only to speak of the church but also to address the world at the heart of its deepest need, for human beings long for true community in freedom, justice and peace and for the respect of human dignity.

4. Furthermore to understand the church in terms of communion confronts Christians with the scandal of our divisions. Christian disunity obscures God's invitation to communion for all humankind and makes the gospel we proclaim harder to hear. But the consideration of communion also enables Christians to recognize that certain yet imperfect communion they already share. Christians of many traditions are coming to acknowledge the central place of communion in their understanding of the nature of the church and its unity and mission. This is the communion to the study of which this document is devoted.

5. After a survey of how communion is unfolded in scripture, we explore the way in which the church as communion is sacrament of the merciful grace of God for all humankind. Then follows a treatment of the relationship of communion to the apostolicity, catholicity and holiness of the church and a consideration of the necessary elements required for unity and ecclesial communion. Finally, we affirm the existing communion between our two churches and outline some of the remaining issues which continue to divide us.

I. Communion unfolded in scripture

6. The relationship between God and his creation is the fundamental theme of holy scripture. The drama of human existence, as expounded in scripture, consists in the formation, breakdown and renewal of this relationship. The biblical story opens with God establishing this relationship by creating human beings in his image and likeness; God blesses and honours them by inviting them to live in communion both with him and with one another as stewards of his creation. In the unfolding saga of Genesis the disobedience of Adam and Eve undermines both their relation with God and their relation with each other: they hide from God; Adam blames Eve; they are expelled from the garden; their relationship with the rest of creation is distorted. What ensues in Genesis illustrates this recurrent pattern in human history.

7. In the variety of literary styles and theological traditions coming from every period of the long history of the people of Abraham, the books of the Old Testament bear witness to the fact that God wants his people to be in communion with him and with each other. God's purpose is reaffirmed in covenant with his people. Through Abraham God gives the promise of blessing to all the nations (Gen. 12:1-3). Through Moses God establishes a people as his own possession, a community in a covenant relationship with him (Ex. 19:5-6). In the promised land the temple becomes the place where God chooses to set his name, where he dwells with his people (Deut. 12:5). The prophets consistently denounce the community's faithlessness as threatening this relationship. Nevertheless, God's fidelity remains constant and he promises through the prophets that his promise will be accomplished. Although division and exile follow upon the sins of the chosen people, reconciliation of the scattered people of God will spring from a radical transformation within a new covenant (Jer. 31:31ff.).

God will raise up a servant to fulfil his purpose of communion and peace for his chosen people and also for all the nations (Isa. 49:6; cf. also Micah 4:1-4).

8. In the fullness of time, God sends his Son, born of a woman, to redeem his people and bring them into a new relationship as his adopted children (cf. Gal. 4:4-5). When Jesus begins his ministry he calls together a band of disciples with whom he shares his mission (Mark 3:14; cf. John 20:21). After Easter they are to be witnesses to his life, teaching, death and resurrection. In the power of the Spirit given at Pentecost they proclaim that God's promises have been fulfilled in Christ. For the apostolic community the baptism of repentance and faith bestowed in this new covenant does more than restore that which was lost: by the Spirit believers enter Christ's own communion with the Father. In the eucharist, the memorial of the new covenant, believers participate in the body and blood of Christ (1 Cor. 11:23-27) and are made one body in him (1 Cor. 10:16-17). It is communion with the Father, through the Son, in the Holy Spirit which constitutes the people of the new covenant as the church, "a people still linked by spiritual ties to the stock of Abraham".[2]

9. On Calvary the hideous nature of sin and evil is clearly exposed. In the cross are found God's judgment upon the world and his gift of reconciliation (2 Cor. 5:14-19). Through the paschal victory all estrangement occasioned by differences of culture, class, privilege and sex is overcome. All those who are united with the death and resurrection of Christ have equal standing before God. Moreover, because Christ is the one in whom and through whom all things are created and reconciled, the proper relationship between humanity and the rest of creation is restored and renewed in him (Col. 1:15-20; Gal. 3:27-29).

10. However, the life of communion is still impaired by human sin (1 Cor. 1:10ff.). The failure of Christians to respond to the demands of the gospel gives rise to divisions among Christians which obscure the church's witness. The New Testament affirms that there is a constant need for recourse to the repentance and reconciliation offered by Christ through the church (Matt. 18:15-20; cf. 1 John 1:5-10).

11. In the writings of the New Testament the failures of the disciples and the divisions among them are fully recognized. Nevertheless the reign of God is already perceived as a reality in the world (Mark 1:15; Luke 11:20), even though it will be perfectly realized only in the fullness of the kingdom of God. Its culmination is described as a feast, "the wedding supper of the Lamb" (Rev. 19:9), a vivid image of communion deeply rooted in human experience. This feast is spoken of by Jesus in the parables (Matt. 22:1-10), and foreshadowed in the feeding of the multitudes (John 6). The celebration of the eucharist prefigures and provides a foretaste of this messianic banquet (Luke 22:30). In the world to come, such signs will cease since the sacramental order will no longer be needed, for God will be immediately present to his people. They will see him face to face and join in endless praise (Rev. 22:3-4). This will be the perfection of communion.

12. In the New Testament the word "koinonia" (often translated "communion" or "fellowship") ties together a number of basic concepts such as unity, life together, sharing and partaking. The basic verbal form means "to share", "to participate", "to have part in", "to have something in common" or "to act together". The noun can signify fellowship or community. It usually signifies a relationship based on participation in a shared reality (e.g. 1 Cor. 10:16). This usage is most explicit in the Johannine writings: "We proclaim to you what we have seen and heard, so that you also may have fellow-

ship with us. And our fellowship is with the Father and with his Son Jesus Christ" (1 John 1:3; cf. 1 John 1:7).³

13. In the New Testament the idea of communion is conveyed in many ways. A variety of words, expressions and images points to its reality: the people of God (1 Pet. 2:9-10); flock (John 10:14; Acts 20:28-29; 1 Pet. 5:2-4); vine (John 15:5); temple (1 Cor. 3:16-17); bride (Rev. 21:2); body of Christ (1 Cor. 12:27; 1 Cor. 10:17; Rom. 12:4-5; Eph. 1:22-23). All these express a relationship with God and also imply a relationship among the members of the community. The reality to which this variety of images refers is communion, a shared life in Christ (1 Cor. 10:16-17; cf. John 17) which no one image exhaustively describes. This communion is participation in the life of God through Christ in the Holy Spirit, making Christians one with each other.

14. It is characteristic of the apostle Paul to speak of the relationship of believers to their Lord as being "in Christ" (2 Cor. 5:17; Col. 1:27-28; Gal. 2:20; cf. also John 15:1-11) and of Christ being in the believer through the indwelling of the Holy Spirit (Rom. 8:1-11). This relationship Paul also affirms in his description of the church as the one body of Christ. This description is integrally linked with the presence of Christ in the eucharist. Those who share in the supper of the Lord are one body in Christ because they all partake of the one bread (1 Cor. 10:16-17). This description underlines the intimate, organic relationship which exists between the risen Lord and all those who receive new life through communion with him. Equally it emphasizes the organic relationship thus established among the members of the one body, the church. All who share in the "holy things" of the sacramental life are made holy through them: because they share in them together they are in communion with each other.

15. The New Testament reflects different dimensions of communion as experienced in the life of the church in apostolic times.

At the centre of this communion is life with the Father, through Christ, in the Spirit. Through the sending of his Son the living God has revealed that love is at the heart of the divine life. Those who abide in love abide in God and God in them; if we, in communion with him, love one another, he abides in us and his love is perfected in us (cf. 1 John 4:7-21). Through love God communicates his life. He causes those who accept the light of the truth revealed in Christ rather than the darkness of this world to become his children. This is the most profound communion possible for any of his creatures.

Visibly, this communion is entered through baptism and nourished and expressed in the celebration of the eucharist. All who are baptized in the one Spirit into one body are united in the eucharist by this sacramental participation in this same one body (1 Cor. 10:16-17; 12:13). This community of the baptized, devoted to the apostolic teaching, fellowship, breaking of bread and prayer (cf. Acts 2:42), finds its necessary expression in a visible human community. It is a community which suffers with Christ in anticipation of the revelation of his glory (Phil. 3:10; Col. 1:24; 1 Pet. 4:13; Rom. 8:17). Those who are in communion participate in one another's joys and sorrows (Heb. 10:33; 2 Cor. 1:6-7); they serve one another in love (Gal. 5:13) and share together to meet the needs of one another and of the community as a whole. There is a mutual giving and receiving of spiritual and material gifts, not only between individuals but also between communities, on the basis of a fellowship that already exists in Christ (Rom. 15:26-27; 2 Cor. 8:1-15). The integrity and building up of that fellowship require appropriate structure, order and discipline (cf. 1 Cor. 11:17-34 and the pastoral epistles *passim*).

Communion will reach its fulfilment when God will be all in all (1 Cor. 15:28). It is the will of God for the whole creation that all things should be brought to ultimate unity and communion in Christ (Eph. 1:10; Col. 1:19-20).

Already in the New Testament these different dimensions of communion are discernible, together with a striving towards their ever more faithful realization.

II. Communion: sacramentality and the church

16. God's purpose is to bring all people into communion with himself within a transformed creation (cf. Rom. 8:19-21). To accomplish this the eternal Word became incarnate. The life and ministry of Jesus Christ definitively manifested the restored humanity God intends. By who he was, by what he taught, and by what he accomplished through the cross and resurrection, he became the sign, the instrument and the first-fruits of God's purpose for the whole of creation (Col. 1:15-17). As the new Adam, the risen Lord is the beginning and guarantor of this transformation. Through this transformation, alienation is overcome by communion, both between human beings and above all between them and God. These two dimensions of communion are inseparable. This is the mystery of Christ (Eph. 2:11-3:12).

17. Communion with God through Christ is constantly established and renewed through the power of the Holy Spirit. By the power of the Spirit, the incomparable riches of God's grace are made present for all time through the church. Those who are reconciled to God form "one body in Christ and are individually members one of another" (Rom. 12:5). By the action of the same Spirit, believers are baptized into the one body (1 Cor. 12:13) and in the breaking of the bread they also participate in that one body (1 Cor. 10:16-17; 11:23-29). Thus the church "which is Christ's body, the fullness of him who fills all in all", reveals and embodies "the mystery of Christ" (cf. Eph. 1:23; 3:4,8-11). It is therefore itself rightly described as a visible sign which both points to and embodies our communion with God and with one another; as an instrument through which God effects this communion; and as a foretaste of the fullness of communion to be consummated when Christ is all in all. It is a "mystery" or "sacrament".

18. The church as communion of believers with God and with each other is a sign of the new humanity God is creating and a pledge of the continuing work of the Holy Spirit. Its vocation is to embody and reveal the redemptive power of the gospel, signifying reconciliation received through faith and participation in the new life in Christ. The church is the sign of what God has done in Christ, is continuing to do in those who serve him, and wills to do for all humanity. It is the sign of God's abiding presence, and of his eternal faithfulness to his promises, for in it Christ is ever present and active through the Spirit. It is the community where the redemptive work of Jesus Christ has been recognized and received, and is therefore being made known to the world. Because Christ has overcome all the barriers of division created by human sin, it is the mission of the church as God's servant to enter into the struggle to end those divisions (cf. Eph. 2:14-18; 5:1-2).

19. The Holy Spirit uses the church as the means through which the word of God is proclaimed afresh, the sacraments are celebrated, and the people of God receive pastoral oversight, so that the life of the gospel is manifested in the life of its members. The church is both the sign of salvation in Christ, for to be saved is to be brought into communion with God through him, and at the same time the instrument of salvation,

as the community through which this salvation is offered and received. This is what is meant when the church is described as an "effective sign", given by God in the face of human sinfulness, division and alienation.[4]

20. Human sinfulness and Christian division obscure this sign. However, Christ's promise of his abiding presence in the midst of his people (Matt. 18:20; 28:20) gives the assurance that the church will not cease to be this effective sign. In spite of the frailty and sinfulness of its members, Christ promises that the powers of destruction will never prevail against it (Matt. 16:18).

21. Paradoxically it is pre-eminently in its weakness, suffering and poverty that the church becomes the sign of the efficacy of God's grace (cf. 2 Cor. 12:9; 4:7-12). It is also paradoxical that the quality of holiness is rightly attributed to the church, a community of sinners. The power of God to sanctify the church is revealed in the scandal of the cross where Christ in his love gave himself for the church so that it might be presented to him without spot or wrinkle, holy and without blemish (Eph. 5:26-27). God was in Christ reconciling the world to himself, making him who knew no sin to be sin for us so that in him we might become the righteousness of God (cf. 2 Cor. 5:19-21).

22. The communion of the church demonstrates that Christ has broken down the dividing wall of hostility, so as to create a single new humanity reconciled to God in one body by the cross (cf. Eph. 2:14-16). Confessing that their communion signifies God's purpose for the whole human race, the members of the church are called to give themselves in loving witness and service to their fellow human beings.

This service is focused principally in the proclaiming of the gospel in obedience to the command of Christ. Having received this call, the church has been entrusted with the stewardship of the means of grace and with the message of salvation. In the power of Christ's presence through the Spirit it is caught up in the saving mission of Christ. The mandate given to the church to bring salvation to all the nations constitutes its unique mission. In this way the church not only signifies the new humanity willed by God and inaugurated by Christ. It is itself an instrument of the Holy Spirit in the extension of salvation to all human beings in all their needs and circumstances to the end of time. To speak of the church as sacrament is to affirm that in and through the communion of all those who confess Jesus Christ and who live according to their confession, God realizes his plan of salvation for all the world. This is not to say that God's saving work is limited to those who confess Christ explicitly. By God's gift of the same Spirit who was at work in the earthly ministry of Christ Jesus, the church plays its part in bringing his work to its fulfilment.

23. To be united with Christ in the fulfilment of his ministry for the salvation of the world is to share his will that the church be one, not only for the credibility of the church's witness and for the effectiveness of its mission, but supremely for the glorification of the Father. God will be truly glorified when all peoples with their rich diversity will be fully united in one communion of love. Our present communion with God and with each other in the Holy Spirit is a pledge and foretaste here and now of the ultimate fulfilment of God's purpose for all, as proclaimed in the vision of "a great multitude which none could number, from every nation, from all tribes and peoples and tongues... crying out with a loud voice, 'Salvation belongs to our God who sits upon the throne, and to the Lamb!'" (Rev. 7:9-10).

24. The sacramental nature of the church as sign, instrument and foretaste of communion is especially manifest in the common celebration of the eucharist. Here, cele-

brating the memorial of the Lord and partaking of his body and blood, the church points to the origin of its communion in Christ, himself in communion with the Father; it experiences that communion in a visible fellowship; it anticipates the fullness of the communion in the kingdom; it is sent out to realize, manifest and extend that communion in the world.

III. Communion: apostolicity, catholicity and holiness

25. The church points to its source and mission when it confesses in the creed, "we believe in one holy catholic and apostolic church". It is because the church is built up by the Spirit upon the foundation of the life, death and resurrection of Christ as these have been witnessed and transmitted by the apostles that the church is called *apostolic*. It is also called apostolic because it is equipped for its mission by sharing in the apostolic mandate.

26. The content of the faith is the truth of Christ Jesus as it has been transmitted through the apostles. This God-given deposit of faith cannot be dissociated from the gift of the Holy Spirit. Central to the mission of the Spirit is the safeguarding and quickening of the memory of the teaching and work of Christ and of his exaltation, of which the apostolic community was the first witness. To safeguard the authenticity of its memory the church was led to acknowledge the canon of scripture as both test and norm. But the quickening of its memory requires more than the repetition of the words of scripture. It is achieved under the guidance of the Holy Spirit by the unfolding of revealed truth as it is in Jesus Christ. According to the Johannine gospel the mission of the Holy Spirit is intimately linked with all that Christ Jesus said, did and accomplished. Christ promised that the Father will send the Holy Spirit in his name to teach the disciples all things and to bring to remembrance all that he has said (cf. John 14:26). To keep alive the memory of Christ means to remain faithful to all that we know of him through the apostolic community.

27. Such faithfulness must be realized in daily life. Consequently in every age and culture authentic faithfulness is expressed in new ways and by fresh insights through which the understanding of the apostolic preaching is enriched. Thus the gospel is not transmitted solely as a text. The living Word of God, together with the Spirit, communicates God's invitation to communion to the whole of his world in every age. This dynamic process constitutes what is called the living tradition, the living memory of the church. Without this the faithful transmission of the gospel is impossible.

28. The living memory of the mystery of Christ is present and active within the church as a whole; it is at work in the constant confession and celebration of the apostolic faith and in the insights, emphases and perspectives of faithful members of the church. And since faith seeks understanding, this includes an examination of the very foundations of faith. As the social setting of the Christian community changes, so the questions and challenges posed both from within and from without the church are never entirely the same. Even within the period covered by the New Testament this process is evident when new images and fresh language are used to express the faith as it is handed on in changing cultural contexts.

29. If the church is to remain faithfully rooted and grounded in the living truth and is to confess it with relevance, then it will need to develop new expressions of the faith. Diversity of cultures may often elicit a diversity in the expression of the one gospel; within the same community distinct perceptions and practices arise. Nevertheless these

must remain faithful to the tradition received from the apostles (cf. Jude 3). Since the Holy Spirit is given to all the people of God, it is within the church as a whole, individuals as well as communities, that the living memory of the faith is active. All authentic insights and perceptions, therefore, have their place within the life and faith of the whole church, the temple of the Holy Spirit.

30. Tensions inevitably appear. Some are creative of healthy development. Some may cause a loss of continuity with apostolic tradition, disruption within the community, estrangement from other parts of the church. Within the history of Christianity, some diversities have become differences that have led to such conflict that ecclesial communion has been severed. Whenever differences become embodied in separated ecclesial communities, so that Christians are no longer able to receive and pass on the truth within the one community of faith, communion is impoverished and the living memory of the church is affected. As Christians grow apart, complementary aspects of the one truth are sometimes perceived as mutually incompatible. Nevertheless the church is sustained by Christ's promise of its perseverance in the truth (cf. Matt. 16:18), even though its unity and peace are constantly vulnerable. The ultimate God-given safeguard for this assurance is the action of the Spirit in preserving the living memory of Christ.

31. This memory, realized and freshly expressed in every age and culture, constitutes the apostolic tradition of the church. In recognizing the canon of scripture as the normative record of the revelation of God, the church sealed as authoritative its acceptance of the transmitted memory of the apostolic community. This is summarized and embodied in the creeds. The Holy Spirit makes this tradition a living reality which is perpetually celebrated and proclaimed by word and sacrament, pre-eminently in the eucharistic memorial of the once-for-all sacrifice of Christ, in which the scriptures have always been read. Thus the apostolic tradition is fundamental to the church's communion which spans time and space, linking the present to past and future generations of Christians.

32. Responsibility for the maintenance of the apostolic faith is shared by the whole people of God. Every Christian has a part in this responsibility. The task of those entrusted with oversight, acting in the name of Christ, is to foster the promptings of the Spirit and to keep the community within the bounds of the apostolic faith, to sustain and promote the church's mission, by preaching, explaining and applying its truth. In responding to the insights of the community, and of the individual Christian, whose conscience is also moulded by the same Spirit, those exercising oversight seek to discern what is the mind of Christ. Discernment involves both heeding and sifting in order to assist the people of God in understanding, articulating and applying their faith. Sometimes an authoritative expression has to be given to the insights and convictions of the faithful. The community actively responds to the teaching of the ordained ministry, and when, under the guidance of the Spirit, it recognizes the apostolic faith, it assimilates its content into its life.

33. Succession in the episcopal ministry is intended to assure each community that its faith is indeed the apostolic faith, received and transmitted from apostolic times. Further, by means of the communion among those entrusted with the episcopal ministry the whole church is made aware of the perceptions and concerns of the local churches: at the same time the local churches are enabled to maintain their place and particular character within the communion of all the churches.

34. In the creeds the church has always confessed its *catholicity*: "I believe in... the holy catholic church". It gets this title from the fact that by its nature it is to be scat-

tered throughout the world, from one end of the earth to the other, from one age to the next. The church is also catholic because its mission is to teach universally and without omission all that has been revealed by God for the salvation and fulfilment of humankind; and also because its vocation is to unite in one eucharistic fellowship men and women of every race, culture and social condition in every generation. Because it is the fruit of the work of Christ upon the cross, destroying all barriers of division, making Jews and Gentiles one holy people, both having access to the one Father by the one Spirit (cf. Eph. 2:14-18), the church is catholic.

35. In the mystery of his will God intends the church to be the recreation in Christ Jesus of all the richness of human diversity that sin turns into division and strife (cf. Eph. 1:9-10). In so far as this recreation is authentically demonstrated in its life, the church is a sign of hope to a divided world that longs for peace and harmony. It is the grace and gospel of God that brings together this human diversity without stifling or destroying it; the church's catholicity expresses the depth of the wisdom of the Creator. Human beings were created by God in his love with such diversity in order that they might participate in that love by sharing with one another both what they have and what they are, thus enriching each other in their mutual communion.

36. Throughout its history the church has been called to demonstrate that salvation is not restricted to particular cultures. This is evident in the variety of liturgies and forms of spirituality, in the variety of disciplines and ways of exercising authority, in the variety of theological approaches, and even in the variety of theological expressions of the same doctrine. These varieties complement one another, showing that, as the result of communion with God in Christ, diversity does not lead to division; on the contrary, it serves to bring glory to God for the munificence of his gifts. Thus the church in its catholicity is the place where God brings glory to his name through the communion of those he created in his own image and likeness, so diverse yet profoundly one. At every eucharistic celebration of Christian communities dispersed throughout the world, in their variety of cultures, languages, social and political contexts, it is the same one and indivisible body of Christ reconciling divided humanity that is offered to believers. In this way the eucharist is the sacrament of the church's catholicity in which God is glorified.

37. In the eucharist the church also manifests its solidarity with the whole of humanity. This is given expression in intercession and thanksgiving, and in the sending out of the people of God to serve and to proclaim the message of salvation to the world. The church's concern for the poor and oppressed is not peripheral but belongs to the very heart of its mission (cf. 2 Cor. 8:1-9).

Moreover, for the church effectively to carry out its ministry of reconciliation, it is necessary that its members and communities display in their common life the fruits of Christ's reconciling work. As long as Christians are divided, they do not fully manifest the catholic nature of the church.

38. Catholicity is inseparable from holiness, as is evident from the early liturgical traditions which often speak of "the holy catholic church", and from early forms of the creed which include the words "we believe in the Holy Spirit in the holy catholic church". The church is *holy* because it is "God's special possession" (1 Pet. 2:9-10), endowed with his Spirit (Eph. 2:21-22), and it is his special possession since it is there that "the mystery of his will, according to his good pleasure" is realized, "to bring all things in heaven and on earth together under one head, Christ" (Eph. 1:9-10).

Being set apart as God's special possession means that the church is the communion of those who seek to be perfect as their heavenly Father is perfect (Matt. 5:48). This implies a life in communion with Christ, a life of compassion, love and righteousness. The holiness of the church does not mean that it is to be cut off from the world (John 17:15ff.). Its vocation is to be, through its holiness, salt of the earth, light to the world (Matt. 5:13-16). In this way the church declares the praises of him who called his people out of darkness into his marvellous light (cf. 1 Pet. 2:9).

39. The catholicity of God's purpose requires that all the diverse gifts and graces given by God to sanctify his people should find their proper place in the church. Every Christian is called to be consecrated to the life and service of the communion (1 Pet. 4:10ff., 1 Cor. 12:4ff.). And what is true of the individual is equally true of the local churches. Communion with other local churches is essential to the integrity of the self-understanding of each local church, precisely because of its catholicity. Life in self-sufficient isolation, which rejects the enrichment coming from other local churches as well as the sharing with them of gifts and resources, spiritual as well as material, is the denial of its very being. It is the particular ministry of oversight to affirm and order the diverse gifts and graces of individuals and communities; to effect and embody the unity of the local church and its unity with the wider communion of the churches. By the example of their lives those who bear oversight are to witness to the holiness of the church and in their ministry foster holiness amongst its members.

Amid all the diversity that the catholicity intended by God implies, the church's unity and coherence are maintained by the common confession of the one apostolic faith, a shared sacramental life, a common ministry of oversight, and joint ways of reaching decisions and giving authoritative teaching.

40. The catholicity of the church is threatened, in the first place, when the apostolic faith is distorted or denied within the community. It is also threatened whenever the faith is obscured by attitudes and behaviour in the church which are not in accord with its calling to be the holy people of God, drawn together by the Spirit to live in communion. Just as the church has to distinguish between tolerable and intolerable diversity in the expression of the apostolic faith, so in the area of life and practice the church has to discover what is constructive and what is disruptive of its own communion. Catholicity and holiness are also impaired when the church fails to confront the causes of injustice and oppression which tear humanity apart or when it fails to hear the cries of those calling for sustenance, respect, peace and freedom.

41. When the creed speaks of the church as holy, catholic and apostolic, it does not mean that these attributes are distinct and unrelated. On the contrary, they are so interwoven that there cannot be one without the others. The holiness of the church reflects the mission of the Spirit of God in Christ, the holy One of God, made known to all the world through the apostolic teaching. Catholicity is the realization of the church's proclamation of the fullness of the gospel to every nation throughout the ages. Apostolicity unites the church of all generations and in every place with the once-for-all sacrifice and resurrection of Christ, where God's holy love was supremely demonstrated.

IV. Unity and ecclesial communion

42. The church, since apostolic times, has always included belief in its unity among the articles of faith (e.g. 1 Cor. 12:12ff.; Eph. 4:4-6). Because there is only one Lord, with whom we are called to have communion in the one Spirit, God has given his

church one gospel, one faith, one baptism, one eucharist and one apostolic ministry through which Christ continues to feed and guide his flock.

43. For a Christian the life of *communion* means sharing in the divine life, being united with the Father, through his Son, in the Holy Spirit, and consequently to be in fellowship with all those who share in the same gift of eternal life. This is a spiritual communion in which the reality of the life of the world to come is already present. But it is inadequate to speak only of an invisible spiritual unity as the fulfilment of Christ's will for the church; the profound communion fashioned by the Spirit requires visible expression. The purpose of the visible ecclesial community is to embody and promote this spiritual communion with God (cf. §§16-24).

For a local community to be a *communion* means that it is a gathering of the baptized brought together by the apostolic preaching, confessing the one faith, celebrating the one eucharist, and led by an apostolic ministry. This implies that this local church is in communion with all Christian communities in which the essential constitutive elements of ecclesial life are present.

For all the local churches to be *together in communion*, the one visible communion which God wills, it is required that all the essential constitutive elements of ecclesial communion are present and mutually recognized in each of them. Thus the visible communion between these churches is complete and their ministers are in communion with each other. This does not necessitate precisely the same canonical ordering: diversity of canonical structures is part of the acceptable diversity which enriches the one communion of all the churches.

44. The *constitutive elements* essential for the visible communion of the church are derived from and subordinate to the common confession of Jesus Christ as Lord. In the picture of the Jerusalem church in the Acts of the Apostles we can already see in nascent form certain necessary elements of ecclesial communion which must be present in the church in every age (cf. §15).

45. In the light of all that we have said about communion it is now possible to describe what constitutes ecclesial communion. It is rooted in the confession of the one apostolic faith, revealed in the scriptures and set forth in the creeds. It is founded upon one baptism. The one celebration of the eucharist is its pre-eminent expression and focus. It necessarily finds expression in shared commitment to the mission entrusted by Christ to his church. It is a life of shared concern for one another in mutual forbearance, submission, gentleness and love; in the placing of the interests of others above the interests of self; in making room for each other in the body of Christ; in solidarity with the poor and the powerless; and in the sharing of gifts both material and spiritual (cf. Acts 2:44). Also constitutive of life in communion is acceptance of the same basic moral values, the sharing of the same vision of humanity created in the image of God and recreated in Christ, and the common confession of the one hope in the final consummation of the kingdom of God.

For the nurture and growth of this communion, Christ the Lord has provided a ministry of oversight, the fullness of which is entrusted to the episcopate, which has the responsibility of maintaining and expressing the unity of the churches (cf. §§33 and 39 and *The Final Report*, ministry and ordination). By shepherding, teaching and the celebration of the sacraments, especially the eucharist, this ministry holds believers together in the communion of the local church and in the wider communion of all the churches (cf. §39). This ministry of oversight has both collegial and primatial dimensions. It is grounded in the life of the community and is open to the community's participation in the discovery of God's will. It is exercised so that unity and communion are expressed, preserved and fostered at every level – locally, regionally and universally. In the context of the communion of all the churches the episcopal ministry of a universal primate finds its role as the visible focus of unity.

Throughout history different means have been used to express, preserve and foster this communion between bishops: the participation of bishops of neighbouring sees in episcopal ordinations; prayer for bishops of other dioceses in the liturgy; exchanges of episcopal letters. Local churches recognized the necessity of maintaining communion with the principal sees, particularly with the see of Rome. The practice of holding synods or councils, local, provincial, ecumenical, arose from the need to maintain unity in the one apostolic faith (cf. *The Final Report*, authority in the church, I.19-23, II.12).

46. All these inter-related elements and facets belong to the visible communion of the universal church. Although their possession cannot guarantee the constant fidelity of Christians, neither can the church dispense with them. They need to be present in order for one local church to recognize another canonically. This does not mean that a community in which they are present expresses them fully in its life.

47. Christians can never acquiesce with complacency in disunity without impairing further their communion with God. As separated churches grow towards ecclesial communion it is essential to recognize the profound measure of communion they already share through participation in spiritual communion with God and through those elements of a visible communion of shared faith and sacramental life they can already recognize in one another. If some element or important facet of visible communion is judged to be lacking, the communion between them, though it may be real, is incomplete.

48. Within the pilgrim church on earth, even when it enjoys complete ecclesial communion, Christians will be obliged to seek even deeper communion with God and one another. This is also expressed through faith in the "communion of saints", whereby the church declares its conviction that the eucharistic community on earth is itself a participation in a larger communion which includes the martyrs and confessors and all who have fallen asleep in Christ throughout the ages. The perfection of full communion will only be reached in the fullness of the kingdom of God.

V. Communion between Anglicans and Roman Catholics

49. The convictions which this commission believes that Anglicans and Roman Catholics share concerning the nature of communion challenge both our churches to move forward together towards visible unity and ecclesial communion. Progress in mutual understanding has been achieved. There exists a significant degree of doctrinal agreement between our two communions even upon subjects which previously divided us. In spite of past estrangements, Anglicans and Roman Catholics now enjoy a better understanding of their long-standing shared inheritance. This new understanding enables them to recognize in each other's church a true affinity.

50. Thus we already share in the communion founded upon the saving life and work of Christ and his continuing presence through the Holy Spirit. This was acknowledged jointly in the common declaration of Pope John Paul II and Archbishop Robert Runcie of 2 October 1989:

We also urge our clergy and faithful not to neglect or undervalue that certain yet imperfect communion we already share. This communion already shared is grounded in faith in God our Father, in our Lord Jesus Christ, and in the Holy Spirit; our common baptism into Christ; our sharing of the holy scriptures, of the Apostles' and Nicene Creeds; the Chalcedonian definition and the teaching of the fathers; our common Christian inheritance for many centuries. This communion should be cherished and guarded as we seek to grow into the fuller communion Christ wills. Even in the years of our separation we have been able to recognize gifts of the Spirit in each other. The ecumenical journey is not only about the removal of obstacles but also about the sharing of gifts.

51. One of the most important ways in which there has already been a sharing of gifts is in spirituality and worship. Roman Catholics and Anglicans now frequently pray together. Alongside common participation in public worship and in private prayer, members of both churches draw from a common treasury of spiritual writing and direction. There has been a notable convergence in our patterns of liturgy, especially in that of the eucharist. The same lectionary is used by both churches in many countries. We now agree on the use of the vernacular language in public worship. We agree also that communion in both kinds is the appropriate mode of administration of the eucharist. In some circumstances, buildings are shared.

52. In some areas there is collaboration in Christian education and in service to local communities. For a number of years, Roman Catholic and Anglican scholars have worked together in universities and other academic institutions. There is closer cooperation in ministerial formation and between parochial clergy and religious communities. The responsibility for the pastoral care of interchurch families is now increasingly entrusted to both churches. Meetings of Roman Catholic and Anglican bishops are becoming customary, engendering mutual understanding and confidence. This often results in joint witness, practical action and common statements on social and moral issues. The growing measure of ecclesial communion experienced in these ways is the fruit of the communion we share with the Father, through the Son, in the Holy Spirit.

53. We cannot, however, ignore the effects of our centuries of separation. Such separation has inevitably led to the growth of divergent patterns of authority accompanied by changes in perceptions and practices. The differences between us are not only theological. Anglicans and Roman Catholics have now inherited different cultural traditions. Such differences in communities which have become isolated from one another have sometimes led to distortions in the popular perceptions which members of one church have of the other. As a result visible unity may be viewed as undesirable or even unattainable. However, a closer examination of the developments which have taken place in our different communities shows that these developments, when held in complementarity, can contribute to a fuller understanding of communion.

54. In recent years each communion has learnt from its own and each other's experiences, as well as through contact with other churches. Since the Second Vatican Council, the principle of collegiality and the need to adapt to local cultural conditions have been more clearly recognized by the Roman Catholic Church than before. Developing liturgical diversity, the increasing exercise of provincial autonomy, and the growing appreciation of the universal nature of the church have led Anglicans to develop organs of consultation and unity within their own communion. These developments remind us of the significance of mutual support and criticism, as together we seek to understand ecclesial communion and to achieve it.

55. Developments in the understanding of the theology of communion in each of our churches have provided the background for the commission's reflections on the nature of communion. This statement intends to be faithful to the doctrinal formulations to which Anglicans and Roman Catholics are each committed without providing an exhaustive treatment of the doctrine of the church.

56. Grave obstacles from the past and of recent origin must not lead us into thinking that there is no further room for growth towards fuller communion. It is clear to the commission, as we conclude this document, that, despite continuing obstacles, our two communions agree in their understanding of the church as communion. Despite our distinct historical experiences, this firm basis should encourage us to proceed to examine our continuing differences.

57. Our approach to the unresolved matters we must now face together will be shaped by the agreed understanding of communion we have elaborated.

An appreciation both of the existing degree of communion between Anglicans and Roman Catholics as well as the complete ecclesial communion to which we are called will provide a context for the discussion of the long-standing problem of the reconciliation of ministries which forms part of ARCIC II's mandate. This will build upon ARCIC I's work on ministry and ordination, which provides a new context for discussion of the consequences of the bull *Apostolicae Curae* (1896).

In the light of our agreement we must also address the present and future implications of the ordination of women to the priesthood and episcopate in those Anglican provinces which consider this to be a legitimate development within the catholic and apostolic tradition. The Lambeth conference of 1988, while resolving that "each province respect the decision and attitudes of other provinces in the ordination or consecration of women to the episcopate", also stressed the importance of "maintaining the highest possible degree of communion with the provinces that differ" (Resolution 1, 1).

Writing to the archbishop of Canterbury shortly after the Lambeth Conference, Pope John Paul II said of the ordination of women that "the Catholic church, like the Orthodox church and the ancient Oriental churches, is firmly opposed to this development, viewing it as a break with Tradition of a kind we have no competence to authorize". Referring to ARCIC's work in the reconciliation of ministries the pope said that "the ordination of women to the priesthood in some provinces of the Anglican communion, together with the recognition of the right of individual provinces to proceed with the ordination of women to the episcopacy, appears to pre-empt this study and effectively block the path to the mutual recognition of ministries" (letter of Pope John Paul II to the archbishop of Canterbury, 8 December 1988).

Another area which the commission is currently engaged in studying is that of moral issues. Our distinct cultural inheritances have sometimes led us to treat of moral questions in different ways. Our study will explore the moral dimension of Christian life and seek to explain and assess its significance for communion as well as the importance of agreement or difference on particular moral questions.

It is evident that the above issues are closely connected with the question of authority. We continue to believe that an agreed understanding of the church as communion is the appropriate context in which to continue the study of authority in the church begun by ARCIC I. Further study will be needed of episcopal authority, particularly of universal primacy, and of the office of the bishop of Rome; of the question of provincial autonomy in the Anglican Communion; and the role of the laity in decision-making within the church. This work will take into account the response of the Lambeth Conference 1988 and the response of the Roman Catholic Church to *The Final Report* of ARCIC I.

58. Serious as these remaining obstacles may seem, we should not overlook the extent of the communion already existing between our two churches, which we have described in the last part of this statement. Indeed, awareness of this fact will help us to bear the pain of our differences without complacency or despair. It should encourage Anglicans and Roman Catholics locally to search for further steps by which concrete expression can be given to this communion which we share. Paradoxically, the closer we draw together the more acutely we feel those differences which remain. The forbearance and generosity with which we seek to resolve these remaining differences will testify to the character of the fuller communion for which we strive. Together with all Christians, Anglicans and Roman Catholics are called by God to continue to pursue the goal of complete communion of faith and sacramental life. This call we must obey until all come into the fullness of that divine Presence, to whom, Father, Son, and Holy Spirit, be ascribed all honour, thanksgiving and praise to the ages of ages. Amen.

NOTES

[1] Cf. "Common Declaration", Pope John Paul II and the Archbishop of Canterbury, Robert Runcie, 2 October 1989.
[2] Second Vatican Council, *Nostra Aetate*, 4.
[3] Communion has been treated in many ecumenical documents including the final report of ARCIC I (introduction). Cf. also *Communion-Koinonia*, a study by the Institute for Ecumenical Research, Strasbourg, 1990.
[4] The language of "effective sign" and "instrument" is known to Anglicans in the catechism of the Book of Common Prayer and in the Articles of Religion, in which baptism and the eucharist are said to be "not only a sign... but rather... a sacrament", "sure witnesses, and effectual signs of grace", "as a means whereby we receive" grace, "as by an instrument", and which "be effectual because of Christ's institution and promise" (The Catechism; articles 25, 26, 27, 28). For the Roman Catholic Church, similarly, instrumental language was largely developed in relation to the sacraments rather than the church. But reflection on the mystery of Christ and the church led to the development of its self-understanding in terms of itself being "in Christ... in the nature of sacrament – a sign and instrument, that is, of communion with God and of unity among all people", and "as the universal sacrament of salvation" (*Lumen Gentium* 1, 48).

36. Life in Christ: Morals, Communion and the Church

Venice, Italy, 5 September 1993

Preface

As we reach the end of ten years in the life of ARCIC II, it may be opportune to recall the words of Pope John Paul II and Archbishop Robert Runcie in their common declaration at Canterbury in May 1982:

> The new international commission is to continue the work already begun; to examine, especially in the light of our respective judgments on the *Final Report*, the outstanding doctrinal differences which still separate us, with a recognition of the ministries of our communions, and to recommend what practical steps will be necessary when, on the basis of our unity in faith, we are able to proceed to the restoration of full communion. We are well aware that this new commission's task will not be easy but we are encouraged by our reliance on the grace in the ecumenical movement of our time.

We repeat these words in order to assure both our communions that the work of the commission, however long or difficult it may be, must continue and is continuing.

Among the many international dialogues, bilateral and multilateral, between divided Christians, the Anglican-Roman Catholic International Commission is the first to have directly attempted the subject of morals. We have prepared this statement in response to requests from authorities of both our communions. These requests have given voice to a widespread belief that Anglicans and Roman Catholics are as much, if not more, divided on questions of morals as on questions of doctrine. This belief in turn reflects the profound and true conviction that authentic Christian unity is as much a matter of life as of faith. Those who share one faith in Christ will share one life in Christ. Hence the title of this statement: "Life in Christ: Morals, Communion and the Church".

The theme of this statement was already adumbrated in our previous work on "Church as Communion". In describing the "constitutive elements essential for visible communion of the church", we wrote: "Also constitutive of life in communion is acceptance of the same basic moral values, the sharing of the same vision of humanity created in the image of God and recreated in Christ, and the common confession of the one hope in the final consummation of the kingdom of God" (44,45).

As Christians we seek a common life not for our own sakes only, but for the glory of God and the good of humankind. In the face of the world around us, the name of God is profaned whenever those who call themselves Christians show themselves divided in their witness to the objective moral demands which arise from our life in Christ. Our search for communion and unity in morals as in faith is therefore a form of the Lord's own prayer to his Father:

Hallowed be thy name,
thy kingdom come,
thy will be done,
on earth as it is in heaven.

        Bishop Cormac Murphy-O'Connor   Bishop Mark Santer
        Co-chairman   *Co-chairman*

                                                                           Venice, 5 September 1993

A. INTRODUCTION

1. There is a popular and widespread belief that the Anglican and Roman Catholic communions are divided most sharply by their moral teaching. Careful consideration has persuaded the commission that, despite existing disagreement in certain areas of practical and pastoral judgment, Anglicans and Roman Catholics derive from the scriptures and Tradition the same controlling vision of the nature and destiny of humanity and share the same fundamental moral values. This substantial area of common conviction calls for shared witness, since both communions proclaim the same gospel and acknowledge the same injunction to mission and service. A disproportionate emphasis on particular disagreements blurs this important truth and can provoke a sense of alienation. There is already a notable convergence between the two communions in the witness they give, for example, on war and peace, euthanasia, freedom and justice, but exaggeration of outstanding differences makes this shared witness – a witness which could give direction to a world in danger of losing its way – more difficult to sustain and at the same time hinders its further development. Such a shared witness is, in today's society, urgent. It is also, we believe, possible. The widespread assumption, therefore, that differences of teaching on certain particular moral issues signify an irreconcilable divergence of understanding, and therefore present an insurmountable obstacle to shared witness, needs to be countered. Even on those particular issues where disagreement exists, Anglicans and Roman Catholics, we shall argue, share a common perspective and acknowledge the same underlying values. This being so, we question whether the limited disagreement, serious as it is, is itself sufficient to justify a continuing breach of communion.

2. In presenting this statement on morals, we are responding, not simply to popular concern, but also to requests from the authorities of both communions. In the past, ecumenical dialogue has concentrated on matters of doctrine. These are of primary importance and work here still remains to be done. However, the gospel we proclaim cannot be divorced from the life we live. Questions of doctrine and of morals are closely interconnected, and differences in the one area may reflect differences in the other. Common to both is the matter of authority and the manner of its exercise. Although we shall not here be addressing the issue of authority directly, nevertheless we hope that an understanding of the relationship between freedom and authority in the moral life may contribute to our understanding of their relationship in the life of the church.

3. In what follows we shall attempt to display the basis and shape of Christian moral teaching and to show that both our communions apprehend it in the same light. We begin by reaffirming our common faith that the life to which God, through Jesus

Christ, calls women and men is nothing less than participation in the divine life, and we spell out some of the characteristics and implications of our shared vision of life in Christ. We go on to remind ourselves of our common heritage and of the living tradition through which both communions have sought to develop a faithful and appropriate response to the good news of the gospel. Next we review the ways in which this tradition has diverged since the break in communion, at the same time drawing attention to signs of a new convergence, not least in our emphasis on the common good. We fasten upon the two particular issues of marriage after divorce and contraception – issues upon which the two communions have expressed their disagreement in official documents and pastoral practice – in order to determine as precisely as we can the nature and extent of our moral disagreement and to relate it to our continuing agreement on fundamental values. In our last section we return to the theme of communion and, in the light of what has gone before, show how communion determines both the structure of the moral order and the method of the church's discernment and response. Finally, we reaffirm our belief that differences and disagreements are exacerbated by a continuing breach of communion, and that integrity of moral response itself requires a movement towards full communion. We conclude by suggesting steps by which we may move forward together along this path to the greater glory of God and the well-being of God's world.

B. SHARED VISION

4. The Christian life is a response in the Holy Spirit to God's self-giving in Jesus Christ. To this gift of himself in incarnation, and to this participation in the divine life, the scriptures bear witness (cf. 1 John 1:1-3; 2 Pet. 1:3-4). Made in the image of God (cf. Gen. 1:27), and part of God's good creation (cf. Gen. 1:31), women and men are called to grow into the likeness of God, in communion with Christ and with one another. What has been entrusted to us through the incarnation and the Christian tradition is a vision of God. This vision of God in the face of Jesus Christ (cf. 2 Cor. 4:6; compare Gen. 1:3) is at the same time a vision of humanity renewed and fulfilled. Life in Christ is the gift and promise of new creation (cf. 2 Cor. 5:17), the ground of community, and the pattern of social relations. It is the shared inheritance of the church and the hope of every believer.

5. God creates human beings with the dignity of persons in community, calls them to a life of responsibility and freedom, and endows them with the hope of happiness. As children of God, our true freedom is to be found in God's service, and our true happiness in faithful and loving response to God's love and grace. We are created to glorify and enjoy God, and our hearts continue to be restless until they find in God their rest and fulfilment.

6. The true goal of the moral life is the flourishing and fulfilment of that *humanity* for which all men and women have been created. The fundamental moral question, therefore, is not "What ought we to do?", but "What kind of persons are we called to become?" For children of God, moral obedience is nourished by the hope of becoming like God (cf. 1 John 3:1-3).

7. True personhood has its origins and roots in the life and love of God. The mystery of the divine life cannot be captured by human thought and language, but in speaking of God as Trinity in unity, Father, Son and Holy Spirit, we are affirming that the

Being of God is a unity of self-communicating and interdependent relationship. Human persons, therefore, made in this image, and called to participate in the life of God, may not exercise a freedom that claims to be independent, wilful and self-seeking. Such a use of freedom is a distortion of their God-given humanity. It is sin. The freedom that is properly theirs is a freedom of responsiveness and interdependence. They are created for communion, and communion involves responsibility in relation to society and nature as well as to God.

8. Ignorance and sin have led to the misuse and corruption of human freedom and to delusive ideas of human fulfilment. But God has been faithful to his eternal purposes of love and, through the redemption of the world by Jesus Christ, offers to human beings participation in a new creation, recalling them to their true freedom and fulfilment. As God remains faithful and free, so those who are in Christ are called to be faithful and free, and to share in God's creative and redemptive work for the whole of creation.

9. The new life in Christ is for the glorification of God. Living in communion with Christ, the church is called to make Christ's words its own. "I have glorified you on earth" (cf. John 17:4). The new life has also been entrusted to the church for the good of the whole world (cf. "Church as Communion", 18). This life is for everyone and embraces everyone. In seeking the common good, therefore, the church listens and speaks not only to the faithful, but also to women and men of goodwill everywhere. Despite the ambiguities and evils in the world, and despite the sin that has distorted human life, the church affirms the original goodness of creation and discerns signs and contours of an order that continues to reflect the wisdom and goodness of the Creator. Nor has sin deprived human beings of all perception of this order. It is generally recognized, for example, that torture is intrinsically wrong, and that the integration of sexual instincts and affections into a lifelong relationship of married love and loyalty constitutes a uniquely significant form of human flourishing and fulfilment. Reflection on experience of what makes human beings, singly and together, truly human gives rise to a natural morality sometimes interpreted in terms of natural justice or natural law, to which a general appeal for guidance can be made. In Jesus Christ this natural morality is not denied. Rather, it is renewed, transfigured and perfected, since Christ is the true and perfect image of God.

10. Christian morality is one aspect of the life in Christ which shapes the tradition of the church, a tradition which is also shaped by the community which carries it. Christian morality is the fruit of faith in God's word, the grace of the sacraments, and the appropriation, in a life of forgiveness, of the gifts of the Spirit for work in God's service. It manifests itself in the practical teaching and pastoral care of the church and is the outward expression of that continual turning to God whereby forgiven sinners grow up together into Christ and into the mature humanity of which Christ is the measure and fullness (cf. Eph. 4:13). At its deepest level, the response of the church to the offer of new life in Christ possesses an unchanging identity from age to age and place to place. In its particular teachings, however, it takes account of changing circumstances and needs, and in situations of unusual ambiguity and perplexity it seeks to combine new insight and discernment with an underlying continuity and consistency.

11. Approached in this light the fundamental questions with which a Christian morality engages are such as these:

- What are persons called to be, as individuals and as members one of another in the human family?
- What constitutes human dignity and what are the social as well as the individual dimensions of human dignity and responsibility?
- How does divine forgiveness and grace engage with human finitude, fragility and sin in the realization of human happiness?
- How are conditions and structures of human life related to the goal of human fulfilment?
- What are the implications of the creatureliness which human beings share with the rest of the natural world?

At this fundamental level of inquiry and concern, we believe, our two communions share a common vision and understanding. To affirm our agreement here will prove a significant step towards the recovery of full communion. It will put in proper perspective any disagreement that may continue to exist in official teaching and pastoral practice on particular issues, such as divorce and contraception. The crisis of the modern world is more than a crisis of sexual ethics. At stake is our humanity itself.

C. COMMON HERITAGE

1. A shared tradition

12. Anglicans and Roman Catholics are conscious that their respective traditions, rooted in a shared vision, stem from a common heritage, which in spite of stress and strain, within and without, shaped the church's life for some fifteen hundred years. Drawing upon the faith of Israel, this common heritage springs from the conversion of the disciples to faith in Jesus Christ and their mission to share that faith with others. Fullness of life in Christ in the kingdom of God is its goal. It is also the norm by which the Tradition in all its varied manifestations is to be judged. Any manifestation that no longer has the power to nurture and sustain the new life in Christ is thereby shown to be corrupt. Anglicans and Roman Catholics firmly believe that their respective traditions continue to nourish and support them in their daily discipleship, but they are aware of the impairment to their common heritage caused by the breach in their communion, and they look forward to the time when both traditions will again flow together for their mutual enrichment and for their common witness and service to the world.

13. The shared Tradition was richly woven from many strands. These include faith in God, Father, Son and Holy Spirit, publicly professed in baptism; a common life, founded on love, centred in eucharistic prayer and worship, expressed in service; the teaching and nourishment of the scriptures; an ordered leadership, entrusted with guarding and guiding the Tradition through the conflicts of history; a sense of discipleship, manifested in the lives of the saints and acknowledged by devotion and piety; the proscription of deeds that undermine the values of the gospel and threaten to destroy the new life in Christ; ways of reconciliation, by which sinners may be brought back into communion with God and with one another. At the same time the Tradition drew upon the inherited wisdom and culture of the world in which it was embedded.

14. This common Tradition carried with it a "missionary imperative" – a call to preach the gospel, to live the life of the gospel in the world, and to work out a faithful

and fruitful response to the gospel in encounter with different cultures. Both Anglicans and Roman Catholics have understood the missionary task in this way, and both have been eager to fulfil the claims of their earthly citizenship (cf. Rom. 13:4-5), while remembering that they are citizens of heaven (cf. Phil. 3:20). They have attempted to carry out Christ's missionary injunction accordingly, though sometimes they have interpreted their involvement in the cultural life of the world in very different ways. In their engagement with culture they have been led to give careful thought to the practical expression of the new life in Christ and to provide specific teaching on some of its moral and social aspects.

15. This openness to the world, which has characterized both our traditions, has shaped the pattern of life which these traditions have sustained. It is not the life of an inwardly pious and self-regarding group, withdrawn from the world and its conflicts. It is, rather, a life to be lived out amidst the ambiguities of the world and its conflicts. Yet it is also a pilgrim life which, while seeking the welfare of the world, has a destiny which transcends the present age. Admittedly, this involvement with the world has from time to time led the church into compromise and alliance with corrupt principalities and powers. At other times, however, cooperation with secular authorities has borne good fruit, and the conviction that the church is called to live in the world and to work for the salvation of the world has remained strong. Thus, while both our communions retain painful memories of occasions of betrayal and sin, both put their trust, not in human strength, but in the saving power of God.

16. Both our traditions draw their vision from the scriptures. To the scriptures, therefore, we now turn, to discover the origins of our common heritage in the gospel of Jesus Christ and the faithful response of the Christian community.

2. The pattern of our life in Christ

17. The good news of the gospel is the coming of the kingdom of God (cf. Mark 1:15), the redemption of the world by our Lord Jesus Christ (cf. Gal. 4:4-5), the forgiveness of sins and new life in the Spirit (cf. Acts 2:38), and the hope of glory (cf. Col. 1:27).

18. The redemption won by Jesus Christ carries with it the promise of a new life of freedom from the domination of sin (cf. Rom. 6:18). Through his dying on the cross Christ has overcome the powers of darkness and death, and through his rising again from the dead he has opened the gates of eternal life (cf. Heb. 10:19-22). No longer are men and women alienated from God and from one another, enslaved by sin, abandoned to despair and destined to destruction (cf. Eph. 2:1-12). The entail of sin has been broken and humanity set free – free to enter upon the liberty and splendour of the children of God (cf. Rom. 6:23; 8:21).

19. The liberty promised to the children of God is nothing less than participation, with Christ and through the Holy Spirit, in the life of God. The gift of the Spirit is the pledge and first instalment of the coming kingdom (cf. 2 Cor. 1:21-22). Patterned according to Christ, the wisdom of God, and empowered by the Holy Spirit of God, the church is called not only to proclaim God's kingdom, but also to be the sign and firstfruits of its coming. The unity, holiness, catholicity and apostolicity of the church derive their meaning and reality from the meaning and reality of God's kingdom. They reflect the fullness of the life of God. They are signs of the universal love of God, Father, Son and Holy Spirit, the love poured out upon the whole creation. Hence the

life of the church, the body of Christ, the community of the Holy Spirit, is rooted and grounded in the eternal life and love of God.

20. It is this patterning power of the kingdom that gives the church its distinctive character (cf. Rom. 14:17). The new humanity, which the gospel makes possible, is present in the community of those who, already belonging to the new world inaugurated by the resurrection, live according to the law of the Spirit written in their hearts (cf. Jer. 31:33). However, the church has always to become more fully what its title deeds proclaim it to be. It exists in the "between-time", between the coming of Christ in history and his coming again as the Christ of glory. Insofar as it remains in the world, it too has to learn obedience to its living Lord, and to work out in its own life in community the matter and manner of its discipleship.

21. The earliest disciples devoted themselves to the "apostles' teaching and fellowship, the breaking of bread and prayers" (Acts 2:42). In the portrayal of this communion the disciples were said to have had "all things in common", selling their possessions and sharing their goods "as any had need" (Acts 2:44-45). This striking example of community care and concern has, down the ages, prompted a critique of every form of society based on the unbridled pursuit of wealth and power. It has challenged Christians to use their gifts and resources to equip God's people for the work of service (cf. Eph. 4:12). Its deep significance is disclosed in the claim that the whole company of believers was "of one head and soul... and everything they owned was held in common" (Acts 4:32).

22. This communion in heart and soul is inspired by the Holy Spirit and manifested in a life patterned according to the mind of Christ. As Paul puts it, "if there is any encouragement in Christ, any incentive of love, any participation in the Spirit, any affection and sympathy, complete my joy by being of the same mind, having the same love, being in full accord and of one mind... that same mind which was in Christ Jesus" (Phil. 2:1-2:5). The distinctive mark of the mind of Christ, Paul goes on to explain, is humble obedience and self-emptying love (cf. Phil. 2:7-8).

3. The mind of Christ

23. The mind of Christ remains in the church through the presence of the Paraclete/Spirit (cf. John 14:26). It is mediated through the remembered teaching of Jesus and the prayerful discernment of the body of Christ and its members, and gives shape and direction to the practical life of Christian community. This teaching is expressed in Jesus' summary of the law in the twofold commandment of love (cf. Matt. 5:3-12,21-48). It has a dual focus in the radical command "love your enemies" (cf. Matt. 5:43) and the new commandment "love one another as I have loved you" (cf. John 13:34). The mind of Christ, so disclosed, determines the character of renewed humanity, forms the pattern of Christian obedience, and establishes the universe of shared moral values. In this important sense there is a givenness within the Christian response, which the changes of history and culture cannot impair.

24. The mind of Christ, who is the Way as well as the Truth and the Life (cf. John 14:6; Matt. 7:14), also shapes the process by which Christians approach the challenge of new and complex moral and pastoral problems. Because they worship the same God and follow the same Lord, with the guidance of the Holy Spirit they approach these problems with similar resources and concerns. The method of arriving at practical decisions may vary, but underlying any differences of method there is a shared under-

standing of the need to use practical reason in interpreting the witness of the scriptures, Tradition and experience.

25. The mind of Christ also exposes the continuing threat of sin – sins of ignorance and neglect as well as deliberate sins. A knowing and willing disregard of the pattern of life which Christ sets before us is deliberate sin. But people can also drift into sin without any perception of what they are doing. Distorted structures of common life prompt a sinful response. Habits of sin then dull the conscience, until sinners come to prefer darkness to light. So solidarity in sin threatens to disrupt the fellowship of the Holy Spirit.

26. In Christ freedom and order are mutually supportive. The obedience of Christian discipleship is neither the mechanical application of regulation and rule, nor the wilful decision of arbitrary choice. In the freedom of a faithful and obedient response the disciples of Christ seek to discern Christ's mind rather than express their own. In exercising its authority to remit and retain sins (cf. John 20:23), the church has a twofold task of guarding against the power of sin to destroy the life of the community, and of fostering the freedom of its members to discern what is "good and acceptable and perfect" (Rom. 12:2).

4. Growing up into Christ

27. The salvation which God has secured for us once and for all, through the death and resurrection of Jesus Christ, he has now to secure in us and with us through the power of the Holy Spirit. We have to become what, in Christ, we already are. We have to "grow up in every way into him who is the head, into Christ" (Eph. 4:15). We have to "work out (our) own salvation with fear and trembling; for God is at work in (us), both to will and to work for his good pleasure" (Phil. 2:12-13).

28. The lived response of the church to the grace of God develops its own shape and character. The pattern of this response is fashioned according to the mind of Christ; the raw material is the stuff of our everyday world. In Johannine language, believers are still "in" the world, but are not "of" the world (cf. John 17:13-14). In Pauline language, they continue to live "in the body" (2 Cor. 5:6), but no longer "in the flesh" (Rom. 8:9). Christians are to continue in their secular roles and relationships according to the accepted social codes of behaviour, but are to do so as "in the Lord" (cf. Eph. 5:21-6:11; Col. 3:18-4:1). Their new intention and motivation, while affirming the need for these social structures, contain the seeds of radical critique and reappraisal.

29. The fidelity of the church to the mind of Christ involves a continuing process of listening, learning, reflecting and teaching. In this process every member of the community has a part to play. Each person learns to reflect and act according to conscience. Conscience is informed by, and informs, the tradition and teaching of the community. Learning and teaching are a shared discipline, in which the faithful seek to discover together what obedience to the gospel of grace and the law of love entails amidst the moral implications of the gospel which calls for continuing discernment, constant repentance, and "renewal of the mind" (Rom. 12:2), so that through discernment and response men and women may become what in Christ they already are.

30. As part of its missionary imperative and pastoral care, the church has not only to hand on from generation to generation its understanding of life in Christ, but also from time to time to determine how best to reconcile and support those members of the community who have, for whatever reason, failed to live up to its moral demands. Its

aim is twofold: on the one hand, both to minimize the harm done by their falling away and to maintain the integrity of the community, and on the other, to restore the sinner to the life of grace in the fellowship of the church.

5. Discerning the mind of Christ

31. Christian morality is an authentic expression of the new life lived in the power of the Holy Spirit and fashioned according to the mind of Christ. In the tradition common to both our communions, discerning the mind of Christ is a patient and continuing process of prayer and reflection. At its heart is the turning of the sinner to God, sacramentally enacted in baptism and renewed through participation in the sacramental life of the church, meditation on the scriptures, and a life of daily discipleship. The process unfolds through the formation of a character, individual and communal, that reflects the likeness of Christ and embodies the virtues of a true humanity (cf. Gal. 5:19-24). At the same time shared values are formulated in terms of principles and rules defining duties and protecting rights. All this finds expression in the common life of the church as well as in its practical teaching and pastoral care.

32. The teaching developed in this way is an essential element in the process by which individuals and communities exercise their discernment on particular moral issues. Holding in mind the teaching they have received, drawing upon their own experience, and exploring the particularities of the issue that confronts them, they have then to decide what action to take in these circumstances and on this occasion. Such a decision is not only a matter of deduction. Nor can it be taken in isolation. It also calls for detailed and accurate assessment of the facts of the case, careful and consistent reflection and, above all, sensitivity of insight inspired by the Holy Spirit.

6. Continuity and change

33. Guided by the Holy Spirit, believer and believing community seek to discern the mind of Christ amidst the changing circumstances of their own histories. Fidelity to the gospel, obedience to the mind of Christ, openness to the Holy Spirit – these remain the source and strength of continuity. Where there has been an actual break in communion, this difference cannot but be the more pronounced, giving rise to the impression, often mistaken, that there is some fundamental disagreement of understanding and approach.

34. Moral discernment is a demanding task both for the community and for the individual Christian. The more complex the particular issue, the greater the room for disagreement. Christians of different communions are more likely to agree on the character of the Christian life and the fundamental Christian virtues and values. They are more likely to disagree on the consequent rules of practice, particular moral judgments and pastoral counsel.

35. In this chapter we have been concerned to reaffirm the heritage which Anglicans and Roman Catholics share together. We believe that the elements of this heritage provide the basis for a common witness to the world. But since the Reformation the traditions of our two communions have diverged, and there are now differences between them which we must acknowledge and face with honesty and patience. Left unacknowledged, they remain a threat to any common task we might undertake. Faced together with honesty and integrity, they will, we believe, be seen at a deeper level to reflect different aspects of a living whole.

D. PATHS DIVERGE

36. For some fifteen centuries the church in the West struggled to maintain a single, living tradition of communion in worship, faith and practice. In the 16th century, however, this web of shared experience was violently broken. Movements for reform could no longer be contained within the one communion. The Roman Catholic Church and the churches of the Reformation went their different ways and fruits of shared communion were lost. It is in this context of broken communion and diverging histories that the existing differences between Anglicans and Roman Catholics on matters of morality must be located if they are to be rightly understood.

37. These differences, we believe, do not derive from disagreement on the sources of moral authority or on fundamental moral values. Rather, they have arisen from the different emphases which our two communions have given to different elements of the moral life. In particular, differences have occurred in the ways in which each, in isolation from the other, has developed its structures of authority and has come to exercise that authority in the formation of moral judgment. These factors, we believe, have contributed significantly to the differences that have arisen in a limited number of important moral issues. We cannot, of course, hope to do justice to the complex histories that have shaped our two communions and given to each its distinctive ethos. However, we wish to draw attention to two strands in our histories which, for present purposes, are of special significance. First, structures of government and the voice of the laity, and secondly, processes of moral formation and individual judgment.

1. Structures of government and the voice of the laity

38. At the Reformation the Church of England abjured papal supremacy, acknowledged the sovereign as its supreme governor (cf. article 37), and adopted English as the language of its liturgy (cf. article 24). Thus the life of the church, the culture of the nation and the law of the land were inextricably combined. In particular, the lay voice was given, through parliament, a substantial measure of authority in the affairs of the church. With the growth of the Anglican Communion as a worldwide body, patterns of synodical government developed in which laity, clergy and bishops shared the authority of government, the bishops retaining a special voice and responsibility in safeguarding matters of doctrine and worship.

39. As the Anglican Communion has spread, provinces independent of the Church of England have come into being, each with its own history and culture. English culture has become less and less of a common bond as other cultures have exercised an increasing influence. Each province is responsible for the ordering of its own life and has independent legislative and juridical authority; yet each continues in communion with the Church of England and with one another. Every ten years since 1867 the bishops of the Anglican Communion have met together at Lambeth at the invitation of the archbishop of Canterbury, to whom they continue to ascribe a primacy of honour. The resolutions of their conferences have a high degree of authority, but they do not become the official teaching of the individual provinces until these have formally ratified them. In recent times regular meetings of the primates of the Anglican Communion, as well as of the Anglican Consultative Council, in which laity, clergy and bishops are all represented, have contributed to this network of dispersed authority. Whether existing instruments of unity in the Anglican Communion will prove adequate

to the task of preserving full communion between the provinces, as they develop their moral teaching in a rapidly changing and deeply perplexing world, remains to be seen.

40. The Reformation and its aftermath also had repercussions in the government of the Roman Catholic Church. Some of the European rulers who maintained allegiance to Rome found this relationship strained and frustrating, especially since, in certain areas, the papacy also exercised temporal power. The church reacted strongly, however, to any attempt by a secular power to arrogate to itself prerogatives that it believed were rightfully its own. This concern of the church to uphold its independence from the state, together with its need to reaffirm and strengthen its unity in the face of divisive forces, lent to the papal office a renewed significance, and provided the context for the solemn definition of the first Vatican Council which clarified the universal jurisdiction of the bishop of Rome and his infallibility

41. A further development in the Roman Catholic Church since Vatican I has clarified the teaching role of the college of bishops in communion with its head, the bishop of Rome. Bishops are not only the chief teachers in their own diocese, but they also share responsibility for the teaching of the whole church. For Roman Catholics, government and teaching continue to be the prerogative of the episcopal office. Their experience has been that these structures of authority have served the church well in maintaining a fundamental unity of moral teaching.

42. There has also been a significant development in the Roman Catholic Church in the ways by which the laity participate in the discernment and articulation of the church's faith. Laypersons have taken on new roles in liturgy, catechesis and pastoral work, and have come to be involved with their pastors in a variety of consultative and advisory bodies at parochial, diocesan and national levels. This collaboration has been enhanced by their involvement in theological education.

2. Processes of moral formation and individual judgment

43. After the breakdown in communion, Anglicans and Roman Catholics continued to develop, in related but distinctive ways, their common tradition of moral theology and its application by a process of casuistry to specific moral problems. This process has its roots in the New Testament and in the writings of the church fathers. In the late middle ages, however, certain widespread philosophical views diverted attention from the controlling moral vision and concentrated on the obligations of the individual will and the legality of particular acts. What is intended to be a painstaking search for the will of God in the complex circumstances of daily life ran the danger of becoming either meticulous moralism or a means of minimizing the challenge of the gospel.

44. Developments in Roman Catholic moral theology after the council of Trent were not altogether free from this danger. In the 17th century papal authority countermanded both rigorism and laxity. It sought to re-establish a vision of the moral life which respected the demands of the gospel while, at the same time, acknowledging the costliness of discipleship and the frailties of the human condition. During this and subsequent periods, moral theology and spiritual theology were treated as two disciplines, the former tending to restrict itself to the minimal requirements of Christian obedience. In the second half of the present century the Roman Catholic Church, in its desire to set the moral life within a comprehensive vision of life in the Spirit, has witnessed a renewal of moral theology. There has been a return to the scriptures as the central source of moral insight. Older discussions, based on the natural law, with the scriptures

cited solely for confirmation, have been integrated into a more personalistic account of the moral life, which itself has been grounded in the vocation of all human persons to participate in the life of God. An emphasis on the community of persons has led to significant developments, not only in the church's teaching on personal relationships, but also in its teaching on the economic and social implications of the common good.

45. The Anglican tradition of moral theology has been varied and heterogeneous. In the 17th century Anglican theologians of both catholic and puritan persuasion produced comprehensive works of "practical divinity". Drawing on the scholastic tradition, and determined to hold together the moral and spiritual life, they developed this tradition, within a context of Christian vocation of personal holiness. Thus they rejected any approach to the moral life that smacked of moral laxity, and mistrusted any casuistry that, in the details of its analysis of the moral act, threatened to destroy an integral spirit of genuine repentance and renewal. In subsequent centuries the practice of casuistry fell largely into disuse, to be replaced by teaching on "Christian ethics". The aim of this discipline was to set forth the ideal character and pattern of the Christian life and so to prepare Christians for making their own decisions how best to realize that ideal in their own circumstances. The present century has seen a renewal among Anglicans of the discipline of moral theology, sustained by a growing recognition of the need for systematic reflection on the difficult moral issues raised by new technologies, the limits of natural resources, and the claims of the natural environment. In recent times, in response to widespread appeals for guidance on issues of public and social morality, representatives of Christian bodies and other persons of good will have been brought together to study these issues and to suggest how society might best respond to them for the sake of the common good.

46. Anglicans and Roman Catholics have both used a variety of means to strengthen Christian discipleship in its moral dimension. These have included preaching, regular use of catechisms and public recitation of the commandments. In one matter of special significance, however, the Reformation and the consequent Counter-Reformation moved the Church of England and the Roman Catholic Church in different directions. The Reformers' emphasis on the direct access of the sinner to the forgiving and sustaining word of God led Anglicans to reject the view that private confession before a priest was obligatory, although they continued to maintain that it was a wholesome means of grace, and made provision for it in the Book of Common Prayer for those with an unquiet and sorely troubled conscience. While many Anglicans value highly the practice of private confession to a priest, others believe with equal sincerity that it is for them unhelpful and unnecessary. It is sufficient for themselves, they say, that the word of God, expressed in the scriptures and appropriated in the power of the Holy Spirit, speaks authoritatively to their conscience, offering both assurance of forgiveness and practical guidance. For both those who do, and for those who do not, confess their sins privately, general confession and absolution by the priest remains an integral part of the regular Anglican liturgy, a ministry designed to cover both individual and corporate sin. Furthermore, Anglicans often turn to their pastors and advisers, lay and ordained, for moral and spiritual counsel.

47. The Roman Catholic Church, on the other hand, has continued to emphasize the sacrament of penance and the obligation, for those conscious of serious sin, of confessing their sins privately before a priest. Indeed, the renewal of private confession was a major concern of the council of Trent. Since Vatican II the development of the

ministry of forgiveness and healing has led to new forms of sacramental reconciliation, both individual and communal. For centuries the discipline of the confession of sins before a priest has provided an important means of communicating the church's moral teaching and nurturing the spiritual lives of penitents.

3. Moral judgment and the exercise of authority

48. Reflection on the divergent histories of our two communions has shown that their shared concern to respond obediently to God's word and to foster the common good has nevertheless resulted in differing emphases in the ways in which they have nurtured Christian liberty and authority. Both communions recognize that liberty and authority are essentially interdependent, and that the exercise of authority is for the protection and nurture of liberty. It cannot be denied, however, that there is a continuing temptation which the continued separation of our two communions serves only to accentuate – to allow the exercise of authority to lapse into authoritarianism and the exercise of liberty to lapse into individualism.

49. All moral authority is grounded in the goodness and will of God. Our two communions are agreed on this principle and on its implications. Both our communions, moreover, have developed their own structures and institutions for the teaching ministry of the church, by which the will of God is discerned and its implications for the common good declared. Our communions have diverged, however, in their views of the ways in which authority is most fruitfully exercised and the common good best promoted. Anglicans affirm that authority needs to be dispersed rather than centralized, that the common good is better served by allowing to individual Christians the greatest possible liberty of informed judgment, and that therefore official moral teaching should as far as possible be commendatory rather than prescriptive and binding. Roman Catholics, on the other hand, have, for the sake of common good, emphasized the need for a central authority to preserve unity and to give clear and binding teaching.

4. Differing emphases, shared perspectives

50. In our conversations together we have made two discoveries: first, that many of the preconceptions that we brought with us concerning each other's understanding of moral teaching and discipline were often little more than caricatures; and secondly, that the differences which actually exist between us appear in a new light when we consider them in their origin and context.

51. Some of these differences lend themselves to misperception and caricature. It is not true, for instance, that Anglicans concern themselves solely with liberty, while Roman Catholics concern themselves solely with law. It is not true that the Roman Catholic Church has predetermined answers to every moral question, while the Anglican church has no answers at all. It is not true that Roman Catholics always agree on moral issues, nor that Anglicans never agree. It is not true that Anglican ethics is pragmatic and unprincipled, while Roman Catholic moral theology is principled but abstract. It is not true that Roman Catholics are always more careful of the institution in their concern for the common good, while Anglican moral teaching is utilitarian. Caricature, we may grant, is never totally contrived; but caricature it remains. In fact, there is good reason to hope that, if they can pray, think and act together, Anglicans and Roman Catholics, by emphasizing different aspects of the moral life, may come to complement and enrich each other's understanding and practice of it.

52. Nevertheless, differences there are and differences there remain. Both Anglicans and Roman Catholics are accustomed to using the concept of law to give character and form to the claims of morality. However, this concept is open to more than one interpretation and use, so causing real and apparent differences between our two traditions. For example, a notable feature of established Roman Catholic moral teaching is its emphasis on the absoluteness of some demands of the moral law and the existence of certain prohibitions to which there are no exceptions. In these instances, what is prohibited is intrinsically disordered and therefore objectively wrong. Anglicans, on the other hand, while acknowledging the same ultimate values, are not persuaded that the laws as we apprehend them are necessarily absolute. In certain circumstances, they would argue, it might be right to incorporate contextual and pastoral considerations in the formulation of a moral law, on the grounds that fundamental moral values are better served if the law sometimes takes into account certain contingencies of nature and history and certain disorders of the human condition. In so doing, they do not make the clear-cut distinction, which Roman Catholics make, between canon law, with its incorporation of contingent and prudential considerations, and the moral law, which in its principles is absolute and universal. In both our communions, however, there are now signs of a shift away from a reliance on the concept of law as the central category of providing moral teaching. Its place is being taken by the concept of "persons-in-community". An ethic of response is preferred to an ethic of obedience. In the desire to respond as fully as possible to the new law of Christ, the primacy of persons is emphasized above the impersonalism of a system of law, thus avoiding the distortions of both individualism and utilitarianism. The full significance of this shift of emphasis is not yet clear, and its detailed implications have still to be worked out. It should be emphasized, however, that whatever differences there may be in the way in which they express the moral law, both our traditions respect the consciences of persons in good faith.

53. We hope we have said enough in this chapter to explain how a deeper understanding of our separated histories has enabled us to appreciate better the real character of our divergences, and has persuaded us that it has been our broken communion, more than anything else, that has exacerbated our disagreements. In recent times there has been a large measure of cross-fertilization between our two traditions. Both our communions, for example, have shared in the renewal of biblical, historical and liturgical studies, and both have participated in the ecumenical movement. Our separated paths have once again begun to converge. It is in the conviction that we also possess a shared vision of Christian discipleship and a common approach to the moral life, that we take courage now to look directly at our painful disagreement on two particular moral issues.

E. AGREEMENT AND DISAGREEMENT

54. The moral issues on which the Anglican and Roman Catholic communions have expressed official disagreement are the marriage of a divorced person during the life-time of a former partner; and the permissible methods of controlling conception. There are other issues concerning sexuality on which Anglican and Roman Catholic attitudes and opinions appear to conflict, especially abortion and the exercise of homosexual relations. These we shall consider briefly at the end of this section; but because

of the official nature of the disagreement on the former two issues, we shall concentrate on them.

1. Human sexuality

55. Before considering the points of disagreement, we need to emphasize the extent of our agreement. Both our traditions affirm with scripture that human sexuality is part of God's good creation (cf. Gen. 1:27; see further Gen. 24; Ruth 4; the Song of Songs; Eph. 5:21-32; etc.). Sexual differentiation within the one human nature gives bodily expression to the vocation of God's children to interpersonal communion. Human sexuality embraces the whole range of bodily, imaginative, affective and spiritual experiences. It enters into a person's deepest character and relationships, individual and social, and constitutes a fundamental mode of human communication. It is ordered towards the gift of self and the creation of life.

56. Sexual experience, isolated from the vision of the full humanity to which God calls us, is ambivalent. It can be as disruptive as it can be unitive, as destructive as it can be creative. Christians have always known this to be so (cf. Matt. 5:28). They have therefore recognized the need to integrate sexuality into an ordered pattern of life, which will nurture a person's spiritual relationships both with other persons and with God. Such integration calls for the exercise of the virtue traditionally termed chastity, a virtue rooted in the spiritual significance of bodily existence (cf. 1 Thess. 4:1-8; Gal. 5:23; Cor. 6:9,12-20).

57. Both our traditions offer comparable accounts of chastity which involves the ordering of the sexual drive either towards marriage or in a life of celibacy. Chastity does not signify the repression of sexual instincts and energies, but their integration into a pattern of relationships in which a person may find true happiness, fulfilment and salvation. Anglicans and Roman Catholics agree that the new life in Christ calls for a radical break with the sin of sexual self-centredness, which leads inevitably to individual and social disintegration. The New Testament is unequivocal in its witness that the right ordering and use of sexual energy is an essential aspect of life in Christ (cf. Mark 10:9; John 8:11; 1 Cor. 7:1; Pet. 3:1-7; Heb. 13:4), and this is reiterated throughout the common Christian tradition, including the time since our two communions diverged.

58. Human beings, male and female, flourish as persons in community. Personal relationships have a social as well as a private dimension. Sexual relationships are no exception. They are bound up with issues of poverty and justice, the equality and dignity of women and men, and the protection of children. Both our traditions treat of human sexuality in the context of the common good, and regard marriage and family life as institutions divinely appointed for human well-being and happiness. It is in the covenanted relationship between husband and wife that the physical expression of sexuality finds its true fulfilment (cf. Gen. 2:18-25), and in the procreation and nurturing of children that the two persons together share in the life-giving generosity of God (cf. Gen. 1:27-29).

2. Marriage and family

59. Neither of our two traditions regards marriage as a human invention. On the contrary, both see it as grounded by God in human nature and as a source of community, social order and stability. Nevertheless, the institution of marriage has found dif-

ferent expression in different cultures and at different times. In our own time, for instance, we are becoming increasingly aware that some forms, far from nurturing the dignity of persons, foster oppression and domination, especially of women. However, despite the distortions that have affected it, both our traditions continue to discern and uphold in marriage a God-given pattern and significance.

60. Marriage gives rise to enduring obligations. Personal integrity and social witness both require a life-long and exclusive commitment, and the "good" which marriage embodies includes the reciprocal love of husband and wife, and the procreation and raising of children. When these realities are disregarded, a breakdown of family life may ensue, carrying with it a heavy burden of misery and social disintegration. The word "obligation", however, is inadequate to express the profound personal call inherent in the Christian understanding of marriage. Both our traditions speak of marriage as a "vocation to holiness" (Lambeth 1958, resolution 112 as quoted in Lambeth 1968, resolution 22), as involving an "integral vision of... vocation" (*Familiaris Consortio*, 32). When God calls women and men to the married estate, and supports them in it, God's love for them is creative, redemptive and sanctifying (cf. Lambeth, *ibid.*).

61. The mutual pact, or covenant, made between the spouses (cf. *Gaudium et Spes*, 47-52, and *Final Report on the Theology of Marriage and its Application to Mixed Marriages*, 1975, 21) bears the mark of God's own abundant love (cf. Hos. 2:19-21). Covenanted human love points beyond itself to the covenantal love and fidelity of God and to God's will that marriage should be a means of universal blessing and grace. Marriage, in the order of creation, is both sign and reality of God's faithful love, and thus it has a naturally sacramental dimension. Since it also points to the saving love of God, embodied in Christ's love for the church (cf. Eph. 5:25), it is open to a still deeper sacramentality within the life and communion of Christ's own body.

62. So far, we believe, our traditions agree. Further discussion, however, is needed on the ways in which they interpret this sacramentality of marriage. The Roman Catholic tradition, following the common tradition of the West, which was officially promulgated by the council of Florence in 1439, affirms that Christian marriage is a sacrament in the order of redemption, the natural sign of the human covenant having been raised by Christ to become a sign of the irrevocable covenant between himself and his church. What was sacramental in the order of creation becomes a sacrament of the church in the order of redemption. When solemnized between two baptized persons, marriage is an effective sign of redeeming grace. Anglicans, while affirming the special significance of marriage within the body of Christ, emphasize a sacramentality of marriage that transcends the boundaries of the church. For many years in England after the Reformation, marriages could be solemnized only in church. When civil marriage became possible, Anglicans recognized such marriages, too, as sacramental and graced by God, since the state of matrimony had itself been "adorned and beautified" by Christ by his presence at the marriage at Cana of Galilee (cf. BCP 1662, *Introduction to the Solemnization of Matrimony*). From these considerations it would appear that, in this context, Anglicans tend to emphasize the breadth of God's grace in creation, while Roman Catholics tend to emphasize the depth of God's grace in Christ. These emphases should be seen as complementary. Ideally, they belong together. They have, however, given rise to differing understandings of the conditions under which the sacramentality of a marriage is fulfilled.

63. The vision of marriage as a fruitful, life-long covenant, full of the grace of God, is not always sustained in the realities of life. Its very goodness, when corrupted by human frailty, self-centredness and sin, gives rise to pain, despair and tragedy, not only for the couple immediately involved in marital difficulty or breakdown, but also for their children, the wider family and the social order. Faced with such situations, the church endeavours to minister the grace and discipline of Christ himself. Anglicans and Roman Catholics have both sought to act in obedience to the teaching of Christ. However, in their separation their practice and pastoral discipline came to differ and diverge. In order to elucidate the significance of such differences and divergences we shall now turn to the two issues on which disagreement has been officially voiced, namely, marriage after divorce and contraception.

3. Marriage after divorce

64. Before the break in communion in the 16th century, the church in the West had come to derive a doctrine of indissolubility from its interpretation of the teaching of Jesus concerning marriage. The official church teaching included two affirmations: not only was it the case that the marriage bond *ought not* to be dissolved; but it was also the case that it *could not* be dissolved. At the Reformation, continental Protestant Reformers interpreted the teaching of Jesus (cf. Matt. 5:32; 19:9) differently, and urged that divorce was permissible on grounds of adultery or desertion. The council of Trent, on the other hand, reaffirmed the teaching, first, that the marriage bond could not be dissolved, even by adultery, and secondly, that neither partner, not even the innocent one, could contract a second marriage during the life-time of the other.

a) The Anglican Communion

65. The development of a distinctive marriage discipline within Anglicanism can be understood only in the context of the development of diverse civil jurisdictions. This is true both of the Church of England and of other Anglican provinces. At the time of the Reformation the Church of England passed no formal resolution on marriage and divorce. It never officially accepted the teaching of the continental Reformers, but despite attempts to introduce an alternative discipline, held to the older belief and practice. Revisions of canon law in 1597 and 1604 established no change in teaching or discipline, although, in the centuries that followed, theological opinion varied and even in practice was not completely uniform. Up to the middle of the 19th century divorce, with the consequent freedom to marry again, was available only to the rich and influential few by act of parliament. In 1857, when matrimonial matters were transferred from ecclesiastical to civil jurisdiction, divorce on grounds of adultery was legalized. Although clergy were given the right to refuse to solemnize the marriage of a divorced person in the life-time of a former partner, the Church of England as a whole came to accept de facto the new state of affairs: marriages after divorce occurred, but the church refused to give official approval to their solemnization.

66. As Anglican provinces were inaugurated outside England, each had to formulate its own pastoral marriage discipline in the light of local civil law and marriage customs. In an attempt to secure a coherent policy among the provinces, the Lambeth conference of 1888 reaffirmed the life-long intention of the marriage covenant, but accepted that the clergy should not be instructed to refuse the sacraments to those who were remarried "under civil sanction". It left open the question whether or not the inno-

cent party was free to enter a second marriage. Since then, theological opinion has varied. Some Anglicans have continued to hold the traditional view of indissolubility. Others have argued that, once the married relationship has been destroyed beyond repair, the marriage itself is as if dead, the vows have been frustrated and the bond has been broken. The Lambeth Conference of 1978 reaffirmed the "first-order principle" of life-long union, but it also acknowledged a responsibility for those for whom "*no course absolutely* consonant with the first order principle of marriage as a life-long union may be available" (resolution 34). Subsequent practice has varied. Different provinces of the Anglican Communion have devised different marriage disciplines. Among some of them permission is granted, on carefully considered pastoral grounds, for a marriage after divorce to be solemnized in church, although even in these cases practice varies concerning the precise form the complete service takes. In other cases, after a civil ceremony, a service of prayer and dedication may be offered instead. The practical decision normally lies with the bishop and the bishop's advisers.

b) The Roman Catholic Church

67. In the period following the breach of communion, the Roman Catholic Church continued to uphold the doctrine of indissolubility reaffirmed at Trent. At the same time it developed a complex system of jurisprudence and discipline to meet its diverse practical and pastoral needs and to provide a supportive role for those whose faith was threatened by a destructive marital relationship.

68. A distinction is made between marriages that are sacraments – those in which both partners are baptized – and marriages that are not sacraments ("natural marriages") – those in which one or both partners are unbaptized. In Roman Catholic teaching both forms of marriage are in principle indissoluble. A sacramental marriage which has been duly consummated cannot be dissolved by any human power, civil or ecclesiastical. Where such a marriage, however, has not been consummated, it can be dissolved. On the other hand, it has come to be accepted that a non-sacramental marriage, whether consummated or not, can in certain cases be dissolved.

69. The history of these matters is long and complex. In his first letter to the Corinthians, St Paul deals with the case of a married couple, one of whom is a believer, the other a non-believer. If the non-believer refuses to stay with the believer, then, he says, "the brother or sister is not bound" (1 Cor. 7:15; cf. 12-15). This was later interpreted in canon law to mean that the partner who had become a Christian was free to leave an unbelieving spouse who was unwilling to continue married life "in peace", and to marry again. There are several references to this "Pauline text" in the writings of the early church fathers dealing with the dissolution of marriage. It became part of church legislation in 1199, but was fully clarified only in the code of canon law of 1917. It is still part of Roman Catholic practice (cf. *Codex Iuris Canonici* [CIC] Can. 1143).

70. The exercise of the "Pauline privilege" is not the only occasion when the power to dissolve a marriage is invoked. In the course of the missionary expansion of the church other situations have prompted similar action. From 1537 popes used their powers to dissolve the natural marriages of inhabitants of Africa and the Indies who wished to convert to the Catholic faith. In 1917 this practice "in favour of the faith" (or, as it is sometimes called, the "Petrine privilege") was extended to other parts of the world and applied to similar situations. The "privilege of the faith" is still recognized today,

and subject to certain conditions a dissolution of a non-sacramental marriage may, by way of exception, be granted on these grounds by the holy see.

71. Other elements in Roman Catholic doctrine and practice have been prompted by particular practical problems. For example, it was the problem of clandestine marriages, valid but not proved to be so, that prompted the council of Trent to promulgate the decree *Tametsi* (1563). This required that marriages be celebrated before the pastor (or another priest delegated by him or the ordinary) and two or three witnesses. With certain modifications, this "form" is still binding, and failure to observe it, without due dispensation, renders a marriage null and void (cf. CIC Can. 1108). A partner to such a union, therefore, is not considered in canon law to be held by a marital bond and is free to contract a valid marriage. In the case of an intended marriage between a Roman Catholic and a person who is not a Roman Catholic, the church today often grants a dispensation from the "form", out of respect for the beliefs, conscience and family ties of the person concerned.

72. Another development in Roman Catholic jurisprudence concerns the practice of annulment, that is, the declaration of the fact that a true marriage never existed. The marriage contract requires full and free consent. If this is lacking, there can be no marriage. It has always been recognized that there can be no marriage if a person is forced to enter it against his or her will. More recent reflection has analyzed in greater depth the nature of consent. It is now recognized that there may be serious psychological as well as physical defects. If such defects can be demonstrated to have existed when verbal consent was exchanged, it can be declared, according to Roman Catholic teaching, that there was never a marriage at all (cf. CIC Can. 1095). Serious defect is also present if, at the time of exchanging consent, there is a deliberate rejection of some element essential to marriage (cf. CIC Can. 1056; 1101, §2).

c) The situation today

73. Clearly there are differences of discipline and pastoral practice between Anglicans and Roman Catholics. Some of the factors in our traditions are the result of responses to contingent historical circumstances, for example, the Roman Catholic Church's requirement of the "form" for valid marriage. However, other elements have deeper roots. When we explore our differences it is to these, in particular, that we must direct our attention. Before doing so, however, it is important to note that both communions make provision for marital separation, without excluding the persons concerned, even after civil divorce, from the eucharist.

74. In accord with the Western tradition, Anglicans and Roman Catholics believe that the ministers of the marriage are the man and woman themselves, who bring the marriage into being by making a solemn vow and promise of life-long fidelity to each other. Anglicans and Roman Catholics both regard this vow as solemn and binding. Anglicans and Roman Catholics both believe that marriage points to the love of Christ, who bound himself in an irrevocable covenant to his church, and that therefore marriage is in principle indissoluble. Roman Catholics go on to affirm that the unbreakable bond between Christ and his church, signified in the union of two baptized persons, in its turn strengthens the marriage bond between husband and wife and renders it absolutely unbreakable, except by death. Other marriages can, in exceptional circumstances, be dissolved. Anglicans, on the other hand, do not make an absolute distinction between marriages of the baptized and other marriages, regarding all marriages as

in some sense sacramental. Some Anglicans hold that all marriages are therefore indissoluble. Others, while holding that all marriages are indeed sacramental and are in principle indissoluble, are not persuaded that the marriage bond, even in the case of marriage of the baptized, can never in fact be dissolved.

75. Roman Catholic teaching that, when a sacramental marriage has been consummated, the covenant is irrevocable, is grounded in its understanding of sacramentality, as already outlined. Further, its firm legal framework is judged to be the best protection for the institution of marriage, and thus best to serve the common good of the community, which itself redounds to the true good of the persons concerned. Thus Roman Catholic teaching and law uphold the indissolubility of the marriage covenant, even when the human relationship of love and trust has ceased to exist and there is no practical possibility of recreating it. The Anglican position, though equally concerned with the sacramentality of marriage and the common good of the community, does not necessarily understand these in the same way. Some Anglicans attend more closely to the actual character of the relationship between husband and wife. Where a relationship of mutual love and trust has clearly ceased to exist, and there is no practical possibility of remaking it, the bond itself, they argue, has also ceased to exist. When the past has been forgiven and healed, a new covenant and bond may in good faith be made.

76. Our reflections have brought to the fore an issue of considerable importance. What is the right balance between regard for the person and regard for the institution? The answer must be found within the context of our theology of communion and our understanding of the common good. For the reasons which have been explained, in the Roman Catholic Church the institution of marriage has enjoyed the favour of the law. Marriages are presumed to be valid unless the contrary case can be clearly established. Since Vatican II renewed emphasis has been placed upon the rights and welfare of the individual person, but tensions still remain. A similar tension is felt by Anglicans, although pastoral concern has sometimes inclined them to give priority to the welfare of the individual person over the claims of the institution. History has shown how difficult it is to achieve the right balance.

77. Our shared reflections have made us see more clearly that Anglicans and Roman Catholics are at one in their commitment to following the teaching of Christ on marriage; at one in their understanding of the nature and meaning of marriage; and at one in their concern to reach out to those who suffer as a result of the breakdown of marriage. We agree that marriage is sacramental, although we do not fully agree on how, and this affects our sacramental discipline. Thus, Roman Catholics recognize a special kind of sacramentality in a marriage between baptized persons, which they do not see in other marriages. Anglicans, on the other hand, recognize a sacramentality in all valid marriages. On the level of law and policy, neither the Roman Catholic nor the Anglican practice regarding divorce is free from real or apparent anomalies and ambiguities. While, therefore, there are differences between us concerning marriage after divorce, to isolate those differences from this context of far-reaching agreement and to make them into an insuperable barrier would be a serious and sorry misrepresentation of the true situation.

4. Contraception

78. Both our traditions agree that procreation is one of the divinely intended "goods" of the institution of marriage. A deliberate decision, therefore, without justifi-

able reason, to exclude procreation from a marriage is a rejection of this good and a contradiction of the nature of marriage itself. On this also we agree. We are likewise at one in opposing what has been called a "contraceptive mentality", that is, a selfish preference for immediate satisfaction over the more demanding good of having and raising a family.

79. Both Roman Catholics and Anglicans agree, too, that God calls married couples to "responsible parenthood". This refers to a range of moral concerns, which begins with the decision to accept parenthood and goes on to include the nurture, education, support and guidance of children. Decisions about the size of a family raise many questions for both Anglicans and Roman Catholics. Broader questions concerning the pressure of population, poverty, the social and ecological environment, as well as more directly personal questions concerning the couple's material, physical and psychological resources, may arise. Situations exist in which a couple would be morally justified in avoiding bringing children into being. Indeed, there are some circumstances in which it would be morally irresponsible to do so. On this our two communions are also agreed. We are not agreed, however, on the methods by which this responsibility may be exercised.

80. The disagreement may be summed up as follows. Anglicans understand the good of procreation to be a norm governing the married relationship as a whole. Roman Catholic teaching, on the other hand, requires that each and every act of intercourse should be "open to procreation" (cf. *Humanae Vitae*, 11). This difference of understanding received official expression in 1930. Before this, both churches would have counselled abstinence for couples who had a justifiable reason to avoid conception. The Lambeth Conference of Anglican bishops, however, resolved in 1930 that "where there is a clearly felt moral obligation to limit or avoid parenthood, and where there is a morally sound reason for avoiding complete abstinence... other methods may be used" (resolution 15). The encyclical of Pope Pius XI (*Casti Connubii*, 1930), which was intended among other things as a response to the Lambeth resolution, renewed the traditional Roman Catholic position. In 1968 the teaching was further developed and clarified in Pope Paul VI's encyclical, *Humanae Vitae*. The Lambeth Conference of 1968 reaffirmed the position that had been taken by the 1958 Lambeth Conference. The Roman Catholic position has been frequently reaffirmed since, for example, in the documents *Familiaris Consortio*, 1981, and *Catechism of the Catholic Church*, 1992. This teaching belongs to the ordinary magisterium calling for "religious assent".

81. The immediate point at issue in this controversy would seem to concern the moral integrity of the act of marital intercourse. Both our traditions agree that this involves the two basic "goods" of marriage, loving union and procreation. Moral integrity requires that husband and wife respect both these goods together. For Anglicans, it is sufficient that this respect should characterize the married relationship as a whole; whereas for Roman Catholics, it must characterize each act of sexual intercourse. Anglicans understand the moral principle to be that procreation should not arbitrarily be excluded from the continuing relationship; whereas Roman Catholics hold that there is an unbreakable connection, willed by God, between the two "goods" of marriage and the corresponding meanings of marital intercourse, and that therefore they may not be sundered by any direct and deliberate act (cf. *Humanae Vitae*, 12).

82. The Roman Catholic doctrine is not simply an authoritative statement of the nature of the integrity of the marital act. The whole teaching on human love and sexual-

ity, continued and developed in *Humanae Vitae*, must be taken into account when considering the Roman Catholic position on this issue. The definition of integrity is founded upon a number of considerations: a way of understanding human fruitfulness and divine creativity; the special vocation of the married couple; and the requirements of the virtue of marital chastity. Anglicans accept all of these considerations as relevant to determining the integrity of the marital relationship and act. Thus they share the same spectrum of moral and theological considerations. However, they do not accept the arguments Roman Catholics derive from them, nor the conclusions they draw from them regarding the morality of contraception.

5. Other issues

83. So far in this section we have argued that our disagreements in the areas of marriage, procreation and contraception, areas in which our two communions have made official but conflicting pronouncements, are on the level of derived conclusions rather than fundamental values. However, as we observed earlier, there are other important issues in the area of sexuality where no official disagreement has been expressed between our two communions, but where disagreement is nonetheless perceived to exist. Although Anglicans and Roman Catholics may often achieve a common mind and witness on many issues of peace and social justice, nevertheless, it is said, their teaching is irreconcilable on such matters as abortion and homosexual relations. What is more, there are other difficult and potentially divisive issues in the offing, as scientific and technological expertise develops the unprecedented power to manipulate the basic material, not only of the environment, but also of human life itself.

84. This is not the time or place to discuss such further issues in detail. However, confining ourselves to the two issues of abortion and homosexual relations, we would argue that, in these instances too, the disagreements between us are not on the level of fundamental moral values, but on their implementation in practical judgments.

85. Anglicans have no agreed teaching concerning the precise moment from which the new human life developing in the womb is to be given the full protection due to a human person. Only some Anglicans insist that in all circumstances, and without exception, such protection must extend back to the time of conception. Roman Catholic teaching, on the other hand, is that the human embryo must be treated as a human person from the moment of conception (cf. *Donum Vitae*, 1987, and Declaration on Procured Abortion, 1974). Difference of teaching on this matter cannot but give rise to difference of judgment on what is morally permissible when a tragic conflict occurs between the rights of the mother and the rights of the foetus. Roman Catholic teaching rejects all direct abortion. Among Anglicans the view is to be found that in certain cases direct abortion is morally justifiable. Anglicans and Roman Catholics, however, are at one in their recognition of the sanctity, and right to life, of all human persons, and they share an abhorrence of the growing practice in many countries of abortion on grounds of mere convenience. This agreement on fundamentals is reflected both in pronouncements of bishops and in official documents issued by both communions (cf. *Catechism of the Catholic Church*, 1992, 2270, and Lambeth Conference Report, 1930, 16, and 1978, 10).

86. We cannot enter here more fully into this debate, and we do not wish to underestimate the consequences of our disagreement. We wish, however, to affirm once again that Anglicans and Roman Catholics share the same fundamental teaching con-

cerning the mystery of human life and the sanctity of the human person. They also share the same sense of awe and humility in making practical judgments in this area of profound moral complexity. Their differences arise in the way in which they develop and apply fundamental moral teaching. What we have said earlier about our different formulations of the moral law is here relevant (see §52). For Roman Catholics, the rejection of abortion is an example of an absolute prohibition. For Anglicans, however, such an absolute and categorical prohibition would not be typical of their moral reasoning. That is why it is important to set such differences in context. Only then shall we be able to assess their wider implications.

87. In the matter of homosexual relationships a similar situation obtains. Both our communions affirm the importance and significance of human friendship and affection among men and women, whether married or single. Both affirm that all persons, including those of homosexual orientation, are made in the divine image and share the full dignity of human creatureliness. Both affirm that a faithful and lifelong marriage between a man and a woman provides the normative context for a fully sexual relationship. Both appeal to scripture and the natural order as the sources of their teaching on this issue. Both reject, therefore, the claim, sometimes made, that homosexual relationships and married relationships are morally equivalent, and equally capable of expressing the right ordering and use of the sexual drive. Such ordering and use, we believe, are an essential aspect of life in Christ. Here again our different approaches to the formulation of law are relevant (cf. §52). Roman Catholic teaching holds that homosexual activity is "intrinsically disordered", and concludes that it is always objectively wrong. This affects the kind of pastoral advice that is given to homosexual persons. Anglicans could agree that such activity is disordered; but there may well be differences among them in the consequent moral and pastoral advice they would think it right to offer to those seeking their counsel and direction.

88. Our two communions have in the past developed their moral teaching and practical and pastoral disciplines in isolation from each other. The differences that have arisen between them are serious, but careful study and consideration has shown us that they are not fundamental. The urgency of the times and the perplexity of the human condition demand that they now do all they can to come together to provide a common witness and guidance for the well-being of humankind and the good of the whole creation.

F. TOWARDS SHARED WITNESS

89. We have already seen how divergence between Anglicans and Roman Catholics on matters of practice and official moral teaching has been aggravated, if not caused, by the historic breach of communion and the consequent breakdown in communication. Separation has led to estrangement, and estrangement has fostered misperception, misunderstanding and suspicion. Only in recent times has this process been reversed and the first determined steps taken along the way to renewed and full communion.

90. The theme of communion illumines, we believe, not only the reality of the church as a worshipping community but also the form and fullness of Christian life in the world. Indeed, since the church is called in Christ to be a sign and sacrament of a renewed humanity, it also illumines the nature and destiny of human life as such. As ARCIC has affirmed in *Church as Communion*:

To explore the meaning of communion is not only to speak of the church but also to address the world at the heart of its deepest need, for human beings long for true community in freedom, justice and peace and for respect of human dignity (§3).

In this final section, therefore, we return once again to the theme of communion and consider the light it sheds both on the moral order and on the church's moral response.

1. Communion and the moral order

91. Communion, we have argued, is a constitutive characteristic of a fully human life, signifying "a relationship based on participation in a shared reality" (cf. *Church as Communion*, §12). From this perspective the moral dimension of human life is itself perceived to be fundamentally relational, determined both by the nature of the reality in which it participates and by the form appropriate to such participation.

92. Participation of human beings in the life of God, in whom they live and move and have their being (cf. Acts 17:28), is grounded in their creation in God's image (cf. *Church as Communion*, 6). The fundamental relationship in which they stand, therefore, is their relationship to God, Creator and goal of all that is, seen and unseen. Created and sustained in this relationship, they are drawn towards God's absolute goodness, which they experience as both gift and call. Moral responsibility is a gift of divine grace; the moral imperative an expression of divine love. When Jesus bids his disciples before all else to seek the kingdom of God (cf. Matt. 6:33), he tells them also that they are to reflect in their own lives the "perfection" which belongs to the divine life (cf. Matt. 5:48). This call to "perfection" echoes the Lord's call to the people of Israel to participate in his holiness (cf. Lev. 19:2). As such, it does not ignore human fragility, failure and sin; but it does lay bare the full dimensions of a response that reflects the height and breadth and depth of the divine righteousness and love (cf. Rom. 8:1-4).

93. Human beings are not purely spiritual beings; they are fashioned out of the dust (cf. Gen. 2:7). Created in the image of God, they are shaped by nature and culture, and participate in both the glory and the shame of the human story. Their responsibility to God issues in a responsibility for God's world, and their transformation into the likeness of God embraces their relationships both to the natural world and to one another. Hence no arbitrary boundaries may be set between the good of the individual, the common good of humanity, and the good of the whole created order. The context of the truly human life is the universal and all-embracing rule of God.

94. The world in which human beings participate is a changing world. Science and technology have given them the power, to a degree unforeseen in earlier centuries, to impress their own designs on the natural environment, by adapting the environment to their own needs, by exploiting it and even by destroying it. However, there are ultimate limits to what is possible. Nature is not infinitely malleable. Moreover, not everything that is humanly possible is humanly desirable, or morally right. In many situations, what is sometimes called progress is, as a consequence of human ignorance, degrading and destructive The moral task is to discern how fundamental and eternal values may be expressed and embodied in a world that is subject to continuing change.

95. The world in which human beings participate is not only a changing world; it is also a broken and imperfect world. It is subject to futility and sin, and stands under the judgment of God. Its human structures are distorted by violence and greed. Inevitably, conflicts of value and clashes of interest arise, and situations occur in which the requirements of the moral order are uncertain. Law is enacted and enforced to pre-

serve order and to protect and serve the common good. Admittedly, it can perpetuate inequalities of wealth and power, but its true end is to ensure justice and peace. At a deeper level, the moral order looks for its fulfilment to a renewal of personal freedom and dignity within a forgiving, healing and caring community.

2. Communion and the church

96. Life in Christ is a life of communion, to be manifested for the salvation of the world and for the glorification of God the Father. In the fellowship of the Holy Spirit the church participates in the Son's loving and obedient response to the Father. But even if, in the resurrection of Christ, the new world has already begun, the end is not yet. So the church continues to pray and prepare for the day when Christ will deliver the kingdom to the Father (cf. 1 Cor. 15:24-28) and God will be all in all. In the course of history Anglicans and Roman Catholics have disagreed on certain specific matters of moral teaching and practice, but they continue to hold to the same vision of human nature and destiny fulfilled in Christ. Furthermore, their deep desire to find an honest and faithful resolution of their disagreements is itself evidence of a continuing communion at a more profound level than that on which disagreement has occurred.

97. The church as communion reflects the communion of the triune God, Father, Son and Holy Spirit (cf. John 17:20-22; 14:16f., 2 Cor. 13:13), and anticipates the fullness of communion in the kingdom of God. Consequently, communion means that members of the church share a responsibility for discerning the action of the Spirit in the contemporary world, for shaping a truly human response, and for resolving the ensuing moral perplexities with integrity and fidelity to the gospel. Within this shared responsibility, those who exercise the office of pastor and teacher have the special task of equipping the church and its members for life in the world, and for guiding and confirming their free and faithful response to the gospel. The exercise of this authority will itself bear the marks of communion, insofar as a sustained attentiveness to the experience and reflection of the faithful becomes part of the process of making an informed and authoritative judgment. One such example of this understanding of the interaction of communion and authority, we suggest, is the careful and sustained process of listening and public consultation which has preceded the publication of some of the pastoral letters of bishops' conferences of the Roman Catholic Church in different parts of the world.

98. Communion also means that, where there has been a failure to meet the claims of the moral order to which the church bears witness, there will be a determined attempt to restore the sinner to the life of grace in the community, thereby allowing the gospel of forgiveness to be proclaimed even to the greatest of sinners. Anglicans and Roman Catholics share the conviction that God's righteousness and God's love and mercy are inseparable (cf. *Salvation and the Church*, 17 and 18), and both communions continue to exercise a ministry of healing, forgiveness and reconciliation.

3. Towards moral integrity and full communion

99. Anglicans and Roman Catholics share a deep desire, not only for full communion, but also for a resolution of the disagreement that exists between them on certain specific moral issues. The two are related. On the one hand, seeking a resolution of our

disagreements is part of the process of growing together towards full communion. On the other hand, only as closer communion leads to deeper understanding and trust can we hope for a resolution of our disagreements.

100. In order to make an informed and faithful response to the moral perplexities facing humanity today, Christians must promote a global and ecumenical perception of fundamental human relationships and values. Our common vision of humanity in Christ places before us this responsibility, while at the same time requiring us to develop a greater sensitivity to the different experiences, insights and approaches that are appropriate to different cultures and contexts. The separation that still exists between our two communions is a serious obstacle to the church's mission and a darkening of the moral wisdom it may hope to share with the world.

101. Our work together within this commission has shown us that the discernment of the precise nature of the moral agreement and disagreement between Anglicans and Roman Catholics is not always an easy task. One problem we faced was the fact that we often found ourselves comparing the variety of moral judgments present and permissible among Anglicans with the official, authoritative teachings of the Roman Catholic Church. This feature of our discussions was inevitable, given the differences between our two communions in the way they understand and exercise authority. Working together, however, has convinced us that the disagreements on moral matters, which at present exist between us, need not constitute an insuperable barrier to progress towards fuller communion. Painful and perplexing as they are, they do not reveal a fundamental divergence in our understanding of the moral implications of the gospel.

102. Continuing study is needed of the differences between us, real or apparent, especially in our understanding and use of the notion of "law". A clearer understanding is required of the relation of the concept of law to the concepts of moral order and the common good, and the relation of all these concepts to the vision of human happiness and fulfilment as "persons-in-community" that we have been given in and through Jesus Christ. However, Anglicans and Roman Catholics do not talk to each other as moral strangers. They both appeal to a shared tradition, and they recognize the same scripture as normative of that tradition. They both respect the role of reason in moral discernment. They both give due place to the classic virtue of prudence. We are convinced, therefore, that further exchange between our two traditions on moral questions will serve both the cause of Christian unity and the good of that larger society of which we are all part.

103. We end our document with a specific practical recommendation. We propose that steps should be taken to establish further instruments of cooperation between our two communions at all levels of church life (especially national and regional), to engage with the serious moral issues confronting humanity today. In view of our common approach to moral reflection, and in the light of the agreements we have already discovered to exist between us, we believe that bilateral discussions between Anglicans and Roman Catholics would be especially valuable.

104. We make this proposal for the following reasons:

> Working together on moral issues would be a practical way of expressing the communion we already enjoy, of moving towards full communion, and of understanding more clearly what it entails; without such collaboration we run the risk of increasing divergence.

Moving towards shared witness would contribute significantly to the mission of the church and allow the light of the gospel to shine more fully upon the moral perplexities of human existence in today's world.

Having shared vision of a humanity created in the image of God, we share a common responsibility to challenge society in places where that image is being marred or defaced.

105. We do not underestimate the difficulties that such collaboration would involve. Nevertheless, we dare not continue along our separated ways. Our working and witnessing together to the world is in itself a form of communion. Such deepening communion will enable us to handle our remaining disagreements in a faithful and more creative way. "He who calls you is faithful, and he will do it" (1 Thess. 5:24).

XVII. ANGLICAN-ROMAN CATHOLIC DIALOGUE

37. Common Declaration
George Carey, Archbishop of Canterbury, and Pope John Paul II

Vatican, 5 December 1996

Once again in the city of Rome an archbishop of Canterbury, His Grace George Carey representing the Anglican Communion, and the bishop of Rome, His Holiness Pope John Paul II, have met together and joined in prayer.

Conscious that the second Christian millennium, now in its closing years, has seen division, even open hostility and strife, between Christians, our fervent prayer has been for the grace of reconciliation. We have prayed earnestly for conversion – conversion to Christ and to one another in Christ. We have asked that Catholics and Anglicans may be granted the wisdom to know, and the strength to carry out, the Father's will. This will enable progress towards that full visible unity which is God's gift and our calling.

We have given thanks that in many parts of the world Anglicans and Catholics, joined in one baptism, recognize one another as brothers and sisters in Christ and give expression to this through joint prayer, common action and joint witness. This is a testimony to the communion we know we already share by God's mercy and demonstrates our intention that it should come to the fullness willed by Christ. We have given particular thanks for the spirit of faith in God's promises, persevering hope and mutual love which has inspired all who have worked for unity between the Anglican Communion and the Catholic church since our predecessors Archbishop Michael Ramsey and Pope Paul VI met and prayed together. In the Church of St Gregory on the Celian Hill, we have remembered with gratitude the common heritage of Anglicans and Catholics rooted in the mission to the English people which Pope Gregory the Great entrusted to St Augustine of Canterbury.

For over 25 years a steady and painstaking international theological dialogue has been undertaken by the Anglican-Roman Catholic International Commission (ARCIC). We affirm the signs of progress provided in the statements of ARCIC I on the eucharist and on the understanding of ministry and ordination, which have received an authoritative response from both partners of the dialogue. ARCIC II has produced further statements on salvation and the church, the understanding of the church as communion, and on the kind of life and fidelity to Christ we seek to share. These statements deserve to be more widely known. They require analysis, reflection and response. At present the international commission is seeking to further the convergence on authority in the church. Without agreement in this area we shall not reach the full visible unity to which we are both committed. The obstacle to reconciliation caused by the ordination of women as priests and bishops in some provinces of the Anglican Communion has also become increasingly evident, creating a new situation. In view of this, it may be opportune at this stage in our journey to consult further about how the relationship between the Anglican Communion and the Catholic church is to progress. At the same time, we encourage ARCIC to continue and deepen our theological dialogue, not only over issues connected with our present difficulties but also in all areas where full agreement has still to be reached.

We are called to preach the gospel, urging it "in season and out of season" (2 Tim. 4:2). In many parts of the world Anglicans and Catholics attempt to witness together in the face of growing secularism, religious apathy and moral confusion. Whenever they are able to give united witness to the gospel they must do so, for our divisions obscure the gospel message of reconciliation and hope. We urge our people to make full use of the possibilities already available to them, for example in the Catholic Church's *Directory for the Application of Principles and Norms on Ecumenism* (1993). We call on them to repent of the past, to pray for the grace of unity and to open themselves to God's transforming power, and to cooperate in all appropriate ways at local, national and provincial levels. We pray that the spirit of dialogue may prevail which will contribute to reconciliation and prevent new difficulties from emerging. Whenever actions take place which show signs of an attitude of proselytism they prevent our common witness and must be eliminated.

We look forward to the celebration of 2000 years since the Word became flesh and dwelt among us (cf. John 1:14). This is an opportunity to proclaim afresh our common faith in God who loved the world so much that he sent his Son, not to condemn the world but so that the world might be saved through him (cf. John 3:16-17). We encourage Anglicans and Catholics, with all their Christian brothers and sisters, to pray, celebrate and witness together in the year 2000. We make this call in a spirit of humility, recognizing that credible witness will only be fully given when Anglicans and Catholics, with all their Christian brothers and sisters, have achieved that full, visible unity that corresponds to Christ's prayer "that they may all be one... so that the world may believe" (John 17:21).

38. Summons to Witness to Christ in Today's World
A Report on Conversations 1984-1988

Atlanta, USA, 23 July 1988

Preface

This report which we here present is the result of five meetings between Baptists and Roman Catholics in the years 1984-88. The conversations were sponsored by the Commission on Baptist Doctrine and Interchurch Cooperation of the Baptist World Alliance and the Vatican Secretariat for Promoting Christian Unity. They were the first international conversations between our two bodies.

Our overall theme was "Christian Witness in Today's World". Our primary goal was to come to a mutual understanding of certain convergences and divergences between the Baptist and Roman Catholic world confessional families. Additional goals included:
1) to establish relations and maintain a channel of communication through conversation for mutual as well as self-understanding;
2) to identify new possibilities as well as to clarify existing difficulties in regard to a common witness in view of the current world situation and the mandate of Christ to proclaim the gospel;
3) to address existing prejudices between our two world confessional families.

During these initial conversations, where we experienced God's presence and God's blessings, these objectives were in large part fulfilled. What we achieved in these conversations is an encouragement to similar efforts at various levels in church life.

At each session the main work was theological discussion. Scholarly papers were presented and discussed by participants. Bible studies related to the selected themes, and visits to local communities in the places where the meetings took place enriched our conversations. In each location, leaders of the Baptist and Roman Catholic communities visited the group and shared with them the support of their good wishes and their prayers.

We offer this report, with thanks, to the bodies that sponsored our conversations. The sixteen of us who have been participants have been conscious of the Spirit of God at work among us, and formed in the course of three years' friendships that have been full of encouragement and edification. As this report is completed, we remember fondly one of our members, Rev. Jerome Dollard, OSB, who was suddenly called from this life on 26 December 1985.

Those of us who took part in the conversations regard our experience together as a great gift from God. We hope other Baptists and Roman Catholics will have the grace of a similar experience. In that spirit we offer this report to Baptists, Roman Catholics, and others for their study and their prayerful reflection.

> Bishop Bede Heather
> Roman Catholic Church
> *Co-chairman*

> Dr David Shannon
> Baptist Church
> *Co-chairman*

I. The conversations in review

1. Since the Second Vatican Council (1962-65), Baptists and Roman Catholics have entered into conversations with one another at numerous levels. Only in the past five years, however, have they undertaken a series of conversations at the international level. Jointly sponsored by the Commission on Baptist Doctrine and Interchurch Cooperation of the Baptist World Alliance and the Vatican Secretariat for Promoting Christian Unity, these conversations have focused on a subject of concern to both bodies, namely, "Christian Witness in Today's World".

2. In this series of five conversations, Baptist and Roman Catholic participants, composed of church leaders and scholars, discovered a remarkable amount of consensus on both general and specific issues. Agreement centred on God's saving revelation in Jesus Christ, the necessity of personal commitment to God in Christ, the ongoing work of the Holy Spirit, and the missionary imperative that emerges from God's redemptive activity on behalf of humankind. There were, of course, some significant differences on both general and specific issues. We often noted that divergences appeared among representatives of the same communion as well as among those of the two communions.

3. The conversations, held annually in various locations, explored the following topics relative to common witness. The first, meeting in West Berlin, 18-21 July 1984, focused on "Evangelism/Evangelization: The Mission of the Church". The second, assembled in Los Angeles, 24-30 June 1985, addressed the issues of "Christology" and "Conversion/Discipleship", aspects of "Witness to Christ". The third, convened in New York City, 2-7 June 1986, explored ecclesiological issues under the title of "The Church as Koinonia of the Spirit". The fourth, held in Rome, 13-18 July 1987, directed itself to specific issues standing in the way of improving common Christian witness, that is, proselytism and restrictions on religious freedom. The fifth, located in Atlanta, Georgia, 18-23 July 1988, sought to gather the fruit of the entire series.

II. Common statement

4. This statement does not offer a summary of the individual sessions. It attempts, rather, to synthesize the discussions over five years and to articulate our shared response to the revelation of God in Jesus Christ as this has been given to us in the Bible and in the faith and practice of our respective communities.

A. *Our witness to Christ*

5. Our common witness rests on shared faith in the centrality of Jesus Christ as the revelation of God and the sole mediator between God and humankind (1 Tim. 2-5). We come to know Jesus Christ through the scriptures, especially of the New Testament, which we share in common as the source and sustainer of our faith. That knowledge is experientially confirmed by the internal witness of the Holy Spirit, is handed down by

the community of believers, and is certified by the authoritative witness of the church throughout the ages. We are also aware that God set forth in Christ "the mystery of his will" (Eph. 1:9). All human language is inadequate to express the mystery of God's grace and love manifested in the life, death and resurrection of Jesus. We strive, with Paul as our guide, to gain "insight into the mystery of Christ" (Eph. 1:4).

6. The distinction between the person and the work of Christ, while helpful to later theology, does not capture the riches of the biblical testimony to Jesus Christ. The christological statements in the New Testament express the faith of individuals and groups. In their earliest forms, such as we find in Paul's resurrection *paradosis* (1 Cor. 15:1-11) and in the "kerygmatic" speeches of Acts (e.g., 2:22-24; 3:14-16; 4:10-12; 10:40-43), Jesus is proclaimed as the one who God raised up (or made Lord and Messiah) for our sins or in whose name we are saved. The doctrine of the person of Christ cannot be separated from the message of the saving work which God accomplished in and through Christ.

7. The New Testament speaks of Jesus in different ways. The synoptic gospels present Jesus as the one who proclaims the advent of God's reign and enacts it in his ministry (Mark 1:14-15). He calls sinners to repentance (Luke 5:32) and conquers the power of evil (Luke 11:19f.). He takes the side of the sick and the marginal in his society (Luke 4:16-19). He gathers disciples who were to be with him and to be sent by him (Mark 3:13-15). He possesses a unique familiarity with God and teaches those who follow him to pray to God as Father (Matt. 6:25-33). He summons those who would follow him to love God and neighbour with whole heart, mind and soul (Mark 12:28-34) and gives his life as a ransom that others may be free (Mark 10:45).

8. The gospel of John is a rich source for understanding Christ, and its language and perspective gave shape to the christological formulation of the councils. It was written in order that people might believe that Jesus was the Christ, the Son of God, and that believing they might have life in his name (John 20:31). Jesus is presented as the Word who was with God from the beginning and through whom all things were made (John 1:1-3). This Word became flesh and dwelt among us so that his glory could be seen. He was full of grace and truth (John 1:14). Eternal life was to know the one true God and Jesus Christ whom God had sent (John 17:3). Access to this eternal life was by way of faith. The Christian was summoned to confess with Martha, "Lord, I believe that you are the Christ, the Son of God, he who is coming into the world" (John 11:27). Through the death and resurrection of Jesus, the Holy Spirit was given for the remission of sin (John 20:22-23). Through the witness of the Paraclete, the disciples were made witness to Christ (John 15:26-27). Jesus in dying prayed for them that the Father keep them in his name and make them one (John 17:11).

9. Jesus is proclaimed as the one who descended from David according to the flesh and is designated Son of God in power according to the Spirit of holiness by his resurrection from the dead (Rom. 1:4). He is also the suffering servant and the Son of Man who came not to be served but to serve (Mark 10:45). He is the Saviour born for us in the city of David (Luke 2:11) and the one who, though equal to God, emptied himself, taking on the form of a servant, being born in human likeness (Phil. 2:7).

10. The work of Christ is presented under a variety of metaphors such as justification (Gal. 2:16; Rom. 3:26-28; 5:18), salvation (2 Cor. 7:10; Rom. 1:16; 10:10; 13:11), expiation and redemption (Rom. 3:24-25; 8:32), and reconciliation (2 Cor. 5:18-20; Rom. 5:10-11). These expressions point to the ontological, objective event

wherein God has begun the restoration of a fallen humanity to relationship with himself and has inaugurated a renewal of creation through Christ's death on the cross and resurrection from the dead. The offer of salvation from God in Christ is received in faith, which is a gift of God "who desires all people to be saved and to come to the knowledge of the truth" (1 Tim. 2:4).

11. Discussion of our witness to Christ has revealed that our two communions are one in their confessions of Jesus Christ as Son of God, Lord and Saviour. The faith in Christ proclaimed in the New Testament and expressed in the first four ecumenical councils is shared by both of our churches. Our discussion uncovered no significant differences with regard to the doctrine of the person and work of Christ, although some did appear with regard to the appropriation of Christ's saving work. We believe that this communion of faith in Christ should be stressed and rejoiced in as a basis for our discussions of other areas of church doctrine and life, where serious differences may remain.

12. While affirming that the scriptures are our primary source for the revelation of God in Jesus, we give different weight to creeds and confessional statements. Roman Catholics affirm that sacred scripture and sacred Tradition "flow from the same divine wellspring" and that "the church does not draw her certainty about all revealed truths from the holy scriptures alone" (DV, no. 9). The faith of the church expressed in its creeds through the ages is normative for Catholics. Baptists, while affirming the creeds of the first four ecumenical confessional statements in their history, do not hold them as normative for the individual believer or for subsequent periods of church life. For Baptists, scriptures alone are normative.

B. The call to conversion

13. Jesus inaugurated his public ministry by announcing the advent of God's reign and by summoning people to be converted and to believe in the gospel (Mark 1:14-15). He immediately summoned disciples to follow him (Mark 1:16-20). Saul, the persecutor of the early Christians, through a revelation of the gospel of Jesus becomes Paul, the apostle to the Gentiles (Gal. 2:1-10). The mystery of who Jesus is and what he did for us can ultimately be grasped only in faith and in the practice of Christian discipleship through hope and love (1 Thess. 1:3).

14. After his resurrection Jesus announced to his disciples that "repentance and forgiveness of sins should be preached in his name to all nations" (Luke 24:47). Before he departed from his disciples, Jesus commissioned them to make disciples of all nations, baptizing them and teaching them to observe all that he commanded them (Matt. 28:16-20). After Pentecost the disciples began to proclaim repentance and forgiveness of sins to all nations (Acts 2:5-13). Under the guidance of the same Spirit that was given to the disciples at Pentecost, in its preaching and witness the church strives to fulfill the mandate of Jesus and through the ages renews this proclamation of conversion and forgiveness.

15. Conversion is turning away from all that is opposed to God, contrary to Christ's teaching, and turning to God, to Christ, the Son, through the work of the Holy Spirit. It entails a turning from the self-centredness of sin to faith in Christ as Lord and Saviour. Conversion is a passing from one way of life to another new one, marked with the newness of Christ. It is a continuing process so that the whole life of a Christian should be a passage from death to life, from error to truth, from sin to grace. Our life in Christ

demands continual growth in God's grace. Conversion is personal but not private. Individuals respond in faith to God's call, but faith comes from hearing the proclamation of the word of God and is to be expressed in the life together in Christ that is the church.

16. Conversion and discipleship are related to one another as birth to life. Conversion is manifested in a life of discipleship. In the gospels Jesus summoned disciples to be with him and to share his ministry of proclaiming the advent of God's reign and bringing the healing power of this reign into human life. He also summoned them to be like him in taking up their crosses and in living in loving service to others. After Easter and Pentecost the early community continued to announce and spread the good news and to witness to the saving power of God. Like Jesus, the disciples were persecuted, but through the gift of the Spirit they remained faithful and continued to proclaim the gospel.

17. Throughout history God continues to summon people to follow Jesus, and by the gift of the Spirit and the power of faith the risen Lord continues his ministry. Discipleship consists in personal attachment to Jesus and in commitment to proclamation of the gospel and to those actions which bring the healing and saving power of Jesus to men and women today. The disciple is nurtured by scriptures, worship, prayer in all its forms, works of mercy towards others, proclamation, instruction and the witness of daily life. The church, which can be called a community of disciples, is gathered in the name and presence of the risen Christ. This community is summoned to share the gift it has received. The gift is thus a mandate for a tireless effort to call all people to repentance and faith. A community of disciples of Jesus is always a community in mission.

18. As Baptists and Catholics we both strive to "be converted and believe in the good news" (Mark 1:14). Yet, conversion and discipleship are expressed differently in our ecclesial communions. Baptists stress the importance of an initial experience of personal conversion wherein the believer accepts the gift of God's saving and assuring grace. Baptism and entry into the church are testimony to this gift, which is expressed in a life of faithful discipleship. For Catholics baptism is the sacrament by which a person is incorporated into Christ and is reborn so as to share in the divine life. It is always consequent upon faith; in the case of an infant, this faith is considered to be supplied by the community. Catholics speak of the need for a life of continual conversion expressed in the sacrament of reconciliation (penance), which in the early church was sometimes called a "second baptism". In both of our communions changes in church practice challenge us to consider more deeply our theology of conversion and baptism. In the recently instituted "Rite for the Christian Initiation of Adults", Roman Catholics affirm that the baptism of adults is the paradigm for a full understanding of baptism. In some areas of the world Baptists receive baptism at a very early age.

C. Our witness in the church

19. "Koinonia of the Spirit" (Phil. 2:1; cf. 2 Cor. 13:14) is a helpful description of our common understanding of the church. Koinonia suggests more than is implied by English terms used to translate it, such as "fellowship" or "community". Based on the root idea of "sharing in one reality held in common", it was used in a variety of ways by early Christians. According to 1 Corinthians 1:9, Christians are "called into the fellowship of the Son", which means the same as being "in Christ" or being a member of the body of Christ (1 Cor. 12:12ff.). As we participate in Christ, we participate in the

gospel (1 Cor. 9:23; Phil. 1:5) or in faith (Philemon 6) or in the Lord's supper (1 Cor. 10:16ff.). To share in the supper is to share in Christ's body and blood (v.21). Fellowship with Christ entails participation in his life (Rom. 6:8; 2 Cor. 7:3), sufferings (Rom. 8:17; 2 Cor. 7:3; Gal. 2:19-20), resurrection (Col. 2:12; 3:1; Eph. 2:6), and eternal reign (Rom. 8:17; 2 Tim. 2:12). For Paul koinonia with the risen Christ is the same as koinonia with the Spirit (2 Cor. 13:14) and with other Christians. This is more than a bond of friendship. All share together in the spiritual blessings of the Spirit and are thus obligated to help one another (Rom 12:13) in their afflictions (Phil. 4:14) as well as in their blessings. In 1 John, to be a Christian means to have koinonia with God – Father and Son (1:3,6) – and with other believers (1:3,7). The accent is placed on active participation – "walking" and "doing" – as an expression of this fellowship.

20. Discussion of the passages cited above led to the following conclusions: (1) that in and through Christ God has laid down the foundation of the church, (2) that koinonia both between God and human beings and within the church is a divine gift, and (3) that the Spirit effects the continuity between the church and Jesus. The uniting of a diverse humanity – Jews and Greeks, males and females, slaves and masters (Gal. 3:28) – in one body could not have occurred on human initiative. It depended, rather, on God's action through Jesus Christ – dead, buried and risen. We are now called into communion with God and with one another in the risen One. God actually binds us together in an intimate fellowship through the Holy Spirit. God offers the Spirit as a gift to the whole community of faith to guide it and nurture it and bring it to maturity.

21. Koinonia, whether between God and humanity or among human beings, must be regarded as a gift of God. Though made "in the image of God", both male and female (Gen. 1:27), to dwell in community, Adam, humanity, has ruptured the relationship with God and with one another that would make such community possible. God's long-suffering love alone sufficed to salvage a broken humanity, through Israel and above all through God's Son, Jesus Christ, the new Adam. In the Son God did for us what we could not do for ourselves. The free gift of God in Christ surpassed by far the effects of Adam's transgression (Rom. 5:15-17).

22. The Spirit continues in the church the redemptive work God began in the Son. In baptism the Spirit unites the diverse members – Jew and Gentile, slave and freedom, male and female and, we could add, black and white, rich and poor, etc. – into a single body (1 Cor. 12:12-13; Gal. 3:28). The Spirit is the ground of every dimension of the church's life – worship, interior growth, witness to an unbelieving world, and proclamation of the gospel (Acts 2:42-47; 4:32-37). The Spirit apportions different "gifts" with which the members may build up the body of Christ and carry out the mission of the church (1 Cor. 12:4-11,27-30; Rom. 12:4-8).

23. Koinonia, which is at the heart of the church, is the result of the manifold activity of the Spirit. In the church there are varieties of gifts, but the same Spirit, and varieties of service, but the same Lord, and varieties of working, but the same God, and, though composed of many members, the church is the body of Christ (1 Cor. 12:4; Rom. 12:5). When Baptists speak of church, they refer primarily to the local congregation gathered by the Spirit in obedience and service to God's word. Catholics by "church" refer to the community of faith, hope and charity as a visible structure established and sustained on earth by Christ (*"LG"*, no. 8). While both Baptists and Catholics admit the presence of Christ in the church (Matt. 18:20; 28:20), they understand this in different ways. Catholics believe that the church is a "society furnished

with hierarchical organs and the mystical body of Christ [which] are not to be considered two realities... Rather, they form one interlocked reality which is comprised of a divine and a human element" (*ibid.*). Baptists affirm that the church is divine as to its origin, mission and scope; human as to its historical existence and structure.

D. Our witness in the world

24. The gift of faith we have received is a gift to be shared with others. Jesus was sent by God to proclaim the good news of God (Mark 1:14; cf. Luke 4:18; 7:22). He sent the twelve (Matt. 10:5ff.) and the seventy (Luke 10:1ff.) to carry the same message. After the resurrection he directed his followers to go into all the world and make disciples (Matt. 28:16-20) and commissioned them to be witness to the ends of the earth (Acts 1:8). The church has engaged in this task throughout its history.

25. Both Baptists and Roman Catholics respond to this summons through a ministry of evangelism or evangelization. Baptists typically emphasize free personal response of individuals to the gospel, often to the neglect of corporate responsibility. In more recent years, however, some Baptist groups have focused less on the individual and more on the corporate and social implications of evangelism/evangelization.

26. Roman Catholics apply the term "evangelization" to the "first proclamation" of the gospel to non-believers (EN, no. 21) and also in the wider sense of the renewal of humanity, witness, inner adherence, entry in the community, acceptance of signs and apostolic initiative. These elements are complementary and mutually enriching (*ibid.*, no. 24). Christ is the centre and end of missionary effort. Catholic emphasis upon incarnation, however, encourages a greater concern for "inculturation" than does Baptist emphasis upon redemption of fallen humanity from sin. It also opens the way for assigning sacraments a more prominent place in the evangelization task.

27. Recent ecumenical developments have led to increased appreciation by Roman Catholics and Baptists for each other and for other Christian bodies and may open the way to common witness. Documents of the Second Vatican Council and after speak of many factors uniting Catholics and Protestants: faith, baptism, sharing in the life of grace, union in the Holy Spirit, the Christian life and discipleship. While Vatican II maintained that the church of Christ "constituted and organized in the world as a society, subsists in the Catholic Church" (LG, no. 8), it also acknowledged that "some, even very many, of the most significant elements or endowments which together go to build up and give life to the church herself can exist outside the visible boundaries of the Catholic Church" (UR, no. 3).

28. Baptists and Roman Catholics differ among themselves about salvation within non-Christian religions. The Second Vatican Council brought to an end the negative attitude towards them that had prevailed in the church and made it possible to enter into dialogue with them about some of the common problems of the present which need global attention. The council expressed its high regard for the manner of life, precept and doctrines of these religions which "often reflect a ray of truth which enlightens all men" (NA, no. 2). At the same time the council made it clear that the church "proclaims and is in duty bound to proclaim without fail, Christ who is 'the way, the truth and the life' (John 14:6), in whom men find the fullness of religious life and in whom God reconciled all things to himself (2 Cor. 5:18-19)" (*ibid.*). Baptists have issued no major statements on salvation through other religions but must construe the biblical pronouncement, "for there is no other name under heaven given among humankind by

which we must be saved" (Acts 4:12), in a rather strict fashion. They frequently cite also, "I am the way, and the truth, and the life; no one comes to the Father, but by me" (John 14:6), and apply it in the narrow sense. Some Baptists, nevertheless, have engaged in dialogue or conversations with representatives of the other major world religions. Similarly, they discern the need for cooperation among world religions to solve urgent human problems.

E. Challenges to common witness

29. We respond to the summons to be heralds of the good news by proclaiming the name of Jesus to humankind in such a manner that people will be led to believe in Jesus Christ and to live as true Christians. As we strive to make our lives a witness of the faith that sustains us, certain issues emerge which are of common concern.

30. An important area of common concern is the language we use in speaking of our common witness. "Common witness" means that Christians, even though not yet in full communion with one another, bear witness together to many vital aspects of Christian truth and Christian life. We affirm that it embraces the whole of life: divine worship, responsible service, proclamation of the good news with a view to leading men and women, under the power of the Holy Spirit, to salvation and gathering them into the body of Christ.

31. Realizing that "for freedom Christ has set us free" (Gal. 5:1), we seek ways that people may respond to the gospel in freedom and love. We also confess that competition and bitterness among Christian missionaries have often been a stumbling block for those to whom we seek to proclaim the gospel. Often Christian missionaries are accused of "proselytism", which in both secular and religious circles has taken on the pejorative connotation of the use of methods which compromise rather than enhance the freedom of the believer and of the gospel.

32. A historical overview shows that the understanding of "proselytism" has changed considerably. In the Bible it was devoid of negative connotations. A "proselyte" was someone who, by belief in Yahweh and acceptance of the law, became a member of the Jewish community. Christianity took over this meaning to describe a person who converted from paganism. Mission work and proselytism were considered equivalent concepts until recent times.

33. More recently the term "proselytized" in its pejorative sense has come to be applied by some to the attempts of various Christian confessions to win members from each other. This raises the delicate question regarding the difference between evangelism/evangelization and proselytism.

34. As Baptists and Catholics we agree that evangelization is a primary task of the church and that every Christian has the right and obligation to share and spread the faith. We also agree that faith is the free response by which people, empowered by the grace of God, commit themselves to the gospel of Christ. It is contrary to the message of Christ, to the ways of God's grace, and to the personal character of faith that any means be used which would reduce or impede the freedom of a person to make a basic Christian commitment.

35. We believe that there are certain marks which should characterize the witness we bear in the world. We affirm:
– that witness must be given in a spirit of love and humility;
– that it leaves the addressee full freedom to make a personal decision;

- that it does not prevent either individuals or communities from bearing witness to their own convictions, including religious ones.

36. We also admit that there are negative aspects of witness which should be avoided, and we acknowledge in a spirit of repentance that both of us have been guilty of proselytism in its negative sense. We affirm that the following things should be avoided:
- every kind of physical violence, moral compulsion, and psychological pressure (for example, we noted the use of certain advertising techniques in mass media which might bring undue pressure on readers/viewers);
- explicit or implicit offers of temporal or material advantages, such as prizes for changing one's religious allegiance;
- improper use of situations of distress, weakness or lack of education to bring about conversion;
- using political, social and economic pressure as a means of obtaining conversion or hindering others, especially minorities, in the exercise of their religious freedom;
- casting unjust and uncharitable suspicion on other denominations;
- comparing the strengths and ideals of one community with the weaknesses and practices of another community.

37. On the basis of this understanding of proselytism just given, we agree that the freedom of the gospel and the individual must be respected in any process of evangelism/evangelization. We are aware, however, that often the charge of "proselytism" in a negative sense can be made when one communion comes in contact with the evangelization/evangelism of the other. Every effort must be made to increase mutual knowledge and understanding and to respect the integrity and rights of other individuals and communities to live and proclaim the gospel according to their own traditions and convictions. In an increasingly secularized world, division and religious strife between Christian bodies can be such a scandal that non-believers may not be attracted to the gospel.

38. From the time of Constantine until the modern period, the Christian church has experienced a wide variety of relationships to secular authority where, by custom, law and concordat, civil authority and church have been intertwined in many areas of life. Unfortunately, these inter-relationships have sometimes led to intolerance and consequent suffering. In some traditionally Roman Catholic countries, Baptists were sometimes deprived of their full civil and religious rights and freedom. On the other hand, in areas where Baptists were a numerical majority or enjoyed greater economic or social power, Roman Catholics, although supposedly enjoying all civil rights, sometimes suffered discrimination, injustice and intolerance.

39. Baptists were among the first to advocate the separation of church and state. Having taken shape in an age of religious strife and persecution, Baptists have historically advocated freedom of conscience and practice in religious matters, not simply for Baptists but for all persons.

40. Historically, Roman Catholics and Baptists have differed over the relation of the church to civil authority and on the question of religious liberty. With the Declaration on Religious Liberty of the Second Vatican Council, Roman Catholicism affirmed strongly that "the human person has the right to religious freedom" (no. 2) and that this freedom means that all men and women "are to be immune from coercion on the part of individuals or of social groups and of any human power, in such wise that in mat-

ters religious no one is to be forced to act in a manner contrary to his or her own beliefs" (*ibid.*). The council states that this freedom is "based on the very dignity of the human person as known through the revealed Word of God and by reason itself" (no. 2). Since religious liberty is a right which flows from the dignity of the person, civil authorities have an obligation to respect and protect this right.

41. Both Baptists and Catholics agree that religious freedom is rooted in the New Testament. Jesus proclaimed God's reign and summoned people to a deep personal conversion (Mark 1:14-15), which demands that a person be able to respond freely to God's offer of grace. The apostle Paul resisted all those who attempted to coerce the churches into practices or beliefs which he felt contrary to the freedom won by the death and resurrection of Christ.

42. In the area of religious freedom Roman Catholics and Baptists can fruitfully explore different forms of common witness. Both groups struggle to exist in situations where religious freedom is not respected. Both are concerned about those who suffer persecution because of their faith.

43. In certain traditionally Roman Catholic countries, civil constitutions and laws enacted prior to the Second Vatican Council have not been changed to reflect the teaching of the Council. In some settings with a dominant Baptist majority, the traditional Baptist stress on separation of church and state as a means to assure religious freedom has been weakened. Both groups need to exercise greater vigilance to assure respect for religious liberty.

44. Christians have a right and duty to bring their religious insights and values to the public debate about the structure and direction of a society. This may also include the effort to embody their values in civil law. As they do so, however, they should always be sensitive to and considerate of the rights of individual conscience and of minorities and the welfare of the society as a whole. They should measure their efforts against Jesus' command to love one's neighbour as oneself, his proclamation that both the just and the unjust have the same loving Father, and his own concern for marginal groups in his society.

III. Areas needing continued exploration

A. Theological authority and method

45. These conversations between Baptists and Roman Catholics have frequently surfaced different views and uses of theological authority and method. The theoretical reason for that is clear. Baptists rely on scriptures alone, as interpreted under the guidance of the Holy Spirit, the Reformation principle. Roman Catholics receive God's revelation from the scriptures interpreted in the light of the Tradition under the leadership of the magisterium, in a communal process guided by the Holy Spirit.

46. In fact, however, the differences are not as sharp as this formulation would suggest. At the Second Vatican Council the Roman Catholic Church dealt carefully and in detail with the relationship between scripture and Tradition (DV, no. 2). It endeavoured to reach and express an understanding of the relationship between scripture, Tradition and the teaching office of the church (magisterium). Each of these has its own place in the presentation of the truth of Jesus Christ. The place of one is not identical with that of the other, yet in the Roman Catholic view these three combine together to present divine revelation. On the other hand, Baptists invoke the Baptist heritage as decisively

as Roman Catholics cite Tradition, usually disclaiming that it bears the same authority as scripture but holding on to it vigorously nonetheless.

47. Theory and fact need to be brought together in such a way as to alleviate some anxiety on both sides. Roman Catholics often ask how Baptists regard crucial theological statements which the church has issued in its walk through history, e.g., the great christological statements of Nicea and Constantinople. In brief, do they subscribe to orthodoxy of any kind? Baptists, looking at certain dogmas which they regard as grounded in Tradition rather than in scripture, e.g., the immaculate conception and the assumption of Mary, ask whether Roman Catholics set any limits to what can be defined. Can the church simply approve anything it wants as official doctrine? The key issue needing discussion here is that of development of doctrine.

B. The shape of koinonia

48. Another issue which distinguishes our communions is the different ways in which the koinonia of the Spirit is made concrete. Baptists and Catholics obviously conceive of the Spirit working through different structures. For Baptists, koinonia is expressed principally in local congregations gathered voluntarily under the lordship of Jesus Christ for worship, fellowship, instruction, evangelism and mission. In accordance with their heritage they recognize the Spirit's direction through the interdependency of associations, conventions, alliances, and other bodies designed to proclaim the good news and to carry out the world mission of Christ. However, they have sought to avoid development of structures which would threaten the freedom of individuals and the autonomy of local congregations. For Roman Catholics, the koinonia which the Spirit effects in the local congregation is simultaneously a koinonia with the other local congregations in the one universal church. Correspondingly, they recognize the Spirit's activity in the spiritual and institutional bonds which unite congregations into dioceses presided over by bishops and which unite dioceses into the whole church presided over by the bishop of Rome. Vital to future ecumenical progress would be further discussion of the relationship between the Spirit and structures.

C. Relationship between faith, baptism and Christian witness

49. The conversations revealed growing common concern among Baptists and Roman Catholics about authenticity of faith, baptism and Christian witness. There are, however, obvious divergences. Baptists, viewing faith primarily as the response of the individual to God's free gift of grace, insist that the faith response precede baptism. Baptist congregations, however, vary in the way they receive persons baptized as infants in other congregations. Practices range from rebaptism of all persons who have not received baptism at the hands of a Baptist minister to acceptance of all persons baptized by any mode, whether as infants or as adults. Roman Catholics regard the sacraments, such as baptism, in a context of faith, as an exercise of the power of the risen Christ, comparable to that exercised by Jesus when he cured the sick and freed the possessed. Emphasizing the corporate as well as the individual nature of faith, they baptize infants and catechize them through a process culminating in full participation in the church.

50. Both approaches present some difficulties. Baptists are not one on how children relate to the church prior to baptism. Some churches now have "child dedication" rites, but most have not dealt with the issue at all. Baptist "rebaptisms" (viewed by them as

a first baptism) can offend Christians of other communions, because they suggest the others are not really Christian and because they seem to violate the scriptural call for "one baptism". Roman Catholics and others who practise infant baptism, on the other hand, confront the problem that there is little clear evidence in the scriptures for this practice. The baptizing of infants thus seems to be sustained principally by tradition and a more corporate understanding of faith.

51. The heart of the problem to be addressed here seems to be the nature of faith and the nature of the sacraments (called "ordinances" by most Baptists), which raise a number of questions Baptists and Catholics must deal with together. Is faith solely an individual's response to God's gift? Can the faith of the community supply for the personal faith of an infant? May one speak of a "community of faith", that is, of the body of Christ as itself a subject of a common faith in which individual believers participate? Are the sacraments outward signs of a preceding inner commitment? Are they the means through which Christ himself effects his healing and saving work? What does it mean to say that baptism is "the sacrament of faith"? The issues between us are unlikely to be resolved without addressing these questions.

D. Clarification of key terms

52. We are aware that religious tension between communities can arise from different understanding and use of similar terms. A fundamental concept in both our communities is that of "mission". In its most extensive sense Baptists speak of the mission of the church to glorify God by making him known through faith in Jesus Christ. Roman Catholics also speak of "mission" in its broadest sense as everything that the church does in service of the kingdom of God. Baptists understand missions (plural, in the sense of the outward movement of the church) as one of the means by which the church accomplishes its mission in the world.

53. Baptists almost never use the term "evangelization" but prefer the term evangelism to describe how believers, individually or collectively, take the gospel of Christ to the world, "going everywhere preaching the word" (Acts 8:4). "Evangelization" until recent years was not frequently used within Roman Catholicism. The best working definition can be found in the apostolic exhortation of Pope Paul VI, On Evangelization in the Modern World (1975): "... if it had to be expressed in one sentence the best way of stating it would be to say that the church evangelizes when she seeks to convert, solely through the divine power of the message she proclaims, both the personal and collective consciences of people, the activities in which they engage, and the lives and concrete milieu which are theirs" (no. 18). Evangelization is, therefore, a broad concept comprising three major activities: (a) evangelism, understood as the proclamation of the gospel to the unchurched within one's own society or culture; (b) missionary activity, which involves cross-cultural proclamation of the gospel; and (c) pastoral activity – nourishing and deepening the gospel among those already committed to it.

54. Even with a growing convergence in terminology, evangelism/evangelization assumes different forms within our two communions. The Baptist stress on conversion as an act of personal faith and acceptance of Jesus as Lord and Saviour gives precedence to leading people to an explicit confession of faith through proclamation of the gospel. Roman Catholics stress that by baptism a person is made new in Christ in the church and stress the establishment of Christian community through proclamation of the word and through a ministry of presence and service.

55. Within these different emphases, however, there are strong similarities. Both communions stress the need for unbelievers and the unchurched to hear and live the message of salvation expressed in the scriptures, and both strive to fulfill Jesus' command to love the neighbour by engaging in works of mercy and charity both at home and in "mission" countries.

E. The place of Mary in faith and practice

56. Devotion to Mary has traditionally been an area of great difference between Roman Catholics and Baptists. It also emerged in our discussions as a challenge to common witness. Baptists in general have two major problems with Marian devotion: (1) it seems to compromise the sole mediatorship of Jesus as Lord and Saviour; and (2) Marian doctrines such as the immaculate conception and the assumption, which are proclaimed by Catholics as infallible and hence to be believed in faith, seem to have little explicit grounding in the Bible. According to Roman Catholics, devotion to Mary does not compromise the unique role of Christ, is rooted in her intimate relationship to Jesus, reflects her continuing role in salvation history, and has a solid basis in the New Testament.

57. Because of the long history of misunderstanding and the theological difficulties and subtleties inherent in Marian doctrines, we do not expect consensus in the foreseeable future. In an area such as devotion to Mary, which evokes both strong emotions and strong convictions from both communions, the quest for mutual understanding and respect is put to the test. Roman Catholics must attempt to understand and sympathize with the serious problems Baptists have with Marian devotion and doctrine. Baptists must try to understand not only the biblical and the theological grounds of Marian doctrine and devotion, but its significance in popular piety and religious practice.

F. Concrete ways to offer a common witness to the gospel

58. Conversations between Baptists and Roman Catholics will not lead in the near future to full communion between our two bodies. This fact, however, should not prevent the framing of concrete ways to witness together at the present time. It will be helpful to think of several different levels – international, national, regional and local – in which Catholics and Baptists could speak or act in concert. Such cooperation is already taking place in a variety of ways: translation of the scriptures into indigenous languages, theological education, common concern and shared help in confronting famine and other natural disasters, health care for the underprivileged, advocacy of human rights and religious liberty, working for peace and justice, and strengthening of the family. Baptists and Catholics could enhance their common witness by speaking and acting together more in these and other areas. A whole row of issues vital to the survival of humankind lies before us.

The prayer of Jesus, "that they may all be one; even as thou, Father, are in me and I in thee, that they also may be in us, so that the world may believe that thou hast sent me" (John 17:21), has given a sense of urgency to our conversations. We testify that in all sessions during the past five years there has been a spirit of mutual respect and growing understanding. We have sought the guidance of the Lord of the church and give honour and glory to him for the presence and guidance of the Holy Spirit. We pray that God, who has begun this good work in us, may bring it to completion (cf. Phil. 1:6).

XIX. DISCIPLES OF CHRIST-ROMAN CATHOLIC DIALOGUE

39. The Church as Communion in Christ

St Louis, Missouri, USA, 7 December 1992

Preface

Begun in 1977, the Disciples of Christ-Roman Catholic international dialogue has reached a place of maturity among the various bilateral dialogues and within the whole ecumenical movement. While its work has not yet reached the advanced levels of consensus some of the bilaterals have attained, this dialogue has achieved substantial agreements in several areas that give assurance of the unity that is already given to these two traditions and of the fuller unity that will be God's gift some day in the future. This common theological work between Disciples and Roman Catholics also offers unique ecumenical insights that we believe will be helpful to the other dialogues and efforts in the wider search for visible ecclesial unity.

The first report from the international commission for dialogue, "Apostolicity and Catholicity", was published in 1982, and is sometimes referred to as the Ardfert (Ireland) text, the site of the commission's meeting in 1982. This second report, "The Church as Communion in Christ" (1993), is the product of the ten years (1983-92) of intensive theological work, the building of friendship and common prayer. This St Louis (USA) text is offered for study and reception by Roman Catholics and Disciples throughout the world and to our brothers and sisters in other churches who seek to be faithful to Christ's prayer for the unity of the church.

We rejoice in the measure of agreement – however partial – we are able to record. We look forward with promise to the future issues we shall address. We hope and pray this report and the years of dialogue ahead will deepen our communion (koinonia), broaden the exchanges between our churches locally and globally, and strengthen our common witness and service to the world in the name of the triune God – Father, Son and Holy Spirit.

Samuel E. Carter, SJ   Paul A. Crow Jr
Bishop of Kingston   Disciples of Christ
Co-chairman   *Co-chairman*

Introduction

1. After the completion of the first stage of the dialogue between the Disciples of Christ and the Roman Catholic Church (1977-81) and its agreed account, "Apostolicity and Catholicity" (1982), it was understood that the current state of ecumenism required serious study of the nature of the church. This came from our conviction that the Christian identity in itself and Christian mission in the world are inseparable from a clear and deep understanding of the church.

2. The choice we made to focus on the church coincides with the choice made by many ecumenical dialogues today: the Anglican-Roman Catholic, Orthodox-Roman Catholic, Anglican-Reformed and Disciples-Reformed international commissions and the Lutheran-Roman Catholic commission in the USA. The same focus is found in the Faith and Order commission of the World Council of Churches and the Joint Working Group between the World Council of Churches and the Roman Catholic Church. This is a sign of our day that reveals the ecumenical movement to be in the midst of a deep probing of the link between ecumenism and the nature of the church.

3. For this second stage of discussions, our dialogue met ten times: in Venice, Italy (1983); Nashville, Tennessee (1984); Mandeville, Jamaica (1985); Cambridge, England (1986); Duxbury, Massachusetts (1987); Gethsemani, Kentucky (1988); Venice, Italy (1989); Toronto, Canada (1990); Rome, Italy (1991) and St Louis, Missouri (1992). In every meeting we prayed together, we met with members of local congregations, and we studied and discussed together the similarities and differences that characterize our two communities. In our meetings we focused on how the church as communion is linked to the new creation that God wills. We studied the visibility of the church's communion (koinonia) as revealed in the celebration of the eucharist and maintained through continuity with the apostolic Tradition. And we focused on the role of the ministry and the involvement of the whole church in maintaining the faith of the apostles.

I. The specific nature of this dialogue within the ecumenical movement

4. The dialogue between the Disciples of Christ and the Roman Catholic Church has a specific character. This character may be described in sociological categories by saying that it comes not only from an encounter between a Catholic and a Protestant ethos,[1] but more particularly from the ways in which Disciples understand themselves to express a Protestant ethos and Roman Catholics understand themselves to express a Catholic ethos.

5. Generally in a Catholic ethos great emphasis is placed on sacraments and liturgy. The corporate character of the faith in both the definition of doctrine and its continuing affirmation in the life of the church is stressed. Episcopal oversight, rooted in apostolic continuity and succession, is regarded as necessary for the preservation of the gospel and the life of the church.

6. Generally in a Protestant ethos great emphasis is placed on the proclamation of the word, the necessity of the judgment of each individual's conscience as it is bound by the gospel, and the individual's responsibility for the appropriation of the word of God. Episcopal oversight may be considered desirable for the well-being of the church but not essential. Sometimes it has been denied that a specific form of oversight originates in the will of Christ for the church. The test of church structures is the extent to which they are faithful to the gospel and facilitate authentic proclamation and Christian living.

7. These general differences between a Catholic and a Protestant ethos explain important differences between Disciples and Roman Catholics. Not only are their theological traditions and ecclesial structures different, but they have ways of appropriating the Christian mystery in daily life that are not the same. Nevertheless, on some vital issues what they share in common is more determinative for them than their belonging to a Protestant or a Catholic ethos. The customary vocabulary of division between

Protestant and Catholic does not apply exactly to the specific priorities of Disciples and Roman Catholics.

8. The Disciples movement emerged out of 19th-century Protestantism, but it had nothing to do with a deliberate break from the Roman Catholic Church and lacked the memories of 16th- and 17th-century controversies. Moreover, some of its most specific concerns were criticisms of the way in which contemporary Protestantism understood and lived out fidelity to the apostolic witness. It came from the desire to lead the church towards a unity rooted in the weekly celebration of the Lord's supper. Alexander Campbell was convinced that "the union of Christians is essential to the conversion of the world", an insight which has lost none of its force in the 20th century.[2] The Roman Catholic Church too proclaims that it has a specific mission for the unity of the world, and affirms that this unity is signified and given by the eucharistic communion. It too teaches that the restoration of unity among all Christians is linked with the salvation of the world. Indeed Disciples and Roman Catholics pursue these goals in ways deeply marked by their different histories. But they have to discern whether all these affirmations and convictions are not in fact the expression of a very profound communion in some of the most fundamental gifts of the grace of God.

9. This is why, after a certain agreement had been expressed in "Apostolicity and Catholicity", Disciples and Roman Catholics continued their dialogue in order to discover the degree of communion they already share. Their goal is to be together, growing in this communion and fostering it, and to be with all Christians (as the First Letter of Peter puts it) "God's own people, in order that you may proclaim the mighty acts of him who called you out of darkness into his marvellous light" (1 Pet. 2:9 NRSV).

10. To be honest and not lead to a "cheap ecumenism", this dialogue required two important and complementary investigations. It was necessary first to discuss clearly the issues on which, because of their history and ethos, Disciples and Roman Catholics are different. But then it was necessary to discern in what measure these differences are really divisive. Are they only two diverse ways of manifesting or living out the same basic conviction? If that should be the case, another question has to be asked: How would it be possible to express visibly this existing communion? More precisely: What kind of changes would be required to enable this existing communion to contribute to the full restoration of Christian unity?

Differences in Christian faith and life

11. At first glance the historic differences between the Roman Catholic Church and Disciples of Christ seem to make the division between them irreconcilable. Roman Catholics have understood themselves in the context of the continuous history of the church; Disciples have understood themselves in the context of their origin as a reform movement (developing out of the Presbyterian church) committed to find a way to overcome denominationalism. Hence, where Roman Catholics have seen the church throughout its history as continuous with the teaching of the apostles, Disciples have considered that some discontinuities in the life of the church have been necessary for the sake of the gospel. Roman Catholics have found in creeds and doctrinal definitions a sign of the assistance of the Holy Spirit to bind the church into one and to lead it into all truth. Disciples have wanted to remain faithful to the apostolic church of the New Testament with its vision of unity in Christ but have been distrustful of many of the creeds, confessions and doctrinal teachings within Christian tradition, finding in the

way they have been used a threat to unity. This has led them to be suspicious as well of the structure of episcopal authority, which Roman Catholics believe is a necessary means for maintaining continuity with the apostles and with their teaching. Roman Catholics have been convinced that the college of bishops in communion with the see of Rome, teaching in conjunction with other ordained ministers and with the whole church, is a necessary means of preserving the church in continuity with the apostles.

12. The celebration of the eucharist (also called the Lord's supper or mass) has been central to both Roman Catholics and Disciples, but the eucharist has been understood in different ways.

13. For Disciples the centrality of the Lord's supper has been highlighted by its celebration every Lord's day. In obeying the Lord's commandment, "Do this in memory of me", Disciples have understood themselves to be in communion with the faithful in all places and all ages. Hence, they have called all the baptized to the communion table and in particular have eschewed any formal creeds that kept Christians from taking communion together. However, they generally did not recognize the validity of infant baptism until the present century. Understanding themselves as a believers' church after the pattern of the New Testament church, the Disciples have practised baptism upon confession of faith in Christ and have looked upon faith more as a trusting attitude and a life of witness than as assent to doctrinal formulations. They have emphasized the role of the whole eucharistic congregation in witnessing to the apostolic faith, and they have felt free to designate, as part of their church order, members of the community other than ordained ministers and ordained elders to preside at the eucharist, especially if no regular minister or elder should be present. In the practice of believers' baptism and in the recovery of the weekly celebration of the eucharist, Disciples have claimed to be in continuity with the faith of the apostles.

14. In celebrating the eucharist, Roman Catholics also have claimed to be in continuity with the faith of the apostles. Indeed, they have seen the celebration of the eucharist as a way to enter into communion with the whole body of Christ. They have emphasized that the eucharist signifies the unity of the church and so they have invited to the eucharistic celebration only those in communion with the bishop and through him in communion with all the local churches in communion with the bishop of Rome throughout the world. They have practised infant baptism and have emphasized the role of the whole community in supporting and nurturing the faith. In using ancient creeds and traditional liturgies, Roman Catholics have understood themselves to be in continuity with the generations of Christians who have gone before them since the apostles. Faith for Roman Catholics is not limited to the assent to such formulations, but it cannot be recognized without such assent. While different members have different gifts in the life of the church, only the bishop or an ordained minister in communion with him is empowered to preside over the celebration of the eucharist.

15. Disciples have been readily critical of some developments in the history of the church, even seeing in these developments errors needing correction, because of their awareness of human finitude. They have been inclined to recognize sin in many aspects of the institutional church. Roman Catholics have recognized sin within individual members of the church but because they believe the church belongs to Christ and has received the gifts of the Spirit that maintain it in holiness and truth, they are slow to find sin and error in the church's actions and teachings and quick to see continuity with the apostolic teaching.

16. Both Disciples and Roman Catholics approach church teachings with appreciative yet critical eyes. Their two different general attitudes about the church as an institution lead Roman Catholics to be more appreciative and Disciples to be more critical. For this reason they differ on the relative weight given, on the one hand, to individual discernment and conscience and, on the other hand, to the communal mind. It can be said that Roman Catholics are convinced that, although they must decide for themselves, they cannot decide by themselves. Disciples, on the other hand, are convinced that, although they cannot decide by themselves, they must decide for themselves.

17. Indeed, Roman Catholics and Disciples appear so different and live in such different ways that for many of their members the proposal that their differences could be overcome is nearly incredible.

A convergence of vision?

18. Through our dialogue we nevertheless discovered that, despite these real and continuing differences, our understanding of the church converges on some notable points which both Disciples and Roman Catholics believe necessary for the visible unity of the church. We are convinced that these convergences are important not only for our two traditions but also for all the communities in dialogue to achieve this goal.

19. We had already begun to discover this convergence in the first stage of our dialogue. In "Apostolicity and Catholicity", we saw that our two traditions had sometimes pursued the same goal using different means. We became convinced that "the Spirit of God has already brought us into Christ and continues to move us towards full visible unity" (p. 4). We recognized that "each Christian's faith is inseparable from the faith of the community" (p. 9), and agreed that "every generation must come to faith anew through the power of the Holy Spirit and hand on this faith to succeeding generations" (p. 10). We were convinced that "there can be only one church of God" (p. 11) which cannot be destroyed by divisions among Christians. We were able "to affirm the mutual recognition of baptism administered by Roman Catholics and Disciples, convinced that the oneness we received by the grace of God in baptism must find its completion in visible ecclesial unity" (p. 8). We affirmed a common belief "that the church takes visible shape in history and that one sign of this visibility is the common profession of the gospel with reception of baptism" (p. 11). The restoration of "the unique unity of the one church of God is the goal", we agreed, and "we are already on the way" (p. 11); we sought a renewed fidelity to actions that would intensify and deepen our relationship.

20. In the second stage of our dialogue together we deepened our conviction that we are one on some crucial issues; and the goal of this statement of convergence is to elucidate a shared vision of the church. We do not intend to discuss the extent of communion between Disciples and Roman Catholics. Nor will we focus, one by one, on a number of separate issues that have divided us. Instead, we want to present our shared understanding of the whole plan of God to draw together and redeem the human family, and the essential role of the church in manifesting and bringing about this plan. By beginning with God's offer of salvation to the whole of humanity and the means God gives to remember and announce this offer, we have been able to discover that we share the same understanding of the basic nature of the church.

II. New creation and communion

21. Christians confess that the same God who created human beings has also redeemed them. God has not abandoned humanity to its sinfulness but, through the plan of salvation, has given the possibility of forgiveness of sin and new life. This plan of salvation culminates in Christ Jesus. In the Spirit through the Son, the Father gathers into fellowship all those who had been alienated. By drawing people out of isolation and into communion (koinonia) God makes a new creation – a humanity now established as children of God, a people who know themselves to have received forgiveness of sin and to have put away the old and put on the new, even as they await the consummation still to come (Rom. 8:18-25).

22. This activity of God – the forgiveness of sins and making a new creation – and the response to it in thanks and praise is fundamental to the experience and understanding of koinonia. Various meanings of koinonia are found in the New Testament. Paul uses koinonia to describe sharing in the eucharist (1 Cor. 10:14-20). In breaking the bread and blessing the cup, Christians have koinonia with the body and blood of Christ. The communities which contributed to the collection for the saints in Jerusalem were bound in koinonia (partnership) with them through the sharing of material goods (1 Cor. 8:3-4; Rom. 15:26-27; Phil. 1:5). Yet another use of koinonia stresses the fellowship of those who walk in the light because they are in communion with the Father and the Son and consequently with one another (1 John 1:3,7).

23. To speak of communion (koinonia) is to speak of the way human beings come to know God as God's purpose for humanity is revealed. God in Christ through the Holy Spirit calls human beings to share in the fellowship within the divine life, a call to which they respond in faith. Thus, communion refers first to the fellowship with God and subsequently to sharing with one another. Indeed, it is only by virtue of God's gift of grace through Jesus Christ that deep, lasting communion is made possible: by baptism, persons participate in the mystery of Christ's death, burial and resurrection and are incorporated into the one body of Christ, the church.

24. The new creation is a foretaste of what will come in fullness through the Spirit at the end of time. The Spirit of God, acting in history, is the main agent of that communion which is the church. Persons are brought into living relationship with the Father through the Son by the power of the Spirit. Human relationships are thus set in a new context so that people may recognize one another as equally God's children and come to acknowledge the bonds that link them as a gift from God. People who have come to this new self-understanding see all other human beings as men and women whom God wills also to save. God's redeeming act in Christ demands that all humanity be united.

Eucharist and continuity with the apostolic community

25. To be the communion God wills, the church has to live in the memory of its origin, remembering with thanksgiving what God has done in Christ Jesus. That memory sustains and nourishes its life. The church in fulfilment of its mission proclaims the good news of the gracious, saving acts of God as the word of God is preached, the sacraments are celebrated, and the new life shared with God is given.

26. To live in this memory means for Disciples and Roman Catholics to be in continuity with the witness of the apostolic generation. The New Testament speaks of those called apostles in the earliest period in a variety of ways, and they played a

unique and essential role in formulating and communicating the gospel. The church is founded on their proclamation. They began or nurtured the early communities, and they soon chose collaborators in the first generation of Christians to share the apostolic work of preaching, teaching and pastoral guidance.

27. Both Disciples and Roman Catholics share an intention to live and teach in such a way that, when the Lord comes again, the church may be found witnessing to the faith of the apostles. By preserving the memory of what the apostles taught, and by proclaiming and living it anew for the present day, both Disciples and Roman Catholics believe that they maintain continuity with the apostolic witness, forming a living tradition that is "built upon the foundation of the apostles and prophets, Christ Jesus himself being the cornerstone" (Eph. 2:20).

28. Memory, as in biblical usage, is more than a recalling to mind of the past. It is the work of the Holy Spirit linking the past with the present and maintaining the memory of that on which everything depends – the faith itself and the church which embodies that faith. Through the Spirit, therefore, the power of what is remembered is made present afresh, and succeeding generations appropriate the event commemorated. The Spirit keeps alive the sense of the faith in the whole community and lavishes a variety of *charisma* that enable it to live in the memory of Jesus Christ. In the eucharist especially, the Spirit makes Christ present to the members of the community.

29. Both Disciples of Christ and Roman Catholics celebrate the eucharist regularly and frequently – at least every Sunday. Although they have differences in the understanding of the eucharist, they are one in the conviction that the communion willed by God takes on a specific reality at the Lord's supper. In fact, the celebration of the eucharist renews, makes real and deepens visible fellowship with God. In the eucharistic gathering, they celebrate God's salvation given through Christ as a gift, a gift which empowers for service. To participate in the eucharistic celebration is to be reaffirmed in membership of the people of God, to be empowered by Christ through the Holy Spirit, and so to be made a part of the work of reconciliation in the world.

30. The eucharist is an act through which a divine reality otherwise more or less hidden emerges and is made present. What is revealed is the plan of salvation, the good news that Jesus Christ reconciles humanity to the Father. The eucharist both symbolizes and makes present, together with the gift of Christ himself, the salvation offered through him. In it faith is freshly evoked and is further nourished in the participant; for the community the essential elements of Christian faith and life are expressed.

31. The eucharist is a communal event. In it Christians are bound with Christ and with one another. It is the action that most fully expresses the fellowship that is the church. Here also Christians know more deeply and strengthen the bonds that unite their local community with other local Christian communities. Furthermore, they find themselves impelled by eucharistic communion to extend themselves in care for all those in God's creation, especially those who suffer. Indeed, the eucharist is essential to the being and mission of the church of God in the world. Christians acknowledge that a test of their credibility to the world as a symbol of God's presence can be found in the quality of the communion among themselves and with others.

32. God in Christ invites to the eucharist, and through the Holy Spirit binds together into one body all who break the one loaf and share the one cup. At the Lord's table the unity of the church is accomplished, for believers are joined to Christ and to one another. Thus, precisely because the celebration of the eucharist is the climax of the

church's life, disunity among Christians is felt most keenly at the eucharist; and their inability to celebrate the Lord's supper together makes them less able to manifest the full catholicity of the church.

Teaching and continuity with the apostolic community

33. Disciples and Roman Catholics are convinced that in their faith they must remain in continuity with the apostles, even if they understand what this demands in different ways. This common conviction challenges them to explore the ways in which each has remained in continuity with the apostolic community, and to explore as well the possibility that each might be enriched by gifts remembered and exercised more fully by the other. As they have come to understand each other better, they have realized that each continues to retain many of the ways in which apostolic Tradition is maintained.

34. Both receive the scriptures as a normative witness to the apostolic faith. Both agree as well that the history of the church after the writing and formation of the New Testament canon belongs to the church's continuity in apostolic Tradition, even though they have different emphases in understanding the significance of that history. Both find within this history many developments which, because they are the work of the Holy Spirit, are normative for the church. Both affirm that the gospel is embodied in the Tradition[3] of the church.

35. When Roman Catholics and Disciples evaluate earlier formulations of doctrine, both are committed to continuity with the church's history, though in different ways – a significant difference which requires further investigation. Both agree that doctrinal statements never exhaust the meaning of the word of God and that they may need interpretation or completion by further formulations to be clear. Both also agree that fresh doctrinal statements may be needed to preserve the gospel when it is endangered or to preach it in a new cultural context.

36. Human memory can be deficient and selective because of finitude and sin, and the pilgrim church is affected by these limitations. But both Roman Catholics and Disciples are agreed that the Holy Spirit sustains the church in communion with the apostolic community because Christ promised that the Spirit "will teach you everything and remind you of all that I have said to you" (John 14:26 NRSV). The Spirit guides the church to understand its past, to recall what may have been forgotten and to discern what renewal is needed for the gospel to be proclaimed effectively in every age and culture. This underlines the importance of reflection and study in the life of the church to keep alive the memory.

37. Continuity with the apostolic Tradition calls for fresh understandings or practices of discipleship, which the church adopts in order to transmit the same apostolic faith effectively in new times and places. As the church receives the apostolic Tradition in different contexts and circumstances, the Spirit enables it to hold fast to the apostolic faith and to discern authentic developments in its thought and practice. The Holy Spirit guarantees that the church shall not in the end fail to witness faithfully to the divine plan.

38. Thus the church not only remembers (in the biblical sense) what was done in the past, the saving act in Jesus Christ. Neither does it only remember what is promised in the age to come (cf. § 28). At the very heart of the church's memory, God's saving acts in the past provide a foretaste of transformation so that the future breaks in already

to the present. Salvation seen from the perspective of the scriptures reaches out from the past into the future.

The gifts of the Spirit for the church

39. The Holy Spirit not only gives the church that memory which enables it to remain in the apostolic Tradition, but is also present in the church leading Christians and the whole community of the baptized deeper into the mystery of Christ. Both Disciples and Roman Catholics recognize this as a constitutive gift of God to the church. Through the Holy Spirit the believer is drawn into union with the love of Christ for his Father, for humanity, and for the whole of creation. The will of the believer is also led to unite itself with the will of Christ in obedience to the Father. Thus, the individual believer is drawn into deeper communion with the movement of Christ's self-offering, embodied in the eucharist. This in turn becomes the centre of a life of witness to Christ.

40. A Christian receives the gift of faith within and for the communion (koinonia) which is the church. Hence, the sense of faith *(sensus fidei)* in the life of an individual Christian is a reflection of the extent to which, by the same Spirit, each one shares in the life of the ecclesial body as such; it becomes an expression of the instinct for faith of the whole body. The inner dynamism of the gift of faith – the power of the Holy Spirit which draws believers into spiritual unity – sustains the interaction of the faith of the individual and the faith of the community.

41. The Spirit gives a variety of gifts or charisma which enable the church as a whole to receive and hand on the apostolic Tradition. At the heart of these are the gifts appropriate to worship, particularly in the celebration of the Lord's supper. In the act of celebrating the eucharist the whole community of the baptized is drawn together by the Holy Spirit in a visible unity of faith, hope and love. Together with the charisma of the one who presides at the celebration, many other charisma can be exercised in service of the church in the central action of its life. Then there are charisma of Christian formation, such as the witness to the faith given by parents to their children, and by those who teach in schools and congregations.

42. Moreover, the memory of the apostolic faith is maintained in lives lived according to the gospel. The faithful have a sense of care for all humankind, responsibility for their well-being, and sharing in their suffering, sorrow and oppression as well as in their joy, good fortune and liberation. The charisma which enable the work of mercy – with the poor, the needy, the homeless, the sick and the aged – recall the whole community to the gospel imperative of love.

43. In addition there are extraordinary gifts which are found in the lives of people who give vivid witness to the gospel and capture the imagination of the community of the baptized in such a way that it is recalled to the gospel and the apostolic Tradition. These gifts, like all gifts, must be tested in the church for authenticity.

44. Within the mutuality and complementarity of the different charisma which are given to and for the church, there is a particular charisma given to the ordained ministry to maintain the community in the memory of the apostolic Tradition. Both Disciples and Roman Catholics affirm that the Christian ministry exists to actualize, transmit and interpret with fidelity the apostolic Tradition which has its origin in the first generation. It also has a special responsibility in serving and showing forth the unity of the church. The intention of the apostolic community in establishing ministries in other places was initially to establish collaborators rather than to choose successors: what

began as an expansion of communion over distance became later on an expansion over time. We have found this a helpful insight in enabling us to affirm a common understanding of the importance of succession.

45. Although historically Disciples came from those traditions which at the Reformation rejected episcopacy as the Reformers knew it in the Roman Catholic Church, Disciples have always recognized that the work of the ministry, shared in the local congregation by ordained ministers and ordained elders, is essential to the being of the church and is a sign of continuity with the apostolic Tradition. Roman Catholics believe that the bishop, acting in collaboration with presbyters, deacons and the whole community in the local church, and in communion with the whole college of bishops throughout the world united with the bishop of Rome as its head, keeps alive the apostolic faith in the local church so that it may remain faithful to the gospel.[4] Both Disciples and Roman Catholics affirm that the whole church shares in the priesthood and ministry of Christ. They also affirm that ordained ministers have the specific charisma of representing Christ to the church and that their ministries are expressions of the ministry of Christ to the whole church. They believe that God has given to the church all the gifts needed for the proclamation of the gospel, but this does not mean that every member has received every charism or authority for doing so. Rather, it is the corporate shaping of the whole people of God by the gospel which enables them to hold fast to "the faith which was once for all delivered to the saints" (Jude 3, RSV). The ordained ministry is specifically given the charisma for discerning, declaring and fostering what lies in the authentic memory of the church. In this process this charism of the service of memory is in communion with the instinct for faith of the whole body. Through this communion the Spirit guides the church.

The church
46. We thus discover that our diversities are real but not all of them are necessarily signs of division. Roman Catholics and Disciples have more in common than might be expected after the exposition of their differences. We are now sure that in confessing together that the church is communion, we are in agreement on a very crucial issue, which is not isolated from many central issues of the faith. We agree – together with many other Christians – on important truths:
- A person is saved by being introduced into this communion of believers, described in the New Testament by images of the body of Christ, the temple of God, the vine, the household of God.
- This communion is never given to the believer without the involvement of other believers, some of them being the ministers of the church, having a specific responsibility for preaching the word of God and presiding at the celebration of the sacraments. Through the word and the sacraments the church is the servant or instrument of God's plan of salvation.
- This communion is ultimately with the apostolic community, whose memory is constantly kept alive and made present, especially thanks to the work of the ordained ministry, the witness of the holy and committed members of the community, and the expression of the mind of the church by all the members trying to be faithful to their vocation.

47. We therefore come to a very important agreement concerning the nature and mission of the church. The church of God is that part of humanity which through faith

and in the power of the Holy Spirit responds to God's plan of salvation revealed and actualized in Jesus Christ. Consequently, it becomes the community of all those who in Christ, by the gift of God, are bound into a communion with the Father and with one another. Its members are called to live in such a way that, in spite of their failures and their weakness, this communion becomes visible and is constantly in search of a more perfect realization.

48. This visibility is realized especially in the celebration of the eucharist. There, gathered together and after having confessed their faith, the baptized people receive the body and blood of Christ, the Son of God who reconciled humanity to God in one body through the cross. There they enter into communion with the saints and members of the whole household of God. Moreover, what is celebrated at the eucharist has to be actualized in a life of common prayer and faith, of faithfulness to the gospel, of sharing the spiritual and even material goods of the community, and of commitment to the will of God that the saving work of Christ be extended as offer to all.

49. Participation in this communion begins through baptism and is sustained in continuing eucharistic fellowship. The Holy Spirit uses the church as the servant by which the word of God is kept alive and constantly preached, the sacraments are celebrated, the people of God are served by the ministers with responsibility for oversight, and the authentic evangelical life is manifested through the life of holy and committed members of Christ. This is why Disciples and Roman Catholics agree that the church is the company of all the baptized, the community through which they are constantly kept in the memory of the apostolic witness and nourished by the eucharist. The eucharist is never celebrated and received by a member isolated from an ecclesial community gathered around its ministers. The church is therefore at the same time the sign of salvation (to be saved is to be in communion) and the community through which this salvation is offered.

50. By this communion – which is the church – an effective sign is given by God also to the world. This sign stands in contrast to the divisions and hatred within humanity. Even if it is always stamped by the deficiencies of its members, the church of God demonstrates that the division of humanity created by the corruption of the human heart with its egoism and desire for possessions or power has been overcome through the life, death and resurrection of Christ. A new life is made possible, the life of the children of God whose bonds of relationship are a gift coming from the Father.

51. Moreover, because Christians come to know that God wants all other human beings also to become members of Christ, they are drawn to give themselves in loving witness and service to humanity. This service culminates when they commit themselves to the preaching of the gospel, being obedient to the command of Christ, their Lord. The church is in that way not only a sign of the new humanity God wants but also an instrument the Holy Spirit uses in order to extend salvation to all human situations and needs, in all places until the end of history.

52. Hence, we are able to affirm gladly the traditional conviction that the church is at one and the same time an epiphany of the destiny which God wills for all humanity and a means to achieve that destiny. These inseparable functions of sign and instrument, epiphany and means, are contained in the expression "the church is the sacrament of God's design", as used in the Roman Catholic and Orthodox traditions. This phrase signifies that God realizes the plan of salvation in and through the communion of all those who confess Jesus Christ and live according to this confession. We know,

indeed, that this saving work is not limited to those who confess Christ explicitly, but that the benefits of Christ's work are offered to all human beings. In hope we expect that these benefits may be accepted by many who do not fully confess the Giver of their gifts. Nevertheless, we do believe that the church, by making visible God's reconciling work and being the servant of God in the accomplishment of this work, stands as a light on the mountain-top, awakening the world to a recognition of its true destiny. The communion that is the church allows people to witness what Christian faith confesses: there is salvation and it comes from God through Christ.

Future work
53. We have not yet, indeed, discussed some of the most important points which continue to divide us. For we believe that these issues can be fairly and deeply treated only on the basis of the kind of agreement we have reached in the document we are now publishing. Moreover we are convinced that they are to be treated in conjunction with the work of other bilateral ecumenical dialogues, which are also struggling with them. They will be proposed for the agenda of our future discussions. Among them four have a very specific meaning for the visible unity of the church:

a) First, our dialogue has made us aware of a point we need to consider more deeply. Even if we agree on the signification and function of the eucharist, we feel that we still have to discuss our traditional teaching and practice concerning the presence of the Lord in the celebration of the supper, its sacrificial nature, the role of the ordained minister and the role of the community. This is important, given the emphasis that both Disciples and Roman Catholics put on the weekly celebration of the Lord's supper and its link with the visible unity of Christians.

b) A second issue is the way we understand the fundamental structure of the church gathered around the eucharist and the Catholic tradition's understanding of episcopacy – given through a sacrament – as the institution necessary for an authentic eucharist to be celebrated.

c) A third issue is the nature of the rule of faith in a changing history. In what sense is "the faith which was once for all delivered to the saints" expressed in the teaching of the church throughout the ages?

d) Lastly, an issue which requires to be explored by all the churches and communities in dialogue with the Roman Catholic Church is the primacy of the bishop of Rome and the affirmation that it is founded in the will of Christ for the church.

54. These are difficult issues. Nevertheless we believe – after these ten years of dialogue on the church – that it will be possible to clarify many misinterpretations (on both sides) and possibly to discover ways of growing towards the kind of mutual metanoia (repentance) and coming together which will allow very profound communion in some of the most important gifts of the grace of God, and make possible important and irreversible steps on our road towards the full unity God intends.

NOTES

[1] By ethos is meant the social, mental, religious and philosophical atmosphere surrounding a group and influencing its way of life.

[2] A. Campbell, "Foundation of Christian Union", *Christianity Restored*, Bethany, Va. 1835, 103-4 (more commonly cited in the 2nd ed., *The Christian System*, 1839, 115). Alexander Campbell (1788-1866), son of the Rev. Thomas Campbell, a Seceder Presbyterian minister from Ahorey, Ireland, who emigrated to the USA in 1807, was president of Bethany College, West Virginia, and one of the leading figures in the emergence of Disciples of Christ as a distinctive religious movement.

[3] The use of a capital T follows the definition agreed at the Montreal Faith and Order conference in 1963: "By the Tradition is meant the gospel itself, transmitted from generation to generation in and by the church, Christ himself present in the life of the church" *(Report of the Fourth World Conference on Faith and Order,* no. 39, p.50).

[4] Cf. *LG*, no. 22; Norman P. Tanner, ed., *Decrees of the Ecumenical Councils*, 1990, ii, 866.

40. The Evangelical-Roman Catholic Dialogue on Mission

1977-1984

Introduction

The Evangelical–Roman Catholic dialogue on mission was a series of three meetings which took place over a period of seven years. The first was held at Venice in 1977, the second at Cambridge in 1982, and the third at Landévennec in France in 1984.

1. The participants

Those who took part in the dialogue were theologians and missiologists from many parts of the world. Six of us (three from each side) attended all three meetings; others were able to come to only one or two of them.

The evangelical participants were drawn from a number of churches and Christian organizations. They were not official representatives of any international body, however. For the evangelical movement has a broad spectrum, which includes evangelical denominations (both within and outside the World Council of Churches), evangelical fellowships (within mainline, comprehensive denominations), and evangelical parachurch agencies (specializing in tasks like Bible translation, evangelism,[1] cross-cultural mission, and third-world relief and development), which accept different degrees of responsibility to the church.[2]

It is not easy to give a brief account of the distinctive beliefs of evangelical Christians, since different churches and groups emphasize different doctrines. Yet all evangelicals share a cluster of theological convictions which were recovered and reaffirmed by the 16th-century Reformers. These include (in addition to the great affirmations of the Nicene Creed) the inspiration and authority of the Bible, the sufficiency of its teaching for salvation, and its supremacy over the traditions of the church; the justification of sinners (i.e., their acceptance by God as righteous in his sight) on the sole ground of the sin-bearing – often called "substitutionary" – death of Jesus Christ, by God's free grace alone, apprehended by faith alone, without the addition of any human works; the inward work of the Holy Spirit to bring about the new birth and to transform the regenerate into the likeness of Christ; the necessity of personal repentance and faith in Christ ("conversion"); the church as the body of Christ, which incorporates all true believers, and all of whose members are called to ministry, some being "evangelists, pastors, and teachers"; the "priesthood of all believers", who (without any priestly mediation except Christ's) all enjoy equal access to God and all offer him their sacrifice of praise and worship; the urgency of the great commission to spread the gospel throughout the world, both verbally in proclamation and visually in good works of love; and the expectation of the personal, visible and glorious return of Jesus Christ to save, to reign and to judge.

The Roman Catholic participants, who spoke from the point of view of the official teaching of their church, were named by the Vatican Secretariat for Promoting Christian Unity. The existence of the secretariat is evidence of the effective renewal of attitude towards other Christians, which has taken place among Roman Catholics as a result of the Second Vatican Council twenty years ago and which is still having its effects. In that Council it was acknowledged that "Christ summons the church, as she goes her pilgrim way, to that continual reformation of which she always has need, insofar as she is an institution of men here on earth".[3] As a result, Roman Catholics have been able to acknowledge joyfully "the riches of Christ and virtuous works in the lives of others who are bearing witness to Christ".[4] This same renewal turned the attention of Roman Catholics to the scriptures in a new way, exhorting the church "to move ahead daily towards a deeper understanding of the sacred scriptures" which "contain the word of God and, since they are inspired, really are that word".[5] And it led to a better expression of the relation between scripture and Tradition in communicating God's word in its full purity. Here indeed are the elements which have enabled Roman Catholics to acknowledge common ground with other Christians, and to assume their own responsibility for overcoming divisions for the sake of the mission of God and the fullness of his glory.

2. The background

It is the will of God that "all men be saved and come to the knowledge of the truth. For there is one God, and there is one mediator between God and men, the man Christ Jesus, who gave himself as a ransom for all" (1 Tim. 2:4-5); "there is salvation in no one else" (Acts 4:12). Mission begins in the activity of God himself who sent his Son, and whose Son sent his Spirit. All who belong to God in Jesus Christ must share in this mission of God.

A dialogue on mission between evangelicals and Roman Catholics has been possible for two reasons. First, both constituencies have recently been concentrating their attention on evangelism. In July 1974 the evangelical International Congress on World Evangelization took place in Switzerland and issued the Lausanne Covenant.[6] A few months later the third general assembly of the Roman Catholic Synod of Bishops studied the same topic, and at their request Pope Paul VI issued in December 1975 his apostolic exhortation entitled *Evangelii Nuntiandi*, or Evangelization in the Modern World.[7]

Secondly, a study of these two documents reveals a measure of convergence in our understanding of the nature of evangelism, as the following quotations show: "To evangelize is to spread the good news that Jesus Christ died for our sins and was raised from the dead according to the scriptures... Evangelism itself is the proclamation of the historical, biblical Christ as Saviour and Lord."[8] Again, witness must be "made explicit by a clear and unequivocal proclamation of the Lord Jesus. There is no true evangelization if the name, the teaching, the life, the promises, the kingdom and the mystery of Jesus of Nazareth, the Son of God, are not proclaimed."[9]

3. The experience

In our time there are many possible forms of dialogue. Some are undertaken with an immediate view to working for organic unity between the bodies which the participants represent. Others do not exclude this purpose but begin from where they are with a more general purpose. Still others begin by stating that they do not envisage organic or structural unity but aim rather at an exchange of theological views in order to increase mutual understanding and to discover what theological ground they hold in common. ERCDOM has been a dialogue of the latter kind. It was not conceived as a step towards church unity negotiations. Rather it has been a search for such common ground as might be discovered between evangelicals and Roman Catholics as they each try to be more faithful in their obedience to mission. It was also undertaken quite consciously in the knowledge that there are still both disagreements and misrepresentations between evangelicals and Roman Catholics which harm our witness to the gospel, contradict our Lord's prayer for the unity of his followers, and need if possible to be overcome.

During the three meetings friendships were formed, and mutual respect and understanding grew, as the participants learned to listen to one another and to grapple with difficult and divisive questions, as well as rejoice in the discovery of some common understandings.

It was a demanding experience as well as a rewarding one. It was marked by a will to speak the truth, plainly, without equivocation, and in love. Neither compromise nor the quest for lowest common denominators had a place; a patient search for truth and a respect for each other's integrity did.

4. The report

This report is in no sense an "agreed statement", but rather a faithful record of the ideas shared. It is not exhaustive, for more questions were touched on than could be described in this brief compass. Yet enough has been included to give a substantial idea of how the dialogue developed and to communicate something of it without creating misunderstandings or false expectations.

An effort has been made to convey what went on at all three meetings, bearing in mind that in none was a complete exposé given of most issues. ERCDOM was only a first step, even if not a negligible one.

Our report, as far as it goes, gives a description of some areas in which evangelicals and Roman Catholics hold similar or common views, which we are able to perceive more clearly as we overcome the stereotypes and prejudiced ideas which we have of each other. In addition, it sets out some of the serious matters on which evangelicals and Roman Catholics differ, but about which in the last seven years the participants in ERCDOM have begun to learn to speak and listen to each other.

Although all those who participated in the three meetings contributed richly, the responsibility for the final form of the report rests with those who were at Landévennec. Publication is undertaken on the general endorsement of the 1984 participants, although it is not the kind of document to which each was asked to subscribe formally. Nevertheless, it is their express hope that it may be a means of stimulating local encounters in dialogue between evangelicals and Roman Catholics. Our report is far from being definitive; the dialogue needs to be continued and developed.

The participants in ERCDOM offer this report to other evangelicals and Roman Catholics as a sign of their conviction that fidelity to Jesus Christ today requires that we take his will for his followers with a new seriousness. He prayed for the truth, holiness, mission and unity of his people. We believe that these dimensions of the church's renewal belong together. It is with this understanding that we echo his prayer for ourselves and each other:

> Sanctify them in the truth; thy word is truth. As thou didst send me into the world, so I have sent them into the world. I pray... that they may all be one; even as thou, Father, art in me, and I in thee, that they also may be in us, so that the world may believe. (John 17:17-21)

1. Revelation and authority

It may well be asked why participants in a dialogue on mission should spend time debating theological questions concerned with divine revelation, the scriptures, the formulation of truth, principles of biblical interpretation, and the church's magisterium or teaching authority. For these topics may not appear to be directly related to our Christian mission in the world. Yet we judged a discussion of them to be indispensable to our task for two main reasons. The first and historical reason is that the issue of authority in general, and of the relation between scripture and Tradition in particular, was one of the really major points at issue in the 16th century. Indeed, the evangelical emphasis on *sola scriptura* has always been known as the "formal" principle of the Reformation. So Roman Catholics and evangelicals will not come to closer understanding or agreement on *any* topic if they cannot do so on *this* topic. Indeed in every branch of the Christian church the old question "by what authority?" (Mark 11:28) remains fundamental to ecumenical discussion. Our second reason for including this subject on our agenda was that it has a greater relevance to mission than may at first appear. For there can be no mission without a message, no message without a definition of it, and no definition without agreement as to how, or on what basis, it shall be defined.

1. Revelation, the Bible, and the formulation of truth

Roman Catholics and evangelicals are entirely agreed on the necessity of revelation, if human beings are ever to know God. For he is infinite in his perfections, while we are both finite creatures and fallen sinners. His thoughts and ways are as much higher than ours as the heavens are higher than the earth (Isa. 55:9). He is beyond us, utterly unknowable unless he should choose to make himself known, and utterly unreachable unless he should put himself within our reach. And this is what together we believe he has done. He has revealed the glory of his power in the created universe[10] and the glory of his grace in his Son Jesus Christ, and in the scriptures which he said bear witness to him (e.g., John 5:39).

This process of special revelation began in the Old Testament era. "God spoke of old to our fathers by the prophets" (Heb. 1:1). He fashioned Israel to be his people and taught them by his law and prophets. Old Testament scripture records this history and this teaching. Then the Father sent his Son, who claimed to be the fulfilment of prophecy, himself proclaimed the good news of salvation, chose the twelve apostles to be his special witnesses, and promised them the inspiration of his Spirit. After Pentecost they went everywhere preaching the gospel. Through their word Christian communities came into being, nourished by the Old Testament and the gospel. The apostles' teaching was embodied in hymns, confessions of faith, and particularly their letters. In due time the church came to recognize their writings as possessing unique authority and as handing down the authentic gospel of Jesus Christ. In this way the canon of the New Testament was constituted, which with the Old Testament comprise the Christian scriptures.

We all recognize that in the scriptures God has used human words as the vehicle of his communication. The Spirit's work of inspiration is such, however, that what the human authors wrote is what God intended should be revealed, and thus that scripture is without error. Because it is God's word, its divine authority and unity must be recognized, and because he spoke through human beings, its original human context must also be taken into account in the work of interpretation.

But are human words adequate to describe God fully, even if they are inspired? No. The infinite reality of the living God is a mystery which cannot be fully communicated in words or fully comprehended by human minds. No verbal formulation can be coextensive with the truth as it is in him. Nevertheless, God has condescended to use words as well as deeds as appropriate media of his self-disclosure, and we must struggle to understand them. We do so in the confidence, however, that though they do not reveal God fully, they do reveal him truly.

Roman Catholics and evangelicals differ slightly in their understanding of the nature of scripture, and even more on what the proper process of interpretating this word should be. Both groups recognize that God spoke through the human authors, whose words belonged to particular cultures.

Roman Catholics speak of this relationship between the divine and the human in scripture as being analogous to the divine and the human in Christ. As the Second Vatican Council put it, "Indeed the words of God, expressed in the words of men, are in every way like human language, just as the Word of the eternal Father, when he took on himself the flesh of human weakness, became like man."[11] Thus the written testimony of the biblical authors is inscribed within the logic of the incarnation.

Evangelicals also sometimes use this analogy, but they are not altogether comfortable with it. Although it has some validity, they do not believe it is exact since there is no hypostatic union between the human and the divine in scripture. They usually emphasize instead the model of God's providence, namely, that he is able even through fallen human beings to accomplish his perfect will. So he has spoken through the human authors of the Bible in such a way that neither did he suppress their personality nor did they distort his revelation.

Thus together we affirm that the written word of God is the work of both God and human beings. The divine and the human elements form a unity which cannot be torn asunder. It excludes all confusion and all separation between them.

With respect to the process of interpretation, Roman Catholics affirm that scripture must be seen as having been produced by and within the church. It is mediated to us by the inspired witness of the first Christians. The proper process of interpretation is determined by the process of scripture's creation. We cannot understand it in its truth unless we receive it in the living faith of the church which, assisted by the Holy Spirit, keeps us in obedience to the word of God.

Evangelicals acknowledge the wisdom of listening to the church and its teachers, past and present, as they seek to understand God's word, but they insist that each believer must be free to exercise his or her personal responsibility before God, in hearing and obeying his word. While the church's interpretations are often helpful, they are not finally necessary because scripture, under the Spirit's illumination, is self-interpreting and perspicuous (clear).

Thus, contemporaneity has come to mean different things in our two communities. Each recognizes that the word of God must be heard for and in our world today. For Roman Catholics God's word is contemporary in the sense that it is heard and interpreted within the living church. For evangelicals it is contemporary in the sense that its truth has to be applied, by the illumination of the Holy Spirit, to the modern world.

Despite these differences, we are agreed that since the biblical texts have been inspired by God, they remain the ultimate, permanent and normative reference of the revelation of God. To them the church must continually return, in order to discern more clearly what they mean, and so receive fresh insight, challenge and reformation. They themselves do not need to be reformed, although they do need constantly to be interpreted, especially in circumstances in which the church encounters new problems or different cultures. Roman Catholics hold that "the task of giving an authentic interpretation of the word of God whether in its written form or in the form of Tradition has been entrusted to the living teaching office of the church alone."[12] This seems to evangelicals to derogate from scripture as "the ultimate, permanent and normative reference". Nevertheless, both sides strongly affirm the divine inspiration of scripture.

2. Principles of biblical interpretation

Our understanding of the nature of the Bible determines our interpretation of it. Because it is the word of God, we shall approach it in one way; and because it is also the words of men, in another.

a) Humble dependence on the Holy Spirit

Because the Bible is the word of God we must approach it with reverence and humility. We cannot understand God's revelation by ourselves, because it is "spiritually discerned" (1 Cor. 2:14). Only he who spoke through the prophets and apostles can interpret to us his own message. Only the Spirit of truth can open our hearts to understand, to believe and to obey. This is "wisdom", and the Holy Spirit is the "Spirit of wisdom and of revelation" in our knowledge of God (Eph. 1:17). Moreover, the Spirit operates within the body of Christ, as we shall elaborate later.

b) The unity of scripture

Because the Bible is the word of God, it has a fundamental unity. This is a unity of origin, since he who has revealed himself does not contradict himself. It is also a unity of message and aim. For our Lord said the scriptures "bear witness to me" (John 5:39; cf. Luke 24:25-27). Similarly we read that "the sacred writings... are able to instruct you for salvation through faith in Christ Jesus" (2 Tim. 3:15). Thus, God's purpose through scripture is to bear testimony to Christ as Saviour, to persuade all men and women to come to him for salvation, to lead them into maturity in Christ, and to send them into the world with the same good news.

In the midst of great diversity of content, therefore, scripture has a single meaning, which permeates and illuminates all the partial meanings. We renounce every attempt to impose on scripture an artificial unity or even to insist on a single overarching concept. Instead, we discover in scripture a God-given unity, which focuses on the Christ who died and rose again for us and who offers to all his people his own new life, which is the same in every age and culture. This centrality of Christ in the scriptures is a fundamental hermeneutical key.

c) Biblical criticism

Since the Bible is God's word through human words, therefore under the guidance of the Holy Spirit, who is the only one who leads us into the understanding of scripture, we must use scientific critical tools for its elucidation, and we appreciate the positive gains of modern biblical scholarship. Human criticism and the Spirit of God are not mutually exclusive. By "criticism" we do not mean that we stand in judgment upon God's word, but rather that we must investigate the historical, cultural and literary background of the biblical books.

We must also try to be aware of the presuppositions we bring to our study of the text. For none of us lives in a religion- or culture-free vacuum. What we must seek to ensure is that our presuppositions are Christian rather than secular. Some of the presuppositions of secular philosophy which have vitiated the critical study of the Bible are (a) evolutionary (that religion developed from below instead of being revealed from above), (b) anti-supernatural (that miracles cannot happen and that therefore the biblical miracles are legendary), and (c) demythologizing (that the thought-world in which the biblical message was given is entirely incompatible with the modern age and must be discarded). Sociological presuppositions are equally dangerous, as when we read into scripture the particular economic system we favour, whether capitalist or communist or any other.

One test by which our critical methodology may be assessed is whether or not it enables people to hear the biblical message as good news of God revealing and giving himself in the historic death and resurrection of Christ.

d) The "literal" sense

The first task of all critical study is to help us discover the original intention of the authors. What is the literary genre in which they wrote? What did they intend to say? What did they intend us to understand? For this is the "literal" sense of scripture, and the search for it is one of the most ancient principles which the church affirmed. We must never divorce a text from its biblical or cultural context but rather think ourselves back into the situation in which the word was first spoken and heard.

e) A contemporary message

To concentrate entirely on the ancient text, however, would lead us into an impractical antiquarianism. We have to go beyond the original meaning to the contemporary message. Indeed, there is an urgent need for the church to apply the teaching of scripture creatively to the complex questions of today. Yet in seeking for relevance, we must not renounce faithfulness. The ancient and the modern, the original and the contemporary, always belong together. A text still means what its writer meant.

In this dialectic between the old and the new, we often become conscious of a clash of cultures, which calls for great spiritual sensitivity. On the one hand, we must be aware of the ancient cultural terms in which God spoke his word, so that we may discern between his eternal truth and its transient setting. On the other, we must be aware of the modern cultures and world-views which condition us, some of whose values can make us blind and deaf to what God wants to say to us.

3. The church's teaching authority

It is one thing to have a set of principles for biblical interpretation; it is another to know how to use them. How are these principles to be applied, and who is responsible for applying them?

a) The individual and the community

Evangelicals, who since the Reformation have emphasized both "the priesthood of all believers" and "the right of private judgment", insist on the duty and value of personal Bible study. The Second Vatican Council also urged that "easy access to sacred scripture should be provided for all the Christian faithful".[13]

Both evangelicals and Roman Catholics, however, recognize the dangers which arise from making scripture available to all Christian people and from exhorting them to read it. How can they be protected from false interpretations? What safeguards can be found? Whether we are evangelicals or Roman Catholics, our initial answer to these questions is the same: the major check to individualistic exegesis is the Holy Spirit who dwells and works in the body of Christ which is the church. The scriptures must be interpreted within the Christian community. It is only "with all the saints" that we can comprehend the full dimensions of God's love (Eph. 3:18).

Roman Catholics also say that scripture is interpreted by the church. Yet the church's task, paradoxically speaking, is at one and the same time to submit totally to the witness of scripture in order to listen to God's word and to interpret it with authority. The act of authority in interpreting God's word is an act of obedience to it.

But how in practice does the Christian community help us towards truth and restrain us from error? We are agreed that Christ has always intended his church to have gifted and authorized teachers, both scholars and pastors. When Philip asked the Ethiopian whether he understood the Old Testament passage he was reading, he replied, "How can I, unless someone guides me?" (Acts 8:31).

Many of our teachers belong to the past. Both evangelicals and Roman Catholics have inherited a rich legacy of tradition. We cherish creeds, confessions and conciliar statements. We peruse the writings of the fathers of the church. We read books and commentaries.

Christ also gives his church teachers in the present (Eph. 4:11), and it is the duty of Christian people to listen to them respectfully. The regular context for this is public worship in which the word of God is read and expounded. In addition, we attend church synods and councils, and national, regional and international conferences at which, after prayer and debate, our Christian understanding increases.

Respectful listening and mutual discussion are healthy; they are quite different from uncritical acquiescence. Both evangelicals and Roman Catholics are troubled by the authoritarian influence which is being exerted by some strong, charismatic leaders and teachers of different backgrounds. The kind of thoughtless submission which is sometimes given to such was firmly discouraged by the apostles. The people of Beroea were commended because they examined the scriptures to see whether Paul's preaching was true (Acts 17:11). Paul urged the Thessalonians to "test everything", and John to "test the spirits", i.e., teachers claiming inspiration (1 Thess. 5:21; 1 John 4:1). Moreover, the criterion by which the apostles exhorted the people to evaluate all teachers was the deposit of faith, the truths which they had heard "from the beginning" (1 John 2:24; 2 John 9).

b) The regulation of Christian belief

We all agree that the fact of revelation brings with it the need for interpretation. We also agree that in the interpretative task both the believing community and the individual believer must have a share. Our emphasis on these varies, however, for the evangelical fears lest God's word be lost in church traditions, while the Roman Catholic fears it will be lost in a multiplicity of idiosyncratic interpretations.

This is why Roman Catholics emphasize the necessary role of the magisterium, although evangelicals believe that in fact it has not delivered the Roman Catholic Church from a diversity of viewpoints, while admittedly helping to discern between them.

Evangelicals admit that in their case, too, some congregations, denominations and institutions have a kind of magisterium. For they elevate their particular creed or confession to this level, since they use it as their official interpretation of scripture and for the exercise of discipline.

Both Roman Catholics and evangelicals cherish certain creeds and confessions which summarize their beliefs. They also agree that new formulations of faith may be written and affirmed for our times. Other doctrinal statements may be either revised or replaced by better statements, if this seems to be required by a clearer proclamation of the good news. All of us accept responsibility to listen ever more attentively to what the Spirit through the word is saying to the churches, so that we may grow in the knowledge of God, in the obedience of faith and in a more faithful and relevant witness.

What, then, evangelicals have asked, is the status (and the authority for Roman Catholics) of the various kinds of statements made by those with a ministry of official teaching? In reply, Roman Catholics say that the function of the magisterium is to regulate the formulations of the faith, so that they remain true to the teaching of scripture. They also draw a distinction. On the one hand, there are certain *privileged formulations*, e.g., a formal definition in council by the college of bishops, of which the pope is the presiding member, or a similar definition by the pope himself, in special circumstances and subject to particular conditions, to express the faith of the church. It is conceded that such definitions do not necessarily succeed in conveying all aspects of the truth they seek to express, and while what they express remains valid, the way it is expressed may not have the same relevance for all times and situations. Nevertheless, for Roman Catholics they do give a certainty to faith. Such formulations are very few, but very important. On the other hand, statements made by those who have a special teaching role in the Roman Catholic Church have different levels of authority (e.g., papal encyclicals and other pronouncements, decisions of provincial synods or councils, etc.). These require to be treated with respect, but do not call for assent in the same way as the first category.

We all believe that God will protect his church, for he has promised to do so and has given us both his scriptures and his Spirit; our disagreement is on the means and the degree of his protection.

Roman Catholics believe that it is the authoritative teaching of the church which has the responsibility for oversight in the interpretation of scripture, allowing a wide freedom of understanding, but excluding some interpretations as inadmissible because erroneous.

Evangelicals, on the other hand, believe that God uses the Christian community as a whole to guard its members from error and evil. Roman Catholics also believe in this *sensus fidelium*. For in the New Testament, church members are urged: "Let the word of Christ dwell in you richly; teach and admonish one another" (Col. 3:16). They are also exhorted to "see to it that their brothers and sisters stand firm in truth and righteousness".[14]

4. Can the church be reformed?

a) The need for reform

So far in this first section of our report we have concentrated on the church's responsibility to teach. Can it also learn? Can the church that gives instruction receive it? More particularly, can scripture exercise a reforming role in the church? Is the church itself under the scripture it expounds?

These are questions which the Roman Catholic Church put to itself anew during the Second Vatican Council, and has continued to ask itself since (UR, no. 6).

Evangelicals, however, to whom continuous reformation by the word of God has always been a fundamental concern, wonder whether the reform to which the Roman Catholic Church consented at Vatican II was radical enough. Has it been more than an *aggiornamento* of ecclesiastical institutions and liturgical forms? Has it touched the church's theological life or central structures? Has there been an inner repentance?

At the same time, Roman Catholics have always asked whether evangelicals, in the discontinuity of the 16th-century Reformation, have not lost something essential to the gospel and the church.

Yet we all agree that the church needs to be reformed, and that its reformation comes from God. The one truth is in God himself. He is the reformer by the power of his Spirit according to the scriptures. In order to discern what he may be saying, Christian individuals and communities need each other. Individual believers must keep their eyes on the wider community of faith, and churches must be listening to the Spirit, who may bring them correction or insight through an individual believer.

b) Our response to God's word

We agree on the objectivity of the truth which God has revealed. Yet it has to be subjectively received, indeed "apprehended", if through it God is to do his reforming work. How then should our response to revelation be described?

We all acknowledge the difficulties we experience in receiving God's word. For as it comes to us, it finds each of us in our own social context and culture. True, it creates a new community, but this community also has its cultural characteristics derived both from the wider society in which it lives and from its own history, which has shaped its understanding of God's revelation. So we have to be on the alert, lest our response to the word of God is distorted by our cultural conditioning.

One response will be intellectual. For God's revelation is a rational revelation, and the Holy Spirit is the Spirit of truth. So the Christian community is always concerned to understand and to formulate the faith, so that it may preserve truth and rebut error. Response to God's truth can never be purely cognitive, however. Truth in the New Testament is to be "done" as well as "known", and so to find its place in the life and experience of individuals and churches. Paul called this full response "the obedience of faith" (Rom. 1:5; 16:26). It is a commitment of the whole person.

Understanding, faith and obedience will in their turn lead to proclamation. For revelation by its very nature demands communication. The believing and obeying community must be a witnessing community. And as it faithfully proclaims what it understands, it will increasingly understand what it proclaims.

Thus reform is a continuous process, a work of the Spirit of God through the agency of the word of God.

2. The nature of mission

The very existence of the Evangelical–Roman Catholic Dialogue on Mission testifies to our common commitment to mission. One of the factors which led to its inauguration was the publication of the Lausanne covenant (1974) and of *Evangelii Nuntiandi*, Pope Paul VI's apostolic exhortation Evangelization in the Modern World (1975). These two documents supplied some evidence of a growing convergence in our understanding of mission. Not that evangelicals or Roman Catholics regard either of these statements as exhaustive, but they consider them valuable summaries and teaching tools.

1. The basis of mission

In response to the common criticism that we have no right to evangelize among all peoples, we together affirm the universality of God's purposes. God's creation of the world and of all humankind means that all should be subject to his lordship (Ps. 24:1-2; Eph. 3:8-11). The call of Abraham and of Israel had the wider purpose that all nations might see God's glory in his people and come to worship him. In the New Testament Jesus sends his disciples out in proclamatory witness, leading to the apostolic mission to all nations. In his Epistle to the Romans, Paul teaches that, since all without distinction have sinned, so all without distinction are offered salvation, Gentiles as well as Jews (3:22f.; 10:12).

We are agreed that mission arises from the self-giving life and love of the triune God himself and from his eternal purpose for the whole creation. Its goal is the God-centred kingdom of the Father, exhibited through the building of the body of Christ and cultivated in the fellowship of the Spirit. Because of Christ's first coming and the outpouring of the Holy Spirit, Christian mission has an eschatological dimension: it invites men and women to enter the kingdom of God through Christ the Son by the work and regeneration of the Spirit.

We all agree that the arrival of the messianic kingdom through Jesus Christ necessitates the announcement of the good news, the summons to repentance and faith, and the gathering together of the people of God. Sometimes Jesus clearly used "the kingdom of God" and "salvation" as synonyms.[15] For to announce the arrival of the kingdom of God is to proclaim its realization in the coming of Jesus Christ. And the church witnesses to the kingdom when it manifests the salvation it has received.

At the same time, long-standing tensions exist between Roman Catholics and evangelicals. While both sides affirm that the pilgrim church is missionary by its very nature, its missionary activity is differently understood.

Vatican II defines the church for Roman Catholics as "the sacrament of salvation", the sign and promise of redemption to each and every person without exception. For them, therefore, "mission" includes not only evangelization but also the service of human need, and the building up and expression of fellowship in the church. It is the mission of the church to anticipate the kingdom of God as liberation from the slavery of sin, from slavery to the law, and from death; by the preaching of the gospel, by the forgiveness of sins, and by sharing in the Lord's supper.[16] But the Spirit of God is always at work throughout human history to bring about the liberating reign of God.

Evangelization is the proclamation (by word and example) of the good news to the nations. The good news is that God's actions in Jesus Christ are the climax of a divine revelation and relationship that has been available to everyone from the beginning. Roman Catholics assert that the whole of humanity is in a collective history which God makes to be a history of salvation. The *mysterion* of the gospel is the announcement by the church to the world of this merging of the history of salvation with the history of the world.

Evangelicals generally, on the other hand, do not regard the history of salvation as coterminous with the history of the world, although some are struggling with this question. The church is the beginning and anticipation of the new creation, the firstborn among his creatures. Though all in Adam die, not all are automatically in Christ. So life in Christ has to be received by grace with repentance though faith. With yearning evangelicals plead for a response to the atoning work of Christ in his death and resurrection. But with sorrow they know that not all who are called are chosen. Judgment (both here and hereafter) is the divine reaction of God to sin and to the rejection of the good news. "Rich young rulers" still walk away from the kingdom of grace. Evangelization is therefore the call to those outside to come as children of the Father into the fullness of eternal life in Christ by the Spirit, and into the joy of a loving community in the fellowship of the church.

2. Authority and initiative in mission

Primary Christian obedience, we agree, is due to the Lord Jesus Christ and is expressed in both our individual and our common life under his authority. Roman Catholics and evangelicals recognize that the tension between ecclesiastical authority and personal initiative, as also between the institutional and the charismatic, has appeared throughout biblical and church history.

While for Roman Catholics hierarchical structures of teaching and pastoral authority are essential, the servant church, as described by the Second Vatican Council, is called to express herself more fully in the exercise of apostolic collegiality and subsidiarity (the principle that ecclesial decisions are made at the lowest level of responsibility).

Evangelicals have traditionally emphasized the personal right of every believer to enjoy direct access to God and the scriptures. There is also among them a growing realization of the importance of the church as the body of Christ, which tempers personal initiative through the restraint and direction of the fellowship.

This issue of authority has a bearing on mission. Are missionaries sent, or do they volunteer, or is it a case of both? What is the status of religious orders, mission boards or missionary societies, and para-church organizations? How do they relate to the churches or other ecclesial bodies? How can a preoccupation with jurisdiction (especially geographical) be reconciled with the needs of subcultures, especially in urban areas, which are often overlooked?

Although our traditions differ in the way we respond to these questions, we all wish to find answers which take account both of church structures and of the liberty of the Spirit outside them.

3. Evangelization and socio-political responsibility

The controversy over the relationship between evangelization and socio-political responsibility is not confined to Roman Catholics and evangelicals; it causes debate between and among all Christians.

We are agreed that "mission" relates to every area of human need, both spiritual and social. Social responsibility is an integral part of evangelization, and the struggle for justice can be a manifestation of the kingdom of God. Jesus both preached and healed, and sent his disciples out to do likewise. His predilection for those without power and without voice continues God's concern in the Old Testament for the widow, the orphan, the poor, and the defenceless alien.

In particular we agree:
a) that serving the spiritual, social and material needs of our fellow human beings together constitutes love of neighbour and therefore "mission";
b) that an authentic proclamation of the good news must lead to a call for repentance, and that authentic repentance is a turning away from social as well as individual sins;
c) that since each Christian community is involved in the reality of the world, it should lovingly identify with the struggle for justice as a suffering community;
d) that in this struggle against evil in society, the Christian must be careful to use means which reflect the spirit of the gospel; the church's responsibility in a situation of injustice will include repentance for any complicity in it, as well as intercessory prayer, practical service, and prophetic teaching which sets forth the standards of God and his kingdom.

We recognize that some Roman Catholics and some evangelicals find it difficult to subscribe to any inseparable unity between evangelization and the kind of socio-political involvement which is described above. There is also some tension concerning the allocation of responsibility for social service and action. Roman Catholics accept the legitimacy of involvement by the church as a whole, as well as by groups and individuals. Among evangelicals, however, there are differences between the Lutheran, Reformed and Anabaptist traditional understandings of church and society. All would agree that Christian individuals and groups have social responsibilities; the division concerns what responsibility is assigned to the church as a whole.

4. God's work outside the Christian community

We have written about the church and the kingdom. We are agreed that the concept of the church implies a limitation, for we talk about "church members", which infers that there are "non-members". But how widely should we understand the kingdom of God? We all agree that God works within the Christian community, for there he rules and dwells. But does he also work outside, and if so, how?

This is a question of major missiological importance. All of us are concerned to avoid an interpretation of the universal saving will of God, which makes salvation automatic without the free response of the person.

At least four common convictions have emerged from our discussions. They concern the great doctrines of creation, revelation, salvation and judgment.

1. *Creation:* God has created all humankind and by right of creation all humankind belongs to God. God also loves the whole human family and gives to them all "life and breath and everything" (Acts 17:25).
2. *Revelation:* There are elements of truth in all religions. These truths are the fruit of a revelatory gift of God. Evangelicals often identify their source in terms of general revelation, common grace, or the remnant image of God in humankind. Roman Catholics more frequently associate them with the work of the Logos, the true light

coming into the world and giving light to every man (John 1:9), and with the work of his Holy Spirit.
3. *Salvation:* There is only one Saviour and only one gospel. There is no other name but Christ's through whom anyone may be saved (Acts 4:12). So all who receive salvation are saved by the free initiative of God through the grace of Christ.
4. *Judgment:* While the biblical concept of judgment refers to both reward and punishment, it is clear that those who remain in sin by resisting God's free grace (whether they are inside or outside the visible boundaries of the church) provoke his judgment, which leads to eternal separation from him. The church itself also stands under the judgment of God whenever it refuses or neglects to proclaim the gospel of salvation to those who have not heard Christ's name.

The sphere for missionary activity is described differently within each tradition. Roman Catholics would expect God's mercy to be exercised effectively in benevolent action of his grace for the majority of humankind, unless they specifically reject his offer. Such a position gives them cause for confidence. Evangelicals consider that this view has no explicit biblical justification and that it would tend to diminish the evangelistic zeal of the church. Evangelicals are therefore less optimistic about the salvation of those who have no personal relationship to God through Jesus Christ.

We all affirm that the missionary enterprise is a participation in the mission of Jesus and the mission of his church. The urgency to reach all those not yet claimed by his lordship impels our mission.

Whether or not salvation is possible outside the Christian community, what is the motivation for mission work? We agree that the following strong incentives urgently impel Christians to the task of mission:

a) to further the glory of God: the earth should be a mirror to reflect his glory;
b) to proclaim the lordship of Jesus Christ: all men and women are called to submit to his authority;
c) to proclaim that Christ has struggled with Satan and dethroned him: in baptism and conversion we renounce Satan's rule and turn to Christ and righteousness;
d) to proclaim that man does not live by bread alone: the gospel of salvation is the perfect gift of God's loving grace;
e) to hasten the return of the Lord – the eschatological dimension: we look for the day of the Lord when the natural order will be completely redeemed, the whole earth will be filled with the knowledge of the Lord, and people from every nation, people, tribe and tongue will praise the triune God in perfection.

3. The gospel of salvation

Roman Catholics and evangelicals share a deep concern for the content of the good news we proclaim. We are anxious on the one hand to be faithful to the living core of the Christian faith, and on the other to communicate it in contemporary terms. How then shall we define the gospel?

1. Human need

Diagnosis must always precede prescription. So, although human need is not strictly part of the good news, it is an essential background to it. If the gospel is good news of salvation, this is because human beings are sinners who need to be saved.

In our description of the human condition, however, we emphasize the importance of beginning positively. We affirm that all men and women are made by God, for God, and in the image of God, and that sin has defaced but not destroyed this purpose and this image (Gen. 9:6; James 3:9). Therefore, as the creation of God, human beings have an intrinsic worth and dignity. Also, because of the light which lightens everybody, we all have within us an innate desire for God which nothing else can satisfy. As Christians, we must respect every human being who is seeking God, even when the search is expressed in ignorance (Acts 17:23).

Nevertheless, original sin has intervened. We have noted Thomas Aquinas's description of original sin, namely "the loss of original justice" (i.e., a right relationship with God) and such "concupiscence" as constitutes a fundamental disorder in human nature and relationships, so that all our desires are inclined towards the making of decisions displeasing to God.

Evangelicals insist that original sin has distorted every part of human nature, so that it is permeated by self-centredness. Consequently, the apostle Paul describes all people as "enslaved", "blind", "dead", and "under God's wrath", and therefore totally unable to save themselves.[17]

Roman Catholics also speak of original sin as an injury and disorder which has weakened – though not destroyed – human free will. Human beings have lifted themselves up against God and sought to attain their goal apart from him.[18] As a result this has upset the relationship linking man to God and "has broken the right order that should reign within himself as well as between himself and other men and all creatures".[19] Hence human beings find themselves drawn to what is wrong and of *themselves* unable to overcome the assaults of evil successfully, "so that everyone feels as though bound by chains".[20]

Clearly there is some divergence between Roman Catholics and evangelicals in the way we understand human sin and need, as well as in the language we use to express them. Roman Catholics think evangelicals overstress the corruption of human beings by affirming their "total depravity" (i.e., that every part of our humanness has been perverted by the fall), while evangelicals think Roman Catholics underestimate it and are therefore unwisely optimistic about the capacity, ability and desire of human beings to respond to the grace of God. Yet we agree that all are sinners, and that all stand in need of a radical salvation which includes deliverance from the power of evil, together with reconciliation to God and adoption into his family.

2. The person of Jesus Christ

The radical salvation which human beings need has been achieved by Jesus Christ. Evangelicals and Roman Catholics are agreed about the centrality of Christ and of what God has done through him for salvation. "The Father has sent his Son as the Saviour of the world" (1 John 4:14). But who was this Saviour Jesus?

Jesus of Nazareth was a man who went about doing good, teaching with authority, proclaiming the kingdom of God, and making friends with sinners to whom he offered pardon. He made himself known to his apostles, whom he had chosen and with whom he lived, as the Messiah (Christ) promised by the scriptures. He claimed a unique filial relation to God whom in prayer he called his Father ("Abba"). He thus knew himself to be the Son of God, and exhibited the power and authority of God over nature, human beings and demonic powers. He also spoke of himself as the Son of man. He fulfilled the perfect obedience of the Servant in going even to death on the cross. Then God raised him from the dead, confirming that he was from the beginning the Son he claimed to be (Ps. 2:7). Thus he was both descended from David "according to the flesh" and "designated Son of God in power according to the Spirit of holiness by his resurrection from the dead" (Rom. 1:3-4). This is why his apostles confessed him as Lord and Christ, Son of God, Saviour of humankind, sent by the Father, agent through whom God created all things, in whom we have been chosen from before the foundation of the world (Eph. 1:4), the Word made flesh.

The incarnation of the Son was an objective event in history, in which the divine Word took upon himself our human nature. Within a single person were joined full divinity and full humanity. Although this understanding of him was not precisely formulated until the theological debates of the early centuries, we all agree that the Chalcedonian definition faithfully expresses the truths to which the New Testament bears witness.

The purposes of the incarnation were to reveal the Father to us, since otherwise our knowledge of God would have been deficient; to assume our nature in order to die for our sins and so accomplish our salvation, since he could redeem only what he had assumed; to establish a living communion between God and human beings, since only the Son of God made human could communicate to human beings the life of God; to apply the basis of the *imitatio*, since it is the incarnate Jesus we are to follow; to reaffirm the value and dignity of humanness, since God was not ashamed to take on himself our humanity; to provide in Jesus the first-fruits of the new humanity, since he is the "firstborn among many brethren" (Rom 8:29), and to effect the redemption of the cosmos in the end.

So then, in fidelity to the gospel and in accordance with the scriptures, we together confess the person of Jesus Christ as the eternal Son of God, who was born of the Virgin Mary and became truly man, in order to be the Saviour of the world.

In our missionary task, we have not only to confess Christ ourselves, but also to interpret him to others. As we do so, we have to consider, for example, how to reconcile for Jews and Muslims the monotheism of the Bible with the divine sonship of Jesus, how to present to Hindus and Buddhists the transcendent personality of God, and how to proclaim to adherents of traditional religion and of the new religious consciousness the supreme lordship of Christ. Our Christology must always be both faithful to scripture and sensitive to each particular context of evangelization.

3. The work of Jesus Christ

It was this historic person, Jesus of Nazareth, fully God and fully human, through whom the Father acted for the redemption and reconciliation of the world. Indeed, only a person who was both God and man could have been the mediator between God and human beings. Because he was human he could represent us and identify with us in our weakness. Because he was God he could bear our sin and destroy the power of evil.

This work of redemption was accomplished supremely through the death of Jesus Christ, although we acknowledge the unity of his incarnate life, atoning death and bodily resurrection. For his death completed the service of his life (Mark 10:45) and his resurrection confirmed the achievement of his death (Rom. 4:25).

Christ was without sin, and therefore had no need to die. He died for our sins, and in this sense "in our place". We are agreed about this basic truth and about other aspects of the atonement. But in our discussion two different emphases have emerged, which we have summarized by the words "substitution" and "solidarity", although these concepts are not altogether exclusive.

Evangelicals lay much stress on the truth that Christ's death was "substitutionary". In his death he did something which he did not do during his life. He actually "became sin" for us (2 Cor. 5:21) and "became a curse" for us (Gal. 3:13). Thus God himself in Christ propitiated his own wrath, in order to avert it from us. In consequence, having taken our sin, he gives us his righteousness. We stand accepted by God in Christ, not because Christ offered the Father our obedience, but because he bore our sin and replaced it with his righteousness.

Roman Catholics express Christ's death more in terms of "solidarity". In their understanding, Jesus Christ in his death made a perfect offering of love and obedience to his Father, which recapitulated his whole life. In consequence, we can enter into the sacrifice of Christ and offer ourselves to the Father in and with him. For he became one with us in order that we might become one with him.

Thus the word "gospel" has come to have different meanings in our two communities.

For evangelicals, it is the message of deliverance from sin, death and condemnation, and the promise of pardon, renewal and indwelling by Christ's Spirit. These blessings flow from Christ's substitutionary death. They are given by God solely through his grace, without respect to our merit, and are received solely through faith. When we are accepted by Christ, we are part of his people, since all his people are "in" him.

For Roman Catholics the gospel centres in the person, message and gracious activity of Christ. His life, death and resurrection are the foundation of the church, and the church carries the living gospel to the world. The church is a real sacrament of the gospel.

So the difference between us concerns the relationship between the gospel and the church. In the one case, the gospel reconciles us to God through Christ and thus makes us a part of his people; in the other, the gospel is found within the life of his people, and thus we find reconciliation with God.

Although pastoral, missionary and cultural factors may lead us to stress one or other model of Christ's saving work, the full biblical range of words (e.g., victory, redemption, propitiation, justification, reconciliation) must be preserved, and none may be ignored.

The resurrection, we agree, lies at the heart of the gospel and has many meanings. It takes the incarnation to its glorious consummation, for it is the human Christ Jesus who reigns glorified at the Father's right hand, where he represents us and prays for us. The resurrection was also the Father's vindication of Jesus, reversing the verdict of those who condemned and crucified him, visibly demonstrating his sonship, and giving us the assurance that his atoning sacrifice had been accepted. It is the resurrected and exalted Lord who sent his Spirit to his church and who, claiming universal authority, now sends us into the world as his witnesses. The resurrection was also the beginning of God's new creation, and is his pledge both of our resurrection and of the final regeneration of the universe.

4. The uniqueness and universality of Jesus Christ

In a world of increasing religious pluralism, we affirm together the absolute uniqueness of Jesus Christ. He was unique in his person, in his death and in his resurrection. Since in no other person has God become human, died for the sins of the world, and risen from death, we declare that he is the only way to God (John 14:6), the only Saviour (Acts 4:12) and the only Mediator (1 Tim. 2:5). No one else has his qualifications.

The uniqueness of Jesus Christ implies his universality. The one and only is meant for all. We therefore proclaim him both "the Saviour of the world" (John 4:12) and "Lord of all" (Acts 10:36).

We have not been able to agree, however about the implications of his universal salvation and lordship. Together we believe that "God... desires all men to be saved and to come to the knowledge of the truth" (1 Tim. 2:4), that the offer of salvation in Christ is extended to everybody, that the church has an irreplaceable responsibility to announce the good news of salvation to all peoples, that all who hear the gospel have an obligation to respond to it, and that those who respond to it are incorporated into God's new worldwide, multiracial, multicultural community which is the Father's family, the body of Christ, and the temple of the Holy Spirit. These aspects of the universality of Christ we gladly affirm together.

Roman Catholics go further, however, and consider that, if human sin is universal, all the more is Christ's salvation universal. If everyone born into the world stands in solidarity with the disobedience of the first Adam, still the human situation as such has been changed by the definitive event of salvation, that is, the incarnation of the Word, his death, his resurrection and his gift of the Spirit. All are now part of the humanity whose new head has overcome sin and death. For all there is a new possibility of salvation which colours their entire situation, so that it is possible to say: "Every person, without exception, has been redeemed by Christ, and with each person, without any exception, Christ is in some way united, even when that person is not aware of that."[21] To become beneficiaries of the obedience of the Second Adam, men and women must turn to God and be born anew with Christ into the fullness of his life. The mission of the church is to be the instrument to awaken this response by proclaiming the gospel, itself the gift of salvation for everyone who receives it, and to communicate the truth and grace of Christ to all.[22]

Evangelicals, on the other hand, understand the universality of Christ differently. He is universally present as God (since God is omnipresent) and as potential Saviour (since he offers salvation to all) but not as actual Saviour (since not all accept his offer). Evangelicals wish to preserve the distinction, which they believe to be apostolic, between those who are in Christ and those who are not (who consequently are in sin and under judgment), and so between the old and new communities. They insist on the reality of the transfer from one community to the other, which can be realized only through the new birth: "If anyone is in Christ, he is a new creation" (2 Cor. 5:17).

The relationship between the life, death and resurrection of Jesus and the whole human race naturally leads Roman Catholics to ask whether there exists a possibility of salvation for those who belong to non-Christian religions and even for atheists. Vatican II was clear on this point: "Those also can attain to everlasting salvation who through no fault of their own do not know the gospel of Christ or his church." On the one hand, there are those who "sincerely seek God and, moved by his grace, strive by their deeds to do his will". On the other, there are those who "have not yet arrived at an explicit knowledge of God, but who strive to live a good life, thanks to his grace".[23] Both groups are prepared by God's grace to receive his salvation either when they hear the gospel or even if they do not. They can be saved by Christ, in a mysterious relation to his church.

Evangelicals insist, however, that according to the New Testament, those outside Christ are "perishing" and that they can receive salvation only in and through Christ. They are therefore deeply exercised about the eternal destiny of those who have never heard of Christ. Most evangelicals believe that, because they reject the light they have received, they condemn themselves to hell. Many are more reluctant to pronounce on their destiny, have no wish to limit the sovereignty of God, and prefer to leave this issue to him. Others go further in expressing their openness to the possibility that God may save some who have not heard of Christ, but immediately add that, if he does so, it will not be because of their religion, sincerity or actions (there is no possibility of salvation by good works), but only because of his own grace freely given on the ground of the atoning death of Christ. All evangelicals recognize the urgent need to proclaim the gospel of salvation to all humankind. Like Paul in his message to the Gentile audience at Athens, they declare that God "commands all men everywhere to repent, because he has fixed a day on which he will judge the world in righteousness by a man whom he has appointed" (Acts 17:30-31).

5. The meaning of salvation

In the Old Testament, salvation meant rescue, healing and restoration for those already related to God within the covenant. In the New Testament, it is directed to those who have not yet entered into the new covenant in Jesus Christ.

Salvation has to be understood in terms of both salvation history (the mighty acts of God through Jesus Christ) and salvation experience (a personal appropriation of what God has done through Christ). Roman Catholics and evangelicals together strongly emphasize the objectivity of God's work through Christ, but evangelicals tend to lay more emphasis than Roman Catholics on the necessity of a personal response to, and experience of, God's saving grace. To describe this, again the full New Testament vocabulary is needed (for example, the forgiveness of sins, reconciliation with God, adoption into his family, redemption, the new birth – all of which are gifts brought to us by the Holy Spirit), although evangelicals still give paramount importance to justification by grace through faith.

We agree that what is offered us through the death and resurrection of Christ is essentially "deliverance", viewed both negatively and positively. Negatively, it is a rescue from the power of Satan, sin and death, from guilt, alienation (estrangement from God), moral corruption, self-centredness, existential despair and fear of the future, including death. Positively, it is a deliverance into the freedom of Christ. This freedom brings human fulfilment. It is essentially becoming "sons in the Son" and therefore brothers to each other. The unity of the disciples of Jesus is a sign both that the Father sent the Son and that the kingdom has arrived. Further, the new community expresses itself in eucharistic worship, in serving the needy (especially the poor and disenfranchized), in open fellowship with people of every age, race and culture, and in conscious continuity with the historic Christ through fidelity to the teaching of his apostles. Is salvation broader than this? Does it include socio-political liberation?

Roman Catholics draw attention to the three dimensions of evangelization which *Evangelii Nuntiandi* links. They are the *anthropological*, in which humanity is seen always within a concrete situation; the *theological*, in which the unified plan of God is seen within both creation and redemption; and the *evangelical*, in which the exercise of charity (refusing to ignore human misery) is seen in the light of the story of the Good Samaritan.

We all agree that the essential meaning of Christ's salvation is the restoration of the broken relationship between sinful humanity and a saving God; it cannot therefore be seen as a temporal or material project, making evangelism unnecessary.

This restoration of humanity is a true "liberation" from enslaving forces; yet this work has taken on an expanded and particular meaning in Latin America. Certainly God's plan of which scripture speaks includes his reconciliation of human beings to himself and to one another.

The socio-political consequences of God's saving action through Christ have been manifest throughout history. They still are. Specific problems (e.g., slavery, urbanization, church-state relations and popular religiosity) have to be seen both in their particular context and in relation to God's overall plan as revealed in scripture and experienced in the believing community through the action of the Spirit.

Appendix: The Role of Mary in Salvation

Roman Catholics would rather consider the question of Mary in the context of the church than of salvation. They think of her as a sinless woman, since she was both overshadowed by the Spirit at the incarnation (Luke 1:35) and baptized with the Spirit on the day of Pentecost (Acts 1:14f. and 2:14). She thus represents all Christians who have been made alive by the Spirit, and Roman Catholics speak of her as the "figure" or "model" of the church.

The reason why we have retained this section on Mary within the chapter on "The Gospel of Salvation" (albeit as an appendix) is that it is in the context of salvation that evangelicals have the greatest difficulty with Marian teaching and that we discussed her role at ERCDOM II.

The place of Mary in the scheme of salvation has always been a sensitive issue between Roman Catholics and evangelicals. We have tried to face it with integrity.

a) The interpretation of scripture

It raises in an acute form the prior question how we use and interpret the Bible. We are agreed that biblical exegesis begins with a search for the "literal" sense of a text, which is what its author meant. We further agree that some texts also have a "spiritual" meaning, which is founded on the literal but goes beyond it because it was intended by the divine – though not necessarily the human – author (e.g., Isa. 7:14). This is often called the *sensus plenior*. The difference between Roman Catholics and evangelicals lies in the degree to which the spiritual sense may be separated from the literal. Both sides agree that, whenever scripture is not explicit, there is need for some check on the extravagances of interpreters. We are also agreed that this check is supplied by the context, both the immediate context and the whole of scripture, which is a unity. Roman Catholics, however, say that scripture must be read in the light of the living, developing Tradition of the church, and that the church has authority to indicate what the true meaning of scripture is. Thus, in relation to Mary, Roman Catholics concede that devotion to Mary was a post-apostolic practice but add that it was a legitimate development, whereas evangelicals believe it has been unwarrantably imported into the Roman Catholic interpretation of scripture.

b) Mary and salvation

In one of our ERCDOM II sessions, entitled "The Place of the Virgin Mary in Salvation and Mission", an evangelical response was made to Pope Paul VI's 1974 apostolic exhortation *Marialis Cultus* (To Honour Mary). Evangelical members of the dialogue asked for an explanation of two expressions in it which, at least on the surface, appeared to them to ascribe to Mary an active and participatory role in the work of salvation.

The first (I.5) describes the Christmas season as a prolonged commemoration of Mary's "divine, virginal and salvific motherhood". In what sense, evangelicals asked, could Mary's motherhood be called "salvific"? The Roman Catholics replied that the explanation of the term was to be found in the text itself, namely, that she "brought the Saviour into the world" by her obedient response to God's call.

The second passage (I.15) refers to "the singular place" that belongs to Mary in Christian worship, not only as "the holy Mother of God" but as "the worthy associate of the Redeemer". In what sense, evangelicals asked, could Mary properly be described as the Redeemer's "worthy associate?" It did not mean, the Roman Catholics responded, that she was personally without need of redemption, for on the contrary she was herself saved through her Son's death. In her case, however, "salvation" did not signify the forgiveness of sins, but that because of her predestination to be the "Mother of God", she was preserved from original sin ("immaculate conception") and so from sinning. Positively, she could be described as the Redeemer's "associate" because of her unique link with him as his mother. The word should not give offence, for we too are "associates of the Redeemer", both as recipients of his redemption and as agents through whose prayers, example, sacrifice, service, witness and suffering his redemption is proclaimed to others.

The evangelicals made a double response to these explanations. First, they still found the language ambiguous, and considered this ambiguity particularly unfortunate in the central area of salvation. Secondly, they felt the whole Roman Catholic emphasis on Mary's role in salvation exaggerated, for when the apostles John and Paul unfold the mystery of the incarnation, it is to honour Christ the Son, not Mary the mother. At the same time, they readily agreed that in Luke's infancy narrative, Mary is given the unique privilege of being the Saviour's mother and on that account is addressed as both "highly favoured" and "blessed among women" (1:28-42). If evangelicals are to be true to their stance on sola scriptura, they must therefore overcome any inhibitions they may have and faithfully expound such texts.

Our discussion also focused on the use of the term "cooperation". For example, it is stated in *Lumen Gentium*, chapter VIII, that Mary is rightly seen as "cooperating in the work of human salvation through free faith and obedience" (II, no. 56), and again that "the unique mediation of the Redeemer does not exclude but rather gives rise... to a manifold cooperation which is but a sharing in this unique source" (III, no. 62). The evangelicals agreed that the notion of cooperation with God is biblical (e.g., "workers together with him", 2 Cor. 6:1), but pointed out that this refers to a divine-human partnership in which our share lies in the proclaiming – and not in any sense in the procuring – of salvation. The Roman Catholics agreed. The "cooperation" between Christ and us, they said, does not mean that we can add anything to Christ or his work, since he is complete in himself, and his work has been achieved. It means rather that we share in the benefits of what he has done (not in the doing of it) and that (by his gift alone, as in the case of Mary) we offer ourselves to him in gratitude, to spend our lives in his service, and to be used by him as instruments of his grace (cf. Gal. 1). The evangelicals were relieved but still felt that the use of the word "cooperation" in this sense was inappropriate.

Another word we considered was "mediatrix", the feminine form of "mediator". The evangelicals reacted with understandable vehemence against its application to Mary, as did also some Roman Catholics. She must not be designated thus, they insisted, since the work of mediation belongs to Christ alone. In reply, the Roman Catholics were reassuring. Although the word (or rather its Greek equivalent) was used of Mary from the 5th century onwards, and although some bishops were pressing at Vatican II for its inclusion in the text, the Council deliberately avoided it. It occurs only once, and then only in a list of Mary's traditional titles. Moreover, in the same section of *Lumen Gentium* (III, nos 60-62) Christ is twice called "the one Mediator" in accordance with 1 Timothy 2:5-6, and his unique mediation is also referred to twice, which (it is added) Mary's maternal ministry "in no way obscures or diminishes".

The final document of the Puebla conference of the evangelization of Latin America (1979), which contains a long section entitled "Mary, Mother and Model of the Church" (§§282-303), was cited by evangelical participants. Paragraph 293 declares that Mary "now lives immersed in the mystery of the Trinity, praising the glory of God and interceding for human beings". Evangelicals find this a disturbing expression, and not all Roman Catholics are happy with it, finding it too ambiguous (if indeed "immersed" is an accurate translation of the Spanish original *immersa*; there has been some controversy about this). Roman Catholics explain that the notion of Mary's "immersion" in the Trinity means that she is the daughter of the Father, the mother of the Son, and the temple of the Holy Spirit (all three expressions being used in §53 of *Lumen Gentium*). But they strongly insist that, of course, she cannot be on a level with the three persons of the Trinity, let alone a fourth person. In addition, they point out that Roman Catholics' understanding of the role of Mary should be determined by the whole of chapter VIII of *Lumen Gentium*, and other official statements of Roman Catholic belief, rather than by popular expressions of Marian piety.

The fears of evangelicals were to some extent allayed by these Roman Catholic explanations and assurances. Yet a certain evangelical uneasiness remained. First, the traditional Catholic emphasis on Mary's role in salvation (e.g., as the "New Eve", the life-giving mother) still seemed to them incompatible with the much more modest place accorded to her in the New Testament. Secondly, the vocabulary used in relation to Mary seemed to them certainly ambiguous and probably misleading. Is it not vitally important, they asked, especially in the central doctrine of salvation through Christ alone, to avoid expressions which require elaborate explanation (however much hallowed by long tradition) and to confine ourselves to language which is plainly and unequivocally Christ-centred?

At the same time Roman Catholics are troubled by what seems to them a notable neglect by evangelicals of the place given by God to Mary in salvation history and in the life of the church.

4. Our response in the Holy Spirit to the gospel

We agree that evangelism is not just a proclamation of Christ's historic work and saving offer. Evangelism also includes a call for response which is often called "conversion".

1. The work of the Holy Spirit

This response, however, does not depend on the efforts of the human person but on the initiative of the Holy Spirit. As is stated in the scripture, "for by grace you have been saved through faith; and this is not your own doing, it is the gift of God – not because of works, lest any man should boast" (Eph. 2:8-9). There is therefore a trinitarian dimension to the human person's response: it is the Father who gives; his supreme gift is his Son, Jesus Christ, for the life of the world (John 6:23); and it is the Holy Spirit who opens our minds and hearts so that we can accept and proclaim that Jesus Christ is Lord (1 Cor 12:3) and live as his disciples. This means that the Holy Spirit guarantees that the salvation which the Father began in Jesus Christ becomes effective in us in a personal way.

When human persons experience conversion, the Holy Spirit illumines their understanding so that Jesus Christ can be confessed as the Truth itself revealed by the Father (John 14:6). The Holy Spirit also renders converted persons new creatures who participate in the eternal life of the Father and the Son (John 11:25-26). Furthermore, the Holy Spirit, through the gifts of faith, hope and love, already enables converted persons to have a foretaste of the kingdom which will be totally realized when the Son hands over all things to the Father (1 Cor. 15:28).

Thus, the work of the Holy Spirit in Christian conversion has to be seen as the actual continuation of his previous creative and redemptive activity throughout history. Indeed, at the beginning the Holy Spirit was present at the act of creation (Gen. 1:2), and he is continually sent forth as the divine breath by whom everything is created and by whom the face of the earth is renewed (Ps. 104:29-30). Although all persons are influenced by the life-giving Spirit of God, it is particularly in the Old Testament, which he inspired, that the recreative work of the Holy Spirit after the fall of humankind is concretely manifested. In order to ground the divine plan to recreate humanity, the Holy Spirit first taught the patriarchs to fear God and to practise righteousness. And to assemble his people Israel and to bring it back to the observance of the covenant, the Holy Spirit raised up judges, kings and wise men. Moreover, the prophets, under the guidance of the Spirit, announced that the Holy Spirit would create a new heart and bestow new life by being poured out in a unique way on Israel and, through it, on all humanity (Ezek. 36:24-28; Joel 2:28-29).

The recreative work of the Holy Spirit reached its culminating point in the incarnation of Jesus Christ who, as the New Adam, was filled with the Holy Spirit without measure (John 3:34). Because Jesus Christ was the privileged bearer of the Holy Spirit, he is the one who gives the Holy Spirit for the regeneration of human beings: "He on whom you see the Spirit descend and remain, this is he who baptizes with the Holy Spirit" (John 1:33). Through his death on behalf of sinful humankind and his rising up to glory, Jesus Christ communicates the Holy Spirit to all who are converted to him, that is, receive him by faith as their personal Lord and Saviour. This new life in Jesus Christ by the Holy Spirit is signified by baptism and by membership in the body of

Christ, the church. Furthermore, through his indwelling in converted persons, the Holy Spirit attests that they are co-heirs with Christ of eternal glory.

2. Conversion and baptism

We have been agreeably surprised to discover a considerable consensus among us that repentance and faith, conversion and baptism, regeneration and incorporation into the Christian community all belong together, although we have needed to debate their relative positions in the scheme of salvation.

"Conversion" signifies an initial turning to Jesus Christ in repentance and faith, with a view to receiving the forgiveness of sins and the gift of the Spirit, and to being incorporated into the church, all signed to us in baptism (Acts 2:38-39). The expression "continuous conversion" (if used) must therefore be understood as referring to our daily repentance as Christians, our response to new divine challenges, and our gradual transformation into the image of Christ by the Spirit (2 Cor. 3:18). Moreover, some who have grown up in a Christian home find themselves to be regenerate Christians without any memory of a conscious conversion.

We agree that baptism must never be isolated, either in theology or in practice, from the context of conversion. It belongs essentially to the whole process of repentance, faith, regeneration by the Holy Spirit, and membership of the covenant community, the church. A large number of evangelicals (perhaps the majority) practise only "believer's baptism". That is, they baptize only those who have personally accepted Jesus Christ as their Saviour and Lord, and they regard baptism both as the convert's public profession of faith and as the dramatization (by immersion in water) of his or her having died and risen with Christ. The practice of infant baptism (practised by some evangelicals, rejected by others) assures both that the parents believe and will bring their children up in the Christian faith and that the children will themselves later come to conscious repentance and faith.

We rejoice together that the whole process of salvation is the work of God by the Holy Spirit. And it is in this connection that Roman Catholics understand the expression *ex opere operato* in relation to baptism. It does not mean that the sacraments have a mechanical or automatic efficacy. Its purpose rather is to emphasize that salvation is a sovereign work of Christ, in distinction to a Pelagian or semi-Pelagian confidence in human ability.

There is a further dimension of the work of the Holy Spirit in our response to the gospel to which we have become increasingly sensitive, and which we believe belongs within our understanding of the work of the Spirit in mission.

In the light of biblical teaching, particularly in the Epistle to the Ephesians,[24] and also in view of the insights gained through Christian missionary experience, we believe that, although the revelation of Jesus Christ as the Truth by the Holy Spirit is in itself complete in the scriptures, nevertheless he is wanting to lead the church into a yet fuller understanding of this revelation. Hence we rejoice that in the various cultural contexts in which men and women throughout nearly twenty centuries of Christian history have been enabled by the Holy Spirit to respond to the gospel, we can perceive the many-sidedness of the unique Lord Jesus Christ, the Saviour of all humankind.

Accordingly, we hope that the Holy Spirit will make us open to such new and further insights into the meaning of Jesus Christ, as he may wish to communicate by means of various manifestations of Christian life in our Christian communities, as well as in human societies where we earnestly desire that he will create a response to the gospel in conversion, baptism and incorporation into Christ's body, the church.

3. Church membership

Conversion and baptism are the gateway into the new community of God, although evangelicals distinguish between the visible and invisible aspects of this community. They see conversion as the means of entry into the invisible church, and baptism as the consequently appropriate means of entry into the visible church. Both sides agree that the church should be characterized by learning, worship, fellowship, holiness, service and evangelism (Acts 2:42-47). Furthermore, life in the church is characterized by hope and love, as a result of the outpouring of the Holy Spirit: "And hope does not disappoint us, because God's love has been poured into our hearts through the Holy Spirit which has been given to us" (Rom. 5:5). It is the Holy Spirit who arouses and sustains our response to the living Christ. Through the power of the Holy Spirit, the unity of the human family, which was disrupted by sin, is gradually being recreated as the new humanity emerges (Eph. 2:15).

The issue of church membership has raised in our dialogue the delicate and difficult question of the conversion of those already baptized. How are we to think of their baptism? And which church should they join? This practical question can cause grave problems in the relationship between Roman Catholics and evangelicals. It is particularly acute in places like Latin America, where large numbers of baptized Roman Catholics have had a minimal relationship with the Roman Catholic Church since their baptism.

When such Roman Catholics have a conversion experience, many evangelical churches welcome them into membership without rebaptizing them. Some Baptist churches, however, and some others would insist on baptizing such converts, as indeed they baptize Protestant converts who have been baptized in infancy.

Then there is the opposite problem of Protestant Christians wishing to become members of the Roman Catholic Church. Since Vatican II, the Roman Catholic Church has recognized other Christians as being in the first place "brethren", rather than subjects for conversion. Nevertheless, since the Roman Catholic Church believes that the one church of Christ subsists within it in a unique way, it further believes it is legitimate to receive other Christians into its membership. Such membership is not seen as an initial step towards salvation, however, but as a further step towards Christian growth. Considerable care is taken nowadays to ensure that such a step is not taken under wrong pressure and for unworthy motives. In other words, there is an avoidance of "proselytism" in the wrong sense. Then, provided that there is some proof of valid baptism having taken place, there is no question of rebaptism.

Church members need constantly to be strengthened by the grace of God. Roman Catholics and evangelicals understand grace somewhat differently, however; Roman Catholics thinking of it more as divine life and evangelicals as divine favour. Both sides agree that it is by a totally free gift of the Father that we become joined to Christ and enabled to live like Christ through the power of the Holy Spirit. Both sides also understand the eucharist (or Lord's supper) as a sacrament (or ordinance) of grace. Roman Catholics affirm the real presence of the body and blood of Jesus Christ and emphasize the mystery of Christ and his salvation becoming present and effective by the working of the Holy Spirit under the sacramental sign,[25] whereas evangelicals (in different ways according to their different church traditions) view the sacrament as the means by which Christ blesses us by drawing us into fellowship with himself, as we remember his death until he comes again (1 Cor. 11:26).

Despite the lack of full accord which we have just described, both evangelicals and Roman Catholics agree that the eucharist is spiritual food and spiritual drink (1 Cor. 10:3-4,16), because the unifying Spirit is at work in this sacrament. As a memorial of the new covenant, the eucharist is a privileged sign in which Christ's saving grace is especially signified and/or made available to Christians. In the eucharist the Holy Spirit makes the words Jesus spoke at the last supper effective in the church and assures Christians that through their faith, they are intimately united to Christ and to each other in the breaking of the bread and the sharing of the cup.

4. Assurance of salvation

It has always been traditional among evangelicals to stress not only salvation as a present gift, but also the assurance of salvation enjoyed by those who have received it. They like, for example, to quote 1 John 5:13: "I write this to you who believe in the name of the Son of God, that you may know that you have eternal life." Thus eternal life begins in us now through the Spirit of the risen Christ, because we are "raised with him through faith in the working of God, who raised him from the dead" (Col. 2:12). Yet in daily life we live in the tension between what is already given and what is still awaited as a promise, for "your life is hid with Christ in God. When Christ who is our life appears, then you will also appear with him in glory" (Col. 3:3-4).

Roman Catholics and evangelicals are agreed that the only ground for assurance is the objective work of Christ; this ground does not lie in any way in the believer. We speak somewhat differently about the work of Christ, however, and relate it differently in terms of practical piety. Evangelicals refer to the "finished" work of Christ on the cross and rest their confidence wholly upon it. Roman Catholics also speak of Christ's work as having been done "once for all"; they therefore see it as beyond repetition. Nevertheless, they understand that through the eucharist Christ's unique, once-for-all work is made present, and that by this means they maintain a present relationship to it. The relationship to Christ's finished work which evangelicals enjoy is maintained by faith, but it is faith in what was done, and what was done is never re-presented.

Roman Catholics and evangelicals both claim an authentic religious experience, which includes an awareness of the presence of God and a taste for spiritual realities. Yet evangelicals think Roman Catholics sometimes lack a visible joy in Christ, which their assurance has given them, whereas Roman Catholics think evangelicals are sometimes insufficiently attentive to the New Testament warnings against presumption. Roman Catholics also claim to be more realistic than evangelicals about the vagaries of religious experience. The actual experience of evangelicals seldom leads then to doubt their salvation, but Roman Catholics know that the soul may have its dark nights. In summary, evangelicals appear to Roman Catholics more pessimistic about human nature before conversion but more optimistic about it afterwards, while evangelicals allege the opposite about Roman Catholics. Roman Catholics and evangelicals together agree that Christian assurance is more an assurance of faith (Heb. 10:22) than of experience, and that perseverance to the end is a gratuitous gift of God.

5. The church and the gospel

Evangelicals, because of their emphasis on the value of the individual, have traditionally neglected the doctrine of the church. The topic was not neglected in our dialogue, however. We found ourselves united in certain convictions about the church, and in our commitment to it. We were able to agree on a fourfold relationship between the church and the gospel.

1. The church is a part of the gospel

The redemptive purpose of God has been from the beginning to call out a people for himself. When he called Abraham, he promised to bless all nations through his posterity, and has kept his promise. For all those who are united to Christ, Gentiles as well as Jews, are Abraham's spiritual children and share in the promised blessing.[26]

This wonderful new thing, namely the abolition of the dividing wall between Jews and Gentiles and the creation of a single new humanity, was at the heart of Paul's gospel (Eph. 2:14,15). He called it "the mystery of Christ", which having been made known to him, he must make known to others (Eph. 3:3-9).

Both evangelicals and Roman Catholics are conscious of past failure in their understanding of the church. Roman Catholics used to concentrate on the church as a hierarchical institution, but now (since Vatican II) see it in new perspective by stressing the important biblical images such as that of the people of God. Evangelicals have sometimes preached an excessively individualistic gospel, "Christ died for me". This is true (Gal. 2:20), but it is far from the whole truth, which is that Christ gave himself for us "to purify for himself a people..." (Titus 2:14).

Thus both Roman Catholics and evangelicals agree that the church as the body of Christ is part of the gospel. That is to say, the good news includes God's purpose to create for himself through Christ a new, redeemed, united and international people of his own.

2. The church is a fruit of the gospel

The first clear proclamation of the good news in the power of the Holy Spirit resulted in the gathered community of God's people – the church (Acts 2:39-42). This was to become the pattern for subsequent apostolic and missionary endeavours with the gospel. The condition for membership of the community is *repentance* (chiefly from the sin of unbelief and rejection of Christ), and *faith* in the Lord Jesus Christ, witnessed to in submission to baptism in his name (Acts 2:38). The benefits of membership include the personal enjoyment of the forgiveness of sins, and participation in the new life of the Spirit (Acts 2:38-39; 1 Cor. 12:13).

From the beginning, the community of God's people was marked by a devotion to the apostolic teaching, to fellowship (a sharing which extended to practical loving care), to the breaking of bread (the Lord's supper), and to the prayers or public worship (Acts 2:42). To this *believing, worshipping, caring and witnessing* community, "the Lord added to their number day by day those who were being saved" (Acts 2:47).

Evangelicals on the whole have tended to emphasize personal salvation almost to the point of losing sight of the central place of the church. The multiplication of evangelistic organizations and agencies which are not church-based has contributed to this distortion. There is, however, a growing desire to correct it. For wherever the gospel goes, it bears fruit in the spread and growth of the church.

3. The church is an embodiment of the gospel

The very life of the church as God's new community becomes itself a witness to the gospel. "The life of the community only acquires its full meaning when it becomes a witness, when it evokes admiration and conversion and when it becomes the preaching and proclamation of the good news."[27] Thus the church is the sign of the power and the presence of Jesus, the light of Christ shining out visibly to bring all men to that light.[28]

As a fellowship of communities throughout the world, the church is to be "a people brought into unity from the unity of the Father, Son and Holy Spirit" (Cyprian). This was why Jesus had come into the world and why the living communion of believers between themselves and the Lord of life, and between each other, is to be the proclamation that will move people's hearts to belief (John 13:34-35, 17:23).

In every place the believing community speaks to the world by an authentically Christian life given over to God in a communion that nothing should destroy and at the same time given to one's neighbour with limitless zeal (cf. 1 Pet. 2:12).

It is also the community of peace which makes Jew and Gentile one, in which by the power of the broken body of Christ, the enmity which stood like a dividing wall between them has been broken down and a single new humanity brought into being (Eph. 2:15-16). The church cannot with integrity preach the gospel of reconciliation unless it is evidently a reconciled community itself.

It is a community that makes present the obedient Lord who underwent death for us. It is founded upon him (Eph. 2:20), he is its Lord (Eph. 1:22), and its power to speak of him comes from the manner in which it reproduces in all its members and in its common life his obedience to the saving plan of God.

This unity, holiness, love and obedience are the alternative sign that Christ is not an anonymous or remote Lord. They are the mark of the community given over to God, and they speak about the good news of salvation in Jesus Christ.

4. The church is an agent of the gospel

That the church must be an agent of the gospel overflows from its internal life. The church which receives the word must also sound it forth (1 Thess. 1:5-8). The church which embodies its message visually must also declare it verbally.

First, the church continues and prolongs the very same mission of Christ.[29]

Secondly, the church received Christ's command to be his witnesses in the power of the Spirit to the end of the earth (Acts 1:8).

Thirdly, the church proclaims the message with the authority of the Lord himself, who gave her the power of the Spirit. As to the qualified subjects of this authority, there are divergences between evangelicals and Roman Catholics. For evangelicals, the agent of the proclamation is the whole community of believers, who are equipped for this task by those appointed to the pastoral ministry (Eph 4:11-12). For Roman Catholics also, the evangelistic task belongs to the whole people of God, but they believe bishops have a special role and responsibility both to order the life of the community for this task and, as successors to the ministry of apostolic times, to preach the good news of the kingdom.

To sum up, the church and the gospel belong indissolubly together. We cannot think of either apart from the other. For God's purpose to create a new community through Christ is itself an important element in the good news. The church is also both the fruit and the agent of the gospel, since it is through the gospel that the church spreads, and through the church that the gospel spreads. Above all, unless the church embodies the gospel, giving it visible flesh and blood, the gospel lacks credibility and the church lacks effectiveness in witness.

More and more Christians are recognizing this lack of a fully credible, effective witness because of divisions among themselves. They believe that Christ has called all his disciples in every age to be witnesses to him and his gospel to the ends of the earth (cf. Acts 1:8). Yet those who profess such discipleship differ about the meaning of the one gospel and go their different ways as if Christ himself were divided (cf. 1 Cor. 1:13).

To be sure, Christian separations and divisions have often been due to conscientiously held convictions, and Christian unity must not be sought at the expense of Christian truth. Nevertheless, the divisions and their causes contradict the will of Jesus Christ, who desires his people to be united in truth and love. They also hinder the proclamation of his good news of reconciliation. Therefore the gospel calls the church to be renewed in truth, holiness and unity, in order that it may be effectively renewed for mission as well.

6. The gospel and culture

The influence of culture on evangelism, conversion and church formation is increasingly recognized as a topic of major missiological importance. The Willowbank report *Gospel and Culture* (1978) defines culture as "an integrated system of beliefs (about God or reality or ultimate meaning), of values (about what is true, good, beautiful and normative), of customs (how to behave, relate to others, talk, pray, dress, work, play, trade, farm, eat, etc.), and of institutions which express these beliefs, values and customs (government, law courts, temples or churches, family, schools, hospitals, factories, shops, unions, clubs, etc.), which binds a society together and gives it a sense of identity, dignity, security and continuity".[30] Viewed thus, culture pervades the whole of human life, and it is essential for Christians to know how to evaluate it.

It is acknowledged that evangelicals and Roman Catholics start from a different background. Evangelicals tend to stress the discontinuity, and Roman Catholics the continuity, between man unredeemed and man redeemed. At the same time, both emphases are qualified. Discontinuity is qualified by the evangelical recognition of the image of God in humankind and continuity by the Roman Catholic recognition that human beings and societies are contaminated by sin. The Lausanne covenant summarized this tension as follows: "Because man is God's creature, some of his culture is rich in beauty and goodness. Because he is fallen, all of it is tainted with sin and some of it is demonic."[31]

We have particularly concentrated on the place of culture in four areas – in the Bible, in cross-cultural evangelism, in conversion and in church formation.

1. Culture and the Bible

We have already affirmed that the Bible is the word of God through the words of human beings. Realizing that human language and human thought-forms reflect human cultures, we saw the need to explore two major questions: (a) What was the attitude of the biblical authors to their cultures?(b) How should we ourselves react to the cultural conditioning of scripture?

In answer to the first question, we considered the New Testament. Its message comes to us from the context of the first-century world, with its own images and vocabulary, and is thus set in the context of that world's culture. The culture has become the vehicle of the message.

Yet within that first-century culture there were elements which the Christian and the church were required to resist, out of loyalty to the Lord Jesus. Distinctions between the new community and the surrounding culture were clearly drawn. At the same time, the Christian and the church enjoyed a new freedom in Christ, which enabled them to discern those elements in the culture which must be rejected as hostile to their faith and those which were compatible with it and could on that account be affirmed. Blindness, which leads Christians to tolerate the evil and/or overlook the good in their culture, is a permanent temptation.

Our other question was concerned with how we ourselves should react to the cultural conditioning of scripture. It breaks down into two subsidiary questions which express the options before us. First, are the biblical formulations (which we have already affirmed to be normative) so intrinsically conditioned by their mode of specific cultural expression that they cannot be changed to suit different cultural settings? Put another way, has biblical inspiration (which evangelicals and Roman Catholics both acknowledge) made the cultural forms themselves normative? The alternative is to ask whether it is the revealed teaching which is normative, so that this may be re-expressed in other cultural forms. We believe the latter to be the case, and that such re-expression or translation is a responsibility laid both on cross-cultural missionaries and on local Christian leaders.[32]

2. Culture and evangelism

Christian missionaries find themselves in a challenging cross-cultural, indeed tri-cultural, situation. They come from a particular culture themselves, they travel to people nurtured in another, and they take with them a biblical gospel which was originally formulated in a third. How will this interplay of cultures affect their evangelism? And how can they be simultaneously faithful to scripture and relevant to the local culture?

In the history of mission in this century, a progress is discernible. The successive approaches may be summarized as follows:

a) In the first period, the missionary brought along with the gospel message many of the cultural trappings of his or her own situation. Then culture, instead of being (as in the New Testament) a vehicle for the proclamation of the gospel, became a barrier to it. Accidentals of teaching and practice were taught as if they were essentials, and a culture-Christianity was preached as if it were the gospel.

b) In the second period, the gospel message was translated into terms (language and thought-forms, artistic symbols and music) appropriate to those to whom it was brought, and the cultural trappings began to be left behind. Now local cultures, instead of being neglected, were respected and, where possible, used for the better communication of the gospel. In a word, the gospel began to be "contextualized".

c) In the third period, in which we are living, missionaries bring both the biblical gospel and an experience of life in Christ. They also endeavour to take seriously the people to whom they have come, with their world-view and way of life, so that they may find their own authentic way of experiencing and expressing the salvation of Christ. This kind of evangelism tries to be both faithful to the biblical revelation and relevant to the people's culture. In fact it aims at bringing scripture, context and experience into a working relationship effective for presenting the gospel.

3. Culture and conversion

We are clear that conversion includes repentance and that repentance is a turning away from the old life. But what are the aspects of the old life from which a convert must turn away? Conversion cannot be just turning away from "sin" as this is viewed in any one particular culture. For different cultures have different understandings of sin, and we have to recognize this aspect of pluralism. So missionaries and church leaders in each place need great wisdom, both at the time of a person's conversion and during his or her maturing as a Christian, to distinguish between the moral and the cultural, between what is clearly approved or condemned by the gospel on the one hand and by custom or convention on the other. The repentance of conversion should be a turning away only from what the gospel condemns.

4. Culture and church formation

In the development of the Christian community in each place, as in the other areas we have mentioned, missionaries must avoid all cultural imperialism; that is, the imposition on the church of alien cultural forms. Just as the gospel has to be inculturated, so must the church be inculturated also.

We all agree that the aim of "indigenization" or "inculturation" is to make local Christians congenial members of the body of Christ. They must not imagine that to become Christian is to become Western and so to repudiate their own cultural and national inheritance. The same principle applies in the West, where too often to become Christian has also meant to become middle-class.

There are a number of spheres in which each church should be allowed to develop its own identity. The first is the question of certain forms of organization, especially as they relate to church leadership. Although Roman Catholics and evangelicals take a different approach to authority and its exercise, we are agreed that in every Christian community (especially a new one), authority must be exercised in a spirit of service. "I am among you as one who serves," Jesus said (Luke 22:27). Yet the expression given to leadership can vary according to different cultures.

The second sphere is that of artistic creativity – for example, church architecture, painting, symbols, music and drama. Local churches will want to express their Christian identity in artistic forms which reflect their local culture.

A third area is theology. Every church should encourage theological reflection on the aspirations of its culture and seek to develop a theology which gives expression to these. Yet only in such a way as to apply, not compromise, the biblical revelation.

Two problems confront a church which is seeking to "inculturate" itself, namely, provincialism and syncretism. "Provincialism" asserts the local culture of a particular church to the extent that it cuts itself adrift from, and even repudiates, other churches. We are agreed that new expressions of local church life must in no way break fellowship with the wider Christian community.

Syncretism is the attempt to fuse the biblical gospel with elements of local culture which, being erroneous or evil, are incompatible with it. But the gospel's true relation to culture is discriminating, judging some elements and welcoming others. The criteria it applies to different elements or forms include the questions whether they are under the judgment of Christ's lordship and whether they manifest the fruit of the Spirit.

It has to be admitted that every expression of Christian truth is inadequate and may be distorted. Hence the need for mutually respectful dialogue about the relative merits of old and new forms, in the light of both the biblical revelation and the experience of the wider community of faith.

The Second Vatican Council addressed itself to these important matters. It recognized that in every culture there are some elements which may need to be "purged of evil association" and to be restored "to Christ their source, who overthrows the rule of the devil and limits the manifold malice of evil". In this way "the good found in people's minds and hearts, or in particular customs and cultures, is purified, raised to a higher level and reaches its perfection..."[33]

Hence it is not a question of adapting things which come from the world usurped by Satan, but of repossessing them for Christ. To take them over as they are could be syncretism. "Repossession", on the other hand, entails four steps: (a) the selection of certain elements from one's culture; (b) the rejection of other elements which are incompatible with the essence of the biblical faith; (c) the purification from the elements selected and adopted of everything unworthy; (d) the integration of these into the faith and life of the church.

The age to come has broken into this present age in such a way as to touch our lives with both grace and judgment. It cuts through every culture. Vatican II referred to this discontinuity and also emphasized the need for "the spiritual qualities and endowments of every age and nation" to be fortified, completed and restored in Christ.[34]

For Jesus Christ is Lord of all and our supreme desire vis-a-vis each culture is to "take every thought captive to obey Christ" (2 Cor. 10:5).

7. The possibilities of common witness

We turn in our last chapter from theological exploration to practical action. We have indicated where we agree and disagree. We now consider what we can do and cannot do together. Since our discussion on this topic was incomplete, what follows awaits further development.

1. Our unity and disunity

We have tried to face with honesty and candour the issues which divide us as Roman Catholics and evangelicals. We have neither ignored, nor discounted, nor even minimized them. For they are real and, in some cases, serious.

At the same time, we know and have experienced that the walls of our separation do not reach to heaven. There is much that unites us and much in each other's different manifestations of Christian faith and life which we have come to appreciate. Our concern throughout our dialogue has not been with the structural unity of churches, but rather with the possibilities of common witness. So when we write of "unity", it is this that we have in mind.

To begin with, we acknowledge in ourselves and in each other a firm belief in God, Father, Son and Holy Spirit. This faith is for us more than a conviction; it is a commitment. We have come to the Father through the Son by the Holy Spirit (Eph. 2:18).

We also recognize that the gospel is God's good news about his Son Jesus Christ (Rom. 1:1-3), about his godhead and manhood, his life and teaching, his acts and promises, his death and resurrection, and about the salvation he has once accomplished and now offers. Moreover, Jesus Christ is our Saviour and our Lord, for he is the object of our personal trust, devotion and expectation. Indeed, faith, hope and love are his gifts to us, bestowed on us freely without any merit of our own.

In addition, God's word and Spirit nourish this new life within us. We see in one another "the fruit of the Spirit", which is "love, joy, peace, patience, kindness, goodness, faithfulness, gentleness, self-control" (Gal. 5:22-23). No wonder Paul continues in this text with an exhortation that there be among us "no self-conceit, no provoking of one another, no envy of one another" (5:26).

There is therefore between us an initial if incomplete unity. Nevertheless, divisions continue even in some doctrines of importance, as we have made clear in earlier chapters of our report. Our faith has developed in us strong convictions (as it should), some uniting us, others dividing us. The very strength of our convictions has not only drawn us together in mutual respect, but has also been a source of painful tension. This has been the price of our encounter; attempts to conceal or dilute our differences would not have been authentic dialogue but a travesty of it. So would have been any attempt to magnify or distort our difference. We confess that in the past members of both our constituencies have been guilty of misrepresenting each other, on account of either laziness in study, unwillingness to listen, superficial judgments or pure prejudice. Whenever we have done this, we have borne false witness against our neighbour.

This, then, is the situation. Deep truths already unite us in Christ. Yet real and important convictions still divide us. In the light of this, we ask: What can we do together?

2. Common witness

"Witness" in the New Testament normally denotes the unique testimony of the apostolic eye-witnesses who could speak of Jesus from what they had seen and heard. It is also used more generally of all Christians who commend Christ to others out of their personal experience of him and in response to his commission. We are using the word here, however, in the even wider sense of any Christian activity which points to Christ, a usage made familiar by the two documents jointly produced by the World Council of Churches and the Roman Catholic Church, which are entitled "Common Witness and Proselytism" (1970) and "Common Witness" (1980).

a) Common witness in Bible translation and publishing

It is extremely important that Roman Catholics and Protestants should have an agreed, common text in each vernacular. Divergent texts breed mutual suspicion; a mutually acceptable text develops confidence and facilitates joint Bible study. The United Bible Societies have rendered valuable service in this area, and the Common Bible (RSV), published in English in 1973, marked a step forward in Roman Catholic-Protestant relationships.

The inclusion of the Old Testament Apocrypha (books written in Greek during the last two centuries before Christ), which the Roman Catholic Church includes as part of the Bible, has proved a problem, and in some countries evangelicals have for this reason not felt free to use this version. The United Bible Societies and the Secretariat for

Promoting Christian Unity have published some guidelines in this matter,[35] which recommend that the Apocrypha be printed "as a separate section before the New Testament" and described as "deutero-canonical". Many evangelicals feel able to use a Common Bible in these circumstances, although most would prefer the Apocrypha to be omitted altogether.

b) Common witness in the use of media
Although we have put down the availability of a common Bible as a priority need, evangelicals and Roman Catholics are united in recognizing the importance of Christian literature in general and of Christian audiovisual aids. In particular, it is of great value when the common Bible is supplemented by common Bible reading aids. In some parts of the world, Bible atlases and handbooks, Bible dictionaries and commentaries, and explanatory notes for daily Bible reading are available in a form which betrays no denominational or ecclesiastical bias. The same is true of some Christian films and filmstrips. So evangelicals and Roman Catholics may profitably familiarize themselves with each other's materials with a view to using them whenever possible.

In addition, the opportunity is given to the churches in some countries to use the national radio and television service for Christian programmes. We suggest, especially in countries where Christians form a small minority of the total population, that the Roman Catholic Church, the Protestant churches and specialist organizations cooperate rather than compete with one another in the development of suitable programmes.

c) Common witness in community service
The availability of welfare varies greatly from country to country. Some governments provide generous social services, although often the spiritual dimension is missing, and then Christians can bring faith, loving compassion and hope to an otherwise secular service. In other countries the government's provision is inadequate or unevenly distributed. In such a situation the churches have a particular responsibility to discover the biggest gaps and seek to fill them. In many cases the government welcomes the church's contribution.

In the name of Christ, Roman Catholics and evangelicals can serve human need together, providing emergency relief for the victims of flood, famine and earthquake, and shelter for refugees; promoting urban and rural development; feeding the hungry and healing the sick; caring for the elderly and the dying; providing a marriage guidance, enrichment and reconciliation service; a pregnancy advisory service and support for single-parent families; arranging educational opportunities for the illiterate and job creation schemes for the unemployed; and rescuing young people from drug addiction and young women from prostitution. There seems to be no justification for organizing separate Roman Catholic and evangelical projects of a purely humanitarian nature and every reason for undertaking them together. Although faith may still in part divide us, love for neighbour should unite us.

d) Common witness in social thought and action
There is a pressing need for fresh Christian thinking about the urgent social issues which confront the contemporary world. The Roman Catholic Church has done noteworthy work in this area, not least through the social encyclicals of recent popes. Evangelicals are only now beginning to catch up after some decades of neglect. It should be

to our mutual advantage to engage in Christian social debate together. A clear and united Christian witness is needed in face of such challenges as the nuclear arms race, North-South economic inequality, the environmental crisis and the revolution in sexual mores.

Whether a common mind will lead us to common action will depend largely on how far the government of our countries is democratic or autocratic, influenced by Christian values or imbued with an ideology unfriendly to the gospel. Where a regime is oppressive, and a Christian prophetic voice needs to be heard, it should be a single voice which speaks for both Roman Catholics and Protestants. Such a united witness could also provide some stimulus to the quest for peace, justice and disarmament; testify to the sanctity of sex, marriage and family life; agitate for the reform of permissive abortion legislation; defend human rights and religious freedom; denounce the use of torture, and campaign for prisoners of conscience; promote Christian moral values in public life and in the education of children; seek to eliminate racial and sexual discrimination; contribute to the renewal of decayed inner cities; and oppose dishonesty and corruption. There are many such areas in which Roman Catholics and evangelicals can both think together and take action together. Our witness will be stronger if it is a common witness.

e) Common witness in dialogue

The word "dialogue" means different things to different people. Some Christians regard it as inherently compromising, since they believe it expresses an unwillingness to affirm revealed truth, let alone to proclaim it. But to us "dialogue" means a frank and serious conversation between individuals or groups, in which each is prepared to listen respectfully to the other, with a view to increased understanding on the part of both. We see no element of compromise in this. On the contrary, we believe it is essentially Christian to meet one another face to face rather than preserving our isolation from one another and even indifference to one another, and to listen to one another's own statements of position, rather than relying on second-hand reports. In authentic dialogue we struggle to listen carefully not only to what the other person is saying but to the strongly cherished concerns which lie behind his or her words. In this process our caricatures of one another become corrected.

We believe that the most fruitful kind of Evangelical-Roman Catholic dialogue arises out of joint Bible study. For, as this report makes clear, both sides regard the Bible as God's word, and acknowledge the need to read, study, believe and obey it. It is surely through the word of God that, illumined by the Spirit of God, we shall progress towards greater agreement.

We also think that there is need for Evangelical-Roman Catholic dialogue on the great theological and ethical issues which are being debated in all the churches, and that an exchange of visiting scholars in seminaries could be particularly productive.

Honest and charitable dialogue is beneficial to those who take part in it; it enriches our faith, deepens our understanding, and fortifies and clarifies our convictions. It is also a witness in itself, inasmuch as it testifies to the desire for reconciliation and meanwhile expresses a love which encompasses even those who disagree.

Further, theological dialogue can sometimes lead to common affirmation, especially in relation to the unbelieving world and to new theological trends which owe more to contemporary culture than to revelation or Christian tradition. Considered and

f) Common witness in worship

The word "worship" is used in a wide range of senses from the spontaneous prayers of the "two or three" met in Christ's name in a home to formal liturgical services in church.

We do not think that either evangelicals or Roman Catholics should hesitate to join in common prayer when they meet in each other's homes. Indeed, if they have gathered for a Bible study group, it would be most appropriate for them to pray together for illumination before the study and after it for grace to obey. Larger informal meetings should give no difficulty either. Indeed, in many parts of the world evangelicals and Roman Catholics are already meeting for common praise and prayer, both in charismatic celebrations and in gatherings which would not describe themselves thus. Through such experiences they have been drawn into a deeper experience of God and so into a closer fellowship with one another. Occasional participation in each other's services in church is also natural, especially for the sake of family solidarity and friendship.

It is when the possibility of common participation in the holy communion or eucharist is raised that major problems of conscience arise. Both sides of our dialogue would strongly discourage indiscriminate approaches to common sacramental worship.

The mass lies at the heart of Roman Catholic doctrine and practice, and it has been emphasized even more in Catholic spirituality since the Second Vatican Council. Anyone is free to attend mass. Other Christians may not receive communion at it, however, except when they request it in certain limited cases of "spiritual necessity" specified by current Roman Catholic legislation. Roman Catholics may on occasion attend a Protestant communion service as an act of worship. But there is no ruling of the Roman Catholic Church which would permit its members to receive communion in a Protestant church service, even on ecumenical occasions. Nor would Roman Catholics feel in conscience free to do so.

Many evangelical churches practise an "open" communion policy, in that they announce a welcome to everybody who "is trusting in Jesus Christ for salvation and is in love and charity with all people", whatever their church affiliation. They do not exclude Roman Catholic believers. Most evangelicals would feel conscientiously unable to present themselves at a Roman Catholic mass, however, even assuming they were invited. This is because the doctrine of the mass was one of the chief points at issue during the 16th-century Reformation, and evangelicals are not satisfied with the Roman Catholic explanation of the relation between the sacrifice of Christ on the cross and the sacrifice of the mass. But this question was not discussed at our meetings.

Since both Roman Catholics and evangelicals believe that the Lord's supper was instituted by Jesus as a means of grace[36] and agree that he commanded his disciples to "do this in remembrance" of him, it is a grief to us that we are so deeply divided in an area in which we should be united and that we are therefore unable to obey Christ's command together. Before this becomes possible, some profound and sustained theological study of this topic will be needed; we did not even begin it at ERCDOM.

g) Common witness in evangelism

Although there are some differences in our definitions of evangelism, Roman Catholics and evangelicals are agreed that evangelism involves proclaiming the gospel, and that therefore any common evangelism necessarily presupposes a common commitment to the same gospel. In earlier chapters of this report we have drawn attention to certain doctrines in which our understanding is identical or very similar. We desire to affirm these truths together. In other important areas, however, substantial agreement continues to elude us, and therefore common witness in evangelism would seem to be premature, although we are aware of situations in some parts of the world in which evangelicals and Roman Catholics have felt able to make a common proclamation.

Evangelicals are particularly sensitive in this matter, which is perhaps not surprising, since their very appellation "evangelical" includes in itself the word "evangel" (gospel). Evangelicals claim to be "gospel" people, and are usually ready, if asked, to give a summary of their understanding of the gospel. This would have at its heart what they often call "the finished work of Christ", namely, that by bearing our sins on the cross, Jesus Christ did everything necessary for our salvation and that we have only to put our trust in him in order to be saved. Although many evangelicals will admit that their presentation of the gospel is often one-sided or defective, yet they could not contemplate any evangelism in which the good news of God's justification of sinners by his grace in Christ through faith alone is not proclaimed.

Roman Catholics also have their problems of conscience. They would not necessarily want to deny the validity of the message which evangelicals preach but would say that important aspects of the gospel are missing from it. In particular, they emphasize the need both to live out the gospel in the sacramental life of the church and to respect the teaching authority of the church. Indeed, they see evangelism as essentially a church activity done by the church in relation to the church.

So long as each side regards the other's view of the gospel as defective, there exists a formidable obstacle to be overcome. This causes us particular sorrow in our dialogue on mission, in which we have come to appreciate one another and to discover unexpected agreements. Yet we must respect one another's integrity. We commit ourselves to further prayer, study and discussion in the hope that a way forward may be found.

3. Unworthy witness

We feel the need to allude to the practice of seeking to evangelize people who are already church members, since this causes misunderstanding and even resentment, especially when evangelicals are seeking to "convert" Roman Catholics. It arises from the phenomenon which evangelicals call "nominal Christianity" and which depends on the rather sharp distinction they draw between the visible church (of professing or "nominal" Christians) and the invisible church (of committed or genuine Christians) – that is, between those who are Christian only in name and those who are Christian in reality. Evangelicals see nominal Christians as needing to be won for Christ. Roman Catholics also speak of "evangelizing" such people, although they refer to them as "lapsed " or "inactive" rather than as "nominal", because they do not make a separation between the visible and invisible church. They are understandably offended whenever evangelicals appear to regard all Roman Catholics as *ipso facto* unbelievers, and when they base their evangelism on a distorted view of Roman Catholic teaching and practice. On the other hand, since evangelicals seek to evangelize the nominal members of their own churches, as well as of others, they see this activity as an authentic concern for the gospel, and not as a reprehensible kind of "sheep-stealing". Roman Catholics do not accept this reasoning.

We recognize that conscientious conviction leads some people to change from Catholic to evangelical or evangelical to Catholic allegiance, and leads others to seek to persuade people to do so. If this happens in conscience and without coercion, we would not call it proselytism.

There are other forms of witness, however, which we would all describe as "unworthy", and therefore as being "proselytism" rather than "evangelism". We agree, in general, with the analysis of this given in the study document entitled "Common Witness and Proselytism" (1970), and in particular we emphasize three aspects of it.

First, proselytism takes place when our *motive* is unworthy, for example when our real concern in witness is not the glory of God through the salvation of human beings but rather the prestige of our own Christian community or indeed our personal prestige.

Secondly, we are guilty of proselytism whenever our *methods* are unworthy, especially when we resort to any kind of "physical coercion, moral constraint or psychological pressure", when we seek to induce conversion by the offer of material or political benefits or when we exploit other people's need, weakness or lack of education. These practices are an affront both to the freedom and dignity of human beings and to the Holy Spirit whose witness is gentle and not coercive.

Thirdly, we are guilty of proselytism whenever our *message* includes "unjust or uncharitable reference to the beliefs or practices of other religious communities in the hope of winning adherents". If we find it necessary to make comparisons, we should compare the strengths and weaknesses of one church with those of the other, and not set what is best in the one against what is worst in the other. To descend to deliberate misrepresentation is incompatible with truth and love.

Conclusion

We who have participated in ERCDOM III are agreed that every possible opportunity for common witness should be taken, except where conscience forbids. We cannot make decisions for one another, however, because we recognize that the situation varies in different groups and places. In any case, the sad fact of our divisions on important questions of faith always puts a limit on the common witness which is possible. At one end of the spectrum are those who can contemplate no cooperation of any kind. At the other are those who desire a very full cooperation. In between are many who still find some forms of common witness conscientiously impossible, while they find others to be the natural, positive expression of common concern and conviction. In some third-world situations, for example, the divisions which originated in Europe are felt with less intensity, and mutual trust has grown through united prayer and study of the word of God. Although all Christians should understand the historical origins and theological issues of the Reformation, yet our continuing division is a stumbling block and the gospel calls us to repentance, renewal and reconciliation.

We believe that the Evangelical-Roman Catholic Dialogue on Mission has now completed its task. At the same time we hope that dialogue on mission between Roman Catholics and evangelicals will continue, preferably on a regional or local basis, in order that further progress may be made towards a common understanding, sharing, and proclaiming of "the faith which was once for all delivered to the saints" (Jude 3). We commit these past and future endeavours to God, and pray that by "speaking the truth in love, we are to grow up in every way into him who is the head, into Christ" (Eph. 4:15).

NOTES

[1] "Evangelism" and "evangelization" are used indiscriminately in this report. The former is commoner among evangelicals, the latter among Roman Catholics, but both words describe the same activity of spreading the gospel.

[2] Given the diversity of the evangelical constituency as well as the differences of understanding between evangelicals and Roman Catholics, the use of the word "church" in this paper inevitably carries some ambiguity. Further conversations would be required before it would be possible to arrive at greater clarity and common terms of ecclesiological discourse.

[3] *UR*, 6, in *The Documents of Vatican II*, ed. Walter M. Abbott, Geoffrey Chapman, 1967.

[4] *Ibid.*, no. 4.

[5] *DV*, nos 23,24.

[6] *The Lausanne Covenant: An Exposition and Commentary by John Stott*, World Wide Publications, 1975, Lausanne Occasional Paper no. 3.

[7] *EN*.

[8] Lausanne Covenant, no. 4.

[9] EN, no. 22.

[10] E.g., Ps. 19:1-6; Rom. 1:19-20.

[11] *DV*, no. 13.

[12] *Ibid.*, no. 10.

[13] *Ibid.*, no. 22.

[14] E.g., 1 Thess. 5:14-15; Heb. 3:12-13; 12:15.

[15] E.g., Mark 10:23-27; cf. Isa. 52:7.

[16] In this report we use "the Lord's supper", "the holy communion", and "the eucharist" indiscriminately; no particular theology is implied by these terms. The mass is limited to Roman Catholic contexts. Similarly we use "sacrament" or "ordinance" in relation to baptism and eucharist without doctrinal implications.

[17] E.g., Eph. 2:1-3; 4:17-19; 2 Cor. 4:3-4.

[18] *GS*, no. 13.

[19] *Ibid.*

[20] *Ibid.*

[21] Encyclical *Redemptor Hominis*, Pope John Paul II, Catholic Truth Society, 1979, 14.

[22] *LG*, no. 8.

[23] *LG*, no. 16.

[24] Cf. Eph. 3:10; 3:18; 1:13.

[25] *SC*, nos 7,47.

[26] E.g., Rom. 4; Gal. 3.

[27] *EN*.

[28] *LG*, chap. I.

[29] John 20:21-22; cf. Matt. 28:16-20; Luke 24:46-49.

[30] *The Willowbank Report: Consultation on Gospel and Culture*, Lausanne Committee for World Evangelization, 1978, Lausanne Occasional Paper no. 2.

[31] Lausanne Covenant, no. 10.

[32] Here Roman Catholics will want to make reference to the encyclical of Pope John Paul II, *Slavorum Apostoli*, 2 June 1985.

[33] *AG*, no. 9.

[34] *GS*, no. 58.

[35] Guiding Principles for Interconfessional Cooperation in Translating the Bible (1968).

[36] See ch. 4 (3).

41. Martin Luther – Witness to Jesus Christ

Kloster Kirchberg, Germany, 6 May 1983

I. From conflict to reconciliation

1. This year our churches celebrate the 500th anniversary of the birth of Martin Luther. Christians, whether Protestant or Catholic, cannot disregard the person and the message of this man. Standing on the threshold of modern times, he has had, and still has, a crucial influence on the history of the church, of society, and of thought.

2. For centuries opinions about Luther were diametrically opposed to one another. Catholics saw him as the personification of heresy and blamed him as the fundamental cause of schism between the Western churches. Already in the 16th century the Protestants began to glorify Luther as a religious hero and not infrequently also as a national hero. Above all, however, Luther was often regarded as the founder of a new church.

3. The judgment of Luther was closely connected with each church's view of the other: they accused one another of abandoning the true faith and the true church.

4. In the churches of the Reformation and in theology, the rediscovery of Luther began in the early days of this century. Soon afterwards, intensive study of the person of Luther and his work started on the Catholic side. This study has made notable scholarly contributions to Reformation and Luther research and, together with the growing ecumenical understanding, has paved the way towards a more positive Catholic attitude to Luther. We see on both sides a lessening of outdated, polemically coloured images of Luther. He is beginning to be honoured in common as a witness to the gospel, a teacher in the faith, and a herald of spiritual renewal.

5. The recent celebrations of the 450th anniversary of the Augsburg confession (1980) have made an essential contribution to this perspective. This confession of faith is inconceivable without the person and theology of Luther. Furthermore, the insight that the Augsburg confession reflects "a full accord on fundamental and central truths" (Pope John Paul II, 17 November 1980) between Catholics and Lutherans facilitates the common affirmation of fundamental perceptions of Luther.

6. Luther's call for church reform, a call to repentance, is still relevant for us. He summons us to listen anew to the gospel, to recognize our own unfaithfulness to the gospel, and to witness credibly to it. This cannot happen today without attention to the other church and to its witness and without the surrender of polemical stereotypes and the search for reconciliation.

II. Witness to the gospel

7. In criticizing various aspects of the theological tradition and church life of his time, Luther considered himself a witness to the gospel – an "unworthy evangelist of our Lord Jesus Christ". He appealed to the biblical apostolic testimony which, as a "doctor of holy scripture", he was committed to interpret and proclaim. He took his stand consciously on the confession of the early church to the triune God and to Christ's person and work, and saw in this confession an authoritative expression of the biblical message. In his striving for reformation, which brought him external persecution and inner tribulation, he found assurance and comfort in his call by the church to study and teach the scriptures. In this conviction he felt himself supported by the Lord of the church himself.

8. Knowing his responsibility as a teacher and pastor, and at the same time personally experiencing the anguished need for faith, he was led by his intense study of the scriptures to a renewed discovery of God's mercy in the midst of the fears and uncertainties of his time. According to his own testimony, this "Reformation discovery" consisted in recognizing that God's righteousness is, in the light of Romans 1:17, a bestowal of righteousness, not a demand that condemns the sinner. "He who through faith is righteous shall live", i.e., he lives by the mercy granted by God through Christ. In this discovery, confirmed for Luther by the church father Augustine, the message of the Bible became a joyful message, that is, "gospel". It opened for him, as he said, "the gate of paradise".

9. In his writings, as in his preaching and teaching, Luther became a witness to this liberating message. As the "doctrine of the justification of the sinner through faith alone", it was the central point of his theological thinking and of his exegesis of scripture. Those whose consciences suffered under the dominion of the law and human ordinances, and who were tormented by their failures and by concern for eternal salvation could gain assurance through faith in the gospel of the liberating promise of God's grace.

10. Historical research has shown that the beginnings of an agreement on this fundamental concern of Luther's were already apparent in the theological discussions at the time of the Reformation. But this agreement was not effectively accepted by either side, and was obscured and nullified by later polemics.

11. In our time, Luther research and biblical studies on both sides have again opened the way for a mutual understanding of the central concerns of the Lutheran Reformation. Awareness of the historical conditionedness of all forms of expression and thought has contributed to the widespread recognition among Catholics that Luther's ideas, particularly on justification, are a legitimate form of Christian theology. Thus in summarizing what had already been jointly affirmed by Catholic and Lutheran theologians in 1972 ("The Gospel and the Church"), the Catholic-Lutheran statement on the Augsburg confession says that: "A broad consensus emerges in the doctrine of justification, which was decisively important for the Reformation: it is solely by grace and by faith in Christ's saving work and not because of any merit in us that we are accepted by God and receive the Holy Spirit who renews our hearts and equips us for and calls us to good works" (*All Under One Christ*, 1980).

12. As witness to the gospel, Luther proclaimed the biblical message of God's judgment and grace, of the scandal and the power of the cross, of the lostness of human beings, and of God's act of salvation. As an "unworthy evangelist of our Lord Jesus

Christ", Luther points beyond his own person in order to confront us all the more inescapably with the promise and the claim of the gospel he confessed.

III. Conflict and the schism in the church

13. Luther's interpretation and preaching of justification by faith alone came into conflict with the prevailing forms of piety which obscured God's gift of righteousness. Luther believed that his protests were in conformity with the teaching of the church and, indeed, even defended that teaching. Any thought of dividing the church was far from his mind and was strongly rejected by him. But there was no understanding for his concerns among the ecclesiastical and theological authorities either in Germany or in Rome. The years following the famous "Ninety-five Theses" of 1517 were marked by increasing polemics. As the disputes intensified, Luther's primarily religious concerns were increasingly intertwined with questions of church authority and were also submerged by questions of political power. It was not Luther's understanding of the gospel considered by itself which brought about conflict and schism in the church, but rather the ecclesial and political concomitants of the Reformation movement.

14. When Luther was threatened with excommunication and summoned to revoke what for him were essential theological convictions, he saw in this the refusal of the secular and church authorities to discuss his theological reasoning. The conflict turned more and more on the question of final authority in matters of faith. Luther appealed to scripture in this dispute, and came to doubt that all doctrinal decisions of the popes and councils were binding in conscience. Yet his emphasis on the sola scriptura and on the clarity of scripture included acceptance of the creeds of the early church and respect for traditions which were in accordance with scripture. He maintained throughout all conflicts his trust in God's promise to keep his church in the truth.

15. As the hostility of the church authorities increased, so did Luther's polemical attitude. The pope was rejected as "Antichrist", the mass condemned as idolatry. In turn, Luther and his followers were categorized as heretics and sometimes even accused of apostasy. The hope that agreement could be reached at the Diet in Augsburg in 1530 was not fulfilled. Luther considered the rejection he met with as a sign of the approaching apocalypse. He could see no way back from the attitude of reciprocal condemnation.

16. Luther was claimed by a great variety of groups and tendencies in church and society in pursuit of their special interests (anti-clerical, revolutionary or enthusiast). He himself fought against these pressures, but his image suffered from distortions which still persist to this day.

17. These historical events cannot be reversed or undone. We can, however, seek to remove their negative consequences by investigating their origins and admitting culpable failures. Ultimately, however, they will only be healed when the positive aims of the Reformation become the joint concern of Lutherans and Roman Catholics.

IV. Reception of Reformation concerns

18. The Lutheran churches have tried over the centuries to conserve Luther's theological and spiritual insights. Not all his writings, however, have influenced the Lutheran churches to the same degree. There has often been a tendency to give more importance to his polemical works than to his pastoral and theological writings. Those writings which were given the status of confessional documents are of special ecclesial significance. Among these, his two catechisms occupy a special position in the life

of the churches. Together with the *Confessio Augustana*, they form an appropriate basis for an ecumenical dialogue.

19. Nevertheless, Luther's heritage has suffered various losses and distortions in the course of history:
- the Bible was increasingly isolated from its church context, and its authority was legalistically misunderstood because of the doctrine of verbal inspiration;
- Luther's high estimate of sacramental life was largely lost during the Enlightenment and in pietism;
- Luther's concept of human beings as persons before God was misinterpreted as individualism;
- the message of justification was at times displaced by moralism;
- his reservations about the role of political authorities in church leadership were silenced for long periods of time; and
- his doctrine of the twofold nature of God's rule (the doctrine of "the two kingdoms") was misused to legitimate the church's denial of responsibility for social and political life.

20. Together with their gratitude for Luther's contributions, Lutheran churches are in our day aware of his limitations in person and work and of certain negative effects of his actions. They cannot approve his polemical excesses; they are aghast at the anti-Jewish writings of his old age; they see that his apocalyptic outlook led him to judgments which they cannot approve, e.g., on the papacy, the Anabaptist movement, and the peasants' war. In addition, certain structural weaknesses in Lutheran churches have become obvious, especially in the way in which their administration was taken over by princes or the state – which Luther himself wanted to think of as simply an emergency arrangement.

21. A defensive attitude towards Luther and his thinking was in some respect determinative for the Roman Catholic Church and its development since the Reformation. Fear of the distribution of editions of the Bible unauthorized by the church, a centralizing over-emphasis on the papacy, and a one-sidedness in sacramental theology and practice were deliberately developed features of Counter-Reformation Catholicism. On the other hand, some of Luther's concerns are taken into account in such Tridentine reforming efforts as, for example, the renewal of preaching, the intensification of religious instruction, and the emphasis on the Augustinian doctrine of grace.

22. There has developed in our century – first of all in German-speaking areas – an intensive Catholic re-evaluation of Luther the man and of his Reformation concerns. It is widely recognized that he was justified in attempting to reform the theology and the abuses in the church of his time and that his fundamental belief – justification given to us by Christ without any merit of our own – does not in any way contradict genuine Catholic tradition, such as is found, for example, in St Augustine and Thomas Aquinas.

23. This new attitude to Luther is reflected in what Cardinal Willebrands said at the Lutheran World Federation's fifth assembly: "Who... would still deny that Martin Luther was a deeply religious person who with honesty and dedication sought for the message of the gospel? Who would deny that in spite of the fact that he fought against the Roman Catholic Church and the apostolic see – and for the sake of truth one must not remain silent about this – he retained a considerable part of the old Catholic faith? Indeed, is it not true that the Second Vatican Council has even implemented requests that were first expressed by Martin Luther, among others, and as a result of which many aspects of Christian faith and life now find better expression than they did

before? To be able to say this in spite of all the differences is a reason for great joy and much hope."

24. Among the insights of the Second Vatican Council which reflect elements of Luther's concerns may be numbered:
- an emphasis on the decisive importance of holy scripture for the life and teaching of the church (DV);
- the description of the church as "the people of God" (LG, ch. II);
- the affirmation of the need for continued renewal of the church in its historical existence (LG, no. 8; UR, no. 6);
- the stress on the confession of faith in the cross of Jesus Christ and of its importance for the life of the individual Christian and of the church as a whole (LG, no. 8; UR, no. 4; GS, no. 37);
- the understanding of church ministries as service (CD, no. 16; PO);
- the emphasis on the priesthood of all believers (LG, nos. 10-11; AA, no. 24);
- commitment to the right of the individual to liberty in religious matters (DH).

25. There are also other requests of Luther's that can be regarded as fulfilled in the light of contemporary Catholic theology and church practice: the use of the vernacular in the liturgy, the possibility of communion in both kinds, and the renewal of the theology and celebration of the eucharist.

V. Luther's legacy and our common task

26. It is possible for us today to learn from Luther together. "In this we could all learn from him that God must always remain the Lord, and that our most important human answer must always remain absolute confidence in God and our adoration of him" (Cardinal Willebrands).
- As a theologian, preacher, pastor, hymn writer and man of prayer, Luther has, with extraordinary spiritual force, witnessed anew to the biblical message of God's gift of liberating righteousness and made it shine forth.
- Luther directs us to the priority of God's word in the life, teaching and service of the church.
- He calls us to a faith which is absolute trust in the God who in the life, death and resurrection of his Son has shown himself to be gracious to us.
- He teaches us to understand grace as a personal relationship of God to human beings, which is unconditional and frees from fear of God's wrath and for service of one another.
- He testifies that God's forgiveness is the only basis and hope for human life.
- He calls the churches to constant renewal by the word of God.
- He teaches us that unity in essentials allows for differences in customs, order and theology.
- He shows us as a theologian how knowledge of God's mercy reveals itself only in prayer and meditation. It is the Holy Spirit who persuades us of the truth of the gospel and keeps and strengthens us in that truth in spite of all temptations.
- He exhorts us to remember that reconciliation and Christian community can only exist where not only "the rule of faith" is followed, but also the "rule of love", "which always thinks well of everyone, is not suspicious, believes the best about its neighbours and calls anyone who is baptized a saint" (Martin Luther).

27. Trust and reverent humility before the mystery of God's mercy are expressed in Luther's last confession which, as his spiritual and theological last will and testament, can serve as a guide in our common search for unifying truth "We are beggars. This is true."

42. Facing Unity

Rome, Italy, 3 March 1984

Preface
Unity in the truth, the elimination of divisive differences, and thus the achievement of church fellowship – these have been and are the main concerns in the dialogue initiated in 1967 between the Lutheran World Federation and the Roman Catholic Church.

With the publication of the Malta report *The Gospel and the Church* in 1972, a first round of discussions was completed. This established an extensive consensus in the interpretation of justification and also a convergence of views in the controversial question of the relationship between scripture and Tradition.

With a view to settling problems which it had been impossible to deal with adequately in the Malta report, a new stage of the dialogue was launched. In 1978, the Roman Catholic-Lutheran Joint Commission was able to adopt the statement on "The Eucharist", in which serious differences were eliminated and a common witness formulated in fundamental questions. In 1981, the document *The Ministry in the Church* was published, which shows convergences and agreements in the understanding of the common priesthood, the ordained ministry, ordination and the apostolic succession.

A year earlier, in 1980, there had been the common statement on the *Confessio Augustana* – the basic confession of all Lutheran churches. On the basis of an evaluation of careful studies, the commission was able to affirm that we are "all under one Christ". For it was not only the declared intention of the Augsburg confession of 1530 to remain in accord with the faith of the early church and the Roman church: its statements in great measure realize this intention. The "newly discovered agreement in central Christian truths" gave "good ground for the hope that in the light of this basic consensus answers will also be forthcoming to the still unsettled questions and problems, answers which will achieve the degree of unanimity required if our churches are to make a decisive advance from their present state of division to that of sister churches" (*All Under One Christ*, no. 25).

In 1983, the 500th anniversary of the birth of Martin Luther provided the opportunity for a joint statement, "Martin Luther – Witness to Jesus Christ".

The documents and statements just mentioned served indirectly the goal of church fellowship. The latter was dealt with directly and explicitly in a document, *Ways to Community*, published in 1980. "Christian Unity is a blessing of the triune God, a work which he accomplishes, by means he chooses, in ways he determines" (no. 8). These considerations proceed from the unity already given in Christ, focus attention on the barriers which still remain, and point out what is already now possible and necessary; they encourage us to take those steps together which can bring us nearer to the goal.

Finally, in 1984 the commission completed its work on a document on which it had worked for many years: *Facing Unity: Models, Forms and Phases of Catholic–Lutheran Church Fellowship*. This document strives for clarity regarding the nature of church unity and a concept of that goal which implies neither absorption nor return, but rather a structured fellowship of churches. The prerequisite is community in confessing the one faith and in sacramental life. A solution must be found for still existing divisive differences. The dialogue documents require to be examined, perhaps corrected and supplemented, and finally given authority in the churches. This is a condition for complete church fellowship in word, sacrament and ministry. The document presented here seeks to outline step by step how such church fellowship could become a reality. The commission is conscious that the latter part of its considerations, in particular, is venturesome and provisional in character. We have always to remain open for God's ways and dispensations. All our reflections are, in the end, "a prayer to the Lord who knows ways which surpass our vision and are beyond our power", as the document says in conclusion.

Hans L. Martensen, George A. Lindbeck,
Bishop of Copenhagen, Denmark Professor, Yale University, USA
Co-chairman *Co-chairman*

Introduction

1. The full realization of unity given in Christ and promised by him calls for concrete forms of ecclesial life in common. Of what sort could and should these be? What is their relationship to our present ecclesial realities? What challenges are connected with this? What concrete steps have to be taken? We pose these questions by considering in Part I the key term "models of unity", and in the light of our substantially common understanding of the nature of unity, we examine the forms or models of church unity found in the history of the church, particularly the recent ecumenical discussions. In Part II we deal specifically with the relationship between the Roman Catholic Church and the Lutheran churches and with the question of forms and phases of Catholic-Lutheran church fellowship.

Part I: Concept of Unity and Models of Union

2. For us "models of union" are not arbitrary constructions. We see in them realizable forms of the fundamental understanding of unity described in our document *Ways to Community* (Roman Catholic-Lutheran Joint Commission, Geneva, 1981).

3. The unity of the church given in Christ and rooted in the triune God is realized in our unity in the proclaimed word, the sacraments, and the ministry instituted by God and conferred through ordination. It is lived both in the unity of the faith to which we jointly witness, and which together we confess and teach, and in the unity of hope and love which leads us to unite in fully committed fellowship. Unity needs a visible outward form which is able to encompass the element of inner differentiation and spiritual diversity as well as the element of historical change and development. This is the unity

of a fellowship which covers all times and places and is summoned to witness and serve the world.[1]

4. It is our conviction that in its essential aspects, this view of unity corresponds with the formulation adopted by the third assembly of the World Council of Churches at New Delhi in 1961: "We believe that the unity which is both God's will and his gift to his church is being made visible as all in each place who are baptized into Jesus Christ and confess him as Lord and Saviour are brought by the Holy Spirit into one fully committed fellowship, holding the one apostolic faith, preaching the one gospel, breaking the one bread, joining in common prayer, and having a corporate life reaching out in witness and service to all and who at the same time are united with the whole Christian fellowship in all places and all ages in such wise that ministry and members are accepted by all, and that all can act and speak together as occasion requires for the tasks to which God calls his people."[2]

A. The church as fellowship

5. The one church of Jesus Christ assumes concrete form in local churches which participate in the diversity of historical, cultural and racial situations in which the people live to whom the gospel is proclaimed in word and sacrament. The church is therefore a communion *(communio)* subsisting in a network of local churches. "This church of Christ is truly present in all legitimate local congregations of the faithful which, united with their pastors, are themselves called churches in the New Testament. For in their own locality these are the new people called by God, in the Holy Spirit and in much fullness (cf. 1 Thess. 1:5). In them the faithful are gathered together by the preaching of the gospel of Christ, and the mystery of the Lord's supper is celebrated... In these communities, though frequently small and poor, or living far from any other, Christ is present. By virtue of him the one, holy, catholic and apostolic church gathers together."[3]

6. This view of church unity as communion *(communio)* goes back to the early days of Christianity. It is determinative for the early church as well as for the life and ecclesiology of the Orthodox churches. In recent times it has been particularly stressed in Catholic ecclesiology. Part of the fundamental stress of the Second Vatican Council is that the one church exists in and consists of particular churches.[4] "By divine providence it has come about that various churches established in diverse places by the apostles and their successors have in the course of time coalesced into several groups, organically united, which, preserving the unity of faith and the unique divine constitution of the universal church, enjoy their own discipline, their own liturgical usage, and their own theological and spiritual heritage... This variety of local churches with one common aspiration is particularly splendid evidence of the catholicity of the undivided church."[5] This view is regarded as both giving rise to and determining the re-establishment of unity. "The deepening... of an ecclesiology of communion is... perhaps the greatest possibility for tomorrow's ecumenism... So far as the reintegration of the churches into unity is concerned, we have to follow the line of this ecclesiology, which... is both very ancient and yet very modern."[6]

7. This view of the church and of ecclesial unity is also in accord with Lutheran ecclesiology.[7] The local communities gathered around word and sacrament do not remain isolated as visible forms of the church of Jesus Christ, but rather live in such larger and organically united communities as regional churches, national churches, folk

churches, etc. The worldwide Lutheran community, which has the Lutheran World Federation as an instrument, is made up of churches that are bound together by a common understanding of the gospel and by participation in the sacraments which that includes.

B. Models of partial union

8. On the basis of our understanding of the nature of unity, those models appear inadequate which are determined only by concepts of church unity which are only partial. In the opinion of some, however, they can play an important transitional role in certain situations if they are understood either as "steps" on the way to unity or as "partial" expressions of unity; moreover, they can also draw attention to important components of unity.

9. (1) For instance, one can wish to achieve mere *"spiritual"* unity by deliberately dispensing with common ecclesial structures and visible organization. Since the visible manifestations of unity – understood as an essentially spiritual, inward possession – are not expected until the end of time, external features and structures are considered not only superfluous but even as false and harmful. Although such a posture may well remind us of the essential and irrevocable spiritual dimension of all ecumenical efforts,[8] and also of the provisional nature of our expressions of church unity, it nevertheless fails to see the essential visible character of the church and of its unity to such an extent that it cannot be considered as a valid model of unity.

10. (2) This also applies when the unity of the church is expressed in the form of a mere *fellowship-in-dialogue*, where formerly separate communities, delimited and mutually condemnatory, engage in lively questioning of each other, in listening and speaking. Although dialogue is an essential phase in efforts towards church unity, and although the dialogue momentum must not disappear even in a united church, a mere fellowship-in-dialogue falls short of being a full expression of church unity.

11. (3) Furthermore, a form of union which understands itself essentially as *fellowship-of-action* takes seriously the element of common service that is indispensable for a Christian concept of unity, but at the same time (measured by the understanding of unity in no. 3 above) lacks certain essential elements that do not permit it to be seen as a fully valid model of unity. This is true not only of ad hoc fellowship-of-action, but also of such structured church unions as Christian "councils" or "study groups", and church "federations" or "alliances", whose purpose is primarily to facilitate practical cooperation.

12. (4) The practice of *intercommunion* or the proffering of eucharistic hospitality between divided churches must also be seen as only a partial way of expressing unity. The ecumenical and pastoral value of intercommunion or eucharistic hospitality is assessed differently. Some people see in them a step on the way to unity, others regard them as a problematical attempt to realize unity. But it is clear to all that, at the very most, we are here concerned with a provisional expression of unity that will be endangered time and time again, and that it is essential to go further.

C. Models of comprehensive union

13. In recent ecumenical discussions a series of models of union has been developed and partly practised in the life of the churches. These models correspond more closely to our understanding of unity than the ones mentioned above. They go beyond

partial aspects and bring the whole of unity into view. Endeavours to give concrete shape to Catholic-Lutheran church fellowship cannot ignore such discussion and experiences; they are fulfilled in the framework of these discussions, are co-determined by them, and can receive from them important directives and impulses. Below we describe and briefly analyze the most important and best known of these models. The order in which they are here treated follows an historical rather than systematic sequence.

14. A description of these models must allow for a particular difficulty. Although individual models can be clearly distinguished from each other or can be related to each other, there is often considerable confusion on the level of terminology. This confusion is partly because in some cases a different meaning may be given to the model than is inherent in it. This can be noted, for example, in the case of the model of "conciliar fellowship" and the model of "church fellowship". Therefore, when giving a detailed account of each particular model one should seek to avoid private interpretations. One should always refer to those texts which may be regarded as the most original, representative or official in character (for example, reports of the commission on Faith and Order of the World Council of Churches, the conference of secretaries of Christian world communions, the assemblies of the World Council of Churches, or individual Christian world communions).

15. The terminological confusion, however, has sometimes found its way even into these more representative texts – for example, concepts of "organic union" or "organic unity" and "corporate fellowship". In each particular instance one should explain how the same concept can refer to differing realities. It helps to clarify the situation and the concepts if a sketch – at least in outline – is given of the motivation and context which have contributed to the development of a model.

1. Organic union

16. The concept "organic union" or "organic unity" is one of the oldest ecumenical concepts, and it can refer either to a specific understanding of unity or to a particular model of union. The concept which refers to the unity of the church as the "body of Christ" was taken over by the church union movements at the beginning of the century in order to describe their ecumenical goal. In the course of time, it received a specific meaning that it had not had originally and, as far as many are concerned, still does not yet have (see also §§19-22 below).

17. According to this specific meaning – which has become increasingly common in the terminology of the Faith and Order movement and then in the World Council of Churches – the model of "organic union" reflects a thinking which regards the existence of different confessional churches as a decisive obstacle to attaining true Christian unity and therefore takes the view that unity can be realized only by surrendering traditional ecclesial and confessional allegiance and identity. "Organic union", which generally comprises the working out of a common confession of faith, agreement about sacraments and ministry, and a homogeneous organizational structure, therefore arises out of the union of existing churches and ecclesial identities to form a "new fellowship with its own new name" and an "identity of its own".[9] It is "costly" and involves "surrender of the denominational identities" through merging "to form one body", "a kind of death" of the denominations which existed before; but it is nevertheless regarded as the way "to receive a fuller life".[10]

18. The use of this model of "organic union" has hitherto been concentrated mainly on the local, national and regional levels.

2. Corporate union

19. Like the concept of "organic union" or "organic unity", the concept of "corporate union" has a long history. In addition, both concepts seem to have been at first identical in content and therefore interchangeable,[11] and indeed many today still regard them as such. At any rate, one must take care to note that "corporate" or "organic" unity or union do not mean here the same thing as the concept of "organic union" in the sense just described (cf. §§16-18 above). The danger here of terminological confusion and factual misunderstanding is particularly great.

20. The concept "corporate union" and the corresponding concept "organic union" confront us, inter alia, in Catholic theologians and the Anglican-Catholic dialogue. There they precisely do not mean realizing unity by surrendering existing ecclesial tradition. Rather, different church communities form in "corporate union" – on the basis of an essential consensus on questions of faith and a joint episcopal constitution as in the early church – a fellowship of faith and life in which they as relatively independent corporate members retain a permanent place. They have thereby the possibility and the duty of preserving what in view of the apostolic witness they consider to be of permanent value in their theology and piety, placing it in the service of the fellowship as a whole.

21. A merger or mutual absorption of existing ecclesial traditions is rejected because "every church fellowship would lose its character in a fusion of this kind".[12] "Corporate union" is therefore "union in diversity"[13] or, as is said, a unity of churches "which remain churches and nevertheless become one church".[14]

22. This model of "corporate union" has now become the declared aim of the Anglican-Catholic dialogue, though with the label "organic unity".[15] In this sense Paul VI, in an address on the occasion of the visit of the archbishop of Canterbury and referring to the Anglican-Catholic conversations at Malines, said, "The pace of this movement (Anglican-Catholic rapprochement) has quickened marvellously in recent years, so that these words of hope 'the Anglican church united not absorbed' are no longer a mere dream."[16]

3. Church fellowship through agreement (concord)

23. A model of union has been developed and become operative among the Lutheran, Reformed and United churches in Europe which is described as "church fellowship". Substantially it is based on a doctrinal agreement (the Leuenberg agreement, 1973) jointly drawn up and ratified by these churches.

24. In this context church fellowship means: "On the basis of the consensus they have reached in their understanding of the gospel" and on the basis of having determined that "the doctrinal condemnations expressed in the confessional documents no longer apply to the contemporary doctrinal position of the assenting churches", the various churches accord each other "fellowship in word and sacrament" ("table and pulpit fellowship") and also fellowship in the ecclesial ministry ("mutual recognition of ordination and the freedom to provide for intercelebration").[17] The doctrinal agreement here involved does not imply a "new confession of faith".[18] Rather, the church fellowship made possible by this agreement is a fellowship among "churches with different confessional positions" in continuing "loyalty to the confessions of faith which bind them, or with due respect for their traditions".[19]

25. Although such a church fellowship understands itself as the realization of church unity in the full sense, it does not consider itself as something sealed and static. Rather, it contains a dynamic element in as much as the churches constituting the fellowship pledge themselves to "strive for the fullest possible cooperation in witness and service to the world".[20] Furthermore, this orientation towards a continual confirmation and deepening of the fellowship is expressed in the fact that the churches "pledge themselves to their common doctrinal discussions".[21]

26. Although this model of a church fellowship through agreement (concord) was first developed and practised in the context of the Lutheran, Reformed and United churches in Europe, it is fundamentally open and applicable also to other churches and other geographical regions. Indeed, it is no longer limited to Europe.

4. Conciliar fellowship

27. By taking up and purposely elaborating the statements made at New Delhi and Uppsala, the commission on Faith and Order developed the concept of "conciliar fellowship", which was received by the WCC assembly in Nairobi, 1975. Although "conciliar fellowship" can also "refer to a quality of life within each local church",[22] in the true sense this concept denotes a detailed model of union.

28. This "conciliar fellowship" model finds its application not so much at the level of the local churches but "in the first place it expresses the unity of church separated by distance, culture and time".[23] It intends to be, therefore, a model of union on a wider level, ultimately on the level of the universal church. The definition says: "The one church is to be envisioned as a conciliar fellowship of local churches which are themselves truly united."[24]

29. In this "conciliar fellowship" the various local churches "recognize the others as belonging to the same church of Christ", confess the same apostolic faith, have full communion with one another in baptism and eucharist, recognize each other's members and ministries, and are one in witness and service in and before the world. The structural bond necessary for the "conciliar fellowship" is provided primarily by "conciliar gatherings",[25] i.e., by means of "representative gatherings".[26] Both Catholics and Orthodox stress thereby that "conciliar fellowship" necessarily encompasses also the ministry transmitted in apostolic succession.

30. "Conciliar fellowship" does not mean a monolithic unity,[27] but rather a "diversity" which must "not only be admitted but actively desired".[28] For a long time it was not at all clear what place amid these diversities would be accorded the individual church or confessional traditions, especially since the "conciliar fellowship" model seemed to be very closely connected with the model of "organic union" (see §§16-18 above).[29] Indeed, it seemed to presuppose "organic union".[30] In the meantime these considerations have been further developed by the commission on Faith and Order[31] and also by other bodies[32] in such a way that confessional traditions can undoubtedly retain an identifiable life in this "conciliar fellowship", provided that this will not call into question the basic elements of "conciliar fellowship".

5. Unity in reconciled diversity

31. There have always been tendencies within the ecumenical movement that aimed at an ecumenical fellowship in which the existing ecclesial traditions with their particularity and diversity would remain in integrity and authenticity. The above

described models of "corporate union" (see §§19-22 above) and of "church fellowship by means of agreement" (see §§23-26 above) are examples of this.

32. In this sense, and against the background of intensified ecumenical commitment on the part of the churches and Christian world communions, the model of "unity in reconciled diversity" has recently been developed.[33] It is based on the idea that "the variety of denominational heritages [is] legitimate" and forms part of "the richness of life in the church universal". When "in the open encounter with other heritages" the existing traditions and denominations lose their "exclusive" and "divisive character, there emerges a vision of unity that has the character of a 'reconciled diversity'".[34]

33. The idea of "unity in reconciled diversity" means that "expression would be given to the abiding value of the confessional forms of the Christian faith in all their variety" and that these diversities, "when related to the central message of salvation and Christian faith" and when they "ring out, [are] transformed and renewed" in the process of ecumenical encounter and theological dialogue; they "lose their divisive character and are reconciled to each other... into a binding ecumenical fellowship in which even the confessional elements" are preserved.[35] "Unity in reconciled diversity" therefore does not mean "mere coexistence". It means "genuine church fellowship, including as essential elements the recognition of baptism, the establishing of eucharistic fellowship, the mutual recognition of church ministries, and a binding common purpose of witness and service".[36]

34. The model of "unity in reconciled diversity" comes "very close to the concept of 'conciliar fellowship'... and cannot be put forward as a rival to this concept". The tension felt occasionally in the beginning vis-a-vis the model of "conciliar fellowship" – "that the latter seems to take insufficiently into account the legitimacy of the confessional differences and therefore the need to preserve them"[37] – seems to have been largely overcome in the meantime.[38]

D. The example of the union of Florence

35. For possible church union without merger or absorption, the example of Florence is important.

36. The union between the Latin and Byzantine churches formed at the council of Florence did not represent a merger. Without prejudicing the unity of faith basic to the fellowship, each church preserved its own liturgical, canonical and theological tradition. This common faith could be expressed in various formulations (for example, as regards the "procession" of the Holy Spirit) and tolerate diversities of discipline (for example, the toleration of remarriage of divorced Christians of the Greek but not of the Latin rites, a differentiation still operative at Trent).

37. Even though this attempt failed, impulses from Florence did not remain without effect. It is due to them that the Roman Catholic Church can no longer be identified by its Latinism. Following Vatican II, however, the model of sister churches applies, a model that is inspired by the relationships that existed during the first millennium.[39]

38. Moreover, several statements made by Vatican II about the united Eastern churches are of great importance in the search for a model of unity in diversity. There we read: "That church, holy and catholic, which is the mystical body of Christ, is made up of the faithful who are organically united in the Holy Spirit through the same faith, the same sacraments, and the same government and who, combining into various

groups held together by a hierarchy, form separate churches or rites."[40] "Such individual churches, whether of the East or of the West... differ somewhat among themselves in what are called rites (that is, in liturgy, ecclesiastical discipline and spiritual heritage)..."[41] "Therefore, attention should everywhere be given to the preservation and growth of each individual church. For this purpose, parishes and a special hierarchy should be established for each where the spiritual good of the faithful so demands. The ordinaries of the various individual churches which have jurisdiction in the same territory should, by taking common counsel in regular meetings, strive to promote unity of action."[42]

39. Vatican II, therefore, does not call for a single jurisdiction or a single bishop in each particular case. Moreover, the council considers it to be legitimate for the church of one particular rite, i.e., a church with its own spiritual, theological and canonical tradition, to reach out everywhere, even beyond its original geographical limits. Admittedly, it is a question here of provisional measures in the expectation of the restoration of unity between the Roman Catholic Church and the Eastern churches which are not yet in full fellowship with it.[43]

40. The example of Florence shows that it is possible for the Roman Catholic Church to unite with another church without merger if that church confesses the same faith and if the mutual recognition of ministries can be achieved. For this example shows:
– the possibility, at least temporarily, of the presence of two bishops at the same place, and
– the justification of different theological, canonical and spiritual traditions carried by these different episcopal jurisdictions.

E. Fellowship of sister churches

41. Without being able to refer to them as "models" of union in the strict sense, two concepts merit particular attention, which have proved to be important and useful in endeavours to conceive of and practise models of union. Both concepts, each in its own way, express and underscore the idea of unity in diversity as emphasized particularly by some of the models of union described above ("corporate union", see §§19-22 above; "church fellowship through agreement", see §§23-26 above).

1. Ecclesial "types"

42. The view was taken repeatedly in the past that the ecumenical problem derives from the fact that, ever since the early days, distinct basic types and archetypes of the faith have existed within Christianity; these types, though fundamentally interconnected, differ distinctively from each other with regard to specific characteristics of piety, doctrine ethos, ecclesial structures, etc., and manifest themselves to some extent in the existing churches. The ecumenical task, then, would not consist of eliminating these different basic types or of merging them, but rather of making visible their legitimacy and of preserving and keeping them together in the fellowship of the one church for which we strive.

43. The view that within Christianity there exist different ecclesial types *(typoi)* has also been presented in more recent times. The term *typos*, for example, has been defined as follows: "Where there is a long coherent tradition, commanding men's love and loyalty, creating and sustaining a harmonious and organic whole of complemen-

tary elements, each of which supports and strengthens the other, you have the reality of a typos." The elements that constitute each ecclesial typos are a "characteristic theological method and approach", "a characteristic liturgical expression", a specific "spiritual and devotional tradition", a "characteristic canonical discipline". "The life of the church needs a variety of *typoi* which would manifest the full catholic and apostolic character of the one and holy church."[44]

2. Sister churches

44. Recently the concept of "sister churches" has become even more important. As an expression of the fellowship between individual local churches, it has a long tradition that goes right back to the early church and was used in this sense by the Second Vatican Council.[45] For some time this concept has also been used to describe fellowship that has been regained or aspired to between separated churches, especially in the ecumenical relations between the Roman Catholic Church and the Orthodox churches.

45. This new usage goes back above all to the message that Pope Paul VI sent to Ecumenical Patriarch Athenagoras I. It reads as follows: "Now, after a long period of division and reciprocal incomprehension the Lord grants us that we rediscover ourselves as sister churches despite the obstacles which were then raised between us. In the light of Christ, we see how urgent is the necessity of surmounting these obstacles in order to succeed in bringing to its fullness and perfection that unity – already so rich – which exists between us." This fellowship between "sister churches" is a fellowship in diversity. "It is a matter of knowing and of respecting each other in the legitimate diversity of liturgical, spiritual, disciplinary and theological traditions (cf. UR, §§14,17) by means of a frank theological dialogue, made possible by the re-establishment of brotherly charity in order to attain accord in the sincere confession of all revealed truths."[46]

Part II: Forms and Phases of Catholic-Lutheran Fellowship

ON THE WAY TO CHURCH FELLOWSHIP

46. All the models of union described above undoubtedly contain valuable pointers for shaping Catholic-Lutheran church fellowship. Nevertheless, none of these models was worked out in a specifically Catholic-Lutheran context. One must therefore ask whether, in envisioning a promising form of Catholic-Lutheran fellowship, one should not consider more closely the particularities of that relationship. One should by no means assume, however, that there exists one single model which can lead us to fellowship.

47. What is significant and useful in the foregoing description and analysis of the various models of union for the shaping of the Catholic-Lutheran fellowship is: The unity we seek will be a unity in diversity. Particularities developed within the two traditions will not merely be fused, nor their differences completely given up. "This is underscored by the models of 'unity in reconciled diversity', 'corporate union', and 'church fellowship through agreement', as well as by the concepts of typos and 'sister churches'."

What is really at stake is that a theologically based agreement of the type that already exists in the Catholic-Lutheran dialogue should work through divergences to the point where they lose their church-divisive character. At the same time it should both clarify and make certain that remaining differences are based on a fundamental consensus in understanding the apostolic faith and therefore are legitimate. "This aspect is particularly stressed by the models of 'unity in reconciled diversity' and 'church fellowship through agreement'."

Once the divergences of both traditions have lost their divisive force, they can no longer be the subject of mutual condemnation. It should be publicly declared that they are now groundless. "This is emphasized, above all, by the model of 'church fellowship through agreement'."

The unity we seek must be rooted in common sacramental life. "This is implied by all models, but is particularly implicit in the understanding of unity as *communio*."

The unity we seek must assume concrete form in suitable structures that would enable our hitherto separated communities to lead a truly common life and to make joint action possible both at the level of the local churches and at the universal level. "This is stressed particularly by the models of 'organic union' and 'conciliar fellowship'."

In our endeavours to find the appropriate structures needed for full and binding fellowship, we shall have to face up to the question of jointly exercising the ministry of church leadership, present in the office of bishop in the early church. "This is one of the presuppositions of the model of 'corporate union'."

48. Christian reconciliation plays an important part in all the forms and phases of the unity we seek. We jointly confess that we have been reconciled with God through Christ. As we acknowledge this with thanksgiving and praise, we must also confess our sins and errors and know ourselves to be called to be reconciled with others.

The mutual reconciliation which we seek as Christians of different churches, and which stands entirely under the reconciliation that occurred in Christ, does not simply eliminate our differences. There are differences that stem from error and weakness of faith and which cannot therefore be overcome without repentance, self-criticism and renewal. Here reconciliation has its price. But there are also differences between us that derive from the fact that the one church of Christ exists in various places, and that one and the same faith can be expressed and lived in different ways. We can recognize such differences as legitimate, yes, even accept them with joy, as far as they enable us to learn from each other, correct, stimulate or enrich us.

This mutual recognition, which can be achieved step by step, is decisive for the process of reconciliation. Reconciliation cannot happen without the freedom, given us through Christ's reconciliation, from our instinctive fear of the other as stranger and our anxious concern for our own identity.

Reconciliation is not possible without dialogue and constant communication. It is a process of discerning the spirits and of searching for steps along a pathway known only to God. Reconciliation is thus a dynamic process, even where church unity exists or has been re-established. For as long as sin and conflict remain and as long as Christians and churches live in changing times and in a diverse world, this process will not be completed.

49. The dynamic inherent in the process of reconciliation and the realizing of church fellowship unfolds itself more clearly in the efforts for:
a) fellowship in confessing the one apostolic faith (community of faith);
b) fellowship in sacramental life (community in sacraments);
c) fellowship as a structured fellowship in which community of faith and community in sacraments find adequate ecclesial form and in which common life, common

decisions and common action are not only possible; they are required (community of service).

During this process of realizing church fellowship, there is no sequential or gradational relationship between the achievement of community of faith, community in sacraments, and community of service. According to our understanding of unity (see §3 above), the concretization of church fellowship rather constitutes an integral process in which each of these three elements achieves full realization only together with the others. This process is characterized by the two inter-related aims of "recognition" and "reception".[47]

GROWTH OF CHURCH FELLOWSHIP THROUGH MUTUAL RECOGNITION AND RECEPTION

50. The stage of full mutual recognition has not yet been attained between our churches, although it is beginning to reveal itself.

In recent years a broad process of comprehension and rapprochement embracing all levels of church life has led to the fact that our churches see each other in a completely different way than before. Likewise, recent decades have seen positive changes, with regard to forms of thought and life of our churches, which shaped them and greatly influenced their relationship with each other.

51. True to the spirit of Vatican II (see §53 below), the Roman Catholic Church has changed its view vis-a-vis the Lutheran churches. A reassessment both of the common past and of the Lutheran heritage has taken place. This is clearly expressed by the words of Pope John Paul II on the occasion of his visit to the land of Luther in 1980.

With regard to the history of our separation, the pope said: "'Let us no more pass judgment on one another' (Rom. 14:13). Let us rather recognize our guilt. 'All have sinned' (Rom. 3:23) applies also with regard to the grace of unity. We must see and say this in all earnestness and draw our conclusions from it." "If we do not evade the facts we realize that the faults of men led to the unhappy division of Christians, and that our faults again hinder the possible and necessary steps towards unity. I emphatically make my own what my predecessor Hadrian VI said in 1523 at the Diet of Nuremberg: 'Certainly the Lord's hand has not been shortened so much that he cannot save us, but sin separates us from him... All of us, prelates and priests, have strayed from the right path and there is not anyone who does good (cf. Ps. 14:3). Therefore we must all render honour to God and humble ourselves before him. Each of us must consider why he has fallen and judge himself rather than be judged by God on the day of wrath.'"[48]

On the occasion of Martin Luther's 500th anniversary, the pope wrote: "In fact, the scientific researches of evangelical and Catholic scholars, researches whose results have already reached notable points of convergence, have led to the delineation of a more complete and more differentiated picture of Luther's personality and of the complex texture of the social, political and ecclesial historical realities of the first half of the 16th century. Consequently there is clearly outlined the deep religious feeling of Luther who was driven with burning passion by the question of eternal salvation."[49]

Concerning the Catholic-Lutheran dialogue, particularly the conversation on the Augsburg confession, the pope took up the statement of the German Catholic bishops: "Let us rejoice to discover not only partial consent on some truths, but also agreement on the fundamental and central truths. That lets us hope for unity also in the areas of our faith and our life in which we are still divided up to now."[50]

52. In the Lutheran churches, likewise, there has been a profound change of attitude vis-a-vis the Catholic church. With reference to the plea for forgiveness of Pope Paul VI and in answer to it, the fifth LWF assembly (1970) stated: "It is... in accordance with this commandment of truth and love that we as Lutheran Christians and congregations be prepared to acknowledge that the judgment of the Reformers upon the Roman Catholic Church and its theology was not entirely free of polemical distortions, which in part have been perpetuated to the present day. We are truly sorry for the offence and misunderstanding which these polemic elements have caused our Roman Catholic brethren. We remember with gratitude the statement of Pope Paul VI to the Second Vatican Council in which he communicates his plea for forgiveness for any offence caused by the Roman Catholic Church.... Together with all Christians [we] pray for forgiveness in the prayer our Lord has taught us."[51]

The presence of official Lutheran observers at all the sessions of the Second Vatican Council, the subsequent beginning of bilateral dialogues both at the world level and in many countries, closer life together and increased cooperation with local Catholic churches, parishes and Catholic Christians have led Lutherans to a new understanding of Catholic piety, church life and teaching. The Roman Catholic Church is no longer regarded as "false church". Many differences have lost their former unfamiliarity and divisive rigour as far as Lutheran sensitivity is concerned. One now encounters a general readiness to abandon long-standing negative prejudices and to examine doctrinal condemnations pronounced in the past to see whether they are still valid today. Thus, for example, the papal office and its holders appear in a new light that makes former condemnations and the hostile images of the past untenable. In view of common theological understandings and liturgical developments in both churches, the sharp condemnation of Catholic mass is considered to belong to the past, as is shown, for example, by the decisions of some Lutheran churches in favour of reciprocal eucharistic hospitality.[52]

53. The Roman Catholic Church has not only changed its attitude vis-a-vis the Lutheran churches but with Vatican II has also renewed its forms of thought and life.
- Vatican II adopted an understanding of church that does not exclusively identify the Roman Catholic Church with the church of Jesus Christ, but also recognizes the church of Jesus Christ outside its bounds in other churches and ecclesial communities.[53]
- Attention to the "hierarchy of truths", as called for by the Decree on Ecumenism,[54] implies that every theological statement must be related to the foundation of the Christian faith. Lutherans have similar concerns.[55]
- Moreover, in its forms of piety, its liturgical life (celebration of mass, for example), and its government (for example, by the general development of synodal elements at all levels of church life), the Catholic church is reflecting on its origins, thereby showing concretely that in each of these areas it understands itself as a church in need of "continual reformation".[56]

54. A renewal of the forms of theological thinking and ecclesial life is also taking place in the Lutheran churches.
- The renewed orientation in the early decades of this century to the Reformation and Reformation theology, accompanied by a historical examination of developments in the early church and the middle ages, has led in recent decades to a deepened understanding of church, ecclesial ministry and worship.

- The sacramental dimension of worship, preserved during the Reformation but often diminished later, is again emphasized without weakening the stress on the word. In many respects this emphasis has reshaped the liturgical life of the Lutheran churches.
- The normative function of scripture in the life, teaching and proclamation of the church continues to be maintained; an exclusivistic understanding of scripture, detached from the transmission process and church tradition, seems to have been overcome.
- Continuity with the early church, which was preserved and indeed stressed by the Reformers, is again seen more clearly and is creating an enhanced awareness of the ecumenicity and catholicity of the Lutheran confession.

A. Community of faith

55. For Catholics and Lutherans alike the common confession of the one apostolic faith means (1) bearing joint witness to this faith, (2) taking account of legitimate differences, and (3) overcoming the obstacles raised by earlier mutual condemnations.

1. Joint witness to the apostolic faith

56. For the unity of our churches and especially for our task of preaching, common witness to the apostolic faith is of fundamental importance. If we apply the principle of the "hierarchy of truths", the christological and trinitarian centre or "foundation of the Christian faith" is primarily at stake.[57] It is from there that the full catholicity of the faith is again to be mutually comprehended. Such an endeavour will bring about shifts of emphasis and changes in the self-understanding of our churches: overcoming of one-sidedness, loosening of constraints, correction of certain exaggerations.

57. This process is already under way:
- The starting point is the common affirmation of the faith of the early church, formulated by the early councils in obedience to holy scripture and witnessed to in the creeds of the early church (Apostles' Creed, Nicene Creed, Athanasian Creed).[58] "Together we confess the faith in the triune God and the saving work of God through Jesus Christ in the Holy Spirit.... Through all the disputes and differences of the 16th century, Lutheran and Catholic Christians remained one in this central and most important truth of the Christian faith."[59]
- The process of growth in common witness is advanced by a new consensus regarding the relationship between holy scripture and Tradition, long the subject of controversy: "This poses the old controversial question regarding the relationship of scripture and Tradition in a new way. The scripture can no longer be exclusively contrasted with Tradition, because the New Testament itself is the product of primitive tradition. Yet as the witness to the fundamental Tradition, scripture has a normative role for the entire later tradition of the church."[60]
- It extends to our understanding of the gospel expressed during the Reformation, particularly in the doctrine of justification: "Today, however, a far-reaching consensus is developing in the interpretation of justification. Catholic theologians also emphasize in reference to justification that God's gift of salvation for the believer is unconditional as far as human accomplishments are concerned. Lutheran theologians emphasize that the event of justification is not limited to individual forgiveness of sins, and they do not see in it a purely external declaration of the justifica-

tion of the sinner. Rather the righteousness of God actualized in the Christ event is conveyed to the sinner through the message of justification as an encompassing reality basic to the new life of the believer."[61] "It is solely by grace and by faith in Christ's saving work and not because of any merit in us that we are accepted by God and receive the Holy Spirit who renews our hearts and equips us for and calls us to good works."[62]

– It entails a far-reaching consensus regarding the understanding and the celebration of the eucharist (see no. 76 below).[63]

– It has led to a basic, though not yet complete, consensus in the understanding of church: "By church we mean the communion of those whom God gathers together through Christ in the Holy Spirit, by the proclamation of the gospel and the administration of the sacraments, and the ministry instituted by him for his purpose. Though it always includes sinners, yet in virtue of the promise and fidelity of God it is the one, holy, catholic and apostolic church which is to continue forever."[64] "It stands under the gospel and has the gospel as its superordinate criterion";... its "authority... can only be service of the word and... it is not master of the word of the Lord."[65]

– It extends also to the understanding and exercise of the ordained ministry in the church: The special ecclesial ministry, which is transmitted by ordination (see §71 below), "is instituted by Jesus Christ"[66] and as such "is constitutive for the church".[67] Its specific function is "to assemble and build up the Christian community by proclaiming the word of God, celebrating the sacraments and presiding over the liturgical, missionary and diaconal life of the community".[68] In performing this function the ministry stands "in the midst of the whole people and for the people of God", but "inasmuch as the ministry is exercised on behalf of Jesus Christ and makes him present, it has authority over against the community".[69]

58. Even though efforts towards consensus regarding the apostolic faith must be continued, as was shown particularly clearly in our common reflection on the Augsburg confession, one may already say that we can "discover not simply a partial consensus on some truths, but rather a full accord on fundamental and central truths",[70] to put it in the words of Pope John Paul II and of the German Catholic bishops.

59. The executive committee of the Lutheran World Federation took this up and announced: "We... agree that... Roman Catholics and Lutherans 'have discovered that they have a common mind on basic doctrinal truths which points to Jesus Christ, the living centre of our faith' (*All Under One Christ*, no. 17) and that therefore with regard to the Augsburg confession one may and should speak of 'a full accord on fundamental and central truths'... or respectively of a 'basic consensus' of faith (*ibid.*, nos. 18,25)."[71]

60. To reach the goal in this effort towards consensus in the apostolic faith, one must take account of how our two churches understand and practise doctrinally authoritative teaching, and which office holders may therefore in the name of our churches pronounce an official judgment about the theological consensus attained in our dialogue.

In the Roman Catholic Church the function of authoritative teaching is in a special manner the task of the bishops, who discharge this task "in a many-sided exchange regarding faith with believers, priests and theologians".[72] Doctrinal decisions of the church are ultimately binding when "the bishops interpret the revealed faith in universal agreement with each other and in communion with the bishop of Rome".[73]

In the Lutheran interpretation, too, "the holders of the episcopal office are... entrusted in a special manner with the task of watching over the purity of the gospel".[74] But in most Lutheran churches authoritative teaching is effected more in a process of consensus-building in which church leaders or bishops, teachers of theology, pastors and non-ordained members of the congregation participate with basically equal rights. Usually this process has synodal forms.[75]

Authoritative teaching in both churches is subject to the norm of the gospel[76] and is oriented to past doctrinal decisions recognized as binding. In both churches doctrinal decisions, if they are to become fruitful and develop their full situational force, depend on far-reaching reception in the consciousness and life of the local churches, congregations and believers.[77]

It can therefore be seen that both churches can and do teach in an authoritative way, and that in spite of existing differences, there are important parallels in achieving authoritative teaching. Thus, it is possible for both churches, each in its own way, to accord authoritative character to the agreements in their understanding of the apostolic faith which they have attained. It would be important to ensure that this process, going on within the two churches, even now proceeds with a certain degree of synchronization and as much commonality as possible.

2. Unity of faith in the diversity of its forms of expression

61. Unity in the same faith does not mean uniformity in the way it is articulated and expressed. This is one of the basic presuppositions of the ecumenical movement of our century.[78]

Whenever the reference is to doctrine and life, Reformation theology reiterates the conviction that complete conformity is not a condition for church unity.[79]

62. Vatican II states: "While preserving unity in essentials, let all members of the church, according to the office entrusted to each, preserve a proper freedom in the various forms of spiritual life and discipline, in the variety of liturgical rites, and even in the theological elaborations of revealed truths."[80]

In this sense Pope Paul VI expressed himself repeatedly and, in doing so, gave even more concrete shape to the idea of unity of faith in the diversity of its forms of expression. In his speech in the cathedral of Phanar (1967) he said:

> In the light of our love for Christ and of our brotherly love, we perceive even more clearly the profound identity of our faith, and the points on which we still differ must not prevent us from seeing this profound unity. And here, too, charity must come to our aid, as it helped Hilary and Athanasius to recognize the sameness of the faith underlying the differences of vocabulary at a time when serious disagreements were creating divisions among Christian bishops. Did not pastoral love prompt St Basil, in his defence of the true faith in the Holy Spirit, to refrain from using certain terms which, accurate though they were, could have given rise to scandal in one part of the Christian people? And did not St Cyril of Alexandria consent in 433 to abandon his beautiful formulation of theology in the interest of making peace with John of Antioch, once he had satisfied himself that in spite of divergent modes of expression, their faith was identical?[81]

Somewhat similarly, on the occasion of the 1600th anniversary of the death of St Athanasius (1973), Pope Paul VI said in an address to Patriarch Shenouda: "He [Athanasius] in turn recognized in the church of the West a secure identity of faith despite differences in vocabulary and in the theological approach to a deeper understanding of the mystery of the triune God."[82]

63. Diversities be they diversities of church traditions or diversities caused by specific historic, ethnic and cultural contexts – can be understood and lived as different forms of expressing the one and the same faith when they are "related to the central message of salvation and Christian faith" and do not endanger this centre,[83] and when they are therefore sustained by one and the same gospel. It is not necessary that each church adopt the specific forms of belief, piety or ethics of the other church and make them its own. But each church must recognize them as specific and legitimate forms of the one, common Christian faith. Then it is "justified to recognize a legitimate diversity in the plurality of traditions and to assess them positively".[84]

64. In this sense, for example, the Catholic-Lutheran dialogue on the eucharist has led to the result that the existing differences in the statements about the manner in which Christ is present in the eucharist "must no longer be regarded as opposed in a way that leads to separation", but that in common, albeit in different ways, "the reality of the eucharistic presence" is testified to.[85] Similarly, the Catholic–Lutheran dialogue document on the ministry in the church, with a view to the different interpretations and statements regarding "sacramentality" and "uniqueness" of ordination, was of the opinion that it could speak of a "consensus on the reality" as follows: "Wherever it is taught that through the act of ordination the Holy Spirit gives grace strengthening the ordained person for the lifetime ministry of word and sacrament, it must be asked whether differences which previously divided the churches on this question have not been overcome."[86]

65. In the area of ethical decisions it appears important that the Catholic church right up to and including the council of Trent[87] did not condemn the practice of divorced persons remarrying in the Eastern Orthodox churches, although it did reject this practice for itself.

66. The joint Catholic-Lutheran reflection on the Augsburg confession must be seen in this context, as it proceeded during recent years and when it had become clear that as far as this confession is concerned – including its diverse expressions and approaches – one could note "full accord on fundamental and central truths".[88] Likewise, quite a few dogmatic decisions of the Catholic church need a common and, if possible, binding interpretation that would bring out more clearly the common ground of our faith. This would be particularly true for the more recent dogmas relating to Mary and to the papacy, because for Lutheran churches and Christians to accept that they are in accordance with scripture and gospel represents a serious problem.[89]

3. Removal of doctrinal condemnations

67. Our ecclesial awareness has been traumatized by mutual condemnations. These may have been uttered as formal, reciprocal, doctrinal condemnations, but they can also be seen as general prejudices that have taken root in the consciousness of the members of our churches. It is precisely in this form that they have had particularly widespread and fateful repercussions. In order to return to a common confession of the one faith and a true communal relationship, it is necessary that each of our churches declare officially, in all points where this is possible in view of the current teaching of the other church, that these condemnations have become meaningless.

68. Past doctrinal condemnations cannot be rendered ineffectual through a relativizing of truth. Rather, it is the duty to be truthful which calls us to act.

Theological-historical research and more recent ecclesial developments lead us even now to the insight that in important questions those reciprocal doctrinal condemnations are not or are no longer applicable. Thus, for example, the necessary rejection by the Reformation of the "Pelagians and others who teach that, without the Holy Spirit and by the power of nature alone, we are able to love God above all things and can also keep the commandments of God in so far as the substance of the acts is concerned",[90] does not affect the official teaching of the Catholic church.[91] Vice versa, the equally necessary Catholic rejection of those who hold that "Christians are not concerned with the ten commandments"[92] or that "anyone who has become justified once can no longer sin or lose his state of grace"[93] is not applicable to the position of the Lutheran confessions.[94] Similarly, the Reformation condemnation of "those who teach that the sacraments justify by the outward acts" and "without the proper attitude in the recipient"[95] is not applicable to Catholic teaching,[96] and vice versa, the Catholic rejection of those who say that "the sacraments of the new covenant do not communicate grace *ex opere operato*, but that the faith alone is sufficient to obtain the grace of divine promise"[97] does not apply to the Lutheran confessions.[98] Moreover, the Reformation's condemnation of the sacrifice of the mass as a denial of the once-for-all sacrifice of the cross[99] does not touch the teaching of the Catholic church[100] any more than Catholic condemnation of those who deny the real presence of Christ in the eucharist[101] or call it into question by rejecting the doctrine of transubstantiation[102] need apply to the Lutheran church and its teaching.[103]

69. To be sure, agreement that earlier doctrinal condemnations are no longer applicable cannot be achieved by mere statements of consensus issued by theologians. What is really needed are official declarations by the chief teaching authorities of each of the churches concerned, each according to its own procedures. In the Catholic church this falls within the competence of the holy see in agreement with the episcopate as a whole. In the Lutheran churches the most appropriate procedure would be one analogous to what was done in accepting the Leuenberg agreement, i.e., a form of synodal process in the individual churches (see nos. §§23-26 above).

Official declarations of this type, however, will gain their true ecclesial importance and find their way into the life of the people of God only if they happen in the framework of liturgical celebrations that give expression to both penitence and thanksgiving.

B. Community in sacraments

70. Community with Christ and community of Christians with each other are mediated through word and sacrament in the Holy Spirit. Where Christians and churches desire full community with each other, it follows that their joint understanding of the apostolic witness and their common testimony to the Christian faith (see §§55ff. above) must go hand in hand with a common sacramental life.[104] We can note gratefully that in this respect important things have happened recently. (1) Our churches have a more intensive sacramental life. (2) With regard to understanding and celebration of the sacraments, a growing agreement can be noted. The requirements for a common sacramental life have, however, not yet been fully met. (3) Within the fundamental consensus, open questions remain.

1. Growth of sacramental life in our churches

71. In both the consciousness of Lutheran and Roman Catholic churches, the sacramental dimension of the Christian life has in recent times once again come to the fore. Growing out of the sacrament of baptism (Rom. 6:3ff.), Christian life in its deepest

sense is the gift of sharing in the death and resurrection of Jesus Christ. This sharing is mediated through proclamation of the word and celebration of the sacraments equally.[105] In the sacraments it occurs in a manner which accents the corporeality, the personal character, and the community dimension of this sharing, whereby it should be noted that for Lutherans as well as for Catholics the word belongs to the nature of the sacraments themselves.[106]

72. The deepened consciousness of the sacramental dimension of Christian existence has also reshaped the life and practice of our churches.

In several respects the last few centuries have seen a renewal of sacramental life in the Roman Catholic Church:
– New emphasis has been placed on the interrelatedness of sacrament, proclaimed word and faith that the Reformers felt necessary to stress again.[107] This has influenced the reform of the liturgical orders for the celebration of the sacraments.
– The primary importance of baptism[108] and of the eucharist[109] has been stressed, especially by reshaping their celebration.
– A comprehensive view of the sacramental life of the church has been given precedence over an isolated approach to individual sacraments, by understanding the church in Christ as "the universal sacrament of salvation",[110] as "the 'sacrament of unity'".[111]

These tendencies have led to liturgical developments which parallel many Lutheran concerns: greater space for the proclamation of the word of God, use of the vernacular, more frequent communion under both kinds, curtailing of masses without the participation of the people, to mention only the most important reforms.

73. Parallelling this, an intensification of sacramental life in the Lutheran churches has developed.
– Regarding baptism, which in the Lutheran tradition has always been considered fully a sacrament and a fundamental and permanent point of reference of Christian existence, there is renewed appreciation of its place in the Sunday gathering for worship.
– The eucharist is today being celebrated more frequently at the regular Sunday worship service than was the case in the past. The Reformation had stressed that Lutheran communities celebrated it with particular devotion and reverence, expressly urging believers to communicate.[112]
– It is stressed that as far as the Lutheran tradition is concerned, the sacramental dimension of Christian life was never called into question and, indeed, was expressly defended in inter-Reformation disputes. It was thus possible for the Lutheran Reformers – following the scriptures (Col. 1:27; 1 Tim. 3:16) – to speak of Christ as the one sacrament[113] or to attribute "sacramental" character to the word of the scripture and the proclaimed word as bearers of the presence of Christ and as efficacious word.[114]

74. The linkages of the sacraments and their liturgical celebrations both with the world and with all humanity have again been discovered by Lutheran and Catholic traditions together.[115]

2. Increasing agreement in understanding and celebration of the sacraments

75. Lutherans and Catholics are conscious that they participate in one and the same *baptism*.[116] In keeping with the statement *BEM*, we jointly confess that "Christian bap-

tism is rooted in the ministry of Jesus of Nazareth, in his death and in his resurrection. It is incorporation into Christ, who is the crucified and risen Lord; it is entry into the new covenant between God and God's people."[117] This common understanding of baptism is expressed in the manner in which baptism is administered, and is confirmed by the fact that almost everywhere our churches have officially recognized each other's baptism. Moreover, our churches are faced by common or similar pastoral tasks concerning the understanding of baptism and how it is expressed and concretized in baptismal practice, faith-life, and the piety of congregations and the faithful.

76. A great deal of progress towards a common understanding and celebration of the *eucharist* has been made in recent years as a result of numerous dialogues between our churches at various levels. In the course of these dialogues, it proved possible to reconcile positions with regard to the understanding of the eucharist that had previously been thought to be in conflict and were therefore seen as divisive (sacrifice of the mass, eucharistic presence); many of the remaining differences are within the common sphere, thus depriving them of their divisive force.[118] Regarding liturgical form, both churches are moving towards growing consensus in the basic elements of eucharistic celebration.[119]

77. Theological endeavours have also led to a better reciprocal understanding regarding the other sacraments in the Catholic church, whose sacramental character has hitherto been admitted only hesitantly or not at all by the Lutheran churches.

78. Various Catholic-Lutheran dialogues on the ordained ministry in the church have shown that, even though Lutherans do not speak of *ordination* as a sacrament, there is yet "substantial convergence" between the Catholic and Lutheran understanding and practice wherever ordination is celebrated through the laying-on of hands and prayer (epiclesis) as act of blessing, and wherever it is taught "that through the act of ordination the Holy Spirit gives grace strengthening the ordained person for the lifetime ministry of word and sacrament".[120] Lutheran tradition has taken account of this even though it does not include ordination among the sacraments in the strict sense. "In principle... [it does] not reject" the sacramental understanding of ordination.[121]

79. The Augsburg confession and both of Luther's catechisms treat *confession* (of sin) in close connection with the baptismal and eucharistic sacraments. In the apology of the Augsburg confession, they are even expressly included among the sacraments.[122] Present-day Catholic-Lutheran research with regard to the understanding of confession in the Augsburg confession, moreover, has brought to light misunderstandings of each other's position that existed on both sides in the 16th century.[123] The Roman Catholic liturgy of penitence, which places the accent on the remission of sins and on personal guidance, together with the more frequent celebration of penitence, foreseen in the new Catholic liturgy, help to promote understanding between our two churches. The difficulties encountered today by the practice of personal confession in certain areas of the Catholic church and the widespread lack of understanding among many Lutherans make confession a common pastoral task for both churches.

80. Our dialogue about marriage and mixed marriages has revealed a "view of marriage which is in a profound sense a common one". We affirm together that the event of salvation in Christ affects Christians also in their conjugal life which can never be without reference to it. The relationship is nothing other than the grace "as a lasting promise", which Christ grants people in their married life, a grace that "is not simply an idea" but "reality". This means, however, attributing to marriage a "sacramental"

aspect, a "sacramental power", even though the Reformation churches do not consider it "to be a sacrament in the full sense of the word".[124]

81. Confirmation and the anointing of the sick have received hardly any consideration in the Catholic-Lutheran dialogue.

Since in the Western churches *confirmation* developed into a rite distinct from baptism, the questions regarding the necessary age for its administration and its precise function have been discussed again and again. In the Lutheran Reformation confirmation disappeared completely. Later it was reintroduced as a rite of admission to the Lord's supper and/or the celebration of coming of age. As such it was closely linked with previous catechetical instruction. In the Catholic church confirmation is understood to be an integral part of sacramental initiation into the church, although here, too, it is not devoid of catechetical aspects. In both churches the promise of the gifts of the Holy Spirit is central. Even in the Lutheran understanding confirmation is an act of blessing performed through the prayer of the congregation, and in which grace is promised and granted to the confirmand. Catholics and Lutherans both participate in the ecumenical discussion of the questions about a proper relationship of confirmation to baptism and Christian witness.[125]

82. In the course of post-conciliar reforms in the Catholic church, the *anointing of the sick* was emphasized more strongly than before as a special help for the sick and the dying, and it was linked with the proclamation of the word. Lutherans have seldom practised the anointing of the sick. They have, however, attributed great importance to the pastoral care of sick people. In some Lutheran churches this has recently led to attempts to reintroduce anointing of the sick.[126] This could therefore become the subject of a promising dialogue between Catholics and Lutherans, if one bears in mind the common pastoral tasks and the emerging rapprochement. Both Catholics and Lutherans are now finding a point of encounter inasmuch as the former are gradually getting away from an isolated understanding of the individual sacraments, and the latter are more and more abandoning a narrow use of the concept of sacrament. This, in order to understand and live together the sacramental dimension of Christian existence in a new and better way. Particularly in the present situation where people experience social isolation and personal loneliness, both traditions have a special pastoral task towards the sick and the dying.

3. Open questions, remaining differences, basic agreements

83. In spite of an enhanced common awareness of the sacramental dimension of Christian and ecclesial life, and in spite of a deepened consensus in the understanding and praxis of the sacraments, there remain open questions that must be answered with a view to the common sacramental life that belongs to full church fellowship. Clarification of these questions must be brought about in joint dialogue and in the life and praxis of each of the two churches. In this connection the agreements which already exist, or which we have now reached, give us the freedom to challenge each other and to ask reciprocally critical questions regarding teaching and praxis.

84. Nevertheless, even here we must not strive after a questionable homogeneity. Just as in the case of the understanding of faith, the common sacramental life needed for unity must not be mistaken for uniformity. Room must be left for legitimate diversities. This is true not only in relation to the understanding and shaping of the individual sacraments or sacramental ecclesial acts, but also in relation to the concept of sacra-

ment as such. The open questions remaining, especially regarding the number of sacraments, are ultimately rooted in an open concept of sacrament. Not only between our two churches, but also within our churches, the concept of sacrament is not fixed in every last detail. A certain fluctuation historically in determining the number of sacraments – as well as the differentiation between or "ranking" of the sacraments[127] (and a conjunctive "analogue-use" of the sacramental concept) – all point in this direction.

85. For an understanding and the celebration of the individual sacraments and therefore also for the common sacramental life of our two churches, it has to be taken into account that the sacraments are part of God's trinitarian act of salvation: the work that God performed in Christ once for all for the salvation of the world is mediated by the Holy Spirit, who works through word and sacrament so that *communio sanctorum* is formed, i.e., church as participation in the gifts of salvation and as communion of the faithful.

This makes it clear once more how important it is for a proper understanding and conservation of the sacramental dimension of Christian existence and church life when both our traditions are able to speak of Christ as the one sacrament and therefore as the source of the individual sacraments (see §§72 and 73 above). At the same time it becomes clear why on the Catholic side one speaks today of the church as the "sacrament".[128] The Lutheran tradition is not yet very familiar with this thought, and it is often inclined to criticize it. But its intention should be acceptable for Lutherans: as the body of Christ and "koinonia" of the Holy Spirit, the church is the sign and instrument of God's grace, an instrument that of itself can do nothing. The church lives by the word as it lives by the sacraments, and at the same time stands in their service.

C. Community of service

86. The church lives by word and sacrament and also stands in their service. It has therefore a structured form in which the service of the whole people of God and the service of those who have been entrusted with the special ordained ministry can act together. Consequently, in our search for church fellowship, it is not possible to separate the efforts for community of faith (II/a) and sacramental life (II/b) from efforts for a structured church fellowship (community of service) that would permit and ensure common life, common decisions and common action (see §49 above).

1. Commitment to a structured fellowship (community of service)

87. If, in the present process of growing reciprocal recognition and reception, our two churches affirm increasingly that they confess the same faith and share a common understanding of the sacraments, then they are also entitled and obliged to enter into structured fellowship with each other. With the New Testament we confess the church as "people of God", as "body of Christ", and as "temple of the Holy Spirit". This confession does not permit us to limit the relationship between our churches to be a mere reciprocally respectful coexistence or internalization. This confession calls us to live out the existing community of faith and sacrament also in a structured ecclesial fellowship. Each of these images of the church, found in the New Testament, confronts us with this commitment.

88. The church as *people of God* is called to live in unity, for God does not lead Christians to himself and to salvation in isolation or independently of each other. Faith, without ceasing to be personal faith, is always a faith that lives in the community and

is transmitted, preserved and renewed in it. Just as the people of the old covenant encompassed different tribes and yet was one single people of God, the new people of God has been called together from all nations of the earth, embraces all the diversity of the human world, lives in many places, and listens to God's calling in many languages and in many different ways. It is nevertheless a single undivided people, called by the one Lord, in the one Spirit, to one faith, to solidarity and love for each other, and to common witness and service in the world.

89. The church, the new "people of God", is the *body of Christ*. "For by one Spirit we were all baptized into one body" (1 Cor. 12:13). Elsewhere, speaking of the eucharist, St Paul says: "The bread which we break, is it not a participation in the body of Christ? Because there is one bread, we who are many are one body" (1 Cor. 10:16ff.). Just as the eucharist is not a part of the body of Christ but the whole Christ, so also the local church is not only a part of the whole, but a realization of the church of God.[129] If therefore according to the New Testament the individual local church is church of God in the *full* sense, it is yet not the whole church of God. This limited nature of the individual churches and their necessary solidarity with each other calls for a concrete and lived-out fellowship which embraces all aspects of ecclesial life. It corresponds to the nature of the church which as "body of Christ" is an organic whole.

90. Just as the church is called to be "people of God" and "body of Christ", it is also called to be *temple of the Holy Spirit*. Since the plenitude of the gifts of the Spirit is given only in the fellowship of all local churches, no church can claim the Holy Spirit for itself alone.[130] Such a claim would contradict the fellowship instituted by the Holy Spirit. The same would be true if one single church wanted to live a life independent of the other churches, if it wanted to dominate them, or even if it were indifferent towards the faith of these churches. Confessing the church as "temple of the Holy Spirit" and recognizing the other church as "temple of the Holy Spirit" means therefore entering into active fellowship with this church. If one and the same spirit of love and unity lives in the churches, all are obliged to pray for each other, to work together and to care for each other.

91. The growing reciprocal recognition as church thus leads us to binding common life, to active exchange, and to mutual acceptance in witness, service and solidarity according to the nature of the church as "people of God", "body of Christ", and "temple of the Holy Spirit". It commits our churches at both the local and the universal levels not only to an occasional fellowship, practised from time to time, but to a fully lived-out fellowship that requires for its realization a structured form.

2. Structured church fellowship and a common ordained ministry

92. The dialogue between our churches and, in general, ecumenical efforts for visible unity of the church have shown that the structured form needed for full and binding fellowship between churches can be manifold and variable. It is not limited to the hierarchical dimension of the church but rather embraces the service of the whole people of God, includes the charisma of all the faithful, and expresses itself in synodal structures and processes. At the same time, fellowship in the ordained ministry forms an essential part of the structured church fellowship.

This fellowship in the ordained ministry, though not yet fully realized, is nevertheless basically present in the mutual recognition of ministries as forms of the ministry instituted by Christ.[131] The coexistence of ministries mutually recognized must be transformed into a common exercise of ordained ministry appropriate to its nature, whereby particular importance is attached to the common exercise of the "ministry of leadership and of pastoral supervision *(episcope)*".[132]

Only in a church fellowship so structured is it possible to take joint decisions to preserve and further the apostolicity, catholicity and unity of the church and to act jointly in witness and service.

93. There already exists today a broad area in which a partial common exercise of ordained ministry and also of ecclesial *episcope* is possible, desirable and even necessary. It is carried out between our two churches, for example, in the area of social responsibility, in the ethical, diaconal and charitable fields, or in evangelization.

94. But yet these forms of cooperation between ordained ministries are far from a comprehensive fully common exercise of the ordained ministry. In order to have progress one must look at three factors:
1) the statement of Vatican II which, regarding the ordained ministry of the Reformation churches, speaks of a "lack of the sacrament of orders";[133]
2) a certain "asymmetry" in the more precise definition of the theological value assigned to the ministry, particularly of the historic episcopacy in the understanding of the church;
3) the close bond that exists in the Catholic church between the bishops and the pope.

95. (1) While according to the Lutheran understanding of church the existence of the ministry in the Catholic church is not to be called into question,[134] Catholics cannot yet fully recognize the ordained ministry in Lutheran churches because, according to their view, these churches lack the fullness of the ordained ministry since they "lack of the sacrament of orders".[135] This would only be possible through a process of "acceptance of full church communion"[136] of which fellowship in the historical episcopacy is an essential part.

96. (2) Catholics and Lutherans share the conviction that the ordained ministry of the church, which because it is "instituted by Jesus Christ"[137] "stands over against the community as well as within the community",[138] is "essential" for the church.[139] Nevertheless it is *possible* for Lutherans – and in this they differ from Catholics – to give a theological description of the church without making explicit mention of the ministry because it is either "presupposed"[140] or implied by the proclamation of the word and the administration of the sacraments.

97. Lutherans, like Catholics, can recognize as "the action of the Spirit"[141] the historical differentiation of the one apostolic ministry into more local ministry and more regional forms, and they can consider "the function of *episcope*... as necessary for the church".[142] Likewise Lutherans feel free "to face up to the call for communion with the historic episcopal office"[143] (i.e., the historically evolved pattern of episcopal ministry in the form of the office of bishop standing in apostolic succession). Nevertheless Lutherans and Catholics place different accents on the significance of that historic episcopal office for the church.[144]

98. The two problems are closely related. The "lack of the sacrament of orders" that the Catholic side claims to be inherent in the ministry of the Lutheran churches cannot, because of its very nature, be annulled solely by theological insights and agreements or by ecclesiastical or canonical declarations and decisions, as, for example, by the theological and canonical act of recognizing these ministries. What is needed rather is acceptance of the fellowship in ecclesial ministry, and this, ultimately, means accep-

tance of the fellowship in episcopal ministry which stands in apostolic succession. Lutherans are fundamentally free and open to accept such fellowship in the episcopal office. Yet within this understanding of the importance or significance of the episcopal office for the catholicity, apostolicity and unity of the church, Lutherans are inclined to place the accent differently from Catholics.

99. The problems mentioned here need not block the road to fellowship in the church ministry and therefore to a fully structured ecclesial fellowship. But it does call for renewal and deepening of the understanding of the ordained ministry, particularly the ministry serving the unity and governance *(episcope)* of the church.

100. (3) In connection with the above mentioned, it has to be borne in mind that as far as Catholics are concerned, fellowship in the ordained ministry is expressed by the college of all bishops with the pope at its head.

101. A Roman Catholic bishop or a group of Catholic bishops do not exercise their *episcope* without involving the whole of the episcopate.[145] When bishops intend to take a decision committing them and their church to a process which has as its goal full church fellowship with Lutheran churches, they can only do this in community with the whole of the Catholic episcopate. The same is true if within their own church they wish to concretize a common exercise of *episcope* with their Lutheran partners.

102. In concrete terms this means that the bishops exercise *episcope* in the fellowship collegially with the first among them, the pope. They recognize the supreme jurisdictional authority of the pope over the universal church and all the faithful, an authority that – according to Vatican I – is of an episcopal, ordinary and direct nature.[146]

103. The process that is to lead to a common ordained ministry via the joint exercise of the *episcope* therefore necessarily requires the participation of the pope. He can, in the face of the entire Roman Catholic Church, guarantee the propriety of this process. He can help assure that the unity re-established in one place will not lead to new divisions in another. Thus, according to its mission, the Petrine ministry can not only protect fellowship but further it.

3. Joint reflection on the early church

104. The understanding of a ministry serving the unity of the church and *episcope*, on which Catholics and Lutherans diverge to some extent, can be deepened and gain in commonality if the two sides reflect together about how this ministry was seen and practised in the early church. Both sides have good reasons for participating in such a reflection.

105. According to the statements of Vatican II on the sacramentality and collegiality of the episcopal office,[147] Catholics no longer follow the view that prevailed in the middle ages. Taking the presbyterate *(sacerdotium)* as point of departure, it differentiated the episcopate only by virtue of its greater dignity and jurisdictional authority. One indication of this is the fact that in the 1968 edition of the *Pontificale Romanum*, the former prayer accompanying the imposition of hands is replaced by the prayer taken from Hippolytus's *Apostolic Tradition*. Within Catholic theology this return to the early church fathers is also a call to emphasize more strongly the collegiality of the bishops as an expression of the fellowship of local churches.

106. The Lutheran Reformation basically affirmed the episcopal office of the early church.[148] There was readiness to retain the episcopal office in its traditional form, even though there was criticism of the manner in which the office was exercised at that

time. To some extent this criticism was explicitly associated with and legitimated by references to the early church.[149] Thus it is clear that also on the Lutheran side, the question of episcopal ministry is dealt with in reference to the early church.

107. The understanding of the nature of episcopal ministry which then prevailed becomes obvious in the rite of ordination of a bishop. Essential aspects of this are also significant for us today:

108. (a) Ordination is at the same time a charismatic, liturgical and ecclesial event.

The early church did not separate the charismatic event (gift of the Spirit) from the liturgical ceremony (imposition of hands as part of the eucharistic service on Sundays) nor from its ecclesial context (commissioning and jurisdiction). In the worshipping community and by the imposition of hands of the bishops, the new bishop receives the gift of the Spirit.[150] This gift contains a special charism of presiding over his church.[151]

109. The bishop is a baptized member of the local koinonia.[152] In the ordination he, as one who is baptized, receives the call of the church and induction into an office. These two aspects are linked by the action of the Holy Spirit, through which the new bishop receives a gift of grace, which is not intended for his own well-being and does not separate him from the congregation, but which is rather for the benefit of the congregation and which places him in its service.[153]

At the local level bishops stand in their churches and serve them as a personal responsibility. The particular responsibility of one bishop is thus linked with the responsibility of all, as is also shown by the ordination liturgy.

110. (b) The vigilance with regard to the apostolicity of the faith that belongs to the bishop's duty is bound up with the responsibility for the faith borne by the whole Christian people.

Members of the church participate in the election of their bishop and receive the person who is to exercise the apostolic ministry. In addition, when the candidate answers the ordination questions and confesses his faith in the presence of the congregation, the congregation is witness that the bishop represents the authentic apostolic faith. All this shows that the apostolic succession is not really to be understood as a succession of one individual to another,[154] but rather as a succession in the church, to an episcopal see and to membership of the episcopal college,[155] as shown by the lists of bishops.[156]

The responsibility of the congregation is not limited to the moment of ordination. Its full scope is illustrated by the exception "that one must deny one's consent even to bishops when it happens that they err and speak in a manner that contradicts the canonical texts".[157] This means that the *episcope* is not exercised in isolation but normally in concert with the community of the believers, i.e., within a diversity of ministries and services and in the *synodal* life of the local church.

111. (c) The bishops are servants of unity and of the fellowship among churches.

Even though the Christians in a given place must give their consent in the election of their bishop, they do not impose their hands at his ordination. That is done by the leaders of the neighbouring churches.

Bishops thus both represent the universal church in their own church and represent their own church among all other churches.[158] This mediating position corresponds to the task of the new bishop in the realm of faith, which is expressly emphasized by the confession-like structure of his ordination. As leader of his own church together with the other bishops (collegiality), he is to bear witness to the faith received from the apostles and to watch over it.

Furthermore, the bishops are those who primarily, though not exclusively, ensure regular communication between the churches. This is done formally in regional or even universal conciliar life that serves to further or re-establish fellowship among the churches.

Finally, bishops are obliged to promote the common action and common witness of the churches. All this indicates that the episcopal office, as understood in the light of ordination, must be exercised collegially if it is to serve the fellowship of the churches.

4. The significance of reflection on the early church for church fellowship between Catholics and Lutherans

112. This understanding by the early church of the episcopal office as a service to the koinonia can stimulate, correct and enlarge the view of Catholics and Lutherans in their endeavours for a commonly exercised *episcope*. It becomes particularly clear that *episcope* is exercised in concert with the church as a whole in a personal, collegial and communal way. Consequently, the exercise of the *episcope* cannot be separated from the responsibility of the laity or from "synodality" or conciliarity.

113. In the sense of the early church, the episcopal office is to serve the koinonia of the local church in a threefold manner:

- *Personal:* Christ "came not to be served but to serve" (Mark 10:45). This is the duty of all Christians. It is particularly applicable to bishops in an office for which they have received grace, authority and responsibility. This personal dimension of *episcope* excludes any purely administrative or functional interpretation of this ministry. Since it serves the diversity of gifts granted to Christians and the mission of the people of God, the incumbents themselves are not in the centre. Accordingly the linkage between the person of the incumbent and the commission of the office is properly balanced, and former misunderstandings can be eliminated.[159]
- *Collegial*, in the sense that one is never bishop for oneself, but in collegiality with the priests and deacons and in a college with the fellow bishops. On the basis of ordination a bishop becomes bishop of the church over which he presides, and at the same time is recognized as bishop by the whole church and shares responsibility for it. When churches are in communion, ordination and full ecclesial recognition go hand in hand. From this follows the fully sanctioned participation of the bishops in the conciliar life of the church of God at both its regional and universal levels.
- *In cooperation with the congregation*, inasmuch as the bishop's ministry, even though it is not exercised in the name of the people, is generally exercised in fellowship with the people and respects the diversity of the ministries and charisma given by the Spirit.[160] Thus absolute sovereignty either on the part of the congregation or the bishop is excluded.

114. These three ways of exercising the bishop's ministry correspond to what the New Testament teaches us about the manner in which the apostles themselves exercised their ministry.[161] They have also been underscored repeatedly in the wider ecumenical endeavours.[162] Also within our churches corresponding new deliberations are taking place.

115. Since the Second Vatican Council the Catholic church has been introducing institutional changes which stress the coresponsibility of parishioners in the local churches. Various councils have been set up to bring together the local pastors and

members (parish councils), the bishop and the faithful in his diocese (pastoral councils), and the bishop and the presbyters (presbyteral councils). Likewise, diocesan and regional synods have been held with the participation of laity. The functions of the bishops are thus being combined in a structured manner with the responsibility of the whole people of God and its various members.

116. The realization of a true communal life which corresponds to the nature of the church as a fellowship (koinonia) is an important current concern of the Lutheran churches. Efforts are thus being made – partly by referring to the insights of the Reformation, which stress again the early church's concept of the priesthood of all the baptized – to meet the dangers of a "clerical church" by trying to further the participation and active responsibility of all parish members. In the emphasis on the local congregation assembled by God through word and sacrament, which is characteristic of the Lutheran understanding of church, evidences of a congregational narrowness are today seen with a more critical eye than in former times, and efforts are being made to counteract them theologically and practically. The enhanced awareness of the importance of the *episcope*, clearly to be seen among Lutherans, must be noted in this connection. It is understood, however, not as a mere administrative office but as a ministry of word and sacrament, and particularly as ministry of the *pastor pastorum*, which serves the wider ecclesial fellowship and becomes its effective representative.

5. Approach to a jointly exercised ministry of fellowship

117. Common reflection about the early church brings to light a way to a jointly exercised ministry which requires careful examination. The following considerations may be of help. The proposed process is not necessarily the only possible one, though it does seem to avoid obstacles which have, up to now, impeded the way to church fellowship. The description here given may be modified in many of its details. It is neither a rigid nor a final plan. Preserving its central intention, however, is what is important.

118. The process leading to full realization of church fellowship as a structured community is, strictly speaking, a correlated and integral process involving reciprocally recognized ministries and the joint exercise of ministries, especially of the ministry of the episcope.[163] Fully spelled out, it has the following structure.

An officially declared mutual recognition of ordained ministries opens the way by means of an initial act to the joint exercise of *episcope*, including ordaining. A series of such ordinations would eventually lead to a common ordained ministry. The process could function at the universal level, but could also be set in motion at local, regional or national ecclesial levels.

The process would thus have the following phases:
- preliminary forms of a joint exercise of episcope (ch. 6);
- initial act of recognition (ch. 7);
- collegial exercise of *episcope* (ch. 8);
- transition to a common ordained ministry (ch. 9).

119. It is of decisive importance for understanding and implementing this process that one attend to and preserve its integral and correlative character. It is not a matter of isolated acts or of phases in a gradual process. Rather the reciprocal recognition of ministries means essentially enabling and initiating the joint exercise of *episcope* out of which then the ordained ministry arises. And therefore a mutual recognition of min-

istries which does not initiate the joint exercise of *episcope* and the common ordained ministry growing out of it is insufficient for the realization of structured church fellowship. Furthermore, a joint exercise of *episcope*, including ordaining, is inconceivable without the act of mutual recognition of the ministries, an act which by its nature enables and initiates the joint exercise of *episcope*.

6. Preliminary forms of the joint exercise of episcope

120. As a rule a preparatory process will be needed before the above described correlative and integral process of mutual recognition of ministries[164] and joint exercise of *episcope* begins in its strict sense, a process during which a gradual recognition of ministries and the appropriate prototypical forms of a joint exercise of ministries, especially the ministry of *episcope*, are developed.

121. Such preliminary forms are, for example:
- working groups or Christian councils which already exist in many countries;
- mutual invitation of church leaders, pastors and laity to synods of the two churches, with a right to speak;
- development of more solid forms of working relationship, at the local or regional levels, between those who exercise *episcope* in the two churches so that even now they can speak and act jointly where conscience does not require them to speak and act separately;
- creation, in a country or a region, of conciliar organs for the exchange of experiences and for common consultation in order to arrive at common decisions in such matters as evangelization, social service, public responsibility.

122. Also in these preliminary forms or steps on the way to joint exercise of the *episcope*, the main point will always be inter-relating of both dimensions of the process, i.e., mutual recognition and joint exercise of the ministries, in which the participation and active cooperation of the entire ecclesial community should also be ensured.

7. Initial act of recognition

123. If a fundamental consensus is reached on faith, sacramental life and ordained ministry such that remaining differences between Catholics and Lutherans no longer can appear as church-dividing, and reciprocal doctrinal condemnations no longer have any basis, then a mutual act of recognition should certainly follow.

124. This act entails a recognition of the fundamental consensus which is ecclesially binding and, at the same time, a mutual recognition that in the other church, the church of Jesus Christ is actualized. It declares and confirms the will of both churches to relate to each other as churches of Jesus Christ and to live in full fellowship *(communio ecclesiarum)*. Concerning the common ministry needed for full church fellowship, this means:
- on the Catholic side, affirmation of the existence in the Lutheran churches of the ministry instituted by Christ in his church, while at the same time pointing to a lack of fullness of the ordained ministry as a *defectus* which, for the sake of church fellowship, has jointly to be overcome;
- an enabling and concurrent authoritative beginning of a joint exercise of *episcope* which progressively brings about and implies fellowship in the fully structured ordained ministry.

125. The act of recognition should be appropriate to the binding, ecclesial and integral character of the process of realizing church fellowship. To it belong a binding confessional declaration and an appropriate liturgical celebration in which, if possible, the first joint ordination should be held, thus marking the beginning of the joint exercise of *episcope*.

Church fellowship begun in this manner opens possibilities of sacramental and particularly eucharistic fellowship, the modalities of which have to be clarified on the Catholic side according to the existing canon law.[165]

126. Church fellowship between Catholics and Lutherans is ultimately sought as a fellowship between the whole Catholic church and the totality of the Lutheran churches. Any act of initial recognition – whether it involves the churches at the local, regional, national or international levels – must have this as its goal.

On the Lutheran side, in view of these considerations, the relevant decisions would be taken by the independent churches (for example, *Landeskirchen* or national churches, or their associations). In this respect forms must be found which ensure that action is being taken in solidarity with the other churches of the Lutheran communion.

On the Catholic side, note must be taken of the requirements of the episcopate as a whole. Depending on the circumstances at any given time, local bishops, bishops of a church province, or an episcopal conference would have to take primary responsibility. If a positive judgment is arrived at, the act of initial recognition must occur in cooperation with the pope, because such an act concerns the whole Catholic church. On the basis of his particular responsibility for the unity of Christians and the fellowship of the churches, it is the task of the pope to approve or encourage such a local act in the name of the Catholic church.

8. A single episcope *in collegial form*

127. The common exercise of *episcope*, including ordaining – made possible by the recognition of ministries – through which community of faith and sacraments between Lutherans and Catholics becomes structured church fellowship, will initially take *the shape of a single* episcope *exercised in collegial form*.

In places where they exist together, the churches would provide for themselves a single episcopate in collegial form. It would go beyond all preliminary forms of parallel or partial joint exercise of *episcope*, but without merging the two episcopates. This single episcopate would at the same time ensure necessary unity and legitimate diversity. What is foreseen is a form of local church in which our churches would truly be one without having been absorbed. This is the case, for example, with the united churches of the East (see §§35-40 above), and is the intention of the model of "unity in reconciled diversity" (see §§31-34 above).[166] In such a situation, the Catholic or Lutheran congregations would preserve their existing links with their bishop. Moreover, the collegial exercise of *episcope* in a region or a country can be furthered by the presence of a regional primate to whom his episcopal colleagues grant certain privileges, as for example convening and chairing of an assembly, or under certain conditions representation of the church of the region or country vis-a-vis civil authorities.[167]

128. Such a form of jointly exercised *episcope* is most readily derived from the *ductus* of the preceding considerations, commends itself on the basis of the nature of the growing understanding and convergence between Catholics and Lutherans, and corresponds most clearly and honestly to the mutual recognition of ministries already set

forth. This form of jointly exercised *episcope* is also in basic agreement with the understanding of the unity of the local church as it was held and practised in the early church.

The unity of the local church found expression in the early church through a single bishop exercising jurisdiction in one and the same territory.[168] The catholicity and apostolicity of the church as well as its unity was thus to be demonstrated and preserved.

Neither race nor language nor class nor any other human condition can be the principle of church unity. The "localness" of the church, linked with a single bishop, makes clear that thereby Christians are one with each other and that, on the basis of one faith and one baptism, they gather around one eucharist. This eucharist is always celebrated in unity with the bishop.

129. There are, therefore, multiple reasons for the traditional principle of a single bishop in one local church. However, in a situation in which – as in ours – the concern is the realization of church fellowship between hitherto separated churches, forms of local church structure seem possible which ensure and testify to the unity, catholicity and apostolicity of these churches without in each case being presided over by only one single bishop.

130. That does not exclude the question whether, following the creation of the common ministry to which the jointly exercised *episcope* would lead (see ch. 9 below), there can or shall be also other forms of jointly exercised *episcope* than the collegial one (see ch. 10 below).

131. Whatever the precise procedures for the common exercise of *episcope* may be, the nature and the content of the decisions to be taken must be subject to an evaluation process which could extend over several years. On the Catholic side, churches engaged in such a process must account before the whole Catholic church for their initiatives, the difficulties encountered and their positive experiences. Other Catholic churches, in contact with Lutheran churches somewhere in the world, will listen to them attentively. The indispensable discussion partner for them will be the Roman see because of its special role within the Catholic church.

9. Transition from joint exercise of episcope *to a common ordained ministry*

132. The joint exercise of the ministry of episcope, which includes ordaining, leads to the gradual establishment of a common ordained ministry.

133. The formation of the ordained church ministry would be the result of individual ordinations which would take place whenever there is a candidate to ordain. All neighbouring bishops, Lutherans and Catholics, on the basis of the jointly exercised *episcope* would ordain the new minister together. At the end of this process – within a reasonable space of time – the common ordained ministry would be realized.

134. Each of these ordinations must be understood and undertaken as an event which is at the same time (a) confessional, (b) epicletic, (c) communal, and (d) juridical:

a) At the moment of taking up his ministry, the new minister confesses the apostolic faith before the entire worshipping community which, together with the Catholic and Lutheran bishops (or other ministers exercising *episcope*) present on that occasion, witnesses to the correctness of his faith.

b) The entire action of ordination is embraced by the invocation of the Holy Spirit by the whole worshipping community.[169] Within this liturgical action the gift of the

Spirit, necessary for the exercise of the ministry, is imparted through the imposition of hands by the Catholic and Lutheran bishops.
c) Not everything, however, can depend on the common imposition of hands. The whole congregation is also involved. It could in one way or another participate in the election of the ordinand. As a rule, members of the church or congregation testify to the faith and morals of the candidate. The church or congregation for which the minister is being ordained engages in an act of acceptance (reception). Finally, ordination also concerns the fellowship among the churches, since it is one of the tasks of those ordained to further this fellowship.
d) Ordination sets one immediately into the service of the church and confers the authority inherent in such service. In the Catholic church, a new bishop has to be appointed or confirmed by the pope. As various current concordats indicate, or as in the election of the patriarchs of the united churches of the East, the Catholic church can adopt various procedures that do not necessarily eventuate in direct appointment.

135. It must be clearly understood that at stake in joint ordinations by Catholic and Lutheran bishops is a gift of grace of the Holy Spirit received in common by Catholics and Lutherans. In a confession of gratitude the two partners recognize together that the common and collegial ordained ministry is a gift of the Spirit to the apostolic church. At this juncture it would therefore be wrong to pose the question of what the one partner has given to the other.

136. A common ordained ministry would thus grow out of the jointly exercised *episcope*. This transition would be a *process* which is so irrevocably rooted in a truly joint exercise of *episcope* that, should it not take place or be discontinued, one could no longer really speak of a jointly exercised *episcope*. Ordination constitutes one of the most important functions of *episcope*.[170]

137. This transition to a common ordained ministry is pre-eminently a *gift of God*. Understood as epicletic and confessional events, the ordinations through which our churches receive the ministry show that this common ordained ministry also is not the result of human efforts, but God's gift given through God's Spirit.

138. The *dimension of ecclesial reconciliation* inherent in this event should be expressed in all local congregations through preparation marked not only by joy and gratitude, but also by penitence, both sides confessing their sins against koinonia.

139. In this act of reconciliation and penitence, as is generally characteristic of the path we have proposed, our churches turn resolutely towards the future and leave it to God to judge the past. This implies that the time elapsing between the reciprocal recognition of ministries and the beginning of the jointly exercised *episcope* on the one hand, and the establishing of the common ministry on the other, be considered or declared a time of real but growing and deepening church fellowship. It is *a period of transition vouchsafed by God.*[171]

140. The form described here for realizing a common ordained ministry is not intended to exclude other forms. Rather, it appears to us to be the most appropriate one for the relationship between Lutheran churches and the Roman Catholic Church. In filling vacant posts by new ordinations, one avoids problems which could encumber other procedures which have been discussed or could allow for misinterpretations:
a) *Reordination:* Its problems are not only terminological: one would properly speak of "ordination" in the case of an ordination considered null and void. Reordination

is primarily a problem because the church whose ministers were newly ordained would have to admit the invalidity of all previous ordinations.

b) *Supplementary ordination:* In view of the fact that previous ordinations were intended for a particular church and not for the universal church, a "supplementary ordination" has been considered. The problem here is that existing ordinations are not then taken seriously. For the Catholic church, therefore, a "supplementary ordination" is inconceivable when it recognizes the ordination of a previously separated church as, for example, the Orthodox church.

c) *Act of "reconciliation of ministries":* What is meant here is a comprehensive act of worship during which, by mutual imposition of hands, forgiveness is asked and the Holy Spirit is invoked in prayer that it would grant to all the gifts they need. The problematic of such a broad act of "reconciliation of ministries" derives from its ambiguity and, consequently, from its unclarity. Is there implicitly an ordination or a supplementary ordination? Is the validity of previous ordinations taken seriously?

d) *Mutual commissioning:* If previous ordinations in the other church are considered valid, a mutual commissioning of ordained ministers would be conceivable in order to achieve a common church ministry. The problematic here is that this would be a mere administrative act, while the establishment of a ministerial fellowship cannot be reduced to a legal action. Moreover, mutual commissioning would be an act among ordained ministers with no attention to the role of the people of God.

141. For the transition period, the way proposed makes it imperative to determine precisely the juridical status of the jointly ordained as well as of those bishops and ministers (presbyters) not yet jointly ordained.

10. Exercise of the common ordained ministry

142. After the realization of a common ordained ministry, the exercise of the episcopate need not be uniform for each place. Specific historical, social and cultural situations, as well as the diversity of spiritual traditions, can speak in favour of exercising that ministry in different ways. According to local circumstances, one can imagine at least three forms of the exercise of the episcopate and, consequently, of a truly united local church.

143. *First form: a single* episcope *in collegial form.* In this case the mode of exercising the *episcope* already practised during the transition period would be continued (see §§119-122 above).

144. *Second form: a single bishop for differently structured parishes.* Parishes which differ on the basis of their spiritual and theological traditions live under one bishop who cares for the fellowship among them and also protects their legitimate differences. Thus in the united evangelical *Landeskirchen* of Germany, for example, there are Reformed and Lutheran parishes which have a common bishop or church president and are subject to a common church authority. Also, Catholic Armenians or Maronites living under a bishop of the Latin rite have the possibility of maintaining their religious identity outside their native country by having their own parishes. In the framework of church fellowship, a similar practice would be conceivable between Catholics and Lutherans.

145. *Third form: merger.* The churches unite into a single church in which the parishes are also merged. The merged church would have only a single bishop. This form which is foreseen, for example, by the model of "organic union" (see §§16-18

above) seems legitimate and feasible – if it is desired – especially in the case of churches which live in a non-Christian environment.[172]

11. Indivisibility of the koinonia

146. The realization of church fellowship in which community of faith and community in the sacraments attain ecclesial shape confronts both Lutherans and Catholics with the question of the indivisibility of the koinonia, even though the problem does not present itself in a completely symmetrical manner for the two sides.

147. From the Lutheran point of view, if a Lutheran church enters into full fellowship with the Catholic church, it does not mean:
a) that this church enters ipso facto into fellowship with those churches which are already in fellowship with the Catholic church;
b) that this Lutheran church forgoes ipso facto its fellowship with the other Lutheran churches and with other churches not in fellowship with the Catholic church;
c) that the remaining Lutheran churches, in fellowship with this church but not with the Catholic church, enter ipso facto into fellowship with the Catholic church or renounce their fellowship with this church.[173]

But it does mean:
a) that for this church the question of fellowship with those churches which are in fellowship with the Catholic church is raised on a new level, under new presuppositions, and with greater urgency than previously;
b) that this church affirms as its task and responsibility working towards fellowship of all other Lutheran churches with the Catholic church;
c) that the remaining Lutheran churches also consider and affirm the possibility of a fellowship with the Catholic church as their own possibility to a greater extent than previously.

148. On the Catholic side this question arises: Is it possible for the Catholic church to be in full fellowship with a church which is itself in fellowship with another church with which the Catholic church is not in fellowship?

Only a few insignificant historical precedents can be cited. In the early church, for example, perhaps the schism of Meletius of Antioch and the special position of St Basil; in more recent times (17th/18th century), fellowship with Orthodox church groups of the Greek islands without these churches becoming united churches. A remote analogy is the mutual admission to the eucharist in emergency situations by the patriarchate of Moscow and the Catholic church without this agreement being extended to the whole Orthodox church.

Whatever historical precedents there may be, it is especially necessary to answer authoritatively the questions raised above. In doing so, it is assumed:
a) that the third church holds no doctrines which clearly contradict central truths of faith;
b) that even if there is agreement in the central truths of faith, this church and its members are not admitted ipso facto to the eucharist in the whole Catholic church.

Future perspective

149. At the end of our description of how to achieve Catholic-Lutheran church fellowship, many questions still remain open. The origins and the history of our ecclesial separation are too complex for us to be able to describe clearly and without ambiguity

the process of overcoming it. Only as we continue along the road which we have started together will the obscurity disappear and answers be found to still-open questions. We are sure to find in our churches many partners who will accompany us on this road with additions and corrections, encouragement and reassurance.

We hope to find also in other churches people who accompany us on this road. It could be that our reflections will help them, just as we have received and continue to expect valuable impulses from them. Even as our efforts have their presuppositions in specific Catholic–Lutheran realities and have their goal in Catholic-Lutheran church fellowship, still we must not lose sight of the task and the aim of wider Christian unity. It is our deep conviction that each individual step towards unity must be understood as a step taken towards the unity of all churches. This unity remains always "a blessing of the triune God, a work which he accomplishes, by means he chooses, in ways he determines".[174] Consciousness of that has been strengthened and deepened in us in the course of efforts to describe our common path. Seen in this way, all our reflections are a prayer to the Lord who knows ways which surpass our vision and are beyond our power.

NOTES

[1] "Ways to Community", Roman Catholic-Lutheran Joint Commission, Geneva, 1981, especially nos. 4–52.
[2] *The New Delhi Report*, London, 1962, report of section III, no. 2, p.116.
[3] *Vatican II*, LG, no. 26.
[4] *Ibid.*, no. 23; cf. CIC, can. 368f.
[5] *LG*, no. 23.
[6] J. Willebrands, "The Future of Ecumenism", in *One in Christ*, 4, p.323.
[7] Cf. W. Elert, *Abendmahl und Kirchengemeinschaft in alten Kirche hauptsächlich des Ostens,* Berlin, 1954; *Koinonia – Arbeilen des Ökumenischen Ausschusses der Vereiniglen Evangelisch-Lutherischen Kirche Deutschlands zur Frage der Kirchen- und Abendmahlsgemeinschaft*, Berlin, 1957.
[8] *UR*, no. 8.
[9] "Concepts of Unity and Models of Union", a preliminary study document of the Faith and Order commission, Oct. 1972, FO/72:20, IIId and IVb.
[10] *Breaking Barriers: Nairobi, 1975*, London/Grand Rapids, 1976, report of section II, pp.65 and 63, nos 14 and 10.
[11] *The Second World Conference on Faith and Order, Edinburgh, 1937*, London, 1937, pp.252f.
[12] H. Tenhumberg, "Kirchliche Union bzw. korporative Wiedervereinigung", in *Kirche und Gemeinde*, ed. W. Danielsmeyer and C.H. Ratschow, Witten, 1974, pp.24f.
[13] J. Ratzinger, *Theologische Prinzipienlehre: Bausteine zur Fundamentaltheologie*, Munich, 1981, p.121.
[14] J. Ratzinger, "Die Kirche und die Kirchen", in *Reformatio*, 1964, p.105.
[15] *The Final Report of the Anglican-Roman Catholic International Commission*, 1981, conclusion in *GA*, p.116.
[16] AAS, 1977, no. 5, p.284.
[17] Leuenberg agreement, nos. 29-33.
[18] *Ibid.*, no. 37.
[19] *Ibid.*, nos. 29 and 30.
[20] *Ibid.*, no. 29
[21] *Ibid.*, no. 37.
[22] Nairobi, *op. cit.*, p.60, no. 4.
[23] *Ibid.*
[24] *Ibid.*, no. 3; cf. definition of "local church", "The Unity of the Church – Next Steps", in *What Kind of Unity?*, Faith and Order Paper no. 69, WCC, Geneva, 1974, p.123.
[25] Nairobi, *op. cit.*, p.60, no. 3.
[26] "The Unity of the Church – Next Steps", op. cit., A.III.3, p.122.

[27] Nairobi, op. cit., p.60, no. 4.
[28] *Ibid.*, p.61, no. 7.
[29] "The Unity of the Church – Next Steps", *op. cit.*, A.IV, pp.123ff.
[30] Accra Report, "The Unity of the Church: The Goal and the Way", in *Uniting in Hope: Accra, 1974*, Faith and Order Paper No. 72, p.114.
[31] *Sharing in One Hope*, commission on Faith and Order, Bangalore, 1978, Faith and Order Paper no. 92, Geneva, pp.235-42.
[32] For example, at the first forum on bilateral conversations (April 1978) or at the consultation between the World Council of Churches and the world confessional families (Geneva, Oct. 1978); see *LWF Report*, no. 15, June 1983, Gunther Gassmann/Harding Meyer, "The Unity of the Church – Requirements and Structure", pp.33-39,50-54.
[33] "The Ecumenical Role of the World Confessional Families in the One Ecumenical Movement", discussion paper from two consultations with representatives from world confessional families (Geneva, 1974), nos. 17-21, *LWF Report*, no. 15, June 1983, pp.27f.
[34] *Ibid.*, no. 30, p.31.
[35] *In Christ – A New Community*, proceedings of the sixth assembly of the Lutheran World Federation, Dar-es-Salaam, 1977; Geneva, 1977, Statement on Models of Unity, p.174.
[36] *Ibid.*, p.174; cf. "Ecumenical Relations of the Lutheran World Federation", report of the working group on the inter-relations between the various bilateral dialogues, Geneva, 1977, no. 154.
[37] *In Christ – A New Community*, *op. cit.*, p.174.
[38] See above, no. 30; cf. G. Gassmann/H. Meyer; "The Unity of the Church", *op. cit.*, pp.15ff.
[39] *Tomos Agapis. Dokumentation zum Dialog der Liebe zwischen dem Hl. Stuhl und dem Ökumenischen Patriarchat 1958-1976*, edited on behalf of the Stiftungsfonds Pro Oriente, Vienna (Innsbruck/Vienna/Munich, 1978), passim.
[40] *OE*, no. 2.
[41] *Ibid.*, no. 3
[42] *Ibid.*, no. 4.
[43] Cf. *ibid.*, no. 30.
[44] Jan Cardinal Willebrands, in an address given to representatives of the Anglican Communion in Cambridge, England, January 1970; text published in *Documents on Anglican-Roman Catholic Relations*, Washington, 1972, pp.39ff.
[45] *UR*, no. 14.
[46] Message of Pope Paul VI to Patriarch Athenagoras I on July 25 1967, *Information Service*, Secretariat for Promoting Christian Unity, 1967/3, pp.12f.; AAS 59, 1967, pp.852-54.
[47] The two concepts must be distinguished from each other. Each of them has a distinct meaning and conceptual history. Cf. in the vast literature, for example: A. Grillmeier, "Konzil und Rezeption. Methodische Bemerkungen zu einem Thema der ökumenischen Diskussion der Gegenwart", *Theologie und Philosophie*, 45, 1970, pp.321-52; Y. Congar, "La 'reception' comme réalité ecclésiologique", *Revue des sciences philosophiques et théologiques*, 56, 1972, pp.369-403; G. Gassmann, "Rezeption im ökumenischen Kontext", *Ökumenische Rundschau*, 76, 1977, pp.314-27; H. Meyer, "'Anerkennung'- Ein ökumenischer Schlüsselbegriff", Dialog und Anerkennung. Beiheft zur *Ökumenischen Rundschau*, no. 37 (Frankfurt, 1978), pp.25-41; M. Garijo, "Der Begriff der 'Rezeption' und sein Ort im Kern der katholischen Ekkiesiologie", *Theologischer Konsens und Kirchenspaltung*, P. Lengsfeld and H.G. Stobbe, eds, Stuttgart, 1981, pp. 97-109, and Anmerkungen, pp.167-72; E. Lanne, "La 'réception,'" *Irénikon*, vol. LV, 1982, pp.199-213.

The term "reception" is often used with regard to accepting specific statements or documents, but here we intend both terms, "reception" and "recognition", to be designations of interchurch relations and actions: "Recognition" means basically a theological and spiritual affirmation of the other church in its special emphases, which confers on this church – as a whole or in individual elements of its belief, life or structure – legitimacy and authenticity. "Reception" means basically a theological and spiritual affirmation of the other church – as a whole or in individual elements of its belief, life, or structure – which accepts and appropriates the special emphases of the other church either as its own or as contributions (in the sense of correction or complement).

Therefore "recognition" and "reception" each involve a specific emphasis: "Recognition" stresses more strongly the special character of the other in its independence, an independence capable of fellowship. "Reception" emphasizes more strongly the special character of the other as containing elements to be adopted and integrated into a church's own life and thinking and into its fellowship with the other church. "Recognition" and "reception" must go hand in hand and complement each other in efforts for church fellowship. There can be no "reception" without recognition of the legitimacy and authenticity of the other. "Recognition" calls for beginning the process of accepting and adopting the particular features of the other in as much as they represent a contribution to the life and thinking of the partner and are considered as necessary for realizing the fellowship.

[48] Pope John Paul II in Germany, *Information Service*, Secretariat for Promoting Christian Unity, no. 45, 1981/I, cf. p.7.

[49] Pope John Paul II's Letter on Fifth Centenary of Birth of Martin Luther to Cardinal Willebrands, President of the Secretariat for Promoting Christian Unity, *Information Service*, op. cit., no. 52, 1983/III, p.83.

[50] Pope John Paul II in Germany, *Information Service*, op. cit., no. 45, 1981/I, p.6.; cf. Pastoral Letter of German Bishops, "Thy Kingdom Come" (20 Jan. 1980), *KNA-Dokumentation*, no. 5, 23 Jan. 1980; and *Lutheran–Roman Catholic Discussion on the Augsburg Confession*, Documents 1977-1981, ed. Harding Meyer, LWF Report, no. 10, Aug. 1980, pp.55,64.

[51] *Sent into the World*, proceedings of the fifth assembly of the Lutheran World Federation, Evian, 1970; Minneapolis, 1971, pp.156f.

[52] Cf. the recommendations regarding eucharistic hospitality by the Church of the Augsburg Confession of Alsace and Lorraine, Dec. 1973, *Lutheran World*, 22, 1975, pp.152ff., and the "Pastoraltheologische Handreichung der Vereinigten Evangelisch-Lutherischen Kirche Deutschlands" regarding the question of the participation of Lutheran Christians in the celebration of the eucharist by other confessions, 1975. Cf. also *A Statement on Communion Practices*, ALC/LCA, 1978, p.7, "Intercommunion".

[53] The affirmations that the church of Christ "subsists in the Catholic Church" (*LG*, no. 8) and that the Spirit of Christ has not refrained from using "these separated churches and communities... as means of salvation" (*UR*, no. 3) show that the Catholic church does not identify the church of God with its own visible boundaries. This constitutes a considerable change in attitude. It indicates a recognition that "some, even very many, of the most significant elements or endowments which together go to build up and give life to the church herself can exist outside the visible boundaries of the Catholic church" (*ibid.*) and an awareness "that whatever is wrought by the grace of the Holy Spirit in the hearts of our separated brethren can contribute to our own edification" (*ibid.*, no. 4).

[54] *Ibid.*, UR, no. 11.

[55] Cf. "The Gospel and the Church", Malta report, no. 25.

[56] UR, no. 6; cf. also LG, no. 8.

[57] *Ibid.*, UR, no. 11; cf. Malta report, nos. 24f.

[58] Cf. BC, pp.17ff.

[59] "All Under One Christ", no. 13; cf. Lutherans and Catholics in Dialogue 1, "The Status of the Nicene Creed as Dogma of the Church", Washington DC, 1965; and "Erklarung zur 1600-Jahr-Feier des Glaubensbekenntnisses von Nizäa-Konstantinopel" of the joint commission of representatives from the Evangelical Church in Germany and the Catholic church, *KNA Dokumentation*, no. 16, 3 June 1981.

[60] Malta report, no. 17.

[61] *Ibid.*, no. 26.

[62] "All Under One Christ", no. 14.

[63] Cf. "The Eucharist", nos. 1-45 and 76; cf. also "The Liturgical Celebration of the Eucharist", *ibid.*, pp.29ff.

[64] "All Under One Christ", no. 16.

[65] Malta report, nos. 48 and 21.

[66] "The Ministry in the Church", no. 20.

[67] "All Under One Christ", no. 18; cf. The Ministry in the Church, no. 17.

[68] *Ibid.*, no. 31.

[69] *Ibid.*, nos. 14 and 23.

[70] See footnote 50 above.

[71] "Lutheran-Roman Catholic Discussion on the Augsburg Confession Documents 1977-1981", op. cit., p.76.

[72] "The Ministry in the Church", no. 51.

[73] *Ibid.*, no. 52.

[74] *Ibid.*, no. 53.

[75] Cf. *Ibid.*, no. 55.

[76] *Ibid.*, no. 57.

[77] Cf. *ibid.*, nos. 52 and 54.

[78] Already during the first world conference on Faith and Order it was said that "unity... does not mean uniformity". *Reports of the World Conference on Faith and Order*, Lausanne, Aug. 1927; Boston, 1928, report on Subject VII, p.20.

[79] AC, VII, BC, p.32; cf. Luther's comment to the confession of the Bohemian Brethren, WA 50, p.380; *Confessio Helvetica Posterior*, XVII; 39 Articles, Art. 19.

[80] *UR*, no. 4; cf. LG, no. 23.

[81] *Information Service*, Secretariat for Promoting Christian Unity, 1967/3, p.10. Similarly it is reported in the message of the holy father to the ecumenical patriarch that "it is a matter of knowing and of respecting each other in the legitimate diversity of liturgical, spiritual disciplinary and theological traditions (cf. *UR*, nos. 14 and 17) by means of a frank theological dialogue, made possible by the re-establishment of brotherly charity in order to attain accord in the sincere confession of all revealed truths. In order to restore and preserve communion and unity, care must indeed be taken to 'impose no burden beyond what is indispensable' (Acts 15:28; *UR*, no. 18)."

[82] *Information Service*, Secretariat for Promoting Christian Unity, no. 22, Oct. 1973/IV, p.7.

[83] Statement on "Models of Unity", *In Christ – A New Community, op. cit.*

[84] Gemeinsame Synode der Bistümer der BRD, 1974, no. 4.33. The assembly of the Lutheran World Federation (1977) spoke in this connection of "a way of living encounter, spiritual experience together, theological dialogue and mutual correction, a way on which the distinctiveness of each partner is not lost sight of but brings out, is transformed and renewed, and in this way becomes visible and palpable to the other partners as a legitimate form of Christian existence and of the one Christian faith." *In Christ – A New Community*, p.174. Cf. no. 33 above.

[85] "The Eucharist", no. 51; cf. nos. 48-51 and 16.

[86] "The Ministry in the Church", no. 33; cf. nos. 32 and 39.

[87] Cf. Tridentinum, Sess. XXIV, canon 7; DS 1807 and note 1.

[88] Cf. no. 51 above; cf. "All Under One Christ", particularly nos. 14f.

[89] With a view to Eastern Orthodox churches, Joseph Cardinal Ratzinger says regarding the doctrine of primacy: "Rome does not have to require of the East more regarding the primacy doctrine than was formulated and practised during the first thousand years." Basically it can be said "that what was possible for a thousand years, cannot be impossible for Christians today" ("Die Frage der Wiedervereinigung zwischen Ost und West", *Theologische Prinzipienlehre, op. cit.*, 209).

[90] CA XVIII, Ed. 1531, DC, p.40.

[91] Cf. DS, 1551-1553.

[92] DS, 1569.

[93] DS, 1573.

[94] Cf. CA XX, 1f., BC, p.41; CA XII, 7; BC, p.35; SA, Part III, III, 42-45, BC, pp.309f.

[95] CA XIII, Ed. 1531, BC, p.36; Apol IV, 63; BC, p.115.

[96] Cf. "The Eucharist", no. 61, pp.69-75.

[97] DS, 1651.

[98] Cf. CA V, 2, VIII, 2; XIII BC, pp.31,33,35f. "The Eucharist", pp.70-73.

[99] SA, Part II, II, BC, pp.293ff.

[100] Cf. "The Eucharist", nos. 56-61.

[101] DS, 1651.

[102] Cf. DS, 1652.

[103] Cf. "The Eucharist", nos. 14-17,50-51.

[104] Cf. "Ways to Community", nos. 14ff.

[105] Cf. Apol XII, 5; BC, pp.211f.; DV, no. 2; PO, nos. 2 and 4; SC, no. 7.

[106] Cf. SC, no. 35; on the Lutheran side the reception of the sentence of St Augustine: *Accedat verbum ad elementum et fit sacramentum* ("when the word is added to the element or the natural substance, it becomes a sacrament"), for example in the Large Catechism IV, 18, BC, p.438, and in the Smalcald Articles, Part III, V, 1, BC, p.310.

[107] SC, nos. 24, 35, 51, 52; "The Eucharist", nos. 7 and 61.

[108] LG, no. 15, UR, no. 22.

[109] *Ibid.*, AG, no. 9, PO, no. 5.

[110] *Ibid.*, LG, no. 48, cf. 1 and 9.

[111] *Ibid.*, SC, no. 26. In this respect present-day theology can speak of the church as the "primordial sacrament" and of Christ as the "proto-sacrament" in whom and through whom the church is the universal sacrament of salvation (LG, nos. 1 and 48).

[112] CA XXIV, 1 and 4; BC, p.56.

[113] WA 6, 86; WA 6, 501, LW, vol. 36, p.18; cf. Melanchthon's *Loci communes theologici*, Library of Christian Classics, Melanchthon and Bucer, London, 1969, vol. XIX, p.135.

[114] WA 9, 440-442.

[115] Cf. for example "The Eucharist", nos. 38-41.

[116] Cf. LG, no. 15, UR, nos. 3, 4 and 22.

[117] *Baptism, Eucharist and Ministry*, Faith and Order Paper No. 111, Geneva, 1982, Baptism, 1,1.

[118] Cf. "The Eucharist", and the document of the Catholic–Lutheran dialogue in the USA: "The Eucharist: A Lutheran-Roman Catholic Statement", *Lutherans and Catholics in Dialogue, III, "The Eucharist as Sacrifice"*, Washington/New York, 1967.

119 Cf. "The Eucharist", nos. 75 and 76; "The Liturgical Celebration of the Eucharist", *ibid.*, pp.29ff.
120 "The Ministry in the Church", no. 33; cf. no. 32; also Malta report, no. 59; and the document of the Catholic–Lutheran dialogue in the USA: "Eucharist and Ministry: A Lutheran–Roman Catholic Statement", *Lutherans and Catholics in Dialogue*, IV, Washington/New York, 1970, no. 16.
121 "The Ministry in the Church", no. 33.
122 Apol. XIII, no. 4; BC, p.211.
123 H. Fagerberg/H. Jorissen, "Busse und Beichte", *Confessio Augustana – Bekenntnis des einen Glaubens*, eds H. Meyer and H. Schütte, Paderborn/Frankfurt, 1980, pp.228ff.
124 "Theology of Marriage and the Problems of Mixed Marriages", Geneva, 1977, nos. 16-21 and 29.
125 *BEM*, op. cit., Baptism, 14.
126 *Occasional Services*, a companion to Lutheran book of worship, Minneapolis/Philadelphia, 1982, "Service of the Word for Healing", pp.89-102.
127 Baptism and eucharist as "chief basic sacraments", "Ways to Community", no. IX; cf. Tridentinum, DS, 1603; LG, no. 7, and the concept of *potissima sacramenta* of Thomas Aquinas (S.Th. III q. 62, a. 5) or the *sacramenta majora*.
128 Cf. LG, nos. 1, 9,48; SC, no. 26.
129 This theological principle describes the relationship among the local churches in New Testament times and also the relationship of the local churches within the Catholic church according to the understanding of Vatican II: "This church of Christ is truly present in all legitimate local congregations of the faithful, which, united with their pastors, are themselves called churches" (LG, no. 26). "In and from such individual churches there comes into being the one and only Catholic church" (*ibid.*, no. 23; cf. CD, no. 11). The application of this principle to the Catholic church and the Lutheran churches must be regarded as legitimate from the moment – but only from the moment – they have found their way back to community in faith and sacramental life universally or locally.
130 LG, no. 13 interprets the words (1 Pet. 4:10): "As each has received a gift, employ it for one another as good stewards of God's varied grace" pneumatologically and applies them to the local churches. In the spirit of this theological principle, the Dogmatic Constitution on the Church, no. 13, adds that in the people of God "each individual part of the church contributes through its special gifts to the good of the other parts and of the whole church. Thus through the common sharing of gifts and through the common effort to attain fullness in unity, the whole and each of the parts receive increase." Such a theological principle can be applied to the relationship between the Catholic church and the Lutheran churches. Re-established unity in faith and in the sacraments enables them jointly to share in the dynamic which the Dogmatic Constitution on the Church, no. 13, describes as follows: "Moreover, within the church particular churches hold a rightful place. These churches retain their own traditions without in any way lessening the primacy of the chair of Peter. This chair presides over the whole assembly of charity and protects legitimate differences, while at the same time it sees that such differences do not hinder unity but rather contribute towards it. Finally, between all the parts of the church there remains a bond of close communion with respect to spiritual riches, apostolic workers, and temporal resources."
131 Cf. "The Ministry in the Church", no. 85.
132 *Ibid.*, nos. 42, 43 and 44.
133 UR, no. 22.
134 The "Ministry in the Church", no. 79.
135 *Ibid.*, nos. 75, 78.
136 *Ibid.*, no. 82.
137 *Ibid.*, no. 20.
138 *Ibid.*, no. 23.
139 *Ibid.*, no. 17.
140 *Ibid.*, no. 30.
141 *Ibid.*, no. 45.
142 *Ibid.*, no. 43.
143 *Ibid.*, no. 80.
144 Cf. *ibid.*, nos. 43 and 66.
145 Cyprian said: "The episcopate is one, each part of which is held by each one for the whole", "The Treatises of Cyprian", 1, 5, *The Writings of the Ante-Nicene Fathers*, vol. 5, Grand Rapids, 1965, p.423.
146 With respect to Catholic ecclesiology these terms have to be understood as follows:
- They do not mean that the pope became the bishop of the Catholic church as a result of the First Vatican Council. The signature of Paul VI under the documents of Vatican II identifies him as the bishop of the Catholic church in Rome (cf. H. Marot, "Note sur l'expression 'episcolus ecclesiae catholicae'", Irénikon, 37, 1964, pp.221-26; again mentioned in Y. Congar ed., "La collégialité épiscopale. Histoire et théologie", *Unam Sanctam*, 37, Paris, 1965, pp.94-98.

- Nor do they mean that the pope can take the place of the local bishops daily and permanently because, like the primacy, the episcopate exists by "the same divine institution" (cf. the collective declaration of the German episcopate regarding the circular letter of the German chancellor concerning the future election of the pope, DS, 3112-3116, and the letter of approval by Pius IX).
- Finally they do not mean that there is no distinction between his commission as primate of the Catholic church and his task as patriarch of the West. Thus, for example, the code *Juris Canonici* promulgated in 1983 is valid only for the Latin church. The bilateral dialogue between the Catholic church and the Orthodox churches will probably induce the holy see to determine which of its present functions belong to the primacy and which to the Patriarchate of the West.

And yet these expressions confirm the fact that the Catholic bishops always exercise their ministries in fellowship with the bishop of Rome and that the pope, in turn, exercises his ministry of unity and leadership within the college of bishops and the community of the churches thanks to the universal jurisdictional authority that is associated with his commission. This authority is defined as "ordinary" not in the sense of "daily" but in the sense of "not delegated", because it is part of his commission. The point of the primacy is not the day-to-day government of the church but to serve its unity.

[147] LG, nos. 21f.

[148] Apol. XIV, 1; BC, p.214; SA, Part III, X; BC, p.314; FC SD, X, 19; BC, p.614; cf. "The Ministry in the Church", no. 42.

[149] CA XXVIII, 28; BC, p.85; SA, Part II, IV; BC, pp.298ff.; Treatise on the Power and Primacy of the Pope, 13-15, 62f., 70f., BC, pp.322,330f.,331f.

[150] That all may be "praying in their heart for the descent of the Spirit", *The Apostolic Tradition of Hippolytus*, Archon Books, Ann Arbor, Michigan, 1962, no. 2, p.33.

[151] "Pneuma hegemonikon", *ibid.*, no. 3, pp.34f.

[152] Cf. Augustine: *Pro vobis episcopus, vobiscum christianus* (PL, nos. 38, 1483).

[153] Cf. the continuation of the quotation of Augustine: *Illud est nomen suscepti officii, illud gratiae* (PL, nos. 38, 1483).

[154] The canons do not permit a bishop to ordain his successor (cf. canon 75 of the so-called Apostolic Canons, Bruns 1, 11; Synod of Antioch, 341, canon 23, Bruns 1, 86; Synod of Caesarea, 393, see E.W. Brooks, *The Sixth Book of the Letters of Severus Patriarch of Antioch*, London, Oxford, 1903, vol. 11, pp.223-24; Roman Synod, 465, canon 5, Bruns 11, pp.283-84). See also the statement made by Augustine who found himself in an embarrassing situation, since his bishop Valerian had asked him to be not "his successor, but... be associated with him as coadjutor", and he had been ordained by Megalius, primate of Numidia. Augustine excuses Valerian on the grounds that canon 8 of Nicea, which does not allow the coexistence of two Catholic bishops in the same town, was not known in Hippo *(The Fathers of the Church: Early Christian Biographies*, Washington DC, 1952, "The Life of St Augustine by Bishop Possidius", ch. 8, p.82; PL, nos. 32,39-40).

[155] Cf. "The Ministry in the Church", no. 62.

[156] Episcopal lists are lists of those who preside over a church (cf. L. Koep, *Bischofslisten*, RAC 2, pp.410-15). This connection between succession and tradition within a church has always been stressed jointly by Catholics and Orthodox (cf. the second session of the joint international commission for theological dialogue between the Roman Catholic Church and the Orthodox church, Munich, 1982: "The minister is also the one who 'receives' from his church, which is faithful to tradition, the word he transmits" *(Information Service*, op. cit., no. 49, 1982, 11/III, p.110).

[157] Augustine, *De unitate ecclesiae* II, 28; PL, no. 43, 410-11. Cf. also Thomas Aquinas, *De veritate quaestia*, q. 14, a. 10 ad 11: "And we believe the successors of the apostles and the prophets only in so far as they tell us those things which the apostles and prophets have left in their writings" (Truth, Chicago, 1952/4, vol. 2, p.258).

[158] Vatican II says: "Each individual bishop represents his own church, but all of them together in union with the pope represent the entire church" (LG, no. 23).

[159] Approaches in this direction can be found in P.E. Persson, *Kyrkans ämbete som Kristusrepresentation*, Lund, 1961 (shortened German version *Representatio Christi. Der Amtsbegriff in der neueren römisch-katholischen Theologie*, Göttingen, 1966), and in L.M. Dewailly, "La personne du ministre et l'objet du ministère" (about Persson's book), RSPhTh 46, 1962, pp.650-57.

[160] Note how Cyprian wanted to exercise his authority together with the Christians of his community, priests and deacons, and the college of bishops, i.e., in a synodal and collegial manner: "From the beginning of my episcopate, I decided to do nothing of my own opinion privately without your advice and the consent of the people" (St Cyprian, *Letters 1-81*, Washington DC, 1964, Letter 14,4, p.43). "I think that I alone ought not to give a decision in this matter... since this examination of each one must be discussed and investigated more fully not only with my colleagues, but with the whole people themselves" (*ibid.*, Letter 34,4, p.89; cf. Letter 19,2, pp.52f.). Regarding the relationship between the bishop and his congrega-

tion in a number of large episcopal sees in the time of the early church, see L. Scipioni, *Vescovo e popolo*, Milano, Vita e Pensiero, 1977; regarding the middle ages, see Y. Congar, "Quod omnes tangit ab omnibus tractari ac approbari debet", *RHDFE* 4e série, 36, 1958, pp.210-59, reprinted in *Droit ancien et structures ecclésiales*, Variorum Reprints, London, 1982.

[161] Their ministry can be exercised in a personal manner, which is shown very clearly in the letters of St Paul. Behind the statements and instructions of Paul lie the grace and function given to him personally (cf. the expression "by the grace given to me" in Rom. 12:3 and 15:15; 1 Cor. 3:10; Gal. 2:9; see also Col. 1:25; Eph. 3:2,7f., and from the greetings Rom. 1:1; 1 Cor. 1:1; 2 Cor. 1:1; Gal. 1:1 [cf. also Col. 1:1; Eph. 1:1] regarding the topic, cf. Gal 1). Paul also needs the koinonia of the other apostles if his preaching is to be not in vain (cf. Gal 2:1-10, especially verse 9; 1 Cor. 15:7f.).

This collegiality of the (twelve) apostles appears particularly in the Acts of the Apostles which speaks stereotypically of "the apostles" (in plural – 26 times) and where they are often presented as a body acting homogeneously (cf. Acts 2:42f.; 4:33,35,36f.; 5:12; 6:6; 8:14, 18; 11:1. Occasionally Peter appears as protagonist of the apostles: cf. Acts 2:14,37; 5:2f.,29). It is noteworthy that the exercise of authority by the apostles by no means excludes the cooperation of the presbyters and the congregation, but proceeds in "concerted action", as is expressly the case at the election of the "seven" (Acts 6:2-6) and is shown even more clearly in connection with the so-called council of apostles (cf. Acts 15:2,4,22f.; 16:4). Note also the justification of Peter before "the apostles and the brethren who were in Judea" (Acts 11:1-18). This koinonia with the congregation in the exercise of the ministry is less directly expressed but is substantially present in a more nuanced way in the letters of Paul. These letters give evidence of great respect for the responsibility of the congregation in spite of their stress on the authority of the apostle. Paul (usually) does not decree, but argues (indicative – imperative!) and thus takes the congregation at their word regarding their own Christian freedom. It is striking that apart from specific questions of faith, Paul hardly ever gives his own instructions regarding the concrete ordering of the practical life of the congregation, but only intervenes when the praxis of the congregation errs. That in this respect Paul understands his authority as subsidiary to the authority of the congregation is expressed clearly in 1 Cor. 5 and 6:1-12, where he does not appeal to the "offenders", but to the congregation which should really have acted on its own.

[162] The BEM statement on the Ministry (1982) notes: "The ordained ministry should be exercised in a personal, collegial and communal way" (no. 26). This is developed by stressing the complementarity of these three aspects, and it is added: "An appreciation of these three dimensions lies behind a recommendation made by the first world conference on Faith and Order at Lausanne in 1927: 'In view of (i) the place which the episcopate, the council of presbyters and the congregation of the faithful, respectively, had in the constitution of the early church, and (ii) the fact that episcopal, presbyteral and congregational systems of government are each today, and have been for centuries, accepted by great communions of Christendom, and (iii) the fact that episcopal, presbyteral and congregational systems are each believed by many to be essential to the good order of the church, we therefore recognize that these several elements must all, under conditions which require further study, have an appropriate place in the order of life of a reunited church...'" (Commentary, no. 26).

[163] Cf. remarks on "recognition" and "reception" as "inter-related aims" (§49 above and note 47).

[164] "The Ministry in the Church", nos. 74-86; esp. nos. 83-85.

[165] Cf. particularly CIC, can. 844, §§1-3, pp.156f.

"1. Catholic ministers may lawfully administer the sacraments only to catholic members of Christ's faithful, who equally may lawfully receive them only from catholic ministers, except as provided in paras. 2, 3 and 4 of this canon and in can. 861, para. 2.

"2. Whenever necessity requires or a genuine spiritual advantage commends it, and provided the danger of error or indifferentism is avoided, Christ's faithful for whom it is physically or morally impossible to approach a catholic minister, may lawfully receive the sacraments of penance, the eucharist and anointing of the sick from non-catholic ministers in whose churches these sacraments are valid.

"3. Catholic ministers may lawfully administer the sacraments of penance, the eucharist and anointing of the sick to members of the eastern churches not in full communion with the catholic church, if they spontaneously ask for them and are properly disposed. The same applies to members of other churches which the apostolic see judges to be in the same position as the aforesaid eastern churches so far as the sacraments are concerned."

[166] In connection with such a situation Pierre Duprey writes: "It is possible that what the council of Chalcedon and tradition as a whole regarded as essential, that is that there should be one bishop in a single place, may be impossible to realize, at least in the first stage, a stage which may be very long. But... it is of capital importance to achieve the unity of *episcope*: if it cannot be personal, it can be collegial" (*Midstream*, vol. XVII, no. 4, Oct. 1978, p.384).

[167] Some Lutheran churches, for example in Sweden and Finland, have an episcopal primate by established custom and consider this order as helpful. A resident bishop acting in concert with suffragans is a manner of exercising *episcope* often encountered in the Catholic church.
[168] Nicea, c. 8 (COD, 9); Constantinople 1, c. 2 (COD, 27-28); Lateran IV, c. 9 (COD, 215).
[169] Hippolytus, *op. cit.*, no. 2, p.33.
[170] Cf. "The Ministry in the Church", nos. 29, 43-44.
[171] Hesitations expressed in the BEM statement on the Ministry lose their point: churches that are willing "to accept episcopal succession as a sign of the apostolicity of the life of the whole church... yet... cannot accept any suggestion that the ministry exercised in their own tradition should be invalid until the moment that it enters into an existing line of episcopal succession" (no. 38).
[172] Cf. the statement concerning the attitude of the LWF to churches in union negotiations, *Sent into the World, op. cit.*, pp.142f.
[173] Compare, for example, the situation that has been created by the establishment of church fellowship between Lutheran, United and Reformed churches in Europe – Leuenberg agreement, 1973.
[174] "Ways to Community", no. 8.

XXI. LUTHERAN-ROMAN CATHOLIC DIALOGUE

43. Church and Justification

Wurzburg, Germany, 11 September 1993

Foreword

Visible unity has always been and continues to be the ultimate goal of the international dialogue between the Roman Catholic Church and the Lutheran communion. In 1992 this dialogue, sponsored by the Lutheran World Federation and the Pontifical Council for Promoting Christian Unity, celebrated its twenty-fifth anniversary, having begun its work in Zurich in 1967, just after the close of the Second Vatican Council.

With this document the dialogue completes the third phase of its work, a phase which has addressed an issue at the heart of Lutheran-Roman Catholic relations: the role of the church in salvation. This theme grew organically out of the reports of the first two phases.

The Malta report, *The Gospel and the Church* (1972), marked the end of the initial phase of dialogue. It ascertained a "far-reaching consensus" in the doctrine of justification and demonstrated a convergence of views in the area of scripture and Tradition. The Malta report became the foundation for further dialogue, establishing its direction and demonstrating its feasibility. The breadth of its scope led naturally to a series of documents in the second phase dealing with more particular dogmatic issues seen as church-dividing since the 16th-century Reformation.

Having before it not only the confessional documents of the Reformation era, but also the documents of Vatican II, and benefiting from the labours of theologians in biblical, liturgical, dogmatic and historical studies, the Lutheran-Roman Catholic Joint Commission was able, in its second phase, to transmit to the churches common documents on *The Eucharist* (1978) and *The Ministry in the Church* (1981). It also produced statements marking two Reformation anniversaries: *All Under One Christ* was a common statement on the *Confessio Augustana* in observance of the 450th anniversary of its presentation in 1530, and "Martin Luther – Witness to Jesus Christ" was issued in 1983, the 500th anniversary of the Reformer's birth. Both documents and the many other articles and addresses that these anniversaries also occasioned are important contributions towards the goal of Catholic-Lutheran unity.

Two further documents from the second phase of dialogue addressed themselves to how visible unity might be realized in concrete ways: *Ways to Community* (1980) and *Facing Unity – Models, Forms, and Phases of Catholic-Lutheran Church Fellowship* (1984).

When in 1985 the question of how to proceed to a third phase was addressed, a joint memorandum began with this judgment:

The dialogue has brought us to a point from which it is no longer possible to go back. Thus the question about the actualization of Catholic-Lutheran church fellowship should be the framework for the further dialogue....

A statement from the seventh assembly of the Lutheran World Federation (1984) was then quoted with approval:

In the third phase of the continuing theological dialogue, the themes must be so formulated that the implications for church fellowship of the consensus expressed or the convergence achieved are clearly sought.

After a reference to the doctrinal condemnations of the Reformation era, the joint memorandum concludes:

It can be observed that... Catholics and Lutherans keep coming back to the question about the understanding of the church, more precisely to the central question of the church and the nature of its instrumentality in the divine plan of salvation (church as sign and instrument; "sacramentality" of the church)... This question immediately raises again, especially for the Lutheran side, the question of the doctrine of justification. It is less a matter of the understanding of justification as such... rather it is a matter of the implications of the mutual relationship of justification and the church.

It was noted how this brings the discussion back to an issue present already in the first phase of dialogue. Almost two decades later, however, the new joint commission had to take account of how the issue of justification had surfaced again in its documents on eucharist and ministry and be aware of the growing intensity of a new debate as to whether a "fundamental difference" between Protestantism and Catholicism really exists.

The third phase of dialogue was instructed to deal with the question of the church in light of sacramentality and justification. It began its work in the spring of 1986, completing it in 1993. Plenary sessions were held annually. In most years there was a drafting meeting scheduled between plenary sessions.

Once the work had begun it was the responsibility of the joint commission to shape, clarify and determine its own course. Though the joint statement here presented clearly follows the original mandate in the joint memorandum of 1985, two developments should be noted which may assist the reader in understanding our work. First, because of the developments between 1972 (Malta report) and 1986, the joint commission found itself compelled to test the claim of a "far-reaching consensus" on justification. In so doing they relied heavily on the comprehensive American dialogue statement, *Justification by Faith* (1985), and on the justification chapter of *The Condemnations of the Reformation Era – Do They Still Divide?* (1986).

Second, as work progressed on what has become *Church and Justification*, ecclesiological themes not originally part of the schema required attention. The scope of the project had to grow if the result was to be persuasive. Thus it has become the most extensive statement to be presented by the international dialogue to date.

In submitting its work the joint commission asks that this report be seen together with the documents from the second phase, *The Eucharist* and *The Ministry in the Church*, as well as *Ways to Community* and *Facing Unity*. It asks whether, taken together, these documents constitute the sufficient consensus which would enable our churches to embark upon concrete steps towards visible unity which have become more and more urgent.

Paul-Werner Scheele	James R. Crumley, Jr, Bishop (retired)
Bishop of Würzburg, Germany	Lutheran Church in America, USA
Co-chairman	*Co-chairman*

1. Justification and the Church

1. Catholics and Lutherans in common believe in the triune God who for Christ's sake justifies sinners by grace through faith and makes them members of the church in baptism. Thus faith and baptism link justification and the church; the justified sinner is incorporated into the community of the faithful, the church, and becomes a member of it. Justification and the church thus stand in a vital relationship and are fruits of the saving activity of God.

2. According to Lutheran tradition the justification of sinners is the article of faith by which the church stands or falls.[1] Thus Luther says in the exposition of Psalm 130:4, which for him is the epitome of the doctrine of justification: "For if this article stands, the church stands; if it falls, the church falls."[2] This is the background against which the Catholic-Lutheran dialogue has as its theme the relation between justification and the church. A consensus in the doctrine of justification – even if it is nuanced – must prove itself ecclesiologically. Everything that is believed and taught about the nature of the church, the means of salvation, and the church's ministry must be founded in the salvation-event itself and must be marked by justification-faith as the way in which the salvation-event is received and appropriated. Correspondingly, everything that is believed and taught about the nature and effect of justification must be understood in the overall context of statements about the church, the means of salvation, and the church's ministry. This is the necessary precondition by which all the life and activity of the church must constantly be checked, as was stressed in the USA dialogue, *Justification by Faith*. "Catholics as well as Lutherans can acknowledge the need to test the practices, structures and theologies of the church by the extent to which they help or hinder 'the proclamation of God's free and merciful promises in Christ Jesus which can be rightly received only through faith'."[3]

3. At the beginning of this dialogue document on the church in the light of justification-faith, it should be emphasized that justification and the church are truths of faith (1.1) because both are grounded in faith in Christ and the Trinity (1.2) and are an unmerited gift of grace which becomes at the same time a challenge in our world (1.3).

1.1. Justification and the church as truths of faith

4. Catholics and Lutherans together testify to the salvation that is bestowed only in Christ and by grace alone and is received in faith. They recite in common the creed, confessing "one holy catholic and apostolic church". Both the justification of sinners and the church are fundamental articles of faith. In faith in the triune God, we confess that this God justifies us by grace without our meriting it and gathers us together in his church. His mercy is and remains the source of our life. "Solely by grace and by faith in Christ's saving work and not because of any merit in us... we are accepted by God and receive the Holy Spirit who renews our hearts and equips us for and calls us to

good works."[4] It is by God's incomprehensible "glorious grace" that we have access through Christ in one Spirit to the Father, "are citizens with the saints and also members of the household of God", and "are built together spiritually into a dwelling place for God" (Eph. 2:18-22; cf. Eph. 1:5f.).

5. Strictly and properly speaking, we do not believe in justification and in the church but in the Father who has mercy on us and who gathers us in the church as his people; and in Christ who justifies us and whose body the church is; and in the Holy Spirit who sanctifies us and dwells in the church. Our faith encompasses justification and the church as works of the triune God which can be properly accepted only in faith in him. We believe in justification and the church as a *mysterium*, a mystery of faith, because we believe solely in God, to whom alone we may completely consign our lives in freedom and love and in whose word alone, which promises salvation, we can establish our whole life with complete trust. Consequently we can say in common that justification and the church both guide us into the mystery of the triune God and are therefore *mysterium*, the mystery of faith, hope and love.

1.2. Justification and the church founded in the mystery of Christ and of the Trinity

6. According to the witness of the New Testament, our salvation, the justification of sinners and the existence of the church are indissolubly linked with the triune God and are founded in him alone. This is attested in various but consistent ways. "God... proves his love for us in that while we still were sinners Christ died for us... Now that we have been justified by his blood, will we be saved through him from the wrath of God. For if while we were enemies, we were reconciled to God through the death of his Son, much more surely, having been reconciled, will we be saved by his life" (Rom. 5:8-10). "For God so loved the world that he gave his only Son, so that everyone who believes in him may not perish but may have eternal life" (John 3:16). "In this is love, not that we loved God but that he loved us and sent his Son to be the atoning sacrifice for our sins" (1 John 4:10). In short, God "first loved us" (1 John 4:19). Our salvation in the triune God is founded in the sending of the Son and of the Holy Spirit (cf. Gal. 4:4-6; John 14:16f.,26; 16:7-15).

7. Accordingly, the church has its foundation in the sacrifice of the Son and the sending of the Spirit. God "obtained" his church "with the blood of his own Son" (Acts 20:28). Christ has saved the church for it is his body (cf. Eph. 5:23). Christ "loved the church and gave himself up for her, in order to make her holy by cleansing her with the washing of water by the word" (Eph. 5:25f.). By virtue of the sending of the Holy Spirit the young church appears publicly on the day of Pentecost (cf. Acts 2). Especially in Paul's letters, the relation of the church to the triune God becomes clear, when he describes it as the pilgrim people of God the Father, as the body of Christ, the Son, and as the temple of the Holy Spirit.

1.3. Justification and the church as unmerited gift of grace and challenge

8. When Paul describes God's church in Corinth as "those who are sanctified in Christ Jesus, called to be saints" he shows by this that the church and its members live entirely by the unmerited gift of Christ's grace, for which he expressly gives thanks (1 Cor. 1:2-4). In the Letter to the Ephesians the unmerited gift of grace which constitutes both Christian existence and the church becomes an occasion for the praise of God's

majesty and grace (cf. Eph. 1:3-14). "For by grace you have been saved through faith, and this is not your own doing; it is the gift of God – not the result of works, so that no one may boast" (Eph. 2:8f.). The mystery of Christ and of the Trinity is the foundation for this unmerited gracious gift of justification and the church: "But when the goodness and loving kindness of God our Saviour appeared, he saved us, not because of any works of righteousness that we had done, but according to his mercy, through the water of rebirth and renewal by the Holy Spirit. This Spirit he poured out on us richly through Jesus Christ our Saviour, so that, having been justified by his grace, we might become heirs according to the hope of eternal life" (Titus 3:4-7). It corresponds to the graciousness of this gift that human beings contribute nothing but can only receive it in faith: "For by grace you have been saved through faith" (Eph. 2:8; cf. Rom. 3:28).

9. Lutherans and Catholics together acknowledge the biblical witness on justification and the church as an unmerited gift of grace; they see in this witness a tremendous challenge in our world. God "desires everyone to be saved and to come to the knowledge of the truth" (1 Tim. 2:4). The message of justification is an expression of God's universal saving will. It promises salvation and the right to life without regard to merit and worthiness. God accepts the sinful creature in pure mercy and thus cancels out the law of works and achievement as the basis for life. God thus opens up a way of life, which most profoundly contradicts that which prevails in the world: the life of love. This love arises out of faith and passes on the boundless mercy which it has received. It suffers from the distress and injustice that others experience and meets it with self-sacrifice and renunciation. And it urges the members of the church to promote justice, peace and the integrity of creation together with all people of good will, amid the glaring contrast between poor and rich, and in the conflicts between ideologies and interests, races, nations and sexes. Thus the church is both a contradiction and a challenge in our world – as the place where merciful justification is proclaimed, as the locus for community and love, as co-shaper of a more just and humane world.

2. The Abiding Origin of the Church

2.1. Jesus Christ as the only foundation of the church

10. "No one can lay any foundation other than the one that has been laid; that foundation is Jesus Christ" (1 Cor. 3:11). In all its trenchancy this statement is to be evaluated and heeded as the fundamental principle of ecclesiology. "The one and only foundation of the church is the saving work of God in Jesus Christ which has taken place once for all."[5] Everything that is to be said on the origin, nature and purpose of the church must be understood as an explanation of this principle. As an essential mark of the church, its unity – which since the very beginning of church history has existed only as a unity under threat, challenged by fragmentation (cf. 1 Cor. 1:10ff.) – is to be understood solely in the light of this principle.

11. "Jesus the Christ" or "Jesus is Lord" is the original form of the Christian confession of faith. The author of this confession, through which the church as community becomes heard in this world, is the Holy Spirit, in whose power Christ is known as the Lord (1 Cor. 12:3), and God the Father, who by his revelation gives us faith in the Messiah and Son (cf. Matt. 16:17). The church owes its origin "not to a single, isolated act by which it was established" but is "founded in the totality of the Christ-event... start-

ing from the election of the people of God of the Old Testament, in the work of Jesus, in his proclamation of the kingdom and in the gathering of the disciples through his call to conversion and discipleship,... in the institution of the Lord's supper, in the cross and resurrection of Christ, in the outpouring of the Holy Spirit and in the fact that this whole path is directed towards eschatological consummation in the parousia of the Lord".[6] In this comprehensive sense, the term "founding or institution of the church by Jesus Christ" is a meaningful explication of the ecclesiological principle in 1 Corinthians 3:11, which cannot be abandoned.

12. Jesus' whole work is determined and permeated by the mystery of the Trinity. It was always in obedience to the Father who sent him (cf. John 5:19); it was also filled with the authority and power of the Holy Spirit through whom Jesus had his existence (cf. Luke 1:35), who showed him to be the Son of God from his baptism onwards (cf. Luke 3:22), and who revealed him with power by resurrection from the dead (cf. Rom. 1:4). Thus the trinitarian confession was already included in the original form of the confession of Christ, as a doxology of the work of salvation which has taken place once for all.

2.2. The election of Israel as the abiding presupposition of the church

13. The church of the New Testament was always aware that the history of the people of God did not begin with itself. The God who raised Jesus from the dead is the same God who called Abraham to be the father of all who believe, who elected Israel from among all the nations to be his treasured possession, and who entered into an enduring covenant with it (cf. Rom. 9:6). In salvation-history the church thus presupposes the history of Israel (cf. Acts 13:16ff.; Heb. 1:1f.). "The church ever keeps in mind the words of the apostle about his kinsmen, 'who have the adoption as sons, and the glory and the covenant and the legislation and the worship and the promises; who have the fathers, and from whom is Christ according to the flesh' (Rom. 9:4-5), the son of the Virgin Mary."[7] The church must always remain conscious of the fact that "she received the revelation of the Old Testament through the people with whom God in his inexpressible mercy deigned to establish the ancient covenant. Nor can she forget that she draws sustenance from the root of that good olive tree onto which have been grafted the wild olive branches of the Gentiles (cf. Rom. 11:17-24)."[8]

2.2.1. GOD'S GRACE AS THE CONTINUUM OF ISRAEL'S HISTORY

14. God communicated to Israel the mystery of his name and assured them "I am the Lord your God" (Ex. 20:2). "You only have I known of all the families of the earth" (Amos 3:2; cf. Deut. 7:6). For that purpose God already called Abraham from his father's house and his homeland (cf. Gen. 12:1) into a path of obedient faith in him who called him (cf. Gen. 15:6; 17:1). Israel's faithfulness was not to be divided: "You must remain completely loyal to the Lord your God" (Deut. 18:13). Israel shall therefore not have any other gods but serve only the one and only true God (cf. Ex. 20:3-5). "Hear, O Israel: the Lord is our God, the Lord alone. You shall love the Lord your God with all your heart, and with all your soul, and with all your might" (Deut. 6:4f.). This was and is Israel's fundamental confession.

15. God's choice of Israel from among all the nations as his own people is not based on its merits or outstanding achievements. "It was not because you were more numerous than any other people that the Lord set his heart on you and chose you – for you

were the fewest of all peoples. It was because the Lord loved you... that the Lord has brought you out with a mighty hand" (Deut. 7:7f.). This love remains steadfast. Though Israel often broke its covenant faith with God, God remained open to its conversion. Where God might have rightly terminated the covenant or said to Israel, as to an adulterer, "You are not my people", he called them to himself with the loving words, "Children of the living God" (Hos. 1:10; cf. Rom. 9:25f.). Thus the miracle of the forgiveness of sins belongs to the gifts of God's love for his people (cf. Isa. 44:2). From the start God's covenant of faithfulness includes the forgiveness of sins. Many psalms testify to this, just as the prophets not only proclaim judgment but repeatedly testify also to grace and return. God's grace is the origin and foundation of the old and the new covenants and the basis for the expectation of eternal glory.

2.2.2. THE ELECTION OF ISRAEL FOR THE NATIONS

16. Although God's saving concern was repeatedly rejected and the covenant broken, God himself preserved the continuity of his gracious care by ever-renewed saving initiatives. And just as the covenant with Noah established a new start in humanity's history with God, so too the election of Israel from the beginning aimed at the inclusion of all nations in God's salvation history.

17. The blessing God promised Abraham is not limited to making his descendants a great nation but has its climax in the promise, "... in you all the families of the earth shall be blessed" (Gen. 12:3; cf. Gal. 3:8). The prophets see as the final act of salvation history the nations of the earth moving to Jerusalem like a star-shaped pilgrimage from every direction, to receive a common salvation in God's universal kingdom of peace (cf. Isa. 2:1-5; Micah 4:1-4). Zion as the centre of Israel is to become the centre of the messianic kingdom of peace for the whole world of nations, and a descendant of David, the great king of Israel, is to be the king of peace ruling over all the nations (cf. Isa. 9:5f.). As the chosen servant of God, he himself will bring the justice of God to the peoples of the whole earth (cf. Isa. 42:1-12; 49:6).

2.3. The foundation of the church in the Christ-event

18. "But when the fullness of time had come, God sent his Son, born of a woman, born under the law, in order to redeem those who were under the law, so that we might receive adoption as children. And because you are children, God has sent the Spirit of his Son into our hearts, crying, 'Abba! Father!'" (Gal. 4:4-6). Jesus' mother was a Jewish woman. As the Messiah of Israel, Jesus is descended from the family of David (cf. Luke 1:32f.; Rom. 1:3f.). The God whose rule Jesus proclaimed is the God of Abraham, Isaac and Jacob. It was to the people of Israel that Jesus directed this proclamation (cf. Matt. 15:24; 10:6). Jesus proclaimed God's love in an unheard-of radical way: "I have come to call not the righteous but sinners" (Mark 2:17). In line with this he taught love for this God whose kingly rule is consummated in mercy and the love of one's neighbour, including enemies (cf. Matt. 5:44). On these two fundamental commandments "hang" all the law and the prophets (Matt. 22:40; cf. Deut. 6:5; Lev. 19:18).

19. That Jesus as Son of God is the Messiah and that in him the eschatological rule of God has dawned is the unique saving event which effects a definitive salvation for all the nations, going beyond all the saving gifts in the history of his people. All the promises of the prophets are fulfilled in him: he is the light that illumines all darkness, the life that overcomes all the power of death, the righteousness that cancels out all sin.

According to the witness of the New Testament the "new covenant" (Jer. 31:31-34) has been inaugurated in his "blood" (1 Cor. 11:25; Luke 22:20), and his blood is the "blood of the covenant" (Ex. 24:8) which was poured out for all "for the forgiveness of sins" (Matt. 26:28; cf. Mark 14:24). In Jesus is perfected God's faithfulness to the covenant. From the beginning God has held fast to his will to save, against all human unfaithfulness: "... God has imprisoned all in disobedience so that he may be merciful to all" (Rom. 11:32).

2.3.1. THE PROCLAMATION OF THE REIGN OF GOD IN WORD AND DEED

20. What Jesus proclaimed was the dawn of the exclusive reign of God (cf. Ps. 97), which was looked for by Israel, sung in the "new song" (Ps. 96), but effected in an entirely unexpected way. In many parables Jesus speaks pointedly of its nearness in figures of speech. It is like a tiny seed out of which a great tree will grow (cf. Matt. 13:31f.). It is like a "treasure hidden in a field" or an incomparably beautiful pearl, which should be acquired here and now and for which one will spend no less than everything one has (Matt. 13:44-46). It comes up and grows "of itself"; human effort can neither aid it in any way (Mark 4:26-29) nor prevent what it does (cf. Matt. 13:24-26). It is God's action alone. But all those who accept it from Jesus' words and deeds must allow themselves to be wholly taken into service by it and must subordinate everything else to it (cf. Luke 9:57-62).

21. The reign of God is present in Jesus' words and deeds. By virtue of "the Spirit of God" he expels demons (Matt. 12:28) and frees human beings from their power (cf. Mark 5:1ff.). It is the saving power of God's eschatological reign that Jesus promises to sinners (cf. Mark 2:10f.). "I have come to call not the righteous but sinners" (Mark 2:17; cf. Luke 18:9ff.). In common meals in which eschatological joy of salvation prevails, he celebrates the miracle of the presence of the kingdom of God with "tax collectors and sinners" (Mark 2:15f.). These meals are also harbingers of the eucharistic community of the church after Easter.

22. What Jesus proclaims as the power of God's reign is his justifying love, which creates salvation: his unlimited mercy, with which he receives the lost into his Father's house and bestows rich gifts on them (cf. Luke 15:11ff.), forgives sinners their guilt (cf. Matt. 18:23ff.), promises salvation to the poor, the hungry and the suffering (cf. Luke 6:20-23), and gives the last the same share in his salvation as the first (cf. Matt. 20:1ff.). Correspondingly, the unlimited love of one's neighbour is the real meaning of the righteousness that God calls for from his elect (cf. Luke 10:25-37). Thus, in the Sermon on the Mount Jesus shows us the actual intention of God's law in its individual commandments. Just as the reign of God redeems the lost, so too it lays on those who are saved the duty of solidarity with the lost as "peace-makers" (Matt. 5:9), and prepares them to accept persecutions, slanders and sufferings "for righteousness' sake" (Matt. 5:10-12).

23. Jesus called specific persons to follow him as his disciples. Thus, they became personal witnesses to the nearness of the reign of God. That reign is to be accepted at once, without delay and apprehensiveness (cf. Luke 14:15ff.; 17:28ff.). The disciples are to leave everything (cf. Mark 1:16ff.; 10:29f.) in order to be fully with Jesus (cf. Mark 3:14) and follow him wherever he goes. Self-denial is as much a mark of citizenship in the kingdom of God (cf. Matt. 18:3f.) as following Jesus (cf. Mark 8:34).

24. Jesus called twelve disciples as his particular followers. He sent them out and empowered them as his messengers (apostles) to proclaim his message of the kingdom

of God to the whole people of Israel and, as a sign of its nearness, to heal the sick and free the possessed from the power of the demons just as he had done (cf. Mark 3:14f.; 6:7; Matt. 10:7f.). That the apostles numbered twelve corresponds to the full complement of the tribes of Israel. Thus, their ministry has a meaning in terms of salvation history: in the proclamation of Jesus the kingdom of God has definitively dawned, that kingdom which is the consummation of God's history with his chosen people, however much its ultimate manifestation on the last day is still pending. But at the same time, the ministry of the twelve apostles also has a fundamental ecclesial significance. The apostles are to preach the gospel after Easter so that their witness is foundational and normative for the whole church. According to Luke 10:1, Jesus also sent out seventy (or seventy-two) other disciples with the same mission. Their number matches that of "the elders of Israel" (Ex. 24:1; Num. 11:16f.) and relates likewise to the people of Israel as a whole and to the full complement of the nations (cf. Gen. 10).

25. The kingdom of God is the eschatological saving reality that affects the whole world. In earthly terms it is unattainable. Nevertheless, because it is there in Jesus, it is present among his disciples (cf. Luke 17:20f.). The same is also true of the church: it is not identical with the kingdom of God, which even after Easter remains hidden in the eschatological future. The kingdom is entirely God's affair, not that of any human being, nor is it at the disposal of anyone in the church. And yet its eschatological saving reality can already be experienced in the church in the "righteousness and peace and joy" which, imparted by word and sacrament, take effect in the common life of Christians "in the Holy Spirit" (Rom. 14:17). In this sense it can be said that the church is the kingdom of God already present but "hidden"[9] "in mystery".[10]

2.3.2. CROSS AND RESURRECTION

26. Jesus, who taught his disciples to pray for protection from eschatological sufferings (cf. Matt. 6:13; Luke 11:4), who was aware of the provocation of his message (cf. Matt. 10:34-39), and who proclaimed the reign of God in weakness (cf. Matt. 11:12; Mark 4:30-32 par.), was himself willing to accept the consequences arising from his preaching. He himself lived out the willingness to serve to the end and the readiness for martyrdom which he demanded from his disciples (cf. Luke 22:27; Mark 9:35 par.; Mark 8:34f.). When he journeyed up to Jerusalem, he knew what had befallen John the Baptist and was aware of the fate of the prophets (cf. Mark 6:14-29; 9:13; Matt. 23:34-39). In regard to the aim of his mission he was able to say: "For the Son of Man came not to be served but to serve, and to give his life a ransom for many" (Mark 10:45; cf. 1 Tim. 2:5).[11] In unwavering confidence that the reign of God was coming (cf. Mark 14:25), he voluntarily took upon himself (cf. Matt. 26:39,42) his death on the cross as a necessity (cf. Mark 8:31; 9:31; 10:32f.) laid upon him in accordance with God's saving will and suffered the distress of being forsaken by God (cf. Mark 15:34; Matt. 27:46). In this he fulfilled the prophecy of the Servant of God who "bore the sin of many" (Isa. 53:12): "But he was wounded for our transgressions, crushed for our iniquities; upon him was the punishment that made us whole, and by his bruises we are healed" (Isa. 53:5; cf. 1 Pet. 2:24; Rom. 4:25).

27. In the night before his death, at supper together with the Twelve, Jesus "took a loaf of bread and after blessing it he broke it, gave it to them, and said, 'Take, this is my body.' Then he took a cup, and after giving thanks he gave it to them, and all of them drank from it. He said to them, 'This is my blood of the covenant, which is poured

out for many'" (Mark 14:22-24). Thus, with effective signs Jesus gave his disciples an anticipatory share in the saving event of his atoning death as a once-for-all sacrifice, through which all who believe in him have been redeemed from sin (cf. Matt. 26:28) and freed for life in the Spirit. According to the formulations in Mark and Matthew, that which happened for Israel in the action of the covenant made at Sinai (Ex. 24:8) now happens "for many". According to the formulations in Luke and Paul (cf. 1 Cor. 11:25), the prophetic promise of the new covenant (cf. Jer. 31:31-34) is realized. The meaning is the same: the eschatological miracle of a universal "eternal redemption" (Heb. 9:12) takes place in Jesus' sacrificial death on the cross. With the command, "Do this in remembrance of me" (1 Cor. 11:24f.; Luke 22:19), Jesus promises his church that in every celebration of the Lord's supper he himself will be present as the one who was sacrificed for us, in the same way as in this meal with the apostles on the passover eve before his death: "For as often as you eat this bread and drink the cup, you proclaim the Lord's death until he comes" (1 Cor. 11:26).

28. For the disciples the story of Jesus' passion becomes the story of their denial. They fell asleep while Jesus, in his prayer that night, struggled with the will of his heavenly Father (cf. Mark 14:37-41). Upon his arrest they all fled (cf. Mark 14:50). Even Simon, the "Rock", goes back on his word: having just been willing to share death and prison with his Master (cf. Luke 22:23), he denies him three times (cf. Mark 14:66ff.). Only Jesus' prayer for him keeps him from falling into Satan's control and brings him back to faith, thereafter to strengthen his brothers (cf. Luke 22:31ff.; John 21:15ff.). Abandoned by everyone in Gethsemane, Jesus accepted his own death, surrendering in complete faith to his Father, so that "he became the source of eternal salvation for all who obey him" as "a high priest according to the order of Melchizedek" (Heb. 5:7-10). Thus, in every act of worship Christ's congregation goes to that cross "outside the gate" that there they may bear his shame (Heb. 13:10-12) and have that communion with the crucified, which takes us beyond earthly time into the "city that is to come" (Heb. 13:14).

29. Jesus' mother stands below the cross with two other women and the "disciple whom he loved" (John 19:25-27). Jesus commends them to each other: the disciple to Mary as her son in his stead and Mary to the disciple as his mother. Thus, in the form of these two a small community stands under Jesus' cross as archetype of the church whose permanent place is the cross of its Lord whence it has its life. After Jesus' death a soldier pierced his side "and at once blood and water came out" (John 19:34) – a sign that the saving effect of his death would benefit his church through the sacraments of baptism and the Lord's supper (cf. 1 John 5:5-8).

30. In the early hours of Easter morning three women disciples find Jesus' grave empty, and an angel announces his resurrection (cf. Mark 16:1ff.). The risen Christ himself "appeared to Cephas, then to the twelve" (1 Cor. 15:5) and frequently to still others, men and women. The resurrection of the crucified is God's central eschatological miracle, the breakthrough of the eschaton: Jesus is "the first-fruits of those who have died", the first to experience resurrection (1 Cor. 15:20; cf. Col. 1:18): he is God's act of new creation, through which he has procured victory for the love with which his Son gave himself to us (cf. 1 Cor. 15:57; Rom. 8:31-39; Col. 2:13f.). By this act of God's power, the death of Christ has acquired saving power: as the justification of sinners (cf. Rom. 4:25) and as reconciliation with God (cf. 2 Cor. 5:18-21) as well as a new creation – life in the power of the Spirit (cf. 2 Cor. 5:17; Rom. 8:9-11; Eph. 2:5f.;

1 Pet. 1:2). In his exaltation above "every name" (Phil 2:9-11) the risen Lord has become "head of the body, the church" (Col. 1:18) and has become lord over the entire universe, a lordship which will last till he hands over the universe – reconciled and at peace – to his Father, and God becomes "all in all" (1 Cor. 15:25-28).

31. Before his exaltation to the Father, for his disciples Jesus opened up the understanding of scripture as witness to Christ, its centre being his suffering on the cross and his resurrection (cf. Luke 24:45f.). He gave the apostles the commission and authority to preach the gospel of repentance for "the forgiveness of sins... to all nations" (Luke 24:47): "Go therefore and make disciples of all nations, baptizing them in the name of the Father and of the Son and of the Holy Spirit, and teaching them to obey everything that I have commanded you. And remember, I am with you always, to the end of the age" (Matt. 28:19f.). As a legacy he gave his church the Holy Spirit which was to "guide" them "into all the truth" (John 16:13), empower them to forgive sins (cf. John 20:23), and enable them to preach and bear witness among all the nations (cf. Acts 1:8). In the power of the Spirit of God the church was to abide in the love of Christ as he abides in his Father's love (cf. John 14:16f.; 15:10) – "that they may all be one" so that the world may know that Jesus Christ is the Son sent by the Father who loves his own as the Father loves him (John 17:21-23).

2.3.3. THE CHURCH AS THE PEOPLE OF GOD FROM ALL NATIONS

32. The wonderful plan of God's salvation history is that in Jesus' mission that purpose is also fulfilled which from the beginning God had linked to the election of Israel: the inclusion of all nations in the promised salvation and the foundation of the church as God's eschatological community of salvation. Just as at the beginning God recognized Abraham's righteousness without merit or worthiness but on the basis of faith alone (cf. Gen. 15:6; Rom. 4:3-8), so too he has made the same justification "by faith apart from works prescribed by the law" (Rom. 3:28) the entrance into his church for everyone (cf. Rom. 4:16f.; Gal. 3:6-9). Jesus Christ is the one Lord of the one church from among all the nations (cf. Acts 10:34-36), the one foundation and cornerstone of what God has built (cf. Eph. 2:20f.). Abraham's faith in the God who justifies sinners is fulfilled in the faith of Christians in Jesus Christ (cf. Rom. 4:3).

33. In the outpouring of the Spirit on the day of Pentecost, God confirms that the assembly of those who believe in Jesus as the Christ is God's messianic people of the last days (cf. Acts 2; 1 Cor. 12-14; John 14:15-31; 16:4-15; 20:19-23). Therefore the apostle's proclamation of the gospel "concerning his Son" (Rom. 1:3) serves to "bring about the obedience of faith among all..." (Rom. 1:5). Paul is not ashamed of the gospel, which "is the power of God for salvation to everyone who has faith, to the Jew first and also to the Greek. For in it the righteousness of God is revealed through faith for faith; as it is written, 'The one who is righteous will live by faith'" (Rom. 1:16f.). In this way Paul unfolds the gospel concerning the Son, identifying it with the gospel of the righteousness of God.

2.4. The church as "creature of the gospel"

2.4.1. THE PROCLAMATION OF THE GOSPEL AS FOUNDATION OF THE CHURCH

34. As on earth the Lord called and gathered people by the proclamation of the "good news of the kingdom" (Matt. 4:23; 9:35; 24:14; Mark 1:14), so too after Pente-

cost the calling and the fresh gathering of God's people is continued by the proclamation of the "good news of Christ" (Rom. 15:19; cf. 1:16; 1:1-9). For this purpose the risen Lord chooses his witnesses and sends them into the world (cf. Matt. 28:19; Mark 16:15; Acts 1:8; John 20:21). When they proclaim the gospel of "Jesus as the Messiah" (Acts 5:42) and people hear that gospel and accept it in faith as a promise of salvation, congregations are constituted from Jerusalem as far as Rome. The commission laid upon the apostles is "to proclaim the gospel" (Rom. 1:15; 1 Cor. 1:17; 9:16). This gospel, as "God's word" (1 Thess. 2:13) or the "word of the Lord" calls people to be "imitators of... the Lord" (1 Thess. 1:5-8), and brings the church into being (cf. 1 Cor. 15:1f.).

35. At the side of the audible word of gospel proclamation stand baptism and the Lord's supper as visible means of God's saving acts and of the gathering of his people (cf. 1 Cor. 10:1-13). Just as a rescued Israel emerges out of the Red Sea, so the Christian community emerges out of baptism; as the manna was for Israel in the desert, so now the Lord's supper is the pilgrim food for God's new people. Through baptism all are bound together with Christ (cf. Rom. 6:3ff.) and form the one "body of Christ" (1 Cor. 12:27). The Lord's supper is par excellence the visible and effectual expression of the congregation as a "sharing in the body of Christ" (1 Cor. 10:16f.).

36. The 16th-century Reformation highlighted with utmost emphasis the fact that the church lives on the basis of the proclamation of the gospel. It reproached the church of that time for not corresponding to that fundamental dependence on the gospel in its life and doctrine, and for having to a great extent withdrawn itself from subordination to the gospel. Consequently the main ecclesiological concern of the Reformation was perpetual dependence on the gospel and subordination to it. This was concentrated in the formula that the church is *creatura evangelii*.[12] Already in 1517 the sixty-second of Luther's ninety-five theses spoke of "the most holy gospel"[13] as "the true treasure of the church"[14] and one of the key principles of Lutheran ecclesiology takes this up: "The entire life and nature of the church is in the word of God."[15] Article 7 of the Augsburg confession corresponds to this, describing the church as "the assembly of all believers among whom the gospel is preached in its purity and the holy sacraments are administered according to the gospel".[16]

37. The conviction that the church lives out of the gospel also determines the Roman Catholic understanding of the church. In Vatican II's Dogmatic Constitution on the Church we read, "... the gospel... is for all time the source of all life for the church";[17] and the Decree on the Church's Missionary Activity says that the "chief means of this implantation [i.e., of the church] is the preaching of the gospel of Jesus Christ".[18] The apostolic exhortation of Pope Paul VI, Evangelization in the Modern World, states: "The church is born of the evangelizing activity of Jesus and the Twelve... Having been born consequently out of being sent, the church in her turn is sent by Jesus... Having been sent and evangelized, the church herself sends out evangelizers. [They are] to preach not their own selves or their personal ideas, but a gospel of which neither she nor they are the absolute masters and owners, to dispose of it as they wish, but a gospel of which they are the ministers, in order to pass it on with complete fidelity."[19]

38. In the Malta report Catholics and Lutherans together said that the church "as *creatura et ministra verbi*... stands under the gospel and has the gospel as its superor-

dinate criterion".[20] There was agreement that "the authority of the church can only be service of the word and... it is not master of the word of the Lord".[21] This primacy of the gospel over the church was also attested jointly in regard to church order and the ministry.[22]

39. For the Reformation it was self-evident that the proclamation of the gospel as the imparting of grace and salvation does not take place only in the preached word. Even when the Reformers were particularly stressing the importance of proclaiming the word, they held fast to the idea that the gospel is also communicated through the sacraments and that the preached word and administered sacraments belong together. The Smalcald articles state that the "gospel" is not proclaimed "in... one way" but "through the spoken word", "through baptism", "through the holy sacrament of the altar", and "through the power of the keys".[23] The definition of the church as *creatura evangelii* therefore means that the church lives on the basis of the gospel that is communicated in word and sacrament and accepted through faith.

40. Imparting the gospel in word and sacrament implies the ministry of proclaiming the word and administering the sacraments. This corresponds to the biblical witness according to which the message of reconciliation implies the "ministry of reconciliation" (2 Cor. 5:18ff.). Proclaiming the word and administering the sacraments are therefore not merely momentary acts but fundamental realities which permanently define the church. While all believers are to communicate the gospel in their own spheres of life, the proclamation of the word and the administration of the sacraments as public acts are perpetually assigned to the ministry instituted by God. A basic agreement exists here between Catholic and Lutheran teaching, notwithstanding the existing differences in how this ministry is understood and organized. This has been repeatedly ascertained by the Catholic-Lutheran dialogue: "By church we mean the communion of those whom God gathers together through Christ in the Holy Spirit, by the proclamation of the gospel and the administration of the sacraments, and the ministry instituted by him for this purpose."[24]

2.4.2. THE PROCLAMATION OF THE GOSPEL IN THE HOLY SPIRIT

41. We share the belief that the Holy Spirit creates the church as the communion of believers through faith in the gospel and works through this communion. The proclamation of the gospel takes place in the power of the Holy Spirit (cf. Acts 1:8). It comes "in power and in the Holy Spirit and with full conviction" and makes those who accept the word themselves messengers of the gospel (1 Thess. 1:5-8). The Holy Spirit who is promised and given to those who bear witness to the gospel (cf. John 20:22) empowers them for their witness (cf. 2 Cor. 4:13), keeps them with Christ (cf. John 14:26; 15:26f.), and gives them the certainty of acting not in their own strength but "for Christ" (2 Cor. 5:20) and with his authority (cf. John 20:23).

42. The Holy Spirit who calls and empowers witnesses for gospel testimony also awakens and sustains the faith which responds to the proclaimed gospel, faith which accepts it as the promise of salvation (cf. 1 Thess. 1:5f.; 1 Tim. 1:14). It is the Spirit who enables those who hear the message to confess Christ as Lord (cf. 1 Cor. 12:3; Rom. 10:9f.). In this "Spirit of adoption", they have access to God through Christ and call him "Father" (Rom. 8:14-16; Eph. 2:18).

43. In awakening faith through the proclaimed gospel, the Holy Spirit brings the church into being (cf. Acts 2) as congregations who are known and commended for

their faith (cf. Rom. 1:8; 1 Thess. 1:8). Through the Spirit all are "baptized into one body" (1 Cor. 12:13). In the variety of gifts the Spirit binds the individual believers together as living members (cf. 1 Cor. 12:4ff.). The unity of the Spirit is also the principle of the unity of this body that is the church (cf. 1 Cor. 12:13; Eph. 4:3f.), which as a whole is a "dwelling place for God" in the Spirit (Eph. 2:22).

2.4.3. THE PROCLAMATION OF THE GOSPEL BY THE APOSTLES

44. That Jesus Christ is the church's "foundation" (1 Cor. 3:11) and that the church lives on the basis of the gospel of Christ is concretized in the fact that the apostles called by Christ are also the church's "foundation" (Eph. 2:20). This they are not of themselves but by the power of the gospel which they have received and to which they are primary witnesses – the gospel transmitted in word and sacrament that creates, sustains and governs the church. This has permanent eschatological validity. The twelve apostles of Jesus will "sit on twelve thrones, judging the twelve tribes of Israel" (Matt. 19:28 par.), and the "twelve foundations" bear "the twelve names of the twelve apostles of the Lamb" (Rev. 21:14).

45. In the ancient church, appealing to the apostles and their testimony was the decisive defence against false doctrine. "We have learned from none others the plan of our salvation, than from those [i.e., the apostles] through whom the gospel has come down to us."[25] As the apostles received the revelation from Christ, so too the church receives it through the apostles,[26] and the "rule of faith" acquires its binding nature through its faithful reflection of this apostolic tradition.[27] Augustine sums up: "What the whole church believes is wholly rightly believed, even if it has not been directly decided by councils, but has been transmitted only on apostolic authority as belonging to the unquestioned substance of the faith."[28] The title of the creed as the "Apostles Creed"[29] expresses this conviction of the abiding, binding nature of the apostolic witness.

46. This apostolic testimony – according to the common conviction of our churches – has its normative expression in the New Testament canon. All subsequent church proclamation, doctrine and tradition is interpretation. As apostolic writings the scriptures of the New Testament, together with those of the Old Testament, are "the only rule and norm according to which all doctrines and teachers alike must be appraised and judged" say the Lutheran confessions.[30] The Dogmatic Constitution on Divine Revelation of Vatican II states that the apostles had the commission to "preach to all men the gospel" as "the source of all saving truth and moral teaching".[31] Hence "apostolic preaching, which is expressed in a special way in the inspired books" must be "preserved by a continuous succession of preachers until the end of time".[32] Though Lutherans and Catholics think differently in many respects about the way in which the apostolic norm is safeguarded, the shared conviction nevertheless is that "apostolicity" is an essential attribute of the church and the criterion par excellence of its faith, its proclamation, its teaching and its life.

47. In the Lutheran-Roman Catholic dialogue to date, this common conviction that the apostolic witness is the normative origin of the church has repeatedly been expressed and confirmed: The church stands for all time on the foundation of the apostles; it is in "all historical changes in its proclamation and structures... at all time referred back to its apostolic origin".[33]

3. The Church of the Triune God

3.1. The trinitarian dimension of the church

48. It is our common confession that the church is rooted in God's election of Israel as well as being founded in the Christ-event and the proclamation of the gospel by the apostles in the Holy Spirit. So long, however, as this confession does not recognize the profound relationship of the church to God as Holy Trinity it remains inadequate and open to misunderstandings. This relationship of the church to the triune God is both causal and substantive, involving the differentiated yet reciprocal unity of Father, Son and Holy Spirit.

49. The church is the communion of believers called into existence by the triune God. As such it is a divinely created, human reality. That the church is anchored in the divine life of the triune God does not thereby negate its human dimension nor open the way to ecclesial presumptuousness. But it does preclude an understanding of the church which tends to regard it merely or even primarily as a human societal phenomenon. God allows the church to share in the triune divine life: the church is God's own people, the body of the risen Christ himself, the temple of the Holy Spirit (3.2). The church's unity or communion *(koinonia, communio)* partakes of and reflects the unity of the triune God (3.3).

50. This biblical view of the substantive relation of the church to the triune God, which is developed in what follows, was profoundly familiar to the ancient church. It is alive in the more recent Roman Catholic understanding of the church, as is shown for instance by Vatican II's Dogmatic Constitution on the Church,[34] and the Orthodox-Roman Catholic dialogue.[35] But this trinitarian view is also at home in the Reformation view of the church. The Catholic-Lutheran dialogue to date has repeatedly shown this,[36] as has the statement of the Lutheran World Federation assembly in 1984, "The Unity We Seek": the church and its unity "participates in the unity of the Father, Son and Holy Spirit".[37]

3.2. The church as God's pilgrim people, body of Christ and temple of the Holy Spirit

3.2.1. THE CHURCH AS GOD'S PILGRIM PEOPLE

51. When the church of the New Testament applies to itself the honorific title of Israel, "people of God", it is not using merely comparative language, nor is it simply referring to the sum of individual believers. Neither does "people of God" mean only that it is God who summons and holds this "people" together. Besides all these things it means that this people has its "holiness" and its fundamental character as a "chosen race" of God the Father by really belonging to God (1 Pet. 2:9; cf. Ex. 19:5f.). As such, this "people", in its historical-terrestrial existence, is by no means immune to temptation, error and sin. It is the "pilgrim" people of God standing under God's judgment for the duration of its earthly pilgrimage and depending upon God's daily renewal of grace and fidelity. Therefore, it needs confession of sin and constant renewal. Nevertheless and precisely because of this, it is and remains the people who belong to God the Father.

52. Since the coming of Jesus Christ, the community of those who have been baptized in his name, who confess Christ and call upon him, has been the chosen people

of God, a title hitherto applied only to the people of Israel. Two things are therein expressed simultaneously: the church's continuity with Israel and the dawn of a new stage of salvation history in which faith in the one God takes shape as faith in the triune God, and the community of God's elect expands to include believers in Christ from all peoples. The invitation to Israel remains open to join the chorus of faith in God's eschatological saving action in the proclamation, passion and resurrection of Jesus, the Messiah and the Son of God, and thus to belong to the communion of the church. In the picture of the old covenant pilgrim people of God, the church may recognize itself as the people of the new covenant moving towards entry into the kingdom of God, the aim of its earthly pilgrimage. "People of God" thus expresses the intimate relationship of the church with Israel and of Israel with the church in the history of salvation.

53. People from all nations belong together as Christians in the one universal church. As the people of God in the midst of all peoples, the church embraces all the diversity of the human world. It lives in many places and hears God's call in many languages and in a multiplicity of ways. Nevertheless, it is a single undivided people, called by the one Lord, in one Spirit, to one faith, to solidarity and mutual love, to common witness and service in the world, and to be for people of all races and social classes. Thus, in its being and its mission the church is a sign for the future unity of humanity.

54. Through baptism the people of God is called to be a priestly people: "But you are a chosen race, a royal priesthood, a holy nation, God's own people, in order that you may proclaim the mighty acts of him who called you out of darkness into his marvellous light" (1 Pet. 2:9). In both the Lutheran and the Catholic traditions, therefore, we rightly speak of the "priesthood of all the baptized" or the "priesthood of all believers".[38] What constitutes this priesthood is that all the baptized have access to God through Christ, the "one mediator" (1 Tim. 2:5) and "high priest" (Heb. 4:14), that all confess their faith in the one Lord, call upon him in prayer, serve him with their whole life, and witness to all people everywhere (cf. 1 Pet. 3:15).[39]

55. Within the church as people of the new covenant, all social, racial and sexual divisions have in principle been overcome (cf. Gal. 3:26-28). There are no privileges nor any precedence of some over the others (cf. Matt. 23:8; Mark 9:35). In the world with its struggles for power, racial conflicts and social tensions, Christians are therefore in duty bound together with all people of good will to contribute to reconciliation and peace. Like their Lord they are to care for the poor and the oppressed, to seek fellowship with them and to intervene publicly on their behalf. As witnesses to their Lord who is "the resurrection and the life" (John 11:25) Christians should everywhere be a light of hope for all "who have no hope" (1 Thess. 4:13).

3.2.2. THE CHURCH AS BODY OF CHRIST

56. Also the New Testament references to the church as a "body" go far beyond the limits of a mere comparison. As a result of baptism all Christians become one body in the one faith through the one Spirit. The many members of that body do indeed have different tasks but they are nonetheless "individually... members one of another" (Rom. 12:4-5). This social reality of the church as a spiritual organism (cf. 1 Cor. 12:14-26) has its actual basis in the sacramental reality of real participation in Christ and the linking of the lives of all Christian believers in and with Christ, the crucified and risen Lord: "Do you not know that all of us who have been baptized into Christ Jesus were

baptized into his death? Therefore we have been buried with him by baptism into death, so that, just as Christ was raised from the dead by the glory of the Father, so we too might walk in newness of life" (Rom. 6:3f.). Consequently all are together not only "one body" (1 Cor. 12:12) but also "the body of Christ" (1 Cor. 12:27). Christ himself "is the head... from whom the whole body, joined and knit together by every ligament... promotes the body's growth in building itself up in love" (Eph. 4:15f.). Thus, baptism is the entry into the Christian life in the sense of participation in Christ himself. It is the abiding foundation of all life and of all common life in the church.

57. Rooted in baptism, this reality of the church as "Christ's body" finds ever new expression in the Lord's supper. When the Lord says: "This is my body that is for you" (1 Cor. 11:24), the broken bread becomes for us all a "sharing in the body of Christ. Because there is one bread, we who are many are one body, for we all partake of the one bread" (1 Cor. 10:16f.). The designation of the church as "body of Christ" indicates, therefore, the elementary and vital bond between Christ, the Lord's supper, and the church: "Baptized by the one Spirit into the one body (cf. 1 Cor. 12:13) believers – nourished by the body of Christ – become ever more one body through the Holy Spirit."[40] Christ who is himself really present in the celebration of the Lord's supper, "nourishes and tenderly cares for" his church as his body (Eph. 5:29f.), after making "her holy by cleansing her with the washing of water by the word" (Eph. 5:26). Just as in anticipation the people in the wilderness "all ate the same spiritual food and all drank the same spiritual drink... Christ" (1 Cor. 10:3f.), so the church lives through its Lord, present in the holy supper as the "bread of life" (John 6:35), "the living bread that came down from heaven" so that the promise holds: "Whoever eats of this bread will live forever" (John 6:51). "Those who eat my flesh and drink my blood have eternal life... [they] abide in me, and I in them" (John 6:54-56).

58. It is from this sacramental reality of the church as "Christ's body" that the spiritual-diaconal reality of its common life flows. As Paul describes it, all Christians are equipped and called by God's Spirit to fulfill the membership given to them in the body of Christ in a distinctive way (cf. 1 Cor. 12:4-6; Rom. 12:6-8). Each one is needed and all need each other (cf. 1 Cor. 12:14ff.). "Like good stewards of the manifold grace of God, serve one another with whatever gift each of you has received" (1 Pet. 4:10; cf. Eph. 4:7). All are to serve "the building up" of the church and its unity (Eph. 4:12) with their gifts and are to contribute to peace (cf. Eph. 4:3), which means concretely "for the common good" of all (1 Cor. 12:7). Thus, the principle of all living together in the church is love (cf. 1 Cor. 13:13–14:1). This finds expression in the structures of the church's life.

3.2.3. THE CHURCH AS TEMPLE OF THE HOLY SPIRIT

59. Reference to the constitutive relation between church and Holy Spirit runs through the whole New Testament witness concerning the church. Here too the question is not only that of a causal relation – in the sense that the Holy Spirit makes the church of the new covenant come into existence, that the proclamation of the gospel takes place in the power of the Spirit, that it is the Spirit who awakens faith in those who hear the gospel, and that the Spirit bestows on the church his manifold gifts. The Holy Spirit does all that by remaining in the church and entering into a close and substantive relation with the church. It is part of the mystery of the church that the Spirit of God is its spirit. This finds expression in the image of the church as "temple of the

Holy Spirit". Even if the direct application of this concept to the church is not found in the New Testament, it is nevertheless quite clear that the New Testament statements regarding the Holy Spirit and his relation to the church have this intention.

60. The Holy Spirit is "poured out" on the disciples and on all who accept the message of Christ in faith (Acts 2:17f.; 10:45); the Spirit is "distributed"[41] (Heb. 2:4) and "given" (e.g., 2 Cor. 1:22; Eph. 1:17), and they "receive" (e.g., Acts 1:8; 2:38; 1 Cor. 2:12; Gal. 3:14) and "have" (Rom. 8:9) the Spirit. Believers are "filled" with the Holy Spirit (e.g., Acts 2:4; 9:17; Eph. 5:18), so that they are now in "the spirit" and live, walk and serve (e.g., 1 Cor. 14:16; Gal. 5:16; 5:25; 1 Pet. 4:6) "in" the Spirit – i.e., "in the new life of the Spirit" (Rom. 7:6). So it can then be said that the Holy Spirit "dwells" (1 Cor. 3:16; James 4:5) in the believers and that they are "the temple of the living God" (2 Cor. 6:16; cf. 1 Cor. 3:16), "a temple of the Holy Spirit" (1 Cor. 6:19).

61. That which is true of believers as individuals is also true of the community of believers as a whole, the church: they are to be "built together spiritually into a dwelling place for God" (Eph. 2:22), into a "spiritual house" (1 Pet. 2:5), and they are to grow "into a holy temple in the Lord" (Eph. 2:21). The greeting and the blessing of the apostle is addressed to the community as a whole: "the communion of the Holy Spirit be with all of you" (2 Cor. 13:13). This Holy Spirit, with whom the community has "communion" and who dwells in the church as in a holy temple, leads men and women to faith by the proclamation of the gospel (cf. 1 Thess. 1:5), acts in baptism (cf. Acts 2:38; 1 Cor. 6:11), and in the Lord's supper (cf. 1 Cor. 10:1-4; 12:13) for their salvation, supports them in their prayer (cf. Rom. 8:26), and through Christ gives them access to God the Father (cf. Rom. 8:14-16; Eph. 2:18). The Spirit strengthens the witnesses of the gospel (cf. 1 Thess. 1:5-7), maintains the church in truth (cf. John 14:26), and bestows upon it the manifold riches of his gifts (cf. 1 Cor. 12:4-6). The one Spirit is the principle of the church's unity (cf. 1 Cor. 12:13; Eph. 4:3f.). As God's power, through which Jesus was raised from the dead (cf. Rom. 1:4), the Spirit is, amidst the earthly life of the church, the "first instalment" of the future fullness of salvation (2 Cor. 1:22), in which the faithful already participate and which is the goal of their earthly pilgrimage.

62. Catholics and Lutherans both teach that the church as a community of believers is called and gathered together by the Holy Spirit through the proclamation of the gospel in word and sacrament, and is empowered by the Holy Spirit who works in and through it. The statements contained in Luther's Small and Large Catechisms[42] here coincide with those of the Dogmatic Constitution on the Church[43] of Vatican II.

3.3. The church as koinonia/communio founded in the Trinity

3.3.1. THE UNITY OF THE CHURCH SUSTAINED AND FORMED BY THE TRIUNE GOD

63. Participation in the communion of the three divine persons is constitutive for the being and life of the church as expressed in the three New Testament descriptions of it as "people of God", "body of Christ", and "temple of the Holy Spirit". Thus the church also shares in the communion of the Father with the Son and of both with the Holy Spirit. The unity of the church as communion of the faithful has its roots in the trinitarian communion itself, as this is expressed in the greeting of the first letter of John: "... so that you also may have fellowship with us; and truly our fellowship is with the Father and with his Son Jesus Christ" (1 John 1:3; cf. John 17:21).

64. This can already be seen in the fact that the three designations of the church are not simply interchangeable, while being intimately linked together and referring to each other. This corresponds to the inseparable but at the same time differentiated unity of the three divine persons and their activity.
– The church as "people of God" of the new covenant is the communion of those who have been baptized in Christ's name and have received the Holy Spirit.
– As "body of Christ", the faithful and the church have a share in Christ who was raised from the dead "by the glory of the Father" (Rom. 6:3f.); and through the Holy Spirit the faithful are incorporated into the body of Christ, and they receive their gifts for the building up of the body.
– In the church as "temple of the Holy Spirit", it is the Spirit who as "the Spirit of Christ" (Rom. 8:9; cf. 2 Cor. 3:17) binds the faithful to Christ, the mediator of all salvific gifts, and who through him gives them access to the Father, whom they may invoke as "Abba, Father" in the same Spirit.

65. However one looks at the church, whether as "people of God" or "body of Christ" or "temple of the Holy Spirit", it is rooted in the inseparable communion or koinonia of the three divine persons and is thereby itself constituted as koinonia. It is not primarily the communion of believers with each other which makes the church koinonia; it is primarily and fundamentally the communion of believers with God, the triune God whose innermost being is koinonia. And yet the communion of believers with the triune God is inseparable from their communion with each other.

3.3.2. KOINONIA/COMMUNIO THROUGH PREACHING, BAPTISM AND THE LORD'S SUPPER

66. That the church as koinonia is based in the trinitarian koinonia is shown and realized in the proclamation of the gospel, baptism and the Lord's supper.

67. The preaching of the gospel, from which the church as fellowship of believers lives, can be rightly understood only in its trinitarian frame of reference. But it also links the individual believer and all believers with God in the divine trinitarian koinonia. The church's preaching proclaims the "good news of Christ" (Rom. 15:19; cf. 1:16). In their preaching the apostles and with them all witnesses to the gospel are "ambassadors for Christ" (2 Cor. 5:20). They "teach" what Jesus Christ – who will remain with them "always, to the end of the age" – has "commanded" them (Matt. 28:20). The preaching of the gospel of Christ takes place in the "power" of the "Holy Spirit" (Acts 1:8). The Spirit calls and empowers the witnesses for their ministry (cf. John 20:22f.; 2 Cor. 4:13). The Spirit awakens and sustains the faith which accepts the gospel that is preached as the promise of salvation (cf. 1 Thess. 1:5f.; 1 Tim. 1:14) and which responds to it in confession (cf. 1 Cor. 12:3). In this proclamation by the apostles and all the witnesses – a proclamation which is sustained by the Holy Spirit – Jesus' preaching of the "good news of the kingdom of God", by which he called people to him and gathered them around him, is continued after Easter and Pentecost. Jesus' preaching in word and deed acquired its authority solely from the fact that his words and deeds were identical with those of the Father who had sent him (cf. John 14:10,24; 8:28; 10:15). Of Jesus as "beloved" Son of the Father can it be said, "listen to him!" (Matt. 17:5 par.).

68. Baptism in the name of the Father, Son and Holy Spirit (Matt. 28:19) leads us into communion with the triune God and into sharing in his blessings and thus also knits believers together into a communion. Baptism is calling and election by God and

makes us God's possession: thus also creating the community of those who are called and chosen, "God's own people" (1 Pet. 2:9). In baptism we are baptized into Christ's body, partaking of his death and resurrection, and putting on Christ: consequently the baptized also constitute "one body... one with another" (Rom. 12:4f.) and are one communion in which creaturely and social divisions no longer count for anything (cf. Gal. 3:26-28). The baptized receive the Holy Spirit: they are thus also bound together into one communion "in the one Spirit" (1 Cor. 12:12f.; Eph. 4:3f.).

69. The celebration of the Lord's supper draws believers into the presence and communion of the triune God through thanksgiving *(eucharistia)* to the Father, remembrance (anamnesis) of Christ and invocation (epiclesis) of the Holy Spirit. In a special way the celebration is the koinonia of believers with the crucified and risen Lord present in the supper, and for that very reason it also creates and strengthens the koinonia of the faithful among and with each other. Paul says: "The cup of blessing that we bless, is it not a sharing in the blood of Christ? The bread that we break, is it not a sharing in the body of Christ? Because there is one bread, we who are many are one body, for we all partake of the one bread" (1 Cor. 10:16f.). His rebuke of the Corinthians follows this dialectic precisely; when their practice of the Lord's supper violates their koinonia, they profane their eucharistic communion with the Lord (cf. 1 Cor. 11:20-29).

70. It is the common conviction of our churches that in and through the eucharistic koinonia with Christ, ecclesial koinonia is established and strengthened. On the Catholic side one can point, for instance, to Vatican II, especially to its Dogmatic Constitution on the Church,[44] or to Thomas Aquinas, for whom the reality *(res)* of the Lord's supper is "the mystical body of Christ" in which we are strengthened "through unity with Christ and with his members".[45] On the Lutheran side this conviction is expressed, for instance, in Luther's sermon on "The Blessed Sacrament of the Holy and True Body of Christ and the Brotherhoods 1519",[46] which is important for his ecclesiology, or in Martin Chemnitz's commentary on 1 Corinthians 10 in which, adopting the trinitarian standpoint, he says, "In the Lord's supper... we all receive one and the same body of Christ... and because in this way the members of the church are fused into one body of Christ, they are also bound up with each other and become one body whose head Christ is. Thus when we receive the body and blood of Christ in the Lord's supper, we are closely bound up with Christ... and through Christ we are united with the Father... Thus we become partakers (koinonia) of the Father, the Son and the Holy Spirit. This all comes about from the saving communion (koinonia) of the body and blood of the Lord...."[47]

71. In these explanations based on the New Testament witness, both our traditions understand themselves to be in agreement with the ancient church for which the Pauline statements on koinonia in Christ were decisive. St John of Damascus summarizes this patristic theological tradition as follows: "It [the eucharist] is also called communion, and truly is so, because of our having communion through it with Christ and partaking both of his flesh and his divinity, and because through it we have communion with and are united to one another. For, since we partake of one bread, we all become one body of Christ and one blood and members of one another and are accounted of the same body with Christ."[48]

3.3.3. KOINONIA/COMMUNIO AS ANTICIPATORY REALITY

72. The three biblical designations of the church as "people of God", "body of Christ" and "temple of the Holy Spirit" all interpret its trinitarian basis in anticipatory fashion:

- The universal people of God will first gather in its entirety on the last day; only in anticipation of that ultimate gathering can the church be the people of God today who live already on the basis of what God will make of them.
- The church is the body of the crucified and risen Christ for whose return in glory we still wait.
- The church is the temple of the Holy Spirit whose reality among us is "down payment" *(arrabón)* of eschatological reality.

Thus, the church is already everything the biblical designations of it say it is – but in such a way that it awaits in anticipation what is most profoundly its being and the source of its life.

73. This also holds good for the church as koinonia. It is already a partaking in the koinonia of the Father, Son and Holy Spirit; but as the pilgrim church it is such provisionally and in fragmentary fashion; and this means in anticipation and expectation of its final destination, which is still pending: consummation in the kingdom of God, in which the triune God will be "all in all" (1 Cor. 15:24-28).

3.4. Ecclesial communion – communion of churches

3.4.1. COMMON WITNESS

74. On both the Catholic and the Lutheran side, the concept of koinonia/communio has once more become important ecclesiologically; indeed, it has become central. In Lutheranism this becomes clear in the increasing use, and above all theological deepening, of the term "church fellowship/communion", which it has been possible to observe more or less since the 1950s. The term is understood as an acceptance of the concept of koinonia/communio in the early New Testament church as described above, and it can also claim the support of the Reformation view of the church and incorporate specific aspects of it. Especially since Vatican II, the idea of koinonia/communio and the term itself have become determinative for the Catholic view of the church. In this we see "the central and fundamental idea" of the ecclesiology developed by the council.[49]

75. On the basis of a concept of koinonia derived from the New Testament and the early church, Lutherans and Catholics agree that the church is a koinonia/communio rooted in the mystery of the holy Trinity. Proof of that assertion is found both in the Lutheran confessions and documents of Vatican II.

76. According to the teaching of the Council "human dignity lies in man's call to communion with God".[50] The Council refers to 1 John 1:2f., according to which believers are to attain koinonia with the Father and the Son, for God has revealed himself so that "through Christ... man has access to the Father in the Holy Spirit and comes to share in the divine nature".[51] God thus seeks "to establish peace or communion between sinful human beings and himself, as well as to fashion them into a fraternal community".[52] In this way the mystery of the church is indicated, for according to the council the communion with God in the body of Christ effected through the Holy Spirit is the foundation for the koinonia of the church. The Spirit dwells in the faithful, guiding and governing the church. It establishes the "communion of the faithful and joins them together... in Christ".[53]

77. The Lutheran confessions indicate the chief meaning of church fellowship by designating the nature of the church as the communion of the faithful[54] which origi-

nates in communion with Christ through the Holy Spirit, and which lives from faithful hearing of the word and receiving of the sacraments. When CA 7 describes the "one holy Christian church" as the "assembly of all believers",[55] it means that "communion of saints"[56] of which the Apostles' Creed speaks.[57] The fact that "communio" is understood and translated as "assembly" or "congregation" and not, for linguistic reasons, rendered "community" in German, should not cause the term to lose any of its New Testament or early church content or meaning. There is no sociological reductionism involved. Instead, the fellowship *(communio)* is an assembly or congregation "under one head, Christ, called together by the Holy Spirit", in which "I also am a part and member, a participant and co-partner in all the blessings *[Güter]* it possesses. I was brought to it by the Holy Spirit and incorporated into it through the fact that I have heard and still hear God's word, which is the first step in entering it."[58] "To have communion or fellowship" therefore does not simply mean "having some relationship with another person" but rather that "many persons share or eat or partake of one common thing".[59] Just as the communion of Christians with each other is grounded in their common sharing in Christ, so it is for them a communion of mutual sharing and mutual help and service: "This fellowship is twofold: on the one hand we partake of Christ and all saints; on the other hand we permit all Christians to be partakers of us, in whatever way they and we are able."[60]

78. According to the Second Vatican Council, it is through the word of preaching and the celebration of the sacraments, of which the eucharist is the "centre and summit", that Christ, the author of our salvation, becomes present in the church.[61] "From the table of both the word of God and of the body of Christ" the "bread of life" is offered the faithful.[62] In the breaking of the eucharistic bread they actually gain a share in the Lord's body and are raised to communion with him and among one another, for communion in the body of Christ makes those who receive the one bread into the body of the Lord.[63] The eucharist is therefore the summit of ecclesial *communio*[64] and "the very heartbeat of the congregation of the faithful".[65]

79. Catholics and Lutherans together understand that the communion with God mediated through word and sacrament leads to communion of the faithful among themselves. This takes concrete shape in the communion of the churches: the one, holy, catholic and apostolic church, the una sancta of the creed, is realized in the *communio ecclesiarum* as local, regional and universal communion, and so as church fellowship.

80. There is only one church of God. In the New Testament the same word *ecclesia* signifies both the whole church (e.g., Matt. 16:18; Gal. 1:13) and the church of a region (e.g., Gal. 1:2), the church of a city (e.g., Acts 8:1; 1 Cor. 11:18) or of a house (e.g., Rom. 16:5). Accordingly, Lutherans and Catholics see the church of God in local, regional and universal terms, but these different ways in which the church becomes a reality must be understood on the basis of the one, holy, catholic and apostolic church, the una sancta of the creed.

81. Because the church, as communion of the faithful, is based in communion with Christ, the one Lord, there is only one single church. According to the Lutheran confessions the promise that it will "remain forever" applies only to that *una sancta ecclesia*.[66] That church is "a holy Christian people",[67] persons "scattered throughout the world who agree on the gospel and have the same Christ, the same Holy Spirit, and the same sacraments".[68] The church "is mainly an association of faith and of the Holy Spirit in men's hearts".[69]

82. According to the Second Vatican Council, "God has gathered together as one all those who in faith look upon Jesus as the author of salvation and the source of unity and peace, and has established them as the church, that for each and all she may be the visible sacrament of this saving unity. While she transcends all limits of time and of race, the church is destined to extend to all regions of the earth, and so to enter into the history of mankind."[70] "The church, then, God's only flock, like a standard lifted high for the nations to see, ministers the gospel of peace to all mankind, as she makes her pilgrim way in hope towards her goal, the fatherland above."[71]

83. Looked at diachronically – through all time – the una sancta as an eschatological reality pervades the whole of history, from the first days *(ecclesia ab Abel)* to the last, the time of Christ's return in glory. It has taken shape especially since the elect people of God has become the body of Christ and the temple of the Holy Spirit, and hence represents for the faithful the place of new life and of that communio with God which finds expression in communion with each other.

3.4.2. THE LUTHERAN UNDERSTANDING OF LOCAL CHURCH

84. Differences between the Catholic and Lutheran position appear when the question is posed about the realization of the church from a synchronic – here and now – point of view. For Lutherans the local congregation is church in the full sense; for Catholics it is the local church led by its bishop.

85. Lutherans understand the *una sancta ecclesia* to find outward and visible expression wherever people assemble around the gospel proclaimed in sermon and sacrament. Assembled for worship the local congregation therefore is to be seen, according to the Lutheran view, as the visible church, *communio sanctorum*, in the full sense. Nothing is missing which makes a human assembly church: the preached word and the sacramental gifts through which the faithful participate in Christ through the Holy Spirit, but also the minister who preaches the word and administers the sacraments in obedience to Christ and on his behalf, thus leading the congregation.

86. The understanding of the church as communion of persons based on communion with the one Lord includes the communion of separate congregations bound together in true communion with Christ. Therefore congregations may not distance themselves nor isolate themselves from one another. The communion they have in Christ must be visible.

87. Lutheran congregations are part of larger fellowships which are themselves constitutionally structured. According to geographical, historical, national or political realities they form dioceses or juridically autonomous provincial or national churches. These larger communities are held together by communion in Christ, and that shows itself in their common understanding of the apostolic faith (confessional communion), in word and sacrament (pulpit and altar fellowship), and in a mutually recognized ministry.

88. In the second half of the 19th century, consciousness of the global dimension of ecclesial communion grew stronger among the Lutheran churches. First came regional[72] and finally worldwide Lutheran associations.[73] For decades the Lutheran World Federation understood itself as a "free association of churches" – having common confessions but without having declared pulpit and altar fellowship. The concept of "church fellowship" played an increasingly important role as the Federation responded to repeated questions about its ecclesial character. "Church fellowship"

combined the New Testament/patristic concept of koinonia/communio with the Lutheran understanding of church.[74] More recently it was the concept of communion itself which became the leitmotif of efforts towards the clarification and new definition of the nature of the Lutheran World Federation, efforts which came to their conclusion in the decision of the Federation's 1990 assembly. Now the constitution states: "The Lutheran World Federation is a communion of churches which confess the triune God, agree in the proclamation of the word of God and are united in pulpit and altar fellowship."[75]

89. It therefore becomes clear what, according to Lutheran understanding of the church as koinonia, is constitutive, irrespective of whether the expression is congregational, territorial/national or global: the common understanding and confession of the apostolic faith (confessional communion) and communion in preaching and the sacraments (pulpit and altar fellowship), including by implication the ministry of proclamation and the administration of the sacraments (recognition of ministries).

90. This understanding of church as koinonia was and is determinative for ecumenical efforts of the Lutheran churches. The sought-for visible unity of the church is, in this sense, understood as ecclesial communion.[76] The statement of the 1984 Lutheran World Federation assembly, "The Unity We Seek", is developed by explicit use of the concept of communion.[77]

3.4.3. THE ROMAN CATHOLIC UNDERSTANDING OF LOCAL CHURCH

91. When Catholics view the church synchronically and spatially, they understand that it expresses itself throughout the earth as local church, regional church and universal church, but that none of these expressions can be exclusively identified with the una sancta. Rather the una sancta is for each expression the criterion for unity in the truth.[78]

92. In Catholic ecclesiology the local church is essentially neither a part of the universal church nor an administrative or canonical district of it. According to the teaching several times stated at Vatican II, the church of God is truly present and effective in the local church, i.e., diocese.[79] The decree on the bishops' pastoral office states: "A diocese is that portion of God's people which is entrusted to a bishop to be shepherded by him with the cooperation of the presbytery. Adhering thus to its pastor and gathered together by him in the Holy Spirit through the gospel and the eucharist, this portion constitutes a particular church in which the one, holy, catholic and apostolic church of Christ is truly present and operative."[80] The theology of the local church here presented coheres with the conciliar theology of the people of God.[81] The expression "portion" *(portio)* was deliberately preferred to "part" *(pars)*, because a "portion" contains all the essential features of the whole – which is not the case with "part". In other words the local church has all the qualities of the church of God, and one must not therefore look upon it as a branch office of the universal church. The mention of the bishop points to the structural fellowship of the local churches with each other, for as a result of his ordination the bishop functions as a connecting link of the church, both as the representative of the whole church in his church and as the representative of his church in relation to all the others.[82] The reference to the presbytery points to the collegial nature of the ministry in the local church.

93. On the level of the diocese one finds a full presence of the church of God. Moving out from this level, the fundamental conciliarity of the church is expressed in the

participation of the bishop in a council. Since however parishes also have the structural characteristics of the church of God ("portion" of the people of God, Holy Spirit, gospel, eucharist and ministry), the Second Vatican Council recognizes: "Parishes set up locally under a pastor who takes the place of the bishop... in a certain way represent the visible church as it is established throughout the world."[83] In actual fact it is the parish, even more than the diocese, which is familiar to Christians as the place where the church is to be experienced.

94. Each of the constitutive elements of the local church ("portion" of the people of God, Holy Spirit, gospel and eucharistic presidency of the bishop) and their presence together show that the local church is indeed the church of God in the full sense, but that it cannot be regarded as the whole church of God. "The local church is not a free-standing, self-sufficient reality. As part of a network communion, the local church maintains its reality as church by relating to other local churches."[84] Part of its nature is to be in real fellowship with other local churches and with the church as a whole.

95. This fellowship of the local church with the church universal is not an abstract, purely theoretical reality. In the local church one encounters the essential mystery of the church; in the local church one is instructed in the faith and led to a confession of the apostolic faith and only there can one be baptized, confirmed, ordained, married and receive the Lord's body at his table. Only through the local church is one a member of the Catholic church. Nor can one conceive of the universal church apart from the local churches, as if the whole church could exist apart from the local churches. In actuality, "in and from such individual churches there comes into being the one and only Catholic church".[85] In both terms – "in these" and "out of them" – the reciprocal nature of the relationship is expressed, not the priority of one over the other. If "out of them" is deleted, the universal church would disintegrate into separate particular churches; if one removes "in these", the local church is degraded into nothing but an administrative unit of the universal church.

96. The relation of "reciprocal inherence"[86] or "mutual indwelling"[87] which exists between the local and the universal church neither dissolves the independence of the local church nor its essential inclusion in the universal church but consolidates both, in the same way as the ultimate responsibility of each bishop to God for his local church and for his faithful does not call in question his inclusion in the college of bishops with the pope. According to the teaching of the council the bishop is the "visible source and foundation" for the unity of the local church and the "Roman pontiff... is the visible source and foundation of the unity of the bishops and of the multitude of the faithful", while the local churches are fashioned after the model of the universal church.[88] Thus the church is a unity in and out of diversity, it is a body of churches,[89] or a *communio* of churches.

97. The fellowship of local churches, that is to say the church universal, is therefore not a platonic entity. It is what supports each individual church. Only for the church universal does the promise hold good of remaining in the truth. That cannot be said of any local church. In periods of great crisis where the specific expression of faith was at stake, only the fellowship of all the churches, and especially the ecumenical councils, succeeded in working out answers in spite of the well-known communication difficulties. The contributions and initiatives which single local churches made towards resolving disputed questions had their full impact only in the framework of reception by the communion of churches. Generally it is true that "mutual solicitude, support,

recognition and communication are essential qualities among local churches. Even from earliest times, the local churches felt themselves linked to one another. This koinonia was expressed in a variety of ways: exchange of confessions of faith; letters of communion as a kind of 'ecclesiastical passport'; hospitality; reciprocal visits; mutual material help; councils; and synods."[90]

98. A consequence of the universal character of the great commission in the New Testament (cf. Matt. 28:19; Acts 1:8; 2:1-12) is the pluriformity of the local churches within the church catholic. It is also a matter of experience that effective evangelization has been possible only through the formation of regional churches strong enough to influence a whole culture. An image in the Decree on the Church's Missionary Activity of Vatican II makes it plain how the universality of mission calls for the involvement of human cultures in the faith and thus requires as well the specific characteristics of the particular churches as conditioned by their cultural context: it is the church which after Pentecost "speaks all tongues, which lovingly understands and accepts all tongues, and thus overcomes the divisiveness of Babel".[91] This church is entrusted with a universal yet unique message. Consequently, it must avoid the danger of particularism; that is, it must be ready to understand and respect as valid the language of the other. At the same time, the church's missionary task is to follow Christ who committed himself "in virtue of his incarnation, to the definite social and cultural conditions of those human beings among whom he dwelt".[92] In this sense the "congregation of the faithful, endowed with the riches of its own nation's culture, should be deeply rooted in the people".[93]

99. Thus the particular churches are catholic in the full sense only if they have gone through a process of critical inculturation which requires them, within the culture and society in which they live, to examine what has to be affirmed, purified and integrated.[94] In "each major socio-cultural area" the emergence of particular churches presupposes that "every appearance of syncretism" be excluded and that "particular traditions, together with the individual patrimony of each family of nations, can be illumined by the light of the gospel, and then be taken up into Catholic unity. Finally, the individual young churches, adorned with their own traditions, will have their own place in the ecclesiastical communion...."[95] Thus, the catholicity of the whole church will be enriched by the catholicity of the particular churches. Accordingly, the Dogmatic Constitution on the Church sketches this ideal: "In virtue of this catholicity each individual part of the church contributes through its special gifts to the good of the other parts and of the whole church. Thus through the common sharing of gifts and through the common effort to attain fullness in unity, the whole and each of the parts receive increase."[96]

100. As a result of taking seriously the special character of particular churches, Vatican II also hopes for a stimulus for the restoration of unity among the separated Christians. The Constitution on the Church states that "this variety of local churches with one common aspiration is particularly splendid evidence of the catholicity of the undivided church",[97] and the Decree on Ecumenism says: "Let all members of the church, according to the office entrusted to each, preserve a proper freedom in the various forms of spiritual life and discipline, in the variety of liturgical rites, and even in the theological elaborations of revealed truth. In all things let charity be exercised. If the faithful are true to this course of action, they will be giving ever richer expression to the authentic catholicity of the church and, at the same time, to her apostolicity."[98]

101. Because cultural units are usually more comprehensive than a diocese, it is necessary that this definition of particular churches be actualized by associations of local churches, for example in the classical form of patriarchates, or in the modern form of churches *sui iuris* and by conferences of bishops of the same or several nations, or on the level of a whole continent, e.g., CELAM.[99] One must further note patriarchal, provincial and plenary synods as well as the declarations of the bishops' conferences. It is also the task of the papal primate to protect proper diversity. "Moreover, within the church particular churches hold a rightful place. These churches retain their own traditions without in any way lessening the primacy of the chair of Peter. This chair presides over the whole assembly of charity and protects legitimate differences, while at the same time it sees that such differences do not hinder unity but rather contribute towards it."[100]

102. The gospel of salvation is directed to the whole of humanity: God created the church with a view to universal reconciliation and unity, and Jesus promised to remain with his church to the end of the age (cf. Matt. 16:18; 18:20; 28:20; Eph. 4:1-13). In this sense the una sancta and the church universal will always have precedence over the local churches. At the same time it is true that the church of God has always assumed a local shape; for Christians receive baptism, celebrate the eucharist, and give a socially identifiable witness always in a particular place. In this sense there will always be a priority of the local churches over the church as a whole, but not over the eschatological una sancta. Consequently, we may speak of a reciprocity in the relations between the local and the universal church. But it is different with the una sancta, which permeates the whole of history as an eschatological reality and with which no realization of the church of God as a local, regional or universal church can be exclusively identified.

103. The eucharist best expresses the reciprocal relation between the local churches, the universal church and the eschatological church. "Since Pentecost the church celebrates the eucharist as the one, holy, catholic and apostolic church. The eucharistic celebration, therefore, embraces the church both in its local and universal dimension. It thus affirms a mutual presence of all the churches in Christ and in the Spirit for the salvation of the world."[101]

104. In the documents of Vatican II the designation "mother church" is not applied to any local church nor even to the church of Rome, but is strictly reserved for the una sancta. This demonstrates that the fellowship of all the churches makes them sisters in its bosom. As the Decree on Ecumenism puts it, there is that "communion of faith and charity... which ought to thrive between local churches, as between sisters".[102]

3.4.4. TASKS OF FURTHER DIALOGUE

105. The Catholic view of the church as koinonia/communio may be made fruitful for ecumenical endeavour,[103] and it too – like the Lutheran view of a "church fellowship" – has its specific emphases and configurations. However, the fundamental idea in both cases is the same and is ecclesiologically determinative in the same way. It is part of the nature of every local church to be open towards the other local churches. Catholicity requires that.

106. According to the belief of the Catholic church, of course, the primatial function of the bishop of Rome is an essential element of the church, with the consequence that each local church must be related to the primacy of the church of Rome and its

bishop in order to be in the full communion of churches. But on the other hand it must not be forgotten that the Roman primacy is also related to the koinonia of the local churches. The Catholic-Lutheran dialogue must deal with the question of the ministry of oversight in the whole church in the context of ecclesial koinonia in general, but also in the particular context of the Roman Catholic understanding of the relationship between the episcopal college and the papal office. To be sure a problem thereby arises in regard to the Catholic ecclesiology of communion to which the ecumenical dialogue has, in various ways, called attention. In spite of Catholic adherence to the principle of a ministry of unity in the universal church, the challenge to self-criticism cannot be ignored. The doctrine of primacy must be further developed, and primatial practice must be shaped accordingly. One hopes, therefore, that in its further work the Catholic-Lutheran dialogue on ecclesiology will take up the theme of a ministry of leadership for the universal church within the framework of communion ecclesiology.

4. The Church as Recipient and Mediator of Salvation

107. In the summary of the biblical witness on the abiding origin of the church, it was stressed that the proclamation of the gospel by the apostles in the Holy Spirit is the foundation of the church, and that as *creatura evangelii* the church is committed to serving the gospel.[104] Thus the church is the recipient and mediator of salvation. In the great biblical images of the people of God, the body of Christ, and the temple of the Holy Spirit, the church shows itself to be a koinonia founded in the life of the triune God from whom it receives life and salvation, and the church imparts life and salvation in faithfulness to its task of mission, which it has received from God.[105]

4.1. The church as *congregatio fidelium*

108. A comparison of Lutheran and Catholic views of the church cannot disregard the fact that there are two fundamentally inseparable aspects of being church: on the one hand, the church is the place of God's saving activity (the church as an assembly, as the recipient of salvation) and on the other it is God's instrument (the church as ambassador, as mediator of salvation). But it is one and the same church which we speak of as the recipient and mediator of salvation. In the course of the history of theology, the emphases have been variously placed. While Lutherans see the church mainly as the recipient of salvation, as the "congregation of the faithful", *congregatio fidelium*, contemporary Catholic theology emphasizes more the church as the mediator of salvation, as "sacrament" of salvation.[106]

4.1.1. THE LUTHERAN VIEW

109. "The creed calls the holy Christian church a *communio sanctorum*, 'a communion of saints'."[107] Luther thus repeats in the Large Catechism what he had already set out in *A Brief Explanation... of the Creed*: "I believe that there is on earth, through the whole wide world, no more than one holy, common Christian church, which is nothing else than the congregation, or assembly of the saints, i.e., the pious, believing men on earth, which is gathered, preserved and ruled by the Holy Ghost, and daily increased by means of the sacraments of the word of God."[108] Thus, the church is not simply the sum of its individual members, for it is founded on the very word of God that faith receives, and individuals belong to it by receiving the word and sacrament in

faith. The power of the Holy Spirit is what produces and sustains this assembly of believers among whom the individual is reckoned.

110. According to the Augsburg confession the church is "the assembly of all believers among whom the gospel is preached in its purity and the holy sacraments are administered according to the gospel".[109] The Apology explains this: "The church is... mainly[110] an association of faith and of the Holy Spirit in men's hearts. To make it recognizable, this association has outward marks, the pure teaching of the gospel[111] and the administration of the sacraments in harmony with the gospel of Christ."[112] The context makes clear that "pure doctrine and conformity to the gospel" indicates the message of justification by which the church's life must be evaluated and to which the church as a whole is subordinated. In this the Augsburg confession restates the teaching of the ancient, but also the medieval church.[113] The church receives its whole life and being from Christ, whose body it is, and who "renews, consecrates and governs [it] by his Spirit".[114] It can live only on the basis of this promise of the forgiveness of sins and the fellowship of salvation which has been bestowed on it. The church is gift in every respect because it lives by the Spirit of God and from the Lord present in it.

111. The proclamation of the gospel and the celebration of the sacraments characterize the church as communion of salvation where Christ is present and where we can find him: "Those who are to find Christ must first find the church.... But the church is not wood and stone but the mass of people who believe in Christ; one must hold to it and see how they believe and pray and teach; they assuredly have Christ with them."[115] Luther emphasizes the necessity of the church for the salvation of individuals so strongly that he can say, "I believe that no one can be saved who is not found in this congregation, holding with it to one faith, word, sacraments, hope and love."[116] Similarly the church is highlighted in the Apology as the place of the promise of salvation for children. They are to be baptized, so that they will share Christ's promise, which "does not apply to those who are outside of Christ's church, where there is neither word nor sacrament, because Christ regenerates through word and sacrament".[117] "For the kingdom of Christ is only where the word of God and the sacraments are to be found."[118] Faith and listening to the voice of the good shepherd, Jesus Christ, distinguish the church as God's people from every other people; for, "thank God, a seven-year-old child knows what the church is, namely, holy believers and sheep who hear the voice of their Shepherd".[119] The church is therefore the *congregatio fidelium*, the congregation of salvation as a faith-congregation, founded by God's word and bound to it: "God's word cannot be present without God's people, and God's people cannot be without God's word."[120]

112. Faith in the gospel allows believers to place their salvation entirely in God's hands and makes them free to serve God and humanity. The gift of the faith-community becomes the task of acting in line with koinonia; everything is common to everyone in the congregation of salvation. Luther says: "I believe that in this congregation or church, all things are common [cf. Acts 2:44], that everyone's possessions belong to the others and no one has anything of his own; therefore, all the prayers and good works of the whole congregation must help, assist and strengthen me and every believer at all times, in life and death, and thus each bear the other's burden, as St Paul teaches" (cf. Gal. 6:2).[121] The "communion of believers", *communio credentium*, finds concrete expression in the general priesthood of all believers. By baptism all believers receive a share in the priesthood of Christ. They can and should therefore witness to

the gospel and intercede for each other before God. "Therefore because he [a Christian] is a priest and we are his brothers, all Christians have power and authority and must so act that they preach, and come before God each asking for the other and offering themselves up to God."[122] In the general priesthood a representational authority is given; for one is always a priest for others. Understood in this way, being a Christian is a social charisma, a service before God for and to others.

4.1.2. THE CATHOLIC VIEW

113. *Congregatio fidelium* was the predominant definition for the church in the late medieval theology. The *Catechism of the Council of Trent (Catechismus Romanus)* too speaks of the church as "the congregation of the faithful".[123] To it belong all "who were called by faith to the light of truth and the knowledge of God, that... they may worship the living and true God piously and holily, and serve him from their whole heart".[124] The catechism also refers to Augustine's words with regard to Psalm 140: "The church... consists of the faithful people, dispersed throughout the world."[125] In reference to the Apostles' Creed, the catechism sees a statement about the church[126] in the words "communion of saints".[127] As communion on the basis of the confession of faith and the sacraments as well as the communion of life, this "communion of saints" is described as mutual love and mutual helping in sorrow and need. For this view the catechism has recourse above all to the Pauline statements on the church as the body of Christ; the gifts of God are given for the use of the whole church and should benefit everyone.[128]

114. The church is the assembly of those who believe in Christ. Vatican II describes the whole church as "all those, who in faith look upon Jesus as the author of salvation"[129] and calls the individual congregation the "congregation of the faithful";[130] it thus appropriates the terminology of Augustine, who describes the church as redeemed community,[131] the "community and society of the saints".[132] *Communio* is the fundamental ecclesiological concept of the Council even if it uses the idea of *communio* on many levels and nowhere defines it. The church was established by Christ as "fellowship of life, charity and truth"[133] and the Holy Spirit "gives her a unity of fellowship and service".[134] The entire saving work of Jesus Christ and therefore the church is founded in the mystery of the triune God; "in order to establish peace or communion between sinful human beings and himself, as well as to fashion them into a fraternal community, God determined to intervene in human history in a way both new and definitive".[135] This communion with God and of human beings among themselves is brought about by God's word and the sacraments. "For those who believe in Christ, who are reborn not from a perishable but from an imperishable seed through the word of the living God (cf. 1 Pet. 1:23), not from flesh but from water and the Holy Spirit (cf. John 3:5-6), are finally established as 'a chosen race, a royal priesthood'... (1 Pet. 2:9-10)."[136] The Council states that in Christ "all the faithful are made a holy and royal priesthood. They offer spiritual sacrifices to God through Jesus Christ, and they proclaim the perfections of him who has called them out of darkness into his marvellous light. Hence, there is no member who does not have a part in the mission of the whole body."[137] The Council calls this priesthood the "common priesthood"[138] to distinguish it from the "ministerial priesthood".[139] The eucharist is pre-eminent among the sacraments; "the eucharistic action is the very heartbeat of the congregation of the faithful over which the priest presides".[140] "Truly partaking of the body of the Lord in the

breaking of the eucharistic bread, we are taken up into communion with him and with one another."[141]

115. The Council states equally clearly that "the people of God finds its unity first of all through the word of the living God... For through the saving word the spark of faith is struck in the hearts of unbelievers, and fed in the hearts of the faithful."[142] The proclamation of the word is essential for the right administration of the sacraments; "for these are sacraments of faith, and faith is born of the word and nourished by it".[143]

116. The Decree on the Church's Missionary Activity describes pointedly the power of God's word to justify and awaken faith: "The Holy Spirit, who calls all men to Christ by the seeds of the word and by the preaching of the gospel, stirs up in their hearts the obedience of faith. When in the womb of the baptismal font He begets to a new life those who believe in Christ, He gathers them into the one people of God."[144] Nor is the judging power of God's word in any way ignored. "The words of Christ are at one and the same time words of judgment and grace, of death and life. For it is only by putting to death what is old that we are able to come to a newness of life... By himself and by his own power, no one is freed from sin or raised above himself, or completely rid of his sickness or his solitude or his servitude. On the contrary all stand in need of Christ, their Model, their Mentor, their Liberator, their Saviour, their Source of life."[145] Thus, the church lives as a communion of believers, not by its own strength but entirely from God's gift. This of course becomes its task in passing on the faith and mediating salvation.

4.1.3. COMMON WITNESS

117. Both Lutherans and Catholics understand the church as the assembly of the faithful or saints which lives from God's word and the sacraments. Seen thus, the church is the fruit of God's saving activity, the community of his truth, his life and his love. Christ who acts in his saving word and sacrament confronts the church, which is the recipient of his and the Holy Spirit's activity. The presence of Christ marks the church as the place where salvation takes place. The gift of salvation however becomes the task and mission of the church as the community which has received salvation. Thus, the church is taken by its Lord into the ministry of mediating salvation. That holds good in association and mutual support within the congregation of the faithful itself but also particularly in confronting the world, especially all who still do not believe and still do not belong to the assembly of the faithful.

4.2. The church as "sacrament" of salvation

4.2.1. THE CHURCH UNDER THE GOSPEL AND THE TWOFOLD SALVIFIC MEDIATION OF THE GOSPEL

118. The Lutheran-Roman Catholic dialogue has stated that the church "stands under the gospel and has the gospel as its superordinate criterion".[146] For this one can appeal both to Luther, who sees the church as "creature of the gospel"[147] and to Vatican II according to which "the gospel... is for all time the source of all life for the church".[148] The gospel by which the church was created and lives is mediated externally and corporally in dual form: by word and by sacrament. Both modes of mediation however are connected in fundamentally indissoluble fashion without doing away with their specific characteristics. The word proclaimed is an audible sign, the sacra-

ments are a visible word. These are the two modes in which the transmission of the gospel is saving in its effect. Thus, not only is attention drawn to salvation or information given about it, but the gospel thus confronts people in their inmost selves as effectual externally and corporally by its presence, bringing them to faith, justifying and sanctifying them.

119. Because in this way the church lives from the gospel and is taken into the service of the dual mediation of the gospel that effects salvation, Catholic talk of the church as "sacrament" can be described in terms of its purpose: "As the body of Christ and koinonia of the Holy Spirit, the church is the sign and instrument of God's grace, an instrument that of itself can do nothing. The church lives by the word as it lives by the sacraments and at the same time stands in their service."[149] The meaning of what is said about the church as the "sacrament" of salvation will be worked out below with reference to the Catholic and Lutheran traditions and their common foundation in the Bible.

4.2.2. THE CATHOLIC VIEW

120. In the documents of Vatican II the church is referred to as "sacrament" – a sign and instrument of salvation – especially where the nature of the church and its universal mission are explained in considerable detail. At the beginning of the Constitution on the Church there is a programmatic statement, "Christ is the light of all nations".[150] By the church's proclamation of the gospel to all creatures (cf. Mark 16:15), all people are to be illumined by the radiance of Christ, which "brightens the countenance of the church"; for "by her relationship with Christ, the church is a kind of sacrament of intimate union with God, and of the unity of all mankind, that is, she is a sign and an instrument of such union and unity".[151] The Council underlines very distinctly the church as centred in Christ, when it sees its "sacramentality" to be completely "in Christ". Catholic theology therefore speaks also of the "primal sacrament" *(Ursakrament)* which Jesus Christ himself is. The Council takes this direction when it speaks in the Constitution on the Sacred Liturgy of the "Mediator between God and man:... for his humanity, united with the person of the Word, was the instrument of our salvation. Thus in Christ 'there came forth the perfect satisfaction needed for our reconciliation, and we received the means for giving worthy worship to God'."[152]

121. Of the church as the "messianic people" we also read: "Established by Christ as a fellowship of life, charity and truth, it is also used by him as an instrument for the redemption of all, and is sent forth into the whole world as the light of the world and the salt of the earth (cf. Matt. 5:13-16)."[153] The Council sees the establishment of the church as rooted in the whole mystery of Christ[154] but links the statement of the church as "sacrament" in a special way with the resurrection of Christ and the sending of the Spirit: "Rising from the dead (cf. Rom. 6:9), He sent his life-giving Spirit upon his disciples and through this Spirit has established his body, the church, as the universal sacrament of salvation. Sitting at the right hand of the Father, He is continually active in the world, leading men to the church, and through her joining them more closely to himself..."[155]

122. The term "sacrament", as a sign and instrument of salvation, gives expression to the universal mission of the church and its radical dependence on Christ. It thus becomes clear that neither the foundation of the church nor its goal lies in the church itself, and that it therefore does not exist by itself or for itself. Only in and through Christ, only in and through the Holy Spirit is the church effectual as a mediator of sal-

vation. That is especially important when theologians speak of the sacraments as self-actualizations of the church, in order to prevent a purely outward understanding of the church as simply the steward of sacraments as means of grace, and instead to set forth an inner affinity, which though is not an identity, between the church and the sacraments, both being signs and instruments of salvation. As a "communion of life, love and truth" on the one hand and as an "instrument for the salvation of everyone" and as "universal sacrament of salvation" on the other hand, the church is the actual place and instrument of the universal saving will of God "who desires everyone to be saved and to come to the knowledge of the truth" (1 Tim. 2:4). God's will that all should be saved becomes for the individual a gracious promise when the church testifies to the truth of Christ and celebrates and proffers the sacraments, i.e., when Christ's salvation is present in the witness and sacramental celebration of the church done in and through Christ and thus in and through the Holy Spirit. In the church – his body and his bride – Christ himself remains thus present for all people of the world through his saving acts.

123. In Catholic thought the concept of "sacrament" is constantly applied to the church analogically.[156] Church is not "sacrament" in the same sense as the sacraments of baptism and the eucharist. That is already clear in reference to how they function: the individual sacraments develop their saving efficacy "on the basis of their being celebrated";[157] their efficacy is not dependent on the worthiness of the minister or the recipient, because it is Christ who effects salvation in the sacraments. That cannot be said about the church as "sacrament" in the same way. Rather, one applies the concept of sacrament to the church to aid theological reflection, for it clarifies the inner connection between outward, visible structure and hidden, spiritual reality. Just as the sacraments in scholastic thinking are described as visible signs and instruments of invisible grace, Vatican II sees the church as "one interlocked reality which is comprised of a divine and a human element" in which "the communal structure of the church serves Christ's Spirit, who vivifies it by way of building up the body (cf. Eph. 4:16)".[158] But this view of the church as "sacrament" also stands in the context of the effective imparting of salvation to all people: "The one Mediator... communicates truth and grace to all" through the church.[159] Speaking of the church as "sacrament" in the context of salvation for all people and of mission theology shows especially that Vatican II did not simply take over such earlier theories as "primal sacrament". Rather, the Council's own theological point of departure is a further development of earlier considerations.

124. Here again we see that although it is his body, the church cannot be simply identified with Christ absolutely. It is taken into his service to mediate salvation to all people and needs the constant vivifying power of the Holy Spirit. In influencing its own members, it is Christ who as head grants participation in his Spirit and who thus causes the life and growth of the body.[160] It is part of the logic of such a sacramental concept of the church that the church in its human weakness must "incessantly pursue the path of penance and renewal"[161] and be called to "continual reformation".[162] Even outside the "visible structure" of the church, "many elements of sanctification and of truth can be found"[163] and God's saving activity is visibly and latently at work at the same time among "those who have not yet received the gospel".[164]

4.2.3. THE LUTHERAN VIEW

125. For Lutheran theology it is of fundamental and crucial importance that God bestows forgiveness, life and the bliss of salvation on every believer through word and

sacraments as means of grace[165] and that the church as the "assembly of all believers" is the place "in" which these means of grace are effectual.[166] This means that preaching as "the living voice of the gospel"[167] itself has "sacramental" character, given that within the audible word lies the power to impart to the faithful that reality of salvation to which the words of the proclamation point. "When I preach, Christ himself preaches in me."[168] Thus, the "external word",[169] as an "effectual word",[170] stands alongside the sacraments as means of grace. We "must constantly maintain that God will not deal with us except through his external Word and sacrament".[171] The teaching of the Anabaptists "that the Holy Spirit comes to us... without the external word of the gospel"[172] is therefore expressly condemned as such. The condemnation of the Donatists – for whom the sacraments become useless and ineffectual when administered by "wicked priests" – likewise points to the objective efficacy of word and sacrament, which remain "efficacious even if the priests who administer them are wicked men",[173] because they are instituted and enjoined by Christ.

126. But if the church is the place where these means of grace become effectual, it follows that the church itself is in a derivative sense an instrument of salvation. On the one hand it is called into being as a *congregatio fidelium*, a church, through the event of the "means of grace" so that it is itself a *creatura evangelii*; on the other, it is the place where people participate in salvation – there is no alternative. In this sense it is true for Reformation theology too that there is no salvation outside the church.[174]

127. As mediator of word and sacrament the church is the instrument through which the Holy Spirit sanctifies; "it is the mother that begets and bears every Christian through the word of God",[175] but in such a way that Jesus Christ himself is working and becomes salvifically present in its preaching and administration of the sacraments. In other words, however much the mediating activity of the church and the saving activity of God coincide in what happens there, they are nevertheless plainly different in this: while it is true that the church imparts participation in salvation to believers, nevertheless it is Christ alone and not the church who has gained salvation for the world and who bestows on believers participation in this salvation through word and sacrament. In what it does, the church is totally the servant of Christ, its Lord, being called to this service and given authority for it by Christ, its Lord.

128. Against this background, Lutherans note affinities but also questions regarding the new Catholic understanding of the church as "sacrament". Lutheran thought corresponds more closely to the designation of Jesus Christ as "sacrament" found in Augustine[176] and later Roman Catholic theology. Christ is the "single sacrament"[177] of God, because he himself is the means par excellence of salvation. The individual sacraments are means of salvation because through them Jesus Christ accomplishes salvation and thus establishes and preserves the church. This means that the church does not actualize its own existence in the sacraments; rather the church receives salvation and its very being from Christ and only as recipient does it mediate salvation. In this perspective, the individual sacraments are linked with Christ as he faces the church. One should be reticent about language which blurs this distinction. Talk about the church actualizing itself in the sacraments is open to serious misunderstanding and is better avoided. Lutheran theology points to the fact that calling the church "sacrament" must be clearly distinguished from the way "sacrament" is applied to baptism and the Lord's supper.

129. The first Lutheran query entails a second: how does the understanding of the church as "sacrament" relate to that of the church as holy and sinful? Differently from

baptism and the Lord's supper, which exist wholly in their instrumentality and sign-character, the church is instrument and sign of salvation as the community of those who receive salvation. In other words, the church is instrument and sign as the community of believers, who as people justified by God are at the same time holy and sinful. Lutherans point out that Catholic references to the church as "sacrament" must not contradict the fact that the church is at the same time holy and sinful.[178]

130. There are certainly Lutheran theologians who apply "sacrament" to the church. Yet reservations about references to the church as "sacrament" remain in Lutheran theology, since such references can lead to misunderstandings on both the points just explained. Therefore many confine themselves to speaking of the church as sign and instrument of salvation in the sense already outlined.

4.2.4. THE UNITY AND DISTINCTNESS OF CHRIST AND THE CHURCH

131. We can leave it to further theological reflections to determine how Christ and the church are one in sacramental activity without thereby being identified, and how a possible sacramental view of the church therefore has its roots in the fundamental description of Christ as the "primal sacrament" and is limited by that statement. Talk of the church as "sacrament" is in fact foreign to the Lutheran ecclesiological tradition and is acceptable only under the reservations just set forth – reservations which Catholic theologians also take seriously. Nevertheless, harking back to the biblical witness we can together state the following.

132. The New Testament sees the mystery of the relationship between Christ and the church in unity and diversity. The unity is highlighted in a series of statements, for instance, when Paul not only sees baptized believers as "one in Christ" but addresses them as such (Gal. 3:28). According to Paul, the community is "one body in Christ" (Rom. 12:5), and as "body of Christ" (1 Cor. 12:27) is in fact "Christ" (1 Cor. 12:12). It becomes clear that this unity in Christ does not imply an undifferentiated identity when Christ is described as "head of the body, the church" (Col. 1:18; cf. Eph. 1:22f.; 4:14ff.; 5:23). We are to distinguish head from body but on no account to separate them, for the "building up [of] the body of Christ" (Eph. 4:12-16) proceeds from Christ, the head, who has saved the church as his body (cf. Eph. 5:23). "The church is subject to Christ" always (Eph. 5:24) and linked to him in love (cf. Eph. 4:16). The interlinking of unity and diversity becomes clear especially in the image of the bride and bridegroom (cf. 2 Cor. 11:2; Eph. 5:22ff.; Rev. 19:7f.; 21:2; 22:17).

133. Of course the personal relation between Christ and church must not obscure the different quality of relations between the two; for from the start the church is the redeemed, receiving church and remains so forever. Precisely in the light of the doctrine of justification it becomes plain that the church owes its existence and activity solely to the mercy of God in Jesus Christ and to the breath of the Spirit. Only so is Christ able to make salvation effectual through the church in proclamation and the sacraments. Both the Lutheran and Catholic understandings of the church's salvific service through word and sacrament are based on this biblical foundation. We can leave it to theological reflection to explain in greater detail how this works, if only it becomes and remains clear that God's eschatological promise of grace really determines the church's activity and guides it from within, and that salvation thus appears palpably in history. Nevertheless it must be evident that salvation can never be effected by human beings or be at their disposal, but even in the activity of the church it remains the gift of God.

134. On the basis of the stipulations mentioned, there is agreement among Lutherans and Catholics that the church is instrument and sign of salvation and, in this sense, "sacrament" of salvation. To be sure the reservations are taken seriously by both sides, and one must strive for a theological language that is unambiguous.

4.3. The church visible and hidden

135. The view has often been advanced that the terms "visible church" and "invisible church" point to a disagreement between Roman Catholic and Lutheran ecclesiologies. Often one appeals to Luther's saying, the holy church "is invisible, dwelling in the Spirit, in an 'unapproachable' place".[179] Post-Reformation Catholic ecclesiology reacted polemically to such an understanding of the church and focused almost exclusively on the church as an external, visible entity marked out by creed, sacramental structure and hierarchical leadership. Thus, Bellarmine stressed that as an "association"[180] the church was "just as visible and palpable as the Republic of Venice".[181] In the 19th century especially, Lutherans and Catholics both thought that this was the essential difference in their ecclesiologies.

136. But the assumed disagreement often lost its sharp contours, since each side repeatedly denied that it taught what the other side condemned. Thus, Melanchthon in the *Apology of the Augsburg Confession* utterly rejected the reproach that the church was, in the Lutheran Reformation view, only a kind of "Platonic republic".[182] Nor – in the light of the pronouncements of Vatican II – can the reproach be sustained that the one holy church is equated undialectically on the Catholic side with its empirical historical form. For there it is said of the church that while "the visible assembly and the spiritual community" are indeed "not to be considered as two realities", they are nevertheless linked together asymmetrically: "... the communal structure of the church serves Christ's Spirit, who vivifies it by way of building up the body (cf. Eph. 4:16)".[183]

137. It seems that oversimplified formulations have led, wrongly, to the view that here the two churches are at odds. In what follows the aim is to examine whether there is ultimately a conflict between the two positions.

138. On the Lutheran side the Augsburg confession by no means describes the church as an invisible entity. Rather it describes the church as an "assembly"[184] to which a "ministry" constitutively belongs.[185] Also, regarding the words of Luther quoted above[186] one must note that they continue, "... therefore its [the church's] holiness cannot be seen".[187] For Luther the word "church" here does not denote an invisible entity. His point is that the church does not display visibly the essential marks that qualify it as church – in this instance "holiness". That the word "church" nevertheless means a visible assembly becomes evident in the fact that there are "marks" of the church, "that is, word, confession and sacraments",[188] all of which represent extremely visible realities.

139. The Lutheran view of the church is of course marked by a tension which may easily evoke misunderstanding of the "invisibility" of the church. According to the Apology, "hypocrites and evil men are... members of the church according to the outward associations of the church's marks... especially if they have not been excommunicated".[189] Thus, it might seem as if there were on the one hand the invisible "association of the faith" and on the other the "outward association" which is recognizable by "marks". But Lutherans have rejected that view ever since the Apology.[190]

140. Lutheranism sees the church as an "assembly". An assembly is not as such invisible. Invisible rather is the fact that this assembly really is church, i.e., that this visible body is the "body of Christ", that God really is at work in the word and in the sacraments that are its visible marks, and that its ministers are servants of the Holy Spirit. The predicate "invisible" is appropriate for the church insofar as it is an object of faith. This is also shown by the statement of Luther which has been quoted, in which he says "anyone who thinks this way turns the article of the creed 'I believe a holy church' upside down; he replaces 'I believe' with 'I see'".[191] The same purpose is clearly revealed where Luther dissociates himself polemically from abuses of the ambiguous word "church" in ecclesiastical politics. "If these words had been used in the creed: 'I believe that there is a holy Christian people', it would have been easy to avoid all the misery that has come in with this blind, obscure word 'church'."[192]

141. In the Lutheran view, certain aspects of the church's visibility are what it makes invisible: only to the eye of faith is an assembly recognizable as the assembly of the people of God, and yet – between the times – the church has to be visible. In this world what makes it a hidden church is the same as what made Christ on the cross a hidden God, i.e., that he was only all too visible in and for this world. The passage often quoted from Luther's Large Commentary on Galatians makes this clear. The crucial section reads: "God conceals and covers [the church] with weaknesses, sins, errors and various offences and forms of the cross in such a way that it is not evident to the senses anywhere."[193]

142. The tension characteristic of the Lutheran understanding of the hiddenness of the church manifests a recurring problematic which all traditions have wrestled with in understanding the church and which they must continue to deal with. That is why Vatican II says that "possessing the Spirit of Christ" is fundamental to being "fully incorporated into the society of the church". Those are not saved, however, who do "not persevere in charity", though they remain "indeed in the bosom of the church" but "only in a 'bodily' manner and not 'in their hearts'".[194] In its Constitution on the Church the Council does not solve the problem. The difficulty of the relationship between church membership "according to the heart" and membership only "according to the body", and thus between the church as spiritual and as visible corporeal entity, is for us a common difficulty. To be sure, the Lutheran emphasis that the hiddenness of the church corresponds to a specific characteristic of the Christian faith, namely recognizing God at work in that which seems opposed to him, introduces a dimension which goes beyond the problem of the recognition of church membership.

143. In statements quoted from Vatican II's Dogmatic Constitution on the Church, Lutherans discern important convergences in the way the church is understood. The constitution sees the church unambiguously in the context of the mystery of the universal bestowal of the saving love of God the Father, as that is revealed in the history of Jesus as the Christ[195] and made effective by the Holy Spirit in election, reconciliation and communion, so that "all believers would have access to the Father through Christ in the one Spirit".[196] The constitution resolutely maintains that the church is the "body of Christ". In so doing it follows the Pauline statements, but it avoids precise definition of membership in this body.[197]

144. The Constitution on the Church produces a synthesis, which is new for Catholic theology, between the spiritual or transcendent reality of the church and its visible social reality. The spiritual community of faith, hope and love lives on the basis of the Father's

gift. Through the one bread which Christ proffers, believers are made into one body, and as temple of the Holy Spirit, the church is above all a mystery of communion with the triune God himself.[198] At the same time the church is also a historical reality. It began with Jesus' proclamation of the reign of God and the founding of the messianic people of the new covenant, and this community of disciples has had unmistakable elements of social organization since the apostolic age.[199] The visible congregation stands in a complex relation to the mystery of the koinonia in which it has its origin and to which it seeks to give credible shape. Because the Council posits an indissoluble link between the church as a visible assembly and the mystery of life shared in communion with God, it is possible to speak of the church as a "sacrament".[200]

145. Crucial here is the analogy between the visible communal structure serving the life-giving Spirit, by which it is vivified, and the assumed human nature of Christ serving the eternal Word.[201] By the very fact of its service, the social community is involved in a constant struggle as it journeys through history. Again and again it is in need of cleansing and renewal;[202] and this continuous reform encompasses all the moral, disciplinary and doctrinal witness of the church to God's grace.[203]

146. A simple identification of the salvation-community with the empirical church, such as would place the empirical church beyond reform, is clearly labelled by Vatican II as an error which Catholic teaching should avoid.

147. Catholics and Lutherans are in agreement that the saving activity of the triune God calls and sanctifies believers through audible and visible means of grace which are mediated in an audible and visible ecclesial community. They also agree that in this world the salvation-community of Christ is hidden, because as a spiritual work of God it is unrecognizable by earthly standards, and because sin, which is also present in the church, makes ascertaining its membership uncertain.

4.4. Holy church/sinful church

148. With the creeds of the early church we confess in common that the church is "holy". This holiness essentially consists in the fact that the church participates in the triune God, who alone is holy (cf. Rev. 15:4), from whom it derives and to whom it is journeying:

– The church is holy through the gracious election and faithfulness of God. Just as the people of the old covenant were a "holy nation" because they had been chosen to be God's "treasured possession" (Ex. 19:5f.; cf. Lev. 11:44f.; Deut. 7:6), so too by virtue of the new covenant of grace the church is God's "holy nation", the people who became his special possession (1 Pet. 2:9).
– The church is holy through the saving work of Christ. Christ sanctified himself for his own, "so that they also may be sanctified in truth" (John 17:19); he sacrificed himself for the church, his "bride", "in order to make her holy" (Eph. 5:25f.).
– The church is holy through the presence of the Holy Spirit. The Holy Spirit dwells in believers as in a temple (cf. 1 Cor. 3:16; 6:19; Eph. 2:22); they are "sanctified by the Holy Spirit" (Rom. 15:16; cf. 1 Cor. 6:11); the Holy Spirit builds up the church and equips it by means of the gifts of the Spirit (cf. 1 Cor. 12; Eph. 4:11f.); the Holy Spirit gives life to the church and strengthens it through spiritual fruits (cf. Gal. 5:22).

149. In so far as the holiness of the church continues to be rooted in the holiness of the triune God, we make common confession that the church in its holiness is indestructible. Christ has promised his presence to his disciples "to the end of the age"

(Matt. 28:20) and has promised his church that "the gates of Hades will not prevail against it" (Matt. 16:18).

150. Vatican II's Dogmatic Constitution on the Church states: "The church... is holy in a way which can never fail. For Christ, the Son of God,... loved the church as his bride, delivering himself up for her. This he did that he might sanctify her (cf. Eph. 5:25-26). He united her to himself as his own body and crowned her with the gift of the Holy Spirit, for God's glory."[204]

151. This belief in the indestructibility and abiding existence of the church as the one holy people of God is an essential element in Luther's ecclesiology and is fundamental for a correct understanding of his struggle for reform. "The Children's creed [catechism] teaches us (as was said) that a Christian holy people is to be and to remain on earth until the end of the world. This is an article of faith that cannot be terminated until that which it believes comes, as Christ promises, 'I am with you always, to the close of the age'."[205] In this sense the Augsburg confession says, "It is also taught... that one holy Christian church will be and remain forever."[206]

152. This belief in the indestructibility of the one holy church includes the idea that in the ultimate sense the church cannot apostatize from the truth and fall into error. In this conviction the Reformation understands itself to be in continuity with the prior theological and ecclesiastical tradition; thus, it has always understood the biblical promises in this way (cf. Matt. 16:18; 28:20; John 16:13). So "the church cannot err"[207] repeatedly occurs in the Reformers in this or a similar form,[208] and the Catholic-Lutheran dialogue has also referred to this shared conviction.[209]

153. Of course, the confession of the church's holiness has always gone hand in hand with the knowledge that the power of evil and sin, although it will not overcome the church, is nevertheless at work in it. The church "without a spot or wrinkle or anything of the kind" (Eph. 5:27) will appear only at the end of its earthly pilgrimage, when "Christ will present her to himself in all her glory".[210] The holiness of the church therefore exists both "already" and "not yet". It is a "genuine though imperfect holiness".[211]

154. It is part of the theological tradition of our churches to apply the biblical pictures and parables of the weeds among the wheat (cf. Matt. 13:38), the wise and foolish bridesmaids (cf. Matt. 25:1ff.) or the net and the fish (cf. Matt. 13:47f.), to the church in its visible and temporal reality: the church in its concrete form always includes good and evil people, believers and unbelievers, true and false teachers. The ancient church's condemnation of the Novatian and Donatist views of the church was adopted by the Reformation. The statement in article 8 of the Augsburg confession, that in the church, which is "properly speaking nothing else than the assembly of all believers and saints", there are nevertheless still "many false Christians, hypocrites and even open sinners... among the godly",[212] expresses a conviction shared equally by Catholics and Lutherans.

155. As especially the Lutheran-Roman Catholic dialogue on justification has shown, there is also agreement that all believers as members of the church are involved in a relentless struggle against sin and are in need of daily repentance and the forgiveness of sins. They depend constantly on justifying grace and rely on the promise which is given them in the struggle against evil.

156. With this in mind, it is not in dispute between us that the church is "holy" and "sinful" at the same time and that the imperative calling to holiness is always a con-

comitant of the indicative that holiness has been bestowed (cf. 1 Thess. 4:3f.,7; 2 Cor. 7:1). Thus, the church is in constant need of repentance and the forgiveness of sins, and of cleansing and renewal. Vatican II stated this repeatedly, even if it does not use the term "sinful" of the church. The Dogmatic Constitution on the Church says: "While Christ, 'holy, innocent, undefiled' (Heb. 7:26), knew nothing of sin (2 Cor. 5:21), but came to expiate only the sins of the people (cf. Heb. 2:17), the church, embracing sinners in her bosom, is at the same time holy and always in need of being purified, and incessantly pursues the path of penance and renewal."[213] And the Decree on Ecumenism states, "Christ summons the church, as she goes her pilgrim way, to that continual reformation of which she always has need, insofar as she is an institution of men here on earth."[214]

157. Differences between our churches emerge in answering the question: Where does the idea of the church's need for renewal or of its sinfulness find its necessary limit, by reason of the divine pledge that the church abides in the truth and that error and sin will not overcome it?

158. The Lutheran Reformation no less emphatically than Roman Catholic theology stresses the fact that there is and must be such a limit. Thus, Luther is able to distinguish between "erring" and "remaining in error". By this he wishes to show how abiding in the truth, which is promised to the church, is not a reality in peaceful possession but, under the faithfulness and forgiveness of God, is realized in ongoing struggle against error.[215] Even more important is the distinction he makes between the teaching and the life of the church. Whereas in regard to its life the "holy church is not without sin, as it confesses in the Lord's prayer 'Forgive us our sins'",[216] the opposite is true of its teaching, i.e., of its obedient proclamation of the gospel, insofar as the gospel is preached, the sacraments are administered, and absolution is given "on behalf of Christ" (2 Cor. 5:20)[217] and by his authority. "The teaching must be neither sinful nor reprehensible and it does not have its place in the Lord's prayer in which we say 'Forgive us our sins'. For it is not our doing, but God's own word which cannot sin or do wrong."[218]

159. In this conception the Lutheran Reformation lies wholly in the realm of what is also maintained on the Catholic side. The conviction that the church's abiding in the truth – its indefectibility – is not a reality held in peaceful possession is also shared on the Catholic side. Therefore, Catholics and Lutherans can say in common that "the church's abiding in the truth should not be understood in a static way but as a dynamic event which takes place with the aid of the Holy Spirit in ceaseless battle against error and sin in the church as well as in the world".[219] Luther's distinction between the life and the teaching of the church corresponds to the Catholic distinction between the "members" of the church, who in their constancy in faith, their life and their deeds are always in need of the forgiveness of sins and of renewal,[220] and the church itself, which in teaching and proclamation expounds the unalterable "deposit of faith";[221] between the church as an "institution of men here on earth", which "Christ summons... to... continual reformation",[222] and the church as "enriched with heavenly things", as a divine creation with the "elements of sanctification and of truth" given to it by Christ.[223]

160. From the Lutheran standpoint serious questions to the Catholic view first present themselves where the God-given indestructible holiness of the church and God's promise that the church will abide in the truth are so objectivized in specific ecclesial

components that they appear to be exempt from critical questioning. Above all this, Lutheran query is directed at ecclesial offices and decisions which serve people's salvation and sanctification. The question arises when the Holy Spirit's aid is attributed to them in such a way that as such they appear to be immune from the human capacity for error and sinfulness and therefore from needing to be examined. That will be dealt with in what follows.[224] Similar questions are also directed at the institution of the canonization of saints.

161. These Lutheran questions cannot be regarded as superfluous, even in the light of the fact that in the Catholic view these ecclesial offices and decisions have their historically variable forms and are carried out by sinful human beings. For that reason they continue to be imperfect, can obscure the indestructible holiness of the church,[225] and therefore are in need of reform.[226]

162. In fact these Lutheran queries touch directly on the self-understanding of the Roman Catholic Church at a decisive point; but they suggest conclusions which as such were not there from the beginning.

163. The Lord's promise that it will abide in the truth is the basis for the Catholic church's belief that the truth can be articulated in propositions and can lead to forms of expressing the gospel which are inerrant and infallible.[227] Further, it believes that there are abiding, established ecclesial offices which are willed by God's providence.[228] Also that the saints perfected by God are not all anonymous but are named by canonization as those who may be addressed as the perfected of God.[229]

164. Thereby very diverse areas are addressed of which the first, inerrant truth, and the last, perfected holiness, have one thing in common: they express the fact that God's activity in this world – in its decisive and definitive quality – is incarnational and anticipates the eschaton. They of course represent such diverse levels that they should not simply be mentioned in one breath. Catholic thinking finds it hard to see why the effects of divine decisiveness should be intrinsically open to criticism and why it is not enough to distinguish between human sinfulness and the divine saving activity in such a way that, although they remain exposed to human inadequacy and sinfulness, God's works are inherently good and cannot be rendered ineffectual.

165. In spite of the above questions one may, regarding the overarching problematic of the holiness of the church and its need for renewal, speak of common Lutheran-Roman Catholic basic convictions. Taken together they constitute a broad consensus within which remaining differences are neither abolished nor denied. Still only in discussing each of the relevant ecclesiological points in question is it possible to discover their theological and ecumenical importance.

4.5. The significance of the doctrine of justification for the understanding of the church

4.5.1. THE PROBLEM AND THE ORIGINAL CONSENSUS

166. Many of the questions which Catholics and Lutherans address to one another regarding the relation between the doctrine of justification and the understanding of the church emerge from two different concerns, which may be summarized as follows: Catholics ask whether the Lutheran understanding of justification does not diminish the reality of the church; Lutherans ask whether the Catholic understanding of church does not obscure the gospel as the doctrine of justification explicates it. Neither con-

cern is unfounded, but needs to be clarified, especially because the New Testament knows of no opposition between gospel and church.

167. In dealing with the relationship between the doctrine of justification and the understanding of the church, it is important to note which perspective on justification is employed. It is not primarily a matter of how the saving event can be rightly described and how God communicates his righteousness to the sinner. This indeed stands at the centre of Reformation arguments but, as such, has no immediate critical implications for ecclesiology. These emerge only when – as happened especially in the Lutheran Reformation – justification is seen both as centre and criterion of all theology. Therefore the doctrine of the church must correspond to justification as criterion. The reciprocal questions of Catholics and Lutherans mentioned above arise only from such a perspective.

168. The far-reaching consensus in the understanding of justification noted during this and other Lutheran-Roman Catholic dialogues leads to testing the consensus on the critical significance of the doctrine of justification for all church doctrine, order and practice. Everything which is believed and taught regarding the nature of the church, the means of grace, and the ordained ecclesial ministry must be grounded in the salvation event itself and bear the mark of justification-faith as reception and appropriation of that event. Correspondingly, all that is believed and taught regarding the nature and effects of justification must be understood in the total context of assertions about the church, the means of grace, and the church's ordained ministry. Expressing the Lutheran position, the Malta report of 1972, *The Gospel and the Church*, stated: "... all traditions and institutions of the church are subject to the criterion which asks whether they are enablers of the proper proclamation of the gospel and do not obscure the unconditional character of the gift of salvation".[230] In the United States, the Lutheran-Roman Catholic dialogue took over this assertion as its common declaration: "Catholics as well as Lutherans can acknowledge the need to test the practices, structures and theologies of the church by the extent to which they help or hinder 'the proclamation of God's free and merciful promises in Christ Jesus which can be rightly received only through faith'."[231]

4.5.2. COMMON BASIC CONVICTIONS

169. Just as the New Testament does not acknowledge a fundamental contradiction between gospel and church, so we too must beware lest we see justification and the church as being from the outset in conflict with each other, let alone as being incompatible. Three basic convictions, shared by Catholics and Lutherans, and which lead from the doctrine of justification into ecclesiology, prevent that.

170. First, the gospel, as the Reformation doctrine of justification understands it, is essentially an "external word". That is to say it is always mediated through one or more individuals addressing one or more other individuals. The gospel is not a doctrine that can be internalized as one's own in such a way that thereafter no further address from other persons is needed. It remains a message "from outside", and hearers remain dependent on its communication by one who proclaims it. This is expressed, for instance, in article 7 of the Augsburg confession, which describes the church not simply as the "assembly of all believers" or *congregatio sanctorum* but also links this "assembly of all believers" constitutively to the "external" witness of the gospel in preaching and the sacraments, which conversely can have their place only in the

church, "the assembly of all believers".[232] On the one hand, the church lives from the gospel; on the other, the gospel sounds forth in the church and summons into the community of the church.

171. Second, the gospel which is proclaimed in the Holy Spirit is according to its nature a creative word. If belief in the gospel is our righteousness, then the gospel does not merely inform us about righteousness but makes us through the Holy Spirit into new, justified persons who already "walk in newness of life" (Rom. 6:4). This conviction, common to Catholics and Lutherans, leads into the understanding of church. For if we confess in common that the gospel that gathers the church really is God's creative word, then we must also confess in common that the church itself really is God's creation and as such is a social reality that unites people.

172. Third, God, who creates the church through his word and has promised that it will abide in the truth and will continue to exist, is faithful to his word and his promise. In the interim, until this promise attains its eschatological goal in the consummation of all things, God effects his faithfulness in the historical form of the church also through structures of historical continuity. Previously, Old Testament Israel was a real historical people which lived from God's promises. To them he gave structures of historical continuity. To be sure, the continuity of the church appears especially to Lutherans to be a constant struggling against the dangers of error and apostasy and finally a victory of God's faithfulness over the constantly recurring unfaithfulness of human beings. This view rests on constitutive ecclesial experiences which are not without their ecclesiological relevance. But Lutherans nonetheless hold that the church will continue in existence and that there are structures which contribute to this continuity, without of course being able to guarantee it.

4.5.3. THE AREAS OF CONTROVERSY

173. The questions which arise regarding the relationship between justification and the church may be presented and discussed in four areas: (1) the institutional continuity of the church, (2) the ordained ministry as ecclesial institution, (3) the teaching function of the church's ministry, and (4) the jurisdictional function of the church's ministry. Each of these areas relates to the above-mentioned reciprocal questioning by Catholics and Lutherans: whether the Lutheran doctrine of justification diminishes the reality of the church; whether the Catholic understanding of the church obscures the gospel as it is explicated by the doctrine of justification.

4.5.3.1. *Institutional continuity of the church*

174. As a creature of the gospel and its proclamation, which is always "external", creative, and sustained by God's faithfulness, the church exists continuously through the ages: "one holy Christian church will be and remain forever".[233] Just as everything God creates through his word and sustains in faithfulness to his word has its history, so too the church has its history. It is historical like other creatures, though in a unique way: only the church is promised that it will endure and that the gates of hell will not overcome it.

175. The historicity of the church is most profoundly bound up with that of the gospel which calls it into being and from which it lives. As the proclaimed and transmitted external word the gospel mediates the abiding faithfulness of God in the midst of the history of this world.

176. The church created by the gospel is more than the total sum of persons who belong to it here and now. The church is "assembly" not only as congregation which gathers for worship at a particular time and in a particular place. At the same time it is "assembly" in a sense transcending time and place, as church of all people and generations, as the church founded in the Christ-event and existing in the pre-existent reality of fellowship in the body of Christ. In this sense the church is a communal, social reality of singular character and continuous existence.

177. If God creates the church as an historical community with a continuous existence by means of the external gospel, this activity of God has its counterpart in the establishment of structural and institutional realities. These serve the continuity of this community, are an expression of it and therefore themselves have a continuous existence. The founding of the church, i.e., its institution in the Christ-event and the establishment of such structural and institutional realities, are therefore indissolubly linked together.

178. Apostolic preaching, which has its precipitate in the New and the Old Testament canons, together with the sacraments of baptism and the Lord's supper and the divinely empowered "ministry of reconciliation" (2 Cor. 5:18), are such God-appointed means and signs of the continuity of the church which, according to Reformation conviction too, remain constantly in the church.[234] They are institutions in which God makes his creative grace and sustaining faithfulness visible and effective, and which for their part effect and testify to the permanence of the church by their continuity. Their perpetual continuity and that of the church are inseparable.

179. These realities, which were established along with the foundation of the church, have taken on specific forms in the course of history or have produced other realities which in turn testify to the continuity of the church and serve it, and which therefore likewise have a long-term purpose or have proven themselves to be enduring. This is particularly true regarding the forms which the "ministry of reconciliation" took on very early in the history of the church. But it also holds good for the creeds, dogmas or confessional writings which have arisen in history as an expression of the apostolic faith, and which have their basis in the biblical writings, especially in the confessions of faith found in the New Testament. Our two churches give in part different and indeed controversial responses to the question of how far and to what degree these ecclesiastical realities which have arisen in history share in the enduring quality of the realities established when the church was founded. The reasons for the differences are certainly theological and ecclesiological, but very often they also reflect different experiences of the church. But it is not in dispute that (1) these realities arose in the history of the church and were not directly and explicitly established when it was founded; (2) they can certainly give expression to the continuity of the church and be of service to it; and (3) they nevertheless remain capable of renewal and in need of renewal.

180. Above all, however, it is agreed that all institutional or structural elements of church continuity are and remain instruments of the gospel, which alone creates and sustains the church, not in their own right but only insofar and as long as they testify to the continuity of the church and serve that continuity. Their effectiveness as signs and means of the continuity of the church is limited and called in question when and for as long as their relatedness to and transparency for that gospel are diminished or obscured.

181. This is true regarding how the church deals with the realities which are integral to its foundation and – according to our common conviction – are indispensable to it, such as the word of God available in the canon of holy scripture, the sacraments of baptism and the Lord's supper, and the ministry of reconciliation. But this is especially true of the signs and means of continuity in the church which have emerged in history. Here the idea of the indispensable nature of these signs and instruments of institutional continuity for the church, as advocated not only but especially on the Catholic side, may itself evoke the concern, and indeed reproach that the gospel of the radical gratuitousness of the gift of salvation and unconditional nature of the reception of salvation is being obscured. Consequently, special care is needed to see to it that these instruments and signs of institutional continuity in the church do not cease to function as servants of the gospel, not even when one seems obligated to grant them an ecclesially indispensable and binding character.

4.5.3.2. Ordained ministry as institution in the church

182. It has already been said in common[235] that the "ministry of reconciliation" which proclaims reconciliation with God "on behalf of Christ" (2 Cor. 5:18-20) is one of the indispensable institutional realities given to the church from the beginning to express and serve its continuity.[236] It was also said in common that these realities built into the church, and also their further configurations in history, do not in themselves testify to the church's continuity or bring it about, except insofar as they serve the gospel through which the Holy Spirit creates and sustains the church. The more these institutional realities are thus subordinated to the justification criterion, the less we can say that they as such contradict the doctrine of justification and are condemned by it.

183. This is true also of the ordained ministry insofar as it is by its nature, according to our churches' view, that "ministry of reconciliation" (2 Cor. 5:18). The critical assertion that the ordained ministry as an institution of continuity by its very existence runs counter to the doctrine of justification is thus repudiated fundamentally.

184. However, the fact that the Reformation doctrine of justification and its emphasis on the unconditionality of the gift of salvation has at times been understood as questioning the necessity of the ordained ministry and the legitimacy of its institutional, ecclesial form calls for an even more pointed rejoinder.

185. First of all it must be stressed, as the previous Roman Catholic-Lutheran dialogue has done, that the Lutheran Reformation knows no such ecclesiological consequence of the doctrine of justification. There is no contradiction between the doctrine of justification and the idea of an ordained ministry instituted by God and necessary for the church. Quite the opposite. The Augsburg confession already makes this clear, with its characteristic transition from the article on justification[237] to that on the church's ministry.[238] There justifying faith is grounded in the gospel, which the ordained ministry is to proclaim in word and sacraments. Article 14 of the Augsburg confession excludes the idea, which only arose in the 19th century, that "the church's ministry" or the "preaching ministry" could mean anything other than the ecclesiastical institution of the ordained ministry. For Luther and the Lutheran confessions, the church's ministry and the gospel are so closely united that they can both be spoken of in identical terms[239] and can let the church be founded on the ministry.[240] In a similar sense Lutheran orthodoxy taught that the triune God is "the primary efficient cause" of

the church and that the church's ministry is the "efficient cause which God uses to gather his church".[241]

186. In agreement with the Reformation, and without contradicting the Reformation doctrine of justification, we can therefore repeat what has already been said in the Lutheran-Roman Catholic dialogue on the ministry: "... the existence of a special ministry is abidingly constitutive for the church".[242]

187. These points show that Reformation thought provides no basis for fearing that the very existence of an ordained ministry as necessary institution for the church obscures the gospel. Above all it must be seen how the institution of the ministry is positively in line with the gospel and its explication through the doctrine of justification.

188. If the New Testament – and with it the Lutheran Reformation – sees the special character of the ordained ministry in the fact that ministers are called to preach reconciliation publicly "on behalf of Christ" (2 Cor. 5:20),[243] and thus stand "over against the community" even while "within the community",[244] this corresponds directly to the inmost concern of the doctrine of justification itself. At stake is that God in Christ approaches human beings "from outside" for their salvation notwithstanding everything they know, are capable of, and are. Human beings – even believers – cannot say to themselves what God has to say to them and cannot bring themselves to that salvation which God alone has prepared for them. This structural movement "outside us and for us"[245] is constitutive of the saving revelation of God in Christ. It is continued in the proclamation of the gospel and must continue there if the gospel is not to be obscured. For this, God establishes the ordained ministry, and consequently, from among his many followers, Jesus calls his emissaries, in whom his mission from the Father is continued (cf. John 20:21; 17:18) and of whom it is true to say "whoever listens to you listens to me" (Luke 10:16) and "whoever welcomes you welcomes me, and whoever welcomes me welcomes the one who sent me" (Matt. 10:40).

189. Thus, not only does the institution of the ordained ministry not contradict the gospel as it is explicated by the doctrine of justification, but corresponds to it and in the last analysis receives its character of indispensability for the church from that correspondence. The Lutheran-Roman Catholic dialogue on the church's ministry had drawn attention to this also when it stated with the Accra document of that time and with the later BEM statement[246] that "the presence of this ministry in the community 'signifies the priority of divine initiative and authority in the church's existence'".[247]

190. It is no contradiction of the close connection between the ministry and the gospel but is rather in line with it, that for the ministry and for ordained ministers the doctrine of justification as explication of the gospel must be the criterion for their own self-understanding and actions. For although the connection between the ministry and the gospel certainly exists, it is no guarantee against abuse and false doctrine. Just as the New Testament knows of and warns against "false teachers"[248] and "false apostles"[249] (2 Pet. 2:1; 2 Cor. 11:13), it is also part of the historical experience of the church that the office, in its bearers and their ministry, may come to contradict the gospel (cf. Gal 1:6ff.; 2:14). The way this experience registers in the ecclesiology and church law of our two churches differs in part. The possibility of a conflict between the ministry and the gospel and thus the need for the church to stand guard over the primacy of the gospel are however seen and affirmed on both sides.

191. The conviction that the doctrine of justification must, as an explication of the gospel, be the critical yardstick for our understanding and exercise of the ministry is applied in the Lutheran Reformation and the Lutheran churches in a special and for them significant way. It relates to the specific forms which the divinely instituted ministry has assumed in the course of history. This is true above all in regard to the specific formation of the ecclesial ministry of leadership *(episcope)*. The development of the ministry into an episcopate standing in a historic succession, i.e., the continuity of apostolic succession which occurred already very early in history,[250] was fully affirmed by the Lutheran Reformation and emphatically championed,[251] just as other church realities were affirmed and conserved which had come into being in the course of history (e.g., the biblical canon, the creeds of the ancient church). For Lutheran thinking too it is entirely possible to acknowledge that the historical development of an episcopate in a historic succession was not something purely within the sphere of history, set in motion only by sociological and political factors, but that it "has taken place with the help of the Holy Spirit" and that it "constitutes something essential for the church".[252]

192. However, Lutherans cannot agree when something is seen in this historically developed formation of the ministry whose existence plays a part in determining the very being of the church. The reason is not simply the ecclesial experience of the Reformation, namely that, at least in central Europe, the Reformation struggled for the truth of the gospel not only without the support of the church's episcopate but even against its resistance. The deeper reason is the concern that putting episcopacy on such a level endangers the unconditional nature of the gift of salvation and its reception. And that is precisely what is at stake in the Reformation doctrine of justification. For this unconditionality necessarily implies that only that may be considered necessary for the church to be church which is already given by Jesus Christ himself as means of salvation. If ecclesial structures, which emerged in history, are elevated to that level, they become preconditions for receiving salvation and so, in the Lutheran view, are put illegitimately on the same level with the gospel proclaimed in word and sacrament, which alone is necessary for salvation and the church.

193. Here a clear difference between Catholics and Lutherans reveals itself in the theological and ecclesiological evaluation of the episcopal office in historic succession, a difference which has been repeatedly noted in the Catholic-Lutheran dialogue up to now.[253]

194. According to Roman Catholic understanding, there is an historic development of the then-permanent form of the ordained ministry. This is especially true of its post-apostolic organization into "bishops, priests and other ministers".[254] Here of course we have to consider that this post-apostolic organization and identification of distinctions in the ministry is already attested to incipiently in the Bible and was introduced in the transition from the "emerging" to the "developed" church.

195. The shared Catholic-Lutheran conviction that the historical emergence of the ministry's structure is not simply to be traced back to human – sociological and political – factors but "has taken place with the help of the Holy Spirit"[255] is, in the Catholic view, understood and prioritized differently than in Lutheran thought. Unlike the Lutherans, Catholics see a "divine institution" in the organization of the ministry as it has developed through history, i.e., a development led, willed and testified to by divine providence.[256] Under the operation of the Holy Spirit within the apostolic tradition,

episcopacy and apostolic succession as orderly transmission of the ordained ministry have developed as the expression, means and criterion of the continuity of the tradition in post-apostolic times. Thus, in the providence of God the bishops "by divine institution"[257] are successors to the apostles. The task of the apostles to tend the church of God continues in the episcopacy, and bishops are to exercise it continually.

196. The episcopate and apostolic succession as the orderly transmission of the ordained ministry in the church are therefore in the Catholic view essential for the church as church, and so are necessary and indispensable. Nevertheless, word and sacrament are the two pillars of the church which are necessary for salvation. The episcopate and apostolic succession stand in service as ministry to what is necessary for salvation, so that the word will be authentically preached and the sacraments rightly celebrated. The episcopate and apostolic succession serve to safeguard the apostolic tradition, the content of which is expressed in the rule of faith. The Spirit of God uses the episcopate in order to identify the church in every historical situation with its apostolic origin, to integrate the faithful in the one universal faith of the church, and just so through the episcopate to make its liberating force effective. In this sense the episcopate is in the Catholic view a necessary service of the gospel, which is itself necessary for salvation.

197. The difference between the Catholic and Lutheran views on the theological and ecclesiological evaluation of the episcopate is thus not so radical that a Lutheran rejection or even indifference towards this ministry stands in opposition to the Catholic assertion of its ecclesial indispensability. The question is rather one of a clear gradation in the evaluation of this ministry, which can be and has been described on the Catholic side by predicates such as "necessary" or "indispensable", and on the Lutheran side as "important", "meaningful" and thus "desirable".[258]

198. For a proper understanding of this Catholic-Lutheran difference in the evaluation of the episcopate, it is necessary to observe that behind it lie two different correlations of salvation and church.

199. According to the Lutheran doctrine of justification and the Lutheran understanding of the church, it is only through the proclamation of the gospel in word and sacraments, which ordained ministers are called to do, that the Holy Spirit effects justifying faith[259] and that the church is created and preserved.[260] The church exists in the full sense of the word where this saving gospel proclamation takes place.[261]

200. Following this ecclesiological line, nothing good and "profitable"[262] for ecclesial communion which exists alongside the gospel proclaimed in word and sacraments may be considered ecclesially necessary, in the strict sense of that word, lest the one thing necessary for salvation – the gospel – be endangered.[263]

201. According to the Catholic understanding of faith, there is also a stable correlation of church and salvation which cannot be dissolved. Therefore Vatican II calls the church "the universal sacrament of salvation".[264] It is sign and instrument of salvation for all humanity, so that without the church there is no salvation. Within this context, however, Catholic thinking further differentiates the subjective and personal consideration of human salvation by reason of God's grace and the objective and ecclesiological view of the church as recipient and mediator of salvation. Therefore, the Second Vatican Council maintains with regard to non-Catholic Christians that "many elements of sanctification and of truth can be found outside of her visible structure"[265] and that the non-Catholic churches and communities are used by Christ's Spirit as "means of

salvation".[266] In addition, Vatican II says in relation to non-Christians that God's saving activity is at once visibly and invisibly at work among those who have not yet received the gospel, and that God "can lead those inculpably ignorant of the gospel to that faith without which it is impossible to please him".[267] To this extent there is, according to Catholic understanding, a correlation between salvation and church consisting not only in the church membership of those who hear the word in faith and receive the sacraments fruitfully, but there is also an ordination to the church on the basis of the visible and hidden saving work of God's grace outside the church which can lead to saving faith.

202. This differentiation is also expressed regarding the ecclesial necessity of the episcopal office in apostolic succession, something which is not necessary for the salvation of individual persons. Because of such a differentiation it is possible for Catholics to assert the necessity of this office without thereby contradicting the doctrine of justification. Thus the episcopal office is understood in the church as a necessary ministry of the gospel, which itself is necessary for salvation.

203. Even so, Catholics will have to take seriously and answer the Lutheran question. If Catholics hold that the Lord's supper celebrated in Lutheran churches has "because of the lack *[defectus]* of the sacrament of orders... not preserved the genuine and total reality *[substantia]* of the eucharistic mystery",[268] does that not, after all, show that they regard the episcopal office in historic succession as the regular transmitter of the ordained ministry in the church, and so indirectly as necessary for salvation? Catholics must answer that an ecclesiology focused on the concept of succession, as held in the Catholic church, need in no way deny the saving presence of the Lord in a eucharist celebrated by Lutherans.

204. The difference in the theological and ecclesiological evaluation of the episcopal office in historic succession loses its sharpness when Lutherans attribute such a value to the episcopate that regaining full communion in this office seems important and desirable, and when Catholics recognize that "the ministry in the Lutheran churches exercises essential functions of the ministry that Jesus Christ instituted in his church"[269] and does not contest the point that the Lutheran churches are church.[270] The difference in evaluating the historic episcopate is thereby interpreted in such a way that the doctrine of justification is no longer at stake and consequently it is also possible to advocate theologically the regaining of full communion in the episcopate.[271]

4.5.3.3. Binding church doctrine and the teaching function of the ministry

205. The church's abiding in the truth, which is God's promise and also his commission to the church, requires inescapably that the church must distinguish the truth of the gospel from error. That means, however, the church must teach. This does not at all contradict the Reformation doctrine of justification because its own claim is to promote this very distinction between truth and error in a fundamental way.

206. The commission to continue in the truth, like the promise to bring this about, holds good for the church as a whole. Our churches are agreed on this. We also agree that it is primarily the Spirit of God, promised to the church and dwelling in it,[272] who enables it so to continue and gives it the authority to distinguish truth and error in a binding way, that is, to teach.[273] Finally, we agree that for his activity God in the Holy Spirit makes use of temporal instruments and circumstances which he himself has bestowed upon the church as a temporal and creaturely entity;[274] and that the ministry

is one of these instruments and circumstances.²⁷⁵ There is no tension between this and the doctrine of justification as criterion for the church's life and activity.

207. It is in fact true of the Lutheran as much as of the Roman Catholic Church that like the church in every age, it is a teaching church which sees itself under the continuing commission to preserve the truth of the gospel and to reject error. Its catechisms, especially Luther's Large Catechism, and most particularly the confessions with their "teaching" and "rejecting" exemplify this.²⁷⁶

208. The difference between our churches only begins to surface where the issue is how the church's responsibility for teaching is exercised. When the Roman Catholic Church attributes a special responsibility and authority for teaching to the ministry and in particular to the episcopate, this in itself still does not imply any essential difference from the Lutheran view and practice. For in the Lutheran view too the ministry, along with its mission and authority to preach the gospel and inseparably from them, is given a responsibility for the "purity" of the proclaimed gospel and the "right" administration of the sacraments "according to the gospel".²⁷⁷ It was also axiomatic for the Reformation that there are ordered ministries in the church such as the teaching office of theologians and faculties who had the right and duty to distinguish truth and error in a special way. Luther was himself able to assert his rights as a theological teacher in face of the ecclesiastical authorities who had themselves appointed him as such.

209. Following the medieval tradition, it was extremely common for the theological faculties in areas of the Lutheran Reformation to exercise something like an ecclesial teaching function. Nor was it contested on the Reformation side that a special responsibility for teaching belongs to the bishops: they are entitled "according to divine right... to... judge doctrine and condemn doctrine that is contrary to the gospel", and congregations are therefore in duty "bound to be obedient to the bishops according to the saying of Christ in Luke 10:16, 'He who hears you hears me'."²⁷⁸ The episcopal structure was however not preserved in most churches of the Reformation.²⁷⁹ Very early in the German lands (about 1527) there developed within the framework of ecclesial governance by princes an alternative system for supra-parish doctrinal oversight by creating superintendents, visitors or visitation commissions. They exercised the function of a teaching office by seeing to it that parish preaching and the administration of the sacraments were true to the gospel. "Also in our day there is interpretation and development of church doctrine in Lutheran churches through the decisions of the appropriate ecclesial authorities" (bishops' synods, church councils) in which office-bearers, church members, and theological teachers together play a part.²⁸⁰ Nevertheless, significant differences appear here too.

210. The Reformers thought that the promise and responsibility which held good for the whole church was concentrated to such an extent in the teaching ministry exercised by bishops and the pope in the Roman church that the inerrancy promised to the church as a whole had shifted to the bishops and the pope. This, so it was said, revealed the new Roman "definition of the church", which was rejected.²⁸¹ Regarding the promise and commission to abide in the truth the following principle held good for the Reformation: "Nor should that be transferred to the popes which is the prerogative of the true church: that they are pillars of the truth and that they do not err."²⁸²

211. Here, according to Reformation conviction, the critical function of the doctrine of justification comes into play. In this, the primary question is not that the church as the congregation of the faithful *(congregatio fidelium)* might take second place to the

church as "supreme outward monarchy";[283] or that the equality of the people of God might be cancelled out. And it certainly is not a question of a modern ideal of freedom or the application to the church of the idea of the sovereignty of the people. The issue is, first and foremost, the primacy of the gospel over the church – the freedom, sovereignty and ultimate binding nature of the gospel as God's word of grace.

212. The Reformation conviction is that this gospel, even if proclaimed in the church and by ministers called to serve "in Christ's place and stead",[284] cannot without reservations and with no questions asked be consigned to an ecclesiastical ministry to preserve. For insofar as this ministry, like every church institution, is carried out by human beings who are capable of error, not only would the danger of error be increased thereby, because the error would then take on binding force in the church, but also and above all a sovereignty and ultimate binding force would attach to the decisions and stipulations of this ministry and its representatives which are reserved for the gospel alone. That is why what people teach in the church must ultimately be measured against the gospel alone. Only then is it certain that the church relies on God's word and not human words.

213. For the sake of the gospel, the Reformation doctrine of justification therefore requires that the church's ministry and its decisions should as a matter of principle be open to examination by the whole people of God. As a matter of principle justification debars them from insulating themselves from such an examination. In regard to its decisions the teaching ministry must permit "question or censure",[285] as the Apology says, by the church as a whole, for which the promise of abiding in the truth holds good, and which is the people of God, the body of Christ, and the temple of the Holy Spirit. Otherwise it seems doubtful from a Reformation perspective that the teaching ministry serves the word of God and is not above it.[286]

214. The binding nature of church teaching is not cancelled out by this but is made subject to a reservation. In the Reformation view the teaching of the church or of a teaching ministry must take place precisely in this dialectical tension between the claim of its binding nature and the reservation relating to that binding nature. This will demonstrate that the teaching ministry respects the independence of the gospel and its ultimate binding nature, which is nothing other than the independence and binding nature of the grace of God. In this, church teaching as such demonstrates its own conformity with the gospel.

215. It is thus clear that the doctrine of justification certainly does not lead Reformation thinking into a depreciation, far less a rejection, of binding church teaching and of a teaching ministry of the church. The churches of the Lutheran Reformation themselves carry out binding teaching and themselves have organs or ministries for the church's teaching. They even have displayed the willingness and indeed the "deep desire"[287] to recognize for themselves the church's teaching ministry in its traditional form.[288] What they insist on is solely that this teaching and this teaching ministry be in accordance with the gospel in their self-understanding and exercise and do not contradict the gospel.[289]

216. The problem of a tension between the claim to and the reservation related to binding teaching arises for Catholics too. Admittedly from their point of view the matter has a different weight and value. According to Catholic teaching the church as a whole is "the pillar and bulwark of the truth" (1 Tim. 3:15). "The body of the faithful as a whole... cannot err in matters of belief" as it receives the "supernatural sense of

the faith" from the Spirit of truth.²⁹⁰ Within the people of God, the bishops in communion with the bishop of Rome are the authentic teachers of the faith by virtue of their episcopal ordination as successors in the presiding ministry of a local church.²⁹¹ But their teaching office remains anchored in the life of faith of the whole people of God, who share in the discovery of and in witnessing to the truth. Thus "the vigilance with regard to the apostolicity of the faith that belongs to the bishop's duty, is bound up with the responsibility for the faith borne by the whole Christian people",²⁹² and thus bishops exercise their teaching ministry "only in community with the whole church" and "in a many-sided exchange regarding faith with believers, priests and theologians",²⁹³ for the whole "people of God shares also in Christ's prophetic office".²⁹⁴

217. "While it is possible for the individual bishop to fall away from the continuity of the apostolic faith... Catholic tradition holds that the episcopate as a whole is nevertheless kept firm in the truth of the gospel."²⁹⁵ The bishops have to watch over the continuity of the apostolic faith, while being bound to the canon of scripture and the apostolic tradition: the "teaching office is not above the word of God but serves it, teaching only what has been handed on".²⁹⁶ It has the task of listening reverently to the word of God, preserving it in holiness and expounding it faithfully.²⁹⁷ The same is valid for the priest. "The task of priests is not to teach their own wisdom but God's word."²⁹⁸ This submission to the canon of the scriptures and the apostolic tradition is the basic criterion for the response of faith, especially in borderline cases, so that according to Augustine and Thomas Aquinas it can be said: "One must deny one's consent even to bishops when it happens that they err and speak in a manner that contradicts the canonical texts."²⁹⁹

218. The church can make infallible decisions on doctrine, as happened in the early church at ecumenical councils.³⁰⁰ These decisions explicate the revelation that has taken place once for all, and are made in harmony with the faith of the entire people of God, certainly not against them.³⁰¹ These decisions, when made under specific conditions, are valid of themselves and do not need any subsequent formal approval, though they of course "depend on extensive reception in order to have living power and spiritual fruitfulness in the church".³⁰²

219. Decisions of the church's teaching ministry are indeed binding – as dogma, even definitively binding. But the church knows it is the pilgrim people of God on the march. Hence recognition of the truth in theology and dogma is fragmentary and often one-sided, since it is frequently a response to errors that have taken an extreme position. Dogma is historically conditioned and therefore open to corrections, deeper understanding and "new expressions".³⁰³ The church nevertheless believes that the Holy Spirit guides it into the truth and preserves it from error when solemn definitions are made. When the teaching ministry appeals to the Holy Spirit (cf. Acts 15:28), this does not run counter to the criterion of the doctrine of justification. For the question here is not about conditions for salvation, but the criteria of our knowledge of revelation. The message of the radical gratuity of the gift of salvation, and of the unconditionality of the reception of salvation, is not obscured by the institution of councils, because their role is to witness to the truth of revelation and to protect this truth against erroneous opinions.

220. The Catholic understanding of faith holds that the gospel is interpreted by the consensus of a council and this can therefore in special cases bring forth a definitively binding statement (a dogma in the Catholic view) on which members of the church can

rely as an expression of the gospel. Even if faith does not rest in the formulation but in the reality, that is, in the truth of the gospel, it nevertheless needs the formulation in which the gospel is expressed, the wording of which must be very carefully heeded in a critical situation (cf. 1 Cor. 15:2; 4:6).

221. On the other hand, also in Catholic understanding, a dogmatic statement is not simply a given about which no further questions may be asked. "The tradition which comes from the apostles develops in the church with the help of the Holy Spirit. For there is a growth in the understanding of the realities and the words which have been handed down. This happens through the contemplation and study made by believers, who treasure these things in their hearts..., through the intimate understanding of spiritual things they experience, and through the preaching of those who have received through episcopal succession the sure gift of truth. For, as the centuries succeed one another, the church constantly moves forward towards the fullness of divine truth until the words of God reach their complete fulfilment in her."[304] Looked at in this light, the transmission of faith, official doctrinal proclamation, and the history of dogma are complex hermeneutical processes in which all the faithful, members of the teaching office, and theologians are participants even if in differing ways.[305] Abiding in the truth of the gospel does not exclude the painstaking quest for the truth. It is not carried out alone by one component of the church but is due in the last analysis to the support and guidance of God's Spirit who exercises control through the fellowship of the whole people of God.

222. This comparison of the Lutheran and Catholic understanding of binding doctrines shows, despite all the different emphases and a fair number of critical questions, that binding teaching need not contradict justification. Catholics and Lutherans agree that binding teaching illuminates the truth of the gospel, on which truth alone members of the church may and should rely in living and dying and which alone sustains their faith. They agree that, for example, in the councils that confess the faith in the Trinity and in Jesus Christ the truth of the gospel is explicated. There are considerable differences, to be sure, as to how the truth of the gospel is affirmed. Even if Catholics cannot in the same way appropriate the Lutheran dialectic in which the claim to a binding character for doctrine contrasts with a reservation as to that binding character, and if they ask whether there is not a danger here that the opinion of individuals will be identified with the truth of the gospel, they too are aware of the provisional nature of human knowledge of the truth, even in the ultimately binding decisions of the teaching office. If Lutherans pose the above-mentioned question concerning the Catholic form of binding teaching, they are nevertheless faced with the task of rethinking "the problem of the teaching office and the teaching authority" and of reflecting especially on the council as an institution, that is, as "the locus for the expression of the consensus of all Christendom",[306] and of its importance to which the Reformation always firmly held.[307]

4.5.3.4. Church jurisdiction and the jurisdictional function of the ministry

223. The questions of doctrine and the church's teaching office, and of ecclesial jurisdiction and the jurisdictional function of the ministry are very close to each other and show clear parallels. In part the two questions even overlap, in so far as decisions of the church's teaching ministry are juridically binding.

224. Catholics and Lutherans together say that God, who establishes institutional entities in his grace and faithfulness, and who uses them to preserve the church in the truth of the gospel, also uses church law and legal ordinances for this purpose.

225. Thus, Lutherans cannot say that gospel and church on one side and ecclesiastical law on the other are mutually exclusive or that the doctrine of justification prohibits the development of binding ecclesial law. The very fact that in Reformation lands legally binding church orders *(Kirchenordnungen)* came into being at a very early date, and that in their doctrinal sections *(corpora doctrinae)*, which were replaced later by the confessions, the doctrine of justification has a central place, shows that justification itself participated in the juridically binding nature of these church orders. Constitutions of today's Lutheran churches indicate this also.

226. When, however, it comes to the understanding of church law and its binding nature; when the question is raised to what extent and in what sense the church, and especially the ordained ministry, have the authority to make legally binding decisions and regulations; and when it is asked to what extent such decisions, once taken, can be critically examined on the basis of the gospel – then a difference between Catholics and Lutherans becomes evident, just as it does with the question of doctrine and the teaching ministry.

227. This difference, however, is to be seen in the context of common basic convictions which have already been highlighted in the Lutheran-Roman Catholic dialogue.

- In regard to church law as a whole the principle holds good for both churches that "the salvation of souls... must always be the supreme law".[308]
- That in turn means that according to common conviction all church law and all development of ecclesial law are related and subordinated to the service of the gospel. "The church is permanently bound in its ordering to the gospel which is irrevocably prior to it"; the gospel is "the criterion for a concrete church order".[309]
- Even where, in line with the traditional view and terminology, the character of "divine law", a *ius divinum*, is attributed to church legislation, it has a historical shape and form, and it is therefore both possible and necessary to renew and reshape it.[310]

228. These common basic convictions show that church law, notwithstanding its claim to be binding, is by its nature and by definition subject to a reservation as to its binding nature. This is of crucial importance, because it is precisely the critical demand raised by the doctrine of justification regarding all church legislation and so also to all church legal authorities. No church legislation can claim to be binding in such a manner that it is necessary for salvation, thus equalling the ultimate binding nature of the gospel, which is itself the binding nature of grace. Insofar as this demand is not met, church law becomes subject to criticism from the doctrine of justification. On this our churches agree in principle. It is important that this agreement should also be maintained in church practice; but whether, how and to what extent this happens in our churches must be verified from one case to another.

229. These basic convictions apply also to the question to what extent and in what way a jurisdictional function is appropriate to the ordained ministry. The Reformation too can in fact attribute a jurisdictional function to the ministry, but in so doing it emphasizes the primacy of the gospel and, essentially, those limitations which are recognized in common by Catholics and Lutherans.[311]

230. This is the overall intention of article 28 of the Augsburg confession.[312] It develops a view of the power *(potestas)* of the bishops, which unequivocally includes jurisdictional functions. At the same time it seeks to guarantee the harmony of this min-

istry and its exercise with the gospel, doing this essentially in the framework of the basic convictions outlined above.

231. The proper tasks of the bishop, which appertain basically to the pastor also – because of a theological lack of clarity in the differentiation between bishop and pastor – are, according to CA 28, "to preach the gospel", "to forgive... sins", "to administer... the sacraments", to "condemn doctrine that is contrary to the gospel", and to "exclude from the Christian community".[313] They can be summed up in the terms "power of keys",[314] "the office of preaching",[315] or "jurisdiction".[316] These show that according to the Reformation view, the ministry as a pastoral office includes jurisdictional functions, certainly in such a way that these functions do not become autonomous but remain bound up in the total pastoral responsibility of the ministry and so preserve their pastoral character.

232. Over against these functions of the ordained ministry which are "necessary for salvation"[317] and are in this sense by "divine right"[318] but which must be exercised "not by human power but by God's word alone",[319] the duty of the congregation to obey holds good.[320] It is an obligation, however, which is paired with the duty to refuse obedience should the ministry violate the gospel in its exercise of these functions.[321]

233. Alongside this the bishops can undoubtedly exercise yet another kind of jurisdiction,[322] from marriage legislation through ceremonial laws and regulations for worship to decrees for fasts and so on. Such regulations in the last analysis serve the orderly common life of the congregation,[323] and they may be changed, replaced and even abrogated.[324] Here too indeed a duty on the part of the congregation to obey holds good,[325] but it is fundamentally different in kind. It does not end only where these regulations of the ministry which relate to church law violate the gospel in their content. It already ends where they are imposed as "necessary for salvation"[326] and binding on the conscience,[327] and here changes into a duty to refuse obedience. For these regulations are already contradicting the "teaching concerning faith", that is, of the "righteousness of faith"[328] and "Christian liberty", i.e., the freedom of the Christian from the law,[329] and they thereby become subject to criticism by the doctrine of justification.

234. It is a Lutheran conviction that there is a legitimate jurisdictional function of the ordained ministry in this context which is defined by the doctrine of justification.

235. According to the Catholic view the above-mentioned common basic convictions also mark the jurisdictional authority of the episcopate.[330] The exercise of law and canonical practice is always to be seen in its pastoral intention and within a concern for the salvation of humanity.

236. The authority and power of bishops is part of their being shepherds and presiders over the church. It is founded in the divine mission that Christ entrusted to the apostles,[331] to hand on the gospel which "is for all time the source of all life for the church".[332] This power also includes the right and the duty to regulate everything in the church which pertains to the ordering of worship and of the apostolate. But it should be carried out in accordance with the example of the Good Shepherd, Jesus Christ.[333] Bishops exercise their pastoral and jurisdictional authority in the name of Christ and personally, i.e., as their special, regular and direct power, in communion with the bishop of Rome.[334] In this connection they have always to take into account the fact that every ordering of the church develops from a permanently given basis, namely, that the church is a community of faith and sacraments. The proclamation of the word of God and the celebration of the sacraments constitute the church and determine its

nature, because the Lord of the church effects salvation in them. The binding force of a church law therefore presupposes the conviction that the church is a faith and sacramental community. The aim of the law and canons of the church is to serve the church's order and to express its unity while contributing to the good order of the care of souls. Thus church order, with law and canons, arises out of the nature of the church as a faith and sacramental community.

237. Catholic teaching insists that no one may be coerced into believing nor be "forced to act in a manner contrary to his own beliefs" in religious matters.[335] Even the call of God to serve him in spirit and in truth, though it binds human beings in their conscience to obey that call, does not coerce them into doing so.[336] And while church norms and laws can indeed be binding in conscience on Christians as members of the church, they cannot "release a member of the church from his direct responsibility to God".[337]

238. The Catholic-Lutheran dialogue has stressed that "the church is permanently bound in its ordering to the gospel which is irrevocably prior to it... The gospel, however, can be the criterion for a concrete church order only in living relationship with contemporary social realities. Just as there is a legitimate explication of the gospel in dogmas and confessions, so there also exists a historical actualization of law in the church."[338] In this sense the *Codex Iuris Canonici* of 1983 also attempts a reordering of Catholic church legislation in the light of Vatican II, in order to correspond better with the church's mission of salvation. In particular the ecclesiological guidelines of the dogmatic constitution *Lumen Gentium* and the pastoral constitution *Gaudium et Spes* constitute the hermeneutical framework for this. "Over the course of time, the Catholic church has been wont to revise and renew the laws of its sacred discipline so that, maintaining always fidelity to the divine Founder, these laws may be truly in accord with the salvific mission entrusted to the church... This new code can be viewed as a great effort to translate the conciliar ecclesiological teaching into canonical terms."[339]

239. Catholic theology draws attention to the fact that it is God's saving activity, not ecclesiastical law-givers with their legislation, which establishes the fellowship of believers and therefore brings people into a new social situation with obligations: that of the believers' fellowship with each other and with God. This new social situation is expressed by the ecclesiastical law-giver in legal ordinances. The point of ecclesiastical legislation is to help believers perceive and fulfill their rights and duties as well as possible in the light of the faith, and thus to contribute to the realization of the saving mission of the church.

240. Because church legislation can be seen as a normative function of the tradition of faith, and because the binding force of church laws is ultimately founded in the binding force of faith, church law differs from every other law. Because of the binding force of faith, the church legislator addresses the religious conscience, and thus ecclesiastically binding norms presuppose a free decision of faith. Consequently, it is possible for a discrepancy and thus a case of conflict to arise between the obligation of a church law and the conscience of the individual Christian believer. Catholic theology, of course, does not generally speak of a "reservation" regarding the binding character of church laws, but in individual cases it does take into account the possibility of conflict. The salvation of human beings counts as supreme law. If in a concrete instance the application of the existing canons may prejudice or even endanger a person's salvation, that consti-

tutes a case in which Christian believers who are quite willing to obey church law and have also shown this in practical living may, and even must, nevertheless come to a decision which is against the letter of the law, because on the basis of faith they see themselves entitled or even obliged to make that decision as a matter of conscience.

241. Despite different ecclesiological starting points and a different frame of reference, fundamental common elements and correspondences do exist between Lutherans and Catholics on the matter of the doctrines of justification and salvation and their relation to the jurisdictional authority of the ordained ministry. The task of church laws is to serve the salvation of the individual.

242. We may sum up by saying that in regard to all the problem areas discussed here (4.5.3.1-4), we may not speak of a fundamental conflict or even opposition between justification and the church. This is quite compatible with the role of the doctrine of justification in seeing that all the church's institutions, in their self-understanding and exercise, contribute to the church's abiding in the truth of the gospel which alone in the Holy Spirit creates and sustains the church.

5. The Mission and Consummation of the Church

243. As the recipient and mediator of salvation the church has its enduring foundation in the triune God. Its ultimate goal is consummation in God's kingdom. God will create his eternal and universal kingdom of righteousness, peace and love, and himself will bring about his own definitive reign and salvation. God has chosen and established the church by grace in this age and for this age, so that it may proclaim his gospel to all creatures (cf. Mark 16:15), worship him unceasingly, and praise him for the "riches of his grace" (cf. Eph. 1:3-14), and in witness and service make known to all people his loving kindness and goodness of heart (cf. Titus 3:4-6), until he himself dwells ultimately in our midst and makes all things new (cf. Rev. 21:3-5). Thus, while in this age the church does indeed have its responsible missionary task of proclaiming the gospel (cf. 1 Cor. 9:16) and serving God and humanity (cf. Matt. 22:37-40), it also goes on its way through this age in the certainty of God's mercy and grace (cf. 2 Cor. 12:9) and in joyful confidence in the return of the Lord. Jesus has said to us, "But strive first for the kingdom of God and his righteousness, and all these things will be given to you as well" (Matt. 6:33); and he has taught us to pray, saying "Father, hallowed be your name. Your kingdom come" (Luke 11:2).

5.1. The church's mission

244. Everywhere Lutherans and Catholics find themselves repeatedly confronted by the same challenges – challenges which vary greatly in the different regions of the world and can also change very quickly (5.1.1). This leads Lutherans and Catholics to address these challenges together and to reflect afresh on the mission of the church in the light of the message of justification (5.1.2). We are agreed that our missionary task represents a true if limited participation in God's own realization of his plans as Creator, Redeemer and Sanctifier (5.1.3). Regarding the most important elements in our task as churches – evangelization, worship and service to humanity – no essential differences divide us (5.1.4). Such a broad consensus demands of our churches that we intensify and expand their field of practical cooperation on every level in serving the gospel of Jesus Christ.

5.1.1. COMMON CHALLENGES TO OUR CHURCHES IN A CONSTANTLY CHANGING WORLD

245. The challenges facing the churches throughout the world are often quite varied, corresponding to the different regional contexts; but in a given place they confront Lutherans and Catholics and in the same way. In South Africa racist thinking has not stopped at the doors of just one church. In other countries of Africa and in parts of Asia, Christians of all confessions see themselves threatened or even persecuted by a militant Islam. In the southeast part of Europe, the churches face the challenge to overcome extreme ethnic and national allegiances in a situation of flagrant violation of human dignity up to genocide. In the countries of Latin America, the incredible differences between poor and rich cut across all the churches and confessions. Religious alienation in the secular context of many European countries never affects only one church by itself.

246. Many problems arise not only in the one or the other context; they confront our churches worldwide: the reawakening of nationalism, extreme rightist tendencies, increasing readiness for violence, and violence itself. These and similar common challenges make the churches look afresh at their missionary task and confront them with the inescapable question, how far they can and really want to make common cause in the face of such challenges. An example of a common quest for answers to today's questions in the light of the gospel and of the various church traditions is the conciliar or ecumenical "process of mutual commitment to justice, peace and the integrity of creation" to which the assembly of the World Council of Churches in Vancouver called in 1983. That led to the European Ecumenical Assembly "Peace with Justice" in Basel in 1989 and the world convocation in Seoul in 1990, as well as to activities in many countries and regions of the world.

247. How quickly contexts can change has become very clear in those countries of Eastern Europe that have in virtually bloodless revolutions liberated themselves from many years of one party's and ideology's position of supremacy. The complexity of human living conditions and the speed of social change in our age call for the churches to test constantly the challenges of the changing contexts in the light of the gospel in order to fulfill their task of mission authentically and contextually. The "signs of the times" are thus a call to the churches to reflect on their own origins and to make appropriate responses. Together they can contribute to perceiving present forms of the enduring struggle between faith and unbelief, sin and justice, the old and the new creation, correctly. In so doing the church must pay particular attention to how people today express both their distress and their hopes.

248. A church which has been called together by Christ to serve his work on earth will therefore always have to make an effort to realize to the utmost its missionary opportunities. The gospel message of grace and reconciliation compels those who have heard and accepted it to bring it to those who have not yet heard it or who have still had no proper opportunity to accept it. We must be alarmed when we think about those who have forgotten or estranged themselves from God's good news. Catholics and Lutherans together must accept their missionary calling as disciples of Jesus Christ. They must in common face the challenges of constant renewal in their churches under the influence of the Holy Spirit, so that they become common instruments for God's saving plan in ever more authentic ways.

249. In reflecting on the common challenges we are fully aware of the inner relationship between church and unity. The existing separations between Lutherans and

Church and Justification 543

Catholics are an obstacle for the one ministry of reconciliation to which we are called. Discord among Christians openly contradicts – as Vatican II says – "the will of Christ, provides a stumbling block to the world, and inflicts damage on the most holy cause of proclaiming the good news to every creature".[340] Therefore, the changing world in which we live offers a great challenge to our churches to pursue with new energy our ecumenical pilgrimage towards visible unity.

5.1.2. REFLECTION ON THE CHURCH'S MISSION IN LIGHT OF THE MESSAGE OF JUSTIFICATION

250. The late prophetic testimonies of Israel already give us an inkling of a fundamental dimension of our life and calling in the church. The Lord God showed his saving power by gathering his people from the countries to which they had been dispersed and re-establishing them as his chosen servants (cf. Isa. 41:8-10; 43:1-7). But God's salvation is intended to reach all the ends of the earth (cf. Isa. 45:22f.), and one day all peoples are to flock into the city of the Lord (cf. Isa. 60:3f.,10,14). At the same time those who belong to the people of Israel are described as "witnesses" who are to testify to the mercy of the Lord and the almighty work by which he realizes his plan of salvation (cf. Isa. 43:10,12; 44:8). And finally some of those gathered by the Lord from different nations and tongues shall be sent to "the coast lands far away" in order to proclaim the glory of the Lord and bring new worshippers into the house of the Lord (cf. Isa. 66:18-21).[341]

251. What was already in evidence in Israel in the period after the Exile reached its consummation in Jesus Christ. As church we find our identity in him, especially in his own mission to preach the gospel (cf. Mark 1:15; 1:28f.), to call not the righteous but sinners (cf. Mark 2:17), and to give his life as a ransom for many (cf. Mark 10:45). Jesus found his own task of mission outlined by the prophets, to "bring good news to the poor" and "to proclaim release to the captives" (Luke 4:18); and this has continuing relevance for us as his disciples, as a guideline for our own decisions and preferences in the service of love.

252. Jesus sent out his disciples to spread his message and healing ministry throughout Galilee (cf. Luke 9:1f.). Thus, at the same time he anticipated what was still to come. After his resurrection Jesus passed on his mission to the disciples, which still today is his legacy for Christians: "As the Father has sent me, so I send you" (John 20:21). In all the gospels we find this commission of the risen Lord, which defines the church. "Go into all the world and proclaim the good news to the whole creation" (Mark 16:15). "Go therefore and make disciples of all nations, baptizing them in the name of the Father and of the Son and of the Holy Spirit, and teaching them to obey everything that I have commanded you" (Matt. 28:19f.). "Thus it is written, that the Messiah is to suffer and to rise from the dead on the third day, and that repentance and forgiveness of sins is to be proclaimed in his name to all nations, beginning from Jerusalem" (Luke 24:46f.; cf. Acts 1:8).

253. As individuals and communities we know ourselves to be addressed by these words, and in obedience we accept the commission of our Lord to evangelize, to win new disciples, and to spread his healing presence throughout the world. The full significance of this commission passes our understanding. But we know that we live through him who died "to gather into one the dispersed children of God" (John 11:52). The church has received "fellowship... with the Father and with his Son Jesus Christ" (1 John 1:3), a fellowship which is meant for all people. As the church we are chosen

and destined to go out into the world and bear fruit (cf. John 15:16) by spreading the knowledge of the one true God and Jesus Christ, who is eternal life (cf. John 17:3).

254. This call to service, so emphatically entrusted to us by the Lord, plainly exceeds our human striving and performance. The missionary sending of the church is at all times made possible by the power of the Holy Spirit, just as that power was given to the apostolic community for their witness to the risen Christ (cf. Acts 2:33-36; 3:12-15; 5:30-32; 13:1-4,30-33). The church knows that it is filled with "power from on high" and that it is thus enabled to proclaim God's own conquest of human wickedness and his call to repentance (cf. Luke 24:47-49; Acts 2:23f.). In the spirit of Pentecost the church summons men and women to baptism and to new life in congregations of apostolic teaching, to the sharing of resources and gifts, to the breaking of bread and to prayer, praise and intercession (cf. Acts 2:42-47; 4:32-35). Further evangelizing must still be carried out in our world, and our churches are confident that the Holy Spirit which was once poured out will continue to overcome human obstacles (cf. Acts 10:44-48), open hearts to the gospel (cf. Acts 16:14), and create new congregations which are brought to life by the apostolic witness to Jesus Christ.

255. In faith we look back on these unrepeatable beginnings through which God has deeply impressed the missionary command on the nature of the church. We bear a treasure for the world. We stand together in that ministry of reconciliation which affects the whole world. Although as individuals and communities we are only earthen vessels, we are encouraged by the Spirit of God to accept the missionary task of speaking about him in whom we believe, Jesus Christ. We have the task of preparing the ways by which he can come to human beings as their reconciler, as God's own righteousness and as the beginning of the new creation (cf. 2 Cor. 5:17-21).

5.1.3. MISSION AS SHARING IN GOD'S ACTIVITY IN THE WORLD

256. Catholics and Lutherans are agreed that the mission of the church to proclaim the gospel and serve humanity is a true – even if also limited – sharing in God's activity in the world towards the realization of his plan as Creator, Redeemer and Sanctifier. Reflection on the nature of our calling and authority as church has priority, and we are grateful that our dialogue enables us to do this together (5.1.3.1). But God's activity in the world is more comprehensive than what he carries out through the church. And the commission to Christians to let themselves be taken by him into service goes beyond the sphere of the church. Both our traditions have developed their own ideas about this: the Lutheran doctrine of God's two kingdoms and the Catholic doctrine of the rightful autonomy of creation,[342] of earthly spheres and realities (5.1.3.2).

5.1.3.1. Common understanding

257. We have learned to understand the nature of our missionary task in the church by considering the activity of our God whom holy scripture reveals as Creator of heaven and earth, Redeemer of lost humanity, and Sanctifier of those who are brought to the Lord Jesus Christ. Through God's grace and call, the mission of the church shares in the continuing activity of Father, Son and Holy Spirit. The church serves God's missionary activity in his world. Our ministry is therefore characterized by what we ascribe to the divine persons, i.e., their respective activities in creation, redemption and sanctification. God graciously accepts our words and deeds by accomplishing his own plan to save and to bless.

258. In effectual and sustaining love God the Creator is devoted to everything he has created, and he shows his special love for human beings, whom he has made in his image (cf. Gen. 1:26). Conversely, human beings are called to be God's fellow workers. As stewards they are entrusted with care for creation, and to them is committed the promotion of justice and well-being for all, for which purpose God has given them reason and conscience as well as specific institutional structures as instruments of his creative and sustaining love. We know of course from the teaching of the faith and from our own experience that this love has to operate in the context of the fallen world, which is characterized by sin. Justice and protective measures, which must be established here, can do no more than limit the effects of evil; they cannot uproot it.

259. The call and commitment to serve God's creative and sustaining will applies to everyone, both Christians and non-Christians. They are to strive together for peace, justice and the integrity of creation. With the aid of their reason they must together look for practical ways and for a mode of organizing the institutional order which in their period of history will best serve to realize those purposes that God has appointed. Here church members have no greater competence than their non-Christian sisters and brothers who are made in the image of God; on the other hand there may be differences of opinion between them regarding the best way to achieve common objectives.

260. In relation to the creative and sustaining will of God, church members have no additional call to obedience and no special competence beyond that of their fellow humans. But in view of the obscuring of the creative and sustaining will of God in this sinful world, they have a special responsibility. Transformed by the gospel, individual Christians – already a new creation in faith – have, like the church as a whole, a sharpened awareness of the standards and tasks that hold good for all human beings, and advocate them with unprejudiced hearts. Where necessary, vis-a-vis other persons as well as on their behalf, Christians are to step in both by admonition, advice and action and by their own style of life in the cause of human dignity, fundamental human rights, and for freedom, justice and the integrity of creation. They are to alleviate distress and suffering. Thus, as individuals and as a church community they point to God-given values and standards of creation. At the same time they draw the attention of their fellow creatures to the limited objectives and possibilities of their social and political activities and preserve them from excessive ideological demands and from the temptation to totalitarianism.

261. God sent the Son as Redeemer in order to proclaim unconditional divine grace for sinful humanity. In the form of a servant, Jesus took sin upon himself in order to conquer it and make available to all believers a share of his righteousness and of new life and access to the Father in the Holy Spirit. Jesus Christ is the centre of the missionary task of the church, which recognizes that he has commissioned it to bring his liberating message and grace to all peoples. Here lies the special mission of the church: to fulfill Jesus' commission, to missionize the world, and to build up communities of disciples who, transformed by faith already here on earth, radiate the firm hope of future fulfilment of the kingdom of God on the day of eschatological consummation. Church members rejoice in their regeneration through baptism, in which they have been anointed in Christ through the Holy Spirit to be members of a priestly, prophetic and royal people. From baptism they receive their supreme dignity and their responsibility to serve the mission of Jesus Christ in dependence on him and conformed to him. This includes the priestly ministry of praise, self-sacrifice and intercession. Part of this

is the prophetic commission to expose evil, proclaim salvation and also witness to the hope of glory in the midst of the afflictions of this age. Royal dignity is therein epitomized by living in Christian freedom from sin and from the contrarieties of the world (cf. Rom. 8:31-39), and thus serving humanity fearlessly by word and deed, so that the dominion of sin will be overcome, creation will serve human welfare, and preferential love will be shown to our weak and ill-treated brothers and sisters.

262. God sent the Spirit into the world to bring people to faith by means of word and sacrament, to justify sinners, and to call together the church as a koinonia, in this way attaining the ends of the mission of the Son. Thus, in the midst of the old world the new creation is already raised up in holiness. In baptism, through the Spirit, men and women are made members of a community which acts as instrument of the Spirit's mission. Through proclamation in different forms, through actions which testify to the new world which has dawned – though still marked by ambiguity and limitation – and, where necessary, through acting representatively and critically for the present world, Christians implement this task and thus minister to the saving rule of God, which has already begun with the death and resurrection of Jesus and with the outpouring of the Holy Spirit.

5.1.3.2. Two traditions

263. Lutherans and Catholics understand the mission of the church as sharing in God's activity in the world; they also know, however, that God's activity in the world goes beyond the sphere of the church. Even if bounds are set to the God-given task of the church, Christians are aware that they must serve God in all areas of society. How this is understood and practised is differently expressed in our two traditions.

5.1.3.2.1. The Lutheran teaching on the two kingdoms

264. In order to do justice theologically and pastorally to this situation, the Lutheran tradition developed the doctrine of the "two kingdoms (realms)" of God. This is not a concrete socio-ethical programme, but it does define an ethical locus for Christians who already live their lives as citizens of the new world while also continuing as citizens of the old world. How can Christians, whose rule of life is the Sermon on the Mount, hold responsible positions in politics, administration of justice, law enforcement, economy or the military? The two kingdoms cannot be equated with the distinction between the church and the world; they are also to be found within the church, because the church is a *corpus permixtum* and every Christian is still a sinner.

265. The real-life context of Christians is the spiritual kingdom of the *communio sanctorum*. Here Christ is head of a spiritual realm, as through word and sacrament in the Holy Spirit he brings people to faith and preserves that faith.[343] The behaviour appropriate to this kingdom is the radical love that corresponds to the Sermon on the Mount,[344] a love that arises out of faith and is made possible by the Holy Spirit: unreserved readiness to serve, waiving one's own rights, non-resistance, non-violence in following Jesus Christ and in his strength. Such love makes visible already in the present world the new world desired by God.

266. Because this love is the fruit of the heart transformed in faith, it cannot be elevated to the status of law nor advocated as a general standard for social life. Indeed, in the context of the fallen world that would mean giving evil the upper hand and handing over human society to the selfishness and arbitrariness of the powerful.[345] Where

faith does not prevail, that is, among non-Christians but also in regard to Christians themselves, since they too remain sinners, it is necessary to have a social order which checks evil, and which despite evil guarantees the best possible life. This will be an order which cares for the protection of life and limb and for civic justice.[346] Its instruments are not the word and the Spirit but the law[347] and institutions which are equipped with power and make use of force where there is no other possibility.[348] The social order does not operate through the transformation of hearts but by imposing obligations and calling for obedience, and in the last resort through compulsion.

267. Although this ordering of life does not correspond to God's real intentions for humanity, it is nevertheless also an instrument of his love, as his "worldly kingdom", through which he preserves and forms creation even in its fallen state. Such ordering of life must therefore be affirmed as "instituted and ordained by God for the sake of good order".[349] As distinct from the spiritual kingdom, the instruments of the worldly kingdom are not contingently and particularly effectual; rather, its standards are embedded in the consciences of human beings[350] and established in the institutions of human society.[351] That is to say, they can and must claim universality and prove themselves in human society. Consequently, the actual structuring of political and social life is entrusted in great measure to human reason and expertise, whether of Christians or non-Christians,[352] and may vary according to context and historical perspective.[353] All structuring possibilities aim at and are limited by the contribution they make to the preservation and just ordering of the world.

268. The two kingdoms have to be strictly distinguished with regard to their goals, instruments and methods.[354] If this does not happen, either the spiritual kingdom is robbed of its uniqueness, as the renewed heart and corresponding ethic of radical love and renunciation are reduced to conventional morality and socio-political justice, or conversely the worldly kingdom is ruined. It is ruined because society, thinking its members are already wholly good, dispenses with erecting the barriers of external order, laws and needed institutional force against evil and thus leaves the field open for it, or because the attempt is made to influence hearts and achieve unselfish, idealistic acts – by whatever criteria one measures these – with the use of compulsion.

269. Nevertheless, distinguishing between the two kingdoms does not mean separating them. They cannot be parcelled out between two separate groups, as if the renewed heart and its corresponding ethic were something for only a few, while the mass of Christians could do without them. Rather, they are given with faith itself and are common to all Christians.[355] But all Christians continue to be also citizens of the unredeemed world and as creatures of God together with all other human beings, they have the responsibility of caring for its preservation and organization and of committing themselves to serving God's worldly kingdom. Thus Christians, according to their respective station in society (one's "calling"), will also hold and exercise power, help in promoting and enforcing law, and put down violence – even by the use of disciplined opposing force – instead of renouncing power, law and force in the spirit of the Sermon on the Mount.[356] Whether they act in the one way or the other depends on whether they are acting on their own behalf or for others. Here the spheres frequently overlap so that Christians can decide which principle they must follow according to their own consciences only. But they can be certain that even where because of societal responsibility they exercise or appeal to power, law and force they are not contradicting God's will but serving it.[357] Indeed they have to regard this service as a duty in the practical

and disinterested fulfilment of which they demonstrate their Christianity in the world.[358] In such activity, even if they do nothing other than is done by all persons of good will, they will do it differently, by bringing into evidence something of the love and readiness to forgive which is a special characteristic of Christian faith.[359] But they will also be aware of working to preserve and order a world in which evil still lurks and sets limits to the good that may be achieved.

270. In contrast to the 16th century, the doctrine of the two kingdoms requires modification in many respects today. For historical changes and the unsettled nature of social structures, with the resultant opportunities and difficulties, are more obvious today than before. Also the fact that justice and the ironing out of social inequalities – not only among individuals but also among groups, nations and continents – is perceived in an entirely different way today, as memoranda and other church statements of the last few decades show. But all this does not change anything in the fundamental assertions of the doctrine of God's two kingdoms itself. It continues to show the way by making it possible to maintain the eschatological existence of believers but at the same time to assert their place and responsibility for the world, which remains God's creation but is still unredeemed, without the two spheres being confused or separated.

271. Thus, on the one hand, the doctrine of the two kingdoms secures that the life of faith has another foundation, other instruments, and another shape than socio-political life in the world. Neither are worldly authorities entitled to intervene in spiritual concerns, nor can faith and its ethical fruits become worldly themselves by becoming a social programme, whether utopian or of a clerical and theocratic nature. And on the other hand, it makes clear that the conservation and ordering of the world, even in its unredeemed state, are subordinate to the will of God, but that this is to be worked out in ways which are not specifically Christian and comprehensible only to believers, but which claim to apply for everyone. Thus, the doctrine of the two kingdoms makes it possible to allow autonomy in socio-political actions over against the gospel and to endorse the secular character of the ordinances of the world – though this autonomy may not set itself against God's purpose of conserving and properly ordering the world. Those who are aware that ethical standards are based in the will of God must be especially vigilant in insisting on this, in view of the manifold obscuring elements in the life of society. The doctrine of the two kingdoms imposes on Christians a life and activity in tension between two systems of reference, but this is the same tension present in the very nature of the life of faith, that of being in the world and not of the world. This tension will be resolved only with the full and definitive dawn of the kingdom of God.

5.1.3.2.2. The Roman Catholic teaching on the "proper autonomy of earthly affairs"

272. Catholic teaching also recognizes the limits of the church's task, especially by its acknowledgment of the proper "autonomy of earthly affairs".[360] This autonomy does not leave human activities in the political and economic fields to arbitrary decisions. But neither can these fields be directly explained or shaped by the biblical revelation and the gospel of Jesus Christ. The Catholic view of autonomy rests on the perception that the Creator has endowed all his creatures with their own specific nature and inner development, with their own structures, values and modes of action. Human experience studies and rational reflections are entitled to explore creation. Moreover, the values which permeate this world impinge on the human moral conscience on all levels.

273. Reason and conscience operate together in moulding the order of this world. Nevertheless, Christian faith places the realities of the world in a new horizon of meaning and integrates them there. Christian values, such as the dignity and freedom of each person as well as mercy, kindness and gentleness in social legislation, are to be integrated into responsibility for the world. Therefore, faith makes it possible to challenge critically destructive tendencies in society, politics, economics and culture, and to strengthen the positive impulses of a secular ethic.

274. "Christ, to be sure, gave his church no proper mission in the political, economic or social order. The purpose which he set before her is a religious one."[361] He commissioned his disciples to spread his gospel, build up congregations, promote holiness and guide people to eternal life. These religious priorities free the church from any essential ties with a particular form of human culture or a specific political, economic or social system. The church lays claim to no power over the secular sphere, no matter how much it strives for the freedom to operate in society, to serve selflessly and to testify to Christ's message. Catholic doctrine addresses Christians as "citizens of two cities" and reminds them of the profusion of their professional, political and social duties.[362] Calling people to action in this world is in fact stimulated by Christ's call to conversion and newness of life. Christian formation stimulates new energies and a new sensitivity, which are discernibly advantageous to the secular world. It promotes, for example, a vision of unity which transcends all differences of nationality, race and class, a detachment from possessions as the standard of personal dignity, and a dynamic of love for humanity for whose salvation Christ died.

275. On the basis of new social, political and economic challenges in the last two centuries, challenges which did not previously exist, Catholic theology has developed a social teaching which to a great extent has been received magisterially. This teaching of the popes, the Second Vatican Council and numerous bishops' conferences is primarily directed towards moulding the moral conscience of church members but is also concerned with persuading all people of good will and thus influencing public order. This socio-ethical doctrine has developed, and will go on developing, in the effort to keep pace with the rapid changes in the modern industrial world and the gap between North and South. By nature it is a doctrine regarding human beings in society, human dignity, human rights and the moral values that must determine social action. Pope and bishops have not flinched from denouncing systematic exploitation and injustice. The same socio-ethical doctrine has however refrained from offering ready-made models and promoting the implementation of technical solutions for problems. It has left open the field where rational research and personal values converge as the basis of options for the creation of a social order. It is even officially acknowledged that within the church there can be differences of opinion between honest and faithful Catholics in regard to their individual modes of procedure in the promotion of the common good.[363]

276. This comprehensive body of social teaching, whose individual statements are issued with different degrees of binding character, represents an aspect in contemporary Catholic life and teaching to which, for the theological reasons explained above, nothing in the Lutheran churches corresponds. At a future stage in our dialogue this aspect of asymmetry between our churches must be dealt with in regard to socio-ethical questions and, more fundamentally, in relation to the extent of the church's competence in moral questions.

5.1.4. THE FUNDAMENTAL COMPONENTS OF THE CHURCH'S MISSIONARY TASK

277. Lutherans and Catholics are agreed on the priority of the task of evangelizing the world (5.1.4.1), on the central significance of proclaiming and celebrating the grace of God in worship (5.1.4.2), and on the commandment to serve humanity as a whole (5.1.4.3). They also agree that "martyria, leitourgia and diakonia (witness, worship and service to the neighbour) are tasks entrusted to the whole people of God".[364]

5.1.4.1. Commission to evangelize

278. The essential task which our Lord gave his church is the proclamation of the good news of his saving death and his resurrection. As Christians we share in the Lord's missionary commission and, like the apostolic preaching on the day of Pentecost, our message too contains the invitation to baptism and to sharing in the "promised Spirit of new life and freedom "(cf. Acts 2:38). We are convinced that evangelism brings with it God's unique gift of grace to the world, and we agree with the words of the Apostle Paul, "... woe to me if I do not proclaim the gospel!" (1 Cor. 9:16).

279. Evangelism lays claim to the whole person for witness to Christ; it demands the witness of a life which corresponds to the gospel in faith, hope and love. Here it is not simply a question of the work done by those sent out as missionaries but also of the witness of each individual Christian and each Christian community. Although the specific objective of evangelizing is bringing people to faith and not creating a new order of society, it nevertheless has a profound effect on the life of society. For Christians today insist on the strict observation of freedom of religion and freedom of conscience, and in common with all people of good will, they are especially watchful and zealous in supporting the conservation and humane structuring of the world, and enter the lists against discrimination, oppression and injustice. By the way in which they do these things, they make evident the love and forgiveness of God that has been bestowed on them.

280. We recognize that it is particularly necessary nowadays to enter into inter-religious dialogue, paying respectful heed to those who belong to other religious traditions. It is imperative to respect the convictions of others in order to create a basis for peace in societies where Christians live as neighbours of adherents of other great world religions. We keep ourselves open to the idea that God can be active in hidden ways in non-Christian religions too, and we therefore enter into dialogue with other religions in a trusting readiness to learn. Beyond such dialogue, however, we also see ourselves as obliged by the gospel to bear credible witness to the grace and truth which have been given to the whole world in a unique way in Jesus Christ, and we hope that this witness encounters faith.

281. In our day a special task is the re-evangelizing of traditionally Christian areas where large numbers of the baptized have lapsed into mere nominal Christianity. We are thus commissioned to invite our contemporaries to recognize afresh the glory of God that shines in the face of Jesus and to accept the message of reconciliation (cf. 2 Cor. 4:6; 5:19). A precious treasure has been entrusted to us which we should pass on to all people.

5.1.4.2. Centrality of worship

282. Our dialogue has already expressed a common understanding of our calling to join in the great eucharistic doxology in the presence of our Lord: "through him, with him, in him in the unity of the Holy Spirit all honour and glory is yours, almighty

Father, now and forever". For our unity with Christ leads to the everlasting Father through the power of the Holy Spirit in preaching, thanksgiving and praise, intercession and self-offering.[365] Worship is thus central to our mission as a church, for in it we celebrate our justification in Christ and proclaim as a priestly people the marvellous works of him who has called us "out of darkness into his marvellous light" (1 Pet. 2:9).

283. Common worship is by its nature not a means to any other end. Worship is rather the most important matrix of faith and an essential expression of it, for in worship our faith is induced and nourished through the proclamation of the gospel of Christ and our common sharing with others in the same gospel and the same sacramental life. In worship we are linked with Christians of every age right back to the apostles and joyfully celebrate the grace of communion with the Father and his Son Jesus Christ (cf. 1 John 1:3). Worship may therefore never be made to serve an ideology or be reduced to an educational tool. Services of worship are intended to attract and invite people and to radiate an aura of the kindness and benevolence of our God, who has redeemed us because of his mercy (cf. Titus 3:4-6).

284. In worship our church community, the church at a particular time and in a particular place, becomes concrete and visible in a special way. The annual round of the liturgical seasons and feasts, with their climaxes at Christmas, Good Friday/Easter and Pentecost, deepens our ecclesial identity as the people of God, the body of Christ, and the temple of the Holy Spirit. When we gather together to confess our sins, to hear God's saving word, to remember his great deeds, and to sing hymns and songs, to intercede for a blessing on everyone, and to celebrate the eucharistic meal, we are a people of faith in the most pregnant sense. This is our proper task as church, and we accept it as such with a sense of responsibility to offer our Creator and Redeemer adoration and praise in the name of all creatures, through our Lord Christ. In worship the existence of the church as an existence for others becomes particularly clear in "supplications, prayers, intercessions and thanksgivings" (1 Tim. 2:1f.) for all people, particularly also for those responsible in government, which the congregation assembled in the Holy Spirit in the presence of Christ offers to God. Here too we must remain aware that as justified sinners we ourselves are constantly in need of repentance and conversion. Since we have been called to such a ministry of reconciliation, we lament all the more the scandal of separation and the divisions among us, which are an obstacle to the full expression of the unity of the one priestly people that comes before God to praise him and be renewed through his word and Spirit.

5.1.4.3. Responsibility of the church and the service of humanity

285. Our task must bear the deep imprint of Jesus' view: "For the Son of Man came not to be served but to serve, and to give his life a ransom for many" (Mark 10:45). In following him, who in "the form of a slave" (Phil. 2:7) became the mediator of the grace we have received, we have been called to an attitude and behaviour like his. In obedience to him who affirmed the Creator's will for the world, we must contribute to its preservation and well-being. Thus as Christians and as communities, we are instruments of God in the service of mercy and justice in the world.

286. God's activity in the world is more comprehensive than what he does through the church. Fulfilling the commission of evangelism and worship is the service due to all humanity. By striving in common with all people of good will for healing, protection and promotion of human dignity, for respectful and rational handling of the

resources of creation, for the consolidation of social unity, respect for social diversity, and for deepening of the general sense of responsibility, Christians are servants of the Creator's love for the world. Through their readiness to do without and their unselfish charity, they reflect the light of Christ even where his name is not confessed.

287. Together with their non-Christian brothers and sisters but also where necessary over against them, Christians serve humanity, championing human dignity and inalienable and inviolable human rights. Knowing that these are received by human beings from their Creator, the church interprets them as expressions of an obligation towards God and speaks to others of the transcendent dimension of their lives. If necessary, the church also must address specific political and social problems in the effort to raise consciousness regarding human distress and the demands of civil justice.

288. Christians serve human society by supporting structures in politics, law, administration, education and economics which promote holistic human development. They contribute towards awareness and the strengthening of ties that bind all human beings in one family despite racial, cultural, national and socio-economic differences. They are eager to provide generous aid in situations of special distress, and they work on projects directed towards promoting long-term solutions to overcome misery.

289. The contribution which Christians make in all areas of social life – in politics, education and nurture, health, science, culture and the mass media – is to work like yeast in dough. Such action, determined by competence and dedication, is an essential part of the task which Christians are to fulfill in order to stop the destructive flood of evil and to promote lives in accord with human dignity and reverence towards God.

5.2. The eschatological consummation of the church

290. Reflection on the church as the recipient and mediator of salvation as well as on its mission would remain incomplete if its eschatological consummation were not also taken into account. It is precisely in the eschatological consummation of the church, as seen by the New Testament and expressed in the creed, that we see the convergence in God of all the paths of the church as God's pilgrim people. God himself definitively causes his rule and his salvation to prevail. Thus, the church's role as recipient and mediator of salvation once again becomes plain in terms of its end and consummation. In what follows, the eschatological consummation of the church will be considered from a twofold standpoint: first, in regard to the communion of saints *(sanctorum communio)* as it is confessed in the Apostles' Creed (5.2.1), and second, in regard to the New Testament message of the kingdom and rule of God (5.2.2).

5.2.1. SANCTORUM COMMUNIO

5.2.1.1. Common faith

291. Lutherans and Catholics confess "the communion of saints" *(sanctorum communionem)* in the Apostles' Creed. According to Luther's Large Catechism this means the church: a "Christian congregation or assembly", "a holy Christian people". It is a communion of saints because it lives harmoniously in one faith and in love under one head, Christ and by the Holy Spirit. Through the Holy Spirit every member of this "holy community" shares in everything and especially in the word of God. The Holy Spirit constantly remains with the church, sanctifies it, strengthens its faith and produces its fruits.[366]

292. The *Catechismus Romanus* understands the expression *sanctorum communio* similarly as the explanation of what the church is, for communion "with the Father and with his Son Jesus Christ" is realized in this community of the saints (1 John 1:3). "Communion of saints" means communion on the basis of the confession of faith and the sacraments, especially baptism and the eucharist, and on the basis of the interrelationship of all members of the body of Christ. It is a unity and community brought about by the Spirit, because the Holy Spirit sees to it that whatever gift anyone has belongs to the whole communion.[367]

293. Catholics and Lutherans confess in common that the "communion of saints" is the community of those united in sharing in the word and sacraments (the *sancta*) in faith through the Holy Spirit, the community of "those who are sanctified in Christ Jesus [and] called to be saints [the *sancti*]" (1 Cor. 1:2).

5.2.1.2. Community of perfected saints

294. Beyond the circle of believers in Christ who live on earth, the "communion of saints" is seen as a community of those who have been sanctified, cutting across all the ages and reaching into the eternity of God, a community in which one shares and into which one enters through the church. The patristic church believed "the communion of saints" to the glory of God, honoured God himself in the saints, and thus kept alive the longing for the life to come. In the Lutheran confessions too there is a fundamental adherence to the idea of a living communion with the saints, for despite criticism of invocation of the saints, it is not denied that we should give "honour to the saints": in thanks to God for their gifts of grace, in the strengthening of our faith because of their example, and in "imitation, first of their faith and then of their other virtues, which each should imitate in accordance with his calling".[368] It is granted "that the angels pray for us" and that "the saints in heaven pray for the church".[369] From ancient times therefore in the preface of the liturgy it is said: "Through him the angels praise your majesty, the heavenly hosts adore you, and the powers tremble; together with the blessed Seraphim all the citizens of heaven praise you in brilliant jubilation. Unite our voices with theirs and let us sing praise in endless adoration: Holy, holy, holy."[370] Vatican II placed the ideas of the fathers and the practice of venerating the saints in an ecclesiological context.[371] It stresses the eschatological character of the church as the pilgrim people of God and speaks of that people's "union with the church in heaven".[372]

5.2.1.3. Communion of the church on earth with the perfected saints

295. In confessing the *sanctorum communio*, our common faith in the triune God who will perfect the church finds expression. For the *communio* with God which has already been given and realized on earth through Jesus Christ in the Holy Spirit is the foundation of Christian hope beyond death and of the *communio* between Christ's saints on earth and Christ's saints who have already died. The communion of saints reaches beyond death because it is founded in God himself. Only through death and judgment can individuals and the church as a whole reach consummation (cf. 1 Cor. 4:4f.; 2 Cor. 5:10; Acts 10:42; Heb. 11:6; 9:27; 1 Pet. 4:17). Thus, belief in the communion of saints as the consummation of the church in no way makes light of sin, death and judgment. Because our fellowship with the dead is in God alone, our relations with the dead are in the safe-keeping of the mystery of God. Such an unfathomable differ-

ence exists between the present temporal and the future eternal life (cf. 1 Cor. 15:37-57) that we cannot adequately comprehend eternal life in words. We can express it only in images of hope, as holy scripture indicates (cf. 1 Cor. 2:9). Nevertheless we believe in the fundamental indestructibility of the life given us in Christ through the power of the Holy Spirit even through the judgment and beyond death.

296. Because of the horror of death we mourn the dead at the grave, but because we are Christians we mourn as those who have hope. Our common Christian hope is the crucified and risen Lord through whom God will also lead the dead to glory with Christ (cf. 1 Thess. 4:14). Those who are sanctified in Christ Jesus will be "with the Lord forever" (1 Thess. 4:17) even through death and judgment. Christians believe in God, who is not a God of the dead but of the living (cf. Mark 12:27 par.), for "to him all of them are alive" (Luke 20:38b). Paul confesses that we do not live or die to ourselves but that "whether we live or whether we die, we are the Lord's" (Rom. 14:7-9), and that nothing, not even death, can separate us "from the love of God in Christ Jesus our Lord" (Rom. 8:35-39). Therefore, the pilgrim people of God are aware that they look "for the city that is to come" (Heb. 13:14) of the sanctified church, "the heavenly Jerusalem,... the assembly of the firstborn who are enrolled in heaven,... and to the spirits of the righteous made perfect" (Heb. 12:22f.). The communion of saints, the unity of the pilgrim and heavenly church, is realized especially in worship, in the adoration and praise of the thrice-holy God and the Lamb, our Lord Jesus Christ (cf. Rev. 4:2-11; 5:9-14). The pilgrim church reaches its goal and thus its end and consummation when "the last enemy... death" is deprived of its power and the Son hands over everything to the rule of God the Father so that "God may be all in all" (1 Cor. 15:24-28).

5.2.2. THE CHURCH AND THE KINGDOM OF GOD

5.2.2.1. New Testament view

297. According to the witness of the synoptic gospels, the reign of God is the core of the preaching of Jesus of Nazareth (cf. Mark 1:15; Matt. 4:17), the petition for the coming of his Father's kingdom is the centre and fulcrum of his prayer (cf. Luke 11:2; Matt. 6:9f.), and the reign of God comes to human beings as the reality proclaimed as well by his deeds (cf. Luke 11:20; Matt. 12:28). Thus through and in Jesus himself the reign of God becomes present, and thus God's lordship establishes itself among those whom Jesus healed and who were affected by his preaching (cf. Luke 17:20f.).

298. By his preaching and practice of the kingdom of God, Jesus wished to call all Israel and prepare them to be eschatologically renewed and recreated by God. Especially the calling and sending out of the Twelve (cf. Mark 3:14; 6:7; Matt. 10:6) is a luminous sign that the reign of God presumes an actual people, in and through whom that kingdom can be established. The coming of the kingdom of God and the eschatological new creation of Israel belong inseparably together. Right up to his death Jesus maintained this, as shown by the eschatological perspective of his eucharistic words (cf. Mark 14:25 par.; Luke 13:29; 14:15; 22:30). Jesus' last meal, as an anticipation and interpretation of his death, becomes a bequest ensuring that God's offer is renewed for all Israel through Jesus' death as an atonement. Without merit or limit, sins are forgiven and new life bestowed (cf. Mark 14:24 par.).

299. Even if God has created for himself in the church an actual people made up of Jews and Gentiles (cf. Eph. 2:11-22) who owe their existence to the death and resur-

rection of Jesus and to the sending of the Spirit, this "new" people of God, which believes in the Messiah as having come, is still fundamentally related to Israel as a whole. The will of Jesus to gather Israel together held good then and still does. Seen in this way, Jesus' will to gather the eschatological people of God in wholeness and fullness, and under the rule of God, already includes the post-Easter church. Paul confirms this in his reflections on Israel in relation to salvation history: in the church consisting of Jews and Gentiles it is specifically the Gentile Christians who must never forget the origin of salvation history. Israel became salvation to the nations and will also be saved (cf. Rom. 9-11). For the church this means that it is the actual people of God in whom the reign of God is already kindled and through whom it is to extend. The church is the dawning and the sign of the kingdom of God.

5.2.2.2. Lutheran view

300. Though the Lutheran confessions contain no specific reflections on the theme of the kingdom of God and the church, there are nevertheless enough indications that the church is oriented towards the kingdom of God and taken into service for that kingdom, and that hidden in the church, the kingdom of God or of Christ has already dawned and is at work. In the explanation of the second petition in the Lord's prayer, the Large Catechism equates the kingdom of God with the saving activity of Jesus Christ who was sent "into the world to redeem and deliver us from the power of the devil and to bring us to himself and rule us as a king of righteousness, life and salvation". This he does in the Holy Spirit through his word. This kingdom is a "kingdom of grace" which is already actively present here on earth but will be consummated in eternity and will bring its citizens to their destination there. Coming to us temporally "through the word and faith" it will become manifest "in eternity" and definitively on the return of Christ.[373]

301. According to the *Apology* the church is the kingdom of Christ as the *congregatio sanctorum*, as he rules by the word and by preaching, works through the Holy Spirit, and increases in us faith, the fear of God, love and patience within the heart.[374] The church is not identical with the ultimate and all-embracing kingdom, which God will introduce at the end of the ages, but in the church it already begins here on earth[375] and is already hiddenly present.[376] In good works as fruit of faith it is already visible before the whole world.[377] In itself, however, the kingdom is "hidden under the cross", like Jesus before he entered his heavenly dominion.[378] Mingled with unbelievers (cf. Matt. 13:36ff.,47ff.; 25:1ff.) and still sinners themselves, the holy members of the church cannot yet represent the kingdom of God unambiguously. In spite of the fact that the church is not a "Platonic republic",[379] the kingdom has already broken in. Only the *notae*, the marks of the church, i.e., the "pure teaching of the gospel and the sacraments" are unequivocal. This tension will cease only when at the end of the ages Christ himself totally realizes and reveals the kingdom.[380]

5.2.2.3. Catholic view

302. Catholics are also persuaded that the kingdom of God is inseparably linked with the person of Jesus Christ. "In Christ's word, in his works and in his presence this kingdom reveals itself to men."[381] In Jesus the reign of God has dawned, and he himself is the reign of God in person. The Council speaks in a more nuanced way about the church. On the one hand it says that it receives from the exalted Lord "the mission

to proclaim and to establish among all peoples the kingdom of Christ and of God", but on the other hand it stresses that despite its gradual growth the church "strains towards the consummation of the kingdom".[382] Its destiny is "the kingdom of God which has been begun by God himself on earth, and which is to be further extended until it is brought to perfection by him at the end of time. Then Christ our life (cf. Col. 3:4) will appear."[383] In this way the Council clearly highlights the church's being taken into service for the kingdom of God and on the other hand keeps open, in the eschatological reservation, the fact that the kingdom of God is not at human disposal. God himself will establish and perfect his reign. The church is only "the kingdom of Christ now present in mystery",[384] the "initial budding forth of that kingdom" on earth.[385]

303. Thus, taking up the sacramental ecclesiological thinking of the Council, one can also speak of the church as the sacramental sign of the kingdom of God through the presence of the Lord in the Holy Spirit.[386] Because the crucified and risen Lord is with his church "always, to the end of the age" (Matt. 28:20), it is – with trust in this promise – the sacramental sign of the kingdom of God. The presence of the Lord is made actual in the Holy Spirit and is communicated in the word of God, the celebration of the eucharist and the other sacraments, and in the community of brothers and sisters. The Spirit does indeed "blow where it chooses" (John 3:8) but in and through the church this Spirit accomplishes the saving activity of God and his reign. The Spirit works in the world in the witness and service of the church, and in the Spirit the church fulfills its adoration, its intercessions, and its advocacy for everyone before God. Thus, the church serves the reign of God for the world. It is directed towards the kingdom of God as its eschatological salvation.

304. The kingdom of God is therefore the church's constant orientation, abiding motivation, critical court of appeal and final goal. The power of the coming kingdom is already really present in the church through its Lord in the Holy Spirit. The Holy Spirit effects forgiveness of sins, sanctification and life in the church. The Spirit supports its mission and perfects its catholicity. In the miracle of tongues at Pentecost the "divisiveness of Babel" is indeed fundamentally overcome.[387] Nevertheless the Spirit makes the church repeatedly cry, Come! so that the dispersed children of God may ultimately be gathered together (cf. Rev. 22:17-20; John 11:52). Seen in this way, the church is the place where the reign of God has already dawned, and thus it is the recipient of salvation. But at the same time it is also an instrument and sign for the reign which God himself implements, and thus it is the mediator of salvation. At the end the church will be taken up into the kingdom of God, i.e., it will come to an end because it is no longer needed as sign and instrument. But this end is also the consummation of its earthly form as the place of God's reign and the beginning of its new, definitive existence in the eternal kingdom of God.[388]

5.2.2.4. Perspective in ecumenical dialogue

305. In ecumenical dialogue too the church is seen in various ways as sign and instrument of the presence of Christ, the mission of Christ, and the kingdom. Thus the commission on Faith and Order of the World Council of Churches states that "the church is called to be a visible sign of the presence of Christ, who is both hidden and revealed to faith, reconciling and healing human alienation in the worshipping community".[389] In its report on the meeting in Bangalore the same commission says, "The church is a sign and

instrument of Christ's mission to all humankind."[390] In the message of the 1980 world conference on mission and evangelism in Melbourne, it was said that "the good news of the kingdom must be presented to the world by the church, the body of Christ, the sacrament of the kingdom in every place and time".[391] Despite all the inadequacies of the churches as they actually exist, the reality of their character as signs of the eschatological rule of God is highlighted and stressed: "Yet there is reality here. The whole church of God, in every place and time, is a sacrament of the kingdom which came in the person of Jesus Christ and will come in its fullness when he returns in glory."[392]

306. Similar pronouncements are to be found in the bilateral ecumenical dialogues. Thus in the Lutheran-Roman Catholic dialogue in the USA the mission of the church is seen "to be an anticipatory and efficacious sign of the full unification of all things when God will be all in all".[393] The Anglican-Lutheran dialogue calls the church "an instrument for proclaiming and manifesting God's sovereign rule and saving grace",[394] but also indicates that an "authentic fellowship of the reconciled"[395] is a precondition for the proper exercise of the mission and service of the church. Thus, a necessary reservation is pointed out in order to evaluate realistically talk of the church as a sign of the kingdom of God. It is an ongoing task of the church to be a credible sign of the kingdom. Its credibility will repeatedly be distorted by human weakness and sin and become blurred by lack of contrition. Therefore, the church always needs purification through repentance and renewal. The report of section III of the world conference on mission and evangelism in Melbourne speaks of a frightening claim, "frightening, because it causes every one of us to examine our personal experience of the empirical church and to confess how often our church life has hidden rather than revealed the sovereignty of God the Father whom Jesus Christ made known".[396]

5.2.2.5. Common witness

307. Lutherans and Catholics together regard the church as the dawning and the instrument of the kingdom of God. Two things should be maintained together. On the one hand, there is the reality of the powers of the kingdom of God, especially in the proclamation of the word of God and the celebration of the sacraments as the means of salvation, but also in the reconciled community of sisters and brothers as the place of salvation. On the other hand, there is the interim nature of all words and signs in which salvation is imparted but also the inadequacies in preaching, worship and the serving community as these exist in practice among believers. To this extent the church always lives on the basis of letting itself be lifted up into the coming kingdom, remembering its own provisional nature. The earthly church will find its eschatological consummation only when the kingdom has come. Then when God's kingdom dawns the church will be consummated and all hiddenness fully revealed.

308. The assembly of the faithful as a community of the perfected is the consummation of the church in the unveiled, pure presence and reign of God who is love, with whom and in whom all those made perfect have community and are in constant touch with each other: "God may be all in all" (1 Cor. 15:24-28). "And I heard a loud voice from the throne saying, 'See, the home of God is among mortals. He will dwell with them as their God; they will be his people, and God himself will be with them; he will wipe every tear from their eyes. Death will be no more; mourning and crying and pain will be no more, for the first things have passed away.' And the one who was seated on the throne said, 'See, I am making all things new'" (Rev. 21:3-5a).

NOTES

[1] *Articulus stantis et cadentis ecclesiae.*
[2] WADB 40,111,352,3: *quia isto articulo stante stat Ecclesia, ruente ruit Ecclesia.*
[3] *Justification by Faith*, Lutherans and Catholics in Dialogue VII, Minneapolis, 1985, 153.
[4] *All Under One Christ*, 1980, statement on the Augsburg confession by the Roman Catholic–Lutheran joint commission, 14, in GA, 241-247.
[5] *Kirchengemeinschaft in Wort und Sakrament.* Bilaterale Arbeitsgruppe der Deutschen Bischofskonferenz und der Kirchenleitung der Vereinigten Evangelisch-Lutherischen Kirche Deutschlands, Paderborn/Hannover, 1984, 1 (hereafter *Kirchengemeinschaft*).
[6] *Ibid.*, 2; cf. LG, nos. 3f.
[7] NA, no. 4.
[8] *Ibid.*
[9] Apol 7.17f.; BC, 171.
[10] LG, no. 3.
[11] *Kirchengemeinschaft*, 2; LG, no. 5.
[12] WA 2,430.
[13] WA 1,236: *sacrosanctum evangelium*; LW 31, 31.
[14] *Ibid*: *Verus thesaurus ecclesiae; ibid.*
[15] WA 7,721.
[16] CA 7; BC, 32.
[17] LG, no. 20.
[18] AG, no. 6.
[19] EN, no. 15.
[20] Report of the joint Lutheran–Roman Catholic study commission on *The Gospel and the Church*, 1972 (hereafter Malta report), GA, nos. 169-189.
[21] *Ibid.*, no. 21.
[22] *Ibid.*, nos. 33,47,48,50; cf. 56.
[23] SA, III, 4; BC, 310.
[24] *All Under One Christ*, no. 16.
[25] Irenaeus, "Against Heresies", 111.1.1 in *Ante-Nicene Fathers*, Grand Rapids, Michigan, 1967, 1,414.
[26] Cf. Tertullian, *De praescr.*, 6,37.
[27] Cf. Tertullian, *Adv. Marc.*, 1,21; 4,5.
[28] Augustinus, *De bapt.*, 4, 31: *Quod universa tenet ecclesia, nec conciliis institutum sed semper retentum est nonnisi auctoritate apostolica traditum rectissime creditur.*
[29] Cf. for instance Rufinus, *Expositio Symboli apostolorum*, no. 2: CCL, nos. 20, 134f.
[30] FC Ep 1; BC, 464.
[31] DV, no. 7.
[32] DV, no. 8.
[33] Malta report, no. 57; cf. *The Ministry in the Church*, Roman Catholic-Lutheran joint commission, Geneva, 1982; GA, nos. 248-275.
[34] LG, esp. no. 1.
[35] "The Mystery of the Church and of the Eucharist in the Light of the Mystery of the Holy Trinity", Joint International Commission for Theological Dialogue between the Roman Catholic Church and the Orthodox Church, 1982, esp. 11,1 and 1,5/d.
[36] Cf. *Ways to Community*, Roman Catholic-Lutheran joint commission, Geneva, 1981, 9-13, in GA, nos. 215-240; *The Ministry in the Church*, no. 12; FU, supra.
[37] LWF Report no. 19/20, 1985, 175.
[38] Cf. WA, 16,407, 38,247; LG, nos. 9-17; in the ecumenical dialogue cf. *BEM*, Ministry 1-6 in GA, nos. 465-503; *The Ministry in the Church*, 12-13; *Kirchengemeinschaft*, 61.
[39] See below 5.1.
[40] *The Eucharist*, Lutheran-Roman Catholic joint commission, Geneva, 1980, 25, in GA, nos. 190-214.
[41] *Merismós pneúmatos agioû".*
[42] Cf. BC, 345,415-420.
[43] Cf. LG, no. 4.
[44] E.g., LG, no. 7; cf. LG, no. 3.
[45] Thomas Aquinas, *Summa Theologiae III*, 73a.1; 79a.5.
[46] WA 2, 742-758: LW 35, 45-73.
[47] Martin Chemnitz, "Fundamenta sanae doctrinae de vera et substantiali praesentia... corporis et sanguinis Domini in Coena", IX.

48 St John of Damascus, *The Orthodox Faith* IV 13, *The Fathers of the Church*, vol. 37, Washington, 1958, 361.
49 Documents of the Extraordinary Synod, "The Final Report", Rome, 1985, in *The Tablet*, 14 Dec. 1985, II,C, I.
50 GS, no. 19.
51 DV, no. 2.
52 AG, no. 3.
53 UR, no. 2.
54 *Communio/congregatio sanctsorum/fidelium.*
55 CA 7; BC 32.
56 *Communion sanctorum.*
57 Apol 7,8; BC 169; cf. translation and interpretation of *communio sanctorum* in Luther's Large Catechism as "a communion of saints", as "a little holy flock or community"; BC 416f.
58 LC 11, 3; BC 417; cf. Apol 7, 8: "'Church' means, namely, the assembly of saints who share the association of the same gospel or teaching and of the same Holy Spirit, who renews, consecrates, and governs their hearts." BC 169.
59 Luther to the term koinonia in 1 Corinthians 10:16ff.; WA 26,493; LW 37,356.
60 WA 2,754; LW 35,67.
61 AG, no. 9.
62 DV, no. 21.
63 Cf. LG, no. 7 with reference to 1 Corinthians 10:16f.; cf. LG, no. 3.
64 CF. LG, no. 11.
65 PO, no. 5: *congregatio fidelium.*
66 CA 7; BC 32; cf. Apol 7, 9; BC 169f.
67 LC 11,3; BC 417.
68 Apol 7,10; BC 170.
69 Apol 7,5; BC 169.
70 LG, no. 9.
71 UR, no. 2.
72 North America and Europe.
73 Lutheran world convention, 1923; Lutheran World Federation, 1947.
74 CA 7.
75 LWF constitution 111: Nature and Functions.
76 Cf. Agreement between Reformation churches in Europe (Leuenberg Agreement), 1973, Frankfurt, 1993, 29 and 33; FU, nos. 23-26.
77 LWF Report no. 19/20, Budapest 1984, 175.
78 The terminology for describing the local church and the church as a whole (all the local churches that are in communion with each other) does not derive from a systematic and critical decision. Even Vatican II did not come to such a decision. Consequently in the Council's documents, *ecclesia localis* and *ecclesia particularis* can designate the diocesan church, but with equal frequency the two terms also describe associations of diocesan churches. *Ecclesia universa* (used on twenty-three occasions) and *ecclesia universalis* (used on twenty-five occasions) designate the church as a whole or the universal church. This is never described as the church of Rome.

The *Codex Iuris Canonici* of 1983, which does not have the expressions *ecclesia localis* and *ecclesia universalis*, makes use of the two terms *ecclesia particularis* (diocese) and *ecclesia universa* (the church as a whole). Catholic theologians have not wholly identified themselves with this choice of terms. They prefer to reserve the term "particular church" *(ecclesia parlicularis)* for associations of churches which are characterized by their special cultural features and to describe the church in one place as the "local church" in order to preserve the catholicity of the church.

In German this leads to preferring the term *Ortskirche* ("local church") to "particular church" and likewise to the term "partial church" (which suggests the false idea that the local church is a part of the universal church).
79 Cf. SC, no. 41; LG, nos. 23 and 26; CD, no. 11.
80 CD, no. 11.
81 Cf. LG, chs 2 and 3.
82 Cf. LG, no. 23, and FU, no. 112.
83 SC, no. 42.
84 *The Church: Local and Universal,* 36. JWG, infra.
85 LG, no. 23.
86 International Commission of Theologians: *Themata Selecta de Ecclesiologia* (Documenta 13). Vaticano 1985, 32: *mutua interioritas.*

[87] John Paul II, speech to the Roman Curia, 20 Dec. 1990, AAS 83 (1991), 745-747.
[88] LG, no. 23.
[89] *Corpus ecclesiarum* (LG, no. 23). The reason of the corporeality of the church is the sacramental sharing in the body of Christ; see above 76 and 78.
[90] *The Church: Local and Universal*, 37.
[91] AG, no. 4.
[92] AG, no. 10.
[93] AG, no. 15.
[94] Cf. LG, no. 13.
[95] AG, no. 22.
[96] LG, no. 13.
[97] LG, no. 23.
[98] UR, no. 4.
[99] Consejo Episcopal Latinoamericano (Council of Latin American Bishops).
[100] LG, no. 13.
[101] *The Church: Local and Universal*, 24.
[102] UR, no. 14; cf. FU, nos. 44f.
[103] Cf. FU, no. 5-7.
[104] See above 2.4.
[105] See above 3.3.
[106] See below 4.2.
[107] LC 111.47; BC 416.
[108] WA 7,219; LW Phil.Ed. 11,373.
[109] CA 7 (and 8); BC 32; BSLK 61,1: *Congregatio sanctorum [et vere credentium], in qua evangelium pure docetur et recte administrantur sacramenta.*
[110] *Principaliter*, cf. CA 8: *proprie.*
[111] *Pura evangelii doctrina.*
[112] Apol 7,5; BC 169.
[113] Cf. CA 1 and 3.
[114] Apol 7,5; BC 169.
[115] WA 10,I/1:140, 8.14.
[116] WA 7,219,6; LW Phil.Ed. II,373.
[117] Apol 9,2; BC 178.
[118] *Ibid.*, German text.
[119] SA 111,12; BC 315.
[120] WA 50,629,34: LW Phil.Ed. II, 271.
[121] WA 7,219,11; LW Phil.Ed. II, 373.
[122] WA 12,308,4.
[123] *Catechism of the Council of Trent* 1,10,2; Cat. Rom. 1,10,5: *coetus omnium fidelium.*
[124] *Ibid.*, 1,10,2.
[125] *Ibid.*
[126] *Ibid.*, 1,10,24.
[127] *Communio sanctorum.*
[128] *Catechism of the Council of Trent* 1,10,23-27.
[129] LG, no. 9.
[130] AG, nos. 15,19; PO, no. 4f.
[131] *Civitas redempta.*
[132] PO, no. 2.
[133] LG, no. 9.
[134] LG, no. 4: *in communione et ministratione.*
[135] AG, no. 3.
[136] LG, no. 9.
[137] PO, no. 2.
[138] LG, no. 10.
[139] *Ibid.*
[140] PO, no. 5.
[141] LG, no. 7, referring to 1 Cor. 10:17.
[142] PO, no. 4.
[143] *Ibid.*
[144] AG, no. 15.

[145] AG, no. 8.
[146] Malta report, 48.
[147] WA 2,430,6: *creatura... Evangelii.*
[148] LG, no. 20.
[149] FU, no. 85.
[150] LG, no. 1.
[151] *Ibid.*
[152] SC, no. 5.
[153] LG, no. 9.
[154] Cf, LG, nos. 2-5.
[155] LG, no. 48; cf. LG, nos. 7,59.
[156] Thus the term "sacrament" is always placed within quotation marks when related to the church in order to draw attention to the analogous use of language. This is expressly highlighted in the Dogmatic Constitution on the Church when talking of the church as "a kind of *[veluti]* sacrament... a sign and an instrument...." (LG, no. 1).
[157] *Ex opere operato.*
[158] LG, no. 8.
[159] *Ibid.*
[160] Cf. LG, no. 7, referring to 1 Cor. 12, Eph. 1 and Col. 2.
[161] LG, no. 8; cf. No. 48.
[162] UR, no. 6.
[163] LG, no. 8; cf. UR, no. 3f.
[164] LG, no. 16; GS, no. 22.
[165] Cf. CA 5.
[166] CA 7.
[167] *Viva vox evangelii.*
[168] WA 20,350,6: *Quando ego praedico, ipse [sc. Christus] praedicat in me.*
[169] *Verbum externum.*
[170] *Verbum efficax.*
[171] SA 111,8; BC 313.
[172] CA 5; BC 31.
[173] CA 8; BC 33.
[174] *Extra ecclesiam nulla salus;* cf. Apol 9,2; BC 178.
[175] LC 1,40ff.; BC 416.
[176] Augustine, Ep. 187, CSEL 57,113.
[177] Cf. WA 6,501.37: 86,7f.; LW Phil.Ed. II,177.
[178] See below 4.4.
[179] WA 40/II,106,19; LW 27,84.
[180] *Coetus.*
[181] Bellarmine, *Disputatio de conciliis et ecclesia,* III.ii.
[182] Apol 7,20; BC 171.
[183] LG, no. 8.
[184] CA 7; BC 32.
[185] CA 5, 14; BC 31,36.
[186] See above 135.
[187] WA 40/II,106,20; LW 27,84.
[188] Apol 7,3; BC 169.
[189] *Ibid.*
[190] Apol 7.1-22; BC 168ff.
[191] WA 40/II,106.29; LW 27,85.
[192] WA 50.625,3; LW Phil.Ed. V,265.
[193] WA 40/II,106,21; LW 27,84; cf. Apol 7,19.
[194] LG no. 14.
[195] LG, nos. 1-8.
[196] LG, no. 4.
[197] Cf. LG, no. 7.
[198] Cf. LG, no. 8.
[199] Cf. LG, no. 5:9.
[200] See above 4.2.
[201] Cf. LG, no. 8.

²⁰²*Ibid.*
²⁰³Cf. UR, no. 6.
²⁰⁴LG, no. 39.
²⁰⁵WA 50,628,16; LW 41,148.
²⁰⁶CA 7; BC 32.
²⁰⁷*Ecclesia non potest errare.*
²⁰⁸Cf. WA 18,649f.; 30 III, 408; 51,513 and 515f.; Apol 7,27: BC 173.
²⁰⁹E.g., Malta report, 22f.; *The Ministry in the Church*, 58.
²¹⁰UR, no. 4, cf. Augustine, *Retract.*, lib.II, c. 18.
²¹¹LG, no. 48.
²¹²CA 8; BC 33.
²¹³LG, no. 8; cf. No. 40.
²¹⁴UR, no. 6.
²¹⁵WA 38,215f.
²¹⁶WA 51,516,15.
²¹⁷Cf. Apol 7:28; BC 173.
²¹⁸WA 51,517,19; see also 513ff., esp. 516f.; cf. WA 38,216.
²¹⁹Malta report, 23.
²²⁰Cf. LG, nos. 8; 40; DS 229 and 1537.
²²¹UR, no. 6.
²²²*Ibid.*
²²³LG, no. 8; cf. UR, no. 3.
²²⁴See 4.5.3.1-4.
²²⁵Cf. GS, no. 43.
²²⁶Cf. UR, no. 6.
²²⁷See below 4.5.3.3.
²²⁸See below 4.5.3.2.
²²⁹See below 5.2.1.
²³⁰Malta report, 29.
²³¹Justification by Faith, 153; cf. 28.
²³²CA 7; BC 32.
²³³*Ibid.*
²³⁴WA 401,69; cf. 46,6f.
²³⁵See above 178.
²³⁶Cf. *The Ministry in the Church*, 17.
²³⁷CA 4; BC 30.
²³⁸CA 5; BC 31.
²³⁹Apol 7,20; BC 171; WA 30III, 88.
²⁴⁰*Tractatus*, 25.
²⁴¹Johann Gerhard, *Loci theologici*, XXII,V,37,40.
²⁴²*The Ministry in the Church*, 18.
²⁴³Cf. *Apol* 7,28; BC 173.
²⁴⁴*The Ministry in the Church*, 23.
²⁴⁵*Extra nos pro nobis.*
²⁴⁶Cf. BEM, Ministry, 8,12,42.
²⁴⁷*The Ministry in the Church*, 20.
²⁴⁸*Pseudoapostoloi.*
²⁴⁹*Pseudoapostoloi.*
²⁵⁰Cf. *The Ministry in the Church*, 40-49; 59-66.
²⁵¹Cf. Apol 14; BC 214f.
²⁵²*The Ministry in the Church*, 49; cf.50.
²⁵³*Ibid.*, 46f.; esp. FU, no. 94-98.
²⁵⁴DS 1776.
²⁵⁵*The Ministry in the Church*, 49.
²⁵⁶Cf. DS 1776: *hierarchiam divina ordinatione institutam*; cf. LG, no. 28 "Thus the divinely established ecclesiastical ministry is exercised on different levels by those who from antiquity have been called bishops, priests, and deacons."
²⁵⁷LG, no. 20.
²⁵⁸Cf. Apol 14; BC 214f.; WA 26, 195f.; *The Ministry in the Church*, 65f., 49 and 50; FU, nos. 106, 97.
²⁵⁹Cf. CA 5; BC 31.

²⁶⁰Cf. CA 7; BC 32; WA 7,721; see above 36.
²⁶¹See above 85.
²⁶²Apol 7,34; BC 175.
²⁶³Apol 7,30-37 interprets CA 7: The question in the *nec necesse est* is not whether what is added in the church to proclaim the gospel is "profitable" and "necessary" for the church. The main question is rather whether it is "necessary for righteousness" *(necessarius ad iustitiam)*. BC 173ff.
²⁶⁴LG, no. 48.
²⁶⁵LG, no. 8; cf. UR, no. 3.
²⁶⁶UR, no. 3.
²⁶⁷AG, no. 7.
²⁶⁸UR, no. 22.
²⁶⁹*The Ministry in the Church*, 77.
²⁷⁰Cf. UR, nos. 19-23.
²⁷¹Cf. *Facing Unity*, 117-139.
²⁷²See above 3.2.3.
²⁷³Cf. Malta report, 18.
²⁷⁴See above 4.5.2.
²⁷⁵See above 4.5.3.1.
²⁷⁶CA 1: *Ecclesiae magno consensu apud nos docent...* "Our churches teach with great unanimity..." (BC 27); cf. CA 1-21 (BC 27ff.), and the conclusion in the first part of the *Confessio Augustana* which says: "This is just about a summary of the doctrines that are preached and taught in our churches" (BC 47).
²⁷⁷CA 7; BC 32.
²⁷⁸CA 28,21f.; BC 84.
²⁷⁹Cf. *The Ministry in the Church*, 42.
²⁸⁰Cf. *ibid.*, 55.
²⁸¹Apol 7.23-27, esp. 23; BC 172f.
²⁸²Apol 7,27; BC 173.
²⁸³Apol 7,27; BC 173.
²⁸⁴Apol 7,28; BC 173.
²⁸⁵Apol 7,23; BC 172.
²⁸⁶Cf. DV, no. 10.
²⁸⁷Apol 14,1 and 2; BC 214.
²⁸⁸Cf. Malta report, 66; *The Ministry in the Church*, 65f.,73,80; FU, no. 97.
²⁸⁹Cf. Malta report, 66.
²⁹⁰LG, no. 12.
²⁹¹Cf. LG, no. 25.
²⁹²FU, no. 110.
²⁹³*The Ministry in the Church*, 51.
²⁹⁴LG, no. 12.
²⁹⁵*The Ministry in the Church*, 62; cf. LG, no. 25.
²⁹⁶DV, no. 10; cf. *The Ministry in the Church*, 50.
²⁹⁷Cf. *Ibid.*, 50 and 62.
²⁹⁸PO, no. 4.
²⁹⁹FU, no. 110 and footnote 157.
³⁰⁰Cf. among others DS 265.
³⁰¹DS 3073f.
³⁰²*The Ministry in the Church*, 52.
³⁰³Cf. *Mysterium ecclesiae*, 5. Statement by the Vatican Congregation for the Doctrine of the Faith.
³⁰⁴DV, no. 8.
³⁰⁵Cf. DV, no. 10.
³⁰⁶*The Ministry in the Church*, 56 and 73.
³⁰⁷See above 211-214.
³⁰⁸CIC, Can. 1752: *salus animarum semper suprema lex*; The Code of Canon Law, London, 1983, p.310; Malta report, 32. For church law, "the final decisive viewpoint must be that of the salvation of the individual believer".
³⁰⁹Malta report, 33.
³¹⁰Cf. *Ibid.*, 31 and 33.
³¹¹See above, 227.
³¹²CA 28: The Power of Bishops; BC 81ff.
³¹³CA 28,5 and 21; BC 81 and 84.

[314] CA 28,5 and 8; BC 81.
[315] CA 28,10; BC 82.
[316] CA 28,20f. and 29; BC 84f.
[317] CA 28,8f.; BC 82.
[318] CA 28,21; BC 84.
[319] Ibid.
[320] CA 28,22; ibid.
[321] CA 28,23ff.; ibid.
[322] CA 28,29ff.; BC 85f.
[323] CA 28,53 and 55; BC 89f.
[324] CA 28,66f. and 73f.; BC 92ff.
[325] CA 28,55; BC 90.
[326] CA 28,43-48; 50,53 and frequently; BC 88ff.
[327] CA 28,42,49,53,64,77, and frequently; ibid.
[328] CA 28,37,50,52,66, and frequently; BC 86ff.
[329] CA 28,51,60,64 and frequently; BC 89ff.
[330] See above 227.
[331] LG, no. 27.
[332] LG, no. 20.
[333] LG, no. 27.
[334] LG, no. 27; CD, no. 3.
[335] DH 2 *(in re religiosa neque aliquis cogatur ad agendum contra suam conscientiam)*; 12.
[336] DH 11.
[337] Malta report, 32, referring to DH 2:10-12.
[338] Malta report, 33.
[339] John Paul II, apostolic constitution *Sacrae Disciplinae Leges*, promulgating the new code of 1983; CIC, Xlff.
[340] UR, no. 1.
[341] Cf. *Redemptoris Missio,* no. 12.
[342] Cf. GS, no. 41.
[343] Apol 16, BC 222ff.; cf. also CA 28,8f; LC III, 53.
[344] LC 1, fifth commandment; BC 390f.: WA 6,36f., 43:15,300f.; 11.245, 250; 30/II,111f.
[345] WA 15,302; 11,252f.; cf. Apol 16,6.
[346] CA 28, 11.
[347] *Usus civilis legis.*
[348] CA 28,11.
[349] CA 16; BC 37; cf. Apol 13,15; BC 213.
[350] FC SD 5; BC 564ff.
[351] LC I,141f; 150; BC 384ff.
[352] WA 40,III,221-223.
[353] WA 18,818; 24,6-9.
[354] CA 28.12; BC 83, Apol 16,2: BC 222.
[355] LC 1; BC 390f.; WA 6,37f.;11,245,249f.;18,308f.
[356] Apol 15,25f.; BC 218f.
[357] Apol 16,13; BC 224.
[358] CA 27,49; BC 78f.; Apol 27,37; BC 275.
[359] Apol 4,121f.; BC 124; cf. also WA 11,279;7,544f.,600; 15,293.
[360] GS, no. 36.
[361] GS, no. 42.
[362] GS, no. 43.
[363] GS, no. 43.
[364] *The Ministry in the Church,* 13.
[365] *The Eucharist,* 12; 29-37.
[366] Cf. LC 11.3; BC 417ff.
[367] Cf. *The Catechism of the Council of Trent,* 1:X,23-26.
[368] Apol 21.4-7; BC 229f.
[369] Apol 21, 8f.; BC 230.
[370] *The Eucharist,* 39.
[371] Cf. LG, no. 50f.
[372] Cf. LG, no. 50f.

[373] LC 111,51ff.; BC 426f.
[374] Apol 16.54; BC 222ff.
[375] *Ibid.*
[376] Apol 7.17; BC 171.
[377] Apol 4,189; BC 133.
[378] Apol 7 18f.; BC 171; see above 142f.
[379] Apol 7,20; BC 171; *civitas platonica*.
[380] Apol 7,17-20; BC 171.
[381] LG, no. 5.
[382] *Ibid.*
[383] LG, no. 9.
[384] LG, no. 3.
[385] LG, no. 5.
[386] See above 121-125.
[387] AG, no. 4.
[388] Cf. LG, no. 48f.
[389] *Uniting in Hope: Accra 1974*, 93, Faith and Order Paper 72.
[390] *Sharing in One Hope: Bangalore 1978*, 239, Faith and Order Paper 92.
[391] *Your Kingdom Come*, Geneva, WCC, 1980, pp.235f.
[392] *Ibid.*
[393] "Differing Attitudes Toward Papal Primacy" 1, in *Papal Primacy and the Universal Church*, Minneapolis, 1974.
[394] "Anglican-Lutheran International Conversations", London, 1973 (Pullach report), 59 in GA, 13-34.
[395] *Ibid.*
[396] *Your Kingdom Come*, 193.

44. Joint Declaration on the Doctrine of Justification

Augsburg, Germany, 31 October 1999

Preamble
1. The doctrine of justification was of central importance for the Lutheran Reformation of the 16th century. It was held to be the "first and chief article"[1] and at the same time the "ruler and judge over all other Christian doctrines".[2] The doctrine of justification was particularly asserted and defended in its Reformation shape and special valuation over against the Roman Catholic Church and theology of that time, which in turn asserted and defended a doctrine of justification of a different character. From the Reformation perspective, justification was the crux of all the disputes. Doctrinal condemnations were put forward both in the Lutheran confessions[3] and by the Roman Catholic Church's council of Trent. These condemnations are still valid today and thus have a church-dividing effect.

2. For the Lutheran tradition, the doctrine of justification has retained its special status. Consequently it has also from the beginning occupied an important place in the official Lutheran-Roman Catholic dialogue.

3. Special attention should be drawn to the following reports: "The Gospel and the Church" (1972)[4] and "Church and Justification" (1994)[5] by the Lutheran-Roman Catholic joint commission, "Justification by Faith" (1983)[6] of the Lutheran-Roman Catholic dialogue in the USA and "The Condemnations of the Reformation Era: Do They Still Divide?" (1986)[7] by the ecumenical working group of Protestant and Catholic theologians in Germany. Some of these dialogue reports have been officially received by the churches. An important example of such reception is the binding response of the United Evangelical Lutheran Church of Germany to the "condemnations" study, made in 1994 at the highest possible level of ecclesiastical recognition together with the other churches of the Evangelical Church in Germany.[8]

4. In their discussion of the doctrine of justification, all the dialogue reports as well as the responses show a high degree of agreement in their approaches and conclusions. The time has therefore come to take stock and to summarize the results of the dialogues on justification so that our churches may be informed about the overall results of this dialogue with the necessary accuracy and brevity, and thereby be enabled to make binding decisions.

5. The present joint declaration has this intention: namely, to show that on the basis of their dialogue the subscribing Lutheran churches and the Roman Catholic Church[9] are now able to articulate a common understanding of our justification by God's grace through faith in Christ. It does not cover all that either church teaches about justifica-

tion; it does encompass a consensus on basic truths of the doctrine of justification and shows that the remaining differences in its explication are no longer the occasion for doctrinal condemnations.

6. Our declaration is not a new, independent presentation alongside the dialogue reports and documents to date, let alone a replacement of them. Rather, as the appendix of sources shows, it makes repeated reference to them and their arguments.

7. Like the dialogues themselves, this joint declaration rests on the conviction that in overcoming the earlier controversial questions and doctrinal condemnations, the churches neither take the condemnations lightly nor do they disavow their own past. On the contrary, this declaration is shaped by the conviction that in their respective histories our churches have come to new insights. Developments have taken place which not only make possible, but also require the churches to examine the divisive questions and condemnations and see them in a new light.

1. Biblical message of justification

8. Our common way of listening to the word of God in scripture has led to such new insights. Together we hear the gospel that "God so loved the world that he gave his only Son, so that everyone who believes in him may not perish but may have eternal life" (John 3:16). This good news is set forth in holy scripture in various ways. In the Old Testament we listen to God's word about human sinfulness (Ps. 51:1-5; Dan. 9:5f.; Eccles./Qo 8:9f.; Ezra 9:6f.) and human disobedience (Gen. 3:1-19; Neh. 9:16f.,26) as well as of God's "righteousness" (Isa. 46:13; 51:5-8; 56:1 [cf. 53:11]; Jer. 9:24) and "judgment" (Eccles./Qo 12:14; Ps. 9:5f; 76:7-9).

9. In the New Testament diverse treatments of "righteousness" and "justification" are found in the writings of Matthew (5:10; 6:33; 21:32), John (16:8-11), Hebrews (5:3; 10:37f.), and James (2:14-26).[10] In Paul's letters also, the gift of salvation is described in various ways, among others: "for freedom Christ has set us free" (Gal. 5:1-13; cf. Rom. 6:7), "reconciled to God" (2 Cor. 5:18-21; cf. Rom. 5:11), "peace with God" (Rom. 5:1), "new creation" (2 Cor. 5:17), "alive to God in Christ Jesus" (Rom. 6:11,23), or "sanctified in Christ Jesus" (cf. 1 Cor. 1:2; 1:30; 2 Cor. 1:1). Chief among these is the "justification" of sinful human beings by God's grace through faith (Rom. 3:23-25), which came into particular prominence in the Reformation period.

10. Paul sets forth the gospel as the power of God for salvation of the person who has fallen under the power of sin, as the message that proclaims that "the righteousness of God is revealed through faith for faith" (Rom. 1:16f.) and that grants "justification" (Rom. 3:21-31). He proclaims Christ as "our righteousness" (1 Cor. 1:30), applying to the risen Lord what Jeremiah proclaimed about God himself (Jer. 23:6). In Christ's death and resurrection all dimensions of his saving work have their roots for he is "our Lord, who was put to death for our trespasses and raised for our justification" (Rom. 4:25). All human beings are in need of God's righteousness, "since all have sinned and fall short of the glory of God" (Rom. 3:23; cf. Rom. 1:18-3:20; 11:32; Gal. 3:22). In Galatians (3:6) and Romans (4:3-9), Paul understands Abraham's faith (Gen. 15:6) as faith in the God who justifies the sinner (Rom. 4:5) and calls upon the testimony of the Old Testament to undergird his gospel that this righteousness will be reckoned to all who, like Abraham, trust in God's promise. "For the righteous will live by faith (Hab. 2:4; cf. Gal. 3:11; Rom. 1:17). In Paul's letters, God's righteousness is also God's power for those who have faith (Rom. 1:16f.; 2 Cor. 5:21). In Christ he makes it our

righteousness (2 Cor. 5:21). Justification becomes ours through Christ Jesus "whom God put forward as a sacrifice of atonement by his blood, effective through faith" (Rom. 3:25; see 3:21-28). "For by grace you have been saved through faith, and this is not your own doing; it is the gift of God – not the result of works" (Eph. 2:8f.).

11. Justification is the forgiveness of sins (cf. Rom. 3:23-25; Acts 13:39; Luke 18:14), liberation from the dominating power of sin and death (Rom. 5:12-21) and from the curse of the law (Gal. 3:10-14). It is acceptance into communion with God: already now, but then fully in God's coming kingdom (Rom. 5:1f.). It unites with Christ and with his death and resurrection (Rom. 6:5). It occurs in the reception of the Holy Spirit in baptism and incorporation into the one body (Rom. 8:1f., 9f; 1 Cor. 12:12f.). All this is from God alone, for Christ's sake, by grace, through faith in "the gospel of God's Son" (Rom. 1:1-3).

12. The justified live by faith that comes from the word of Christ (Rom. 10:17) and is active through love (Gal. 5:6), the fruit of the Spirit (Gal. 5:22f.). But since the justified are assailed from within and without by powers and desires (Rom. 8:35-39; Gal. 5:16-21) and fall into sin (1 John 1:8,10), they must constantly hear God's promises anew, confess their sins (1 John 1:9), participate in Christ's body and blood, and be exhorted to live righteously in accord with the will of God. That is why the apostle says to the justified: "Work out your own salvation with fear and trembling; for it is God who is at work in you, enabling you both to will and to work for his good pleasure" (Phil. 2:12f.). But the good news remains: "there is now no condemnation for those who are in Christ Jesus" (Rom. 8:1), and in whom Christ lives (Gal. 2:20). Christ's "act of righteousness leads to justification and life for all" (Rom. 5:18).

2. The doctrine of justification as ecumenical problem

13. Opposing interpretations and applications of the biblical message of justification were in the 16th century a principal cause of the division of the Western church and led as well to doctrinal condemnations. A common understanding of justification is therefore fundamental and indispensable to overcoming that division. By appropriating insights of recent biblical studies and drawing on modern investigations of the history of theology and dogma, the post-Vatican II ecumenical dialogue has led to a notable convergence concerning justification, with the result that this joint declaration is able to formulate a consensus on basic truths concerning the doctrine of justification. In light of this consensus, the corresponding doctrinal condemnations of the 16th century do not apply to today's partner.

3. The common understanding of justification

14. The Lutheran churches and the Roman Catholic Church have together listened to the good news proclaimed in holy scripture. This common listening, together with the theological conversations of recent years, has led to a shared understanding of justification. This encompasses a consensus in the basic truths; the differing explications in particular statements are compatible with it.

15. In faith we together hold the conviction that justification is the work of the triune God. The Father sent his Son into the world to save sinners. The foundation and presupposition of justification is the incarnation, death and resurrection of Christ. Justification thus means that Christ himself is our righteousness, in which we share through the Holy Spirit in accord with the will of the Father. Together we confess: By

grace alone, in faith in Christ's saving work and not because of any merit on our part, we are accepted by God and receive the Holy Spirit, who renews our hearts while equipping and calling us to good works.[11]

16. All people are called by God to salvation in Christ. Through Christ alone are we justified, when we receive this salvation in faith. Faith is itself God's gift through the Holy Spirit who works through word and sacrament in the community of believers and who, at the same time, leads believers into that renewal of life which God will bring to completion in eternal life.

17. We also share the conviction that the message of justification directs us in a special way towards the heart of the New Testament witness to God's saving action in Christ: it tells us that as sinners our new life is solely due to the forgiving and renewing mercy that God imparts as a gift and we receive in faith, and never can merit in any way.

18. Therefore the doctrine of justification, which takes up this message and explicates it, is more than just one part of Christian doctrine. It stands in an essential relation to all truths of faith, which are to be seen as internally related to each other. It is an indispensable criterion which constantly serves to orient all the teaching and practice of our churches to Christ. When Lutherans emphasize the unique significance of this criterion, they do not deny the inter-relation and significance of all truths of faith. When Catholics see themselves as bound by several criteria, they do not deny the special function of the message of justification. Lutherans and Catholics share the goal of confessing Christ in all things, who alone is to be trusted above all things as the one Mediator (1 Tim. 2:5f.) through whom God in the Holy Spirit gives himself and pours out his renewing gifts [cf. sources for section 3].

4. Explicating the common understanding of justification

4.1. Human powerlessness and sin in relation to justification

19. We confess together that all persons depend completely on the saving grace of God for their salvation. The freedom they possess in relation to persons and the things of this world is no freedom in relation to salvation, for as sinners they stand under God's judgment and are incapable of turning by themselves to God to seek deliverance, of meriting their justification before God, or of attaining salvation by their own abilities. Justification takes place solely by God's grace. Because Catholics and Lutherans confess this together, it is true to say:

20. When Catholics say that persons "cooperate" in preparing for and accepting justification by consenting to God's justifying action, they see such personal consent as itself an effect of grace, not as an action arising from innate human abilities.

21. According to Lutheran teaching, human beings are incapable of cooperating in their salvation, because as sinners they actively oppose God and his saving action. Lutherans do not deny that a person can reject the working of grace. When they emphasize that a person can only receive (mere passive) justification, they mean thereby to exclude any possibility of contributing to one's own justification, but do not deny that believers are fully involved personally in their faith, which is effected by God's word [cf. sources for 4.1].

4.2. Justification as forgiveness of sins and making righteous

22. We confess together that God forgives sin by grace and at the same time frees human beings from sin's enslaving power and imparts the gift of new life in Christ.

When persons come by faith to share in Christ, God no longer imputes to them their sin and through the Holy Spirit effects in them an active love. These two aspects of God's gracious action are not to be separated, for persons are by faith united with Christ, who in his person is our righteousness (1 Cor. 1:30): both the forgiveness of sin and the saving presence of God himself. Because Catholics and Lutherans confess this together, it is true to say that:

23. When Lutherans emphasize that the righteousness of Christ is our righteousness, their intention is above all to insist that the sinner is granted righteousness before God in Christ through the declaration of forgiveness and that only in union with Christ is one's life renewed. When they stress that God's grace is forgiving love ("the favour of God"[12]), they do not thereby deny the renewal of the Christian's life. They intend rather to express that justification remains free from human cooperation and is not dependent on the life-renewing effects of grace in human beings.

24. When Catholics emphasize the renewal of the interior person through the reception of grace imparted as a gift to the believer,[13] they wish to insist that God's forgiving grace always brings with it a gift of new life, which in the Holy Spirit becomes effective in active love. They do not thereby deny that God's gift of grace in justification remains independent of human cooperation [cf. sources for section 4.2].

4.3. Justification by faith and through grace

25. We confess together that sinners are justified by faith in the saving action of God in Christ. By the action of the Holy Spirit in baptism, they are granted the gift of salvation, which lays the basis for the whole Christian life. They place their trust in God's gracious promise by justifying faith, which includes hope in God and love for him. Such a faith is active in love and thus the Christian cannot and should not remain without works. But whatever in the justified precedes or follows the free gift of faith is neither the basis of justification nor merits it.

26. According to Lutheran understanding, God justifies sinners in faith alone *(sola fide)*. In faith they place their trust wholly in their Creator and Redeemer and thus live in communion with him. God himself effects faith as he brings forth such trust by his creative word. Because God's act is a new creation, it affects all dimensions of the person and leads to a life in hope and love. In the doctrine of "justification by faith alone", a distinction but not a separation is made between justification itself and the renewal of one's way of life that necessarily follows from justification and without which faith does not exist. Thereby the basis is indicated from which the renewal of life proceeds, for it comes forth from the love of God imparted to the person in justification. Justification and renewal are joined in Christ, who is present in faith.

27. The Catholic understanding also sees faith as fundamental in justification. For without faith, no justification can take place. Persons are justified through baptism as hearers of the word and believers in it. The justification of sinners is forgiveness of sins and being made righteous by justifying grace, which makes us children of God. In justification the righteous receive from Christ faith, hope and love and are thereby taken into communion with him.[14] This new personal relation to God is grounded totally on God's graciousness and remains constantly dependent on the salvific and creative working of this gracious God, who remains true to himself, so that one can rely upon him. Thus justifying grace never becomes a human possession to which one could appeal over against God. While Catholic teaching emphasizes the renewal of life by

justifying grace, this renewal in faith, hope and love is always dependent on God's unfathomable grace and contributes nothing to justification about which one could boast before God (Rom. 3:27) [see sources for section 4.3].

4.4. The justified as sinner

28. We confess together that in baptism the Holy Spirit unites one with Christ, justifies and truly renews the person. But the justified must all through life constantly look to God's unconditional justifying grace. They also are continuously exposed to the power of sin still pressing its attacks (cf. Rom. 6:12-14) and are not exempt from a lifelong struggle against the contradiction to God within the selfish desires of the old Adam (cf. Gal. 5:16; Rom. 7:7-10). The justified also must ask God daily for forgiveness as in the Lord's prayer (Matt. 6:12; 1 John 1:9), are ever again called to conversion and penance, and are ever again granted forgiveness.

29. Lutherans understand this condition of the Christian as a being "at the same time righteous and sinner". Believers are totally righteous, in that God forgives their sins through word and sacrament and grants the righteousness of Christ which they appropriate in faith. In Christ, they are made just before God. Looking at themselves through the law, however, they recognize that they remain also totally sinners. Sin still lives in them (1 John 1:8; Rom. 7:17,20), for they repeatedly turn to false gods and do not love God with that undivided love which God requires as their Creator (Deut. 6:5; Matt. 22:36-40 pr.). This contradiction to God is as such truly sin. Nevertheless, the enslaving power of sin is broken on the basis of the merit of Christ. It no longer is a sin that "rules" the Christian for it is itself "ruled" by Christ with whom the justified are bound in faith. In this life, then, Christians can in part lead a just life. Despite sin, the Christian is no longer separated from God, because in the daily return to baptism, the person who has been born anew by baptism and the Holy Spirit has this sin forgiven. Thus this sin no longer brings damnation and eternal death.[15] Thus, when Lutherans say that justified persons are also sinners and that their opposition to God is truly sin, they do not deny that, despite this sin, they are not separated from God and that this sin is a "ruled" sin. In these affirmations, they are in agreement with Roman Catholics, despite the difference in understanding sin in the justified.

30. Catholics hold that the grace of Jesus Christ imparted in baptism takes away all that is sin "in the proper sense" and that is "worthy of damnation" (Rom. 8:1).[16] There does, however, remain in the person an inclination (concupiscence) which comes from sin and presses towards sin. Since, according to Catholic conviction, human sins always involve a personal element and since this element is lacking in this inclination, Catholics do not see this inclination as sin in an authentic sense. They do not thereby deny that this inclination does not correspond to God's original design for humanity and that it is objectively in contradiction to God and remains one's enemy in lifelong struggle. Grateful for deliverance by Christ, they underscore that this inclination in contradiction to God does not merit the punishment of eternal death[17] and does not separate the justified person from God. But when individuals voluntarily separate themselves from God, it is not enough to return to observing the commandments, for they must receive pardon and peace in the sacrament of reconciliation through the word of forgiveness imparted to them in virtue of God's reconciling work in Christ [see sources for section 4.4].

4.5. Law and gospel

31. We confess together that persons are justified by faith in the gospel "apart from works prescribed by the law" (Rom. 3:28). Christ has fulfilled the law and by his death and resurrection has overcome it as a way to salvation. We also confess that God's commandments retain their validity for the justified and that Christ has by his teaching and example expressed God's will which is a standard for the conduct of the justified also.

32. Lutherans state that the distinction and right ordering of law and gospel is essential for the understanding of justification. In its theological use, the law is demand and accusation. Throughout their lives, all persons, Christians also, in that they are sinners, stand under this accusation which uncovers their sin so that, in faith in the gospel, they will turn unreservedly to the mercy of God in Christ, which alone justifies them.

33. Because the law as a way to salvation has been fulfilled and overcome through the gospel, Catholics can say that Christ is not a law-giver in the manner of Moses. When Catholics emphasize that the righteous are bound to observe God's commandments, they do not thereby deny that through Jesus Christ God has mercifully promised to his children the grace of eternal life[18] [see sources for section 4.5].

4.6. Assurance of salvation

34. We confess together that the faithful can rely on the mercy and promises of God. In spite of their own weakness and the manifold threats to their faith, on the strength of Christ's death and resurrection they can build on the effective promise of God's grace in word and sacrament and so be sure of this grace.

35. This was emphasized in a particular way by the Reformers: in the midst of temptation, believers should not look to themselves but look solely to Christ and trust only him. In trust in God's promise they are assured of their salvation, but are never secure looking at themselves.

36. Catholics can share the concern of the Reformers to ground faith in the objective reality of Christ's promise, to look away from one's own experience, and to trust in Christ's forgiving word alone (cf. Matt. 16:19; 18:18). With the Second Vatican Council, Catholics state: to have faith is to entrust oneself totally to God,[19] who liberates us from the darkness of sin and death and awakens us to eternal life.[20] In this sense, one cannot believe in God and at the same time consider the divine promise untrustworthy. No one may doubt God's mercy and Christ's merit. Every person, however, may be concerned about his salvation when he looks upon his own weaknesses and shortcomings. Recognizing his own failures, however, the believer may yet be certain that God intends his salvation [see sources for section 4.6].

4.7. The good works of the justified

37. We confess together that good works – a Christian life lived in faith, hope and love – follow justification and are its fruits. When the justified live in Christ and act in the grace they receive, they bring forth, in biblical terms, good fruit. Since Christians struggle against sin their entire lives, this consequence of justification is also for them an obligation they must fulfill. Thus both Jesus and the apostolic scriptures admonish Christians to bring forth the works of love.

38. According to Catholic understanding, good works, made possible by grace and the working of the Holy Spirit, contribute to growth in grace, so that the righteousness that comes from God is preserved and communion with Christ is deepened. When

Catholics affirm the "meritorious" character of good works, they wish to say that, according to the biblical witness, a reward in heaven is promised to these works. Their intention is to emphasize the responsibility of persons for their actions, not to contest the character of those works as gifts, or far less to deny that justification always remains the unmerited gift of grace.

39. The concept of a preservation of grace and a growth in grace and faith is also held by Lutherans. They do emphasize that righteousness as acceptance by God and sharing in the righteousness of Christ is always complete. At the same time, they state that there can be growth in its effects in Christian living. When they view the good works of Christians as the fruits and signs of justification and not as one's own "merits", they nevertheless also understand eternal life in accord with the New Testament as unmerited "reward" in the sense of the fulfilment of God's promise to the believer [see sources for section 4.7].

5. The significance and scope of the consensus reached

40. The understanding of the doctrine of justification set forth in this declaration shows that a consensus in basic truths of the doctrine of justification exists between Lutherans and Catholics. In light of this consensus the remaining differences of language, theological elaboration and emphasis in the understanding of justification described in paragraphs 18 to 39 are acceptable. Therefore the Lutheran and the Catholic explications of justification are in their difference open to one another and do not destroy the consensus regarding the basic truths.

41. Thus the doctrinal condemnations of the 16th century, in so far as they relate to the doctrine of justification, appear in a new light. The teaching of the Lutheran churches presented in this declaration does not fall under the condemnations from the council of Trent. The condemnations in the Lutheran confessions do not apply to the teaching of the Roman Catholic Church presented in this declaration.

42. Nothing is thereby taken away from the seriousness of the condemnations related to the doctrine of justification. Some were not simply pointless. They remain for us "salutary warnings" to which we must attend in our teaching and practice.[21]

43. Our consensus in basic truths of the doctrine of justification must come to influence the life and teachings of our churches. Here it must prove itself. In this respect, there are still questions of varying importance which need further clarification. These include, among other topics, the relationship between the word of God and church doctrine, as well as ecclesiology, ecclesial authority, church unity, ministry, the sacraments and the relation between justification and social ethics. We are convinced that the consensus we have reached offers a solid basis for this clarification. The Lutheran churches and the Roman Catholic Church will continue to strive together to deepen this common understanding of justification and to make it bear fruit in the life and teaching of the churches.

44. We give thanks to the Lord for this decisive step forward on the way to overcoming the division of the church. We ask the Holy Spirit to lead us further towards that visible unity which is Christ's will.

Resources for the Joint Declaration on the Doctrine of Justification

In parts 3 and 4 of the joint declaration formulations from different Lutheran-Catholic dialogues are referred to. They are the following documents:

"All Under One Christ", statement on the Augsburg confession by the Roman Catholic/Lutheran joint commission, 1980, in *Growth in Agreement*, Harding Meyer and Lukas Vischer, eds, New York, Ramsey, 1984, pp.241-47.

Denzinger-Schönmetzer, *Enchiridion symbolorum* ...32nd to 36th ed. (hereafter DS).

Denzinger-Hünermann, *Enchiridion symbolorum* ...since the 37th ed. (hereafter DH).

Evaluation of the Pontifical Council for Promoting Christian Unity of the study "Lehrverurteilungen – kirchentrennend?", Vatican, 1992, unpublished document (hereafter PCPCU).

"Justification by Faith", *Lutherans and Catholics in Dialogue VII*, Minneapolis, 1985 (hereafter USA).

Position paper of the joint committee of the United Evangelical Lutheran Church of Germany and the LWF German national committee regarding the document "The Condemnations of the Reformation Era: Do They Still Divide?" in *Lehrverurteilungen im Gespräch*, Göttingen, 1993 (hereafter VELKD).

The Condemnations of the Reformation Era: Do they Still Divide?, Karl Lehmann and Wolfhart Pannenberg, eds, Minneapolis, 1990 (hereafter LV:E)

For 3: The Common Understanding of Justification (§§17 and 18) (LV:E 68f; VELKD 95)

"... a faith centred and forensically conceived picture of justification is of major importance for Paul and, in a sense, for the Bible as a whole, although it is by no means the only biblical or Pauline way of representing God's saving work" (USA, no. 146).

"Catholics as well as Lutherans can acknowledge the need to test the practices, structures, and theologies of the church by the extent to which they help or hinder 'the proclamation of God's free and merciful promises in Christ Jesus which can be rightly received only through faith' (§28)" (USA, no. 153).

Regarding the "fundamental affirmation" (USA, no. 157; cf. 4) it is said:

"This affirmation, like the Reformation doctrine of justification by faith alone, serves as a criterion for judging all church practices, structures, and traditions precisely because its counterpart is 'Christ alone' *(solus Christus)*. He alone is to be ultimately trusted as the one mediator through whom God in the Holy Spirit pours out his saving gifts. All of us in this dialogue affirm that all Christian teachings, practices, and offices should so function as to foster 'the obedience of faith' (Rom. 1:5) in God's saving action in Christ Jesus alone through the Holy Spirit, for the salvation of the faithful and the praise and honour of the heavenly Father" (USA, no. 160).

"For that reason, the doctrine of justification – and, above all, its biblical foundation – will always retain a special function in the church. That function is continually to remind Christians that we sinners live solely from the forgiving love of God, which we merely allow to be bestowed on us, but which we in no way – in however modified a form – 'earn' or are able to tie down to any preconditions or postconditions. The doctrine of justification therefore becomes the touchstone for testing at all times whether a particular interpretation of our relationship to God can claim the name of 'Christian.' At the same time, it becomes the touchstone for the church, for testing at all times whether its proclamation and its praxis correspond to what has been given to it by its Lord" (LV:E 69).

"An agreement on the fact that the doctrine of justification is significant not only as one doctrinal component within the whole of our church's teaching, but also as the touchstone for testing the whole doctrine and practice of our churches, is – from a Lutheran point of view – fundamental progress in the ecumenical dialogue between our churches. It cannot be welcomed enough" (VELKD 95, 20-26; cf. 157).

"For Lutherans and Catholics, the doctrine of justification has a different status in the hierarchy of truth; but both sides agree that the doctrine of justification has its specific function in the fact that it is 'the touchstone for testing at all times whether a particular interpretation of our relationship to God can claim the name of "Christian". At the same time it becomes the touchstone for the church, for testing at all times whether its proclamation and its praxis correspond to what has been given to it by its Lord' (LV:E 69). The criteriological significance of the doctrine of justification for sacramentology, ecclesiology and ethical teachings still deserves to be studied further" (PCPCU 96).

For 4.1: Human powerlessness and sin in relation to justification (§§19-21) (LV:E 42ff; 46; VELKD 77-81; 83f)

"Those in whom sin reigns can do nothing to merit justification, which is the free gift of God's grace. Even the beginnings of justification, for example, repentance, prayer for grace, and desire for forgiveness, must be God's work in us" (USA, no. 156.3).

"*Both* are concerned to make it clear that... human beings cannot... cast a sideways glance at their own endeavours... But a response is not a 'work.' The response of faith is itself brought about through the uncoercible word of promise which comes to human beings from outside themselves. There can be '*co*operation' only in the sense that in faith the heart is involved, when the word touches it and creates faith" (LV:E 46f).

"Where, however, Lutheran teaching construes the relation of God to his human creatures in justification with such emphasis on the divine 'monergism' or the sole efficacy of Christ in such a way, that the person's willing acceptance of God's grace – which is itself a gift of God – has no essential role in justification, then the Tridentine canons 4, 5, 6 and 9 still constitute a notable doctrinal difference on justification" (PCPCU 22).

"The strict emphasis on the passivity of human beings concerning their justification never meant, on the Lutheran side, to contest the full personal participation in believing; rather it meant to exclude any cooperation in the event of justification itself. Justification is the work of Christ alone, the work of grace alone" (VELKD 84,3-8).

For 4.2: Justification as forgiveness of sins and making righteous (§§22-24) (USA, nos. 98-101; LV:E 47ff.; VELKD 84ff.; cf. also the quotations for 4.3)

"By justification we are both declared and made righteous. Justification, therefore, is not a legal fiction. God, in justifying, effects what he promises; he forgives sin and makes us truly righteous" (USA, no. 156,5).

"Protestant theology does not overlook what Catholic doctrine stresses: the creative and renewing character of God's love; nor does it maintain... God's impotence towards a sin which is 'merely' forgiven in justification but which is not truly abolished in its power to divide the sinner from God" (LV:E 49).

"The Lutheran doctrine has never understood the 'crediting of Christ's justification' as without effect on the life of the faithful, because Christ's word achieves what it promises. Accordingly the Lutheran doctrine understands grace as God's favour, but nevertheless as effective power... 'for where there is forgiveness of sins, there is also life and salvation'" (VELKD 86,15-23).

"Catholic doctrine does not overlook what Protestant theology stresses: the personal character of grace, and its link with the word; nor does it maintain... grace as an objective 'possession' (even if a conferred possession) on the part of the human being – something over which he can dispose" (LV:E 49).

For 4.3: Justification by faith and through grace (§§25-27) (USA, nos. 105ff; LV:E 49-53; VELKD 87-90)

"If we translate from one language to another, then Protestant talk about justification through faith corresponds to Catholic talk about justification through grace; and on the other hand, Protestant doctrine understands substantially under the one word 'faith' what Catholic doctrine (following 1 Cor. 13:13) sums up in the triad of 'faith, hope, and love'" (LV:E 52).

"We emphasize that faith in the sense of the first commandment always means love to God and hope in him and is expressed in the love to the neighbour" (VELKD 89,8-11).

"Catholics... teach as do Lutherans, that nothing prior to the free gift of faith merits justification and that all of God's saving gifts come through Christ alone" (USA, no. 105).

"The Reformers... understood faith as the forgiveness and fellowship with Christ effected by the word of promise itself... This is the ground for the new being, through which the flesh is dead to sin and the new man or woman in Christ has life *(sola fide per Christum)*. But even if this faith necessarily makes the human being new, the Christian builds his confidence, not on his own new life, but solely on God's gracious promise. Acceptance in Christ is sufficient, if 'faith' is understood as 'trust in the promise' *(fides promissionis)*" (LV:E 50).

Cf. the council of Trent, session 6, chap. 7: "Consequently, in the process of justification, together with the forgiveness of sins a person receives, through Jesus Christ into whom he is grafted, all these infused at the same time: faith, hope and charity" (DH 1530).

"According to Protestant interpretation, the faith that clings unconditionally to God's promise in word and sacrament is sufficient for righteousness before God, so that the renewal of the human being, without which there can be no faith, does not in itself make any contribution to justification" (LV:E 52).

"As Lutherans we maintain the distinction between justification and sanctification, of faith and works, which however implies no separation" (VELKD 89,6-8).

"Catholic doctrine knows itself to be at one with the Protestant concern in emphasizing that the renewal of the human being does not 'contribute' to justification, and is certainly not a contribution to which he could make any appeal before God. Nevertheless it feels compelled to stress the renewal of the human being through justifying grace, for the sake of acknowledging God's newly creating power; although this renewal in faith, hope, and love is certainly nothing but a response to God's unfathomable grace" (LV:E 52f).

"Insofar as the Catholic doctrine stresses that grace is personal and linked with the word, that renewal... is certainly nothing but a response effected by God's word itself, and that the renewal of the human being does not contribute to justification, and is certainly not a contribution to which a person could make any appeal before God, our objection... no longer applies" (VELKD 89,12-21).

For 4.4: the justified as sinner (§§28-30) (USA, nos. 102ff.; LV:E 44ff.; VELKD 81ff.)
"For however just and holy, they fall from time to time into the sins that are those of daily existence. What is more, the Spirit's action does not exempt believers from the lifelong struggle against sinful tendencies. Concupiscence and other effects of original and personal sin, according to Catholic doctrine, remain in the justified, who therefore must pray daily to God for forgiveness" (USA, no. 102).

"The doctrines laid down at Trent and by the Reformers are at one in maintaining that original sin, and also the concupiscence that remains, are in contradiction to God... object of the lifelong struggle against sin... [A]fter baptism, concupiscence in the person justified no longer cuts that person off from God; in Tridentine language, it is 'no longer sin in the real sense'; in Lutheran phraseology, it is *peccatum regnatum*, 'controlled sin'" (LV:E 46).

"The question is how to speak of sin with regard to the justified without limiting the reality of salvation. While Lutherans express this tension with the term 'controlled sin' *(peccatum regnatum)* which expresses the teaching of the Christian as 'being justified and sinner at the same time' *(simul iustus et peccator)*, Roman Catholics think the reality of salvation can only be maintained by denying the sinful character of concupiscence. With regard to this question a considerable rapprochement is reached if LV:E calls the concupiscence that remains in the justified a 'contradiction to God' and thus qualifies it as sin" (VELKD 82,29-39).

For 4.5: Law and gospel (§§31-33)
According to Pauline teaching this topic concerns the Jewish law as means of salvation. This law was fulfilled and overcome in Christ. This statement and the consequences from it have to be understood on this basis.

With reference to canons 19f. of the council of Trent, the VELKD (89,28-36) says as follows: "The ten commandments of course apply to Christians as stated in many places of the confessions... If canon 20 stresses that a person... is bound to keep the commandments of God, this canon does not strike us; if however canon 20 affirms that faith has salvific power only on condition of keeping the commandments this applies to us. Concerning the reference of the canon regarding the commandments of the church, there is no difference between us if these commandments are only expressions of the commandments of God; otherwise it would apply to us."

The last paragraph is related factually to 4.3, but emphasizes the 'convicting function' of the law which is important to Lutheran thinking.

For 4.6: Assurance of salvation (§§34-36) (LV:E 53-56; VELKD 90ff.)
"The question is: How can, and how may, human beings live before God in spite of their weakness, and with that weakness?" (LV:E 53).

"The foundation and the point of departure [of the Reformers is]... the reliability and sufficiency of God's promise, and the power of Christ's death and resurrection; human weakness, and the threat to faith and salvation which that involves" (LV:E 56).

The council of Trent also emphasizes that "it is necessary to believe that sins are not forgiven, nor have they ever been forgiven, save freely by the divine mercy on account of Christ"; and that we must not doubt "the mercy of God, the merit of Christ and the power and efficacy of the sacraments; so it is possible for anyone, while he regards himself and his own weakness and lack of dispositions, to be anxious and fearful about his own state of grace" (council of Trent, session 6, ch. 9, DH 1534).

"Luther and his followers go a step farther. They urge that the uncertainty should not merely be endured. We should avert our eyes from it and take seriously, practically and personally the objective efficacy of the absolution pronounced in the sacrament of penance, which comes 'from outside'... Since Jesus said, 'Whatever you loose on earth shall be loosed in heaven' (Matt. 16:19), the believer... would declare Christ to be a liar... if he did not rely with a rock-like assurance on the forgiveness of God uttered in the absolution... This reliance can itself be subjectively uncertain – that the assurance of forgiveness is not a security of forgiveness *(securitas)*; but this must not be turned into yet another problem, so to speak: the believer should turn his eyes away from it, and should look only to Christ's word of forgiveness" (LV:E 53f.).

"Today Catholics can appreciate the Reformer's efforts to ground faith in the objective reality of Christ's promise, 'whatsoever you loose on earth ....' and to focus believers on the specific word of absolution from sins... Luther's original concern to teach people to look away from their experience, and to rely on Christ alone and his word of forgiveness [is not to be condemned]" (PCPCU 24).

A mutual condemnation regarding the understanding of the assurance of salvation "can even less provide grounds for mutual objection today – particularly if we start from the foundation of a biblically renewed concept of faith. For a person can certainly lose or renounce faith, and self-commitment to God and his word of promise. But if he believes in this sense, he *cannot at the same time* believe that God is unreliable in his word of promise. In this sense it is true today also that – in Luther's words – faith *is* the assurance of salvation" (LV:E 56).

With reference to the concept of faith of Vatican II, see Dogmatic Constitution on Divine Revelation, no. 5: "'The obedience of faith'... must be given to God who reveals, an obedience by which man entrusts his whole self freely to God, offering 'the full submission of intellect and will to God who reveals', and freely assenting to the truth revealed by him."

"The Lutheran distinction between the certitude *(certitudo)* of faith which looks alone to Christ and earthly security *(securitas)*, which is based on the human being, has not been dealt with clearly enough in the LV. The question whether a Christian "has believed fully and completely" (LV:E 53) does not arise for the Lutheran understanding, since faith never reflects on itself, but depends completely on God, whose grace is bestowed through word and sacrament, thus from outside *(extra nos)*" (VELKD 92,2-9).

For 4.7: The good works of the justified (§§37-39) (LV:E 66ff, VELKD 90ff.)

"But the Council excludes the possibility of earning *grace* – that is, justification – (can. 2; DS 1552) and bases the earning or merit of *eternal life* on the gift of grace itself, through membership in Christ (can. 32: DS 1582). Good works are 'merits' as a *gift*. Although the Reformers attack 'Godless trust' in one's own works, the council explicitly excludes any notion of a claim or any false security (cap. 16: DS 1548f). It is evident... that the council wishes to establish a link with Augustine, who introduced the concept of merit, in order to express the responsibility of human beings, in spite of the 'bestowed' character of good works" (LV:E 66).

If we understand the language of "cause" in canon 24 in more personal terms, as it is done in chapter 16 of the Decree on Justification, where the idea of communion with Christ is foundational, then we can describe the Catholic doctrine on merit as it is done in the first sentence of the second paragraph of 4.7: growth in grace, perseverance in righteousness received from God and a deeper communion with Christ.

"Many antitheses could be overcome if the misleading word 'merit' were simply to be viewed and thought about in connection with the true sense of the biblical term 'wage' or reward" (LV:E 67).

"The Lutheran confessions stress that the justified person is responsible not to lose the grace received but to live in it... Thus the confessions can speak of a preservation of grace and a growth in it. If righteousness in canon 24 is understood in the sense that it affects human beings, then it does not strike us. But if 'righteousness' in canon 24 refers to the Christian's acceptance by God, it strikes us; for this righteousness is always perfect; compared with it the works of Christians are only 'fruits' and 'signs'" (VELKD 94,2-14).

"Concerning canon 26, we refer to the Apology where eternal life is described as reward: '... We grant that eternal life is a reward because it is something that is owed – not because of our merits but because of the promise'" (VELKD 94,20-24).

Official Common Statement
by the Lutheran World Federation and the Catholic Church

1. On the basis of the agreements reached in the *Joint Declaration on the Doctrine of Justification (JD)*, the Lutheran World Federation and the Catholic church declare together: "The understanding of the doctrine of justification set forth in this Declaration shows that a consensus in basic truths of the doctrine of justification exists between Lutherans and Catholics" (JD 40). On the basis of this consensus the Lutheran World Federation and the Catholic church declare together: "The teaching of the Lutheran churches presented in the declaration does not fall under the condemnations from the council of Trent. The condemnations in the Lutheran confessions do not apply to the teaching of the Roman Catholic Church presented in this declaration" (JD 41).

2. With reference to the resolution on the joint declaration by the council of the Lutheran World Federation of 16 June 1998 and the response to the joint declaration by the Catholic Church of 25 June 1998 and to the questions raised by both of them, the annexed statement (called "Annex") further substantiates the consensus reached in the joint declaration; thus it becomes clear that the earlier mutual doctrinal condemnations do not apply to the teaching of the dialogue partners as presented in the joint declaration.

3. The two partners in dialogue are committed to continued and deepened study of the biblical foundations of the doctrine of justification. They will also seek further

common understanding of the doctrine of justification, also beyond what is dealt with in the joint declaration and the annexed substantiating statement. Based on the consensus reached, continued dialogue is required specifically on the issues mentioned especially in the joint declaration itself (JD 43) as requiring further clarification in order to reach full church communion, a unity in diversity, in which remaining differences would be "reconciled" and no longer have a divisive force. Lutherans and Catholics will continue their efforts ecumenically in their common witness to interpret the message of justification in language relevant for human beings today, and with reference both to individual and social concerns of our times.

By this act of signing the Catholic Church and the Lutheran World Federation confirm the joint declaration on the doctrine of justification in its entirety

Annex to the Official Common Statement

1. The following elucidations underline the consensus reached in the *Joint Declaration on the Doctrine of Justification (JD)* regarding basic truths of justification; thus it becomes clear that the mutual condemnations of former times do not apply to the Catholic and Lutheran doctrines of justification as they are presented in the joint declaration.

2. "Together we confess: By grace alone, in faith in Christ's saving work and not because of any merit on our part, we are accepted by God and receive the Holy Spirit, who renews our hearts while equipping and calling us to good works" (JD 15).

a) "We confess together that God forgives sin by grace and at the same time frees human beings from sin's enslaving power (...)" (JD 22). Justification is forgiveness of sins and being made righteous, through which God "imparts the gift of new life in Christ" (JD 22). "Since we are justified by faith we have peace with God" (Rom. 5:1). We are "called children of God; and that is what we are" (1 John 3:1).We are truly and inwardly renewed by the action of the Holy Spirit, remaining always dependent on his work in us. "So if anyone is in Christ, there is a new creation: everything old has passed away; see, everything has become new!" (2 Cor. 5:17). The justified do not remain sinners in this sense.

Yet we would be wrong were we to say that we are without sin (1 John 1:8-10, cf. JD 28). "(A)ll of us make many mistakes" (James 3:2). "Who is aware of his unwitting sins? Cleanse me of many secret faults" (Ps. 19:12). And when we pray, we can only say, like the tax collector, "God, be merciful to me, a sinner" (Luke 18:13). This is expressed in a variety of ways in our liturgies. Together we hear the exhortation "Therefore, do not let sin exercise dominion in your mortal bodies, to make you obey their passions" (Rom. 6:12). This recalls to us the persisting danger which comes from the power of sin and its action in Christians. To this extent, Lutherans and Catholics can together understand the Christian as *simul justus et peccator,* despite their different approaches to this subject as expressed in JD 29-30.

b) The concept of "concupiscence" is used in different senses on the Catholic and Lutheran sides. In the Lutheran confessional writings "concupiscence" is understood as the self-seeking desire of the human being, which in light of the Law, spiritually understood, is regarded as sin. In the Catholic understanding concupiscence is an inclination, remaining in human beings even after baptism, which comes from sin and presses towards sin. Despite the differences involved here, it can be recognized from a Lutheran perspective that desire can become the opening through which sin attacks. Due to the power of sin the entire human being carries the tendency to oppose God. This tendency, according to both Lutheran and Catholic conception, "does not correspond to God's original design for humanity" (JD 30). Sin has a personal character and, as such, leads to separation from God. It is the selfish desire of the old person and the lack of trust and love towards God.

The reality of salvation in baptism and the peril from the power of sin can be expressed in such a way that, on the one hand, the forgiveness of sins and renewal of humanity in Christ by baptism is emphasized and, on the other hand, it can be seen that the justified also "are continuously exposed to the power of sin still pressing its attacks (cf. Rom. 6:12-14) and are not exempt from a lifelong struggle against the contradiction to God (...)" (JD 28).

c) Justification takes place "by grace alone" (JD 15 and 16), by faith alone, the person is justified "apart from works" (Rom 3:28, cf. JD 25). "Grace creates faith not only when faith begins in a person but as long as faith lasts" (Thomas Aquinas, S. Th. II/II 4, 4 ad 3). The working of God's grace does not exclude human action: God effects everything, the willing and the achievement, therefore, we are called to strive (cf. Phil. 2:12ff.). "As soon as the Holy Spirit has initiated his work of regeneration and renewal in us through the word and the holy sacraments, it is certain that we can and must cooperate by the power of the Holy Spirit..." (The Formula of Concord, FC SD II,64f.; BSLK 897,37ff.).

d) Grace as fellowship of the justified with God in faith, hope and love is always received from the salvific and creative work of God (cf. JD 27). But it is nevertheless the responsibility of the justified not to waste this grace but to live in it. The exhortation to do good works is the exhortation to practise the faith (cf. BSLK 197,45). The good works of the justified "should be done in order to confirm their call, that is, lest they fall from their call by sinning again" (Apol. XX,13, BSLK 316,18-24; with reference to 2 Pet. 1:10. Cf. also FC SD IV,33; BSLK 948,9-23). In this sense Lutherans and Catholics can understand together what is said about the "preservation of grace" in JD 38 and 39. Certainly, "whatever in the justified precedes or follows the free gift of faith is neither the basis of justification nor merits it" (JD 25).

e) By justification we are unconditionally brought into communion with God. This includes the promise of eternal life; "[I]f we have been united with him in a death like his, we will certainly be united with him in a resurrection like his" (Rom. 6:5, cf. John 3:36, Rom. 8:17). In the final judgment, the justified will be judged also on their works (cf. Matt. 16:27; 25:31-46; Rom. 2:16; 14:12; 1 Cor. 3:8; 2 Cor. 5:10, etc.). We face a judgment in which God's gracious sentence will approve anything in our life and action that corresponds to his will. However, everything in our life that is wrong will be uncovered and will not enter eternal life. The Formula of Concord also states: "It is God's will and express command that believers should do good works which the Holy Spirit works in them, and God is willing to be pleased with them for Christ's sake and he promises to reward them gloriously in this and in the future life" (FC SD IV,38). Any reward is a reward of grace, on which we have no claim.

3. The doctrine of justification is measure or touchstone for the Christian faith. No teaching may contradict this criterion. In this sense, the doctrine of justification is an

"indispensable criterion which constantly serves to orient all the teaching and practice of our churches to Christ" (JD l8). As such, it has its truth and specific meaning within the overall context of the church's fundamental trinitarian confession of faith. We "share the goal of confessing Christ in all things, who is to be trusted above all things as the one Mediator (1 Tim. 2:5-6) through whom God in the Holy Spirit gives himself and pours out his renewing gifts" (JD 18).

4. The response of the Catholic church does not intend to put in question the authority of Lutheran synods or of the Lutheran World Federation. The Catholic church and the Lutheran World Federation began the dialogue and have taken it forward as partners with equal rights *(par cum pari)*. Notwithstanding different conceptions of authority in the church, each partner respects the other partner's ordered process of reaching doctrinal decisions.

NOTES

[1] The Smalcald Articles, II,1; Book of Concord, 292.
[2] *Rector et judex super omnia genera doctrinarum,* Weimar ed. of Luther's Works (WA), 39,I,205.
[3] It should be noted that some Lutheran churches include only the Augsburg confession and Luther's Small Catechism among their binding confessions. These texts contain no condemnations about justification in relation to the Roman Catholic Church.
[4] Report of the Joint Lutheran-Roman Catholic study commission, published in *Growth in Agreement*, New York, Geneva, 1984, pp.168-89.
[5] Published by the Lutheran World Federation, Geneva, 1994.
[6] *Lutheran and Catholics in Dialogue VII*, Minneapolis, 1985.
[7] Minneapolis, 1990.
[8] "Gemeinsame Stellungnahme der Arnoldshauner Konferez der Vereinigten Kirche und des Deutschen Nationalkomitees des Lutherischen Weltbundes zum Dokument 'Lehrverurteilungen – kirchentrennend?'", *Ökumenische Rundschau*, 44, 1995, 99-102; including the position papers which underlie this resolution, cf. *Lehrverurteilungen im Gespräch, Die ersten offiziellen Stellungnahmen aus den evangelischen Kirchen in Deutschland*, Göttingen, Vandenhoeck & Ruprecht, 1993.
[9] The word "church" is used in this declaration to reflect the self-understandings of the participating churches, without intending to resolve all the ecclesiological issues related to this term.
[10] Cf. Malta report, §§26-30; "Justification by Faith", §§122-47. At the request of the US dialogue on justification, the nonPauline New Testament texts were addressed in *Righteousness in the New Testament* by John Reumann, with responses by Joseph A. Fitzmyer and Jerome D. Quinn, Philadelphia, New York, 1982, pp.124-80. The results of this study were summarized in the dialogue report "Justification by Faith" in §§139-42.
[11] "All Under One Christ", §14, in *Growth in Agreement*, 241-47.
[12] Cf. WA 8:106; American ed. 32:227.
[13] Cf. DS 1528.
[14] Cf. DS 1530.
[15] Cf. Apology II:3845; Book of Concord, 105f.
[16] Cf. DS 1515.
[17] Cf. DS 1515.
[18] Cf. DS 1545.
[19] Cf. DV 5
[20] Cf. DV 4.
[21] Condemnations of the Reformation Era, 27.

XXII. METHODIST-ROMAN CATHOLIC DIALOGUE

45. Towards a Statement on the Church
Fourth Series 1982-1986

Nairobi, Kenya, 1986

Preface

Over the past twenty years, successive joint commissions between the Roman Catholic Church and the World Methodist Council have reported to their respective churches at five-year intervals through the Vatican Secretariat for Promoting Christian Unity and the World Methodist Council. A significant body of material has been considered by Methodists and Roman Catholics meeting annually since the commencement of these bilateral discussions in 1967.

The first report issued by a joint commission was known as *The Denver Report* (so named for the city where the World Methodist Council met in 1971). Covering the period of 1967-70, the report addressed the following subjects: Christianity and the contemporary world, spirituality, Christian home and family, eucharist, ministry and authority.

As will be readily understood, some of these areas were only examined in a cursory way and were taken up by *The Dublin Report* (1972-75). Taking the Denver document as a point of departure, the commission advanced joint exploration in the areas of spirituality and some moral issues, while pressing on to consider in greater depth the doctrines of the eucharist and the ordained ministry.

During the next quinquennium, a significant agreed statement on the Holy Spirit was issued in *The Honolulu Report* (1977-81). This was written in a more popular style. It was during this time that another change was introduced – the periodic publication of parts of the report, for study and comment, as they were developed in the course of the five years. Sections on Christian experience and Christian moral decisions covered new ground, and discussions begun on authority were reported as requiring fuller development.

The text of *The Nairobi Report*, which follows, represents the work of the present 1982-85 joint commission, which met on four occasions. The first session at Reuti-Hasliberg, Switzerland, in 1982, established "The Nature of the Church" as the theme for the quinquennium. Building upon a careful outline, preparations were made for research and the writing of papers to explore the various sub-themes. Subsequent meetings in Milan, Lake Junaluska and Venice explored the nature of the church, sacraments, episcopacy, and "ways of being one church"; Peter in the New Testament and the Petrine ministry; and authority in the church, under the heads of jurisdiction and the teaching office. In the light of the work done at the final meeting in Venice, a proposal at the conclusion of the text suggests that the next commission proceed to address the general theme of the apostolic tradition.

In Venice tribute was paid the late Msgr Richard Stewart for his faithful and effective service as the Roman Catholic co-secretary of the commission for the past seven years. Msgr Stewart died unexpectedly at age fifty-eight in July 1985 while on holiday in England. He was for seven years a member of the Vatican Secretariat. The joint commission, recognizing his theological acumen, his careful concern for every detail of the work, his boundless energy and profound commitment to the cause of Christian unity, wishes to dedicate this report to him.

The Nairobi report deals with some of the most difficult questions Roman Catholics and Methodists have faced together. Although there are similarities in the order and structure of the two churches, Methodists and Catholics at present differ in their doctrine of the ministry and of the teaching office. The commission has started to address these divergences, exploring their origins in history and seeking perspectives for agreement. It has reaffirmed those things already held in common with regard to the role of leadership in the church and the quest for Christian unity.

We now make this report available in the hope that it will stimulate wide study, discussion and reactions among both Catholics and Methodists. Such discussion and reaction at this stage of our dialogue will be invaluable for our continued progress on the path towards that fullness of fellowship and communion which is our aim and objective.

Bishop William R. Cannon
World Methodist Council
Co-chairman

Bishop J. Francis Stafford
Roman Catholic Church
Co-chairman

Towards a Statement on the Church

1. Because God so loved the world, he sent his Son and the Holy Spirit to draw us into communion with himself. This sharing in God's life, which resulted from the mission of the Son and the Holy Spirit, found expression in a visible koinonia[1] of Christ's disciples, the church.

I. The nature of the church

2. Christianity arose because of the life, death and resurrection of Jesus. Although it is possible to speak of a "people of God" from the time of Abraham, the expression "Christian church" designates the assembly of the Christian faithful. The ministry of Jesus himself was addressed to *a people*, so that the first persons who heard and accepted the proclamation of the kingdom were already oriented to one another by their relationship within Israel. As is shown by this gathering of those who walked with him and shared a common life with him, especially the Twelve, the ministry of Jesus created a community. After the resurrection this community shared the new life conferred by the Spirit, and very soon came to be called the church. Baptized into the faith and proclaiming the crucified and risen Lord, the members were united to one another by the Spirit in a life marked by the apostolic teaching, common prayer, the breaking of bread, and often by some community of goods; and those who were converted and drawn to them became part of this koinonia.

3. As the assembly of God's people gathered in Christ by the Holy Spirit, the church is not a self-appointed, self-initiated community. It originated in the redemptive act of

God in Christ; and it lives in union with Christ's death and resurrection, comforted, guided and empowered by the Holy Spirit (see further in the Honolulu report, 1981, nos. 19-21, "The Holy Spirit in the Christian Community").

4. The church is a complex reality. The New Testament provides a great variety of images for the church (body of Christ, people of God, bride of Christ, temple, flock or sheepfold, royal priesthood, etc. – many of these reflecting Old Testament imagery), and theologians have offered other images and models. None of these can express exhaustively or even adequately exactly what the church is, the whole of its mystery. Nevertheless, each has purpose since different images illustrate different aspects of the church. For instance, as the Second Vatican Council exemplifies, it is easier to think of reform, change and repentance if one speaks of the church as the people of God (cf. Vatican Council II, *LG*, ch. 3), because this connotes among other things a pilgrim people still full of imperfections and liable to sin. Notwithstanding our sinfulness, the risen Christ unites us with himself as his body, and some of the other images we have listed illustrate the holiness of the church as the people he has made his own.

5. In the New Testament period, diversity of time, place and circumstances produced diversity among groups of believers — diversity of community structures, diverse formulations of the faith, diverse traditions shaped by different histories and problems, diverse house meeting places within the same city, diverse Christian centres. Nevertheless, passages in the New Testament, such as the account in Acts 15 of the council of Jerusalem, attest to koinonia among such diversities, and to a sense of *the* church to which all Christians belong. There are also passages, such as 1 John 2:19, that suggest the breaking of the koinonia because certain diversities were deemed intolerable distortions of what was from the beginning.

6. Just as the Old Testament represents the tradition of the people of Israel, so the New Testament scriptures, which have become normative and corrective for all Christian traditions in every age, themselves arose from the life and tradition of the apostolic and early church. They should be read with reverence and prayer. Yet an important task of scholarship in all Christian churches is to examine critically the biblical material in order to hear the scriptures in their own terms and to help the church discern the word of God for its life today (see also the Honolulu report, no. 34).

7. The church is judged, transformed and empowered for mission by the word of God as appropriated through the Spirit. The reforming power of the word is evident in such instances as some of the medieval reforms (monastic, papal, mendicant), the Reformation and the Catholic renewal of the 16th and 17th centuries, the evangelical revival of the 18th century, the ecumenical movement of the 20th, and many other movements of renewal.

8. The church lives between the times of the life, death, resurrection and exaltation of Jesus Christ and his future coming in glory. The Spirit fills the church, empowering it to preach the word, celebrate the eucharist, experience fellowship and prayer, and carry out its mission to the world: thus the church is enabled to serve as sign, sacrament and harbinger of the kingdom of God in the time between the times.

9. Christ works through his church, and it is for this reason that Vatican II speaks of the church as a kind of sacrament, both as an outward manifestation of God's grace among us and as signifying in some way the grace and call to salvation addressed by

God to the whole human race (cf. *LG*, no. 1). This is a perspective that many Methodists also find helpful.

10. The mystery of the word made flesh and the sacramental mystery of the eucharist point towards a view of the church based upon the sacramental idea, i.e., the church takes its shape from the incarnation from which it originated and the eucharistic action by which its life is constantly being renewed.

II. Church and sacraments

11. Being a Christian has necessarily both a personal and a communal aspect. It is a vital relationship to God in and through Jesus Christ in which faith, conversion of life and membership in the church are essential. Individual believers are joined in a family of disciples, so that belonging to Christ means also belonging to the church which is his body.

12. Both the personal and communal aspects of the Christian life are present in the two sacraments that Methodists and Roman Catholics consider basic. Baptism initiates the individual into the koinonia of the church; in the eucharist, Christ is really present to the believer (cf. Dublin report, 1976, no. 54), who is thus bound together in koinonia both with the Lord and with others who share the sacramental meal.[2]

13. It is by divine institution that the church has received baptism and the eucharist, outward signs of inward grace consisting of actions and words by which God encounters his people; these signs are recognized as sacraments by both churches. The church has authority to institute other rites and ordinances, which are valued as sacred actions and signs of God's redeeming love in Christ (cf. Honolulu report, no. 49, concerning marriage). Some of these the Roman Catholic Church recognizes as sacraments, since it sees them as ultimately derived from the will of Christ. Methodists, while using the term "sacrament" only of the two rites for which the gospels explicitly record Christ's institution, do not thereby deny sacramental character to other rites.

14. Sacraments are to be seen in the wider context of God's action in salvation history, in the church, and in individual human lives. The grace which comes through the sacraments is the grace of Christ, the visible image of the unseen God, in whom divine and human natures are united in one person; the church proclaims the action of the same Christ at work within us; and the individual sacraments likewise convey the reality of his action into our lives.

15. The sacraments are effective signs by which God gives grace through faith. Their efficacy should not be conceived in any merely mechanical way. God works through his Spirit in a mysterious way beyond human comprehension, but he invites a full and free human response.

16. Salvation is ultimately a matter of our reconciliation and communion with God — a sharing in God's life which is effected through real union with Christ. Those actions of the church that we call sacraments are effective signs of grace because they are not merely human acts. By the power of the Holy Spirit, they bring into our lives the life-giving action and even the self-giving of Christ himself. It is Christ's action that is embodied and made manifest in the church's actions which, responded to in faith, amount to a real encounter with the risen Jesus. And so, when the church baptizes, it is Christ who baptizes. Likewise it is Christ who says: "This is my body... this is my blood" and who truly gives himself to us. The fruit of such encounters is our sanctification and the building up of the body of Christ.

III. Called to unity

17. Already in the New Testament the term *ecclesia* is used for the community of those who accepted Jesus' proclamation of the kingdom, transmitted by apostles and disciples. In this church their response of faith was sealed in baptism, as they confessed their sins and were forgiven, received the Holy Spirit and were joined together in Christ.

18. More specifically, ecclesia or church is applied in the New Testament to Christians meeting together in a house or living in the same city. We also find the term "the church" used in a more universal way for the body of Christ which is the fullness of him who fills all in all, the communion of the saints on earth and in heaven.

19. All these usages of the word "church" have continued throughout Christian tradition. In addition, as a result of further factors, geographical and historical, the term came to be used in other ways. Some of these usages arose because of diversities of language or rite, such as Syrian church, Coptic church or Latin church. Others came about because of fundamental differences in doctrine, faith or ecclesial polity, such as Lutheran church, Methodist church, or Roman Catholic church.

20. As Methodists and Roman Catholics, we recognize that the divisions underlying this last usage are contrary to the unity Christ wills for his church. In obedience to him who will bring about this unity, we are committed to a vision that includes the goal of full communion in faith, mission and sacramental life.

21. Such communion, which is the gift of the Spirit, must be expressed visibly. This visible unity need not imply uniformity, nor the suppression of the gifts with which God has graced each of our communities.

IV. Ways of being one church

22. As we reflect on a reunited church, we cannot expect to find an ecclesiology shaped in a time of division to be entirely satisfactory. Our explorations towards a more adequate ecclesiology have begun and are helping us to give proper recognition to each other's ecclesial or churchly character. They will also assist in overcoming our present state of division.

23. We have found that koinonia, both as a concept and an experience, is more important than any particular model of church union that we are yet able to propose. Koinonia is so rich a term that it is better to keep its original Greek form than bring together several English words to convey its meaning. For believers it involves both communion and community. It includes participation in God through Christ in the Spirit, by which believers become adopted children of the same Father and members of the one body of Christ sharing in the same Spirit. And it includes deep fellowship among participants, a fellowship which is both visible and invisible, finding expression in faith and order, in prayer and sacrament, in mission and service. Many different gifts have been developed in our traditions, even in separation. Although we already share some of our riches with one another, we look forward to a greater sharing as we come closer together in full unity (cf. *UR*, no. 4).

24. In our discussion we found that the following, each in its own way, offered elements for a model of organic unity in the koinonia of the one body of Christ:

a) Considerable value was found in the notion of what have come to be called *typoi*. This implies that within the one church in which there is basic agreement in faith, doctrine and structure essential for mission, there is room for various "ecclesial traditions", each characterized by a particular style of theology, worship, spirituality and discipline.

b) From one perspective the history of John Wesley has suggested an analogy between his movement and the religious orders within the one church. Figures such as Benedict of Nursia and Francis of Assisi, whose divine calling was similarly to a spiritual reform, gave rise to religious orders, characterized by special forms of life and prayer, work, evangelization and their own internal organization. The different religious orders in the Roman Catholic Church, while fully in communion with the pope and the bishops, relate in different ways to the authority of pope and bishops. Such relative autonomy has a recognized place within the unity of the church.

c) A third train of ideas is suggested by the term "sister churches". In its original usage, the expression contained a strong geographical component (e.g., church of Rome, church of Constantinople). But more recent usage, as when Paul VI looked forward to the Roman Catholic Church embracing "the Anglican church" as an "everbeloved sister", hints that it may be possible to envisage reunion among divided traditions as a family reconciliation (cf. Pope Paul VI's letter to Patriarch Athenagoras, Anno Ineunte, 25 July 1967, in *Tomos Agapis* [1958-82], English tr. E.J. Stormon SJ, New York, Paulist Press, 1986, no. 176).

d) The relations between churches of the Roman (Latin) rite and those of various oriental rites also in communion with the bishop of Rome afford a further possible model for the retention of different styles of devotion and church life within a single communion.

25. In trying to take these ideas further, we began to explore the acceptable range of variety and uniformity in the church.

26. Christians, sharing the same faith, relate to God in a great variety of ways, often helped by spiritual traditions which have developed, under the providence of God, in the course of history. Some of these traditions are embodied in and furthered by religious societies, renewal movements and pious associations or institutes. The church should protect legitimate variety both by ensuring room for its free development and by directly promoting new forms of it.

27. We broached the question whether such varying needs can be provided for within the framework of the local congregation and how far a particular tradition or form of prayer and worship may require special provisions (parishes, ministries, other organizations). How far would the pastoral care of such groups require separate, possibly overlapping jurisdictions, or could it be provided by one, single, local form of *episcope* (supervision or oversight)?

28. There have to be limits to variety; some arise from the need to promote cohesion and cooperation, but the basic structures of the church also set limits that exclude whatever would disrupt communion in faith, order and sacramental life.

V. Structures of ministry

29. We have reflected on the structure of ministry in the church. An examination of the New Testament evidence and of subsequent history shows that the church has always needed a God-given ministry. From the written data alone it cannot be ascertained with certainty whether the threefold ministry of bishop, presbyter and deacon, which developed from the New Testament (cf. Dublin report, no. 83) was established in the first century. It is acknowledged that it became generally established in the 2nd and 3rd centuries and was clearly universal in the same post-New Testament period in which the scriptural canon was established and the classical creeds were formed. Roman Catholics and some Methodists would see a similarity in these three develop-

ments under the guidance of the Holy Spirit. But we are not agreed on how far this development of the ministry is now unchangeable and how far loyalty to the Holy Spirit requires us to recognize other forms of oversight and leadership that have developed, often at times of crisis or new opportunity in Christian history. Practically, however, the majority of Methodists already accept the office of bishop, and some Methodist churches that do not have expressed their willingness to accept this for the sake of unity.

30. A stable pattern of ordained ministry (e.g., the threefold one) has never prevented a variation of the ways pastoral care has actively been exercised, and there is no reason to suppose that such flexibility will cease when Methodists and Catholics are united in faith, mission and sacramental life.

31. Unity in faith, mission and sacramental life can be achieved only on an apostolic basis. As the Dublin report already recognized, "we all agree that the church's apostolicity involves continuous faithfulness in doctrine, ministry, sacrament and life to the teaching of the New Testament" (no. 84). At present, however, we differ in the account we give of the apostolic succession. For Roman Catholics, the graded threefold ministry is derived from the teaching of the New Testament through the living tradition of the church. The succession in ministry is guaranteed by episcopal laying-on of hands in historical succession and authentic transmission of the whole faith within the apostolic college and the communion of the whole church (cf. Dublin report, no. 85). "Methodists... preserve a form of ministerial succession in practice and can regard a succession of ordination from the earliest times as a valuable symbol of the church's continuity with the church of the New Testament, though they would not use it as a criterion" (Dublin report, no. 87).

32. In Roman Catholic teaching (see *LG*, nos. 18-29), bishops are ordained to the fullness of the sacrament of order for a pastoral and priestly ministry which is responsible for the authentic teaching of the truths of salvation, and for the rule of the churches entrusted to them. Therefore, as successors of the apostles, they preach the gospel and preside at the celebration of the sacraments, fostering the unity of the people of God in a given place, that the church may increase to the glory of God. In collegial communion with fellow bishops and with the bishop of Rome, they cement and express the bond of the universal fellowship.

33. Broadly speaking, there are in World Methodism two basic patterns of church government, one deriving from North America and one from Britain. From its inception, American Methodism has been episcopal in constitution, not claiming apostolic succession in the sense of the Roman Catholic Church but laying stress on the teaching, preaching, pastoral, sacramental and governing aspects of the episcopal office. British Methodism has a single order of ordained ministry and in those churches which have followed the British pattern, *episcope* (pastoral oversight) is exercised through the conference and, by authority of the conference, is shared among chairmen of districts and superintendent ministers. The British Methodist Church did not in its origin reject episcopacy but developed without it because of the historical circumstances of its origin. In recent years it has expressed the willingness in principle to embrace episcopacy, for it has done so in certain reunion schemes outside Britain and was willing to do so in England in certain schemes which did not eventually succeed.

34. Both Roman Catholics and Methodists believe that *episcope* of the churches is a divinely given function. The Roman Catholic Church and many Methodist churches

express *episcope* through bishops. It is the belief of the Roman Catholic Church and these Methodist churches that for the exercise of their ministry the bishops receive special gifts from the Holy Spirit through prayer and the laying-on of hands.

35. Methodist churches which have an ordained ministry but do not have bishops, believing them not to be essential to a church, have considered adopting them as an enrichment of their own life and to promote the unity of Christians; such bishops would be a focus of unity and a sign of the historic continuity of the church.

36. It is Roman Catholic teaching that "to ensure the indivisible unity of the episcopate, [Jesus Christ] set St Peter over the other apostles" (*LG*, no. 18) as a "fundamental principle of unity of faith and communion". This is basic to Catholic belief in the primacy of the bishop of Rome. This primacy is exercised in a collegial relation with the other bishops of the church and finds a privileged expression in councils of the church.

37. For Methodists the concept of primacy is unfamiliar, even if historically John Wesley exercised a kind of primacy in the origins of the Methodist church. In his day this was carried out in the context of his conference of preachers; today's conference continues to embody certain elements of this function.

38. Since Catholics and Methodists have committed themselves to seeking full unity in faith, mission and sacramental life, we now have to turn to questions of the Petrine office and the primacy of the bishop of Rome.

VI. The Petrine office

39. We begin with the New Testament, in which the Twelve, and also Paul and other apostles, fulfilled important functions. But in the light of the questions which subsequently arose, we naturally concentrate on Peter even though we do not wish to isolate him from the other apostles, seeking to give a factual account of the relevant New Testament material.

40. With this background in mind, we shall then turn to consider subsequent history by starting from the nature of leadership and primacy in the church. Discernment of the various factors in scripture and history might contribute to an agreed perception of what functions the see of Rome might properly exercise in a ministry of universal unity, by what authority, and on what conditions.

a) Peter in the New Testament

41. Simon Peter had a special position among the Twelve: he is named first in the lists and is called "first" (Matt. 10:2); he is described as among the first called; he is among the three or four associated with Jesus on special occasions; at times he is portrayed as spokesman for the others, either answering or asking questions; he is named as the first of the apostolic witnesses to the risen Jesus; he is remembered as having confessed Jesus during the ministry (even if the gospels differ in their presentation of that confession); he is renamed by Jesus. However, his misunderstanding of Jesus, his failure to heed warnings and his denials are also narrated.

42. Special sayings in the gospels point to a distinctive church-oriented role for Peter (Matt. 16:18-19; Luke 22:31-32; John 21:15-17). In Acts, chapters 1-15, after the resurrection, Peter exercises a certain leadership in the affairs of the early church. In the scene of Acts 10 it is revealed to him that the church must be open to the Gentiles, a position he had to defend in Jerusalem (Acts 11:2ff.). Paul's Letter to the Galatians

shows Peter as an important figure at Jerusalem, as having an apostolate to the circumcised, and as agreeing with Paul that Gentile converts need not be compelled to conform to Jewish circumcision. However, it also shows Peter as yielding to the "men who came from James" on the issue of not eating with the Gentiles — a concession that Paul describes as not being straightforward about the truth of the gospel (2:14).

43. Acts 15 shows Peter, Barnabas, Paul and James as all speaking to the issue of the admission of Gentile converts without circumcision, but indicates that James insisted on their observance of specific purity laws. Galatians 2 and Acts 15 have led many to suspect that Peter's position in relation to Judaism stood in between that of James on the one side and of Paul on the other. Some would regard the failure to mention Peter in the second half of the Book of Acts as a sign that his authority had declined; others would regard the fact that Luke concentrates on Peter first and then on Paul as reflecting the author's purpose to show how Christianity gradually moved from Jerusalem and the mission to the Jews, towards Rome and the Gentile mission.

44. First Corinthians shows a party loyal to Peter (Cephas) in a Greek city in the 50s (1 Cor. 1:12; 3:22); it also raises the possibility that Peter's activities had brought him to Corinth (9:5). After mentioning the appearances of the risen Jesus to Peter and to others (1 Cor. 15:5-8), Paul says, "Whether then it was I or they so we preach and so you believed." This is seen as an indication of basic elements shared by Peter's and Paul's preaching, in spite of the disagreement described in Galatians 2:14.

45. First Peter portrays Peter as an apostle writing from Babylon (by which is meant Rome), instructing Christians in Asia Minor, and as a presbyter exhorting fellow presbyters to be good shepherds (5:1-3). Second Peter 3:15-16 portrays Peter as advising people how to interpret the letters of "our beloved brother Paul".

46. Many scholars think the Petrine letters were written after Peter's life-time; some or all of the special gospel sayings about Peter referred to in no. 42 may also have been committed to writing after Peter's death. Therefore an evaluation of the New Testament evidence concerning Peter must take into account not only Peter's relationship to Jesus before the resurrection, and Peter's career in the early church, but also how Peter was regarded after his death.

47. The New Testament depicts Peter in a plurality of images and roles: missionary fisherman (Luke 5; John 21); pastoral shepherd (John 21; Luke 22:32; 1 Pet. 5); witness and martyr (1 Cor. 15:5; cf. John 21:15-17; 1 Pet. 5:1); recipient of special revelation (Matt. 16:17; Acts 10:9-11; 2 Pet. 1:16-17); the "rock" named by Jesus (Matt. 16:18; John 1:42; Mark 1:42); recipient of the keys of the kingdom of heaven (Matt. 16:18); confessor and preacher of the true faith (Matt. 16:16; Acts 2); guardian against false teaching (2 Pet. 1:20-21; 3:15-16; Acts 8:20-23); and weak human being and repentant sinner, rebuked by Christ and withstood by Paul (Mark 8:33; Matt. 16:23; Mark 14:31,66-72; John 21:15-17; Gal. 2:5). Most of these images persist through two or more strands of the New Testament tradition, and several recur in subsequent church history.

b) Primacy and the Petrine ministry

48. In looking at the question of universal primacy one may begin with the desirability of unity focused around leadership.

49. All local churches need a ministry of leadership. In early church development such leadership came to be exercised by the bishop, who was a focus of unity. Even-

tually churches were grouped in provinces, regions and patriarchates, in which archbishops, primates and patriarchs exercised a similar unifying role in service to the koinonia.

50. Analogously the question arises whether the whole church needs a leader to exercise a similar unifying role in service to the worldwide koinonia.

51. Given this context, one then has to face the claim that the Roman see already exercises such a ministry of universal unity. As the Roman claim was essentially complete by the 5th century, it may be helpful to examine the lines of development which led in that direction. The special position and role of the Roman see in the early church depended on the convergence of several factors. Some of these factors had to do with the particular city in which the church was located, some with the development of the episcopate (cf. no. 29), and others with the relation of the bishop of Rome to Peter and Paul. For Roman Catholics the decisive factor for the special position and role of the Roman see is the relation of the bishop of Rome to Peter.

52. As the capital city of the empire, Rome's strategic importance for the worldwide mission of Christianity was recognized already in New Testament times (cf. Acts). Paul looked for the support of the Roman church in his preaching of the gospel, and Peter, as we have seen, is portrayed as writing from Rome to Christians in Asia Minor. In the 2nd century Rome was already recognized as an apostolic church. Both I Clement, written from Rome, and Ignatius, writing to Rome, mention Peter and Paul. Irenaeus of Lyons acknowledged the outstanding force of Rome's testimony to the apostolic tradition on account of its dual foundation *(fundata et constituta)* upon Peter and Paul (cf. *Adv. Haereses* III, iii). That both of them suffered martyrdom there no doubt gave Rome an advantage over Antioch or Corinth, churches which also rejoiced in the same twofold apostolic connection. By the latter half of the 2nd century, the lists of the bishops of Rome mention Peter first, although from I Clement and the Shepherd of Hermas it is not clear precisely when a sole bishop was recognized as a figure distinct from the other presbyters.

53. By the middle of the 3rd century (cf. Cyprian, *De catholicae ecclesiae unitate*, no. 4), "Petrine" texts from the gospels had begun to be applied, *mutatis mutandis*, to the bishop of Rome. The fact that Peter's ministry in the life of the church is emphasized even in New Testament passages written after his death indicates that images of Peter had continued importance for the church. The application of the Petrine texts in the 3rd century could be seen as reflecting this ongoing importance. Luke 22 has Jesus, with his own death in view, charging Peter to strengthen the brethren. In John 21, the risen Lord commands Peter to tend and feed the flock. In Matthew 16, Peter, who confessed his faith in Jesus as "the Christ, the Son of the living God", is named the rock on which Christ will build his church, and he is given the power to bind and loose, and the very keys of the kingdom. In Acts, Peter at Pentecost correspondingly takes the lead in proclaiming the Lordship of the crucified and risen Jesus. Peter's mediating position in New Testament controversies between the positions of Paul and James (cf. no. 43) made him a figure for fostering unity in the essentials of the faith. The Petrine role of enunciating the faith, sometimes at points of conflict, was illustrated at the council of Chalcedon when the bishops approved the doctrine of Leo I of Rome: "This is the faith of the fathers; this is the faith of the apostles; this is the faith of us all; Peter has spoken through Leo."[3]

54. In the early centuries many had been willing, more or less spontaneously, to accord to the Roman church a respect of the kind reflected in the phrase of Ignatius of

Antioch, "presiding in love" (Ad Rom., Introd.). In the 2nd century Rome's repudiation of Marcion and Valentinus helped to establish orthodoxy for the whole church. On the other hand, Roman involvement in controversies was not always appreciated nor the Roman solution accepted (e.g., the response of the Asian churches to Victor over the date of Easter). In the 4th and 5th centuries, with Christianity established as the religion of the empire, the popes began to make more frequent use of the language of Roman law in their interventions, supported by the bishops in closest geographical proximity (i.e., within the Western patriarchate). This more juridical turn sharpened the issue of authority. On the one hand the authority of the Roman church promoted missionary activity, monastic life, and doctrinal and liturgical cohesiveness, and after the collapse of the Western empire helped to preserve and shape European civilization. On the other hand, increasingly developed formulation and application of the Roman claims, and more vigorous resistance to them, alike contributed to the origin and continuation of divisions in Christianity, first in the East and eventually in the West.

55. From this survey it will be seen that the primacy of the bishop of Rome is not established from the scriptures in isolation from the living tradition. When an institution cannot be established from scripture alone, Methodists, in common with other churches which stem from the Reformation, consider it on its intrinsic merits, as indeed do Roman Catholics; but Methodists give less doctrinal weight than Roman Catholics to long and widespread tradition.

56. The Roman Catholic members are agreed that being in communion with the see of Rome has served as the touchstone of belonging to the church in its fullest sense. This commission is agreed that not being in communion with the bishop of Rome does not necessarily disqualify a Christian community from belonging to the church of God (cf. "The Roman Catholic Church has continued to recognize the Orthodox churches as churches in spite of divisions concerning the primacy", Anglican-Roman Catholic International Commission, Authority II, no. 12). Likewise, Methodist members are agreed that Catholic acceptance of the Roman primacy is not an impediment to churchly character.

57. The positions stated in the previous paragraph, however, do not justify acquiescence in our present division. For Roman Catholics reconciliation with the see of Rome is a necessary step towards the restoration of Christian unity. Others see the claim of the bishop of Rome as an obstacle to Christian unity. It is now necessary to re-examine these claims in the hope of furthering unity. In a period when Christians of all communions frequently meet and cooperate and are often highly critical of divisions in the church, such an examination has fresh urgency.

58. Methodists accept that whatever is properly required for the unity of the whole of Christ's church must by that very fact be God's will for his church. A universal primacy might well serve as focus of and ministry for the unity of the whole church.

59. From history it can be shown that some of the current functions carried out by the bishop of Rome pertain to his diocesan see or to his office as patriarch of the Latin church and do not pertain to the essence of his universal ministry of unity. A clearer recognition of this today would make it easier for Methodists to reconsider whether the bishop of Rome might yet exercise this ministry for other Christians as well as for those who already accept it.

60. In considering the possible exercise of the ministry of the bishop of Rome among Christians who do not at present accept it, questions about jurisdiction and

infallibility are both understood by Roman Catholics as aspects of the primacy which the bishop of Rome has among other bishops in virtue of his special relation to Peter and the special position of the church in Rome deriving from the witness of Peter and Paul.

c) Jurisdiction[4]

61. It is within an understanding of the episcopal office, as outlined above (nos. 31-38), that Roman Catholics see the special role of the bishop of Rome. Just as each bishop is a focus of unity in his own diocese, so the bishop of Rome is such a focus in the communion of dioceses of the whole church. In regard to the diocese of Rome, the pope has the authority or jurisdiction that the bishops have in their dioceses. Roman Catholics believe that he also has ordinary jurisdiction throughout the church in the sense that he acts by virtue of his office and not by delegation. This is an immediate episcopal jurisdiction in all dioceses, in the exercise of which he is required to respect each local church and the authority of each bishop. Catholics recognize that theological exploration of the relation between the authority of the pope and that of the local bishop remains unfinished. The authority of the pope should not in any case, they say, be described exclusively or primarily in jurisdictional terms. Just as many images are used of Peter in the New Testament (see no. 47), so a variety of images may be used of the pope. It may be said that he is called to be an effective symbol of the unity of the church in faith and life. He is a reminder of the apostles witnessing to the resurrection, of Paul preaching to the Gentiles, and of Peter professing faith in Christ and being sent to feed the sheep. In a particular way the pope is a sign of Peter. "Vicar of Peter" is an ancient title that indicates that Peter, a saint in heaven, is present in the church on earth and is, as it were, made visible in the pope. As the papal legate said at the council of Ephesus (A.D. 431), "Peter... lives, presides and judges... in his successors."[5]

62. It would not be inconceivable that at some future date in a restored unity, Roman Catholic and Methodist bishops might be linked in one episcopal college and that the whole body would recognize some kind of effective leadership and primacy in the bishop of Rome. In that case Methodists might justify such an acceptance on different grounds from those that now prevail in the Roman Catholic Church. Moreover, as said above, some of the current functions carried out by the bishop of Rome pertain to his diocesan see or to his office as patriarch of the Latin church rather than to his universal ministry of unity. Further joint study would need to be done on the nature of episcopacy and on the precise nature and extent of the authority which properly belongs to the pope's universal ministry.

d) Authoritative teaching

63. Because God wills the salvation of all men and women, he enables the church, by the Holy Spirit, so to declare the truth of the divine revelation in Jesus Christ that his people may know the way of salvation.

64. The scriptures bear permanent witness to the divine revelation in Christ and are normative for all subsequent tradition.

65. At different moments of history it is sometimes necessary to clarify the contents of Christian faith, and even to define the limits of orthodoxy. For this reason the Christian church convenes in councils, whose purpose it is to bring into sharper focus various aspects of Christian belief. Properly understood, the decisions of the ecumenical

councils which met in the first centuries command assent throughout the whole church, and there is no reason to think that at the end of the patristic era God stopped enabling his church to speak in such a way. Other occasions have called, and may still call for such authoritative guidance.

66. According to Catholic belief, the authority of such councils derives from the charisma of teaching and discernment which the Spirit gives for the building up of the body. The episcopal college exercises this teaching ministry through discerning the faith of Christians, present and past, and always with reference to the supreme norm of the scriptures. To the extent that the church in any era teaches the truths of salvation that were originally taught in the scriptures, that teaching is binding. To definitions of a council "the assent of the church can never be wanting, on account of the action of the Holy Spirit, by which the universal flock of Christ is kept and makes progress in the oneness of faith" (*LG*, no. 25).

67. It is acknowledged that a general council would take on new and greater significance if convened in a situation in which all Christians were united and represented. It is also acknowledged that many councils of the early church were not recognized as genuine councils and their teaching did not have the guarantee of truth (e.g., Robber Synod of Ephesus in 449).

68. Roman Catholics believe that the bishops of the church enjoy the special assistance of the Holy Spirit when, by a collegial act with the bishop of Rome in an ecumenical council, they define doctrine to be held irrevocably.

69. As understood by Roman Catholics, papal infallibility is another embodiment of the infallibility with which the church has been endowed. Christ's promise of sure guidance and the gift of the Spirit were to the whole church and result in the church's capacity to formulate the faith in a manner that is beyond doubt. In carefully defined and limited circumstances, the pope exercises this capacity in and for the whole church.

70. Catholics understand that he does this when, as teacher and pastor of all the faithful, he is to be understood as teaching that some particular matter of faith or morals is part of divine revelation requiring the assent of believers. In this case reception of the doctrine by the assent of the faithful cannot be lacking.

71. When the pope teaches infallibly, infallibility is, properly speaking, not attributed to the pope, nor to the teaching, but rather to this particular act of teaching. It means that he has been prevented by God from teaching error on matters relating to salvation. It does not mean that a particular teaching has been presented in the best possible way, nor does it mean that every time he teaches he does so infallibly.

72. Methodists have problems with this Roman Catholic understanding of infallibility, especially as it seems to imply a discernment of truth which exceeds the capacity of sinful human beings. Methodists are accustomed to see the guidance of the Holy Spirit in more general ways: through reformers, prophetic figures, church leaders and Methodist conferences for example, as well as through general councils. Methodist conferences, exercising their teaching office, formulate doctrinal statements as they are needed, but do not ascribe to them guaranteed freedom from error. Nevertheless Methodists always accept what can clearly be shown to be in agreement with the scriptures. The final judge of this agreement must be the assent of the whole people of God, and therefore Methodists, in considering the claims made for councils and for the pope, welcome the attention which Roman Catholic theologians are giving to the understanding of the reception of doctrine.

73. Methodists have further difficulty with the idea that the bishop of Rome can act in this process on behalf of the whole church. We have not yet discussed together the content of the doctrines of the immaculate conception and assumption of the blessed virgin Mary, but from the Methodist point of view, whether they are true or not, they are not regarded as essential to the faith. It therefore seems to Methodists that these dogmas lack assent and reception by all Christian people. In any case, it can be expected that further study on the reception of doctrine will throw more light on the subject of infallibility.

74. An approach towards convergence in thinking about infallibility may perhaps be reached by considering the Methodist doctrine of assurance. It is the typical Methodist teaching that believers can receive from the Holy Spirit an assurance of their redemption through the atoning death of Christ and can be guided by the Spirit who enables them to cry "Abba, Father" in the way of holiness to future glory.

75. Starting from Wesley's claim that the evidence for what God has done and is doing for our salvation, as described above, can be "heightened to exclude all doubt", Methodists might ask whether the church, like individuals, might by the working of the Holy Spirit receive as a gift from God in its living, teaching, preaching and mission, an assurance concerning its grasp of the fundamental doctrines of the faith such as to exclude all doubt, and whether the teaching ministry of the church has a special and divinely guided part to play in this. In any case, Catholics and Methodists are agreed on the need for an authoritative way of being sure, beyond doubt, concerning God's action insofar as it is crucial for our salvation.

Proposals for future work

76. In light of the work done so far we make the following proposal, for the topics of the next quinquennium. Grouped under the general heading "The Apostolic Tradition", they could include: the apostolic faith; its teaching, transmission and reception; the sacramental ministry, ordination and apostolic succession; Mary; and the church.

NOTES

[1] Cf. no. 23.
[2] Our discussions revealed that we must still examine and resolve persisting differences concerning the efficacy of baptism, particularly of infants. Neither of us believes that a non-baptized person is by that very fact excluded from salvation, nor that baptism automatically ensures perseverance unto salvation. Both in this paragraph and the succeeding one the references to the eucharist emphasize only certain communal and personal aspects which are immediately relevant to this discussion of the church. In the Dublin report, nos. 47-74, the commission has given a much fuller account of the present areas of agreement and of remaining disagreement concerning this sacrament.
[3] See E. Schwartz, ed., *Acta Conciliorum Oecumenicorum*, II/I, ii. 81(277); cf. Leo, Epistle 98 (Migne, PL 54, 951).
[4] For an explanation of this item, cf. ARCIC I, Authority II, no. 16.
[5] Cf. Schwartz, *op. cit.*, I/I, iii, 60.

XXII. METHODIST-ROMAN CATHOLIC DIALOGUE

46. The Apostolic Tradition
Fifth Series 1986-1991

Paris, France, 15 April 1991

Preface

The theological dialogue between the Roman Catholic Church and the World Methodist Council has now been going on for twenty-five years. The early years of this dialogue dealt with a wide range of issues, doctrinal, ethical and pastoral. In the last fifteen years, the dialogue has focused on a series of inter-related doctrinal issues which have also been the subject of attention in other ecumenical dialogues. In 1981 we produced a report on *The Holy Spirit* and in 1986 *Towards a Statement on the Church*. To these documents we now add our text on *The Apostolic Tradition*. In it we seek to address some of the questions that are outstanding, following on previous studies.

It is important to note that this report has deliberately not addressed all the differences of doctrine or practice that exist between us in respect of the questions it deals with. For example, there is no detailed examination of the question of apostolic succession; we do not investigate the different ways in which Catholics and Methodists actually teach and hand on the faith. Nor do we evaluate the ecclesiological self-understanding that is specific to either Catholics or Methodists. Our concern, rather, has been to set out theological perspectives within which such more specific questions may be viewed. We propose these perspectives as consistent with the doctrinal positions of both churches but not as full expositions of them. What we hope is that a careful reading of this report may enable Catholics and Methodists to see their own and each other's doctrine and practice in a wide theological and historical perspective, and to discern convergences between them.

This approach is consistent with our conviction that we already share a certain though as yet imperfect communion. It is a staging post at which we areware of much that we hold in common and respect the gifts that have been bestowed on one another in our time of separation. But we are also "committed to a vision that includes the goal of full communion in faith, mission and sacramental life" (*Towards a Statement on the Church*, no. 21). The gradual realization of that vision requires us to explore critically and constructively the theological bases which underpin our present positions. This report is a contribution to that process.

This document was completed at a plenary meeting of the commission which took place at the house of the Filles du Cœur de Marie at the rue Notre-Dame-des-Champs in Paris. The members of the commission wish to express their appreciation of the hospitality they received from the sisters there.

Bishop James W. Malone	Dr Geoffrey Wainwright
Catholic Church	World Methodist Council
Co-chairman	*Co-chairman*

The Apostolic Tradition

Because God so loved the world, he sent his Son and the Holy Spirit to draw us into communion with himself. This sharing in God's life, which resulted from the mission of the Son and the Holy Spirit, found expression in a visible koinonia [communion, community] of Christ's disciples, the church.

Report of the joint commission between the
Roman Catholic Church and World Methodist Council,
Fourth Series 1982-1986

Introduction

1. Jesus Christ was sent among us by God the Father to make known and to bring to completion the divine purpose of salvation, the "mystery of Christ" hitherto hidden and "now revealed in the Spirit" (Col. 1:26 and Eph. 3:5). In the power of the Holy Spirit, this mission continues in and through the church, the family Christ gathers together in common obedience to the Father's will. As Christ's servant, the church proclaims to the world the message of his victory over sin and death, provides a living sign of that victory, and summons everyone to repent and believe the gospel and so receive the promised Spirit.

2. It is Christ's will that his disciples should live at peace with one another; he binds them together through the gift of divine grace. The New Testament documents do not present us with an unattainable ideal but describe the actual life of a real society brought into being by Christ. This society is not a closed fellowship of perfect observance; its members have not already attained all that God intends, and it is open to all the world. It acknowledges that by his grace true followers of Christ may be found everywhere and welcomes them into its company as they affirm their Christian discipleship.

3. This Roman Catholic-Methodist dialogue, and the whole movement for unity in the faith, follows the path Christ set for his church in obedience to the mission he himself received from God the Father and transmitted to us (Matt. 28:18-20). It is a movement that breaks down the barriers sin has set up between Christians, drawing all believers into a single fellowship of praise and forming life-long enemies into friends for eternity. Today as Catholics and Methodists we both face the urgent task of evangelizing a world deeply affected by superstition and secularism, by indifference and injustice; we must look together to the one Lord who sends the Spirit upon us all that we may go out and witness in his name. Doing this with credibility entails a common understanding of the gospel and the ability to recognize in each other's lives and confessions an authentic witness to the faith.

4. In order to build on previous work in the dialogue, the commission pursued a theme which has proved increasingly important throughout the whole ecumenical movement, namely the apostolic tradition, understood as the teaching, transmission

and reception of the apostolic faith. It is hoped that this approach may set the difficult problem of ministry in a new light, since this topic has hitherto been predominantly considered in its relationship to the administrative and sacramental life of the church rather than in relation to its teaching.

5. In the overall title of this report, "The Apostolic Tradition", the word "Tradition" signifies the living transmission of the gospel of Christ, by manifold means, for the constant renewal of every generation. Christians do not order the life of the church by the fixed repetition of rigid routine laid down in the past. Rather, by recalling and holding fast to the treasured memory of the events of our salvation, we receive light and strength for our present faith as, under God, we seek to meet the needs of our own time. It is Christian hope that makes possible our whole-hearted and active contribution to the continued handing-on of the transforming power contained in the gospel.

6. Our knowledge of the past life of the people of God, witnessing to their experience of God's action among them, enables us to recognize and to comprehend the risen Christ as he speaks to us today. We learn to express ourselves in his language in the midst of the people he has made; he sends the Spirit to us to open our understanding and to guide our words and actions in the service of his loving purpose for the extension and completion of God's kingdom. We enter into his loving purpose as, by God's grace, we receive in faith the benefits of Christ's saving death on the cross and with him, dying to self, are raised to new life (Rom. 6:3-4). This is the mystery that constitutes the true life of every believer and gives meaning and effect to all preaching and teaching of the church, to every practice, ministry and ordinance.

Part One: The Apostolic Faith – Its Teaching, Transmission, and Reception

7. In the New Testament description of the birth of the church, a role is attributed to each of the three persons of the Trinity, which is both distinct and inseparable from the role of the other two. To the Father is attributed the gracious purpose by which we were chosen for filial adoption in union with the eternal Word before the foundation of the world. The actual work of founding the church is attributed to the Son and to the Holy Spirit. The Son founds the church by his act of redemption. The Spirit is co-founder of the church with the Son, by being the church's principle of sanctification. The two divine missions – the sending of the Son and of the Spirit by the Father – are extensions in our world of time of the two eternal processions in the Trinity. The new relationship, both individual and corporate, which they bring about in human beings towards God, is none other than what the New Testament calls the church.

8. The indivisible relationship between these two divine missions is everywhere present in the patterns which govern every aspect of the life of the church: its confession of faith, the discipleship of its members, and their communion with one another. It is the Holy Spirit who enables us to confess the truth revealed in the Son, to be united to him in a relationship as adopted children of the Father, and to live in charity in the one body of Christ.

I. Word and church

9. "In many and various ways God spoke of old to our ancestors by the prophets; but in these last days he has spoken to us by the Son, whom he appointed the heir of

all things, through whom also he created the world" (Heb. 1:1-2). The church of God has been brought into being by the same creative and self-revealing activity of God. In the Son, God has spoken definitively to us: the Son who is so completely the expression of his heavenly Father that he is called God's Word (John 1:1-18). He makes known God's purpose and carries it out. For the Word of God, now made flesh, speech and action are intrinsically connected; his words take effect and his deeds have meaning.

10. It is the cross and resurrection of Christ that supremely reveal him to us, achieving his purpose and making him our Saviour. When the apostles preached Christ, they proclaimed Christ crucified and risen. When the church preaches Christ today, it is the same proclamation that is made. Christ, the Word of God incarnate, still has the same message for us and the same gifts of grace by which he saves us.

11. The apostolic mission, the charge laid on the apostles to transmit the message of Jesus Christ to their own and to all successive generations, is precisely the service of the Word. The person of Christ, his teaching and his work for us: it was to all this that the apostles bore witness, for all this is God's Word.

12. As the gospel was preached by the apostles, the church was called together and built up. Service of the word was their over-riding responsibility (Acts 6:2-4), a service of Christ himself and of the community that by faith came to be identified with him (Acts 6:7; 12:24; 19:20).

13. A profound understanding of the church must begin with a reflection on the word of God, who brings the church into being and continues to make the church what it is. The word spoken to us in Christ calls forth our response. Thus, the church is sustained by a conversation, initiated by the Lord. God, who called all worlds into being by the power of his word, speaks to us kindly and with sternness, gently and with thunderous warnings, with laws and with love, in proclamation to his people and heart-to-heart to each and every one. By calling together a messianic community in which the promises were fulfilled, Christ made himself known as Messiah. As he called his flock to follow him, he showed himself to be the Good Shepherd.

14. That which the church was to become as a consequence of the apostolic mission is discernible in its first coming to birth, and to discern that coming to birth, one must be aware of the extent to which Christ by deed and by word engaged his followers in communication with himself.

15. Christ was content to speak with other audiences and with later generations through those who became his first disciples. Only this degree of confidence invested by Christ in his followers could match the free self-communication of God to the world and to those whom he had made in his own image. To draw all to himself, the Son died upon the cross. He gave us his words and his very self and waits patiently for us to understand. Any other way would have frustrated his own purpose: to draw us to love him. In order to fulfill this saving purpose, he called into being the church where the word's recreating power is evident, remaking people into a community that could share his life and live in harmonious relationships with one another. Thus the church is the place where the word of God is spoken, heard, responded to and confessed (Rom. 10:8-17). The law of God, so the prophets said, was to become a law not written externally on tablets of stone but written on our hearts, taken in, and made heart-knowledge: it was to be our second nature (Jer. 31:31-34).

16. The Tradition received by the apostles itself continues an unbroken process of communication between God and human beings. Every possible human resource is

employed to sustain and deepen this process: linguistic, ritual, artistic, social and constitutional. The written word of scripture is its permanent norm. Through the sacraments of baptism and the eucharist, the memory of the events whereby the church came into being is preserved. The living Word has made a living community in which men and women converse with God and speak their faith to one another. Guided by its pastors and teachers, the church continues to communicate with all generations, preserves its own identity and message, and is daily renewed in its obedience.

17. Through the living Word, recalling and renewing the acts of Christ's life for us, his history becomes our history. We celebrate our new birth; we are forgiven, strengthened and healed; we are united with one another; we find our vocation for ministry; and we give thanks to God through the power of Christ's death and living victory. In his life on earth, the Word confirmed his words by his actions for us; the same is true today.

18. The growth of the church comes about through a continued hearing and assimilation of the word of God. To be sure that we are hearing the word, we maintain communion with those who have heard and obeyed the word before us. But we will not be saved simply by repeating what other generations have said and done. We must express for ourselves, act for ourselves, and ourselves be transformed through the renewal of our minds and hearts, if the living Tradition of Christ and his apostles is to be continued. The faith must be handed on.

19. In every time and in every place, the church lives and moves by calling to mind all that it has seen and heard of the marvels of God's word in his created world and in the history he is making with us. But we do not live in the past. Memory enables us to recognize the Lord as he comes to us today. His presence in the events of our lives proves to us that his words are true. His deeds for us today make possible our own words of praise and our own acts of service by which God is glorified.

20. But the word of God, with us today, does not tell us, any more than the apostles were told, what comes next in our story. Since the gospel tradition looks to the future, we live in hope. And Christian hope is the strength that enables us, claiming his promises, to be totally committed to the present. We know that we are travelling towards the one whose memory we cherish and whose presence we know. By confessing our faith in living words, we learn how to die with Christ, to hide our life in him, so that when he appears we too will be made known in glory.

21. In conclusion, we recall that the search for ecumenical reconciliation has revealed only too clearly the difficulty of reuniting scripture and Tradition once they have been notionally separated. Scripture was written within Tradition, yet scripture is normative for Tradition. The one is only intelligible in terms of the other. We do not claim to have resolved here all the ecumenical problems that arise in relation to this issue. What we have sought to do is to ask ourselves how the Christian of today can confess with Christians of all time the one true faith in Jesus Christ, the same yesterday, today and forever.

II. Spirit and church

22. In the New Testament the action of the sovereign and life-giving Spirit is closely related to the action of the word. What God does through the word is done in the Spirit, so that the same effect can often be attributed to the word, or to the Spirit, or to both. It is God's action that is perceived in all cases.

23. Thus the Spirit appears in the New Testament narrative as early as the annunciation: the angel assures Mary that "the Holy Spirit will come" upon her and "the power of the Most High will overshadow" her (Luke 1:35). Therefore her Son will be called Son of the Most High and will be recognized by the prophet Simeon, inspired by the Holy Spirit, as the one through whom God has prepared his salvation (2:30).

24. As Jesus' ministry begins at his baptism by John, the Spirit descends upon him in the form of a dove, and leads him to the desert where he rejects the temptation from the evil one to carry out this ministry in ways disobedient to the will of the Father (Mark 1:10; Matt. 3:16). At Nazareth, Jesus affirms that the prophecy of Isaiah 61:1-2 ("The Spirit of the Lord is upon me...") is now fulfilled in him (Luke 4:18-21). At the heart of Jesus' ministry, Luke places the promise of an outpouring of the Spirit (Luke 11:13).

25. The gospel of John emphasizes particularly the promise and presence of the Spirit. The Baptist identifies Jesus as one who "baptizes in the Holy Spirit" (John 1:33). True worship will be "in Spirit and in truth" (John 4:23). The promised Spirit is the Paraclete (Advocate) and the Spirit of truth (14:15-17; 15:26). This promise is fulfilled when Jesus is glorified on the cross (7:37-39).

26. The outpouring of the Spirit is presented in several ways in the New Testament. For John, the Spirit is given by the risen Christ on the evening of the resurrection and empowers the disciples to forgive and to retain sins (20:22-23). For Luke in Acts (2:1-11), the Spirit is given on the day of Pentecost, and the Spirit's presence is manifested in extraordinary ways. In Acts, the manifestation of the Spirit is seen as a proof that baptism has been received: those who have been baptized must receive the Spirit (the sealing). The Spirit is received by all those who "hear the word", both Jews and Gentiles (Acts 10:45). The Spirit leads Paul in his missionary journeys (Acts 13:2-5).

27. The Spirit distributes gifts to all for the good of the koinonia (1 Cor. 12:1-11). The Spirit is the inner power of the new life in Christ. Because the faithful are in Christ and with Christ, they receive the Spirit and are in the Spirit. There is a diversity of gifts, yet these are united in their source, the one Spirit, and in their purpose, the koinonia. Yet the Spirit "blows where it wills", and the faithful cannot put limits to the Spirit's action in humankind.

28. The Holy Spirit, the third person of the Trinity, acts not as an impersonal force but personally inspires and guides those who come to believe. The Spirit seeks the unbelievers and reaches them in ways that are often mysterious, transforming their hearts. The Holy Spirit prepares the way for the preaching of the word to those who do not believe, enabling them to respond in faith and to know the saving grace of God. The Spirit thus creates and maintains the oneness of the church, bringing the many into unity and joining to their head the members of the body of Christ. Believers recognize one another as members of the body, share in one ministry of word and sacrament, and partake of the eucharistic meal, where through and with Christ, in the Spirit, they offer a sacrifice of praise and thanksgiving to the Father.

29. As the Spirit abides in the community where the faith is confessed in fidelity to Christ, the Spirit makes the faithful aware of the presence among them and within them of Christ and of the Father. God dwells in the faithful, and they dwell in God, in whom they "live and move and have their being". This spiritual presence is pure, unmerited gift. It calls the faithful to holiness, brings them to and keeps them in the justice that is of Christ, sets them on the way to perfection, and empowers them to act through the

Spirit's many gifts. As the faithful use their gifts of the Spirit for the good of the community and the spread of the gospel, they also receive the fruits of the Spirit (Gal. 5:22-23), which build up the life of the church in peace and joy.

30. Yet the gifts can be neglected and abused. In their sinfulness, the believers can resist and grieve the Spirit. But the Holy Spirit is also the Paraclete or Advocate who pleads for them and brings about repentance, forgiveness and reconciliation.

31. The Holy Spirit reminds the disciples of the message and words of the Lord and enables them to participate in the saving events of the life, death and rising of Christ. The Holy Spirit is invoked in the supper of the Lord; and, in preaching and proclamation, it is the Spirit, moving the hearts and minds of the hearers, who leads them into the fullness of truth. The Spirit's abiding presence in the church through the ages is enlivened by moments of abundant outpouring, times when the faithful have the impression of living through "a new Pentecost". Thus the Spirit guides the church in recognizing the word in the scriptures, so that they become the document and charter of its life. The Spirit enables the people of God and their ministers to understand and interpret the word in the scriptures, to transmit and explain it verbally, to hear it and receive it with faith. When it becomes necessary, the same Spirit leads the church to self-criticism and so to reform and renewal, in greater fidelity to its memory of Christ. The Spirit thus writes the gospel in the hearts of the faithful, and this gospel in the heart inspires the members of the koinonia to let the word which they believe give form to their prayer of praise and thanksgiving. In all these ways the Spirit continues to shape and enrich the memory of the community.

32. The power and presence of the Spirit lead the faithful from grace to grace. As the Holy Spirit leads them to reflect on their memory of Christ, to partake of his memorial, and to experience Christ as a present reality, they are opened to God's purpose both for themselves and for the whole of creation. The Spirit inspires them to pray and strive for the welfare of all of God's creatures, and so to protect and promote the habitat that God has given them. In ways that are known to God alone, the Spirit is also present and active among those who have not heard the gospel or have not believed it. The Christian believers trust in God's hidden action transforming the world according to God's ultimate purpose. They seek to discern God's saving power at work. The Spirit makes them eager to see the fulfilment of all of God's promises and to pray for the coming of God's kingdom. The same Spirit gives them the certainty that the obstacles and evils that are symbolized in "the world, the flesh, and the Devil" will be overcome by God's power in God's own time. But the Christian hope that is nurtured by the Spirit also looks further than this earth and the present life. It looks forward to the eternal kingdom, where God reigns among the saints of all ages and nations and tongues. In this final transformation the Spirit will bring to an end the trials of the church on earth, the sufferings of the saints, and will bring the elect into the glory that the Father has reserved for those who love him (1 Cor. 2:9).

III. The pattern of Christian faith

33. In John's gospel, Jesus says, "I am the way, the truth and the life", and goes on to affirm that though he is to go away, he leaves his Spirit who will witness to him. The Spirit will convince us of sin and lead us into the truth. Since the truth is always Christ's, there is a continuum of faith with the past. Thus, the Holy Spirit has enabled the faithful to confess Christ in every generation, and the church continues in this com-

munion of saints. It is this permanence in Christ and in the Spirit which gives the church its identity and self-understanding and keeps it in the gospel which it has to proclaim to the world.

34. In each generation the church inherits a history in which earlier Christians have sought to express the truth of God in their own time and place, and in that history an important place is given to those theologians who provided the earliest elucidations of the faith. The church also knows that God will provide witnesses to the faith in the future, but the present church has its own particular responsibility to the word and the Spirit now.

35. We know from past history and present experience that Christ's Spirit of truth works in a dynamic of continuity and change. The Holy Spirit brings home to us the truth of the gospel in a variety of ways. For while the Spirit never changes, the manner of the Spirit's operation may vary with each group of believers. The Spirit moves in a gracious and positive manner, even when demanding costly discipleship. And we have the injunction laid on us not to grieve the Spirit; rather, we must cooperate with the Spirit.

36. What cooperation is thus demanded? Referring to the Holy Spirit's role in binding us to Christ, St Irenaeus maintained that through God alone can God be known. Developing the same theme, St Athanasius asserts that the divine Word became human so that we, in some sense, might become divine. Thus, we cooperate with the Spirit as we take to ourselves this self-giving of God in the mystery of the incarnation. This, according to biblical witness, is the way God has chosen from all eternity for the salvation of humankind. Therefore, every ordered expression of the gospel is an attempt to proclaim this mystery – the love of God who saves in Christ – and all our efforts to discern and describe Christian belief must find their focus here. Since the heart of the gospel and the core of the faith is the love of God revealed in redemption, then all our credal statements must derive from faith in Christ, who is our salvation and the foundation of our faith. Thus, as Vatican II recognized, "there exists an order or 'hierarchy' of truths since they vary in their relation to the foundation of the Christian faith" (*Unitatis Redingratio*, no. 11). Likewise Methodists, following Wesley, recognize an "analogy of faith" among the major doctrines of the church.

37. The faith which is believed is believed within particular settings. The expression of the faith has been shaped by cultures before us, and we in turn seek to speak it in the language of our time and place. Inculturation conveys the faith authentically only when what is contextual, be it language or any other form of cultural expression, is itself transformed by the transcendent truth of the gospel. It then in turn becomes an effective means of transforming the lives of those who belong to this culture. Affirmations about God made by the believing community are active symbols, calling for realization in the lives of its members. Therefore, when Christians recite the creed within a liturgical setting, they do more than list a set of beliefs – they identify themselves with that great company "whose lives are hid with Christ in God" (Col. 3:4). Because the Spirit provides in the church such abundant gifts of perception and understanding, the recitation of the creed engenders in every age a great diversity and richness of faith. We say "we believe", and the life of the church is deepened and renewed.

38. The Nicene Creed, used by both Catholics and Methodists in their liturgy and teaching, is a comprehensive and authoritative statement of Christian faith. It was the text upon which John Wesley based his explication when, in his Letter to

a Roman Catholic, he summarized "the faith of a true Protestant". We include the text of the creed, known as the Nicene Creed, since it constrains us to take very seriously the degree of communion that Catholics and Methodists already share. In a world deeply affected by superstition and by unbelief, our proclamation of this common faith must be an occasion for giving thanks and a stimulus to deepen our unity in Christ:

> We believe in one God, the Father, the Almighty, maker of heaven and earth, of all that is seen and unseen.
> We believe in one Lord, Jesus Christ, the only Son of God, eternally begotten of the Father, God from God, Light from Light, true God from true God, begotten, not made, of one Being with the Father. Through him all things were made. For us men and for our salvation he came down from heaven: by the power of the Holy Spirit he became incarnate from the Virgin Mary, and was made man. For our sake he was crucified under Pontius Pilate; he suffered death and was buried. On the third day he rose again in accordance with the scriptures; he ascended into heaven and is seated at the right hand of the Father. He will come again in glory to judge the living and the dead, and his kingdom will have no end.
> We believe in the Holy Spirit, the Lord, the giver of life, who proceeds from the Father and the Son. With the Father and Son he is worshipped and glorified. He has spoken through the prophets.
> We believe in one, holy, catholic and apostolic church. We acknowledge one baptism for the forgiveness of sins. We look for the resurrection of the dead, and the life of the world to come. Amen.

IV. The pattern of Christian life

1. The gift of new life

39. Faith in Jesus Christ involves assent to the truths of the gospel. In confessing these truths we likewise confess our new identity as sons and daughters of God. As our minds are filled with the truths of the gospel, they are transformed, and that transformation brings about a new life. St Paul tells his converts to be "transformed by the renewing of their minds" (Rom. 12:2). Through the hearing of and response to the gospel a crucial change of both heart and mind takes place. So it is that Paul prays to God for his new converts "that you may be filled with knowledge of God's will in all spiritual wisdom and understanding, so that you may lead lives worthy of the Lord, fully pleasing to him, as you bear fruit in every good work and as you grow in knowledge of God" (Col. 1:9-10).

40. Through Christ's death and resurrection the way is opened for reconciliation to the Father in the Holy Spirit. Baptism, the sacrament of faith, is the sign of that new life which the Father gives us through Christ in the Spirit. Christ's death has put to death sin in our lives; it has freed us from the bondage of sin and death. The new life that replaces the old is a life of love: it is a sharing in the inner life of God that is communicated to us by the Holy Spirit: "God's love has been poured into our hearts through the Holy Spirit that has been given to us" (Rom. 5:5). This love is pure gift, and in virtue of it we are drawn ever more deeply into the inner life of God and are able to cry "Abba, Father" (Gal. 4:6). It is other-centred and boundless in its range and scope, directed to the whole world. In particular, it pushes us out to the poor, the weak, and the unloved. It is love without preference and without distinction, since because of the work of Christ, there is no longer Jew or Greek, slave or free, male or female (Gal. 3:28).

2. The challenge of new life

41. This gift is also call and responsibility. Paul tells the Colossians that it is precisely because they have died and been raised to new life that they must put to death those features of their old way of life which still persist. They must put away their old garments and "put on the garment of God's chosen people" (cf. Col. 3:12). The obligation of Christians to change their lives is rooted and grounded in what God has done for them. For a few, the transformation comes quickly, as John Wesley noted in his "Plain Account of Christian Perfection". But for most the putting to death of the old way of life and the taking on of the new involves Christians in a long and painful process of maturing in love. It is a costly journey and inevitably involves suffering, since the pattern of Christian life will reflect the pattern of Christ's dying and rising. It was the constant concern of Paul to foster and nurture this growth. Individuals, then, are changed by the saving action of God in Christ that is appropriated through the power of the Holy Spirit. But the bestowal of the gift of new life on individuals constitutes a new principle of unity. The baptized share together in the life of love, and this sharing is a vital dimension of the koinonia which is the church.

3. The communion of new life

42. By allegiance to Christ the believer becomes part of the community in which Christ is remembered (anamnesis). Christ's words to his disciples are relevant here. The Christian is brother, sister, mother to Christ in community with others (Mark 3:31-35; Matt. 12:46-60; Luke 8:19-21).

43. The early Christian believers were part of a community where life was lived in common with others, the disunity of Babel being reversed by the events of and after Pentecost (Acts 2:44; 4:32). In Acts 2:42 we read of the four fundamental elements in their life together: hearing the teaching of the apostles, communion (koinonia), breaking of bread and the prayers.

44. In their worship on the Lord's day they experienced his presence and renewing grace as they celebrated the eucharist together. In the service itself, the profound nature of their relation to each other was manifested in the giving of the peace and pre-eminently in the holy communion: "The bread which we break, is it not a sharing in the body of Christ? Because there is one bread, we who are many are one body, for we all partake of the one bread" (1 Cor. 10:16-17). The eucharist remains the focus where the pattern of life specific to Christians is shown forth.

45. It has been customary to state that Methodists regard the preaching of the word as the central act of worship, while for Catholics the eucharist is "the centre and culmination" of Christian life (*Presbyterium Ordinis*, no. 5). This contrast should not be put too strongly. In the beginnings of Methodism, the Wesleys encouraged and practised a much more frequent observance of the Lord's supper than was customary in the Anglican church of the time, and in recent decades Methodists are increasingly appreciating the centrality of the eucharist and Catholics the fundamental importance of the preaching of the word.

4. The source of new life

46. By baptism we are received into the community of belief and are nurtured there as the faith is passed on to us ("traditioned" to us) through the family and the church. Unless this "traditioning" takes place, we receive little of the Christian faith. Each gen-

eration and each person must claim for themselves the life of faith. We receive the faith in more explicit terms through hearing the preached word, Sunday schools, catechism classes, first communion classes, confirmation classes and church-sponsored schools. Sustained growth in the Christian faith requires time spent in study of the scriptures and in prayer based on the scriptures. The faith is nourished in both our traditions by devotional life that plays a significant part in its growth. There are also many ways in which the spiritual life has been nurtured among us, e.g., Christian family life, Methodist class meetings, various lay apostolates, and renewal movements in the Catholic church, the practice of retreats, ecumenical house groups and marriage enrichment courses. In all these situations "heart speaks to heart" *(cor ad cor loquitur).*

5. The practice of new life
47. The Christian hope is that humanity will one day be gathered into Christ when the gospel has been preached to all nations (Matt. 24:14; 28:19). In the widest sense of the mission of the church, there is the mandate to feed the hungry, clothe the naked, visit the sick and the prisoners, welcome the stranger (Matt. 25:31-46). These "works of mercy" belong to the Christian mission in the widest sense, and Catholic-Methodist cooperation has often been most successful in this area. In particular, both churches have tried to promote true Christian community without respect of race, sex or class. In places that are hostile to Christianity, missionary endeavour has been difficult, and fidelity to the gospel has proved very costly. The picture in Hebrews of the saints who watch from heaven and encourage us is pertinent here (Heb. 12:1).

48. The proclamation of the gospel by words is an essential task for each generation of believers. Christians also bear witness when they seek to let their light shine before others, so that their conduct as well as their words may bring others to glorify God (Matt. 5:16; 1 Pet. 2:12). Personal evangelism contributes to the corporate mission and is vitally important in making new believers.

V. The pattern of Christian community
49. The real relationships existing within the Godhead, Father, Son and Holy Spirit, are reflected within the ordered life of creation and still more clearly revealed to the eye of faith in the pattern they establish and make possible for the community life of God's people.

50. Whenever the word of God is truly heard, the church shapes its life in due obedience; the pattern thus brought into being becomes in its turn a means of showing forth the word. As individuals are healed and remade by Christ, so also are the relationships within which their life is brought to fulfilment. When, for example, the community of Christians at Philippi was told to have the mind of Christ, who emptied himself and took the form of a servant, this was not just an instruction to private individuals but an exhortation for the benefit of their common life. Further still, it was not just for their own health and happiness as a community, but for making known the word to the world: it was a setting forth of the word through an effective embodiment of the servanthood of the incarnate one. One passage in the New Testament – 1 John 1:1-3 – dares to suggest that the life of the Christian community is a reflection of the life of the Godhead: thus the communal life of Christians has a vertical as well as a horizontal dimension. They do not merely enjoy fellowship with each other; their life together is a sharing in the life of the Father and his Son Jesus Christ.

51. The Saviour rescues us from loneliness and sets us within the infinitely diverse security of his friends. The images used in the gospels and in the apostolic preaching give indications relating to the ordered life brought into being by Christ. The images are corporate as well as individual. They evoke the bridegroom as well as the bride, the good shepherd's care, the growth and pruning of the vine, the manifold activities and talents of the body, family life in the home, good stewardship, the tender care of the Samaritan, the touch of the healer, the watchful love of the father. In the light of the Lord's supper, the image of the body has inspired profound insights and reflections on the church as the body of Christ.

52. It must also be remembered that in the New Testament, the actions that allow the church to grow in strength and ordered life – the setting apart of new ministers or corporate decisions and teaching, for example – are always accompanied by the action of the Holy Spirit, who makes it possible for us to live in communion and harmony with one another (Acts 13:2; 15:28; 16:6-7; 2 Tim. 1:14). The Spirit is the invisible thread running through the work of the church in the world, enabling our minds to hear and receive the word, enlightening them to understand the word, and giving us tongues to speak the word (John 14:26; 16:13-14; Acts 4:31). Relating us to one another and to Christ our Head, the Holy Spirit gives coherent shape and variety to the people of God. Within that people as they are, and for that people as they shall be, the Holy Spirit invites us all to share in the service of the one who came to serve.

Part Two: Ministry and Ministries:
Serving within the Apostolic Tradition

53. The life of the church, of the human race as it is gathered together and renewed by Christ, is a life of worship, by which believers share in the exchange of love that is the life of the blessed Trinity, Father, Son and Holy Spirit. With Christ our Head and in the power of his Spirit, we serve God in a variety of ways for God's glory and for making known God's loving purpose.

I. Service of the word

54. As the apostle sent by God (Heb. 3:1), Christ shared his carrying-out of the Father's will with others. These he sent into the world to serve the gospel, just as he himself had been sent into the world to serve (John 20:21-23). They were given the formal title of apostle. Theirs was a ministry of ministries: they were sent out to make him known and to care for his people. The apostles, already joined together in the public ministry of Christ, continued after the ascension to be his friends and servants, fully aware of their appointed responsibility to tell everyone of what God had done for them in Christ.

55. In the Book of Acts, the apostles are described as "servants of the word" (Acts 6:4; cf. Luke 1:2). This phrase holds a rich meaning, conveying all that is said in scripture about God's action through his word in creation and in his saving purpose in history. What he says he does. What he does makes him known to us. There is a solidarity between word and deed. This complete interdependence of word and deed in God's action for us culminates in the coming of the person who, in his entire being, is the word of God. "Service of the word" implies the service of a living person, whose words are always fruitful and whose deeds make him known. Supremely in Christ, words and

actions are one. Through the Spirit these deeds and words culminate in the living presence of Jesus in us. It is in this context that the sermon and the sacrament must be understood. In preaching, the Word of God himself addresses us through the preacher: "Whoever hears you hears me" (Luke 10:16). In the eucharist, our Lord's words, "This is my body", "This is my blood", convey both his meaning and the actual giving of himself.

56. The "servants of the word" are therefore those who bring the whole of this divine life into the world, enabling all of us, in our turn, to become servants, each one unique and different but all gathered together in perfect harmony.

57. The present disharmony among Christians is crucially reflected in divisions of doctrine and practice concerning this service of the word. An arrival at a common mind over Christ's purpose for ministry would therefore have a far-reaching effect in the promotion of unity throughout the Christian churches.

II. Gifts of the Spirit

58. The entire Christian community has the responsibility of spreading the gospel and witnessing to the Lord's work of salvation until he comes. This task has "its origins in the mission of the Son and that of the Holy Spirit according to the purpose of God the Father" (*Ad Gentes*, no. 2).

59. Throughout the ages the Holy Spirit has poured out gifts on those who have been baptized in the name of Christ. These gifts are for the building up of the church, which is charged with proclaiming the good news for the salvation of the world, so that all people may come to faith and share in the worship of the triune God (cf. Rom. 15:7-16; 2 Cor. 4:13-15). Thus, each charism that is given elicits a response that must be lived out in ministry and in service: "And his gifts were that some should be apostles, some prophets, some evangelists, some pastors and teachers, to equip the saints for the work of ministry for the building up of the body of Christ until we all attain to the unity of the faith and of the knowledge of the Son of God" (Eph. 4:11-13). The gifts of the Spirit, therefore, are for communion (koinonia): for the drawing of humanity into communion with the Father and the Son, and for the building up and strengthening of communion among those who believe.

60. Among the gifts bestowed by the Spirit there is the specific charism received by those who are called to the ordained ministry. This charism is directed towards the ordering and harmony which must prevail in the exercise of all the gifts. Properly to understand the relationship between the ministries of the ordained and the non-ordained, it is vital to see in both of them the activity of the Spirit who enlivens and unifies the church through the gifts: "Now there are a variety of gifts but the same Spirit; and there are varieties of service, but the same Lord; and there are varieties of working, but it is the same God who activates them all in everyone" (1 Cor. 12:4-7). The same Spirit operates among all the baptized and across all the generations.

61. The New Testament describes the Spirit-filled life in the early Christian communities. The origins of the ordained ministry are found in the commission that Christ gave to his apostles (Matt. 28:18-20). While there was at the beginning no single pattern, the ordained ministry was a gift to the church for leadership in its corporate and worshipping life, for the maintenance and deepening of its order and structure, for the organization of its missionary witness, and for discernment in understanding and applying the gospel. As time passed, the church was led by the Spirit to recognize the

threefold ministry of bishop, presbyter and deacon as normative; some other patterns of ministry that may be discerned in the New Testament became assimilated to the threefold one. While not all the many gifts of the Spirit for ministry have figured equally throughout the history of the church, all have been bestowed afresh at times of crisis and opportunity. Yet the testimony of the New Testament must continue to throw light on the ways in which the ordained ministry has developed and to challenge the ways it functions in our different communions.

III. The church, a living body

62. The community of the faithful is brought into existence by the Holy Spirit. The Spirit relates the faithful to one another, distributing gifts among them. Thus the community receives a living structure. Some of the New Testament images – a body, a household, a people, a vineyard – point to dynamics of growth and to a reality with many aspects and dimensions. Others – the bride, the flock – imply also that it has its own definite identity and is the centre of God's attention, called to share the divine love and opened to the Holy Spirit in whom the faithful experience God's love. As it spreads abroad the good news, the community calls all people to conversion and new life. Led by the Spirit, it extends throughout the many and varied cultures of the world and is sustained through time from year to year, generation after generation. Through the centuries it is rejuvenated as the gospel strikes the imagination and the Spirit stirs up the love of new and younger members. Like the sap of the vine that brings greenness to all branches and twigs, the church is an overflowing source of life. From the human environment it receives new riches that nurture it and which it in turn transforms, opening up the many cultures of the world to intimations of the kingdom of God. The Holy Spirit directs the course of the Christian community by bringing to it the harvest of love, joy, peace, patience, kindness, goodness, fidelity, gentleness and self-control (Gal. 5:22-25). The community is a living organism, not a collection of individuals; it is a place of meeting where people exchange things old and new, not a museum where things are looked at. What is handed on by its tradition in the form of memory acts as a leaven among those who receive it, who then enrich it as they cherish it and pass it on again to their successors. There are times, of course, when Christians do not respond as they ought to the Spirit's guidance. They lack fidelity to Christ, they are lukewarm in the worship of God, they do not show love towards one another, they fail in missionary outreach. So, like all living organisms, Christian communities go through periods of dormancy and decline. But even then hope is held out for vigorous and healthy life because the church is sustained by the Spirit of God who never leaves himself without witnesses.

1. The community of faith and baptism

63. The Spirit calls people to this new life, as those who have heard the word come to Christ, the only Saviour and Mediator. Baptism is given in the midst of the community to new Christians who, at their baptism, confess the faith they have received. Symbolically they are plunged in the cleansing waters where they receive the Holy Spirit and are given the garment of faith "in the name of the Father, the Son and the Holy Spirit". United to Christ in his dying and his rising, they bear witness that they are reborn in him. In the administration of baptism, the community testifies to its faith with the words of the traditional creed. For example, the Apostles' Creed had its origin in

the candidates' confession of faith. Methodists and Catholics agree that Christians are baptized into the faith that has been received from the apostles and obediently preached by the community and its members. In both our traditions it has been the normal practice for the pastors of the community to preside over the entire process of Christian initiation. Both the Methodist and the Catholic churches consider it right to baptize the infants born to believers. They encourage their members to take the opportunities presented to them to renew the vows that they made, or that were made for them, in baptism.

64. Those who confess their faith, endorsed by the community, are brought through the baptismal waters into the life of God that is communicated through Christ in the Holy Spirit. This life, being the very life of the divine persons, is itself a life of communion and involves participating in the bond of love established by the Spirit between God and creation. The baptized become sisters and brothers in Christ. They are constituted as the family of God, sharing in its privileges and responsibilities.

65. By baptism, the community of the believers shares in the holiness of God, a holiness that is manifested in the Christian life of the faithful. The community feeds on the memory of the Lord, celebrates his abiding presence, and looks forward in hope to the continuing service of God and of neighbour until the end of time, thus affirming its trust in the ultimate victory of Christ over the power of evil. It is itself a sign and instrument of God's kingdom.

66. Thus, the baptized and believing community is a communion. Holding in common the faith in which they are baptized and all the holy things that are God's gifts, they grow into a communion of the people who are made holy by God's grace and power. While all the baptized thus make up "the communion of saints", they also recognize the conspicuous presence of divine grace in specific persons – the saints – whose lives and example testify, even to the shedding of their blood for Jesus, to the transforming action of the Spirit of God in every generation. The "cloud of witnesses" transcends denominational barriers.

2. The community of worship

67. The Christian community continues to flourish by virtue of the common baptism and faith of its members. But it is also sustained and nurtured by the celebration of the memorial of the Lord, the service of thanksgiving in which it experiences, as the Spirit is invoked, the presence of the risen Christ. There the word of God is heard in the scriptures and the proclamation of the gospel. Through the holy meal of the community, the faithful share "a foretaste of the heavenly banquet prepared for all mankind" (British *Methodist Service Book*, 1975). As they receive the sacrament of his body and blood offered for them, they become the body through which the risen Lord is present on earth in the Holy Spirit (1 Cor. 10:16-17). As they share his body and blood that have brought to the sinful world salvation and reconciliation, they proclaim today the past events of the Lord's death and resurrection, and as they do so they present to the world their confidence and hope that Christ who "has died and is risen" will also "come again".

68. This experience of the presence of the Lord in the setting of worship attunes the hearts and minds of the faithful to all other aspects of his presence. They return to him the love they have received from him, when they serve the poor and when they struggle for social justice. In the sick and suffering they see the sufferings of Christ. In their

own pains and sorrows endured for the sake of the gospel they share in the passion of Christ. In all this the faithful experience the wonderful exchange by which in Christ and the Holy Spirit, all is common to all. And they present to God all that they have and all that they are as their own sacrifice of praise.

69. In the worshipping fellowship, the community confesses Jesus Christ as Lord, shares the peace which Christ gives, and so anticipates the heavenly kingdom where the risen Christ fills all things to the glory of God the Father. The community of the faithful is thus the proclaiming, celebrating and serving community which gives glory to God in the name of all creatures. By its gatherings on the Lord's day the community shapes the life of its members, helping them to make their weekly and daily tasks expressions of the royal priesthood of the believers gathered together under the high priesthood of the risen Lord. Thus, the community provides for its members a pattern of life consecrated to God and directed towards fulfilment in the final manifestation of Christ.

3. The ordained minister in the community

70. Ever since the time of the apostles, ministers have led the community in the worship of God, in proclaiming Christ and receiving him, in organizing the community's life of service in the Spirit. Worship, witness and service join hands in word and sacrament: this has served as the central model for what Christian ministers must both be and do.

71. Chosen from among the people, the ordained ministers represent the people before God as they bring together the prayers of the community. Entrusted with the pastoral care of the community, they act in Christ's name and person as they lead the people in prayer, proclaim and explain the word, and administer the sacraments of faith.

72. In each place the pastor gathers the faithful into one, and as all the ministers relate to one another and transmit the same gospel, they ensure a universality of conviction and communion among all the faithful. They transmit what they have received: the good news as taught from apostolic times, the sacraments as signs and instruments of the Lord's saving presence and action, the call to holiness that the Holy Spirit addresses to all.

73. United around their minister in worship and in witness, and in the carrying out of their vocational tasks, the faithful know themselves to be gathered in Christ by the Holy Spirit. In the pastoral care that is extended to them, the faithful perceive themselves to be led by the Good Shepherd who gave his life for the sheep.

74. As the community is renewed from one Lord's day to the next, it is nourished by the tradition it has received, and responsibility for this is especially entrusted to those ministers who inherit the apostolic function of oversight in the community. The function of oversight entails on the part of the ministers a solicitude for all the churches: they are charged to ensure that the community remain one, that it grow in holiness, that it preserve its catholicity, and that it be faithful to apostolic teaching and to the commission of evangelization given by Christ himself.

75. These four "marks" of the Christian community should be exemplified at each moment of its existence. They should also be effectively transmitted from one generation to the next. The saints who have passed into the fullness of the mystery of God's grace are forever part of the community: the witness and examples of the past continue

to be cherished; the saints in heaven are held as instances of Christ's "closest love" and as present tokens of the ultimate fulfilment of all God's promises.

76. The transmission of the gospel is the work of the whole assembly of the faithful under the guidance and with the encouragement of their pastors. The living presence of the Lord among his people is the source of the Christian life. The pastors of the community are his servants as he provides grace and spiritual strength to his people and leads them to the goal of their earthly pilgrimage.

77. The transmission of the gospel in word and sacraments is itself the work of the Spirit. As they urge the faithful to Christian perfection, the ordained ministers obey the call of Christ, and they help the community in its search for the forms of Christian holiness that are appropriate to different periods, ages and conditions of life. Catholics and Methodists are at one in seeing in a divinely empowered ministry the guidance of the Holy Spirit and are moving in the direction of greater shared understanding of the nature of ordination and of the structure of the ministry in regard to the responsibility to teach and to formulate the faith.

IV. The ordained ministry: call and empowerment

78. We consider now the call to the ordained ministry, ordination to the ministry, and continuance in it.

1. Call

79. Both Methodists and Catholics recognize the power of God in the enabling of all ministry. During his earthly ministry the Lord Jesus himself in his sovereign freedom appointed twelve. The experience of Paul, who according to his own words received the call to be an apostle direct from the risen Christ, attests to the freedom and movement of the Holy Spirit to call persons at will into ministry. This call may be experienced in several ways: as an internal compulsion that we feel found to obey; through the convergence of several external factors, all of which indicate its possibility; through the influence of the church and its people, which exercises a claim upon us; or through the indication of a need and the ability under God to fulfill that need. Whichever way the call is experienced, it does not remain an inward compulsion but is tested by the church and finally confirmed before the candidate is ordained. The different ways in which this judgment is made in the Catholic and Methodist contexts reflect the different understanding and experience of being churches that have developed during centuries of independent growth.

2. Ordination

80. Both our traditions retain the practice, attested in the New Testament documents, of setting apart for ministry by the laying-on of hands with prayer; prayer is made for the gift of the Holy Spirit appropriate to the particular form of ministry. Ordination takes place in an assembly of the church in which the people give their assent to the candidates, appropriate scriptures are read, and candidates profess their adherence to the faith of the church. Through the laying-on of hands, ordinands are incorporated into the existing body of ministers.

81. In the Catholic understanding and practice of apostolic succession, the bishops through the act of ordination share ministerially the high priesthood of Christ, in one degree or another, with other ministers (bishops, presbyters and deacons), who are their

fellow workers in carrying out the apostolic duties entrusted to them (cf. *Presbyterium Ordinis*, no. 2).

82. In Methodist understanding and practice, including those Methodist churches that are episcopally ordered, candidates for ordination are accepted by the conference after examination as to the genuineness of their call, their spiritual fitness and their capacity for ministry. They are then ordained by prayer and the imposition of hands by the bishop, or by the president of the conference, and given the tasks of declaring the gospel, celebrating the sacraments and caring pastorally for Christ's flock.

3. Continuance in the ministry

83. Within the community of the people of God, under the guidance of the Holy Spirit, an authentic ministry, of the ordained as of all the people of God, communicates Christ to persons, edifies them and builds them up in the faith. In one way or another, it is shown by its fruits.

84. All ministry continues to depend entirely upon God's grace for its exercise. The God who calls crowns his call with gifts for ministry. It is not only the use of the personal gifts of the minister which is at issue here. The minister lives constantly in the grace of God by means of prayer, study of the scripture and participation in the sacraments. As an instrument in God's hands, the ordained minister imparts the word of God to God's people, both by speech and by the sacraments of the church. Both Methodists and Catholics maintain the principle that while the preached word and the acted word call for holiness in the minister, it is not the ministers' worthiness that makes them effective, but the transforming power of the Holy Spirit.

85. The call of God is seen to be a stable and permanent one by both Catholics and Methodists. The ordained person is committed to a life-long ministry; therefore, just as baptism and confirmation are not repeated, neither is ordination. Both communions are here faithful to the constant practice of the church.

V. Convergences and divergence

86. Previous paragraphs make it clear that Methodists and Catholics share a fundamentally important perspective on ministry, affirming that the ordained ministry is essentially pastoral in nature. Ordained ministers have the special responsibility of exercising and holding together the functions of proclaiming the gospel, calling people to faith, feeding the flock with word and sacrament, and making Christ known through the ministry of servanthood to the world. The ordained ministry is a representative one, in the sense expounded in paragraph 71 above.

87. Within this perspective there remain several unresolved issues related to ordained ministry which call for further examination.

1. Sacramentality

88. For Catholics, ordination is a sacrament. Methodists are accustomed to reserve the term sacrament for baptism and the Lord's supper. They do, however, with Catholics look upon ordination as an effective sign by which the grace of God is given to the recipient for the ministry of word and sacrament.

89. A way forward may lie in deeper common reflection on the nature of sacrament. Christ, "the image of the invisible God" (Col. 1:15), may be thought of as the primary

sacrament, revealing God's nature and purpose and enabling us to know and serve him. We may also discern within his action on our behalf certain gifts by which our lives are ordered, nourished and sustained. These have traditionally been classified by Catholics as sacraments in a more specific use of the word.

90. Both Methodists and Catholics see the Holy Spirit as the one who empowers all ministry, both ordained and lay. Further, both Methodists and Catholics would agree that all the people of God must be a sign of Christ in a real sense and that all ministry must be exemplary of Christ and the gospel. Thus, a life clearly in consonance with Christ is a vocation for all Christians.

91. At Vatican II the Roman Catholic Church referred to the church in terms of a "sacrament of salvation" (*Ad Gentes*, no. 5; cf. *Lumen Gentium*, no. 1). Methodists would prefer the word "sign" to sacrament, but the meaning in each case is essentially the same, because the church obeys the mandate of its founder to preach to all nations the gospel of salvation it has received.

2. Episcope

92. Methodists and Catholics can acknowledge together the reality of *episcope* (oversight) in the New Testament and can agree that an ordained ministry which exercises *episcope* is vital for the life of the church. Without the exercise of this gift of oversight, disorder and therefore disunity are inevitable. Koinonia and *episcope* imply one another. In a Catholic perspective this mutual implication reaches its culmination when the bishop presides over liturgical worship, in which the preaching of the gospel and the celebration of the Lord's supper weld together into unity the members of Christ's body.

93. Central to the exercise of *episcope* is the task of maintaining unity in the truth. Thus, teaching is the principal part of the task of *episcope*. In a Catholic understanding the church is united through its unity in faith and sacramental communion. The teaching of a common faith by the college of bishops in union with the successor of Peter ensures unity in the truth. The succession of bishops through the generations serves the continued unity of the church in the faith handed on from the apostles. In the Methodist tradition, Wesley accepted and believed in the reality of *episcope* within the Church of England of which he was a minister. In relation to the Methodist societies, he exercised *episcope* over the whole; all his followers were bound to be in connection with him. He expounded the main teachings of the church by means of his sermons, notes on the New Testament, and conference minutes, and made available to his people authorized abridgements of doctrinal and spiritual work. His appointment of Francis Asbury and Thomas Coke to the superintendency in America was rooted in his belief that the Holy Spirit wished to bestow the gift of *episcope* at that time and in that place for the sake of maintaining unity of faith with the church of all ages. It was part of a fresh and extraordinary outpouring of the gift of the Spirit who never ceases to enliven and unify the church.

94. As we continue to consider remaining differences over the sacramental nature of ordination and the forms of succession and oversight, we rejoice in the work of the Spirit who has already brought us this far together, recognizing that the ecumenical movement of which we are part is itself a grace of the Holy Spirit for the unity of Christians. When the time comes that Methodists and Catholics declare their readiness for that "full communion in faith, mission and sacramental life" towards which they

are working ("Towards a Statement on the Church", no. 20), the mutual recognition of ministry will be achieved not only by their having reached doctrinal consensus, but it will also depend upon a fresh creative act of reconciliation which acknowledges the manifold yet unified activity of the Holy Spirit throughout the ages. It will involve a joint act of obedience to the sovereign word of God.

3. Who may be ordained

95. In the New Testament record there is strong evidence that the pastoral ministry was exercised by both married and unmarried people. By long-standing tradition the Latin rite of the Catholic Church, seeing a positive congruence between celibacy and the ordained priesthood, requires that priests remain unmarried, although exceptions to this practice have been allowed. Methodists, in common with other Protestant churches, ordain both married and unmarried people, but no ultimate doctrinal obstacle divides Methodists and Catholics here.

96. Methodists ordain women because they believe that women also receive the call, evidenced by inward conviction and outward manifestation of the gifts and graces and confirmed by the gathering of the faithful.

97. Catholics do not ordain women, believing that they have no authority to change a practice that belongs to the sacrament of order as received in the Tradition of the church.

98. Our general reflections on the nature of ordained ministry and our treatment of this particular question will need to be mutually illuminating. Further thought will be of benefit to both traditions.

Conclusion

99. Together Catholics and Methodists confess the church as part of the triune God's eternal purpose for the salvation of humankind. The church is the communion of those who have received, receive and will receive through faith the benefits of the redemptive work of God accomplished in the life, death and resurrection of the Word made flesh. In the Holy Spirit they acknowledge the lordship of Christ to the glory of the Father. Thus constituted and sustained by the Word and the Spirit, the church is both a sign and an instrument of the Father's good pleasure for the world: it is a sign, because it is the first-fruits of God's gracious purpose and work; it is an instrument because it has the task of further proclaiming the gospel and doing the works that belong to God's kingdom. By its own communal life it bears witness to that society of love in which the city of God will consist.

100. Catholic and Methodist formularies differ over the concrete location of the church which they both confess. While Wesley and the early Methodists could recognize the presence of Christian faith in the lives of individual Roman Catholics, it is only more recently that Methodists have become more willing to recognize the Roman Catholic Church as an institution for the divine good of its members. For its part, the Roman Catholic Church since Vatican II certainly includes Methodists among those who, by baptism and faith in Christ, enjoy "a certain though imperfect communion with the Catholic Church"; and it envisages Methodism among those ecclesial communities which are "not devoid of meaning and importance in the mystery of salvation" (*Unitatis Redingratio*, no. 3).

101. In the quarter-century since its inception, the joint commission between the Roman Catholic Church and the World Methodist Council has contributed to the degree of mutual recognition which now exists. It has done so by the clarification of Methodist and Catholic positions and traditions, especially as these impinge on each other. A large measure of common faith has been brought to light, so that the increase in shared life that has begun may confidently be expected to continue. The need now is to consolidate the measure of agreement so far attained and to press forward with work on those areas in which agreement is still lacking. Continuing doctrinal progress should both encourage and reflect the growth in mutual recognition and in sharing in the life of the triune God.

47. The Word of Life: A Statement on Revelation and Faith
Sixth Series (1991-1996)

Baar, Switzerland, 15 November 1995

Preface

In every country of the world, men and women, old and young, are found worshipping in churches, cathedrals, chapels and house groups, confessing in a great variety of cultures and in many tongues "Jesus Christ is Lord". They have discovered the Redeemer of the world to be their own Saviour, and their commitment to Christ gives meaning and purpose to their lives.

In Asia and Africa, the number of Christians has doubled in recent years as seeds sown in earlier times come to fruition. Indigenous evangelizers have taken responsibility in the creation and animation of new church communities. New ecclesial communities are also being born in places thought by some to have moved into a "post-Christian" era. In countries of Eastern Europe, believing people have lived their faith with tenacity in the face of atheism and oppression and now bear dynamic witness to the way faith continues to outlive all forces that would destroy it. New signs of life are appearing in Western countries where Christians are confessing their faith as a thoughtful alternative to prevailing materialistic values and the full flowering of secularism that had seemed an inevitable trend in the modern world.

Catholics and Methodists participate in this astonishing persistence and explosive growth of Christian presence and witness in the world. Whether in a Catholic parish in Zaire or in an urban Methodist congregation in Korea, whether at the preaching of the word or in the celebration at the table, the common acclamation rings out: "Christ has died, Christ is risen, Christ will come again." Praise issues in evangelistic testimony and caring service as believing Methodists and Catholics disperse to bear witness to the Lord among their neighbours.

The heart of the faith is common to Catholics and Methodists; but while they sometimes share in prayer and witness together, often they proceed on their own more or less parallel lines. The current situation calls into question the separation that we have inherited and spurs us on to work for our eventual full communion in Christ. The work done by this commission up to now has been directed towards this end. Our previous document, *The Apostolic Tradition*, studied the source of our faith and the means by which it has been communicated to us.

God's word, revealing God to us, and God's Spirit, enabling us to know God, have led us now to study more closely the ways in which God gives himself to us and the response that we make. God's revelation comes for our reception as the word of life, to be confessed, propagated and celebrated. The more we can do these things together, the more we shall be in harmony with the gospel of reconciliation, and the more credible will be our witness, to the glory of God, Father, Son and Holy Spirit. Therefore, we seek full communion in faith, mission and sacramental life. This report is offered as a contribution towards the achievement of the doctrinal agreement necessary to that end.

        Bishop James W. Malone   Dr Geoffrey Wainwright
        Roman Catholic Church   World Methodist Council
        Co-chairman   *Co-chairman*

The Word of Life

INTRODUCTION

1. In the continuing search for the doctrinal agreement necessary to full communion between Catholics and Methodists, the joint commission now treats what are usually called, in theological terms, "revelation" and "faith". We are looking for commonly acceptable ways of expounding the historical self-disclosure and indeed self-gift of the triune God, focused in Jesus Christ, the Word made flesh, and brought home to successive generations of believers by the Holy Spirit, released in power at Pentecost. We are seeking a common account of how men, women and children, opened to the gracious presence of God, are enabled to commit themselves, body and soul, heart and mind and will, to their Maker and Redeemer and, in communion with him, become renewed in the divine image, in the holiness and happiness which is God's intention for humankind. God's revelation and the human response to it constitute the substance of the church's faith, mission and sacramental life; and the more common the account we can give of these things, the closer we may come to one another in our understanding and practice of them and so be readier for full communion between us.

2. Seeking to place its work under the word of God, the commission heard anew the opening words of the First Letter of St John:

> That which was from the beginning, which we have heard, which we have seen with our eyes, which we have looked upon and touched with our own hands, concerning the word of life – the life was made manifest, and we saw it, and testify to it, and proclaim to you the eternal life which was with the Father and was made manifest to us – that which we have seen and heard we proclaim also to you, so that you may have fellowship with us; and our fellowship is with the Father and with his Son Jesus Christ. (1 John 1:1-3)

This sacred text starts from the particularity of the God of Israel's self-revelation in Christ; the divine Word, who was in the beginning with God and has led the history of the chosen people, has been made flesh in Jesus. That sheer self-gift of God is a word of life to humankind: God so loved the world that he gave his only Son, that whoever believes in him should not perish but have eternal life. In Christ, in his words, his deeds, his entire existence, God has been revealed in audible, visible, palpable form: God has been received by human ears, eyes and hands. What the first believers have taken in, they then bear witness to and transmit, for the message spreads the offer of a life shared with God. The modes of the announcement will appropriately reflect, echo and hand on what was seen, heard and touched in the embodied manifestation of God in Jesus Christ. Accepted in faith, the words, signs and actions of the gospel will become the means of communion with the one true God, Father, Son and Holy Spirit. The divine life into which the Spirit introduces believers will be a common life, as each transmits and receives what is always the gift of God.

3. In this passage from scripture, we find already indicated all the main themes of the commission's deliberations and report: the gift of the revelation of the triune God; the human response of faith; the proclamation, as missionary message, of what has been received in faith; word and sacrament as the intelligible and tangible means of grace; communion with the triune God as the very life of the church, the community of believers which in God's name offers to the world the salvation that the church already anticipates with joy.

4. The revelation of the triune God is the source of the church's faith, the church's mission and the church's sacramental life. These are three essential ingredients in the full communion our commission has declared is the final goal of our dialogue (cf. *Towards a Statement on the Church*, §20; *The Apostolic Tradition*, §94).

5. Revelation is God's self-disclosure to human creatures. Having already left a divine mark in all that he has made, God initiated a more direct self-revelation by speaking to Abraham, who was called to the land where his descendants would dwell. The Creator became known as the God of Abraham, Isaac and Jacob. Abraham and Sarah, who received the promise of God, have been seen as models for all believers. Giving the law through Moses and leading the chosen people through judges, kings and prophets, God was known to the people of Israel in a unique way among the nations. And this knowledge of God and of our human condition before him has been conveyed to later ages by the scriptures of the Old Testament.

6. In the midst of this chosen people, at the appointed time, God sent the divine Word, who took flesh from the Virgin Mary as Jesus, the Christ, the Redeemer and Mediator, in whom the divine revelation was fully embodied. The first response to this revelation in Christ is formulated in the scriptures of the New Testament, which are thus normative for all later ages.

7. The scriptures attest that it is by the Spirit of God that human beings see God manifest in history. Thus, their response to revelation is more than a mere reaction to extraordinary events; it is "faith", that is, a knowledge that involves complete personal commitment, body and soul, heart and mind, to the divine self-disclosure – of the one whom Jesus called "Abba, Father", of the Word whose presence and action is perceived in the words and acts of Jesus Christ, and of the Spirit, the Enabler and Supporter of all who believe.

8. Revelation and faith are thus correlative events and moments. What God reveals through Jesus is apprehended in faith through the power of the Holy Spirit. While this faith was, in the Old Testament, an inspired response to God made known as the Creator and the Law-giver who also spoke through the prophets, it is, in the New Testament, shaped by the fundamental awareness of the tri-unity of God that has been preserved and continues to be experienced in the Christian community. That witness to this trinitarian faith has been handed on in the apostolic tradition. It has been preserved in successive ages by baptism in the threefold name of God, "the Father, the Son, and the Holy Spirit", formulated in the traditional creeds, and reflected in the decisions and exhortations of the great councils of the church. Catholics and Methodists are in full agreement on this christological and trinitarian dimension of revelation and of faith.

9. God's revelation aims to bring about communion between humankind and God. The faithful response to God's gift of himself is fundamentally one of grateful acceptance and loving self-surrender. All who have welcomed the revelation of the Father, Son and Holy Spirit feel bound to celebrate together the wonderful deeds of God and to declare them in mission to the world:
- Christians have always been ready to give an account of the hope they share (cf. 1 Pet. 3:15) and have professed their faith publicly. United with Christ through baptism and the Lord's supper, they are called to make their own the faith of the whole community of believers. Sunday after Sunday, Methodists and Catholics make the same fundamental affirmations of faith during worship, and this realization impels them to work towards *unity of faith* in every aspect of Christian life.
- From the day of Pentecost, believers have gone out in the power of the Spirit to share what they have seen and heard and handled. They have done so aware that the gift they have received is not for themselves only; that Christ through his Spirit has commissioned them to make disciples of all the nations. Faith flows out in mission. Catholics and Methodists recognize that they have to overcome everything that prevents them from bearing *united witness* to the one God revealed in Jesus Christ.
- The community that professes its faith and reaches out in mission to the world experiences the reality of Christ's promise "I am with you always, yes, to the end of time" (Matt. 28:20). Its life together, above all its worship, manifests this grace of God. In its prayer, preaching and sacramental rites it is nourished in communion with God and offers an invitation to humankind to accept the salvation offered in Jesus Christ. Here, too, Christ's Spirit challenges us to be reconciled *at one table* in a unity of worship and praise so that the world may believe.

10. By baptism and the faith in Christ which it signifies, Catholics and Methodists already enjoy a certain measure of ecclesial communion. The purpose of the dialogue between us is to increase and deepen our relationship until we reach sufficient agreement in the Christian truth that our common baptism can without equivocation be completed in our mutual participation in the meal to which the one Lord invites us and all his followers. The unity we seek to promote is not solely for our own enjoyment but for the sake of a credible witness to the reconciliation that God in Christ has wrought for the world and therefore among humankind. Our unity is to allow us to "glorify with one mind and one voice the God and Father of our Lord Jesus Christ" (Rom. 15:6), in anticipation of the day when every knee will bow, and every tongue confess that "Jesus is Lord", to the glory of God the Father (cf. Phil. 2:10). As Catholics and Methodists, we are inspired and sustained by a vision of the crowning moment when "there will be a deep, an intimate, an uninterrupted union with God; a constant communion with the Father and his Son Jesus Christ, thought the Spirit; a continual enjoyment of the Three-One God, and of all the creatures in him!" (John Wesley, Sermon 64, "The New Creation", 1785).

SECTION ONE: REVELATION

I. God's self-giving

11. "Canst thou by searching find out God?" (Job 11:7). The biblical answer is clear: God cannot be found by our efforts to seek him out. The mystery of his being cannot be penetrated by human endeavour alone. Indeed, although human beings have

been made in God's image, they have been blind to the light of his mystery in the order of created things. Our knowledge of God is entirely dependent on the Creator's free and gracious choice to make himself known, which he has continued to do in pursuit of his good purpose for us.

12. We call this self-communication of God "revelation" because of the recurrent biblical pictures of one who is hidden taking action to disclose himself, at the same time pointing people in the right direction and opening their eyes so that they may truly see him. Yet in this self-communication not all was revealed. Even Jacob, who wrestled with God, saw him face to face and lived, gaining the new name "Israel" (cf. Gen. 32:30), still did not know God in his fullness; God's name was withheld. "I appeared to [them] as God Almighty", Moses is reminded, "but by my name 'the *Lord*' I did not make myself known to them" (Ex. 6:3).

13. Jacob's change of name to Israel, and before him Abram's to Abraham, reminds us that when God is known or seen through revelation, more is gained than information. In biblical thought a name is more than a label; it actually conveys the being and character of the one thus named. So, with knowledge of God in his revelation comes new relationship, new possibility, even in Paul's words "a new creation" (2 Cor. 5:17). When Simon recognizes Jesus as the Son of the living God he becomes Peter on whom the church is to be built. When the light of revelation breaks through to Saul on the Damascus road he becomes Paul, the apostle to the Gentiles. Those who take to themselves God's revelation in Jesus Christ are conformed to his image and receive his name.

II. God's revelation in history

A. THE HISTORY OF SALVATION

14. That God reveals himself in history is a central theme in the church's preaching and teaching, referring as it does to the events which made Israel a people through whom all the nations would be blessed. Some events in particular are emphasized, such as the call of Abraham, the exodus and Sinai events, settling in the promised land and returning from captivity in Babylon. These are seen as paradigmatic manifestations of God as Creator, Redeemer, Sustainer and Liberator.

15. It is important to note, however, two things.

First, that these occurrences by themselves did not necessarily amount to revelation. It was not always clear at the time who this self-revealing God was or what the events implied for the way the participants were to respond. Did the Egyptians acknowledge God's hand in the Exodus? "Is the Lord among us or not?" the people demanded of Moses in the wilderness (Ex. 17:7). How could they sing the Lord's song in the alien Babylon? Thus, along with occurrence there was needed the interpreting word – sometimes directly from God, more often through the prophets, and especially in the Torah with its commandments from God revealing his will.

Second, the history in which God is revealed is not limited to these special events. God is present in all history – to Israel as judge even when it seems he has deserted them; Lord over all the nations even if they do not acknowledge him; reflected in creation even if not clearly perceived; imaged in his human creatures even if they have distorted that image.

16. Revelation then has this comprehensive relation to history; for those who have eyes to see and hearts to know, the destiny of all individuals and nations is with the

Creator-God, and will be fulfilled when his day comes, unexpected through the terms of such a day may be, as Amos reminds us (cf. 5:18).

B. JESUS CHRIST, THE DECISIVE EVENT OF REVELATION

17. The New Testament writers affirm, in their different ways, that God's self-revelation in history reaches its climax in Jesus Christ. In his life, death and resurrection he reveals God in a unique way. Jesus does more than announce and point to the coming kingdom; in his powerful deeds and life of loving obedience to the Father, the kingdom is already present (Luke). As proclaimer of the word he is more than the last in a long line of prophets, more even than the prophet whose coming would herald the last days; he conveys the word of God by being its embodiment (John). He is greater than priests and angels, as well as prophets; he is the eternal Son through whom the world was founded and to whom all things are now in subjection (Hebrews).

18. In echoing the same theme Paul continues the image of "uncovering that which has been concealed". In Jesus is unveiled the mystery previously hidden of God's purpose that all nations might be brought to obedience (cf. Rom. 16:25). And Jesus does more than simply announce this intention; he reveals God's righteous purpose by fulfilling it, dying so that even the ungodly may be reconciled to God (cf. Rom. 5:7-8) and that the reordering of the whole cosmos may begin (cf. Col. 1:18-20).

C. REVELATION AS WORD AND ACT

19. It is obvious that it is only because of these earliest witnesses to Jesus that we know him as the self-revelation of God. We are dependent upon those who came to faith in him at the time and spread the word about him, on those who later wrote their accounts not just of what happened but of its meanings and significance, and on those in the community of faith from then until now – lively and faithful interpreters of the tradition.

20. Significantly, this link between event and interpreting word goes back to the actions and speech of Jesus. Reading the gospels, we see that his words and mighty deeds became witnesses to Jesus himself, inviting people to recognize in him the power and authority of God.

21. So, for example, Jesus' ethical teachings on murder and adultery call not just for renunciation of anger and lust but for decision about who it is that claims authority to go beyond earlier authorities, and hence decision about whether Jesus is to be accepted as authentic revealer of God. In the same way, Jesus' healing miracles come to bear witness to him as they call for faith, not just so that they will work but so that he will be recognized as exercising power and authority from none other than God. Along with the deed, therefore, goes the interpreting word. The casting out of the demon, for example, is linked with Jesus' authority as teacher (cf. Mark 1:21-28); healing the paralytic goes along with his authoritative word of forgiveness (cf. Mark 2:1-12); the implication of his healing on the sabbath is made clear by his word "the Son of Man is Lord even of the sabbath" (Mark 2:28). John too makes it clear that the revelation occurs when deed and word are brought together: the feeding of the multitude with "I am the bread of life" (John 6); healing the blind man with "I am the light of the world" (John 9); the raising of Lazarus with "I am the resurrection and the life" (John 11). Thus the words and the deeds of Jesus alike gain their full significance from their source and power in God.

22. God's purpose was also made known through those who came to have faith in Jesus. As the believing community proclaimed the gospel of God's love revealed in Jesus the Christ and manifested the gifts of the Spirit in their lives, other people came to believe in Jesus, to know his risen presence and to follow his way. This revelation comes not simply through words but also by what believers have become through their calling by Jesus and empowering by the Holy Spirit. "The light of the knowledge of the glory of God in the face of Christ" that has come to Paul and the others now shines through them, earthen vessels though they are, so that the transcendent power may be known, so that "the life of Jesus may be manifested" (2 Cor. 4:5-10; cf. 1 Thess. 1:5).

23. So it is in the ongoing life of the church. When there is faithful witness to Jesus Christ, people hear through the words of witness the word of God and know through deeds of love the God of love. To such witness in word and deed all the faithful are called, but not in isolation from each other. To be "in Christ" is already to belong not only to him but also to the whole company of believers that lives by his grace. From the beginning of his ministry Jesus called others to him in order to embody God's loving purpose for the world. So Paul, after the resurrection, was able to call the church both the body of Christ and the community of the Holy Spirit.

III. Revelation of God: Father, Son and Holy Spirit

24. From the beginning, the disciples of Jesus recognized that his life and work could not be accounted for in merely human terms. So the questions arose: What was his relation to the Maker of heaven and earth? And to the Spirit who moved over the waters at creation and inspired the words and actions of the prophets? Integrally related to these questions about his person were others about his work: What has he done? How are his death and resurrection God's work for our salvation?

25. The biblical witness has led the church to the conviction that Father and Son and Spirit were giving themselves for the redemption of us all. On the cross Jesus suffered and died, evoking the Father's compassion as his Son endured the full extent of human alienation in order to redeem it. Just as we see Jesus' relation to the one he called Father in sharpest focus around his death, so his relation to the Spirit is clearly seen in the witness to his life. It was by the Spirit that he was conceived, anointed at baptism for his vocation as Son, and led into the wilderness to face the alternative ways, advocated by the Tempter, of being Son. In the Spirit he taught; by the Spirit he healed and so revealed the presence of the kingdom; with the Spirit he endowed his followers for their ministry in his name.

26. This testimony to the life of Jesus, as part of the history of Father, Son and Holy Spirit, is confirmed by the resurrection. For the resurrection testifies both to the victory of the Father, who raised Jesus from darkness and death, and to the power of the Spirit, who conforms believers to the image of Christ. Living in the presence of the risen Lord, we know by faith the transforming power of the Holy Spirit and are enabled to live as grateful children of the Father. Thus the church gives glory to the one God, Father, Son and Holy Spirit.

SECTION TWO: FAITH

27. God's revelation is received by the faith it prompts; and the act of faith is traditionally styled "the faith by which we believe" *(fides qua creditur)*. Correspondingly,

believing faith is directed towards God, the story of his revelation, its results and its expected completion; and the content of faith is styled "the faith which is believed" *(fides quae creditur)*. As living response to the living God, faith grows and produces fruits, its authenticity being tested in a process of discernment. These three facets of faith are treated in what follows: the faith by which we believe, the faith which is believed, and the fruitfulness of faith.

I. The faith by which we believe

28. The gospel invites all human beings to join the first disciples in receiving God's revelation in Jesus Christ. It is in a situation of sin that his revelation is received. All of humanity has been so infected by self-centredness, self-reliance and the search for false gods that, facing the total holiness of Jesus, humanity is seen as having sinned in Adam. The basic sinfulness is experienced in many ways, and especially in the insecurity and distress that follow a continual failure to do good and a recurrent choice of what is evil. In the midst of this sinfulness, Jesus comes as the only Saviour, God's revelation acquires the dimension of redemption, and faith is offered by the Spirit as saving faith, by which those who believe the gospel receive forgiveness, justification, sanctification, and all the graces that are needed to persevere in God's ways.

29. Individual believers profess this saving faith as members of a community, the community of those who, like Mary at the annunciation (cf. Luke 1:38), have consented to God's design for their life and who, like Peter, have confessed Jesus to be "the Christ, the Son of the Living God" (Matt. 16:16). The church, as the community of salvation, gathers in itself all those who have effectively been called "out of darkness into God's own marvellous light" (1 Pet. 2:9). Through sharing the word and participating in the sacraments of faith, the church's members experience the healing hand of Christ when they struggle with the many obstacles that scripture designates as the world, the flesh and the devil (cf. 1 John 2:13-16); and already they are given a taste of Christ's victory over death (cf. Heb. 6:4-5).

30. It is not by human power that the believers perceive the word addressed to them through Christ, believe it, and come to salvation (cf. Matt. 16:17). Faith is God's gift, which they accept. Finding in Jesus "the pioneer and perfecter of their faith, who for the joy that was set before him endured the cross" (Heb. 12:2), the faithful undergo conversion, learn fidelity and witness to the one they trust. They strive to practise a loving and willing obedience. Because they believe in Christ, they obey him. Because they hear and confess the truth of his revelation, they seek to live by it. Because they trust in his promises, they abandon themselves to God and they work towards the perfection to which they are called. In their life of fidelity and obedience, they are led by the prompting of the Holy Spirit.

31. While it is entirely God's gift, faith is inseparably a free act and an attitude of grateful reception of God's grace and revelation and of self-commitment to the living Lord, who from first to last is the guide of the faithful through the action of the Holy Spirit (cf. 1 Cor. 12:3). Freely given, it is freely received. As faith transforms human life it enables the mind to discern God's plan of salvation as this is described in the scriptures and delineated in the creeds in which the church has from time to time formulated its faith in unanimity of hearts and minds (cf. Acts 4:32). In this fidelity, revelation feeds the intellect with heartfelt convictions.

II. The faith which is believed

32. To speak in the same breath of faith "transforming human life" and "enabling the mind to discern God's plan", of "heartfelt conviction" and "feeding the intellect", of "unanimity of heart and mind" confirms the inseparability of the life of faith and statements of faith. The faith that receives God's revelation, the faith by which we believe, is more than a dimension of human feeling, accompanied through response that is shaped by the nature and being of God who gives himself in revelation. Thus what is believed is an integral part of faith, and it is this that gives content to that life of fidelity and obedience to which the faithful are led by the promptings of the Holy Spirit.

33. Already in the New Testament there is a clear link between the faith by which we believe, the faith which is believed, and the faithful action consistent with such belief. In the Letter to the Philippians (2:6-8), Paul includes an early hymn about Jesus Christ, "who, though he was in the form of God, did not count equality with God a thing to be grasped, but emptied himself, taking the form of a servant, being born in the likeness of men. And being found in human form he humbled himself and became obedient to death, even death on a cross." This was used, not only to enable Paul and the community to give unified verbal expression to their faith, but also to provide the pattern for their ongoing life as the body of Christ, obedient to the way of their living Lord. Thus, the affirmation of faith is prefaced with the words, "have this mind among yourselves which you have in Christ Jesus". The faith by which we believe and the faith which is believed come together in the life of faithful obedience.

34. Historically the church has always expressed this faith in credal form. As noted above, the affirmations in the Letter to the Philippians are made in the context of the giving of life to the believer. That the early church understood its own more formally developed statements of the faith in the same way is shown by its universal use of the name "symbol" for the creed. This reflected a common practice of the time when contracts were made. Each party took a piece of broken clay vessel, later to be fitted together to confirm the identity of the parties to the contract. These interlocked parts were called a symbol (from the Greek *symbolon*, a putting together). So, to call the creed "symbol" was to emphasize the way it brings together God's gift and the church's response, believers too being brought together by affirming the sign of having faith. Therefore, during the rites of initiation, the bishop gave the creed to persons to be baptized as a symbol of active participation in the believing community, to be reappropriated as the creed was recited thereafter within the context of worship.

35. Thus the creeds are one component, along with sacraments and authority, of what St Augustine considered the universally recognized ways *(catholica)* of taking to ourselves the self-giving of God in Christ. It is therefore a mistake to view the creeds simply as collections of propositional statements requiring no more than intellectual assent. They convey the gospel message in a way the Catholics and Methodists accept as authoritative and life-giving, as is shown by their being regularly prayed in the liturgy. For both our churches, therefore, what is believed is a matter of glad assurance, leading on to a path of faith to be followed.

36. In his *Letter to a Roman Catholic*, John Wesley affirms the faith to which true Protestants and true Catholics both subscribe, faith which is believed and faith by which we believe, leading on to faithful action. He follows the outline of the Nicene Creed: God the Father of all, who "of his own goodness created heaven and earth, and

all that is therein"; Jesus Christ, "conceived by the singular operation of the Holy Ghost and born of the blessed Virgin Mary", joining "the human nature with the divine in one person; dying on the cross, risen and ascended" as "Mediator till the end of the world"; "the infinite and eternal Spirit of God, equal with the Father and the Son,... not only perfectly holy in himself but the immediate cause of holiness in us"; the holy catholic church gathered by Christ through his apostles; the forgiveness, justification and resurrection of the faithful. Then Wesley goes on to insist on the practice of such faith by those who believe. Thus the appeal for unity, that Protestants and Catholics should "help each other on in whatever we are agreed leads to the kingdom", is based on the conviction that what is believed and affirmed in common must be embodied in the life both of the believer and the community of faith. It is with this conviction that Methodists and Catholics continue in dialogue, "that we may not fall short of the religion of love, and thus be condemned in what we ourselves approve". Faith is tested by the fruit it bears.

III. The fruitfulness of faith

A. THE GROWTH OF FAITH

37. The living response to the living God revealed in the Bible engages the whole person, and so we may speak of a variety of ways in which the response is lived and expressed within the church. We respond to God's self-disclosure not only by simple assent to what he has done for us in Christ but by a return to our original calling through a life of faith lived in history. Revelation is transmitted by people of flesh and blood in a variety of situations. This brings forth a creative and dynamic fruitfulness so that the church as a living body always develops new expressions of faith, hope and love.

1. History and development

38. In the course of its development, the Christian community has gained new insights into the revelation once given. The tradition shows its fruitfulness in the richly varied expression of these insights. Since this is a historical process, we are in a dialogue not only with our contemporaries but with our predecessors in the faith. We must hear what has already been said, and in doing so we recognize the dynamic character of revelation, as the past enters the present and prepares for the future. Coherent development illustrates the fruitfulness of revelation.

39. The church itself, as a seed which grows with support of the Holy Spirit and in response to God, has an inherent dynamic. There is no way of understanding the fruitfulness of revelation save in the community of faith. Development is an ecclesial process based on the experience and holiness of the faithful. It is seen by both Methodists and Catholics as a more comprehensive phenomenon than the development of doctrine. St John's gospel, in speaking of fruitfulness, points to ecclesial perspectives: the Father is the husbandman, Christ is the vine and we are his branches; and it is the Holy Spirit who will guide the community into the fullness of truth. Since the Holy Spirit shows the way, no limits can be set to God's assistance in this process. Developments as the fresh interpretation of faith means allowing our minds in each generation to be formed according to the mind which was in Christ Jesus.

2. The church and its environment

40. Since the church is made up of human beings, its growth in understanding takes place through human interaction. Christians exercise their freedom in creative dialogue with the world. Fruitfulness occurs not only as the result of the church's own internal pondering on its origin and destiny but also in response to external stimuli. The perception of the truth grows and is tested by the challenges of successive ages.

41. To live the gospel implies taking up those challenges, in the certainty that Jesus Christ is Lord of history and knowing that the Spirit of God is active in human life, inspiring and leading in the quest for justice, freedom, peace and human dignity. The church, as it shares in this human endeavour, under the guidance of the Holy Spirit and attentive to the word of God manifested in the scriptures and in its own historical experience, tries to identify what is good and should be defended and promoted, and to call attention to and resist ideas and courses of action opposed to the gospel and detrimental to human life. This process, which has always been present in the life of the churches, has been sometimes called "discerning the signs of the times".

42. The church often enters into discussion with different schools of thought as it considers new theories, questions and discoveries. It listens to friends, rivals and enemies. But there are times when it must also resist ideas that are opposed to the gospel. Revelation itself provides the motivation and guidance for this ministry of the word.

B. THE FRUITS OF FAITH

43. Faithfulness assumes many forms. They certainly include the following.

1. Confession

People have witnessed to their faith in Jesus Christ, the Incarnate Word, even to the point of martyrdom. In baptism this same faith has been confessed in the midst of the believing community. When necessity arose, the church formulated its belief through the Nicene-Constantinopolitan Creed. From time to time in subsequent centuries, synods and councils have again confessed the faith in formulas adapted to new circumstances and in new languages.

44. The developing fruitfulness of the faith has at times led to a refocusing of the understanding of the gospel. This was notably the case with confessions produced at the time of the Reformation, which centred on the experience of being justified by grace through faith. In them and in the subsequent teaching of the council of Trent, the Christian and trinitarian heart of the faith was placed in the context of the sovereign action of God alone in bringing sinners to justification and salvation.

45. The very fruitfulness of faith means it is also exposed to the diverse influences of the cultures and philosophies it encounters. The desire to increase faith by understanding and to protect it from variations and deviations has led to the formulation of doctrines. Some of these have served in turn as standards of faith and orthodoxy (as in the traditional creeds), while others have been used to build up theological systems that would be intellectually satisfying and would provide apologetical arguments for the defence and further proclamation of the faith. Different doctrinal emphases and diverse theological syntheses, however, have counted among the many facets that have estranged churches from one another and eventually led to conflicting doctrines and confessions. The attempt to overcome such estrangement ecumenically is itself a fruit of the continuing development of faith.

2. Spiritual life

46. The manifold fruitfulness of faith has been manifest at the level of thought, in the careful elaboration of doctrine, and also at the level of personal experience. The truths that are implied in the gospel have been sensed to be living truths leading to newness of life and to deep experiences of God in Christ, present in the heart by the testimony of the Spirit. Ways of spiritual life have been explored and described. The writings of the Syriac, Greek and Latin fathers, the monastic rules and the theology of the early middle ages, the more scholastic descriptions of ways of ascent to God, the documents of the *devotio moderna* at the time of the Renaissance, are monuments and instruments of the fruitfulness of faith. As they discovered and followed the examples of great saints, the faithful have explored new paths to God and found new evidences of the divine presence in their lives, in the community and in the world around them. For example, the Virgin Mary, *theotokos*, has come to be seen, especially by the Orthodox and Catholic tradition, as an icon of the companion in pilgrimage. Devotion to a disciplined life of prayer and commitment to the works of mercy stood at the origin of the Methodist movement. The untiring efforts of John Wesley to proclaim the gospel to all, especially the neglected and the poor, and to call them to a life of holiness and a desire for perfection, were themselves a precious evidence of the fruitfulness of faith.

47. Devotion is the form that faith takes in prayer. It inspires new life and manifests the Spirit's enablement of weak human wills to do good. It leads on to discipline, when the desire to follow the Lord organizes personal life, regulates the use of resources, and places personal enthusiasm and passion at the service of the gospel.

48. In the search for perfection, Christians have found help from outside the Christian tradition, formerly in neo-platonism and recently, for example, in various Asian schools of wisdom. This has not been without its dangers. Yet sources of spiritual life and devotion to counterbalance the danger of deviation have always been available in scripture, especially in the New Testament and the psalms. Personal life and devotion find their proper setting in the light of the word faithfully preached and of the sacraments administered in accordance with the gospel. Thus faith, devotion and discipline are located within the worship and liturgy of the community.

3. Worship

49. In the presence of the self-revealing God, people feel awe and joy and are moved to express this in praise, prayer, confession and commitment. They wish to recall the message of grace they have heard; to celebrate the acts of God with words, gestures and song; to express in prayer their fears, needs and hopes; and to re-enact the story of salvation in liturgy and drama.

50. The scriptures amply attest the centrality of private and public worship for God's people. When God's revelation of himself came to its fulfilment in Jesus Christ, the people of the new covenant held on to their heritage of worship in a new way. The psalms became a hymnal for the Christian church; the passover meal acquired fuller meaning as a sacrament of salvation in Jesus Christ. Moreover, new hymns were formed (cf. Phil. 2:6-11; Col. 1:15-20), and baptism in the name of the triune God became the sign of new creation in Christ and incorporation in his body.

51. As the gospel spreads, entering new cultures, different languages and expressions are used and the church's worship is enriched and diversified. The church welcomes both developments in liturgical traditions and new and spontaneous expressions

of faith and worship as signs of the fruitfulness of God's message and the ever-present action of the Holy Spirit. At the same time the church seeks to ensure that they are genuine manifestations of the Spirit and faithfully reflect and proclaim the gospel.

4. Service

52. The faithful community claims to follow the one who came not to be served but to serve (cf. Mark 10:45). The model for all ministry is found in the Lord himself. In his earthly ministry he proclaimed the coming kingdom and "went about doing good" (Acts 10:38) – healing the sick, calling the dispossessed and marginalized, demanding justice and restoring life. In a variety of ways the church not only proclaims the message with words but also ministers to the spiritual and material needs of all – in caring for the poor, the stranger and the neglected. This service of charity has been an essential part of its mission. Having experienced the loving mercy of God, the church also feels bound to denounce injustice and oppression, to work for peace, and to articulate the ethical consequences of God's love for humankind. To all cultures, the church offers the "leaven" of the gospel.

C. THE DISCERNMENT OF FAITH

53. It is the Holy Spirit who makes the revelation given in the very person of Jesus Christ fruitful for building up the church as a whole and for the spiritual journey of each of its members. The Holy Spirit is the source of all authentic discernment. "Do not quench the Spirit, do not despise prophesying, but test everything; hold fast what is good, abstain from every form of evil" (1 Thess. 5:19-22). There are several ways and means of "testing" all things, a variety of principles of discernment provided by the Spirit.

1. Criteria for discernment

1) Fidelity to scripture

54. Because the scriptures are the normative witness to the revelation in Christ, they are central to Christian discernment. The Christian believer must become acquainted with their content, reflect on their meaning and apply their teaching in daily life. "From childhood you have been acquainted with the sacred writings which are able to instruct you for salvation through faith in Christ Jesus. All scripture is inspired by God and profitable for teaching, for reproof, for correction, and for training in righteousness, that the man of God may be complete, equipped for every good work" (2 Tim. 3:15-17).

55. Fidelity to the scriptural word is also exercised by those who, in virtue of their ministry, assist the faithful in this scriptural discernment. Thus the Second Vatican Council stated that the "magisterium is not above God's word: it rather serves the word, teaching only what has been transmitted, as by divine mandate and with the Holy Spirit's assistance, it listens to God's word with piety, keeps it in awe and expounds it with fidelity" (*Dei Verbum*, §10). Wesley was able to spread scriptural holiness throughout the land because he made scriptural truth run with the oil, and burn with the fire, of the Holy Spirit.

2) *Sentire cum ecclesia*

56. This Latin phase is often used in Roman Catholic theology to denote an inner harmony between personal conviction in faith and the teaching of the church. The con-

viction is designated by a word for *feeling (sentire)* rather than for *thinking*, because it is a kind of spiritual instinct, antecedent to any discursive reflection on the truth to which it adheres or on rational proof of that truth. It derives not only from intellectual capacity, but also from moral uprightness and graced spiritual goodness.

57. Wesley was well aware of the paramount importance of such conviction for giving living witness to the basic Christian doctrines handed on from generation to generation by the church. Contemporary divines frequently accused him of irresponsibility in authorizing for preaching men whom they regarded as theological ignoramuses. He retorted that a morally upright tradesman who prayerfully frequents the scriptures can much more easily attain that level of conviction indispensable for effective witness and preaching than a dissolute clergyman who relies on a purely academic biblical and theological expertise. Wesley knew that, in the mind and the heart of the deeply convinced Christian believer, the Holy Spirit is ever at work, bonding the exercise of particular spiritual gifts into unity with the exercise of complementary gifts in all the other members of the body of Christ, the church.

58. In the perspective of Vatican II, this action of the Spirit brings about an interdependence in communion between the spiritual instinct of the whole body of the faithful and those who are empowered to make normative acts of discernment of what is, or is not, faithful to Christian Tradition. "Thus the remarkable harmony of bishops and faithful comes into being in the preservation, the practice and the confession of the traditional faith" (*DV*, §10). The Latin for "harmony" is *con-spiratio*, that is, a "convergence of inspiration", brought about by the Holy Spirit between the *sentire* of the faithful and discernment by the magisterium.

3) Reception

59. One criterion by which new developments in Christian teaching or living may be judged consonant with the gospel is their long-term reception by the wider church. Such reception sometimes will take place in theological discussion and sometimes in the practical life of the local churches or of the individual believer. In every case reception of what is true is a spiritual process. The deep conviction of gaining the truth, however, can be an occasion for struggle and separation, when conflicting opinions claim to be true. The process of reception, therefore, calls also for a careful listening to the insights of others. Only the truth itself brings about conformity to Christ in the Spirit. To be anointed with scriptural truth by the Spirit of Jesus (cf. 1 John 2:20-21) is to let his truth seep into every area of Christian living. It is to assimilate it into the very being of the church and its members, to receive it in the fullest sense of the word. Those who are rooted in the biblical truth by the work of the Spirit not only know the truth, but they know that they know it.

4) By their fruits

60. Conformity in deep conviction to Christian doctrinal and moral truth bears fruit in holiness. It produces that spiritual holiness which, in his successive descriptions of the character of a Methodist, Wesley so often described as "walking even as Christ walked". This vital link between truth and holiness makes holiness a criterion of the existence of truth in the process of interpretation and development of doctrine. This process involves not just one individual but whole generations in succession to one another. Towards the end of his life, Wesley attempted several times a history of the

Methodist movement. He considered that the truth of the most precious insights of Methodism was demonstrated by the flowering of scriptural holiness in every part of the land. The quality of Methodism's fruits proved the health of the original tree.

61. The Second Vatican Council speaks of a growth in insight into what is passed on by Christian Tradition, coming about through a pondering which unites the heart and the head, in a way characteristic of the *sentire cum ecclesia* referred to earlier. Growth in insight "comes through the contemplation and study of believers who ponder these things in their hearts (cf. Luke 2:19 and 51)" (*DV*, §8). There must be growth in love to achieve more insightful knowledge of the riches of faith. In other words, there must be growth in holiness. Holiness is therefore an ecclesial life; it is a source of such development in its forming of the convictions and insights of believers and their interaction on each other.

2. Agents of discernment

62. The criteria by which the church discerns the will of God have been applied in several ways and at several levels of the life of the people of God. One may list the following:

1) Discernment by the people of God

63. According to scripture the discernment of God's will is the task of the whole people of God. The admonition to prove and to approve *(dokimazein)* what is good in the eyes of God is a major theme within the letters of the apostles (cf. Rom. 12:2; Eph. 5:10-17; Phil. 1:9f.; 1 Thess. 5:21; 1 John 4:1f.). Paul prays for the church in Philippi, "that your love may abound more and more, with knowledge and all discernment, so that you may approve what is excellent, and may be pure and blameless for the day of Christ, filled with the fruits of righteousness which come through Jesus Christ, to the glory and praise of God" (Phil. 1:9). The people of God in their daily life have "to learn what is pleasing to the Lord" (Eph. 5:10) and what will meet the needs of their neighbours. In this discernment, God's love is the leading power, and the needs of the community of the believers and the sufferings of the people around them are pointers to the right direction. Such active openness in love to the very truth which is Jesus and to the disinherited people of their times drove many of the saints in our two communions to new forms of piety and service in the world. By this kind of discernment, Wesley taught that it was not enough that masters should treat their slaves justly and fairly, but that it was God's will that slavery be abolished.

2) Prophetic discernment

64. At times in the history of the people of God, shepherds and flock have gone astray. Through the prophets God called his people back to the way. This was not only true for Israel but also for the church of the New Testament. The letters to the seven churches witness to the exalted Lord telling his church what to do and what to abstain from (cf. Rev. 1:4-3:22). In the history of the church, prophetic voices of warning and admonition have arisen, some of which were readily listened to and some not. The prophetic call is not based on approval by official authorities or on reception by the whole people of God. It claims to be directly authorized by God.

65. Because there have been cases of false prophecy, St Paul refers to the necessity of "discerning spirits", distinguishing between spirits (cf. 1 Cor. 12:10) and weighing

what is said by prophets (cf. 1 Cor. 14:29). The gift of prophecy should be exercised according to the analogy of faith (cf. Rom 12:6), in accordance with the basic truth of the apostolic message. Wesley saw such an "analogy of faith" in the basic subjects of biblical preaching: original sin, justification by faith, and present inward salvation. This may be related to the christological criterion: "Every spirit which confesses that Jesus Christ has come in the flesh is from God, and every spirit which does not confess Jesus is not of God" (1 John 4:2-3). God's saving and redeeming act has in fact reached human nature and existence in their entirety. This is what links faith in the incarnation of Christ with the message of the justification and sanctification of sinners by faith through God's saving grace. This is the criterion, this is the "analogy of faith", according to which prophecy should be exercised and tested.

66. The difficulty of "weighing" or even "discerning" the words of prophets has to be acknowledged, but this should not diminish the challenge to listen to prophetic voices. This difficulty has sometimes occasioned divisions, and it is only with hindsight that those who have been so divided have been able to begin to distinguish the true from the false in what was at issue.

3) Pastoral discernment

67. There are times when the church needs a formal decision about whether some doctrines are right or wrong, or which actions are appropriate to the needs of the time as well as to the calling of the church. Already the Acts of the Apostles tells us that the "apostles and the elders gathered together to consider this matter" (15:6). It is the common belief of our churches that there are those who are authorized to speak for the church as a whole and who, after having carefully listened to scripture and Tradition and the experience of believers trying to live out the gospel, and after a reasonable and prayerful discussion, may say "it has seemed good to the Holy Spirit and to us" (Acts 15:28a; cf. 1 Cor. 7:40b).

68. Both the Roman Catholic Church and the Methodist churches hold that the first ecumenical councils defined a fundamental, genuine and valid formulation and interpretation of the apostolic faith.

69. Within the Roman Catholic Church, the teaching office of the bishops in unity with the bishop of Rome is exercised in the name of Jesus Christ. While their teaching office "is not superior to the word of God, but is its servant" (*DV*, §10), the bishops "have received the sure charism of truth", which may authorize them to define the doctrines drawn from the divine revelation.

70. Within Methodism, the teaching office is exercised by the conferences. When Wesley in 1744 first met with some of his preachers for such a conference, he asked them to decide on the following questions: (1) what to teach, (2) how to teach, (3) what to do. Basic for the decision was the testimony of scripture, but they also looked into the treasures of Christian tradition, especially from the earliest times, and they listened to the experience of those engaged in the work of evangelism and reflected rationally on the questions facing them. On this basis and with these guidelines in mind, Methodist conferences discern what God wants to be preached and done in today's world.

71. The differences between these approaches and their implications for the communion of faith will have to be dealt with at a later stage of the dialogue between Methodists and Catholics.

4) Convergence in discernment

72. St Paul himself writes to the Corinthian church with which he is in controversy over the interpretation of the gospel: "Not that we lord it over faith; we work with you for your joy, for you stand firm in your faith" (2 Cor. 1:24). Every formal expression of pastoral authority, whether the teaching office of the bishops or the power of councils, synods and conferences, and every expression of prophetic challenge, is to serve the upbuilding of the whole people of God under the lordship of Christ himself. This should lead to a growing interdependence and mutual recognition of those who exercise pastoral authority within the church, those who offer prophetic vision, and all those who, by their response to revelation and their inspiration through the creative love of God, participate in the active tradition of the gospel and compassionate discernment of the will of God for his church and the world.

SECTION THREE: MISSION

I. The mission of the church comes from God

A. THE SOURCE OF MISSION

73. The church's missionary activity takes many forms but ultimately has only one source. Mission springs from the triune God's loving design for all humanity. God's act of creating and his concern for his creatures are expressions of his outgoing love. When the Father chose to make himself known, and when he revealed and inaugurated his loving purpose for a world marked by sin, he did this through sending his Son and the Holy Spirit. "When the fullness of time had come, God sent his Son" and "the Spirit of his Son" (Gal. 4:4-6). In many places in St John's gospel Jesus is designated as the one "the Father has sent" and he himself promises that the Father and he will send the Spirit. It is, therefore, a fundamental Christian conviction that the very nature of the church is missionary, and that the church's mission is none other than a sharing in the continuing mission of the Son and the Holy Spirit expressing the Father's love for all humankind.

B. COMMISSIONED BY CHRIST

74. The risen Christ himself calls on those who follow him to share in his mission. Addressing his disciples, he says: "As the Father sent me, so I send you" (John 20:21). They are to carry forward his once-for-all redemptive mission in space and time, to all peoples and all ages. He prays also "on behalf of those who will believe in [him] through their word" (John 17:20-23). They must all be sanctified by his truth, holding fast to what the Word himself has given them (John 17:17; 17:14). As they proclaim Jesus Christ, whose person and mission were totally one, those who follow him spend themselves even to the point of laying down their lives for the gospel.

C. MISSION EMPOWERED BY THE HOLY SPIRIT

75. Such participation in the mission of Christ is possible only because of the outpouring of the Holy Spirit. The infant church, gathered behind closed doors, was empowered to go out and speak effectively of the mighty deeds God had done through Jesus Christ only after it had received the Holy Spirit at Pentecost (Acts 2; cf. Luke 24:48-49; cf. also John 20:22). What happened in Jesus Christ, in a particular time and

place, is henceforward communicated to people of every language and culture. In the Spirit, the proclaiming community itself becomes a living gospel for all to hear.

D. THE BAPTIZED AND MISSION

76. The great commissioning at the end of St Matthew's gospel is addressed to the apostles and to all who will share their faith (Matt. 28:16-20). All nations are to come to the fullness of life in the triune God in whose name they will be baptized. Those who accept the gospel will become members of the body of Christ, and a dwelling place of the Holy Spirit, knowing and loving God as their Father. As they are united with Christ, they are also joined to his mission. All aspects of their common life serve to build up the body and its members in holiness. They are thereby enabled to reach out in word and witness to all who have not yet heard the gospel.

II. Mission: word and act

77. Jesus' mission was to proclaim God's saving acts: "The Spirit of the Lord is upon me, because he has anointed me to preach good news to the poor. He has sent me to proclaim release to the captives and recovering of sight to the blind, to set at liberty those who are oppressed, to proclaim the acceptable year of the Lord" (Luke 4:18-19). Jesus was sent to announce that God was coming to release the people from captivity to the powers of evil, sin and death and to heal their suffering and wounds. What Jesus said, he did. He set those free who were possessed by evil spirits and released those who suffered from guilt and alienation. On the other hand, his preaching reached beyond the present moment. In blessing the poor he gave them the assurance that God was with them and his kingdom would belong to them.

78. Because the ministry of the church derives from the mission of Jesus, his ministry must serve as the paradigm for the mission of the church. The church proclaims what God has done to save humankind through the life, death and resurrection of Jesus Christ. He is the Word of life, which God has spoken; he is the witness to all human beings that God has come and, from within their limitations, shared the abundance of his love. Taking upon himself the burden and curse of the law, he reconciled us to God and took away our sins, making peace by the blood of his cross. To proclaim God's love in Jesus Christ is more than to remember and tell the story of Jesus and what he has done for us; wherever this story is told, those who hear are empowered by the Holy Spirit to open their hearts to the love of God so that they may live in a community of love, reconciliation and peace.

79. People who have experienced God's faithfulness and righteousness will share what they have received by deeds of mercy and justice. Moreover, they will seek to shape society according to the pattern of the kingdom of God. Theirs is the fellowship of the new creation, of which they have received a foretaste by the gift of the Holy Spirit. Never claiming to build the kingdom by their own efforts, they will give all the glory to God.

80. Every facet of the church's mission – witness, service and worship – embraces both word and act:
– Witness requires the public proclamation of the gospel, telling the story and inviting response and acceptance. It includes testimony from person to person and the silent and yet telling faithfulness of those who suffer and even die for their Lord and his love.

- Service is expressed in care for the sick and needy and all who long for healing; in counselling the troubled; in advocacy for the poor; and in work for peace, justice and the preservation of creation.
- In worship, the manifold gifts of God's grace are celebrated within the body of Christ. The community that gathers around word and sacrament draws into fellowship people from different backgrounds, with different abilities and gifts, all being made one in Jesus Christ.

All this has been recognized in both our traditions at their best. But we often fall short in practice of what we maintain in principle. This gives a reason for repentance and change of heart, for the integrity of the gospel demands our full commitment to witness, service and worship.

III. Mission and community

81. Since the church is missionary by its very nature, mission is by its very nature ecclesial. Built by the Holy Spirit, the community will be the instrument for the proclamation and acting out of the gospel, the place where people will grow in faith and holiness, and a paradigm of the new life of joy, peace, solidarity and service which Jesus Christ offers to all humankind.

82. The church's mission involves prophetic and priestly service. Its message relays God's demand for mercy, justice and peace in human society, particularly in regard to the weakest and the least privileged. In a world of brokenness and estrangement, the Christian fellowship, as a community of acceptance, forgiveness, freedom and love, can function as a sacrament of Christ's healing presence.

83. The existence of such a community is the fruit of the Spirit who gathers, sustains, nourishes and endows the faithful with the diverse gifts which enable them to witness to the gospel. This requires that the community and its members make constant use of the means of grace God has provided, not least among which are ecumenical sharing, fellowship and cooperation. Through these means all are called to daily repentance, continual renewal and the search for holiness. Being thus strengthened by the Spirit, the faithful witness to Christ by word, example and action, even as they are scattered into the world for their daily life and duties. In turn, their witness, shared in fellowship, prayer and praise, builds, strengthens and deepens the community.

IV. The apostolic mission

84. The whole people of God has been sent by Christ into the world to witness to the love of the Father in the power of the Holy Spirit. In this sense it is apostolic. All its members are gifted by the Spirit, and there is no gift without its corresponding service. Within that service of the whole there has been, from the beginning, a ministry uniquely called and empowered to build up the body of Christ in love. This is "apostolic" in the specific sense, because it began with Christ's choosing from among his disciples the twelve "whom he named apostles" (Luke 6:13). It has continued through the ages in those who follow them in that ministry. After his death and resurrection Christ confirmed the commission of the apostles and sent them out as messengers by whom the gospel, spoken and lived, would be preserved and proclaimed throughout the whole world (cf. Matt. 28:19-20). Their consistent witness, in obedience, was to be a sign of the continuing presence of Christ (cf. Acts 1:8). In the mission of the church, their special place has been remembered and acknowledged. The first history of the

spread of Christ's teaching is entitled the Acts of the Apostles; the baptismal confession is called the Apostles' Creed; the handing-on of that faith from generation to generation is known as the apostolic tradition.

85. In their imperfections, their slowness of understanding and their wavering faith, as well as in their ultimate loyalty, the apostles are representative of the humanity Christ came to save. Their life with him became a model for the life of the church; they began to grasp the revelation; they were held together by a common hearing of the word; they were sent out with a common purpose, to enable all teaching; the recognizable pattern of their fellowship (Acts 2:41-47) has persisted in the life of the church.

86. The church is like a living cell with Christ as its centre; the community, as it grows and multiplies, retains its original pattern. Apostolic communities need people to do for their own time what the apostles did in theirs: to pastor, teach and minister under the authority of the Good Shepherd and Teacher, the Servant Lord.

87. All those to whom the apostles transmit their faith have a share in their work. All are called to witness. All are called to glorify God and intercede for the world. All are called to serve their neighbour.

88. In the Methodist and Catholic churches some receive by ordination a special calling and are consecrated and authorized to proclaim and teach the gospel of God's love in Jesus Christ, to lead the worshipping community to the throne of grace and administer the sacramental gifts of God, and to guide the life of the church, its care for the needy, and its missionary outreach. In the Catholic tradition, these tasks are entrusted to the bishops ordained in the apostolic succession, along with their presbyters and deacons. In the Methodist tradition, following Wesley, ordained ministry is held to be in succession to the apostles, although not dependent in the same way on the succession of bishops.

V. Mission and ecumenism

89. The gospel of reconciliation requires a reconciled and reconciling community. The Christian churches are not yet able to carry out God's mission in unity, and this is a serious obstacle to mission. We acknowledge gratefully the fruits that our ecumenical relationships have brought in building up our communities for mission and in the missionary activity of our churches. Our churches should take every opportunity for cooperation, and work and pray to overcome the difficulties which stand in the way. We should explore the possibilities for cooperation in service and, whenever possible, in proclamation. The more we overcome differences in doctrine and polity, the stronger will be our witness and the easier it will be to avoid even the suggestion of proselytism. Nearly thirty years of dialogue between Catholics and Methodists have revealed sufficient agreement in faith for our churches to recognize integrity and faithfulness in each other's proclamation of the gospel. While large areas of agreement between Roman Catholics and Methodists about our responsibilities in society make much common action possible, differences remain concerning some areas of personal and social ethics. A careful and responsible dialogue about those differences would be fruitful, not only for our churches but for our mission in society.

VI. Mission and cultures

90. According to both Methodists and Catholics, the message of the gospel is meant for all times. It transcends all cultures. Yet the gospel – which arose in a Palestinian

matrix – has been announced in the languages of many cultures. Since salvation is intended for people where they are, it is relevant to all cultures, and it should be proclaimed in ways that are appropriate to each. Evangelization as proclamation of the gospel is clearly distinct from inter-religious dialogue, in which competent Christians meet with members of other religions in order to reach better mutual understanding. Yet inter-religious dialogue itself pertains to the process of mission and the inculturation of the gospel, since evangelization brings Christians into contact with cultures that have been largely shaped by other religions.

91. One may see a certain analogy between the mystery of the incarnation and the inculturation of the gospel. The culture that the gospel ought to enter and transform has, as it were, a body and a soul. The body of a culture includes the web of social, economic and political structures that provide the stability without which the higher forms of creativity could not develop. These forms – intellectual, artistic, religious – are like the soul of a culture, a response to the attraction of truth, beauty and goodness for the human spirit. They come from a thirst for a spiritual fullness which no merely human values can provide.

92. Both the Christian evangelist and the converts coming from non-Christian religions are challenged with an unavoidable process of discernment. What in the cultural values, rooted in religious aspirations, are authentic expressions of the movement of transcendence towards the absolute truth and goodness of God? What are the deviations from it, imposing limitations on it, or even wounding some of the deepest aspirations of the human heart?

93. The evangelist must never seek to impose the answer to this question. He must have with his hearers the patience which God showed to his people in the Old Testament. Through the prophets, God gave a partial revelation of his saving purpose for the human race before finally communicating the fullness of that purpose in the gift of his only Son (Heb. 1:1-2; John 3:16). In any case the direct proclamation of the message should not be abandoned. Inter-religious dialogue is not a substitute for evangelization, which remains an imperative of the gospel.

SECTION FOUR: SACRAMENTAL LIFE

I. The mystery of God in Christ and the church

94. In its 1991 report on "The Apostolic Tradition", the commission sensed the need for deeper common reflection on the nature of sacrament, starting from the idea of Christ himself as "the primary sacrament" (§89). Bearing in mind that one of the oldest names for sacrament is "mystery" *(mysterion)*, Christians find a direct scriptural basis for viewing Christ in this way in 1 Timothy 3:16, where Christ is referred to as "the mystery of our religion":

> He was manifested in the flesh,
> vindicated in the spirit,
> seen by angels,
> preached among the nations,
> believed on in the world,
> taken up in glory.

95. The "mystery" of God is God's eternal purpose, which has now been revealed in the person and work of Jesus Christ, a saving design which embraces Jew and Gen-

tile alike in the goodness of God's final kingdom (Mark 4:11; Rom. 16:25-27; 1 Cor. 2:7-10; Eph. 3:1-20; Col. 1:25-27; 2:2-3). Christ is "the image of the invisible God" (Col. 1:15), the Father's Son upon whom the Holy Spirit always rests (John 1:33). Having taken our humanity into his own person, the Son is both the sign of our salvation and the instrument by which it is achieved.

96. As the company of those who have been incorporated into Christ and nourished by the life-giving Holy Spirit (1 Cor 12:13), the church may analogously be thought of in a sacramental way. Precisely as the body of Christ and the community of the Holy Spirit, the church may be spoken of "as a kind of sacrament, both as an outward manifestation of God's grace among us and as signifying in some way the grace and call to salvation addressed by God to the whole human race."[1] Constituted by God's saving grace, the church becomes the instrument for extending the divine offer as widely as the scope of God's eternal purpose for humankind.

97. In such an approach, the sacraments of the church may be considered as particular instances of the divine mystery being revealed and made operative in the lives of the faithful. Instituted by Christ and made effective by the Spirit, sacraments bring the mystery home to those in whom God pleases to dwell.

98. The particular sacraments flow from the sacramental nature of God's self-communication to us in Christ. They are specific ways, in which, by the power of the Holy Spirit, the risen Jesus makes his saving presence and action effective in our midst. Thus, in his public ministry Jesus did not communicate the good news of our salvation in words alone; he addressed himself in signs and actions to those who came to him in faith. Moreover such signs and actions were addressed to both body and spirit. Thus, he healed the paralytic and forgave him his sins. After Christ's passion, death and resurrection, the Saviour continues his words and actions among us by means of sacramental signs.

99. There is a two-way connection between the church and the sacraments. On the one hand, the sacraments build up the church as the body of Christ until its members come to their full stature; on the other hand, the church is at work through the sacraments by virtue of the mission received from the Holy Spirit.

II. The sacraments and other means of grace

100. By virtue of their ecclesial nature, the sacraments are organically related to each other. In the celebration of the eucharist, as both word and table, the church is built up as the body of Christ. Into the eucharistic community one is admitted by baptism, which identifies the believer with the death and resurrection of Christ. Methodists and Catholics emphasize this vital connection between ecclesial communion and the sacraments of baptism and eucharist in different but analogous ways. Methodist affirm the full sacramental nature of the rites of baptism and eucharist, by attributing to Christ their direct institution. At the same time, they consider other Christian practices, listed by Wesley himself, to be specific means of grace. Catholics attribute primacy to baptism and eucharist among seven sacramental rites which sustain the life of faith.

101. It is our common belief that baptism is an action of God by which the baptized begin their life with Christ the Redeemer and participate in his death and resurrection. As Christ is received in faith, original sin is erased, sins are forgiven, the baptized are justified in the eyes of God and become a new creation; with all believers they share the communion of the Spirit; and they are called to seek perfection in hope and in love

through faithful response to God's continuing gifts of grace. Through the ministry of the church, baptism is given with water "in the name of the Father, the Son and the Holy Spirit". Baptism is irrevocable and is not repeated. While it is received in the context of a local church and in a specific Christian community, it introduces people into the universal church of Christ and the gathering of the saints.

102. With the whole Christian tradition, Methodists and Catholics find in the New Testament the evidence that baptism is the basic sacrament of the gospel. They also agree that Jesus Christ instituted the eucharist as a holy meal, the memorial of his sacrifice. As the baptized partake of it they share the sacrament of his body given for them and his blood shed for them; they present and plead his sacrifice before God the Father; and they receive the fruits of it in faith. Proclaiming, in his risen presence, the death of the Lord until he comes, the eucharistic assembly anticipates the final advent of Christ and enjoys a foretaste of the heavenly banquet prepared for all peoples. In the words of the Wesleys' *Hymns on the Lord's Supper*:

> He bids us eat and drink
> Imperishable food,
> He gives his flesh to be our meat,
> And bids us drink his blood:
> What'er the Almighty can
> To pardoned sinners give,
> The fullness of our God made man
> We here with Christ receive.[2]

103. Meanwhile, as believers we seek to enact throughout our lives that which we celebrate in the sacraments. Thus prayers of the Roman Missal ask that the sacraments received at Easter may "live forever in our minds and hearts", and that "we who have celebrated the Easter ceremonies may hold fast to them in life and conduct".[3]

104. Baptism, received once, and holy communion, received regularly in the church's liturgical festivals, are at the heart of the life of holiness to which the faithful are called. While they are the two biblical sacraments recognized by the Methodist tradition, the Catholic tradition regards other holy actions of the church as also sacraments of the gospel instituted by the Saviour: in them also God's grace reaches the faithful in keeping with some of the acts and words of Jesus to which the New Testament bears witness.

105. Catholics believe that in confirmation the gift of the Spirit confirms what was done in baptism. The faithful who are aware of sinning and are contrite have access to Christ the healer and forgiver in the sacrament of reconciliation. When they are sick, they also receive in the anointing the touch of Christ the healer. When they marry, they marry in the Lord through a sacrament of mutual communion, in which they are given an image of the communion of all the saints in Christ and a promise of the graces that are needed for the fidelity which they themselves promise. In the sacrament of orders, some of the believers are chosen and empowered to act for Christ in the spiritual guidance of the faithful through the preaching of the word and the administration of the sacraments. In all sacraments the power of the Spirit is at work, inviting the believers to closer union with their Redeemer, to the glory of God the Father.

106. Although Methodists do not recognize these rites as sacraments of the gospel, they too affirm the active presence of the Holy Spirit in the life of the faithful, the necessity of repentance for sins, the power of prayer for healing, the holiness of mar-

riage, and the enablement by the Spirit of those who are called and ordained for the tasks of the ministry.

107. Catholics and Methodists both recognize other "means of grace" than those they count as sacraments. These include public and private prayer, the reading of scripture, the singing of hymns, fasting, and what Methodists refer to as "Christian conversation". In the same category one may reckon the traditional works of mercy, such as visiting the sick and serving the poor. As the faithful meet the image of Christ in their neighbour, they acquire and develop a sense of the pervading sacramentality of the life of faith.

SECTION FIVE: KOINONIA–COMMUNION

I. Communion through the apostolic witness

108. The opening passage of St John's First Letter, already quoted to indicate what is meant by revelation (see introduction, §2), constitutes also the most complete statement of what the New Testament writers understand by the Greek word *koinonia* (communion). The beginning of the passage describes in poignant terms the privilege enjoyed by the apostles of intimate contact with the incarnate Son of God. St John wants us to grasp, albeit in our limited human perspective, something of the richness of the infinite and life-giving love which the Father has poured out on us in the sending of the Son and the Holy Spirit for our redemption and sanctification. He then addresses directly those whose discipleship of Christ is to bring them, throughout the ages and in union with the apostles, into an intimate sharing in the communion in love of the three persons of the Trinity: "that which we have seen and heard we proclaim also to you, so that you may have fellowship (koinonia) with us; and our fellowship (koinonia) is with the Father and with his Son Jesus Christ" (1 John 1:3).

109. It is of the essence of the church to be a sharing in this communion of love between the three persons of the Trinity. The phrase "communion with us" underlines that our own personal sharing in this love is inseparable from our communion with each other, because it is the nature of this love to bring about a mutual relationship between persons created in the image and likeness of the triune God. The "us" here referred to are those who have the responsibility of bringing the visible Christian community into being through an apostolic preaching which includes word and sacrament. The very existence of the church as a visible institution in this world becomes a manifestation of communion with the persons of the Trinity. Koinonia is thus both invisible and visible communion in love.

110. Entering into this koinonia involves travelling the road of the one whom the apostles heard, saw and touched. It means, to use other words of St John's Letter, which John Wesley never tired of repeating in his sermons, abiding in Christ and therefore in the Trinity, by walking even as Christ walked (cf. 1 John 2:6). It means entering into the glory of trinitarian love by the way of suffering characteristic of the paschal mystery. We can become, through the Holy Spirit, joint heirs of God with Christ, says St Paul, "if we suffer with him in order that we may also be glorified with him" (Rom. 8:17). In other words, the mystery of trinitarian communion in love, when it touches our lives, changes our way of living into conformity with Christ. The change must penetrate every area of our lives and, in particular, the practicalities of the service of others, by which Christ is still visible to us: "As you did it to one of the least of these my brethren, you did it to me" (Matt. 25:40).

II. Basic expressions of communion in our churches

111. Our life with the triune God and with one another is expressed in various embodiments of communion in our churches. To some extent our living of this communion is restricted to the still separate lives of our Catholic and Methodist communities. Our ultimate goal is that there should be full ecclesial communion between us. As a move in that direction, we should acknowledge some of the vital elements in the partial communion we already enjoy, while also delineating some of the problematic differences on which further work needs to be done.

A. Faith

112. As Roman Catholics and as Methodists we live from the same gospel, the apostolic message of God's saving acts in Jesus Christ, and we share the same faith. This faith is rooted in the scriptures, which are the common ground of our preaching and teaching as Christian churches. It is summarized by the creeds of the early church, especially the Apostles' Creed and the Nicene Creed, which we confess regularly in our worship.

113. But we share not only a common root or source of our faith; we recognize in each other the same readiness to respond to the proclamation of the gospel. In the past, Methodists tended to see the faith of Roman Catholics merely as an assent to what the church teaches, whereas Catholics sometimes thought Methodist belief to be a purely emotional personal conviction. These prejudices have been overcome. Faith is always personal but never private, for faith incorporates the believing individual into the community of faith. Therefore, his or her faith is both a personal conviction and also a sharing of what is held by the "community of the believers". At the same time, to believe in God and the salvation which he has wrought for us is the living response of the whole life of the believer and changes our lives in every respect; it is personal, living faith. Our traditions may stress the corporate and the individual aspects of faith differently, but both are common to us.

114. While we are agreed on the existence of a common faith between us (cf. §§32-36), problems arise when we seek to define the distinctive teachings which are necessary to constitute the full communion of faith which would unite our churches.

115. Methodists have learned from John Wesley to discern between, on the one hand, different "opinions" about manners of worship, about ecclesiastical polity, or even about the exposition of certain spiritual truths and, on the other, the essential doctrines of the gospel. "Opinions" are by no means unimportant and at least within the Methodist connection there should be as much agreement on them as possible. But for the communion of faith with other Christians, the unity in regard to the "essentials" is decisive, and not the differences of "opinions". Such essential doctrines are: the three-one God; the divine creation of the world and the vocation of humankind to holiness and happiness; the incarnation and atoning work of God the Son; the work of the Spirit as source of all truth, renewal and communion; the need of fallen humankind to repent and to believe the gospel; the divine provision of grace through word and sacrament and the institution and gathering of the church; the summons to love of God and neighbour; and the promise of a final judgment and victory, where all the redeemed will share in glorifying and enjoying God forever. The Methodist churches did not establish a fixed "canon" of these essentials of Christian faith; but whenever the question of the communion of faith with other churches is put, these elements will be vital for the conversation.

116. The Roman Catholic Church is at one with the Methodists over these essential doctrines, but emphasizes that the whole teaching of the church constitutes an organic unity. Its members are therefore called upon to believe the full teaching of the church. But within the ecumenical dialogue also the "'hierarchy of truths' of Catholic doctrine should always be respected; truths all demand due assent of faith, yet are not all equally central to the mystery revealed in Jesus Christ, since they vary in their connection with the foundation of the Christian faith".[4] This may be helpful when we discuss those doctrines which are important for the teaching and spirituality of the Catholic church, but which will not be easily accepted by Methodists, e.g., the teaching about Mary in relation to Christ and the church. We will be able to deal with controversial issues without concealing or diminishing what has been already achieved in a common understanding of the gospel despite some differences which still remain. These should be the subject of further investigation.

B. WORSHIP

117. Communion with God and with one another is lived and experienced by word and sacrament in the worship of the Christian community. In praise and prayer we share the wonderful deeds of God as well as all human joy and the needs which arise among us. Listening to the word of God brings us together as a community of those who look to God's creative and redemptive word for all their needs.

118. The sacramental life of the church expresses this communion with God and with one another in a profound way. The sacraments are at one and the same time effective signs of God's fellowship with his people and of the fellowship of the people of God with one another. Baptism and eucharist, the sacraments which are common to almost all Christian churches, show this most clearly. Those who are baptized receive a share in the death of the one Lord Jesus Christ and in the power of his resurrection; at the same time they are baptized into the one body, the body of Christ with its many members who suffer and rejoice together. At the table of the Lord's supper, the "cup of blessing" is "a participation in the body of Christ", therefore "we who are many are one body, for we all partake of the one bread" (1 Cor. 10:16-17). "Discerning the body" (1 Cor 11:29) means both to recognize the reality of our communion with Christ and to be responsible for the fellowship with brothers and sisters in the Lord.

119. We encourage ongoing discussion at the appointed levels wherever formal mutual recognition of baptism between our churches is still lacking. We are happy that this recognition has already taken place in many regions. Methodists welcome Roman Catholics to their celebration of the Lord's supper, but they have to respect the fact that participation in communion is still not permissible for Roman Catholics. In some pastoral circumstances Catholics are able to invite Methodists to take part in their eucharist.[5] The very desire of many people to take part at the Lord's table with Christians of other churches is a sign of a fellowship which looks forward with longing to a full communion not yet attained.

120. Roman Catholics and Methodists are agreed on the provision of an ordained ministry within the communion of the church to safeguard and foster its common life. Together we recognize that Christ the Good Shepherd shares his pastoral care with others. Those who are called to exercise this care in the ordained ministry receive their particular responsibility from him. They are appointed as witnesses to the living truth of the message entrusted to them, guides of the community that responds to the gospel they proclaim, and providers of the life of worship that should be offered in commu-

nion by the whole church. Yet the communion that we seek to establish between Roman Catholics and Methodists finds at this point its most visible obstacle: we cannot share in eucharistic communion because we identify differently the ministers who bear this corporate responsibility in space and time, and the kind of teaching authority committed to them. Progress towards full communion depends on the results that can be obtained from the study of this issue.

121. Behind our differences we thankfully confess that we are able to see common ground: all our sacramental life is rooted in Jesus Christ, the "primary sacrament", whose incarnation and death is the deepest sign of God's communion with all the anxieties and needs of humankind and whose life and resurrection is the model and the source of power for our living together in love and mutual compassion.

122. Christian worship is not only constituted by word and sacrament but also by the mutual care of brothers and sisters for one another and for all who are in need. "God's love has been poured into our hearts through the Holy Spirit" (Rom. 5:5), and this love binds us together and enables us to love our neighbour as ourselves. This aspect of Christian communion has been especially important for the Methodist movement since the days of John Wesley. Methodists have tried to fulfill this task in small groups gathering regularly for mutual confession, exhortation, encouragement and prayer. The forms have changed over the years, but the challenge to live this dimension of Christian fellowship is as urgent as ever. We are happy to see that in both our churches this task has been recognized and efforts have been made, sometimes jointly, to meet the need for such a worship in the midst of our daily life.

C. MISSION

123. Christian communion as koinonia necessarily includes communion in mission. It is communion with God, who sent his Son to reconcile the world and sent his Spirit to restore in human beings the image of God. Communion in mission is at the same time the fellowship of those who are sent by their risen Lord and who are empowered by his Spirit to be witnesses of God's love and peace throughout the world. Our proclaiming of God's love includes witness of word and deed, by preaching and serving, by struggling for justice and suffering with the oppressed. We draw attention to what we have already said above in section three.

124. We readily admit that in the past we have so often worked without one another or even against one another. This has weakened our witness and has hindered the mission of God. We seek God's forgiveness for our faults and our shortcomings.

125. We have found considerable convergence in our understanding of the church's mission in the world, such that increasingly Methodists and Catholics are able to work together for those they are called to serve. And we hope that communion in mission will also further our communion in worship and in faith. We work and pray for a growing communion between our churches, not because such unity is an end in itself, making life more comfortable and easy for us. Its goals are "that the world may believe" (John 17:21) and "that together [we] may with one voice glorify the God and Father of our Lord Jesus Christ" (Rom. 15:6).

III. The church universal

126. Christian communion is more than the fellowship of the members of the same congregation or the same local community. The church of God has universal dimen-

sions in regard to both time and space. Our Lord's prayer for his disciples, "that they may be one" (John 17:11) was not only meant to bring unity to these Christian disciples who lived together at the same time. When Jesus prayed "for those who believe in me through their word" (John 17:20), he spoke about the unity and continuity of the church throughout the generations. Communion means therefore also communion with the church of those who preceded us in the faith throughout the ages.

127. Although we may differ in our evaluations about what have been signs of faithfulness and perseverance in the church's history, we certainly agree that God's faithfulness has preserved his church despite the faults, errors and shortcomings evident in its history.

128. In the same way, we acknowledge the importance of a structure which binds together local churches to testify to the global nature of the gospel and of the church universal. But we have different perceptions about the nature and the theological weight of those structures.

129. The Roman Catholic Church relies on the promise which it believes to have been given to St Peter and the apostles (see, e.g., Matt. 16:18) and to have been fulfilled throughout history in the apostolic succession and the episcopal college together with its head, the bishop of Rome as the successor of St Peter. The hierarchical structure of the church is an important means and guarantee given by God's grace to preserve the continuity and the universality of the Catholic church.

130. Methodist churches see the continuity of the apostolic tradition preserved by the faithfulness to the apostolic teaching. The teaching office which decides what is faithful and what is not lies in the hands of conciliar bodies, the conferences. All Methodist churches recognize the necessity of a ministry of *episcope*, "oversight", and in many Methodist churches this is expressed in the office of bishop (cf. "Towards a Statement on the Church", §§31-34). Local churches are bound together by connexional structures which have to mediate the needs of local churches and of the church as a whole. Methodists anticipate that more unity and a growing communion between churches of different traditions may be achieved by new conciliar structures. Obviously, Roman Catholics and Methodists share a common concern regarding the church universal as an expression of communion in Christ. But they differ widely in their beliefs about the means which God has given to attain or preserve this goal. These differences may be the greatest hindrances on the way to full communion.

CONCLUSION

131. The joint commission between the Roman Catholic Church and the World Methodist Council has existed for thirty years. Its work has passed through at least two generations. The first need was for mutual acquaintance; and for a decade and more, the commission engaged in this by way of self-introduction and the preliminary tackling together of doctrinal, ethical and pastoral issues that were being faced on the wider ecumenical scene. A second state developed as the attempt was made to sketch broad theological perspectives, acceptable to both Roman Catholics and Methodists, in which it would eventually become possible to treat the matters which divide us. The commission believes that a considerable commonality of outlook has been established in the areas of pneumatology (1981 report), ecclesiology (1986 report), the apostolic tradition (1991 report), and now revelation and faith (1996 report).

132. The time may have come for concentration, in the directions thus shown, on some of those more detailed questions that have recurrently caused difficulty among us. In particular, future study could address the related topics of pastoral and doctrinal authority, the offices of oversight in the church and succession in them, and the offer made by Rome of a Petrine ministry in the service of unity and communion. We should thus be encouraged to pursue, more immediately and at a deeper level, the understanding that we both have of ourselves and of our partners in respect to the one church of Jesus Christ and the communion which belongs to the body of Christ.

NOTES

[1] "Towards a Statement on the Church", 1986, §9, referring to Vatican II's Dogmatic Constitution on the Church, *Lumen Gentium*, §1.
[2] John and Charles Wesley, *Hymns on the Lord's Supper*, 1745, no. 81.
[3] See the prayer after communion for the second Sunday of Easter *(ut paschalis perceptio sacramenti continua in nostris mentibus perseveret)*, and the opening prayer for Saturday in the seventh week of Easter *(ut qui paschalia festa peregimus haec moribus et vita teneamus)*.
[4] Pontifical Council for Promoting Christian Unity, *Directory for the Application of Principles and Norms on Ecumenism*, 1993, §75, cf. *Unitatis Redintegratio*, §11.
[5] See the principles and norms which Catholic bishops apply in this matter, in *Directory for the Applications of Principles and Norms on Ecumenism*, §§104-107,129-131.

XXIII. EASTERN ORTHODOX-ROMAN CATHOLIC DIALOGUE

Historical Introduction

The theological dialogue between the Orthodox and Roman Catholic churches began after long and fruitful preparation by: (1) official and unofficial ecclesial contacts and theological discussions; (2) the favourable decrees of the Second Vatican Council and the pan-Orthodox conferences; (3) the "dialogue of love" between the Old Rome and the New; and (4) the work of both the technical theological commissions and the joint coordinating committee. The official beginning of the theological dialogue was marked by the convening of the first meeting of this joint theological commission, held on Patmos and Rhodes (1980).

In the course of the work, which was marked by splendid festivities, the commission evaluated the positive results of the dialogue of love in regard to relations between the two churches; it decided on the basic principles that would govern the working method of the joint theological commission; and it chose as the first theme of study and theological preparation "The mystery of the church and of the eucharist in the light of the mystery of the Holy Trinity".

The second plenary session was held in Munich (1982). Its work consisted chiefly of a study of the text drafted by the joint coordinating committee (Venice 1981), which in turn was based on texts drafted by three sub-committees (1980, 1981). The discussions of the full commission focused on: the nature of the eucharist; the relation between eucharist and Holy Trinity; the action of the Trinity through the eucharist as well as through the church and the communion of local churches. The theological discussion of these subjects produced significant fruits; it brought out important elements of agreement that could serve in the further work of the joint commission and that were set down in the common declaration subsequently approved. In keeping with the schedule of work drawn up at Rhodes the commission also decided on the next subject to be discussed: "Faith, sacraments and the unity of the church".

The third plenary session took place at the Orthodox Academy in Crete (1984). The work of the commission was conducted in accordance with the method that had been established for the dialogue. The joint sub-commissions did their own work after the Munich meeting and prepared draft texts that were then evaluated by the joint coordinating committee, which met in Nicosia, Cyprus (1983). The texts drafted by the sub-commissions dealt especially with the following specific themes: (1) faith and communion in the sacraments; (2) the sacraments of initiation and their connection with the unity of the church. In choosing these themes, the sub-commissions were acting in accord with the wishes of the plenary assembly of Munich. During the work of the joint coordinating committee an intense effort was made to draw up a unified draft text that could serve as the basis for the work of the third plenary session. But the lengthy theological debates among members of this committee on certain points of the draft text caused difficulties for the preparation and approval of the document by the full joint theological commission. In the end the latter handed the document back to the joint coordinating committee with instructions to seek a resolution through theological discussion of the points disputed (liturgical administration of the sacraments of initiation; relation between baptism, confirmation and eucharist; and so on). And in fact the joint coordinating committee met again in Opole, Poland (1985), and managed to solve the problems raised by the theological formulation of the text through dialogue, which means the following of a common path in the search for the unity of faith. The agreements achieved there were to be presented to the plenary assembly of the joint theological commission, which was scheduled for Bari in the following year.

The fourth plenary session was held at Bari (1986). The joint theological commission continued to discuss the subject of the previous, third session ("Faith, sacraments and the unity of the church"). The absence, for various ecclesial and non-ecclesial reasons, of some local church representatives (Jerusalem, Russia, Greece, Georgia) on the inter-Orthodox commission caused difficulties for the continuation of the joint theological commission's work. The commission decided to send the final text to these absent members. During the discussions the question of investigating the problems of proselytism and uniatism was raised, and methods were suggested for dealing with these problems. On this point the statement in the Bari communique is characteristic:

> This meeting was devoted principally to a final discussion and approval of an agreed statement on the subject of "Faith, sacraments and the unity of the church"; this statement represents a continuation of the agreed statement already approved by the commission: "The mystery of the church and of the eucharist in the light of the mystery of the Holy Trinity". These studies are part of a series undertaken in support of a dialogue that is aimed at the restoration of full communion in faith and sacramental life between the two churches.
>
> The text has two parts. The first describes elements essential to the restoration of complete unity: the confession of a common faith; the liturgical manifestation of faith; conditions for a communion of faith; true faith and communion in the sacraments; the unity of the church in faith and sacraments. The second part studies the sacraments of Christian initiation and their connection with the unity of the church. The administration of these sacraments differs in the Orthodox and Catholic churches: immersion or pouring in baptism; the temporal separation of baptism, confirmation and eucharist; the more recent practice of inverting of the traditional order by the admission of baptized Christians to the eucharist without previous confirmation. These differences are a problem for the Orthodox, because they represent a changing of the tradition and the admission of theological and liturgical principles that justify such changes.
>
> Progress was made in dealing with these subjects and in recognition of the permissible existence of divergent traditions in each church. The commission realized, however, that the theological and liturgical themes which had emerged from the discussion required further serious study.
>
> One of the working principles which the commission had adopted at its first meeting in Rhodes (1980) was that the dialogue of love must constantly accompany the theological dialogue; this would make it easier to resolve difficulties and would strengthen fraternal relations between the two churches at both the local and the universal levels. In the spirit of this principle the members of the commission once again condemn proselytism, as official leaders and groups of both churches have already done on several occasions. Every kind of proselytism must be avoided in relations between our faithful; where it is found it must be renounced.

It is in relation to this development in the dialogue that the appraisal given by His Holiness Pope John Paul II, at St Peter's in Rome on the Vigil of the Feast of Peter and Paul (28 June 1985), is to be understood. He said: "The church must learn to breathe once again with both lungs, the Eastern and the Western... The principal dialogue in which the Catholic church is engaged is the theological dialogue which it is now carrying on with the venerable Orthodox churches, its sister churches, in the context of the dialogue of love." In the same spirit the third preconciliar pan-Orthodox conference (November 1986) greeted "with satisfaction the positive advances made... but it also recognized the existence of problems regarding subject matter, method and other points, which hinder the rapid and successful development of the dialogue". It suggested that the subjects to be discussed be taken "not only... from those areas in which the two churches are 'united', but also from those in which they are 'separated' from one another, and in particular the area of ecclesiology". In addition, it recommended some methodological improvements (composition of separate drafts of documents by each side; critique of the original text; acceptance of texts from the two commissions and not from individuals; etc.), and it urged the necessity of addressing "the negative effects of uniatism and proselytism".

The fifth plenary session took place at Valamo, Finland (1988). Its task was to continue discussion with a view to producing a joint draft on the subject of "the sacrament of order in the sacramental structure of the church, with particular reference to the importance of apostolic succession for the sanctification and unity of the people of God".

This topic had been determined by the third plenary session (Crete 1984) and had been studied by three sub-commissions, which composed three draft versions. The joint coordinating committee (Opole 1985) revised the three drafts and then composed a preliminary document, the main lines of which were discussed at the fourth plenary session in Bari (1986). As the fifth session carried on its work in Valamo, it undertook a systematic revision of the entire text and made many suggestions for improvements in substance and language. Finally, the document was unanimously accepted by the members of the commission. In its communique the commission emphasized the point that "the working method adopted earlier has been followed. The purpose was not to produce a complete and systematic theology of the subject. Rather, the document gives information about those aspects of the sacramental laying-on of hands, the structure of the church and apostolic succession, regarding which there is either agreement between the two churches or differences of view."

In addition, it was decided to establish a joint sub-committee that would carry on the study of the ecclesiological and practical aspects of uniatism and proselytism. This sub-commission in turn decided to entrust this study to specialists on the subject who were not members of the commission. The special sub-commission would then make a report to the joint theological commission, which would evaluate the recommendations presented to it.

At this third session the subject for the next plenary session was chosen: "Ecclesiological and canonical consequences of the sacramental structure of the church: conciliarity and authority in the church". The theme was to be developed by the three sub-commissions, while the joint theological commission itself was to combine their work into a unified draft document. The latter was in turn to be discussed at the sixth plenary session (Munich 1990), first by each side separately, and then by the body as a whole with a view to final approval. The communique of the fifth meeting in Valamo had this to say on the subject: "Both churches have traditions of conciliarity; these should be studied with the expectation of finding points of agreement, or at least with the hope that divergences will no longer be obstacles to full communion. The authority of the church, and episcopal authority in particular, should be studied not only at the level of the churches generally and of particular regions, but also at the level of the individual or local church."

The dialogue ran into new difficulties which can be traced back to the violent accusations and conflicts which pitted the uniates against the Orthodox in Czechoslovakia, Yugoslavia and the Ukraine during the political and social changes in Eastern Europe. These conflicts elicited unequivocal reactions within the church of Russia and other local Orthodox churches. The ecumenical patriarchate followed all these developments closely. The seriousness of the problem was brought home to participants in the meeting of representatives of the Roman Catholic Church and the Church of Russia in Moscow (12-17 January 1990). The representatives expressed their disquiet at the tension caused by the accusations from both sides, and they came to the conclusion that the resolution of the problem must be looked for in the light of evangelical love and in the spirit of dialogue between the two churches. Only if those involved renounce hostile utterances and any use of force will it be possible for the Orthodox and for all who in any way belong to the Roman Catholic Church to bear peaceful witness to their faith at their traditional places of worship. This renunciation will in turn be possible only if the two churches together bear witness to the love and peace of Christ for the salvation of the world.

Continuing accusations caused contention and a break in the official dialogue between the two churches. The sub-commission charged with studying the subject met in Vienna (26-30 January 1990). It rejected uniatism as a way of recovering church unity, and it composed a paper on the subject that was discussed at the meeting of the joint theological commission for dialogue in Freising/Munich (6-15 June 1990). After lengthy discussion a joint communique was issued which, together with the report drawn up by the special sub-commission in Vienna, was to serve the special sub-commission as a basis for working on the topic and then submitting a draft text to the joint coordinating committee before 1 May 1991. The first recommendations for doing away with the accusations levelled by each confession at the other reject any and every form of physical or moral force and every kind of proselytism; they recommend dialogue as the only appropriate way of dealing with all these problems and especially with the problems of uniatism. For this reason, they also stress the need of continuing the dialogue in order to resolve all the causes of crisis in relations between the two churches.

1991 *Damaskinos Papandreou*

Thus the question of uniatism was submitted to three sub-commissions, and the coordinating committee, meeting at Ariccia, Italy, in June 1991, drafted a text for consideration at the seventh plenary session. It took place in June 1993 at the Balamand school of theology in Lebanon, under the auspices of the Orthodox Patriarchate of Antioch. There was a reduced Orthodox presence because of the absence of representatives of six Orthodox churches. Nevertheless, the draft was examined and amended, and was adopted on 23 June.

The full title of the Balamand document is "Uniatism, method of union in the past, and the present search for full communion". It hinges on two central affirmations: on one hand, "the method which has been called uniatism" is rejected because it is "opposed to the common tradition of our churches". On the other hand, it unequivocally affirms that the Eastern Catholic churches "have the right to exist and to act in response to the spiritual needs of their faithful". The bulk of the document is divided into two sections, the first dealing with ecclesiological principles, and the second with practical recommendations.

The document ends with an expression of the hope that since the document excludes all proselytism by Catholics at the expense of the Orthodox, the obstacles that prevented six autocephalous Orthodox churches from attending the dialogue will have been overcome, and that the work "already so happily begun" might continue.

Reactions to the Balamand document, however, have been mixed. On the Catholic side it has been widely accepted, but criticized in some conservative circles. The bishops of the Romanian Greek Catholic Church wrote a letter to Pope John Paul II in July 1993 rejecting Balamand and all the other documents produced by the dialogue, but the head of the Ukrainian Greek Catholic Church, Cardinal Myroslav Lubachivsky, issued an encyclical in April 1994 in which he accepted the document and pledged to implement it in the life of his church. On the Orthodox side, the Romanian Orthodox holy synod officially approved the document in July 1993, and the theological commission of the holy synod of the Russian Orthodox Church in April 1997 gave it cautious acceptance but called for further clarifications. The holy synod of the Orthodox Church of Greece rejected Balamand out of hand in December 1994, however, and it has been denounced violently in old-calendar circles.

Given the uneven response to the document, the Orthodox side requested that the same theme be taken up again at the eighth plenary session, with a focus on the canonical and ecclesiological implications of uniatism. A draft document was produced at Ariccia, Italy, in June 1998, and the eighth session was scheduled for July 2000 at Mount St Mary Seminary in the Archdiocese of Baltimore, USA.

1999   *Ronald Roberson*

48. The Mystery of the Church and of the Eucharist in the Light of the Mystery of the Holy Trinity

Munich, Germany, 30 June-6 July 1982

Faithful to the mandate received at Rhodes, this report touches upon the mystery of the church in only one of its aspects. This aspect, however, is particularly important in the sacramental perspective of our churches, that is, the mystery of the church and of the eucharist in the light of the mystery of the holy Trinity. As a matter of fact the request was made to start with what we have in common and, by developing it, to touch upon from inside and progressively all the points on which we are not in agreement.

In composing this document we intend to show that in doing so we express together a faith which is the continuation of that of the apostles.

This document makes the first step in the effort to fulfil the programme of the preparatory commission, approved at the first meeting of the commission for dialogue.

Since there is question of a first step, touching upon the mystery of the church under only one of its aspects, many points are not yet treated here. They will be treated in succeeding steps as has been foreseen in the programme mentioned above.

I

1. Christ, Son of God incarnate, dead and risen, is the only one who has conquered sin and death. To speak, therefore, of the sacramental nature of the mystery of Christ is to bring to mind the possibility given to man, and through him to the whole cosmos, to experience the "new creation", the kingdom of God here and now through material and created realities. This is the mode *(tropos)* in which the unique person and the unique event of Christ exists and operates in history starting from Pentecost and reaching to the parousia. However, the eternal life which God has given to the world in the event of Christ, his eternal Son, is contained in "earthen vessels". It is still only given as a foretaste, as a pledge.

2. At the last supper, Christ stated that he "gave" his body to the disciples for the life of "the many", in the eucharist. In it this gift is made by God to the world, but in sacramental form. From that moment the eucharist exists as the sacrament of Christ himself. It becomes the foretaste of eternal life, the "medicine of immortality", the sign of the kingdom to come. The sacrament of the Christ event thus becomes identical with the sacrament of the holy eucharist, the sacrament which incorporates us fully into Christ.

3. The incarnation of the Son of God, his death and resurrection were realized from the beginning, according to the Father's will, in the Holy Spirit. This Spirit, which pro-

ceeds eternally from the Father and manifests himself through the Son, prepared the Christ event and realized it fully in the resurrection. Christ, who is the sacrament par excellence, given by the Father for the world, continues to give himself for the many in the Spirit, who alone gives life (John 6). The sacrament of Christ is also a reality which can only exist in the Spirit.

4. The church and the eucharist

a) Although the evangelists in the account of the supper are silent about the action of the Spirit, he was nonetheless united closer than ever to the incarnate Son for carrying out the Father's work. He is not yet given, received as a person, by the disciples (John 7:39). But when Jesus is glorified then the Spirit himself also pours himself out and manifests himself. The Lord Jesus enters into the glory of the Father and, at the same time, by the pouring out of the Spirit, into his sacramental *tropos* in this world. Pentecost, the completion of the paschal mystery, inaugurates simultaneously the last times. The eucharist and the church, body of the crucified and risen Christ, become the place of the energies of the Holy Spirit.

b) Believers are baptized in the Spirit in the name of the holy Trinity to form one body (cf. 1 Cor. 12:13). When the church celebrates the eucharist it realizes "what it is", the body of Christ (1 Cor. 10:17). By baptism and chrismation (confirmation) the members of Christ are "anointed" by the Spirit, grafted into Christ. But by the eucharist the paschal event opens itself out into church. The church becomes that which it is called to be by baptism and chrismation. By the communion in the body and blood of Christ, the faithful grow in that mystical divinization which makes them dwell in the Son and the Father, through the Spirit.

c) Thus, on the one hand, the church celebrates the eucharist as expression here and now of the heavenly liturgy; but on the other hand, the eucharist builds up the church in the sense that through it the Spirit of the risen Christ fashions the church into the body of Christ. That is why the eucharist is truly the sacrament of the church, at once as sacrament of the total gift the Lord makes of himself to his own and as manifestation and growth of the body of Christ, the church. The pilgrim church celebrates the eucharist on earth until her Lord comes to restore royalty to God the Father so that God may be "all in all". It thus anticipates the judgment of the world and its final transfiguration.

5. The mission of the Spirit remains joined to that of the Son. The celebration of the eucharist reveals the divine energies manifested by the Spirit at work in the body of Christ.

a) The Spirit prepares the coming of Christ by announcing it through the prophets, by directing the history of the chosen people towards him, by causing him to be conceived by the Virgin Mary, by opening up hearts to his word.

b) The Spirit manifests Christ in his work as saviour, the gospel which is he himself. The eucharistic celebration is the anamnesis (the memorial). Truly, but sacramentally, the *ephapax* (the "once and for all") is and becomes present. The celebration of the eucharist is par excellence the kairos (proper time) of the mystery.

c) The Spirit transforms the sacred gifts into the body and blood of Christ *(metabole)* in order to bring about the growth of the body which is the church. In this sense the entire celebration is an epiclesis, which becomes more explicit at certain moments. The church is continually in a state of epiclesis.

d) The Spirit puts into communion with the body of Christ those who share the same bread and the same cup. Starting from there, the church manifests what it is, the sacrament of the trinitarian koinonia, the "dwelling of God with men" (cf. Rev. 21:4).

The Spirit, by making present what Christ did once for all – the event of the mystery – accomplishes it in all of us. The relation to the mystery, more evident in the eucharist, is found in the other sacraments, all acts of the Spirit. That is why the eucharist is the centre of sacramental life.

6. Taken as a whole, the eucharistic celebration makes present the trinitarian mystery of the church. In it one passes from hearing the word, culminating in the proclamation of the gospel – the apostolic announcing of the word made flesh – to the thanksgiving offered to the Father and to the memorial of the sacrifice and to communion in it thanks to the prayer of epiclesis uttered in faith. For the epiclesis is not merely an invocation for the sacramental transforming of the bread and cup. It is also a prayer for the full effect of the communion of all in the mystery revealed by the Son.

In this way the presence of the Spirit itself is extended by the sharing in the sacrament of the word made flesh to all the body of the church. Without wishing to resolve yet the difficulties which have arisen between the East and the West concerning the relationship between the Son and the Spirit, we can already say together that this Spirit, which proceeds from the Father (John 15:26) as the sole source in the Trinity and which has become the Spirit of our sonship (Rom. 8:15) since he is also the Spirit of the Son (Gal. 4:6), is communicated to us particularly in the eucharist by this Son upon whom he reposes in time and in eternity (John 1:32).

That is why the eucharistic mystery is accomplished in the prayer which joins together the words by which the word made flesh instituted the sacrament and the epiclesis in which the church, moved by faith, entreats the Father, through the Son, to send the Spirit so that in the unique offering of the incarnate Son, everything may be consummated in unity. Through the eucharist believers unite themselves to Christ, who offers himself to the Father with them, and they receive the possibility of offering themselves in a spirit of sacrifice to each other, as Christ himself offers himself to the Father for the many, thus giving himself to men.

This consummation in unity brought about by the one inseparable operation of the Son and the Spirit, acting in reference to the Father in his design, is the church in its fullness.

II

1. If one looks at the New Testament one will notice first of all that the church describes a "local" reality. The church exists in history as local church. For a region one speaks more often of churches, in the plural. It is always a question of the church of God but in a given place.

Now the church existing in a place is not formed, in a radical sense, by the persons who come together to establish it. There is a "Jerusalem, from on high" which "comes down from God", a communion which is at the foundation of the community itself. The church comes into being by a free gift, that of the new creation.

However, it is clear that the church "which is in" a given place manifests itself when it is "assembled". This assembly itself, whose elements and requirements are indicated by the New Testament, is fully such when it is the eucharistic synaxis. When the local church celebrates the eucharist, the event which took place "once and for all" is made present and manifested. In the local church, then, there is neither male nor female, slave nor free, Jew nor Greek. A new unity is communicated which overcomes divisions and restores communion in the one body of Christ. This unity transcends psychological, racial, socio-political or cultural unity. It is the "communion of the Holy Spirit" gathering together the scattered children of God. The newness of baptism and of chrismation then bears its fruit. And by the power of the body and blood of the Lord, filled with the Holy Spirit, there is healed that sin which does not cease to assault Christians by raising obstacles to the dynamism of the "life for God in Christ Jesus" received in baptism. This applies also to the sin of division, all of whose forms contradict God's design.

One of the chief texts to remember is 1 Corinthians 10:15-17: one sole bread, one sole cup, one sole body of Christ in the plurality of members. This mystery of the unity in love of many persons constitutes the real newness of the trinitarian koinonia communicated to men in the church through the eucharist. Such is the purpose of Christ's saving work, which is spread abroad in the last times after Pentecost.

This is why the church finds its model, its origin and its purpose in the mystery of God, one in three persons. Further still, the eucharist thus understood in the light of the trinitarian mystery is the criterion for functioning of the life of the church as a whole. The institutional elements should be nothing but a visible reflection of the reality of the mystery.

2. The unfolding of the eucharistic celebration of the local church shows how the koinonia takes shape in the church celebrating the eucharist. In the eucharist celebrated by the local church gathered about the bishop, or the priest in communion with him, the following aspects stand out, interconnected among themselves even if this or that moment of the celebration emphasizes one or another.

The koinonia is eschatological. It is the newness which comes in the last times. That is why everything in the eucharist as in the life of the church begins with conversion and reconciliation. The eucharist presupposes repentance (metanoia) and confession *(exomologesis)*, which find in other circumstances their own sacramental expression. But the eucharist forgives and also heals sins, since it is the sacrament of the divinizing love of the Father, by the Son, in the Holy Spirit.

But this koinonia is also kerygmatic. This is evident in the synaxis not only because the celebration "announces" the event of the mystery, but also because it actually realizes it today in the Spirit. This implies the proclamation of the word to the assembly and the response of faith given by all. Thus the communion of the assembly is brought about in the kerygma, and hence unity in faith. Orthodoxy (correct faith) is inherent in the eucharistic koinonia. This orthodoxy is expressed most clearly through the proclamation of the symbol of faith which is a summary of the apostolic tradition of which the bishop is the witness in virtue of his succession. Thus the eucharist is inseparably sacrament and word since in it the incarnate word sanctifies in the Spirit. That is why the entire liturgy and not only the reading of holy scriptures constitutes a proclamation of the word under the form of doxology and prayer. On the other hand, the word proclaimed is the word made flesh and become sacramental.

Koinonia is at once ministerial and pneumatological. That is why the eucharist is its manifestation par excellence. The entire assembly, each one according to rank, is *leiturgos* of the koinonia. While being a gift of the trinitarian God, koinonia is also the response of men. In the faith which comes from the Spirit and the word, these put in practice the vocation and the mission received in baptism: to become living members, in one's proper rank, of the body of Christ.

3. The ministry of the bishop is not merely a tactical or pragmatic function (because a president is necessary) but an organic function. The bishop receives the gift of episcopal grace (1 Tim. 4:14) in the sacrament of consecration effected by bishops who themselves have received this gift, thanks to the existence of an uninterrupted series of episcopal ordinations, beginning from the holy apostles. By the sacrament of ordination the Spirit of the Lord "confers" on the bishop, not juridically as if it were a pure transmission of power, but sacramentally, the authority of servant which the Son received from the Father and which he received in a human way by his acceptance in his passion.

The function of the bishop is closely bound to the eucharistic assembly over which he presides. The eucharistic unity of the local church implies communion between him who presides and the people to whom he delivers the word of salvation and the eucharistic gifts. Further, the minister is also the one who "receives" from his church, which is faithful to tradition, the word he transmits. And the great intercession which he sends up to the Father is simply that of his entire church praying with him. The bishop cannot be separated from his church any more than the church can be separated from its bishop.

The bishop stands at the heart of the local church as minister of the Spirit to discern the charisma and take care that they are exercised in harmony, for the good of all, in faithfulness to the apostolic tradition. He puts himself at the service of the initiatives of the Spirit so that nothing may prevent them from contributing to building up koinonia. He is minister of unity, servant of Christ the Lord, whose mission is to "gather into unity the children of God". And because the church is built up by the eucharist, it is he, invested with the grace of priestly ministry, who presides at the latter.

But this presidency must be properly understood. The bishop presides at the offering which is that of his entire community. By consecrating the gifts so that they become the body and blood the community offers, he celebrates not only for it, nor only with it and in it, but through it. He appears then as minister of Christ fashioning the unity of his body and so creating communion through his body. The union of the community with him is first of all of the order of *mysterion* and not primordially of the juridical order. It is that union expressed in the eucharist which is prolonged and given practical expression in the "pastoral" relations of teaching, government and life. The ecclesial community is thus called to be the outline of a human community renewed.

4. There is profound communion between the bishop and the community in which the Spirit gives him responsibility for the church of God. The ancient tradition expressed it happily in the image of marriage. But that communion lies within the communion of the apostolic community. In the ancient tradition (as the apostolic tradition of Hippolytus proves) the bishop elected by the people – who guarantee his apostolic faith, in conformity with what the local church confesses – receives the ministerial grace of Christ by the Spirit in the prayer of the assembly and by the laying-on of hands *(chirotonia)* of the neighbouring bishops, witnesses of the faith of their own churches. His charism, coming directly from the Spirit of God, is given him in the apostolicity of his church (linked to the faith of the apostolic community) and in that of the other churches represented by their bishops. Through this his ministry is inserted into the catholicity of the church of God.

Apostolic succession, therefore, means something more than a mere transmission of powers. It is succession in a church which witnesses to the apostolic faith, in communion with other churches which witness to the same apostolic faith. The see *(cathedra)* plays an essential role in inserting the bishop into the heart of ecclesial apostolicity. On the other hand, once ordained, the bishop becomes in his church the guarantor of apostolicity and the one who represents it within the communion of churches. That is why in his church every eucharist can only be celebrated in truth if presided over by him or by a presbyter in communion with him. Mention of him in the anaphora is essential.

Through the ministry of presbyters, charged with presiding over the life and the eucharistic celebration of the communities entrusted to them, those communities grow in communion with all the communities for which the bishop has primary responsibility. In the present situation the diocese itself is a communion of eucharistic communities. One of the essential functions of presbyters is to link these to the eucharist of the bishop and to nourish them with the apostolic faith of which the bishop is the witness and guarantor. They should also take care that Christians, nourished by the body and blood of him who gave his life for his brethren, should be authentic witnesses of fraternal love in the reciprocal sacrifice nourished by the sacrifice of Christ. For, according to the word of the apostle, "if someone sees his brother in need and closes his heart against him, how does God's love abide in him?" The eucharist determines the Christian manner of living the paschal mystery of Christ and the gift of Pentecost. Thanks to it there is a profound transformation of human existence always confronted by temptation and suffering.

III

1. The body of Christ is unique. There exists then only one church of God. The identity of one eucharistic assembly with another comes from the fact that all with the same faith celebrate the same memorial, that all by eating the same bread and sharing in the same cup become the same unique body of Christ into which they have been integrated by the same baptism. If there are many celebrations, there is nevertheless only one mystery celebrated in which all participate. Moreover, when the believer communicates in the Lord's body and blood, he does not receive a part of Christ but the whole Christ.

In the same way, the local church which celebrates the eucharist gathered around its bishop is not a section of the body of Christ. The multiplicity of local synaxes does not divide the church, but rather shows sacramentally its unity. Like the community of the apostles gathered around Christ, each eucharistic assembly is truly the holy church of God, the body of Christ, in communion with the first community of the disciples and with all who throughout the world celebrate and have celebrated the memorial of the Lord. It is also in communion with the assembly of the saints in heaven, which each celebration brings to mind.

2. Far from excluding diversity or plurality, the koinonia supposes it and heals the wounds of division, transcending the latter in unity.

Since Christ is one for the many, as in the church which is his body, the one and the many, the universal and local are necessarily simultaneous. Still more radically, because the one and only God is the communion of three persons, the one and only church is a communion of many communities and the local church a communion of persons. The one and unique church finds her identity in the koinonia of the churches. Unity and multiplicity appear so linked that one could not exist without the other. It is this relationship constitutive of the church that institutions make visible and, so to speak, "historicize".

3. Since the universal church manifests itself in the synaxis of the local church, two conditions must be fulfilled above all if the local church which celebrates the eucharist is to be truly within the ecclesial communion.

a) First, the identity of the mystery of the church lived by the local church with the mystery of the church lived by the primitive church – catholicity in time – is fundamental. The church is apostolic because it is founded on and continually sustained by the mystery of salvation revealed in Jesus Christ, transmitted in the Spirit by those who were his witnesses, the apostles. Its members will be judged by Christ and the apostles (cf. Luke 22:30).

b) Today mutual recognition between this local church and the other churches is also of capital importance. Each should recognize in the others through local particularities the identity of the mystery of the church. It is a question of mutual recognition of catholicity as communion in the wholeness of the mystery. This recognition is achieved first of all at the regional level. Communion in the same patriarchate or in some other form of regional unity is first of all a manifestation of the life of the Spirit in the same culture, or in the same historical conditions. It equally implies unity of witness and calls for the exercise of fraternal correction in humility. This communion within the same region should extend itself further in the communion between sister churches.

This mutual recognition, however, is true only under the conditions expressed in the anaphora of St John Chrysostom and the first Antiochene anaphoras. The first condition is communion in the same kerygma, and so in the same faith. Already contained in baptism this requirement is made explicit in the eucharistic celebration. But it also requires the will for communion in love (agape) and in service (diakonia), not only in words but in deeds.

Permanence through history and mutual recognition are particularly brought into focus in the eucharistic synaxis by the mention of the saints in the canon and of the heads of the churches in the diptychs. Thus it is understood why these latter are signs of catholic unity in eucharistic communion, responsible, each on its own level, for maintaining that communion in the universal harmony of the churches and their common fidelity to the apostolic tradition.

4. We find then among these churches those bonds of communion which the New Testament indicated: communion in faith, hope and love, communion in the sacraments, communion in the diversity of charisms, communion in the reconciliation, communion in the ministry. The agent of this communion is the Spirit of the risen Lord. Through him the church universal, catholic, integrates diversity or plurality, making it one of its own essential elements. This catholicity represents the fulfilment of the prayer of chapter 17 of the gospel according to John, taken up in the eucharistic epicleses.

Attachment to the apostolic communion binds all the bishops together, linking the *episcope* of the local churches to the college of the apostles. They too form a college rooted by the Spirit in the "once for all" of the apostolic group, the unique witness to the faith. This means not only that they should be united among themselves by faith, charity, mission, reconciliation, but that they have in common the same responsibility and the same service to the church. Because the one and only church is made present in his local church, each bishop cannot separate the care for his own church from that of the universal church. When, by the sacrament of ordination, he receives the charism of the Spirit for the *episcope* of one local church, his own, by that very fact he receives the charism of the Spirit for the *episcope* of the entire church. In the people of God he exercises it in communion with all the bishops who are here and now in charge of churches and in communion with the living tradition which the bishops of the past have handed on. The presence of bishops from neighbouring sees at his episcopal ordination "sacramentalizes" and makes present this communion. It produces a thorough fusion between his solicitude for the local community and his care for the church spread throughout the world. The *episcope* for the universal church is seen to be entrusted by the Spirit to the totality of local bishops in communion with one another. This communion is expressed traditionally through conciliar practice. We shall have to examine further the way it is conceived and realized in the perspective of what we have just explained.

49. Faith, Sacraments and the Unity of the Church

Bari, Italy, June 1987

The international joint commission for theological dialogue between the Catholic church and the Orthodox church at its plenary meeting in Bari (9-16 June 1987) approved a new statement on "Faith, Sacraments and the Unity of the Church".

This topic had been agreed on at the Munich plenary of 1982. After parallel study by three joint sub-commissions the joint coordinating committee at Nicosia, Cyprus, 1983, produced a synthesis of their work, which was presented and discussed at the Crete plenary meeting in 1984. The same committee then revised the draft, (Opole, Poland, 1985) in accordance with the modifications asked for by the plenary. The text which resulted was examined afresh during the plenary which spread over two sessions, that of 1986 and that 1987. The approved text, now about to be published, is the joint commission's second statement. It follows and is closely linked with "The Mystery of the Church and of the Eucharist" in the light of the mystery of the Holy Trinity.

These two statements answer to the requirements of the "plan for embarking on theological dialogue between the Catholic church and the Orthodox church" at the first plenary session in Patmos, Rhodes (1980). This joint preparatory document considers that "study of the sacraments of the church is helpful for examining the problems of dialogue positively and in depth".

Introduction

1. After our meeting in Munich in 1982 and in accord with the "plan" adopted by our commission during its first meeting at Rhodes in 1980, this fourth session of the commission has undertaken to consider the question of the relation between faith and sacramental communion.

2. As was stated in the "plan" of our dialogue, which was approved at Rhodes, unity in faith is a presupposition for unity in the sacraments, and especially in the holy eucharist. But this commonly accepted principle raises some fundamental issues which require consideration. Does faith amount to adhering to formulas or is it also something else? Faith, which is a divine gift, should be understood as a commitment of the Christian, a commitment of mind, heart and will. In its profound reality it is also an ecclesial event which is realized and accomplished in and through the communion of the church, in its liturgical and especially in its eucharistic expression. This ecclesial and liturgical character of the faith must be taken seriously into consideration.

3. Given this fundamental character of faith, it is necessary to affirm that faith must be taken as a preliminary condition, already complete in itself, which precedes sacra-

mental communion; and also that it is increased by sacramental communion, which is the expression of the very life of the church and the means of the spiritual growth of each of its members. This question has to be raised in order to avoid a deficient approach to the problem of faith as a condition for unity. It should not, however, serve to obscure the fact that faith is such a condition, and that there cannot be sacramental communion without communion in faith both in the broader sense and in the sense of dogmatic formulation.

4. In addition to the question of faith as a presupposition of sacramental communion and in close connection with it, following the "plan" of the dialogue, we have also considered in our meetings the relation of what are called sacraments of initiation i.e. baptism, confirmation or chrismation and eucharist – to each other and to the unity of the church. At this point it is necessary to examine if our two churches are confronted simply with a difference in liturgical practice in doctrine, since liturgical practice and doctrine are linked to one another. Should we consider these three sacraments as belonging to one sacramental reality or as three autonomous sacramental acts? It should also be asked if for the sacraments of initiation a difference in liturgical practice between the two traditions raises a problem of doctrinal divergence, which could be considered as a serious obstacle to unity.

I. Faith and communion in the sacraments

5. Faith is inseparably both the gift of God who reveals himself and the response of the human person who receives this gift. This is the synergy of the grace of God and human freedom. The locus of this communion is the church. In the church, revealed truth is transmitted according to the Tradition of the apostles based on the scriptures, by means of the ecumenical councils, liturgical life, and the fathers of the church; and is put into practice by the members of the body of Christ. The faith of the church constitutes the norm and the criterion of the personal act of faith. Faith is not the product of an elaboration or of a logical necessity, but of the influence of the grace of the Holy Spirit. The apostle Paul received grace "in the obedience of faith" (Rom. 1:5). St Basil says on this subject: "Faith precedes discourse about God; faith and not demonstration. Faith which is above logical methods leads to consent. Faith is born not of geometric necessities, but of the energies of the Spirit" (in Ps. 115:1).

6. Every sacrament presupposes and expresses the faith of the church which celebrates it. Indeed, in a sacrament the church does more than profess and express its faith: it makes present the mystery it is celebrating. The Holy Spirit reveals the church as the body of Christ which he constitutes and makes grow. Thus the church nourishes and develops the communion of the faith of its members through the sacraments.

1. True faith is a divine gift and free response of the human person

7. Faith is a gift of the Holy Spirit. Through faith God grants salvation. Through it, humanity has access to the mystery of Christ who constitutes the church and whom the church communicates through the Holy Spirit who dwells in it. The church can only transmit what causes it to exist. Now, there is only one mystery of Christ and God's gift is unique, whole and irrevocable (Rom. 11:29). As for its content, faith embraces the totality of doctrine and church practice relating to salvation. Dogma, conduct and liturgical life overlap each other to form a single whole and together constitute the treasure of faith. Linking in a remarkable fashion the theoretical and practical character of faith,

St John Damascene says: "This [faith] is made perfect by all that Christ decreed, faith through works, respect for and practice of the commandments of the One who has renewed us. Indeed, the one who does not believe according to the tradition of the catholic church or who by unseemly works is in communion with the devil, is an infidel" (*De fide orthodoxa* IV, 10, 83).

8. Given by God, the faith announced by the church is proclaimed, lived and transmitted in a local, visible church in communion with all the local churches spread over the world, that is, the catholic church of all times, and everywhere. The human person is integrated into the body of Christ by his or her koinonia (communion) with this visible church which nourishes this faith by means of the sacramental life and the word of God, and in which the Holy Spirit works in the human person.

9. One can say that, in this way, the gift of faith exists in the single church in its concrete historical situation, determined by the environment and the times, and therefore in each and all of the believers under the guidance of their pastors. In human language and in a variety of cultural and historical expressions, the human person must always remain faithful to this gift of faith. Certainly, one cannot claim that the expression of the true faith, transmitted and lived in the celebration of the sacraments, exhausts the totality of the richness of the mystery revealed in Jesus Christ. Nevertheless, within the limits of its formulation and of the persons who receive it, it gives access to the whole truth of the revealed faith, that is, to the fullness of salvation and life in the Holy Spirit.

10. According to the Letter to the Hebrews, this faith is "the substance of things to be hoped for, the vision of unseen realities" (11:1). It grants a share in divine goods. It is also understood in terms of an existential confidence in the power and love of God, in acceptance of the eschatological promises as fulfilled in the person of Jesus Christ. Yet, as this Letter to the Hebrews further indicates, faith also requires an attitude towards the milieu of existence and the world. This attitude is marked by readiness to sacrifice one's own will and to offer one's life to God and to others as Christ did on the cross. Faith brings one into association with the witness of Christ and with "a cloud of witnesses" (12:1) which envelop the church.

11. Faith therefore involves a conscious and free response from the human person and a continual change of heart and spirit. Consequently, faith is an interior change and a transformation, causing one to live in the grace of the Holy Spirit who renews the human person. It seeks a reorientation towards the realities of the future kingdom which, even now, is beginning to transform the realities of this world.

12. Faith is a presupposition of baptism and the entire sacramental life which follows it. Indeed, one participates through baptism in the death and resurrection of Jesus Christ (Rom. 6). Thus begins a process which continues all through Christian existence.

2. The liturgical expression of the faith

13. In the church, the sacraments are the privileged place where the faith is lived, transmitted and professed. In the Byzantine liturgical tradition the first prayer for entrance into the catechumenate asks the Lord for the candidate: "Fill him/her with faith, hope and love for you that he/she may understand that you are the one true God, with your only Son our Lord Jesus Christ and your Holy Spirit." Similarly the first question the church puts to the candidate for baptism in the Latin liturgical tradition is:

"What do you ask of the church?" and the candidate answers: "Faith." "What does faith give you?" "Eternal life."

14. Our two churches express their conviction in this matter by the axiom *lex orandi lex credendi*. For them the liturgical tradition is an authentic interpreter of revelation and hence the criterion for the expression of the true faith. Indeed, it is in the liturgical expression of the faith of our churches that the witness of the fathers and of the ecumenical councils celebrated together continues to be for believers the sure guide of faith. Independently of diversity in theological expression, this witness, which itself renders explicit the "kerygma" of the holy scriptures, is made present in the liturgical celebration. In its turn, the proclamation of the faith nourishes the liturgical prayer of the people of God.

3. The Holy Spirit and the sacraments

15. The sacraments of the church are "sacraments of faith" where God the Father hears the *epiclesis* (invocation) in which the church expresses its faith by this prayer for the coming of the Spirit. In them, the Father gives his Holy Spirit who leads us into the fullness of salvation in Christ. Christ himself constitutes the church as his body. The Holy Spirit edifies the church. There is no gift in the church which cannot be attributed to the Spirit (Basil the Great, *PG* 30, 289). The sacraments are both gift and grace of the Holy Spirit, in Jesus Christ in the church. This is expressed very concisely in an Orthodox hymn of Pentecost: "The Holy Spirit is the author of every gift. He makes prophecies spring forth. He renders priests perfect. He teaches wisdom to the ignorant. He makes fishermen into theologians and consolidates the institution of the church."

16. Every sacrament of the church confers the grace of the Holy Spirit because it is inseparably a sign recalling what God has accomplished in the past, a sign manifesting what he is effecting in the believer and in the church, and a sign announcing and anticipating the eschatological fulfilment. In the sacramental celebration the church thus manifests, illustrates and confesses its faith in the unity of God's design.

17. It will be noted that all sacraments have an essential relationship to the eucharist. The eucharist is the proclamation of faith par excellence from which is derived and to which every confession is ordered. Indeed, it alone proclaims fully, in the presence of the Lord which the power of the Spirit brings about, the marvel of the divine. For the Lord sacramentally makes his work pass into the church's celebration. The sacraments of the church transmit grace, expressing and strengthening faith in Jesus Christ, and are thus witnesses of faith.

4. The faith formulated and celebrated in the sacraments: the symbols of faith

18. In the eucharistic assembly the church celebrates the event of the mystery of salvation in the eucharistic prayer (anaphora) for the glory of God. The mystery it celebrates is the very one which it confesses, while receiving the saving gift.

19. Although the content and finality of this eucharistic celebration have remained the same in the local churches, they have however used varied formulas and different languages which, according to the genius of different cultures, bring into relief particular aspects and implications of the unique salvation event. At the heart of ecclesial life, in the eucharistic *synaxis* (assembly), our two traditions, Eastern and Western, thus experience a certain diversity in the formulation of the content of the faith being celebrated.

20. From earliest times there has been joined to the administration of baptism a formulation of faith by means of which the local church transmits to the catechumen the essential content of the doctrine of the apostles. This "symbol" of the faith enunciates in compact form the essentials of the apostolic tradition, articulated chiefly in the confession of faith in the holy Trinity and in the church. When all the local churches confess the faith, they transmit, in the rite of baptism, this one faith in the Father, Son and Holy Spirit. Nevertheless, at different times and in different places, the formulation has been expressed differently as circumstances required, using terms and propositions which were not identical from one formulary to another. All, however, respected the content of faith. The Eastern church in its baptismal rite uses the Nicene-Constantinopolitan Creed. Faithful to its own tradition, the Western church conveys to the catechumen the text called the Apostles Creed. This diversity of formulas from one church to another does not in itself indicate any divergence about the content of the faith transmitted and lived.

5. Conditions for communion of faith

21. The first condition for a true communion between the churches is that each church makes reference to the Nicene-Constantinopolitan Creed as the necessary norm of this communion of the one church spread throughout the whole world and across the ages. In this sense the true faith is presupposed for a communion in the sacraments. Communion is possible only between those churches which have faith, priesthood and the sacraments in common. It is because of this reciprocal recognition that the faith handed down in each local church is one and the same (as are the priesthood and the sacrament as well), that they recognize each other as genuine churches of God and that each of the faithful is welcomed by the churches as a brother or sister in the faith. At the same time, however, faith is deepened and clarified by the ecclesial communion lived in the sacraments in each community. This ecclesial designation of faith as the fruit of sacramental life is verified at various levels of church life.

22. In the first place, by the celebration of the sacraments, the assembly proclaims, transmits and assimilates its faith.

23. Furthermore, in the celebration of the sacraments, each local church expresses its profound nature. It is in continuity with the church of the apostles and in communion with all the churches which share one and the same faith and celebrate the same sacraments. In the sacramental celebration of a local church, the other local churches recognize the identity of their faith with that church's and by that fact are strengthened in their own life of faith. Thus the celebration of the sacraments confirms the communion of faith between the churches and expresses it. This is why a member of one local church, baptized in that church, can receive the sacraments in another local church. This communion in the sacraments expresses the identity and unicity of the true faith which the churches share.

24. In the eucharistic concelebration between representatives of different local churches identity of faith is particularly manifested and reinforced by the sacramental act itself. This is why councils, in which bishops led by the Holy Spirit express the truth of the church's faith, are always associated with the eucharistic celebration. By proclamation of the one mystery of Christ and sharing of the one sacramental communion, the bishops, the clergy and the whole Christian people united with them are able to witness to the faith of the church.

6. True faith and communion in the sacraments

25. Identity of faith, then, is an essential element of ecclesial communion in the celebration of the sacraments. However, a certain diversity in its formulation does not compromise the koinonia between the local churches when each church can recognize, in the variety of formulations, the one authentic faith received from the apostles.

26. During the centuries of the undivided church, diversity in the theological expression of a doctrine did not endanger sacramental communion. After the schism occurred, East and West continued to develop, but they did this separately from each other. Thus, it was no longer possible for them to take unanimous decisions that were valid for both of them.

27. The church as "pillar and bulwark of truth" (1 Tim. 3:15) keeps the deposit of faith pure and unaltered while transmitting it faithfully to its members. When the authentic teaching or unity of the church was threatened by heresy or schism, the church, basing itself on the Bible, the living tradition and the decisions of preceding councils, declared the correct faith authentically and infallibly in an ecumenical council.

28. When it is established that these differences represent a rejection of earlier dogmas of the church and are not simple differences of theological expression, then clearly one is faced with a true division about faith. It is no longer able to have sacramental communion. For faith must be confessed in words which express the truth itself. However, the life of the church may occasion new verbal expressions of "the faith once and for all delivered to the saints" (Jude 3), if new historical and cultural needs call for them, as long as there is explicit desire not to change the content of the doctrine itself. In such cases, the verbal expression can become normative for unanimity in the faith. This requires criteria for judgment which allow a distinction between legitimate developments, under the inspiration of the Holy Spirit, and other ones.

Thus:

29. The continuity of the tradition: the church ought to give suitable answers to new problems, answers based on the scriptures and in accord and essential continuity with the previous expressions of dogmas.

30. The doxological meaning of the faith: even liturgical development in one local church should be able to be seen by the others as in conformity with the mystery of salvation as it has received that mystery and celebrates it.

31. The soteriological meaning of the faith: expression of the faith should envision the human being's final destiny, as a child of God by grace, in his or her deification *(theosis)* through victory over death and in the transfiguration of creation.

32. If a formulation of the faith contradicts one or other of these criteria, it becomes an obstacle to communion. If, on the other hand, such a particular formulation of the faith contradicts none of these criteria, then this formulation can be considered as a legitimate expression of faith, and does not make sacramental communion impossible.

33. This requires that the theology of *theologoumena* be seriously considered. It is also necessary to clarify what concrete development occurring in one part of Christianity can be considered by the other as a legitimate development. Furthermore, it should be recognized that often the meaning of terms has changed in the course of time. For this reason an effort should be made to understand every formula according to the intention of its authors so as not to introduce into it foreign elements or eliminate elements which, in the mind of the authors, were obvious.

7. The unity of the church in faith and sacraments

34. In the church the function of ministers is above all to maintain, guarantee and promote the growth of communion in faith and sacraments. As ministers of the sacraments and doctors of the faith, the bishops, assisted by other ministers, proclaim the faith of the church, explain its content and its demands for Christian life and defend it against wrong interpretations which would falsify or compromise the truth of the mystery of salvation.

35. Charitable works of ministers, or their taking positions on the problems of a given time or place, are inseparable from the two functions of the proclamation and teaching of the faith, on the one hand, and the celebration of worship and sacraments, on the other.

36. Thus, unity of faith within a local church and between local churches is guaranteed and judged by the bishop, who is witness to the tradition, and in communion with his people. It is inseparable from unity of sacramental life. Communion in faith and communion in the sacraments are not two distinct realities. They are two aspects of a single reality which the Holy Spirit fosters, increases and safeguards among the faithful.

II. The sacraments of Christian initiation: their relation to the unity of the church

37. Christian initiation is a whole in which chrismation is the perfection of baptism and the eucharist is the completion of the other two.

The unity of baptism, chrismation and the eucharist in a single sacramental reality does not deny, however, their specific character. Thus, baptism with water and the Spirit is participation in the death and resurrection of Christ and new birth by grace. Chrismation is the gift of the Spirit to the baptized as a personal gift. Received under the proper conditions, the eucharist, through communion in the body and blood of the Lord, grants participation in the kingdom of God, including forgiveness of sins, communion in divine life itself and membership in the eschatological community.

38. The history of the baptismal rites in East and West, as well as the way in which our common fathers interpreted the doctrinal significance of the rites, shows clearly that the three sacraments of initiation form a unity. That unity is strongly affirmed by the Orthodox church. For its part, the Catholic church also preserves it. Thus, the new Roman ritual of initiation declares that "the three sacraments of Christian initiation are so closely united that they bring the faithful to full capability for carrying out, through the Spirit, the mission which in the world belongs to the entire assembly of the Christian people" (*Prenotanda Generalia*, n. 2).

39. The pattern of administration of the sacraments which developed very early in the church reveals how the church understood the various stages of initiation as accomplishing, theologically and liturgically, incorporation into Christ by entering into the church and growing in him through communion in his body and his blood in this church. All of this is effected by the same Holy Spirit who constitutes the believer as a member of the body of the Lord.

40. The early pattern included the following elements:

41.1: for adults, a period of spiritual probation and instruction during which the catechumens were formed for their definitive incorporation into the church;

42.2: baptism by the bishop assisted by his priests and deacons, or administered by priests assisted by deacons, preceded by a profession of faith and various intercessions and liturgical services;

43.3: confirmation or chrismation in the West by the bishop, or in the East by the priest when the bishop was absent, by means of the imposition of hands or by anointing with holy chrism, or by both;

44.4: the celebration of the holy eucharist during which the newly baptized and confirmed were admitted to the full participation in the body of Christ.

45. These three sacraments were administered in the course of a single, complex liturgical celebration. There followed a period of further catechetical and spiritual maturation through instruction and frequent participation in the eucharist.

46. This pattern remains the ideal for both churches since it corresponds the most exactly possible to the appropriation of the scriptural and apostolic tradition accomplished by the early Christian churches which lived in full communion with each other.

47. The baptism of infants, which has been practised from the beginning, became in the church the most usual procedure for introducing new Christians into the full life of the church. In addition, certain local changes took place in liturgical practice in consideration of the pastoral needs of the faithful. These changes did not concern the theological understanding of the fundamental unity, in the Holy Spirit, of the whole process of Christian initiation.

48. In the East, the temporal unity of the liturgical celebration of the three sacraments was retained, thus emphasizing the unity of the work of the Holy Spirit and the fullness of the incorporation of the child into the sacramental life of the church.

In the West, it was often preferred to delay confirmation so as to retain contact of the baptized person with the bishop. Thus, priests were not ordinarily authorized to confirm.

49. The essential points of the doctrine of baptism on which the two churches are agreed are the following:
1) the necessity of baptism for salvation;
2) the effects of baptism, particularly new life in Christ and liberation from original sin;
3) incorporation into the church by baptism;
4) the relation of baptism to the mystery of the Trinity;
5) the essential link between baptism and the death and resurrection of the Lord;
6) the role of the Holy Spirit in baptism;
7) the necessity of water which manifests baptism's character as the bath of new birth.

50. On the other hand, differences concerning baptism exist between the two churches: (1) the fact that the Catholic church, while recognizing the primordial importance of baptism by immersion, ordinarily practises baptism by infusion; (2) the fact that in the Catholic church a deacon can be the ordinary minister of baptism.

51. Moreover, in certain Latin churches, for pastoral reasons, for example in order to better prepare confirmands at the beginning of adolescence, the practice has become more and more common of admitting to first communion baptized persons who have not yet received confirmation, even though the disciplinary directives which called for the traditional order of the sacraments of Christian initiation have never been abrogated. This inversion, which provokes objections or understandable reservations both by Orthodox and Roman Catholics, calls for deep theological and pastoral reflection

because pastoral practice should never lose sight of the meaning of the early tradition and its doctrinal importance. It is also necessary to recall here that baptism conferred after the age of reason in the Latin church is now always followed by confirmation and participation in the eucharist.

52. At the same time, both churches are preoccupied with the necessity of assuring the spiritual formation of the neophyte in the faith. For that, they wish to emphasize on the one hand that there is a necessary connection between the sovereign action of the Spirit, who realizes through the three sacraments the full incorporation of the person into the life of the church, the latter's response and that of his community of faith and, on the other hand, that the full illumination of the faith is only possible when the neophyte, of whatever age, has received the sacraments of Christian initiation.

53. Finally, it is to be recalled that the council of Constantinople, jointly celebrated by the two churches in 879-880, determined that each see would retain the ancient usages of its tradition, the church of Rome preserving its own usages, the church of Constantinople its own, and the thrones of the East also doing the same (cf. Mansi XVII, 489 B).

(translation from the original French text)

50. Common Declaration
Pope John Paul II and Patriarch Dimitrios I

Vatican, 7 December 1987

At the conclusion of the patriarch's visit on Monday 7 December and just before his departure for London, the pope and the patriarch signed a common declaration.

For this event, Pope John Paul II went to the Torre San Giovanni where the patriarch had resided during his stay.

The text of the declaration is as follows:

We, Pope John Paul II and the Ecumenical Patriarch Dimitrios I, give thanks to God who has granted us to meet in order to pray together with the faithful of the church of Rome, venerable by the memory of the principal apostles Peter and Paul, and to converse with one another concerning the life of Christ's church and its mission in the world.

Our meeting is a sign of the fraternal spirit which exists between the Catholic church and the Orthodox church. This brotherly spirit which has been manifested on numerous occasions and in diverse ways, does not cease to grow and to bear fruit for the glory of God. We experience again the joy of being together as brothers (cf. Ps. 133). As we give thanks "to the Father of lights from whom every perfect gift comes" (cf. James 1:17), we pray and we invite all the faithful of the Catholic church and of the Orthodox church to intercede with us before God: may he bring to perfection the work which he has begun among us! In making our own St Paul's words, we exhort them: "Make my joy complete by living in full harmony" (Phil. 2:2). May the heart of all be constantly disposed to receiving unity as a gift which the Lord makes to his church!

We express our joy and satisfaction in taking note of the first results and the positive evolution of the theological dialogue announced at the time of our meeting at the Phanar on 30 November 1979. The documents accepted by the mixed commission constitute important points of reference for the continuation of the dialogue. Indeed, they seek to express what the Catholic church and the Orthodox church can already profess together as their common faith regarding the mystery of the church and the bond between faith and sacraments. Since each of our churches has received and celebrates the same sacraments, they perceive better that, when unity in faith is assured, a certain diversity of expressions, often complementary, and of proper usages does not create an obstacle but enriches the life of the church and the understanding, always imperfect, of the mystery revealed (cf. 1 Cor. 13:12).

In view of these first results of the effort undertaken in common, in "the obedience of faith" (Rom. 1:5), to re-establish full communion between the Catholic church and the Orthodox church, we thank and encourage the members of the mixed commission for theological dialogue. We desire that the faithful be informed of this in order that they may give thanks to God, may join in prayer to the Lord "that all may be one" (John 17:21), may remain vigilant in intercession and may grow together in faith and hope. We desire as well that advances of the dialogue may bring Catholics and Orthodox to grow in better mutual understanding and in greater charity. By preaching, catechesis and theological formation oriented in this direction, the dialogue will bear all its fruits in the people of God.

We beseech the Spirit of the Lord, who at Pentecost manifested unity in the diversity of tongues, to "lead us to the whole truth" (cf. John 16:13) and to ensure that solutions will be found to the difficulties which still hinder the full communion which will be made manifest in the eucharistic celebration.

Our meeting takes place in this year of the twelfth centennial of the second council of Nicea prepared by a long collaboration without rift between the church of Rome and the church of Constantinople, which caused the Orthodox faith to triumph. The churches of East and West, through the centuries, have celebrated together the ecumenical councils which have proclaimed and defended "the faith handed on to the saints once and for all" (Jude 3). "Called to one single hope" (Eph. 4:4), we await the day willed by God when refound unity will be celebrated and when full communion will be established by a concelebration of the Lord's eucharist.

We renew before God our common commitment to promote the dialogue of charity in every possible manner, following the example of Christ in nourishing his church and surrounding it with the solicitude of his charity (cf. Eph. 5:29). In this spirit, we reject every form of proselytism, every attitude which would or could be perceived as a lack of respect.

This creative charity leads us to collaborate for justice and peace both on the global as well as on the regional and local level. It urges us not to limit this collaboration but to open it out beyond Christians to all those who, in other religions, search for God, his justice and his peace. It makes us ready to work together for the welfare of humanity with all people of good will. Indeed, the church's mission towards the world which Christ comes to save implies the defence of human dignity wherever it is directly or indirectly called into question in a multitude of ways: among others, by the misery which hinders a decent life; by everything which impedes the life of couples and of families, the basis of the whole of society; by the limitation of the freedom of individuals and communities to live and profess their faith and develop according to their own culture; by the use of and traffic in human beings, youths in particular, in order to gratify the lust of others or to make them slaves to drug addiction; by a pursuit of pleasure beyond moral limits; by the fear which generates the existence of means which gravely damage the integrity of creation; by racist ideologies denying the fundamental equality of all before God, ideologies particularly inadmissible for Christians who must reveal to the world the face of Christ the Saviour and thus aid it to overcome its contradictions, its tensions and its anguish because they believe that God so loved the world that he gave his own Son in order that all might be saved by him (cf. John 3:16-17) and become in him one single body where they are members one of another (cf. Rom. 12:5).

In these moments full of joy when we experience a profound spiritual communion which we wish to share with the pastors and faithful both of the East and the West, we raise our hearts to him who is the Head, Christ. It is from him that the whole body acts in harmony and agreement thanks to the structures which serve it according to an activity divided in keeping with the capacity of each one. Thus the body realizes its proper growth. Thus it builds itself up in love (cf. Eph. 4:16).

May all glory be given to God through Christ in the Holy Spirit!

XXIII. EASTERN ORTHODOX-ROMAN CATHOLIC DIALOGUE

51. The Sacrament of Order in the Sacramental Structure of the Church

New Valamo, Finland, 26 June 1988

Introductory note

The joint international commission for theological dialogue between the Roman Catholic Church and the Orthodox church approved in its fifth plenary session at the monastery of New Valamo, Finland, 19-27 June 1988, a new common statement entitled "The Sacrament of Order in the Sacramental Structure of the Church, with Particular Reference to the Importance of the Apostolic Succession for the Sanctification and Unity of the People of God".

This theme was chosen by the joint commission during its third session in Crete in 1984. Immediately afterwards, in 1984 and 1985, the theme was studied simultaneously by three sub-commissions. In June 1985 in Opole, Poland, the joint coordinating committee, on the basis of the studies produced by the sub-commissions, elaborated an organic synthesis.

The proposed document was given a preliminary examination by the joint commission in the first phase of the fourth plenary session in Bari in June 1986 and a number of amendments were proposed. Therefore the draft was revised by a joint editorial committee which met in Rome, 22-26 September 1986.

Consequently the draft of the document reached the fifth plenary session of the commission in Finland already in a highly developed form. Nevertheless, the joint commission re-examined it paragraph by paragraph before approving it unanimously.

This is the third document produced by the joint commission, in which the fourteen autocephalous and autonomous Orthodox churches are taking part, and which was created on the occasion of the visit of His Holiness John Paul II to the ecumenical patriarchate on 30 November 1979.

With strict theological coherence, the document on the sacrament of order and apostolic succession is linked to the first two already published, the first entitled *The Mystery of the Church and of the Holy Eucharist in the Light of the Mystery of the Holy Trinity* (Munich, 1982), and the second entitled *Faith, Sacraments and the Unity of the Church* (Bari, 1987).

The joint commission for theological dialogue between the Catholic church and the Orthodox church chose as the theme of the first phase of the dialogue a study of the sacraments in their relation to the unity of the church, proposing and desiring the use of a positive method, intending, that is, to begin with those common elements which unite Catholics and Orthodox.

The document which is now being published is, along with the two earlier ones, a valuable result of the work of this international joint commission. As such, for the time being it engages the responsibility only of the members of the commission.

The competent authorities of the Catholic church, for their part, while permitting publication of the document as an encouragement to the conversations underway, reserve to themselves the right to express in the future their official position on the results already obtained, on the possible need to subsequently clarify some aspects, and on the need to address other points in the dialogue. The authorities of the various Orthodox churches engaged in this dialogue will do the same.

The Sacrament of Order in the Sacramental Structure of the Church

with Particular Reference to the Importance of Apostolic Succession for the Sanctification and Unity of the People of God

Introduction

1. Having expressed our idea of the mystery of the church as a communion of faith and sacraments, pre-eminently manifested in the eucharistic celebration, our commission now addresses the crucial question of the place and role of ordained ministry in the sacramental structure of the church. We will deal, then, with the sacrament of order as well as with ordination to each of the three degrees of episcopate, presbyterate and diaconate. We rely on the certitude that in our churches apostolic succession is fundamental for the sanctification and the unity of the people of God.

2. Our churches affirm that ministry in the church makes actual that of Christ himself. In the New Testament writings, Christ is called apostle, prophet, pastor, servant, deacon, doctor, priest, *episcopos*. Our common tradition recognizes the close link between the work of Christ and that of the Holy Spirit.

3. This understanding prevents us seeing in the economy Christ in isolation from the Spirit. The actual presence of Christ in his church is also of an eschatological nature, since the Spirit constitutes the earnest of the perfect realization of God's design for the world.

4. In this perspective the church appears as the community of the new covenant which Christ through the Holy Spirit gathers about himself and builds up as his body. Through the church, Christ is present in history; through it he achieves the salvation of the world.

5. Since Christ is present in the church, it is his ministry that is carried out in it. The ministry in the church therefore does not substitute for the ministry of Christ. It has its source in him. Since the Spirit sent by Christ gives life to the church, ministry is only fruitful by the grace of the Spirit. In fact, it includes many functions which the members of the community carry out according to the diversity of the gifts they receive as members of the body of Christ. Certain among them receive through ordination and exercise the function proper to the episcopate, to the presbyterate and to the diaconate. There is no church without the ministries created by the Spirit; there is no ministry without the church, that is to say, outside and above the community. Ministries find their meaning and grounds for existence (raison d'etre) only in it.

I. Christ and the Holy Spirit

6. The Spirit, which eternally proceeds from the Father and reposes on the Son, prepared the Christ event and achieved it. The incarnation of the Son of God, his death and his resurrection, were accomplished in fact according to the will of the Father, in the Holy Spirit. At the baptism, the Father through the manifestation of the Spirit inaugurates the mission of the Son. This Spirit is present in his ministry: the announcing of the good news of salvation, the manifesting of the coming of the kingdom, the bearing witness to the Father. Likewise, it is in the same Spirit that, as the unique priest of the new covenant, Christ offers the sacrifice of his own life and it is through the Spirit that he is glorified.

7. Since Pentecost, in the church which is his body, it is in the Spirit alone that those who are charged with ministry can carry out the acts which bring the body to its full stature. In the ministry of Christ as in that of the church, it is the one and the same Spirit which is at work and which will act with us all the days of our life.

8. In the church ministry should be lived in holiness, with a view towards the sanctification of the people of God. So that the whole church and especially its ordained ministers might be able to contribute to "the perfecting of the saints for the work of ministry for building up the body of Christ", different services are made possible by many charisms (Eph. 4:11-12; cf. 1 Cor. 12:4-28; Rom. 12:4-8).

9. The newness of the church's ministry consists in this: Christ, servant of God for humanity, is present through the Spirit, in the church, his body, from which he cannot be separated. For he himself is "the first-born amongst many brothers". It is according to this sacramental way that one must understand the work of Christ in history from Pentecost to the parousia. The ministry of the church as such is sacramental.

10. For this reason Christ's presence in the church is also eschatological. Wherever the Spirit is at work, he actually reveals to the world the presence of the kingdom in creation. Here is where ecclesial ministry is rooted.

11. This ecclesial ministry is by nature sacramental. The word sacramental is meant to emphasize here that every ministry is bound to the eschatological reality of the kingdom. The grace of the Holy Spirit, earnest of the world to come, has its source in the death and resurrection of Christ and is offered, in a sacramental manner, by means of sensible realities. The word "sacramental" likewise shows that the minister is a member of the community whom the Spirit invests with proper functions and power to assemble it and to preside in the name of Christ over the acts in which it celebrates the mysteries of salvation. This view of the sacramentality of ministry is rooted in the fact that Christ is made present in the church by the Spirit whom he himself has sent to the church.

12. This nature of ecclesial ministry is further shown in the fact that all ministries are intended to serve the world so as to lead it to its true goal, the kingdom of God. It is by constituting the eschatological community as body of Christ that the ministry of the church answers the needs of the world.

13. The community gathered in the Spirit around Christ exercising his ministry for the world has its foundation in Christ, who is himself the cornerstone, and in the community of the Twelve. The apostolic character of churches and their ministry is understood in this light.

14. On the one hand, the Twelve are witness of the historic life of Jesus, of his ministry and of his resurrection. On the other, as associated with the glorified Christ, they

link each community with the community of the last days. Thus the ecclesial ministry will be called apostolic because it is carried out in continuity and in fidelity to what was given by Christ and handed on in history by the apostles. But it will also be apostolic because the eucharistic assembly at which the minister presides is an anticipation of the final community with Christ. Through this double relationship the church's ministry remains constantly bound to that of the Twelve, and so to that of Christ.

II. The priesthood in the divine economy of salvation

15. The entire divine economy of salvation culminates in the incarnation of the Son, in his teaching, his passion, his glorious resurrection, his ascension and his second coming. Christ acts in the Holy Spirit. Thus, once and for all, there is laid the foundation for re-establishing the communion of man with God.

16. According to the epistle to the Hebrews, Christ by his death has become the one mediator of the new covenant (Heb. 9:15) and having entered once for all into the holy place with his own blood (Heb. 9:12), he is forever in heaven the one and eternal High Priest of this new covenant "so as to appear now in the presence of God on our behalf" (Heb. 9:24) to offer his sacrifice (Heb. 10:12).

17. Invisibly present in the church through the Holy Spirit, whom he has sent, Christ then is its unique High Priest. In him, priest and victim, all together, pastors and faithful, form a "chosen race, a royal priesthood, a holy nation, a people he claims as his own" (1 Pet. 2:9; cf. Rev. 5:10).

18. All members of the churches, as members of the body of Christ, participate in this priesthood, called to become "a living sacrifice holy and acceptable to God" (Rom. 12:1; cf. 1 Pet. 2:5). Head of the church, Christ has established, to make himself present, apostles chosen among the people, whom he endowed with authority and power by strengthening them through the grace of the Holy Spirit. The work and mission of the apostles are continued in the church by the bishops with the priests and deacons who assist them. By ordination, the bishops are established successors of the apostles and direct the people along the ways of salvation.

19. Grouped around the glorified Lord, the Twelve give witness to the presence of the kingdom already inaugurated and which will be fully manifested at the second coming. Christ has indeed promised them that they would sit on twelve thrones, judging with the Son of Man the twelve tribes of Israel (Matt. 19:28).

20. As historic witness of what the Lord accomplished, the ministry of the Twelve is unique and irreplaceable. What they laid down was founded therefore once for all and no one in the future could build except on the foundation thus established (Eph. 2:20; Rev. 21:14).

21. But the apostles remain at the same time the foundations of the church as it endures through the ages, in such a way that the mission they received from the Lord always remains visible and active, in expectation of the Lord's return (cf. Matt. 18:18 and, earlier, 16:19).

22. This is why the church, in which God's grace is at work, is itself the sacrament par excellence, the anticipated manifestation of the final realities, the foretaste of God's kingdom, of the glory of the God and Father, of the eschaton in history.

23. Within this sacrament which is the church, the priesthood conferred by ordination finds its place, being given for this church. In fact, it constitutes in the church a charismatic ministry *(leitourgema)* par excellence. It is at the service of the church's

life and continued existence by the Holy Spirit, that is to say, of the unity in Christ, of all the faithful living and dead, of the martyrs, the saints, the just of the Old Testament.

III. The ministry of the bishop, presbyter and deacon

24. In the celebration of the eucharist, the entire assembly, each according to his or her status, is "liturge" of the koinonia, and is so only through the Spirit. "... there are varieties of ministries, but the same Lord... To each is given the manifestation of the Spirit for the common good" (1 Cor. 12:5,7). The various ministries converge in the eucharistic synaxis, during which they are conferred. However, their diversity is ordered to the entire life of the community: fidelity to the word of God, abiding in harmony and fraternal charity, witness before "those outside", growth in holiness, constancy in prayer, care for the poorest.

25. Since it culminates in the celebration of the eucharist in which Christian initiation is completed, through which all become one body of Christ, the ministry of the bishop is, among all the charisms and ministries which the Spirit raises up, a ministry of presiding for gathering in unity. In fact, bearing the variety of gifts of the Spirit, the local church has at its centre the bishop, whose communion realizes the unity of all and expresses the fullness of the church.

26. This unity of the local church is inseparable from the universal communion of the churches. It is essential for a church to be in communion with the others. This communion is expressed and realized in and through the episcopal college. By his ordination, the bishop is made minister of a church which he represents in the universal communion.

27. Episcopal ordination, which according to the canons is conferred by at least two or three bishops, expresses the communion of the churches with that of the person selected: it makes him a member of the communion of bishops. In the ordination the bishops exercise their function as witnesses to the communion in the apostolic faith and sacramental life not only with respect to him whom they ordain, but also with respect to the church of which he will be bishop. What is fundamental for the incorporation of the newly elected person in the episcopal communion is that it is accomplished by the glorified Lord in the power of the Holy Spirit at the moment of the imposition of hands.

Here we are only considering ordination under its sacramental aspect. The problems raised by the manner of electing a bishop will be studied later.

28. Episcopal ordination confers on the one who receives it by the gift of the Spirit, the fullness of the priesthood. During the ordination the concelebration of the bishops expresses the unity of the church and its identity with the apostolic community. They lay hands and invoke the Holy Spirit on the one who will be ordained as the only ones qualified to confer on him the episcopal ministry. They do it, however, within the setting of the prayer of the community.

29. Through his ordination, the bishop receives all the powers necessary for fulfilling his function. The canonical conditions for the exercise of his function and the installation of the bishop in the local church will be further discussed by the commission.

30. The gift conferred consecrates the recipient once for all to the service of the church. This is a point of the traditional doctrine in East and West, which is confirmed by the fact that in the event of disciplinary sanctions against a bishop followed by

canonical reintegration, there is no reordination. On this subject, as on all the essential points concerning ordination, our churches have a common doctrine and practice, even if on certain canonical and disciplinary requirements, such as celibacy, customs can be different because of pastoral and spiritual reasons.

31. But ecclesial ministry is exercised through a variety of functions. These are exercised in interdependence; none could replace another. This is especially true of the fundamental ministries of the bishop, the presbyter and the deacon, and of the functions of the laity, all of which together give structure to the eucharistic community.

32. Throughout the entire history of our churches, women have played a fundamental role, as witnessed not only by the most holy Mother of God, but also by the holy women mentioned in the New Testament, by the numerous women saints whom we venerate, as well as by so many other women who up to the present day have served the church in many ways. Their particular charisms are very important for the building up of the body of Christ. But our churches remain faithful to the historical and theological tradition according to which they ordain only men to the priestly ministry.

33. Just as the apostles gathered together the first communities, by proclaiming Christ, by celebrating the eucharist, by leading the baptized towards growing communion with Christ and with each other, so the bishop, established by the same Spirit, continues to preach the same gospel, to preside at the same eucharist, to serve the unity and sanctification of the same community. He is thus the icon of Christ the servant among his brethren.

34. Because it is at the eucharist that the church manifests its fullness, it is equally in the presiding at the eucharist that the role of the bishop and of the priest appears in its full light.

35. In the eucharistic celebration, in fact, believers offer themselves with Christ as a royal priesthood. They do so thanks to the ministerial action which makes present in their midst Christ himself who proclaims the word, makes the bread and the cup become through the Spirit his body and blood, incorporating them in himself, giving them his life. Moreover, the prayer and the offering of the people incorporated in Christ are, so to speak, recapitulated in the thanksgiving prayer of the bishop and his offering of the gifts.

36. The eucharist thus realizes the unity of the Christian community. It also manifests the unity of all the churches which truly celebrate it and further still the unity, across the centuries, of all the churches with the apostolic community from the beginnings up to the present day. Transcending history, it reunites in the Spirit the great assembly of the apostles, of martyrs, of witnesses of all periods gathered around the Lamb. Indeed, as the central act of episcopal ministry it makes clearly present the world to come: the church gathered in communion, offering itself to the Father, through the Son, in the Holy Spirit.

37. He who presides at the eucharist is responsible for preserving communion in fidelity to the teaching of the apostles and for guiding it in the new life. He is its servant and pastor. The bishop is also the guide of the entire liturgical life of his local church and, following his example, this church becomes a community of prayer. He presides at its praise and at its intercession, and he himself prays unceasingly for all those entrusted to him by the Lord, knowing that he is responsible for each one before the tribunal of God.

38. It also rests with him to see to it that there be given to his people, by preaching and catechesis, the authentic content of the word of God given to the apostles "once for

all". He is in fact the primary one responsible for the preaching of the word of God in his diocese.

39. To him also belongs the task of leading this people towards proclaiming to all human beings salvation in Jesus Christ, and towards a witness which embodies that proclamation. Therefore, it is for him to govern his church in such a way that it always remains faithful to its Christian vocation and to the mission deriving therefrom. In all this, however, he remains a member of the church called to holiness and dependent on the salvific ministry of this church, as St Augustine reminds his community: "For you I am a bishop, with you I am a Christian." At his ordination the bishop makes his own the faith of the whole church by solemnly confessing it and thus becomes father to the extent that he has fully become its son by this confession. It is essential for the bishop to be the father of his people.

40. As successor of the apostles, bishops are responsible for communion in the apostolic faith and fidelity to the demands of a life lived according to the gospel.

41. It is in presiding over the eucharistic assembly that the role of the bishop finds its accomplishment. The presbyters form the college grouped around him during that celebration. They exercise the responsibilities the bishop entrusts to them by celebrating the sacraments, teaching the word of God and governing the community, in profound and continuous communion with him. The deacon, for his part, is attached to the service of the bishop and the priest and is a link between them and the assembly of the faithful.

42. The priest, ordained by the bishop and dependent upon him, is sent to fulfil certain definite tasks; above all he is sent to a parish community to be its pastor: he presides at the eucharist at the altar (consecrated by the bishop), he is minister of the sacraments for the community, he preaches the gospel and catechizes; it is his duty to keep in unity the charisms of the people (laos) of God; he appears as the ordinary minister of the local eucharistic community, and the diocese is thus a communion of eucharistic communities.

43. The diaconate is exercised at the service of the bishop and the priest, in the liturgy, in the work of evangelization and in the service of charity.

IV. Apostolic succession

44. The same unique ministry of Christ and his apostles remains in action in history. This action is, through the Spirit, a breakthrough to "the world to come", in fidelity to what the apostles transmitted about what Jesus did and taught.

45. The importance of this succession comes also from the fact that the apostolic tradition concerns the community and not only an isolated individual, ordained bishop. Apostolic succession is transmitted through local churches ("in each city", according to the expression of Eusebius of Caesarea; "by reason of their common heritage of doctrine", according to Tertullian in the *De Praescriptione*, 32, 6). It is a matter of a succession of persons in the community, because the una sancta is a communion of local churches and not of isolated individuals. It is within this mystery of koinonia that the episcopate appears as the central point of the apostolic succession.

46. According to what we have already said in the Munich document, "apostolic succession, therefore, means something more than a mere transmission of powers. It is succession in a church which witnesses to the apostolic faith, in communion with the other churches, witnesses of the same apostolic faith. The 'see' *(cathedra)* plays an

important role in inserting the bishop into the heart of ecclesial apostolicity" (Munich document, II, 4). More precisely, the term *cathedra* is used here in the sense of the presence of the bishop in each local church.

47. "On the other hand, once ordained, the bishop becomes in his church the guarantor of apostolicity, the one who represents it within the communion of churches, its link with the other churches. That is why in his church every eucharist can only be celebrated in truth if presided over by him or by a presbyter in communion with him. Mention of him in the anaphora is essential" *(ibid.)*.

48. "Attachment to the apostolic communion joins together all the bishops, maintaining the *episcope* of the local churches, to the college of the apostles" *(ibid.,* III, 4). The bishops are thus rooted in the "once for all" of the apostolic group through which the Holy Spirit gives witness to the faith. Indeed, as the foundation of the church, the Twelve are unique. Even so, it was necessary that other men should make visible their irreplaceable presence. In this way the link of each community would be maintained with both the original community and the eschatological community.

49. Through his ordination each bishop becomes successor of the apostles, whatever may be the church over which he presides or the prerogatives ($\pi\rho\epsilon\sigma\beta\epsilon\tau\alpha$) of this church among the other churches.

50. Incorporated into the number of those to whom the particular responsibility for the ministry of salvation has been entrusted, and so placed in the succession of the apostles, the bishop ought to pass on their teaching as well as model his whole life on them. Ireneaeus of Lyons puts it thus: "It is where the charisms of God have been planted that we should be instructed in the truth, that is among those in whom are united succession in the church from the apostles, unassailable integrity of conduct and incorruptible purity of doctrine" (*Adv. Haer.* IV, 26, 5). Among the essential functions of the bishop is that of being in his church through the Spirit a witness and guarantor of the faith and an instrument for maintaining it in apostolic fidelity. Apostolic succession is also a succession in the labours and sufferings of the apostles for the service of the gospel and in the defence of the people entrusted to each bishop. According to the words of the first letter of St Peter, the apostolic succession is also a succession in the presence of mercy and understanding, of defence of the weak, of constant attention to those entrusted to their charge, with the bishop thus being a model for the flock (cf. 1 Pet. 5:1-4; 2 Cor. 4:8-11; 1 Tim. 4:12; Titus 2:7).

51. Furthermore it belongs to the episcopal ministry to articulate and organize the life of the church with its service and offices. It is his task also to watch over the choice of those who are to carry out responsibilities in his diocese. Fraternal communion requires that all the members, ministers or laypeople, listen to each other for the good of the people of God.

52. In the course of its history, the church in East and West has known various forms of practising communion among bishops: by exchange of letters, by visits of one church to another, but principally by synodal or conciliar life. From the first centuries a distinction and a hierarchy was established between churches of earlier foundation and churches of more recent foundation, between mother and daughter churches, between churches of larger cities and churches of outlying areas. This hierarchy of *taxis* soon found its canonical expression, formulated by the councils, especially in the canons received by all the churches of the East and West. These are, in the first place, canons 6 and 7 of the first council of Nicea (325), canon 3 of the first council of Con-

stantinople (second ecumenical council, 381), canon 28 of Chalcedon (fourth ecumenical council, 451), as well as canons 3, 4 and 5 of Sardica (343) and canon 1 of the council of Saint Sophia (879-880). Even if these canons have not always been interpreted in the same way in the East and in the West, they belong to the heritage of the church. They assigned to bishops occupying certain metropolitan or major sees a place and prerogatives recognized in the organization of the synodal life of the church. Thus was formed the pentarchy: Rome, Constantinople, Alexandria, Antioch and Jerusalem, even if in the course of history there appeared apart from the pentarchy other archbishops, metropolitans, primates and patriarchs.

53. The synodal character of episcopal activity showed itself especially in questions under discussion which interested several local churches or the churches as a whole. Thus in each region different types of synods or local and regional councils and conferences of bishops were organized. Their forms could change according to different places and times, but their guiding principle is to manifest and make efficacious the life of the church by joint episcopal action, under the presidency of the one whom they recognized as the first among them. In fact, according to canon 34 of the apostolic canons, belonging to the canonical tradition of our churches, the first among the bishops only takes a decision in agreement with the other bishops and the latter take no important decision without the agreement of the first.

54. In ecumenical councils, convened in the Holy Spirit at times of crisis, bishops of the church, with supreme authority, decided together about the faith and issued canons to affirm the Tradition of the apostles in historic circumstances which directly threatened the faith, unity and sanctifying work of the whole people of God, and put at risk the very existence of the church and its fidelity to its Founder, Jesus Christ.

55. It is in this perspective of communion among local churches that the question could be addressed of primacy in the church in general and, in particular, the primacy of the bishop of Rome, a question which constitutes a serious divergence among us and which will be discussed in the future.

52. Uniatism: Method of Union of the Past, and the Present Search for Full Communion

Balamand, Lebanon, 23 June 1993

Introduction

1. At the request of the Orthodox churches, the normal progression of the theological dialogue with the Catholic church has been set aside so the immediate attention might be given to the question which is called "uniatism".

2. With regard to the method which has been called "uniatism", it was stated at Freising (June 1990) that "we reject it as a method for the search for unity because it is opposed to the common tradition of our churches".

3. Concerning the Oriental Catholic churches, it is clear that they, as part of the Catholic communion, have the right to exist and to act in answer to the spiritual needs of their faithful.

4. The document prepared at Ariccia by the joint coordinating committee (June 1991) and finished at Balamand (June 1993) states what is our method in the present search for full communion, thus giving the reason for excluding "uniatism" as a method.

5. This document is composed of two parts: (1) ecclesiological principles, and (2) practical rules.

Ecclesiological principles

6. The division between the churches of the East and of the West has never quelled the desire for unity wished by Christ. Rather this situation, which is contrary to the nature of the church, has often been for man the occasion to become more deeply conscious of the need to achieve this unity, so as to be faithful to the Lord's commandment.

7. In the course of the centuries various attempts were made to re-establish unity. They sought to achieve this end through different ways, at times conciliar, according to the political, historical, theological and spiritual situation of each period. Unfortunately, none of these efforts succeeded in re-establishing full communion between the church of the West and the church of the East, and at times even made oppositions more acute.

8. In the course of the last four centuries, in various parts of the East, initiatives were taken within certain churches and impelled by outside elements, to restore communion between the church of the East and the church of the West. These initiatives led to the union of certain communities with the see of Rome and brought with them, as a consequence, the breaking of communion with their mother churches of the East.

This took place not without the interference of extra-ecclesial interests. In this way Oriental Catholic churches came into being. And so a situation was created which has become a source of conflicts and of suffering in the first instance for the Orthodox but also for Catholics.

9. Whatever may have been the intention and the authenticity of the desire to be faithful to the commandment of Christ "that all may be one" expressed in these partial unions with the see of Rome, it must be recognized that the re-establishment of unity between the church of the East and the church of the West was not achieved and that the division remains, embittered by these attempts.

10. The situation thus created resulted in fact in tensions and oppositions.

Progressively, in the decades which followed these unions, missionary activity tended to include among its priorities the effort to convert other Christians, individually or in groups, so as "to bring them back" to one's own church. In order to legitimize this tendency, a source of proselytism, the Catholic church developed the theological vision according to which she presented herself as the only one to whom salvation was entrusted. As a reaction, the Orthodox church, in turn, came to accept the same vision according to which only in her could salvation be found. To assure the salvation of the "separated brethren" it even happened that Christians were rebaptized and that certain requirements of the religious freedom of persons and of their act of faith were forgotten. This perspective was one to which that period showed little sensitivity.

11. On the other hand, certain civil authorities made attempts to bring back Oriental Catholics to the church of their fathers. To achieve this end they did not hesitate, when the occasion was given, to use unacceptable means.

12. Because of the way in which Catholics and Orthodox once again consider each other in their relationship to the mystery of the church and discover each other once again as sister churches, this form of "missionary apostolate" described above, and which has been called "uniatism", can no longer be accepted either as a method to be followed nor as a model of the unity our churches are seeking.

13. In fact, especially since the Pan-Orthodox conferences and the Second Vatican Council, the rediscovery and the giving again of proper value to the church as communion, both on the part of Orthodox and of Catholics, has radically altered perspectives and thus attitudes. On each side it is recognized that what Christ has entrusted to his church – profession of apostolic faith, participation in the sacraments, above all the one priesthood celebrating the one sacrifice of Christ, the apostolic succession of bishops – cannot be considered the exclusive property of one of our churches. In this context, it is clear that any rebaptism must be avoided.

14. It is in this perspective that the Catholic churches and the Orthodox churches recognize each other as sister churches, responsible together for maintaining the church of God in fidelity to the divine purpose, most especially in what concerns unity. According to the words of Pope John Paul II, the ecumenical endeavour of the sister churches of East and West, grounded in dialogue and prayer, is the search for perfect and total communion which is neither absorption nor fusion but a meeting in truth and love (cf. *Slavorum Apostoli*, no. 27).

15. While the inviolable freedom of persons and their obligation to follow the requirements of their conscience remain secure, in the search for re-establishing unity there is no question of conversion of people from one church to the other in order to ensure their salvation. There is a question of achieving together the will of Christ for

his own and the design of God for his church by means of a common quest by the churches for a full accord on the content of the faith and its implications. This effort is being carried on in the current theological dialogue. The present document is a necessary stage in this dialogue.

16. The Oriental Catholic churches who have desired to re-establish full communion with the see of Rome and have remained faithful to it have the rights and obligations which are connected with this communion. The principles determining their attitude towards Orthodox churches are those which have been stated by the Second Vatican Council and have been put into practice by the popes who have clarified the practical consequences flowing from these principles in various documents published since then. These churches, then, should be inserted, on both local and universal levels, into the dialogue of love, in mutual respect and reciprocal trust found once again, and enter into the theological dialogue, with all its practical implications.

17. In this atmosphere, the considerations already presented and the practical guidelines which follow, insofar as they will be effectively received and faithfully observed, are such as to lead to a just and definitive solution to the difficulties which these Oriental Catholic churches present to the Orthodox church.

18. Towards this end, Pope Paul VI affirmed in his address at the Phanar in July 1967: "It is on the heads of the churches, of their hierarchy, that the obligation rests to guide the churches along the way that leads to finding full communion again. They ought to do this by recognizing and respecting each other as pastors of that part of the flock of Christ entrusted to them, by taking care for the cohesion and growth of the people of God, and avoiding everything that could scatter it or cause confusion in its ranks" (*Tomos Agapis*, no. 172). In this spirit Pope John Paul II and Ecumenical Patriarch Dimitrios I together stated clearly: "We reject every form of proselytism, every attitude which would be or could be perceived to be a lack of respect" (7 December 1978).

Practical rules

19. Mutual respect between the churches which find themselves in difficult situations will increase appreciably in the measure that they will observe the following practical rules.

20. These rules will not resolve the problems which are worrying us unless each of the parties concerned has a will to pardon, based on the gospel and, within the context of a constant effort for renewal, accompanied by the unceasing desire to seek the full communion which existed for more than a thousand years between our churches. It is here that the dialogue of love must be present with a continually renewed intensity and perseverance which alone can overcome reciprocal lack of understanding and which is the necessary climate for deepening the theological dialogue that will permit arriving at full communion.

21. The first step to take is to put an end to everything that can foment division, contempt and hatred between the churches. For this the authorities of the Catholic church will assist the Oriental Catholic churches and their communities so that they themselves may prepare for full communion between Catholic and Orthodox churches. The authorities of the Orthodox church will act in a similar manner towards their faithful. In this way it will be possible to take care of the extremely complex situation that has been created in Eastern Europe, at the same time in charity and in justice, both as regards Catholics and Orthodox.

22. Pastoral activity in the Catholic church, Latin as well as Oriental, no longer aims at having the faithful of one church pass over to the other, that is to say, it no longer aims at proselytizing among the Orthodox. It aims at answering the spiritual needs of its own faithful and it has no desire for expansion at the expense of the Orthodox church. Within these perspectives, so that there will no longer be a place for mistrust and suspicion, it is necessary that there be reciprocal exchanges of information about various pastoral projects and that this cooperation between bishops and all those with responsibilities in our churches can be set in motion and develop.

23. The history of the relations between the Orthodox church and the Oriental Catholic churches has been marked by persecutions and sufferings. Whatever may have been these sufferings and their causes, they do not justify any triumphalism; no one can glory in them or draw an argument from them to accuse or disparage the other church. God alone knows his own witnesses. Whatever may have been the past, it must be left to the mercy of God, and all the energies of the churches should be directed towards obtaining that the present and the future conform better to the will of Christ for his own.

24. It will also be necessary – and this on the part of both churches – that the bishops and all those with pastoral responsibilities in them scrupulously respect the religious liberty of the faithful. These, in turn, must be able to express freely their opinion by being consulted and by organizing themselves to this end. In fact, religious liberty requires that, particularly in situations of conflict, the faithful are able to express their opinion and to decide without pressure from outside if they wish to be in communion either with the Orthodox church or with the Catholic church. Religious freedom would be violated when, under the cover of financial assistance, the faithful of one church would be attracted to the other, by promises, for example, of education and material benefits that may be lacking in their own church. In this context, it will be necessary that social assistance as well as every form of philanthropic activity be organized with common agreement so as to avoid creating new suspicions.

25. Furthermore, the necessary respect for Christian freedom – one of the most precious gifts received from Christ – should not become an occasion for undertaking a pastoral project which may also involve the faithful of other churches, without previous consultation with the pastors of these churches. Not only should every form of pressure, of any kind whatsoever, be excluded, but respect for consciences, motivated by an authentic exigency of faith, should be one of the principles guiding the pastoral concern of those responsible in the two churches and should be the object of their common reflection (cf. Gal. 5:13).

26. That is why it is necessary to seek and to engage in an open dialogue, which in the first place should be between those who have responsibilities for the churches at the local level. Those in charge of the communities concerned should create joint local commissions or make effective those which already exist, for finding solutions to concrete problems and seeing that these solutions are applied in truth and love, in justice and peace. If agreement cannot be reached on the local level, the question should be brought to mixed commissions established by higher authorities.

27. Suspicion would disappear more easily if the two parties were to condemn violence wherever communities of one church use it against communities of a sister church. As requested by His Holiness Pope John Paul II in his letter of 31 May 1991, it is necessary that all violence and every kind of pressure be absolutely avoided in

order that freedom of conscience be respected. It is the task of those in charge of communities to assist their faithful to deepen their loyalty towards their own church and towards its traditions and to teach them to avoid not only violence, be that physical, verbal or moral, but also all that could lead to contempt for other Christians and to a counter-witness, completely ignoring the work of salvation which is reconciliation in Christ.

28. Faith in sacramental reality implies a respect for the liturgical celebrations of the other church. The use of violence to occupy a place of worship contradicts this conviction. On the contrary, this conviction sometimes requires that the celebration of other churches should be made easier by putting at their disposal, by common agreement, one's own church for alternate celebration at different times in the same building. Still more, the evangelical ethos requires that statements or manifestations which are likely to perpetuate a state of conflict and hinder the dialogue be avoided. Does not St Paul exhort us to welcome one another as Christ has welcomed us, for the glory of God (Rom. 15:7)?

29. Bishops and priests have the duty before God to respect the authority which the Holy Spirit has given to the bishops and priests of the other church and for that reason to avoid interfering in the spiritual life of the faithful of that church. When cooperation becomes necessary for the good of the faithful, it is then required that those responsible for an agreement among themselves establish for this mutual assistance clear principles which are known to all, and act subsequently with frankness, clarity, and with respect for the sacramental discipline of the other church.

In this context, to avoid all misunderstanding and to develop confidence between the two churches, it is necessary that Catholic and Orthodox bishops of the same territory consult with each other before establishing Catholic pastoral projects which imply the creation of new structures in regions which traditionally form part of the jurisdiction of the Orthodox church, in view to avoid parallel pastoral activities which would risk rapidly degenerating into rivalry or even conflicts.

30. To pave the way for future relations between the two churches passing beyond the outdated ecclesiology of return to the Catholic church connected with the problem which is the object of this document, special attention will be given to the preparation of future priests and of all those who, in any way, are involved in an apostolic activity carried on in a place where the other church traditionally has its roots. Their education should be objectively positive with respect to the other church. First of all, everyone should be informed of the apostolic succession of the other church and the authenticity of its sacramental life. One should also offer all a correct and comprehensive knowledge of history aiming at a historiography of the two churches which is in agreement and even may be common. In this way, the dissipation of prejudices will be helped, and the use of history in a polemical manner will be avoided. This presentation will lead to an awareness that faults leading to separation belong to both sides, leaving deep wounds on each side.

31. The admonition of the apostle Paul to the Corinthians (1 Cor. 6:1-7) will be recalled. It recommends that Christians resolve their differences through fraternal dialogue, thus avoiding recourse to the intervention of the civil authorities for a practical solution to the problems which arise between churches or local communities. This applies particularly to the possession or return of ecclesiastical property. These solutions should not be based only on past situations or rely solely on general juridical prin-

ciples, but they must also take into account the complexity of present realities and local circumstances.

32. It is in this spirit that it will be possible to meet in common the task of re-evangelization of our secularized world. Efforts will also be made to give objective news to the mass media, especially to the religious press, in order to avoid tendentious and misleading information.

33. It is necessary that the churches come together in order to express gratitude and respect towards all, known and unknown – bishops, priests or faithful, Orthodox, Catholic whether Oriental or Latin – who suffered, confessed their faith, witnessed their fidelity to the church and, in general, towards all Christians, without discrimination, who underwent persecutions. Their sufferings call us to unity and, on our part, to give common witness in response to the prayer of Christ "that all may be one, so that the world may believe" (John 17:21).

34. The international joint commission for theological dialogue between the Catholic church and the Orthodox church, at its plenary meeting in Balamand, strongly recommends that these practical rules be put into practice by our churches, including the Oriental Catholic churches who are called to take part in this dialogue, which should be carried on in the serene atmosphere necessary for its progress, towards the re-establishment of full communion.

35. By excluding for the future all proselytism and all desire for expansion by Catholics at the expense of the Orthodox church, the commission hopes that it has overcome the obstacles which impelled certain autocephalous churches to suspend their participation in the theological dialogue, and that the Orthodox church will be able to find itself altogether again for continuing the theological work already so happily begun.

53. Common Declaration
Pope John Paul II and Bartholomew, Ecumenical Patriarch
Vatican, 29 June 1995

On the evening of Thursday, 29 June, Pope John Paul II and Ecumenical Patriarch Bartholomew I signed a common declaration in the Vatican at their last meeting before the patriarch's departure from Rome. The following is a translation of the declaration, which was written in Italian.

"Blessed be the God and Father of our Lord Jesus Christ, who has blessed us in Christ with every spiritual blessing" (Eph. 1:3).

1. We also thank God for this brotherly meeting of ours which took place in his name and with the firm intention of obeying his will that his disciples be one (John 17:21). Our meeting has followed other important events which have seen our churches declare their desire to relegate the excommunications of the past to oblivion and to set out on the way to re-establishing full communion. Our venerable predecessors Athenagoras I and Paul VI became pilgrims to Jerusalem in order to meet in the Lord's name, precisely where the Lord, by his death and resurrection, brought humanity forgiveness and salvation. Subsequently, their meetings at the Phanar and in Rome have initiated this new tradition of fraternal visits in order to foster a true dialogue of charity and truth. This exchange of visits was repeated during the ministry of Patriarch Dimitrios when, among other things, the theological dialogue was formally opened. Our new-found brotherhood in the name of the one Lord has led us to frank discussion, a dialogue that seeks understanding and unity.

2. This dialogue – through the joint international commission – has proved fruitful and has made substantial progress. A common sacramental conception of the church has emerged, sustained and passed on in time by the apostolic succession. In our churches, the apostolic succession is fundamental to the sanctification and unity of the people of God. Considering that in every local church the mystery of divine love is realized and that this is how the church of Christ shows forth its active presence in each one of them, the joint commission has been able to declare that our churches recognize one another as sister churches, responsible together for safeguarding the one church of God, in fidelity to the divine plan, and in an altogether special way with regard to unity.

We thank the Lord of the church from the bottom of our hearts because these affirmations we have made together not only hasten the way to solving the existing difficulties, but henceforth enable Catholics and Orthodox to give a common witness of faith.

3. This is particularly appropriate on the eve of the third millennium when, 2000 years after the birth of Christ, all Christians are preparing to make an examination of conscience on the reality of his proclamation of salvation in history and among men.

We will celebrate this great jubilee on our pilgrimage towards full unity and towards that blessed day, which we pray is not far off, when we will be able to share the same bread and the same cup, in the one eucharist of the Lord.

Let us invite our faithful to make this spiritual pilgrimage together towards the jubilee. Reflection, prayer, dialogue, reciprocal forgiveness and mutual fraternal love will bring us closer to the Lord and will help us better to understand his will for the church and for humanity.

4. In this perspective we urge our faithful, Catholics and Orthodox, to reinforce the spirit of brotherhood which stems from the one baptism and from participation in the sacramental life. In the course of history and in the more recent past, there have been attacks and acts of oppression on both sides. As we prepare, on this occasion, to ask the Lord for his great mercy, we invite all to forgive one another and to express a firm will that a new relationship of brotherhood and active collaboration will be established.

Such a spirit should encourage both Catholics and Orthodox, especially where they live side by side, to a more intense collaboration in the cultural, spiritual, pastoral, educational and social fields, avoiding any temptation to undue zeal for their own community to the disadvantage of the other. May the good of Christ's church always prevail! Mutual support and the exchange of gifts can only make pastoral activity itself more effective and our witness to the gospel we desire to proclaim more transparent.

5. We maintain that a more active and concerted collaboration will also facilitate the church's influence in promoting peace and justice in situations of political or ethnic conflict. The Christian faith has unprecedented possibilities for solving humanity's tensions and enmity.

6. In meeting one another, the pope of Rome and the ecumenical patriarch have prayed for the unity of all Christians. In their prayers, they have included all the baptized who are incorporated into Christ, and they have asked for an ever deeper fidelity to his gospel for the various communities.

7. They bear in their heart a concern for all humanity, without any discrimination according to race, colour, language, ideology or religion.

They therefore encourage dialogue, not only between the Christian churches, but also with the various religions, and above all with those that are monotheistic.

All this doubtless represents a contribution and a presupposition for strengthening peace in the world, for which our churches pray constantly. In this spirit, we declare, without hesitation, that we are in favour of harmony among peoples and their collaboration, especially in what concerns us most directly; we pray for the full realization of the European Union, without delay, and we hope that its borders will be extended to the East.

At the same time, we make an appeal that everyone will make a determined effort to solve the current burning problem of ecology, in order to avoid the great risk threatening the world today due to the abuse of resources that are God's gift.

May the Lord heal the wounds tormenting humanity today and hear our prayers and those of our faithful for peace in our churches and in all the world.

XXIV. ORIENTAL ORTHODOX-ROMAN CATHOLIC DIALOGUE

Historical Introduction

The theological dialogue between the Oriental Orthodox churches and the Roman Catholic Church began on two levels simultaneously:
a) unofficial ecumenical meetings in which prominent theologians and members of the hierarchy took part; and
b) concrete official common declarations issued by the head of the Roman Catholic Church and the heads of the several Oriental Orthodox churches.

The first four ecumenical theological conferences were held at the Pro Oriente Ecumenical Institute in Vienna (1971, 1973, 1976, 1978). The work done at these conferences was based on theological papers presented by both sides on a wide range of subjects. At the first two meetings the Christology of the two churches was the main topic of discussion; the following two meetings dealt with ecclesiological and historico-canonical problems. Both the theological papers and the ensuing discussion of them were on a very high level. The meetings were also marked by a very special effort of the two sides to draw closer to each other amid inherited theological and ecclesiological differences. The theological discussions brought to light important elements in a convergence and even an agreement of the two theological traditions, especially in the area of Christology. The exclusively theological character of this convergence was recognized at the first four ecumenical meetings and especially at the fifth (1988). At the same time, these meetings emphasized the contribution thereby made to the promotion of official initiatives on the part of the churches: for example, the official common declarations of Pope Paul VI and Shenouda III, Patriarch of the Coptic Orthodox Church (1973), and of Pope John Paul II and Ignatius Zakka I, Patriarch of the Syrian Orthodox Church (1984). Of like importance was the agreement reached on a number of subjects at the meeting between Pope Paul VI and Mar Ignatius Jacob III, Patriarch of the Syrian Orthodox Church (27 October 1971). The heads of the two churches recognized "the deep spiritual communion" that existed between the two churches and agreed that "there is no difference in the faith they profess concerning the mystery of the Word of God made flesh and become really man" (*Doing the Truth in Charity* [Ecumenical Documents I], pp.237-38).

The common declaration (1984) of Pope John Paul II and Ignatius Zakka I, Patriarch of the Syrian Orthodox Church, made it quite clear that the above-mentioned two heads of the churches had in 1971 "denied that there was any difference in the faith they confessed in the mystery of the Word of God made flesh and become truly man".

The official theological convergence and rapprochement in the area of inherited differences in the Christology by which the two churches live served to remove theological misunderstandings on both sides and created a common basis for agreement on christological questions. This basis was recorded in the Declaration of Agreement on Christology between the Coptic Orthodox Church and the Roman Catholic Church. The declaration was drawn up by the joint theological commission of the two churches and then accepted unanimously by the full membership of the commission (12 February 1988). The statement says:

> We believe that our Lord, God and Saviour Jesus Christ, the Incarnate Logos, is perfect in his divinity and perfect in his humanity. He made his humanity one with his divinity without mixture nor mingling, nor confusion. His divinity was not separated from his humanity even for a moment or twinkling of an eye.
> At the same time, we anathematize the doctrines of both Nestorius and Eutyches.

The Armenian church joined this growing consensus in Christology when Catholicos Karekin I of Etchmiadzin visited Rome in December 1996. In a common declaration with Pope John Paul II, the two church leaders spoke of their "fundamental common faith in God and in Jesus Christ", and declared their hope that past christological controversies "should not continue to influence the life and witness of the church today".

Those participating in the third ecumenical conference had become aware of the tendency whereby unofficial ecumenical conferences lead to an official theological dialogue. In its communique the conference noted that "as an unofficial consultation, we are not in a position to act as though we were the official representatives of our churches, or to make decisions in their name". Among the recommendations of the unofficial conference, however, was the resolution that the churches should discuss the establishment of a "joint commission". This should be made up of bishops, theologians and canonists, so that the points of agreement and disagreement raised by the unofficial ecumenical conference might be studied more fully and the causes of friction in relations between the two churches might be investigated. Be that as it may, the fourth unofficial ecumenical conference focused its work on a study of the following subjects: the primacy question; synodality and the assent of the faithful. In the course of the discussion important differences emerged in regard to the primacy and infallibility of the pope and to their exercise in the church. All these points were set down in the communique of this conference.

A joint commission for theological dialogue was not in fact established in the case of the Oriental Orthodox churches as a group and the Roman Catholic Church, as it had been in the dialogue between the Orthodox church and the Roman Catholic Church. The way was initially prepared for the formation of such a comprehensive joint commission when a bilateral dialogue was begun between the Roman Catholic Church and some individual churches in the family of Oriental Orthodox churches. Thus a joint commission was established for theological dialogue between the Coptic Orthodox Church and the Roman Catholic Church. This was considered to be the first official meeting between representatives of the two churches in almost fifteen hundred years; its first phase ended with the above-cited short formula of agreement on Christology. The common declaration which the heads of the two churches had issued in 1973 (*Doing the Truth in Charity*, pp.246-48) served as the basis for the agreement. This point was emphasized in the letter of Pope John Paul II to Shenouda III, Patriarch of the Coptic Orthodox Church (30 April 1988), in which he refers to the text of the agreement on Christology and remarks that this "summarizes the essential points of the document signed by Your Holiness and my predecessor, Pope Paul VI, on 10 May 1973. It was good that their common declaration should be given a simpler and more popular form, thus making it accessible to all the faithful in Egypt."

A comparable acknowledgment of agreement was voiced in the common declaration of Pope John Paul II and Ignatius Zakka I, Patriarch of the Syrian Orthodox Church (23 June 1984), which proclaims the identity of the faith of both churches in the areas of Christology, the church, the holy eucharist and the sacraments. The differences that still existed did not, of course, permit the restoration of full communion. In cases, however, in which no clerics of one or other church were available, and in order to provide pastoral service to the faithful of either church, it was allowed that the faithful of the one church might receive the sacraments of penance, eucharist and anointing of the sick in the other church. We "authorize them [the faithful] in such cases to ask for the sacraments of penance, eucharist and anointing of the sick from lawful priests of either of our two sister churches, when they need them". This ecclesial practice in exceptional cases did not, however, do away with the need of opening a bilateral theological dialogue on the theological or ecclesiological differences that had come to light; on the contrary, the practice demanded that such a dialogue be begun immediately and in an orderly manner.

The Malankara Syrian Orthodox Church of India and the Roman Catholic Church, on the other hand, pushed the idea that an international joint commission should be established to carry on an official bilateral theological dialogue. The commission met in Kottayam (Kerala), India, 22-25 October 1989, and unanimously accepted a joint statement on faith and specifically on the mystery of the incarnation of the Word of God. This was meant to put an end to such differences as still existed between the two churches in the area of Christology. This agreement was presented to the respective agencies of the two churches. These in turn accepted it and decided to publish the text as a Statement of the Joint Commission for dialogue (3 June 1990).

This joint statement limits itself to expressing agreement on Christology. In the process it sets down, with unusual clarity, the points on which there had traditionally been theological disagreement (nos 4-6). By way of Christology a rapprochement was also achieved regarding the mystery of the church (no. 7). The members of the joint commission also made the point that the remaining differences between the two churches are purely historical differences of confessional formulation and of emphases within a common faith. They also expressed their conviction that "these differences are such as can co-exist in the same communion and therefore need not and should not divide us" (no. 8). This means, however, either that the entire task of the joint commission was already accomplished at this first meeting, or that the ecclesiological and canonical differences expounded at the unofficial ecumenical conferences (1971, 1973, 1976, 1978, 1988) are not a hindrance to ecclesial communion between the two churches.

In 1993 the same commission produced an important set of pastoral guidelines dealing with marriages between the faithful of their two churches that may serve as a model for the work of other bilateral commissions in the future.

Damaskinos Papandreou

54. Common Declaration
John Paul II and Mar Ignatius Zakka I Iwas

Vatican, 23 June 1984

1. His Holiness John Paul II, Bishop of Rome and Pope of the Catholic Church, and His Holiness Moran Mar Ignatius Zakka I Iwas, Patriarch of Antioch and All the East and Supreme Head of the Universal Syrian Orthodox Church, kneel down with full humility in front of the exalted and extolled heavenly throne of our Lord Jesus Christ, giving thanks for this glorious opportunity which has been granted them to meet together in his love in order to strengthen further the relationship between their two sister churches, the church of Rome and the Syrian Orthodox Church of Antioch – the relationship already excellent through the joint initiative of their holinesses of blessed memory Pope Paul VI and Patriarch Moran Mor Ignatius Yacoub III.

2. Their holinesses Pope John Paul II and Patriarch Zakka I wish solemnly to widen the horizon of their brotherhood and affirm herewith the terms of the deep spiritual communion which already unites them and the prelates, clergy and faithful of both their churches, to consolidate these ties of faith, hope and love, and to advance in finding a wholly common ecclesial life.

3. First of all, their holinesses confess the faith of their two churches, formulated by the Nicene council of 325 A.D. and generally known as the Nicene Creed. The confusions and schisms that occurred between their churches in the later centuries, they realize today, in no way affect or touch the substance of their faith, since these arose only because of differences in terminology and culture and in the various formulae adopted by different theological schools to express the same matter.

Accordingly, we find today no real basis for the sad divisions and schism that subsequently arose between us concerning the doctrine of incarnation.

In words and life we confess the true doctrine concerning Christ our Lord, notwithstanding the differences in interpretation of such a doctrine which arose at the time of the council of Chalcedon.

4. Hence we wish to reaffirm solemnly our profession of common faith in the incarnation of our Lord Jesus Christ, as Pope Paul VI and Patriarch Moran Mor Ignatius Yacoub III did in 1971.

They denied that there was any difference in the faith they confessed in the mystery of the Word of God made flesh and become truly man. In our turn we confess that he became incarnate for us, taking to himself a real body with a rational soul. He shared our humanity in all this except sin. We confess that our Lord and our God, our Saviour and the King of all, Jesus Christ, is perfect God as to his divinity and perfect man as to his humanity. In him his divinity is united to his humanity. This union is real, perfect, without blending or mingling, without confusion, without alteration, without division, without the least separation. He who is God eternal and indivisible, became visible in the flesh and took the form of servant. In him are united, in a real, perfect, indivisible and inseparable way, divinity and humanity, and in him all their properties are present and active.

5. Having the same conception of Christ, we confess also the same conception of his mystery. Incarnate, dead and risen again, our Lord, God and Saviour has conquered sin and death. Through him during the time between Pentecost and the second coming, the period which is also the last phase of time, it is given to man to experience the new creation, the kingdom of God, the transforming ferment (cf. St Mt. XIII, 33) already present in our midst. For this God has chosen a new people, his holy church which is the body of Christ. Through the word and through the sacraments the Holy Spirit acts in the church to call everybody and make them members of this body of Christ. Those who believe are baptized in the Holy Spirit in the name of the Holy Trinity to form one body and through the holy sacrament of the anointing of confirmation their faith is perfect and strengthened by the same Spirit.

6. Sacramental life finds in the holy eucharist its fulfilment and its summit, in such a way that it is through the eucharist that the church most profoundly realizes and reveals its nature. Through the holy eucharist the event of Christ's pascha expands throughout the church. Through holy baptism and confirmation, indeed, the members of Christ are anointed by the Holy Spirit, grafted on to Christ; and through the holy eucharist the church becomes what she is destined to be through baptism and confirmation. By communion with the body and blood of Christ the faithful grow in that mysterious divinization which by the Holy Spirit makes them dwell in the Son as children of the Father.

7. The other sacraments, which the Catholic Church and the Syrian Orthodox Church of Antioch hold together in one and the same succession of apostolic ministry, i.e. holy orders, matrimony, reconciliation of penitents and anointing of the sick, are ordered to that celebration of the holy eucharist which is the centre of sacramental life and the chief visible expression of ecclesial communion.

This communion of Christ with each other and of local churches united around their lawful bishops is realized in the gathered community which confesses the same faith, which reaches forward in hope of the world to come and in expectation of the Saviour's return and is anointed by the Holy Spirit who dwells in it with charity that never fails.

8. Since it is the chief expression of Christian unity between the faithful and between bishops and priests, the holy eucharist cannot yet be concelebrated by us. Such celebration supposes a complete identity of faith such as does not yet exist between us. Certain questions, in fact, still need to be resolved touching the Lord's will for his church, as also the doctrinal implications and canonical details of the traditions proper to our communities which have been too long separated.

9. Our identity in faith, though not yet complete, entitles us to envisage collaboration between our churches in pastoral care, in situations which nowadays are frequent both because of the dispersion of our faithful throughout the world and because of the precarious conditions of these difficult times. It is not rare, in fact, for our faithful to find access to a priest of their own church materially or morally impossible. Anxious to meet their needs and with their spiritual benefit in mind, we authorize them in such cases to ask for the sacraments of penance, eucharist and anointing of the sick from

lawful priests of either of our two sister churches, when they need them. It would be a logical corollary of collaboration in pastoral care to cooperate in priestly formation and theological education. Bishops are encouraged to promote sharing of facilities for theological education where they judge it to be advisable.

While doing this we do not forget that we must still do all in our power to achieve the full visible communion between the Catholic Church and the Syrian Orthodox Church of Antioch, and ceaselessly implore our Lord to grant us unity which alone will enable us to give to the world a fully unanimous gospel witness.

10. Thanking the Lord who has allowed us to meet and enjoy the consolation of faith we hold in common (cf. Rom. 1:12) and to proclaim before the world the mystery of the Person of the Word incarnate and of his saving work, the unshakeable foundation of that common faith, we pledge ourselves solemnly to do all that in us lies to remove the last obstacles still hindering full communion between the Catholic church and the Syrian Orthodox Church of Antioch, so that with one heart and voice we may preach the word: "The True Light that enlightens every man" and "that all who believe in his name may become the children of God" (cf. St John 1:9-12).

55. The Continuation of the Dialogue

Cairo, Egypt, 12 February 1988

In the love of God, the Father, by the grace of the Only Begotten Son, and by the gift of the Holy Spirit.

On Friday, 12 February 1988, the mixed commission of the dialogue between the Catholic church and the Coptic Orthodox Church met in the Monastery of St Bishoy, Wadi El Natrun, in Egypt.

His Holiness Pope Shenouda III opened the meeting by prayer. His Excellency Giovanni Moretti, the Apostolic Pro Nuncio in Egypt, and Rev. Fr Pierre Duprey, secretary of the Vatican Secretariat for Promoting Christian Unity, attended this meeting representing His Holiness Pope John Paul II and enabled to sign this agreement. Also bishops delegated by His Beatitude Stephanos II Ghattas, Patriarch of the Coptic Catholic Church, were present and delegated to sign this agreement.

We have rejoiced at the historical meeting that happened in the Vatican in May 1973 between His Holiness Pope Paul VI and His Holiness Pope Shenouda III. This was the first meeting since about 15 centuries between our two churches.

In that meeting we found ourselves in agreement on many issues of faith. In that meeting also a mixed commission was formed to discuss the issues of difference of doctrine and faith between the two churches aiming at church unity. Previously in Vienna, September 1971, Pro Oriente arranged a meeting between theologians of the Catholic Church and those of the Oriental Orthodox churches: the Coptic, the Syrian, the Armenian, the Ethiopian and the Indian. They achieved an agreement concerning Christology.

We are grateful to God that we are now able to sign a common formula expressing our official agreement on Christology which was already approved by the holy synod of the Coptic Orthodox Church on 21 June 1986.

All other issues of difference between our churches will be discussed successively according to God's will.

56. Report of the International Joint Commission for Dialogue

between the Coptic Orthodox Church and the Roman Catholic Church

Monastery of St Bishoy, Egypt, 27 April 1990

In the name of the Father, Son and Holy Spirit, one God, Amen.

The international joint commission between the Catholic Church and the Coptic Orthodox Church held its regular study meeting from 23 to 27 April 1990 in the Monastery of St Bishoy. The main theme of discussion was the procession of the Holy Spirit and the controversy over the filioque in the text of the creed.

His Holiness Pope Shenouda III, after welcoming the members of the commission, presented a general view of the subject and indicated the points which His Holiness felt needed discussion and solution.

Papers were presented to consider both churches' views concerning (1) the history of the filioque controversy, (2) biblical, theological and patristic aspects of the procession of the Holy Spirit, and (3) the addition of the formula "filioque – and the Son" to the text of the Nicene-Constantinopolitan Creed.

The work of this meeting of the commission was primarily concerned with clarifying each side's understanding of the other's positions. For the Coptic Orthodox Church the filioque should not be in the creed or in the liturgy or in the theological teaching for doctrinal and canonical reasons. The Catholic Church believes that this addition is admissible for both reasons. There was a full discussion of the terminology used by both churches and the principal official declarations made by the Catholic Church in this matter.

While each side expressed and clarified what its church considers to be its own authentic belief, it is the unanimous conviction of the members of the commission that further studies must be made in each of the three areas mentioned above. These studies will be prepared for distribution and reflection before the next meeting of the commission, scheduled for 15 to 19 April 1991.

The intensive work of the commission could not have been carried out without the prayers and fraternal concern of many people at the monastery of St Bishoy. Strongly encouraged by His Holiness Pope Shenouda, the bishops, monks and staff, clerical and lay, showed a spirit of Christian love and dedication which impressed those coming from outside and helped inspire the members of the commission in their search for that light and strength of the Holy Spirit which will lead both churches to the fullness of communion in faith and love.

57. Statement of the Joint Commission
between the Roman Catholic Church and the Malankara Orthodox Syrian Church

Kottaya, India, 3 June 1990

The joint international commission for dialogue between the Roman Catholic Church and the Malankara Orthodox Syrian Church of India met for the first time from 22 to 25 October 1989 at Kottayam, Kerala.

The members of this commission unanimously adopted a common text concerning their faith in the mystery of the incarnate Word in order to put an end to the christological disagreement which existed between the two churches. This doctrinal agreement was submitted to the authorities of the Roman Catholic Church and the Malankara Orthodox Syrian Church, who have approved it and decided that it should be made public on 3 June 1990, the feast of Pentecost.

Statement

1. In our first meeting, which was characterized by a spirit of concord, mutual trust, fraternal love and desire to overcome division and misunderstandings inherited from the past, we found our common ground in the one, holy, catholic and apostolic faith, held by the one and undivided church of the early centuries, the faith in Christ always affirmed by both sides.

2. Above all we thank the Lord our God for having brought us together for a cordial and sincere dialogue on some doctrinal and pastoral problems which can stand in the way of our mutual ecclesial relations and communion.

3. In this atmosphere we have worked out this brief statement to be submitted to our respective church authorities for their approval, wherein we seek to express our common understanding of, and our common witness to, the great and saving mystery of our Lord Jesus Christ, the Word of God incarnate; we hope this statement can lead us to the restoration of full communion between our churches. Our work was made much easier by the painstaking documentation and detailed discussions held at an unofficial level by our theologians during the past twenty-five years.

4. We affirm our common faith in Jesus Christ, our Lord and Saviour, the eternal Logos of God, the Second Person of the Most Holy Trinity, who for us and for our salvation came down from heaven and was incarnate by the Holy Spirit from the Blessed Virgin Mary, Mother of God. We believe that our Lord Jesus Christ, the Word made flesh, is true God and true man. The Word of God has taken a human body with a rational soul, uniting humanity with divinity.

5. Our Lord Jesus Christ is one, perfect in his humanity and perfect in his divinity – at once consubstantial with the Father in his divinity, and consubstantial with us in

his humanity. His humanity is one with his divinity – without change, without commingling, without division and without separation. In the Person of the eternal Logos incarnate are united and active in a real and perfect way the divine and human natures, with all their properties, faculties and operations.

6. Divinity was revealed in humanity. The glory of the Father was manifest in the flesh of the Son. We saw the Father's love in the life of the Suffering Servant. The incarnate Lord died on the cross that we may live. He rose again on the third day, and opened for us the way to the Father and to eternal life.

7. All who believe in the Son of God and receive him by faith and baptism are given power to become children of God. Through the incarnate Son into whose body they are integrated by the Holy Spirit, they are in communion with the Father and with one another. This is the heart of the mystery of the church, in which and through which the Father by his Holy Spirit renews and reunites the whole creation in Christ. In the church, Christ the Word of God is known, lived, proclaimed and celebrated.

8. It is this faith which we both confess. Its content is the same in both communions; in formulating that content in the course of history, however, differences have arisen, in terminology and emphasis. We are convinced that these differences are such as can co-exist in the same communion and therefore need not and should not divide us, especially when we proclaim him to our brothers and sisters in the world in terms which they can more easily understand.

9. It is the awareness of our common faith that leads us to pray that the Holy Spirit of God may remove all remaining obstacles and lead us to that common goal – the restoration of full communion between our churches.

58. Report of the Second Meeting
Joint International Commission between the Roman Catholic Church and the Malankara Orthodox Syrian Church[1]

Manganam, Kottayam, India, 9-12 December 1990

The joint international commission of the Roman Catholic Church and the Malankara Orthodox Syrian Church had been set up in 1988. Its first meeting was held in October 1989. The second meeting was held at the Spirituality Centre, Manganam, Kottayam, from 9 to 12 December 1990. Bishop Pierre Duprey and Metropolitan Paulos Mar Gregorios presided over the meeting.

In the inaugural session, greetings from His Holiness Pope John Paul II were conveyed by Bishop Pierre Duprey and greetings from His Holiness Catholicos Baselius Mar Thoma Mathews I were conveyed by the Catholicos-Designate Metropolitan Mathews Mar Coorilos. The condolence resolution over the demise of one of the joint commission members, Fr Dr E.R. Hambye, was passed. Bishop Pierre Duprey was felicitated for having been ordained as bishop. Ramban Fr Dr M.A. Mathai was congratulated for being elected to the bishopric.

Bishop Pierre Duprey, Metropolitan Paulos Gregorios and Fr Dr Xavier Koodapuzha presented papers on ecclesial communion. Fr Dr Mathew Vellanickal's and Fr Dr V.P. Varghese's papers on communion in the sacramental mysteries were also presented.

The joint commission also considered the statement prepared by the sub-commission on marriage between members of both churches.

In their discussions and deliberations, the joint commission agreed upon two statements: (1) the issue of marriages between members of both churches (appendix), (2) the issue of ecclesial-eucharistic communion (appendix). The statements are to be submitted to the respective authorities for approval and subsequent action.

The joint commission also decided to continue the study and discussions on the following issues through the sub-commissions, so that the sub-commissions could present their reports to the next meeting of the joint commission:
1) sub-commission on marriage issues to continue;
2) sub-commission on Indian church history in relation to unity and separation of our churches – to be appointed;
3) sub-commission to discuss the theme "the role of the episcopate in the unity of the church" – to be appointed.

---

[1] This joint commission must be clearly distinguished from the joint commission between the Catholic Church and the Malankara Jacobite Syrian Orthodox Church, which is a different commission that also met in India on 15 December 1990.

All the sub-commissions will be chaired by Archbishop Mar Joseph Powathil and Metropolitan Paulos Mar Gregorios.

The joint commission also identified certain areas where practical collaboration between the two churches could be made more effective. The joint commission appealed to the authorities of both the churches to initiate and strengthen meaningful cooperation at least in the following areas:
1) joint action to face the challenges of sectarianism;
2) joint action against alcoholism and drug abuse;
3) common study-research programmes for music, art and architecture;
4) institutional collaboration in the fields of education and health care;
5) media cooperation (literature, audio and video);
6) collaboration in social, developmental programmes;
7) cooperation in efforts for communal harmony and national integration.

The next meeting of the joint commission will meet from 9 to 14 December 1991, at the Bombay Orthodox Centre. (There is the possibility of the change of venue, for the convenience of the commissioners.) The main theme for the next meeting will be "The Role of the Episcopate in the Unity of the Church".

His Grace Mar Kuriakose Kunnacherry hosted the dinner on Monday 10 December at the bishop's house, Kottayam. The commissioners visited His Holiness the Catholicos at the Devalokam Catholicate Palace on Tuesday, 11 December. On the same day, on behalf of His Holiness the Catholicos, the Catholicos-Designate His Grace Mathews Mar Coorilos, hosted a dinner to the commissioners at the Sophia Centre. His Grace Archbishop Mar Joseph Powathil hosted the dinner on Wednesday, 12 December, at the archbishop's house, Changanacherry.

The second meeting of the joint commission concluded at 6.00 pm on Wednesday, 12 December 1990.

Appendix 1: Interim Report on Marriage

Joint international commission for dialogue between the Roman Catholic Church and the Malankara Orthodox Syrian Church of India

The commission in its first meeting held at Sophia Centre, Kottayam, from 22 to 25 October 1989 had set up a sub-commission to study the issue of marriages between the members of the Catholic Church and the Malankara Orthodox Syrian Church. The sub-commission presented its study report to the commission in its second meeting held at Spirituality Centre, Manganam, Kottayam, from 9 to 12 December 1990. Having discussed the report, the commission agreed upon the following points:

1. Both our churches affirm their common loyalty to the catholic and apostolic Tradition. This living Tradition is always an open, growing and dynamic reality, with both a universally common core and specific ways of understanding, expression and practice which have become part of the reality of the church for Christians living in various localities.

2. In the matter of matrimony as a Christian sacrament, while we recognize that the historical record is not always clear, and that some of the present practices and beliefs are the result of long developments which are not uniform in all localities, we agree, along with all ancient churches, that matrimony is a holy sacramental mystery of the

church; the church itself is the great sacramental mystery of Christ's incarnation. While our practices vary, even within one church, in regard to the sacrament of matrimony, we confess that it is the church which administers all sacramental mysteries enabling the faithful to share in the mystery of the kingdom of God.

3. The man-woman relationship is integral to the original creation (Gen. 1:26-28). Our Lord himself taught us that in the beginning the twain were one and that it is ultimately God who joins together man and woman in marriage to become one flesh (Matt. 19:4-6). Christian marriage derives its meaning from the great mystery of the union of Christ with his bride, the church (Eph. 5:22-32).

4. We agree that the marriage between Christians is a sacrament, is for life and is indissoluble. Differences of practice prevail among our various traditions in relation to the impediments to marriage, declaration of the nullity of marriage and separation of married couples. These differences need to be further studied by the sub-commission to see to what extent, if any, they affect marriages between Catholics and Orthodox.

5. We recognize that the mutual consent of the marriage partners is a constitutive element in the sacrament of matrimony. However, the expression of that mutual consent seems to take different forms in the canonical practices of our ecclesial traditions.

6. We are also agreed that the eucharist is the crown of all sacramental mysteries. Hence in Christian married life the communion of husband and wife in the eucharistic body and blood of Christ is of central importance.

7. Our two churches are not now in eucharistic communion with each other. This situation makes it difficult for members of the two different churches to be united in matrimony and to continue in one eucharistic fellowship. The Roman Catholic Church has special provisions for "mixed marriages" and for pastoral care of the "mixed" married couple and their children. The Malankara Orthodox Church does not now permit its members to continue in that church after marrying someone not in that communion. Each church justifies its present practice on theological and canonical grounds.

8. The commission, based on the report of the sub-commission, discussed various possibilities of finding a mutually acceptable interim arrangement for marriages between members of the two churches until eucharistic communion is restored between them. The discussion led to the elaboration of certain principles, on the basis of which the sub-commission should make further studies and bring specific proposals to the next meeting of the commission.

9. The main principles are the following:
a) Marriages between members of two churches not in eucharistic communion with each other are not normal, and should be allowed only in exceptional circumstances, and be treated as special cases.
b) The two churches recognize two fundamental considerations for making interim provisions in such marriages:
   i) the church has a God-given responsibility to be faithful to the apostolic Tradition it has inherited, and to maintain it in its integrity without compromise;
   ii) the church has also a similarly God-given responsibility for the pastoral nurture and care of its members through word and sacrament, and to provide for their spiritual growth and general welfare.

When these considerations seem to come in conflict with each other in some cases, special measures have to be devised.

c) In devising any interim measures, not only should the two principles be held in view; it should be recognized that the Malankara Orthodox Church and the Roman Catholic Church hold in common a very large area of the Christian faith and tradition. Arrangements made between these churches may or may not be applicable in the case of other churches.
d) There are differences of practice even within the Roman Catholic Church.

This interim report is submitted to our respective authorities; a further report with specific proposals will be prepared by the sub-commission in order to be considered by the next plenary meeting of the commission.

Appendix 2: Interim Report on Ecclesial Eucharistic Communion

Joint international commission between the Roman Catholic Church and the Malankara Orthodox Syrian Church of India

1. We give thanks to God for having brought us together again to pray and work for the advancement of unity and for the strengthening of relations between our two churches, on our way to the restoration of eucharistic communion. We experienced again the presence of the Holy Spirit among us, leading us in Christ to that unity for which he prayed.

2. Our previous agreement on our common understanding of the great central mystery of the incarnation was the foundation and basis for our discussion, particularly since christological disputes were the occasion for the original breach of communion, centuries ago, between the Roman Catholic Church and the Oriental Orthodox churches. The Christ whom we jointly confess is the One who also prays for us "that they all be one; even as thou, Father, art in me, and I in thee, that they also may be in us, so that the world may believe, that thou has sent me" (John 17:21).

3. The unity of faith is a necessary condition for common participation in the sacramental life of the church, and particularly for the common celebration of the eucharist. The fact that we have been able to make a common confession of our faith in the incarnate Lord Jesus Christ encourages us to go forward to identify and articulate other areas of agreement, and to examine again any divergences, real or apparent, that may seem to stand in the way of restoring communion. Our common loyalty and commitment to the one apostolic tradition of the church gives us hope that, by the grace of God, all obstacles can be overcome.

4. We agree that the life of the triune God, which is communion in love, is the prototype and source of true Christian unity and of ecclesial-eucharistic communion. The church itself, which is communion in Christ by the Holy Spirit, is the great sacramental mystery by which the whole creation is brought into communion with the triune God.

5. The holy eucharist is the central experience and summit of communion, and unfortunately also the place where our divisions are most evident, and where our witness to the world is most clearly impaired by our disunity. It is important therefore to remove all obstacles to communion, so that our witness to the world may be one.

6. Communion in the church is both in the Holy Spirit who creates the communion and indwells it, and also in the sacramental mysteries of the church. This unity is a

lived unity, marked by the presence of the Holy Spirit and by common adherence to the same faith, same sacramental life, and same apostolic ministry.

7. All of us agree that the unity of the church involves communion among many churches united by the same faith and the same sacramental-ministerial structure of the church. But there are obvious divergences in our perception of how that ecclesial structure is to be manifested. These divergences will need to be examined, in order to remove all obstacles to restoring communion.

8. A variety of liturgical forms, sacramental practices, disciplinary procedures, and streams of theological and spiritual traditions, co-exist within the Roman Catholic communion. These are no impediment to communion. Communion does not demand uniformity in all respects. The Malankara Catholic Church is almost identical with the Malankara Orthodox Church in their liturgical and canonical practices, and yet they are not in communion. The reasons need to be studied, and the conditions for restoring communion to be made more precise.

59. Pastoral Guidelines
on Marriages between Members of the Catholic Church and the Malankara Syrian Orthodox Church[1]

Ernakulam, India, November 1993

This agreement between the Catholic Church and the Malankara Syrian Orthodox Church on interchurch marriages has been prepared taking into account the following elements of the common declaration of Pope John Paul II and Syrian Orthodox Patriarch Zakka I Iwas of Antioch, dated 23 June 1984:
1) the common profession of faith between the pope and the patriarch on the mystery of the incarnate Word;
2) the common affirmation of their faith in the mystery of the church and the sacraments;
3) the possibility given by the declaration for a pastoral collaboration, including the mutual admission of the faithful belonging to both churches to the reception of the sacraments of penance, eucharist and anointing of the sick for a grave spiritual need.

Having considered the above mentioned events and declaration, the Malankara Syrian Orthodox Church and the Catholic Church agreed on the following considerations and norms.

As our two churches believe in and confess the mystery of the church and its sacramental reality, we consider it our duty to specify the areas of agreement in cases of marriages between the members of our two churches.

Man and woman created in the image of God (Gen. 1:26-27) are called to become sharers of the eternal divine communion. The sacrament of marriage is an image of this divine communion. Marital intimacy and self-effacing sharing are reflections of the deepest interpersonal sharing within the trinitarian communion. Hence this intimate marital communion is divinely confirmed by Christ with the seal of unity and of indissolubility, and ordered towards the good of the spouses and the generation and education of the offspring.

> He answered, "Have you not read that he who made them from the beginning *made them male and female*, and said, For this reason *a man shall leave his father and mother and be joined to his wife and the two shall become one flesh?*" What therefore God has joined together, let no man put asunder (Matt. 19:46).

Marriage is a great sacrament of divine communion, and St Paul compares the mutual relationship of the husband and wife to the mystery of communion between

---

[1] This agreement, along with the attached pastoral guidelines, was drafted in November 1993 by the commission for dialogue between the Catholic Church and the Malankara Syrian Orthodox Church. It was released on 25 January 1994, after it was approved by the competent authorities of both churches.

Jesus Christ and his church (cf. Eph. 5:21-26; Titus 2:3f., 1 Pet. 3:1f.; Rev. 18:7; 21:2). St Paul calls it a great mystery: "This mystery is a profound one, and I am saying that it refers to Christ and the church" (Eph. 5:32). Hence we believe that the sacrament of marriage bearing the image of the eternal divine communion is also an image of the most intimate communion between the risen bridegroom with his bride, the church.

The church is the primordial sacrament of the eternal divine communion and, through the celebration of her sacramental mysteries, she deepens her communion with the divine spouse and enables her members to participate in the divine life.

Our two churches accept the sacredness and indissolubility of the sacramental bond of marriage and consider the conjugal relationship as an expression of the above communion and a means to achieve self-effacing mutual love and freedom from selfishness, which was the cause of the fall of humanity.

In this theological perspective, taking into account the question of the marriages between the members of our two churches, we consider it a matter of our pastoral concern to provide the following directives.

Our two churches desire to foster marriages within the same ecclesial communion and consider this the norm. However, we have to accept the pastoral reality that interchurch marriages do take place. When such occasions arise, both churches should facilitate the celebration of the sacrament of matrimony in either church, allowing the bride/bridegroom the right and freedom to retain her/his own ecclesial communion, by providing necessary information and documents. On the occasion of these celebrations, the couple as well as their family members belonging to these two churches are allowed to participate in the holy eucharist in the church where the sacrament of matrimony is celebrated. We consider it also the great responsibility of the parents to pay special attention to impart to the extent possible and in mutual accord proper ecclesial formation to their children in full harmony with the tradition of the ecclesial communion to which they have to belong.

Pastoral Guidelines on Marriages between Members of the Catholic Church and of the Malankara Syrian Orthodox Church[2]

1. These guidelines are framed on the basis of the common declaration of His Holiness Pope John Paul II and His Holiness Patriarch Ignatius Zakka I Iwas.

2. Commissions were appointed by both churches to explore ways and means to foster the existing common affirmation of the faith and sacramental unity between the churches.

3. Having considered the above-mentioned declaration and the unity that exists between the two churches in faith and sacraments, both churches have agreed to accept the reality of interchurch marriages taking place between their members.

4. The two churches desire to foster marriages with ecclesial communion and consider this as the norm. However, accepting the reality that interchurch marriages do take place at times, the two churches have decided to facilitate the celebration of the sacrament of matrimony in either church, allowing the bride/bridegroom the right and freedom to retain her/his own ecclesial communion, by providing necessary information and documents.

---

[2] Applies to the Catholic Church.

Preparation for interchurch marriages

5. When the parties apply for an interchurch marriage they should be told that the marriage within the same faith is better for the harmony of the family and the upbringing of the children.

6. If they insist on conducting the interchurch marriage they should be instructed properly about the agreement reached between the Syrian Orthodox Church and the Catholic Church on interchurch marriages.

7. It should be stressed that, while each partner holds his/her ecclesial faith as supreme or paramount, he/she should respect the ecclesial faith of his/her partner.

8. A pre-marriage preparatory course and a premarital counselling session are highly recommended.

9. The bride/bridegroom shall produce her/his baptism certificate.

10. The priest must ensure that the bride/bridegroom is eligible for marriage.

11. The priest should ensure that the bride/bridegroom has paid the church donations in connection with marriages according to the practice of the churches.

12. The bride and bridegroom, after mutual consultation, may select the church in which the marriage is to be celebrated.

13. Written permission for interchurch marriage from the respective bishops should be obtained by the bride/bridegroom.

14. Banns should be published in the respective churches, which also announce that it is an interchurch marriage.

15. Once the permission is obtained from the bishops, the respective parish priests are expected to issue the necessary documents for the conduct of marriage.

16. Marriage in the Lent or Advent seasons is only to be conducted with the permission of the bishops.

Celebration of interchurch marriages

17. The liturgical minister should be the parish priest of the church where the marriage is celebrated, or his delegate from the same ecclesial communion.

18. There is to be no joint celebration of marriage by the ministers of both churches. The marriage is to be blessed either by the Catholic or by the Syrian Orthodox minister. However, there could be some kind of participation at the liturgical service by the other minister who could read a scriptural passage or give a sermon.

19. On the occasion of these celebrations, the couple and any members of their families who belong to these churches are allowed to participate in the holy eucharist in the church where the sacrament of matrimony is being celebrated.

20. Proper entries must be made in the church registers, and marriage certificates should be issued for a record to be made in the register of the other church.

Pastoral care of Catholic-Syrian Orthodox interchurch families

21. The Catholic partner is to be reminded that he or she has to commit him-/herself to imparting to their children proper Catholic formation, to the extent possible and in agreement with his/her partner (cf. *Directory for the Application of Principles and Norms on Ecumenism*, no. 150-151). Such formation should be fully in harmony with the Catholic tradition to which he/she belongs.

22. The pastors of both partners are bound in conscience to provide continued pastoral care to the interchurch families in such a way as to contribute to their sanctity, unity and harmony.

23. Each partner is to be advised to attend the liturgical celebrations of his/her respective church, but the couple may be allowed to participate jointly in the eucharistic celebration on special occasions when this joint participation is socially required.

24. Any declaration of the nullity of such marriages is only to be considered with the consent of the bishops concerned from both churches.

25. The funeral service should as far as possible be conducted according to the rite of the dead person's church, even though he/she may be buried in either of the cemeteries, especially if the other partner is already buried there in a family tomb.

60. Common Declaration
Pope John Paul II and Catholicos Karekin I

Vatican, 13 December 1996

As they bring to a close their solemn meeting which they are deeply convinced has been of particular significance for the ongoing relations between the Catholic Church and the Armenian Apostolic Church, His Holiness John Paul II, Bishop of Rome and Pope of the Catholic Church, and His Holiness Karekin I, Supreme Patriarch and Catholicos of All Armenians, give humble thanks to the Lord and Saviour Jesus Christ who has enabled them to meet in his love for prayer together, for a fruitful discussion of their common desire to search out a more perfect unity in the Holy Spirit, and for an exchange of views about how their churches may give a more effective witness to the gospel in a world approaching a new millennium in the history of salvation.

Pope John Paul II and Catholicos Karekin I recognize the deep spiritual communion which already unites them and the bishops, clergy and lay faithful of their churches. It is a communion which finds its roots in the common faith in the holy and life-giving Trinity proclaimed by the apostles and transmitted down the centuries by the many church fathers, church doctors, bishops, priests and martyrs who have followed them. They rejoice in the fact that recent developments of ecumenical relationships and theological discussions carried out in the spirit of Christian love and fellowship have dispelled many misunderstandings inherited from the controversies and dissensions of the past. Such dialogues and encounters have prepared a healthy situation of mutual understanding and recovery of the deeper spiritual communion based on the common faith in the holy Trinity that they have been given through the gospel of Christ and in the holy Tradition of the church.

They particularly welcome the great advance that their churches have registered in their common search for their unity in Christ, the Word of God made flesh. Perfect God as to his divinity, perfect man as to his humanity, his divinity is united in him to his humanity in the Person of the only begotten Son of God, in a union which is real, perfect, without confusion, without alteration, without division, without any form of separation.

The reality of this common faith in Jesus Christ and in the same succession of apostolic ministry has at times been obscured or ignored. Linguistic, cultural and political factors have immensely contributed towards the theological divergences that have found expression in their terminology of formulating their doctrines. His Holiness John Paul II and His Holiness Karekin I have expressed their determined conviction that because of the fundamental common faith in God and in Jesus Christ, the controversies and unhappy divisions which sometimes have followed upon the divergent ways in expressing it, as a result of the present declaration, should not continue to influence the life and witness of the church today.

They humbly declare before God their sorrow for these controversies and dissensions and their determination to remove from the mind and memory of their churches the bitterness, mutual recriminations and even hatred which have sometimes manifested themselves in the past, and may even today cast a shadow over the truly fraternal and genuinely Christian relations between leaders and the faithful of both churches, especially as these have developed in recent times.

The communion already existing between the two churches and the hope for and commitment to the recovery of full communion between them should become factors of motivation for further contact, more regular and substantial dialogue, leading to a greater degree of mutual understanding and recovery of the communality of their faith and service.

Pope John Paul II and Catholicos Karekin I give their blessing and pastoral support to the further development of existing contacts and to new manifestations of that dialogue of charity between their respective pastors and faithful which will bear fruit in the fields of common action on the pastoral, catechetical, social and intellectual levels.

Such a dialogue is particularly imperative in these present times when the churches are faced with new challenges to their witness to the gospel of Jesus Christ arising out of the rapidly changing situations in the modern world so deeply affected by an extreme secularistic and secularizing pace of life and culture. It requires closer collaboration, mutual confidence and a greater degree of concern for common action. It presumes and requires an attitude of service which is not self-seeking and which is characterized by a mutual respect for the fidelity of the faithful to their own churches and Christian traditions.

They appeal to their clergy and laity to carry out more actively and effectively their full cooperation in all fields of diakonia, and to become agents of reconciliation, peace and justice, struggling for the true recognition of human rights and dedicating themselves to the support of all those who are suffering and are in spiritual and material need throughout the world.

John Paul II and Karekin I express a particular pastoral concern for the Armenian people, both those living in their historic motherland where freedom and independence were once more recovered and re-established recently through the creation of the new independent state of Armenia, those living in Nagorno Karabagh in need of permanent peace, and those who live in a state of worldwide diaspora. Amid upheavals and tragedies, especially during this century, these people have remained faithful to the apostolic faith, the faith of martyrs and confessors, the faith of millions of unnamed believers for whom Jesus Christ, the Son of God incarnate and Saviour of the world, has been the foundation of their hope, and whose Spirit has guided them across the centuries. As they approach the 17th centenary of the official establishment of the church in Armenia, may they receive the special blessings of the triune God for peace with justice and for a renewed dedication to witnessing faithfully to the Lord Jesus Christ.

XXV. ASSYRIAN CHURCH OF THE EAST-ROMAN CATHOLIC DIALOGUE

Historical Introduction

After many centuries of isolation, relations between the Assyrian Church of the East and the Catholic Church began to improve dramatically in the 1980s. The Assyrian Patriarch, Mar Dinkha IV, visited Pope John Paul II in Rome in 1984 and participated in the day of prayer for peace at Assisi in 1986. Subsequent occasional informal contacts culminated in the signing of a common declaration by Mar Dinkha and Pope John Paul II in the Vatican on 11 November 1994. The text affirms that Catholics and Assyrians are "united today in the confession of the same faith in the Son of God" and envisages broad pastoral cooperation between the two churches, especially in the areas of catechesis and the formation of future priests. The pope and patriarch also established a mixed committee for theological dialogue and charged it with overcoming the obstacles that still prevent full communion.

The first session of the dialogue took place in Rome in November 1995. It focused on the sacraments and especially the eucharist, and noted that the christological agreement had been received positively in both churches. The second meeting was held in Beirut in October 1996, and dealt with the theology of marriage and the sacrament of the sick. The third meeting took place in Rome in October 1997. It continued its study of the sacraments, and took up consideration of the Nicene-Constantinopolitan Creed and the Catholic doctrines on the immaculate conception and assumption of Mary.

The rapprochement between the two churches has found concrete expression in increased contacts and cooperation between the Assyrian Church of the East and its Catholic counterpart, the Chaldean Catholic Church. Mar Dinkha IV and Chaldean Patriarch Raphael Bidawid met in Detroit, Michigan, USA, on 29 November 1996, and issued a joint patriarchal statement. The two patriarchs pledged to work for the reunification of their churches by forming a joint commission for unity that was to elaborate a common catechism, oversee the foundation of a seminary in the United States for both churches, and develop common pastoral programmes.

On 15 August 1997, the two patriarchs met again, on the occasion of a joint blessing of a new Assyrian parish in Roselle, Illinois, USA, and ratified a joint synodal decree for promoting unity, that had been signed by the members of both holy synods. It restated the areas of pastoral cooperation envisaged in the joint patriarchal decree, recognized that Assyrians and Chaldeans should come to accept their diverse practices as legitimate, formally implemented the establishment of an Assyrian-Chaldean joint commission for unity, and declared that each side recognized the apostolic succession, sacraments and Christian witness of the other. The text also spelled out the central concerns of both sides in the dialogue. While both churches wanted to preserve the Aramaic language and culture, the Assyrians were intent on preserving their freedom and self-governance, while the Chaldeans affirmed that the preservation of full communion with Rome was among its basic principles.

Ronald Roberson

61. Common Christological Declaration
between the Catholic Church and the Assyrian Church of the East

Rome, Italy, 11 November 1994

His Holiness John Paul II, Bishop of Rome and Pope of the Catholic Church, and His Holiness Mar Dinkha IV, Catholicos-Patriarch of the Assyrian Church of the East, give thanks to God who has prompted them to this new brotherly meeting.

Both of them consider this meeting as a basic step on the way towards the full communion to be restored between their churches. They can indeed, from now on, proclaim together before the world their common faith in the mystery of the incarnation.

* * *

As heirs and guardians of the faith received from the apostles as formulated by our common fathers in the Nicene Creed, we confess one Lord Jesus Christ, the only Son of God, begotten of the Father from all eternity who, in the fullness of time, came down from heaven and became man for our salvation. The Word of God, second Person of the Holy Trinity, became incarnate by the power of the Holy Spirit in assuming from the holy Virgin Mary a body animated by a rational soul, with which he was indissolubly united from the moment of his conception.

Therefore our Lord Jesus Christ is true God and true man, perfect in his divinity and perfect in his humanity, consubstantial with the Father and consubstantial with us in all things but sin. His divinity and his humanity are united in one person, without confusion or change, without division or separation. In him has been preserved the difference of the natures of divinity and humanity, with all their properties, faculties and operations. But far from constituting "one and another", the divinity and humanity are united in the person of the same and unique Son of God and Lord Jesus Christ, who is the object of a single adoration.

Christ therefore is not an "ordinary man" whom God adopted in order to reside in him and inspire him, as in the righteous ones and the prophets. But the same God the Word, begotten of his Father before all worlds without beginning according to his divinity, was born of a mother without a father in the last times according to his humanity. The humanity to which the Blessed Virgin Mary gave birth always was that of the Son of God himself. That is why the Assyrian Church of the East is praying to the Virgin Mary as "the Mother of Christ our God and Saviour". In the light of this same faith the Catholic tradition addresses the Virgin Mary as "the Mother of God" and also as "the Mother of Christ". We both recognize the legitimacy and rightness of these expressions of the same faith and we both respect the preference of each church in her liturgical life and piety.

This is the unique faith that we profess in the mystery of Christ. The controversies of the past led to anathemas, bearing on persons and on formulas. The Lord's Spirit permits us to understand better today that the divisions brought about in this way were due in large part to misunderstandings.

Whatever our christological divergences have been, we experience ourselves united today in the confession of the same faith in the Son of God who became man so that we might become children of God by his grace. We wish from now on to witness together to this faith in the One who is the Way, the Truth and the Life, proclaiming it in appropriate ways to our contemporaries, so that the world may believe in the gospel of salvation.

* * *

The mystery of the incarnation which we profess in common is not an abstract and isolated truth. It refers to the Son of God sent to save us. The economy of salvation, which has its origin in the mystery of communion of the Holy Trinity – Father, Son and Holy Spirit – is brought to its fulfilment through the sharing in this communion, by grace, within the one, holy, catholic and apostolic church, which is the people of God, the body of Christ and the temple of the Spirit.

Believers become members of this body through the sacrament of baptism, through which, by water and the working of the Holy Spirit, they are born again as new creatures. They are confirmed by the seal of the Holy Spirit who bestows the sacrament of anointing. Their communion with God and among themselves is brought to full realization by the celebration of the unique offering of Christ in the sacrament of the eucharist. This communion is restored for the sinful members of the church when they are reconciled with God and with one another through the sacrament of forgiveness. The sacrament of ordination to the ministerial priesthood in the apostolic succession assures the authenticity of the faith, the sacraments and the communion in each local church.

Living by this faith and these sacraments, it follows as a consequence that the particular Catholic churches and the particular Assyrian churches can recognize each other as sister churches. To be full and entire, communion presupposes the unanimity concerning the content of the faith, the sacraments and the constitution of the church. Since this unanimity for which we aim has not yet been attained, we cannot unfortunately celebrate together the eucharist which is the sign of the ecclesial communion already fully restored.

Nevertheless, the deep spiritual communion in the faith and the mutual trust already existing between our churches entitle us from now on to consider witnessing together to the gospel message and cooperating in particular pastoral situations, including especially the areas of catechesis and the formation of future priests.

In thanking God for having made us rediscover what already unites us in the faith and the sacraments, we pledge ourselves to do everything possible to dispel the obstacles of the past which still prevent the attainment of full communion between our churches, so that we can better respond to the Lord's call for the unity of his own, a unity which has of course to be expressed visibly. To overcome these obstacles, we now establish a mixed committee for theological dialogue between the Catholic Church and the Assyrian Church of the East.

62. Final Report

Dialogue between the Secretariat for Promoting Christian Unity and Leaders of the Some Pentecostal Churches and Participants in the Charismatic Movement within Protestant and Anglican Churches

1972-1976

Introduction

1. The series of talks described as the Roman Catholic-Pentecostal dialogue had its beginning in the contacts made by individual members of the Pentecostal churches with the Vatican Secretariat for Promoting Christian Unity in 1969 and 1970. With the assistance of the Rev. David J. du Plessis, an international Pentecostal leader, noted figure among Pentecostals, and a guest at the Second Vatican Council, and Fr Kilian McDonnell, OSB, director of the Institute for Ecumenical and Cultural Research, Collegeville, Minnesota, USA, the initial impulse was clarified and concrete proposals began to emerge.

2. In 1970 the first of two exploratory meetings was held to see if a serious theological discussion between Roman Catholics and Pentecostals on the international level would be possible. The first gathering was largely an occasion for beginning to know one another. At the second meeting in 1971 each side put "hard" questions to the other, a more purposeful conversation resulted, and it became clear that it would be possible to undertake discussions of a more systematic kind.

3. Therefore, later in 1971, a small steering committee with members from both sides worked out a programme of topics which could be treated at meetings over a five-year period.

4. The dialogue has a special character. The bilateral conversations which the Roman Catholic Church undertakes with many world communions (e.g., the Anglican Communion, the Lutheran World Federation, etc.) are prepared to consider problems concerning church structures and ecclesiology and have organic unity as a goal or at least envisage some kind of eventual structural unity. This dialogue has not. Before it began it was made clear that its immediate scope was not "to concern itself with the problems of imminent structural union", although of course its object was Christians coming closer together in prayer and common witness. Its purpose has been that "prayer, spirituality and theological reflection be a shared concern at the international level in the form of a dialogue between the Secretariat for Promoting Christian Unity of the Roman Catholic Church and leaders of some Pentecostal churches and participants in the charismatic movements within Protestant and Anglican churches".

5. The dialogue has sought "to explore the life and spiritual experience of Christians and the churches", "to give special attention to the meaning for the church of fullness of life in the Holy Spirit", attending to "both the experiential and theological dimensions" of that life. "Through such dialogue" those who participate "hope to share

in the reality of the mystery of Christ and the church, to build a united testimony, to indicate in what manner the sharing of truth makes it possible... to grow together".

6. Certain areas of doctrinal agreement have been looked at with a view to eliminating mutual misunderstandings. At the same time, there has been no attempt to minimize points of real divergence. One of these, for example, is the importance given to faith and to experience, and their relation in Christian life.

7. The dialogue has been between the Roman Catholic Church and some Pentecostal churches. Here, too, there have been special features. On the Roman Catholic side, it has had the usual authorization given by the Secretariat for Promoting Christian Unity to such meetings on an international scale and the participants were appointed officially by the Secretariat. The Pentecostal participants were appointed officially by their individual churches (and in several cases are leaders of these churches) or else came with some kind of approbation of their churches. Therefore, it has been a dialogue with some Pentecostal churches and with delegates of others. These are churches which came into being over the last fifty or sixty years when some Protestant churches expelled those who made speaking in tongues and other charismatic manifestations an integral part of their spirituality.

8. In addition, there were participants in the charismatic movement who were invited by the Pentecostals. They belong to Anglican or Protestant churches which already have bilateral dialogues in progress with the Roman Catholic Church. Therefore, it is as participants in the charismatic movement and not primarily as members of their own churches that they share in the dialogue.

9. It was also pointed out in the beginning that "this dialogue is not directly concerned with the domestic pastoral question of the relationship of the charismatic movement among Catholics to the Catholic church. The dialogue may help indirectly to clarify this relationship but this is not the direct concern of our deliberations."

10. At the first meeting of the dialogue in Horgen, Switzerland, June 1972, an exegetical approach was taken in order to study "baptism in the Holy Spirit" in the New Testament, its relation to repentance and the process of sanctification, and the relation of the charismata to it. At Rome in June 1973 the second meeting was devoted to the historic background of the Pentecostal movement, the relation of baptism in the Holy Spirit to the rites of Christian initiation, and the role of the Holy Spirit and the gifts of the Spirit in the mystical tradition. The third meeting, held at Schloss Craheim, West Germany, June 1974, focused on the theology of Christian initiation, the nature of sacramental activity, infant and adult baptism. At the fourth meeting, held in Venice, May 1975, the areas of public worship (especially eucharistic celebration), the human dimension in the exercise of the spiritual gifts, and discerning of spirits were the main concern. In Rome, May 1976, the final session was devoted to the topic of prayer and praise.

Baptism in the Holy Spirit

11. In the New Testament the expression "to baptize in the Holy Spirit" (Mark 1:8) is used to express, in contrast to the baptism of John (John 1:33), the baptism by Jesus who gives the Spirit to the new eschatological people of God, the church (Acts 1:5). All men are called to enter into this community through faith in Christ who makes them disciples through baptism and sharers of his Spirit (Acts 2:38-39).

12. In the Pentecostal movement "being baptized in the Spirit", "being filled with the Holy Spirit", and "receiving the Holy Spirit" are understood as occurring in a deci-

sive experience distinct from conversion whereby the Holy Spirit manifests himself, empowers and transforms one's life, and enlightens one as to the whole reality of the Christian mystery (Acts 2:4; 8:17; 10:44; 19:6).

13. It is the Spirit of Christ which makes a Christian (1 Cor. 12:13) and that life is "Christian" inasmuch as it is under the Spirit and is characterized by openness to his transforming power. The Spirit is sovereignly free, distributing his gifts to whomsoever he wills, whenever and howsoever he wills (1 Cor. 12:11; John 3:7-8). There is also the human responsibility to seek after what God has promised (1 Cor. 14:1). This full life in the Spirit is growth in Christ (Eph. 4:15-16) which must be purified continually. On the other hand, due to one's unfaithfulness to the promptings of the Spirit (Gal. 6:7-9; 1 John 3:24) this growth can be arrested. But also new ways open up and new crises occur which could be milestones of progress in the Christian life (2 Cor. 3:17-18; 2 Cor. 4:8-11).

14. The participants are conscious that during the nineteen centuries other terms have been used to express this experience called "baptism in the Holy Spirit". It is one used today by the Pentecostal movement. Other expressions are "being filled with the Holy Spirit", "receiving the Holy Spirit". These expressions should not be used to exclude traditional understandings of the experience of and faith in the reality of Christian initiation.

15. The Holy Spirit gratuitously manifests himself in signs and charisma for the common good (Mark 16:17-18), working in and through but going beyond the believer's natural ability. There is a great variety of ministries in which the Spirit manifests himself. Without minimizing the importance of these experiences or denying the fruitfulness of these gifts for the church, the participants wished to lay stronger stress on faith, hope and charity as sure guides in responding to God (1 Cor. 13:13-14:1; 1 Thess. 1:3-5). Precisely out of respect for the Spirit and his gifts, it is necessary to discern between true gifts and their counterfeits (1 Thess. 5:22; 1 John 4:1-4). In this discernment process the spiritual authority in the church has its own specific ministry (1 John 4:6; Acts 20:28-31; 1 Cor. 14:37-38) because it has special concern for the common good, the unity of the church, and her mission in the world (Rom. 15:17-19; Acts 1:8).

Christian initiation and the gifts

16. From the earliest non-canonical texts of the church there is witness to the celebration of Christian initiation (baptism, laying-on of hands/chrismation, eucharist) as clearly expressing the request for and the actual reception of the Holy Spirit. The Holy Spirit dwells in all Christians (Rom. 8:9), and not just in those "baptized in the Holy Spirit". The difference between a committed Christian without such a Pentecostal experience and one with such an experience is generally not only a matter of theological focus, but also that of expanded openness and expectancy with regard to the Holy Spirit and his gifts. Because the Holy Spirit apportions as he wills in freedom and sovereignty, the religious experiences of persons can differ. He blows where he wills (John 3:8). Though the Holy Spirit never ceased manifesting himself throughout the entire history of the church, the manner of the manifestations has differed according to the times and cultures. However, in the Pentecostal movement, the manifestation of tongues has had, and continues to have, particular importance.

17. During times of spiritual renewal when charismatic elements are more manifest, tensions can arise because of prejudice, lack of mutual understanding and communi-

cation. Also, at such times as this, the discerning of spirits is more necessary than ever. This necessity should not lead to discernment being misused so as to exclude charismatic manifestations. The true exercise of the charisma takes place in love and leads to a greater fidelity to Christ and his church. The presence of charismatic gifts is not a sign of spiritual maturity, and those who lack experience of such gifts are not considered to be inferior Christians. Love is the context in which all gifts are rightly exercised, love being of a more definitive and primary order than the spiritual gifts (1 Cor. 13). In varying degrees all the charisma are ministries directed to the building up of the community and witness in mission. For this reason mystical experiences, which are more generally directed towards personal communion with God, are distinguished from charismatic experiences which, while including personal communion with God, are directed more to ministerial service.

The giving of the Spirit and Christian initiation
18. The Holy Spirit, being the agent of regeneration, is given in Christian initiation, not as a commodity but as he who unites us with Christ and the Father in a personal relationship. Being a Christian includes the reception of grace through the Holy Spirit for one's own sanctification as well as gifts to be ministered to others. In some manner all ministry is a demonstration of the power of the Spirit. It is not agreed whether there is a further imparting of the Spirit with a view to charismatic ministry, or whether baptism in the Holy Spirit is, rather, a kind of release of a certain aspect of the Spirit already given. An inconclusive discussion occurred on the question as to how many impartings of the Spirit there were. Within classical Pentecostalism some hold that through regeneration the Holy Spirit comes *into* us, and that later in the baptism in the Spirit, the Spirit comes *upon* us and begins to flow from us. Finally, charisma are not personal achievements but are sovereign manifestations of the Holy Spirit.

Baptism
19. Baptism involves a passing over from the kingdom of darkness to Christ's kingdom of light, and always includes a communal dimension of being baptized into the one body of Christ. The implications of this concord were not developed.

20. In regard to baptism, the New Testament reflects the missionary situation of the apostolic generation of the church and does not clearly indicate what may have happened in the second and following generation of believers.

21. In that missionary situation, Christian initiation involved a constellation normally including proclamation of the gospel, faith, repentance, baptism in water, the receiving of the Spirit. There was disagreement as to the relationship of these items, and the order in which they may or should occur. In both the Pentecostal and Roman Catholic tradition, laying-on of hands may be used to express the giving of the Spirit. Immersion is the ideal form which most aptly expresses the significance of baptism. Some, however, regard immersion as essential; others do not.

22. In discussing infant baptism, certain convergences were noted: (a) Sacraments are in no sense magical and are effective only in relationship to faith.

23. (b) God's gift precedes and makes possible human receiving. Even though there was disagreement on the application of this principle, there was accord on the assertion that God's grace operates in advance of our conscious awareness.

24. (c) Where paedo-baptism is not practised and the children of believing parents are presented and dedicated to God, the children are thus brought into the care of the Christian community, and enjoy the special protection of the Lord.

25. (d) Where paedo-baptism is practised it is fully meaningful only in the context of the faith of the parents and the community. The parents must undertake to nurture the child in the Christian life, in the expectation that, when he or she grows up, the child will personally live and affirm faith in Christ.

26. Representatives of the charismatic movement in the historic churches expressed different views on baptism. Some agreed substantially with the Roman Catholic, others with the classical Pentecostal view.

27. Attention was drawn to the pastoral problem of persons baptized in infancy seeking a new experience of baptism by immersion later in life. It was stated that in a few traditions rites have been devised, involving immersion in water in order to afford such an experience. The Roman Catholics felt there were already sufficient opportunities within the existing liturgy for reaffirming one's baptism. Rebaptism in the strict sense of the word is unacceptable to all. Those participants who reject paedo-baptism, however, explained that they do not consider as rebaptism the baptism of a believing adult who has received infant baptism. This serious ecumenical problem requires future study.

Scripture, Tradition and developments
28. The church is always subject to sacred scripture. There was, however, considerable disagreement as to the role of Tradition in interpretation of scripture.

29. The Pentecostal and charismatic movements have brought to the understanding of scripture a new relevance and freshness to confirm the conviction that scripture has a special message, vital to each generation. Moreover, these movements challenge the exegetes to take a new look at the sacred text in the light of the new questions and expectations the movements bring to scripture.

30. It was agreed that every church has a history and is inevitably affected by its past. Some developments in that past are good, some are questionable; some are enduring, some are only temporary. A discernment must be made on these developments by the churches.

Charismatic renewal in the historic churches
31. The dialogue considered that in the context of the charismatic movement in the historic churches there was justification for new groups and communities within the churches. Though such movements have a legitimate prophetic character, their ultimate purpose is to strengthen the church, and to participate fully in her life. Therefore, the charismatic movement is not in competition with the churches, nor is it separate from them. Further, it should recognize the church authorities. In a word the charismatic renewal is a renewal in the body of Christ, the church, and is, therefore, in and of the church.

Public worship
32. Public worship should safeguard a whole composite of elements: spontaneity, freedom, discipline, objectivity. On the Roman Catholic side, it was noted that the new revised liturgy allows for more opportunities for spontaneous prayer and singing at the

eucharist and in the rites of penance. The Pentecostal tradition has come to accept a measure of structure in worship and recognizes the development in its own history towards some liturgy.

33. In the Roman Catholic context the phrase *ex opere operato* was discussed in relation to the celebration of the sacraments. The disquiet of some participants was removed by the explanation of the Roman Catholic doctrine of grace, which stresses that the living faith of the recipient of a sacrament is of fundamental importance.

Public worship and the gifts

34. Corporate worship is a focal expression of the worshipper's daily life as he or she speaks to God and to other members of the community in songs of praise and words of thanksgiving (Eph. 5:19-20; 1 Cor. 14:26). Our Lord is present in the members of his body, manifesting himself in worship by means of a variety of charismatic expressions. He is also present by the power of his Spirit in the eucharist. The participants recognized that there was a growing understanding of the unity which exists between the formal structure of the eucharistic celebration and the spontaneity of the charismatic gifts. This unity was exemplified by the Pauline relationship between chapters 11 and 14 of 1 Corinthians.

35. There exists both a divine and human aspect to all genuinely charismatic phenomena. So far as concerns the human aspect, the phenomena can rightly be subject to psychological, linguistic, sociological, anthropological and other investigations which can provide some understanding of the diverse manifestations of the Holy Spirit. But the spiritual aspect of charismatic phenomena ultimately escapes a purely scientific examination. While there is no essential conflict between science and faith, nevertheless, science has inherent limitations, particularly with regard to the dimensions of faith and spiritual experience.

36. A survey of the scientific literature on speaking in tongues was presented. Another presentation outlined a Jungian psychological evaluation of the phenomenology of the Holy Spirit. However, neither of these topics was developed adequately in discussion, and they await more extended consideration. This could be done in the context of a future treatment of the place of speaking in tongues as an essential factor in the Pentecostal experience.

37. The relationship between science and the exercise of the spiritual gifts, including that of healing, was discussed. Classical Pentecostals, as well as other participants, believe that through the ministry of divine healing can come restoration to sound health. Full agreement was not reached in this matter in view of the importance of the therapeutic disciplines, and the participants recommended further in-depth study.

Discernment of spirits

38. The New Testament witnesses to the charism of the discerning of spirits (1 Cor. 12:10), and also to a form of discernment through the resting of the spirits (1 John 4:1), and the proving of the will of God (Rom. 12:2), each exercised in the power of the Spirit. There are different aspects of discernment of spirits which allow for human experience, wisdom and reason as a consequence of growth in the Spirit, while other aspects imply an immediate communication of the Spirit for discernment in a specific situation.

39. Discernment is essential to authentic ministry. The Pentecostal tradition lays stress on the discerning of spirits in order to find "the mind of the Spirit" for ministry

and public worship. It is also understood as a diagnostic gift which leads to the further manifestation of other charismata for the edification of the body of Christ and the work of the gospel. The operation of this gift in dependence upon the Spirit develops both in the believer and community a growth in a mature sensitivity to the Spirit.

40. Normally, but not absolutely, expectancy is a requisite for the manifestations of the Spirit through human acts on the part of the believer and the community, that is, an openness which nevertheless respects the sovereignty of the Spirit in the distribution of his gifts. Because of human frailty, group pressure and other factors, it is possible for the believer to be mistaken or misled in his awareness of the Spirit's intention and influence in the believer's acts. It is for this reason that criteria are essential to confirm and authenticate the genuine operation of the Spirit of truth (1 John 4:1-6). These criteria must be based upon the scriptural foundation of the incarnation, the lordship of Christ, and the building up of his church. The important element of community criteria involves common wisdom of a group of believers, walking and living in the Spirit, when, led by those exercising the ministry of discernment, a mature discipline results and the group is capable of discerning the mind of God.

41. The Roman Catholic tradition understands such community discernment to be exercised by the whole church of which her leaders receive a special charism for this purpose. All traditions find a confirmatory individual criterion in the extent to which the believer is influenced in his daily life by the Spirit of Christ who produces love, joy, peace: the plenitude of the fruit of the Spirit (Gal. 5:22).

Prayer and praise

42. The relationship between the objective and the subjective aspects of Christian life was raised. Prayer has two main forms: praise and petition. Both have an objective and a subjective aspect.

In the prayer of praise the essential aspect is worship itself, the adoration of the Father in the Spirit and in the truth of Christ (cf. John 4:23-24). One of the expressions of this prayer of praise is the gift of tongues, with joy, enthusiasm, etc.

In the prayer of petition, the believer has always to distinguish between God the giver, and the gift of God.

43. Also discussed was the relationship between the word of God and our experience of the Spirit. The Bible must always be a control and a guide in the Christian experience; but on the other hand, the spiritual experience itself constantly invites us to read the Bible spiritually, in order that it become living water in our Christian life.

44. We recognize multiple aspects of the total Christian experience, which embraces the presence of God (joy, enthusiasm, consolation, etc.), and also the experience of our own sin and the experience of the absence of God, with Christ dying on the cross (Mark 15:34; Phil. 3:10), desolation, aridity, and the acceptance of our personal death in Christ as an integral part of the authentic Christian life and also of the true praise of God.

Topics for further discussion

45. In the course of conversations, a number of areas were touched on which are recommended for further study. Among them were the following: (a) speaking in tongues as a characteristic aspect of the experience in the Pentecostal movement; (b) the subjective dispositions relative to the baptism in the Holy Spirit; (c) the rela-

tionship between the faith of the individual and the faith of the community in terms of content; (d) the relationship between faith and experience; (e) the psychological dimension of charismatic experience; (f) an examination of the charismata of healing and the casting out of demons; (g) the relationship between the sacraments and a conscious personal response of God; (h) the nature of the sacramental event and, in this context, the nature of the church; (i) the problem of interpreting scripture; (j) the ministries and the ministry gifts: their purpose and operation; and (k) the social implications of spiritual renewal.

Character of the final report
46. The character of the final report compiled by the steering committee which has served the dialogue does not represent the official position of the classical Pentecostal churches, or of the Roman Catholic Church. Rather, it represents the content of the discussion. Though the conclusions are the result of serious study and dialogue by responsible persons, it does not commit any of the churches or traditions to the theological positions here expressed, but is submitted to them for suitable use and reaction.

It has been the consensus of all participants that the dialogue has been an occasion of mutual enrichment and understanding and offers the promise of a continuing relationship.

63. Final Report
Dialogue between the Secretariat for Promoting Christian Unity and Some Classical Pentecostals

1977-1982

Introduction

1. The following is a report of conversations at the international level which represent a second five-year series that had its beginnings in informal talks in 1969 and 1970 between the Vatican Secretariat for Promoting Christian Unity and some members of the classical Pentecostal churches. The co-chairmen of this quinquennium were the Rev. David du Plessis of Oakland, California, USA, and the Rev. Kilian McDonnell, OSB, of Collegeville, Minnesota, USA. The conversations took place according to the indications agreed to by the Secretariat for Promoting Christian Unity and the Pentecostal representatives in 1970.

2. This dialogue has its own specific quality. Growth in mutual understanding of classical Pentecostal and Roman Catholic theologies and spiritual practice rather than organic or structural unity is the special object of these bilateral conversations.

3. It is a concern of the dialogue to seek out those areas where classical Pentecostals and Roman Catholics represent divergent theological views and spiritual experiences, and in this way to foster mutual understanding in what distinguishes each partner, such as faith/experience and its role in the Christian life. Without minimizing these differences, the dialogue also seeks common theological ground where "the truth of the gospel" is shared (Gal. 2:14).

4. The Roman Catholic participants were officially appointed by the Secretariat for Promoting Christian Unity. There were various kinds of representation on the classical Pentecostal side. Some were appointed by their individual churches, a few were church officials, others were members who came with the approbation of their churches, and in still other cases they came as members in good standing with their churches.

5. Besides the classical Pentecostals, there were in the first five-year series (1972-76) participants from the charismatic movement in various Protestant churches. These were members of the Anglican or Protestant communions with whom the Roman Catholic Church was already in formal contact through bilateral dialogues. These Anglican and Protestant participants took part primarily because of their involvement in the charismatic renewal rather than as members of their own churches. The first five-year series of conversations extended from 1972 through 1976. In those meetings the following topics were discussed: "Baptism in the Holy Spirit" in the New Testament and its relation to repentance, sanctification, charisma, rites of initiation; the historic background of the classical Pentecostal movement; the role of the Holy Spirit and the gifts of the Spirit in the mystical tradition; the theology of the rites of initiation; the

nature of sacramental activity; infant and adult baptism; public worship, with special attention given to eucharistic worship; discernment of spirits; and the human dimension in the exercise of the spiritual gifts, prayer and praise.

6. In 1977 a second five-year series was initiated. This second series, 1977-82 (no session was held in 1978 because of the death of the pope), had a different character than the first series. In order to more clearly focus the conversations, it was decided that this second series should be exclusively a conversation between the classical Pentecostals and the Roman Catholic Church. Therefore, participants in the charismatic renewal who were members of the Anglican and Protestant churches were not included in the dialogue in a systematic way.

7. At the first meeting of the second series of talks, held in Rome, October 1977, the dialogue discussed speaking in tongues and the relation of experience to faith. The second meeting in Rome, October 1979, discussed the relation of scripture and Tradition, and the ministry of healing in the church. In Venice, October 1980, the meeting focused on church as a worshipping community, and Tradition and traditions. The meeting in Vienna in October 1981 focused on the role of Mary. The last meeting of the series was held at Collegeville, Minnesota, in October 1982, where ministry was the area of concentration.

Speaking in tongues

8. A personal relationship with Jesus Christ belongs to the definition of a Christian. Classical Pentecostals have never accepted the position or taught that this relationship must necessarily be expressed through speaking in tongues in the sense that one could not be a Christian without speaking in tongues.

9. The manifestation of tongues was never entirely absent in the history of the church, and is found in a notable way among Roman Catholics and other Christians involved in charismatic renewal, as well as among classical Pentecostals.

10. It was agreed that every discussion about Christian *glossolalia* should be founded on scripture. That some New Testament authors saw tongues as playing a role in the Christian life is indicated in various books of the Bible. "And they were all filled with the Holy Spirit and began to speak in other tongues as the Spirit gave them utterance" (Acts 2:4; 10:46; 19:6; Mark 16:17; 1 Cor. 12:4,10,18; 14:2,5,22; Rom. 8:26).

11. The teaching of the classical Pentecostals on the charismata seeks to be faithful to the picture of the New Testament church as reflected in 1 Cor. 12-14. Classical Pentecostals have rendered a service by encouraging the various communions to be open and receptive to those spiritual manifestations to which they claim to have been faithful.

Faith and experience

12. By experience the dialogue understands the process or event by which one comes to a personal awareness of God. The experience of God's "presence" or "absence" can be a matter of *conscious awareness*. At the same time, and at a deeper level, there remains the constant abiding faith-conviction that God's loving presence is revealed in the person of his Son, through the Holy Spirit.

13. A Christian is one who experiences not only Easter and Pentecost, but also the cross. The experience of God's "absence" can lead a Christian to a sense of being abandoned, as Jesus himself experienced on the cross. The death of Christ is to be found at

the heart of our Christian experience, and therefore we too experience a death: "I have been crucified with Christ; it is no longer I who live but Christ who lives in me" (Gal. 2:20).

14. There was no unanimity whether non-Christians may receive the life of the Holy Spirit. According to contemporary Roman Catholic understanding, to which Vatican II gives an authoritative expression, "All must be converted to Jesus Christ as he is made known by the church's preaching" (*Ad Gentes*, §7). "The church... is necessary for salvation" (*Lumen Gentium*, §14). But Vatican II also says that all without exception are called by God to faith in Christ and to salvation (*Lumen Gentium*, §§1,16; *Nostra Aetate*, §§1,2). This is brought about "in an unseen way... known only to God" (*Gaudium et Spes*, §22; *Ad Gentes*, §7). This theology is seen as a legitimate development of the total New Testament teaching on God's saving love in Christ. The classical Pentecostal participants do not accept this development but retain their interpretation of the scripture that non-Christians are excluded from the life of the Spirit: "Truly, truly I say unto you, unless one is born anew, he cannot see the kingdom of God" (John 3:3).

15. In the immediacy of the Holy Spirit's manifestation in persons, he engages the natural faculties. In the exercise of the charisma, human faculties are not set aside, but used. The action of the Spirit is not identical with the forces inherent in nature.

16. Individual spiritual experience is seen as part of the communitarian dimensions of the gospel. Persons live in community, and the church should be a lived experience of community. There is rich history of community experience in the church.

17. No matter how vivid or powerful the individual's spiritual experience may be, it needs to be discerned and judged by the community. Love, which is the normative bond of community life, is the biblical criterion of all spiritual experience (cf. 1 Cor. 13).

Scripture and Tradition

18. Both Pentecostals and Roman Catholics hold that the books of the Old Testament were accepted by the early church as inspired. The primitive church existed for a period without its own Christian scriptures. Of the early Christian writings, a certain number were accepted by the church, in the light of the Holy Spirit, as inspired.

19. Roman Catholics believe that these scriptures have been handed down through the centuries in a tradition of living faith, a tradition which has been experienced by the whole church, guided by church leaders, operative in all aspects of Christian life, and on occasion expressed in written form in creeds, councils, etc. This tradition is not a source of revelation separate from scripture, but scripture responded to and actualized in the living tradition of the church.

20. Pentecostals maintain that there are not two authorities (i.e., scripture plus church tradition), but one authority, that of scripture. However, scripture must be read and understood with the illumination of the Holy Spirit. Pentecostals believe that the interpretation of scripture can only be discerned through the Holy Spirit. In Pentecostal movements there is a broad consensus of what elements are fundamental to the Christian faith. But there is a reluctance to give this consensus a status of tradition, because of a fear that religious tradition operates against the gospel.

21. Pentecostals feel that further dialogue will be needed to discuss how the Roman Catholic Church can propose, as a matter of faith, doctrines such as the assumption of

Mary, which go beyond the letter of scripture and which Pentecostals believe to be unacceptable tradition.

Exegesis

22. In contemporary Roman Catholic scholarship, the historical-critical method is the accepted framework within which exegesis is done. In this method emphasis is given to understanding an ancient author in his own idiom, cultural context and religious background.

23. Pentecostals reject the philosophical and theological principles of form and redaction criticism as militating against the plenary inspiration of scripture. They insist on the necessity of the light given by the Holy Spirit if the reader is to respond with faith and understanding to the word of God. It was a consensus of the participants that this discussion was a valuable contribution to the dialogue.

24. Roman Catholics believe that the light of the Holy Spirit given in and through the church is the ultimate principle of interpretation of scripture. They reject any exegetical method that would deny this. However, they believe that critical methods are compatible with a Spirit-inspired exegesis and consider them necessary for a proper understanding of the text.

25. The Pentecostal form of exegesis, while having its roots in evangelicalism, is not specifically defined. It is admittedly in a formative stage. Current exegesis would tend to be a pneumatic literal interpretation.

Biblical interpretation

26. In the event of conflicting interpretation of scripture texts, Roman Catholics accept the guidance of the Spirit as manifested in the living tradition. While the teaching of the church stands under the word of God, this same teaching serves the authoritative and authentic communication of the word of God to the people (*Dei Verbum*, § 10). While Catholics believe both scripture and Tradition cohere in each other and thus transmit the word of God, they do accord a priority to scripture.

27. In the event of conflicting interpretation of scripture texts, Pentecostals rely on the Holy Spirit's guidance without the developed dogmatic structure found in the Roman Catholic Church. While there may be some danger of subjectivism, God is trusted to provide the guidance of the Spirit within the local body of believers (John 14:26; 15:26; 16:13; 2 John 2:27).

Faith and reason

28. In the determination of the limits and validation of religious knowledge, it was agreed that faith and reason cannot be polarized. However, Pentecostals place a greater emphasis upon pneumatic inspiration and supernatural manifestations than on reason for determining the limits and validity of religious knowledge.

29. In spite of the differences mentioned above, it is seen that classical Pentecostals and Roman Catholics agree on the basic elements of the Christian faith, e.g., Trinity, incarnation, resurrection, inspiration of scripture, the preaching of the gospel as an integral part of the ministry of the church, and the guidance of the body of Christ by the Holy Spirit.

30. Still needing clarification in this dialogue is the relation between scripture and Tradition. In this relationship, Roman Catholics do grant a priority to scripture. But

according to Vatican Council II, Decree on Divine Revelation (§10), "sacred Tradition and sacred scripture make up a single sacred deposit of the word of God. Hence both scripture and Tradition must be accepted and honoured with equal feelings of devotion and reverence." Also in need of further discussion is whether the various methods of exegesis – for example, the form-critical method which most Catholic exegetes use – are compatible with classical Pentecostal principles.

Healing in the church

31. The ministry of healing in the church is practised in both the Roman Catholic Church and the Pentecostal churches as part of their total ministry. Both Pentecostals and Roman Catholics agree that through prayerful petition they seek the healing of the whole person's physical, spiritual and emotional needs. Catholics consider the "anointing of the sick" a sacrament. Pentecostals accept anointing with oil as a part of the commission to minister healing with the preaching of the gospel. (In the Roman Catholic Church, the sacrament of anointing of the sick was formerly named "extreme unction".)

32. In the life of the Roman Catholic Church there have been, and are, those who dedicate their lives to the care of and ministry to the sick. Pentecostals are becoming increasingly involved in this important aspect of ministry to the sick and suffering.

33. There are attitudinal differences with regard to healing. Roman Catholic practice regards healing of the body as one outcome of the ministry to the sick in the church. Pentecostals place more emphasis on the expectation of healing in the afflicted through preaching and praying. There is a basic difference in each approach to healing. Roman Catholics may seek healing in sacramental rites, in healing services, novenas and similar forms of devotion. They also go on pilgrimage to shrines where healing may take place. At these places many seek and experience a deepening of faith and a spiritual healing. Pentecostals teach people to expect healing anywhere at any time.

34. Both, in their official teaching, recognize and accept that Jesus is the Healer and that faith looks to Jesus for this grace. Pentecostals as well as Roman Catholics exercise reserve in making judgments about miraculous manifestations and healings.

35. There is a difference in expectation – that of Catholics being more passive while that of Pentecostals being more aggressive. There is admittedly a new awareness of the reality of the healing in the Roman Catholic Church, both within and outside the sacramental order. On the other hand, the dialogue is aware of the existence of some popular religious expressions that may lack sufficient theological understanding.

36. The place of suffering in this life is looked upon by Roman Catholics and some Pentecostals as a means of grace, as a purifying of the soul, and as an instrument for opening one to God's spiritual strength, which sustains one and causes one to rejoice in affliction. Both Roman Catholics and Pentecostals believe that suffering may lead one to understand and be comforted (Phil. 3:10) by the redemptive suffering of Jesus. However, Pentecostals continue to expect healing unless there is a special revelation that God has some other purpose. Both Roman Catholics and Pentecostals accept that the will of God is pre-eminent in the whole matter of healing.

37. Although there appears to be some similarity in lay participation in the ministry of healing, the discussions revealed that there is still a wide gap between Catholics and Pentecostals. Catholics, singly and in community, pray for the sick and with the sick. However, only the priest may administer the anointing of the sick, which is a sacra-

ment. Pentecostals anoint with oil (James 5:14-15) but do not confine the anointing with oil to the ordained ministry. The ministry to the sick, with the laying-on of hands by all believers (Mark 16:17-18), is commonly practised.

38. In contemporary Roman Catholic theology, the necessity for healing is applied to a broader spectrum of social ills. In this application of healing to problems of social injustice, Roman Catholics and classical Pentecostals have widely divergent views. Because of economic and cultural exploitation, many people live in sub-human economic disease. Roman Catholics and Pentecostals have different approaches to the mandate to heal the social conditions which hinder good health.

39. Classical Pentecostals are reluctant to apply divine healing to such a broad range of social injustices. Though they believe exploitative conditions should be rectified, they would emphasize the priority of direct evangelism as the best means of effecting social change.

40. There are a number of areas where there is agreement between Roman Catholics and Pentecostals: the necessity of the cross, healing as a sign of the kingdom, healing of the total person, the involvement of the laity in prayer for healing, the expectation of healing through the eucharist/Lord's supper, and Christ as the Healer.

Community, worship and communion

41. Pentecostals insist on a personal confession of faith in Jesus Christ as the basis of Christian community, rather than on a sacramental and ecclesial approach to the mediating work of Christ. They hold that the believer experiences Christ in every aspect of the worshipping community: singing, praying, testimony, preaching, the ordinance of baptism, the celebration of holy communion, and also in daily living.

42. Roman Catholics insist on conversion to the living God by personal encounter with the living Christ. This conversion often takes place gradually. For Roman Catholics, the church, its ministry and sacraments, are the normal instruments and manifestations of Christ's action and presence, and of the gift of his Spirit. The sacraments are acts of Christ which make present and active the saving power of the paschal mystery.

43. For membership in a Pentecostal church, individuals are expected to have experienced a personal confession of faith in Jesus Christ; and then participate in the life, follow the leadership, and be willing to accept responsibility in the church. In some Pentecostal churches, membership is concurrent with one's water baptism by immersion. Membership in the Roman Catholic Church requires baptism, profession of Roman Catholic faith, and active communion with the local community, the bishops and the successor of St Peter.

44. Both among Pentecostals and Roman Catholics, members may lose their fellowship in the community for serious deviation in doctrine or practice. This penalty of severance from the church is intended to be remedial, a reminder of one's guilt before God and the need for repentance.

45. Both Pentecostals and Roman Catholics celebrate the Lord's supper/eucharist with notable difference in doctrine and practice. Roman Catholics regard the eucharist as a sacramental memorial of Christ's sacrifice on Calvary in the biblical sense of the word anamnesis. By God's power, in the eucharistic celebration Jesus is present in his death and resurrection. This sacred rite is for Roman Catholics a privileged means of grace and the central act of worship. It is celebrated frequently, even daily. Among Pen-

tecostals, the Lord's supper does not hold an equally predominant place in their life of worship. Most Pentecostals celebrate the Lord's supper as an ordinance in obedience to the command of the Lord. Other Pentecostal churches believe this memorial to be more than a reminder of Jesus' death and resurrection, considering it a means of grace.

46. Generally Pentecostals practise "open communion", that is, anyone may participate in the Lord's supper provided they acknowledge the lordship of Christ and have examined their own dispositions (1 Cor. 11:28). Except in certain cases of spiritual necessity determined by the church, the Roman church admits to communion only its own members provided they are free from serious sin. This is not meant to be a refusal of fellowship with other Christians, but rather expresses the Roman Catholic Church's understanding of the relationship between the church and the eucharist.

47. The justification for this practice by Catholics was contested by Pentecostals. This was found to be painful on both sides, and the dialogue agrees that the subject with regard to admission to communion requires a great deal of further discussion.

48. Both Pentecostals and Roman Catholics agree that a common faith is the basis of communion in the body of Christ. For Roman Catholics, full communion means the collegial unity of the heads of the local churches (namely, the bishops, with the bishop of Rome who exercises the primacy). Pentecostals would not attach the same significance to structural bonds between churches and will welcome fellowship with many autonomous churches. The Roman Catholic Church recognizes the mediation of Christ at work in churches which are not in full communion with it, through the word that is preached and believed, the sacraments that are celebrated and the ministry that is exercised. If it considers that these gifts are not found in their fullness in a particular church, it does not thereby make any judgment on the actual holiness of the members of that church. The Roman Catholic Church describes the relationship of other Christians with Catholics as that of brothers and sisters in an incomplete communion *(Unitatis Redintegratio)*.

Tradition and traditions

49. Our views concerning the sacredness and importance of holy scripture allowed us to sense immediately that we had much more to affirm in one another than to question. Both sides of the dialogue agreed as to the inspired nature of both the Old Testament and the New Testament, thus giving scripture a privileged place in both churches.

50. The canonicity of the New Testament is agreed upon in terms of selection and the process of its establishment by the church. Both Pentecostals and Roman Catholics recognize the role of the church in the composition of the books of the New Testament and in the formation of the canon and both acknowledge that the church preceded the written New Testament.

51. The Pentecostal representatives stress that the church itself was created by the calling (election) of Christ, and formed by the doctrinal sayings of Jesus and the messianic interpretation of the scriptures of Jesus himself (Luke 24:45ff.). In this sense, according to Pentecostals, the church itself was formed by the word of God. The church's role in the formation of the New Testament is then essentially that of one who transmits, interprets and applies the salvific message of Jesus Christ. Roman Catholics emphasize more the role of the church as having an authority recognizing and enunciating the truth of the gospel in doctrinal pronouncements.

52. Both sides recognize that scripture is of necessity linked to interpretation. Both agree that scriptural content itself includes interpretation; that it requires interpretation, and thus an authoritative interpreter. There is significant divergence as to the degree of interpretation within scripture and the kind of interpretation by the church necessary in order to understand scripture accurately. Disagreement centres around what or who is an authoritative interpreter. To the Pentecostal it is the right interpretation under the illumination of the Holy Spirit leading to consensus. To the Roman Catholic, it is the church interpreting scripture as understood by the people of God and discerned by the teaching office of the church. Both Pentecostals and Roman Catholics see interpretative authority as an expression of the activity of the Spirit in the church.

53. Both Roman Catholics and Pentecostals recognize the existence of a process of theological discernment in the ongoing life of the church. The Roman Catholics affirm the ministry of discernment by the teaching office of the church and also recognize that a ministry of discernment may exist outside the Roman Catholic Church. The sharpest disagreement arose concerning the irreformable character of some of these discernments. Roman Catholics hold that the faithful will not be led into error when the authority of the church is fully engaged in enunciating the faith. Pentecostals make no such claim.

54. Pentecostals recognize the strength of the Roman Catholic understanding of corporate and collegial interpretation of scripture. However, Pentecostals would like to share with Roman Catholics their characteristic experience of direct dependence upon the Holy Spirit for illumination and interpretation of scripture.

55. A major difference was encountered in the understanding of the role of tradition. Roman Catholics in the dialogue explain Tradition in a twofold sense, each sense related to the other. Tradition, here spelled with a capital T, stands for everything that is being and has been handed down, the once-for-all revelation made by God in Jesus Christ, the word of God proclaimed in written and oral form, and the whole of the Spirit-filled community's response to the truth of the gospel. As such, Tradition contains both an active element of handing down by the church and a passive one of the material handed down. Within Tradition in this sense, the word of God as scripture has a kind of primacy. In this understanding Tradition is a continuous process.

56. Tradition in this sense is not to be confused with traditions. These are various ways of practice and teaching whereby Tradition is transmitted. These traditions become binding only when they are made the object of a special decision of church authority.

57. Classical Pentecostals would not place the same value upon Tradition (or tradition) as Roman Catholics, unless grounded in the express witness of scripture. The Pentecostals, while acknowledging the accumulation of traditions in their own history, would say that these traditions apart from scripture have little authority in the church.

Perspectives on Mary

58. Since Catholic doctrine concerning Mary was perceived as a point of divergence, it was important to classical Pentecostals to discuss this topic. Considerable time was needed to treat the various issues: the doctrine itself, the method by which the doctrine is justified, and the practical consequences at the popular level. The time devoted to the issues is reflected in the space given this topic in the report.

59. Both classical Pentecostals and Roman Catholics agree that the various biblical texts which mention Mary witness to the importance of Mary in the New Testament. The point of divergence was the doctrinal development which took place on the basis of these texts. Classical Pentecostals insist that they cannot go beyond the clear meaning of the text which is normative for all doctrine and experience. Roman Catholics also maintain that scripture is normative for any and all later doctrinal development. But they further hold that the church, praying and preaching the scriptures, can, through the guidance of the Holy Spirit who leads into all truth, find in the biblical texts and in complete fidelity to them a meaning which goes beyond the classical Pentecostals' interpretation.

60. Behind the differences between classical Pentecostals and Roman Catholics in interpretation of specific Marian texts in the scriptures lie doctrinal differences, often implicit and unexpressed. Possibly the most important of these are in the area of Mary's relationship to the church and her role in the communion of saints.

61. Both classical Pentecostals and Roman Catholics were surprised that they had entertained unreal perceptions of the other's views on Mary. Classical Pentecostals were pleased to learn of the concern of authorities in the Roman Catholic Church to be prudent in appraising Marian doctrinal development which claims a biblical basis. Classical Pentecostals, while recognizing that doctrinal development that is clearly based on scriptural evidence is not entirely absent from Pentecostal history, admit no doctrinal development with regard to Mary.

The motherhood of Mary

62. Both Roman Catholics and Pentecostals agree that Mary is the Mother of Jesus Christ, who is the Son of God, and as such she occupies a unique place. Both Roman Catholics and classical Pentecostals recognize the historical origins of the title "Mother of God" *(theotokos)* arising from the christological disputes at the council of Ephesus (A.D. 431). In order to preserve the unity of the one person having two natures to which the Virgin gave birth, the council approved the title *"theotokos"* ("God-bearer" or "Mother of God"). This was not a Marian definition, concerned to give Mary a new title, but a christological definition concerned with the identity of Jesus Christ. It is only at the moment of the incarnation that she becomes the Mother of God. She is not the Mother of God in his eternal triune existence, but the Mother of God the Son in his incarnation.

The veneration of Mary

63. Roman Catholics and classical Pentecostals concur in the special respect due to Mary as the mother of Jesus. Both view her as the outstanding example or model of faith, humility and virtue. Both Roman Catholics and Pentecostals share a concern for the necessity of a correct perspective on Mary. However, there are significant differences in the understanding of the veneration to be given to Mary.

64. Pentecostals expressed concern about what they consider to be excesses in contemporary veneration of Mary. For Pentecostals, certain Roman Catholic practices of Marian veneration appear to be superstitious and idolatrous. For Roman Catholics, there is an apparent failure among Pentecostals to take account of the place of Mary in God's design as indicated in holy scripture.

65. Roman Catholics, while admitting the occurrence of certain excesses in the practice of veneration of Mary, were careful to point out that proper veneration of Mary

is always christological. In addition, Roman Catholics gave evidence that practical steps are being taken to correct excesses where they occur, in line with the norms of the Second Vatican Council, *Lumen Gentium* §8, and Pope Paul VI in his encyclical *Marialis Cultus* (1974), §§24-36.

The intercession of Mary

66. Both Pentecostals and Roman Catholics teach that Mary in no way substitutes for or replaces the one Saviour and Mediator, Jesus Christ. Both believe in direct, immediate contact between the believer and God. Both pray to God the Father, through the Son, in the Holy Spirit. Catholics believe that intercessory prayers directed to Mary do not end in Mary, but in God himself. Pentecostals would not invoke the intercession of Mary or other saints in heaven, because they do not consider it a valid biblical practice.

Catholic doctrine on the graces given to Mary

67. Roman Catholics believe that Mary always remained a virgin, that she was conceived free from all stain of sin, and that at the end of her life she was assumed body and soul into heaven. Pentecostals reject these beliefs.

68. Roman Catholics claim that belief about these graces given to Mary belongs to the Tradition of the church in which the word of God is unfolded. Pentecostals can find no warrant for these beliefs in scripture. As well as questioning the value of Tradition as a basis for the doctrines of faith, Pentecostals would suggest that these traditions about perpetual virginity, immaculate conception and assumption are without scriptural basis.

69. In the "hierarchy of truths" of faith held by the Roman Catholics, these three doctrines are placed among the truths that are integral to the Roman Catholic faith. Roman Catholics do not believe that those outside the Roman Catholic Church who do not hold these truths are, on that account, excluded from salvation.

The virginity of Mary

70. Both Pentecostals and Roman Catholics agree that Mary was a virgin in the conception of Jesus and see in the texts that state it an important affirmation of the divine sonship of Christ. Roman Catholics believe that Mary remained a virgin after the birth of Jesus and did not have other offspring. Pentecostals commonly maintain that scripture records she had other offspring and lived as the wife of Joseph in the full sense.

71. Roman Catholics take the evidence of scripture as being open to the developments concerning the virginity of Mary, which they find expressed in the earliest fathers of the church. They found in Tradition (understood in the total experience and response of the church as she prays and preaches the word of God) evidence of Mary's virginity.

The immaculate conception of Mary

72. Roman Catholics hold the doctrine of the immaculate conception to be founded on the church's reflection on the Bible, both the Old and New Testaments. This doctrine is seen to follow upon consideration of her role as the Mother of the Saviour and of texts which present her as the perfect fulfilment of Old Testament types, etc.: "the

virgin daughter of Sion" (Luke 1:26-38; cf. Zeph. 3:14-20; Zech. 2:10; 9:9), the "woman" (John 2:1-11; 19:25-27; cf. Gen. 3:15). These texts form a biblical theology of Mary, which provides a basis for the development of the doctrine of the immaculate conception. The explicit development of the doctrine in the life of the church led to its definition by Pope Pius IX in 1854.

73. Pentecostals acknowledge Catholic assurances that the special grace claimed for Mary is a redeeming grace that comes from Jesus. She stands among the redeemed and is a member of the church. However, Pentecostals cannot find any basis for the doctrine of Mary's immaculate conception in scripture. Furthermore, Pentecostals do not see any value for salvation in this doctrine. Roman Catholics see in the Pentecostal attitude a failure to appreciate fully the implications of the incarnation and the power of Christ's saving and sanctifying grace.

74. Further clarification of issues arising from this doctrine would entail a wider discussion by us of pneumatology, christology and ecclesiology. Roman Catholics believe a basic distortion takes place when this doctrine is considered in isolation.

The assumption of Mary

75. Roman Catholics see the doctrine of the assumption, which was explicitly affirmed in the fathers of the church as early as the 6th century, to be in accordance with basic biblical doctrines. The risen Christ is the beginning of the new creation, which is born from above in the death and resurrection of Christ. In Mary, because of her unique relationship with Christ, this new creation by the Spirit was achieved to the point that the life of the Spirit triumphed fully in her. Consequently she is already with her body in the glory of God, with her risen Son.

76. The Pentecostal difficulty rests in the absence of biblical evidence. There is a generally accepted view that Mary, as one of the faithful, awaits the day of resurrection when she, along with all Christians, will be united bodily with her Son in glory. Pentecostals see a parallel between Mary's "assumption" and the Pentecostal understanding of the "bodily resurrection" or the "rapture of the church" (1 Thess. 4:13-18, cf. esp. v.17), but differ as to when this will take place for Mary.

Ministry in the church

77. While it is recognized that the word *ministry* in the New Testament covers many activities, the focus of the dialogue bears upon how ministry in the church continues the ministry of the apostles.

78. Such ministry includes all that pertains to the preaching and proclamation of God's word on which the churches are founded and all that is required for the building up of the church in Christ.

79. For Roman Catholics, all ministries contribute to these ends, but particular importance is attached to the ministry of bishops, and to that of the presbyters and deacons who collaborate with them. Classical Pentecostals find an exercise of apostolic ministry wherever through the preaching of God's word churches are founded, persons and communities are converted to Jesus Christ, and manifestations of the Holy Spirit are in evidence. Within the variety of polity found in Pentecostal circles, biblical terms such as elder, deacon, bishop and pastor are used to designate a variety of offices and ministries, and are not always given the same meaning.

80. It is agreed by both sides of the dialogue that order and structure are necessary to the exercise of ministry.

81. In the development and structuring of ministry, there is no single New Testament pattern. The Spirit has many times led churches to adapt their ministries to the needs of place and time.

82. Roman Catholics see evidence of ministerial office in the New Testament and find in such office part of God's design for the early church, but find in the gradual emergence of the threefold ministry of bishop, presbyter and deacon the way in which God's design is fulfilled and structural and ministerial needs are met in the church.

83. The positions of classical Pentecostals are more varied. Although there is reluctance in some Pentecostal circles to speak of the ministries of apostle and prophet because of the historical abuse sometimes associated with these ministries, they are recognized as existing and important to the life of the church. Even though there is no uniformity in the way that the New Testament depicts ministry, it is the desire of Pentecostals to seek guidelines for ministry and office in the New Testament.

84. Pentecostals appeal primarily to the priesthood of all believers, which connotes access to God and a participation in ministry on the part of all believers. Pentecostals point to a problem of over-institutionalization of ministry. They believe that they find evidence of this in the history and practice of the Roman Catholic Church.

85. Roman Catholics place emphasis on the need for the institution of ecclesial offices as part of the divine plan for the church. They also see such institutions and ministries as related to and aiding the priesthood and ministry of all within the one body. At the same time they are aware of the dangers of institutionalism. In recent decades, there has been a renewed concern in the Roman Catholic Church for the development of the ministry of all believers. Roman Catholics, furthermore, feel that Pentecostals fail to give due acknowledgment to the visible aspect of the church or to the sacrament of order and the sacramental ministry.

Ordination

86. Pentecostals see ordination as a recognition of spiritual gifts already imparted. For Pentecostals, ministry is always initiated by a divine call and attended by evidence of reception of necessary gifts and graces. Ordination of one who has received appropriate gifts provides denominational authority for his continuing function in the ministry to which he has been called.

87. For Roman Catholics, the ministry of ecclesial office is given by God who calls a candidate and pours out his Spirit upon him and gives him a special share in the priesthood of Christ. This gift must be discerned by the church, in the form laid down by church discipline. Ordination is considered a sacrament, which imparts grace, gifts and authority for the ministry of the word, sacrament and pastoral office.

Apostolic succession

88. Both Roman Catholics and Pentecostals believe that the church lives in continuity with the New Testament apostles and their proclamation, and with the apostolic church. A primary manifestation of this is to be found in fidelity to the apostolic teaching.

89. For Roman Catholics, the succession of bishops in an orderly transmission of ministry through history is both guarantee and manifestation of this fidelity.

90. For Pentecostals, the current dynamic of the Spirit is regarded as a more valid endorsement of apostolic faith and ministry than an unbroken line of episcopal succession. They look to apostolic life and to the power of preaching which leads to conversions to Jesus Christ as an authentication of apostolic ministry. They question Roman Catholics as to whether in their insistence on episcopal succession they have at times ignored the requirements of apostolic life. Roman Catholics hold the necessity of apostolic life for an effective ministry. However, they maintain that the sovereignty of God's act in the transmission of the word and the ministry of sacrament is not nullified by the personal infidelity of the minister.

91. Both partners to the dialogue strongly assert that holiness of life is essential to an effective ministry and recognize that the quality of apostolic life of the minister has an effect on the quality of his ministry. Both, by their respective discipline and practice, seek to provide seriously for the holiness of ministers. Both recognize that at times, the power and sovereignty of God is operative in the ministry of a weak and sinful minister, although the discipline of both classical Pentecostals and Roman Catholics provides for the removal from office of anyone who is plainly unworthy.

Recognition of ministries
92. Each partner to the dialogue recognizes that God is at work through the ministry of the other and recognizes that the body of Christ is being built up through it (*Unitatis Redintegratio*, §§3,22). The issue of recognition depends on ecclesiological questions that still need elucidation. However, serious disagreements still remain.

Topics for further discussion
93. During our conversations we touched on a number of topics which could not be discussed adequately and would have to be taken up at a later date. Among them were the following: (a) the personal moment of faith; (b) the communion of saints in relation to Mariology and the intercession of the saints; (c) the development of doctrine in its relation to scripture and Tradition; (d) the inadequacy and limitation in doctrinal formulations marked with the stamp of a certain historical moment; (e) the binding force of the Marian doctrines which have been defined as they relate to salvation within the Roman Catholic Church.

Character of the final report
94. This international dialogue with representatives of classical Pentecostals and Roman Catholics has been characterized by the seriousness of the exchange, as participants seek to reflect in all fidelity the doctrine of their church and at the same time to learn from their opposite partners in dialogue what their true faith stance is. These responsibilities have been exercised with candour and earnestness and have resulted in this final report. Clearly, the report does not commit any church or tradition to any theological position but is offered to them for their reflection and evaluation.

Conclusion
95. The members of the dialogue have experienced mutual respect and acceptance, hoping that the major points of difference will provide an occasion for continuing dialogue to our mutual enrichment.

96. It is the consensus of the participants that the dialogue should continue in this same spirit. Every effort will be made to encourage opportunities for similar bilateral theological conversation at the local level.

97. To that end, the dialogue enters into a period of assimilation to digest the results of the first two phases of exchange and to give broader exposure to mutual efforts undertaken to promote better understanding.

98. Finally, the participants wish to affirm the dialogue as an ongoing instrument of communication between the two traditions.

64. Perspectives on Koinonia

Report from the Third Quinquennium of the Dialogue between the Pontifical Council for Promoting Christian Unity and Some Classical Pentecostal Churches and Leaders

1985-1989

Introduction

1. This is a report of conversations held on the international level between the Pontifical Council for Promoting Christian Unity[1] and some classical Pentecostal churches and leaders. It contains the results of the third phase of dialogue held 1985-89.

2. Contacts for the dialogue were initiated in 1969 and 1970. Among the topics discussed during the first quinquennium (1972-76) were baptism in the Holy Spirit, Christian initiation and the charisms, scripture and Tradition, and the human person and the gifts. In the second quinquennium (1977-82) consideration was given to faith and religious experience, speaking in tongues, and Mary. The co-chairpersons during this third quinquennium, 1985-89, were the Rev. Kilian McDonnell, OSB, Collegeville, Minnesota, USA, and the Rev. Justus T. du Plessis of the Apostolic Faith Mission of South Africa. The conversations dealt with the subject of the church as koinonia.

3. The Rev. David J. du Plessis chaired the Pentecostal delegation during the first two phases of the dialogue. Indeed, the origin of the international Pentecostal-Roman Catholic dialogue, almost twenty years ago, owes much to initiatives he took during and after the Second Vatican Council. David du Plessis continued to take part in the third phase of the dialogue, providing important insights to our deliberations, until his death in 1987. The dialogue commission acknowledges, with gratitude to God, David du Plessis' important contribution to the origin and continuation of our work.

4. This particular series of discussions has been noted for the growing acceptance of the dialogue by the worldwide Pentecostal community. For the first time several Pentecostal churches authorized the participation of officially appointed representatives to the dialogue. These churches include: the Apostolic Church of Mexico (1986); the Apostolic Faith Mission of South Africa (1985-89); the Church of God (Cleveland, Tennessee, USA) (1985-88); the Church of God of Prophecy, USA (1986-88); the Independent Assemblies of God International, USA (1987); the International Church of the Foursquare Gospel, USA (1985-89); the International Communion of Charismatic Churches, USA (1986).

5. Although the unity of the church is a concern of Pentecostals and Roman Catholics alike, the dialogue has not had as its goal or its subject either organic or structural union. These discussions were meant to develop a climate of mutual understanding in matters of faith and practice: to find points of genuine agreement as well as to indicate areas in which further dialogue is required. We hope that further theological convergence will appear as we continue to explore issues together.

6. Building upon the groundwork laid in the previous two series of discussions, this phase of dialogue focused upon the theme of koinonia. At its 1985 meeting in Riano, Italy, discussion was directed to the subject of the communion of the saints. In Sierra Madre, California, USA, during 1986, the subject was the Holy Spirit and the New Testament vision of koinonia. Discussion was directed towards the relationship of sacraments to koinonia in 1987 and 1988. At the meeting in Venice, Italy, in 1987, the dialogue focused upon koinonia, church and sacraments, emphasizing the place of the eucharist, while in its 1988 meeting at Emmetten, Switzerland, the discussion was on koinonia and baptism. During the 1989 meeting in Rome we summarized our findings in this report. The presentation of the findings in this report follows a more systematic order than the chronological sequence in which the topics were discussed.

7. The theme of koinonia was chosen for several reasons. First, the subject of communion of saints emerged from the portions of the discussions in the second phase of dialogue which had centred on Mary. Participants in the second phase believed that the topic of communion was pregnant with possibilities. Second, they also realized that the larger worldwide ecumenical dialogue was viewing the topic of communion with interest and expectation.

8. Koinonia has been an important topic for discussion in a number of international dialogues, for example, in the Orthodox-Roman Catholic dialogue, the second phase of the Anglican-Roman Catholic international dialogue, the Methodist-Roman Catholic dialogue; the Lutheran-Roman Catholic dialogue; the Baptist-Roman Catholic dialogue; and the Disciples of Christ-Roman Catholic dialogue.

9. The theme of koinonia is proving fruitful in the reflection about ecclesiological self-understanding in many Christian churches and communions, as for example in the Anglican Communion and the Lutheran World Federation.[2]

10. During the Second Vatican Council, the Roman Catholic Church emphasized the ecclesiology of communion. The extraordinary synod of bishops, which met in 1985 to celebrate the 20th anniversary of the closing of the Second Vatican Council, recognized the importance given to the notion of communion by the Council. In Pentecostal teaching, koinonia is understood as an essential aspect of church life as it relates to the church's ministry to the world and to the relationships of Christians to one another. Both the Roman Catholics and Pentecostals, therefore, have come to appreciate the biblical importance of koinonia as portrayed in Acts 2:42: "They [Christians] devoted themselves to the apostles' teaching and fellowship [koinonia], to the breaking of bread and the prayers."[3]

11. One of the difficulties we faced in our discussions was the historical difference between the development of the doctrine of the church in Roman Catholicism and in the various Pentecostal traditions. Roman Catholics have a centuries-long tradition of ecclesiological reflection; the Pentecostal movement is less than a century old and has had little opportunity to engage in sustained theological reflection on ecclesiology. Although Pentecostals do not possess a developed ecclesiology, they do embrace a variety of ecclesiological polities, and they hold strongly to certain basic ecclesiological convictions (e.g., the importance of the local congregation). These convictions have been brought to bear on the various issues discussed.

12. While all dialogue participants have sought to represent their church's positions faithfully, the views expressed in this document are those of the joint commission, which now offers its work to the sponsoring bodies.

I. Koinonia and the word of God

13. Though the focus of our dialogue was church as koinonia, the question of scripture and Tradition kept surfacing in all our discussions. We found that much of the agreement and also the disagreement stemmed from the similarities and differences in our understandings of the ultimate bases on which doctrine and practice of the church should rest. Even though we discussed the topic of scripture and Tradition more extensively in previous phases of the dialogue,[4] we offer the following brief summary of our respective views on scripture and Tradition because of its link to the topic of this particular dialogue.

A. Jesus Christ, the perfect Word of God

14. After speaking in many places and in a variety of ways through the prophets, God has now "in these last days... spoken to us by a Son" (Heb. 1:1-2). He sent his Son, the eternal Word of God, who became flesh (cf. John 1:14).

15. Together we believe that our Lord Jesus Christ revealed God in a perfect way through his whole ministry: through his words and deeds, his signs and wonders, but especially through his death and glorious resurrection from the dead, and finally by sending the Spirit of truth (cf. John 15:26; 16:7,12).

16. Jesus Christ is the ultimate and permanent Word of God. The Christian dispensation, as the new and definitive covenant, will never pass away, and we now await no further revelation before the glorious manifestation of our Lord Jesus Christ (1 Tim. 6:14; Titus 2:13).

B. The written word of God

17. We believe together that the books of both the Old and New Testaments have been written, in their entirety, under the inspiration of the Holy Spirit (cf. John 20:31; 2 Tim. 3:16; 2 Pet. 1:19,21; 3:15-16). Scripture is the word of God written in human words in history.

18. Without suppressing the humanity of the biblical writers, God used them to express God's perfect will to God's people. The scripture teaches faithfully and without error that truth which God wanted put into the sacred writings for our salvation (cf. 2 Tim. 3:16).

19. We disagree on the limits of the canon of scriptures. Roman Catholics and Orthodox have the same canon. Pentecostals agree with the Reformation churches in their view of the canon as limited to the sixty-six books of the Old and New Testaments. While Pentecostals do not deny that the books which Roman Catholics treat as deutero-canonical are valuable for the edification of God's people, they do not consider them as normative for faith and practice.

20. Catholics argue that it is significant that the church precedes chronologically the writings of the New Testament. These writings collectively bring together the message transmitted orally by the early apostolic Christian community, filled with the Holy Spirit, and constitute also the witness and response of the people of God to the truth of the gospel.

21. The Roman Catholic Church sees in the texts of the New Testament – whose authors were inspired – the normative expression of revelation which closed with the death of the last apostle. The writings of the New Testament thus express, in a normative fashion, the apostolic Tradition. The determination of the canon of scripture by the

church is also an act of that Tradition. The proper interpretation of scripture has to be made in the communion of the believers, within the living Tradition which is guided by the Holy Sprit. The same Spirit who inspired the scriptures also opens the sense of the scripture to the people of God, so that it nourishes their faith.

22. Both Roman Catholics and Pentecostals recognize that the chosen vessels of God who wrote the New Testament belonged to the church, and they stress that the New Testament biblical authors had a unique place in the history of revelation. Since the church inherited the scripture from the Old Testament people of God, Israel, and from Jesus himself, and since the church rose out of the proclamation of Christ's chosen apostles, it must be considered the creation of the word of God. The church can live in accordance with the will of God only as it submits itself to the prophetic and apostolic testimony contained in the scriptures. By accepting the books of the New Testament into the canon of scriptures, the church *recognized* the New Testament writings as the word of God addressed to humanity.

23. Pentecostals believe that some traditions express correctly the saving truth to which scripture testifies (e.g., Apostles' and Nicene Creeds), but they seek to evaluate all traditions in the light of the word of God in scripture, the ultimate norm of faith and practice in the church.

24. Both Pentecostals and Roman Catholics agree that scripture, inspired by the Spirit, can be properly interpreted only with the help of the Holy Spirit. "So also no one comprehends the thoughts of God except the Spirit of God" because spiritual things "are spiritually discerned" (1 Cor. 2:11,14).

25. There is, however, a significant divergence as to the nature of interpretation which is necessary to understand scripture accurately. In Roman Catholicism the interpretation of the scripture goes on daily in the lives of the faithful at many levels, such as in the family, in the pulpit and in the classroom. The whole body of the faithful who have an anointing that comes from the Holy One cannot err in matters of belief (cf. 1 John 2:20,27). This characteristic is shown in the supernatural appreciation of the faith *(sensus fidei)* of the whole people, when "from the bishops to the last of the faithful" they manifest a universal consent in matters of faith and morals *(Lumen Gentium* §12).[5] Roman Catholics hold that the teaching office of the church "is not above the word of God, but serves it, teaching only what has been handed on, listening to it devoutly, guarding it scrupulously, and explaining it faithfully by divine commission and with the help of the Holy Spirit" *(Dei Verbum,* §10).

26. Pentecostals appreciate the work of interpretation of scripture going on in the Catholic church; however, they look with scepticism on any claim that the whole body of faithful cannot err in matters of belief. Pentecostals also believe that God has given special gifts of teaching to the believing community (1 Cor. 12:28; Eph. 4:12). But, because Pentecostals hold that scripture is clear in all essential points, they believe that each Christian can interpret scripture under the guidance of the Spirit and with the help of the discerning Christian community. Thus, Christians can make responsible judgments for themselves in matters of faith and practice through their use of scripture.

27. Roman Catholics encourage Pentecostals to develop greater contact with the wider Christian community's historical interpretation and biblical hermeneutics. Both Roman Catholics and Pentecostals are together growing in respect for the exegetical endeavour and its enriching findings.

28. Since the beginning of this century, Roman Catholics have been according a greater place to scripture in preaching, liturgy, personal reading and prayer. Pentecostals in recent years have come to appreciate the importance of the faithful teachers of the word of God through church history. The aspiration of all parties in the dialogue is that, under the guidance of the one Holy Spirit, there will be an increasingly common insight into the meaning of scripture, which would help overcome the divisions between Christians.

II. The Holy Spirit and the New Testament vision of koinonia

A. *Koinonia with the triune God*

29. Both Pentecostals and Roman Catholics believe that the koinonia between Christians is rooted in the life of Father, Son and Holy Spirit.[6] Furthermore, they believe that this trinitarian life is the highest expression of the unity to which we together aspire: "that which we have seen and heard we proclaim also to you, so that you may have fellowship with us; and our fellowship is with the Father and with his Son Jesus Christ"(1 John 1:3).

30. Both Roman Catholics and Pentecostals agree that the Holy Spirit is the source of koinonia, or communion. The church has been gathered in the Holy Spirit (cf. 2 Cor. 13:13). They differ, however, in their points of departure and in their emphases.

31. Roman Catholics, on the one hand, stress the God-givenness of the koinonia and its trinitarian character. Their point of departure is the baptismal initiation into the trinitarian koinonia by faith, through Christ in his Spirit. Their emphasis is also on the Spirit-given means to sustain this koinonia (e.g., word, ministry, sacraments, charisma).

32. Pentecostals, on the other hand, stress that the Holy Spirit convicts people of sin, bringing them through repentance and personal faith into fellowship with Christ and one another (cf. 1 Cor. 1:9). As believers continue to be filled with the Spirit (cf. Eph. 5:18), they should be led to seek greater unity in the faith with other Christians. The Holy Spirit is the Spirit of unity (cf. Acts 2:1ff.). Just as the Spirit fell on Gentiles and showed the church to be a universal community, made of both Jews and Gentiles (cf. Acts 10), so also today God is bestowing his Spirit everywhere on Christians from different churches, promoting unity around our common Lord. The common experience of the Holy Spirit challenges us to strive for greater visible unity as we reflect on the shape God wants this unity to take.

33. Our dialogue has helped both partners to discover and appreciate each other's specific emphases. On the one hand, by listening to the Roman Catholic participants, Pentecostals have been reminded of the importance of the communitarian dimension of the New Testament understanding of koinonia. Roman Catholics, on the other hand, have been reminded of the importance of the personal dimension of the same koinonia with God which comes from the Holy Spirit who convicts persons of sin and brings them to faith in Jesus Christ. We believe that these two emphases are not mutually exclusive but rather that they are complementary.

B. *Oneness of the church*

34. Roman Catholics and Pentecostals believe that there is only "one holy catholic apostolic church" made of all believers (cf. Eph. 4:4-6). They differ, however, in their understanding of that one church and of the way one belongs to it. Roman Catholics

consider the establishment of denominations which result from the lack of love and/or divergence in matters of faith as departures away from the unity of the one church, which in fulfilment of the command of the Lord always remains visibly one and subsists in the Roman Catholic Church (*Lumen Gentium*, §8). Pentecostals tend to view denominations as more or less legitimate manifestations of the one universal church. Their legitimacy depends on the degree of their faithfulness to the fundamental doctrines of the scripture. We both agree that the Holy Spirit is the Spirit of unity in diversity (cf. 1 Cor. 12:13ff.) and not the Spirit of division.

35. By appealing to Jesus' teaching on the wheat and tares (Matt. 13:24-30), some Christians distinguish between an invisible church (which is one) and a visible church (which may be divided). While this distinction can be of use in distinguishing between sincere and insincere members of the church, it can cause misunderstanding, since both Pentecostals and Roman Catholics affirm that the church is both a visible and an invisible reality. Neither should the distinction between visible and invisible dimensions of the church be used to justify and reinforce *separation* between Christians.

36. The essential unity of the church neither implies nor mandates uniformity. "For just as the body is one and has many members, and all the members of the body, though many, are one body, so it is with Christ" (1 Cor. 12:12). The diversity is due to the Spirit. "Now there are varieties of gifts, but the same Spirit; and there are varieties of service, but the same Lord; and there are varieties of working, but it is the same God who inspires them all in every one. To each is given the manifestation of the Spirit for the common good" (1 Cor. 12:4-7). The unity which the Spirit forges is resplendent with diversity. The basis of this unity is the lordship of Jesus Christ. No one can confess this lordship except in the Holy Spirit (cf. 1 Cor. 12:3). The unity which the Spirit gives must not be identified simply with like-mindedness, sociological compatibility, or the felt-need for togetherness.

C. Koinonia and gospel witness

37. The present state of visible separation in Christianity is a contradiction of the unity into which we are called by Christ. Fidelity to the concept of koinonia places upon all Christians the obligation of striving to overcome our divisions, especially through dialogue. We need to discern alertly, and in an ongoing way, the character and shape of the visible unity demanded by koinonia.

38. Roman Catholics and Pentecostals lament the scandal of disunity between Christians. The lack of agreement on how koinonia should be lived out in the church, and our resulting divisions, cloud the world's perception of God's work of reconciliation. Insofar as koinonia is obscured, the effectiveness of the witness is impaired. For the sake of giving an effective gospel witness, the issue of Christian unity must be kept before us. For our Lord has prayed for his disciples "that they may all be one; even as thou, Father, art in me, and I in thee, that they also may be in us, *so that the world may believe that thou has sent me*" (John 17:21; cf. John 13:34).

III. Koinonia and baptism[7]

A. The meaning of baptism

39. Pentecostals and Roman Catholics agree that baptism is prefigured in Old Testament symbolism, e.g., in the salvation of Noah and his family (cf. 1 Pet. 3:20-21); the

Exodus through the Red Sea (cf. 1 Cor. 10:1-5); washing as a symbol of the cleansing power of the Holy Spirit (cf. Ez. 36:25).

40. They further agree that baptism was instituted by Christ, and that he commanded his disciples to go "and make disciples of all nations, baptizing them in the name of the Father and of the Son and of the Holy Spirit" (Matt. 28:19). In accordance with the Lord's commission, his disciples baptized those who were added to the fellowship of believers (cf. Acts 2:41).

41. Pentecostals and Roman Catholics differ in that Roman Catholics understand baptism to be a sacrament, while most Pentecostals understand it in terms of an ordinance (i.e., a rite that the Lord has commanded his church to perform). Some Pentecostals, however, do use the term sacrament to describe baptism. These differences illustrate the need for further discussion between Roman Catholics and Pentecostals on the meaning of the terms "sacrament" and "ordinance".

42. Most Pentecostals hold that believers' baptism is clearly taught in scripture (cf. Mark 16:16; Acts 2:38; 8:12,36-39; 10:34-48) and, therefore, believe that baptism of infants should not be practised. Roman Catholics admit that there is no incontrovertible evidence for baptism of infants in the New Testament, although some texts (notably the so-called household baptism texts, e.g., Acts 16:15 and 16:31-33) are understood as having a reference in that direction. Roman Catholics note, however, that through a process of discernment during the early centuries of the church, a development took place in which infant baptism became widely practised within the church; was seen as being of apostolic origin; was approved by many of the fathers of the church; and was received by the church as authentic.

B. Faith and baptism

43. Pentecostals and Roman Catholics agree that faith precedes and is a precondition of baptism (cf. Mark 16:16), and that faith is necessary for baptism to be authentic. They also agree that the faith of the believing community, its prayer, its instruction, nurture the faith of the candidate.

44. Roman Catholics believe that the faith of an infant is a covenant gift of God given in the grace of baptism, cleansing the child from original sin and introducing it to new life in the body of Christ. Infant baptism is the beginning of a process towards full maturity of faith in the life of the Spirit, which is nurtured by the believing community.

45. The majority of Pentecostals practise believers' baptism exclusively, rather than infant baptism. They affirm that faith is the gift of God (cf. Eph. 2:8), but at the same time stress that it is essentially a personal response of an individual. The scripture says: "If you confess with your lips that Jesus is Lord and believe in your heart that God raised him from the dead, you will be saved" (Rom. 10:9). Because they believe that faith must be personally expressed, Pentecostals maintain that an infant cannot receive the impartation of faith unto salvation (Eph. 2:8) or the Holy Spirit. And because they believe that a conscious faith response to the proclamation of the gospel on the part of the candidate is a necessary precondition for baptism, they do not baptize infants.

46. The general refusal of the Pentecostals to practise infant baptism notwithstanding, Roman Catholics and Pentecostals affirm that the grace of God is operative in the life of an infant. It is God who takes initiative for our salvation, and God does so not only in the life of adults but also in the life of infants. Scripture tells us, for instance,

that John the Baptist was filled with the Holy Spirit from his mother's womb (cf. Luke 1:15; cf. also Jer. 1:5).

47. Pentecostals and Roman Catholics differ over when one "comes to Christ" and about the significance of baptism itself. For all Pentecostals, there is no coming to Christ apart from a person's turning away from sin in repentance and towards God in faith (cf. 1 Thess. 1:9), through which they become a part of the believing community. Baptism is withheld until after a person's conscious conversion. Most Pentecostals regard the act of baptism as a visible symbol of regeneration. Other Pentecostals have a sacramental understanding of baptism.

48. Roman Catholics describe conversion as a process incorporating the individual in the church by baptism. Even in infant baptism, a later personal appropriation or acceptance of one's baptism is an absolute necessity.

49. Roman Catholics and Pentecostals agree that a deep personal relationship to Christ is essential to Christian life. They also see how conversion is not only a personal or individual act, but an act that presupposes a proclaiming community before conversion and requires a nurturing community for growth after conversion. Further discussion is needed, however, on the nature of faith, the sense in which faith precedes baptism, and the meaning of corporate faith in Roman Catholic teaching. What is the nature of the gift of faith given to the infant born into the covenant community by baptism?

50. In the Roman Catholic understanding, one is incorporated into the death and resurrection of Christ through baptism, thereby also entering into the koinonia of those saved by Christ. Pentecostals affirm a relationship between baptism and incorporation into the death and resurrection of Christ (Rom. 6:3ff.). Even if Pentecostals do not consider baptism, which makes possible incorporation into the koinonia, as a sacrament, most of them would not see baptism as an empty church ritual. It serves to strengthen the faith of those who have repented and believed in Christ through the Holy Spirit. Often a person will have a deep spiritual experience at baptism (manifested sometimes, for instance, by speaking in tongues). Provided that the person who is being baptized has experienced conversion, some Pentecostals would even speak of baptism as a "means of grace". Without denying the salvation of the unbaptized, all Pentecostals would consider baptism to be an integral part of the whole experience of becoming Christian.

51. Roman Catholics and Pentecostals agree that faith is indispensable to salvation. Pentecostals disagree with the Roman Catholic teaching that baptism is a *constitutive* means of salvation accomplished by the life, death and resurrection of Christ. Nevertheless, Pentecostals do feel the need to investigate further the relationship between baptism and salvation in light of specific passages which appear to make a direct link between baptism and salvation (e.g., John 3:5; Mark 16:16; Acts 22:16; 1 Pet. 3:21). Further discussion is also needed on the effect of baptism.

C. Baptism and the church

52. For Roman Catholics, baptism is the sacrament of entry into the church, the koinonia of those saved in Christ and incorporated into his death and resurrection. For Pentecostals, baptism publicly demonstrates their personal identification with the death and resurrection of Christ (cf. Rom. 6:3ff.), and their incorporation into the body of Christ. In keeping with the long tradition of the catechumenate, some Pentecostals

believe that baptism is a precondition for full church membership to the extent that unbaptized converts are not, strictly speaking, called "brothers and sisters in Christ" but "friends".

53. For both Roman Catholics and Pentecostals, the believing community is important in the preparation for baptism, in the celebration of baptism, and in nurturing the faith of the one baptized. It is essential for the newly baptized believer to continue to grow in faith and love and to participate in the full life of the church.

54. For the Roman Catholic Church, the basis of ecumenical dialogue with Pentecostals, properly speaking, is found in the Catholic recognition of the baptism performed by Pentecostals in the name of the Father, Son and Holy Spirit. This implies a common faith in the Lord Jesus Christ. This recognition by Roman Catholics of Pentecostal baptism means, in consequence, that Roman Catholics believe that they share with Pentecostals a certain, though imperfect, koinonia (cf. *Unitatis Redingratio*, §3). The unity of baptism constitutes and requires the unity of the baptized (cf. *Unitatis Redingratio*, §22). Our agreement on the trinitarian basis of baptism draws and impels us to unity.

55. Pentecostals do not see the unity between Christians as being based in a common water baptism, mainly because they believe that the New Testament does not base it in baptism. Instead, the foundation of unity is a common faith and experience of Jesus Christ as Lord and Saviour through the Holy Spirit. This implies that to the extent that Pentecostals recognize that Roman Catholics have this common faith in and experience of Jesus as Lord, they share a real though imperfect koinonia with them. "For just as the body is one and has many members, and all the members of the body, though many, are one body, so it is with Christ. For by one Spirit we were all baptized into one body – Jews or Greeks, slaves or free – and all were made to drink of one Spirit" (1 Cor. 12:12-13, a passage Pentecostals tend to interpret as not referring to water baptism). Insofar as baptism is related to this experience of Christ through the Spirit, it is also significant for the question of unity between Christians.

D. Baptismal practice

56. Roman Catholics and most Pentecostals agree that a person is to be baptized in water in the name of the Father, Son and Holy Spirit. Roman Catholics and most Pentecostals disagree with those Pentecostals who do not baptize according to the trinitarian formula, especially if in baptizing only in Jesus' name (e.g., Acts 2:38) they deny the orthodox understanding of the Trinity.[8]

57. Baptism by immersion is the most effective visible sign to convey the meaning of baptism. Most Pentecostals hold that immersion in water is the only biblical way to baptize. Roman Catholics permit immersion and pouring as legitimate modes of baptism.

58. Pentecostals and Roman Catholics agree that baptism, when it is discerned as properly administered, is not to be repeated.

59. In addition to theological difficulties, Pentecostals perceive certain pastoral difficulties with the practice of infant baptism. These difficulties commonly associated with the practice of infant baptism are significant enough for Pentecostals to suggest that Roman Catholics continue to examine this practice.

60. Roman Catholics freely acknowledge the possible pastoral difficulties (e.g., creation of a body of baptized but unchurched people) inherent in the misuse of the

practice of infant baptism. But infant baptism often provides a pastoral opportunity to help those parents weak in faith and practice and is the beginning of a whole process of Christian life for the child. "Conversion" in this sense becomes a series of grace-events throughout life, resulting in a commitment equally as firm as that stemming from a sudden conversion in adulthood.

61. Roman Catholics point out that there is a new emphasis upon adult initiation among Roman Catholics in the post-Vatican II rites, without denying the value of infant baptism. Indeed, because adult baptism is now expressed as the primary theological model, the theology and practice of infant baptism is itself enriched. Not only is faith given to the infant through the sacrament, but the parents themselves are fortified as the ones responsible for the infant's future growth, and so are caught up in the grace-giving event, frequently having their own faith strengthened.

62. Roman Catholics and Pentecostals agree that instruction in the faith necessarily follows upon baptism in order that the life of grace may come to fruition. In this connection a pastor should delay or refuse to baptize an infant if the parents (or guardians) clearly have no intention of bringing up the infant in the practice of faith. To baptize under those circumstances would be to act in a manner contrary to the canon law of the Roman Catholic Church.

63. There are some parallels between the Roman Catholic practice of infant baptism and the common practice of infant dedication in Pentecostal churches in terms of the activity of grace and the role of the Christian community in the life of an infant. In infant dedication, as in infant baptism, the parents of the infant and the believing community publicly covenant together with God to bring the infant up so that he or she will come into a personal relationship with Christ. Though Pentecostals do not believe that dedication mediates salvation to an infant or makes him/her a member of the Christian church, they do believe that because of the prayer and the faith of the believing community, a blessing of God rests upon the dedicated infant. Both practices acknowledge in their own way the presence of the grace of God in the infant and are concerned with creating an atmosphere in which the child may grow in the grace and knowledge of the Lord Jesus Christ.

E. Baptism and the experience of the Spirit

64. Roman Catholics and Pentecostals agree that all of those who belong to Christ "were made to drink of one Spirit" (1 Cor. 12:13). We agree that God intends that each follower of Jesus enjoy the indwelling of the Holy Spirit (Rom. 8:9). This indwelling of the Spirit is not the fruit or product of human works, but is due to the unmerited, efficacious action of grace by which each person responds to the special initiative of God.

65. We acknowledge that Roman Catholics and Pentecostals have different understandings of the role of the Spirit in Christian initiation and life, but may nonetheless enjoy a similar experience of the Spirit. Our experience of the Holy Spirit, furthermore, heightens our mutual awareness of the need for unity.

66. We agree that the experience of the Holy Spirit belongs to the life of the church. Wherever the Spirit is genuinely present in the Christian community, its fruit will also become evident (cf. Gal. 5:22-23). Genuine charismata mentioned in scripture (e.g. 1 Cor. 12:8-10,28-30; Rom. 12:6-8; etc.) also indicate the presence of the Spirit. All such manifestations, however, call for discernment by the community (cf. 1 Thess. 5:19-22; 1 Cor. 14; 1 John 4).

67. Generally, Roman Catholics have tended to be cautious about accepting the more spectacular manifestations of the Spirit such as speaking in tongues and prophecy, although the charismatic renewal has helped them to rediscover ways in which such gifts are rooted in their oldest tradition.

68. Roman Catholics fear that Pentecostals limit the Spirit to specific manifestations. Pentecostals fear that Roman Catholics confine the Spirit's workings to sacraments and church order. Therefore, we share a mutual concern not to confine or to limit the Holy Spirit whom Jesus described by the imagery of the freely blowing wind (cf. John 3:8). Each of us seems more worried about the other limiting the Spirit than ourselves. Still, we have learned through our discussions together that there is greater freedom for the Holy Spirit in both of our traditions than we expected to find, and our fears, once shared, have made us more aware of our shortcomings in this regard.

69. Our discussions, too, have made us more aware about the ways in which we use language related to the Holy Spirit. We agree that such ideas as what it means to be "baptized in the Spirit" or "filled with the Spirit" would be fruitful fields for mutual exploration.

IV. Koinonia in the life of the church

A. *Koinonia in the life of God*

70. Both Pentecostals and Roman Catholics recognize that believers have a share in the eternal life which is koinonia with the Father and with his Son Jesus Christ (cf. 1 John 1:2-3), and a communion in the Holy Spirit whom God's Son, Jesus Christ, has given to them (cf. 1 John 3:24; 2 Cor. 13:14). This, the deepest meaning of koinonia, is actualized at various levels. Those who believe and have been baptized into Christ's death (cf. Mark 16:16; Rom. 6:3-4) have koinonia in his sufferings and become like him in his death and resurrection (cf. Phil. 3:10). The next step is the eucharist or the Lord's supper. "The cup of blessing which we bless, is it not a participation [koinonia] in the blood of Christ? The bread which we break, is it not a participation [koinonia] in the body of Christ?" (1 Cor. 10:16). All believers, furthermore, who have koinonia in the eternal life of Father, Son and Holy Spirit and who have koinonia in Christ's death and resurrection are bound together in a koinonia too deep for words. We look forward to the day when we will also have koinonia in his body and blood (1 Cor. 10:16).

71. While both Roman Catholics and Pentecostals teach the indwelling of the Father, Son and the Holy Spirit in the believer (cf. John 17:21; Rom. 8:9), the emphasis on the indwelling of the Trinity in believers is more explicitly articulated in the Roman Catholic faith than in that of the Pentecostals. The nature of the language used to describe it is in need of further exploration together.

72. Together with Roman Catholics, most Pentecostals have a strong commitment to the trinitarian understanding of God. They believe, for instance, that at baptism the trinitarian formula should be used because of Jesus' mandate: "Go therefore and make disciples of all nations, baptizing them in the name of the Father, and of the Son, and of the Holy Spirit" (Matt. 28:19).[9] The Pentecostals do, however, feel challenged by Roman Catholics to develop all the implications for faith and piety which their full trinitarian commitment implies.

B. Church as koinonia

73. The importance of an active response to the gifts of God in the service of koinonia requires mutuality in its many dimensions. Some of these dimensions are the assumption and sharing of responsibility, and a fuller participation in the life of the local congregation. When church members of whatever rank act arbitrarily without taking into account this sharing, their actions obscure the expression of communion. For Roman Catholics and Pentecostals, koinonia in the church is a dynamic concept, implying a dialogical structure of both God-givenness and human response. Mutuality has to exist on every level of the church, its source being the continuing presence of the Holy Spirit.

74. Roman Catholics must often confess to a lack of mutuality at the local and universal levels, even though mutuality is recognized as a criterion for fellowship. Difficulties surrounding lay participation in decision-making processes and the lack of sufficient involvement of women in leadership were examples cited by participants in this dialogue. Roman Catholics, however, would insist that order and hierarchy do not in themselves imply such a defect in mutuality.

75. At the same time, Pentecostals acknowledge both the reluctance that many of their members have in submitting to ecclesial authority and the difficulty which their charismatic leaders have in working through existing ecclesial institutional channels which could protect them from acting irresponsibly or in an authoritarian manner.

76. The difficulties of some Pentecostals with their ecclesial institutions stem in part from frequent emphasis on their direct relation to the Spirit. They forget that the Spirit is given not only to individual Christians, but also to the whole community. An individual Christian is not the only "temple of the Holy Spirit" (1 Cor. 6:19). Roman Catholics have rightly challenged Pentecostals to think of the whole community, too, as a "temple of God" in which the Spirit dwells (1 Cor. 3:16). If Pentecostals were to take the indwelling of the Spirit in the community more seriously, they would be less inclined to follow the personal "leadings of the Spirit" in disregard of the community. Rather they would strive to imitate the apostles who, at the first church council, justified their decision with the following words: "... it has seemed good to the Holy Spirit and to *us*..." (Acts 15:28).

77. In their theology, both Pentecostals and Roman Catholics see themselves standing in a dependent relationship to the Spirit. They acknowledge the need to invoke the Holy Spirit. In accordance with this invocation, they believe in the presence of God whenever two or three are gathered in Christ's name (cf. Matt. 18:20).

78. Pentecostals recognize that while there is an emphasis on holiness in the Roman Catholic Church, they observe that it seems possible for some Roman Catholics to live continuously in a state of sin, and yet be considered members in the church. This seems to the Pentecostals to undermine the concept of Christian discipleship. Though they are mindful of John's words that if "we say we have not sinned, we make him [God] a liar" (1 John 1:10), Pentecostals want to take seriously the warning of the same apostle concerning the unrepentant sinner, namely that "no one who sins has either seen him [the Father] or known him" (1 John 3:6).

79. Roman Catholics wonder how Pentecostals deal with the sins of their own members. Do they have an adequate tradition of bringing those who have fallen into sin into a process of repentance and a sense of God's forgiveness? Without such a tra-

dition how can they avoid harshness when a sinner fails to live up to the congregation's ideal of holiness?

80. Both bodies would do well to recall the scriptural warnings that we must try to see the log in our own eye rather than the speck in our brother's or sister's eye (cf. Matt. 7:4). We should reflect, too, on the Lord's caution against trying to have a wheat field from which all tares have been removed (cf. Matt. 13:24ff.).

C. Koinonia, sacraments and church order

81. Roman Catholics hold that a basic aspect of koinonia between local churches is expressed in the celebration of the sacraments of initiation, namely, by the same baptism, the same confirmation, the same eucharist. Moreover, the celebration of these sacraments requires ordained ministers to preside,[10] ordination being also a sacrament, i.e., an act of Christ in the Spirit celebrated in the communion and for the communion of the church. Furthermore, according to the Catholic tradition, only ordained ministers – principally the bishop – can preside over a local church or diocese.

82. According to Catholic understanding, koinonia is rooted in the bonds of faith and sacramental life shared by congregations united in dioceses pastored by bishops. Through their bishops, the local churches are in communion with one another by reason of the common faith, the common sacramental life and the common episcopacy. Among the fellowship of bishops, the bishop of Rome is recognized as the successor of Peter and presides over the whole Catholic communion. Through their day-to-day teaching, and more specifically through local and universal councils, bishops have responsibility to articulate clearly the faith and discipline of the church. Church order is thus grounded in the koinonia of faith and the sacraments; church order is at the same time an active expression of koinonia.

83. Roman Catholics hold that some existing ecclesiastical structures (such as the office of a bishop) are "God-given", and that they belong to the very essence of church order, rather than serving only its well being.

84. While Pentecostals disagree among themselves concerning how the church should best be ordered (the views range from congregational to episcopal), they accept the full ecclesial status of the churches ordered in various ways. Observing the diversity of the church structures in the New Testament, they believe that the contemporary church should not be narrower in its understanding of the church order than the sacred scriptures themselves.

85. Although Pentecostals do not limit celebration of the sacraments and leadership in the church to the ordained ministers, they do recognize the need for and the value of ordination for the life of the church. Pentecostals do not consider ordination to be a sacrament. Ordinarily Pentecostals recognize that a charism of teacher/pastor is recognized or *can* be given to a person at the laying-on of hands, but they do not consider that at ordination the power of the Holy Spirit is bestowed to the person being ordained. Instead, ordination is a public acknowledgment of a God-given charism which a person has received prior to the act of ordination.

86. Some Pentecostals observe what appears to be a "mechanical" or "magical" understanding of the sacraments, especially among Roman Catholic laity, and do not accept the grace-conveying role of the sacraments distinct from their function as a visible word of God. Roman Catholic theology, however, maintains that the sacraments are not "mechanical" or "magical", since they require openness and faith on the part of

the recipient. In Catholic understanding, the grace of the sacraments is not bestowed automatically or unconditionally, irrespective of the dispositions of the recipient. What Paul says in 1 Corinthians 11:27 ("profaning the body and blood of the Lord") is common teaching in the Roman Catholic Church. Sacramental actions can produce "shrivelled fruit", as Augustine describes it, when the recipients are not in right relation to the Lord.[11] Furthermore, the efficacy of the sacraments is not dependent upon the personal piety of those who minister them, but rather is ultimately dependent upon the grace of God.

87. Pentecostals believe that church order demanded by koinonia is not satisfactorily expressed in some important aspects of Roman Catholic ecclesiology. Even within the context of collegiality, examples which seem to bear this out include those passages where it is stated that "the episcopal order is the subject of this supreme and full power over the universal church", and even more importantly, when it is stated that "the Roman Pontiff has full, supreme and universal power over the church" which "he can always exercise... freely" (*Lumen Gentium*, no. 22). On the whole, Pentecostals propose that presbyterial and/or congregational ecclesial models express better the mutuality or reciprocity demanded by koinonia.

88. Roman Catholics are more inclined to see the Spirit operating through certain ecclesial structures, although Pentecostals, too, recognize that the Spirit may work through ecclesial structures and processes.

89. Both Roman Catholics and Pentecostals are troubled by the discrepancy between the theology and the practice of their own parishes or congregations.

D. The church and salvation

90. According to Roman Catholic ecclesiology, the church can be considered both a *sign* and an *instrument* of God's work in the world. This formulation from the 19th century is still very useful for understanding the role of the church in the world.

91. The church is a sign of the presence of God's saving power in the world. It is also a sign of the eschatological unity to which all peoples are called by God. It is to be this sign both through its individual members and its gathered communities. Insofar as Christians are divided from one another, they are a countersign, a sign of contradiction to God's reconciling purpose in the world.

92. The church is also an instrument of God for announcing the saving news of grace and the coming of God's kingdom. The church is God's instrument in making disciples of all nations preaching the good news of Jesus' life, death and resurrection and baptizing them (cf. Matt. 28:19).

93. In recent years, Roman Catholics have come to describe the church as "a kind of a sacrament" (*Lumen Gentium* §1). This new insight is consistent with its past understanding of the sacraments as signs and instruments of God's saving power.

94. Though Pentecostals do not accept the Roman Catholic understanding of sacraments and the Roman Catholic view of the church as "a kind of sacrament", in their own way they do affirm that the church is both a sign and an instrument of salvation. As the new people of God, the church is called both to reflect the reality of God's eschatological kingdom in history and to announce its coming into the world, insofar as people open their lives to the in-breaking of the Holy Spirit. In Pentecostal understanding, the church as a community is an instrument of salvation in the same sense in which each one of its members is both a sign and instrument of salvation. In their own

way, both the community as a whole and the individual members that comprise it give witness to God's redeeming grace.

V. Koinonia and the communion of the saints

A. *The church as communio sanctorum*

95. God calls us into communion with himself (*communio* with the Holy One), into communion in the body and blood of Christ *(communio in sanctis)*, and into communion between Christians (fellowship of the saints: *communio sanctorum*). In the Nicene Creed, the phrase *communio sanctorum* has eschatological significance: the saints on earth and those in heaven, marked by the same Spirit, are a single body.

96. In terms of the sharing in holy things *(communio in sanctis)*, for Roman Catholics participation in baptism, confirmation and eucharist is constitutive of the church. For Pentecostals, the central element of worship is the preaching of the word. As persons respond to the proclamation of the word, the Spirit gives them new birth, which is a pre-sacramental experience, thereby making them Christians and in this sense creating the church. Of secondary importance are participation in baptism and the Lord's supper, spontaneous exercise of the charismata and the sharing of personal testimonies.

97. Pentecostals would like Catholics to share more among themselves the private devotional reading of the scriptures. Pentecostals ask Roman Catholics whether they could not deepen the experiential dimension of koinonia through spontaneous exercise of the gifts and the sharing of personal testimonies. Convinced that word and sacrament cannot be separated in worship, Catholics ask Pentecostals to re-examine the dynamic relationship between these two in the celebration of baptism and the Lord's supper.

98. The relation between koinonia, sacraments and church order (see above, nos. 81-89) explains why both the sharing in the same eucharistic faith and also in full communion are normal prerequisites for receiving the eucharist in the Roman Catholic Church. Since for Catholics the eucharist is essential and central in the life of the church, participation in the eucharist means and requires unity of faith. Catholics would like to see Pentecostals express clearly what is required for full communion in their churches.

99. According to the Roman Catholic view, the *communio sanctorum* includes a relationship to all the holy ones of God, the saints on earth and also the saints in heaven. Members of the church are given koinonia in the very holiness of God. As a result, they form "a great cloud of witnesses" (Heb. 12:1), a "great multitude which no man could number, from every nation, from all tribes and peoples and tongues" (Rev. 7:9).

100. In Roman Catholic faith and practice, God alone is the object of worship *(latria)*. However, veneration *(doulia)* is given to saints who have "run the race", "finished the course", and have received "a crown of life". It is also important to realize that no Catholic has an obligation *jure divino* of venerating either relics, icons or saints. While this kind of devotion is not necessary for salvation, the church recognizes the usefulness of such forms of devotion, recommends them to its members, and resists any condemnation or contempt of such practices (cf. Council of Trent, session 25).

101. Pentecostals find reassuring the stress in Roman Catholic theology that worship belongs only to God. It is, however, the Pentecostal teaching that the unique medi-

atorial role of Christ positively excludes veneration of relics, icons and saints. Pentecostals do, however, affirm that in their worship the earthly saints join in worship with saints in heaven and with them comprise the one, holy, catholic and apostolic church. As the scripture says: "we are surrounded by so great a cloud of witnesses" (Heb. 12:1) who have lived in history from the beginning of God's dealing with the human race.

B. Holiness, repentance and ministry in history

102. All the baptized are called to be "saints", and indeed, according to scripture, they called themselves such in the early church (e.g., Acts 9:13; 26:10; Rom. 15:25-26; 2 Cor. 8:4; 9:1; etc.).

103. We agree that because of sin, the church is always in need of repentance. It is at once holy and in need of purification. The church is a "holy penitent", and is ever in need of renewal both in its persons and in its structures. Both Catholics and Pentecostals recognize the fact that their respective theologies of koinonia are all too seldom reflected in the empirical reality of the life in their respective communities.

104. Both sides of this dialogue agree on the fundamental demands for holiness in the minister and agree that the unworthiness of a minister does not invalidate the work of the Holy Spirit. For Roman Catholics, God's acts in the sacraments are effective because they are based on God's faithfulness. They believe that the Holy Spirit works with consistency in ministering to those who come in faith. The church gives serious attention to church discipline because human weakness and sin can become obstacles to the effectiveness of ministry. Pentecostals, too, believe that God can work through the ministers of the word of God in spite of their grave failures and sin in their lives. "Some indeed preach Christ from envy and rivalry, but others from good will... What then? Only that in every way, whether in presence or in truth, Christ is proclaimed: in that I rejoice" (Phil. 1:15,18). Pentecostals also believe that the ordinances administered by an unworthy minister are valid (in the sense that, for instance, baptism need not be repeated). Together we believe, however, that the unworthiness of ministers is often a stumbling block that prevents non-believers from coming to faith in a true and living God, and it frequently hinders the work of the Spirit in the believing community.

105. Although Pentecostals stress the freedom of the Spirit to act in the community and emphasize the need for active participation of all members of the church, they do acknowledge the necessity of church order. They affirm church order (which can legitimately take different forms) as the will of the Lord for his church, since they observe from the New Testament that the earliest church has not "been without persons holding specific authority and responsibility" (*BEM*,[12] Ministry, 9) (cf. Acts 14:23; 20:17; Phil. 1:1). Since Pentecostals do not reject ecclesial institutions, they recognize that the Spirit operates not only through charismatic individuals but also through the permanent ministries of the church.

106. There is agreement that the offices and structures of the church, as indeed every aspect of the church, are in a continual need of renewal insofar as they are institutions of men and women here on earth. This presumes that the Spirit can breathe new life into the church's offices and structures when these become "dry bones" (Ezek. 37). This ongoing effort at renewal has important ecumenical implications. This is an essential dynamism of "the movement towards unity" of the people of God (*Unitatis Redintegratio*, §6).

107. Pentecostals and Roman Catholics appear to view the history of the church quite differently. The members of this dialogue believe that the differences in these per-

spectives deserve further mutual exploration. Both Pentecostals and Roman Catholics recognize that continuity in history by itself is no guarantee of spiritual maturity or of doctrinal soundness. Increasingly, both traditions are coming to share a genuine appreciation for the value that church history reveals to them today.

108. Roman Catholics believe that the contemporary church is in continuity with the church in the New Testament. Pentecostals, influenced by restorationist perspectives, have claimed continuity with the church in the New Testament by arguing for discontinuity with much of the historical church. By adopting these two positions, one of continuity, the other of discontinuity, each tradition has attempted to demonstrate its faithfulness to the apostolic faith "once for all delivered to the saints" (Jude 3). The significance of this for the welfare of the whole church urges upon us the need of further common theological reflection on the history of the church.

Conclusion

109. It is hoped that this dialogue might inspire dialogues on national or local levels between Roman Catholics and classical Pentecostals. The participants recommend to their parent bodies that the dialogue continue into a fourth round of discussions.

110. The members of the dialogue during this quinquennium visited worship services representing both traditions. Learning was not confined only to the dialogue table, but also took place in local Catholic parishes and Pentecostal congregations visited during this series of discussions and at informal conversations between sessions.

111. We have explored the subject of koinonia and have been richly rewarded as together we affirmed the lordship of Jesus. We felt his pain as we understood our part in the ongoing brokenness of his body. Nonetheless, that we could spend day after day together sharing in great detail and depth our most dearly held Christian convictions, and come away closer to our risen Lord and to each other, we understand is possible only by the grace and mercy of God.

112. The prayer of Jesus, "that they all may be one" (John 17:21) has become increasingly important to us, and the cause for much prayer and repentance still. Nevertheless, we are heartened by the realization that fresh winds of the Spirit are blowing in the church universal, and we are waiting expectantly to see what in the providence of God is yet to come. Our prayer continues to be "Come, Holy Spirit!"

NOTES

[1] Until 1989, the Pontifical Council was known as the Secretariat for Promoting Christian Unity.
[2] At its eighth general assembly in February 1990, the Lutheran World Federation voted to change its constitution. It now describes itself as a "communion of churches".
[3] Scripture quotations in this text are from the Revised Standard Version of the Bible copyrighted 1946, 1952, 1971, 1973 by the Division of Christian Education of the National Council of the Churches of Christ in the USA.
[4] Final Report (1972–76), document 62 above, nos 28-30; Final Report (1977-82), document 63 above, nos 18-21; 49-57. These reports are also published in Kilian McDonnell, ed., *Presence, Power, Praise*, Collegeville, MN, Liturgical Press, 1980, 3:373–395, and in Arnold Bittlinger, *Papst und Pfingstler*, Frankfurt am Main, Peter Lang, 1978. For the report of the 1977-82 discussions, see Jerry L. Sandidge, *Roman Catholic-Pentecostal Dialogue (1977-1982): A Study in Developing Ecumenism*, Frankfurt am Main, Peter Lang, 1987.

[5] All quotations from the Second Vatican Council are from Walter M. Abbott, ed., *The Documents of Vatican II*, Piscataway, NJ, New Century, 1966.
[6] A segment of Pentecostals known as "Oneness" or "Jesus Name" Pentecostals are opposed to the trinitarian formulation of the faith. Their view of God tends towards modalism, and the baptismal formula that they pronounce is "in the name of Jesus Christ" (Acts 2:38), instead of the traditional trinitarian appeal to Matthew 28:19. Most Pentecostals, however, strongly disagree with this position.
[7] We devote a special section to baptism because of the difficulty which baptism and the practice of baptism have in our dialogue.
[8] See note 6.
[9] See note 6.
[10] This relationship between church order and ordained ministry presiding over a community is well illustrated in the celebration of water baptism, although in cases of necessity every Christian is requested to baptize. Until 1923 even the deacons were not allowed to be the ordinary ministers of baptism. Presently bishops retain for themselves the baptism of adults, and parish priests must have their bishop's permission to perform such a baptism.
[11] The later distinction made between "fruitful" and "unfruitful" sacraments is another way by which the Roman Catholic teaching asserts the same understanding.
[12] Editor's note: The designation BEM refers to the important convergence document of the World Council of Churches titled *Baptism, Eucharist and Ministry* (Geneva, WCC, 1982). It is sometimes known as the Lima document. It is an attempt by member churches of the WCC to reach a significant level of theological convergence on three important aspects of doctrine and practice. This study, Faith and Order Paper no. 111, is currently in the process of "reception" in the member churches, before receiving final implementation. All churches, including non-member churches, have been invited to provide official responses to the document. To date, there has been no official Pentecostal response.

65. Evangelization, Proselytism and Common Witness

1990-1997

Introduction

1. This is a report from the participants of the fourth phase of the international dialogue (1990-97) between the Pontifical Council for Promoting Christian Unity and some classical Pentecostal denominations and leaders. The dialogue began in 1972. The co-chairpersons in the fourth phase were the Rev. Kilian McDonnell, OSB, of Collegeville, Minnesota, USA, and the Rev. Justus du Plessis, of Faerie Glen, South Africa, who was succeeded in 1992 by the Rev. Cecil M. Robeck, Jr, of Pasadena, California, USA.[1]

2. The unity of the church is a concern for Pentecostals and Catholics alike. The particular purpose of these discussions is to develop a climate of mutual respect and understanding in matters of faith and practice, to find points of genuine agreement as well as indicate areas in which further dialogue is required.

The goal is not structural unity, but rather the fostering of this respect and mutual understanding between the Catholic church and classical Pentecostal groups.

3. As we, the participants, have come to the task before us, we have done so as peers. Nevertheless, we have recognized that there is at least one important difference between the Catholic and the Pentecostal teams that bears mention. The Roman Catholic Church possesses that which may be described as official teaching on some of these topics, teaching that has been expressed in various authoritative texts such as the conciliar documents of Second Vatican Council and in papal encyclicals. The Pentecostals possess no comparable body of teaching which may serve as a resource for their position. The diversity of the Pentecostal movement mitigates against a single position on certain topics. When the Pentecostal participants speak as a single voice throughout this document, then, they do so by gathering together what they believe to be the common consensus, held by the vast majority of Pentecostals worldwide.

4. We, the participants, have sought to represent faithfully the positions held by our churches. However, we have made no decisions for the churches since we have no authority to make such decisions. The churches are free to accept or reject the report either in whole or in part. Yet as responsible persons, representing our traditions either officially or in some other way, we have come together over a period of years to study the issues of evangelization, proselytism and common witness. In accordance with our understanding of the gospel we are making proposals to our churches. We, the participants, hereby submit our findings to our respective churches for review, evaluation, correction and reception.

5. Since many Christians have seen the last decade of the second millennium as one in which to emphasize evangelization, and since significant tensions exist between Pentecostals and Catholics on this issue, it appeared appropriate to concentrate on this topic. The previous three phases focused on (1) the baptism in the Holy Spirit, Christian initiation, and the charisms, scripture and Tradition and the human person and the gifts (1972-76), (2) faith and religious experience, speaking in tongues, and the role of Mary (1977-82), and (3) koinonia (Christian communion and fellowship) (1985-89).

6. Specific themes which helped us reach our conclusions in this phase of the dialogue included: the meaning of mission and evangelization (1990, Emmetten, Switzerland); the biblical and systematic foundation of evangelization (1991, Venice, Italy); evangelization and culture (1992, Rocca di Papa, Italy); evangelization and social justice (1993, Paris, France); evangelization/evangelism, common witness and proselytism (1994, Kappel am Albis, Switzerland); and common witness (1995, Brixen/Bressanone, Italy). The dialogue members convened once again in Brixen/Bressanone, Italy, in 1996 to examine a first draft of the report of this dialogue. They continued their drafting in Rome, Italy, in June 1997. The steering committee was then authorized to make the final editorial decisions in keeping with the mind of the participants. This they did in Geneva, Switzerland, in November 1997.

7. The procedure used throughout this phase included the discussion of papers presented by members of each side. Each team then asked the other to respond to a limited number of questions which arose from the discussions of the paper. These questions were designed to challenge participants to think creatively and substantively about the emerging issues. The substance of these discussions were recorded in most years in an "agreed account", which took note of areas of agreement or disagreement, areas of possible convergence, and topics which might need further study. These materials, together with continuing conversations, provided the basis for the final report.

8. Both Pentecostals and Catholics recognize as an essential part of the mission of the church the call to evangelize. As the two teams explored the topic together, they were encouraged by new perspectives and they gained clarity on problematic issues. They hope that their work together points towards possibilities of cooperation in mission for the sake of the gospel.

9. Both the Catholic and the Pentecostal participants of the dialogue have become increasingly aware of the scandal of a divided witness. It is a scandal when unbelievers are more aware of those things which separate these churches than those things they hold in common. It is a scandal, too, when Catholics and Pentecostals demonstrate a lack of love or trust by speaking negatively about one another or acting in ways that antagonize or exclude one another. Because of their divisions, Catholics and Pentecostals are unable to participate together at the table of the Lord. Furthermore, they make evident their division insofar as they proclaim the Lord's death in isolation from one another.

10. Touched by this divided witness, the participants of this dialogue have experienced and expressed to one another their sorrow over this state of affairs. It is a sorrow which has, in part, moved them to search for ways in which these divisions might be resolved, following the Pauline exhortation to "make every effort to maintain the unity of the Spirit in the bond of peace" (Eph. 4:3).

I. Mission and evangelization[2]

11. Both Pentecostals and Catholics believe that God has charged all Christians to announce the gospel to all people, in obedience to the great commission given by Christ (cf. Matt. 28:18-20). Proclaiming God's reconciliation of the world through Christ is central to the church's faith, life and witness (cf. 2 Cor. 5:18-19).

12. The mission and the task of evangelization – proclaiming "the name, teaching, life, promise, the kingdom and the mystery of Jesus of Nazareth, the Son of God" (Evangelization in the Modern World[3] (1975, 22) – lies at the heart of the Catholic faith. Mission has been part of the life of the church throughout the ages. Catholic women and men, especially those in religious orders, have gone to the ends of the earth proclaiming the good news of Jesus Christ. The Second Vatican Council's Decree on the Church's Missionary Activity (1965, 2) taught that "the church on earth is by its very nature missionary since, according to the plan of the Father, it has its origin in the mission of the Son and the Holy Spirit". Following in the path of the Council, both Paul VI and John Paul II in their teaching insist on the need to pursue a "new evangelization".

13. Pentecostals place special emphasis on the proclamation of Jesus as Saviour and Lord resulting in a personal, conscious acceptance and conversion of an individual; a "new birth" as in John 3:3. Pentecostals are also concerned to evangelize the world in these "last days" before Christ returns (cf. Acts 2:14-17; Joel 2:28-32), making disciples as Jesus instructed in the great commission.

14. Both Pentecostals and Catholics agree that "evangelization will... always contain – as the centre and at the same time the summit of its dynamism – a clear proclamation that, in Jesus Christ, the Son of God made man, who died and rose from the dead, salvation is offered to all humankind, as a gift of God's grace and mercy" (Evangelization in the Modern World, 27; cf. Eph. 2:8; Rom. 1:16). From this divine initiative arises the church as an eschatological community, a koinonia. To the extent that Christians participate in this koinonia, they share deep bonds of unity in the Spirit even now despite divisions which continue. The eschatological nature of this koinonia, which fosters unity in diversity, serves as a prophetic sign towards divided humankind (cf. John 17:21).

15. While Catholics and Pentecostals agree on the essential core of the gospel, namely that "in Christ God was reconciling the world to himself" (2 Cor. 5:19), on occasion they differ in practice and language concerning the emphasis they give to certain aspects of evangelization.

Catholics tend to use the term to indicate proclamation of the gospel towards the conversion of persons to Christ. They also acknowledge that evangelization is a complex process made up of various elements including "the renewal of humanity, witness, explicit proclamation, inner adherence, entry into the community, acceptance of signs, apostolic initiative" (Evangelization in the Modern World, 24). Pentecostals have used the terms evangelization and evangelism interchangeably to focus on the proclamation of the gospel towards converting individuals to Christ, followed by their discipling to be effective witnesses for Christ among unbelievers and in society. In short, Pentecostals make a sharper distinction than Catholics between the proclamation of the gospel to those they consider "unsaved" and the discipling of believers or promotion of Christian values in society. Today there is growing convergence between Catholics and Pentecostals in that both see the task as leading individuals to conversion, but also as the transformation of the cultures and the reconciliation of the nations.

16. Catholics and Pentecostals are motivated to evangelize by love for Christ, obedience to the great commission, and the desire that unbelievers may receive the blessings of eternal life now and in the future. While Catholics and Pentecostals teach the second coming of Christ as the blessed hope of the church, Pentecostals stress the urgency of proclamation because many believe in the imminence of that event. Furthermore, Pentecostals view the "baptism in the Spirit" as essential for every believer to receive empowerment for Christian witness (Acts 1:8). While Catholics and Pentecostals express a genuine desire to see the Lord add to the church those who are being saved (cf. Acts 2:47), they also express concern over attitudes expressed by Christian evangelizers which are inconsistent with the central message of the gospel, the great commission (Matt. 28:19-20), the great commandment (Matt. 22:37-39), and the nature of the church. For example, they are troubled when people are dealt with as though they were impersonal objects instead of being respected as individuals who have been created with dignity, in the image of God. They are also troubled when evangelization proceeds exclusively by strategies that aim at limiting the composition of congregations to one race, class, ethnic group or other social groupings resulting in an intended and lasting segregation, which does harm to the nature of Christ's church (cf. Rev. 7:9; 14:1-7). Continued growth, both qualitative and quantitative, will demand more self-criticism and openness to the questions and insights of others in the body of Christ.

17. All Catholics are called to witness to the good news. In practice, over the past few centuries, Catholic evangelization in non-Christian countries has often depended almost exclusively on clergy and religious orders. Most of them received a theological and spiritual formation which prepared them for this mission. In recent years, the Catholic church has also encouraged lay participation in evangelization with the recognition that a proper preparation is necessary for this task (cf. Decree on the Apostolate of Lay People, 28-32).

18. While in recent years Pentecostals have begun to place more attention on the formal training of laypeople and clergy for ministry, Pentecostals have always emphasized that all believers should evangelize, whether formally trained or not, especially by sharing their personal testimony.

19. Both sides understand evangelization as encompassing missionary proclamation to non-Christians, as well as outreach to those who once claimed to have accepted the gospel, but who apparently live a life totally indifferent to the faith they have professed. We need to recognize the delicacy of making judgments as to whether other persons are in fact living indifferently or not.

20. Catholics and Pentecostals both agree that the Holy Spirit prepares individuals and peoples for the reception of the gospel, despite the fallen condition of humankind. While they believe that "ever since the creation of the world, the visible existence of God and his everlasting power have been clearly seen by the mind's understanding of created things" (Rom. 1:20; cf. Ps. 19:1-4), their perspectives diverge over the existence and/or meaning of salvific elements found in non-Christian religions. Catholics and Pentecostals agree that those who are saved have been saved without exception through the death of Jesus Christ. Catholics do not deny that the Spirit may be at work in other religions "preparing the way for the gospel" (cf. Evangelization in the Modern World, 53). Catholics also say, "Those who, through no fault of their own, do not know the gospel of Christ or his church, but who nevertheless seek God with a sincere heart

and, moved by grace, try in their actions to do his will as they know it through the dictates of their conscience – those too may achieve eternal salvation" (Dogmatic Constitution on the Church, 16).

21. Many Pentecostals on the other hand, like many of the early Christians, tend to point out the demonic elements in other religions. While Pentecostals acknowledge the work of the Holy Spirit in the world, convincing people of sin, righteousness and judgment (cf. John 16:8-11), they generally do not acknowledge the presence of salvific elements in non-Christian religions. Some Pentecostals would see a convergence towards the Catholic position above in that the Holy Spirit is at work in non-Christian religions, preparing individual hearts for an eventual exposure to the gospel of Jesus Christ. Pentecostals and Catholics, however, together believe that there is only one Name whereby we can be saved (cf. Acts 4:12). Both believe in the necessity of responding to the divine invitation to seek him and to find him (cf. Acts 17:27).

II. The biblical and systematic foundation of evangelization[4]

22. Catholics and Pentecostals both point to the biblical foundation of evangelization of all people. From the very beginning it was promised to Abraham that through him all generations would be blessed (cf. Gen. 17:1-8). God's covenant with Abraham has a global significance (cf. Gen. 22:18). The prophets show that Israel's election also has importance for all peoples in that they expected the gathering of all peoples at Mount Sion at the coming of the Messiah (cf. Isa. 23; 49:6-8; Joel 3:1-5). Jesus' ministry in his earthly life was focused on Israel, not excluding others in special cases (cf. Matt. 15:21-28), but he came for the salvation of the whole world (cf. John 3:15-17; Matt. 26:28). Paul emphasizes the universal and cosmic dimensions of Jesus' death and resurrection (cf. 2 Cor. 5:19; Rom. 8:21). Then, receiving the Spirit from the Father, Jesus pours out that same Spirit as the agent through whom the work of redemption is being carried out throughout the whole world until the end of time (cf. Acts 2:33). Therefore, the biblical mandate for mission is grounded in the redemptive purpose of God.

23. The content of the message of salvation is Jesus Christ himself, the way to reconciliation with the Father; he is the good news (cf. Gal. 1:16), which he entrusted to his disciples (cf. Matt. 28:19f.). The Holy Spirit, poured out on all people (cf. Acts 2:17; Joel 3:1), is to be understood as giving the inner dynamism of the process of evangelization and salvation. The transmission of the Christian faith consists in proclaiming Jesus Christ in order to lead others to faith in him. From the beginning, the first disciples burned with the desire to proclaim Christ: "We cannot but speak of what we have seen and heard" (Acts 4:20). And they invite people of every era to enter into the joy of their communion with Christ and the Father which is the basis of fellowship among Christians (cf. 1 John 1:1-4).

24. Catholics and Pentecostals agree that the proclamation of Jesus Christ is necessary for the liberation of humanity from sin and the attainment of salvation, because all are subject to "the fall", all are "lost". This condition results in alienation from God and also in alienation from others. Deliverance from oppression and domination of "the principalities and powers", including exorcism in certain cases, is an important part of gospel proclamation.

25. In the process of salvation, God always takes the initiative through grace which frees human hearts to respond (Acts 2:37). He acts through the Word and through the

exercise of "signs and wonders" according to his sovereign will (cf. 1 Cor. 2:4; Rom. 15:18f.). The only role humans have in reconciliation with God is to respond positively and constantly in the power of the Holy Spirit to God's initiatives through Jesus Christ, who is the only Mediator (1 Tim. 2:5) and the Head of the church (Col. 1:18).

26. The ordinary context in which salvation is worked out is the church, the community of believers. Koinonia is to be lived out for the mutual enrichment of the members of the body (1 Cor. 12:26), which in turn makes it possible for the church to become a servant, gift and sign to the world. Acknowledging this and acting accordingly would counteract individualism and total independence of individual communities on the one hand and the tendency towards sterile formalism in personal and institutional life on the other.[5]

27. The life of koinonia is empowered by the Holy Spirit; in recent times many have experienced that power through "the baptism in the Holy Spirit".[6] This presence of the Spirit has been shown in a fresh activity of biblical charisms or gifts (cf. 1 Cor. 12:8-11) reminding all Christians to be open to charisms as the Spirit gives to everyone individually, whether these gifts are more or less noticeable. Some of the charisms are given more for personal edification (cf. 1 Cor. 14:4a), while some provide service to others, and some especially are given to confirm evangelization (cf. Mark 16:15-20). All of them are intended to help build up the koinonia.

III. Evangelization and culture[7]

28. Both Catholics and Pentecostals recognize the complexity of the relationship between church and culture. The faith community evangelizes through its proclamation and through its common life: this means that our proclamation and our Christian lifestyle are always embodied in a specific culture. We accept that there is considerable good in cultures, notwithstanding the fact of humanity's fall from grace. Pentecostals emphasize the changing of individuals who, when formed into a body of believers, bring change into the culture from within. Catholics emphasize that culture itself in its human institutions and enterprises can also be transformed by the gospel.

29. Pentecostals and Catholics agree that when the gospel is introduced into a dominant non-Christian culture, a twofold attitude is required. On the one hand, we have to respect, affirm and support the positive elements in it, elements which will have prepared the people in advance for the reception of the gospel or which are good in themselves. On the other hand, we may have to try to transform this non-Christian culture from within. To do this the local people may be in a better position than foreign missionaries who may be tempted to impose their own culture as a substitute for the gospel.

30. Pentecostals and Catholics also agree that both evangelizers and evangelized need to realize that neither operate in a cultural vacuum. Evangelizers act unjustly towards peoples and cultures if they import political, economic or social ideologies alongside the gospel. The evangelized, too, must be aware of their own culture and religious history and discern how their response to evangelizers is faithful to the gospel as embodied in their own religious history and culture.

31. Pentecostals point out that in recent years an intentional and concentrated focus on "unreached peoples" has arisen. Some Evangelical Christian and Pentecostal movements have targeted the parts of the globe roughly fitting with the longitude/latitude configuration (the 10/40 window) for a significant emphasis of missionary personnel

and finances. The 10/40 window includes regions in which the gospel has never historically made significant inroads and shows Pentecostal consciousness that the so-called "unreached people" have been neglected.

32. Pentecostals in this dialogue wish to observe that in some cultural contexts, such as in Africa, or Asia or even Latin America, Pentecostals have actively and successfully engaged in mission without the benefit of any formal training on issues related to the inculturation of the gospel. They have actually communicated their Christian spirituality, worship and forms of evangelization through their local cultures. Pentecostals believe that this process has been facilitated by their emphasis upon the freedom of the Holy Spirit, with their consequent openness to the diversity of forms of expression in the worship and praise of God (e.g. their recognition of dance as a genuine form of spiritual worship). Their missionary work has been effective because they have a missionary model based on the recognition that all members of the community have been given the gifts or charisms of the Spirit necessary to share the full message of the gospel.

33. Catholics not only see the need to evangelize persons, but also see the need to evangelize cultures, for example through educational institutions. Furthermore, they have often evangelized through aesthetics embodying religious values. However, the ultimate focus of evangelization is the person. Catholics acknowledge instances of shortcomings in their evangelization, for instance, by insufficient Christian initiation and discipleship formation and by not always bringing parishioners to a personal faith commitment. Shortcomings, however, can often be better understood if concrete conditions, such as poverty, illiteracy, a shortage of ministers and the structures of oppression are known.

34. Both Catholics and Pentecostals recognize that the great social changes in Western society result in secularization processes and consequently a decline in religious practice. We deplore and condemn this secularization process, especially when these attitudes become part of a political agenda which promotes a value-free society in the name of tolerance and liberalism. To deplore and condemn are not enough. More positively, as Christians, we have to understand these new challenges and help our people to find new ways and insights to face them in light of Christian values. The fact is that many people face new challenges without guidelines in the fields of religion and ethics.

35. For example, over the past thirty years, technological and scientific innovations have radically changed the concrete conditions in which human beings are born and die in the "Western world". Progress in medicine far more than philosophical ideology has influenced our way of seeing the beginning and end of human life. In former times, procreation and the birth of a child depended much more on "chance", and consequently parents placed their trust in divine providence in this matter. Today an increasing ability to regulate birth allows a child to be "planned". Well before birth, through the pictures we see, we know whether the child is a boy or a girl. Further, the birth of a child takes place in a medical environment, far from the family home.

36. In the same way, at the other end of existence, no society before has ever seen such longevity, such a high proportion of elderly people. And none has taken death away from the family environment to such an extent: some 70 percent of all people in Western societies die in a hospital, in a medical and technical environment. Such far-reaching changes require that we actively engage in these challenges and learn as a Christian community how to respond to them in our preaching, our liturgy and our ser-

vice. In a way, we have to reformulate the everlasting message of salvation in a convincing way for contemporary men and women and not simply repeat it in antiquated language.

IV. Evangelization and social justice[8]

37. Since our traditions have approached the linkages between these two subjects in such different ways we have decided to have each side elaborate the connection in its own way before we show our convergences and differences.

1. Pentecostal reflections on evangelization and social justice

38. Pentecostal churches believe that they have been called by God in the "last days" (Acts 2:17) to be Christ-like witnesses in the power of the Spirit. One of the major contributions of Pentecostals to other Christian communities is an understanding of the church as a Spirit-filled missionary movement which not only founds communities but also cultivates them, while the Holy Spirit empowers them with the charisms.

39. Pentecostals have sometimes been accused of emphasizing evangelization to the exclusion of helping people in their practical needs. The sense of urgency which Pentecostals have concerning witness and salvation of the lost, like that of the early church, is not inconsistent with love and care for one another and for others. There are many examples of their sacrificial care throughout the world. The hope in the imminent coming of the Lord has sustained Pentecostals during persecution, harassment, imprisonment and martyrdom during this century. They have consistently taught that the church must be ready for the coming of the Lord by means of faithful witness and holy living. They have taught that all will have to give account to the righteous Judge for those things which have been done or left undone.

40. Pentecostals have a great concern for the eternal salvation of the soul, but also for the present welfare of the body as is readily apparent in the high priority they give to the doctrine of divine healing. In addition, they have had a real concern for the social as well as for the spiritual welfare of their members, especially in the third world. Theologically, the rebirth of a person by the Spirit is the anticipation of the transformation of the cosmos (cf. 2 Cor. 5:17; Rom. 8:21). This is why conversion and incorporation into the community of faith cannot be seen apart from the transformation of society. The person filled by the Spirit of God is impelled by that same Spirit to cooperate with God in the work of evangelism and social action in the anticipation of the new creation.

41. With their increasing numerical strength and upward social mobility, Pentecostal communities are now confronted by greater challenges for the kinds of social justice and human-rights concerns which the Catholic dialogue partners rightfully voice. Pentecostals continue to believe that intense hope has been and will continue to be necessary for endurance, healing and engagement of the forces – both social and spiritual – which oppress and violate people.

42. If it seems to Catholics that Pentecostals have reflected too little on problems related to social structures, Pentecostals suggest that social conditions under which they existed during early stages of their corporate experience be kept in mind. They had no access to structures of power by which they could influence public policy directly. This has meant that:

a) Most Pentecostals do not give priority to systematic reflection on problems related to social structures. They place more attention on the ways people experience those problems in their own lives and communities.
b) Pentecostalism, for the most part, has not existed until recently among "well educated" people who are able to reflect more systematically on structural dimensions of social justice.
c) Pentecostals do not read the New Testament as placing high priority on structural change; rather, they read it as emphasizing personal conversion and commitment to the communities of faith, and through that process they effect social change.

43. The perceived lack of stress on structural change does not, however, imply a lack of interest in social issues. Pentecostal conversion, while being personal, is not simply an individual experience, but also a communal one. In the life of the community, Pentecostals have found a new sense of dignity and purpose in life. Their solidarity creates affective ties, giving them a sense of equality. These communities have functioned as social alternatives that protest against the oppressive structures of the society at large. Along with some social critics, Pentecostals have discovered that effective social change often takes place at the communal and micro-structural level, not at the macro-structural level.

44. Pentecostals have continued to speak and act on behalf of those victimized by abortion, pornography, violence, oppression, etc. They have been concerned with feeding the hungry, clothing the naked, and providing emergency disaster relief. They have expanded their educational efforts and have begun to address issues of social-structural evil more explicitly. They are discovering their responsibility for those structures and their ability to influence them for good. This awareness was particularly fostered in situations of political and economic oppression.

45. From their earliest existence, Pentecostals have been active in missionary endeavours in the so-called two-thirds world. The churches established there have opposed social evils from the pulpit and on an interpersonal level in the oral fashion typical of the non-literary culture of Pentecostals. This concerns evils such as the caste system in India, polygamy in Africa and the Pacific, and genital mutilation in some African countries. Here exists a difficulty of perception. For older, more literary publics, only what is written and documented is perceived as having real existence. Pentecostals have begun to document work being done on these kinds of social issues in which they may have participated for many years.

46. In recent years and in various parts of the world, there have been a number of attempts to formulate Pentecostal social ethics which address the issues of structural change. Some Pentecostals have used the category of the new creation/kingdom of God with its characteristics of justice and peace to develop criteria for structural change. This has been connected with passages such as Luke 4:16-18 which demands the liberation of the oppressed in the power of the Spirit. Other Pentecostals speak more in terms of principalities and powers, of demonic forces which are present in the structures of the oppressive systems (cf. Eph. 6:12; Col. 2:13-15), that need to be fought with prayer and prophetic denunciation.

47. But even prior to these efforts, Pentecostals sometimes consciously, but usually unconsciously, have long used a number of significant theological criteria for taking social responsibility. More specifically, the ongoing narrative or story of Pentecostal communities has functioned to move people from their experience of the biblical wit-

ness to serious and often successful attempts to solve social problems. Likewise, ethical concerns about matters of justice and peace have developed in Pentecostal communities as they have correlated specific biblical injunctions with the reading of the Bible as a whole.

48. In summary, the emphasis Pentecostals place on personal evangelism and incorporation into Christian communities as a means of cultivating, pursuing and even propagating social structures may differ in method or emphasis from other Christian communities. Certainly as these relatively young churches continue to grow and mature, they will need to grow also in their capacity to address social issues on the societal level from their own perspective and identity. Nevertheless, up to this point these emphases in Pentecostal ministry have not been without impact, and not just in terms of generating and supporting acts of mercy. All this being said, however, we would anticipate that the Pentecostal style of engaging in justice will continue to differ from that of other Christian traditions.

2. Catholic reflections on evangelization and social justice

49. Catholics tend to view the questions of societal change, church and state relationships and human rights from the perspective of a complex and rich Catholic social teaching which is more than a century old in its development. It has its roots in the scriptures, reached its highpoint at Vatican II, and continues on in the Pontificate of John Paul II. For example, two of these documents from Vatican II, the Pastoral Constitution on the Church in the Modern World and the Decree on Religious Liberty, put the Catholic church on record as representing legitimate pluralism, religious liberty and the rights of people to be politically and civilly self-determining. It furthermore holds that they have socio-economic rights. It sees the human person as the inviolable subject of these rights, which include religious liberty. Human freedom is the condition not only of civil liberty, but is fundamental to accepting the gospel in the first place.

50. The synod of bishops of 1971, which focused on the question of justice, spoke of the way in which the quest for justice is an important part of the mission of the church in these words: "Action on behalf of justice and the transformation of society is integral to the mission of the church and the preaching of the gospel or, in other words, of the church's mission for the redemption of the human race and its liberation from every oppressive situation" ("Justice in the World", introduction).

51. All believers are called by God to engage in works of charity and to strive for social justice. According to the Decree on the Apostolate of Lay People of Vatican II, the laity, within the church as a whole, led by the light of the gospel and according to the mind of Christ, are called to renew the temporal order as their own special obligation (Decree on the Apostolate of Lay People, 7). The decree points to the need to change unjust structures, stating that "the demands of justice should first be satisfied. Not only the effects but also the causes of various ills must be removed. Help should be given in such a way that recipients may gradually be freed from dependence on others and become self-sufficient" (Decree on the Apostolate of Lay People, 8).

52. The transforming power of the gospel on individuals, communities and society is the grace of God, especially as mediated through word and sacraments. It is in the prayer of the church, (i.e., in the eucharist, in the other sacraments, as well as in the daily prayer of the people) that we are united to the transforming prayer of Christ. He taught us to pray for the coming of the kingdom (Matt. 6:10), which by its very nature

is God's gift and work. We do not construct the kingdom but rather ask for it, welcome it and rejoice in its growth within us. Prayer empowers us, in fact demands, that we strive for just and loving relationships among people, in family, in community and in society. These are all included in Christ's redemptive work.

53. Any account of modern Catholicism's efforts in these matters of evangelization, education and social justice would be incomplete if it did not mention men's and women's religious communities. Many of these religious congregations view their doing works of justice and faith as intrinsic to their particular calling. Many of their members live out this vision at great sacrifice – even of their lives.

54. To speak of the "kingdom of God" is to speak of the ultimate will of God for the whole of creation. The symbol of the kingdom conveys not only what we hope for but also a sense of urgency about our present responsibilities to be about the work of justice and the ministry of reconciliation between individuals, social classes and racial and ethnic groups. It also furnishes criteria for promoting social well-being on personal, communal, and structural levels.

3. Our common views regarding faith and justice

55. Pentecostals and Catholics agree that the word of God is the foundation of both evangelization and social justice.

56. In the Old Testament there is a strong insistence that the people whom God has freed should live justly (e.g. Jer. 21:12; 22:3; Amos 5:7-12; 8:4-6; Mic. 6:12). One Old Testament passage about justice, in particular (namely Isa. 61:1-3), is quoted by Jesus to characterize his own proclamation (Luke 4:18-21). The fact that we find in the gospel both the great commission to evangelize the nations (Matt. 28:16-20; Mark 16:15-18) and the great commandment to love God and one's neighbour (Matt. 22:34-40; Mark 12:28-34; Luke 10:27-28) suggests that there is a continuum between the two.

57. Koinonia as lived by the early Christians (Acts 2:42-47; 4:32-37) had social implications. Their communities did not act from a concept of social justice. The concern they showed for the poor, widows and strangers was not seen as an entirely separate activity, but rather as an extension of their worship.

58. We agree that:
– evangelization and love for one's neighbour are intrinsically connected and that basic to this love is active work towards social justice;
– even as we engage in evangelization, we need to give due attention to the social welfare of our neighbour;
– both Pentecostals and Catholics need to resist reductionism, anthropocentrism and politicization of Christ or the gospel; and the privatization of the kingdom and individualization of society. Here we see a point of strong convergence.

59. Clearly, any striving for social justice in which our faith communities engage needs to be rooted in the life of God – Father, Son and Holy Spirit. God the Father, who blessed the creation and called it good, commands us to look for justice for our neighbour, particularly orphans, widows and foreigners (Jer. 22:3-5).

God the Son, the Redeemer, who accomplished the work of salvation for the whole world, calls us to imitate his compassionate ministry of preaching the good news of the kingdom, healing the sick and feeding the hungry (Luke 4:16-21). In fact, he identifies himself with them (Matt. 25:31-46).

God the Spirit, who gives life, empowers us to witness to the world – in word and deed (Acts 1:8). Life in the Holy Spirit energizes Christians to engage in evangelization and to work for justice in society. Transformed people are compelled by the Spirit, the Creator and Sanctifier, to transform the world in the light of the in-breaking kingdom of God.

4. Things we have learned together: perceptions and convergences

60. Pentecostals and Catholics exhibit strengths and weaknesses in their understanding and practice of evangelization and social justice. Pentecostals believe that Catholics do not appreciate the social impact of Pentecostal ministry. Though Pentecostals may lack a formal social doctrine, Pentecostal evangelization has arguably a powerful social impact on individuals, on family life and the whole community.

61. We have come to realize that Pentecostals and Catholics have much to bring to one another with regard to social justice. While Catholics believe in the importance of personal faith, they also put great emphasis on the power of the gospel to change societal structures. Pentecostals, on the other hand, have traditionally pursued social change at the individual and communal levels. Catholics wonder whether the Pentecostal theology of evangelization leaves them ill-equipped for engaging in social justice. Pentecostals believe that Catholics should take more seriously the importance of personal and communal transformation for promoting societal change.

62. Catholics realize that in some predominantly Catholic regions of the world there are places where the gospel does not always appear to be effectively proclaimed and/or lived out in daily life.

63. Pentecostals believe that Catholics tend to minimize the impact of the power of the Holy Spirit when it brings concrete changes on the level of the individual, family and community. Pentecostals realize that in the past they were often not sufficiently aware of the implications of the gospel for social systems.

64. Pentecostals and Catholics agree that the regrettable division among Christians is a counter-witness to the credibility of the gospel and a hindrance to the effectiveness of promoting justice in the world. Some non-Christians have used this division as a sign of God's favouring of their own particular faith.

65. In the work of evangelization and social justice, we believe, as we have said above, that our communities are currently undergoing a form of convergence. While the Catholic church is in a process of renewal in evangelization and pastoral formation, Pentecostals are growing in an awareness of their responsibilities in the matter of structures and social systems.

66. Pentecostals and Catholics believe Jesus Christ to be the Lord of the kingdom he came to proclaim, and in our preaching and understanding, the kingdom of God and social justice should not be separated. Churches should strive to be faithful to the demands of the kingdom of God. Scandal is given when the churches, in their social and historical existence, grow slack in pursuing the divine purposes of the kingdom.

67. We differ in our emphases on the sources of evil, specifically, as to what extent they are of human, natural and/or supernatural origin. We also differ in the ways in which to recognize and deal with them. This is an area in which both traditions have much to learn from one another. We see the need to explore together the theological nature of power and its appropriate or inappropriate mediations. We need to ask how

our spiritualities, explicitly or implicitly, empower people to bear witness in evangelization and social justice.

V. Proselytism[9]

1. Moving towards a common position on proselytism

68. Since 1972 members of this dialogue have committed themselves to address the issue of proselytism. That this discussion has at last begun is a sign of the growing trust and maturation of Pentecostal-Catholic relations. Both teams in this international Roman Catholic-Pentecostal dialogue entered into a conversation on this topic with a number of misgivings. It is difficult enough to address this subject as an abstract object of study. But Catholic-Pentecostal relationships in many parts of the world have been troubled at times with accusations of insensitivity to the presence of long-standing Christian communities, charges of proselytism and counter-charges of persecution. Some people, in both traditions, have made it clear that they do not want Catholics and Pentecostals to speak to one another. Others have made it clear that they did not even want the topic of proselytism itself addressed. Both the Catholic and the Pentecostal teams debated within themselves, and then together, the wisdom of undertaking such a discussion in the light of possible repercussions on our mutual and growing relationship. Indeed, even the dialogue itself could suffer, we feared. In spite of these significant concerns, we decided that the urgency of the situation and the need to proclaim the gospel in a credible manner demanded a beginning to this discussion.

69. The members of the dialogue observed that proselytism exists, in large part, because Pentecostals and Catholics do not have a common understanding of the church. To give one illustration, they do not agree on the relationship between the church, on one hand, and baptism as an expression of living faith, on the other.

Nonetheless in our previous discussions we have expressed the ways in which we perceive the bonds between us that already exist. Catholics, for example, hold that everyone who believes in the name of the Lord Jesus and is properly baptized (cf. Perspectives on Koinonia, 54) is joined in a certain true manner to the body of Christ which is the church. For Pentecostals, "the foundation of unity is a common faith and experience of Jesus Christ as Lord and Saviour through the Holy Spirit. This implies that to the extent that Pentecostals recognize that Roman Catholics have this common faith in and experience of Jesus as Lord, they share a real though imperfect koinonia with them" (Perspectives on Koinonia, 55). This is true even though each has different understandings of the church.

70. Still members of the dialogue think that Pentecostals and Catholics already agree on critical points of faith. Recognition of this fact makes it possible for each of our communities to act in ways that do not impede the growth of the other. Lack of mutual recognition, however, has led at times to dismissive charges and counter-charges (e.g. "sects", "unbelievers", "syncretists", etc.) and actions and counteractions (e.g. unilateral decisions for the good of one community, often at the expense of the other community) by members of both communities. These charges and actions have detracted from the ability of Catholics and Pentecostals to witness credibly before the world to the reconciling power of God through Jesus Christ.

71. A primary example of such a conflict may be found in the tensions which exist between Christians who are not in fellowship with one another. It is not our purpose in

this document to give priority to the interests of one particular church over those of another. While in the example given in the following paragraphs, the Catholic church is described as the long-established church and the Pentecostals as the newcomers, such as may be the case in any given European country, there are instances such as in the case of north-east Zimbabwe in which Pentecostals may be described as the long-established church and the Catholics as newcomers. In the use of our example, our concern is merely to illustrate, in concrete terms, the tensions which may arise with respect to mission in a given region between two such churches.

72. Catholics, for instance, may have preached the gospel and established churches in a region centuries ago. Through the centuries these churches have played an important role in the lives of the people of that region. The role which the church has played has extended far beyond the walls of the congregation, permeating every aspect of the culture of the people from art, to music, to social institutions, to festivals and other public celebrations. The lives of the people flow easily between church and the wider culture because the church has impacted the culture in a major way.

73. However, there is another side to this. Often the earlier Christianization of a given culture by Catholicism takes for granted that it remains permeated by faith. As with an individual, so also with a culture, critique by the word and ongoing transformation are necessary.

74. The time and investment in the church by devout Catholics have been significant in many cultures. Sometimes their attempt to live the life of faith has come at a great price – persecution, even martyrdom. Actively embracing the challenges of living and transforming the society to which the gospel has been brought is no small feat. The faithful have struggled to maintain the gospel, even at times when the society has not wanted to hear it. The local church has rejoiced when the gospel has taken root, and sorrowed when it has failed to do so. In other words, evangelization is an ongoing need for any culture.

75. Conflict erupts when another community of Christians enters into the life of an already religiously impacted community and begins to evangelize without due consideration of the price that has been paid for witness to the gospel by believers who have preceded them. Difficulties arise when there is no acknowledgment of the significant role which the church plays in all aspects of the lives of those who are citizens of this region. This conflict comes about because the two Christian communities are separated and have not recognized the legitimacy of one another as members of the one body of Christ. They have been separated from one another. They have not spoken with one another. Certain assumptions have been made by each about the other. Judgments have taken place without proper consultation between them.

76. Even if the motives of newcomers are irreproachable with respect to the welfare of the people in this region, including a genuine concern to see that the citizens of the region have really heard the gospel, their method of entry into the region often contributes to misunderstanding and conflict, and perhaps even to a violent response. Courtesy would seem to call for some communication with the leaders of the older church by the new evangelizers. Without this, the older church and culture are easily violated. The people and church leaders in some of these areas have often been offended by what they see as disrespect or disregard of pastoral activities that have been exercised for a long time. It is easy to see why serious tensions might arise.

77. The conflicts which have occurred between us demonstrate clearly the problem which disunity creates even for well-intentioned Christians. Disunity isolates us from

one another. It leads to suspicion between us. It contributes to a lack of mutual understanding, even to an unwillingness for us to try to understand each other. And all of these things have resulted in a general state of hostility between us in which we even question the Christian authenticity of each other. Our different readings of the gospel reached in our isolated states have led to doctrinal differences which have only further contributed to the question of whether or not the other truly proclaims the gospel.

78. If each perceives the other through the lens of this disunity, the result is all too often that one sees the other as an adversary to its own mission and may, therefore, feel the need to place impediments in the way of the other. There may be public denunciations, even persecution, of one another. Both sides have suffered, Pentecostals in particular since they have usually been the minority. But the main tragedy, and on this both the Catholic and Pentecostal teams agree, is that the conflict resulting from the disunity of Christians always "scandalizes the world, and damages that most holy cause, the preaching of the gospel to every creature" (Decree on Ecumenism, 1). What needs to be faced honestly, and examined with great care, are the reasons behind these conflicts. What we both desire is the pure preaching of the gospel. Most of our conflicts would diminish if we agreed that this is what evangelization is all about.

79. Instead of conflict, can we not converse with one another, pray with one another, try to cooperate with one another instead of clashing with one another? In effect, we need to look for ways in which Christians can seek the unity to which Christ calls his disciples (cf. John 17:21) starting with basic respect for one another, learning to love one another.

2. Replacing dissatisfaction with hope

80. By the 4th century church and state were deeply involved in the life of each other. Since then both have occasionally resorted to coercion to assure political-religious homogeneity in society. This has been expressed in the repression of heresy (inquisition) and of other religions (the expulsion of Jews and Muslims from various European countries). The same concern shaped the principle *cuius regio, eius religio* ("all citizens must accept the religion of their ruler") which was enforced in Europe, especially during the 16th and 17th centuries. The process by which churches and states moved, first, to religious toleration and then to religious freedom only began in the late 18th century and did not become more or less universal in the West until the mid-20th century.

81. In this historical context, Catholics are well aware that attempts at Christianization have often been attached to political and economic expansion (e.g., Latin America) and that sometimes pressure and violence have been used. They also acknowledge that prior to Vatican II, Catholic doctrine has been reluctant to support full religious freedom in civil law.

82. Today Catholics and Pentecostals condemn coercive and violent methods. Nevertheless, all too often aggressiveness still characterizes our interaction. Words have become the new weapons. Catholics are affronted when some Pentecostals assume that they are not even Christians, when they speak disrespectfully of the Catholic church and its leaders or when Pentecostals lead Catholic members into newly established Pentecostal fellowships. Pentecostals are affronted when some Catholics in some parts of the world view them as "rapacious wolves", when they are ridiculed as *panderetas o aleluyas* (tambourines or alleluias), or when they are indiscriminately classified as "sects".

83. Further proof of the fact that neither Catholics nor Pentecostals are satisfied with the state of division which exists between them can be seen in their own discussions of proselytism. An initial working definition of proselytism is that it is a disrespectful, insensitive and uncharitable effort to transfer the allegiance of a Christian from one ecclesial body to another. Actions have already been taken by several traditions which reveal that they believe that "proselytism" is something to be condemned.[10]

84. Pentecostals did not participate directly in the development of those documents, but Pentecostals have also demonstrated their concern over proselytism, on a more limited scale. They have enacted various bylaws, adopted statements on ministerial ethics, and developed other guidelines which provide leadership to their ministers on issues such as how close together congregations can be planted, what permissions need to be obtained from other pastors in the area in which a new work is being planted, and what type of relationship a minister must maintain when working within the parish of another minister of the same denomination, or within a district that is not his or her own. These bylaws, codes of ethics, and other guidelines have been developed to resist any temptation which one minister might have to proselytize (cf. 2 Cor. 10:16). These guidelines work because there is mutual recognition between those who are subject to them.

85. The early writings of Pentecostals reveal a number of rich and fertile visions of unity among Christians, even if at times they were triumphalistic. Among them was the vision of Charles F. Parham who viewed himself as called by the Holy Spirit to serve as an "apostle of unity". Another was repeatedly published by the African-American pastor William J. Seymour of the famous Azusa Street Mission, in the *Apostolic Faith*, that the movement stood for "... Christian unity everywhere". The ministers of the Assemblies of God, in their organizational meeting of April 1914, went so far as to state that they opposed the establishment of "unscriptural lines of fellowship or disfellowship" since such lines stood counter to Jesus' desire for unity as expressed in John 17:21. A number of other early Pentecostal leaders shared these sentiments also, and read this impulse towards unity as one which was birthed by the Holy Spirit.

86. While some Pentecostal bodies, especially some indigenous groups in Latin America and Africa, have retained their original visions for unity, most Pentecostals around the world have chosen to pursue more limited visions of unity. This has happened due to a number of factors. Fundamentalists outside Pentecostalism publicly criticized existing Pentecostal cooperation with many other Christians as inconsistent with biblical teaching. The adoption by some Pentecostals of certain eschatological interpretations popular among fundamentalists and evangelicals led to growing suspicion of the modern movements towards unity among Protestants. Peer pressure which suggested that Pentecostals would be granted acceptance as full members of the evangelical community if they would cut existing ties with certain other Christians, further compromised the original visions of unity.[11] Many Pentecostals also withdrew their support of larger movements towards unity when they believed that their own priorities were not being taken seriously. Vestiges of these original visions of unity are still to be found among the published statements which outline the raison d'etre of many Pentecostal organizations including the Pentecostal World Conference.[12]

87. The Pentecostal members of this dialogue lament the impact of the factors which have led to the loss of the original visions of unity. They would like to challenge

Pentecostals to look once again at their roots that they might rediscover the richness of their earliest call to facilitate unity between all Christians, by internalizing anew the role the Holy Spirit has presumably played in the birth of these deep yearnings.

88. All members of this dialogue also wish to encourage Pentecostals to share their visions of greater Christian unity with other Christians. In turn, we urge the latter to bring their own visions of unity to the discussion. In this way, we believe that together we can "discover the unfathomable riches of the truth" thereby deepening our own understanding of what we believe the Holy Spirit has caused to emerge within us. We are all called to be stewards of this precious gift of unity which we already enjoy and to which we yet aspire in the bond of peace (cf. Eph. 4:3).

89. In the light of these realities which have contributed to our own coming together for dialogue, the members of both teams felt keenly the need to acknowledge that neither Catholics nor Pentecostals have fulfilled sufficiently the demands of the gospel to love one another. While the past cannot be undone and is not even wholly retrievable, we must make every effort to know and express it as accurately as possible.

3. Defining the challenge

90. The term "proselytism" is not found in the Bible, but the term "proselyte" is. It is originally derived from the Old Testament vocabulary relating to those strangers and sojourners who moved into Israel, believed in Yahweh, and accepted the entire Torah (e.g. Ex. 12:48-49). This term carried a positive meaning, i.e., to become a convert to Judaism. In the New Testament, proselytes were present in Jerusalem on the day of Pentecost (cf. Acts 2:11), and at least one of them was chosen to serve the widows (cf. Acts 6:5). But in recent times, "proselytism", as used within Christian circles, has come to carry a negative meaning associated with an illicit form of "evangelism".

91. An issue between Catholics and Pentecostals that relates to the problem of proselytism concerns the way a living faith is perceived in the life of an individual Christian or in a community. Through dialogue we have learned that Pentecostals and Catholics may have different ideas about who is "unchurched", different understandings of how living in a deeply Christian culture can root the Christian faith in someone's life. They may have different ideas of how to assess whether, or in what way, pastoral needs are being met in a Christian community or in a person's life. They may have different ways of interpreting whether or not a person can be considered an evangelized Christian.

92. The dialogue has taught us that because of these differences there is a continual need to learn from one another so as to deepen mutual knowledge and understanding of each other's doctrinal traditions, pastoral practices and convictions. We need to learn to respect the integrity and rights of the other so as to avoid judgments that create unnecessary conflict in regard to evangelization and obstacles to the spreading of the gospel, in addition to those already caused by our divisions.

93. Attempts to define proselytism reveal a broad range of activities and actions that are not easily interpreted. These tend to be identified and evaluated differently by the parties involved. In spite of these difficulties, we have concluded that both for Catholics and for Pentecostals, proselytism is an unethical activity that comes in many forms. Some of these would be:
– all ways of promoting our own community of faith that are intellectually dishonest, such as contrasting an ideal presentation of our own community with the weaknesses of another Christian community;

- all intellectual laziness and culpable ignorance that neglect readily accessible knowledge of the other's tradition;
- every wilful misrepresentation of the beliefs and practices of other Christian communities;
- every form of force, coercion, compulsion, mockery or intimidation of a personal, psychological, physical, moral, social, economic, religious or political nature;
- every form of cajolery or manipulation, including the exaggeration of biblical promises, because these distortions do not respect the dignity of persons and their freedom to make their own choices;
- every abuse of mass media in a way that is disrespectful of another faith and manipulative of the audience;
- all unwarranted judgments or acts which raise suspicions about the sincerity of others;
- all competitive evangelization focused against other Christian bodies (cf. Rom. 15:20).

94. All Christians have the right to bear witness to the gospel before all people, including other Christians. Such witness may legitimately involve the persuasive proclamation of the gospel in such a way as to bring people to faith in Jesus Christ or to commit themselves more deeply to him within the context of their own church. The legitimate proclamation of the gospel will bear the marks of Christian love (cf. 1 Cor. 13). It will never seek its own selfish ends by using the opportunity to speak against or in any way denigrate another Christian community, or to suggest or encourage a change in someone's Christian affiliation. Both the Pentecostal and Catholic members of this dialogue view as proselytism such selfish actions as an illegitimate use of persuasive power. Proselytism must be sharply distinguished from the legitimate act of persuasively presenting the gospel. Proselytism must be avoided.

95. At the same time we acknowledge that if a Christian, after hearing a legitimate presentation of the gospel, freely chooses to join a different Christian community, it should not automatically be concluded that such a transfer is the result of proselytism.

96. For the most part, people hear the preaching of the gospel within their own particular church where their own spiritual needs are also met. It may also happen, on a given occasion, that members of different Christian communities help to organize an evangelistic campaign, in which they also participate. The primary aim of such an evangelistic campaign should always be the proclamation of the gospel. We believe that the Rev. Billy Graham has provided an important model in this regard. Respecting the ecclesial affiliation of the participants, he organizes such campaigns only after he has sought the support and agreement of the churches in the area, including Catholics and Pentecostals. When those who are already part of a Christian community respond to his call to commit themselves more deeply to Christ, the pastoral resources from their own church are immediately made available to help them in their renewed commitment. Thus, proselytism is avoided. The churches involved receive the respect and regard they deserve, illustrating the results of communication and cooperation, demonstrating a measure of real, visible unity.

97. Confusion has resulted when the terms "proselytism" and "evangelism" have been used as though they were synonyms. This confusion has impacted the civil realm. Some countries, for instance, have passed so-called "anti-proselytism" laws which prohibit or greatly restrict any kind of Christian evangelism or missionary activity. We deplore this.

4. Promoting religious freedom

98. Mention of these anti-proselytism laws introduces us to the complex matter of religious freedom. There is general agreement that religious liberty is a civil right. For Christians there is also the religious freedom they are to accord to one another as brothers and sisters in Christ, and to all human beings since they are made in the image and likeness of God.

99. Religious freedom is promoted by both secular society, for example, in statements from the United Nations (cf. United Nations Declaration on Human Rights, 1948; UN Declaration on the Elimination of all Forms of Intolerance and Discrimination Based on Religious Belief, 25 November 1981, art. 1.1) and by the church (e.g. Declaration on Religious Liberty, Vatican II, 1965). Pentecostals and Catholics are in full agreement in the support of religious freedom, whether it is seen as a civil right or as one of the principles that should guide their relationships with each other.

100. Religious freedom as a civil right is very complex in the way it is pursued and resisted in the endlessly varied political situations that have church related to state and state to church. Catholics and Pentecostals need to stand as one in respecting and promoting this civil right for all peoples and for one another.

101. Historically, Pentecostals have not enacted broadly representative resolutions on the subject of religious freedom largely because of their minority status in the societies where they have functioned. They have recently, however, joined with other Christians when issues of religious freedom have been at stake. They have also led efforts to end persecution or to promote legislation towards religious freedom, especially in countries where in the past the rights of their Pentecostal sisters and brothers have been violated (e.g. Italy and a number of Latin American countries). It is clear, therefore, that they believe that the state has a legitimate role in guaranteeing religious freedom.

102. Because of these convictions, members of the dialogue reject:
- all violations of religious freedom and all forms of religious intolerance as well as every attempt to impose belief and practices on others or to manipulate or coerce others in the name of religion;
- inequality in civil treatment of religious bodies, although we affirm, as Vatican II affirmed, that in exercising their rights individuals and social groups "are bound by the moral law to have regard to the rights of others, to their own duties towards others and for the common good of all" (Declaration on Religious Liberty, 7).

103. Catholics believe that the state is obliged to give effective protection to the religious liberty of all citizens by just laws and other suitable means, and to ensure favourable conditions for fostering religious life (cf. Declaration on Religious Liberty, 6).

104. Religious freedom has also been the subject of significant ecumenical dialogue (e.g. "Summons to Witness to Christ in Today's World: A Report on the Baptist-Roman Catholic International Conversations, 1984-1988"[13]). A statement that is even more comprehensive in scope is that of the Joint Working Group between the Roman Catholic Church and the World Council of Churches. With them we agree that "religious freedom affirms the right of all persons to pursue the truth and witness to the truth according to their conscience. It includes the freedom to acknowledge Jesus Christ as Lord and Saviour and the freedom of Christians to witness to their faith in him by word and deed" (Joint Working Group, "The Challenge of Proselytism and the

Calling to Common Witness", 1996, 15). Religious freedom includes the freedom to embrace a religion or to change one's religion without any coercion which would impair such freedom (cf. *ibid.*).

5. Resolving conflicts in the quest for unity

105. Conflicts among Christian groups are not unusual. Difficulties experienced by Protestant missionary movements of the 19th and 20th centuries highlighted the need to resolve tensions among denominations. It became obvious that divisions were obstacles to the preaching of the gospel. These concerns led to the first world missionary conference at Edinburgh, Scotland, in 1910, at which an international body of Protestants and Anglicans assembled to discuss ways to cooperate rather than compete in mission. This conference led to other movements for Christian cooperation. As we approach the end of the century virtually all major Christian families, Anglican, Catholic, Orthodox, Pentecostal and Protestant, are now involved in efforts to find ways to work together, to overcome misunderstandings and to resolve doctrinal differences, so that these will no longer be obstacles to the proclaiming of the gospel of Jesus Christ.

106. These concerns have implications for Pentecostals and Catholics where conflict arises from mission activities. Two points need to be kept in mind. On the one hand, we affirm that the principles of religious freedom are basic for evangelization. On the other hand, divided Christians have real responsibilities for one another because of the bonds of koinonia they already share (cf. Perspectives on Koinonia, 54-55). In facing conflicts, the right to religious freedom must be seen in relationship to the responsibility to respond to Christ's call for the unity of his disciples. Christ calls Christians to live their freedom. At the same time, he calls Christians to unity "so that the world may believe" (John 17:21).

107. The call of the Lord of the church cannot be ignored. It is reinforced by the apostle Paul who exhorted the Ephesians to make "every effort to maintain the unity of the Spirit in the bond of peace" (Eph. 4:3) for "there is one body, and one spirit... one Lord, one faith, one baptism, one God and Father of all" (Eph. 4:4-5). Christians, who have been reconciled to God and entrusted with the ministry of reconciliation (cf. 2 Cor. 5:18), need to be reconciled with each other in order to carry out their ministry effectively. Ongoing division jeopardizes the impact of the gospel.

108. We realize that some of our readers will think that our conclusions are idealistic. We do not agree. We recognize that not everyone has had the same experience and the same opportunity that we have had to work together, to pray together and to learn from one another. We have come to recognize, in a fresh way, that with God all things are possible to those who believe (cf. Mark 9:23). The scriptures teach us that Christ calls us and the apostle invites us to unity (cf. John 17:21; Eph. 4:3). The patterns of our relationships in the past have not reflected this call. We engaged in this dialogue because of what we understand is the will of Christ which our past relationships have not reflected. Our efforts are intended as a contribution to rethinking the lack of conformity between Pentecostal-Catholic relationships and the call of Christ. We commend our findings to our readers recognizing that some will find them to be a real challenge.

109. We look forward to the day when leaders within our two communities will be able to pray together, develop mutual trust, and deal with tensions which arise.

Through our theological dialogue, now twenty-five years old, we have gained a deeper understanding of the meaning of faith in Christ and a mutual respect for one another. We covet for our leaders these same gifts and believe such relationships might yield greater sensitivity on issues of mutual concern. The relationship might even yield a code of ecclesial etiquette to help prevent difficulties from arising.

All of this seems possible and desirable. Are we not, as believers, being prepared for a future in which we will be judges not only of the world but also of the angels (cf. 1 Cor. 6:2-3)? Would it not be a sign of contradiction if we had to hand over our present disputes to the judgment of the world? But this is what is happening when we arrive at impasses. "Can it be", Paul asks, "that there is no one among you wise enough to decide between one believer and another?" (1 Cor. 6:5).

6. Affirming principles for mutual understanding

110. The discussion on the nature of proselytism leads very quickly into practical matters. Even if Pentecostals and Catholics explicitly or implicitly denounce proselytism, many people may need practical guidance on how to live up to this commitment. The members of the dialogue have agreed upon the following principles which seek to express the spirit of Christian love as it is portrayed in scripture (cf. 1 Cor. 13). They submit these principles for consideration by their respective churches.

111. The deep and true source of any Christian witness is the commandment, "You shall love the Lord your God with all your heart, and with all your soul, and with all your mind and you shall love your neighbour as yourself" (Matt. 22:37,39; cf. Lev. 19:18; Deut. 6:5). Christian witness brings glory to God. It is nourished by the conviction that it is the Holy Spirit whose grace and light brings about the response of faith. It respects the free will and dignity of those to whom it is given, whether or not they wish to accept.

112. Pentecostals and Catholics affirm the presence and power of the gospel in Christian communities outside of their own traditions. Pentecostals believe that all Christians, of whatever denomination, can have a living personal relationship with Jesus as Lord and Saviour. Catholics believe that only in their own visible communion "the fullness of the means of salvation can be attained". But they also believe that "some, even very many, of the significant elements and endowments which together go to build up and give life to the church itself, can exist outside the visible boundaries of the Catholic Church" (Decree on Ecumenism, 3). It is the responsibility of all Christians to proclaim the gospel to all who have not repented, believed and submitted their lives to the lordship of Christ. It is imperative for every Christian to speak "the truth in love" (Eph. 4:15) about all Christian communities. We affirm the obligation to portray the beliefs and practices of other Christian communities accurately, honestly and charitably, and wherever possible in cooperative efforts with them. We pray and work "for building up the body of Christ, until all of us come to the unity of the faith and of the knowledge of the Son of God, to maturity, to the measure of the full stature of Christ" (Eph. 4:12b-13).

113. Individual Christians have the right and responsibility to proclaim the gospel boldly (Acts 4:13,29; Eph. 6:19) and persuasively (cf. Acts 17:3; Rom. 1:14). All people have the right to hear the gospel preached in their own "language" in a culturally sensitive fashion. The good news of Jesus Christ addresses the whole person, including his or her behavioural, cognitive and experiential dimensions. We also affirm

responsible use of modern technology as a legitimate means to communicate the gospel.

114. In the light of these issues, we offer the following proposals to our communities:
- to incorporate these principles in our own daily lives and ministries;
- to pursue contacts with Christian leaders for consideration of these issues;
- to conduct our preaching, teaching and pastoral ministry in the light of these principles;
- to invite scholarly and professional societies at all levels to discuss this document;
- to incorporate these insights into the various programmes for educators, ministerial students and other church workers;
- to encourage the development of relationships of mutual understanding and respect which will enable us to work together on these issues.

115. We encourage prayer for and with each other. Above all, we pray that Pentecostals and Catholics will be open to the Holy Spirit who will convince the hearts of all Christians of the urgency and the biblical imperative of these concerns.

116. Without a doubt, proselytism is a sensitive issue among Pentecostals and Catholics, but we believe that through open and honest dialogue and docility to the Spirit, we can respond to the challenge before us. This may not always be easy, but the love of Christ compels us to deal with "a humility and gentleness, with patience, bearing with one another in love, making every effort to maintain the unity of the Spirit in the bond of peace" (Eph. 4:3). It is only then that we will give credible witness to Christ in a world which urgently needs to hear the good news.

VI. Common witness[14]

117. Jesus Christ is the unique witness to the Father, and the Spirit comes from the Father to witness to Jesus Christ. Therefore, witness which belongs to the nature of the Christian life is an imperative of the great commission and is an ideal for which we strive. In different ways, both Pentecostals and Catholics base their witness on Matthew 28. Both consider the Pentecost event as central to their Christian faith. In the biblical sense witness is the unique testimony of the apostles and disciples to what they have seen and heard (1 John 1:1-4). Witness is rooted in the apostles' experience of Jesus who is the image of the Father sent in the power of the Spirit to return all to the source, the Father. Disciples are empowered by the Holy Spirit to proclaim the gospel (Acts 1:8; 4:20).

118. Common witness means standing together and sharing together in witness to our common faith. Common witness can be experienced through joint participation in worship, in prayer, in the performance of good works in Jesus' name and especially in evangelization. True common witness is not engaged in for any narrow, strategic denominational benefit of a particular community. Rather, it is concerned solely for the glory of God, for the good of the whole church and the good of humankind.

119. Common witness requires personal inward conversion, a renewal of heart and mind. This enables all to hear the word of God anew and to listen again to what the Spirit is saying to the churches. Purification of our own hearts and minds and the renewal of our respective communities help make common witness a possibility. One sign that this purification has taken place is that in the process of growing mutual understanding and trust, our stereotypes of one another diminish. In other words, we change, but the change is not compromise.

120. Once mutual trust as persons and reciprocal respect for each other's traditions has been established, then some limited measure of common witness is possible. Are there any precedents? There are innumerable precedents from all over the world. For example when a Pentecostal leader was murdered in Iran in 1995 the eulogy was preached by a Catholic priest. In Berlin the Classical Pentecostals are members of the association of churches and cooperate in its activities. In Munich a Benedictine monastery provided a Pentecostal pastor just starting his ecumenical ministry with meeting rooms in the centre of the city. In the United States a Pentecostal invited a Catholic priest to give a retreat for ministers. A Pentecostal leader was invited to preach in the Catholic cathedral in Los Angeles. The revivals of Billy Graham have long enjoyed both Pentecostal and Catholic participation. In Chile, some Pentecostal leaders participate together with Catholics, Orthodox and other Protestants in the Fraternidad Ecuménica. Pentecostals and Catholics charismatics have for some time now participated together in many ways, including planning such significant international conferences as those held in Jerusalem, Singapore, Bern, Brighton, Port Dickson (Malaysia), Kansas City, New Orleans, Indianapolis and Orlando.

121. Pentecostals and Catholics are still at the beginnings of their relationship and their search for mutual understanding. Some are only now exploring ways of giving common witness. Others do not want to give common witness. As members of the dialogue we believe that a limited common witness is already possible because in many ways a vital spiritual unity exists between us, a real though imperfect communion (Perspectives on Koinonia, 54-55). We already have communion in the grace of Jesus Christ. We both believe in the centrality of scripture. We proclaim together that there is no evangelization unless the name, teaching and life of Jesus Christ, the Son of God, is proclaimed (cf. Evangelization in the Modern World). We share a common belief in the fatherhood of God; the lordship of Jesus Christ, Messiah, Saviour and Coming Lord; the power of the Spirit for witness; the enduring nature of Pentecost; the love of God poured out through the Spirit. We both acknowledge the unique character of salvation, the belief that anyone without exception who is saved attains salvation through Jesus Christ; the forgiveness of sins, the promise of eternal life, the significant role of the charisms, the ten commandments and the beatitudes. Common witness shows the bonds of communion (koinonia) between divided churches.

122. No one is called to compromise. Common witness is not a call to indifference or to uniformity. In fact though division and separation are contrary to the will of God, the diversity within the unity of the one body of Christ is a precious and indispensable gift which is to be recognized, valued and embraced. Common witness prevents neither individuals nor communities from witnessing to their heritage. This can even include our witnessing separately on things over which we seriously disagree. However, this can be done without being contentious, with mutual love and respect.

123. At a deeper level, common witness and forgiveness are intrinsically related to one another. Forgiveness also leads to a more credible common witness. Praying together is a case in point. In fact, mutual forgiveness is itself an act of common witness. Here equity in the recognition of guilt is not the goal. One side may have offended more than the other. That determination is left to God. Rather, as Jesus himself has given us an example, each side takes on the sins of the other. In Christian forgiveness it is not a question of who threw the first stone (John 8:7), of who did what to whom first; rather it is the willingness to make the first step. Both sides should take

the initiative according to gospel norms: Pentecostals should take the initiative for reconciliation because they feel themselves the most aggrieved; Catholics should take the initiative because they are the elder in interchurch relations. In both cases, if asked for our coat, we give also our cloak; if asked to go one mile, we go two (Matt. 5:41).

124. We need to be aware of the dark side of our histories, with full recognition of all the circumstances which gave rise to the distrust. Forgiveness is based on the truth established by both sides. The truth shared by the followers of Christ is not established by judicial procedure (cf. 1 Cor. 6:4-7). There is another way of resolving difficulties, more appropriate for those who are profoundly related to one another in the unity of the Spirit. The offended should not have to prove their position to the last detail. The model here is a more relational one. Once mutual forgiveness has been expressed reconciliation should be effected. In our cases this reconciliation should be expressed publicly in a form acceptable to both groups.

125. Both should have acquaintance with the other's history, and theological positions. Otherwise we will not escape our histories of mutual distrust. Common witness gives Pentecostals and Catholics the opportunity to work together in the writing of our common and separate histories, without excluding different interpretations of the facts. Once Pentecostal and Catholic students have a firm grounding in their own tradition sharing in institutes of higher learning is possible, especially in disciplines such as intellectual history, philosophy, government, law, sociology and medicine. This activity could include not only students but mature scholars. We already share in scholarly biblical research and we participate together in learned societies such as the Society of Pentecostal Studies.

126. We often underestimate the degree of common witness which already exists among Pentecostal and Catholic relatives and neighbours who pray together and cooperate in many ways, including visiting the sick and caring for others. Is it possible that the people in our local congregations and parishes are perhaps more involved in common witness than their pastors and church leaders realize?

127. In our Pentecostal-Catholic dialogue, we have discovered two useful principles:
- we cannot do what conscience forbids;
- we can do together what conscience permits in the area of common witness.

The first principle, "we cannot do what conscience forbids", emphasizes that our witness must be prudent, honest and humble. We recognize today that there are limits as to what we can do together. Both Pentecostals and Catholics have diverse pastoral and worship understandings, as well as doctrinal points which they do not fully share with one another. While we build on those things that unite us, our common witness should also acknowledge our divergences. The present inability of Catholics and Pentecostals to share together at the table of the Lord is a striking example of our divisions and the lack of common witness in this respect (cf. 1 Cor. 11:26). All of us experience this as deeply troubling.

The second principle raises the provocative question: Why do we not do together what we can do together? While recognizing that relations between Pentecostals and Catholics are a matter of a growth progress, what is possible at a later stage of growth may not be possible at an earlier stage. Many Pentecostals and Catholics may not see some of our suggestions as options for today. But both need to know what doors can be opened, if not today, perhaps in the future. Above all, no one wants to close off either the present or future inspiration of the Holy Spirit.

128. Some measure of common prayer seems indispensable for common witness. How can we witness together, if we have not prayed together? To pray together is already common witness. The Week of Prayer for Christian Unity, which is generally celebrated in January or before Pentecost, is a possibility. Pentecostals and Catholic charismatics already share profound experiences in prayer together. There could be exchange of pulpits related to non-eucharistic worship services. We can exchange films, videos and printed materials which explain the faith but betray no denominational animus.

129. We believe that Pentecostals and Catholics can together be proactive in promoting values and positive actions in human society. In the spirit of Matthew 25:31-46, we can stand together against sin in promoting human dignity and social justice. Though with changing times other issues will present themselves, currently there are many examples of the kinds of issues on which we can work together. We can cooperate in such works as the quest for disarmament and peace, providing emergency relief for refugees, for victims of natural disasters, feeding the hungry, setting up educational opportunities for the illiterate, establishing drug rehabilitation programmes and rescuing young women and men from prostitution. We can work together to eliminate racial and gender discrimination, working for the rights and dignity of women, opposing offensively permissive legislation (such as abortion and euthanasia), promoting urban and rural development and housing for the poor, denouncing violations of the environment and the irresponsible use of both renewable and unrenewable natural resources. In some parts of the world, Pentecostals already collaborate with Catholics on many of these issues and others, yet there are still many more opportunities for cooperation, especially in North America. Why do we do apart what we can do together?

130. This document comes out of our experience of dialogue with one another over twenty-five years on a variety of topics, with years of focused discussions on evangelization, proselytism and common witness. Strong bonds of affection and trust between Pentecostals and Catholics in the dialogue have created an atmosphere in which differences have been faced with candour, even when those differences seen to be irreconcilable. We hope that the text conveys something of the frustrating and rewarding moments that have been part of our experience over the years. We also hope that the text will help readers to re-experience what we ourselves experienced, namely, the joy of discovering together astonishing areas of agreement. But the text would lack integrity if it did not also offer to the reader the opportunity to re-experience with us the shocks of the gaps between our positions. Still we hold dear the unity in diversity which exists among us and look forward to the day when we may work more closely together despite our differences. In reality, what unites us is far greater than what divides us. Though the road to that future is not entirely clear to us we are firm in our conviction that the Spirit is calling us to move beyond our present divisions. We invite our readers to travel this road with us.

NOTES

[1] The failing health of the Rev. Justus du Plessis caused him to withdraw from active participation in the dialogue in 1993. The Rev. Jerry Sandidge, who had served as co-secretary on the Pentecostal team, died in 1992 after a lengthy illness with which he had struggled bravely for years. The participants note with

great appreciation their very significant work in promoting this dialogue and other relationships between our communities. We also remember with great appreciation the work of Msgr Heinz-Albet Raem who joined us in 1990 as co-secretary for the Catholic side. He applied his excellent organizational and theological skills in service to this fourth phase for seven years, but he never lived to see its completion because he died in March 1997. Their absence was deeply felt by all members of the dialogue, both Catholic and Pentecostal.

[2] Papers were delivered on this topic by Karl Müller, SVD, of St Augustin, Germany ("A Catholic Perspective of Evangelization: Evangelii Nuntiandi"), and by Dr Gary B. McGee, of the Assemblies of God Theological Seminary, Springfield, MO, USA ("Apostolic Power for End-times Evangelism: A Historical Review of Pentecostal Mission Theology").

[3] A list of official documents of the Roman Catholic Church used in this report is found in Appendix 2, attached to the original published form of this report.

[4] Papers were delivered on this topic by Rev. William Menzies, president and professor of theology at Asia Pacific Theological Seminary, Baguio City, Philippines ("The Biblical Basis for Mission and Evangelism: An Evangelical, Pentecostal Perspective") and Rev. Karl Müller, SVD, St Augustin, Germany ("The Biblical and Systematic Foundation of Evangelization").

[5] For a more complete discussion of koinonia please refer to "Perspectives on Koinonia: The Report from the Third Quinquennium of the Dialogue between the Pontifical Council for Promoting Christian Unity and Some Classical Pentecostal Churches and Leaders, 1985-1989".

[6] Discussion on this issue took place in the first phase of the dialogue.

[7] Papers on this topic were presented by Prof. Hervé Legrand, OP, Institut catholique, Paris ("A Paradigm: Evangelizing in a Secularized and Pluralistic Europe according to some Bishops of the CCEE") and by Everett Wilson (Assemblies of God), Southern California College ("A Paradigm of Latin-American Pentecostalism").

[8] The papers done for this section were by John C. Haughey, S.J. of Loyola University, Chicago ("Evangelization and Social Justice: An Inquiry into Their Relationship"), and by Murl O. Dirkson, PhD, and Karen Carroll Mundy, PhD (Church of God) of Lee University, Cleveland, Tennessee, USA ("Evangelization and Social Justice: A Pentecostal Perspective").

[9] Papers were presented by Rev. Karl Müller, SVD, of St Augustin, Germany ("Proselytism, Common Witness and Evangelization") and by Dr Cecil M. Robeck, Jr (Assemblies of God), Fuller Theological Seminary, Pasadena, CA, USA ("Evangelization, Proselytizing and Common Witness: A Pentecostal Perspective").

[10] On the Catholic side, the theme has been addressed in several international bilateral dialogues in which the Roman Catholic Church has been involved, namely with Evangelicals ("The Evangelical-Roman Catholic Dialogue on Mission, 1977-1984: A Report", here document 40; with Baptists ("Summons to Witness to Christ in Today's World: A Report of the Baptist-Roman Catholic International Conversations, 1984-1988", document 38); with the Orthodox ("Uniatism: Method of Union of the Past, and the Present Search for Full Communion, 1993", document 52). On the multilateral level, the Joint Working Group between the Roman Catholic Church and the World Council of Churches has recently published a study document entitled "The Challenge of Proselytism and the Calling to Common Witness", 1996 (document 72). In so doing, Catholics, like many Protestant and Orthodox groups, have expressed the desire to condemn all proselytism.

[11] Cecil M. Robeck, Jr, "The Assemblies of God and Ecumenical Cooperation, 1920-1965", in Wonsuk Ma and Robert P. Menzies, eds, *Pentecostalism in Context: Essays in Honor of William W. Menzies*, JPT Supplement Series 11, Sheffield, Sheffield Academic Press, 1997, 107-150.

[12] In its 21-29 May 1949 meeting in Paris, the executive committee of the World Pentecostal Conference (now called Pentecostal World Conference), unanimously adopted a two-page "Manifesto and Declaration" in which it outlined its "common purpose and objective". Included as point 6b was the following: "To demonstrate to the world the essential unity of Spirit – baptized believers fulfilling the prayer of the Lord Jesus Christ: 'That all may be one' John 17:21". This action was subsequently announced by the conference secretary, David J. du Plessis, in a report titled "World Pentecost holds its Third International Conference", which appeared in H.W. Greenway, ed., *World Pentecostal Conference – 1952* (no city, British Pentecostal Fellowship, 1952), p.6. A copy of the original "Manifesto and Declaration" is on file in the Archives of David du Plessis Center for Christian Spirituality at Fuller Theological Seminary, Pasadena, CA 91182, USA.

[13] See footnote 10 above.

[14] Papers were delivered on this topic by Kilian McDonnell, OSB, of Collegeville, Minnesota, USA ("Can Classical Pentecostals and Roman Catholics Engage in Common Witness?") and by Prof. Walter J. Hollenweger (Swiss Reformed), Krattigen, Switzerland ("Common Witness"). The Pentecostal team invited participation from Prof. Hollenweger for three reasons. He was formerly a Pentecostal pastor. He was formerly on staff of the Office of Mission and Evangelism of the World Council of Churches. He was for-

merly a professor in the field of mission and evangelism at the University of Birmingham, England, for many years, where his study of global Pentecostalism was a life-long passion. Other dialogue documents which have dealt with common witness are: "The Challenge of Proselytism and the Calling to Common Witness: A Study Document of the Joint Working Group", *The Ecumenical Review*, 48, 2, April 1996, 212-221; the ERCDOM report "The Evangelical-Roman Catholic Dialogue on Mission, 1977-1984", Eerdmans/Paternoster, 1986, and *IS*, 60, 1986/I-II, 71-97, and "Summons to Witness to Christ in Today's World: A Report of the Baptist-Roman Catholic International Conversations, 1984-1988" (see footnote 10 above).

66. Towards a Common Understanding of the Church

Second Phase, 1984-1990

Introduction
1. As representatives of the Reformed churches and of the Roman Catholic Church, we have carried on a dialogue whose purpose has been to deepen mutual understanding and to foster the eventual reconciliation of our two communities. Our conversations have been officially sponsored by the World Alliance of Reformed Churches and the Pontifical Council for Promoting Christian Unity. We have met in Rome, Italy (1984), Kappel-am-Albis, Switzerland (1985), Venice, Italy (1986), Cartigny, Switzerland (1987), and Ariccia, Italy (1988). This report emerged out of these encounters. Joint sub-committees met in Geneva (1989 and 1990) to take into account further suggestions of the commission for the report and to prepare it for publication.

2. An earlier phase of this dialogue took place under the same sponsorship between 1970 and 1977. That series of conversations produced a report entitled "The Presence of Christ in Church and World" (PCCW), which gave attention to issues such as the relationship of Christ to the church, the church as a teaching authority, the eucharist and the ministry. These earlier conversations discovered considerable common ground but left open questions pertaining to such matters as authority, order and church discipline. During approximately these same years representatives of the Lutheran World Federation joined Reformed and Roman Catholic participants in a trilateral dialogue to produce a report titled "The Theology of Marriage and the Problem of Mixed Marriages".[1]

3. In this second phase of dialogue just completed, we have concentrated more directly on the doctrine of the church. Certain ecclesiological issues touched upon in the earlier conversations are further treated. Building on this previous work, we have now gone deeper into the realm of ecclesiology, bringing important aspects of this subject into bilateral conversations for the first time. In this way, we have sought further to clarify the common ground between our communions as well as to identify our remaining differences. We hope these results will encourage further steps towards common testimony and joint ecumenical action.

4. We have discovered anew that the Roman Catholic Church and the Reformed churches are bound by manifold ties. Both communions confess Jesus Christ as Lord and Saviour, affirm the trinitarian faith of the apostolic church through the ages, and observe the one baptism into the threefold name. In recent years Reformed and Roman Catholic Christians have begun, in many places and at many different levels, to share the experience of fellowship and to seek fuller communion in truth and love for the

sake of our common service of Jesus Christ in the world. Our churches share more common ground than previously we were able to see.

5. Yet we have also realized anew that there remain disagreements and divergences between us. Some of these have emerged in the course of this dialogue and have been tackled head-on. Others have been perceived but left for substantive treatment in future dialogue.

6. Our communions are called to live and witness together to the fullest extent possible now and to work together towards future reconciliation. The common ground we share compels us to be open towards one another and to aspire to that communion into which the Spirit seeks to lead us. Each communion is bound in conscience to bear witness to the way in which it understands the gospel, the church, and the relationship between them, but at the same time to bear this witness in dialogue and mutual support. As we articulate our differing positions in love, we are challenged to a deeper fidelity to Jesus Christ.

7. This report presents the results of our dialogue in four chapters. Chapter 1 recalls the 16th-century Reformation and recounts the path taken by each communion since that time. The new openness of ecumenical relationships has helped us to see our respective histories in new perspectives and to clarify our relationships today. A new assessment of our common ground and of our disagreements is now possible; we are moving closer to being able to write our histories together.

8. The existence of this common ground gives us a context for discussing what remains controversial. Thus its content needs careful consideration. Chapter 2 seeks to accomplish this. This chapter focuses upon two areas of fundamental agreement: that our Lord Jesus Christ is the only mediator between God and humankind and that we receive justification by grace through faith. It follows that together we also confess the church as the community of all who are called, redeemed and sanctified through the one mediator.

9. A complete ecclesiology was beyond our scope in this phase of dialogue. But it seemed especially important to reconsider the relation between the gospel and the church in its ministerial and instrumental roles. Chapter 3 takes up this question and carries it through a series of topics: the church as *creatura verbi* and the church as sacrament of grace, continuity and discontinuity in church history, the question of church structure, and the ordering of ministry. Certain convergences are set forth, and the remaining issues noted for future consideration.

10. Finally, Chapter 4 sketches some ways forward. Our churches meet in many settings. In ways appropriate to each situation we may (1) take specific steps to deepen our existing fellowship; (2) address issues in such a way as to come closer to a reconciliation of memories; (3) find arenas for common witness; and (4) consider the nature of the unity we seek.

11. The dialogue commission offers this report to its sponsors in the hope that it may encourage us all to work for the unity of Christians which we believe is God's will.

1. Towards a reconciliation of memories

1.1. WHENCE HAVE WE COME?

12. Whence have our communions come? What paths have they followed – together and apart, interacting, reacting, and going their separate ways – over 450 years

to reach where they are today? This first chapter consists of accounts, written with consultation by each delegation, of our respective histories in relation to one another, as we see them now after five years of annual dialogues.

13. Today, in the late 20th century, our churches are not the same dialogue partners they were even a generation ago, let alone in the 16th century. In the past, we tended to read our histories both selectively and polemically. To some extent, we still do. We see the events through which we have lived through confessionally biased eyes. The present reality of our churches is explained and justified by these readings of the past. Yet we are beginning to be able to transcend these limitations (a) by our common use of the results of objective scholarly inquiry, and (b) by the dialogue our churches have had with each other in this consultation and elsewhere.

14. Historical scholarship today has not only produced fresh evidence concerning our respective roles in the Reformation and its aftermath. It also brings us together in broad agreement about sources, methods of inquiry, and warrants for drawing conclusions. A new measure of objectivity has become possible. If we still inevitably interpret and select, at least we are aware that we do and what that fact means as we strive for greater objectivity and more balanced judgment.

15. The method used in our present dialogue has also deepened our shared historical understanding. We first drafted our respective parts of this chapter separately. Reading and reviewing these drafts together we learned from each other and modified what we had written. We were reminded that over the centuries our forbears had often misunderstood each other's motives and language. We learned that our histories were sometimes a matter of action and reaction, but that at other times we followed separate paths. We occasionally heard each other speak vehemently and felt some of the passions that dictated the course of historical events and still in some ways drive us today.

16. All this has contributed to a certain reassessment of the past. We have begun to dissolve myths about each other, to clear away misunderstandings. We must go on from here, as our conclusion shows, to a *reconciliation* of memories, in which we will begin to share one sense of the past rather than two.

1.2. A REFORMED PERSPECTIVE

1.2.1. The ecclesiological concerns of the Reformers

17. The 16th-century Reformation was a response to a widespread demand for a general renewal of church and society. This demand had begun to be heard long before: it grew more insistent in the 14th and 15th centuries, led to the emergence of Reformed communities such as the earlier Waldensians and the Hussites, and was addressed by several church councils. In the 16th century it resulted in the establishment of the major Protestant churches in various parts of Europe. Thus the unity of the medieval Western church was shattered not only by the separation between the Protestant churches and the see of Rome, but also by the fact that the Reformation consisted of several reforming movements occurring at different times and places, often in conflict with one another, and leading to the different communions and confessional groups we know today.

18. Although the Reformed churches came to form a movement distinct from the Lutheran Reformation in Germany, they shared the same fundamental concerns: to affirm the sole headship of Jesus Christ over the church; to hear and proclaim the mes-

sage of the gospel as the one word of God which alone brings authentic faith into being; to reorder the life, practice and institutions of the church in conformity with the word of God revealed in scripture. In all this there was no intention of setting up a "new" church: the aim was to reform the church in obedience to God's will revealed in his word, to restore "the true face of the church" and, as a necessary part of this process, to depart from ecclesiastical teachings, institutions and practices which were held to have distorted the message of the gospel and obscured the proper nature and calling of the church. For many complex reasons, there resulted new forms of church organization with far-reaching social, political and economic ramifications – forms determined on the one hand by the fresh vision of the church's calling and commission, and on the other hand by rejection of a great deal that had developed in the previous centuries.

19. Among the chief affirmations of early Reformed ecclesiology were:
- the unity and universality of the one true church, to which those belong whom God has called or will call in Jesus Christ;
- the authority of Jesus Christ governing the church through the word in the power of his Spirit;
- the identification of an authentic "visible church" by reference to the true preaching of the word and the right administration of the two dominical sacraments of baptism and the Lord's supper;
- the importance of a proper church order, central to which was the office of the ministry of word and sacrament and, alongside it, the oversight exercised by elders sharing with the ministers of the word in governing the affairs of the church.

20. As a consequence of these affirmations, the Reformers rejected all in the life of the church which, in their understanding, obscured the unique mediatorship of Jesus Christ and seemed to give to the church an excessive role alongside him. The emphasis placed in the ensuing controversy on the authority of the church and its hierarchy led them to question the value of episcopal succession as an expression of the continuity of the church in the apostolic truth through the centuries. In particular, they rejected teachings such as the following:
- the appeal to the church's Tradition as an authority equal to scripture or belonging together with it;
- the universal authority of the pope;
- the claim that church councils constitute an infallible teaching authority;
- the canonical distinction between the office of a bishop and that of any other minister of the word and sacraments.

1.2.2. The emergence and spread of the Reformed churches

21. It is conceivable that many if not all of the Reformers' goals might have been realized without dividing the Western church into different confessional traditions. Their aims and insights could perhaps eventually have been accepted by the entire church and issued in a comprehensive, unified Reformation. In fact, this did not happen. The established leadership of the Western church was not generally prepared to agree to the amendments of doctrine, church order and practice which the Reformers sought. The Reformers for their part were convinced that nothing less than obedience to God and the truth of the gospel was at stake and interpreted resistance as unwillingness to undergo conversion and renewal. In addition, the process of reform proceeded

at different paces and took different forms in different local and national settings. The result was division and much mutual exclusion even among the Reformation churches.

22. In this and in the subsequent development of the Reformed churches, such factors as geography, politics, social and cultural development played a considerable part. The Reformation took place in a period of radical intellectual, cultural and political upheaval, which irreversibly altered the face of Europe and paved the way for the emergence of the modern world. The nascent Reformed churches of the 16th century both contributed to and were moulded by these wider movements. The countries most profoundly influenced by Reformed theology were prominent among those in which, in the 16th and 17th centuries, for better or for worse, the seeds of modern democracy were fostered, new forms of economic order developed, autonomous natural science came to its first great flowering, and the demand for religious tolerance became increasingly insistent. Where it became influential, the Reformed ethos stimulated commerce, challenged despotisms, encouraged parliamentary government and enhanced national consciousness.

23. In these developments, however, the Reformed churches showed that they could, in their own ways, fall victim to many of the same faults they criticized in the Roman Catholic Church. They became legitimators of sometimes oppressive political establishments, fell into clericalism, and grew intolerant of minority viewpoints. They were occasionally guilty of condemnations, burnings and banishment, for example, in regard to the Anabaptists in Switzerland, acts in many cases typical of their times but not to be excused on that account. The Reformed also sometimes lent themselves to various forms of national chauvinism, colonialism and racism. At times their criticisms of opponents (and especially of the papacy) grew intemperate even by the standards of an age given to vituperative language.

24. It has been claimed that the heritage and influence of Reformed thought contributed significantly alongside that of Renaissance and later Humanism to the shaping of modern Western culture. There is less agreement concerning the exact nature of this modernizing influence. It has been argued that in many respects the Reformation was more a medieval than a modern phenomenon, yet it set processes in motion that had far-reaching influence. Even the Enlightenment of the 18th century can properly be seen as owing much to these impulses, albeit in largely secularized form. So, too, can the rise of modern biblical criticism in the 18th century and its rapid development from the 19th onwards.

25. The Reformed churches themselves could not but be affected by all these direct and indirect outworkings of the Renaissance and the Reformation. It must be admitted that they have displayed – especially up to the middle of the 19th century but on occasion also since then as well – a tendency to divide and subdivide on matters of theological or ecclesiological principle. Rationalism, in the guise of a tendency to frame theology in tightly deductive systems, exacerbated this tendency. At times, rationalism gave rise in some Reformed churches to movements which even questioned such fundamental dogmatic convictions as the Trinity and the divinity of Jesus Christ. Another source of diversity lay in varying conceptions of proper church order, e.g., whether the government of the church should be synodal, congregational or episcopal.

26. The family of Reformed churches has continued to grow and spread up to the present. The expansion of the Reformed family is primarily due to the missionary movement of the last two centuries. In 1875, the Alliance of Reformed Churches was

founded as a rallying point for the worldwide Reformed and Presbyterian family. In 1970, it was widened to include the Congregational churches as well. The World Alliance of Reformed Churches counts today about 170 member churches. The majority of the member churches of the Alliance are to be found in Asia, Africa, Latin America and the Pacific. Moreover, the last century has witnessed major efforts towards reunion within the Reformed family, and since 1918 various Reformed churches have entered transconfessional unions. Among the member churches of the Alliance there are today also some 16 united churches, from the Evangelical Church of the Czech Brethren (1918) to the United Reformed Church in the United Kingdom (1981). At the same time it has also become increasingly more aware of the challenge to search after a fuller ecumenical unity. It is mindful of the abiding heritage of the Reformation, but at the same time of the common calling of all Christians today to confess and hold aloft that to which all adhere and in which all believe, namely the good news of Jesus Christ, "the one Word of God which we have to hear and obey in life and in death" (theological declaration of Barmen, 1934).

27. In pursuing its theological task, the World Alliance of Reformed Churches draws on the resources supplied by the rich tradition of Reformed theology through the centuries from Zwingli and Calvin and their contemporary Reformers to such figures of the recent past as Karl Barth, Josef Hromadka and Reinhold Niebuhr. It also stands in the heritage of witness reflected in the confessions of the Reformed churches from the 16th century onwards and seeks to continue that witness faithfully today. It does not do so, however, in the spirit of a narrow traditionalist Reformed confessionalism. Rather, it is open ecumenically and concerned to face contemporary and future social, cultural and ethical challenges. The contribution of Reformed theology to today's churches does not consist merely in the maintenance of theological traditions or in the preservation of ecclesiastical institutions for their own sake, but in being what Karl Barth called "the modest, free, critical and happy science" (*Evangelical Theology*, ch. 1), which enquires into the reality of God in relation to us human beings individually and in community in the light of Jesus Christ, Emmanuel, "God with us".

1.2.3. Contemporary Reformed attitudes towards the Roman Catholic Church

28. Before the Second Vatican Council, with notable exceptions, the general Reformed view was that the Roman Catholic Church had not faced the real challenge of the Reformation and remained essentially "unreformed". This conviction was reinforced in the modern era on the doctrinal level by the definitions of the dogmas of papal infallibility (1870), the immaculate conception of the Virgin Mary (1854), and her bodily assumption (1950). In practical terms, the same conviction grew from the experience of Reformed minorities in countries dominated by Roman Catholicism. Up to this day the memory of the persecution of Reformed minorities plays a significant role. The development of the two traditions largely in isolation – even when alongside each other in the same country – increased the inclination of Reformed Christians and churches to view the Roman Catholic Church in terms of its reaction against the Reformation, and reinforced negative attitudes towards Roman Catholic teaching, piety and practice.

29. Signs of a change in perspective began to appear in the 19th century, but remained sporadic. Contacts increased and the desire for a new mutual understanding became more apparent in the 20th century, not least as an offshoot of the active role

played by many Reformed churches from the beginnings of the ecumenical movement. But it is really only since the pontificate of John XXIII and the events surrounding the Second Vatican Council that a genuinely new atmosphere has developed between the Reformed and the Roman Catholic churches. The presence of Reformed observers at the Council and at other occasions since, the experience of ecumenical contact, shared activity, worship and dialogue at many different levels from the local congregation to international commissions, and increasing cooperation and collaboration between Reformed and Roman Catholic scholars in work of exegetical, historical, systematic and practical theology – all this has helped to break down misunderstandings and caricatures of the present-day reality of the Roman Catholic Church. In particular, these developments have helped the Reformed to appreciate the seriousness with which the Roman Catholic Church has placed the word of God at the centre of its life, not least in modern liturgical reforms.

30. In general it can be said today that a process of reassessment and re-evaluation of the Roman Catholic Church has been taking place among the Reformed churches in the last decades, though not proceeding at the same pace everywhere. There are within the Reformed family those whose attitude to the Roman Catholic Church remains essentially negative: some because they remain to be convinced that the modern development of the Roman Catholic Church has really addressed the issues of the Reformation, and others because they have been largely untouched by the ecumenical exchanges of recent times and have therefore not been challenged or encouraged to reconsider their traditional stance. But this is only one part of the picture. Others in the Reformed tradition have sought to engage in a fresh constructive and critical evaluation both of the contemporary teaching and practice of the Roman Catholic Church and of the classical controverted issues.

31. There is on the Reformed side an increasing sense that while the Reformation was at the time theologically and historically necessary, the division of the Western church should not be accepted as the last word; that it is at best one-sided to read that history as if all the truth lay on the side of the Reformers and none at all on the side of their opponents and critics within the Roman Catholic camp; that there have been both in the more remote and more recent past many positive developments in the Roman Catholic Church itself; that the situation today presents new challenges for Christian witness and service which ought so far as possible to be answered together rather than in separation; and – perhaps most important of all – that Reformed Christians are called to search together with their Roman Catholic separated brothers and sisters for the unity which Christ wills for his church, both in terms of contemporary witness and in terms of reconsidering traditional disagreements. Theological dialogue, joint working groups on doctrinal and ethical issues, and programmes of joint action undertaken by some Reformed churches together with the Roman Catholic Church in recent years – all these reflect this new climate, witness to a new and more positive evaluation of the Roman Catholic Church as an ecumenical partner, and hold out hope of further increase in mutual understanding in the future.

32. This is not to say that all problems between Reformed and Roman Catholic churches have already been resolved; it is to say that a search for solutions is underway and being undertaken together by both sides. One question requiring further consideration is whether our two traditions from their separation in the 16th century onwards need still to be seen as mutually exclusive. Or can they not rather be seen as

reconcilable? Can we not look upon each other as partners in a search for full communion? In that search we may be led to discover complementary aspects in our two traditions, to combine appreciation for the questions and insights of the Reformers with recognition that the Reformed can also learn from the Roman Catholic Church, and to realize that Reformed and Roman Catholics need each other in their attempt to be more faithful to the gospel. Those who have begun to think in this way are attempting to reconcile their heritage as heirs of the Reformation with their experience of fellowship with and learning from their sisters and brothers in the Roman Catholic Church. They are asking: Can our common faith set the questions which have divided and in part still divide us in a wider horizon of reconciliation?

1.3. A ROMAN CATHOLIC PERSPECTIVE

1.3.1. Ecclesiological and reforming concerns of Roman Catholics at the time of the Reformation

33. What was the condition of the Western church on the eve of the Reformation? Contemporaries found much to criticize. So have subsequent historians. Indeed, one of the most striking characteristics of the age was the vehemence of its rhetoric against certain abuses. Efforts were of course being made to change things for the better. Reform within the Catholic church was undertaken in an urgent and more systematic way, however, only after the council of Trent (1545-63) began to address it. But by that time the Protestant Reformation was already well established and underway.

34. Especially denounced at that time were the venality and political and military involvements of some of the popes and members of the curia; the absence of bishops from their dioceses; their often ostentatious wealth and neglect of pastoral duties; the ignorance of many of the lower clergy; the often scandalous lives of clergy, including bishops and certain popes; the disedifying rivalry among the religious orders; pastoral malpractice through misleading teaching about the efficacy of certain rites and rituals; the irrelevance and aridity of theological speculation in the universities and the presence of these same defects in the pulpit; the lack of any organized catechesis for the laity; and a popular piety based to a large extent on superstitious practices. Judgment on the church just before the Reformation has, therefore, been severe – and justly so.

35. Efforts at reform remained sporadic, uncoordinated, or confined to restricted segments of society. Among these efforts was the Observantist movement in the mendicant orders, which sought to restore the simplicity of their original inspiration. Furthermore a reform of the diocesan clergy in Spain was well underway by 1517. The Humanist movement encouraged a reform of theology and ministry that would depend more directly on biblical texts; it advocated a reform of education for both clergy and laity, and proposed an ideal of piety that insisted upon greater interiority and simplicity in religious practice. In the early stages of the Reformation the urgency of the situation was reflected also in the attempts of Pope Adrian VI (1522-23) to implement reform in the curia and elsewhere. The very vehemence with which its abuses were denounced in some sectors of the church and society indicates, moreover, a deepened religious sensitivity. In such a perspective the great leaders of both the Reformation and the Catholic Reform must be seen as products of the concerns of the age into which they were born and, to that extent, in continuity with those concerns and, indeed, with each other.

36. How, then, can we explain the resistance met by the proposals of Reformers like Luther, Zwingli and Calvin? It is at this point that their discontinuity with previous efforts at reform emerges. While those earlier efforts concentrated on discipline, education, pastoral practice and similar matters, Luther addressed himself first and foremost to doctrine, as later did Zwingli and Calvin. Many people, and not only theologians, were taken by surprise and were unwilling to accept this sudden shift to reform of doctrine and especially Luther's emphasis on the doctrine of justification. They were shocked by the implication that the church had for centuries been in error about the true meaning of the gospel. Moreover, Luther's case was soon embroiled in a thicket of personal and theological rivalries and of imperial-papal politics, so that fair procedures and the serenity required for docility to the Spirit were tragically and almost irretrievably compromised at the opening moment. At practically that same moment a vituperative rhetoric from both sides began to dominate theological exchanges.

37. In such an atmosphere the demands and proposals of the Reformers were often also misunderstood by Catholics and then just as often distorted into caricatures. Direct access to their writings was at best piecemeal, at worst thought unnecessary. This meant that almost without exception, the centrality and dramatically evangelical nature of the issue of justification for the Reformers was not grasped. Very few Catholics really understood that for the Reformers what was at stake was not simply this or that doctrine, practice or institution but the very gospel itself. Thus, for Catholics "reform" continued to be conceived in pre-Reformation terms as addressing disciplinary and pastoral issues in their established form. They understood their engagement with the Reformation as refuting its "doctrinal errors".

38. In Catholic circles attention turned more or less immediately to ecclesiological issues. Up to the time of the Reformation reflection on the church had fallen into two main categories. The first consisted of polemical and apologetical works dealing with church order that arose out of conflicts between popes and either bishops or secular leaders. The argumentation was juridical and political. These works, which provided a ready-made, though theologically and biblically inadequate, defence of certain church institutions, were then utilized against the Reformers.

39. The second consisted of assumptions that were more properly theological in nature, but that had become embedded in writings and practice in a much less systematic way. These assumptions were, however, broadly operative in the minds of many persons, and they must be taken into account if we are to understand Catholic resistance to the Reformation. Some of these assumptions and the conclusions drawn from them were as follows:

- Christ founded the church, establishing it on the apostles, who are the basis of the episcopal order of ministry and authority in the church. In this order the bishop of Rome had more than primacy of honour, though the precise nature, extent and function of this primacy was much debated.
  Therefore the proposals of the Reformers concerning church order appeared to be an attack on the apostolic foundation of the church.
- Christ promised unity for the church. Consensus in doctrine, extending through the ages, was a hallmark of the Spirit's work and a sign of Christ's unfailing presence in the church. Therefore the turmoil accompanying the Reformation and the conflict among some of the Reformers themselves were taken as proof positive that the Spirit of God was not at work among them.

- Although the church lived under scripture, the church was chronologically prior to the writings of the New Testament and had recognized since earliest times that it itself as a community, especially when assembled in council, was the authoritative interpreter of the divine word.

  In contrast, the Reformers seemed to arrogate to themselves the right to interpret scripture in a way at variance with the continuing tradition of the community, and they did not seem to provide any warrant for their interpretation that was necessarily grounded in the community.
- Bishops held primary responsibility for church polity.

  In contrast, Luther, Zwingli and the English Reformers appeared to deliver the church into the hands of secular princes and magistrates, thus threatening to reduce the church to a mere instrument of secular politics.

1.3.2. The council of Trent and the Roman Catholic reform

40. Within only a few years after the beginning of the Reformation, the seriousness of the crisis had become apparent to many. Less apparent were the means to address it effectively. Particularly from Germany, however, there soon came the cry for a council. Pope Paul III convoked the council of Trent in December 1645. By that time – a full generation after Luther's Ninety-five Theses – positions had become so hardened and embittered that reconciliation was, humanly speaking, impossible. Responsibility for the long delay in convocation must be ascribed in part to the complex political situation and to the ambivalent or obstructionist attitudes of some Protestant leaders, but lies principally with the fearful, vacillating and self-serving policies of Pope Clement VII (1523-34). By the time Trent began its work, Zwingli had died (1531), Luther had less than a year to live, and other Reformers (such as Calvin) were already utterly convinced that Rome was unwilling to undertake the profound reform they wanted.

41. The council of Trent was destined to last, with long periods of interruption, over eighteen years, finally concluding in December 1563. Attempts to have Protestants participate failed for a number of reasons, with the result that membership in the council was restricted to Catholics. This fact indicated that the religious divisions were already deep and widespread. In a situation like this, the course of the council almost perforce helped confirm and sharpen the divisions, just as the various Protestant confessions of faith had done and would continue to do.

42. Trent addressed both doctrinal and disciplinary issues. Among its doctrinal decrees, the most fully discussed and the most earnestly researched was the decree on justification, approved in 1547. The complaint of Luther and others that the church in its actual practice taught a Pelagian doctrine of justification was taken by the principal authors of the decree with utmost seriousness. Every effort was made to avoid formulations that would fall into that heresy, yet considerable care was also exercised to insist on some measure of human responsibility, under grace, in the process of salvation. In its other doctrinal decrees, Trent gave an extraordinary amount of attention to the sacraments because they were perceived as falling under special attack.

43. The council of Trent was animated by the conviction that it had the special guidance of the Spirit, and it considered itself to be the special vehicle of the continuing action of Christ in the church. Trent's explicit emphasis on the continuity of the church in practice, doctrine and structure with the apostolic age was more pronounced than in any previous council. This emphasis prevented serious consideration of most of the

changes the Reformers found to be required by their reading of the New Testament. At the council a certain reciprocity of word and church was taken for granted, as given and witnessed in both the early and contemporary church. The council, unlike the Reformers, ascribed apostolic authority to certain "traditions", although it refrained from providing a list of them.

44. Trent was notably concerned not to condemn any doctrinal position held by "Catholic theologians" and, although it never mentioned a single Reformer by name, it condemned what it thought were Protestant errors. Its decrees must, therefore, be interpreted with great caution. For several reasons, including the wide range of opinions in the council, Trent made practically no direct and explicit pronouncements about the ecclesiological disputes then raging. However, the very fact that the council took place was itself an expression of the self-understanding of the church.

45. In its decrees "concerning reform", Trent articulated its presumptions in generally juridical terms. It meant these decrees, however, to serve better ministerial practice and more effective care of souls. In reaffirming traditional structures, Trent at the same time undertook a certain redefinition of some of them. Perhaps the most sweeping, though implicit, ecclesiological redefinition in the council and during that era was that the church was primarily a *pastoral* institution. Trent sought especially to direct bishops to a properly pastoral appreciation of their office. It assigned to them the preaching of the word as their principal task, an assignment taken with the utmost seriousness by many post-Tridentine bishops, following the example set by Charles Borromeo and others.

46. Although Trent had given the greatest importance to the responsibility of bishops to proclaim the word of God (cf. Sessio XXIV, 11 Nov. 1563, can. IV De Reformatione; COD [1973] p.763), the doctrine of the sacrament of order promulgated a few months sooner in the same year did not provide any place for the ministry of the word, so much was the council worried about defending the doctrine of sacraments (Sessio XXIII, 15 July 1563, De Ordine, COD [1973], pp.742ff.). This fact masks what was actually happening in Catholicism at the time and for several centuries thereafter. In fact, the ministry of the word was vigorously pursued, not so much because of the criticism of the Reformers as because in this regard the same reforming ideals impelled both Protestants and Catholics, even though much Catholic preaching may not have been biblical in a sense that the Reformed could recognize.

47. This development in the ministry of the word illustrates the fact that Catholic reform in the 16th and 17th centuries was much broader than the council of Trent and cannot be simply equated with it. That reform promoted, among many other things, a great flowering of spiritualities and cultivation of religious experience, a vast programme of catechesis, extensive systems of schools for laity and clergy, as well as other new forms of ministry and evangelization. Impressive though the reform was in so many ways, however, it was not without its failures and false steps. For instance: many earlier abuses like the nepotistic practices of the papal court and the seignorial style of the episcopacy seemed little affected for the better; the various inquisitions had terribly deleterious effects resulting from repressive measures that included confiscation of goods, banishments and executions. The reading of the Bible in the vernacular, although not always forbidden to laity (contrary to that which is often asserted), was subject nevertheless to some extremely strict conditions, which in practice discouraged the laity. Those who were educated were able to read in Latin, as did the clergy, but

those who would read it in the vernacular were often considered suspect. Moreover, the doctrinal and disciplinary decrees of Trent itself often came to be interpreted with a rigour and a partisanship the council did not intend.

1.3.3. From Trent to the present

48. Post-Tridentine partisanship was manifested in various ways, not the least of which was the manner of stressing divergent understandings of the church. For example, when Roman Catholic apologists focused on the notes of the church – *one, holy, catholic and apostolic* – Catholic positions were presented in ways intended to refute the ecclesiological claims of their Protestant contemporaries as well as to convey what Roman Catholics believed about the church. Thus, in contrast to the diversity of Protestant movements, Roman Catholics were united in one, visible church under the pope; where the Reformers championed justification by faith alone, Roman Catholics maintained also the role of good works in sanctification (in being made holy) and insisted on the grace conveyed by a worthy reception of the sacraments; where the newly formed Protestant churches had broken with the apostolic succession of the universal church, the Roman Catholic Church had retained the threefold apostolic ministry of episcopate, presbyterate and diaconate; where the Reformers relied on their individual interpretation of scripture, Roman Catholics claimed to preserve the entirety of catholic doctrine transmitted from Christ through the ages.

49. Such one-sided argumentation (which has generally been abandoned by Roman Catholic theologians since Vatican II) was apologetically successful – if not in convincing Protestants – at least in assuring Roman Catholics that theirs was the one and only true church of Jesus Christ. Moreover, post-Tridentine apologetics capitalized on the divisiveness within Protestantism in contrast to the organic unity of Roman Catholicism. At the same time, post-Tridentine Catholicism became ever more juridical in its approach to a wide range of issues and ecclesiology increasingly institution-oriented and papally centred.

50. This "pyramidal" ecclesiology, which emerged in the context of rising nationalism, received considerable reinforcement in the 19th century when both the spiritual prerogatives and the political power of papacy were subject to repeated attacks. Many ecclesiologists hastened to defend both the spiritual independence and the doctrinal authority of the popes. Simultaneously, on the popular level, the pope was considered the symbol of Roman Catholic unity, his slightest command a matter of unquestioning obedience. In the eyes of many, both within and outside the Roman Catholic Church, papal centrism appeared to have been absolutized by the First Vatican Council's teaching on the "primacy and infallible teaching authority of the Roman pontiff". Due to the adjournment of the council shortly after this definition, Vatican I did not have sufficient opportunity to take up the broader ecclesiological issues in the schema *De Ecclesia*, which was proposed for consideration but never adopted.

51. In fact, the teaching of the First Vatican Council in this regard is much more nuanced than either its ultramontane proponents or its antipapal opponents seem to have realized. For example, Vatican I did not teach that "the pope is infallible", as is popularly imagined. Rather it taught that the pope can, under carefully specified and limited circumstances, officially exercise the infallibility divinely given to the church as a whole, in order to decide questions of faith and morals for the universal church.

52. Forces already then at work have had profound effects on the Catholic church in the 20th century, influencing ecclesiology as well. Renewal movements relating to biblical studies, liturgy, theology, pastoral concerns, ecumenism and other factors paved the way for the Second Vatican Council (1962-65). Influenced also by the ecumenical movement, this council's rich presentation of the church in *Lumen Gentium* differed significantly from apologetical approaches to the past. Concentrating not just on institutional aspects, but on basic biblical and patristic insights on the church, *Lumen Gentium* re-emphasized, among other themes, the notion of the church as the people of God and as a communion. All members of the people of God, it said, participate, even if in different ways, in the life of Christ and in his role as prophet, priest and king (*LG*, nos. 9-13). The council described the dimensions of collegiality in which the bishops of the whole world live in communion with one another and with the pope, the head of the episcopal college. While reiterating again the primacy of the bishop of Rome, the council made clear that the bishops also "exercise their own proper authority for the good of their faithful, indeed even for the good of the whole church" (*LG*, no. 22). In focusing on an ecclesiology of communion, the council was also able to give fresh insights on relations already existing, despite separations, with Christians of other churches and ecclesial communities – a real though imperfect communion that exists because of baptism (*Unitatis Redintegratio*, no. 22).

53. As already seen, Catholics agree that there was need for reform in the church in the 16th century, and acknowledge the fact that church authorities did not undertake the reform which might have prevented the tragic divisions that took place. At the same time the Roman Catholic Church has never agreed with some of the steps taken by the Reformers relating to their separation from the Roman Catholic communion, nor with certain theological positions that developed in Reformed communities, and seeks dialogue with the Reformed on those issues. The various ways in which reform and renewal have taken place within the Catholic church since the 16th century illustrate resources that existed for bringing renewal from within. Thus, while the council of Trent came too late to avoid divisions, it clarified Catholic doctrine and introduced reforms which have had lasting effects in the church. The birth of new religious orders from the 16th century to the 20th, and the renewal of older religious orders, gave fresh impulses to missionary activity. From the 16th century, evangelization has increased. Catholic missionaries, sometimes at the cost of their lives, brought the gospel to lands where it had never been heard before. In traditionally Christian countries, other groups emphasized apostolates of service to the poor and of education of the young or the renewal of contemplative life. Movements of lay spirituality and Catholic action have flourished, especially in the 20th century, along with movements for liturgical, biblical and pastoral renewal. Such developments and many others paved the way for the significant reform and renewal brought about in the Catholic church through the Second Vatican Council which continue to be implemented in the church today.

1.3.4. Contemporary Roman Catholic attitudes towards the Reformed churches

54. The ecumenical experience of Roman Catholics also gradually increased, sometimes intentionally through such efforts as the Week of Prayer for Christian Unity, and sometimes circumstantially as in the experiences of the second world war, when Christians from different churches suffered and died together as prisoners and refugees. While such shared experiences helped to develop the ecumenical climate in which Vat-

ican II met, even the most prophetic could not have predicted that the council would provide what turned out to be a pervasive reorientation in Roman Catholic liturgy and life, theology and thought.

55. Prior to Vatican II, the attitude of most Roman Catholics towards Protestants in general, and members of Reformed churches in particular, was negative, though the degree of negativity ranged from overt hostility in some places to guarded acceptance in others. Friendship between members of the two traditions tended to be based on family, business and social relationships, in which religious differences were frequently left undiscussed. Genuine theological dialogue, though not unknown, was comparatively rare; more common were polemical exchanges in which Roman Catholics criticized and sometimes caricatured the history, doctrine and worship of their Protestant "adversaries".

56. Roman Catholic negativity towards the Reformed churches had a number of intertwined bases. On the ecclesiastical level, the most obvious focus of contention was the Reformed rejection of the episcopacy and the papacy that was also sometimes expressed in terms that Roman Catholics found extremely offensive. Another cause of opposition was the fact that the Reformed principle of sola scriptura resulted in a repudiation of many Roman Catholic teachings and practices, such as the sacrifice of the mass, Marian devotions and the earning of indulgences.

57. These religious differences were further intensified by social, economic and political disparities. In areas where Roman Catholics were a minority, they frequently felt themselves oppressed by members of the "Protestant establishment". The separate and frequently antagonistic development of the Reformed and Roman Catholic communities tended to perpetuate stereotypes and, in some cases, still continues to impede dialogue even today.

58. Although there were some instances of ecumenical dialogue between Reformed and Roman Catholic theologians prior to the Second Vatican Council, it was the Council that provided the significant breakthrough for overcoming the long-standing antagonism in Reformed-Roman Catholic relationships. While the Council primarily aimed at achieving an *aggiornamento* within the Roman Catholic Church, the presence of observers from other Christian communions, including Reformed churches, was a constant reminder that ecclesial reform and renewal are not only internal concerns but have ecumenical implications as well.

59. In particular, *Unitatis Redintegratio* noted that the churches and communities coming from the Reformation "are bound to the Catholic church by an especially close relationship as a result of the long span of earlier centuries when Christian people lived together in ecclesiastical communion" (no. 19). It recognized that the Spirit of Christ has not refrained from using them as a means of salvation (no. 3). The Council encouraged Catholics to work for the reunion of all Christians through ecumenical dialogue, a disavowal of prejudices, and cooperation on projects of mutual concern. Instead of repeating the polemical accusations that charged Protestant Christians with the sin of separation, the Council acknowledged them as "separated brethren" *(fratres seiunucti)*, justified by their faith through baptism, who reverence the written word of God, share in the life of grace, receive the gifts of the Holy Spirit, celebrate Christ's death and resurrection when they gather for the Lord's supper, and witness to Christ through the moral uprightness of their lives, through their works of charity and their efforts for justice and peace in the world.

60. During the years since Vatican II, this process of reconciliation has been carried on in different ways and at various levels – local, national, regional, international. For example, Reformed and Roman Catholics have prayed together, have been involved in theological dialogue at various levels; they have joined in producing Bible translations; they have collaborated on a variety of projects of social concern, economic justice and political witness. At the international level, the efforts of the dialogue co-sponsored by the Vatican Secretariat for Promoting Christian Unity and the World Alliance of Reformed Churches were recognized by Pope John Paul II in a letter to Dr James McCord, president of the World Alliance of Reformed Churches, on the occasion of its general council in Ottawa, in July 1982:

> The way upon which we have embarked together is without return, we can only move forward, that is why we strive to manifest unity more perfectly and more visibly, just as God wants it for all those who believe in him. (Secretariat for Promoting Christian Unity, *Information Service*, 51, 1983, p.30)

61. In the scholarly world, these efforts at reconciliation have been accompanied by new interpretations of Reformation history and theology. For example, Roman Catholic theologians today generally acknowledge that many of the issues raised by the Reformers urgently needed to be faced and resolved. Similarly, Roman Catholic historians, while not agreeing with all aspects of their thought, have become more sympathetic to Zwingli and to Calvin, no longer seeing them chiefly as rebels against ecclesial authority but as Reformers who felt obliged by their understanding of the gospel to continue their efforts to reform the church at all costs. The "zeal that animated these two outstanding religious personalities of Swiss history" was favourably noted by Pope John Paul II on the occasion of his pastoral visit to the Catholic church of Switzerland in 1984:

> The legacy of the thought and ethical convictions particular to each of these two men continues to be forcefully and dynamically present in various parts of Christianity. On the one hand, we cannot forget that the work of their reform remains a permanent challenge among us and makes our ecclesiastical division always present, but on the other hand, no one can deny that elements of the theology and spirituality of each of them maintain deep ties between us. (Secretariat for Promoting Christian Unity, *Information Service*, 55, 1984, p.47)

1.4. CONCLUSION

62. As mentioned at the beginning of this chapter, these reviews of our respective histories, even when sketched so briefly, have shown us "whence we have come", so that we can better understand where we are – so that we can better understand what yet needs to be done in reassessing our past. We see more clearly how our respective self-understandings have been so largely formed by confessional historiographies of the 16th and 17th centuries. These differing self-interpretations have, in turn, fostered the establishment of whole sets of different values, symbols, assumptions and institutions – in a word, different religious and ecclesial cultures. The result is that today, as in the past, the same words, even the same biblical expressions, are sometimes received and understood by us in quite different ways.

63. The very recognition that this is the case marks important progress in our attempt to rid our memories of significant resentments and misconceptions. We need to set ourselves more diligently, however, to the task of reconciling these memories, by writing together the story of what happened in the 16th century, with attention not only

to the clash of convictions over doctrine and church order, but with attention also as to how in the aftermath our two churches articulated their respective understandings into institutions, culture and the daily lives of believers. But, above all, for the ways in which our divisions have caused a scandal, and been an obstacle to the preaching of the gospel, we need to ask forgiveness of Christ and of each other.

2. Our common confession of faith

2.1. OUR LORD JESUS CHRIST: THE ONLY MEDIATOR BETWEEN GOD AND HUMANKIND

64. Before moving on to matters which are still points of disagreement and divergence between our churches, we as a dialogue commission propose to confess together our faith in Christ. We give this affirmation of faith the title "confession" even though it is neither a confession in the ecclesial sense nor a complete statement of faith. We do so because we are convinced that the importance of what we are able to say together merits such a title.

65. We make this confession of faith, wishing to manifest publicly our desire to re-examine the reasons which brought about our separation in the past and to assess whether or not they are still of such a nature as to justify our division. Jesus Christ, in whose name our forbears separated themselves from one another, is also the one who unites us in a community of forgiveness and of kinship. We wish to voice our conviction that what unites us as Christians is more important, more essential, than that which separates us as Roman Catholics and Reformed. Even if full communion is not yet granted us, we cannot define our relations to each other simply in terms of separation and division.

66. We make this confession, moreover, mindful of this world of ours, so as to give common witness before it. With respect for all who seek God, however, God is named for them, or even if for them God cannot as yet be named, we wish to speak the good news of salvation brought in Jesus Christ by God seeking out humankind. In that good news we Christians already find our reconciliation and the strength to work for the fuller reconciliation of all with God and with each other.

67. This confession involves on our part the recognition of the authority of the scriptures, as these have been identified by the early church, to whose teaching we desire to remain obedient. We recall what was said on this subject in the report of the first phase of our dialogue (PCCW, nos. 25-33). In the same way we recognize together in the teaching of the ancient church, the force of a *norma normata*, i.e., an authority which is subject to the authority of the scripture, and we desire to maintain that teaching in its purity. The teaching of the church ought to be an authentic explanation of the trinitarian and christological affirmations of the early confessions of faith and the early councils (cf. on this subject, PCCW, nos. 34-38).

2.1.1. Christ, Mediator and Reconciler

68. Before all humankind, our sisters and brothers, we announce the death of the Lord (cf. 1 Cor. 11:26) and proclaim his resurrection from the dead (cf. Rom. 10:9; Acts 2:32, 3:15). In that mystery of death and resurrection we confess the event which saves humanity, that is, liberates it from the distress in which it is imprisoned by sin and establishes it in communion of life with God. That event reveals *who God is, who we are and who Christ is* as mediator between God and humankind.

69. a) God is the one who "chose us (in Christ) before the foundation of the world... He destined us in love to be his sons through Jesus Christ" (Eph. 1:4-5),[2] a God of tenderness and mercy, who wills not the death of the sinner, but rather that the sinner should be converted and live. God is the one who has loved us unto death: indeed, in the person of Jesus Christ, God himself died on the cross for, "in Christ, God was reconciling the world to himself" (2 Cor. 5:19). But this was not the "death of God" proclaimed in recent times: it was the death of the Just One fallen into the hands of evil persons, and faithful to his mission to the end. Jesus died a death which is a victory over the death which touches all. God's omnipotence is revealed in the deepest weakness of human nature, assumed in solidarity with us. If the death of Jesus is the work of sinners, God from all eternity has made it one with the design of salvation, accomplishing that life-giving work by raising Jesus from the dead. Placed at the heart of human violence, Jesus by his love has transformed the work of death into the work of life.

b) The death and resurrection of Jesus also reveal to us who we are: not merely creatures who are object of God's benevolence, but also human beings capable of sin, historically imprisoned in the bonds of a sin which is our curse. From the beginning we hid ourselves from God, and this is why God is hidden from us. It is not that God is distant and inaccessible, but that we reject the God who is too near and too explicit. This awareness of alienation and exile in the midst of faith we call sin. We recognize that there is a betrayal of God's trust in us and that God's heart is saddened by our separation. From this condition we cannot free ourselves by our own strength. This is why the need and expectation of a mediator are central to the old covenant, where the law, sacrifices, prophecies, wisdom are ways of mediating between a living God and a humanity subject to sin and death. But none of these paths fully reach the goal. Because of sin, the law intended for life judges, condemns and leads to death. Substitute sacrifices are endlessly repeated. Prophecies lag, bide their time, fall silent. Wisdom remains an ideal. In Jesus, the unique mediator, in his death and resurrection we are radically freed from this situation: the way of true life is opened to us anew.

c) The death and resurrection of Jesus finally reveal who Jesus himself is, the one Mediator between God and humanity, that is, the one who comes to reconcile us with God. This is why we accept together the confession of faith of the New Testament. "For there is one God, and there is one Mediator between God and men, the man Christ Jesus, who gave himself as a ransom for all" (1 Tim. 2:5-6). We confess that "there is no other name under heaven given among men by which we must be saved" (Acts 4:12).

70. Mediation and reconciliation have been embodied and located, named and personified in Jesus of Nazareth, whence it was thought at that time nothing good could come; condemned and executed at Jerusalem, which God has since David's time identified as the place of God's peace; resurrected by the power of God; and placed at God's right hand. This is the news, still surprising and overwhelming, which constitutes the gospel; of this the church is the beneficiary and the herald.

71. We therefore confess together that Christ, established as mediator, achieves our reconciliation in all its dimensions: God reconciling humanity; human beings reconciled with each other, and humanity reconciled with God.

– On the one hand, indeed, in and through Jesus Christ we have reconciliation with God. For "every good endowment and every perfect gift is from above, coming

down from the Father of lights" (James 1:17). For "all this is from God, who through Christ reconciled us to himself..." (2 Cor. 5:18); "In him we have redemption through his blood, the forgiveness of our trespasses" (Eph. 1:7).
- On the other hand, in and through Jesus Christ, we have reconciliation among ourselves, "for he is our peace, who has made us both one". In his flesh he "has broken down the dividing wall of hostility... that he might create in himself one new man in place of the two, so making peace, and might reconcile us both to God in one body through the cross, thereby bringing the hostility to an end. And he came and preached peace to you who were far off and peace to those who were near" (Eph. 2:14-17). The vertical and horizontal dimensions of reconciliation are interdependent: just as hostility is the consequence and sign of separation from God, so reconciliation in peace among human beings is the fruit and sign of reconciliation with God. From Christ we receive the gift of reconciliation which aims to extend to all. To this we witness together in faith.
- Finally, thanks to Jesus Christ, Jews and Gentiles "both have access in one Spirit to the Father" (Eph. 2:18). In and through Christ we can offer ourselves "as a living sacrifice, holy and acceptable to God, which is... spiritual worship" (Rom. 12:1). For he "gave himself up for us, a fragrant offering and sacrifice to God" (Eph. 5:2). Jesus, the Christ, marks the end of condemnation by the law, because he is "... our righteousness and sanctification and redemption" (1 Cor. 1:30); he marks the end of the sacrifices of the law because "he entered once for all into the holy place, taking... his own blood, thus securing an eternal redemption" (Heb. 9:12); Christ marks the end of waiting on prophecies because he fulfills all that was written of him "... in the law of Moses, and the prophets and the psalms" (cf. Luke 24:44); Christ marks the end of the anonymity of wisdom, for he himself is the "wisdom of God" (1 Cor. 1:24).

72. We confess together that just as God is unique, the Mediator and Reconciler between God and humankind is unique and that the fullness of reconciliation is entire and perfect in him. Nothing and nobody could replace or duplicate, complete or in any way add to the unique mediation accomplished "once for all" (Heb. 9:12) by Christ, "mediator of a new covenant" (Heb. 9:15; cf. 8:6 and 12:24). This mediation is still present and active in the person of the risen Christ who "is able for all time to save those who draw near to God through him, since he always lives to make intercession for them" (Heb. 7:25).

2.1.2. The work of Christ reveals that he is the Son within the Trinity

73. In his life and in his death Jesus is revealed as the Son par excellence of God, the one who alone knows the Father and whom the Father alone knows (cf. Matt. 11:27), who can address himself to God saying "Abba, Father" (Mark 14:36). Thus in the light of Jesus' resurrection and exaltation, Christians have confessed that he has been made Christ and Lord (cf. Acts 2:36) and that he is the one to whom are applied the words of the Psalm: "Thou art my Son, today I have begotten thee" (Acts 13:33; cf. Heb. 1:5). He is, then, this one whom God has sent us (cf. Gal. 4:4); he who "though he was in the form of God did not count equality with God a thing to be grasped, but emptied himself, taking the form of a servant, being born in the likeness of men. And being found in human form he humbled himself and became obedient unto death, even death on a cross" (Phil. 2:6-8). This is why with the church of every age, we confess

Jesus Christ as at once true God and true human being, at once one with God and joined in solidarity with humankind, not an intermediary between God and humanity but a genuine Mediator, able to bring together God and humanity in immediate communion. His reconciling mediation opens up for us a vision of his mediation in creation: he is "the first-born of all creation; for in him all things were created, in heaven and on earth... all things were created through him and for him" (Col. 1:15-16). He is the Word and "all things were made through him" (John 1:3). The mediation of Christ has thus a cosmic universality: it is directed towards the transformation of our world in God.

74. Finally, the work of Jesus, the Son, reveals to us the role of the Spirit of God who is common to him and to the Father: it reveals to us that God is triune.

75. The Holy Spirit is present and active throughout the history of salvation. In the life of Jesus the Spirit intervenes at all the decisive moments: Jesus was conceived by the Holy Spirit (cf. Luke 1:35; Matt. 1:20); the Spirit descended on him at his baptism (Luke 3:22); he was filled with the Holy Spirit (Luke 4:1); he accomplished his ministry with the power of the Spirit (Luke 4:14). He proclaimed that the prophecy of the Book of Isaiah: "The Spirit of the Lord is upon me, because the Lord has anointed me" (61:1) was fulfilled in him (Luke 4:17-21). He rejoiced in the Holy Spirit (Luke 10:21). No one had ever possessed the Spirit as he did, "not by measure" (John 3:34). Still more, it is he who promises to send the Spirit (John 14:26; 16:7) and invokes the Spirit on his own disciples after the resurrection (John 20:22), because his death had been an act of "giving up" the Spirit to God and at the same time an act of "transmission of the Spirit" (John 19:30). In turn God raises him up and gives him the Spirit, so that he might spread the Spirit among us (cf. Acts 2:32-33). By the life, death and resurrection of Jesus, the Holy Spirit becomes the common gift of the Father and the Son to humanity.

76. Just as the Spirit came upon Jesus at the moment of his baptism, so the Spirit descends upon the disciples gathered in the upper room (Acts 2:1-12) and on the Gentiles who listen to the word (Acts 10:44-48). These three closely linked "Pentecosts" belong to the foundation of the church and make it the "temple of the Spirit". Thus the design pursued from the beginning by God the Creator and Saviour – to bring into being a people – is accomplished.

2.2. JUSTIFICATION BY GRACE, THROUGH FAITH

77. Because we believe in Christ, the one Mediator between God and humankind, we believe that we are justified by the grace which comes from him, by means of faith which is a living and life-giving faith. We recognize that our justification is a totally gratuitous work accomplished by God in Christ. We confess that the acceptance in faith of justification is itself a gift of grace. By the grace of faith we recognize in Jesus of Nazareth, established Christ and Lord by his resurrection, the one who saves us and brings us into communion of life with God. To rely for salvation on anything other than faith would be to diminish the fullness accomplished and offered in Jesus Christ. Rather than completing the gospel, it would weaken it.

78. To speak in this way of our justification and reconciliation with God is to say that faith is above all a reception (Rom. 5:1-2): it is received and in turn it gives thanks for grace. The raising to life, by God alone, of Jesus Christ, put to death by all, is the eschatological event which defines faith as reception of a gift of God, not as any human work (Eph. 2:8-10). We receive from Christ our justification, that is our pardon, our

liberation, our life with God. By faith, we are liberated from our presumption that we can somehow save ourselves; by faith, we are comforted in spite of our terror of losing ourselves. We are set at liberty to open ourselves to the sanctification which God wills for us.

79. The person justified by the free gift of faith, i.e., by a faith embraced with a freedom restored to its fullness, can henceforth live according to righteousness. The person who has received grace is called to bear fruits worthy of that grace. Justification makes him or her an "heir of God, co-heir with Christ" (Rom. 8:17). The one who has freely received is committed to gratitude and service. This is not a new form of bondage but a new way forward. And so, justification by faith brings with it the gift of sanctification, which can grow continuously as it creates life, justice and liberty. Jesus Christ, the one mediator between God and humankind, is also the unique way which leads towards pleasing God. Faith receives freely and bears testimony actively, as it works itself out through love (Gal. 5:6).

2.3. THE CALLING OF THE CHURCH: ITS ROLE IN JUSTIFICATION BY GRACE THROUGH FAITH

80. Together we confess the church, for there is no justification in isolation. All justification takes place in the community of believers or is ordered towards the gathering of such a community. Fundamental for us all is the presence of Christ in the church, considered simultaneously as both a reality of grace and a concrete community in time and space. Christ himself acts in the church in the proclamation of the word, in the celebration of the sacraments, in prayer and in intercession for the world. This presence and this action are enabled and empowered by the Spirit, by whom Christ calls to unite human beings to himself, to express his reality through them, to associate them in the mystery of his self-offering for them.

81. The church's calling is set within the triune God's eternal plan of salvation for humankind. In this sense, the church is already present at creation (Col. 1:15-18). It is present in the history of humankind: "the church from Abel", as it was called in the ancient church. It is also present at the covenant declared to Abraham from which the chosen people would come. Even more, the church is present at the establishment of the people of the covenant. Through the law and the prophets, God calls this people and prepares them for a communion which will be accomplished at the sending of Emmanuel, "God with us" (cf. Matt. 1:23). The novelty introduced by the incarnation of the Word does not call into question the continuity of the history of salvation. Nor does it call into question the significance of the interventions of that same Word and Spirit in the course of the Old Testament revelation. For God has not rejected this people (Rom. 11:1). The continued existence of the chosen people is an integral part of the history of salvation.

82. Nevertheless we believe that the coming of Christ, the Word incarnate, brings with it a radical change in the situation of the world in the sight of God. Henceforth the divine gift which God has made in Jesus Christ is irreversible and definitive. On God's side, salvation is accomplished and is offered to all. The presence of God has become inward among believers (Jer. 31:33; Ezek. 36:26) in a new fashion, by the Holy Spirit which conforms them to the image of Jesus Christ. At the same time, God's presence becomes universal; it is not limited to one people but is offered to all humanity called to be gathered together by Christ in the Spirit.

83. This is why we believe that the people of God gathered together by the death and resurrection of Christ does not live solely by the promise. Henceforth it lives also

by the gift already received through the mystery of the event of Jesus, Christ and Lord, who has sent his Spirit. We therefore confess Jesus Christ as the foundation of the church (1 Cor. 3:11).

84. The inauguration of the church takes place in time and in stages related to the unfolding of the Christ-event. These stages, closely related as they are, are three in number:

a) There is, first, the missionary activity of Jesus "in the days of his flesh" (Heb. 5:7): his preaching of the kingdom, which presupposes the promises of the Old Testament, and his mighty works; the invitation to believe in him and the call to conversion addressed to all; the gathering of the disciples, men and women (Luke 8:1-3), and the appointment of the group of Twelve (Mark 3:13-19); the change of Simon's name to Peter (Matt. 16:18) and the role which is assigned to him in the circle of the disciples (Luke 22:31-32).

b) The second stage is Jesus' celebration of the last supper with these same disciples as a memorial (Luke 22:14-20) of the giving of his life for all; his death on the cross, by which he accomplished the salvation of all (John 12:32); the resurrection of Jesus, which gathers the scattered community of the disciples. The risen Christ for forty days leads his followers into a more profound faith (Acts 1:2-3); in leaving them he gives them the command to baptize (Matt. 28:18), to preach repentance and forgiveness, and to bear witness to him (Luke 24:47-48).

c) The third stage is the sending of the Spirit upon the community of one hundred and twenty gathered on the day of Pentecost (Acts 2:2-4). The disciples are sent out to Israelites and to Gentiles, as is shown by the gift of the Spirit to the Gentiles (Acts 10:44), which may be called a "new Pentecost". Thus, the church is founded once for all, fully constituted and equipped for its universal vocation in the world and for its eschatological destiny. This gift of the Spirit is the first-fruits. The Spirit's work of renewal and gathering will be fully achieved and manifested only when Christ returns in glory.

85. The church is called into being as a community of men and women to share in the salvific activity of Christ Jesus. He has reconciled them to God, freed them from sin, and redeemed them from evil. "They are justified by his grace as a gift, through the redemption which is in Christ Jesus" (Rom. 3:24).

86. The justification of Jesus' disciples, sinful individuals freely justified by grace without any merit on their part, has been one of the constitutive experiences of the Christian faith since the foundation of the church. Justification by grace through faith is given us in the church. This is not to say that the church exercises a mediation complementary to that of Christ or that it is clothed with a power independent of the gift of grace. The church is at once the place, the instrument, and the minister chosen by God to make heard Christ's word and to celebrate the sacraments in God's name throughout the centuries. When the church faithfully preaches the word of salvation and celebrates the sacraments, obeying the command of the Lord and invoking the power of the Spirit, it is sure of being heard, for it carries out in its ministry the action of Christ himself.

87. The ministerial and instrumental role of the church in the proclamation of the gospel and in the celebration of the sacraments in no way infringes the sovereign liberty of God. If God chooses to act through the church for the salvation of believers, this does not restrict saving grace to these means. The sovereign freedom of God can

always call anyone to salvation independently of such actions. But it is true to say that God's call is always related to the church, in that God's call always has as its purpose the building up of the church, which is the body of Christ (1 Cor. 12:27-28; Eph. 1:22-23) (cf. no. 101).

88. This common confession of the church, of its vocation and of its role in justification by grace through faith, provides a positive context for a study of some of the questions which still divide us in our respective understandings of the relationship between Christ's gospel and the church as a community existing in the world.

3. The church we confess and our divisions in history

3.1. INTRODUCTION

89. The difficulties which still separate our communions arise largely from our different understandings of the relationship between that which we confess, on the one hand, concerning the origin and the vocation of the one, holy, catholic and apostolic church in God's plan of salvation and, on the other hand, the forms of its historical existence. Our two communions regard themselves as belonging to the una sancta but differ in their understanding of that belonging.

90. In addressing this subject, we must move beyond comparative ecclesiology. Our method requires us both to say what we can together and to recognize without ambiguity that which cannot yet be the object of consensus.

91. This implies a double challenge. There are, first, *differences* of perspective such that we find in the position of the partner a complementary point of view or a different accent on a single, commonly held truth. In opening ourselves to the partner's critique, we can learn to express our own views in a more balanced way and perhaps find a common frame of reference for understanding each other.

92. Secondly, however, some of our positions seem simply to *diverge*. They appear mutually incompatible or incommensurable. That leaves us, for the present at least, with no choice but to agree to disagree, while seeking clarity about the nature of our disagreements. We find, among other things, that we disagree about what issues are serious enough to be church-dividing. Questions which, from the Roman Catholic side, are obstacles to full communion are not necessarily so from the perspective of the Reformed, and vice versa. This does not dispense us from the responsibility of searching for reconciliation across even the most apparently insurmountable barriers. In the meantime we respect each other, and we are grateful for the measure of community that is possible between us.

93. In this report we do not treat the whole range of ecclesiological issues. We prefer to highlight three particular arenas of discussion because of what is at stake in them, and because of the light they can cast on the way to a fuller consensus. We shall deal, first, with two conceptions of the church which, though different, we consider potentially complementary. We then deal with two areas of apparent divergence or incompatibility: our views of continuity and discontinuity in church history, and of the church's visibility and ministerial order.

3.2. TWO CONCEPTIONS OF THE CHURCH

94. We have already affirmed the ministerial and instrumental role of the church in the proclamation of the gospel and the celebration of the sacraments (nos. 85-86).

Word and sacrament alike are of the very nature of the church. They also provide us with two different conceptions for understanding the church and the way in which it fulfills its ministerial and instrumental role: the first, more "Reformed", the second, more "Roman Catholic".

3.2.1. The church as "creatura verbi"

95. The church existing as a community in history has been understood and described in the Reformed tradition as *creatura verbi*, as "the creation of the word". God is eternally word as well as Spirit; by God's word and Spirit all things were created; reconciliation and renewal are the work of the same God, by the same word and Spirit.

96. God's word in history has taken a threefold form. Primarily it is the Word made flesh: Jesus Christ, incarnate, crucified and risen. Then it is the word as spoken in God's history with God's people and recorded in the scriptures of the Old and New Testaments as testimony to Jesus Christ. Third, it is the word as heard and proclaimed in the preaching, witness and action of the church. The third form depends upon and is bound to the second, through which it has access to the first, the word incarnate in Jesus Christ. This is why the Reformed tradition has insisted so emphatically that the preaching, teaching and witness of the church through the centuries – the church's dogma and tradition – are always to be subordinated to the testimony of the Bible, that scripture rather than Tradition is "the word of God written" and "the only infallible rule of faith and practice". Scripture is the control by which the church's proclamation must be governed if that proclamation is to witness authentically to God's word in Jesus Christ and to be "the word proclaimed". For the word of God is one consistent word: the word of judgment and mercy, the gospel of reconciliation, the announcing of the reign of God. It is a word alive as Jesus Christ himself is alive: it is a word calling to be heard, answered and re-echoed; it is a word claiming response, obedience and commitment as the word of grace which evokes and empowers authentic faith.

97. The church depends upon this word – the word incarnate, the word written, the word preached – in at least three ways:
– the church is founded upon the word of God;
– the church is kept in being as the church by the word of God;
– the church continually depends upon the word of God for its inspiration, strength, and renewal.

98. In each of these aspects, the word and Spirit of God work together, for it is the power of the Spirit that enables the hearing of the word and the response of faith. The word and Spirit of God together establish, preserve and guide the community of the church in and through human history. The church, like faith itself, is brought into being by the hearing of God's word in the power of God's Spirit; it lives *ex auditu*, by hearing.

99. This emphasis upon hearing the word of God has been of central importance in Reformed theology since the 16th century. This is why the Reformed have stressed "the true preaching of the word" together with "the right dispensing of the sacraments according to the institution of Jesus Christ" as a decisive "mark of the true church". Behind this emphasis lies a keen awareness of the way in which the Old Testament proclaimed "the word of the Lord", of the New Testament recognition of Jesus Christ as "the word who was in the beginning with God" – and of the new sense in the 16th cen-

tury that the Bible is a living, contemporary word with which the church's teaching and order, as these had come to develop, were by no means always in harmony. Against the appeal to continuity, custom and institution, the Reformed appealed to the living voice of the living God as the essential and decisive factor by which the church must live, if it will live at all: the church, as *creatura verbi*.

100. Thus far, our exposition has been relatively traditional and familiar. But despite the intended organic relationship between word and church, the Reformed tradition has not always held it steadily in view. It has sometimes inclined to verbalism, to the reduction of the gospel to doctrine, of the divine word incarnate in Jesus Christ to theological theory. Proclamation of the word has been seen simply as an external mark of the church rather than intrinsic to it, the church itself regarded more as the place where scripture is interpreted than as a community living from the word. Such understandings fall short of the full meaning of *creatura verbi* as describing the nature and calling of the church.

101. The church is the creation of the word because the word itself is God's creative word of grace by which we are justified and renewed. The church is the human community shaped and ruled by that grace; it is the community of grace, called to let "this mind be among yourselves, which is yours in Christ Jesus..." (Phil. 2:5). The community of faith is thus not merely the community in which the gospel is preached; by its hearing and responding to the word of grace, the community itself becomes a medium of confession, its faith a "sign" or "token" to the world; it is itself a part of the world transformed by being addressed and renewed by the word of God.

3.2.2. The church as "sacrament of grace"

102. Even before Vatican II, many Roman Catholic theologians described the church as a "sacrament", because this term is associated with the biblical term "mystery". Such a sacramental description highlights the comparison between what the church is and what is enacted in the celebration of the sacraments. The adoption of this term by the Second Vatican Council (*Lumen Gentium I*, no. 1) for speaking of the church has made this usage almost a commonplace in Roman Catholic thought.

103. The Second Vatican Council described the church, because of its relationship with Christ, as "a kind of sacrament, or sign of intimate union with God, and of the unity of all humankind" (*LG*, no. 1). The church is described as the "universal sacrament of salvation" (*LG*, no. 48; *GS*, no. 45; *Ad Gentes*, no. 1), the "visible sacrament of this saving unity" (*LG*, no. 9), and the "wondrous sacrament" (*Sacrosanctum Concilium*, no. 5). In some cases the conciliar text indicates the deep roots of this conception of the church in patristic thinking by referring to some expressions of Cyprian, who speaks of ecclesial unity as a sacrament (*LG*, no. 9 and *SC*, no. 26). It then directly applies these formulas to the church in extending the dynamic of their meaning. At the same time, it refers to a prayer in the Roman missal before the restoration of holy week, which affirms that "from the side of Christ on the cross there came forth the wondrous sacrament which is the whole church" (*SC*, no. 5).

104. The application of the category "sacrament" to the church is doubly analogical. On the one hand, it is analogical with regard to its application to Christ. Christ, indeed, is the primordial sacrament of God in that the logos became flesh, assuming our humanity. Jesus is the full revelation of grace (cf. John 1:14) and "the image of the invisible God" (Col. 1:15), the one who has become "the source of eternal salvation to

all who obey him" (Heb. 5:9). That is why Paul proclaims "the mystery of Christ" (Col. 4:3). Later on, Augustine, for whom the terms "mystery" and "sacrament" are practically equivalent, writes: "There is no other mystery of God than Christ" (*PL*, nos. 33,845). For St Thomas the original sacraments of our salvation are the "mysteries of the flesh of Christ"; in particular, the passion and the resurrection of Christ are sacraments by reason of their double character of being exemplary sign as well as instrumental and effective cause (cf. *Comp. Theol.* 239; *S. Theol.* IIIa, Q. 62, art. 5 and primum). Luther made his own this traditional interpretation of Christ: "The holy scriptures know only one sacrament, which is Christ the Lord himself" (*Disputatio de fide infusa et acquisita*, 1520, 18; *WA*, 6, p.86). All language concerning the sacramentality of the church, then, must respect the absolute lordship of Christ over the church and the sacraments. Christ is the unique foundational sacrament, that is to say, the active and original power of the whole economy of salvation visibly manifested in our world. The church is a sacrament by the gift of Christ, because it is given to it to be the sign and instrument of Christ.

105. In the New Testament the term "mystery" is not directly applied to the church, although Ephesians 5:32 applies this term to Genesis 2:24 and relates that verse to the relationship between Christ and the church (and the Latin Vulgate translated *mysterium* as *sacramentum*). The church then is only a sacrament founded by Christ and entirely dependent on him. Its being and its sacramental acts are the fruit of a free gift received from Christ, a gift in relation to which he remains radically transcendent, but which, however, he commits to the salvation of humankind. That is why, according to the Second Vatican Council, "it is not a vain analogy to compare the church with the mystery of the Word incarnate", for its one complex reality is "constituted from both a human aspect and a divine aspect" (*LG*, no. 8). This analogy should not make us forget the radical difference which remains between Christ and the church. In particular, the church is only the spouse and the body of Christ through the gift of the Spirit.

106. On the other hand, the church is called a sacrament by analogy to the liturgies of baptism and the eucharist, which the Greek fathers called "the mysteries", in a sense already analogous to the Pauline *mysterion*. The sacraments are the gestures and the words which Christ has confided to his church and to which he has linked the promise of grace by the gift of his Spirit.

107. In the church as "sacrament", "a bridge is built between the invisible face of creation and the design of God realized in the covenant" (cf. Groupe des Dombes, *L'Esprit saint, l'Eglise et les sacrements*, 23). Or, in a slightly different register, one can also call the church a "living sign". The terms "sacrament" and "sign" imply coherence and continuity between diverse moments of the economy of salvation, they designate the church at once as the place of presence and the place of distance, and they depict the church as instrument and minister of the unique mediation of Christ. Of this unique mediation the church is the servant, but never either its source or its mistress.

108. As Christ's mediation was carried out visibly in the mystery of his incarnation, life, death and resurrection, so the church has also been established as visible sign and instrument of this unique mediation across time and space. The church is an instrument in Christ's hands because it carries out, through the preaching of the word, the administration of the sacraments and the oversight of communities, a ministry entirely dependent on the Lord, just like a tool in the hand of a worker. So the New Testament describes the ministry of the church as serving as the ministry of Christ. Ministers are

"God's fellow workers" (1 Cor. 3:9), "servants of Christ and stewards of the mysteries of God" (1 Cor. 4:1), "ministers of a new covenant" (2 Cor. 3:6), "ministers of reconciliation" accomplished by Christ (cf. 2 Cor. 5:18) and, more generally, "envoys" or "ambassadors for Christ" (2 Cor. 5:20).

109. The instrumental ministry of the church is confided to sinful human beings. It can therefore be disfigured or atrophied, mishandled and exaggerated. But the reality of God's gift always transfigures human failure, and God's fidelity to the church continually maintains it, according to the promise (Matt. 28:20) which sustains it in its mission of salvation across the ages.

110. The church is thus constituted as a sacrament, an instrument of the unique mediation of Christ, a sign of the efficacious presence of that mediation. The church is such in that it lives out of the word, which has engendered it and which it proclaims, and to the extent that it is open and docile to the Spirit that dwells within it. The Paraclete maintains and continually renews the memory of Christ in the church (John 14:26; 16:15) until the Saviour comes again. This Paraclete accomplishes in the church the ministry of liberty (2 Cor. 3:17), of truth (John 16:13), of sanctification (Rom. 8:12-13), and of transformation (2 Cor. 3:18). In this way, the church is the bearer of the tradition of the word, that is, the sacrament of the word of God; and bearer of transmission of salvation, that is, the sacrament of Christ and of the Spirit.

111. If the church is seen in relation to its source, it may be described as the sacrament of God, of Christ and of the Spirit – as a sacrament of grace. If it is seen in relation to its mission and calling, it may be called the sacrament of the kingdom, or the sacrament of salvation (*LG*, no. 48): "like a sacrament, that is a sign and instrument of intimate union with God and of the unity of the entire human species" (*ibid.*, no. 1).

3.2.3. Questions and reflections

112. We are agreed in recognizing the radical dependence of the church in receiving the transcendent gift which God makes to it, and we recognize that gift as the basis of its activity of service for the salvation of humanity. But we do not yet understand the nature of this salutary activity in the same way. The Reformed commonly allege that Catholics appropriate to the church the role proper to Christ. Roman Catholics, for their part, commonly accuse the Reformed of holding the church apart from the work of salvation and of giving up the assurance that Christ is truly present and acting in his church. Both these views are caricatures, but they can help to focus attention on genuine underlying differences of perspective, of which the themes of *creatura verbi* and *sacramentum gratiae* serve as symbols.

113. The two conceptions, "the creation of the word" and "sacrament of grace", can in fact be seen as expressing the same instrumental reality under different aspects, as complementary to each other or as two sides of the same coin. They can also become the poles of a creative tension between our churches. A particular point at which this tension becomes apparent is reached when it is asked how the questions of the continuity and order of the church through the ages appear in the light of these two concepts.

3.3. THE CONTINUITY OF THE CHURCH THROUGH THE AGES

114. In what sense can it be said that the church has remained one from generation to generation? This question is of immediate relevance for relations between the

Reformed and Roman Catholic churches because the events leading to the Reformation and resulting in division seem to imply a discontinuity in the life of the one church.

3.3.1. God's fidelity and our sinfulness

115. Together we believe that God remains faithful to God's promise and never abandons the people he has called into being. "God is faithful, by whom you were called into the fellowship of his Son, Jesus Christ our Lord" (1 Cor. 1:9). Such is the ground of our conviction that the church continues through the ages to carry out the mission it has received until the end of time, because "the powers of death shall not prevail against it" (Matt. 16:18). Through the church, Christ, who is present with us all days until the end of time (cf. Matt. 28:20), leads us indefectibly to salvation.

116. The continuity of the church has an origin: it is the sending of the apostles on a mission by Christ, a *sending* which makes them "apostles"; it has a purpose – the *mission*, "apostle", to make disciples of all the nations (cf. Matt. 28:19). This is why the church is of its essence apostolic, and its ministry is within an apostolic succession. As was said in our preceding document, this succession "requires at once a historical continuity with the original apostles and a contemporary and graciously renewed action of the Holy Spirit" (PCCW, no. 101). Apostolicity is then a living reality which simultaneously keeps the church in communion with its living source and allows it to renew its youth continually so as to reach the kingdom.

117. God's fidelity is given to men and women who are part of a long history and who, moreover, are sinners. The church's response to God's fidelity must be renewed to meet the challenges of various times and cultures. The church is not worthy of its name if it is not a living and resourceful witness, concretely addressing people's needs. This is also why the church's continuity demands that it recognizes itself as *semper reformanda*. The sinfulness of humanity, which affects not only members of the church but also its institutions, is opposed to fidelity to God. If human sinfulness does not put the church in check, it can nevertheless do grave harm to the church's mission and witness. The constant need for reform in the church is recognized. "Christ summons the church, as it goes on its pilgrim way, to that continual reformation of which it always has need, insofar as it is an institution of human beings here on earth" (*UR*, no. 6). The church must then live within a constant dynamic of conversion.

3.3.2. The need for reform and renewal

118. We acknowledge that at the time of the Reformation the church was in urgent need of reform. We recognize that the various strivings for reform were in their profoundest inspiration signs of the work of the Holy Spirit. In the event of the Reformation, the word of God played a role, that word which is "living and active, sharper than any two-edged sword, piercing to the division of soul and spirit" (Heb. 4:12). Not everything that happened can be attributed to the word because in the division of the Western church human sinfulness also played its part. Our common awareness of this summons us to "discern the spirits", i.e., to distinguish in this process the work of human sinfulness from the work of the Spirit. As Roman Catholics and Reformed, we should not seek to justify ourselves here. We must each assume responsibility for our own past and for that part of the sin which was our own.

119. But that is not all. If it is true that "in everything [even sin, one could say] God works for good with those who love him, who are called according to his purpose"

(Rom. 8:28), we must then recognize the mysterious design of God which moves towards its accomplishment in spite of our division. Our continual conversion to Christ should make us discover and understand the positive meaning of this event in the life of Christ's church. It reminds us of the church's dependence on Christ and the Spirit, who act in it and for it with sovereign liberty. It invites us to recognize new fruits of holiness. It involves us in a Christian striving that impels us to reconcile in our lives complementary aspects of the one gospel. Reflection on the positive meaning of the Reformation, despite the division, concerns us all, because it is a major event in the history of the church.

3.3.3. Questions and reflections
120. Nonetheless, as things are at present, divergences persist between us in our understanding of the continuity of the church and its visibility. The Reformed churches give first consideration to continuity in the confession of faith and in the teaching of gospel doctrine. It is in this sense that the church remains apostolic and the ministers raised up in it by the Spirit form part of the apostolic succession. The Catholic church, for its part, considers that this apostolicity of faith and preaching, as well as that of the administration of the sacraments, are linked to a certain number of visible signs through which the Spirit works, in particular to the apostolic succession of bishops.

121. We both acknowledge the reality of Tradition, but we do not give it the same weight. The Reformed see in holy scripture the sufficient witness of the gospel message, a message that "constantly creates the understanding of itself afresh" (PCCW, no. 29) and is the locus of the immediate communication of the truth. This does not imply disregard for tradition as an expression of faithful communion throughout the centuries. Catholics for their part regard scripture as the *norma normans* of all doctrine of the faith, but they think that scripture, the work of the living tradition of the apostolic generation, is in its turn read and interpreted in a living way in an act of uninterrupted transmission which constitutes the Tradition of the church throughout its history. The authority of this living tradition and of the magisterial decisions which mark it from time to time is founded on submission to the message of scripture. In order to help the people of God be obedient to this message, the church is led to make interpretative decisions about the meaning of the gospel (cf. PCCW, nos. 30,32).

122. Further, we differ in our understanding of the nature of sin in the church. Undoubtedly, we both recognize that, whatever the effect of sin on persons and institutions, the holiness of the preaching of the word and of the administration of the sacraments endures, because the gift of God to the church is irrevocable. In this sense the church is holy, for it is the instrument of that gift of holiness which comes from God. But the Reformed think that God's fidelity is stronger than our infidelity, than the repeated "errors and resistances to the word on the part of the church" (PCCW, no. 42). Hence the church can experience moments when, despite the exemplary witness of individuals, its true identity is obscured by sin beyond recognition. This does not mean that God abandons the church which, for the Reformed, continues in being always and until the end of time. On the Catholic side, it is thought that human sin, even if it goes so far as to mar greatly the signs and institutions of the church, never nullifies its mission of grace and salvation and never falsifies essentially the proclamation of the truth, because God unfailingly guards the church "which he has obtained with the blood of his own Son" (Acts 20:28). The times of the worst abuses were frequently times in

which great sanctity flourished. In other words, we do not think in the same way about the relation of the church to the kingdom of God. The Reformed insist more on the promise of a "not-yet"; Catholics underline more the reality of a gift "already-there".

123. Accordingly, our respective interpretations of the division in the 16th century are not the same. The Reformed consider that the Reformation was a rupture with the Catholic "establishment" of the period. This establishment had become greatly corrupted and incapable of responding to an appeal for reform in the sense of a return to the purity of the gospel and the holiness of the early church. Nevertheless, this does not mean that the resulting division was a substantial rupture in the continuity of the church. For Catholics, however, this break struck at the continuity of the Tradition derived from the apostles and lived through many centuries. Insofar as the Reformed had broken with the ministerial structure handed down by Tradition, they had deeply wounded the apostolicity of their churches. The severity of this judgment is moderated today because ecumenical contacts have made Catholics more aware of the features of authentic Christian identity preserved in those churches.

124. In the future, our dialogue will need to address such still often divisive questions as the following:
1. Considering the interpretation of our positions given above, what can Reformed and Roman Catholics now say together about the reform movements of the 16th century – the reasons behind them, the course they took, and the results that came about?
2. Recognizing (because of baptism and other ecclesial factors) that despite continuing divisions a real though imperfect communion already exists between Reformed and Roman Catholic Christians, what implications does this communion have for our understanding of the continuity of the church?
3. To what extent can we together proclaim the gospel in an idiom intelligible to our contemporaries, even if we differ in some ways in our understanding of the apostolic faith?
4. How can we reconcile the freedom of the individual Christian in appropriating the Christian message with the responsibility of the church for authoritatively teaching that message?

In the past, we have usually answered such questions from our separate ecclesiological perspectives; in the future, we will need to work out a joint response in dialogue.

3.4. THE VISIBILITY AND THE MINISTERIAL ORDER OF THE CHURCH

125. The Reformed and Roman Catholic communions differ in a third way with respect to their understanding of the relation between gospel and church. Our divergence here has to do with the role of visible structure, particularly in relation to mission and ministry. We will look first at visibility and invisibility in the church as such, and then at mission and ministerial order.

3.4.1. The church: visible and invisible

126. In the past, Reformed churches have sometimes displayed a tendency not only to distinguish, but also to separate the invisible church, known to God alone, and the visible church, manifest in the world as a community gathered by the word and sacrament. In fact, such a distinction is not part of genuine Reformed teaching. We can affirm together the indissoluble link between the invisible and the visible. There exists

but one church of God. It is called into being by the risen Christ, forms "one body", is summoned to "one hope", and acknowledges "one Lord, one faith, one baptism, one God and Father of us all..." (Eph. 4:4-6). Christ, through his Spirit, has empowered this church for a mission and a ministry in the world and equipped it to call others to the same unity, hope and faith. From its earliest time, it has been provided through God's grace with ministerial means necessary and sufficient for the fulfilment of its mission.

127. The invisible church is the hidden side of the visible, earthly church. The church is manifest to the world where it is called to share in the kingdom of God as God's chosen people. This visible/invisible church is real as event and institution, wherever and whenever God calls men and women to service.

128. This visible/invisible church lives in the world as a structured community. Gathered around word and sacraments, it is enabled to proclaim God's gospel of salvation to the world. Its visible structure is intended to enable the community to serve as an instrument of Christ for the salvation of the world. It thus bears witness to all human beings of the saving activity of God in Jesus Christ. This testimony of the visible/invisible church often calls it to a confrontation with the world. In such testimony the church sees itself summoned to praise and glorify God. In all its visible activity, its goal is *soli Deo gloria, ad maiorem Dei gloriam*.

129. We diverge, however, on the matter of the closer identification of the church with its visible aspects and structure. Roman Catholics maintain that the church of Christ "subsists" in the Roman Catholic Church (*LG*, no. 8), a formulation adopted at the Second Vatican Council to avoid the exclusive identification of Christ's church with it. They admit likewise that many "elements" or "attributes" of great value, by which the church is constituted, are present in the "separated churches and communities" and that these last are "in no way devoid of significance and value in the mystery of salvation" (*UR*, no. 3). The question is, therefore, to what degree they can recognize that the church of Christ also exists in the Reformed churches. The Reformed for their part do not understand the church as reducible to this or that community, hierarchy or institution. They claim to belong to the church and recognize that others also do. Their chief difficulty is not in extending this recognition to the Roman Catholic Church, but the view that the Roman Catholic Church has of its special relation to the church of Jesus Christ.

3.4.2. Mission and ministerial order

130. Catholics and Reformed agree that the order of the church originates in the gospel which the risen Christ charged his disciples to proclaim. In this perspective, it is given first in word and sacrament: "Go therefore and make disciples of all nations, baptizing them in the name of the Father and of the Son and of the Holy Spirit, teaching them to observe all that I have commanded you; and lo, I am with you always, to the close of the age" (Matt. 28:19-20; cf. Luke 24:47-48; John 20:21b).

131. For those who follow Christ, the word of God contained in scripture and proclaimed, lived and interpreted in the church is the fundamental and inalienable point of reference for the church's order. Scripture bears the word of salvation by which faith is born. Faith leads to baptism, and it is nourished by the celebration of the Lord's supper, the eucharist.

132. This mission, which the risen Christ committed to the "eleven" (Matt. 28:16) and from which the church arose, implies that one should distinguish between those

who announce the gospel ("you") and those to whom it is proclaimed ("make disciples"). It entails, moreover, a ministry of word, sacrament and oversight given by Christ to the church to be carried out by some of its members for the good of all. This triple function of the ministry equips the church for its mission in the world.

133. This ministerial order manifests itself above all in the ministry of the word, i.e. in the preaching of the gospel, "the word of God which you heard from us" (1 Thess. 2:13; cf. 2 Cor. 11:7), the announcing of repentance and forgiveness of sins in the name of Jesus (Luke 24:47-48), and the proclaiming of him as the one anointed with the Spirit "to preach good news to the poor... to set at liberty those who are oppressed" (Luke 4:18). He who was the preacher of God's word par excellence has thus become the Preached One in the word carried to the "ends of the earth" (Acts 1:8) by his chosen witnesses (Acts 10:41-42).

134. The ministerial order also finds expression in the ecclesial rites, traditionally called sacraments. We believe that in them Christ himself acts through the Spirit among his people. The church is ordered through baptism, in which all who believe in Christ are not only washed and signed by the triune God, but are "built into a spiritual house, to be a holy priesthood" (1 Pet. 2:5). Similarly, in the Lord's supper, or the eucharist, the community of faith, hope and love finds its rallying point: "Because there is one bread, we who are many are one body, for we all partake of the one bread" (1 Cor. 10:17). Such rites along with the word of God are fruitful means of grace for those who believe, and by them the whole people of God is built up and nurtured.

135. This order is further manifest in the ministry of oversight *(episcope)*, exercised by church members for the fidelity, unity, harmony, growth and discipline of the wayfaring people of God under Christ, who is "the Shepherd and Guardian *(episcopos)*" of all souls (1 Pet. 2:25). Various "gifts", "services" and "activities" are inspired by God's Spirit in the church (1 Cor. 12:4-6), but all members are called upon to be concerned for that same unity, harmony and upbuilding of the church.

136. Leadership in the New Testament took different forms at various times and places under diverse names (see, e.g., Acts 1:20-25; 20:17;28; 1 Cor. 12:28; Eph. 4:11-13; Phil. 1:1; 1 Tim. 3:1-13; 4:14; 5:3-22; Titus 1:5-9). Paul often refers to himself as the servant/slave of Jesus Christ" (Rom. 1:1; Gal. 1:10; Phil. 1:1) and as such writes to churches that he has founded as one exercising authority in virtue of the gospel that he preaches (1 Thess. 2:9,13; cf. 1 Cor. 15:11: "Whether it was I or they, so we preach and so you believed"). Though we have no direct indication that the communities founded by Paul were presbyterally organized, but only the affirmation of Acts 14:23, where Paul, according to Luke, appoints presbyters "in every church", Paul was at least aware of a structure of leadership in some communities to which he wrote: 1 Thess. 5:12: "respect those who labour among you and are over you in the Lord and admonish you"; Phil. 1:1: greetings are sent to "all the saints in... Philippi, with the overseers and deacons" *(syn episkopois kai diakonois)*. From the various forms of leadership mentioned in the pastorals there emerged a pattern of *episcopoi*, presbyters and deacons, which became established by the end of the 2nd century.

137. This pattern of leadership developed from some New Testament forms, while other (even earlier) New Testament forms did not develop. The spread and theological interpretation of ecclesial leadership in the immediate post-New Testament period must be seen against the background of the wider development of the early church and its articulation of the faith (see 1 Clem 40-44, esp. 42, 1-2, 4; 44, 1-2; Ignatius of Antioch,

Eph 2, 1-5; Magn 2; Hippolytus, *Apost. Trad.*). In the course of history some of the functions of such leaders underwent change; even so the ministry of bishops, presbyters and deacons became in the ancient church the universal pattern of church leadership.

3.5. THE MUTUAL CHALLENGE

138. We have now explored and reflected upon three dimensions of the relation between gospel and church. Despite our agreements, there remain divergences between us which deserve further exploration and offer us new challenges.

139. First, on *the question of doctrinal authority in the church*, the previous report, "The Presence of Christ in Church and World" (nos. 24-42), described our agreement concerning the view that we in large measure share regarding scripture and its canon. In this area, formerly contested matters have been substantially clarified. This document likewise has identified the core of what still separates us in the interpretation of scripture, the authority of confessions of faith and of conciliar decisions, and the question of the infallibility of the church. These divergences still remain to this day. Among the remaining divergences, the following are particularly important. Both sides emphasize the indefectible character of Spirit-guided preaching and teaching that mirrors the gospel and holy scripture. Roman Catholics relate that preaching and teaching to a God-given authority vested in the church which, in service to the word of God in scripture and Tradition, has been entrusted with authentically interpreting it, and which in distinct cases is assisted by the Holy Spirit to pronounce infallibly on matters of faith and morals. Reformed Christians refer such preaching and teaching ultimately to the supreme authority of the word of God in scripture as illuminated by the Holy Spirit.

140. Second, on *the question of the sacraments*, in spite of growing convergence, there still exists between us not only a disagreement concerning their number, but also a divergence in our understanding of "sacrament" and of the competence of the one who ministers. Roman Catholics recognize seven sacraments, according to the council of Trent (DS, 1601), though they give a major importance to baptism and eucharist and recognize in the eucharist the centre of the sacramental life of the church. The Reformed churches recognize baptism and the Lord's supper as sacraments in the ordinary sense, though also recognizing in the laying-on of hands "an efficacious sign which initiates and confirms the believer in the ministry conferred" (PCCW, no. 98). Calvin himself did not object to calling ordination a sacrament, but he did not count it on a level with baptism and eucharist because it was not intended for all Christians (*Institutes* IV:19,28).

141. Third, the earlier document (PCCW, no. 98) provides *a common description of ordination*, putting in relief its double reference to the "historical and present action" of Jesus Christ and to "the continual operation of the Holy Spirit". Nevertheless, the nature of ordination still causes difficulty between us. Is the laying-on of hands a sending on a mission, a passing on of a power, or an incorporation into an order (cf. *ibid.*, no. 108)? On the other hand, can a defect in form put in question or invalidate the ministry as such – or can such a defect be remedied "by reference to the faith of the church" *(ibid.)*?

One further difference concerning the ordained ministry cannot be ignored, especially today. In the Reformed churches, as in many other Protestant communions, it has become increasingly common in recent decades to ordain women without restriction to the ministry of word and sacrament.

142. Fourth, on *the question of how the authority of Christ must be exercised in the church*, we are in accord that the structure of the ministry is essentially collegial (cf. PCCW, no. 102). We agree on the need for *episcope* in the church, on the local level (for pastoral care in each congregation), on the regional level (for the link of congregations among themselves), and on the universal level (for the guidance of the supranational communion of churches). There is disagreement between us about who is regarded as *episcopos* at these different levels and what is the function or role of the *episcopos*.

a) Catholics insist that the ordained ministry is a gift of God given to persons "set apart" (cf. Rom. 1:1) in the community. By the sacrament of ordination the minister is united with Christ, the sole High Priest, in a new way which qualifies him to represent Christ in and for the community. The one ordained can act there *in persona Christi*; his ministry is an embassy in the name of Christ in the service of the word of God (cf. 2 Cor. 3:5). Ordination to the priesthood qualifies one to represent the church before God, in its offering to the Father through Christ in the Spirit. All of these aspects of this ministry are especially realized in the eucharistic celebration. The ordained ministry thus places the church in total and current dependence on its unique Lord.

b) Likewise, for Catholics, at the heart of the ministry, ordained in the succession of the apostles, stands the bishop, who continues in the community the preaching of the apostolic faith and the celebration of the sacraments, either in his own right or through his collaborators, the priests and deacons. His role is also to develop a life of harmony within the community *(homothymadon)*. The bishop also represents his church before other local churches in the bosom of the universal communion. Charged to maintain and deepen the communion of all the churches among themselves, the bishops, with the bishop of Rome who presides over the universal communion, form a "college". This "college" is seen as the continuation of the "college" of the apostles, among whom Peter was the first. The bishop of Rome, understood as the successor of Peter, is the prime member of this college and has the authority necessary for the fulfilment of his service on behalf of the unity of the whole church in apostolic faith and life.

c) Reformed churches also emphasize the importance of the ordained ministry of word and sacrament for the life of the church (cf. Eph. 4:11-16). The Reformed understanding of the ministry is in general more "kerygmatic" than "priestly"; this corresponds to the awareness of the word of God as the power by which the church lives. Within this perspective, however, there is a valid sense in which the Reformed minister acts "in the person of Christ" – e.g., in preaching, in dispensing the sacraments, in pastoral care – and also represents the people, in articulating and leading their worship. For this reason Reformed churches approach the preparation and ordination of ministers with great care, emphasizing the need for a proper order and the laying-on of hands by duly ordained ministers.

d) The Reformed stress the collegial exercise of *episcope*. At the local level the responsibility lies with pastors, elders and/or deacons, with a very important role often played by the church meeting. At regional and national levels it is exercised collectively by synods. The same applies, in principle, to the universal level. The Reformed have never given up hope for a universal council based on the authority of the scriptures. That hope has not yet materialized, though ecumenical world assemblies in our century are an important step towards its fulfillment.

e) The Reformed hold that the 16th century brought into being a new form of church order based on scripture and a practice of the ancient church, adapted to the needs of a new situation. Reformed churches today still maintain that pattern and believe it to be legitimate and serviceable in the life of the church. This does not exclude the possibility of further development in the ecumenical future of the church.

143. Finally, *we have begun to come to terms with the particularly difficult issue of the structure of ministry required for communion in the universal church.* The earlier report (PCCW) made allusion to it. Our discussion of the matter has shown how complex the issues involved are and how different the perspectives in which they are seen on both sides. As we pursue the dialogue on the church's structure and ministry, this theme deserves closer attention.

144. As a programme for future dialogue, we suggest the following questions:
- Our interpretations of scripture are inextricably bound up with our ecclesiological convictions. With what hermeneutical and doctrinal perspectives do we approach the New Testament in the search for guidance on the ordering of the church in the ecumenical future?
- What significance is there for the church today in the role assigned to Peter in several central New Testament passages – and in the way in which that role was interpreted in the ancient church?
- What is the connection between the ministry of leadership described in the New Testament (presidents, leaders, bishops, pastors) and in the ancient church, and (a) Roman Catholic bishops and (b) Reformed ministers of word and sacraments?

4. The way forward

145. Our five years of dialogue have convinced us that a new situation now exists between the Roman Catholic Church and the Reformed churches. It has become apparent that the two confessions share much in common and can, therefore, enter into a living relationship with each other. Encounters in many parts of the world have led to mutual openness and a new understanding. It has become clear that the two sides have much to say to each other and also much to learn from each other.

146. The common ground that unites our churches is far greater than has usually been assumed. We start from the premise that God has already granted us unity in Christ. It is not for us to create unity, for in Christ it is already given for us. It will become visible in our midst as and when we turn to him in faith and obedience and we realize fully in our churches what he expects from us. We firmly believe that the unifying power of the Holy Spirit must prove stronger than all the separation that has occurred through our human sinfulness. This confirms our conviction that we must work for the ultimate goal of full communion in one faith and one eucharistic fellowship.

147. At the same time, however, our dialogue has shown that certain disagreements in understanding the relationship between the gospel and the church have not yet been overcome. It would therefore be unrealistic to suppose that the time has now come for declaring full communion between our churches.

148. But we do believe that the living relationship that has come into being between our churches makes possible a new way of dealing with these divergences. They should not be looked upon primarily as grounds for mutual exclusion but should rather be seen as terrain for mutual challenge. In ecumenical encounter we can deepen our understanding and our obedience. We can discover in the other the gift of God.

149. "Welcome one another, therefore, as Christ has welcomed you, for the glory of God" (Rom. 15:7). On the basis of this appeal of the apostle Paul, we conclude that the Roman Catholic Church and the Reformed churches should no longer oppose each other or even simply live side by side. Rather, despite their divergences, they should live for each other in order to be witnesses to Christ. Guided by this mission, they should open themselves to and for each other.

4.1. THE DIVERSITY OF SITUATIONS

150. In some countries, far-reaching agreement has already been achieved. Official dialogues have taken place and, as a general rule, these have led to results similar to those to be found in the present report. In some other countries the churches maintain close relationships and collaborate regularly, reacting together to important problems of public life. But there are also countries where their relations, even today, hardly go beyond occasional and individual contacts. The mistrust inherited from the past has not yet been overcome. Political situations and sociological factors often play an important part in this mistrust. In some places the Roman Catholic and Reformed churches even find themselves on opposite sides of political conflict. In other places, closer relations are made more difficult by the numerical size of the partners: whenever a large church finds itself faced with a small minority, a great deal of sensitivity and effort are needed if living relationships are to be established. In many places, the diversity of the Reformed churches makes interconfessional dialogue and collaboration more complex.

151. We agree that initiatives should be taken to deepen Christian fellowship in each country. We are grateful for the convergences we have found in the dialogue at the international level and believe that these results can serve as a stimulus for the churches in each country. But the desired living relationship cannot be created only by an agreement at the international level. First, according to the Reformed understanding, each member church is responsible for its own confession, its life and its witness; consequently, the World Alliance of Reformed Churches has no binding authority over its member churches. Secondly, we are convinced that the call for unity must always aim at concrete and lived communion. It is always addressed to "all in each place". But we do believe that the mutual understanding reached in international dialogue should serve as an encouragement to establish more active relations between our churches at the local level.

4.2. STEPS ALONG THE WAY TO UNITY

152. We suggest that dialogues between local churches should keep in mind the following steps on the way to unity:

a) Our churches should give expression to mutual recognition of baptism. In some countries, the Roman Catholic and Reformed churches have already agreed to accept each other's baptism fully and without reserve, provided that it has been celebrated in the name of the Father, the Son and the Holy Spirit and with the use of water. We believe that such agreements can and should be made in all places without delay. Such an agreement implies that under no circumstances can there be a repetition of baptism which took place in the other church. Mutual recognition of baptism is to be understood as an expression of the profound communion that Jesus Christ himself establishes among his disciples and which no human failure can ever destroy.

b) Though mutual recognition of baptism is already possible today, we are not yet in a position to celebrate the eucharist or Lord's supper together. Our different understandings of the relation between the gospel and the church also have consequences as regards admission to communion.

The Reformed churches take the view that, precisely because Christ himself is the host at the table, the church must not impose any obstacles. All those who have received baptism and love the Lord Jesus Christ are invited to the Lord's supper (see the declaration of the World Alliance, Princeton, 1954).

The Roman Catholic Church, on the other hand, is convinced that the celebration of the eucharist is of itself a profession of faith in which the whole church recognizes and expresses itself. Sharing the eucharist therefore presupposes agreement with the faith of the church which celebrates the eucharist.

This difference in the understanding of eucharistic sharing must be respected by both sides. Still, we recall and reaffirm the progress in our common understanding of the eucharist that has already been made in the first phase of dialogue (PCCW, nos. 67-92). Aspects of the common understanding were summarized in these words, which we repeat again here: "... we gratefully acknowledge that both traditions, Reformed and Roman Catholic, hold to the belief in the Real Presence of Christ in the eucharist; and both hold at least that the eucharist is, among other things: (1) a memorial of the death and resurrection of the Lord, (2) a source of living communion with him in the power of the Spirit (hence the epiclesis in the liturgy), and (3) a source of the eschatological hope for his coming again" (PCCW, no. 91)

c) In many countries there has been a rapid rise in the number of confessionally mixed marriages in recent years. It is not therefore surprising that the problem of a more appropriate way of dealing with this new reality has cropped up time and again in the course of bilateral dialogues. We hold that confessionally mixed marriages could be seen as an opportunity of encounter between the two traditions, even though some difficulties cannot be denied. We deem it to be important that the two churches should jointly exercise pastoral responsibility for those who live or grow up in confessionally mixed marriages in a manner which supports the integrity of the conscience of each person and respects their rights. In this respect see also the report of the dialogue between the Roman Catholic Church, the Lutheran World Federation and the World Alliance of Reformed Churches ("The Theology of Marriage and the Problem of Mixed Marriages", cf. no. 2 above).

4.3. TOWARDS THE RECONCILIATION OF MEMORIES

153. In Chapter 1 we tried together to understand our separated histories afresh. Beyond this lies a step not yet taken. From understanding each other's memories we must move to a *reconciliation* of the memories of Roman Catholics with those of Reformed Christians, and vice versa. Shared memories, even if painful, may in time become a basis for new mutual bonding and a growing sense of shared identity.

154. This proposal has been made time and again by both Reformed and Roman Catholic authorities. Pope John Paul II formulated it in the following terms: "Remembrance of the events of the past must not restrict the freedom of our present efforts to eliminate the harm that has been triggered by these events. Coming to terms with these memories is one of the main elements of ecumenical process. It leads to frank recognition of mutual injury and errors in the way the two communities reacted to each other, even though it was the intention of all concerned to bring the church more into line with the will of the Lord" (address to the members of the Swiss Evangelical Church Federation, 14 June 1984).

155. Chapter 1 shows how much has been accomplished in this direction. Mention should be made, for example, of the efforts of Roman Catholic historians to produce a new interpretation of the great Reformers, especially John Calvin, or the attempt of the World Alliance to give a new overtone to the memories of the revocation of the Edict of Nantes. But much yet remains to be done.

156. As illustrations we choose the following:

a) The problem of interpreting the rupture caused by the Reformation has already been touched on. In addition to the theological reflections already offered, serious historical research needs to be jointly undertaken.

b) We must tackle the problem of the condemnations that the Roman Catholic Church and the Reformed churches pronounced against each other. The polemics between the churches found expression in mutual anathematizations, and these continue to make themselves felt today. One need only think, for example, of the condemnation of certain Roman Catholic teachings and practices in such Reformed confessions as the Heidelberg catechism or the Westminster confession, or the identification of doctrines condemned by the council of Trent with certain of the teachings of the Reformers. Conscious efforts at theological and historical research will have to be made in order to distinguish the justified concerns of these declarations from the polemical distortions.

c) Particular attention should be paid to the way in which confessional separation was brought to the Americas, Africa, Asia and Oceania. Churches in these areas had no part in originating the separation. It was only through migration or missionary expansion that European divisions were transplanted to these continents. What in actual fact are the reasons for the separate existence of these churches today? A careful historical analysis might well bring to light new factors of separation which have been added to the inherited confessional differences.

4.4. COMMON WITNESS IN THE WORLD OF TODAY

157. "Living for each other" as churches must also mean "bearing common witness". We take the view that the Roman Catholic Church and the Reformed churches must make every effort to speak jointly to the men and women of today to whom God desires to communicate Christ's message of salvation.

158. Every opportunity for taking common stands with regard to contemporary issues should be taken and used. Our separation must not prevent us from expressing the agreement we have already achieved in our witnessing. For example, the Roman Catholic Church and the World Alliance of Reformed Churches are wholly agreed that every form of racism is contradictory to the gospel and must therefore be rejected. In particular, they see apartheid as a system that the Christian church must condemn if its evangelical credibility is not to be put into jeopardy.

159. Something very similar applies with regard to the witness of the churches on issues of justice, peace and the integrity of God's creation. The most profound convictions of their faith oblige both churches to render decisive witness in these fields. They would imperil the integrity of their teaching if they failed to give it.

160. We also know, however, that challenges which call for common confession in our day and age also generate new divergences and divisions. These could stress and endanger our still fragile fellowship. It is therefore all the more important that we should continually listen anew together to what the Spirit is saying to the church today: the Spirit who will lead us to the fullness of the truth.

4.5. WHAT KIND OF UNITY DO WE SEEK?

161. Even though we are still far from being able to proclaim full communion, it is important for the relations between our churches that we should have an agreed vision of the ultimate goal that should guide our efforts. This is a question that needs further study. Various concepts of unity have been proposed and deserve attention. But we believe that serious consideration should be given in our Reformed-Roman Catholic relationship, and in the ecumenical movement in general, to the description of the "unity we seek", as expressed by the assembly of the World Council of Churches in Nairobi (1975). This text describes what is called "conciliar fellowship", and goes as follows:

> The one church is to be envisioned as a conciliar fellowship of local churches which are themselves truly united.
> In this conciliar fellowship each local church possesses, in communion with the others, the fullness of catholicity, witnesses to the same apostolic faith, and therefore recognizes the others as belonging to the same church of Christ and guided by the same Spirit.
> As the New Delhi assembly pointed out, they are bound together because they have received the same baptism and share in the same eucharist; they recognize each other's members and ministries.
> They are one in their common commitment to confess the gospel of Christ by proclamation and service to the world. To this end, each church aims at maintaining sustained and sustaining relationships with her sister churches, expressed in conciliar gatherings whenever required for the fulfilment of this common calling. (David M. Paton, ed., *Breaking Barriers: Nairobi 1975*, the official report of the fifth assembly of the World Council of Churches, Nairobi, 23 November-10 December 1975, London, SPCK, and Grand Rapids, Eerdmans, 1976, p.60).

162. We see in the Nairobi declaration a sketch of the way in which organic unity could be structured even at the universal level. The statement does not describe the present state of relations between the churches, but rather serves the purpose, without reference to conciliarist controversies of the past, of articulating a concept and vision of unity towards which Christians can move to overcome their divisions.

163. Some of the features described in this text have since been given further attention within our dialogue and within the broader ecumenical movement. A crucial factor in the description is that each local church "witnesses to the same apostolic faith". Without this there can be no unity. In this report, for example, the second chapter, "Our common confession of faith", indicates important aspects of the apostolic faith that we can confess together. Basic for unity too is the need to share the same faith in regard to baptism, eucharist and ministry. An important contribution towards achieving this is the document of the Faith and Order commission on *Baptism, Eucharist and Ministry*, to which the churches have given their official responses.

164. If the living relationship between our churches is to grow, we must consciously foster regular contact with each other. If each church is to consider God's gift in the other, each will have to orientate itself towards the other. Inherited problems of doctrine call for further reflection. Newly arising problems (for example, relationships and dialogue with people of other living faiths, or issues raised by the progress of science and technology) must become subjects of frank and open dialogue. The road to unity can be travelled more readily if both communions can learn to listen together to the word of God and to the questions raised by each other.

165. We pray God to grant us the Spirit to heal wounds, to gather and edify Christ's people, to purify us, and to send us into the world anew.

NOTES

[1] Both reports can be found in Harding Meyer and Lukas Vischer, eds, *Growth in Agreement: Reports and Agreed Statements of Ecumenical Conversations on a World Level*, New York, Paulist/Ramsey, and Geneva, WCC, 1984, pp.433-63 and 277-306 respectively.

[2] Biblical quotations are taken from the *Common Bible: the Holy Bible, Revised Standard Version, Containing the Old and New Testaments with the Apocrypha/Deuterocanonical Books: An Ecumenical Edition*, New York, Collins, 1973.

PART C

XXVIII. WORLD COUNCIL OF CHURCHES AND ROMAN CATHOLIC CHURCH

Historical Introduction

Since the inception of the World Council of Churches in 1948, the Roman Catholic Church has chosen not to be a member. Nevertheless, contacts and cooperation have grown over the years, especially since the Second Vatican Council and especially with the commission on Faith and Order.

The Joint Working Group was established in 1965 by the Roman Catholic Church and the World Council of Churches as their consultative forum. The Joint Working Group is a clear sign that both the Roman Catholic Church and the World Council must work together in the one ecumenical movement.

A major factor in this cooperation is that both are two different entities, the one a worldwide church, the other a council of churches. The Roman Catholic church sees itself as one church with a universal mission and structure of teaching and governance. The World Council recognizes that it is a fellowship of churches, whose members do not take direct and formal responsibility for its studies, actions and statements.

The Joint Working Group understands its mandate to bring to expression the will of its sponsors, to grow in mutual recognition, and to find new ways to stand together in the service of unity and mission. It has sought to bring together the theological, social and pastoral dimensions of ecumenism. The Group endeavours to keep its structure to a minimum and to be flexible in its manner of collaboration. The scope of its activity is reflected in the several statements and reports of the three working groups between 1982 and 1998, which resulted from their annual meetings.[1]

NOTE

[1] See "The History of the RCC-WCC Joint Working Group, in *Joint Working Group between the Roman Catholic Church and the World Council of Churches: Seventh Report*, Geneva, WCC, 1998, pp.24-30.

XXVIII. WORLD COUNCIL OF CHURCHES AND ROMAN CATHOLIC CHURCH

67. Fifth Report of the Joint Working Group

June 1982

Introduction

By the time of the sixth assembly of the World Council of Churches (1983) there will have been over twenty years of official contacts between the World Council of Churches and the Roman Catholic Church. The Joint Working Group, established in 1965 to serve this relationship, has already submitted four official reports to its respective authorities. The first three had simply recorded what had been done in study and collaboration. The fourth report, presented to the fifth assembly in 1975, also looked ahead to what should and could be done. This fifth report is presented in the same spirit.

Further, the last seven years have been crowded with church and world events which have deeply influenced the one ecumenical movement and which call for a more widespread and stronger commitment to its goals and its tasks. These events are first outlined here, in order that realism may mark the evaluation of past collaboration between the Roman Catholic Church and the World Council of Churches and the projections for their relationship during the next decade.

I. The ecumenical situation

1. Changes in the world community

Reflection must begin with a vivid consciousness of those changes in the world community which are transforming the cultural, economic, social and political relations between peoples. The inescapable interdependence of all areas and peoples of the inhabited earth is matched by increasing consciousness of that fact. The human family becomes more aware that it faces either a common future or a common fate. Threats to peace have so critically increased that life itself is at stake. Oppression and violence are destroying the fragile fabric of human communities.

Appalling affluence and consumption of the earth's resources exacerbate growing impatience on the part of the poor and increasing frustration among those not so deprived but who feel themselves powerless to close the gap. New causes of contention continue to arise among nations. Many countries are split within by political and social divisions of great bitterness which lead to confrontation and violence. The precariousness of the economic situation, the breakdown of structures and services, unemployment, and the slowness in finding a new world economic order increase frustration and fear and cynicism. Religion, and its claim to be a source of hope, is questioned and labelled as a way of easy escape from the world's predicament.

Yet, stronger than such events and moods, day by day there is love in the lives of so many people, goodness and selflessness still break through, expectation shines in the eyes of both young and old, the gospel is shared by hungry hearts, hands are joined in confident prayer. Everywhere people begin to be conscious of their solidarity and to stand together in defence of justice and human dignity, their own and that of others.

2. The mission of the church

Such is the context for the mission of the church in the last two decades of this 20th century. More than ever before, the divisions among Christians appear as a scandal. The lack of full visible unity among Christians weakens the church's mission of reconciling human beings to God and to each other (see 2 Cor. 5:18-19), obscures the vision of Christ, the life of the world, and muffles his voice of hope.

More and more, churches are responding by a firm commitment "to the goal of visible unity in one faith and in one eucharistic fellowship expressed in worship and in common life in Christ and to advance towards that unity in order that the world may believe" (constitution of the WCC, art. III). They are being drawn together as agents of reconciliation. In many situations they speak and act together as defenders of human dignity and the rights of peoples and individuals, and to offer hope and purpose by pointing towards "the lamb of God who takes away the sin of the world" (John 1:29), including the sin which causes and perpetuates Christian divisions.

3. The common ground and a common goal

Since the Joint Working Group was set up almost two decades ago, far-reaching developments have taken place in relations between the Roman Catholic Church and the Orthodox, Anglican and Protestant member churches of the World Council. Looking back, one sees the growing awareness of the essential oneness of the people of God in each place and in all places, a oneness based on the real, though imperfect, communion existing between all who believe in Christ and are baptized in his name. Consciousness of this common ground has begun to transform the self-understanding of the churches. Their members are gradually acquiring a new picture of themselves and of their sisters and brothers in other traditions, of the way in which they belong together, of their mutual responsibility and accountability before the world, and of their need "to overcome the obstacles standing in the way to perfect ecclesial communion" (fourth report, Ia).

This common ground is more fully described in the fourth report of the Joint Working Group. Acknowledgment of it strengthens the conviction that the Roman Catholic Church and the member churches of the World Council in their bilateral and multilateral relationships share in one and the same ecumenical movement. More and more they are drawn to a common understanding of the goal of unity. This includes unity in one faith and in one visible ecclesial eucharistic fellowship, "built up into a spiritual house to be a holy priesthood, to offer spiritual sacrifices, acceptable to God through Jesus Christ" (1 Pet. 2:5). And there is growing understanding that this vision of the one church can be manifested as a conciliar fellowship of local churches which are themselves truly united.

4. Internal factors influencing ecumenical relationships

The continued relationship between the Roman Catholic Church and the World Council of Churches and its member churches is sustained by this acknowledged common ground and points to a common goal. But during the last two decades both bodies have undergone profound internal developments of their own, which both ease and hinder many areas of collaboration.

Starting from the integration of the International Missionary Council and the entry of the Eastern European Orthodox churches at the New Delhi assembly (1961), the World Council of Churches has undergone major transformation, growing in membership to more than three hundred churches. More and more it has become a truly worldwide fellowship. At the same time, and building on earlier affirmations about the ministry of the laity, it has reached out through many programmes to make the ecumenical movement a reality among the whole people of God in the whole inhabited earth.

This process of growth and of transformation has faced the World Council with a double task. First, in becoming a truly worldwide fellowship, it had to come to terms with the difficulty of living in a genuine dialogue not only of traditions but also of cultures, with all members participating in each other's lives, sharing burdens and resources, joys and sufferings. Secondly, in addressing itself to the life of its member churches as total communities, it had to respond to the expectations of both women and men, lay and ordained, young and old in their mutual relationships in the ecumenical movement.

In the Roman Catholic Church, the strong call of the Second Vatican Council (1962-65) for renewal in all areas of personal and communal life has awakened new energies whose potential is still in process of being realized. For instance, renewed awareness of the inter-relation of the local church in bonds of communion with the other local churches and with the see of Rome opened up promising possibilities for understanding the place of unity and diversity within the church and the nature of ecclesial communion. But the practical implications of this and of the collegiality it implies are still being worked out in new initiatives and new pastoral structures such as episcopal conferences and other regional and local bodies, and it is these which have primary responsibility for overseeing ecumenical activities.

The patient, unswerving work done under Pope Paul VI to implement the stance of the Second Vatican Council has been followed by the vigorous pastoral leadership of Pope John Paul II; both popes have expressed a strong, clear, ecumenical commitment.

The dramatic and often enthusiastic first steps of Roman Catholic ecumenical involvement were followed by difficulties, some expected, some unforeseen. The scope and complexity of the task is being accepted more realistically, and the differences in structure, history and approach to problems are more honestly taken into account, not least in the relations with the World Council and its member churches.

5. A new "tradition" of ecumenical common witness

It is a cause for joy that some quite notable convergences are emerging in theological understanding of those very issues which had been so divisive; for example, on the nature of the mission of Christ, on the church and its unity, on baptism, eucharist and ministry. Especially there has been a striking convergence in the appreciation of the centrality of the word of God and the eucharist in liturgical worship, and this is being expressed in the similarity of forms used in eucharistic worship. Convergence in forms of social action and common witness has been evident regionally and locally, as churches have become more seriously engaged in trying to do everything together, save what the conviction of faith forbids. There is at present a strong convergence in concern for prayer and spiritual life. This is marked by a number of new movements among laity and clergy which have spread across all traditions.

Indeed one can speak of a new "tradition" of ecumenical understanding, shared concerns and common witness. At the same time, this new heritage is being challenged, because new voices are trying to be integrated into it. Strong accents from the experiences of Christian life and witness in Africa, Asia, Latin America and Oceania join those from Europe and North America. The various ecumenical agendas, which these different Christian traditions work out in their search for an authentic confession of Christ in each place and situation, are not always identical and can cause tensions in the common exploration of the unfathomable riches of the word of God for our times. In face of Christian renewal, there are different judgments about those cherished customs and practices which are so woven into the life of a church that they risk becoming identified with the substance of faith itself. Even the real convergences in theological understanding of faith and order are a strong challenge to churches to find the right ways to enable them to be received by all members. In fact, the remaining causes of division, theological or otherwise, are thrown into starker relief by those very convergences.

So the convergences, which some joyfully welcome as signs of the Spirit's patient work, are questioned by others as inimical to what they believe to be their Christian identity. The dialogue within each church about dialogue between the churches is a constant pastoral necessity.

It is a deep concern that there are groups and whole communities within the structured life of the parent bodies of the Joint Working Group, as well as outside it, which stand apart from the explicit dialogue and from the binding relationship of collaboration. Many of them are distant from both the process and the conclusions of ecumenical reflection, which thus become difficult to communicate in face of an attitude of estrangement.

Many churches, organizations and communities have learned to see the concerns for proclaiming the explicit gospel of Jesus Christ, commitment to social justice, and spiritual renewal as inseparable elements of their total life, mutually nourishing and a part of fidelity to their calling. Yet others want to separate one aspect at the expense of the others, a separation which goes across traditional confessional lines in a way that creates new divisions.

So both the Roman Catholic Church and the member churches of the World Council find in their ecumenical fellowship new kinds of potential divisions, even beyond the confrontation and polarization which mark many societies and the world as a whole. Both face the task of holding together the different elements of Christian witness and of keeping them vitally present in the one ecumenical movement. The common problems they face become a kind of new bond between the Council's member churches and the Roman Catholic Church as they seek to build communion among their own membership and to overcome new kinds of tension and division. With this goes the need for a continued effort of ecumenical awareness-building and formation of a new generation of young church members, who are less aware of the scandal of the divisions which remain, of the goal of unity, and the urgency of the task.

6. Shared concerns and common responses

So in the last decade, the World Council and its member churches and the Roman Catholic Church have found themselves with similar experiences. Under the shock of some of them, they have sometimes been driven inwards to concentrate on their own concerns. Yet in many cases their response to the challenges has been parallel, almost identical.

The reports of the 1973 Bangkok and the 1980 Melbourne conferences, together with the Nairobi section I report on "Confessing Christ Today", and Pope Paul VI's apostolic exhortation *Evangelii Nuntiandi* (Evangelization of the Modern World) affirm the inseparable relationship between proclamation of the gospel and action for justice in all Christian witness. Several papal statements and some WCC programmes, such as those on faith, science and technology, and on good news to the poor, show a convergence in understanding of the witness of the churches and the priorities of mission.

This new perspective on contemporary ways of confessing Christ in word and life has been strengthened through the studies of the WCC commission on Faith and Order on "Giving Account of the Hope That Is in Us", and through the "Common Witness" study of the Joint Working Group, which bring together the search for a common expression of the apostolic faith and the practice of common life and witness among the churches.

There are also similarities in the concern for the role of the laity and the meaning and direction of laity formation in terms of the responsibility of the whole people of God to share the mission of Christ in and to the world.

New insights which women are making known about themselves and their awakened expectations of full participation in the life of church and society pose theological and pastoral challenges and open up new possibilities. These have to be addressed together within the framework of a genuine community of men and women in church and society.

There is the challenge to the churches arising both from the remarkable progress in the multilateral studies of the Faith and Order commission of the World Council and at the same time from the proliferation and intensification of bilateral theological dialogues. Some of the latter, in which the Roman Catholic Church is engaged, have reached a stage that is of considerable significance for the partners and the ecumenical movement as a whole. How the further steps are to be taken will be inevitably a matter affecting all churches and will be of significance for the Faith and Order work where there is active Roman Catholic participation.

7. Acknowledging continuing differences

This brief survey of the relationship since the Joint Working Group came into being indicates progressive growth and convergence as well as the emergence of new problems.

As the JWG moves into a new phase of its work, there is a more realistic assessment of the differences between the two parent bodies, particularly on the international level, which still justify the answer given when the possibility of Roman Catholic membership in the Council was raised in the early 1970s – "not in the immediate future". Nor is it a question which is yet ready to be taken up again.

Among the reasons given are the way in which authority is considered in the Roman Catholic Church. It believes itself to be constituted as a "universal fellowship with a universal mission and structure as an essential element of its identity" (fourth report, II). Thus it gives importance to the differences of structure between itself and the WCC member churches and the differences of operation on a world level. Acknowledging this condition, a sense of realism has developed in the relationship which combines mutual respect and a practical attitude in face of the differences and the convergences achieved by two decades of experience.

The Roman Catholic Church acknowledges its responsibility within the one ecumenical movement and accepts the challenge of undertaking increased collaboration with the World Council of Churches and its member churches, despite its own non-member status.

The question asked in the fourth report remains valid: "How can the Roman Catholic Church and the World Council of Churches, without forming one structured fellowship, intensify their joint activities and thereby strengthen the unity, the common witness and the renewal of the churches?" The guidelines for the Joint Working Group as formulated in the fourth report have provided a clear orientation and framework and are here reaffirmed. If they are fully implemented, the Joint Working Group can be a more visible sign and expression of the relationship, in its role of servant to the two partners.

II. Functions and operations of the Joint Working Group

The description of the function of the JWG given in the fourth report continues to be an adequate indication of what it is and the way it works. It is intended to enable the Roman Catholic Church and the World Council of Churches to evaluate together the development of the ecumenical movement. As before, it will be a joint group with continuity of membership and sufficient breadth of representation from both sides. As an instrument of the parent bodies, it is in close contact with them and accountable to them.

1. Functions

The Joint Working Group aims primarily at discovering and assessing promising new possibilities for ecumenical development. It has the task of stimulating the discussion on the ecumenical movement and of being a challenge to the parent bodies by proposing new steps and programmes.

The Joint Working Group endeavours to interpret the major streams of ecumenical thought and action in the Roman Catholic Church and in the member churches of the World Council of Churches. It facilitates the exchange of information about the progress of the ecumenical movement, especially at the local level.

The Joint Working Group seeks to establish collaboration between the various organs and programmes of the Roman Catholic Church and of the World Council of Churches. In accordance with the principles and procedures of its parent bodies, it encourages the genuine development of a relation which will facilitate such collaboration. To do so it draws upon the insights gained from local experience. As in the past, it remains a consultative group, not an operative agency. It may be empowered by the parent bodies to develop and administer programmes it has proposed when this is called for.

As the Joint Working Group seeks to initiate and help keep alive the discussion on the implications of the ecumenical movement in the Roman Catholic Church and in member churches of the World Council of Churches, it also seeks the best means of communicating its findings and recommendations. An essential aspect of its task is to share its findings with its parent bodies.

2. Collaborators

The Joint Working Group seeks to be in contact with a large number and range of ecumenical organizations and programmes, especially on the local level. It may call upon various offices and programmes of the parent bodies for assistance when special help is needed in certain areas in the process of collaboration. It also seeks information and advice from individuals and organizations which have particular ecumenical experience and competence.

3. Style of operation

As the Joint Working Group seeks to meet the needs of the churches, the style of collaboration must be kept flexible. It must be adaptable to the various and changing needs. Therefore, it seeks to keep new structures to a minimum, while concentrating on ad hoc initiatives, as they are required by the actual developments within the ecumenical movement. On occasion, of course, particular projects may call for some structural organization, which will be set up after due authorization. Flexibility of style does not mean unplanned activity or lack of accountability. Rather it means more careful attention to the setting of priorities and to the use of resources.

III. Activities of the Joint Working Group, 1975-83

In its fourth report the Joint Working Group gave a prospective outline of priorities for collaboration and joint action in the years following 1975. Three of them have engaged the Joint Working Group in a major degree and call for description in this section.

A. PRIORITIES FOR COLLABORATION

1. The unity of the church – the goal and the way

This question had featured prominently in the initial reflections of the Joint Working Group when it was in process of formation. It was introduced again in order to look at new common perspectives coming out of theological discussions involving the Roman Catholic Church and member churches of the World Council of Churches over the preceding decade. For since the Joint Working Group had come into being, a number of old questions concerning unity had been clarified. A study so wide in its implications would need to go on over a number of years and it was to be structured in three parts:
1) identification of the convergences beginning to appear between the RCC and WCC member churches;
2) studies and consultations on the goal of unity, with mention of (a) elements of unity, (b) the church as sign and instrument;
3) consideration of the way to unity, i.e., the visible interim steps that lead to the goal.

The Joint Working Group itself took up the first of these in its meeting in 1977 as it looked at work already done and especially at the convergences in basic areas of faith and order. It had before it this material:
– draft notes on convergences between the RCC and the WCC;
– reactions to the Faith and Order report, "One Baptism, One Eucharist, and a Mutually Recognized Ministry";

– reactions to a survey on the extent to which churches have agreed on the mutual recognition of baptism as administered by each other (the survey was published as Faith and Order Paper no. 90).

The Joint Working Group felt its work on this first part of the topic was only an initial step which would have to be developed in the future and this task still remains to be done.

Since the Joint Working Group is not itself an organ of study, it sought the help of the Faith and Order commission in organizing the second part of the study. Using the plans developed by the Joint Working Group, the commission organized a consultation at Venice in 1978 on the issue of unity in faith. From this came a report which, after revision by the JWG and by a number of theologians from various traditions, was published as the Faith and Order Study Paper no. 100 with the title "Towards a Common Profession of Faith". It makes these points:

- ecumenical growth will require agreement on a common profession of faith;
- the essential elements of such a profession are known to us through the witness of the apostolic community transmitted in the scriptures;
- the ancient professions of faith were developed in response to particular challenges and tensions;
- the needs of the contemporary world could lead the churches to give new emphasis to different aspects of the apostolic texts;
- diversity of doctrinal expressions in the divided churches is not always a sign of dividedness in faith.

The significance of this phase of the study is that a first step has been taken to speak together of the one apostolic faith and of the convergences in theological understanding which can help Christians to move towards professing it together. Thus the study has started with a crucial point from which it can now move to the questions raised originally by the Joint Working Group.

The significance for the study of the other work being done in the Faith and Order commission (where twelve Catholic theologians are members) ought to be noted. Since its 1978 meeting at Bangalore, the commission has had its own long-term study project, "Towards the Common Expression of the Apostolic Faith Today". It had already identified this as one of the requirements for unity, along with the need for agreement on baptism, eucharist and ministry. The study is being continued; preliminary reports have been published and are now being put to WCC member churches and the RCC for response. This is a new and important step for the growth in theological convergence and has implications for the RC relation with the WCC, as member churches and the RCC are invited to look at the implications of this work.

The third part of the study has concentrated on current forms of ecumenical collaboration, especially councils of churches, as illustrating ways to unity. At its meeting in 1979 the Joint Working Group outlined a proposal for developing this theme, and an exploratory consultation was held in Venice in 1982 focusing on the role of councils of churches and "preconciliar structures" in promoting visible interim steps towards unity. The consultation reflected on the role of councils of churches as a means of meeting and mutual recognition, and of growing together towards full communion. It also looked at the importance of RC involvement in councils for fulfilling this role.

There are other elements which relate to the study. One was mentioned by the JWG in its fourth report when it spoke of the need "for an evaluation of the relation of bilateral confessional dialogues to one another and to multilateral conversations". Something was done towards this when, between 1978 and 1980, the secretaries of Christian world communions, the Secretariat for Promoting Christian Unity and the Faith and Order commission organized three sessions of a forum on bilateral dialogues, which has enabled an exchange of information and some reflection on the necessary interaction between multilateral and bilateral approaches to unity within the one ecumenical movement.

2. Common witness

This was the second of the principal questions to engage the Joint Working Group in the period after Nairobi, and it was a major topic for discussion in its meeting in 1977. In the late 1960s, the JWG had already done a study which was published in 1970 under the title "Common Witness and Proselytism". Meanwhile, common witness at all levels had increased greatly and took many new forms. Together with the rapid changes in society and in human relations, this seemed to warrant a new look at the topic. It was decided to begin with actual experience, and the ecumenical and missiological institute of Leiden generously enabled a survey to be made with a reflective analysis of the data obtained. This was the starting point for further work done in small groups and then in a larger consultation at Venice in 1979. The text produced was submitted to the JWG, which authorized its publication at the beginning of 1981 with an appendix which contains examples from several countries of various kinds of common witness. It has been published, not as a definitive document but as a working paper which can stimulate discussion and obtain reactions.

To appreciate the development to which the new study testifies, it may be useful to compare the two studies commissioned by the Joint Working Group. That of 1970 began as an attempt to confront the problem of proselytism. While remaining somewhat marked by its problem-orientation, it was able to move forward to an effort at articulating the value of common Christian witness. This study remains a valuable point of departure and a resource for further work, but it needed to be reviewed in light of what has happened since 1970.

The 1981 study takes up parts of the previous document that had not been sufficiently utilized and expands others that require development. Its major thrust is an attempt to develop the notion of common witness on the basis of a new understanding of unity and mission. The genuine practice of common witness on the local level in so many places has put the problem of proselytism in a different light, even if it is still a difficulty in new ways in some places. The study, in trying to reflect on and evaluate the new rich heritage of common witness, aims at drawing the attention of the churches to the importance of such witness for the unity that is sought and for the ecumenical movement as a whole. It also takes into consideration the factors which have stimulated common witness since 1971 and the difficulties which have impeded it.

The timeliness of the new study and the need for such an instrument of sensitization may be seen by looking at two recent major statements on common witness. The first is taken from the report of the world missionary conference held at Melbourne in May 1980:

> In celebrating, we witness to the power of the gospel to set us free. We can only celebrate in honesty if the churches realize the damage done to their common witness by the scandal of their comfortable life in division – we believe that unless the pilgrimage route leads the churches to visible unity, in the one God we preach and worship, the one Christ crucified for us all, the one Holy Spirit who creates us anew, and the kingdom, the mission entrusted to us in this world will always be rightly questioned. (*Your Kingdom Come*, p. 201)

The second is from an address given by Pope John Paul II:
> ... Yes, the urgent duty of Catholics is to understand what this witness must be, what it implies and requires in the life of the church... In all situations, according to circumstances, it would be necessary to endeavour, with great pastoral wisdom, to discover the possibilities of joint witness of Christians. Doing so, we will come up against the limits that our divergences still impose on this witness and this painful experience will stimulate us to intensify the effort towards a real agreement in faith... It is necessary to advance in this direction with prudence and courage. (address to the plenary of the Secretariat for Promoting Christian Unity, 8 February 1980, *Information Service*, no. 43, 1980, II)

3. Social collaboration

From the time of the Second Vatican Council, there has been quite a range of collaboration in the social field between the Roman Catholic Church and the World Council of Churches. It took place in the context of the whole relationship between the two bodies and of the activity of the Joint Working Group, which concerned itself with this field from the beginning. Hence there was exchange of information, regular consultation, and various contacts and efforts of collaboration between the agencies on each side.

a) A common effort was launched in 1968 with the setting up of SODEPAX as a joint venture of the Pontifical Commission Justice and Peace, and the World Council of Churches. Described as "an ecumenical experiment", it was given a three-year mandate to awaken the Christian churches and their members to a realization of their obligations to promote social justice, human development and peace. With a competent staff, SODEPAX made a widespread response to local initiatives and began to work in six programme areas – social communications, education for development, mobilization for peace, development research, theological reflection, work with peoples of other faiths.

After thorough reassessment, SODEPAX continued with a much smaller staff and programme, for three further mandates until 1980. In this period it concentrated on its programme of education for development in the sense of awareness-building. It served as a liaison between the Pontifical Commission Justice and Peace and the Unit of Justice and Service of the World Council of Churches, stimulating them to extend and intensify the already existing collaboration. In more recent times it issued a regular bulletin, *Church Alert*. SODEPAX maintained its local contacts and continued to act as a catalyst for some initiatives. It has been in making study and information resources for joint initiatives available to local situations that SODEPAX perhaps rendered the greatest service.

However, as a joint venture, SODEPAX continually came up against problems concerning its own structure and function, as well as the limits of the whole relation between the Roman Catholic Church and the World Council of Churches. And this rendered its operation at times unduly difficult. It also happened that the whole wide range of social collaboration tended to become limited to what SODEPAX itself was doing. As a consequence, initiatives that might have been taken up by the various responsible bodies on each side were neglected. Hence in 1980 it was decided that SODEPAX be discontinued.

b) Meanwhile, both within the churches and between them, differences on social ethics became acute in new ways. Different ecclesial presuppositions, divergent attitudes to the role of ideologies, different approaches to methods of social and political changes, different stands on questions of sexual ethics, different understandings of the relation of church and society are some examples. So in 1975 while mapping out its programme for the period after the World Council's Nairobi assembly, the Joint Working Group listed collaboration in social thought and action among its priorities.

The present report deals only with activities between the Roman Catholic Church and the World Council of Churches on the international level. But the ecumenical effort affected concrete situations and attitudes and brought about collaboration at all levels. Hence it is clear that although they are not mentioned in this report, all initiatives at the local, national and regional levels have a special importance. The Joint Working Group, insofar as it is within its competence, wants to promote and sustain them in their development and wider diffusion.

A new discussion began at the JWG meeting at Le Louverain in 1979, when an outline was formulated for a study on collaboration in social thought and action. Three areas for the work were pointed up: (a) the respective characteristics of the two partners as they act in the social field – this would be an attempt to take seriously the difference in nature between them and the different styles of operation it implies; (b) the areas of apparent convergence on issues of social ethics and those of obvious divergence; (c) points on which it is desirable to deepen and enrich the joint reflection of the RCC and the WCC. In specifying this plan further, the JWG in 1980 gave its opinion that the differences in structure and operation need to be taken fully into account if progress is to be made, emphasizing at the same time that "the differences in almost every case are not such as to prevent collaboration but rather call for sensitivity and careful planning to achieve coordination of efforts, participation in each other's studies and programmes, or common action according to the circumstances. For what ultimately matters and indeed determines whether structures and styles of operation are experienced as helps or hindrances is the will to work together effectively" (minutes of the JWG, 1980, Marseilles).

The JWG was aware both that new means of expressing the collaboration would have to be sought, and that it was also necessary to find better instruments for the whole relation in this field. Therefore the JWG proposed a consultation to look at the structures and styles of operation on both sides and to find flexible intermediate instruments to reinforce the collaboration and develop new forms to express it. The consultation took place in March 1981 and the aide-memoire it produced was given to the relevant organisms on each side in the hope that it might enable further steps to be taken together.

c) Until the present, this study has been an effort to respond to the facts of the situation and to find ways to move ahead in developing the partnership between the bodies on each side. Because both the RCC and the WCC wished to find a concrete visible means to foster further collaboration, the JWG developed the idea of a new flexible body, which would assist it in planning, perform a liaison function, and serve as a sign of the ecumenical will to work together. After the conversations of the Joint Working Group on social collaboration at Le Louverain and Marseilles, the executive of the JWG advocated the setting up of a joint consultative group for social thought and action.

The constituent members of this joint consultative group are the sub-units of Unit II: i.e., the Commission on Inter-Church Aid, Refugee, and World Service (CICARWS), the Commission of the Churches on International Affairs (CCIA), the Commission on the Churches' Participation in Development (CCPD), the Christian Medical Commission

(CMC), the Programme to Combat Racism (PCR), as well as one representative of each of the programme units: Faith and Witness, and Education and Renewal. On the Catholic side they are: the Pontifical Commission Justice and Peace, the Pontifical Council Cor Unum, the Pontifical Council for the Laity, the Secretariat for Promoting Christian Unity. It is an interim structure to give visibility to the collaboration between the staffs on each side. It does not make decisions but is to help orientate the collaboration in the social field, to facilitate its coordination, and advise the Joint Working Group, where appropriate, suggesting initiatives to the JWG and to its participating bodies as well as receiving suggestions from them. It is to hold three meetings and then its role and continued existence will be reviewed.

The joint consultative group considers its experience to date a positive one. It has allowed a general exchange of information and has proposed areas to be pursued, notably an effort of catechesis in the field of peace and disarmament and joint reflection on social involvement and proclamation of the gospel. The joint consultative group can also provide a framework within which questions of immediate collaboration between the various commissions concerned with issues of justice and service in the WCC and the corresponding bodies of the RCC can be stimulated, further clarified, and organized on a more regular and organic basis. It seems it may be expected to play a modest but useful role in an area where more needs to be done. It feels that its initial period will help in finding more long-term forms of collaboration and foresees the possibility of its own continuance.

d) Relations between individual offices of the holy see and sub-units of the World Council continued and intensified in the period 1975-83:
- CICARWS, CCPD and the Christian Medical Commission carried on various kinds of collaboration with the Pontifical Commission Justice and Peace, and the Pontifical Council Cor Unum. This included participation in each other's meetings, work groups and study groups as well as providing information and expertise for one another's works. It was helped by means of joint staff meetings between some dicasteries and some of the sub-units, which clarified positions and mutually enriched outlook and programmes. One result of these joint staff meetings is the recent joint publication by CCIA/PCJP of the volume *Peace and Disarmament: Documents of the World Council of Churches and of the Roman Catholic Church.*
- There has been a special relationship between the Christian Medical Commission, the Secretariat for Promoting Christian Unity (since 1971), and Cor Unum. Among other things, this made it possible to have a Roman Catholic consultant with the CMC staff until summer 1979. Since then the position has not been filled. CMC invites Cor Unum, together with other RC participants, to all its meetings. CMC has participated in Cor Unum study groups on health. There is cooperation at national and local levels, which focuses especially on primary health care and is expressed through more than twenty national coordinating offices for health, and through joint efforts in the procurement of pharmaceutical supplies.
- The Commission Justice and Peace has developed a relationship with the Church and Society sub-unit through the latter's study "Faith, Science and Technology".

B. ONGOING COLLABORATION

The mandate of the JWG requires it to initiate and promote collaboration between the organs and programmes of the Roman Catholic Church and the World Council of

Churches. Throughout this past period it has supported many forms of collaboration which give significant expression to the relation between the two parent bodies. In addition to what has already been mentioned in preceding sections, the following are worthy of note.

1. Commission on Faith and Order

For almost fifteen years the commission on Faith and Order has had a number of Roman Catholic theologians among its official members. This has enabled the commission to draw increasingly on RC participation of agreed statements on *Baptism, Eucharist and Ministry* and in the broader effort to explore the conditions of a common confession of the apostolic faith today which incorporates the results of the study initiated by the Joint Working Group.

2. Week of Prayer for Christian Unity

The Secretariat of the Commission on Faith and Order and the Secretariat for Promoting Christian Unity have continued to convene an international group to prepare the common material for the celebration of this week, based on proposals coming each year from an ecumenical group in a particular country. The Week of Prayer continues to be of great significance in stimulating local ecumenical initiatives. The prayer cycle *For All God's People* offers a means of developing a new pattern of mutual intercession.

3. Relationships with the Commission on World Mission and Evangelism (CWME)

For several years, a number of Roman Catholic missionary orders which work with the Congregation for the Evangelization of Peoples have established a consultative relationship with the Conference on World Mission and Evangelism of the WCC. They have also sent observer-consultants to attend the meetings of the Commission on World Mission and Evangelism. This collaboration has been particularly important for RC participation in the world missionary conference of CWME at Melbourne in 1980, as well as for the study on "Common Witness", initiated by the Joint Working Group.

4. Dialogue with People of Living Faiths

Though not structured in ways comparable to the collaboration in the areas of Faith and Order and World Mission and Evangelism, a very fruitful cooperation has developed between the WCC working group on Dialogue with People of Living Faiths and Ideologies and the Vatican Secretariat for Non-Christians. In recent years attention has focused on dialogue with Muslims, and both sides attach great importance to the continuation of this relationship.

5. Ecumenical Institute, Bossey

A new field of collaboration has opened up around the programme of the Ecumenical Institute with the presence of some RC students, an RC board member, and the visit of the Graduate School to Rome each year at the end of its course.

For some time the Secretariat for Promoting Christian Unity has endeavoured to ensure an effective RC presence with the teaching staff of the Ecumenical Institute both for the period of the Graduate School and the major courses sponsored by the Institute.

6. The sixth assembly of the World Council of Churches, Vancouver, July-August 1983

Since the time of the Second Vatican Council, it has become increasingly possible for the Roman Catholic Church and the World Council of Churches to participate and in some way share in each other's great events. The assembly of Vancouver offers also to the Roman Catholic Church the occasion to celebrate the ecumenical movement and renew its ecumenical commitment, even though it will be less directly involved in those aspects of the assembly which make it the highest legislative body of the Council. There will be twenty Roman Catholic delegated observers at the assembly, as well as some advisers and guests. There is a considerable effort being made to inform Roman Catholics on various levels of the assembly and to awaken an intelligent interest in it and to invite them to support it by prayer. By means of reports from several study consultations, an RC contribution is also being made to the study process in the assembly.

IV. Proposals for future work

Before submitting proposals for its future work, the Joint Working Group wants to draw attention to a concern which applies equally to all areas of its activities. In the mandate of the JWG, given in the fourth report and reaffirmed here, hope is expressed that the JWG will "draw upon insights gained from local experience to foster... collaboration". Already in its interim account, published with the agreement of the parent bodies in 1980 (cf. "Deepening Communion: An Account of Current Work", in *The Ecumenical Review*, XXXII, 2, April 1980, pp.179ff.), the JWG expressed its conviction "that it needs to receive greater visibility in order to stimulate local collaboration" (*ibid.*, p.185). Examples were given there of how this objective could be achieved. They included the sharing of results of its deliberations with the constituencies on both sides, even at an interim stage, the sharing of study documents, visible gestures to highlight aspects of collaboration, visits, special meetings, using the Week of Prayer, and highlighting the Joint Working Group meeting itself.

1. The way towards unity

Were a reminder needed, the experience of the past decade would demonstrate that the necessary process of mutual clarification, study and negotiation is not itself enough to achieve unity. The ecumenical movement is an integral part of the whole reconciling work of Christ in which we participate most fruitfully by that holiness of life which is an identification with God's will. Essential to it is a conversion of heart and life both corporate and individual. This must vivify and motivate the necessary renewal of present structures and provide the impulse not only to bring Christians together and enable them to accept each other, but to arrive at a common confession of the one faith and reconciliation in one ministry. It is, in short, the conversion to that which God wills for the church. This is the condition which is indispensable for all the other efforts to be fruitful.

Significant progress has been made in recent years through bilateral and multilateral dialogues, in cooperation between the JWG and Faith and Order, as well as through the forum on bilateral conversations, in sharpening the common understanding of the goal of unity, as well as discerning essential elements and conditions of unity. While the JWG is not itself the place for dialogue as such, it does have to concern itself with the whole relations between the Roman Catholic Church and the member churches of the World Council and must therefore interest itself in the results of the dialogues and their meaning for unity. The JWG should maintain close contact with the work of the commission on Faith and Order, especially in the area of a common expression of the apostolic faith and in the deepening of agreement on the understanding and practice of baptism, eucharist and the ministry. The publication of the convergence statement *Baptism, Eucharist and Ministry* presents a considerable challenge also for the Catholic side as it becomes necessary to determine how far this work does represent a convergence in faith.

In continuing the earlier joint programme on the "Unity of the Church, the Goal and the Way", outlined in 1976, the Joint Working Group proposes to focus attention on those parts which have not been sufficiently taken up, i.e., (1) a renewed reflection on the church as sign and sacrament, coming back after more than a decade to its earlier ecclesiological study on "Catholicity and Apostolicity"; (2) a continuation of the review of ecumenical structures of collaboration, specifically councils of churches and the other interim structures which already express a unity "in via". In pursuing this study, attention should be given to the themes proposed by the exploratory consultation organized by the Faith and Order commission and the Secretariat for Promoting Christian Unity in 1982 on the significance of councils of churches in the ecumenical movement. These include the following:
- the ecclesial importance of the "recognition" and "fellowship" experienced in a council of churches;
- the place of councils on the way towards visible unity and their role in promoting movement from one stage to another;
- the interaction of local, national, regional and world "levels" as these affect the life of councils and their member churches;
- the relation of councils of churches to other forms of ecumenical collaboration.

Further, to emphasize the search for "visible interim steps", the JWG sees potential value in a reflection on the possibilities of common worship, including the sharing of liturgical and devotional resources, the ecumenical significance of the veneration of saints, and the encouragement of informed, mutual intercession (see *For All God's People*, Geneva, 1978).

Finally, in line with the effort of recent years to face together the pastoral care of mixed marriages, it would be valuable to reflect on what has been happening. It might be possible to see how this pastoral collaboration could intensify and become more widespread, so that a better witness be given to the growing unity between churches.

2. Common witness

Work for the visible unity of the church and common witness in the world are intimately related. The two studies published by the Joint Working Group – "Common Witness and Proselytism" (1970), and "Common Witness" (1981) – bring evidence to show that common witness is one of the essential ways of discovering and deepening the unity which is given in Christ, while the strongest form of common witness is the will of the churches to give visible expression to the communion which already exists among them. This communion is not yet complete, but common witness serves to show in striking ways how it is growing and is a means of deepening it. Inevitably in giving witness together, divided Christians are brought in new and painful ways to face the divisions which remain, yet this very experience becomes, through witness given together, an impelling motive to work for the fullness of visible communion. Common witness does not confuse or hide the issue of division but helps the churches live and act together before the world in the name of Jesus Christ as Lord and Saviour. It is thus a test and condition for the ecumenical movement.

Therefore, the JWG affirms common witness as one of its priorities. It will explore ways in which the relationship between the RCC and the WCC may give evidence of it. It has also to work out the implications of the 1981 document for possible action at the world level by the RCC and the WCC. The document is translated into several languages, and it must continue to be the task of the JWG to ensure that it is brought in an adequate way to the attention of the RCC and the WCC member churches for reflection, reaction and implementation, so that they may renew their commitment to witness in unity and may explore fuller possibilities of common witness in their respective situations.

Part of the task is also an articulation of the import of the theological perspectives on common witness, outlined in the study document, for the other studies on the unity of the church, for the reception of the doctrinal convergences being reached by the churches, and ultimately for the achievement of a sharing in eucharistic communion.

In view of the desire expressed at the time of the Second Vatican Council for a common declaration on religious freedom, and giving account to the present situation in the world which elicited the recent statement of the World Council of Churches on religious liberty, it becomes desirable to explore the possibility of working together on the question of religious liberty to secure a common witness.

Recently the Joint Working Group has stressed the need to stimulate ecumenical awareness and to give a new ecumenical formation on regional and local levels by various endeavours of common witness. One means of doing this may be through a series of joint regional consultations over the next few years to explore in a practical way opportunities for common witness.

3. Social collaboration

Common witness includes the efforts of the churches to act together in the defence and promotion of human dignity, the relief of human need, and the affirmation of justice and peace which must be expressed in human relationships and in the structures of society. The concern for Christian social responsibility is an integral part of the apostolic mission of the church. Missionary perspectives necessarily open on to solidarity with the poor, justice, peace and respect for human rights, while the social responsibility of the church has its context in the proclamation of the word and the opening of the human spirit to the transcendent.

This area, however, has also an integrity of its own, and should continue to be seen by the JWG as belonging to its proper field of concern. Recognizing that social collaboration will continue to be conditioned by the differences in structure and method of working in the RCC and the WCC, the Joint Working Group should not cease to encourage the development of flexible forms of collaboration on the international as well as on national and local levels.

Despite the doctrinal differences among the churches, in recent years an ecumenical convergence has been growing in the understanding of several issues in social ethics. Recognizing this convergence, the JWG should look for ways which could help to make visible to a wider audience the joint commitment to these elementary affirmations about Christian social responsibility, which are in conformity with the common Christian faith. In accordance with its earlier discussion at Le Louverain (1979), the JWG sees value in exploring possibilities of common pastoral and catechetical guidance and common work in the following areas:

a) Development: There is, for example, agreement that structural changes are required in the international economic order to correct inequities and spread the use of resources and the benefits of technology among all peoples.
b) Peace: Agreement exists, among other points, that the madness of the arms race diverts resources from development, increases the threat of force in international dispute, and creates the conditions for the destruction of the human race.
c) Human rights: Based on inherent human dignity, the "image of God" in us, and on our common redemption in Christ, the rights (inter alia) to life, to access to health care, to work, to a decent standard of living, to cultural identity, to education, to participation in public life, to dissent for conscience's sake, to physical and psychological integrity, to freedom from torture, and to religious liberty, must be safeguarded by international agreement (see minutes of the JWG, Le Louverain, 1979).

Attention should also be given to the possibility of encouraging initiatives in the area of racism and concerning the role of women.

In addition, the Joint Working Group had noted in 1979 that there are areas on which convergence is lacking and which need to be explored further before common action could be possible. These differences appear among the member churches of the WCC as well as between some of them and the Roman Catholic Church: the pattern of difference changes with the issues and includes aspects of the roles of women and men in the life of the community; patterns of family life, birth control and sexual ethics; forms and means of responding to the need for social change; and methodological approaches to ethics.

Finally, the Joint Working Group should look for ways to enrich and deepen the joint reflection of the WCC and the RCC on basic theological and ecclesiological themes which constitute the necessary background for deeper mutual understanding of ecumenical social responsibilities. Such themes are the relation of the kingdom of God to this world, the role of faith in social problems, the relation between evangelism and struggle for justice in society, the action of the churches and the role of laity, the modes of intervention of the church in the secular realm of society.

On a more practical level, the JWG should encourage appropriate initiatives to come to a closer and more effective coordination between the network of RCC- and WCC-related service agencies at various levels in the area of aid and relief, in order to avoid the possibilities of divisive effects of separate programmes for local communities.

It is important to find ways of sharing information about the considerable volume of ecumenical work going on in local situations and to evaluate this, so that a fruitful interaction may be achieved between initiatives at various levels.

4. Ecumenical formation

The JWG insists on the present urgency of the task of ecumenical formation. It stresses that the improved relations between still separated Christians are not enough. The scandal of Christian division and their deleterious effect on Christian witness continues to obscure the saving power of Christ's grace. God's plan to sum up all things in Christ requires to be shown forth in the common proclamation of the one apostolic faith and in the communion of the one visible eucharistic fellowship, and to be an active power in drawing the human community into reconciliation and oneness. Hence the need to deepen an understanding of the mystery of the church.

Ecumenical formation is a process which includes several elements. It means imparting information about what God is doing through the ecumenical movement to draw his people into one. It entails learning about existing differences between Christians and their churches and about the new convergences being achieved. Such learning comes both from obtaining the relevant information and from involvement in the deeper levels of experience in the life of the Christian community at worship, in service and in witness. It comes, too, in the acknowledgment and practice of responsibility towards each other by communities of separated Christians, as well as by their engagement in various forms of ecumenical dialogue.

The ecumenical dimension is an indispensable part of all processes of Christian formation and nurture, be it the formation of laity, youth work, programmes of catechesis and religious education, or theological training.

Today many people, especially those participating in programmes of laity formation, receive their most significant experience of the ecumenical dimension in the common effort for justice, peace and development. Such initiatives touch on urgent problems and bring Christians together in the exercise of responsibility for building the whole human community, as well as relating global issues to daily action.

Reflection on the nurturing character of all these experiences is needed. It is clear that further ways have to be found of bringing together the different processes of learning, relating formal teaching processes to informal methods of learning (such as conscientization). This can also help Christians to appreciate the necessary relation between the goal of the unity of the church and the concern for the unity of mankind.

Much has to be done if ecumenical formation is to become a full part of the whole Christian ministry. The impact of ecumenical initiatives among educators often remains on the professional level and insufficiently communicates with or benefits from the experience of parish and local communities. Promising new forms of Christian formation at various levels still often do not take sufficient account of the ecumenical movement and its role in the mission of the church. More attention could be given to the ecumenical process found in frequent local and spontaneous efforts of local and spontaneous joint study and action (e.g., during Lent, etc.).

The formal catechetical programmes of various churches often take the ecumenical dimension for granted. It is necessary to spell it out sufficiently and to exploit the new theological convergences. Opportunities of joining in common action with regard to catechetical materials or syllabuses, where this is possible (see the apostolic exhortation of Pope John Paul II, *Catechesi Tradendae*), must not be missed.

Young people have a new experience and often relate to events in the world with a special sensitivity. Better ways must be found of alerting them to the ecumenical dimension and its place in the total responsibility of Christians to and for each other and for the world. As they face life, they need help to discern and to use those living situations where ecumenical learning takes place. In this they will need the wisdom and support of those who have pastoral and teaching roles in the church. Likewise those who have leadership in the churches have to show confidence in young people and react with sensitivity to the contribution which they will make.

Another crucial area is that of theological education and particularly the education of pastors, perhaps the most influential point in ecumenical sensitization. There is a great range of possibilities, but even where there are joint or collaborative faculties and programmes more could be done to draw out their potential with the support and guidance of those responsible in the various churches. In some seminaries homage is paid to ecumenical ideals, while there is an absence of any formal teaching about the ecumenical movement or its history and its theological, spiritual and pastoral significance for the Christian community. As well as trying to include the ecumenical dimension in the courses on theology, it seems still necessary to have also courses which give explicit information and reflection on the ecumenical movement.

At this point in the history of the ecumenical movement and of the relations between the RCC and the WCC and its member churches, a new effort has to be made to assess and use more effectively the resources for this basic task of ecumenical formation.

5. Continuing collaboration

It will be the task of the Joint Working Group to look carefully at what can be done to develop and extend the regular pattern of collaboration and common effort with the various sub-units of the World Council of Churches. In several instances it is substantial and has its own rhythm and style, in others it is still necessary to be on the watch for possibilities of deepening what are as yet only initial contacts. There are several areas where immediate work has to be done.

A. Faith and Order: With completion of the study "Baptism, Eucharist and a Mutually Recognized Ministry", it is now important to find the right ways of obtaining reactions. First steps were taken at an earlier stage in the work, and these did involve some Catholic theological faculties. Now the effort has to be made on a wider scale to have the document known and to test its conclusions so that the convergence in faith which it represents may become part of the consciousness of Christian people. Further necessary progress can take place only if discussion is aroused on all levels, especially on the implications of the convergences for the relationship between the churches.

A similar task has to be done with the study "Towards a Common Expression of the One Apostolic Faith Today", although this is not yet in its final stages.

B. Dialogue with other faiths and ideologies: The pattern of contact and exchange of collaboration now seems to have developed to the point where one or other initiative of the common programme could be undertaken and ways of giving visible and structured expression to the relationship be explored.

C. Community of women and men in church and society: Work on this theme has been done on the Roman Catholic side and is actively being pursued in the World Council of Churches. It involves many of the major issues of today seen from the angle of the involvement and responsible participation of men and women in the life of society. It seems desirable to do more towards a sharing of information and resources and, if possible, coordination of work with consideration given eventually to common efforts in evaluation and follow-up. It could be interesting also, and not only in connection with this question, to look together at the changes on each side in the understanding of the role of the laity over the last thirty years.

D. Joint staff meetings: Meetings between the staff of the individual responsible Roman dicasteries and the corresponding sub-unit of the World Council of Churches have proved their usefulness for exchange of information, mutual sharing of resources, and discovering ways of developing the partnership. They already take place regularly between the Pontifical Commission Justice and Peace and the Churches' Commission on International Affairs and with the Churches' Commission on Participation in Development, between the Dialogue with Living Faiths and Ideologies and the Secretariat for Non-Christians, between the Programme for Theological Education and the Congregation for Catholic Education, between the Pontifical Council for the Laity and the Unit on Education and Renewal. It is important to be alert to new possibilities for bringing other partners from each side into such a regular contact.

V. The future of the Joint Working Group in the ecumenical movement

1. The Joint Working Group was set up in 1965 by the RCC and the WCC as a manifestation of their need to work together in the ecumenical movement.

Its task was described as being to clarify the principles and methods of ecumenical collaboration while giving due account to the differences between its parent bodies, one a worldwide church, the other a council of churches. It has continued to emphasize, as was evident in the fourth report in 1975, the common ground between the churches engaged in the ecumenical movement, and affirmed the real though imperfect communion that already exists between the Roman Catholic Church and the churches in the fellowship of the World Council of Churches.

So the JWG expresses the will of member churches of the WCC and the RCC to meet, to grow in mutual recognition, and to find new ways to be together in the service of unity and mission. Its structure is modest, but with the confidence and support of its parent bodies, it acts as a continuing reminder to the churches engaged in the ecumenical movement that dialogue and action, the restoration of communion and the commitment to common witness, to the unity of the church, and the renewal of the human community belong together. So it attends to both the theological and the social and pastoral dimensions and tries to stimulate the interaction between all levels of ecumenical work. It is an instrument of its parent bodies with the task of keeping prominently before them and before all Christian churches the urgent need to grow in communion and to manifest the existing fellowship of churches through common witness.

2. In the period which lies ahead, the JWG must review the contacts and collaboration taking place between the sub-units of the WCC and partners on the Roman Catholic side and try to find appropriate ways of expressing them. It must continue to be a vantage point from which the whole relationship and its place in the ecumenical movement is surveyed. It will address itself anew to its priorities for the next period – the unity of the church, common witness and social collaboration. Most challenging is the attention it must give to ecumenical formation. This theme reflects a new perspective and is a response to an urgent need in the current ecumenical situation, which calls for the deepening of ecumenical consciousness and the identification of realistic and visible steps which can be taken together.

In all of this, it becomes always more necessary that the JWG draw insights from what is happening locally. Here case studies of ecumenical initiatives will have a larger role to play, and special attention will need to be given to the aspirations and experiences of the major regions, with all their diversity and new promise. In turn the JWG has to make an increasing effort to communicate what it is doing and the significance of this – in the first place always to its parent bodies as it interprets major streams of ecumenical thought and action in the RCC and in member churches of the WCC. Increasingly it must find effective ways to communicate this also to all who have ecumenical and pastoral responsibility, as it discovers and assesses promising new possibilities for ecumenical development. The JWG is in many ways in a unique position both to stimulate its parent bodies by proposing new steps and programmes, and to respond to some of the major streams of ecumenical thought and action, surveying, interpreting, encouraging and challenging. This will meet the demand that the JWG be more and more a point to reflect on and analyze important events that affect the unity willed by Christ for the church and the renewal of the human community. Only so can it have resources to contribute to a new ecumenical mentality among Christians.

3. The Joint Working Group is a small body and its immediate are aims necessarily limited, but the bodies it serves have a wide constituency and broad responsibilities. The time in which we live needs the ecumenical hope which it promotes. It is a sign that new obstacles to ecumenical advances must also be faced without hesitation. With its vivid memories of the past two decades of the ecumenical movement, it can keep Christians from the RCC and the member churches of the WCC aware of the great change that has taken place, helping them to consolidate these gains in the life of the Christian fellowship and to go along joyfully with what God is doing to bring his people into one.

68. Sixth Report of the Joint Working Group

1990

Foreword

The Joint Working Group for relationships between the Roman Catholic Church and the World Council of Churches has just become twenty-five years old – an opportunity for it to take stock of what it has achieved.

The JWG came into existence immediately after Vatican II and the opportunity the latter opened up and endorsed for the Roman Catholic Church. The group was entrusted with studying the conditions for cooperation between the WCC and the Roman Catholic Church and even – in the first few years – with considering the possibility of the latter becoming a member of the WCC. When that prospect proved premature, the WCC turned its attention to furthering relations and practical cooperation between the two partners as far as possible.

In submitting the sixth report of the JWG we wish, first of all, to say how grateful we have been for the experience we have had since it was given its present membership following the 1983 assembly of the World Council of Churches at Vancouver.

Fraternal cooperation among its members has indeed been gradually consolidated till it has become a real fellowship characterized by natural trust and respect. We have learned to talk to each other and listen to each other with real openness. And our awareness of the common mission of our churches in the world has deepened to the point where that mission is seen as the urgent priority.

Reading this sixth report will in itself show the extent to which the productive relations between the WCC and the Roman Catholic Church have multiplied and developed. Setting aside the places in which they have found institutional expression, especially in the commission on Faith and Order, most of the sub-units of the WCC and their Roman Catholic partners have worked out a process of mutual consultation and sometimes common action which must be taken fully into account. The JWG has constantly applied itself to following this process through and expanding it. It has nevertheless not confined itself to this but has also sought to contribute its own bricks to the common structure. The JWG decided to publish as an appendix to this report two documents – on "The Church: Local and Universal" and on the "Hierarchy of Truths" [see following documents in this volume] – which it had ordered and officially received and which demonstrate this. We hope they will make a useful contribution to opening up new stages of fruitful reflection on the journey towards Christian unity.

It is true that we have also had to face certain difficulties – especially as the report shows in the field of social thinking and action. And in the last few years, Roman

Catholic participation in the world convocation on justice, peace and the integrity of creation was subject to a variety of ups and downs on which there is no occasion to go into detail here. We would mention only that this enabled us to realize that, as Cardinal Willebrands put it, "the difference in nature between the WCC and the Roman Catholic Church" represents a continuing obstacle to the full development of their relations. This obstacle must be analyzed more thoroughly. That must be one of the priority tasks of the next JWG.

Above all, however, we wish in submitting this report to state jointly our firm conviction that whatever may be the hazards of the day-to-day history of ecumenism, the search for unity must never cease. We have to be completely and constantly obedient to our Lord's command "that they may all be one". We cannot play fast and loose with that prayer and take up our stance in some status quo. On the contrary we must gratefully appraise the whole way along which the Lord has already brought us over the last fifty years and go forward yet more boldly and hopefully on the path he himself has opened up and in which he constantly walks ahead of us and awaits us!

Bishop Alan Clark
Pastor Jacques Maury
Joint presidents of the Joint Working Group

Introduction

The Joint Working Group of the Roman Catholic Church and the World Council of Churches joyfully celebrates its twenty-five years of ecumenical endeavour. Its mandate to serve the RCC-WCC relationships was given by the central committee of the WCC at Enugu, Nigeria, in 1965 and by the authorities of the RCC in the same year.

Since then the group has made five reports. They reflect the steady growth and maturing in the relations between the RCC and the WCC. The sixth report is prepared in a spirit of gratitude for these fruitful years. It gives an account of the activities of the group since the last assembly of the WCC at Vancouver in 1983. It also looks to the future with hope as the relationships continue and develop.

I. THE ECUMENICAL SITUATION

1. Current development

The life of the churches and the thrust of the ecumenical movement are affected by the situation of our world. Today there are many signs of hope for the human family, not least in places where spiritual forces have helped to break down the forces of tyranny. But we also face many grave problems which threaten the well-being of humanity and call for the concern and solidarity of all people of goodwill. The followers of Jesus Christ have a special duty to be fully present in the world in this time of promise and difficulty. It is a time when the ecumenical movement is more than ever necessary if the churches and Christian communities are to be a sign and seed of the unity, peace and hope which the human family needs.

There is much room for encouragement. An increasing number of Christian communities and ecumenical organizations are active in working for unity among Christians. A number of the essential issues dividing Christians have still to be resolved, but suspicion and hostility have in large part given way to good will and mutual respect. Churches and Christians of different confessions often engage in common witness and in projects of interchurch aid which respond to urgent human need. In a world so often marked by despair, the ecumenical movement itself, as a historic effort to achieve full reconciliation among Christians, is a source of hope. The movement reaches back to the deepest spiritual roots that all Christians share and can be an answer to the spirit of secularism which marks our modern world.

The WCC and the RCC have played an important part in the ecumenical process, not least through their Joint Working Group. The official visit of Pope John Paul II in 1984 to the WCC, as well as the visit of Dr Emilio Castro, general secretary of the WCC, to the Holy See in 1986, have helped consolidate the relationships and the cooperation. In its letter to the extraordinary synod in 1985, the central committee of the WCC could speak of the bonds of "fraternal solidarity" that exist between the two partners. On important ecumenical occasions, each has shared in the initiatives and events of the other. The Assisi Day of Prayer for Peace, called by Pope John Paul II in 1986, was supported by the presence of a high-level delegation from the WCC. There has been notable Roman Catholic presence in the WCC assemblies and conferences.

So the ecumenical task has continued well. However, it has yet to reach its goal of full visible unity. The JWG still has substantial work to do. It is more than ever called to help the RCC and the WCC to strive for the unity of Christians and for the unity and solidarity of all human beings.

2. Patterns of relationships between the WCC and the RCC

Twelve RC theologians are full members of the Faith and Order commission.

Seven others participate as consultants in the commission on World Mission and Evangelism (CWME). An RC representative is on the Bossey board. For a number of years now, three Roman Catholics have worked on the WCC programme staff: in CWME, Bossey and JPIC. Various forms of contact and working relationships have developed also between other WCC sub-units and Vatican offices and missionary societies. There has been useful and continual mutual exchange of information, of newly published documents and of staff visits.

Catholic consultants and observers have participated in a series of WCC conferences, meetings, consultations and seminars.

Many member churches of the WCC and the RCC have close relationships on regional and national levels in taking part in and contributing to ecumenical organizations.

3. Factors that influence the relationships

The above-mentioned patterns are positive factors which promote ecumenical collaboration and strengthen relations not only between WCC sub-units and Vatican departments but also between WCC member churches and the RCC throughout the world. Encouraging statements about the results of this collaboration and achievement of the JWG have been made by Pope John Paul II, representatives of the WCC and leaders of local churches.

Through the agenda of the JWG and other ecumenical endeavours, the RCC and the churches in the WCC fellowship have faced the challenges of division. They have shared in some basic theological reflections on visible unity and contributed to the process of reconciliation, renewal and growing communion. The WCC and the RCC have increased awareness of the need for mission and dialogue, for promoting the values of the gospel in secularized societies, for Christian stewardship of creation, for furthering justice and peace, for the protection of human rights and dignity.

The WCC member churches belong to almost all Christian traditions. They bring a variety of theological streams into the WCC, which has implications for ecumenical dialogue and collaboration.

The diverse understanding of the ecumenical goal and of the means of achieving visible unity may affect ecumenical progress. Acts of proselytism, excessive concern for "confessional identity", lack of awareness about common problems and ecumenical tasks also affect dialogue and rapprochement. Divergencies on basic doctrinal questions, ethical, social and political issues further limit the process of advancing towards full communion and effective common action.

The WCC and the RCC differ in their nature, their structure, their style of operation, their exercise of authority. Sometimes these differences are a hindrance to cooperation. The RCC is a universal church with a strong hierarchical structure fostering unity in diversity. The WCC is a fellowship of autonomous churches bound together in the search for visible unity and common witness. They are not held together by canonical/structural form, but see themselves as belonging to an ecumenical fellowship which enables them to grow together.

The ecumenical partners need to be sufficiently attentive to the use of their own press and other media in portraying the image of the "other". Likewise, more care needs to be taken in the ways the partners speak of some events in the life of the churches and their ecumenical significance.

II. FUNCTIONS AND OPERATIONS OF THE JWG

In its first official report, the JWG stated that "its task, both spiritual and pastoral, is to be undertaken in a spirit of prayer and in the conviction that God is guiding his people... The group is... called on to discern the will of God in the contemporary ecumenical situation" (first report, 1). This has been a guiding principle for the members of the group.

The JWG is a consultative body. It explores new forms of cooperation between the WCC and the RCC and prepares projects but does not make or monitor policy.

At present the JWG consists of twelve members from each side, some of whom are involved in pastoral work in different parts of the world, others are from departments of the Roman curia and units of the WCC. Consultants are co-opted for particular tasks. The JWG normally meets once a year.

A small executive committee is responsible for the ongoing work between annual meetings and prepares the agenda and material for the plenary meetings. At the end of its normal seven-year mandate, the JWG presents an official report to the parent bodies.

Members may also discuss questions and ideas arising from JWG work with their own churches so as to foster dialogue and ecumenical relations.

The JWG is called to help in assessing the ecumenical situation and stimulating the search for visible unity and common witness. It should select those ecumenical issues which require particular care, and promote development of relationships between the WCC and the RCC. This means giving attention, support and encouragement to whatever contributes to wider ecumenical progress, and discerning differences which hinder WCC-RCC relations. By keeping itself informed and stimulating the spread and exchange of information, and sponsoring particular studies, the JWG serves as an instrument of cooperation between the WCC and the RCC. When its findings commend themselves to the parent bodies, the JWG offers its services in helping to present ideas and proposals to the appropriate departments on either side and to such concerned bodies as theological faculties and ecumenical institutes.

III. ACTIVITIES OF THE JWG DURING THE PERIOD 1983-1990

A. Priorities of this period

Since the sixth assembly of the WCC (1983), the JWG has concentrated on four areas: unity of the church – the goal and the way, ecumenical formation, common witness, and social thought and action. Some of these themes, of course, overlap.

1. UNITY OF THE CHURCH – THE GOAL AND THE WAY

The JWG has kept high on its agenda the goal of visible unity of Christians and has regularly undertaken studies of specific importance for this task. A significant role in this work has been carried out by the Faith and Order commission and the Pontifical Council for Promoting Christian Unity. The JWG hopes that by such studies it can be of service in complementing and supporting the ongoing work of bilateral and multilateral dialogues.

In the period 1983-90 five areas of studies relating to unity have been undertaken by the JWG. Two are primarily theological: "The Church: Local and Universal" and "The Hierarchy of Truths". The impetus for work on these two themes came during the visit of Pope John Paul II to the WCC (1984). A third area of study concerns new potential sources of division, especially ethical issues. A fourth relates to the impact of councils of churches on the ecumenical movement. A fifth is concerned with a particular pastoral issue: Christian mixed marriages.

a) The local and universal church

This study document deals with fundamental aspects of the mystery of the church: its local and universal expressions. There is first of all a discussion of the ecclesiology of communion. It is presented as a framework within which the study of the church local and universal takes place. It emphasizes that these two dimensions of the church are not two alternative aspects of the church from which to choose, but must be understood in relationship and seen simultaneously. A second part looks at the church local and universal in ecumenical perspective, presenting the view of Orthodox, Roman Catholic and Protestant positions on this theme. A third section indicates ecclesial elements required for full communion with a visibly united church, which is the goal of the ecumenical movement. This discussion includes a presentation of the way the notion of ecclesial communion has been interpreted by the RCC in the Second Vatican Council (1962-65) and by the New Delhi (1961) and Nairobi (1975) assemblies of the WCC. A fourth section describes the ways in which the different Christian world communions understand and use canonical structures to express and safeguard communion within their churches.

The JWG commissioned and received this study document and presents it with the hope of stimulating further ecumenical reflection on this theme.

b) Hierarchy of truths

The purpose of this study was "an ecumenical attempt to understand and interpret the intention of the Second Vatican Council in speaking of a 'hierarchy of truths', and to examine some implications for ecumenical dialogue and common Christian witness" (no. 3). The result of this work is a study document [see Document 70 in this volume]. It analyzes the conciliar statement, indicates examples of a "hierarchy of truths" in Christian history and in different Christian traditions (even though the expression is not used there), and draws out implications for ecumenical dialogue and for the goal of full communion, as well as for mission, common witness and theological method. It is noteworthy that this study document is the first ecumenical text on this subject.

The JWG commissioned and received this study document and hopes that it will render a service to the wider ecumenical discussion.

c) Ethical issues as new sources of potential divisions

The past twenty-five years have seen more and better multilateral and bilateral dialogues on those *doctrinal* differences which helped to cause and perpetuate divisions among the churches. In many of these dialogues the RCC has been an active partner with member churches of the WCC. Convergence and common affirmations are beginning to form on such classical divisive doctrinal issues as scripture and Tradition, baptism, eucharist and ministry.

But during the same period, personal and social *ethical* questions have appeared, causing disputes and even threatening new divisions within and among churches. All Christian traditions recognize that ethics cannot be separated from revealed doctrine: faith does have ethical consequences. Yet the JWG notes that in fact there is not enough serious, mature and sustained ecumenical discussion on many of these ethical issues and positions, personal and social; for example, nuclear armaments and deterrence, abortion and euthanasia, permanent married love and procreation, genetic engineering and artificial insemination.

The JWG has taken the first steps in exploring the new sources of potential ecumenical divisions. It first asked a few interchurch groups to investigate and illustrate this development in local contexts, and then it convened a small group of specialists to review these studies. The JWG proposes that the subject be a priority for the post-Canberra period. The JWG's intention is not to examine the substance of each of the potentially or actually divisive issues, but to see how they may best be approached in dialogue. Such issues can offer new opportunities for the increase of mutual understanding and respect and, we may hope, for common witness without compromise of a church's convictions or of Christian conscience. The JWG emphasizes the following questions:

1. Why are some ethical issues so emotionally and intellectually divisive that often mature dialogue about them is inhibited, even avoided?
2. In what ways do churches formulate ethical principles and decide on specific issues?

3. Do churches help their members to enlighten and form consciences?
4. In what ways do the churches understand and use their authority to decide on specific issues for all their members?
5. What are the ways in which the churches should humbly enter into public debate, where peoples of other world faiths or of secular persuasions also desire to live together peacefully and justly; how should Christian convictions be presented as a contribution to the common good?
6. When does an ethical issue on which Christians disagree become an obstacle to full ecclesial communion?

In discussing these questions, Christians can rediscover the resources which our church traditions provide for ethical analysis and decision-making. We can better learn to respect the convictions of others who are rooted in their traditions and commitments, and to continue dialogue even in disagreement, without demanding that anyone should compromise convictions "for the sake of unity".

d) Councils of churches

On several occasions the JWG has discussed what councils of churches can do to foster unity and to follow up its own work. A very important contribution during the period under review was the second world consultation for national councils of churches (NCCs), held in Geneva in 1986. This meeting brought together 120 leaders from some seventy NCCs and regional ecumenical bodies:
a) to share their experience and expertise;
b) to encourage the "reception" of recent developments, such as the increased participation of the RCC in NCCs (thirty-five NCCs and three regional councils of churches with RC membership); and
c) to continue reflecting on their ecumenical role and ecclesiological significance.

There were major papers on councils as instruments of unity and in relation to justice, peace and service. One workshop explored specific ecclesiological issues, following on from the theological consultation on "The Significance and Contribution of Councils of Churches in the Ecumenical Movement", which was held in Venice in 1982. Other workshops dealt with the role of NCCs in ecumenism, aspects of mission and dialogue, issues of finance and resource sharing, and councils in their social and political context.

The papers, responses and workshop reports have been published by the WCC in *Instruments of Unity: National Councils of Churches within the One Ecumenical Movement* (Thomas F. Best, ed., Geneva, WCC, 1988).

The vitality and development of NCCs affect the ecumenical movement as a whole. Of particular interest to the JWG are the cases where the RCC is moving to official membership; this at times promotes reflection on crucial ecclesiological and practical issues.

The Geneva consultation touched upon a number of important matters of common concern in the community of national councils. Examples include:
1) the emergence of koinonia as an expression of self-understanding of the councils, affirming unity, diversity and creative interaction;
2) shared life and commitment prompt shared reflection on the nature of the church;
3) people learn more about ecumenism as they take part in the work of NCCs;
4) churches in a council learn together what it means to be "the church in that place";

5) they begin to understand "the instrumental" character of it, but also to appreciate that times have a germinal unity, a certain "ecclesial density" (*Instruments*, pp.42-43);
6) churches in a council will be brought up against the problem of the local and the universal and the relation between authority and autonomy.

e) Christian mixed marriages[1]

In the course of the first years of its existence, the JWG on many occasions considered the pastoral challenges which mixed marriages pose. Its work certainly contributed to the progress represented by Pope Paul VI's *Matrimonia Mixta* (1970), which has been developed in the new code of canon law (1983). Churches normally encourage marriages between persons of the same communion. However, churches and society no longer view mixed marriages as the object of reproach but now consider them with greater appreciation and understanding. The churches still seek more effective pastoral means to assist couples and their children in such marriages – both in preparation for marriage and continuing Christian counselling during the marriage itself. Those couples who take seriously their vocation in marriage as a union in Christ have found it to be an enriching ecumenical experience. Nevertheless, because of the divisions in Christianity, they and their children reflect the sufferings of Christ; with hope and prayer they travel together the road of conversion towards the goal of unity.

Conscious of the increase in mixed marriages and their significance for the ecumenical movement, the JWG held a consultation on this question in 1989. Its report pointed to the rich experience offered by mixed marriages but also to persisting problems such as (1) the mutual recognition by churches of such marriages, (2) differing baptismal practice, (3) the education of children, (4) intercommunion.

The consultation stressed the need for common pastoral care before and during marriage, especially during the early years. It recommended more study of the ecclesiological implications of mixed marriages. Finally, it asked that the next JWG should study the report.

2. ECUMENICAL FORMATION

The fifth report of the JWG emphasized the urgency of the task of ecumenical formation. It stressed that the ecumenical dimension must be an indispensable part of all processes of Christian formation, whether of laity, of youth, in catechesis, in religious education, in theological training.

The subject has been a priority in the subsequent sessions of the JWG. Following discussion and reflection at the Riano meeting (Rome), 1985, a first draft of a possible study document on the subject was prepared. This went through a series of revisions, with texts being prepared for discussion in Bossey, 1987; Venice, 1988; and St. Prix (Paris), 1989. But a primary task remains: to adapt the content, length and style of the draft document to the audience it addresses. After a small consultation in 1990, the executive of the JWG will hand over the unfinished task to the next JWG in the hope that the new group will give the topic priority on its agenda.

---

[1] "Mixed marriages" is used simply to describe the union of spouses of different Christian churches or communions. In more recent times the term "interchurch marriages" is used in some areas to indicate that both parties are clearly committed to their respective churches.

3. COMMON WITNESS

Collaboration between Christians in the search for new ways of rendering common witness has been consistently encouraged by the RCC and the WCC. Pope John Paul II has emphasized that common witness among Christians is a stimulus to the search for full unity. In the joint statement issued by the then general secretary Dr Philip Potter and by Cardinal Willebrands on the occasion of the visit of Pope John Paul II to the WCC (1984), mutual commitment to collaboration in the social field and the need to strengthen cooperation in several other areas was stressed. Pope John Paul II has expressed his conviction that "common witness among Christians is possible in various fields. It is founded on the common faith which exists among them and which the comparison in the dialogue in process has shown in a new light... The common witness which can be given today is a stimulus for the search for full unity" (*L'Osservatore Romano*, 23 January 1986).

The JWG is pleased to note that in many countries important work of common Bible studies, use of the Ecumenical Prayer Cycle, joint Bible translations, publication and distribution is carried out. Very important is also the collaboration between churches in the area of press, radio, television and other means of communication, as well as the training of personnel in specific fields. In some places, the celebration of local, national, regional and international events, the common struggle for human rights, justice and peace (e.g., Basel assembly on "Peace with Justice", 1989), and the sharing of resources, have also contributed to unity, renewal and common Christian witness.

a) Common witness, mission and unity

Following the publication of the "Common Witness" document by the JWG in 1982, steps were taken to distribute it widely and to emphasize its importance both to the visitors to the WCC and to RC groups. The presence of RC consultants in the CWME and their participation in the WCC mission conference in Melbourne (1980) led to the appointment of an RC consultant to the staff of CWME in 1984.

During the period under review, there has been a renewal of CWME staff visits to Rome as well as a visit of Catholics from Rome to Geneva. Members of the staff participated in three Roman Catholic mission seminars. An invitation to the missiological congress at the Urbaniana University (Rome) was also extended to CWME.

A series of visits was made by the RC consultant to both Roman Catholic and Protestant missionary organizations in order to discuss common witness as practised at both national and local levels. An important part of the consultant's work during recent years has involved promoting and organizing RC involvement in work arising from the WCC mission conference in San Antonio, Texas (22 May-1 June 1989). This included a seminar on the conference theme held in Rome with representatives of the WCC, some departments of the Roman curia, and RC missionary organizations. A Vatican delegation of twenty observers was present at the conference itself. The local committee for the conference was chaired by the ecumenical officer of the RC diocese of San Antonio.

Roman Catholic representatives contributed to the discussion on the mission/unity issue at both Faith and Order and CWME meetings.

The question of proselytism has been raised at various meetings and has made the need to promote common witness more urgent. It will be for the next JWG to suggest ways in which common witness, mission and unity can be further promoted. It is important to involve those organizations and groups who share the concern for a common witness to Jesus as Lord and Saviour in today's world. There is also need to continue ecumenical reflection on the challenge of new religious movements.

b) The Week of Prayer for Christian Unity

The Week of Prayer is one of the oldest ways of expressing and celebrating the spiritual communion that binds the churches together in listening to the word of God, in praise, and intercession. The eightieth anniversary of the Week of Prayer, 1987-88, was marked by gratitude for this form of ecumenical fellowship and "spiritual ecumenism", which is generally regarded as an indispensable basis for all other ecumenical endeavours.

Christians are convinced that their efforts to overcome their divisions can only be fruitful through the Lord's blessing. Therefore, prayer should be at the very centre of the ecumenical movement. The various other ecumenical activities that may be occasioned by the Week of Prayer are important, but they should not "obscure" the significance of praying together for unity. In thousands of places all over the world, Christians gather together to pray for Christian unity and the needs of all people. In many places and circumstances this Week remains, for various reasons, the main expression of local ecumenism. The material for the Week of Prayer is prepared each year through joint consultations of the Pontifical Council for Promoting Christian Unity (PCPCU) and the Faith and Order secretariat (WCC). Local churches of different traditions prepare draft texts for these consultations.

At all its meetings, the JWG has heard reports about the Week of Prayer for Christian Unity. It has noted that in several countries, observance of the Week is expanding, while there is a certain stagnation in others. An inquiry undertaken by the PCPCU in 1984 regarding the Week of Prayer showed how vital is the practice of ecumenical prayer for education and renewal, unity and common witness. The considerations and suggestions of the JWG point in the same direction. Churches must be reminded that the Week is not just a prayer for unity once a year, but is an integral part of continuous ecumenical formation and collaboration; that material and proposals for the Week should reflect a wider range of context and opportunities; that more preparation/adaptation should be done at the local level; and that more thought should be given to the relationship between prayer, ecumenical formation and shared activities.

The JWG is convinced that the Week of Prayer can provide one of the most fundamental ecumenical experiences and inspirations and that therefore it deserves the active participation and commitment of all churches.

c) Collaboration in justice, peace and integrity of creation (JPIC)

The initiative for the JPIC programme and convocation came from the sixth assembly at Vancouver (1983). At the 1985 JWG meeting, the PCPCU was asked to investigate the possibility of RC participation in JPIC. In January 1987 the WCC central committee officially invited the RCC to be a "co-inviter" with the member churches of the WCC, non-member churches, and CWCs for the world convocation on JPIC (Seoul, 1990). In December 1987, Cardinal Willebrands informed Dr E. Castro that although the RCC would not be a "co-inviter" because of some unresolved difficulties (for example, "the different nature of the two bodies"), it would collaborate in the project because of the common Christian concerns for justice, peace and integrity of creation.

The RCC sent participants to the preliminary consultations (Geneva, 1986; Glion, 1986; Granvollen, 1988), appointed a staff person to work full-time in Geneva with the JPIC desk, and designated five official representatives on the thirty-member preparatory group.

In September 1988, the WCC general secretary invited Cardinal Willebrands to arrange for the RCC to appoint fifty participants to the Seoul convocation. Cardinal Willebrands and Cardinal Etchegaray (Pontifical Council for Justice and Peace) responded to Dr Castro in November 1989: the RCC would appoint twenty experts to Seoul in the capacity of advisers – the type of participation now customary in WCC assemblies and other major meetings. Meanwhile, the RC staff assigned to JPIC remained; Roman Catholics continued to serve on the local planning committee in Seoul; and the RCC assured financial support for the convocation. Furthermore, local RC churches have fully participated, together with other Christians, in the development of national or regional JPIC programmes, and their representatives attended the convocation in Seoul as members of delegations either of NCCs or of regional ecumenical bodies of which the RCC is a member.

At its January 1990 meeting, the JWG discussed the process that led to the official RC decision. The common preparatory group work and the presence of RC official advisers and others at Seoul, as well as the urgency of common Christian witness in confronting the world's survival issues, will lead the JWG to follow attentively this post-Seoul process, and to be alert to the ways of possible cooperation in the period which leads to the Canberra assembly and thereafter.

4. SOCIAL THOUGHT AND ACTION

At its meetings in Le Louverain (1979) and Marseilles (1980), the JWG accepted a proposal to form a Joint Consultative Group on Social Thought and Action (JCG) that would undertake a study on collaboration in the field of social thought and action. When the mandate of SODEPAX came to an end in 1981, the JCG continued work in this field, focusing first on development, peace and human rights. Later, attention was specifically given to the issues of racism and apartheid (1985-87). At its meeting in Venice (1988), the JWG, with the agreement of the parent bodies, decided not to renew the mandate of the JCG, which ended the same year. The work formerly done by this group is now to be carried out by the JWG itself, with the help of small ad hoc study groups, on basic issues such as development and debt crisis, racism and apartheid, armaments and arms transfers, human rights and religious liberty. At its 1989 meeting, the JWG strongly recommended that it was now time to explore the possibilities of common witness against racism. The Pontifical Council on Justice and Peace (PCJP) and the WCC Programme to Combat Racism (PCR) are working together on a common reflection on the issues of racism and apartheid.

B. Ecumenical collaboration in other areas between WCC and RCC partners

1. MAJOR STUDIES AND OTHER ACTIVITIES IN THE FIELD OF FAITH AND ORDER

Since 1968, the RCC has been officially represented in the commission on Faith and Order; so have several other non-member churches of the WCC. This is the basis for continuing and extensive cooperation, which has enabled Faith and Order to include in its work RC theological perspectives and contributions. Thus, the wider dimensions of current ecumenical endeavours have always been present in this work. In recent years this cooperation and the consequent wider outlook has deepened and led to remarkable results.

The 1982 Lima document on *Baptism, Eucharist and Ministry* was a major result of this cooperation. The document was elaborated with the help of RC theologians and led to convergences on issues that had long been divisive. In the broad discussion process on BEM from 1987 to 1990, the RCC was actively involved at international, national and local levels. Roman Catholics have discussed BEM in ecumenical groups, seminars, commissions, seminaries, theological faculties, publications, etc.

Most importantly, the RCC accepted the invitation of Faith and Order to send a response to BEM at the highest appropriate level. This involved several steps. First, the document was sent to RC bishops' conferences, theological faculties and others, asking them to study it and send their reports to the PCPCU. These reports were analyzed and taken into account by the PCPCU which then, with the help of a team of theological consultants, prepared a draft response to BEM. The response was brought to its final form as a result of collaboration between the PCPCU and the Congregation for the Doctrine of the Faith. In August 1987, it was sent by the PCPCU to the Faith and Order secretariat in Geneva.

The RCC has thus, for the first time, given an official response to an ecumenical document. The response affirms the ecumenical achievement represented by BEM. It contains a positive evaluation of large sections of BEM, points to areas that from an RC point of view need further study, and raises ecclesiological questions which, according to the RCC, need to be faced if ecumenical progress is to be made. It reaffirms the commitment of the RCC to continuing multilateral dialogue.

Pope John Paul II and other RC leaders have repeatedly underlined the importance of BEM in the movement towards visible unity. The BEM process is probably the most significant instance for many years of ecumenical rapprochement between Roman Catholics and Christians of other traditions.

RC theologians have participated in all meetings, consultations and drafting groups of Faith and Order in recent years. They have thus made theological contributions to the major study programmes on "Towards the Common Expression of Apostolic Faith Today" and "The Unity of the Church and the Renewal of Human Community".

The meeting of the Faith and Order commission in Budapest in August 1989 received the results of these studies, which will determine the future direction of the work of Faith and Order. This will include more comprehensive work on ecclesiology, especially a reconsideration of the "unity we seek", for which RC contributions and cooperation are of crucial importance. The same applies to the plan to hold the fifth world conference of Faith and Order in 1993.

2. BILATERAL AND MULTILATERAL DIALOGUES

While the WCC and the RCC cooperate directly through multilateral dialogue in Faith and Order, many member churches of the WCC have been engaged for a long time in bilateral dialogue with the RCC, either through their respective CWCs at the world level or directly at the national level. During the last eight years, both the number and range of bilateral dialogues have increased. They represent an important element of the present ecumenical movement and have led to significant results.

There is common agreement that multilateral and bilateral dialogues have complementary purposes and possibilities. Ways have been developed to further their complementary character and to help to give them common purpose. Thus, the work of Faith and Order has profited from the insights and results of bilateral dialogues, and these in turn have focused attention on the developments and achievements in multilateral dialogues. For example, several bilateral dialogues and many responses of the churches to BEM have seen the BEM document as providing a wider framework within which dialogues can find common aims. The fourth forum on bilateral conversations, sponsored in 1985 by the CWCs and organized by Faith and Order, has confirmed the complementary character of multilateral and bilateral dialogues by evaluating and comparing main elements of multilateral convergence on BEM and the results of bilateral dialogues on the same issues (*Report of the Fourth Forum on Bilateral Conversations*, Faith and Order Paper no. 125, Geneva, 1985). The fifth forum was held in 1990 and focused on the question of consistent ecclesiology in bilateral and multilateral dialogues.

It will also be a task of the next JWG to follow developments in bilateral and multilateral dialogues and help to ensure that they together serve the one ecumenical movement. This corresponds to a request by the WCC central committee in 1988 which was addressed to the JWG and Faith and Order.

3. DIALOGUE AND WITNESS

Cooperation between the WCC Dialogue sub-unit and the Pontifical Council for Interreligious Dialogue (PCID) has continued regularly. There have been yearly joint staff meetings held alternately in Rome and Geneva. Conversations during the past three years have been concerned with:
1) the role of dialogue in relation to religious fundamentalism;
2) dialogue and mission;
3) the place of dialogue in a religiously plural society.

In 1988 a joint meeting was held to discuss the possibilities and problems of tripartite dialogue: Christians, Jews and Muslims. The WCC and its RC partners have also been jointly in contact with Islamic and other organizations.

Roman Catholic groups have participated in the study of the Dialogue sub-unit on "My Neighbour's Faith and Mine", which makes Christians more aware and informed about religious pluralism. Inter-religious dialogue is growing in importance. WCC and RCC partners should discuss the questions it raises and share information, studies and publications.

4. FAITH, SCIENCE AND ETHICS

There are moves towards collaboration on these topics: (1) faith and science, (2) technology and environment, and (3) the theology of creation. For example, Cardinal Sin addressed a Church and Society meeting on technology and its effects on the poor, held in Manila. RC observers attended the working committee meetings of the sub-unit on Church and Society in 1988 and 1989. Further, RC theologians attended consultations on "A Theology of Nature and Theocentric Ethic" (Annecy, September 1988) and on "God, People and Nature – One Community" (Sao Paulo, June-July 1988). Valuable RC contributions on these themes were made.

5. HEALTH CARE, HEALING AND MEDICINE

Since 1982 collaboration in this field has found expression in the presence of RC observers/consultants at the WCC Christian Medical Commission (CMC) meetings. They are appointed jointly by the PCPCU and the Pontifical Council for Health Care Workers. The partners have undertaken joint activities in the field of health care, healing and medicine. For some years there have been mutual invitations to meetings. The exchange of visits between CMC and the Vatican staff have helped further collaboration. One proposal that would augment this cooperation in the future is the appointment of RC consultants to work with the CMC.

6. DIACONAL SERVICE, PEACE AND REFUGEE WORK

The WCC–CICARWS emergencies desk maintains good relations with Caritas Internationalis on disasters and often works closely with national organizations related to Caritas Internationalis, such as Caritas Germany, Caritas Switzerland, Catholic Relief Services, and Secours catholique in France. Effective joint relief work has been done in Ethiopia, and there are plans to support actively long-term reconstruction by the Armenian Apostolic Church. A protocol has been signed by the Armenian Soviet Republic, by WCC/Caritas Internationalis and by the Armenian Apostolic Church.

In the wider context of coordinating agency response to disaster, CICARWS and Caritas Internationalis are members of the LICROSS-Volags steering committee in which six members are engaged, the others being the League of the Red Cross Societies, Oxfam, Catholic Relief Services and the Lutheran World Federation. It, too, should be noted that there was important coordination through the CCDA in 1983-86.

In June 1989 CICARWS visited Rome and met Bishop Alois Wagner, the vice-president of Cor Unum. A number of areas of mutual interest were identified, and an agreement to encourage dialogue on world developments, refugee service and relief operation was warmly welcomed. Sharing information on the position of the two organizations, in the Vatican and the WCC, will help the two bodies in meeting the challenge ahead.

In many parts of the world (Africa, Latin America, Europe), CICARWS partners and networks collaborate with RC colleagues. In Africa there are many NCCs in which Catholics are full members, e.g., Sudan, Botswana, Namibia, Swaziland, Lesotho and Liberia. In these countries there are ongoing refugee programmes in which CICARWS and the RCC participate fully in leadership and funding.

The RCC and the WCC member churches together address issues relating to peace, e.g., in Sudan, and make joint statements. In 1988 a visit to Europe by Sudan church leaders was organized in which Roman Catholics participated. In 1989 a journey was made to North America to explain to churches and human-rights movements the difficult situation in Sudan and its people's deep need for peace. The Namibia repatriation programme, handled by CICARWS, received funds from RC funding agencies. These brief examples – refugee aid, joint projects, peace action, repatriation programmes – indicate that some African Christian councils are active in coordinating essential programmes and need direct funding to be able to offer to their societies leadership and resources. An equitable way must be found by all partners to support ecumenical enterprises.

In 1984 CICARWS refugee service held a consultation of church-related partners in Western countries which had significant RCC participation, to examine the situation of asylum and refugee protection.

In 1986 a global consultation on protection and asylum in Zurich was jointly organized by CICARWS, Swiss Inter-Church Aid (HEKS), and Caritas Switzerland. The consultation brought together representatives of the various Catholic and WCC-related networks. It called for greater collaboration between RC and WCC-related groups serving refugees. An international ecumenical committee on refugee protection was established, to be convened alternately by the WCC and Caritas Internationalis with the participation of other global bodies, such as the LWF, International Catholic Migration Commission, etc.

After this initiative on the international level, efforts have been made to foster collaboration between WCC and RC agencies at the regional levels. The Zurich consultation called for the establishment of joint committees or working groups in each of the regions.

The North American continuation committee for refugee protection is composed of both RC and WCC-related bodies (Canadian Bishops' Conference, Canadian Council of Churches, NCCCUSA, US Catholic Conference) and meets regularly. In Europe, a joint CEC-CICARWS European churches' working group on asylum and refugees was set up and has met every two years since 1988. Catholic participation has been continuous, represented by an observer from the Council of European Bishops' Conferences.

7. INTERNATIONAL ISSUES AND HUMAN RIGHTS

Member churches of the WCC in Latin America and the Caribbean have taken wide-ranging initiatives on human rights, with RC participation at the local level. These are seen as ministries of assistance to victims of human-rights violations, as well as pastoral help. Human Rights Resources on Latin America (HRROLA) has spread ecumenical groups which have RC leadership. It has sought funds from churches and agencies related to CICARWS-WCC for work in which most, if not all, membership in a given ecumenical committee belongs to the RCC.

Examples of cooperation dot the landscape of Latin and Central America. Representatives from *El Salvador* have, with the help of CCIA, appeared before the UN Human Rights Commission. *Chilean experience* includes the work of the committee of cooperation for peace in Chile. This committee, made up of Lutherans, Methodists, Orthodox, Roman Catholics and Evangelicals, has carried out ministries with political prisoners, exiles and families of those who have disappeared.

In *Brazil* the NCC, constituted by the RCC and Protestant churches, has closely followed the situation on human rights, especially in relation to land rights involving several indigenous nations. The Ludigenist missionary council is developing sections and programmes in this connection which are appreciated by the different ethnic groups. The participation of leaders of some Protestant churches in the pastoral commission on land has opened up this section of the national bishops' conference of Brazil to ecumenical dialogue and greater commitment. This progress was confirmed at the seventh inter-ecclesial meeting of basic ecclesial communities in July 1989, where RC, Orthodox and Methodist bishops were present.

WCC and RC-related organizations jointly sponsored a meeting in Brussels, 16-20 May 1988, on the European community and the debt crisis of African, Caribbean and Pacific (ACP) countries.

Representatives of the Vatican PCJP have attended the Commission on Churches' Participation in Development (CCPD) advisory group and economic advisory group meetings. CCPD is a member of the advisory board of the Swiss RC-Protestant initiative regarding the international debt crisis.

8. EDUCATION (GENERAL EDUCATION, THEOLOGICAL EDUCATION, FAMILY EDUCATION)

Collaboration in these areas during most of the period under review was limited to those situations in which the WCC and RC partners in education participated in jointly planned activities with NCCs and regional ecumenical bodies to which local RCCs belong. Examples of this were a workshop held in the Pacific on ecumenical learning for JPIC, in September 1988, and the consultation on the church and persons with disabilities held in Bangkok in March 1989.

Another area of indirect collaboration is in relation to street children. Following the International Year of the Child (1979), a three-year inter-NGO programme on street children and street youth was started on the initiative of the International Catholic Child Bureau (ICCB) in 1982. The WCC and ICCB among others founded a new organization in 1986, called CHILDHOPE, in order to continue the work. The headquarters are in Rio de Janeiro.

Since the beginning of 1988, the scope for joint collaboration, particularly in the field of adult education, increased significantly when an RC priest from Mauritius joined the WCC staff. Because of his previous involvement in ecumenical adult education work in Asia and the Pacific, he has brought the WCC into contact with a new network of RC or RC-related organizations that are open to ecumenical collaboration on justice, peace and development education.

In Eastern and Southern Africa, training for transformation programmes, which were originally started by the RCC, are now being planned ecumenically by NCCs (e.g., Zambia, Zimbabwe) and the All Africa Conference of Churches, with significant RC involvement. The WCC adult education programme is actively participating in this development.

Catholic educators are involved in the work of the Programme on Theological Education (PTE) through the Association of Theological Institutions. RC representatives have attended some consultations sponsored by PTE and other ecumenical partners.

9. RENEWAL AND SPIRITUALITY

Since 1983, spirituality has figured largely in the life and the programmes of the WCC and in cooperation between the WCC and the RCC.

A first step towards "A Spirituality for Our Times" was a consultation held in Annecy (France) in December 1984, in which the RC contribution was substantial. Because of need for further study and reflection on some aspects of spirituality, the sub-unit on Renewal and Congregational Life (RCL), as well as other sub-units of the WCC, have organized a series of seminars and consultations. In all of these the RC participants shared their specific experiences and understanding, making possible creative dialogues between various traditions and cultures of the ecumenical community.

In the period 1985-88, a series of workshops have been held for renewal of worship in Europe, Africa, Asia, Latin America, Caribbean, North America and Australia. Roman Catholics participated in these meetings and, in some cases, shared in the leadership.

10. THE ROLE OF THE LAITY IN CHURCH AND SOCIETY

A good deal of common work in this field has been done on the one hand by the RCL and other sub-units in Programme Unit III "Education and Renewal" and, on the other, by the Pontifical Council for the Laity (PCL).

The sub-unit on RCL has a desk for lay centres. In Asia, Africa, North America, the Caribbean and Europe, networks of ecumenical centres and lay academies include RC centres and staff. RCL and other sub-units in Education and Renewal sent their comments on the Lineamenta document prior to the synod of bishops in October 1987 to the synod secretariat in the Vatican. Moreover, WCC Unit III engaged in a meeting in Geneva on 26-27 February 1987 with representatives of the PCL on the questions raised by the subject of the synod of bishops in 1987.

In November 1988, WCC staff visited the PCL in Rome and discussed the present dialogue and the promotion of this topic. In February 1990, this discussion was carried further in the seminar on "Merging Ecumenical Trends Regarding Laity" organized by Unit III with RC participation. As part of future cooperation between the WCC and the PCL, the RCL has proposed to continue this ecumenical reflection on the role of the laity in church and society.

11. ECUMENICAL INSTITUTE AT BOSSEY

During recent years, the dynamic WCC-RCC collaboration at Bossey has continued. It has been strengthened by the appointment, this time for three years, of an RC professor to the annual graduate school. The participation of an RC observer on the Bossey board, the continued interest of the PCPCU in the graduate school, and the invitation to Bossey staff and students to visit annually various departments of the Roman curia, the unions of superiors general, the missiology department of the Gregorian University, the Dominican house of studies, the Focolare movement, and the St Egidio parish community, have made a positive impact on WCC-RCC relationships and on youth commitment to the ecumenical movement.

12. PREPARATION FOR THE SEVENTH ASSEMBLY OF THE WCC

RC theologians and others have been involved in the preparations for the Canberra assembly through consultations on the theme and sub-themes, several regional meetings, visitors programmes and ecumenical team visits. Twenty RC observers will attend the assembly and contribute to its deliberations. Others are serving on the local committees, and many RC parishes throughout Australia are participating in the preparatory process of study and prayer.

IV. PROSPECTS FOR THE FUTURE (1991-98)

1. Towards a more effective role for the JWG

The JWG is dedicated to its mandate. In a happy atmosphere, it has fulfilled difficult tasks and tried to meet vital priorities. But its status, its heavy agenda, the sensitive nature of the issues it deals with, short annual meetings and limited financial resources do not allow it to cover the whole pattern of relationships between the RCC and the WCC.

Further work is needed to strengthen its role. This could be done. Composition, working methods, financial resources and staffing could be improved. Possibilities should be explored of holding some meetings in different countries. This could stimulate local contacts and make the JWG more effective.

Better communications through publications, special visits and meetings could help the work of the JWG to be better known within its constituencies.

Given the limited time and resources available to the JWG, *its agenda should be more limited in scope*, and better use could be made of the time spent together. While continuing to devote part of its agenda to reviewing cooperation between various programmes of the WCC and the departments of the RCC, the JWG should in future give greater attention to assessing both the ecumenical situation and important developments in various regions of the world, particularly at the local level. In some cases these reviews could be done through written reports. The JWG should concentrate on developing topics of crucial importance for church unity and common Christian witness.

The signs of the times continue to be a challenge to all churches and a call to renewal and unity. The demands of WCC-RCC relationships call for renewed joint efforts to achieve the goal of visible unity of the church and the renewal of human community. Credible Christian witness, mutual respect, and growth in truth and love must be sustained and further developed.

2. Proposals for future work

After assessing its activities over the past seven years, as well as the development in the ecumenical situation, the JWG proposes the following priorities for the next period:
a) ecclesiological dimensions of ecumenical work;
b) ecumenical education and formation;
c) common witness and mission.

The first area provides continuity on the central and ongoing concern for *the unity of the church – the goal and the way*, and places emphasis on ecclesiological issues, such as the ecclesiology of communion and the unity we seek.

The second and the third areas also focus on major ecumenical fields, where joint effort is urgently needed.

a) There are many indications that both in bilateral and multilateral ecumenical dialogues, the understanding of the nature and mission of the church is becoming a central topic. This is so because ecumenical conversations so far have led to the recognition that many of the remaining difficulties in the theological dialogue have their roots in different ecclesiologies, especially in different concepts of the place and mission of the church in God's saving and transforming action. Closely connected with this are (1) the question of authority in the church, (2) the relations between church and humanity, (3) the ecclesiological basis of a common Christian witness and service in a broken world crying out for reconciliation and renewal. "The ecclesiology of communion" integrates a number of basic ecclesiological concerns within a coherent vision.

Through its work on "the church – local and universal" and other topics, the JWG has already been involved in the new ecclesiological debate. This debate will continue, and the JWG should be an active partner in it. The group may again choose a specific aspect of ecclesiology for its own contribution.

The question of "the unity we seek" remains important on the ecumenical agenda. There has been an emerging ecumenical consensus on the conditions and expression of the goal of visible unity, as witness the statements of the WCC assemblies from New Delhi (1961) up to Nairobi (1975). However, since 1975, developments in bilateral dialogues and Faith and Order studies, new relationships between the RCC and other churches, experiences in church union negotiations, changes in ecumenical perspective have all made necessary a restatement of "the unity we seek", which should build on the New Delhi and Nairobi statements.

The 1991 Canberra assembly is expected to take up this task. It will be a major responsibility of the JWG to evaluate such a restatement, to assist in its interpretation and application, and to monitor and support further steps towards this goal.

Among matters needing specific attention are:

- the continuing impact and implication of the BEM process;
- the continuing development of the Faith and Order studies on "Towards the Common Expression of the Apostolic Faith Today" and "The Unity of the Church and the Renewal of Human Community";
- the ecumenical significance and contribution of councils of churches (cf. ch. III, A.1.D. above);
- the possibility of a more comprehensive ecumenical movement and its structures (especially with regard to evangelical and charismatic/Pentecostal movements);
- developments of and input from bilateral multilateral dialogues.

During the next period the JWG should further deepen the study of *new sources of division: ethical issues* (cf. ch. III, A.1.C.).

The report and the recommendations of the consultation (1989) on *mixed marriages* (cf. ch. III, A.1.E.) should be studied particularly for its ecumenical and ecclesiological implications.

Major demographic changes, refugees and migrant workers make more urgent problems of *inter-religious marriages*. A new study on this question should be undertaken in cooperation with the Pontifical Council for Interreligious Dialogue and the WCC sub-unit on Dialogue with People of Living Faiths.

b) Further study on *ecumenical formation* (see ch. III, A.2.) should embrace the wide field of *ecumenical education*. Promoting work for unity, transforming the life of Christians so as to bring about deeper conversion of heart and renewal of the church, should extend to the education of priests, pastors, theologians and laity.

c) During the 1990s the call for common *Christian witness* in missionary endeavours "so that the world may believe" (cf. John 17:21) should continue to be a major task for the JWG (cf. above, ch. III, A.3. and 3a).

The JWG should further explore ecumenical approaches to *dialogue and proclamation of the gospel*. This could be done in collaboration between the WCC sub-units (CWME, Dialogue) and RC partners.

The JWG should also go on moving *towards common perspectives on social thought and action*. During the past period there have been difficulties in tackling some social issues, such as apartheid, JPIC, and with some of the instruments used, e.g., SODEPAX and the JCG. The JWG has called a special meeting to examine these problems, to discern successes and failures, and to make recommendations for the future. Its report will be given to the executive committee of the JWG for consideration in the next steps of collaboration.

The JWG recognized that throughout the world, *ecumenical cooperation at local, national and regional levels* between WCC member churches and the RCC often flourishes, with fruitful results in common witness and mission. The JWG recommends that in the future more account be taken of such ecumenical collaboration and its significance evaluated.

d) Further, the JWG recognized that *new issues are arising in the world which may call for ecumenical collaboration*. These include the considerable spiritual and ideological challenges for the whole world coming from the events in Central and Eastern Europe and in other regions. The response of churches to these theological, economic, political and social issues could be strengthened through ecumenical cooperation. The role of the churches and their life together in such changing societies, and the kinds of solidarity and fellowship they may need from churches elsewhere, could be part of the JWG's future concern. Likewise, the global ecological crisis, newly recognized as an urgent matter of survival, may well call for joint responses. Future decisions about official WCC-RCC cooperation in any of these areas should be carefully considered in the light of the recommendations to come from the meetings on these subjects.

e) Besides these aims, the JWG could continue to monitor *collaboration on matters which may arise from major ecumenical events*. The need to give attention to the results of the JPIC world convocation has already been mentioned. The seventh assembly of the WCC at Canberra in February 1991 will certainly provide new ecumenical impetus. The theme of the assembly, "Come, Holy Spirit – Renew the Whole Creation", can open up fresh dimensions in theological exploration, spiritual understanding, and hope for God's presence and action in the world. Likewise, Roman Catholic events, such as the general synod of bishops in 1990, and the special synod of African bishops, the centenary of the first social encyclical *Rerum Novarum* (1991), can open new paths to explore in this relationship. The JWG encourages openness to the Spirit as we consider the ecumenical implications of these events. They could provide room for increased collaboration between the WCC and RCC.

f) Churches and Christians towards the year 2000: As we approach the end of a millennium, the attention of churches and peoples throughout the world will be focused upon *hope for the future*. This historical turning point will provide a natural occasion for all Christians to reflect on the state of their ecumenical relationships, recommit themselves to unity, and strengthen their common witness for the sake of the world's salvation. The next JWG to serve after the Canberra assembly could take the responsibility of coordinating the responses to the assembly made by the WCC member churches, the RCC and, if possible, other non-member churches. It may be hoped that the churches might offer together to the world a Christian vision of unity and renewal, of social, economic and spiritual life which can contribute to the work for a stable and just world as we enter a new millennium. This goal might be considered by the newly established JWG.

The JWG renews its hope that it will continue to serve as an instrument of unity and ecumenical collaboration between the two partners. It will try to open hearts and minds to the gifts of the Holy Spirit who leads all Christians to unity (cf. Gal. 5:22-23).

69. The Church: Local and Universal
A Study Document Commissioned and Received
by the Joint Working Group

1990

Preface

One of the ways in which the Joint Working Group between the Roman Catholic Church and the World Council of Churches has attempted over the years to fulfill its purpose of fostering closer relations between the two has been to sponsor the joint study of issues that are of great significance in the quest for Christian unity. The theme of "The Church: Local and Universal" is one of these challenging issues.

The JWG has given attention to this theme in the period since the sixth assembly of the World Council of Churches in Vancouver, 1983. The central committee of the WCC asked in 1984 that this theme be studied. The JWG meeting at Riano (Rome), September-October 1985, made plans for "The Church: Local and Universal" to be an important topic for the subsequent meeting in 1987. It asked for three papers to introduce the theme with Catholic, Protestant and Orthodox perspectives, and suggested that these include some consideration of an ecclesiology of communion and also the organization of this communion at the local and universal levels, taking account of diversity within the unity of the church and of cultures. At Bossey, April-May 1987, the JWG heard and discussed these papers which were prepared by Pierre Duprey, Günther Gassmann and Ion Bria. As the process continued, the perspectives of other scholars were collected for continued discussion of the theme at the 1988 meeting. Contributions came from Emmanuel Lanne, OSB, Jean Tillard, OP, Margaret O'Gara and Patrick Granfield, OSB, who had in hand, as they wrote, the three papers mentioned above, as well as the list of questions raised at the discussion at Bossey. These contributions were discussed by the JWG in Venice, April-May 1988, which decided that a consultation on the theme should be held later in 1988. Since all of the contributions for 1988 were from Catholic sources, it asked that theologians belonging to the Orthodox and the Protestant traditions be part of the consultation.

The consultation was convened in Rome during December 1988 by the Secretariat for Promoting Christian Unity and the commission on Faith and Order. Members included Nicholas Lossky, Geoffrey Wainright, Günther Gassmann, Emmanuel Lanne, OSB, Patrick Granfield, OSB, and John A. Radano. The work of the group was facilitated by a draft text prepared beforehand by Patrick Granfield who made use of the papers previously prepared for the JWG meetings of 1987 and 1988. His text was the basis for discussion. The draft resulting was discussed by the JWG in St Prix (Paris) in February 1989. It was further revised by a small committee in September 1989, reviewed by the JWG at its meeting in Rome, January-February 1990, and received there in its present form as a study document.

The Joint Working Group does not intend this study to be an exhaustive presentation on this theme. Rather, it is intended to point to some factors which may help to give support and direction to the continuing ecumenical exploration of this theme. It highlights, for example, the necessity of both the local and the universal expressions of the church, their interdependence, the healthy tension that exists between them, and some aspects of the ecumenical convergence seen today on these notions of the church. It also explores the ecclesiology of communion and its usefulness as a framework for discussing the relationship between the local and universal church, not only within each Christian communion but also in terms of the ecumenical relationship between divided Christian communions. It points to different expressions of ecclesial communion and helps us to see aspects of ecumenical convergence here as well.

This report was prepared with the conviction that the ecclesiology of communion can be a way of expressing and especially of building on the real although imperfect communion already existing between churches despite their continuing division.

Introduction: the church as local and universal communion

1. The church is the icon of the Trinity, and the Trinity is the interior principle of ecclesial communion. From the resurrection to the parousia, communion is willed by the Father, realized in the Son, and caused by the Spirit in and through a community. Every authentic Christian community shares in this communion and is part of the mystery of God unfolded in Christ and the Spirit. Thus, the eschatological reality is already present, and ecclesial communion expresses the "fellowship of the Holy Spirit". At the same time, the church has an inner dynamism towards that unity that rests in the Holy Spirit. In the words of Cyprian, "the church is a people made one with the unity of the Father, the Son, and the Holy Spirit".[1]

2. Different views of the church as local and universal are found among the various Christian communions (cf. below nos. 12-24). Common perspectives on the theological understanding of the local and universal church are therefore critically important for the restoration of Christian unity and have been frequently considered in ecumenical documents.[2] There is only one church in God's plan of salvation. This one church is present and manifested in the local churches throughout the world. It is the same unique church of Jesus Christ, his body, which is thus present in every local church. It is also the same Spirit who from the day of Pentecost gathers together the faithful in the one church and in the individual local churches.

3. Any ecclesiological investigation of the local and universal church must recognize both its christological and pneumatological dimensions, which are reflected in the holy scriptures and the early creeds. The christological dimensions of the church are realized in and through the activity of the Holy Spirit. Thus Ignatius of Antioch could affirm that "where Jesus Christ is, there is the church catholic" (*To the Smyrnaens*, viii, 2) and Irenaeus that "where the church is there is the Spirit, and where the Spirit is, there is the church" (*Adversus haereses*, III, 24, 1). The church is the people of God, the body of Christ, and the temple of the Holy Spirit.

4. This paper will explore in four sections the local and universal aspects of the one church. First, the concept of the ecclesiology of communion as a theological basis and framework for the unity of the church as universal and local; second, the local

and universal communion in ecumenical perspective; third, the ecclesial elements of communion; and fourth, the structuring of communion.

I. The ecclesiology of communion

5. More and more, the concept of *koinonia*[3] or communion is seen as having great value for understanding the multiplicity of local churches in the unity of the one church. Koinonia refers to the source and nature of the life of the church as body of Christ, people of God and temple of the Holy Spirit. In particular, this concept allows us to hold two dimensions of the church – its locality and universality – not as separate entities, but as two integrated dimensions of one reality.

6. The theological meaning of koinonia is rich. Used nineteen times in the New Testament, the term koinonia in its primary sense means participation in the life of God through Christ in the Holy Spirit. Koinonia is the gift of the Holy Spirit: we share in the "fellowship of the Holy Spirit" (2 Cor. 13:14). Koinonia refers to a profound, personal relationship between God and humanity (Acts 2:42 and John 1:3). The Old Testament themes of inheritance and covenant convey similar ideas.[4] Israel is the inheritance of the Lord (Ex. 34:9), and a covenant exists between God and his people (Jer. 24:7). Koinonia rests on God's free choice to communicate himself to us: "We are called into the communion of his (God's) Son, Jesus Christ our Lord" (1 Cor. 1:9). Through baptism believers are called into the fellowship of the Spirit. As a result we share in the passion and consolation of Christ (2 Cor. 1:7; Phil. 3:10); and we participate in the divine nature (2 Pet. 1:4). For St Paul, the sharing of possessions and the financial help for needy churches (koinonia in Rom. 15:26 and 2 Cor. 9:13) are signs of our communion in the life of God.

7. Because it is the result of our union (koinonia) with God, the Christian community can also be called koinonia. The koinonia or bond of union between believers and God establishes a new relationship among believers themselves. It is realized by participating in the life of the triune God through word and sacrament. The church is koinonia precisely because of the fellowship that its members have in the life of the Spirit.[5] Our vertical relationship with God makes possible our horizontal unity with our fellow believers.[6] Koinonia is a dynamic reality that binds us together within the one body of Christ. Our communion with the triune God and with one another develops throughout history and will never be completely realized until we are ultimately united with God in glory. According to Irenaeus, the history of salvation is a progressive introduction of humanity into communion with God (*Adversus haereses*, IV, 14, 2).

8. Does communion relate only to the church? Can it also extend to the world and operate in society? Communion refers primarily to the church, since communion is based on participation in the life of the Trinity. The absence of communion among churches affects the world and society, because it is a negative sign of the gospel message of unity. But growing communion among the churches presents even now a positive sign of Christian unity and an effective way to encourage common Christian witness. Division among Christians is a scandal, but the church's mission to announce the gospel to the world is strengthened as communion grows.

9. In a broader sense a notion of communion can also be related to the whole of humanity. All human beings are created in the image of God and are thus called into communion with God. Because it is God's plan of salvation to reconcile broken humanity and to bring it to fulfilment in the kingdom of God, there is a dynamic in

history towards solidarity and constructive interdependence. The church is called by God to serve this movement of reconciliation and to help break down barriers which prevent that renewed community among human beings willed by God. "By her relationship with Christ, the church is a kind of sacrament or sign and instrument of intimate union with God and of the unity of all humanity"(*Lumen Gentium*, no. 1). "The church is bold in speaking of itself as the sign of the coming unity of mankind" (Uppsala assembly of the WCC, section I).

10. The notion of the ecclesiology of communion has been found helpful in various bilateral conversations. The final report of ARCIC-1 noted that koinonia is the term "that most aptly expresses the mystery underlying the various New Testament images of the church".[7] The Lutheran-Roman Catholic commission described the church as "a communion subsisting in a network of local churches".[8] According to the Nairobi report of the joint commission between the Roman Catholic Church and the World Methodist Council, koinonia "includes participation in God through Christ in the Spirit, by which believers become adopted children of the same Father and members of the one body of Christ sharing in the same Spirit. And it includes deep fellowship among participants, a fellowship which is both visible and invisible, finding expression in faith and order, in prayer and sacrament, in mission and service" (no. 23).[9] The first report of the Catholic-Orthodox joint commission, issued at Munich in 1982 and entitled: "The Mystery of the Church and of the Eucharist in the Light of the Mystery of the Holy Trinity", spoke of the way in which "the unfolding of the eucharistic celebration of the local church shows how the koinonia takes shape in the church celebrating the eucharist". It went on to describe aspects of that koinonia, including that "the koinonia is eschatological... kerygmatic... [and] at once ministerial and pneumatological".[10] The Reformed-Catholic dialogue spoke of the church indicating that "... it comes together for the purpose of adoration and prayer, to receive ever new instruction and consolation and to celebrate the presence of Christ in the sacrament; around this centre, and with the multiplicity of gifts granted by the Spirit... it lives as a koinonia of those who need and help each other" ("The Presence of Christ in Church and World", 1977).[11]

11. Various Christian world communions have also recognized the importance of the ecclesiology of communion. Within the Roman Catholic Church, for example, Cardinal Willebrands said that "the deepening... of an ecclesiology of communion is... perhaps the greatest possibility for tomorrow's ecumenism",[12] and the 1985 synod of bishops called by the pope on the 20th anniversary of the closing of the Second Vatican Council recalled that "the ecclesioiogy of communion is the central and fundamental idea of the Council's documents".[13] In its "Statement on the Self-Understanding and Task of the Lutheran World Federation", the seventh assembly of the LWF (1984) stated that: "We give witness and affirm the communion in which the Lutheran churches of the whole world are bound together."[14] The ecclesiology of communion was also a major consideration of the Anglican Communion within the Lambeth Conference in 1988.

II. Local and universal communion in ecumenical perspective

12. Any discussion of the koinonia in the local and universal church must be first placed in the broader context of the one, holy, catholic and apostolic church, the una sancta of the early Christian creeds.[15] The una sancta in the plan of God is God's

creation – an eschatological reality existing throughout history from the earliest days *(ecclesia ab Abel)* to the return of Christ in glory. The local and universal church are historical manifestations of the una sancta, even though they should not be purely and simply identified with it. They have their unity in the una sancta. There is only one church of God, whether it is expressed locally or universally.

1. The local church

13. The local church is truly church. It has everything it needs to be church in its own situation: it confesses the apostolic faith (with special reference to belief in the Trinity and the lordship of Jesus); it proclaims the word of God in scripture, baptizes its members, celebrates the eucharist and other sacraments; it affirms and responds to the presence of the Holy Spirit and his gifts; announces and looks forward to the kingdom; and recognizes the ministry of authority within the community. All these various features must exist together in order for there to be a local church within the communion of the church of God. The local church is not a freestanding, self-sufficient reality. As part of a network of communion, the local church maintains its reality as church by relating to other local churches. In the words of Vatican II: "The church of Christ is truly present *(vere adest)* in all legitimate local congregations of the faithful which, united with their pastors, are themselves called churches in the New Testament" (*LG*, no. 26).[16]

14. The local church is not an administrative or juridical sub-section or part of the universal church. In the local church the one, holy, catholic and apostolic church is truly present and active (*Christus Dominus*, no. 11). The local church is the place where the church of God becomes concretely realized. It is a gathering of believers that is seized by the spirit of the risen Christ and becomes koinonia by participating in the life of God.

15. All Christian world communions can, in general, agree with the definition of the local church as a community of baptized believers in which the word of God is preached, the apostolic faith confessed, the sacraments are celebrated, the redemptive work of Christ for the world is witnessed to, and a ministry of *episcope* exercised by bishops or other ministers is serving the community. Differences between world communions are connected with the role and place of the bishop in relation to the local church.

16. For churches of the "catholic" tradition, the bishop is essential for the understanding and structure of a local church. Bishops, as successors of the apostles, are "the visible principle and foundation of unity in their own particular churches" (*LG*, no. 23). According to the first report of the Catholic-Orthodox joint commission (Munich, 1982), "the bishop stands at the heart of the local church as minister of the Spirit to discern the charisma, and take care that they are exercised in harmony, for the good of all, in faithfulness to the apostolic tradition" (II/3). The Anglican-Roman Catholic international commission defined the local church as "the unity of local communities under one bishop" (ARCIC-1, final report, p.92). Accordingly, the church is most fully revealed/realized when God's people are united at the eucharistic assembly with the bishop. Consequently, the local church in these traditions is primarily the diocese, but it may also refer to several dioceses.

17. For churches of the Reformation and free-church traditions, which have developed a great variety of institutional structures and forms of self-understanding, the term

"local church" is not so common and therefore also not defined by referring to the office of the bishop. For these churches it is the local Christian community (parish, congregation) for which the above definition would apply and which could, therefore, be called a local church.

18. Yet in addition to the common elements mentioned above in paragraph 15, there are also certain convergences concerning the differences just mentioned within churches characterized by an episcopal concept of the local church. The local congregation or parish is recognized as the local expression of the diocese and the entire church (cf. *Sacrosanctum Concilium*, no. 42). Such communities must, however, be related to the local church, i.e., diocese, and be in communion with it.[17] Reformation and free churches, on the other hand, which put special emphasis on the local congregation, have developed structures which serve a larger community of congregations (e.g., districts, dioceses, circuits) and have developed ministries (e.g., bishops, superintendents, regional pastors) which carry special responsibilities (together with presbyterial-synodical organs) for such larger units. In the past such larger geographical structures were seen mainly under practical aspects. In the present, however, such wider expressions of a local church are seen in a number of churches also in pastoral and ecclesiological terms: as communions of communities.

2. The universal church

19. The universal church is the communion of all the local churches united in faith and worship around the world. However, the universal church is not the sum, federation or juxtaposition of the local churches, but all together are the same church of God present and acting in this world. The issue here is fundamentally ecclesiological and not organizational.[18] The communion of local churches gathered by and around the celebration of word and sacrament manifests the church of God. The concept of the universal church recognizes the diversity of cultural and social conditions. "While preserving unity in essentials", Christians have "a proper freedom in the various forms of spiritual life and discipline, in the variety of liturgical rites, and even in the theological elaborations of revealed truth" (*UR*, no. 4). Catholicity enters into the very concept of church and refers not simply to geographic extension but also to the manifold variety of local churches and their participation in the one koinonia. Each local church contributes its unique gifts for the good of the whole church.

20. The Roman Catholic Church and the Orthodox church understand themselves as representing the church universal. Reformation and free churches, because they had to organize themselves on the national level, often had difficulties in grasping and experiencing the universal dimension of the church. However, through their involvement in the ecumenical movement and their experience within the Christian world communions and the fellowship of the World Council of Churches, they have developed a stronger sense of the universal character of Christ's church, which transcends their own reality as churches organized on a national or regional level. This experience and insight find expression also in the development of Christian world communions which, according to the WCC assembly at Uppsala (1968), provide "some real experience of universality".[19] It is the task of the ecumenical movement to lead the churches to that unity which enables them to confess and express together the universal communion of the church of Jesus Christ.

3. The question of priority

21. In the past, biblical scholars generally held that the term *ecclesia* was first used to designate the local church of a city or region and only later the universal church. Contemporary biblical study, however, raises questions about the earlier view of priority. It presents evidence that suggests a more complex picture of the early Christian community than that indicated by the axiom "first particular, then universal".[20]

22. One way of looking at the question of priority is by using an eschatological and pneumatological ecclesiology. This approach does not assign a priority exclusively to either the local or the universal church, but suggests a simultaneity of both. Both are essential. Thus it must be said, on the one hand, that in God's general plan of salvation the universal has an absolute priority over the local. For Christ came to gather together the dispersed children of God; at Pentecost the Spirit of God was poured out upon all flesh (cf. Acts 2:17). God created the church in the framework of universal reconciliation and unity. The Pentecostal experience and the word and grace of Christ have continual and universal relevance. The gospel of salvation is addressed to humankind as a whole without exception. In this sense the universal has priority and will keep it forever.

23. At the same time, the church began and came into existence at a determined place. "When the day of Pentecost had come, they were all together in one place" (Acts 2:1). From this place the apostles began to preach the gospel to all the nations (cf. Matt. 28:19). In the concrete historical situation of the foundation of the church, the local had priority and will keep it until the second coming of Christ, because the gospel is preached each time in a determined place; the faithful receive baptism and celebrate eucharist in this determined place, even though it is always and necessarily in communion with all the other local churches in the world. There is no local church that is not centred on the gospel and not in communion with all other churches.[21]

24. Since Pentecost, the church celebrates the eucharist as the one, holy, catholic and apostolic church. The eucharistic celebration, therefore, embraces the church both in its local and universal dimension. It thus affirms a mutual presence of all the churches in Christ and in the Spirit[22] for the salvation of the world.

III. The ecclesial elements of communion

25. The ecclesial elements required for full communion within a visibly united church – the goal of the ecumenical movement – are communion in the fullness of the apostolic faith; in sacramental life; in a truly one and mutually recognized ministry; in structures of conciliar relations and decision-making; and in common witness and service in the world. This goal is still to be achieved, and on the way to this goal it is important to note how the notion of ecclesial communion has been interpreted by the Roman Catholic Church in the Second Vatican Council and the way in which it has been interpreted within the World Council of Churches.

1. Interpretations of ecclesial communion

26. The Second Vatican Council described two types of ecclesial communion. The first is full and complete ecclesial communion in which the ecclesial elements of the one, holy, catholic and apostolic church are integrally present. Accordingly the council taught that the unique church of Christ "subsists" in the Catholic Church, "... although many elements of sanctification and of truth can be found outside her visible

structure" (*LG*, no. 8). This leads to the second type, which is partial and incomplete, but nonetheless real ecclesial communion. The essential elements are present in some way in other Christian churches: the written word of God; faith in Christ and in the Trinity; baptism; the sacraments; the life of grace; faith, hope and charity; the interior gifts of the Holy Spirit; and prayer and other spiritual benefits (*UR*, nos. 3,20-23; *LG* no. 15). By their nature these elements tend towards full realization of catholic unity (*LG*, nos. 8,15). Although a non-Catholic community may not have the "institutional" fullness of the ecclesial elements, this does not mean that it does not have an authentic "pneumatic" response to the presence and grace and form a vital communion of faith, hope and charity.[23] The ecclesiology of communion offers a promising way to explain and express the incomplete but real communion that already exists between the Catholic church and the other churches. It allows us to speak of a growing communion.

27. Vatican II, in its teaching on "subsists" and the presence of ecclesial elements outside its visible boundaries, provided sound theological basis for genuine ecumenical commitment. Although it did not resolve the problems, it nevertheless with courage and consistency laid the foundation for further progress. The ecumenical bilateral and multilateral conversations since the council have continued to examine in detail the thorny questions connected with a common profession of faith, the sacramental life and the role of authority.

28. Elements of communion among the churches have been discussed and clarified in the World Council of Churches in the perspective of "the unity we seek". The results of these reflections are formulated in statements of the 1961 New Delhi and 1975 Nairobi assemblies of the WCC.

29. The New Delhi statement said: "We believe that the unity which is both God's will and his gift to his church is being made visible as all in each place who are baptized into Jesus Christ and confess him as Lord and Saviour are brought by the Holy Spirit into one fully committed fellowship, holding the one apostolic faith, preaching the one gospel, breaking the one bread, joining in common prayer, and having a corporate life reaching out in witness and service to all and who at the same time are united with the whole Christian fellowship in all places and all ages in such wise that ministry and members are accepted by all, and that all can act and speak together as occasion requires for the tasks to which God calls his people."[24]

30. Taking up the report of a Faith and Order consultation in Salamanca, the Nairobi assembly stated its vision of unity in the following way: "The one church is to be envisioned as a conciliar fellowship of local churches which are themselves truly united. In this conciliar fellowship, each local church possesses, in communion with the others, the fullness of catholicity, witnesses to the same apostolic faith, and therefore recognizes the others as belonging to the same church of Christ and guided by the same Spirit. As the New Delhi assembly pointed out, they are bound together because they have received the same baptism and share in the same eucharist; they recognize each other's members and ministries. They are in their common commitment to confess the gospel of Christ by proclamation and service to the world. To this end, each church aims at maintaining sustained and sustaining relationships with her sister churches, expressed in conciliar gatherings, whenever required for the fulfilment of their common calling."[25]

31. The two statements from New Delhi and Nairobi refer to ecclesial elements that are generally recognized as being indispensable for any realization of visible church

unity both on the local and universal level. These include the common confession of the apostolic faith; mutual recognition of the apostolicity and catholicity of the other churches and of each other's members, sacraments and ministries; fellowship in the eucharist, in spiritual life, and in mission and service in the world; and the achievement of mutual fellowship, also in conciliar meetings and decisions. Both statements emphasize local unity, but this is inter-related especially in the Nairobi statement, with the universal dimension of unity in the form of a conciliar fellowship (or as a Faith and Order consultation in November 1988 stated: "conciliar communion of common faith and life in the service of God's world"). The descriptions of New Delhi and Nairobi are not limited solely to the goal of visible unity. They express at the same time basic elements of the faith and life of the church, both in its local and universal dimensions.

32. It is obvious that the essential elements of communion or unity stated in these two texts of the WCC correspond to the elements mentioned earlier in this paper. The different Christian traditions believe that these elements, in different forms, are present within their traditions and that, accordingly, full ecclesial communion exists within them. Also between member churches of the WCC different degrees of communion have developed, including, for many, eucharistic hospitality, interim eucharistic sharing, altar and pulpit fellowship understood as full communion. The question then arises as to how the communion can be described between churches which are not yet able to enter into forms of eucharistic fellowship.

33. All churches which participate actively in the ecumenical movement agree that even where eucharistic fellowship and full communion are not yet achieved between churches, nevertheless forms of communion do exist. The churches are no longer living in isolation from each other. They have developed mutual understanding and respect. They pray together and share in each other's spiritual experience and theological insights. They collaborate in addressing the needs of humanity. Through bilateral and multilateral dialogues, they have achieved remarkable convergences with regard to previously divisive issues of doctrine and church order. They share, in different degrees, in the basic elements of communion. It is, therefore, possible to speak of an existing real though imperfect communion among the churches – with the understanding that the degrees and expressions of such communion may vary according to the relationships between individual churches.

34. This recognition of an already existing though imperfect communion is a significant result of ecumenical efforts and a radically new element in 20th-century church history. It provides a basis for renewal, common witness, and service of the churches for the sake of God's saving and reconciling activity for all humanity. And it provides a basis and encouragement for further efforts to overcome those barriers which still prevent the recognition and implementation of full communion between the churches.

2. The interdependence of local and universal in the communion of churches

35. Elements of communion at the local level correspond to and interact with their expression at the universal level, because the Holy Spirit is the same source at both levels. Different churches, however, may have different ways of manifesting the same ecclesial elements. Ecclesial communion is lived and experienced in eucharistic communion. The eucharistic synaxis celebrates both the communion with the eternal life of the triune God, and the link with all worshipping communities, as members of the one body of Christ (cf. 1 Cor. 10:17).

36. "The local church is wholly church, but it is not the whole church."[26] This applies already in the case of existing world communions, even though they may understand "local church" differently. It will continue to apply when full unity among Christians has been realized. The local church should never be seen in isolation but always in a dynamic relationship with other local churches. It has to express its faith in relation to other churches, and in so doing it manifests communion. The catholicity of the church implies an inter-relatedness and interdependence among local churches. Once a local church turns in on itself and seeks to function completely independently from other local churches, it distorts a primary aspect of its ecclesial character. The local church is not a freestanding, self-sufficient reality. As part of a network of communion, the local church maintains its reality as church by relating to other local churches.[27]

37. Mutual solicitude, support, recognition and communication are essential qualities among local churches. Even from earliest times, the local churches felt themselves linked to one another. This koinonia was expressed in a variety of ways: exchange of confessions of faith, letters of communion as a kind of "ecclesiastical passport", hospitality, reciprocal visits, mutual material help, councils and synods.[28]

38. Inter-relatedness is now more evident among local churches of the same world communion. The unity we seek prompts us all to find ways of restoring such koinonia at the local and universal levels with Christian communities, from whom we are at present divided. Ecumenism in its local and universal expression, with its emphasis on dialogue and mutual concern, has already opened up many avenues of collaboration, spiritual and theological exchange, and convergence on essential issues of faith and order.

39. At the same time, however, the growth in the koinonia is especially tested when, locally or universally, the churches are called upon to act together on pressing social issues. Ethical issues can become factors of division, as witnessed in the ongoing discussion on abortion, birth control, divorce and homosexuality. The old slogan that "doctrine divides, service unites" is no longer axiomatic. The impact of socio-cultural challenges and the need for common responses to them is of immense importance for the future of ecumenism.

40. Each Christian world communion has to face specific challenges regarding universality and particularity. The Protestant churches have stressed the importance of the local church, but they face the problem of concretely manifesting universality among their own churches. Participation in the World Council of Churches has heightened the experience of universality among the member churches. In the Roman Catholic Church today dialectical tension between local authority and central authority remains a critical issue.[29]

IV. The structuring of communion

41. The very nature of the church of God, the elements of ecclesial community already discussed, and the lived experience of individual Christian communities all form the basis on which the canonical expression of communion has to be developed. Here are meant questions of polity, order, law, authority and constitution which all refer to the structure of the church and of communion. What has been said above about the nature of communion and its many qualities is presupposed here. The canonical dimension of communion applies to the local and universal framework of one particular

tradition as well as to the already partially existing communion among different churches.

1. Canonical structures

42. Communion, as we have seen, refers to a dynamic, spiritual, objective reality which is embodied in ecclesial structures. The gift of communion from God is not an amorphous reality but an organic unity that requires a canonical form of expression. The purpose of such canonical structuring is to ensure that the local churches (and their members), in their communion with each other, can live in harmony and fidelity to "the faith which has been once and for all entrusted to the saints" (Jude 3).

43. In the Roman Catholic Church, communion with the bishop of Rome is necessary. Vatican II referred on several occasions to "hierarchical communion".[30] It taught that one becomes a member of the college of bishops through sacramental ordination and hierarchical communion with the head and members of the college. At his ordination a bishop receives the office *(munus)* of sanctifying, teaching and governing. But these tasks can be exercised only in hierarchical communion with the head and members of the college of bishops. Furthermore, although bishops possess the threefold *munera* through their ordination, they cannot exercise them in a particular place without a specific determination, a "canonical mission" by the pope. The college of bishops cannot act independently of the pope, since the collegial character of the body would be inoperative without its head.

44. Despite certain differences in the life and the practice of Orthodox churches, they believe on the basis of a common canonical tradition that episcopal ordination confers the functions of sanctifying, teaching and ruling. They have comparable practices dealing with the designation and assignment of bishops. Moreover they agree that the bishops must be in hierarchical communion with the head of the synod. In this context, canon 34 of the "Apostolic Canons" is an appropriate expression of the Orthodox understanding of communion.[31]

45. The Reformation and free churches have developed their canonical structures of expressing and safeguarding communion within their churches. According to their particular heritage, they employ presbyterial and synodical structures for this purpose and, in many cases, integrate into them episcopal ministries under different titles, including the office of bishop. In their respective Christian world communions these churches have also developed canonical structures which enable consultation, cooperation and common witness, but which do not allow for decisions which are binding for the individual member churches of that communion. However, there is a general tendency to strengthen ways in which these communions can express their common faith, life and service on a universal level.

46. The ministry of the bishop of Rome as the minister of universal unity is essential to Roman Catholicism. According to Catholic faith, Peter and his successors, the bishops of Rome, have been entrusted by God to confirm the brethren in the faith "which has been once and for all entrusted to the saints" and in the unity of the one, holy, catholic, and apostolic church (cf. *LG*, no. 25; *CD*, no. 2). The bishop of Rome is seen as the sign and guarantee of the communion of local churches with each other and with the church of Peter and Paul. His ministry is multiple: to protect both unity and legitimate diversity; to offer support and solicitude; to facilitate communication between churches; and to arbitrate differences.

47. The office of the papacy remains a controversial issue in ecumenism, but there are signs of better mutual understanding.[32] On the Orthodox side, Ecumenical Patriarch Dimitrios I, following a deliberation and resolution of his synod, and convinced that it expressed the mind of the early church, stated that the bishop of Rome is marked out as the one who has the presidency of charity and is the first bishop in rank and honour in the whole body of the Lord.[33] The pope can be called *primus inter pares* (first among equals), because this apostolic see has exercised a primacy of love from earliest times.[34] In bilateral dialogues, Lutherans speak of the value of the "Petrine function",[35] and Anglicans have agreed that "a universal primacy will be needed in a reunited church and should appropriately be the primacy of the bishop of Rome".[36] The joint Roman Catholic-World Methodist Council commission noted: "Discernment of the various factors in scripture and history might contribute to an agreed perception of what functions the see of Rome might properly exercise in a ministry of universal unity, by what authority, and on what conditions" (§40).[37] Despite these positive statements, the problems of *ius divinum* (divine right), primacy of jurisdiction, infallibility and the papal teaching authority remain subjects of intense ecumenical dialogue.

2. The shape of future unity

48. If all local churches are to be united to form one *communio ecclesiarum* (communion of churches), there must be an acceptance of the basic ecclesial elements of communion: common profession of the same apostolic faith; proclamation of the word of God; mutual recognition of the sacraments, especially baptism and eucharist; and agreement on the nature and exercise of pastoral leadership. Such agreements and recognitions are necessary for the achievement of visible unity in legitimate diversity.

49. Several models of structured Christian communion have been proposed and critically analyzed within the ecumenical movement. Some of the models of comprehensive union that have been suggested include the following: organic union, corporate union, church fellowship through agreement (concord), conciliar fellowship, communion of communions, and unity in reconciled diversity.[38] Nevertheless, the precise shape the united church of the future should take and the forms of diversity it could embrace is an important but still unresolved question for all Christian communities.

50. Furthermore, the different understandings of the Christian world communions concerning the relationship between the church local and universal clearly affect our approach towards future unity. Questions are raised if ecumenical relations develop rapidly on the local level between traditions which have not achieved full communion on the universal level. For example, what degree of communion can local churches of different traditions achieve in these cases, without breaking communion with churches of their own tradition?

51. In conclusion, it can be said that although canonical communion does not yet exist among local churches of different traditions, the churches are in communion in a profoundly spiritual way. Our churches share the common gospel in the Christian heritage. Because ecclesial communion is a fellowship inspired by the indwelling Spirit, we can say that the barriers of our divisions do not reach to heaven. Christian unity is both a gift and a task. Christians of all communities pray for the unity of all in each place and look forward to that "one visible church of God, truly universal and sent forth to the whole world so that the world may be converted to the gospel and so be saved, to the glory of God" (*UR*, no. 1).

NOTES

[1] Cyprian, *De Orat. Dom.* 23, *PL* 4, 553 and cited in *LG*, no. 4.
[2] For example, see Faith and Order Paper no. 59, report of Joint Working Group on "Catholicity and Apostolicity", 133-58 and 216-17. The individual papers of the group can be found in *One in Christ*, 6, 1970, pp.242-483. Note especially paper by E. Lanne, "The Local Church: Its Catholicity and Apostolicity", 288-313; Secretariat for Promoting Christian Unity [now the Pontifical Council for Promoting Christian Unity], "Ecumenical Collaboration at the Regional, National, and Local Levels", SPCU *Information Service*, 26, 1975, 8-31, esp. part 2; Paul VI, address during the 1973 Week of Prayer for Christian Unity, SPCU *Information Service*, 21, 1973, 3-4; World Council of Churches, *In Each Place: Towards a Fellowship of Local Churches Truly United*, Geneva, WCC, 1977; and Roman Catholic–Lutheran Joint Commission, "Facing Unity", document 42 above.
[3] Koinonia comes from *koinos*, common, the opposite of *idios*: proper, particular, private. Koinoo means to put together or to pool. Koinonia, then, refers to the action of having something in common, sharing in, participating in. It is often rendered in Latin by *communio* or *communicatio*. For studies on koinonia consult P.C. Bori, *Koinonia*, Brescia, Paideia, 1972; J.M. McDermott, "The Biblical Doctrine of Koinonia", *Biblische Zeitschrift*, 19, 1975, 64-77 and 219-233; H.J. Sieben, "Koinonia, communauté-communion", *Dictionnaire de Spiritualité*, Paris, 1975, col. 1743-1745; S. Brown, "Koinonia as the Basis of New Testament Ecclesiology?", *One in Christ*, 12, 1976, 157-167; and J.M.R. Tillard, *Eglise d'Eglises: L'ecclésiologie de communion*, Paris, Cerf, 1987.
[4] See "Héritage et alliance", in *Vocabulaire de théologie biblique*, Paris, 1970.
[5] The *communio sanctorum* in the creed may refer both to the "communion of the saints or holy people" and to "communion in holy things" – sharing the sacraments of baptism and the eucharist. See S. Benko, *The Meaning of Sanctorum Communio: Studies in Historical Theology*, London, SCM, 1964, 3.
[6] John Paul II has used the terms "vertical" and "horizontal". He noted that the vertical dimension of *communio* with God is primary. If it is not deeply experienced, it can weaken the possibility of the horizontal dimension reaching its full potential. Address at the meeting of the US bishops in Los Angeles, 16 September 1987, *Origins*, 17:16, 1 Oct. 1987, 257.
[7] "The Final Report", in *Growth in Agreement* 65.
[8] "Facing Unity" 9.
[9] "Towards a Statement on the Church: Report of the Joint Commission between the Roman Catholic Church and the World Methodist Council", document 45 above.
[10] SPCU *Information Service*, 49, 1982, 109.
[11] GA 447.
[12] "The Future of Ecumenism", *One in Christ*, 11, 1975, 323.
[13] Extraordinary synod of bishops, 1985, "A Message to the People of God and the Final Report", Washington, NCCB, 1986.
[14] Eugene L. Brand, "Toward a Lutheran Communion: Pulpit and Altar Fellowship", LWF *Report*, 26, Geneva, Lutheran World Federation, 1988, 9. This report shows that the ecclesiology of communion has long been a subject of discussion within the Lutheran World Federation.
[15] See Ion Bria, ed., *Jesus Christ – The Life of the World: An Orthodox Contribution to the Vancouver Theme*, Geneva, WCC, 1987, 12-13.
[16] For a discussion of the theology of the local church in Vatican II, see the following: P Granfield, "The Local Church as a Center of Communication and Control", *Proceedings of the Catholic Theological Society of America*, 35, 1980, 256-263; H. Legrand, "La réalisation de l'Eglise en un lieu", in *Initiation à la pratique de la théologie*, B. Lauret and F. Refoulé, eds, Tome III, Dogmatique 2, Paris, Cerf, 1983, 143-345; and J.A. Komonchak, "The Local Realization of the Church", in *The Reception of Vatican II*, G. Alberigo et al., eds, Washington, Catholic University of America Press, 1987, 77-90.
[17] A problem in some parts of the Catholic world is the decrease in the number of ordained ministers. As a consequence there are many parishes where the liturgy of the word is becoming more common than the eucharistic liturgy. When a priest is not available, appointed lay members and religious lead the congregation in prayers and readings and distribute the eucharist. There is great concern that the practice of infrequent eucharistic liturgies could adversely affect the doctrine that the eucharist is central to the Catholic concept of the church.
[18] In the words of J.D. Zizioulas: "There is one church, as there is one God. But the expression of this one church is the communion of the many local churches." See Zizioulas, *Being as Communion*, London, Darton, Longman & Todd, 134-135.
[19] *The Uppsala Report, 1968*, Norman Goodall, ed., Geneva, WCC, 1968, 17.
[20] For further discussion on this point, see R.E. Brown, "The New Testament Background for the Concept of the Local Church", *Proceedings of the Catholic Theological Society of America*, 36, 1981, 1-14,

here 4.
[21] For the New Testament communities of St Paul, the church of the saints of Jerusalem was a reference for communion (cf. 2 Cor. 8-9). This local church was also the test for apostolic faith (cf. Gal. 2:1ff.).
[22] Cf. J.D. Zizioulas, *Being as Communion*, pp.132-33.
[23] It should be noted that the expressions "full and complete communion" and "partial and incomplete communion" are not found as such in Vatican II. They are intended to correspond to" (*UR*, no. 3) and *quaedam communio, etsi non perfecra* (*UR*, no. 3). Some authors prefer to speak of "full and perfect communion", an expression used by Paul VI. This expression assumes the possibility of "incomplete and imperfect communion". Obviously, the use of "perfect" and "imperfect" relates to wholeness or completeness and not to the moral qualities of holiness or goodness.
[24] Lukas Vischer, ed., *A Documentary History of the Faith and Order Movement, 1927-1963*, St Louis, Bethany Press, 1963, pp.144-45.
[25] Davis M. Paton, ed., *Breaking Barriers, Nairobi, 1975*, the official report of the fifth assembly of the WCC, Nairobi, 23 Nov.-10 Dec. 1975, London, SPCK, and Grand Rapids, Eerdmans, 1976, p.60.
[26] J.J. von Allmen, "L'Église locale parmi les autres Eglises locales", *Irénikon*, 43, 1970, 512.
[27] See J. Ratzinger, "The Pastoral Implications of Episcopal Collegiality", *Concilium* (American ed.), vol. 1, 45.
[28] See L. Hertling, *Communio: Church and Papacy in Early Christianity*, Chicago, Loyola UP, 1972; and B.R. Prusak, "Hospitality Extended or Denied: Koinonia from Jesus to Augustine", *The Jurist*, 36, 1976, pp.89-126.
[29] On this issue, see P. Granfield, *The Limits of the Papacy: Authority and Autonomy in the Church*, New York, Crossroad, 1987.
[30] *LG*, nos. 21 and 22; *Nota praevia*, 2 and 4; and *CD*, no. 5.
[31] Canon 34: "The bishops of every region ought to know who is the first one *(protos)* among them, and to esteem him as their head, and not to do any great thing without the consent; but every one ought to manage only the affairs that belong to his own diocese and the territory subject to it. But let him (i.e., the first one) not do anything without the consent of all the other (bishops); for it is by this means that there will be unanimity, and God will be glorified through Christ in the Holy Spirit." Text in F.X. Funk, *Didascalia et constitutiones apostolorum*, 1905, pp.572-74.
[32] See V. von Arosto, et al., *Das Papstamt: Dienst oder Hindernis fur di Oekumene?*, Rosenburg, F. Pustet, 1985.
[33] "Letter of Dimitrios I to Pope Paul VI on the Tenth Anniversary of the Lifting of the Anathemas", 14 Dec. 1975, in E.J. Stormon, SJ, ed., *Towards the Healing of Schism: The Sees of Rome and Constantinople. Public Statements and Correspondence between the Holy See and the Ecumenical Patriarchate 1958-1984*, New York/Mahwah, Paulist Press, 1987, no. 331, pp.279-81.
[34] Ignatius to the Romans I. Also, see J. Meyendorff, et al, *The Primacy of Peter in the Orthodox Church*, Leighton Buzzard, UK, Faith Press, 1963. Also P. Duprey, "Brief Reflections on the Title 'Primus inter Pares'", *One in Christ*, 10, 1974, pp.7-12.
[35] P.C. Empie and T.A. Murphy, eds., *Papal Primacy and the Universal Church: Lutherans and Catholics in Dialogue V*, Minneapolis, Augsburg, 1974.
[36] ARCIC, *The Final Report*, in *GA* 108.
[37] "Towards a Statement on the Church", document 45 above.
[38] Briefly summarized in *Facing Unity* 8-20, with appropriate bibliographical references.

70. The Notion of "Hierarchy of Truths"
An Ecumenical Interpretation

1990

Introduction

1. During Pope John Paul II's visit to the World Council of Churches' offices in Geneva (12 June 1984), Dr Willem A. Visser 't Hooft, former WCC general secretary, suggested a study on the "hierarchy of truths". The expression is in the Second Vatican Council's Decree on Ecumenism (1964). The concept has aroused ecumenical hopes, but the expression still needs clarification of its use in the decree and of its implications for the ecumenical dialogue. The pope immediately favoured the suggestion.

2. The Joint Working Group between the Roman Catholic Church and the World Council of Churches commissioned two consultations on "the hierarchy of truths". The first took place at Bossey, Switzerland, September 1985. After the JWG had commented on the initial report (October 1985), the second consultation met in Rome, March 1987. The draft returned to the JWG meeting in May 1987. A small editorial group incorporated the comments from the JWG and from other consultors. The JWG again reviewed the text in April-May 1988 and in February 1989, and received this present version in January 1990 as a study document to help further reflection on the theme.

3. This report is an ecumenical attempt to understand and interpret the intention of the Second Vatican Council in speaking of a "hierarchy of truths", and to offer some implications for ecumenical dialogue and common Christian witness. The report also relates "hierarchy of truths" to other Christian traditions, although it can do so only in an approximate way. These traditions do not normally use the expression, although they appreciate the insights it contains or they may express them in different terms.

1. The conciliar statement and its contents

4. "In ecumenical dialogue, when Catholic theologians join with separated brethren in common study of the divine mysteries, they should, while standing fast by the teaching of the church, pursue the work with love for the truth, with charity, and with humility. *When comparing doctrines, they should remember that there exists an order or 'hierarchy' of truths in Catholic doctrine, since they vary in their relation to the foundation of the Christian faith.* Thus the way will be open whereby this kind of 'fraternal emulation' will incite all to a deeper awareness and a clearer expression of the unfathomable riches of Christ (cf. Eph. 3:8)" (*Unitatis Redintegratio*, no. 11).

5. The paragraph is in the decree's second chapter, which deals with the practice of ecumenism in the Roman Catholic Church (nos. 5-12). This practice includes the

continual examination of our "own faithfulness to Christ's will for the church", and our efforts "to undertake with vigour, wherever necessary, the task of renewal and reform" (no. 4). Essential in such ecumenical practice is doctrinal dialogue which is carried out "with love for the truth, with charity, and with humility" (no. 11). Therefore, the concept of "the hierarchy of truths" relates directly to the task of ecumenical dialogue.

6. The decree emphasizes the necessity for a clear, full and understandable explanation of Catholic doctrine (no. 11) as a presupposition to "dialogue with our brethren". Then in conversation Christian communions explain their doctrine more profoundly and express it more clearly, in order to achieve a more adequate understanding and accurate judgment about each other's teaching and life (cf. no. 9). Then in the same number 11, the decree broadens this understanding of dialogue: it is a search together into the divine mysteries to incite "a deeper realization and a clearer expression of the unfathomable riches of Christ". One thus has to understand the statement on a "hierarchy of truths" within this broader, never-ceasing investigatory concept of dialogue.

7. Two immediate sources for the teaching about the "hierarchy of truths" indicate its meaning. Archbishop Andrea Pangrazio (Italy) first presented the idea to the Council (November 1963). He noted that "to arrive at a fair estimate of both the unity which now exists among Christians and the divergences which still remain, it seems very important to pay close attention to the hierarchical order of revealed truths which express the mystery of Christ and those elements which make up the church". Later (October 1964), in a written modus or proposed amendment to the decree, Cardinal Franz König (Vienna) proposed the exact phrase, "hierarchy of truths". He emphasized that the truths of faith do not add up in a quantitative way, but that there is a qualitative order among them according to their respective relation to the centre or foundation of the Christian faith (Modus 49).

8. The decree is silent about the meaning of "the foundation of Christian faith". According to the official reason *(ratio)* in Modus 49 for the introduction of the phrase, the importance and the "weight" of truths differ because of their specific links with the mystery of Christ and the history of salvation.

9. Thus by using the words "order" or "hierarchy" the Council intended to affirm the organic nature of faith. Truths are articulated around a centre or foundation; they are not placed side by side.

2. Hierarchy of truths in Christian history

10. "Hierarchy of truths" was a new concept at the Second Vatican Council. But the phrase expresses an insight into a reality which has had different forms in the history of the church. The following serve as examples.

11. Even though the *scriptures* are divinely inspired as a whole and in all its parts, many have seen an order or "hierarchy" in so far as some biblical sections or passages bear witness more directly to the fulfilment of God's promise and revelation in Jesus Christ through the Holy Spirit in the church.

12. One sees several kinds of "hierarchies" in relation to the authority of the church *councils* and to their contents. Most Christian traditions give special priority to the seven ecumenical councils of the early church. Some see also a "hierarchy" among these seven councils, inasmuch as those which have formulated the doctrine of the mystery of Christ and of the Spirit within the communion of the Holy Trinity should as such hold a pre-eminent position in comparison with the other councils.

13. The *sacraments* could provide another example of a "hierarchy" within the same order which directly concerns the faith. Baptism (which for some includes chrismation) as incorporation into the church, and the eucharist as the centre of the life of the church, are regarded as primary, while all other sacramental acts are related to these major sacraments.

14. The mystery of Jesus Christ, particularly seen in his death and resurrection, is at the centre of the *liturgical year*. All the celebrations during the year, such as Christmas and Epiphany, Easter and Pentecost, and feasts of the saints, highlight a different aspect of the one mystery which is always fully present. Thus the various festivals of the liturgical year with their particular emphases are related in different ways *(diversus nexus)* to the centre or foundation – the mystery of Jesus Christ.

15. The churches of the Reformation observe also a kind of "hierarchy" in dealing with the truths of the Christian faith. These churches hold that the gospel of God's saving action in Jesus Christ, witnessed to normatively by holy scripture, is the supreme authority to which all Christian truths should refer. It is in relation to the gospel as the centre of the faith that these churches have summarized the truths of the faith in catechisms meant for the edification of the people of God in their faith, in new liturgical formularies and books, and in confessions of faith which are to guide the pastors in their preaching and the synods in their decisions. All this implies a "hierarchy of truths".

16. The Orthodox tradition refers to the fullness of truth, the totality of the revelation of God. The revealed divine truths constitute an indivisible unity, the coherent apostolic tradition. This holy tradition, on which the church bases its unity, represents the entire content of the divinely revealed faith. There is no distinction between principal and secondary truths, between essential and non-essential doctrines. This position does not mean that within Orthodox theological reflection and formulations, there is no room for differentiation or distinctions. Orthodox theologians suggest that the concept of "hierarchy of truths" could help to distinguish permanent and common teachings of faith, such as the declared symbols (creeds) of the seven ecumenical councils and other credal statements, from those teachings which have not been formulated and sanctioned with the authority of those councils. Here may be room for differentiation. This raises, on the other hand, the problem of the nature of the teaching authority in the church.

Ecumenical discussions on "hierarchy of truths" are thus inseparable from the ways in which the church formulates authoritatively the truths and insights of its faith.

3. Interpretation

a) Hierarchy

17. The Decree on Ecumenism uses "hierarchy of truths" as a metaphor (and places "hierarchy" between quotation marks). This indicates an order of importance (a) which implies a graded structure (b) in which the different decrees serve different functions. The decree applies this to Christian doctrine in two ways. First, there is an order between propositional truths of doctrine and the realities which are known by means of the propositions. Propositional truths of doctrine which articulate the faith, such as the Marian dogmas, refer ultimately to the divine mystery and guide the life of the people of God. Secondly, neither in the life nor the teaching of the whole church is

everything presented on the same level. Certainly all revealed truths demand the same acceptance of faith, but according to the greater or lesser proximity that they have to the basis of the revealed mystery, they are variously placed with regard to one another and have varying connections among themselves (Secretariat for Promoting Christian Unity, "Reflections and Suggestions Concerning Ecumenical Dialogue", 1970, IV, 4 b). Some truths lean on more principal truths and are illumined by them (cf. Congregation for the Clergy, *General Catechetical Directory*, 11 April 1971, no. 43; Congregation for the Doctrine of the Faith, *Mysterium Ecclesiae*, 24 June 1973, no. 4).

18. Some Christian traditions upon reflection perceive two dimensions of a "hierarchy of truths". On the one hand, God's revelation itself exhibits an order, such as the transition from the old covenant to the new covenant. On the other hand, in the continuing response of faith to revelation by God's pilgrim people, one sees an ordering of truth which has been influenced by the historical and cultural contexts of time and place. These varied responses in faith to revelation have resulted in different orderings and emphases in the doctrinal expressions of various churches in their various historical periods, and of groups and even of individuals within churches. The Second Vatican Council recognizes that in the investigation of revealed truth, East and West have used different methods and approaches in understanding and proclaiming divine things, and that sometimes one tradition has come nearer than the other to an appropriate appreciation of certain aspects of a revealed mystery or has expressed them in a clearer manner (*UR*, no. 17).

19. In the ecumenical dialogue, churches may become more aware of existing hierarchies or orderings of truths in their tradition and life. Through dialogue, changes can result also in the ordering of a church's own teachings, and this can facilitate rapprochement. The Reformation churches, for example, increasingly acknowledge the significance of the episcopal ministry in their order of truths; and the Roman Catholic Church is finding a new appreciation of the doctrine of justification by faith. These are signs of convergence.

b) Foundation

20. The Decree on Ecumenism states that "the foundation of Christian faith" determines the different ordering of doctrinal truths (no. 11). What does this term "foundation" mean? The Council's deliberations hint at the meaning by reference to the "mystery of Christ" (Pangrazio) and to the "mystery of Christ and the history of salvation" (Modus, 49). This context clearly indicates that the "foundation" refers primarily to the living and life-giving centre or foundation of the Christian faith itself, and not to any of the formulations which express it. Although many different formulas have witnessed to this centre or foundation, e.g., the Nicene-Constantinopolitan Creed and the Apostles' Creed, no one formula can fully grasp or express its reality.

21. This foundation is primarily that reality on which the entire Christian faith and life rests, and by which the community of Christ's disciples is constituted as his body. It establishes the true nature of the church and sustains it on its pilgrim way. The central place where this foundation is proclaimed, confessed and celebrated is the worship of the church.

22. Any attempt to describe this foundation on a conceptual level should refer to the person and mystery of Jesus Christ, true God and true human being. He is the one who said "I am the way, and the truth, and the life" (John 14:6). In the life, death and

resurrection of the Son of the Father, God has come into our midst for our salvation, and the Holy Spirit has been poured out into our hearts. In the Spirit's power God has established his one church, enables its members to experience Christ in faith and to be witnesses to him, and empowers the church to reach out to all humankind until all have been gathered up in God's kingdom.

23. This foundation is normatively witnessed to by the prophets, apostles and the apostolic communities in the Old and New Testaments. In faithfulness to the original apostolic witness, it is confessed in the ecumenical creeds and handed on by the church through the ages.

c) Nexus

24. The decree bases its affirmation of a "hierarchy of truths" on the fact that these truths have different links *(diversus nexus)* with the foundation of the Christian faith. What is "different"? How do different affirmations of truth relate in different ways to the same foundation?

25. First of all, the Council's sentence does not mean that there is only a more or less incidental relationship between these truths and the foundation, so that a merely relative character stamps them and one can consider them optional in the life of faith. Still less does the decree's sentence consider truths of faith as more or less necessary for salvation or suggest degrees in our obligation to believe in all that God has revealed. When one fully responds to God's self-evaluation in faith, one accepts that revelation as a whole. There is no picking and choosing of what God has revealed, because there is no picking or choosing of what revelation is – our salvation. Hence, there are no degrees in the obligation to believe all that God has revealed.

26. The difference of the link of each truth is in its wider or closer proximity to the foundation of faith. This proximity does not ask us to fit each one of these truths into a static system of ordered concepts. Rather, we are to perceive the dynamic relationship which a given truth entertains with the foundation in the communal and personal faith as it is lived by each member of the body of Christ. We are to see the importance or the proximity or the "weight" which each truth has with the foundation of faith in the existential relationship of Christians and their communities.

27. This presupposes that those truths which serve to explain and protect other more fundamental truths have only an indirect link with the foundation of faith, or at least a link which is less direct than that of other truths. This is important in the search for unity among churches, because each Christian communion establishes a more or less immediate link between this or that truth and the foundation.

4. Ecumenical and theological implications

28. The concept of "hierarchy of truths" has implications for the relations between churches as they seek full communion with one another through such means as the ecumenical dialogue. It can help to improve mutual understanding and to provide a criterion which would help to distinguish those differences in the understanding of the truths of faith which are areas of conflict from other differences which need not be.

a) Implication for the search for full communion

29. The notion of "hierarchy of truths" acknowledges that all revealed truths are related to and can be articulated around the "foundation" – the "mystery of Christ" – through

which the love of God is manifested in the Holy Spirit. All those who accept and confess this mystery and are baptized are brought into union with Christ with each other and with the church of every time and place. This fellowship is based upon the communion of the Holy Spirit, who distributes various kinds of spiritual gifts and ministries and binds the members together in one body which is the church. Thus "the mystery of Christ", "the centre", "the foundation", is not only that which Christians believe but also a life which they share and experience.

30. Those who accept and confess the mystery of Christ and the Holy Trinity and are baptized and thereby share in the fellowship of the Holy Spirit are challenged to manifest that fellowship in shared life, in common witness, in common confession of faith and service to humanity, in shared worship, in joint pastoral care, and in commitment to ecumenical dialogue. Such living-out the degree of communion that already exists excites desire for greater communion.

31. While the common "foundation" and baptism unite Christians with one another in the communion of the Holy Spirit, they have not yet been able in a perfect way to make this communion fully visible. This is due to human weakness and sin, to theological and doctrinal disagreements, to historical factors, and in part also to differences about the ordering of truths around the central mystery.

32. In their common acknowledgment of the "foundation", divided Christians are led to view their differences of ordering the truths around this foundation in a more positive and constructive way; for example, the place in different churches of the doctrine of justification in relation to the "foundation". They understand some differences to be instances of that legitimate diversity of expression of common truth which may always characterize the communion of the church; for example, those differences in theological reflection and devotional practice which may have arisen on account of historical and cultural factors are not necessarily differences with regard to the foundation of the faith. The communion of a visibly united church will certainly include a diversity which is a proper expression of its catholic, apostolic faith.

33. However, there are doctrinal differences which are still decisive obstacles that Christians have to overcome before they can manifest full communion in a shared sacramental and ordered life. These differences vary in importance according to their relation to the central mystery of Christ. Ecumenical dialogue is one of the principal means by which Christians better understand the weight and importance of these differences and their relation to the "foundation" of our common faith. In such dialogue Christians can gain new perspective on their common task to reorder priorities in faith and practice and to take appropriate steps and stages on the way to fuller communion.

34. An appreciation of "hierarchy of truths" could mean that the ecumenical agenda will be based upon a communion in the "foundation" that already exists and will point the way to that ordering of priorities which makes possible a gradual growth into full communion.

b) Implications for ecumenical dialogue

35. If rightly used, the concept of "hierarchy of truths" can help those Roman Catholics who are responsible for teaching the faith eagerly to become more open to fuller communion in the faith of Christ when they are "comparing doctrines" (*UR*, no. 11) in ecumenical dialogue. Those of other Christian confessions also make use of such an ordering of truths and emphasize this method especially in their

ecumenical initiatives. For Protestants, the gospel has a more immediate link with the foundation than does the ministry which serves the gospel. This different link also brings about differences in what we have in common. That there is only partial communion among churches is due not only to their disagreement about certain doctrines but also to the different links they establish between the truths and the foundation of faith. The progress made in ecumenical dialogue leads to convergences which tend to attenuate the differences which the Christian communions have established between the links of certain truths with the foundation of faith. Several churches, by recognizing this in their involvement in bilateral and multilateral dialogues, are experiencing the beginnings of such convergences.

36. By better understanding the ways in which other Christians hold, express and live the faith, each confessional tradition is often led to a better understanding also of itself, and can begin to see its own formulations of doctrine in a broader perspective. This experience and discernment of each other is mutually enriching. The process respectfully approaches the mystery of salvation and its various formulations with no intent to "reduce" the mystery by any or all formulations. The process is a means of more adequately assessing expressions of the truth of revelation, their inter-relation, their necessity, and the possible diversity of formulations. Refocusing on the "foundation", a "hierarchy of truths" may therefore be an instrument of that theological and spiritual renewal which the ecumenical movement requires.

37. The notion of "hierarchy of truths" could be helpful in the area of *mission and common witness*. Especially in secularized and highly complex societies, it is important to proclaim in word and life those foundational truths of the gospel in a way that speaks to the needs of the human spirit. The common discernment of these needs is imperative, and the common use of a "hierarchy of truths" may facilitate an ecumenical discernment of the "foundation" and thus lead to convergence in theological understanding which may clarify the content of a common witness.

38. The contemporary understanding of the missionary task has to respect and take into account the richness, complexity and diversity of cultures. The process by which the Christian faith is interpreted and welcomed in various cultures requires sensitivity to this diversity. A "hierarchy of truths" may also be a means of ensuring that the necessary expressions of the faith in various cultures do not result in any loss of its content or in a separation of Christian truths from the foundation. Both in relating content of faith and culture and in making a distinction between them, the notion of "hierarchy of truths" may play an important part.

39. The notion of "hierarchy of truths" could also be a useful principle in *theological methodology and hermeneutics*. It could provide a way for ordering theological work by acknowledging both the organic wholeness and coherence of the truths of the faith and their different places in relation to the "foundation". It is *dialogical* in spirit inasmuch as it envisages "comparing doctrines" within the specific traditions and within a broader ecumenical context. In directing primary attention to the person and mystery of Jesus Christ, "the one who is, who was and who is to come" (Rev. 1:8), the concept may help theology to respect the *historical dimension* of our search for, and witness to, the truth.

40. By focusing on the "foundation" – the mystery of Christ – the notion of "hierarchy of truths" contains an orientation towards the full realization of the kingdom of God and thereby already now evokes a sense of urgency and responsibility. This can

highlight the dynamic character of the Christian faith, its relevance for every time and age, and therefore serve the pilgrim churches in their task of "discerning the signs of the times" and to give an account of their faith and hope in their concrete situations. In responding to the challenges of the present with an awareness of a "hierarchy of truths", Christians are encouraged both to draw gratefully on the wisdom of their traditions and to be creative by seeking fresh responses in the light of God's coming kingdom.

71. Ecumenical Formation
Ecumenical Reflections and Suggestions

20 May 1993

Preface

It is well accepted that there is an ecumenical imperative in the gospel. However, there is also the indisputable fact that the goal of unity is far from realized. In that context of contradiction, the Joint Working Group between the Roman Catholic Church and the World Council of Churches decided in 1985 to focus on ecumenical formation as a contribution towards conscientizing people with regard to ecumenism. The minutes for that particular meeting of the JWG report:

> It might aim at a more popular readership. The pamphlet should be part of a wider process of promoting the idea of ecumenical formation. It should include an explanation of why ecumenical formation is a priority, along with documentation. Anything produced on ecumenical formation ought to be subtitled "ecumenical reflections and suggestions", to make clear there is no intention of giving directives in a field in which each church has its proper responsibility.

The document is designed to be educational, aimed at stimulating ongoing reflection as an integral part of a process of ecumenical formation. It is rooted in a conviction that there must be a deep spirituality at the heart of ecumenical formation.

With these words, we are happy to recommend this document for study.

Most Rev. Alan Clark His Eminence Metropolitan Elias Audi
Co-moderator *Co-moderator*

I. The ecumenical imperative

1. In his high priestly prayer Jesus prayed for all those who will believe in him, "that they may all be one; as you, Father, are in me and I am in you, may they also be in us, so that the world may believe that you have sent me. The glory that you have given me I have given them, so that they may be one, as we are one" (John 17:89121-22).

The unity to which the followers of Jesus Christ are called is not something created by them. Rather, it is Christ's will for them that they manifest their unity, given in Christ, before the world so that the world may believe. It is a unity which is grounded in and reflects the communion which exists between the Father and the Son and the Holy Spirit. Thus, the ecumenical imperative and the mission of the church are inextricably intertwined, and this for the sake of the salvation of all. The eschatological vision of the transformation and unity of humankind is the fundamental inspiration of ecumenical action.

Disobedience to the imperative

2. However, from very early in her history, the church has suffered from tensions. The earliest Christian community in Corinth experienced tensions and factions (1 Cor. 1:10-17). After the councils of Ephesus (in 431) and Chalcedon (in 451), an important part of the church in the East was no more in communion with the rest of the church.

In 1054 there was the great break between the church of the East and the church of the West. As if those were not enough, the Western church was unhappily divided further at the time of the Reformation. Today we continue to have not only the persistence of those divisions but also new ones.

Whatever the reasons, such divisions contradict the Lord's high priestly prayer, and Paul considers such divisions sinful and appeals "that all of you be in agreement and that there be no divisions among you, but that, you be united in the same mind and the same purpose" (1 Cor. 1:10).

3. Against that background, ecumenical formation is a matter of urgency because it is part of the struggle to overcome the divisions of Christians which are sinful and scandalous and challenge the credibility of the church and her mission.

Some significant responses to the ecumenical imperative

4. If there is a tragic history of disobedience to the ecumenical imperative, there is also heartwarming evidence that time and again the churches, conscious of their call to unity, have been challenged to confront the implications of their divisions. For instance, attempts at reconciliation between the East and the West have taken place in the 13th and 15th centuries. Also in the centuries that followed, there were voices and efforts calling the churches away from divisions and enmity. At the beginning of this century, the modern ecumenical history received significant impulses from the 1910 world missionary conference at Edinburgh. In 1920 the ecumenical patriarchate published an encyclical proposing the establishment of a "koinonia of churches", in spite of the doctrinal differences between the churches. The encyclical was an urgent and timely reminder that "world Christendom would be disobedient to the will of the Lord and Saviour if it did not seek to manifest in the world the unity of the people of God and of the body of Christ". Around the same time, Anglicans and Catholics engaged in theological dialogue at the Malines Conversations, and the first world conferences on Life and Work (Stockholm, 1925) and Faith and Order (Lausanne, 1927) were held.

5. Another recall to the ecumenical imperative in modern times was the meeting held in 1948 at Amsterdam, at which the WCC was formally constituted. The theme of this meeting was very significant: "Man's Disorder and God's Design". The long process which culminated in the birth of the WCC represents a multilateral response to the ecumenical imperative, in which a renewed commitment to the una sancta (the one, holy, catholic and apostolic church) and to making our own the prayer of Jesus that "your will be done on earth as it is in heaven", were openly declared to be on the agenda of the churches.

6. A further important landmark on the ecumenical road was the announcement made by Pope John XXIII, on 25 January 1959, the feast of the conversion of St Paul, to convene the Catholic bishops for the Second Vatican Council, which Pope John XXIII opened in October 1962. This Council, which has been highly significant for ecumenical advance, definitely accelerated the possibilities for the Catholic church to take part in the multilateral dialogue in Faith and Order, and to engage in a range of

bilateral dialogues which are now an important expression of the one ecumenical scene. Various bilateral conversations between various churches attest to growing fruitful relations between churches and traditions which for centuries were at variance.

7. There have also been historic and symbolic actions which are very significant efforts to overcome the old divisions. For example, on 7 December 1965 Pope Paul VI and Patriarch Athenagoras, in solemn ceremonies in Rome and Constantinople, took steps to take away from the memory and the midst of the churches the sentences of excommunication which had been the immediate cause of the great schism between the church of Rome and the church of Constantinople in 1054. Moreover, the icon of the apostles Peter and Andrew in embrace – Peter being the patron of the church of Rome and Andrew the patron of the church of Constantinople – presented by the ecumenical patriarch to the pope, illustrates in graphic and religious form the reconciliation between the churches of the East and the West. The responses of many churches to the Faith and Order document on *Baptism, Eucharist and Ministry*, which was the result of multilateral ecumenical dialogue, is a further illustration of ecumenical advance.

The imperative, a permanent call

8. The foregoing historical moments in the life of the church stand like promontories in the ecumenical landscape and attest to the fact that in spite of persisting divisions, of which there is need for repentance, churches are experiencing a reawakening to the necessity of unity that stands in holy writ and in the Lord's will for the church. Indeed, many have observed that relationships between churches have radically changed from isolation and enmity to mutual respect, cooperation, dialogue and, between several churches from the Reformation, also eucharistic fellowship. The people of God are hearing anew the call "to lead a life worthy of the calling to which you have been called... bearing with one another in love, making every effort to maintain the unity of the Spirit in the bond of peace" (Eph. 4:1-3). These and other developments are steps towards that visible unity, which is a koinonia given and expressed in the common confession of the one apostolic faith; mutual recognition and sharing of baptism, eucharist and ministries; common prayer; witness and service in the world; and conciliar forms of deliberation and decision-making.

II. Ecumenical formation: What is meant by it?

9. That for long periods we have been disobedient to the ecumenical imperative is a reminder that the spirit of ecumenism needs nurturing. Ecumenical formation is an ongoing process of learning within the various local churches and world communions, aimed at informing and guiding people in the movement which – inspired by the Holy Spirit – seeks the visible unity of Christians.

This pilgrimage towards unity enables mutual sharing and mutual critique through which we grow. Such an approach to unity thus involves at once rootedness in Christ and in one's tradition, while endeavouring to discover and participate in the richness of other Christian and human traditions.

A process of exploration

10. Such a response to the ecumenical imperative demands patient, humble and persistent exploration, together with people of other traditions, of the pain of our situation of separation, taking us to both the depths of our divisions and the heights of our

already existing unity in the triune God, and of the unity we hope to attain. Thus, ecumenical formation is also a process of education by which we seek to orient ourselves towards God, all Christians, and indeed all human beings in a spirit of renewed faithfulness to our Christian mission.

A process of learning

11. As a process of learning, ecumenical formation is concerned with engaging the experience, knowledge, skills, talents, and the religious memory of the Christian community for mutual enrichment and reconciliation. The process may be initiated through formal courses on the history and main issues of ecumenism, as well as be integrated into the curriculum at every level of the education in which the church is involved. Ecumenical formation is meant to help set the tone and perspective of every instruction and, therefore, may demand a change in the orientation of our educational institutions, systems and curricula.

12. The language of formation and learning refers to some degree to a body of knowledge to be absorbed. That is important: but formation and learning require a certain bold openness to living ecumenically as well. In 1952 the fourth Faith and Order conference took place in Lund, Sweden. The statement that came from it may be read as a representative text:

> A faith in the one church of Christ which is not implemented by acts of obedience is dead. There are truths about the nature of God and his church which will remain forever closed to us unless we act together in obedience to the unity which is already ours. We would, therefore, earnestly request our churches to consider whether they are doing all they ought to do to manifest the oneness of the people of God. Should not our churches ask themselves whether they are showing sufficient eagerness to enter into conversation with other churches and whether they should not act together in all matters except those in which deep differences of conviction compel them to act separately?... Obedience to God demands also that the churches seek unity in their mission to the world.

A process for all

13. Thus in pursuit of the goal of Christian unity, ecumenical formation takes place not only in formal educational programmes but also in the daily life of the church and people. While the formation of the whole people of God is desired, indeed is a necessity, we also insist on the strategic importance of giving priority to the ecumenical formation of those who have special responsibility for ministry and leadership in the churches. To that extent, theologians, pastors and others who bear responsibility in the church have both a particular need and responsibility for ecumenical formation.

14. The ecumenical formation of those with particular responsibility for forming and animating future church leaders could involve the study of ecumenical history and documents resulting from the ongoing bilateral and multilateral dialogues. In addition, ecumenical gatherings and organizations, particularly of scholars, can provide a useful climate for it. Exchange visits among seminary students in the course of their training may also help this process of deepening the appreciation of other traditions as well as their own.

An expression of ecumenical spirituality

15. It follows from the ecumenical imperative that the process of formation in ecumenism has to be undergirded by and should indeed be an expression of ecumenical spirituality.

It is spiritual in the sense that it should be open to the prayer of Jesus for unity and to the promptings of the Holy Spirit, who reconciles and binds all Christians together.

It is spiritual in yet another sense, of leading to repentance for the past disobedience to the ecumenical imperative, which disobedience was manifested as contentiousness and hostility among Christians at every level. Having ecumenical spirituality in common prayer and other forms as the underpinning of ecumenical formation invites all to conversion and change of heart, which is the very soul of the work for restoring unity.

Furthermore, it is spiritual in the sense of seeking a renewed life-style, which is characterized by sacrificial love, compassion, patience with one another and tolerance. The search for such life-style may include exposing students to the spiritual texts, prayers and songs of other churches with the goal and hope that such familiarity will contribute towards effecting change of heart and attitude towards others, which itself is a gift of the Holy Spirit. Such efforts will help deepen mutual trust, making it possible to learn together the positive aspects of each other's tradition, and thus live constructively with the awareness of the reality and pain of divisions.

16. Ecumenical formation is part of the process of building community in the one household of God, which must be built on trust, centred on Jesus Christ the Lord and Saviour. This demands a spirituality of trust which, among other things, helps to overcome the fear to be exposed to different traditions, for the sake of Christ.

III. Ecumenical formation: How to realize it?

Pedagogy built on communion

17. The renewed emphasis on understanding the church as communion, like the image of the church as the body of Christ, implies differentiation within the one body, which has nevertheless been created for unity. Thus, the very dynamic of ecumenism is relational in character. We respond in faith and hope to God who relates to us first. God relates to us in love, commanding us to love one another (Mark 12:29-31). This response ought to be wholehearted. Therefore, in order to help Christians to respond wholeheartedly to the ecumenical imperative, we must seek ways to relate the prayer of Jesus (John 17:20-24) to all our hearts and minds, to the affective as well as to the cognitive dimensions in them. Christians must be helped to understand that to love Jesus necessarily means to love everything Jesus prayed, lived, died and was raised for, namely, "to gather into one the children of God who are scattered abroad" (John 11:52), the unity of his disciples as an effective sign of the unity of all peoples.

18. The koinonia or communion as the basic understanding of the church demands attempting to develop common ecumenical perspectives on ecclesiology. Unity is not uniformity but a communion of much diversity. Therefore, it is necessary to explore with others the limits of legitimate diversity. In this regard special cognizance must also be taken of the religious and socio-cultural context in which the process of ecumenical formation takes place. Where there is a predominant majority church, ecumenical sensitivity is all the more required.

Going out to each and every one

19. The effectiveness of Christian unity in the midst of a broken world ultimately depends on the work of God's Spirit who wishes each one of us to participate. God

speaks to us today the words which were addressed to Adam and Eve, "Where are you?" (Gen. 3:9) as also the words to Cain, "Where is your brother?" (Gen. 4:9). All Christians should become aware, and make each other aware, of who and where their sisters and brothers are and where they stand in regard to them, whether near or far (Eph. 2:17). They should be helped to go out to meet them, to get involved with them. Involvement and participation in the whole ecumenical formation process is crucial.

20. In a Christian response to God and the ecumenical imperative which comes from God, there is no such thing as "the few for the many". The response to the prayer of Jesus must be the response *of each and every one*. Therefore, the growth into an ecumenical mind and heart is essential for each and for all, and the introduction of, and care for, ecumenical formation are absolutely necessary *at every level* of the church community, church life, action and activities; at *all* educational levels (schools, colleges, universities; theological schools, seminaries, religious/monastic communities, pastoral and lay formation centres; Sunday liturgies, homilies and catechesis).

Commitment to learning in community

21. While ecumenical formation must be an essential feature in every curriculum in theological training, care must be taken that it does not become something intended for individuals only. There must be commitment of learning in community. This has several components: (a) learning about, from and with others of different traditions; (b) praying for Christian unity, and wherever and whenever possible, *together*, as well as praying for one another; (c) offering common Christian witness by acting together, and (d) struggling together with the pain of our divisions. In this regard the participation of different institutions for theological education in a common programme of formation is to be encouraged. Working ecumenically in joint projects becomes another important aspect of ecumenical formation. The reason for such joint action must always be related to the search for Christian unity.

22. Seeking a renewed commitment for ecumenical formation does not imply to gloss over existing differences and to deny the specific profiles of our respective ecclesial traditions. But it may involve a common rereading of our histories and especially of those events that led to divisions among Christians. It is not enough to regret that our histories have been tainted through the polemics of the past; ecumenical formation must endeavour to eliminate polemic and to further mutual understanding, reconciliation and the healing of memories. No longer shall we be strangers to one another but members of the one household of God (Eph. 2:19).

Open to other religions

23. In this world, people are also divided along religious lines. Thus, ecumenical formation must also address the matter of religious plurality and secularism and inform about inter-religious dialogue, which aims at deeper mutual understanding in the search for world community. It must be clear, however, that inter-religious dialogue – with other world religions such as Islam, Buddhism, Hinduism, etc. – has goals that are specifically different from the goals of ecumenical dialogue among Christians. In giving serious attention to this important activity, Christians must carefully distinguish it from ecumenical dialogue.

24. That spirit of tolerance and dialogue must get to the pews and market-places where people feel the strains of the different heritages which encounter each other. The

faith that God is the Creator and Sustainer of all also requires Christians to do everything in their power to promote the cause of freedom, human rights, justice and peace everywhere, and thus actively to contribute to a renewed movement towards human solidarity in obedience to God's will.

Using the instruments of communication

25. In today's search for unity, there is a relatively new factor which must be taken seriously – the scientific technological advances, particularly the communications revolution. The world has become a global village in which peoples, cultures and religions, and Christian denominations which were once far off are now next door one to another. The sense of the "other" is being pressed on us, and we need to relate to one another for mutual survival and peace. Thus, the possibilities of mass communication can be an asset for communicating the ecumenical spirit.

The media can be an extremely important resource for ecumenical formation, and the many possibilities which they offer to promote the ecumenical formation process should be made use of. However, the world of the media has its own logic and values; it is not an unambivalent resource. Critical caution must, therefore, be exercised in availing ourselves of the media for the ecumenical task.

Conclusion: Ecumenical formation and common witness

26. Ecumenism is not an option for the churches. In obedience to Christ and for the sake of the world, the churches are called to be an effective sign of God's presence and compassion before all the nations. For the churches to come divided to a broken world is to undermine their credibility when they claim to have a ministry of universal unity and reconciliation. The ecumenical imperative must be heard and responded to everywhere. This response necessarily requires ecumenical formation, which will help the people of God to render a common witness to all humankind by pointing to the vision of the new heaven and a new earth (Rev. 21:1).

72. The Challenge of Proselytism and the Calling to Common Witness

25 September 1995

Foreword

We would like to present the document "The Challenge of Proselytism and the Calling to Common Witness", which has been prepared by the Joint Working Group between the World Council of Churches and the Roman Catholic Church, in response to concerns expressed by some of our churches in regard to the missionary outreach of other churches that would seem to bear some of the characteristics of proselytism.

It is within the concern for full Christian unity and common Christian witness that the question of proselytism is looked at in this document. There is the common conviction that central to the work of Christian unity is an urgent need for all Christians to be able to give a truly common witness to the whole Christian faith.

In this spirit, the document may help Christian communities to reflect on their own motivation for mission and also on their methods of evangelizing. Dialogue in a truly ecumenical spirit with those considered to be proselytizing is highlighted.

It is our hope, therefore, that this document will be shared at different levels of church life and reflected on by churches, so that it can contribute towards breaking down mistrust, suspicion, misunderstanding or ignorance of the other, where any of these may exist, as well as encourage persevering effort to seek new ways and means of closer collaboration in evangelization, according to the different circumstances of time, place and culture.

All such efforts will mean a deeper commitment to the goal of full communion among Christ's disciples, in the certitude that our fellowship is with the Father, through the Son, in the Holy Spirit. This document is meant as a contribution to that goal.

His Eminence Metropolitan Elias of Beirut
Co-moderator of the
Joint Working Group

Most Rev. Alan C. Clark
Co-moderator of the
Joint Working Group

I. Introduction

1. This document is the result of discussions in the Joint Working Group (JWG) and is presented with the conviction that it is timely, and with the hope that it may serve as an impulse for further reflection and action in the churches. The conversations in the JWG were marked both by the grateful recognition of the increase of common witness of Christians from different traditions, and serious concerns about tensions and conflicts created by proselytism in nearly all parts of the world. It is the new reality of

common witness and a growth in koinonia which forms the backdrop for a critical consideration of proselytism which has been described as conscious efforts with the intention to win members of another church.[1]

2. Even though the JWG has addressed the questions of common witness and proselytism on two previous occasions, recent dramatic events have led it to study these issues once again. Over the past few years we have become more aware of the concern being expressed in new situations and contexts in which people tend to be vulnerable in one way or another, and where proselytizing activity is alleged to be taking place. Some situations invite urgent ecumenical attention, such as:
- within the climate of newly found religious freedom, e.g. in Central and Eastern Europe, where there is a threat felt by some churches that their members are under pressure from other churches to change their allegiance;
- instances in the "developing world" (often easily identified with nations in the Southern hemisphere, though also found elsewhere), in which proselytizing efforts take advantage of people's misfortunes – e.g. in situations of poverty in villages, or in the mass migration to the cities where new arrivals have a sense of being lost in anonymity or marginalized and are frequently outside the pastoral structures of their own church – to induce them to change their church affiliation;
- where people of a particular ethnic group, traditionally members of one church, are said to be encouraged by unfair means to become members of other churches;
- the activity of some new missionary movements, groups or individuals, both within our churches and outside them, especially those originating in the newly industrialized nations which enter countries often uninvited by any church and begin missionary activity among the local people in competition with the local churches;
- in various places the arrival of evangelizing groups making extensive use of the mass media and causing confusion and division among local churches;
- in many parts of the world, the churches are experiencing proselytizing activities of sects and new religious movements.

3. The purpose of this document is to encourage all Christians to pursue their calling to render a common witness to God's saving and reconciling purpose in today's world and to help them to avoid all competition in mission that contradicts their common calling. With this aim the document seeks to facilitate a pastoral response to the continuing challenge of proselytism which not only endangers existing ecumenical relations but is also an additional barrier to our growing together in reciprocal love and trust as brothers and sisters in Christ.

4. Today we thank God for the achievements of ecumenical theological dialogues during recent decades and for a new climate of understanding and friendship in which ecumenical relations are being developed. We are also grateful for all the recent encouraging signs of better mutual understanding and joint perspectives in the area of common witness and proselytism.[2] These are recorded in bilateral and multilateral dialogues among churches and can be seen in significant initiatives of common witness at different levels of church life. These agreements and joint actions provide a basis and encouragement to intensify our efforts to bear together a credible witness to the gospel in the contemporary world.

5. In this study process we wish to affirm what continues to be valid in the two previous WCC-RCC Joint Working Group documents "Common Witness and Proselytism"[3] and "Common Witness".[4] We also want to take into account relevant material

on evangelism and proselytism from some of the aforementioned dialogues. In addition, this study process will be linked with another possible study on proselytism in the World Council of Churches by Unit II.[5]

6. We acknowledge with appreciation similar studies being undertaken by ecumenical bodies such as the Conference of European Churches[6] and the Middle East Council of Churches.[7] Our desire is to invite reflection and action on the part of churches of different traditions in a task to which all are called on our pilgrimage to a fuller expression and experience of visible Christian unity.

II. Mission and unity: The context of common witness

7. An essential element of the church is to participate in the mission of God in Jesus Christ to the world by proclaiming through word and action God's revelation and salvation to all people (1 John 1:1-5). Indeed, God's mission towards a "reconciled humanity and a renewed creation" (cf. Eph. 1:9-10) is the essential content and impulse for the missionary witness of the church.

8. Mission in this sense of being sent with a message that is addressed to the spiritual and also material needs of people is thus an inescapable mandate for the church. This imperative is affirmed today by many churches and is expressed through their regular activities as well as special efforts (New Evangelization, Decades of Evangelism, Mission 2000). Sent to a world in need of unity and greater interdependence amidst the competition and fragmentation of the human community, the church is called to be sign and instrument of God's reconciling love.[8]

9. Ecumenical relationships, however, have from the beginning of the modern ecumenical movement been shaped by the insight that the search for the visible unity of Christ's church must include the commitment to and the practice of a common missionary witness. In the prayer of Jesus "that they all may be one so that the world may believe" (John 17:21), we are reminded that the unity of Christians and the mission of the church are intrinsically related. Divisions among Christians are a counter-witness to Christ and contradict their witness to reconciliation in Christ.

10. In responding to the appeal for the unity of Christians in effective missionary witness, we need to be aware of the reality of diversity rooted in theological traditions and in various geographical, historical and cultural contexts. We recognize, therefore, that the unity we seek is a unity that embraces a legitimate diversity of spiritual, disciplinary, liturgical and theological expressions that enrich common witness. It will include the discovery and appreciation of the many diverse gifts of Christ which we share already now as Christians in "real but imperfect communion", gifts given for the upbuilding of the church (cf. Rom. 12:4-8). Even when churches are not in full communion with each other they are called to be truthful to each other and show respect for each other. Such an attitude does not subvert their self-understanding and their conviction to have received the truth but rather facilitates the common search for unity and common witness to God's love for the world.

11. In the growing ecumenical koinonia there must also be a way of witnessing to the gospel to each other in faithfulness to one's own tradition and convictions. Such mutual witness could enrich and challenge us to renew our thinking and life, and could do so without being polemical towards those who do not share the same tradition. "To speak the truth in love" (Eph. 4:15) is a challenge and an experience long accepted within the ecumenical movement.

12. The recognition of an already existing, though imperfect, communion among churches is a significant result of ecumenical efforts and a new element in 20th-century church history. This existing communion should be an encouragement for further efforts to overcome the barriers that still prevent churches from reaching full communion. It should provide a basis for the renewal, common witness and service of the churches for the sake of God's saving and reconciling activity for all humanity and all creation. It should also provide a basis for avoiding all rivalry and antagonistic competition in mission because "the use of coercive or manipulative methods in evangelism distorts koinonia".[9]

13. When Christians by means of efforts towards common witness struggle to overcome such lack of reciprocal love, of mutual understanding and of trust they will be open to the call for repentance and for the renewal of their efforts. This is the way "to come to the unity of the faith and of the knowledge of the Son of God, to maturity, to the measure of the full stature of Christ" (Eph. 4:13).

14. These efforts include self-critical reflection on our relationships with other churches, openness to appreciate authentically evangelical expressions of life in them, and to be mutually enriched. They will also include engaging in a more authentic dialogue where we can speak meaningfully and honestly to one another, discussing difficulties as they arise and trying to build up relationships (cf. Eph. 4:15).

III. Some basic principles of religious freedom

15. We acknowledge the right of every person "alone or in community with others and in public or in private"[10] to live in accordance with the principles of religious freedom.[11] Religious freedom affirms the right of all persons to pursue the truth and to witness to that truth according to their conscience. It includes the freedom to acknowledge Jesus Christ as Lord and Saviour and the freedom of Christians to witness to their faith in him by word and deed.

Religious freedom involves the right to freely adopt or change one's religion and to "manifest it in teaching, practice, worship and observance"[12] without any coercion which would impair such freedom.

We reject all violations of religious freedom and all forms of religious intolerance as well as every attempt to impose belief and practices on others or to manipulate or coerce others in the name of religion.

16. Freedom of religion touches on "one of the fundamental elements of the conception of life of the person". The promotion of religious freedom contributes also to the harmonious relations between religious communities and is therefore an essential contribution to social harmony and peace. For these reasons, international instruments and the constitutions and laws of almost all nations recognize the right to religious freedom.[13] Proselytism can violate or manipulate the right of the individual and can exacerbate tense and delicate relations between communities and thus destabilize societies.

17. The responsibility of fostering religious freedom and the harmonious relations between religious communities is a primary concern of the churches. Where principles of religious freedom are not being respected and lived in church relations, we need, through dialogue in mutual respect, to encourage deeper consideration and appreciation of these principles and of their practical applications for the churches.

IV. Nature and characteristics of proselytism

18. In the history of the church, the term "proselytism" has been used as a positive term and even as an equivalent concept for missionary activity.[14] More recently, especially in the context of the modern ecumenical movement, it has taken on a negative connotation when applied to activities of Christians to win adherents from other Christian communities. These activities may be more obvious or more subtle. They may be for unworthy motives or by unjust means that violate the conscience of the human person; or even if proceeding with good intentions, their approach ignores the Christian reality of other churches or their particular approaches to pastoral practice.

19. Proselytism as described in this document stands in opposition to all ecumenical effort. It includes certain activities which often aim at having people change their church affiliation and which we believe must be avoided, such as the following:[15]
- making unjust or uncharitable references to other churches' beliefs and practices and even ridiculing them;
- comparing two Christian communities by emphasizing the achievements and ideals of one, and the weaknesses and practical problems of the other;
- employing any kind of physical violence, moral compulsion and psychological pressure, e.g. the use of certain advertising techniques in mass media that might bring undue pressure on readers/viewers;[16]
- using political, social and economic power as a means of winning new members for one's own church;
- extending explicit or implicit offers of education, health care or material inducements or using financial resources with the intent of making converts;[17]
- manipulative attitudes and practices that exploit people's needs, weaknesses or lack of education especially in situations of distress, and fail to respect their freedom and human dignity.[18]

20. While our focus in this document is on relationships between Christians, it is important to seek the mutual application of these principles also in interfaith relations. Both Christians and communities of other faiths complain about unworthy and unacceptable methods of seeking converts from their respective communities. The increased cooperation and dialogue among people of different faiths could result in witness offered to one another that would respect human freedom and dignity and be free of the negative activities described above.

V. Sources of tension in church relationships

21. We need to look at some of the sources of tension in church relationships which could lead to proselytism, in order to ground some of this concern. One is the holding of distorted views of another church's teaching or doctrine and even attacking or caricaturing them, e.g. denouncing prayer for the dead as a denial of the need for personal acceptance of Christ as Lord and Saviour; discrediting the veneration of icons as signs of crude idolatry; interpreting the use of art in church buildings as a transgression of the first commandment.

22. Different understandings of missiology and different concepts of evangelization also underlie some interchurch tensions, e.g. seeing God's gift of salvation as coming exclusively through one's own church; seeing the task of mission as exclusively concerned with social matters or exclusively with spiritual matters, rather than in a holistic way. They can lead to competition or even conflict in missionary practice among the churches rather than a common approach to mission.

23. Different theological and pastoral understandings of the meaning of certain concepts can also contribute to tension in relationships. For example, some aim at the re-evangelization of baptized but non-practising members of other churches. But there are different interpretations of who is "unchurched", or a "true" Christian believer. Efforts to understand the perspectives of other Christian communities on these matters are therefore necessary.

24. The varieties of understanding of membership existing among churches can also be an unnecessary source of tension. There are theological issues involved. The way of becoming a member and even the way of terminating membership in particular churches can be understood very differently. The duties and responsibilities of members also differ from church to church. This diversity of understanding influences the way we see changes in church affiliation.

25. Unfortunately, there are occasions when the personal and cultural confusion of people, their social-political resentments, the tensions within a church, or their hurtful experiences in their own church can be played upon to persuade them to be converted.

26. Sometimes, evangelizers can be tempted to take advantage of the spiritual and material needs of people or their lack of instruction in the faith in order to make them change their church affiliation, because they may interpret this as a lack of pastoral care and attention to these people on the part of churches to which they belong. But in fact, pastoral care, even if it could be more adequate, may be available to the person in his or her own church. Here again there may be different perceptions as to what is adequate and what is inadequate in the field of pastoral care. However the churches must always look for ways to improve the pastoral care they give to their people, especially the quality of instruction in the faith.

27. Tensions also arise on occasion because of the unjust interference on the part of the state in church matters in order to influence people to change church membership.

28. In other situations where a church identifies with the government or works in collusion with it to the extent that it fails to exercise its prophetic role, tensions can arise within the Christian community from what may be seen as preferential treatment by the government for that particular church.

29. Tensions can result in evangelizing activity when there is a lack of sufficient regard for people's culture and religious traditions. There can also be dangers if we lose sight of the fact that the gospel must take root in the soil of different cultures, while it cannot be limited to any culture.

30. Finally, there can be a lack of respect for the beliefs and practices of minority groups in contexts dominated by a majority church, and an inability to see them as full and equal partners in society that causes tensions in relationships. In some cases, a dominant Christian tradition has allowed restrictive laws to be framed by the state which disfavour Christians of another tradition.

VI. Steps forward

31. Despite all efforts to combat it, the problem of proselytism is still with us, causing painful tensions in church relationships and undermining the credibility of the church's witness to God's universal love. Ultimately, proselytism is a sign of the real scandal which is division. By placing the issue of proselytism in the context of church unity and of common witness we suggest a perspective which makes it possible to approach the problem within an adequate theological framework.

32. As responsible ecumenical relationships in many different contexts are a complex reality requiring study and theological dialogue, prayer and practical collaboration, we would like to recommend the following to the churches, keeping in mind that the movement for Christian unity can also contribute to breaking down barriers between people in the wider society as well:
- to encourage churches to pray for one another and for Christian unity in response to the prayer of our Lord, that his disciples "may all be one... so that the world may believe" (John 17:21);
- to prepare more adequate Christian formation programmes within our churches so that people are better equipped to share their own faith, as well as ecumenical programmes that will foster respect for the integrity of other Christian churches and openness to receive from them;
- to develop a sensitivity to existing ecclesial realities in a given area so that, when providing the required pastoral care for one's own church members, it can be done in an atmosphere of communication and appropriate consultation;[19]
- to condemn publication of unverified alleged events or incidents concerning church activities that only fan feelings of fear and prejudice, and of one-sided or prejudicial reports on religious developments which can undercut efforts towards cooperation;[20]
- to try to understand history from the perspective of other churches in order to arrive at a shared common understanding of it and, where necessary, at reconciliation, mutual forgiveness and healing of memories;
- to study together the nature of diakonia in order that the characteristics of Christian service be made clear and transparent; that is, that it may be truly inspired by the love of Christ and that it may not be a reason for tension, nor a means of proselytism;
- to help people to a greater awareness of the phenomenon of sects and new religious movements, through collaborative efforts, and also to consider the question of how to respond pastorally but firmly to coercive religious practices by persons and groups that are not in keeping with the principles of religious liberty;
- to include in any future study of proselytism the significant participation of Christians, both within and outside World Council of Churches and Roman Catholic circles of influence, especially those accused of these practices and those who have changed church affiliation through the efforts of another church.[21]

33. These efforts will be effective and successful to the extent that relationships of reciprocal trust are built between the churches.

VII. Conclusion

34. Knowing that our common faith in Jesus, Lord and Saviour, unites us and that baptism is an effective sign of unity, we are called to live our Christian vocation in unity and to give visible witness to it.

35. Therefore, it is not enough to denounce proselytism. We need to continue to prepare ourselves for genuine common Christian witness through common prayer, common retreats, Bible courses, Bible sharing, study and action groups, religious education jointly or in collaboration, joint or coordinated pastoral and missionary activity,[22] a common service (diakonia) in humanitarian matters and theological dialogue. The immensely rich Christian spiritual patrimony of contemplative prayer can be a resource

for all. We acknowledge that our current divisions limit the extent to which we can engage in common witness. We recall and make our own the principle cited in the third world conference on Faith and Order at Lund, Sweden, 1952:

> We earnestly request our churches to consider whether they are doing all they ought to do to manifest the oneness of the people of God. Should not our churches ask themselves whether they are showing sufficient eagerness to enter into conversation with other churches and whether they should not act together in all matters except those in which deep differences of conviction compel them to act separately...? Obedience to God demands also that the churches seek unity in their mission to the world.23

36. There is also an urgent need to continue to work collaboratively in order to transcend the lines that society draws between those at the centre and those on the peripheries, between those who have an abundance of resources and those marginalized because of race, economics, gender or for other reasons. These societal divisions often provide the context for proselytism and therefore challenge our divided churches to closer collaboration that will be a common Christian witness.[24]

37. In all of these reflections we take our inspiration from the gospel itself:

> This is my commandment: love one another, as I have loved you. No one can have greater love than to lay down his life for his friends... You did not choose me, no, I chose you; and I commissioned you to go out and to bear fruit, fruit that will last; so that the Father will give you anything you ask him in my name. My command to you is to love one another (John 15:12-13,16-17).

NOTES

[1] Cf. also the more detailed description of proselytism in §§18-19.
[2] Among many other examples which could be adduced here are "The Evangelical-Roman Catholic Dialogue on Mission, 1977-1984: A Report", in *Information Service,* Pontifical Council for Promoting Christian Unity, Vatican City, no. 60, 1986, pp.71-97, and document 40 above; "Summons to Witness to Christ in Today's World: A Report on the Baptist-Roman Catholic International Conversations, 1984-1988", in *Information Service,* no. 72, 1990, pp.5-14, and document 38 above; "Letter of Pope John Paul II to Bishops of Europe on Relations between Catholics and Orthodox in the New Situation of Central and Eastern Europe (31 May 1991)", in *Information Service,* no. 81, 1992, pp.101-103; *General Principles and Practical Norms for Coordinating the Evangelizing Activity and Ecumenical Commitment of the Catholic Church in Russia and in the Other Countries of the CIS,* Pontifical Commission for Russia (from the Vatican, 1 June 1992); "Uniatism: Method of Union of the Past, and the Present Search for Full Communion. Report of the Joint International Commission for the Theological Dialogue between the Roman Catholic Church and the Orthodox Church – Balamand, 17-24 June 1993", in *Information Service,* no. 83, 1993, pp.96-99, and document 52 above; "US Orthodox/Roman Catholic Consultation at the Holy Cross Orthodox School of Theology, Brookline, Mass., May 26-28, 1992", in *Origins,* vol. 22, no. 5, 11 June 1992, pp. 79-80; "Towards Koinonia in Faith, Life and Witness", discussion paper for the fifth world conference on Faith and Order, Santiago de Compostela, 3-14 August 1993, published in the conference report, T.F. Best and Günther Gassmann, eds, *On the Way to Fuller Koinonia,* Geneva, WCC, 1994, Faith and Order Paper no. 166, pp.262ff.
[3] Published in *The Ecumenical Review,* vol. 23, no. 1, Jan. 1971, pp.9-20.
[4] "Common Witness: A Study Document of the Joint Working Group of the Roman Catholic Church and the World Council of Churches", Geneva, WCC/CWME, 1982, CWME Series, 1.
[5] Cf. also the report of section IV from the fifth world conference on Faith and Order, "Called to Common Witness for a Renewed World", §14, in *On the Way to Fuller Koinonia,* pp.256f.
[6] Cf. "At Thy Word: Mission and Evangelization in Europe Today", message of the Fifth European Ecumenical Encounter, Santiago de Compostela, 13-17 November 1991, *Catholic International,* vol. 3, no. 2, pp.88-92; *God Unites: In Christ a New Creation,* report of the 10th assembly of CEC, Prague, 1-11 September 1992, pp.182-83, final report of the Policy Reference Committee, appendix 18.

[7] Proselytism, Sects and Pastoral Challenges: Working Document of the Commission of Faith and Unity, MECC, 1989; Signs of Hope in the Middle East, MECC/EMEU Consultation, Cyprus, 1992: history of the dialogue between the MECC and Western Evangelicals.

[8] This perspective is expressed, for example, in Vatican II, *Lumen Gentium*, §1; and in the Faith and Order study document *Church and World: The Unity of the Church and the Renewal of Human Community*, Geneva, WCC, 1990, Faith and Order Paper no. 151.

[9] Report of section IV from the fifth world conference on Faith and Order, §14, *loc. cit.*

[10] Declaration on the Elimination of All Forms of Intolerance and of Discrimination Based on Religion or Belief, 25 November 1981, Art. 1,1.

[11] Cf. Vatican II, Declaration on Religious Liberty *(Dignitatis Humanae)*, Decree on Ecumenism *(Unitatis Redintegratio)*; "Christian Witness, Proselytism and Religious Liberty in the Setting of the World Council of Churches", *The Ecumenical Review*, vol. 13, 1960, pp.79-89; WCC executive committee statement on religious liberty, Geneva, Sept. 1979; "Study Paper on Religious Liberty", WCC/CCIA *Background Information*, 1980/1; "Religious Liberty: Some Major Considerations in the Current Debate", WCC/CCIA *Background Information*, 1987/1.

[12] Declaration on the Elimination of All Forms of Intolerance and of Discrimination Based on Religion or Belief, Art. 7,7 and 7,2.

[13] *Universal Declaration of Human Rights*, Art. 18. Cf. also Conference on Cooperation and Security in Europe: Helsinki Final Agreement.

[14] "A historical overview shows that the understanding of 'proselytism' has changed considerably. In the Bible it was devoid of negative connotations. A 'proselyte' was someone who, by belief in Yahweh and acceptance of the law, became a member of the Jewish community. Christianity took over this meaning to describe a person who converted from paganism. Mission work and proselytism were considered equivalent concepts until recent times." "Summons to Witness to Christ in Today's World: A Report on the Baptist-Roman Catholic International Conversations (1984-1988)", *loc. cit.*, §32.

[15] Cf "Common Witness and Proselytism".

[16] Cf. "Summons to Witness to Christ in Today's World", *loc. cit.*

[17] Cf. "Uniatism: Method of Union of the Past, and the Present Search for Full Communion", *loc. cit.*, §24.

[18] Cf. "The Evangelical-Roman Catholic Dialogue on Mission", *loc. cit.*, section 7.3: Unworthy Witness.

[19] Cf. "Uniatism: Method of Union of the Past, and the Present Search for Full Communion", *loc. cit.*, §22.

[20] Cf. "US Orthodox/Roman Catholic Consultation at the Holy Cross Orthodox School of Theology", *loc. cit.*, §2.

[21] Report of section IV from the fifth world conference on Faith and Order, *loc. cit.*, §14.

[22] "Common Witness", §44.

[23] Oliver S. Tomkins, ed., *The Third World Conference on Faith and Order, Lund, August 15-25, 1952*, London, SCM Press, 1953, p.16.

[24] The theological basis for this common witness and further suggestions may be found in "Common Witness: A Study Document of the Joint Working Group", 1982, *passim*.

73. The Ecumenical Dialogue on Moral Issues
Potential Sources of Common Witness or of Divisions

25 September 1995

Foreword

Already in 1987, the Joint Working Group between the Roman Catholic Church and the World Council of Churches (JWG) began to discuss new potential and actual sources of divisions within and between the churches, and it gradually focused on personal and social ethical issues and positions as potential sources of discord or of common witness.

The JWG summarized its reflections in its 1990 sixth report. The report noted that "in fact there is not enough serious, mature and sustained ecumenical discussion on many ethical issues and positions, personal and social; for example, nuclear armaments and deterrence, abortion and euthanasia, permanent married love and procreation, genetic engineering and artificial insemination" (III.1.c).

The JWG submitted the sixth report to the Roman Catholic authorities and to the seventh assembly of the WCC (Canberra 1991). Both mandated that the JWG should deepen the study as one of the priorities during its next period. It was not to examine the substance of the potentially or actually divisive issues, but it was to describe them and outline how they may best be approached in dialogue, in the hope that such issues can offer new opportunities for the increase of mutual understanding and respect and for common witness, without compromise of a church's convictions or of Christian conscience.

The JWG commissioned consultations, co-directed by Dr Anna-Marie Aagaard (University of Aarhus), one of the WCC presidents, and by Fr Thomas Stransky CSP (Tantur Ecumenical Institute, Jerusalem), a Roman Catholic member of the JWG. The report of the first consultation, held in October 1993 (Rome), was submitted to the JWG plenary in June 1994 (Crete, Greece) for decisions on future procedures. Tantur hosted the second larger consultation in November 1994. A draft received the reactions of the JWG executive (February 1995) and of the Tantur participants. The JWG plenary in May 1995 (Bose, Italy) corrected a new draft, and accepted the text as a study document of the JWG itself.

The study is in two parts: (1) "The Ecumenical Dialogue on Moral Issues: Potential Sources of Common Witness or of Divisions"; (2) "Guidelines for Ecumenical Dialogue on Moral Issues".

The study is intended primarily for those dialogues at local, national and regional levels where Roman Catholics are partners. It may be useful for other bilateral or multilateral discussions.

It is important to understand that the study does not analyze specific controversial issues as such in an attempt to arrive at norms. Rather, it describes present situations and illustrates some underlying contexts which help to place the issues. It suggests possible ways and not the results of dialogue.

The JWG places this study within its general concentration on "The Unity of the Church – the Goal and the Way" (cf. sixth report, III.A) and, more specifically, on new Christian ways of rendering common witness in society at large. Furthermore, the JWG is aware of the study in progress within the WCC (Units I and III) on "Ecclesiology and Ethics", and suggests that it may be complemented by the JWG study document.

His Eminence Metropolitan Elias of Beirut Most Rev. Alan C. Clark
Co-moderator of the *Co-moderator of the*
Joint Working Group *Joint Working Group*

I. Ethics and the ecumenical movement

Of increasing urgency in the ecumenical movement, in the relationships between the churches called to give common witness, is their need to address those moral issues which all persons face and to communicate moral guidance to church members and to society at large.

1. Cultural and social transformations, conflicting basic values and scientific and technological advances are fraying the moral fabric of many societies. This context not only provokes questioning of traditional moral values and positions, but it also raises new complex ethical issues for the consciousness and conscience of all human beings.

2. At the same time, renewed expectations rise in and beyond the churches that religious communities can and should offer moral guidance in the public arena. Christians and those of other faiths or of secular persuasions desire to live peacefully and justly in a humane society. Can the churches together already offer moral guidance as their contribution to the common good, amidst experienced confusion and controversy?

3. Pressing personal and social moral issues, however, are prompting discord among Christians themselves and even threatening new divisions within and between churches. This increases the urgent need for the churches together to find ways of dealing with their controversial ethical issues. By taking the time and care to listen patiently to other Christians, we may understand the pathways by which they arrive at moral convictions and ethical positions, especially if they differ from our own. Otherwise, Christians will continue often to caricature one another's motives, reasonings and ways of behaviour, even with abusive language and acts. Dialogue should replace diatribe.

Other Christians or other churches holding diverging moral convictions can threaten us. They can question our own moral integrity and the foundations of our religious and ethical beliefs. They can demean the authority, credibility and even integrity of our own church. Whenever an individual or a community selects a moral position or practice to be the litmus test of authentic faith and the sole criterion of the fundamental unity of the church, emotions rise high so that it becomes difficult to hear one another.

Christians, while "speaking the truth in charity" (Eph. 4:15), are called upon, as far as possible, "to maintain the unity of the Spirit in the bond of peace" (Eph. 4:3) and avoid wounding further the koinonia which already exists, although imperfectly, among Christians.

4. Therefore, if some ethical issues arouse passionate emotions and create awkward ecumenical relations, the churches should not shun dialogue, for these moral issues also can become church-reconciling means of common witness. A variety of issues are woven into the moral positions of communities. In a prayerful, non-threatening atmosphere, dialogue can locate more precisely where the agreements, disagreements and contradictions occur. Dialogue can affirm those shared convictions to which the churches should bear common witness to the world at large. Furthermore, the dialogue can discern how ethical beliefs and practices relate to that unity in moral life which is Christ's will.

5. Attentive concern for the complexities of the moral life should not cause Christians to lose sight of what is most fundamental for them all: the starting and ending point is the grace of God in Jesus Christ and the Spirit as mediated in the church and in creation. Our life in God is the fundamental continuing source of our movement towards deeper koinonia. Only God's initiating and sustaining grace enables Christians to transcend moral differences, overcome divisions and live their unity in faith.

II. The church as moral environment for discipleship

Included in the call to the church to be the sign and instrument of salvation in a transformed world, is the call to create a moral environment which helps disciples of Christ to shape their personal and communal ethical lives through formation and deliberation.

1. The church has the enduring task to be a community of "the way" (cf. Acts 9:2; 22:4), the home, the family which provides the moral environment of right living and conduct "in Christ", who in the Spirit makes known "the paths of life" to his disciples (Acts 2:28; Ps. 16:11).

Discipleship holds together what Christians believe, how believing Christians act and how they give to fellow Christians and to others an account of why they so believe and so act. Discipleship is the way of believing and acting in the daily struggle to be a faithful witness of Jesus Christ who commissions his community of disciples to proclaim, teach and live "all that I have commanded you" (Acts 1:8; Matt. 28:20).

2. Within the koinonia the disciple of Christ is not alone in the process of discerning how to incarnate in one's life the ethical message of the gospel. Faithful discipleship arises out of private prayer and public worship, of fellowship in sharing each other's joys and bearing each other's burdens. It is nourished by the examples of the saints, the wisdom of teachers, the prophetic vision of the inspired and the guidance of ministerial leaders.

In real but imperfect communion with one another, each church expects itself and other churches to provide a moral environment through formation and deliberation.

3. Formation and deliberation describe the shaping of human character and conduct, the kinds of Christian persons we are and become, and the kinds of actions we decide to do. The scope of Christian morality comprises both our "being" and "doing".

Useful for showing the inseparable dimensions of moral life are the distinctions between moral vision, virtue, value and obligation.

- Moral vision is a person's, a community's or a society's "basic script" of the moral realm, the vision of what belongs to the good, the right and the fitting. A moral vision encompasses, informs and organizes virtues, values and obligations.
- In the Christian moral life various summaries of teaching and different images express the gospel vision itself: the commandments of love of God and of

neighbour; the prophetic teachings on justice and mercy; the Beatitudes; the fruits of the Spirit; ascetic ascent and pilgrimage; costly discipleship and the imitation of Christ; stewarding a good land. These and other biblical images suggest pathways which bring definition and coherence to the moral landscape.
- Moral virtues are desirable traits of a person's moral character, such as integrity, humility and patience, compassion and forgiveness; or prudence, justice, temperance and fortitude. In an analogous way one can predicate these virtues of communities and societies.
- Moral values are not so much these internalized qualities of character but those moral goods which individuals and society prize, such as respect for the dignity of the human person, freedom and responsibility, friendship, equality and solidarity, and social justice.
- Moral obligations are those duties which persons owe one another in mutual responsibility, in order to live together in harmony and integrity, such as telling the truth and keeping one's word; or those imperatives of a biblical moral vision such as loving and forgiving the neighbour, including enemies.

4. This way of describing the scope of morality (vision, virtue, value, obligation) can provide inter-related criteria for the church's moral task: to be ever the witness to "our great God and Saviour Jesus Christ who sacrificed himself for us in order to set us free from all wickedness and to purify a people so that it could be his very own and would have no ambition except to do good" (Titus 2:13-14). A Christian ethic is reductionistic and deficient if it addresses only one or another of these four elements; all of them interact and modify one another. Even when it does address all four, different configurations may characterize its response.

5. The task of moral formation and deliberation is one which the churches share. All churches seek to enhance the moral responsibility of their members for living a righteous life and to influence positively the moral standards and well-being of the societies in which they live.

This identifies an ecumenical objective: the quality of the moral environment that churches create together in and through worship, education and nurture, and social witness. Reverence for the dignity of each person created "in the image of God" (Gen. 1:27), the affirmation of the fundamental equality of women and men, the pursuit of creative non-violent strategies for resolving conflict in human relationships and the responsible stewardship of creation – these are positive contributions of churches through the moral environment they foster. On the other hand, churches can also distort character and malform conscience. They have at times undergirded national chauvinism and ethnocentrism and actively discriminated against persons on the basis of race or nationality, class or gender.

III. Common sources and different pathways of moral deliberation

For those pathways of moral reflection and deliberation which churches use in coming to ethical decisions, the churches share the scriptures and have at their disposal such resources as liturgy and moral traditions, catechisms and sermons, sustained pastoral practices, the wisdom distilled from past and present experiences, and the arts of reflection and spiritual discernment. Yet church traditions configure these common resources in different ways.

1. The biblical vision by itself does not provide Christians with all the clear moral principles and practical norms they need. Nor do the scriptures resolve every ethical

case. Narratives join many instructions about proper conduct – general commandments and prohibitions, prophetic exhortations and accusations, counsels of wisdom, legal and ritual prescriptions and so forth. What moral theology names universal moral principles or norms are in the biblical texts mixed with specific but ever valid commandments and particular provisional prescriptions. The scriptures' use of imagery in provocative, often paradoxical ways further makes interpretations of biblical moral teaching difficult.

Nevertheless, there is general consensus that by prayerfully studying the scriptures and the developing traditions of biblical interpretations, by reflecting on human experiences and by sharing insights within a community, Christians can reach reasonable judgments and decisions in many cases of ethical conduct.

2. Within the history of the church, Christians have developed ways of reflecting systematically on the moral life by the ordering of biblical concepts and images and by rational argument. Such methods intend to introduce clarity and consistency where divergences of discernment threaten to foster confusion and chaos.

For example, one tradition suggests different levels of moral insight and distinguishes between first-order (and unchanging) principles and second-order (and possibly changing) rules. Or more recently, the language of "hierarchy of values" distinguishes between those core values at the heart of Christian discipleship and those other values which are less central yet integral to Christian morality. By emphasizing the "first-order principles" or the "core values", Christians can discover how much they already share, without reducing moral truth or searching for a least common denominator.

3. Christian traditions, however, have different estimates of human nature and of the capacity of human reason. Some believe that sin has so corrupted human nature that reason cannot arrive at moral truths. Others maintain that sin has only wounded human nature, and that with divine grace and human discipline, reason can still reach many universally applicable truths about moral living.

For example, by appealing to scripture and Tradition, to reason and experience, the Roman Catholic Church has developed its understanding of human person and human dignity, of human acts and their goals, and of human rights and responsibilities. In its tradition of moral reflection and teaching, the supreme norm of human life is that universal divine law by which God, in wisdom and love, orders, directs and governs the whole world and all ways of the human community. By nature and through grace, God enables every person intelligently to grasp this divine law, so that all men and women can come to perceive unchangeable truth more fully. Thus the revealed law of God and what one calls "natural law" together express that undivided will of God which obliges human beings to seek and to know it as best they can, and to live as conscience dictates.

4. The tracing of the different pathways which link vision with judgment and decision may help Christians to locate and evaluate some of their differences. For example, Christians who adopt the language of human rights have an effective way of highlighting concern for the powerless, the poor and the marginalized. While different parties may agree on certain fundamental rights, they can reach different, even contradictory applications; for example, rights to religious freedom. Moreover, formulations and extensions of rights have become the subject of much dispute, especially in addressing such ethical issues as human reproduction and abortion.

One Christian vision of the integrity of sexual life links sexual relationship with procreation by an interpretation of natural law and of the biblical accounts of creation. Some churches, such as the Roman Catholic Church, hold this position. Other churches judge it most difficult, even impossible, to affirm such a link. Those which find the appeal to natural law inconclusive accept the possible separation of the good of procreation from the good of sexual relationship, and use this argument to approve contraceptive means in marriage.

5. The Christian stance towards war is another example of different pathways which lead to different conclusions. Every tradition accepts the biblical vision of peace between neighbours and, more specifically, the New Testament witness to non-violent attitudes and acts. A major division has arisen, however, from different judgments concerning the church's collaboration with civic powers as a means of influencing human history. Those churches which have opted for collaboration accept some versions of the "just war" theory; they tolerate, even encourage, the active participation of patriotic Christians in some wars between nations and in armed revolutions within a country. But groups within these same churches agree with those other churches which choose to witness within the political order as non-compromising opponents to all use of military force, because it is contrary to the non-violent, peace-making way of Christ. These Christians abstain from bearing arms, even if that be civil disobedience.

Here one can identify the precise point of difference in major theological options which have fundamental consequences for the policy of a church towards war and the conduct of its members.

IV. Different authoritative means of moral discernment

Different understandings and exercise of church polities and structures of authority mean that moral formation and concrete ethical positions are themselves developed in different ways, even when similar attitudes and outcomes often emerge.

1. The formation of conscience and the development of connected positions on specific ethical issues follow various pathways among different traditions, such as the Orthodox or Roman Catholic, Reformed or Lutheran, Baptist or Friends (Quaker). Every church believes that its members have the task of rightly applying their faith more fully to daily life. All traditions have their own ways of beginning, moving through and concluding their moral deliberations, and of acting upon them. There are different ways of discussing, consulting and arriving at decisions and of transmitting and receiving them.

Influencing this process are the different ways in which they understand the action of the Holy Spirit and the exercise of the specific role of ministerial leadership in moral discernment and guidance.

In the Roman Catholic Church bishops, according to the gift received from the Holy Spirit, and under his guidance, in their ministry of oversight *(episcope)*, are the authoritative guardians and interpreters of the whole moral law, that is, both the law of the gospel and the natural law. Bishops have the pastoral responsibility and duty of offering moral guidance, even sometimes definitive judgment that a specific action is right or wrong. Moral theologians provide ethical discernment within the community. Confessors, pastoral counsellors and spiritual directors seek to take account of the unique needs of the individual person.

In the Orthodox church decisions on ethical issues rest with the hierarchy, whether a synod of bishops or an individual bishop, who are inspired by the scriptures and the long tradition of the church's pastoral care and moral guidance. The main concern is the spiritual welfare of the person in his or her relationship to God and to fellow human beings. The prudential application of church law and general norms (*oikonomia*) sometimes temper strictness, sometimes increase severity. It is a principal means for both spiritual growth and moral guidance. Orthodox tradition cherishes also the role of experienced spiritual fathers and mothers, and in the process of moral reflection, it stresses prayer among both laity and ordained.

Other churches do not ascribe to ministerial leadership this competency in interpretation or such authority of judgment. They arrive at certain ethical judgments by different polities of consulting and decision-making which involve clergy and laity. The Reformed traditions, for example, hold that the living Word of the sovereign God is always reforming the church in faith and life. Doctrinal and ethical judgments should be based on the holy scripture and informed by the whole tradition of the church catholic and ecumenical. But no church body has the final authority in defining the word of God. Redeemed and fallible human beings within the church faithfully rely on the process, inspired by the Holy Spirit, whereby they select their ordained and lay leaders and reach authoritative but reformable expressions of faith and positions on personal and social ethics.

2. Thus, ecumenical dialogue on moral issues should include the nature, mission and structures of the church, the role of ministerial authority and its use of resources in offering moral guidance, and the response to the exercise of such authority within the church. These subjects will in turn help to locate ecumenical gifts and opportunities for common witness, as well as tensions and conflicts.

First, the tensions and conflicts. Is there anxiety and unease because many fear the erosion of the foundational sources of scripture and Tradition, and of church authority which they believe to be most reliable in guiding Christian conscience and conduct? Or are the ways in which particular church traditions understand, accept and use the sources and authorities themselves the source of tension and divisiveness? Does deliberation of ethical issues generate anxiety and anger because some persons negatively experience these sources and their use – for example, the interpretation of scripture and Tradition in such ways that they present the oppressive face of social and theological patriarchy?

One often best understands persistent unchanging stands on a specific issue not by focusing narrowly on it, but by considering what people sense is at stake for life together in society if certain sources, structures and authorities are ignored or even ridiculed. For example, in some settings questions about the beginning and ending of life – abortion and euthanasia – carry such moral freight.

Furthermore, some churches stress more than others the structures of authority and formal detailed statements on belief and morality. This can create an imbalance and lack of realism in the dialogue if one easily compares the official teachings of some churches with the more diffuse estimates of the general belief and practice of others.

Thus, awareness of the moral volatility which surrounds the sources and authorities used – which they are, by whom and how they are interpreted, and with what kinds of concerns they are associated – is critical for understanding why some moral issues are difficult and potentially divisive among Christians.

3. Second, gifts and opportunities. Discerning the gifts in church traditions that may lie unnoticed as treasures for the moral life poses another set of questions for the ecumenical dialogue:

What do inherited understandings and forms of koinonia (communion or fellowship), diakonia (service) and martyria (witness) mean for moral formation today?

Which visions, virtues, values and obligations are nurtured by the *lex orandi, lex credendi, lex vivendi* (the rule of praying, of believing, of living) as particular traditions and structures embody them?

Which practices in the varied traditions contribute to the legitimate difference and authentic diversity of the moral life of the one church? How can both common and distinctive practices contribute to the moral richness of the koinonia?

In dialogue Christians thus need both to recognize the rich resources they share for moral formation and to ask critically how these in fact function in a variety of contexts, cultures and peoples.

V. Ecumenical challenges to moral formation and deliberation

Churches which share real but imperfect koinonia face new challenges as communities of moral formation and deliberation: the pluralism of moral positions; the crisis of moral authority, changing moral judgments on traditional issues, and positions on new ones.

1. Christians agree that there is a moral universe which is grounded in the wisdom and will of God, but they may have different interpretations of God's wisdom, of the nature of that universe and of the degree to which human beings are called to fashion it as co-creators with God.

We cannot deny three facts:

First, Christians do share a long history of extensive unity in moral teaching and practice, flowing in part from a shared reflection on common sources, such as the ten commandments and the beatitudes.

Second, divided Christian communities eventually did acquire some differences in ways of determining moral principles and acting upon them.

Third, these differences have led today to such a pluralism of moral frameworks and positions within and between the ecclesial traditions that some positions appear to be in sharp tension, even in contradiction. The same constellation of basic moral principles may admit of a diversity of rules which intend to express a faithful response to biblical vision and to these principles. Even the explicit divine commandment "Thou shalt not kill" receives conflicting applications; for example, "yes" or "no" to the death penalty as such or for certain crimes.

2. The crisis of moral authority within the churches further complicates effective moral formation and deliberation. Even where a church has an established moral tradition, some members strongly propose alternative positions. In fact, church members are becoming more vocal and persistent in sharp criticism of authoritative moral teaching and practice, and they use the same sources as the basis for differing ethical positions. The fashioning of effective moral formation and deliberation in these settings is an urgent ecumenical task.

3. The process of the formulation and reception of ethical decisions also poses a major challenge of participation: who forms and formulates the churches' moral decisions, using which powers of influence and action and which instruments of consultation? How do church members and the society at large assess, appropriate and respond

to official church pronouncements? What are the channels of such a response, and what kinds of response are encouraged or discouraged?

4. Are not the conditions and structures of dialogue themselves prime ethical issues for churches? They are potentially either divisive or reconciling. They can either enhance or undermine koinonia in faith, life and witness. One starting point is simply to acknowledge that the way in which a church (or churches together) orders and structures its decision-making and then publicly communicates its decisions already embodies a social ethic, and influences moral teaching and practice. Structures, offices and roles express moral values or disvalues. Ways of exercising power, governance and access have moral dimensions. To ignore this is to fail to understand why moral issues and the ways in which they are addressed can be so divisive, even within the same church.

5. The extent to which moral judgments can change needs candid dialogue. For example, until the middle of the 18th century, historical churches, even in their official statements, acquiesced in the practice of slavery; some leaders even proposed biblical and theological arguments to sanction it. Today all churches judge slavery to be an intrinsic evil, everywhere and always wrong. What does this kind of change of a former established teaching of the churches mean for understanding that degree of unity in faithful moral teaching which full communion requires?

Christians in dialogue should not ignore or hide evidence of change in moral teaching or practice. Churches do not always welcome such openness, despite their emphasis on human finitude and sin in the historical development of teachings and practices. Moreover, the interpretation of change in moral teaching is itself a source of disagreement and tension. While some may interpret the change as positive growth in faithful moral understanding, others may judge it as easy compromise or rank failure.

Apartheid is a particular example where, after long deliberation, some families of churches went beyond the rejection of apartheid as inconsistent with the gospel to judge that those who maintained apartheid to be Christian as placing themselves outside the fellowship of the church.

Hence, an ecumenical approach to morality requires the awareness of different evaluations of changing moral traditions.

6. Several *new ethical issues* especially challenge ecumenical collaboration when the churches have no clear and detailed precedents, much less experience and consensus. Only to begin a long list of examples: economic policies in a world of "haves" and "have-nots"; immigration and refugee regulations within and between nations; industrialization and the environment; women's rights in society and in the churches; in vitro fertilization, genetic engineering and other biomedical developments. Christians and others experience the urgency of these unavoidable, complex ethical issues. They expect the churches to offer moral guidance on them.

Even the experts in the empirical sciences may offer conflicting data or disagree on the implications of scientific findings. The ways in which the churches together seek out, gather and order the facts with the best knowledge available from the empirical scientists is already an ecumenical challenge. In the light of this, Christians can responsibly address the moral implications of issues, and offer guidance.

VI. Christian moral witness in a pluralistic society

Christians are called to witness in the public forum to their common moral convictions with humility and with respect for others and their convictions. They should seek dialogue and collaboration with those of other faith communities, indeed with all persons of good will who are committed to the well-being of humanity.

1. In the political process of legislation and judicial decision, churches may rightly raise their prophetic voice in support or in protest. In common witness they can take a firm stand when they believe that public decisions or laws affirm or contradict God's purposes for the dignity of persons or the integrity of creation.

One can highlight the example of common witness of Christians in the struggle against apartheid and "ethnic cleansing". In fact, such moral issues of human rights and equality have been community-building experiences of koinonia in faith and witness, which some perceive as profound experiences of "church".

2. Sometimes churches and Christian advocacy groups may agree on the basic values which they should promote, yet they disagree about the means that should be used, especially in the political arena. In such situations, they should seek collaboration as much as their agreement allows, and at the same time articulate the reasons for their disagreement. Disagreement over some particular points or means to an end should not rule out all collaboration. In these cases, however, it is all the more important to be open and explicit about the areas of disagreement, so as to avoid confusion in common witness.

3. In the public arena, the churches are one family of moral community among others, whether religious or secular. Moral discernment is not the exclusive preserve of Christians. Christian moral understandings and approaches to ethical issues should be open to evaluate carefully the moral insights and judgments of others. Often moral traditions overlap, even when the approaches and idioms of language may be different.

In any case, the manner and the methods by which the churches publicly commend their own moral convictions must respect the integrity of others and their civic rights and liberties. For the authority of the churches in the public moral debate of pluralistic societies is the authority of their moral wisdom, insights and judgments as these commend themselves to the intelligence and conscience of others.

Guidelines for ecumenical dialogue on moral issues

The acceptance and practice of these suggested guidelines for dialogue can promote the goal of the ecumenical movement: the visible unity of Christians in one faith and one eucharistic fellowship, expressed in worship, common life and service, in order that the world may believe.

We assume that churches are seeking to be faithful to God in Christ, to be led by the Holy Spirit and to be a moral environment which helps all members in the formation of Christian conscience and practice. We affirm the responsibility of every church to provide moral guidance for its members and for society at large.

God, who through the Spirit leads Christians to manifest the unity of the church, calls the churches, while still divided, to common witness; that is, together in Christian discipleship they are to manifest whatever divine gifts of truth and life they already share and experience.

A lack of ecumenical dialogue on personal and social moral issues and a weak will to overcome whatever divisiveness they may prompt, place yet another stumbling block in the proclamation of the one gospel of Jesus Christ, who is "the Way, the Truth and the Life" (John 14:6).

Guidelines

1. In fostering the koinonia or communion between the churches, we should as much as possible consult and exchange information with one another, in a spirit of mutual understanding and respect, always "speaking the truth in charity" (Eph. 4:15).

2. In dialogue we should try first to understand the moral positions and practices of others as they understand them, so that each one recognizes oneself in the descriptions. Only then can we evaluate them out of our own tradition and experience.

3. In comparing the good qualities and moral ideals or the weaknesses and practices of various Christian communities, one should compare ideals with ideals and practice with practice. We should understand what others want to be and to do in order to be faithful disciples of Christ, even though those others – as we ourselves – are burdened with weakness and sin.

4. We recognize that Christians enjoy a history of substantial unity in moral teaching and practice. By placing ethical issues within this inheritance of moral unity, we can more carefully understand the origin and nature of any present disagreement or division.

5. We trust that Christians can discover the bases for their moral vision, values and conduct in the scriptures and in other resources: moral traditions (including specific church and interchurch statements), liturgies, preaching and catechetics, pastoral practices, common human experiences and methods of reflection.

6. We should seek from the empirical sciences the best available knowledge on specific issues, and if possible agree on the data and their ethical implications before offering moral guidance.

7. We should acknowledge that various church traditions in fact sometimes agree, sometimes differ in the ways they:
– use scriptures and other common resources, as well as the data of empirical sciences;
– relate moral vision, ethical norms and prudential judgments;
– identify a specific moral issue and formulate the problems;
– communicate within a church those values and disciplines which help to develop its own moral environment in the shaping of Christian character;
– understand and exercise ministerial leadership and oversight in moral guidance.

8. We should be ever alert to affirm whatever is shared in common, and to admit where there are serious divergent, even contrary stances. We should never demand that fellow Christians with whom we disagree compromise their integrity and convictions.

9. In the public arena of pluralistic societies, we should be in dialogue also with others, whether religious or secular. We try to understand and evaluate their moral insights and judgments, and to find a common language to express our agreements and differences.

10. When the dialogue continues to reveal sincere but apparently irreconcilable moral positions, we affirm in faith that the fact of our belonging together in Christ is more fundamental than the fact of our moral differences. The deep desire to find an honest and faithful resolution of our disagreements is itself evidence that God continues to grace the koinonia among disciples of Christ.

XXVIII. WORLD COUNCIL OF CHURCHES AND ROMAN CATHOLIC CHURCH

74. Seventh Report of the Joint Working Group

1998

Foreword

On behalf of the Joint Working Group between the Roman Catholic Church and the World Council of Churches we are pleased to present its seventh report to its parent bodies and recommend its study.

The report results from seven years' work by a dedicated group drawn from the World Council of Churches and the Roman Catholic Church.

The character of the document is intentionally educational. The group believed that it would in this way best serve the interest of all who wish to know not only the Joint Working Group's agenda but the growing relationship of the WCC and the RCC within the broader perspective of the one ecumenical movement which the group has witnessed and in some measure assisted.

In doing so we have gone beyond, both in our report and in our work, a narrow interpretation of our mandate. We believe however that this will be accepted as a measure of the group's deep commitment to the cause of Christian unity.

In thanking all our members for their generous contribution to our common work, we would like to mention in particular those who have accompanied our work and are no longer members of the JWG. We remember with affection Prof. Todor Sabev, Dr Wesley Ariarajah, Sister Monica Cooney and Archbishop Ivan Marin.

We are conscious that this report is published on the eve of the third millennium – a time to turn to God and rejoice in hope. It contains several suggestions for future work intended to cement further the relationship of the WCC and the RCC in our common service of our God, Father, Son and Holy Spirit, to whom be praise for evermore.

His Eminence Elias Audi
Metropolitan of Beirut
Co-moderator of the
Joint Working Group

Most Rev. Mario Conti
Bishop of Aberdeen
Co-moderator of the
Joint Working Group

• There were four appendices to this report. B, C and D are reproduced as documents 73, 72 and 71 in this volume. Appendix A is not included.

I. Introduction

With gratitude this Joint Working Group (JWG) has accepted its mandated responsibilities to serve as an instrument which helps the Roman Catholic Church (RCC) and the World Council of Churches (WCC) to carry out the ecumenical vocation of the churches. The experience of the present members reaffirms our predecessors' conviction expressed in the sixth report (1990): "The ecumenical movement is more than ever necessary if the churches and Christian communities are to be a sign and seed of the unity, peace and hope which the human family needs."

The JWG joyfully looks forward to the celebration in 1998 of the 50th anniversary of the World Council of Churches. The theme of the WCC's eighth assembly (Harare, 3-14 December 1998) is "Turn to God – Rejoice in Hope". As a new millennium dawns the pilgrim people of God turn again to the one triune God with renewed faith and sustain the hope of a restoration of that unity among all Christians which Christ wills. This holy objective, which transcends human power and gifts, engages our renewed efforts towards reconciliation while at the same time opens us to the future inspiration of the Holy Spirit.

Since 1966 the JWG has made six reports. In this seventh report, it offers to its parent bodies an account of its work since the WCC assembly at Canberra in 1991. This report also seeks to inform readers who may be unaware of the history of the JWG and of specific RCC and WCC structures of relationships. [A short history of the JWG is offered as Appendix A.]

II. The collaboration between the RCC and the WCC and its member churches

1. The WCC and the RCC

In 1965 the WCC central committee and the Roman Catholic authorities committed the WCC and the RCC to future collaboration through the visible expression of the JWG. Both partners realized then their differences. As collaborative efforts increased, the JWG came increasingly to respect the ways in which the WCC and the RCC differ in their nature, main structure, exercise of authority and styles of operation.

1. The WCC is a "fellowship" constituted by member churches. Churches which agree with the WCC Basis – that they "confess the Lord Jesus Christ as God and Saviour according to the scriptures and therefore seek to fulfil together their common calling to the glory of the one God, Father, Son and Holy Spirit" – may apply for membership and are accepted if at least two-thirds of the member churches approve.

While the WCC's constitutional documents do not define what is meant by "church" (and the Toronto statement of the 1950 central committee indicates that the WCC "cannot and should not be based on any one particular conception of the church"), its Rules do set forth certain criteria which member churches must satisfy. These include a "sustained independent life and organization", the practice of "constructive ecumenical relations" and a membership of at least 25,000 (10,000 for associate member churches). In fact, nearly all member churches are organized within a single country. The Rules also specify certain "responsibilities of membership", among them participating in the Council's governing bodies and activities, encouraging ecumenical commitment and making an annual financial contribution commensurate with their means.

The constitutional documents specify that the WCC has no legislative authority over its member churches. Organized to "offer counsel and provide opportunity for united action in matters of common interest" (Constitution, art. IV), it may act on behalf of a member church or churches only when that church or those churches request it to do so; and the authority of any public statements it makes consists "only in the weight which they carry by their own truth and wisdom" (Rules, X.2). General policies for the WCC are set by the assembly of official delegates elected by all member churches, which meets every seven years. Implementation of these policies in specific activities is supervised by the central committee of about 150 members elected by each assembly to serve until the next one.

2. The RCC is a communion of local churches or dioceses, each entrusted to a bishop. It is one church with a worldwide mission and structure of sanctifying, teaching and governance through the "college of bishops", with and under the bishop of Rome, the pastor of the whole Catholic church who must ensure the communion of all the churches (cf. Code of Canon Law, canons 331, 375). "The concern for restoring unity involves the whole church, faithful and clergy alike" (Decree on Ecumenism, § 5). But "it pertains *especially to the entire college of bishops and to the apostolic see* to foster and direct among Catholics the ecumenical movement..., which by the will of Christ the church is bound to promote" (canon 755; Code of Canons of the Eastern Churches, canon 902). Conferences of bishops are juridical institutions of a nation or territory, with specific duties and responsibilities designated by canon laws and other decrees; for example, the national conference decides whether or not to be a full member of a national or regional council of churches. No diocese, no conference is autonomous. This "hierarchical communion with the head of the college and its members" (canon 375), which fosters unity in diversity, is an essential element of the RCC's self-identity and of its ecumenical commitment.

2. The Pontifical Council for Promoting Christian Unity (PCPCU) and the WCC

The pope "usually conducts the business of the universal church by means of the Roman curia... for the good and service of the [local or particular] churches" (canon 360). Within the Roman curia is the Pontifical Council for Promoting Christian Unity (PCPCU) which has "the competency and duty of promoting the unity of Christians". The PCPCU is entrusted with the correct interpretation and carrying out of the Catholic principles of ecumenism; and with initiating, promoting or coordinating ecumenical efforts at national, regional and worldwide levels. The PCPCU is responsible for relations with the WCC and for bilateral relations. The PCPCU facilitates WCC relations with other departments of the Roman curia, such as those for the evangelization of peoples, inter-religious dialogue, justice and peace, aid and development, the laity, and Catholic education.

The PCPCU members are from national conferences of bishops and departments of the Roman Curia: over 30 cardinals, archbishops and bishops, and 25 official consultors. They meet in plenary every 18-24 months. The PCPCU has a fulltime staff of 23 persons.

3. Functions, operations and structure of the JWG

The JWG functions according to its original 1966 mandate as modified by the 1975 WCC assembly.

1. The JWG is a consultative forum. It has no authority in itself but reports to its parent bodies – the WCC assembly and central committee, and the PCPCU – which approve policies and programmes.

It undertakes its spiritual and pastoral tasks in a spirit of prayerful conviction that God through Christ in the Spirit is guiding the one ecumenical movement. The group tries to discern the will of God in contemporary situations, and to stimulate the search for visible unity and common witness, in particular through collaboration at world, regional, national and local levels between the RCC, the WCC, and the WCC member churches. This means giving attentive support and encouragement to whatever contributes to ecumenical progress.

The JWG initiates, evaluates and sustains forms of collaboration between the WCC and the RCC, especially between the various organs and programmes of the WCC and the RCC. Its styles and forms of collaboration are flexible, as it discerns similarities and differences which foster or hinder WCC/RCC relations. Concentrating on ad hoc initiatives, it keeps new structures to a minimum in proposing new steps and programmes, carefully setting priorities and using its limited resources of personnel, time and finances.

2. At present the JWG has 17 members, with two co-moderators. Its co-secretaries are a PCPCU staff member and the WCC's deputy general secretary responsible for relations with non-member churches. Most members are involved in pastoral and ecumenical ministries in different regions. Some are from departments of the Roman curia and from the WCC units. The JWG also coopts consultants for its particular tasks. The co-moderators, co-secretaries and four others form the executive, which oversees the JWG between its plenaries and prepares the agenda and materials for them.

Between 1991 and 1997, the JWG has met in plenary six times: Wenningsen, Germany, 1992; Venice, 1993; Crete, 1994; Bose, Italy, 1995; Chambésy, Switzerland, 1996; Venice, 1997.

4. Relationships between the RCC and the WCC (1991-98)

Among the many contacts at various levels have been those between leaders or representatives of the WCC (in Geneva) and the RCC (in Rome) which illustrate their close partnership.

1. *The visit to Rome of WCC general secretary Dr Emilio Castro* (1991) helped to clear up misunderstandings that had arisen around the impression of some that the Canberra assembly was equating the ecumenical movement with the WCC, and around the discussions about the ecclesial nature of the WCC-RCC relationship. Pope John Paul II and Dr Castro exchanged views on the role of the churches in the crisis in Yugoslavia; on the 500th anniversary of the colonization and evangelization of Latin America; and on the re-evangelization of Europe. Discussions with the PCPCU staff focused on specific continuing collaboration with the WCC.

2. *The RC meeting of representatives of the National Episcopal Commissions for Ecumenism* (Rome, 1993), convened by the PCPCU, focused on ecumenical formation and the activities of these commissions. In addition to representatives of 78 episcopal conferences, participants included a WCC member of the JWG and delegates from nine churches and Christian world communions with which the RCC is a partner in bilateral dialogue.

3. *The meeting in Geneva between the WCC officers and PCPCU officials* (November 1993) raised key questions on the role of the JWG: its impact on local ecumenism, its specific contribution in bringing together the work of the national councils of churches (NCCs), and its role in the reception process of various dialogues. With realism on both sides, participants listened to each other's descriptions of the practical differences in the ways they operate. They stressed the important role of the Faith and Order commission in ecumenical dialogue.

4. *A plenary session of the WCC central committee* (Johannesburg, January 1994) discussed the relationship between the RCC and the WCC following presentations on the experiences of the PCPCU by its staff member, Msgr John Mutiso-Mbinda, and on the experiences of RCC membership in national and regional councils of churches such as the Council of Churches in Britain and Ireland and the Caribbean Conference of Churches. Each central committee member received a copy the PCPCU's recent *Directory on Ecumenism* (1993), with a recommendation to read its first chapter on those principles which commit the RCC to ecumenism. The discussion focused on three issues: the potential for local ecumenism, especially in the light of the *Directory*; the new challenges arising from the participation of the RCC in national and regional councils or conferences of churches; the double pattern of relationships, in which it is possible to agree on theological issues and sometimes on socio-political matters, such as churches' attitudes towards war, and yet not be able to dialogue on some other moral questions (cf. minutes of the WCC central committee, Johannesburg, 20-28 January 1995, pp.26-27).

5. *The visit to Rome by general secretary Dr Konrad Raiser and WCC executive staff* (April 1995) affirmed that the JWG is progressing in a trusting atmosphere as it facilitates relationships and cooperation between the two parent bodies. Questions arose: how better to cooperate in responding to problems which face both the WCC member churches and the RCC, for example, on civic religious freedom, Christian witness and proselytism; how better to use the existing links and the findings of many years of collaboration in local situations where most ecumenical expectations emerge; how the JWG can use its experience and instrumentality not only to provoke common thinking but also to prompt joint action in pressing situations related to the daily life and witness of the local churches. In the discussions between Pope John Paul II and Dr Raiser, the general secretary affirmed the WCC's deep commitment to a "culture of life" and to a witness for peace – a major theme of the pope's encyclical *Evangelium Vitae* (1995). The principle of mutual accountability and solidarity among churches on theological, social and ethical questions was underscored as crucial for ecumenical cooperation.

6. *Joint meeting in Rome* (December 1997). In consultation with each other and considering that structural changes in the WCC (cf. below, III.A.5, "Common Understanding and Vision of the WCC") would have consequences on the relationships between the RCC and the WCC, Dr Raiser and Cardinal Cassidy agreed to a meeting between the PCPCU and the WCC in order to share information, to express mutual concerns, and to seek ways to strengthen collaboration.

5. *The PCPCU and Canberra assessments of the JWG's sixth report*

1. In a letter to Dr Emilio Castro prior to the Canberra assembly, PCPCU president Cardinal Edward Cassidy approved the sixth report. He underlined the role of the JWG

as an instrument for the cooperative relationship between the two parent bodies in the common quest for Christian unity. In stressing the Catholic church's conviction of the critical importance of unity of faith for progress towards Christian unity, the cardinal strongly supported the work of Faith and Order; but he also pointed to the necessity of theological foundations in the studies and activities of other WCC programmes and suggested that more development of this dimension could facilitate RCC cooperation in them. The letter recalled the desire of Pope John Paul II that common Christian witness be achieved wherever and as soon as possible. This was especially necessary in common reflection on those issues which tended to divide churches, for example, ethical concerns in which the churches should collaborate in exercising moral leadership.

2. The Canberra assembly received the sixth report with appreciation. The impressive survey of the joint activities between the RCC and the WCC since the 1983 Vancouver assembly did not hide unresolved difficulties and failures. The assembly cited the dissolution of the Joint Consultative Group on Social Thought and Action as an illustration of the particular difficulties facing collaboration in this urgent area. It recommended that the JWG be liberated from monitoring some of the ongoing staff work between Geneva and Rome in order to concentrate on a thorough review of the RCC-WCC relationship and how it might be given more substantial visible expression.

6. Mandated JWG priorities, 1991-98

Both the Canberra assembly and the PCPCU approved and encouraged the priorities which the sixth report had recommended to the next JWG:
– the unity of the church: goal, steps and ecclesiological implications;
– ecumenical formation and education;
– ethical issues as new sources of division;
– common witness in missionary endeavours;
– social thought and action.

The November 1993 meeting between WCC officers and PCPCU officials underlined that the JWG should now focus on its style of working and on identifying those programmatic areas where cooperation was necessary and possible. It acknowledged that in encouraging and facilitating reception of its work, the JWG experiences challenges similar to those faced by the bilateral dialogues.

This seventh report demonstrates that the JWG has offered concrete results in meeting its mandated priorities. The exception is "social thought and action", but even in this case progress has been made in better understanding past difficulties and in opening the way towards new perspectives and possible positive initiatives for future collaboration.

III. Activities of the JWG, 1991-98

A. THE UNITY OF THE CHURCH – THE GOAL AND THE WAY

1. The unity of the church as koinonia

1. The specific focus on the ecclesiology of koinonia (communion) and the unity we seek provides continuity to the central and ongoing JWG concern for "the unity of the church – the goal and the way". This same concern is basic to the mandate of the Faith and Order commission. This commission draws some of its members from

churches which are not WCC members, and since 1968 RC theologians, approved by the PCPCU, have been full commission members. Through Faith and Order the RCC continues to have direct active participation in the WCC.

2. In the period between 1983 and 1990 the JWG itself commissioned and received the study "The Church: Local and Universal" (1990), which was published as an appendix to its sixth report. The document dealt with the fundamental aspects of the mystery of the church as an icon of the Trinity, the ecclesiology of koinonia and the relationship of the church local and universal. It explored the topic from Orthodox, Roman Catholic and Protestant perspectives and indicated the ecclesial elements required for full communion within the visibly united church.

3. Since 1990 this same focus has been developing in: (1) the Canberra assembly statement "The Unity of the Church as Koinonia: Gift and Calling"; (2) the JWG-commissioned study document, a series of reflections by Orthodox, Roman Catholic and Protestants: "Ecumenical Perspectives on the 1991 Canberra Statement on Unity" (Faith and Order paper no. 163); (3) the report of the 1993 fifth world conference on Faith and Order (Santiago de Compostela); (4) the various international bilateral dialogues; (5) the current Faith and Order study "Koinonia: The Nature and Purpose of the Church"; (6) Pope John Paul II's 1995 encyclical *Ut Unum Sint*, on the commitment to ecumenism; (7) the process of study and consultation "Towards a Common Understanding and Vision of the WCC"; and (8) the PCPCU response (April 1997) to this draft (November 1996).

4. The 1991 Canberra statement developed the understanding of koinonia which is a central focus of the JWG's "The Church: Local and Universal". The nature and purpose of the church, as a community which mirrors the reality of the Trinity, is "to unite people with Christ in the power of the Spirit, to manifest communion in prayer and action and thus to point to the fullness of communion with God, humanity and the whole creation in the glory of the kingdom" ("The Unity of the Church as Koinonia: Gift and Calling", Canberra assembly statement, 1.1). Despite the continuing divisions between the churches, they now "recognize a certain degree of communion already existing among them", and they desire to make this communion more visible by seeking consensus on the common confession of the apostolic faith, a common sacramental life, a common mission and moving towards a common ministry and structures of accountability. These elements develop the four classical visible properties or attributes of the church – one, holy, catholic and apostolic.

5. The work of the Faith and Order commission after Canberra has drawn on the impact of its 1982 document *Baptism, Eucharist and Ministry (BEM)* and the responses of the churches to it, including the lengthy one from the RCC. An implicit ecclesiology in BEM requires further clarification: the nature of sacraments and the relation of necessary oversight to be exercised in the church in an office which is personal, collegial and communal. The completed study project "Confessing the One Faith" examines the common apostolic faith through the Nicene Creed, and invites the churches to recognize in their own lives the faith of the church through the ages and to recognize that same faith in other Christian communities (Faith and Order Paper no. 153; cf. the 1996 study guide *Towards Sharing the One Faith*, Faith and Order paper no. 173).

6. The 1993 fifth world conference on Faith and Order in Santiago de Compostela (Spain) drew participants from every continent and ecclesial tradition who are engaged

in Faith and Order concerns in the churches and ecumenical organizations. The conference could rejoice in the results of ecumenical dialogue, particularly since the last world conference in 1963 (Montreal), which was held during the Second Vatican Council when the RCC was only beginning officially and actively to enter the ecumenical movement. The sizeable RC presence in Santiago included the PCPCU President Cardinal Cassidy and 23 delegates, as well as more than 40 others who were hosts, speakers, younger theologians, coopted staff and consultants.

7. Prior to Santiago the Faith and Order commission developed a study process involving a series of regional consultations (RCs took part in many of them), which resulted in the preparatory document "Towards Koinonia in Faith, Life and Witness". The report of the world conference itself explores the nature and meaning of koinonia. The church, as communion rooted in the life of the Holy Trinity, is to be sign and instrument of God's intention for humankind. The report reflects the insights of the bilateral dialogues, including those in which the RCC is a partner; of united and uniting churches; of the Christian world communions (including the RCC); and of regional and national councils of churches (many of which have RCs as full members). It also explores steps towards the manifestation of koinonia, and identifies implications of the understanding of the church as one, holy, catholic and apostolic which are still to be addressed.

8. Clearly in the 1990s, koinonia or ecclesial communion has become central to the discussions of the JWG, of the bilateral dialogues and of the Faith and Order commission. Pope John Paul II wrote in his message to the Santiago conference that "a deepened awareness of the profound mystery of ecclesial communion [koinonia] moves Christians to confess that God and not man is the source of the church's unity; it leads them to repent of their sins against fraternal charity; and it encourages them, under the inspiring work of the Holy Spirit, to work through prayer, word and action to attain that fullness of unity which Jesus Christ desires".

Koinonia is also being used to describe different, and perhaps mutually exclusive, models for the unity of the church, such as communion of communions, reconciled diversity, visible unity of local churches and conciliar fellowship. The implications of koinonia for models of unity require further examination.

2. Major Faith and Order studies

1. Future Faith and Order studies will continue to focus on ecclesiology. A convergence text on the nature and purpose of the church, in a format and style similar to BEM, will draw on other Faith and Order studies – on hermeneutics, worship and ethics – to seek to move forward on the ministry of oversight, the nature of conciliarity and the nature of the church as local and universal. Furthermore, an interdisciplinary process has been initiated on "Ethnic Identity, National Identity and the Search for the Unity of the Church".

2. Common prayer and worship anticipate, express and prepare experiences of Christian communion or koinonia that both reflect and extend beyond theological agreements and convergences. *So We Believe, So We Pray* (Faith and Order paper no. 171) explores a common ordering and scheduling of the primary elements of Christian worship, inculturation and the ways in which worship already actively fosters the search for unity of the church. The baptism study focuses on the continuing pilgrimage

of Christians as they seek to express their incorporation in Christ and their primary consecration as Christians through baptism into the ministry of Christ and the church.

3. Three reports have come out of a collaborative process of reflection between Faith and Order and the WCC's Programme Unit on Justice, Peace and Creation (Unit III) on the relation between ecclesiology and ethics. The Rønde report *Costly Unity* (1993) explores koinonia in relation to the ethical nature and witness of the church as a "moral community" and emphasizes the essential connection between the search for the visible unity of the church and the calling of the churches to prophetic witness and service. The Tantur report *Costly Commitment* (1995) offers a fresh discussion of the relation of eucharist, covenant and ethical engagement. The Johannesburg report *Costly Obedience* (1997) takes up the ethical implications of Christian worship and the role of baptism/Christian initiation in shaping character, and asks: What are the ethical implications of the growing koinonia among the churches? What does the churches' common ethical reflection and action mean for the koinonia which already actively exists among them?

During this same period the JWG published in 1996 its own study, "The Ecumenical Dialogue on Moral Issues: Potential Sources of Common Witness or of Divisions" [cf. document 73 above].

3. Bilateral and multilateral dialogues

1. The RCC cooperates with the WCC through its full membership of the Faith and Order commission; and many WCC member churches are engaged in bilateral dialogues with the RCC, like the Orthodox churches and the ancient Oriental churches. Others are involved in these dialogues either on the national level or internationally through their respective Christian world communions (CWCs), like the Lutherans, the Methodists, the Reformed, the Anglicans, the Baptists and the Disciples of Christ. These multilateral and bilateral dialogues have complementary purposes and thus offer possibilities for coherence in the service of the one ecumenical movement.

2. The conference of general secretaries of the CWCs, at which Bishop Pierre Duprey of the PCPCU represents the RCC, is an informal instrument of information, exchange, reflection and orientation, and organizes periodic forums on the bilateral conversations. The Faith and Order secretariat services these forums.

The fifth bilateral forum (1991) highlighted the common themes and approaches in reference to the church emerging in and through the dialogues (cf. *The Understanding of the Church Emerging in the Bilateral Dialogues: Coherence or Divergence?*, Faith and Order paper no. 156, 1991). The sixth forum (1994) explored the different processes by which churches seek to receive the results of the dialogues and suggested how they might appropriate these results of the dialogues by a process of recognition and reception. This process of recognition also requires attempts to overcome "nondoctrinal" issues which inhibit the movement towards communion, for example, the memory of historical events that have polarized communities, the relations between Orthodox and Eastern Catholic churches, and the relation of majority to minority churches in many areas. The report of this forum also raised the issue of the relation between the local and universal church – in particular, the ability of the local church to take initiatives in furthering ecumenical relations (Faith and Order paper no. 168, 1994).

The seventh bilateral forum (1997) explored "The Emerging Visions of Unity" in the churches through their participation in bilateral dialogues and interfaith dialogues and their common witness on issues of justice and peace. These "emerging visions" were discussed in the light of the Canberra statement "The Unity of the Church as Koinonia: Gift and Calling". The report reaffirms the challenges posed by that statement to the churches, in the dynamic process towards "conciliar unity" (recognizing the ambiguity of the term "council"). Rooted in different cultural and geographical milieus, local churches are interdependent in legitimate diversity. And the strong trends of globalization today prompt fresh insights into the unity of the church and human communities (Faith and Order paper no. 179, 1997).

4. The Ecumenical Directory and the Papal Encyclical Ut Unum Sint

During this period, two authoritative documents have articulated the theological foundations and pastoral directions for the internal ecumenical life and structures of the RCC and for its relations with other churches and ecumenical organizations: the PCPCU's *Directory for the Application of Principles and Norms of Ecumenism* (1993), and Pope John Paul II's encyclical "on the commitment to ecumenism", *Ut Unum Sint* (1995).

1. Approved by the pope, the *Ecumenical Directory* (ED) "gives general norms of universal application to guide Catholic participation in ecumenical activity", so as to guarantee "accordance with the unity of faith and discipline that binds Catholics together". But ED "fully respects the competence of local and territorial church authorities" and recognizes that "many judgments can best be made at the local level".

ED comprehensively presents the RC theological foundations for ecumenical life and action (teaching, attitudes/motivations and spirituality); the ecumenical formation of all the faithful – clergy and laity (studying the scriptures, preaching, catechesis, liturgy) in various settings (family, parish, schools, seminaries, theological faculties, Catholic universities, pastoral ministers' continuing education, hospitals, lay associations and institutes); "spiritual activities" (prayer in common; baptismal celebrations; sharing in sacramental life, especially the eucharist; marriages and mixed marriages; funerals); ecumenical cooperation and common witness (social and cultural life; peace, justice and the stewardship of creation; missionary activities; common Bible translation and distribution; catechetics; medical work; relief and development work; communications media); and church structures (college of bishops, bishops' conferences, patriarchal synods, dioceses and their ecumenical commissions; religious communities and lay organizations; the PCPCU).

2. The encyclical *Ut Unum Sint* emphasizes the RCC's "irrevocable commitment" to ecumenism as "an organic part of her life and work", necessary for credibility in evangelization.

The everyday ecumenical path is by way of repentance for wrongs mutually committed, prayer (especially in common), reciprocal visits, study of shared faith and remaining differences, and cooperation in mission and in service to human needs.

A key word in the encyclical is "dialogue", which is not simply "an exchange of ideas" (n.28) but also an exchange and development of gifts "for the utility and the advantage of all" (n.87). Presupposing loving respect between the partners and a desire for reconciliation, living dialogue includes an examination of conscience by each. The encyclical observes that "certain features of the Christian mystery have at times been more effectively emphasized" in communities other than the RCC (cf. n.14). In "the common quest for truth," sensitivity to different formulations can make possible "surprising discoveries" which enrich the apprehension of revealed truth.

The pope foresees a "continuing and deepening dialogue" (nn.77-79) on the way to "that full communion in the one, holy, catholic and apostolic church which will be expressed in the common celebration of the eucharist" (n.78). Reception of the interim results of dialogue requires a critical analysis and testing for consistency with the apostolic tradition.

The encyclical lists five areas for further work towards "a true consensus of faith": (1) "the relationship between sacred scriptures, as the highest authority in matters of faith, and sacred tradition, as indispensable to the interpretation of the word of God" (a formulation entirely in line with developments in Faith and Order); (2) "the eucharist, as the sacrament of the body and blood of Christ, an offering of praise to the Father, the sacrificial memorial and real presence of Christ and the sanctifying outpouring of the Holy Spirit" (a vision consistent with the Eucharist section of *BEM*); (3) "ordination, as a sacrament, to the threefold ministry of the episcopate, presbyterate and diaconate"; (4) "the magisterium of the church, entrusted to the pope and the bishops in communion with him, understood as a responsibility and an authority exercised in the name of Christ for teaching and safeguarding the faith"; (5) "the Virgin Mary, as mother of God and icon of the church, the spiritual mother who intercedes for Christ's disciples and for all humanity" (cf. n.79).

Declaring the RCC's conviction that in the ministry of the bishop of Rome the church "has preserved the visible sign and guarantor of unity... in fidelity to the apostolic tradition and the faith of the fathers" (n.88), John Paul II acknowledges that "the ministry of unity of the bishop of Rome... constitutes a difficulty for most other Christians" *(ibid.)*. Thus he invites "church leaders and their theologians" to "a patient and fraternal dialogue" concerning the "exercise of this necessary ministry" (cf. n.96). A number of WCC member churches have expressed appreciation for this invitation. For ecclesiological and historical reasons, however, many churches have great difficulty in discussing the primacy of the bishop of Rome and would prefer a wider dialogue on the need, nature and structure of a universal ministry of oversight.

The encyclical spells out the significance of Faith and Order a number of times. It refers in an affirmative way to "the steady work of the commission on Faith and Order" (n.78, note 129). Speaking of the renewal and conversion required in ecumenism, the pope cites various documents which help foster these attitudes, including "the principle documents of the commission on Faith and Order" (n.17) and "in particular, the Lima document *Baptism, Eucharist and Ministry* (January 1982); and *Confessing the One Faith*" (note 28). The contribution of the fifth world conference on Faith and Order is mentioned several times (n.78, note 129; n.45, note 77; n.89).

In 1998, the Faith and Order commission completed its response to *Ut Unum Sint*. The response acknowledges the fine place given to its work in these words: "We in the Faith and Order commission are grateful for the recognition given to our work throughout the encyclical letter. This recognition of Faith and Order work implies a relationship with all ecumenical communities engaged in the ecumenical task." It welcomed the spirit of humility of the encyclical evident in such phrases as "dialogue of consciences" and "dialogue of conversion". The commission highlighted the encyclical's decision on the relation between unity and diversity, and on the recognition of ministries. On the issue of primacy, where satisfaction was expressed for the manner in which this question is treated in the encyclical through emphasis on a ministry of unity – not of power – and of service, the commission affirmed its intention to study the issue in the context of the question of the need for "a universal primacy in the organizational dimension of the life of the church of God on earth".

5. *Common Understanding and Vision of the WCC*

1. Within the World Council of Churches, the meaning of ecumenical commitment and the WCC's role in the ecumenical movement have been the subject of an extended process of study and consultation under the theme "Towards a Common Understanding and Vision of the WCC" (CUV). Mandated by the WCC central committee in 1989, this study has focused on the formulation of a policy document to be presented to the eighth assembly of the WCC in 1998 – on the occasion of the 50th anniversary of the WCC's founding and at the dawn of a new century and a new millennium as a kind of "charter" for ecumenical commitment. The text as adopted by the WCC central committee in September 1997 reflected more than 150 responses to an earlier draft from WCC member churches and ecumenical partners.

The JWG has followed this process closely through briefings by WCC staff, sharing of materials and discussions, recognizing the direct bearing of its results on future working relations between the RCC and the WCC and its member churches.

In mandating the CUV process, the central committee in 1989 referred explicitly to the Council's relationship to churches which are not members. Accordingly, Roman Catholic perspectives were solicited from the beginning; and an observer from the PCPCU attended the December 1995 consultation which produced the original draft of the document. When a second version was shared with WCC member churches and ecumenical partners in November 1996, general secretary Konrad Raiser invited the PCPCU to respond; and an extended response was sent to Geneva in April 1997.

From the perspective of the WCC, the draft (and the text as adopted by the central committee in September 1997) states:

> We give thanks to God that the Roman Catholic Church is, since the Second Vatican Council, an active participant in the ecumenical movement and a valued partner in numerous ways with the WCC (especially through the JWG and participation in the commission of Faith and Order). The member churches of the WCC and the RCC are inspired by the same vision of God's plan to unite all things in Christ. It is inconceivable to us that either the WCC or the RCC could pursue its ecumenical calling without the collaboration of the other, and we firmly hope that both will look for ways to deepen and expand this relationship in the years ahead, particularly since the RCC has in recent years become part of a growing number of local, national and regional ecumenical bodies of which many WCC member churches are also part. While membership in the WCC is by no means the only way for churches to work together on a worldwide level, some member churches of the WCC which already have bilateral relations with the RCC believe that the fellowship of the WCC is impoverished by its absence from this circle of churches.

2. The PCPCU response acknowledges a "developmental continuity" in the RCC's "reception" of "a new ecumenical tradition of reflective experience... with other Christians and communions at the local, national and world levels, and as a result of the RCC's active participation in the WCC", which likewise has experienced "the developmental continuity of its ecumenical vocation during its fifty years of common life".

Especially in the light of *Ut Unum Sint*, the PCPCU response reflects on the common ground or basis of ecumenism and "the one ecumenical movement"; on a common vision seeking to hold together the interrelated dimensions of the churches' faith, life and witness; and on a common calling based on the reality, though imperfect, of the koinonia already existing between the churches.

The PCPCU response concludes that the "ecumenical understanding and commitment of the RCC is, in general, coherent with the present affirmations of the WCC member churches and of the WCC as they are expressed in the proposed Vision Statement".

The PCPCU also responded to proposals in the CUV draft for revisions of present WCC structures and possible new structures, in the light of the implications these would have for future RCC collaboration in the life and work of the WCC and solidarity with the WCC and its member churches.

B. COMMON WITNESS

1. National and regional councils of churches

In February 1993 the WCC and the PCPCU cosponsored the third international consultation of NCCs, held in Hong Kong. The theme was "The NCCs as Servants and Advocates of Unity". Out of the 88 NCCs around the world, 55 include the RCC as full members through its bishops' conferences. Also through the bishops' conferences the RCC is a full member of the regional councils of churches in the Caribbean, the Pacific and the Middle East. Within these national and regional councils the RCC has direct contact with many WCC member churches. Of the 120 participants in Hong Kong, 17 were Roman Catholics, six of them bishops representing their national episcopal conferences.

The consultation considered the NCCs as instruments of expressing communion (koinonia) between the churches and of giving common witness, noting that their work of reconciliation often makes NCCs national advocates in times of social-political crisis. At the same time, there was acknowledgment of the problems facing many NCCs: among them, finding competent resource persons for both the theological and the social ethical reflection; limited financial resources; fostering relations with regional councils of churches and the WCC. Many NCCs must act on a crowded ecumenical stage where more and more agencies with overlapping goals are competing for fewer and fewer resources of personnel and money. Yet the consultation acknowledged that a preoccupation with the sharing of financial resources and development projects too often overshadows the essential task of NCCs to search for Christian unity.

In a written message to the Hong Kong meeting, PCPCU president Cardinal Edward Cassidy observed that collaboration through full RC membership in an NCC causes difficulties if the ecclesiological implications of the fact that local Catholic churches are "within the framework of the communion of faith and discipline of the whole Catholic church" are forgotten. Furthermore, since an NCC should be governed by the norms set down by the member churches and should have only the authority which these constituents give it, an NCC's constitution should "seek to foresee how a satisfactory exercise of common concern can leave room for member churches to dissent from such action when they cannot in conscience be part of the same".

NCCs often engage in joint action or issue statements on difficult ethical and moral questions. "It is important", Cardinal Cassidy noted, "that such issues be studied with due regard for the moral teaching of the member churches, and above all taking into account the objective content of their ethical positions." Regarding this last point, the

JWG recommends that NCCs use its study document "The Ecumenical Dialogue on Moral Issues" (1996; cf. here Document 73).

Nevertheless, as the preparatory document for the Hong Kong conference suggested, the insistence of churches on "greater ownership" of an NCC carries the risk that the council will lose "its ecumenical vocation of being a pioneer that can take on issues and explore new avenues when the churches as such are as yet reluctant to do so"; indeed, the churches may be even content to be "one step removed" from such engagement.

2. Week of Prayer for Christian Unity

The Week of Prayer is one of the oldest and most widespread expressions of that "spiritual ecumenism" which is the heart and wellspring of the ecumenical movement. The preparation of annual materials for the Week of Prayer has created a stable and enduring collaboration between the RCC (through the PCPCU) and the WCC (through the Faith and Order commission).

For many persons the Week of Prayer each year is their main, if not only, ecumenical experience. In the context of frequent talk about the present difficulties and delays in the ecumenical movement, the Week serves as a strong affirmation of the churches' continuing commitment to the search for visible unity and provides a local experience of the catholicity of the universal church.

The annual text originates in the work of ecumenical groups in a single country or region – in recent years, Germany, Belgium, Zaire, Ireland, England, Portugal, Sweden and France. The text they provide is then developed by the international preparatory group and offered to all the churches for responsible local adaptation. This task often inspires fruitful collaboration among the churches within NCCs and other ecumenical bodies. Recent themes reveal an awareness of preparations for the year 2000; but the wide variety of ecumenical and social contexts in which the Week of Prayer is celebrated requires sensitivity and discretion in relating it to the millennium year 2000.

The JWG notes several issues which continue to challenge the churches as they celebrate the Week of Prayer for Christian Unity: how to inspire prayer and work for unity not only during one week, but throughout the whole year; how to encourage creative local adaptation of the material; and how to bring new Christian partners into the experience of common prayer for unity. Attention has been given to broader collaboration in observing the Week and to the fact that there are several widely observed prayer events throughout the year. Thus the material for 1996, "Behold, I stand at the door and knock" (Rev. 3:14-22), was prepared with the participation of official representatives from the world bodies of the YWCA and YMCA.

The JWG affirms the Week of Prayer as one of the most enduring and widespread ecumenical experiences, and urges that all the churches participate actively in the local adaptation, distribution and use of the materials.

3. Cooperation between the PCPCU (Rome) and the WCC's Programme Unit on Churches in Mission: Health, Education and Witness (Unit II)

The PCPCU has continued to facilitate increasing RC collaboration with the work of the WCC's Programme Unit II, through the availability of RC mission experts as consultants and, since 1984, of a full-time RC consultant based in Unit II of WCC staff in Geneva. This latter post has been occupied by a member of a RC missionary community of women; at present the consultant is Sister Elizabeth Moran of the Missionary Sisters of Saint Columban. The role includes liaison with the other appointed RC consultants, and with leaders of RC missionary congregations and RC missiologists in Roman universities and elsewhere. In addition, since 1989 four representatives from the International Unions of Superior Generals of Women and of Men have been full members of the WCC's Conference on World Mission and Evangelism.

These collaborative relationships with WCC staff have been enhanced by an exchange of visits. A delegation of eight persons from Roman curia staff and missionary communities and a professor of missiology visited Geneva in 1995 to become acquainted with the work of the WCC, especially Unit II; in turn, WCC staff concerned with the church's role in education in pluralistic societies visited Rome in 1996 and 1997. The PCPCU and the Unit II stream on education jointly sponsored a 1996 consultation in Rome at which WCC staff met representatives of RC religious congregations of men and of women whose primary ministry is education in schools. Participants listened to one another's experiences in responding to those education challenges which face the churches in increasingly pluralistic societies.

The invited participation of ten official RC consultants to the 1996 conference on world mission and evangelism (Salvador, Brazil) continued this important development of WCC-RCC relationships. The conference theme "Called to One Hope – the Gospel in Diverse Cultures" points to yet another area in which Christians could be seen working together in bringing much-needed hope to a complex, culturally diverse and broken world.

4. The year 2000

1. In its sixth report the JWG highlighted that the end of the millennium provides a natural occasion for all Christians to reflect on the state of their ecumenical relationships, and to recommit themselves to unity and strengthen their common witness. As the new millennium begins, the churches could offer to the world a Christian vision of unity and renewal, of social, economic and spiritual life which contributes to a stable and just world.

2. The JWG considered the celebration of the year 2000, especially in the light of the invitation in Pope John Paul's apostolic letter *Tertio Millennio Adveniente* (1995) to promote ecumenical initiatives of Christians "to turn together to Christ, the one Lord, and to strengthen their common witness; to celebrate the Spirit as the source of hope and unity; and to work together for a 'civilization of love', founded on the universal values of peace, solidarity, justice and liberty, which find the full attainment in Christ".

A WCC representative was invited to participate in the RCC's central committee for the celebration of the jubilee year (February 1996). RC representatives were invited to informal meetings organized by the WCC (June 1996, May 1997) with secretaries of CWCs and ecumenical partners who are planning celebrations to mark the year 2000.

3. The JWG recommends that its parent bodies propose to the local churches ecumenical studies on the significance of common baptism, possibly leading to mutual recognition of baptism in each local place; and on common profession of faith as proposed in both *Tertio Millennio Adveniente* and the Faith and Order study "Confessing the One Faith" (1991). It also raises the question of whether there could not be com-

mon local events for reconciliation among Christian traditions in places where there have been tensions.

4. The JWG has also highlighted the ecumenical potential of a worldwide "common celebration" of the new millennium, noting that its preparation would require careful involvement on the part of all ecumenical partners. Such a celebration, the JWG proposes, could focus on the possibility for Christians to confess together the apostolic faith and could offer common social witness by affirming the principles of the jubilee such as reconciliation, rights to and responsibility for the land, forgiveness of debts and the like.

5. The ecumenical dialogue on moral issues [cf. document 73 above]

1. As noted above, the past 35 years have seen a consistent development of multilateral and bilateral dialogues on those doctrinal differences which helped to cause and perpetuate divisions among the churches. These dialogues, in many of which the RCC has been an active partner with WCC member churches, are revealing convergences and developing common affirmations on such classically divisive issues as scripture and tradition; baptism, eucharist and ministry; the local and universal church; Christian unity and mission.

2. But during these same decades Christian responses to pressing personal and social moral issues were prompting discord, even threatening new divisions within and between the churches. Yet these same issues could become church-reconciling means of common witness. The challenge is urgent for three main reasons: (1) the fraying of the moral fabric of many societies as traditional moral values and positions are questioned and new and complex ethical issues arise, which press upon the consciousness and conscience of all human beings; (2) the genuine expectation, both in and beyond the churches, that they together can and should offer moral guidance to their members and to society at large; (3) the need for the churches, as a family of one moral community in a pluralistic society, to be in dialogue with others and to evaluate their moral insights and judgments – since moral discernment is not the exclusive preserve of Christians.

3. During its present mandate the JWG has offered its own study document "The Ecumenical Dialogue on Moral Issues: Potential Sources of Common Witness or of Divisions" (1996; cf. document 73 above). This document offers ten guidelines for ecumenical dialogue on moral issues.

4. The JWG study does not analyze specific controversial moral issues as such in an attempt to arrive at ethical norms, but rather suggests ways of conducting the dialogue. It outlines the common sources and the different pathways of moral reflection and deliberation, as well as the different authoritative means of moral discernment which churches use in arriving at ethical decisions and in communicating them to their members. While intended primarily for dialogues at local, national and regional levels in which RCs are partners, this document may also be useful for other bilateral and multilateral discussions.

6. Common witness, religious freedom and proselytism [cf. document 72 above]

1. Already during its first five-year mandate, the JWG recognized the urgency of a joint study on Christian witness, common witness, religious freedom and proselytism.

2. The 1970 JWG study document "Common Witness and Proselytism" clarified the meaning of some key terms in this discussion. These descriptions, although they

addressed and reflected the concerns of that time, could be kept in mind in reading the two subsequent JWG study documents "Common Witness" (1982) and "The Challenge of Proselytism and the Calling to Common Witness" (1996; cf. document 72 above):
- By *common witness* is meant the witness that the churches, even while separated, bear together, especially by joint efforts, by manifesting before men and women whatever divine gifts of truth and life they already share and experience in common.
- By *civic religious freedom* is meant that each person or community has the right to be free from any coercion on the part of social groups or human power of any kind; so that no individual or community may be forced to act against conscience or be prevented from expressing belief in teaching, worship or social action.
- By *proselytism* is meant whatever violates the right of the human person, Christian or non-Christian, to be free from external coercion in religious matters, or whatever in the proclamation of the gospel does not conform to the ways God draws free men and women to respond to God's calls to serve in spirit and in truth.

3. The most recent study document has been produced because of the rise of new situations where people are vulnerable in a variety of ways. Allegations are being made about the practice of proselytism and antagonistic competition in missionary activity. For example, those involved in evangelistic activities appear to ignore the Christian reality of other churches, or their particular pastoral approaches. Missionary strategies may include re-evangelizing baptized members of other churches. In the new climate of civic religious freedom in some countries at the present time certain churches maintain that their members are being put under pressure to change their church allegiance.

4. The present study places the problems of civic religious freedom and proselytism in the context of church unity and common witness. Such an approach makes it possible for the churches, in the dialogue of "speaking the truth in love" (Eph. 4:15), to deal with tensions over accusations of proselytism in specific situations with reciprocal trust. The study has in fact been one of the basic texts used by the WCC's Unit II for its own 1997 document "Towards Common Witness", a call to adopt responsible relationships in mission and to renounce proselytism.

5. The JWG recommends the use of its 1996 study document in ecumenical formation programmes, and in the education of missionaries and of those engaged in diaconal service. It may also serve as a basis for conversations with churches and missionary groups who are not in direct relations with the WCC or with national and local councils of churches.

C. ECUMENICAL FORMATION

1. Ecumenical formation [cf. document 71 above]

1. Carrying out a mandate given to it in 1985, the JWG completed in 1993 "Ecumenical Formation: Ecumenical Reflections and Suggestions" (cf. document 71 above).

The perspectives underlying ecumenical formation centre on an understanding of the church as a koinonia which embodies unity and diversity. Ecumenical formation is described in the JWG document as an ongoing process of learning within the various local churches and world communions aimed at informing and guiding people in the one movement which, inspired by the Holy Spirit, seeks the visible unity of Christians.

In this process of formation, mutual sharing and mutual critique take place in the context of the participants' rootedness in Christ and in their own traditions. The document identifies the importance of both informal contacts in daily life and formal courses of study in institutes, focusing on the specific literature of the ecumenical movement, including its history.

2. The JWG's basic concerns are developed further in the 1993 *Ecumenical Directory (ED)*. Exploring the nature and content of ecumenical formation with regard to the whole Christian community, ED emphasizes formation through preaching, catechesis, liturgy and the spiritual life. The PCPCU text also offers guidelines for the formation of those engaged in pastoral work. It emphasizes the ecumenical dimension of theological disciplines, and outlines a specific course in ecumenism for theological faculties, for RC universities and for specialized ecumenical institutes.

3. This section of *ED* was in turn developed in greater detail in a November 1997 document which the PCPCU addressed to each bishop, to the synods of the Eastern Catholic churches and to the national bishops' conferences: "The Ecumenical Dimension in the Formation of Those Engaged in Pastoral Work".

4. Together, *ED* and "The Ecumenical Dimension..." constitute the fullest explication of ecumenical education and formation by any church or Christian world communion. The JWG encourages that wherever prudent and feasible, such RC training be conducted with Christians of other traditions, since this is one of the most fundamental learning experiences. The JWG also suggests that the *Directory* be discussed by religious educators on the local and national levels.

2. Ecumenical Institute, Bossey

1. Since 1946 the WCC's Ecumenical Institute in Bossey, outside Geneva, has provided opportunities of ecumenical formation for thousands of pastors and laypersons from many parts of the world. Its residential sessions create an atmosphere in which mutual understanding of and respect for diverse Christian traditions and a realistic understanding of the ecumenical movement are fostered by living, learning and praying together. The formative element when the students pray together the Lord's prayer or recite together the creed is evident.

The JWG welcomes the recent emphasis on shaping a core curriculum for Bossey which would include exposure to some of the major concerns arising in the ongoing bilateral and multilateral dialogues, among them reflection on the creeds and on baptism, eucharist and ministry.

2. WCC-RCC collaboration at Bossey continues. The faculty of the Ecumenical Institute includes a RC professor, Fr Serapio Kisirinya (Uganda); and a PCPCU staff person (Msgr John Mutiso-Mbinda) sits on the Bossey board as an observer. Since 1978, students of Bossey's annual graduate school of ecumenical studies have enjoyed, as part of the programme, a one-week visit to Rome, prepared by the PCPCU in consultation with the Bossey staff. The students learn more about the RCC through direct contact with persons in various offices of the Roman curia, institutions of higher learning and worldwide religious communities of women and of men whose headquarters are in Rome. Students typically show particular interest in hearing about RC approaches to Christian unity, to issues of justice and peace and to questions related to family life. A private audience with the pope is a high point of the week's experience.

3. Ecumenical Theological Education (ETE)

The WCC's programme on Ecumenical Theological Education (ETE) and its predecessors have worked with the RCC for many years, both directly and indirectly. The most recent visible example of this partnership was the RC participation in the preparatory study process which shaped the agenda of ETE's August 1996 global consultation on the viability of ecumenical theological education today (Oslo, Norway).

The pre-consultation process involved regional colloquia which explored ways of fostering viable ministerial formation and theological education from ecumenical perspectives. ETE's constituency is not only churches but also associations of theological schools in various regions. At every stage RCs in these associations have been visible. The Oslo consultation brought together church leaders, theological educators, students, representatives from funding agencies and from ministerial formation boards. The PCPCU sent a delegation of six persons.

IV. Some other areas of collaboration

1. Interreligious dialogue

1. The WCC's Office for Interreligious Relations (OIRR) and the Pontifical Council for Interreligious Dialogue (PCID) annually hold a joint meeting. Besides information-sharing, these meetings offer an opportunity to examine developments in interreligious relations, assess initiatives for dialogue and reflect on future orientations and priorities. The PCID and OIRR invite each other to take part in their respective activities as well as in the meetings of their advisory bodies. Three joint projects during this period may be highlighted.

2. The OIRR and PCID study document "Reflections on Interreligious Marriages", published in 1997, grew out of a study launched in 1994 by sending questionnaires to different churches and communities and to a number of Christian and non-Christian spouses. The responses to these form the basis of the first part of the document. The second part takes stock of pertinent materials already produced by churches and Christian communities. The third part presents reflections of a pastoral nature. While addressed primarily to pastors, the document may also be useful for other people concerned with interreligious marriages.

3. Interreligious prayer is a growing phenomenon and there is a need to provide pastoral help to the churches. Is it possible to pray with people of other faiths which have different symbol systems – and if so what does this mean? The OIRR-PCID joint study project "Interreligious Prayer and Worship" had three phases: a worldwide survey on the phenomenon with the help of the local churches (completed in 1995); a small consultation of persons who are engaged in the practice of interreligious prayer; and the formulation of conclusions by a consultation of persons with theological expertise (1997). A small number of Christian theologians, including RCs, offered biblical perspectives on interreligious prayer, the different readings of prayer in the churches and in their tradition, and different assessments of interreligious prayer.

4. The Middle East remains a major conflict area in which Jews, Christians and Muslims urgently need together to seek reconciliation, peace and justice. In particular, the city of Jerusalem requires people of these three monotheistic faiths to respond to that common religious call first revealed to Abraham: "to keep the way of the Lord by doing what is right and just" (Gen. 18:19). This is the background of a process initiated by the Lutheran

World Federation and bringing together the OIRR, PCID and the holy see's Commission for Religious Relations with the Jews to co-sponsor two colloquia on Jerusalem.

The first colloquium – on the spiritual significance of Jerusalem for Jews, Christians and Muslims – took place in Glion, Switzerland, in 1993, before the Oslo political agreement between Israel and the Palestinian National Authority. The Jewish, Christian and Muslim participants came mainly from Israel/West Bank-Gaza. By the time of the second colloquium, in Thessaloniki, Greece, in August 1996, the peace process was faltering and pessimism was in the air. The attempts of this colloquium to imagine the future of Jerusalem were unsuccessful. The final message recognizes Jerusalem as a "place of encounter between God and humanity and among human beings in their diversity". Jerusalem "is called to be the City of Peace, but at the moment, there is no peace. Although the peace process between Israelis and Palestinians has been initiated, there is still a long way to go before a just and lasting peace is achieved."

2. Diaconal service

1. Participating in each JWG plenary was the secretary of Cor Unum, the Pontifical Council for Promoting Charitable Works by Catholic Institutes, which finances projects for the needy and facilitates relations with other Christian diaconal and secular international organizations. He kept the JWG up to date on Cor Unum activities and suggested ways of building bridges between it and the WCC's Programme Unit on Sharing and Service (Unit IV).

In February 1997 the Unit IV director and a staff member went to Rome to introduce 1997 as the Ecumenical Year of Churches in Solidarity with Uprooted People in meetings with the Pontifical Councils Cor Unum, for Migration and for Promoting Christian Unity, as well as with Caritas Internationalis. Together they explored areas for dialogue and practical cooperation.

2. The JWG received an extensive report on the main orientations and activities of Unit IV and its understanding of diakonia as an integral part of the churches' witness. This report detailed the established working relationships, in particular with RC international agencies, to assist refugees, uprooted people and migrants; and it identified common concerns for developing cooperation at the regional and national levels within those ecumenical organizations which have local RC churches in their membership.

The JWG observed that although the order of priorities may differ and the language used may not always be the same, both partners deeply shared the fundamental concerns regarding poverty and its root causes. But there is an asymmetry in the visible collaboration between offices concerned with diakonia in Unit IV of the WCC and in the Holy See (as is also the case between Unit III of the WCC and the Pontifical Council for Justice and Peace).

For the JWG two questions remain: (1) How can the dimension of diakonia best be included in encouraging common witness, without disregarding the potential for divisiveness over what is authentic diaconal witness and what is proselytism? (2) How can the JWG take this into account in fulfilling its duty to encourage and facilitate local ecumenism (national and regional councils of churches)?

3. Social thought and action

1. Cooperation between the RCC and WCC member churches in social thought and action is very intense on many levels and in different ways, especially where the RCC

is a member of national councils of churches. Events such as the two European Ecumenical Assemblies (Basel 1989; Graz 1997) show the possibilities of major collaboration and common witness on a regional level.

2. A number of difficulties mark the history of direct collaboration between the offices in Geneva and in Rome. From 1968 to 1980 the coresponsible agency between the holy see and the WCC was the Joint Committee on Society, Development and Peace (SODEPAX). It was replaced, in 1982, by a weaker instrument, the Joint Consultative Group for Social Thought and Action, which became defunct in 1989. Specific tensions arose around efforts at collaboration in the WCC's 1990 world convocation on justice, peace and the integrity of creation (Seoul, Korea), growing out of differences between the WCC and the RCC in their approach to ideological tensions in the world, as well as their differing understandings of and structures for playing a role in international affairs. Also to be taken into account are the many legitimate differences of viewpoint on social and political questions existing within each church.

3. The JWG noted the recent efforts of Unit III of the WCC and the Pontifical Council for Justice and Peace (PCJP) to reinforce their working contacts as the principal central instruments of collaboration in social thought and action. After an interruption of several years, the annual exchange of visits between the two institutions has been revived. These visits are finding new methods for common identification of priorities to be explored together while acknowledging one or the other body might be in a better position to approach a specific subject on its own, with the encouragement and support of the other. In this way it may be possible to test moral principles concerning social questions, using different methodologies while maintaining fellowship.

Among the issues in which future collaboration might be intensified are poverty, economic justice including the international debt, the environment, human rights, and conflict prevention, resolution and reconciliation. Common work, such as a jointly sponsored course of studies on Christian social thought today, could be carried out. The jubilee year 2000 could offer special occasions for collaboration. Unit III and the PCJP have also decided to intensify their exchange of information and to encourage participation in each other's meetings as observers. A PCJP representative already participates in the Unit III commission meetings.

Both sides exchanged texts and documentation on religious freedom. The WCC drew attention to some aspects of the legal position of the Protestant churches in Latin America, where the majority church is Roman Catholic.

4. The PCJP encouraged RC episcopal conferences to take part in the WCC petition campaign on climate change. The PCJP was represented in the WCC consultation on climate change (November 1996); and WCC representatives joined the RCC consultation on social thought and action for the English- and Portuguese-speaking African countries (August 1996) and the European conference on the social teaching of the church (July 1997).

5. The WCC and the PCPCU have also cooperated in projects involving other partners. An example was the March 1993 peace delegation to Guatemala and El Salvador, organized by the Lutheran World Federation and also including representatives from the WCC, the PCPCU, the National Council of Churches of Christ in the USA, and the Latin American Council of Churches. The delegation met with leaders of the RCC and Protestant churches in Guatemala; and a special ecumenical prayer service was organized in the Catholic cathedral in Guatemala City. The group also met with the presi-

dent of Guatemala and other government officials, with the ombudsman for human rights, with widows, refugees and war victims, with the chairman of the reconciliation committee facilitating the negotiations between the government and opposition leaders, and with representatives of the civil sectors.

In December 1996, after 36 years of war, the government of Guatemala and the opposition forces signed a peace treaty. The ecumenical concern which the peace delegation had expressed three years earlier was also a significant gesture which showed the Guatemalans, especially in the churches, the support they were receiving from fellow Christians in other parts of the world.

4. Decade of Churches in Solidarity with Women
1. The WCC inaugurated the Ecumenical Decade of Churches in Solidarity with Women (1988-98) with the goals of encouraging and facilitating responses to women in their efforts to affirm their full, creative empowerment in the life of their churches, through shared leadership and decision-making, theology and spirituality; of giving visibility to women's perspectives and actions in the struggles for justice, peace and the integrity of creation; of denouncing violence against women in its various forms; of considering the effects on women of the global economic crisis and the worldwide upsurge of racism and of xenophobia; and of enabling the churches to free themselves from racism, sexism and classism and from all teachings and practices that discriminate against women.

2. The Decade has given an opportunity for shared reflection and conscientization regarding the realities of the experiences of women as they participate in the life of the churches and in various cultural and political settings. Although the Decade was adopted as a programme for WCC member churches, the RCC has been involved, most noticeably in meeting and acting together at local levels. Participation of RCs in local associations and councils of churches has allowed for joint planning, meetings and celebrations as the Decade progressed. Some RC church leaders were active in inaugurating and promoting the work of the Decade. For example, the RC bishop of Khartoum launched the Decade in the Sudan; and the National Board of Catholic Women acted in a consultative role on the Decade concerns for the bishops' conference of England and Wales.

3. At its midpoint (1994-96), the Decade was "given back to the churches themselves", highlighted in a programme which sent some 75 ecumenical teams to visit nearly every member church of the WCC. RC members of national and local ecumenical groups joined in welcoming and hosting many of these WCC-initiated visits and took an active part in the mid-Decade celebrations and events. For example, in Surinam, RC church workers participated in a series of discussions on the leadership of women in the churches. Awareness of shared concerns among churches was heightened in this way.

During this period some papal documents mirrored concerns regarding women which are closely allied to WCC's goals for the Decade.

4. A summary report *Living Letters* was published by the WCC in 1997 on the basis of the findings from the team visits. Among the insights emerging from the Decade's worldwide activities, the report notes that although the Decade was addressed to the churches, it has in fact been limited mostly to women; the churches have not owned the Decade, nor have they provided the support necessary for it to become a transforming promise to the churches together. Nevertheless, for some the Decade has

offered the opportunity to recognize that issues relating to gender and to community are not simply "women's issues" but belong to the Christian community of women and men – that is, to the whole church.

V. Prospects for the future (1998-2005)

1. Over the seven-year period of its mandate, the JWG has tried to meet its given priorities. But its overloaded agenda, the sensitivity of many of the issues it dealt with, its short annual meetings and the limited financial resources at its disposal did not allow the JWG adequately to assess the ecumenical situation and specific developments at regional, national and local levels, or to cover the whole pattern of relationships between the RCC and the WCC and its member churches.

In the face of its limited resources of time and staff, the JWG had to limit the scope of its agenda and carefully ration the time spent together.

2. The JWG strongly recommends that two general priorities should be continued in the next period.

a) Both the WCC and the RCC are committed to a common, integrated vision of the one ecumenical movement which tries, in its diversity of expressions, emphases and activities, to hold together the interrelated dimensions of the churches' faith and life, mission, witness and service. But, in the words of the PCPCU response to the WCC's draft statement on CUV, "the oneness of the movement is both blessed with authentic diversity and often challenged and burdened with contradictions, even conflicts, and with competing criteria of judgments concerning what are ecumenical successes, standstills and setbacks".

b) The JWG should be alert to those tensions which may threaten the coherence of the movement in its diversity. Addressing the social, economic and political concerns which profoundly affect the quality of life for all human communities is an essential ecumenical task. But attention to these should not come at the expense of attention to the theological divisions and unresolved issues of Christian faith which remain stumbling blocks to achieving the visible unity which is the goal of the ecumenical movement. These are stumbling blocks as well for the churches in carrying out their essential missionary task and in maintaining their dialogue in community with people of other world faiths and secular ideologies.

In this context, the JWG should continue to focus on those fundamental issues which are obstacles to achieving full koinonia of the RCC and the WCC member churches, and on those common concerns which, when addressed by the WCC and the RCC together, manifest common witness to the reconciling love of God.

3. The JWG recommends these specific priorities for the next period of its mandate:

ISSUES AFFECTING KOINONIA
- *The ecclesial consequences of common baptism.* The implications of recognizing the common baptism of Christians on ecclesial communion and liturgical practice.
- *The ecumenical role of interchurch marriages.* The ecclesiological implications of the sacrament of marriage between Christians of different churches and their family life.
- *Local, national and regional councils of churches which have RC churches as full members.* The practical and ecclesiological implications of membership of councils of churches, and their instrumental role in the growth of koinonia.

– *Church and church law.* The impact of ecumenical agreements and dialogues on actual church legislation and on relations between ecclesiology and canon law/church law/church discipline.

COMMON CONCERNS FACING THE WCC AND RCC
– *The stances of conservative evangelicals and charismatic/Pentecostals towards the ecumenical movement and its present structures.* The establishing of dialogue.
– *Christian fundamentalists: an ecumenical challenge?* The impact of fundamentalisms on the ecumenical commitment of churches, and of dialogue with the major issues which Christian fundamentalists address.
– *The place of women in the churches.* The further recognition and integration of the gifts of women in church life and society, and the appropriation of the findings of the Ecumenical Decade of the Churches in Solidarity with Women on the life, structures and witness of the churches.
– *Ecumenical education.* The development of appropriate ecumenical education for church members, students and clergy on the fundamentals of the Christian life in the search for the manifestation of the unity of the church within a pluralist society.

Part D

XXIX. WORLD COUNCIL OF CHURCHES

Historical Introduction

In 1991 the seventh assembly of the World Council of Churches met in Canberra, Australia. One of the most significant documents to emerge from this assembly was the text "The Church as Koinonia: Gift and Calling".[1] This assembly was one of the few times that the World Council of Churches at its highest level of authority had offered an articulation of an understanding of the unity being sought by the member churches.

"The Church as Koinonia" had its origin in the work done by the commission on Faith and Order at the request of the central committee. Thus the commission produced a text for the consideration of the assembly. This text was redrafted and modified in part before it received the approval of the seventh assembly and was transmitted to the churches.

The document, which is quite compressed, brings together what has been said especially recently about the understanding of unity. At the same time it stands in continuity with a long history of World Council statements on the church's unity, that extends back to the New Delhi assembly in 1961.

As its title indicates, it draws on the New Testament and early church concept of koinonia/communio to comprehend the unity of the church in its entirety. In this regard the Canberra text builds on Faith and Order work reaching back at least to the world conference on Faith and Order in Edinburgh in 1937.

By the 1980s koinonia/communio had appeared as an ecclesiological concept in the bilateral dialogues. As an ecumenical concept koinonia/communio has a strong integrative power as the text discloses. The concept brings together diversity and unity in the church. This statement from Canberra indicates how koinonia/communio can be a central notion in the expression of the visible unity of the church. In its conclusion it calls upon the churches to take specific actions towards full expressions of visible unity.

In 1993 the fifth world conference on Faith and Order met in Santiago de Compostela, Spain. At the conclusion of its work the conference issued a message to the churches, "On the Way to Fuller Koinonia". Many of the leading ideas of the Canberra statement found their way into this Faith and Order text and reveal the continuing influence of the concept of koinonia/communio in ecumenical reports.[2]

NOTES

[1] Michael Kinnamon, ed., *Signs of the Spirit: Official Report of the Seventh Assembly of the World Council of Churches*, Geneva, WCC, and Grand Rapids MI, Eerdmans, 1991, pp.172-74.
[2] Thomas F. Best and Günther Gassmann, eds, *On the Way to Fuller Koinonia: Official Report of the Fifth World Conference on Faith and Order*, Faith and Order Paper no. 166, Geneva, WCC, 1994, pp.223-27.

75. The Unity of the Church as Koinonia: Gift and Calling

Canberra, Australia, February 1991

1.1. The purpose of God according to holy scripture is to gather the whole of creation under the lordship of Christ Jesus in whom, by the power of the Holy Spirit, all are brought into communion with God (Eph. 1). The church is the foretaste of this communion with God and with one another. The grace of our Lord Jesus Christ, the love of God, and the communion of the Holy Spirit enable the one church to live as sign of the reign of God and servant of the reconciliation with God, promised and provided for the whole creation. The purpose of the church is to unite people with Christ in the power of the Spirit, to manifest communion in prayer and action and thus to point to the fullness of communion with God, humanity and the whole creation in the glory of the kingdom.

1.2. The calling of the church is to proclaim reconciliation and provide healing, to overcome divisions based on race, gender, age, culture, colour, and to bring all people into communion with God. Because of sin and the misunderstanding of the diverse gifts of the Spirit, the churches are painfully divided within themselves and among each other. The scandalous divisions damage the credibility of their witness to the world in worship and service. Moreover they contradict not only the church's witness but also its very nature.

1.3. We acknowledge with gratitude to God that in the ecumenical movement the churches walk together in mutual understanding. Theological convergence, common suffering and common prayer, shared witness and service as they draw close to one another. This has allowed them to recognize a certain degree of communion already existing between them. This is indeed the fruit of the active presence of the Holy Spirit in the midst of all who believe in Christ Jesus and who struggle for visible unity now. Nevertheless churches have failed to draw the consequences for their life from the degree of communion they have already experienced and the agreements already achieved. They have remained satisfied to coexist in division.

2.1. The unity of the church to which we are called is a koinonia given and expressed in the common confession of the apostolic faith; a common sacramental life entered by the one baptism and celebrated together in one eucharistic fellowship; a common life in which members and ministries are mutually recognized and reconciled; and a common mission witnessing to the gospel of God's grace to all people and serving the whole of creation. The goal of the search for full communion is realized when all the churches are able to recognize in one another the one, holy, catholic and apostolic church in its fullness. This full communion will be expressed on the local and the universal levels through conciliar forms of life and action. In such communion churches are bound in all aspects of their life together at all levels in confessing the one faith and engaging in worship and witness, deliberation and action.

2.2. Diversities which are rooted in theological traditions, various cultural, ethnic or historical contexts are integral to the nature of communion; yet there are limits to diversity. Diversity is illegitimate when, for instance, it makes impossible the common confession of Jesus Christ as God and Saviour the same yesterday, today and forever (Heb. 13:8); and salvation and the final destiny of humanity as proclaimed in holy scripture and preached by the apostolic community. In communion diversities are brought together in harmony as gifts of the Holy Spirit, contributing to the richness and fullness of the church of God.

3.1. Many things have been done and many remain to be done on the way towards the realization of full communion. Churches have reached agreements in bilateral and multilateral dialogues which are already bearing fruit, renewing their liturgical and spiritual life and their theology. In taking specific steps together the churches express and encourage the enrichment and renewal of Christian life, as they learn from one another, work together for justice and peace, and care together for God's creation.

3.2. The challenge at this moment in the ecumenical movement as a reconciling and renewing movement towards full visible unity is for the seventh assembly of the WCC to call all churches:

- to recognize each other's baptism on the basis of the BEM document;
- to move towards the recognition of the apostolic faith as expressed through the Nicene-Constantinopolitan Creed in the life and witness of one another;
- on the basis of convergence in faith in baptism, eucharist and ministry to consider, wherever appropriate, forms of eucharistic hospitality; we gladly acknowledge that some who do not observe these rites share in the spiritual experience of life in Christ;
- to move towards a mutual recognition of ministries;
- to endeavour in word and deed to give common witness to the gospel as a whole;
- to recommit themselves to work for justice, peace and the integrity of creation, linking more closely the search for the sacramental communion of the church with the struggles for justice and peace;
- to help parishes and communities express in appropriate ways locally the degree of communion that already exists.

4.1. The Holy Spirit as promoter of koinonia (2 Cor. 13:13) gives to those who are still divided the thirst and hunger for full communion. We remain restless until we grow together according to the wish and prayer of Christ that those who believe in him may be one (John 17:21). In the process of praying, working and struggling for unity, the Holy Spirit comforts us in pain, disturbs us when we are satisfied to remain in our division, leads us to repentance, and grants us joy when our communion flourishes.

XXIX. WORLD COUNCIL OF CHURCHES

76. Message to the Churches

Santiago de Compostela, Spain, August 1993

1. "The grace of our Lord Jesus Christ and the love of God and the koinonia of the Holy Spirit be with you all" (2 Cor. 13:13).

2. God, who calls all to unity and makes us one in Christ and the Spirit, has drawn us to Santiago de Compostela from around the world. We are a more comprehensive gathering than came together thirty years ago in Montreal at the last world conference on Faith and Order. Far more of us come from Asia, Africa, Latin America, the Caribbean, and the Pacific region. There are more women participants than ever before. The group of younger theologians has eagerly participated in the work. For the first time, the Roman Catholic Church has sent official delegates to a world conference. There is a significant presence of Pentecostal Christians. We have come together, sent by our churches, to further the work of the Faith and Order movement "to proclaim the oneness of the church of Jesus Christ and to call the churches to the goal of visible unity" (Faith and Order commission, by-law 2).

3. We come in joy, giving thanks for the great strides forward that have been made in recent years and for the eagerness of many Christians for a fuller koinonia, but also come in concern for waning commitments to Christian unity. We come in thankfulness for the breakthroughs to freedom that have occurred, for example, in Eastern Europe and Southern Africa. But we also come in concern for a world torn by injustice and strife in such locations as the former Yugoslavia, Somalia and so many other places. We come in pain when we remember what our sin does to humanity and the groaning creation. Our concern and pain become penitence when we think of our failure to do all that is already ecumenically possible and of our silence in the face of hatred and evil, or even worse, our participation in them. We come in hope for the ecumenical future, for the church, and for the world. We now leave Santiago with renewed commitment and enthusiasm for the ecumenical vision. We say to the churches: *there is no turning back*, either from the goal of visible unity or from the single ecumenical movement that unites concern for the unity of the church and concern for engagement in the struggles of the world.

4. *Koinonia* has been the focus of our discussions. This word from the Greek New Testament describes the richness of our life together in Christ: community, communion, sharing, fellowship, participation, solidarity. The koinonia we seek and which we have experienced is more than words. It springs from the word of life, "what we have seen with our eyes, what we have touched with our hands" (1 John 1:1), especially where koinonia is being realized daily in such forms as local ecumenical projects and

base communities. This koinonia which we share is nothing less than the reconciling presence of the love of God. God wills unity for the church, for humanity, and for creation because God is a koinonia of love, the unity of the Father, Son and Holy Spirit. This koinonia comes to us as a gift we can only accept in gratitude. Gratitude, however, is not passivity. Our koinonia is in the Holy Spirit who moves us to action. The koinonia we experience drives us to seek that visible unity which can adequately embody our koinonia with God and one another.

5. The deeper koinonia which is our goal is for the glory of God and for the sake of the world. The church is called to be a sign and instrument of this all-encompassing will of God, the summing up of all things in Christ. Jesus broke down walls of division in his identification with women and with the poor, the outcast and the oppressed. A deeper koinonia will be a sign of hope for all or it will not be a true koinonia in the love of God. Only a church itself being healed can convincingly proclaim healing to the world. Only a church that overcomes ethnic, racial and national hatreds in a common Christian and human identity can be a credible sign of freedom and reconciliation. While our particular focus at this conference has been the visible unity of the church, the horizon of our work has been the wider reach of God's love.

6. One of our tasks in Santiago has been to examine the concrete ecumenical achievements over the past thirty years of the Faith and Order movement, including the bilateral dialogues. We have particularly noted and affirmed the importance of all convergences towards a common understanding and practice of baptism, eucharist and ministry; towards a common confession of the one faith witnessed to in the Nicene-Constantinopolitan Creed; and towards a shared mission and service. The task before the churches now is to receive these convergences into their life. What steps is God leading the churches to take together *now*?

7. The ecumenical movement has changed over the past thirty years. The voices of women and of those from beyond Europe and North America have joined the ecumenical conversation in strength, bringing new insights, new experiences, new diversities. The significance for koinonia of common ethical commitment and action has been firmly placed on the Faith and Order agenda. The many positive movements of evangelical and charismatic renewal still need to be drawn into ecumenical partnership. The transformation is still going on and is at times difficult and controversial. Differences over the goals and methods of ecumenical work and theology have led to intense debates. In these debates, conflicting perspectives often each express significant elements of truth. We are confident we are being led through such tensions into a deeper and broader koinonia in the Spirit. A test of our koinonia is how we live with those with whom we disagree.

8. The ecumenical goal has not yet been reached. The churches still have not come to a full mutual recognition of baptism. There are still obstacles that prevent the sharing together of Christians from all churches at the Lord's table. The obstacles that stand in the way of a fuller koinonia must be felt in all their painfulness and honestly faced in penitence. The way forward will come by new ventures and insights in the faith that unites us, not by compromises that merely obscure the problems. Addressing these obstacles is the specific task of Faith and Order work. This task is more than ever essential to the ecumenical movement. The churches are challenged to an active partnership within the Faith and Order movement in addressing what still divides them.

9. At Santiago, we have again sensed the urgency of our need for greater koinonia in faith, life and witness. The churches have made some progress in implementing the 1952 Lund principle that they should "act together in all matters except those in which deep differences of conviction compel them to act separately". But they must go further. Unity today calls for structures of mutual accountability.

10. Concrete challenges stand before the churches. In relation to *faith*, the churches must continue to explore how to confess our common faith in the context of the many cultures and religions, the many social and national conflicts in which we live. Such confession emphasizes the need for a deeper understanding of the church and its apostolic character in the light of the holy scriptures. In relation to *life*, the churches must dare concrete steps towards fuller koinonia, in particular doing all that is possible to achieve a common recognition of baptism, agreement on a common participation in the eucharist, and a mutually recognized ministry. In relation to *witness*, the churches must consider the implications of koinonia for a responsible care for creation, for a just sharing of the world's resources, for a special concern for the poor and outcast, and for a common and mutually respectful evangelism that invites everyone into communion with God in Christ. But beyond all particular challenges, the churches and the ecumenical movement itself are called to the conversion to Christ that true koinonia in our time demands.

11. The world was made for this koinonia in God, a koinonia that has been won by the life, death, and resurrection of Jesus Christ. We stand before God and our final words must be prayer:

Holy and loving Trinity:

- we come to you in thanksgiving,
    for your gift of koinonia which we now receive as a
    foretaste of your kingdom.
- we come to you in penitence,
    for our failures to show forth koinonia where there is
    division, hostility and death;
- we come to you in expectation,
    that we may enter more deeply into the joy of koinonia;
- we come to you in confidence,
    to commit ourselves anew to your purposes of love;
    justice, and koinonia;
- we come to you in hope,
    that the unity of your church, in all its rich diversity,
    may be ever more clearly manifest as a sign of your love.

Kindle our hearts. Direct our wills. Deepen our understanding. Strengthen our resolve. Help us to be open to you and to our sisters and brothers, that we may together witness to the perfect unity of your love. Amen.